THIRTEENTH STATE CENSUS.

THE

CENSUS OF IOWA,

AS RETURNED IN THE

YEAR 1875,

SHOWING IN DETAIL THE POPULATION, AGRICULTURAL STATISTICS, DOMESTIC AND GENERAL MANUFACTURES, AND OTHER ITEMS OF INTEREST.

PUBLISHED UNDER DIRECTION OF THE EXECUTIVE COUNCIL.

CYRUS C. CARPENTER, Governor.
JOSIAH T. YOUNG, Secretary of State.
BUREN R. SHERMAN, Auditor of State.
WILLIAM CHRISTY, Treasurer of State.

DES MOINES:
R. P. CLARKSON, STATE PRINTER.
Nov. 1, 1875.

TABLE OF CONTENTS.

Number of Dwellings, number of Families; and the Population with the various classifications thereof in the several counties in the State, by Townships 1-69
Acres of improved and unimproved land, with number of acres in cultivation in 1874; rods of fence; number of acres and number of bushels harvested of Spring Wheat, Winter Wheat, Corn, Rye, Oats, Barley, and Buckwheat in the several counties in the State, by Townships 70-128
Statistics concerning Flax, Sorghum, Wild and Tame Grasses, Irish Potatoes, Sweet Potatoes, Onions, Turnips, Beets, Peas, and Beans in the several counties in the State, by Townships 129-187
Number of acres of natural and planted Timber; rods of Hedge; and statistics of the Orchard and Vine in the several counties in the State, by Townships 188-247
Number of Horses of all ages, with number sold for export; number of Mules and Asses, with number sold for export; number of Milch Cows; pounds of Butter made; pounds of Cheese made not at factory; gallons of Milk sold; Work Oxen; all other cattle; Cattle slaughtered or sold for slaughter in 1874; thorough-bred Short-Horns; Hogs on hand, Berkshires, Poland China, and number slaughtered or sold for slaughter in 1874; Sheep on hand, pounds of Wool sheared and sheep slaughtered or sold for slaughter in 1874; with number same killed by dogs, and number of dogs in the several counties in the State, by Townships 248-308
Number of Stands of Bees, pounds of Honey and Beeswax; value of Farm Produce, value of Market Garden Produce, value of Products of the Orchard, value of Small Fruit, value of Products of the Herd, value of Products of the Dairy, and value of Products of the Forest, in the several counties in the State, by Townships 309-346
Number of Dwellings, Families, Population and the various classifications thereof; showing also Nativity of Inhabitants, Foreign Parentage, and number Persons between Five and Twenty-One, in the several counties in the State 347-350
Number of Illiterate Persons, Deaf and Dumb not in State Institution, Blind not in College for the Blind, Insane not in Hospitals, Births and Deaths in 1874, Voters and where Born, Foreigners, and Militia, in the several counties in the State 351-354
Number of Acres of Improved and Unimproved Land, Rods of Fence, Acres in Cultivation in 1874, Acres and Bushels Harvested of Spring Wheat, Winter Wheat, Corn, Rye, Oats, Barley, and Buckwheat, in the several counties in the State 355-358
Number of Acres and Bushels of Flax Seed; acres of Sorghum and Gallons of Syrup from same; gallons of Maple Syrup, pounds of Maple Sugar; Acres of Blue Grass, of Tame Grass and tons of Hay from same; tons of Hay from Wild Grass, bushels of Grass Seed, of Clover Seed; Acres of Hungarian Grass, tons of Hay and bushels of Seed from same; statistics of Hops, Tobacco, Broom Corn and Potatoes, in the several counties in the State 359-362

PAGE.

Number of acres and bushels of Sweet Potatoes, Onions, bushels of Turnips, Beets, Peas and Beans; acres of Natural Timber, of Planted Timber; rods of Hedge; number of Trees in bearing and bushels gathered in 1874 of Apples, Pears, Peaches, Plums, and Cherries, and other Fruit Trees in bearing and number not in bearing; acres of Grapes in Vineyard, pounds of Grapes gathered, gallons of Wine made; number of Vines, pounds gathered and gallons of Wine made of Grapes not in Vineyard, in the several counties in the State 364-369

Number of Horses of all ages, same sold for export; Mules and Asses, same sold export; Milch Cows, pounds of Butter made, pounds of Cheese made not at factory, gallons of Milk sold; Work Oxen; all other Cattle; Cattle slaughtered or sold for slaughter in 1874; Thoroughbred Short-Horns, Devons, Herefords, Ayrshires, Jerseys, Holderness, other improved breeds; Hogs: Berkshires, Poland-China, Chester-White, Magee, Essex, other improved breeds; hogs slaughtered or sold for slaughter in 1874, in the several counties in the State 370-373

Number Sheep on hand, Merino, Cotswold, Leicester, South-down, other improved breeds; pounds of Wool; Sheep slaughtered or sold for slaughter, and number killed by Dogs in 1874; Dogs; stands of Bees; pounds of Honey and Beeswax; value of Farm Produce, Market Garden Produce, Products of the Orchard, Small Fruit, Products of the Herd, Products of the Dairy, and Products of the Forest, in the several counties in the State 374-377

Average yield, per acre, in bushels, of Spring Wheat, Winter Wheat, Corn, Rye, Oats, Barley, Buckwheat, Irish Potatoes, Sweet Potatoes, and Onions, tons of Tame Grass, and in gallons, of Sorghum; also, average number of pounds of wool per Sheep, in the several counties in the State 378-379

Number and character of Manufacturing Establishments, kinds of goods made, kinds of power used, average number of hands employed; tons Pig and Scrap Iron, cubic feet of Wood, pounds of Wool, pounds of Leather, bushels of Flax Seed, Wheat, Corn, and Barley consumed in manufactures in 1874, and value of goods made, in the several counties in the State 380-383

Statistics of Mines and Quarries for 1874, as returned by assessors, in the several counties in the State 384-385

Number and character of Colleges, Academies, Universities, and other Private Schools, with their location; Male and Female Instructors, Studnets, Volumes in Libraries, and amount of income 386-390

Number of acres of Land Assessed, the average value per acre, and aggregate valuation after Equalization; also, the aggregate value of Town Property, Railroad Property, and Personal Property, and total valuation of Taxable Property, and State Tax thereon, in each county for the year 1875 391-394

Number of Acres of Land Assessed, Reported Value per Acre, Equalized Value per Acre, Reported Value of Lands, Reported Value of Town Lots, Reported Value of Lands and Town Lots, and Equalized Value of Lands and Town Lots, Value of Personalty, Reported Total Valuation, Equalized Total Valuation, and State Tax thereon at two mills, in each County in the State, for the Years 1865 and 1875 395-400

Exhibit of aggregates of certain items in the preceding Tables, comparing them with Census of 1865 401-403

Population of the Incorporated Cities and Towns of Iowa, for the Years 1870, 1873, and 1875 404-406

Population of the several Counties in the State at each enumeration since the Organization of the Territory of Wisconsin 407-410

The several Railroads in the State, January 1, 1875, their Length, Assessed Valuation per Mile, and Aggregate Assessed Value, as fixed by the Executive Council, March 1, 1875 411

PAGE.

Statement of the Gross Earnings, Aggregate Gross Earnings, and Gross Earnings per Mile of the several Railroads in the State, in the Years 1873 and 1874 412-413

Statistics of School Districts, Schools, Teachers and their Compensation, Scholars and their Attendance, School-Houses and their Value, Apparatus, Libraries, Expenditures, and Private Schools in the several Counties of the State 414-417

Senators and Representatives from Iowa in the XLIVTH Congress 418

List of Federal Officers in Iowa, together with Time and Place of holding United States Circuit and District Courts 419

Official Register for the Year 1876, giving Names of all State Officers and their Deputies; the Judges of the Supreme, District, and Circuit Courts; the District-Attorneys, and Short-Hand Reporters 420-422

Public Institutions of the State, their Location, Names of Officers and Trustees, 423-428

List of Newspapers and Periodicals Published in the State, November 1st, 1875... 429-439

Alphabetical List of Post-Offices in the State, November 1st, 1875 440-449

List of County Auditors, Clerks of District and Circuit Courts, Treasurers, Recorders, and Sheriffs for 1876 450-453

List of Superintendents of Common Schools, County Surveyors, Coroners, and Members of Boards of Supervisors for 1876 454-456

Times of holding the District and Circuit Courts in the several Counties of the State for the Years 1876 and 1877 457-460

Abstract of Votes Cast at the General Election, October 12th, 1875, for the Offices of Governor and Lieutenant-Governor, by Counties and Townships 461-499

Abstract of Votes Cast at the General Election, October 12th, 1875, for the Offices of Judge of the Supreme Court and Superintendent of Public Instruction, by Congressional Districts and Counties 500-503

List of Members of the Sixteenth General Assembly 504-506

INTRODUCTORY REMARKS.

The census of 1875, the returns of which appear in the following pages, was the thirteenth taken under State authority, and the twenty-first enumeration of the inhabitants of what is now the State of Iowa, by whatever authority made. In 1836, under the provisions of the act of Congress organizing the territory of Wisconsin, Gov. Henry Dodge caused a census of the new territory to be taken. It showed a population of 10,531, found in the counties of "Demoine" and Dubuque, creations of the territorial legislature of Michigan, and comprising all the organized territory north of the northern line of the State of Missouri, from the Mississippi to the Pacific ocean. In 1838, the organic act for Iowa territory provided for an enumeration thereof. This also was taken under the direction of the Governor of the territory, Hon. Robert Lucas. The number of inhabitants ascertained was 22,859, more than double the previous census. The number of counties, by the erection, out of those formerly existing and additional territory, of Cedar, Clayton, Clinton, Henry, Jackson, Johnson, Jones, Lee, Linn, Louisa, Muscatine, Scott, Slaughter (now Washington), and Van Buren, had been increased to sixteen. From this period, the growth of the territory was a steady one, but not marked by the giant strides that characterized the first decade of the State, the annual increase ranging from 6,000 to about 11,000.

The federal census of 1840 showed a population of 43,114 in eighteen counties, Delaware and Jefferson reporting for the first time. Four years later, 75,152 people were found in twenty-one counties: Davis, Kishkekosh (now Monroe), and Wapello appearing in the returns. In 1846, another enumeration was taken preparatory to admission into the Union; showing a population of 97,588. The number of counties reported was now twenty-seven, Appanoose, Benton, Buchanan, Mahaska, Marion, and Polk being added to the list. On the 28th of December following, Iowa entered the Union. From this time forward, its growth, as if stimulated by the change in political relation, was for a dozen years rapid and even prodigious, until, in 1856, 519,055, and in 1859, 638,775, people were found within its borders; while settlement had penetrated into all but seven counties of the State.

The constitution of 1846 provided that within one year after its ratification, and within every subsequent term of two years for eight years, an enumeration of all the white inhabitants should be made. In accordance with this requirement, the First General Assembly provided for a census in each of the years 1847, 1849, and 1851, which were accordingly taken. Up to this time, there seems to have been no effort to gather statistics as to the details of population, or the productions and resources of the State, except for the federal census. A mere counting of the whole number of the people, and except in 1846 only the white people, was all that was attempted. In the Code of 1851 a step further was taken. This provided for a census in 1852, 1854, 1856, and every tenth year thereafter, and required that the return should show, the total number of males, of females, of voters, of militia, and of unnaturalized foreigners. It also created the Census Board to supervise the enumeration, and authorized it to provide for ascertaining and collecting any facts that might be deemed expedient.

The census of 1856 was based upon the plan of that of the United States of 1850. A complete nominal list of all the inhabitants, showing social condition, nativity, occupation, and color, and of the whites the sex, in addition to what the law required, besides an immense mass of information in regard to the productions of the State, were obtained. The law of the Code rendered it more practicable to secure this information, a duplicate of the assessors' blanks being returned to the office of the Secretary of State. This permitted a compilation under one supervision in the same manner as the federal census is collected. The General Assembly, in 1858, saw fit to change this mode, and establish that now in use, which provides that abstracts of the returns shall be prepared by the county auditors respectively and forwarded to the Secretary of State. The act making this change also enlarged the scope of the census, adding several other items to be inquired into, and lodging with the Census Board the same discretionary power as before. This law is the one in force at present.

The constitution of 1857 (the present) provided for an enumeration of all the white inhabitants of the State in 1859, 1863, 1865, 1867, 1869, 1875, and every tenth year thereafter. One of the amendments adopted in 1868 extended the requirement so as to include all inhabitants, regardless of color. The Fourteenth General Assembly provided for an additional census, to be taken in 1873. At each successive enumeration, except the last named, the Census Board has enlarged the field of inquiry until, in 1869, the items about which inquiry was made numbered seventy-six, and in that reported in these pages one hundred and eighty-nine.

The growth which had marked the first ten years of the State was not sustained during the next decade, notably the latter half of it. The financial catastrophe, followed by a failure of crops unparalleled in Iowa, had stopped the flood of immigration into the State; and, the war coming on, the population of the State increased very slowly until 1865, when it reached 754,699, or only 79,214 more than in 1860, a gain of less than 16,000 per annum.

The decade closing with this year, in its first half, witnessed a rapidity of growth surpassed only by that of the years from 1854 to 1858; immigration pouring into the State in vast numbers, and soon occupying all the government lands, and hundreds of thousands of other unimproved acres. The federal census of 1870 showed a population of 1,194,020, indicating an average annual increase, since 1865, greater than the entire growth during the preceding five years; if indeed, the large figures of the census of 1870 are to be relied upon, of which there is some question. Taking the ten years together, there has been an average annual augmentation of population, to the amount of 59,584.5.

The present population of the State, as shown in the following pages, is 1,350,544, an increase, over that of 1873, of 99,211, and over the reported figures of 1870 of 156,524. The population of the State, at each successive enumeration, is presented in full by counties, on pages 407–410 of this book.

The following table shows the varying rate of growth as given by the several enumerations taken under territorial and State authority.

Year of Census.	Population.	Increase from previous Census.	Average annual increase.	Average annual percentage of increase.
1836	10531	....	....	....
1838	22859	12328	6164	58.53
1844	75152	52293	8715	38.56
1846	97588	22436	11218	18.56
1847	116651	19063	19063	19.53
1849	152988	36337	18168	15.58
1851	204774	51786	25893	16.93
1852	230713	25939	25939	12.67
1854	326013	95300	47650	20.69
1856	519055	193042	96521	29.61
1859	638775	119720	39907	7.69
1863	701732	62957	15739	2.46
1865	754699	52967	26483	3.77
1867	902040	147341	73670	9.76
1869	1040819	138779	69389	7.69
1873	1251333	210514	52628	5.06
1875	1350544	99211	49605	3 96

Dividing the space of time embraced in the foregoing figures into four periods, we have the following showing:

Average annual increase during the territorial decade, 8706 or 82.67 per cent.

Average annual increase during first decade of the State.........................42147 or 43.19 per cent.

Average annual increase during period of nine years, 1856–1865.........................26183 or 5.04 per cent.

Average annual increase during decade 1865–1875.......59584 or 7.89 per cent.

The federal enumerations show as follows:

Year.	Population.	Average increase annually.	Average annual rate of increase.
1840	43114	....	......
1850	*192214	14910	34.58
1860	274913	48270	25.11
1870	*1194020	51911	7.96

In preparing the schedules for this census, the Executive Council was deeply impressed with the desirability and importance, in this last enumeration prior to the centennial of American independence, of obtaining such information as to the population, productions, and resources of the State, as would approximate the most closely practicable to absolute accuracy. It was at once seen that this could best be obtained by some plan of operations similar to that of the federal enumeration, and to the State enumeration of 1856. It was suggested to the Council that, while the law contemplated abstracts being prepared of each county's statistics by its auditor, yet this might be complied with in its intent if the assessors' returns were made in duplicate, and one copy sent up by the county auditor in lieu of an abstract. This would permit of the compilation of all the returns under one supervision, which is almost a necessity to the highest accuracy. The Council decided that, however desirable this mode of making the returns evidently was, there was not a sufficient appropriation at its disposal to warrant that body in procuring the clerical force necessary for the labor of arranging and collating the facts contained in the returns from some fifteen hundred townships, towns, and cities, spread over some forty thousand blanks. It was then determined to make the inquiry as thorough as seemed at all likely to be practicable, under the system heretofore prevalent. To this end schedules were prepared embracing—

1. Statistics of Population, with 44 items.
2. Statistics of the Farm, with 48 items.
3. Statistics of Forest and Hedge, with 3 items.
4. Statistics of the Orchard and Vine, with 18 items.
5. Statistics of the Herd, including the Dairy, with 25 items.
6. Miscellaneous statistics, with 3 items.
7. Statistics of Value of Products in 1874, with 7 items.
8. Statistics of Manufactures, with 18 items.
9. Statistics of Mines and Quarries, 9 items.
10. Statistics of Colleges, Seminaries, and other Private Schools, 14 items.

*These figures differ from those appearing in the body of this book, which were taken from first reports of the federal enumeration. The revised report of the census of 1870, which contains also a revision of the former enumerations, gives the footings as above. The error in the census of 1870 in the first report consisted of representing Linn county as having a population of 28,552, (as appears on page 409 of this book,) whereas the number actually ascertained was 31,080.

The Council was fully aware that these schedules presented a formidable array of inquiries to be answered, and largely added to the work of the assessors, already sufficiently great by reason of the duties more closely pertaining to their office in the assessment of property, this being the year for valuation of real estate; but the Council believed it to be imperative that an attempt should be made to get information no less exhaustive than complete answers to all the queries would convey; hence the blanks were prepared as indicated. These schedules contain most of the items included in those of the United States census of 1870; and many, notably in reference to agriculture, not to be found in those schedules. No attempt was made to gather statistics of individual wealth, as was done in the federal census. The officer taking the enumeration was also to assess property; and it was believed to be unwise to try to obtain any data for the census that might seem capable of being used for purposes of assessment. There is frequently much difficulty in getting information for a census for fear such use will be made of it; this difficulty is much greater where the assessor is the enumerating officer. Special care on the part of that officer is therefore necessary to prevent the two classes of information being confounded in the minds of persons visited; while the queries were themselves dissociated, as much as possible, from the idea of data for taxation.

Before another census of the State is taken, the Council believes it to be wise to provide that the enumeration should be made by some person other than the assessor, to be selected with a view to his adaptability to the work. The plan of township, town, and city enumerators, however, should be adhered to. There are none too many, now, for expeditious work; and the value of a census is hightened by every day saved in completing it. The enumeration of Great Britain is taken in one day. Such rapidity, although actually more desirable here than there because of the more frequent changes of residence in a new country and hence greater danger of omissions and duplications, is doubtless impracticable with us; but there would seem to be no reason why the enumeration of inhabitants could not be completed in a week. The data in regard to agriculture, manufactures, mines, private schools, &c., could be obtained at more leisure. Protraction here will not affect reliability. It is believed that with an enumerator in each township and town, two or three in each city of the second class, and one for each ward in a city of the first class, and an additional one for every considerable nationality in any neighborhood speaking a foreign tongue, the number of inhabitants and all the statistics of population could be obtained in so short a time as to insure a degree of accuracy far greater than can be hoped for under a census the taking of which is protracted through several months.

While considering the subject of future enumerations, a few more suggestions are deemed pertinent. The census of the United States is taken as of the first of June; that of this State is taken during the winter and spring months, and as of no particular date. Uniformity in the time of year in which these enumerations are taken is important to their statistical value. There is no perceptible advantage in taking our census in the early months of the year, except that derived in the matter of apparent economy from putting the work in the hands of the assessors, and having it done at the same time as the assessment of property. This saving, whatever it may be, is, as has already been intimated, at the expense of correctness. The amount of work required of the assessor in the odd-numbered years when real as well as personal property is to be valued, a list of the militia prepared, and in the larger cities a register of votes made, is enough for one person to do with any likelihood of accuracy. The conflicting character of the work of the assessor and that of the census-taker, before referred to, enhances the danger of inaccuracy. If the suggestion herein made, that the enumeration be taken by a person specially selected for the work, be adopted, the census can then be taken at the same time of year as that of the United States; which would have a tendency, the time being different from that of the assessment, to keep the queries used for the census from being confounded with those designed to obtain data for taxation.

A further improvement in future enumerations, it is believed, would be found in going back to the plan of duplicate returns made direct to the Secretary of State as in the first enumerations of the State. Compilation could then be under one supervision, which, intelligently collecting and grouping the facts direct from the enumerators' findings, could present results much more satisfactorily, and with far less liability to error, than when the officer making such computation has before him only abstracts of the returns, prepared by ninety-nine officers, whose ordinary duties are sufficient, in most of the counties, to occupy their whole time. Central supervision would materially facilitate the correction of errors appearing on the face of returns, because the enumerators could be reached, and explanations obtained, doubtless, in most cases. Most of the efforts of the Secretary of State to correct evident errors in the returns appearing in this book he has been compelled to abandon, because of being met with the answer, "It is just as the assessor re- "turned it." Further the Secretary could not go; and in some cases the county auditors had already tried and failed to get the matter set right. In one county, 910 acres of natural and 10 of planted timber are reported as within the limits of the town containing the county-seat. This density of forest within an incorporated town naturally excited curiosity, which of course was not at all allayed by the discovery that the corporation contained less than *three hundred acres*, all told! A letter to the county auditor elicited the information that the town assessor had taken it upon himself to include the entire independent district of which the town formed a part, and the smaller territorially, within the field of his labors. Whether the township assessor took the census for his own entire jurisdiction, regardless of the action of the town officer, as it was right he should, does not appear. If he did, the population of the county is of course reported too large; if he did not, the enumerations of the town and township, except as showing the aggregates in both, are worthless. Such evils as this, it is believed, could be reached and remedied under central supervision, invested with proper authority for the purpose, even to requiring new enumerations when apparently needed in any locality.

The attempt to obtain the nativity of the population was not so successful as could be desired; while that to procure a statement of the places of birth of the voters was measurably a failure. It was expected that there would be many whose nativities could not or would not be ascertained, and hence would not be reported. The deficient number would in that case appear in these pages as "Unknown." But, while these deficiencies are much greater than was looked for, there is, in the returns of a large number of the assessors, an actual surplus in the columns of nativities over the whole number of inhabitants; in other words, the number of persons whose birthplaces are reported exceeds that of the whole number of people. This is especially true in the statistics of voters, of which more presently.

Only fourteen counties reported all of whose columns of nativities just balanced the aggregates of population and voters; and this is true of the returns of nativities of every township, town, and ward in those counties. These were: Appanoose, Bremer, Cerro Gordo, Clinton, Dallas, Decatur, Jasper, Madison, Mills, Monona, O'Brien, Polk, Shelby, and Wapello. Besides, Cedar, Floyd, Grundy, Lucas, Page, Ringgold, Story, Webster, and Worth send returns whose columns of nativities of population balance, while those in regard to voters are more or less incorrect. In addition to these, the following counties have returns whose statistics of voters appear entirely correct, but whose nativities of population show either surplus or deficiency, viz.: Adair, surplus of one in Jackson township; Black Hawk, deficiency of three in second ward of Cedar Falls; Davis, 3 surplus in town of Bloomfield and 2 in Perry tp., while the nativities of 100 in Lick Creek tp., and 2 in Union tp., are unreported; Emmet, 7 surplus in High Lake, and 8 deficiency in Center and 3 in Peterson townships; Johnson, surplus of 648 in Iowa City, and 100 in Lucas tp., and deficiencies of 89 in Cedar, Hardin, Oxford, Penn, and Sharon tps.; Linn, 102 surplus in Buffalo township and town of Lisbon, and 2 deficiency in Grant township; Marshall, 1 surplus in first ward of Marshalltown, and 85 deficiency in Minerva, Eden, and Vienna townships; and Sioux, with deficiencies, in every township but Rock, Settler, and Sheridan, amounting in all to 276. The township of Union, Carroll county, made no return of nativities of population. Otherwise, the county is correct. The following counties report deficiencies, with no excess in any township: Calhoun, Mahaska, Muscatine (1 in Orono township), and Taylor (300 in Dallas township). Dubuque, Davenport, Des Moines, Keokuk, and Council Bluffs, in short all the larger cities except Burlington, are in this respect correctly returned, the nativities of all the inhabitants being fully reported. Accuracy in these respects, it is needless to say, is indicative of painstaking care by the assessor in the entire enumeration.

In the nativities of voters, some of the assessors seem to have included those of all the population. The column of surplus or deficiency, on pages 351-354 of this book, indicates this. Clayton county, it will be seen, with 5,272 voters, in all, reports nativities for 11,940; Winneshiek, with 4,117 voters, reports nativities for 10,652; Jackson, with 4,901, has birthplaces for 9,787; Boone reports nativities for 4058 more than its entire number of voters; etc.

The only explanation for this large surplus is the one, above suggested, that these figures in some of the townships really embrace the entire population.

These errors make the returns of nativities of voters therefore almost worthless; while those of population are comparatively unreliable. A nominal list of inhabitants offers the only trustworthy plan of obtaining this class of information correctly.

The general statistics of population and agriculture are believed to approximate correctness as closely as could be expected. They afford gratifying evidence of the growth of our State and the steady development of its resources. The returns of manufactures and mines are less satisfactory than could be desired: one would suppose that these statistics ought to be obtained with more ease than any other. Experience, both in our own and the federal census, fails to sustain this view. The Council has heard of more refusals to impart information on these topics than on all the others upon which the assessors sought it. Unfortunately, there is no authority under the law to compel unwilling persons to give such information. Hence it cannot be obtained, unless those best informed and most interested co-operate with the census-taker in preparing the data.

The majority of the Executive Council avail themselves of this opportunity to say that the work of supervising the taking of the census, compiling the immense mass of returns, arranging them in the perspicuous order in which they appear in the book, and preparing them for publication, has been done entirely under the personal supervision of the Secretary of State, who has been solicitous to make the published report, so far as the data at hand would permit, a complete mirror of the facts, concerning the State's population, wealth, and resources; and has spared no pains to this end. He has also caused to be prepared the very valuable lists and tables, not belonging to the Census, it is true, but of such great utility as fully to justify him in following and enlarging upon the practice which for years has assigned them a place in the Census Report.

C. C. CARPENTER,
JOSIAH T. YOUNG,
BUREN R. SHERMAN,
WILLIAM CHRISTY,
Executive Council.

NOTE.—Since the Errata was printed, some errors have been discovered in Table XIX: "School Statistics;" as follows:—The value of school-houses in Floyd county, on page 517, is given at $999,825, when it should have been $99,982.50. Hamilton county's school-houses, on same page, are valued at $401,135, instead of $40,135, the correct amount. On page 417, the blank line is placed opposite the counties of Muscatine, Osceola, Poweshiek, Ringgold, Story, Taylor, Union, and Van Buren respectively, when it should have been placed in each case one line below. This error makes the statistics on this page, of every county between Montgomery and Wapello in the alphabetical arrangement, appear to be opposite those of the county next below in each case. Bearing this in mind, the statistics in question will be readily traced.

CENSUS RETURNS.

1 *Showing the Population of the several Counties of Iowa for the Year 1875, by Townships, Towns, and Cities.*

ADAIR COUNTY.

Total population.	Names of townships, towns, and cities.	No. of dwelling houses.	Number of families.	White population.			Colored pop'lation			Nativity of inhabitants.				Between 5 and 21 years old.			No. births in 1874.	No. deaths in 1874.	No. of voters.	No. foreigners not naturalized.	No. of militia.
				Male.	Female.	Total.	Male.	Female.	Total.	No. born in Iowa.	No. born in U. S., but not in Iowa.	No. born in foreign countries.	Surplus or deficiency.	No. 5 years old and under 6.	No. 6 years old and under 16.	No. 16 years old and under 21.					
103	Eureka	24	24	55	48	103	......	......	......	25	69	9	......	4	18	14	4	......	29	......	20
416	Fontanelle, town of	96	94	216	200	416	......	......	......	139	268	9	......	21	79	18	22	4	107	1	81
347	Grand River	66	66	180	167	347	......	......	......	157	156	34	......	24	101	24	10	2	65	......	46
480	Greenfield, C. H.	95	95	249	231	480	......	......	......	126	335	19	......	32	105	30	22	8	125	......	107
273	Grove	50	50	139	134	273	......	......	......	297	152	24	......	16	82	9	13	6	56	2	44
590	Harrison	98	100	306	284	590	......	......	......	249	321	20	......	32	158	47	20	11	125	1	95
505	Jackson	83	87	291	214	505	......	......	......	216	246	44	1	30	132	47	32	8	110	5	83
682	Jefferson	129	129	378	304	682	......	......	......	217	397	68	......	23	158	78	19	1	165	5	100
977	Lincoln	178	184	537	440	977	......	......	......	26	663	88	......	44	225	64	33	10	231	6	197
215	Orient	39	39	118	97	215	......	......	......	51	161	3	......	12	44	26	7	3	59	......	48
222	Prussia	41	41	112	110	222	......	......	......	65	113	44	......	11	65	17	8	2	46	8	33
454	Richland	85	85	245	209	454	......	......	......	168	245	41	......	27	106	41	24	10	109	......	65
282	Summerset	65	65	159	123	282	......	......	......	99	148	35	......	13	57	9	13	3	75	......	57
186	Summit	37	37	91	95	186	......	......	......	31	118	37	......	11	44	14	5	3	43	......	41
290	Union	60	60	153	137	290	......	......	......	120	143	27	......	24	51	30	7	10	58	1	38
307	Walnut	62	62	163	144	307	......	......	......	79	199	29	......	17	85	32	14	6	60	1	53
716	Washington	127	127	379	337	716	......	......	......	267	412	37	......	36	173	67	34	7	153	2	136
7045	Total	1335	1345	3771	3274	7045	......	......	......	2332	4146	568	1	377	1683	567	287	94	1616	32	1244

ADAMS COUNTY.

Total population.	NAMES OF TOWNSHIPS, TOWNS, AND CITIES.	No. of dwelling houses.	Number of families.	WHITE POPULATION. Male.	Female.	Total.	COLORED POP'LATION. Male.	Female.	Total.	NATIVITY OF INHABITANTS. No. born in Iowa.	No. born in U. S., but not in Iowa.	No. born in foreign countries.	Surplus or deficiency.	BETWEEN 5 AND 21 YEARS OLD. No. 5 years old and under 6.	No. 6 years old and under 16.	No. 16 years old and under 21.	No. births in 1874.	No. deaths in 1874.	No. of voters.	No. foreigners not naturalized.	No. of militia.
534	Carl	98	98	274	260	534	......	......	......	228	288	18	......	32	161	41	10	3	110	......	93
333	Colony	68	69	182	148	330	2	1	3	108	181	40	— 4	8	67	32	13	1	78	......	62
1055	Corning, town of, C. H.	232	232	434	517	1011	17	27	44	314	682	82	23	36	223	84	35	8	234	......	173
824	Douglas	134	150	445	379	824	......	......	......	294	409	112	— 9	21	186	45	44	12	193	29	148
377	Grant	77	77	207	170	377	......	......	......	142	225	15	5	10	80	21	18	2	83	1	52
722	Jasper	144	144	384	338	722	......	......	......	274	395	51	— 2	28	184	49	30	7	149	1	113
470	Lincoln	84	84	243	227	470	......	......	......	140	256	71	— 3	18	116	36	12	6	109	4	87
304	Mercer	60	60	170	134	304	......	......	......	81	189	32	— 2	13	67	22	15	2	76	......	65
806	Nodaway	143	143	405	392	797	6	3	9	297	455	55	1	43	199	86	39	7	170	5	133
482	Prescott	88	88	266	216	482	......	......	......	134	359	86	97	16	88	37	27	4	125	8	93
552	Quincy, exc. of towns	97	97	273	279	552	......	......	......	195	317	12	— 28	23	99	16	21	11	100	......	77
265	Quincy, town of	71	71	127	138	265	......	......	......	82	177	6	......	7	52	20	8	3	60	1	20
360	Union	62	63	201	159	360	......	......	......	120	235	6	1	19	83	33	18	5	77	6	60
748	Washington	154	154	379	369	748	......	......	......	323	405	20	......	19	176	48	29	7	163	1	107
7832	Total	1512	1530	3990	3726	7776	25	31	56	27[illegible]2	4573	606	......	303	1781	570	319	78	1727	56	1283

ALLAMAKEE COUNTY.

Total population.	NAMES OF TOWNSHIPS, TOWNS, AND CITIES.	No. of dwelling houses.	Number of families.	WHITE POPULATION. Male.	Female.	Total.	COLORED POP'LATION. Male.	Female.	Total.	NATIVITY OF INHABITANTS. No. born in Iowa.	No. born in U. S., but not in Iowa.	No. born in foreign countries.	Surplus or deficiency.	BETWEEN 5 AND 21 YEARS OLD. No. 5 years old and under 6.	No. 6 years old and under 16.	No. 16 years old and under 21.	No. births in 1874.	No. deaths in 1874.	No. of voters.	No. foreigners not naturalized.	No. of militia.
1184	Center	198	198	616	568	1184	......	......	......	525	69	293	—297	72	332	116	46	15	194	54	137
492	Fairview	94	94	255	237	492	......	......	......	221	133	114	— 24	9	150	51	7	......	113	......	71
846	Franklin	162	162	442	404	846	......	......	......	418	331	92	— 5	28	230	98	26	14	174	3	119
751	French Creek	118	118	398	353	751	......	......	......	355	132	215	— 49	12	230	101	28	11	127	18	63
531	Hanover	96	96	287	244	531	......	......	......	322	28	181	......	58	146	41	9	5	88	10	55
683	Iowa	132	132	356	327	683	......	......	......	221	277	179	— 6	22	153	52	31	14	157	13	103
971	Jefferson	170	170	509	462	971	......	......	......	493	293	163	— 22	172	311	88	34	5	193	1	101
1250	Lafayette	216	216	668	582	1250	......	......	......	615	213	442	20	40	331	118	47	15	221	22	181
864	Lansing, exc. of city	145	145	466	398	864	......	......	......	432	139	293	......	67	236	76	33	14	158	19	105

786	Linton	139	139	400	386	786	......	......	......	378	232	231	55	40	247	92	35	17	148	21	86
1015	Ludlow	177	177	529	486	1015	......	......	......	432	301	272	— 10	39	236	2	35	18	161	32	180
1004	Makee, exc town of Waukon	160	160	541	462	1003	1	......	1	455	179	370	— 6	51	297	104	29	4	190	14	73
1120	Paint Creek	192	192	601	519	1120	......	......	......	525	126	472	3	33	330	131	27	15	197	44	149
819	Post, exc. town of Postville	155	155	399	420	819	......	......	......	357	403	90	31	29	204	101	16	3	182	1	106
712	Postville, town of	155	155	342	370	712	......	......	......	294	311	107	......	31	127	47	26	6	166	9	96
932	Taylor	164	164	445	487	932	......	......	......	473	148	207	—104	33	302	121	11	4	189	3	87
405	Union City	71	71	214	191	405	......	......	......	220	54	128	— 3	18	85	25	21	3	72	......	79
854	Union Prairie	142	142	457	397	854	......	......	......	410	180	226	— 38	45	264	112	19	4	163	3	78
860	Waterloo	149	149	442	410	852	4	4	8	358	80	......	—422	38	163	53	41	14	111	......	105
809	Waukon, town of, C. H.	167	167	403	406	809	......	......	......	293	433	77	— 6	23	166	72	23	12	197	1	92
16888	Total	3002	3002	8770	8109	16879	5	4	9	7797	4062	4152		860	4540	1601	544	193	3201	268	2026
	Lansing, city of—																				
377	" First Ward	60	60	187	189	376	1	......	1	131	120	126	......	15	58	42	16	6	62	21	48
685	" Second Ward	98	98	354	331	685	......	......	......	239	196	249	— 1	30	118	48	16	9	148	21	122
936	" Third Ward	138	138	471	465	936	......	......	......	374	245	325	8	34	197	77	34	6	198	15	133
282	" Fourth Ward	41	41	147	135	282	......	......	......	113	62	107	......	22	49	14	8	1	44	4	37
2280	Total of city	337	337	1159	1120	2279	1		1	857	623	807		101	422	181	74	22	452	61	340
19168	Total of county	3339	3339	9929	9229	19158	6	4	10	8654	4685	4959		961	4962	1782	618	215	3653	329	2366

APPANOOSE COUNTY.

708	Bellair	......	130	366	341	707	1	......	1	384	309	15	......	31	185	61	22	9	143	......	85
1414	Caldwell	......	244	749	665	1414	......	......	......	665	712	37	......	62	386	128	57	32	298	1	250
1220	Center, exc. town of Centerville	......	219	639	574	1213	4	3	7	561	587	72	......	47	260	108	51	29	254	9	145
1226	Centerville, town of, C. H.	......	229	603	613	1216	2	8	10	493	686	47	......	42	240	90	44	10	312	......	201
885	Chariton	......	170	441	444	885	......	......	......	434	445	6	......	44	231	95	32	9	186	1	134
540	Douglas	......	102	274	266	540	......	......	......	298	242	......	......	25	142	48	19	15	114	......	81
851	Franklin	......	155	438	413	851	......	......	......	394	435	22	......	28	235	80	23	12	180	1	124
960	Independence	......	170	486	474	960	......	......	......	538	399	23	......	36	256	103	38	15	202	......	118
916	Johns	......	165	486	429	915	1	......	1	436	472	8	......	33	257	87	33	15	190	......	169
596	Lincoln	......	94	321	275	596	......	......	......	289	300	7	......	31	181	68	22	7	131	1	96
753	Moulton, town of	......	179	387	365	752	1	......	1	298	451	4	......	23	163	59	34	13	164	......	141
1093	Pleasant	......	215	555	538	1093	......	......	......	521	543	29	......	41	288	95	30	23	229	3	170
662	Sharon	......	113	358	304	662	......	......	......	367	291	4	......	30	182	87	29	14	125	......	97
958	Taylor	......	177	492	460	952	2	4	6	500	442	16	......	49	257	83	36	19	191	1	101
914	Udell	......	163	462	452	914	......	......	......	515	388	11	......	31	244	119	34	13	185	......	103
619	Union	......	118	319	300	619	......	......	......	340	279	......	......	28	169	60	23	10	136	......	79
772	Walnut	......	134	397	375	772	......	......	......	378	389	5	......	39	183	96	26	16	162	3	118

APPANOOSE COUNTY.—Continued.

Total Population.	Names of Townships, Towns, and Cities.	No. of dwelling houses.	Number of families.	White Population. Male.	White Population. Female.	White Population. Total.	Colored Pop'lation. Male.	Colored Pop'lation. Female.	Colored Pop'lation. Total.	Nativity of Inhabitants. No. born in Iowa.	No. born in U. S., but not in Iowa.	No. born in foreign countries.	Surplus or deficiency.	Between 5 and 21 years old. No. 5 years old and under 6.	No. 6 years old and under 16.	No. 16 years old and under 21.	No. births in 1874.	No deaths in 1874.	No. of voters.	No. foreigners not naturalized.	No. of militia.
1257	Washington, exc. town of Moulton	....	220	637	620	1257	......	......	......	650	578	29	....	50	358	124	50	21	240	2	192
1061	Wells	....	189	557	502	1059	2	......	2	488	562	11	....	40	262	91	47	22	237	4	172
17405	Total	....	3186	8967	8410	17377	13	15	28	8549	8510	346	....	710	4479	1692	650	304	3679	26	2576

AUDUBON COUNTY.

Total Population.	Names of Townships, Towns, and Cities.	No. of dwelling houses.	Number of families.	White Male.	White Female.	White Total.	Colored Male.	Colored Female.	Colored Total.	No. born in Iowa.	No. born in U. S., but not in Iowa.	No. born in foreign countries.	Surplus or deficiency.	No. 5 years old and under 6.	No. 6 years old and under 16.	No. 16 years old and under 21.	No. births in 1874.	No deaths in 1874.	No. of voters.	No. foreigners not naturalized.	No. of militia.
251	Audubon	....	49	128	123	251	......	......	......	107	128	8	— 8	62	65	14	16	4	54	......	46
96	Douglas	....	18	53	43	96	......	......	......	59	52	9	24	13	22	10	4	......	17	......	13
697	Exira, C. H.	....	142	391	306	697	......	......	......	294	351	50	— 2	33	177	55	19	15	171	......	125
145	Greeley	....	35	68	77	145	......	......	......	52	104	10	21	9	36	6	3	1	35	......	31
259	Hamlin	....	45	141	118	259	......	......	......	115	125	32	13	13	77	20	7	3	58	4	46
151	Leroy	....	30	78	73	151	......	......	......	53	97	11	10	8	28	15	11	3	35	2	24
62	Melville	....	13	33	29	62	......	......	......	19	38	5	....	2	17	6	6	1	11	1	10
491	Oakfield	....	100	256	235	491	......	......	......	173	301	17	....	66	64	27	17	9	96	62	36
218	Viola	....	43	120	98	218	......	......	......	82	104	32	....	11	51	14	9	3	50	......	23
2370	Total	....	475	1268	1102	2370	......	......	......	954	1300	174	....	217	535	167	92	39	527	69	354

BENTON COUNTY.

Total Population.	Names of Townships, Towns, and Cities.	No. of dwelling houses.	Number of families.	White Male.	White Female.	White Total.	Colored Male.	Colored Female.	Colored Total.	No. born in Iowa.	No. born in U. S., but not in Iowa.	No. born in foreign countries.	Surplus or deficiency.	No. 5 years old and under 6.	No. 6 years old and under 16.	No. 16 years old and under 21.	No. births in 1874.	No deaths in 1874.	No. of voters.	No. foreigners not naturalized.	No. of militia.
1645	Belle Plain, town of	302	302	786	856	1642	2	1	3	513	784	274	— 74	98	313	108	45	7	338	......	291
679	Benton	123	123	359	320	679	......	......	......	348	309	17	— 5	33	203	73	23	15	144	1	91
768	Big Grove	150	150	414	354	768	......	......	......	261	402	104	— 1	24	166	73	29	13	183	......	144

714	Blairstown, town of	150	150	361	353	714	......	......	......	218	430	37	— 29	32	155	47	19	12	191	......	127
651	Bruce	122	122	343	308	651	......	......	......	252	254	75	— 70	38	147	74	22	11	146	8	120
978	Canton, exc of Shellsburg	186	186	512	466	978	......	......	......	465	450	52	— 11	47	239	80	38	2	216	9	143
1109	Cedar	200	200	580	528	1108	1	......	1	463	559	87	......	40	288	93	37	10	259	7	172
782	Eden	153	153	419	363	782	......	......	......	311	360	102	— 9	33	196	61	30	6	176	2	148
846	Eldorado	158	158	456	390	846	......	......	......	293	262	285	— 6	15	180	79	37	1	141	......	97
1161	Florence	208	208	616	545	1161	......	......	......	446	282	340	— 93	63	304	114	46	14	210	......	150
751	Fremont	129	129	397	354	751	......	......	......	344	154	222	— 31	78	166	63	27	8	100	19	94
540	Harrison	101	101	291	249	540	......	......	......	250	280	10	......	10	151	65	16	8	128	......	97
728	Homer	134	134	387	340	727	1	......	1	248	256	220	— 4	40	192	38	27	7	119	37	68
1152	Iowa, exc. of Belle Plaine	217	217	590	562	1152	......	......	......	505	429	219	1	43	324	102	41	10	225	17	195
988	Jackson	199	199	532	456	988	......	......	......	396	543	58	9	32	238	91	41	7	219	12	117
836	Kane	148	148	443	393	836	......	......	......	269	257	288	— 22	43	202	......	26	17	150	54	92
1082	Leroy, exc. of Blairstown	198	198	580	502	1082	......	......	......	437	416	229	......	30	302	100	38	16	202	20	163
732	Monroe	124	124	393	339	732	......	......	......	278	379	71	— 4	141	203	75	10	11	144	7	104
1279	Polk	269	269	625	654	1279	......	......	......	668	645	86	120	65	362	141	45	11	299	10	212
554	Shellsburg, town of	115	115	287	267	554	......	......	......	228	296	37	13	22	148	37	13	12	137	......	98
817	St. Clair	133	133	442	375	817	......	......	......	334	269	204	— 10	37	232	71	36	9	149	29	79
797	Taylor, exc. of Vinton	153	153	417	380	797	......	......	......	307	431	32	— 27	36	158	84	32	7	171	......	114
829	Union	140	140	468	361	829	......	......	......	215	229	262	—123	56	227	57	26	5	144	6	82
20418	Total	3812	3812	10698	9715	20413	4	1	5	8049	8576	3311		1056	5096	1726	704	219	4191	238	2998
	Vinton, city of, C. H.																				
738	" First Ward	150	150	357	372	729	4	5	9	222	400	17	— 99	15	166	48	19	7	180	1	125
635	" Second Ward	131	131	304	326	630	4	1	5	231	373	39	8	40	105	43	21	4	160	4	93
525	" Third Ward	98	98	269	256	525	......	......	......	145	356	24	......	15	120	33	18	5	131	......	71
491	" Fourth Ward	104	104	237	254	491	......	......	......	195	284	12	......	11	111	50	14	8	108	1	68
2389	Total of city	483	483	1167	1208	2375	8	6	14	793	1413	92		81	502	174	72	24	579	6	357
22807	Total of county	4295	4295	11865	10923	22788	12	7	19	8842	9989	3403		1137	5598	1900	776	243	4770	244	3355

BLACK HAWK COUNTY.

763	Barclay	140	140	403	360	763	......	......	......	301	320	142	......	18	197	78	22	7	157	13	124
735	Bennington	121	121	409	326	735	......	......	......	256	334	145	......	29	215	47	34	8	131	15	111
693	Big Creek, exc. town of La Porte	125	125	385	308	693	......	......	......	227	367	99	......	16	171	75	22	11	168	5	99
763	Black Hawk	140	140	413	350	763	......	......	......	258	353	152	......	33	190	72	29	5	166	11	123
635	Cedar	102	102	339	296	635	......	......	......	269	242	124	......	21	143	79	24	6	119	14	97
1224	Cedar Falls, exc. city of Cedar Falls	192	192	639	584	1223	1	......	1	477	590	157	......	43	457	100	24	8	206	17	127
639	Eagle	108	108	330	309	639	......	......	......	223	239	177	......	28	142	51	33	3	116	24	87
883	East Waterloo, exc. city of Waterloo	163	169	476	407	883	......	......	......	289	483	111	......	27	222	98	19	10	190	16	140
830	Fox	140	140	418	412	830	......	......	......	311	304	215	......	27	237	60	26	4	152	5	78

BLACK HAWK COUNTY.—CONTINUED.

Total population.	NAMES OF TOWNSHIPS, TOWNS, AND CITIES.	No. of dwelling houses.	Number of families.	WHITE POPULATION. Male.	Female.	Total.	COLORED POP'LATION Male.	Female.	Total.	NATIVITY OF INHABITANTS. No. born in Iowa.	No. born in U. S., but not in Iowa.	No. born in foreign countries.	Surplus or deficiency.	BETWEEN 5 AND 21 YEARS OLD. No. 5 years old and under 6	No. 6 years old and under 16.	No. 16 years old and under 21.	No. births in 1874.	No. deaths in 1874.	No. of voters.	No. foreigners not naturalized.	No. of militia.
715	La Porte, town of	172	172	374	341	715	......	......	......	223	421	71	....	35	158	50	18	6	154	4	112
947	Lester	163	163	501	446	947	......	......	......	388	400	159	....	50	279	80	33	6	192	17	96
569	Lincoln	110	110	333	235	568	1	......	1	163	300	106	....	14	128	37	32	6	116	17	90
910	Mt. Vernon	162	162	472	438	910	......	......	......	381	369	160	....	38	214	61	13	4	199	6	121
784	Orange	1[illegible]8	138	431	353	784	......	......	......	292	453	39	....	38	1[illegible]4	74	32	16	175	......	115
1043	Poyner	185	185	531	512	1043	......	......	......	365	519	159	....	51	285	97	36	11	203	15	113
680	Spring Creek	125	125	359	321	680	......	......	......	340	310	30	....	28	202	68	17	7	146	......	61
431	Union	90	90	205	222	427	3	1	4	165	227	39	....	25	83	26	9	3	90	......	65
445	Washington	95	95	239	206	445	......	......	......	156	253	36	....	16	113	46	13	3	118	1	81
446	Waterloo, exc. city of Waterloo	79	79	222	224	446	......	......	......	185	201	57	....	15	110	50	12	6	100	6	55
14135	Total	2550	2556	7479	6650	14129	5	1	6	5269	6688	2178		552	3730	1849	448	130	2908	186	1895
	Cedar Falls, city of—																				
720	First Ward	140	140	354	366	720	......	......	......	199	323	198	....	31	129	59	32	2	143	44	103
823	Second Ward	160	160	387	435	822	......	1	1	298	342	180	— 3	35	215	69	28	8	172	17	113
847	Third Ward	155	155	419	428	847	......	......	......	271	435	141	....	46	210	61	28	3	183	13	119
880	Fourth Ward	168	168	417	460	877	2	1	3	284	454	142	....	48	205	100	35	10	182	8	108
3270	Total of city	623	623	1577	1689	3266	2	2	4	1052	1554	661		160	759	289	123	23	680	82	443
	Waterloo, city of, C. H.																				
1303	First Ward	245	245	640	658	1298	4	1	5	440	681	182	....	61	295	115	37	20	291	12	156
1208	Second Ward	230	230	609	599	1208	......	......	......	599	659	150	....	41	295	1[illegible]7	49	28	275	14	173
1721	Third Ward	324	324	900	821	1721	......	......	......	489	897	335	....	61	389	162	74	19	431	25	156
1276	Fourth Ward	254	254	604	671	1275	1	......	1	419	672	185	....	35	256	119	70	20	292	10	87
5508	Total of city	1053	1053	2753	2749	5502	5	1	6	1747	2909	852		198	1235	523	230	87	1289	61	572
22913	Total of county	4226	4232	11809	11088	22897	12	4	16	8068	11151	3691		910	5724	2061	801	240	4877	329	2910

BOONE COUNTY.

468	Amaqua	92	92	243	225	468	......	......	......	148	228	71	— 21	24	109	37	5	1	106	6	88
195	Beaver	34	34	103	92	195	......	......	......	53	150	32	40	9	3	8	6	......	41	......	32
1532	Boonsboro, town of, C. H.	318	318	743	785	1528	2	2	4	613	817	169	67	71	351	129	73	24	328	12	221
808	Cass	72	72	439	369	808	......	......	......	405	328	41	— 34	84	198	81	31	3	170	2	11
560	Colfax	96	96	295	265	560	......	......	......	167	348	155	110	12	117	38	21	8	115	2	91
1380	Des Moines, exc. of Boone and Boonsboro,	261	261	716	664	1380	......	......	......	534	508	338	......	63	405	124	50	20	254	43	134
1206	Dodge	234	236	615	591	1206	......	......	......	523	509	168	— 6	47	342	81	31	25	236	......	167
891	Douglas	167	167	445	446	891	......	......	......	397	342	153	1	242	95	......	20	70	146	15	109
671	Garden	134	134	364	307	671	......	......	......	236	271	169	5	16	152	47	34	14	142	12	103
411	Grant	85	85	229	182	411	......	......	......	124	75	190	— 22	27	90	24	30	20	65	29	65
441	Harrison	79	79	234	207	441	......	......	......	171	186	74	— 10	15	134	29	18	5	74	12	57
799	Jackson	138	138	417	382	799	......	......	......	277	551	92	121	36	170	88	26	8	162	11	91
2135	Marcy	397	397	1146	989	2135	......	......	......	738	714	661	— 22	80	500	172	99	48	369	264	263
493	Peoples	97	97	279	214	493	......	......	......	262	363	53	185	30	159	55	27	17	154	4	99
697	Pilot Mound	132	132	372	325	697	......	......	......	176	169	157	—195	37	125	47	18	5	89	18	81
445	Union	79	79	247	198	445	......	......	......	151	271	18	+ 2	14	102	43	18	4	107	......	100
733	Worth	140	140	360	373	733	......	......	......	355	318	60	......	32	185	66	33	8	154	37	125
1154	Yell	221	221	595	559	1154	......	......	......	461	550	144	1	56	267	91	48	17	265	16	199
15019	Total	2776	2778	7842	7173	15025	2	2	4	5791	6701	2745	......	898	3545	1170	588	297	2977	483	2135
	Boone, city of																				
502	" First ward	101	101	251	244	495	5	2	7	159	233	110	......	21	102	31	17	1	109	1	65
758	" Second ward	175	175	375	383	758	......	......	......	192	469	97	......	21	107	25	14	1	181	2	76
674	" Third ward	152	152	331	343	674	......	......	......	188	381	107	2	231	39	39	21	2	145	......	69
398	" Fourth ward	70	70	213	185	398	......	......	......	87	147	64	—100	11	75	14	4	2	103	2	40
2332	Total of city	498	498	1170	1155	2325	5	2	7	626	1230	378	......	287	323	109	56	6	538	5	250
17351	Total of county	3274	3276	9012	8328	17340	7	4	11	6417	7931	3123	......	1185	3868	1279	644	303	3515	488	2385

BREMER COUNTY.

518	Dayton	133	133	276	242	518	......	......	......	190	149	179	......	22	129	31	48	9	85	46	31
694	Douglas	139	141	350	344	694	......	......	......	217	297	180	......	24	183	58	15	2	132	30	129
709	Franklin	137	137	365	344	709	......	......	......	261	261	184	......	30	174	50	37	15	131	19	87
440	Frederika	86	87	236	204	440	......	......	......	154	220	66	......	17	117	43	21	5	86	33	48
829	Fremont	147	147	440	388	828	1	......	1	301	352	276	......	48	244	77	37	7	135	48	109
1013	Jackson	195	195	500	506	1006	4	3	7	385	568	60	......	49	259	96	27	6	237	1	148
862	Jefferson	161	161	444	418	862	......	......	......	358	305	199	......	32	225	56	30	8	161	42	102
745	La Fayette	134	134	400	345	745	......	......	......	313	364	68	......	129	61	1	28	8	166	14	104
379	Le Roy	67	67	209	170	379	......	......	......	163	125	91	......	7	130	44	5	3	71	7	26
900	Maxfield	162	162	490	410	900	......	......	......	341	139	420	......	34	244	63	37	12	116	58	67

BREMER COUNTY—Continued.

Total population.	Names of townships, towns, and cities.	No. of dwelling houses.	Number of families.	White population. Male.	White population. Female.	White population. Total	Colored pop'lation. Male.	Colored pop'lation. Female.	Colored pop'lation. Total.	Nativity of inhabitants. No. born in Iowa.	Nativity of inhabitants. No. born in U. S., but not in Iowa.	Nativity of inhabitants. No. born in foreign countries.	Nativity of inhabitants. Surplus or deficiency.	Between 5 and 21 years old. No. 5 years old and under 6.	Between 5 and 21 years old. No. 6 years old and under 16.	Between 5 and 21 years old. No. 16 years old and under 21.	No. births in 1874.	No. deaths in 1874.	No. of voters.	No. foreigners not naturalized.	No. of militia.
1172	Polk	230	233	612	557	1169	2	1	3	381	738	53	....	47	296	82	37	10	285	6	162
704	Sumner	133	133	388	316	704	......	......	......	234	350	120	....	18	157	67	22	4	163	11	95
1002	Warren	170	170	516	486	1002	......	......	......	320	364	318	....	39	313	96	31	16	148	38	91
848	Washington, exc. of Waverly	153	153	435	413	848	......	......	......	315	455	78	....	24	236	85	29	11	193	......	106
10815	Total	2047	2053	5661	5143	10804	7	4	11	3933	4590	2292	....	520	2768	849	404	116	2109	353	1305
	Waverly, city of, C. H.																				
448	" First ward	88	88	229	219	448	......	......	......	135	233	80	....	16	97	48	14	2	95	7	39
452	" Second ward	104	104	225	227	452	......	......	......	157	255	40	....	11	110	29	6	4	108	3	34
590	" Third ward	128	128	286	304	590	......	......	......	180	375	35	....	18	129	53	8	......	134	1	28
569	" Fourth ward	110	110	287	282	569	......	......	......	167	316	86	....	21	120	54	14	3	142	3	56
346	" Fifth ward	62	62	165	171	336	3	7	10	115	189	42	....	29	102	31	6	1	68	3	9
2405	Total of city	492	492	1192	1203	2395	3	7	10	754	1368	283	....	95	558	215	48	10	547	17	166
13220	Total of county	2539	2545	6853	6346	13199	10	11	21	4687	5958	2575	....	615	3326	1064	452	126	2656	370	1471

BUCHANAN COUNTY.

Total population.	Names of townships, towns, and cities.	No. of dwelling houses.	Number of families.	White population. Male.	White population. Female.	White population. Total	Colored pop'lation. Male.	Colored pop'lation. Female.	Colored pop'lation. Total.	Nativity of inhabitants. No. born in Iowa.	Nativity of inhabitants. No. born in U. S., but not in Iowa.	Nativity of inhabitants. No. born in foreign countries.	Nativity of inhabitants. Surplus or deficiency.	Between 5 and 21 years old. No. 5 years old and under 6.	Between 5 and 21 years old. No. 6 years old and under 16.	Between 5 and 21 years old. No. 16 years old and under 21.	No. births in 1874.	No. deaths in 1874.	No. of voters.	No. foreigners not naturalized.	No. of militia.
602	Buffalo	117	117	315	286	601	1	......	1	199	320	83	....	31	140	59	20	4	128	14	78
996	Byron	221	221	593	402	995	1	......	1	389	553	121	67	39	288	96	37	11	244	6	142
576	Cono	111	111	320	256	576	......	......	......	235	268	71	— 2	46	147	46	18	3	123	......	74
1075	Fairbank	139	139	570	505	1075	......	......	......	484	464	149	22	59	280	99	25	10	228	......	124
641	Fremont	117	117	332	309	641	......	......	......	212	370	69	10	34	155	51	18	6	138	9	100
901	Hazleton	149	149	474	427	901	......	......	......	395	409	97	....	85	70	60	18	7	208	2	118
775	Homer	136	136	398	377	775	......	......	......	285	393	97	....	36	158	84	38	9	168	......	102
994	Jefferson	194	194	523	471	994	......	......	......	398	462	122	— 12	49	251	56	32	15	228	11	142
1217	Liberty	234	234	627	590	1217	......	......	......	524	164	83	—446	43	297	111	29	9	280	7	159

612	Madison	122	122	318	294	612	......	......	......	253	283	60	— 16	16	151	78	6	5	131	1	68
695	Middlefield	103	102	379	316	695	......	......	......	262	298	138	3	23	184	78	27	9	155	6	115
909	Newton	154	154	454	455	909	......	......	......	491	264	158	4	47	274	113	33	14	170	5	106
1525	Perry	296	297	757	767	1524	1	......	1	500	812	209	— 4	46	374	114	49	16	345	24	245
562	Sumner	105	105	284	278	562	......	......	......	189	303	6	— 64	88	34	60	3	1	101	......	....
1218	Washington, exc. of Independence	231	228	647	571	1218	......	......	......	478	516	224	....	44	327	136	34	7	255	......	108
593	Westburg	101	101	319	274	593	......	......	......	195	318	80	....	13	166	51	25	3	130	4	98
13891	Total	2530	2527	7310	6578	13888	3	......	3	5489	6197	1767	....	699	3296	1292	412	129	3031	88	1779
	Independence, city of, C. H.																				
1060	" First ward	218	218	530	522	1052	5	3	8	380	512	169	1	107	135	44	43	8	262	18	163
597	" Second ward	122	122	298	299	597	......	......	......	182	289	126	....	35	124	41	21	4	149	2	94
666	" Third ward	129	129	331	335	666	......	......	......	181	431	54	....	137	54	....	23	7	169	......	88
757	" Fourth ward	165	165	359	398	757	......	......	......	261	393	103	....	60	138	49	24	5	194	......	93
344	" Fifth ward	70	70	161	183	344	......	......	......	104	195	45	....	20	62	30	12	2	85	......	50
3424	Total of city	704	704	1679	1737	3416	5	3	8	1108	1820	497	....	359	513	164	123	26	859	20	438
17315	Total of county	3234	3231	8989	8315	17304	8	3	11	6597	8017	2264	....	1058	3809	1456	535	155	3890	108	2217

BUENA VISTA COUNTY.

270	Barnes	50	50	147	123	270	......	......	......	99	52	119	....	11	52	19	10	7	59	4	40
68	Brooks	16	13	33	35	68	......	......	......	17	37	14	....	4	19	6	4	1	15	......	12
239	Coon	56	56	117	122	239	......	......	......	70	136	33	....	10	67	25	7	1	55	......	34
265	Elk	55	55	148	117	265	......	......	......	92	116	57	....	13	61	16	17	1	52	29	45
91	Fairfield	22	24	50	41	91	......	......	......	22	20	49	....	1	16	6	5		24	3	19
115	Grant	27	27	63	52	115	......	......	......	36	55	24	....	4	29	4	4	......	27	2	7
275	Lee—Sioux Rapids, C. H.	56	56	149	126	275	......	......	......	82	142	51	....	9	57	25	5	1	73	......	57
90	Lincoln	16	16	51	39	90	......	......	......	24	46	20	....	4	23	10	5	......	20	......	9
233	Maple Valley	53	53	126	107	233	......	......	......	83	103	47	....	6	60	20	11	3	48	2	34
432	Newell	96	93	230	202	432	......	......	......	114	244	74	....	32	95	21	13	3	99	14	62
410	Nokomis	91	91	221	189	410	......	......	......	96	147	176	9	20	82	32	10	5	72	35	54
83	Poland	19	19	48	35	83	......	......	......	15	60	8	....	1	17	1	4	......	21	1	14
169	Providence	27	27	85	84	169	......	......	......	48	93	28	....	10	53	22	9	2	33	2	19
105	Scott	30	30	51	54	105	......	......	......	39	55	11	....	2	18	....	3	......	26	......	20
237	Storm Lake, exc. of town	54	54	130	107	237	......	......	......	68	137	32	....	16	50	10	11	3	59	1	36
479	Storm Lake, town of	70	70	253	226	479	......	......	......	106	317	56	....	17	94	17	23	7	134	3	101
3561	Total	738	734	1902	1659	3561	......	......	......	1011	1760	799	....	160	793	234	141	35	817	98	563

BUTLER COUNTY.

Total Population.	NAMES OF TOWNSHIPS, TOWNS, AND CITIES.	No. of dwelling houses.	Number of families.	WHITE POPULATION. Male.	Female.	Total.	COLORED POP'LATION Male.	Female.	Total.	NATIVITY OF INHABITANTS. No. born in Iowa.	No. born in U. S., but not in Iowa.	No. born in foreign countries.	Surplus or deficiency.	BETWEEN 5 AND 21 YEARS OLD. No 5 years old and under 6.	No. 6 years old and under 16.	No. 16 years old and under 21.	No. births in 1874.	No. deaths in 1874.	No. of voters.	No. foreigners not naturalized.	No. of militia.
1014	Albion	203	209	533	481	1014	......	......	......	350	546	118	......	34	258	79	26	6	235	12	142
1017	Beaver	189	189	519	498	1017	......	......	......	484	416	117	......	51	246	102	28	9	224	14	156
30[illegible]	Bennezett	58	58	167	135	303	......	......	......	98	156	46	— 2	12	81	31	10	8	68	......	44
807	Butler, exc. of Clarksville	152	152	423	384	807	......	......	......	301	429	74	— 3	29	221	85	23	8	191	......	128
699	Clarksville, town of	137	137	341	358	699	......	......	......	252	404	43	......	47	162	51	21	7	176	......	111
980	Cold Water	196	205	531	449	980	......	......	......	362	552	100	34	17	133	65	36	16	247	......	179
513	Dayton	98	96	251	262	513	......	......	......	165	260	39	— 49	28	127	40	17	6	109	11	84
723	Fremont	139	139	398	325	723	......	......	......	247	338	136	— 2	37	179	57	26	5	119	12	105
594	Jackson	114	114	331	255	586	5	3	8	191	364	3[illegible]	— 6	24	133	50	22	8	145	3	109
677	Jefferson, Butler Center C. H.	1[illegible]3	123	356	321	677	......	......	......	231	255	167	— 24	45	209	10	15	11	149	5	91
401	Madison	72	72	220	181	401	......	......	......	116	144	141	......	13	88	33	20	2	57	35	46
692	Monroe	131	131	364	328	692	......	......	......	207	354	128	— 3	58	155	62	25	6	140	7	114
528	Pittsford	101	101	286	242	528	......	......	......	221	270	33	— 4	23	133	48	26	6	119	2	75
377	Ripley	63	63	203	174	377	......	......	......	163	162	52	......	16	107	21	3	......	75	6	40
1408	Shell Rock	301	301	740	660	1400	4	4	8	441	907	60	......	67	342	123	35	14	358	......	24[illegible]
486	Washington	99	99	262	224	486	......	......	......	118	180	175	— 13	16	103	44	19	8	92	30	63
516	West Point	89	87	289	227	516	......	......	......	195	232	93	4	29	130	47	21	8	95	31	77
11734	Total	2265	2276	6214	5504	11718	9	7	16	4142	5969	1555	......	536	2787	948	373	128	2598	1[illegible]8	1810

CALHOUN COUNTY.

Total Population.	NAMES OF TOWNSHIPS, TOWNS, AND CITIES.	No. of dwelling houses.	Number of families.	WHITE POPULATION. Male.	Female.	Total.	COLORED POP'LATION Male.	Female.	Total.	NATIVITY OF INHABITANTS. No. born in Iowa.	No. born in U. S., but not in Iowa.	No. born in foreign countries.	Surplus or deficiency.	BETWEEN 5 AND 21 YEARS OLD. No 5 years old and under 6.	No. 6 years old and under 16.	No. 16 years old and under 21.	No. births in 1874.	No. deaths in 1874.	No. of voters.	No. foreigners not naturalized.	No. of militia.
247	Butler	56	56	136	111	247	......	......	......	77	124	39	— 7	9	56	20	9	......	59	......	44
828	Calhoun, Lake City, C. H.	123	123	456	372	828	......	......	......	246	536	46	......	34	188	47	25	......	199	......	173
174	Center	3[illegible]	34	85	89	174	......	......	......	38	113	3	— 20	9	53	16	3	......	33	20	20
236	Greenfield	39	39	128	108	236	......	......	......	85	83	19	— 49	10	61	21	14	......	40	2	29
690	Jackson	116	116	365	325	690	......	......	......	257	363	65	— 5	36	184	55	26	......	138	6	116
465	Lincoln	90	90	249	216	465	......	......	......	142	229	64	— 30	16	75	29	16	......	115	2	64

410	Sherman	69	69	207	203	410	......	......	......	111	160	110	— 29	33	78	10	19	......	65	31	21
135	Williams	32	32	65	70	135	......	......	......	44	76	4	— 11	9	22	9	7	......	32	......	21
3185	Total	559	559	1691	1494	3185	......	......	......	1000	168[illegible]	350	......	156	717	207	119	......	681	61	488

CARROLL COUNTY.

511	Arcadia	109	107	289	222	511	......	......	......	120	218	173	......	21	104	22	25	12	90	49	73
196	Carroll, exc. of town	44	50	111	85	196	......	......	......	48	95	53	......	13	40	10	11	......	26	4	35
812	Carroll, town of, C. H.	157	158	420	390	810	......	2	2	193	477	142	......	34	127	36	32	14	224	1	203
172	Eden	33	33	90	82	172	......	......	......	34	104	34	......	14	32	......	5	1	42	3	40
525	Glidden	199	100	300	225	525	......	......	......	150	321	54	......	54	106	47	5	6	122	......	90
16[illegible]	Grant	35	39	92	77	169	......	......	......	48	41	80	......	8	41	14	10	3	30	......	27
244	Jasper	44	44	118	126	244	......	......	......	77	162	5	......	3	74	12	8	6	46	......	32
643	Kniest	111	111	354	289	643	......	......	......	225	132	286	......	41	166	44	27	13	116	27	72
442	Newton	105	105	239	203	442	......	......	......	176	249	17	......	13	98	55	24	11	100	27	84
211	Pleasant Valley	43	43	116	95	211	......	......	......	66	72	73	......	18	42	22	9	1	35	......	45
129	Richland	27	25	75	54	129	......	......	......	49	76	4	......	6	31	8	3	3	35	......	27
32[illegible]	Roselle	62	67	181	143	324	......	......	......	85	127	112	......	12	90	30	18	7	64	......	20
511	Sheridan	102	102	266	245	511	......	......	......	161	236	114	......	27	101	21	32	8	103	......	62
331	Union	79	79	136	195	331	......	......	......	......	......	......	......	25	120	32	10	4	93	......	60
165	Washington	34	34	93	72	165	......	......	......	27	74	64	......	3	25	12	12	4	29	11	38
375	Wheatland	78	78	207	168	375	......	......	......	87	62	226	......	12	67	33	26	11	42	71	27
5760	Total	1262	1175	3087	2671	5758	......	2	2	1546	2446	1437	......	304	1264	398	257	104	1197	193	935

CASS COUNTY.

860	Atlantic, exc. of town	155	155	442	418	860	......	......	......	335	459	67	1	42	210	64	30	7	196	5	93
1832	Atlantic, town of, C. H.	300	351	954	872	1826	4	2	6	171	869	254	—538	64	194	126	57	12	498	1	718
500	Bear Grove	93	93	258	241	·99	1	......	1	144	292	53	— 11	17	111	27	17	3	117	1	91
502	Benton	88	88	270	232	502	......	......	......	175	285	42	......	27	126	65	26	12	108	......	77
617	Brighton	111	111	331	282	613	3	1	4	185	311	121	......	32	141	63	26	6	119	31	95
1008	Cass	186	186	554	454	1008	......	......	......	307	651	156	106	37	262	90	35	13	241	5	164
433	Edna	76	76	219	214	433	......	......	......	137	237	40	— 19	31	126	40	23	5	90	6	70
626	Franklin	124	124	328	298	626	......	......	......	195	336	65	— 30	35	19	35	17	4	151	......	102
526	Grant	108	108	268	258	526	......	......	......	148	313	49	— 16	26	103	25	19	1	104	1	99
310	Lincoln	95	95	166	144	310	......	......	......	104	181	26	1	10	76	20	13	3	71	......	60
184	Massena	40	42	89	95	184	......	......	......	52	123	9	......	5	32	10	11	......	49	......	31
563	Noble	96	96	313	250	563	......	......	......	141	319	106	3	26	82	52	27	7	120	24	121
549	Pleasant	106	106	273	276	549	......	......	......	225	249	52	— 23	16	142	35	29	4	108	19	87
774	Pymosa	137	137	416	358	774	......	......	......	311	368	87	— 8	33	191	60	51	9	164	......	154
284	Union	56	56	147	136	283	1	......	1	96	183	17	12	13	65	13	16	5	71	3	52

CASS COUNTY—Continued.

Total population.	Names of townships, towns, and cities.	No. of dwelling houses.	Number of families.	White population. Male.	White population. Female.	White population. Total.	Colored pop'lation. Male.	Colored pop'lation. Female.	Colored pop'lation. Total.	Nativity of inhabitants. No. born in Iowa.	Nativity of inhabitants. No. born in U. S., but not in Iowa.	Nativity of inhabitants. No. born in foreign countries.	Nativity of inhabitants. Surplus or deficiency.	Between 5 and 21 years old. No. 5 years old and under 6.	Between 5 and 21 years old. No. 6 years old and under 16.	Between 5 and 21 years old. No. 16 years old and under 21.	No. births in 1874.	No. deaths in 1874.	No. of voters.	No. foreigners not naturalized.	No. of militia.
385	Victoria	64	64	217	168	385	......	......	......	49	217	85	— 34	26	97	36	13	4	75	......	58
599	Washington	104	104	328	271	599	......	......	......	202	295	91	— 11	42	118	56	11	5	140	......	109
10552	Total	1939	1992	5573	4967	10540	9	3	12	2977	5688	1320	....	482	2095	817	421	100	2422	96	2181

CEDAR COUNTY.

Total population.	Names of townships, towns, and cities.	No. of dwelling houses.	Number of families.	White population. Male.	White population. Female.	White population. Total.	Colored pop'lation. Male.	Colored pop'lation. Female.	Colored pop'lation. Total.	Nativity of inhabitants. No. born in Iowa.	Nativity of inhabitants. No. born in U. S., but not in Iowa.	Nativity of inhabitants. No. born in foreign countries.	Nativity of inhabitants. Surplus or deficiency.	Between 5 and 21 years old. No. 5 years old and under 6.	Between 5 and 21 years old. No. 6 years old and under 16.	Between 5 and 21 years old. No. 16 years old and under 21.	No. births in 1874.	No. deaths in 1874.	No. of voters.	No. foreigners not naturalized.	No. of militia.
595	Cass	111	111	317	278	595	......	......	......	376	211	8	....	16	136	70	19	10	143	17	102
1542	Center, exc. of Tipton	243	243	803	735	1538	2	2	4	772	685	85	....	54	391	148	39	16	354	2	219
664	Clarence, town of	140	140	330	334	664	......	......	......	195	386	83	....	15	108	49	13	2	177	11	110
715	Dayton, exc. of Clarence	137	137	378	337	715	......	......	......	320	369	26	....	44	209	54	21	6	144	16	83
370	Durant, town of	79	79	192	178	370	......	......	......	113	180	77	....	15	77	35	10	4	84	26	52
702	Fairfield	137	137	371	331	702	......	......	......	308	234	160	....	48	177	58	2[illegible]	3	146	19	117
757	Farmington, exc. of Durant	134	134	398	359	757	......	......	......	296	258	203	....	28	187	49	29	5	132	39	106
1065	Fremont	200	203	548	517	1065	......	......	......	445	493	127	....	74	265	101	33	9	236	6	151
888	Gower	152	152	458	430	888	......	......	......	425	353	110	5	47	225	76	34	11	188	......	115
882	Inland	155	155	477	405	882	......	......	......	432	393	57	....	35	220	69	32	5	179	1	102
1050	Iowa	213	220	531	515	1046	2	2	4	476	520	54	....	36	279	96	29	5	247	4	168
438	Linn	70	72	244	194	438	......	......	......	221	189	28	....	19	102	39	13	2	105	1	75
429	Louden, town of	101	101	228	211	439	......	......	......	172	143	124	....	10	97	42	13	2	73	28	42
826	Massillon	166	166	441	385	826	......	......	......	345	334	147	....	50	155	64	33	10	190	18	157
598	Mechanicsville, town of	140	140	289	304	593	2	3	5	236	313	49	....	7	151	42	6	1	131	......	94
876	Pioneer, exc. of Mechanicsville	170	170	451	425	876	......	......	......	398	455	23	....	55	232	111	38	13	201	2	126
496	Red Oak	93	93	253	243	496	......	......	......	239	189	68	....	20	111	51	6	4	102	12	70
726	Rochester	136	136	387	336	723	1	2	3	377	314	35	....	24	206	83	13	7	151	5	97
1481	Springdale	304	304	727	734	1461	10	10	20	581	822	78	....	43	318	132	33	12	351	5	227
909	Springfield, exc. of Louden	164	169	469	440	909	......	......	......	427	289	193	— 1	28	233	98	26	11	153	38	88

617	Sugar Creek	112	112	308	309	617				375	176	66		61	129	47	20	8	137	11	89
1243	Tipton, town of, C. H.	254	254	577	643	1220	13	10	23	511	653	79		42	265	121	30	25	310	3	210
17879	Total	3411	3428	9177	8643	17820	39	29	59	8040	7959	1880		771	4273	1645	513	171	3934	264	2600

CERRO GORDO COUNTY.

448	Clear Lake, exc. of town	89	89	244	204	448				134	241	73		25	98	33	13	5	99	6	68
622	Clear Lake, town of	127	127	319	301	620		2	2	139	366	117		31	135	43	22	3	146	9	101
141	Daugherty	24	24	84	57	141				55	70	16		11	34	14	6	2	39		34
833	Falls	161	161	429	391	820	8	5	13	256	430	147		39	169	53	43	17	184	4	123
397	Geneseo	85	85	206	191	397				124	216	57		31	96	34	15	8	85	15	60
210	Grant	40	40	109	101	210				50	102	58		34	41	20	10	5	44	7	33
316	Lake	68	68	176	139	315		1	1	90	134	92		34	78	20	1	1	82	2	48
462	Lime Creek	86	90	236	226	462				140	281	41		18	99	44	24	7	107		73
409	Lincoln	74	74	212	197	409				134	228	47		17	112	37	15	4	93		69
447	Mason, exc. of Mason City	85	83	245	202	447				136	260	51		18	109	31	18	8	93	5	82
1703	Mason City, town of, C. H.	349	356	868	834	1702	1		1	468	963	272		113	266	121	60	29	406	26	345
300	Owen	62	62	166	134	300				80	179	41		16	58	28	12	2	67	4	49
397	Portland	85	85	213	184	397				107	223	67		15	90	36	13	7	81	9	44
6683	Total	1335	1344	3507	3161	6668	9	8	17	1913	3693	1079		402	1385	514	252	98	1526	87	1129

CHEROKEE COUNTY.

483	Afton	105	105	270	213	483				170	239	74		21	102	27	18	5	113	29	85
130	Amherst	29	29	70	60	130				16	51	61	— 2	3	29	15	3	1	47	14	20
331	Cedar	69	72	186	145	331				94	256	73	92	15	68	24	16	5	77		59
301	Cherokee, exc. of town	67	66	158	143	301				83	203	28	13	8	54	39	14	3	81		63
841	Cherokee, town of, C H.	165	165	433	408	841				236	493	108	— 4	39	170	67	42	11	209	7	137
118	Diamond	25	25	69	49	118				31	72	9	— 6	6	17	12	12	2	27	2	25
175	Liberty	41	41	97	78	175				35	67	64	— 9	7	45	10	6		31	9	21
44	Marcus	14	14	28	16	44				8	29	7		2	8	4			14	2	8
462	Pilot	101	101	240	222	462				194	246	36	14	23	62	11	14	7	199		86
326	Pitcher	66	66	178	148	326				103	194	47	18	18	44	12	13	5	80	1	68
381	Sheridan	70	70	192	189	381				100	191	85	— 5	18	107	32	20	3	71	1	46
174	Silver	35	35	92	82	174				46	131	6	9	10	36	17	8	7	41		34
96	Spring	27	30	51	45	96				25	44	9	— 18	11	13	1	5	1	22	1	18
183	Tilden	33	33	107	76	183				47	80	56		17	36	16	15	1	36	6	33
200	Willow	35	35	113	87	200				78	107	9	— 6	9	59	15	3	2	43	1	33
4245	Total	882	887	2284	1961	4245				1266	2403	672		207	850	302	189	53	1001	73	736

CHICKASAW COUNTY.

Total population.	NAMES OF TOWNSHIPS, TOWNS, AND CITIES.	No. of dwelling houses.	No. of families.	WHITE POPULATION. Male.	WHITE POPULATION. Female.	WHITE POPULATION. Total.	COLORED POP'LATION Male.	COLORED POP'LATION Female.	COLORED POP'LATION Total.	NATIVITY OF INHABITANTS. No. born in Iowa.	NATIVITY OF INHABITANTS. No. born in U. S., but not in Iowa.	NATIVITY OF INHABITANTS. No. born in foreign countries.	NATIVITY OF INHABITANTS. Surplus or deficiency.	BETWEEN 5 AND 21 YEARS OLD. No. 5 years old and under 6.	BETWEEN 5 AND 21 YEARS OLD. No. 6 years old and under 16.	BETWEEN 5 AND 21 YEARS OLD. No. 16 years old and under 21.	No. births in 1874.	No. deaths in 1874	No. of voters.	No. foreigners not naturalized.	No. of militia.
1077	Bradford, exc. of Nashua	214	214	540	537	1077	......	......	......	400	565	112	......	38	239	103	19	9	241	2	110
1197	Chickasaw	229	229	639	558	1197	......	......	......	474	601	122	......	59	294	105	38	23	260	7	187
624	Dayton	106	106	332	291	623	1	......	1	251	344	139	110	37	177	59	20	7	100	9	102
710	Deerfield	133	133	378	332	710	......	......	......	276	288	146	......	33	189	68	17	4	155	14	110
461	Dresden	100	100	243	218	461	......	......	......	185	248	26	— 2	19	125	54	3	......	100	3	42
642	Fredericksburgh	129	129	330	312	642	......	......	......	212	381	15	— 34	35	148	66	20	4	157	......	70
1039	Jacksonville	186	186	532	507	1039	......	......	......	412	290	340	3	42	26	95	45	5	195	23	120
852	Nashua, town of	186	186	421	431	852	......	......	......	258	506	88	......	30	170	62	20	3	220	......	70
614	New Hampton, exc. of town	110	110	316	298	614	......	......	......	197	246	168	— 3	24	166	56	24	21	115	14	89
623	New Hampton, town of, C. H.	142	142	305	318	623	......	......	......	187	355	63	— 18	37	123	36	5	......	164	2	128
639	Richland	115	115	341	298	639	......	......	......	214	370	74	19	68	184	65	18	8	127	3	90
1139	Stapleton	191	191	605	534	1139	......	......	......	419	494	265	39	110	259	125	49	26	266	7	201
1001	Utica	172	172	530	471	1001	......	......	......	418	198	368	— 17	47	266	125	42	12	145	49	63
782	Washington	136	136	415	367	782	......	......	......	364	228	200	10	46	199	72	30	14	147	......	199
11400	Total	2149	2149	5927	5472	11399	1	......	1	4267	5114	2126	......	625	2565	1091	350	136	2392	133	1581

CLARKE COUNTY.

Total population.	NAMES OF TOWNSHIPS, TOWNS, AND CITIES.	No. of dwelling houses.	No. of families.	WHITE POPULATION. Male.	WHITE POPULATION. Female.	WHITE POPULATION. Total.	COLORED POP'LATION Male.	COLORED POP'LATION Female.	COLORED POP'LATION Total.	NATIVITY OF INHABITANTS. No. born in Iowa.	NATIVITY OF INHABITANTS. No. born in U. S., but not in Iowa.	NATIVITY OF INHABITANTS. No. born in foreign countries.	NATIVITY OF INHABITANTS. Surplus or deficiency.	BETWEEN 5 AND 21 YEARS OLD. No. 5 years old and under 6.	BETWEEN 5 AND 21 YEARS OLD. No. 6 years old and under 16.	BETWEEN 5 AND 21 YEARS OLD. No. 16 years old and under 21.	No. births in 1874.	No. deaths in 1874	No. of voters.	No. foreigners not naturalized.	No. of militia.
716	Doyle, exc. of Hopeville	....	96	365	351	716	......	......	......	279	423	11	— 3	....	152	58	36	5	163	......	82
663	Franklin	....	120	333	330	663	......	......	......	283	371	3	— 6	33	181	67	24	9	144	......	116
572	Fremont	....	113	298	272	570	1	1	2	262	298	12	....	25	145	64	18	8	129	......	86
630	Green Bay	....	113	324	306	630	......	......	......	257	306	15	— 52	17	170	76	27	17	143	1	107
332	Hopeville, town of	....	51	177	155	332	......	......	......	50	43	139	—100	11	80	42	15	2	69	......	....
917	Jackson	....	172	464	453	917	......	......	......	394	473	54	4	58	239	64	35	11	187	5	147
851	Knox	....	149	449	402	851	......	......	......	376	451	24	....	27	227	112	41	11	170	1	140
925	Liberty	....	149	420	505	925	......	......	......	374	547	17	13	22	220	71	37	17	186	......	130
581	Madison	....	108	293	288	581	......	......	......	253	278	43	— 7	18	129	50	20	16	107	4	99

446	Osceola, exc. of town	......	140	234	203	437	4	5	9	257	291	11	113	21	118	50	21	9	122	......	63
1701	Osceola, town of, C. H.	......	300	842	831	1673	17	11	28	690	924	52	— 35	70	341	98	39	28	383	......	227
626	Troy	......	131	331	295	626	......	......	......	216	310	33	— 67	18	140	49	9	4	151	1	129
467	Ward	......	86	239	228	467	......	......	......	169	241	17	— 40	12	123	50	13	3	101	2	85
691	Washington	......	127	358	333	691	......	......	......	365	320	6	......	25	162	67	26	13	158	......	112
10118	Total		1855	5127	4952	10079	22	17	39	4225	5276	437		357	2427	918	361	153	2213	14	1523

CLAY COUNTY.

396	Bridgewater	84	84	208	188	396	......	......	......	113	206	52	— 25	19	79	19	12	1	98	......	62
598	Clay	130	130	310	288	598	......	......	......	178	320	83	— 17	37	134	34	31	16	143	4	105
387	Douglas	78	78	205	182	387	......	......	......	140	188	66	7	16	85	26	15	1	84	......	43
220	Gillett's Grove	49	49	116	104	220	......	......	......	82	126	11	— 1	9	43	25	14	3	54	......	49
146	Herdland	31	31	81	65	146	......	......	......	44	99	3	......	7	42	12	8	3	36	......	27
358	Lincoln	80	80	185	173	358	......	......	......	150	171	1	— 36	18	71	7	23	2	78	2	66
280	Riverton	70	70	147	133	280	......	......	......	84	157	27	— 12	10	44	7	11	4	77	......	53
906	Spencer, C. H.	187	187	499	407	906	......	......	......	246	565	93	— 2	34	195	75	32	7	231	......	170
278	Summit	66	66	143	135	278	......	......	......	62	146	70	......	13	53	22	11	......	67	2	52
3569	Total	775	775	1894	1675	3569				1099	1978	406		163	746	227	157	37	868	8	627

CLAYTON COUNTY.

1709	Boardman, Elkader, C. H.	313	313	890	819	1709	......	......	......	774	485	489	39	99	342	189	62	33	367	21	246
285	Buena Vista	63	63	153	132	285	......	......	......	114	46	28	— 97	8	72	24	6	7	64	8	40
1175	Cass	242	242	610	565	1175	......	......	......	501	551	123	3	36	274	119	34	18	266	6	147
1018	Clayton	185	185	530	488	1018	......	......	......	427	283	310	2	62	252	115	48	3	180	15	124
1022	Cox Creek	188	188	557	465	1022	......	......	......	525	189	308	......	42	273	111	34	18	195	32	86
1049	Elk	196	196	545	504	1049	......	......	......	519	407	123	......	44	271	91	37	19	236	4	173
1194	Farmersburg	213	213	629	561	1190	2	2	4	545	249	400	......	50	284	88	60	24	196	196	102
1182	Garnavillo	215	221	612	570	1182	......	......	......	563	148	471	......	44	326	104	47	18	207	61	134
1261	Girard	212	212	647	614	1261	......	......	......	[illegible]20	273	368	......	60	310	178	30	8	220	105	111
850	Grand Meadow	143	143	447	403	850	......	......	......	382	186	298	16	45	220	79	36	7	136	58	84
1045	Guttenberg, town of	221	221	529	516	1045	......	......	......	485	113	423	— 24	25	264	84	41	13	224	15	99
780	Highland	132	132	405	375	780	......	......	......	360	180	244	4	34	216	93	21	1	154	11	117
1206	Jefferson, exc. of Guttenberg	223	227	656	550	1206	......	......	......	621	56	529	......	58	334	108	56	21	255	41	160
1115	Lodomillo	241	241	577	538	1115	......	......	......	514	522	83	4	177	290	119	25	12	241	4	149
1149	Mallory	210	210	620	529	1149	......	......	......	579	490	74	— 6	89	267	76	38	11	258	6	191
1122	Marion	149	149	601	521	1122	......	......	......	512	62	577	29	42	259	122	49	17	120	97	69
1181	Mendon, exclusive of McGregor and North McGregor	244	244	602	579	1181	......	......	......	453	387	321	— 20	31	334	94	29	3	222	13	128
757	Millville	139	139	391	366	757	......	......	......	402	236	136	17	71	177	85	22	9	144	12	92
1412	Monona	245	245	712	700	1412	......	......	......	507	455	93	—357	84	356	126	19	6	304	4	163

CLAYTON COUNTY—Continued.

Total population.	Names of townships, towns, and cities.	No. of dwelling houses.	Number of families.	White population. Male.	White population. Female.	White population. Total.	Colored pop'lation. Male.	Colored pop'lation. Female.	Colored pop'lation. Total.	Nativity of inhabitants. No. born in Iowa.	Nativity of inhabitants. No. born in U. S., but not in Iowa.	Nativity of inhabitants. No. born in foreign countries.	Nativity of inhabitants. Surplus or deficiency.	Between 5 and 21 years old. No. 5 years old and under 6.	Between 5 and 21 years old. No. 6 years old and under 16.	Between 5 and 21 years old. No. 16 years old and under 21.	No. births in 1874.	No. deaths in 1874.	No. of voters.	No. foreigners not naturalized.	No. of militia.
478	North McGregor, town of	......	104	243	235	478	......	......	......	152	204	132	11	9	96	32	18	7	94	7	84
1040	Read	183	183	538	502	1040	......	......	......	474	103	463	......	41	266	71	33	20	160	58	99
1119	Sperry	226	226	626	573	1199	......	......	......	565	428	206	......	56	296	140	38	17	260	17	171
1214	Volga	237	237	635	579	1214	......	......	......	616	142	130	—326	64	282	120	27	18	213	7	123
889	Wagner	159	159	455	434	889	......	......	......	331	137	214	—207	45	188	86	34	9	145	21	114
25332	Total	4579	4603	12210	12118	25328	2	2	4	11541	6332	6543	......	1316	6249	2454	844	319	4861	819	3006
	McGregor, town of—																				
596	" First ward	......	112	291	303	594	1	1	2	196	264	133	— 3	13	122	52	14	2	141	29	93
651	" Second ward	......	134	312	339	651	......	......	......	238	286	127	......	13	139	44	17	4	152	6	114
368	" Third ward	......	71	190	178	368	......	......	......	152	127	90	1	14	94	33	8	5	74	6	52
237	" Fourth ward	......	43	129	108	237	......	......	......	106	93	38	......	11	71	19	3	......	44	......	24
1852	Total of town	......	360	922	928	1850	1	1	2	692	770	388	......	51	426	148	42	11	411	41	283
27184	Total of county	4579	5053	14132	13046	27178	3	3	6	12233	7102	6931	......	1367	6675	2602	886	330	5272	860	3289

CLINTON COUNTY.

Total population.	Names of townships, towns, and cities.	No. of dwelling houses.	Number of families.	White population. Male.	White population. Female.	White population. Total.	Colored pop'lation. Male.	Colored pop'lation. Female.	Colored pop'lation. Total.	Nativity of inhabitants. No. born in Iowa.	Nativity of inhabitants. No. born in U. S., but not in Iowa.	Nativity of inhabitants. No. born in foreign countries.	Nativity of inhabitants. Surplus or deficiency.	Between 5 and 21 years old. No. 5 years old and under 6.	Between 5 and 21 years old. No. 6 years old and under 16.	Between 5 and 21 years old. No. 16 years old and under 21.	No. births in 1874.	No. deaths in 1874.	No. of voters.	No. foreigners not naturalized.	No. of militia.
740	Berlin	87	87	417	323	740	......	......	......	354	158	228	......	42	185	64	36	5	104	49	66
1364	Bloomfield	270	270	720	643	1363	1	......	1	607	552	205	......	231	366	113	43	27	272	22	158
994	Brookfield	172	172	526	468	994	......	......	......	492	336	166	......	58	270	81	18	2	191	18	132
495	Camanche, exc. of town	95	95	257	238	495	......	......	......	222	192	81	......	18	100	49	13	4	105	10	59
758	Camanche, town of	169	169	395	363	758	......	......	......	285	319	154	......	25	187	76	17	9	187	11	103
1226	Center	210	210	650	576	1226	......	......	......	534	169	523	......	126	278	105	42	9	191	65	120
1346	Clinton, exc. of city	277	277	684	647	1331	5	10	15	419	509	418	......	60	303	114	54	29	236	56	155
7028	Clinton, city of, C. H.	1497	1524	3366	3563	6929	47	52	99	2120	2998	1910	......	149	1397	369	145	56	1363	181	716

987	Deep Creek	165	165	528	459	987	......	......	......	426	170	391	....	41	239	94	32	17	163	57	97
1289	DeWitt, exc. of town	230	230	694	594	1288	1	......	1	558	468	263	....	55	347	130	35	16	276	24	171
1754	DeWitt, town of	320	320	859	876	1735	8	11	19	651	806	297	....	156	310	128	38	15	466	36	189
946	Eden	143	143	518	428	946	......	......	......	399	278	269	....	112	199	87	18	5	185	28	127
1271	Elk River	205	205	716	555	1271	......	......	......	562	229	480	....	51	278	113	39	11	236	87	121
963	Hampshire	169	169	514	449	963	......	......	......	451	102	410	....	33	220	98	39	11	168	56	91
825	Liberty	155	155	442	383	825	......	......	......	326	260	239	....	34	210	76	31	14	154	......	84
363	Lincoln	64	64	193	170	363	......	......	......	174	119	70	....	20	97	52	8	3	76	4	44
382	Lyons, exc. of city	75	75	196	186	382	......	......	......	174	104	104	....	15	55	48	9	4	85	1	24
3784	Lyons, city of	752	752	1845	1925	3770	3	11	14	1681	1182	921	....	186	855	357	99	73	666	105	348
1481	Olive	268	268	785	696	1481	......	......	......	619	405	457	....	63	372	120	56	10	272	193	90
931	Orange	164	164	484	447	931	......	......	......	432	302	197	....	29	243	84	37	12	175	11	108
1199	Sharon	188	188	630	569	1199	......	......	......	557	358	284	....	46	292	111	27	8	238	73	139
804	Spring Rock, exc. of Wheatland	147	147	405	399	804	......	......	......	366	202	236	....	44	232	63	28	6	117	36	64
956	Washington	137	137	488	468	956	......	......	......	449	155	352	....	51	263	92	28	9	174	3	116
828	Waterford	137	137	424	404	828	......	......	......	493	169	166	....	59	261	102	35	11	189	27	120
865	Welton	162	157	463	402	865	......	......	......	408	288	169	....	31	236	89	22	15	151	32	116
716	Wheatland, town of	169	169	362	352	714	1	1	2	291	277	148	....	55	162	55	13	9	129	9	86
34295	Total	6427	6449	17561	16583	34144	66	85	151	14050	11107	9138	....	1790	6957	2870	962	390	5569	1194	3644

CRAWFORD COUNTY.

224	Boyer	38	38	126	98	224	......	......	......	76	103	42	— 3	11	60	17	9	1	41	6	25
63	Charter Oak	12	12	33	30	63	......	......	......	22	36	3	— 2	5	15	5	1	1	17	......	10
1123	Denison, Denison, C H	214	214	583	540	1123	......	......	......	323	556	245	1	57	246	75	52	23	258	20	206
355	East Boyer	62	62	200	155	355	......	......	......	121	153	76	— 5	15	80	32	13	8	75	3	47
258	Goodrich	45	45	142	116	258	......	......	......	55	169	39	5	16	63	20	3	2	46	10	31
36	Hanover	8	8	20	16	36	......	......	......	17	3	16	....	1	5	7	3	......	9	......	7
315	Hays	63	63	173	142	315	......	......	......	96	77	137	— 5	19	70	13	14	8	62	4	46
223	Iowa	77	77	123	100	223	......	......	......	102	74	52	5	6	77	30	9	4	47	1	20
264	Jackson	58	58	141	123	264	......	......	......	97	127	50	10	12	54	27	6	2	70	1	48
643	Milford	127	127	346	297	643	......	......	......	252	351	15	— 25	46	155	46	22	8	144	3	87
91	Morgan	22	22	47	44	91	......	......	......	32	14	43	— 2	4	20	5	6	1	16	8	12
98	Nishnabotany	19	19	44	54	98	......	......	......	29	47	26	4	6	27	7	4	2	25	......	19
361	Otter Creek	69	69	192	169	361	......	......	......	108	61	193	1	17	86	29	23	6	46	29	31
162	Paradise	37	37	82	80	162	......	......	......	44	88	17	— 13	5	40	13	8	5	36	1	24
101	Soldier	20	20	54	47	101	......	......	......	45	44	7	— 5	7	23	10	4	2	18	......	9
334	Stockholm	60	60	180	154	334	......	......	......	78	69	169	— 18	18	47	7	18	1	48	14	23
443	Union	104	120	251	192	443	......	......	......	148	232	45	— 18	17	84	24	14	6	104	15	66
239	Washington	47	47	118	113	232	6	1	7	70	147	18	— 4	12	37	23	12	5	50	......	32
629	West Side	126	126	322	307	629	......	......	......	163	281	185	....	26	191	33	29	8	127	34	95
77	Willow	16	16	39	37	76	1	......	1	26	42	11	2	....	17	2	5	......	15	......	14
6039	Total	1224	1240	3216	2814	6031	7	1	8	1904	2674	1389	....	300	1397	425	255	93	1254	149	852

DALLAS COUNTY.

Total population.	NAMES OF TOWNSHIPS, TOWNS, AND CITIES.	No. of dwelling houses.	Number of families.	WHITE POPULATION. Male.	Female.	Total.	COLORED POP'LATION. Male.	Female.	Total.	NATIVITY OF INHABITANTS. No. born in Iowa.	No. born in U. S., but not in Iowa.	No. born in foreign countries.	Surplus or deficiency.	BETWEEN 5 AND 21 YEARS OLD. No. 5 years old and under 6.	No. 6 years old and under 16.	No. 16 years old and under 21.	No. births in 1874.	No. deaths in 1874.	No. of voters.	No. foreigners not naturalized.	No. of militia.
966	Adams	174	174	497	469	966	......	......	......	451	496	19	......	26	26	114	28	4	216	......	155
1204	Adel, exc. of town	211	211	639	565	1204	......	......	......	489	588	127	......	44	283	103	42	9	274	......	210
815	Adel, town of, C. H.	165	165	405	401	806	5	4	9	320	480	15	......	42	191	68	35	10	194	......	148
427	Beaver	76	75	216	211	427	......	......	......	176	250	1	......	55	62	18	21	7	84	......	69
836	Boone	138	143	447	389	836	......	......	......	346	407	83	......	25	224	69	27	4	185	19	125
666	Colfax	128	128	351	315	666	......	......	......	205	414	47	......	22	169	52	16	12	150	1	115
484	Dallas	92	92	266	218	484	......	......	......	165	289	30	......	20	133	26	23	2	108	......	85
744	Des Moines	133	132	396	347	743	1	......	1	320	368	56	......	30	178	88	21	10	162	4	112
660	Dexter, town of	183	190	337	323	660	......	......	......	203	392	65	......	14	77	49	19	7	141	......	81
529	Grant	92	92	273	256	529	......	......	......	210	229	90	......	29	130	40	26	6	113	5	90
467	Lincoln	86	86	243	224	467	......	......	......	125	311	31	......	20	119	42	14	1	101	1	84
833	Linn	138	138	440	392	832	1	......	1	339	467	27	......	47	196	93	33	12	198	......	139
1142	Spring Valley	237	237	630	512	1142	......	......	......	424	656	62	......	64	244	90	40	11	262	5	183
670	Sugar Grove	137	137	338	325	663	2	5	7	250	336	84	......	53	179	46	21	11	131	30	68
1180	Union, exc. of Dexter	118	118	601	579	1180	......	......	......	479	680	21	......	39	335	132	37	19	255	4	190
1510	Van Meter	290	296	744	748	1492	10	8	18	677	803	30	......	65	349	114	46	13	318	13	247
705	Walnut	132	132	389	316	705	......	......	......	238	484	33	......	45	186	39	15	4	157	6	95
548	Washington	98	98	296	251	547	......	1	1	202	300	46	......	20	150	50	26	11	121	5	89
14386	Total	2628	2644	7508	6841	14349	19	18	37	5619	7900	867	......	660	3231	1233	490	153	3170	93	2285

DAVIS COUNTY.

Total population.	NAMES OF TOWNSHIPS, TOWNS, AND CITIES.	No. of dwelling houses.	Number of families.	WHITE POPULATION. Male.	Female.	Total.	COLORED POP'LATION. Male.	Female.	Total.	NATIVITY OF INHABITANTS. No. born in Iowa.	No. born in U. S., but not in Iowa.	No. born in foreign countries.	Surplus or deficiency.	BETWEEN 5 AND 21 YEARS OLD. No. 5 years old and under 6.	No. 6 years old and under 16.	No. 16 years old and under 21.	No. births in 1874.	No. deaths in 1874.	No. of voters.	No. foreigners not naturalized.	No. of militia.
1570	Bloomfield, exc. of town	300	300	786	772	1558	5	7	12	753	759	58	......	64	392	159	61	21	436	......	180
969	Bloomfield, town of, C. H	199	199	458	484	942	16	11	27	379	520	73	3	9	136	68	4	......	267	......	200
287	Drakeville, exc. of town	63	63	150	137	287	......	......	......	143	131	13	......	12	63	44	10	6	79	......	44
280	Drakeville, town of	58	58	138	142	280	......	......	......	106	160	14	......	13	61	28	10	9	74	......	46
1064	Fabius	196	196	552	512	1064	......	......	......	566	485	13	......	37	309	101	40	15	182	......	188

694	Fox River	109	109	345	349	694	......	......	......	484	259	1	....	33	171	78	23	8	130	......	100
1101	Grove	196	196	546	555	1101	......	......	......	505	517	79	....	34	280	132	35	13	224	12	162
1444	Lick Creek	286	286	720	724	1444	......	......	......	688	608	48	—100	54	393	133	70	27	315	7	183
959	Marion	172	172	474	485	959	......	......	......	500	431	28	....	32	277	92	36	19	194	1	126
699	Perry	134	134	362	337	699	......	......	......	384	311	6	2	25	168	88	36	15	148	......	107
646	Prairie	131	131	331	315	646	......	......	......	317	289	40	....	22	143	69	25	11	138	7	115
629	Roscoe	104	104	321	308	629	......	......	......	352	214	63	....	27	204	66	31	3	102	14	55
947	Salt Creek	179	179	489	458	947	......	......	......	630	301	16	....	53	249	83	50	14	203	....	146
991	Soap Creek	183	183	525	466	991	......	......	......	525	426	40	....	31	250	109	21	13	226	17	163
1158	Union	223	223	581	577	1158	......	......	......	579	537	40	— 2	40	265	131	35	8	259	......	184
1039	West Grove	181	181	520	519	1039	......	......	......	549	479	11	....	....	212	74	37	17	199	......	151
1280	Wyacondah	273	273	543	737	1280	......	......	......	713	560	7	....	46	453	139	45	12	272	......	173
15757	Total	2987	2987	7841	7877	15718	21	18	39	8123	6987	550	....	532	4026	1594	569	211	3448	58	2323

DECATUR COUNTY.

367	Bloomington	70	70	184	179	363	3	1	4	170	180	17	....	24	89	31	5	......	76	......	53
1053	Burrell	201	201	553	500	1053	......	......	......	516	520	17	....	66	308	96	43	19	211	......	144
935	Center, exc. of Leon	158	158	484	451	935	......	......	......	464	464	7	....	123	290	104	9	9	189	......	119
1124	Decatur	208	208	591	533	1124	......	......	......	514	590	20	....	45	295	97	55	23	247	2	190
1108	Eden	209	209	574	531	1105	......	3	3	528	560	20	....	47	333	112	29	17	219	1	155
371	Fayette	64	64	206	165	371	......	......	......	143	206	22	....	13	102	32	18	3	81	2	61
605	Franklin	107	107	302	303	605	......	......	......	274	313	18	....	25	162	72	24	8	125	5	108
1104	Garden Grove	220	220	557	537	1094	7	3	10	408	607	89	....	45	283	88	39	7	253	3	164
506	Grand River	94	94	268	231	499	5	2	7	229	241	36	....	38	124	26	17	10	109	1	72
783	Hamilton	146	146	396	387	783	......	......	......	287	466	30	....	34	195	74	25	12	185	1	137
796	High Point	146	146	390	397	787	4	5	9	394	395	7	....	32	229	73	32	11	171	1	128
889	Leon, town of, C. H.	190	190	444	425	869	14	6	20	364	516	9	....	27	172	73	30	8	234	......	169
745	Long Creek	139	139	375	357	732	7	6	13	343	398	4	....	37	156	57	25	9	161	......	126
519	Morgan	100	100	249	270	519	......	......	......	230	289	....	....	25	134	41	19	6	111	......	80
516	New Buda	98	98	276	240	516	......	......	......	237	271	8	....	13	94	122	13	9	110	......	105
945	Richland	165	165	510	435	945	......	......	......	429	493	23	....	45	251	86	35	14	210	......	165
883	Woodland	137	137	426	457	883	......	......	......	428	412	43	....	34	232	105	37	11	190	......	141
13249	Total	2452	2452	6785	6398	13183	40	26	66	5958	6921	370	....	673	3449	1289	455	176	2882	16	2117

DELAWARE COUNTY.

644	Adams	....	100	343	301	644	......	......	......	305	176	167	4	16	196	77	21	2	121	7	75
838	Bremen	....	139	432	406	838	......	......	......	424	68	192	—154	35	209	70	43	10	130	41	91
954	Coffin's Grove	....	175	501	453	954	......	......	......	392	444	112	— 6	30	224	102	20	14	197	13	102
1264	Colony	....	179	648	616	1264	......	......	......	613	338	248	— 65	34	235	120	37	25	252	36	152
1152	Delaware, exc. of Manchester	....	208	597	555	1152	......	......	......	407	620	125	....	38	293	107	39	12	275	15	165

DELAWARE COUNTY.—Continued.

Total population.	Names of townships, towns, and cities.	No. of dwelling houses	No. of families.	White population. Male.	White population. Female.	White population. Total.	Colored pop'lation. Male.	Colored pop'lation. Female.	Colored pop'lation. Total.	Nativity of inhabitants. No. born in Iowa.	Nativity of inhabitants. No. born in U. S., but not in Iowa.	Nativity of inhabitants. No. born in foreign countries.	Nativity of inhabitants. Surplus or deficiency.	Between 5 and 21 years old. No. 5 years old and under 6.	Between 5 and 21 years old. No. 6 years old and under 16.	Between 5 and 21 years old. No. 16 years old and under 21.	No. births in 1874.	No. deaths in 1874.	No. of voters.	No. foreigners not naturalized.	No. of militia.
1176	Delhi, Delhi, C. H.	....	232	615	553	1172	3	1	4	485	537	154	....	41	266	119	17	6	288	38	189
1008	Elk	....	198	531	477	1008	......	......	......	465	385	118	— 40	42	261	76	30	11	215	......	141
738	Hazel Green	....	129	399	337	738	......	......	......	310	256	125	— 47	31	200	78	19	5	143	8	111
931	Honey Creek	....	189	486	445	931	......	......	......	403	437	91	....	25	246	71	23	9	223	23	175
661	Hopkinton, town of	....	138	331	330	661	......	......	......	259	356	47	1	27	159	48	26	7	166	2	113
1566	Manchester, town of	....	312	766	796	1562	3	1	4	482	892	172	— 20	54	320	155	36	23	404	4	274
719	Milo	....	137	373	346	719	......	......	......	284	342	88	— 5	27	174	88	19	7	166	1	119
824	North Fork	....	155	415	409	824	......	......	......	382	167	266	— 9	36	240	86	31	14	144	26	93
1368	Oneida	....	271	680	688	1368	......	......	......	509	635	234	10	46	297	138	34	8	282	22	166
509	Prairie	....	92	277	235	509	......	......	......	180	226	85	— 18	29	121	49	20	2	116	12	89
744	Richland	....	141	389	355	744	......	......	......	320	275	149	....	24	173	78	24	3	146	24	58
1113	South Fork, exc. of Hopkinton	....	202	572	540	1112	1	......	1	489	1057	183	616	44	277	86	32	14	243	......	145
684	Union	....	137	362	322	684	......	......	......	....	379	88	—217	23	202	75	28	11	151	7	95
16893	Total	....	3134	8717	8164	16884	7	2	9	6709	7590	2644	....	602	4093	1623	499	183	3662	279	2353

DES MOINES COUNTY.

Total population.	Names of townships, towns, and cities.	No. of dwelling houses	No. of families.	White population. Male.	White population. Female.	White population. Total.	Colored pop'lation. Male.	Colored pop'lation. Female.	Colored pop'lation. Total.	Nativity of inhabitants. No. born in Iowa.	Nativity of inhabitants. No. born in U. S., but not in Iowa.	Nativity of inhabitants. No. born in foreign countries.	Nativity of inhabitants. Surplus or deficiency.	Between 5 and 21 years old. No. 5 years old and under 6.	Between 5 and 21 years old. No. 6 years old and under 16.	Between 5 and 21 years old. No. 16 years old and under 21.	No. births in 1874.	No. deaths in 1874.	No. of voters.	No. foreigners not naturalized.	No. of militia.
537	Augusta	107	108	287	250	537	......	......	......	266	171	90	— 10	20	141	48	18	12	114	5	80
1303	Benton	233	244	679	623	1302	......	1	1	697	323	289	6	38	357	112	46	14	253	33	94
2809	Burlington	531	534	1416	1376	2792	11	6	17	1304	614	845	— 46	113	665	212	90	13	473	4	330
1543	Danville	280	280	799	741	1540	2	1	3	808	619	96	— 20	354	323	162	36	24	354	19	250
1342	Flint River	249	243	699	627	1326	10	6	16	769	299	236	— 38	27	319	159	41	5	282	7	173
1448	Franklin	246	242	726	722	1448	......	......	......	822	391	286	51	40	375	151	36	11	289	......	202
861	Huron	165	165	464	397	861	......	......	......	398	290	148	— 25	27	185	94	23	10	176	12	90
148	Jackson	26	26	84	64	148	......	......	......	64	61	16	— 7	7	29	13	2	3	35	1	35
1047	Pleasant Grove	209	209	538	508	1046	......	1	1	601	283	163	....	39	261	117	43	15	214	29	152
1456	Union	271	271	751	697	1448	5	3	8	698	348	339	-- 71	53	271	102	54	21	280	40	177

999	Washington	182	182	536	462	998	1	......	1	536	372	85	— 6	38	261	111	28	2	208	8	161
1626	Yellow Springs	336	335	798	828	1626	......	......	......	868	722	118	82	67	373	144	56	13	368	18	256
15119	Total	2835	2839	7777	7295	15072	29	18	47	7831	4493	2711	....	823	3560	1425	473	143	3046	176	2000
	Burlington, city of, C. H.																				
5644	" First ward	808	885	2688	2905	5593	25	26	51	2316	1680	1688	....	149	1189	464	187	72	799	134	440
2173	" Second ward	274	321	1127	998	2125	29	19	48	787	908	478	....	43	402	185	43	11	473	32	317
3712	" Third ward	496	540	1867	1735	3602	60	50	110	1276	1486	950	....	90	697	390	75	32	633	93	462
2375	" Fourth ward	315	349	1183	1163	2346	11	18	29	825	1024	526	....	53	480	221	48	29	408	59	292
1765	" Fifth ward	217	244	858	876	1734	13	18	31	605	833	317	— 10	33	278	142	34	16	418	15	333
2240	" Sixth ward	469	482	1097	1131	2228	4	8	12	968	809	563	100	102	560	205	105	30	448	52	374
2078	" Seventh ward	418	434	1026	1033	2059	10	9	19	941	746	491	100	80	493	160	103	35	429	50	368
19987	Total of city	2997	3255	9846	9841	19687	152	148	300	7718	7486	5013	....	550	4099	1767	595	225	3608	435	2586
35106	Total of county	5832	6094	17623	17136	34759	181	166	347	15549	11979	7724	....	1373	7659	3192	1068	368	6654	611	4586

DICKINSON COUNTY.

543	Center Grove, Spirit Lake, C. H.	109	109	285	258	543	......	......	......	176	337	36	6	16	126	53	26	5	127	2	103
69	Diamond Lake	15	15	33	36	69	......	......	......	21	39	11	2	2	19	5	2	......	15	......	12
96	Excelsior	29	23	54	42	96	......	......	......	20	63	12	— 1	5	24	5	5	1	23	......	19
102	Lakeville	20	20	64	38	102	......	......	......	27	62	13	....	5	21	6	2	1	25	4	14
133	Lloyd	30	30	76	57	133	......	......	......	43	50	30	— 10	8	32	12	2	2	29	......	17
162	Milford	36	36	86	76	162	......	......	......	25	109	27	— 1	4	47	10	5	2	41	......	32
163	Okoboji	35	35	89	74	163	......	......	......	42	99	18	— 4	5	39	5	6	1	40	......	30
76	Richland	15	13	35	41	76	......	......	......	21	51	2	— 2	7	21	8	3	2	12	......	9
59	Silver Lake	8	8	28	31	59	......	......	......	13	30	16	....	8	20	7	2	......	10	......	7
278	Spirit Lake	46	46	145	133	278	......	......	......	102	134	69	27	44	77	30	......	......	59	......	48
67	Superior	19	19	34	33	67	......	......	......	12	26	28	— 1	7	15	7	4	1	13	......	13
1748	Total	362	354	929	819	1748	......	......	......	502	1000	262	....	111	441	148	57	15	394	6	304

DUBUQUE COUNTY.

1029	Cascade	194	194	505	524	1029	......	......	......	549	224	261	5	44	268	87	28	22	191	17	142
1228	Center	227	227	627	601	1228	......	......	......	666	184	377	— 1	53	334	120	40	10	249	29	179
1030	Concord	181	181	534	496	1030	......	......	......	604	118	279	— 29	51	260	111	37	13	216	11	130
825	Dodge	151	151	451	374	825	......	......	......	424	96	193	—112	79	210	101	40	2	148	4	96
998	Dyersville, town of	201	201	502	496	998	......	......	......	427	188	375	— 8	26	223	69	41	11	215	20	164
842	Iowa	134	134	454	388	842	......	......	......	473	119	237	— 13	39	226	93	26	11	171	12	103
1578	Jefferson	270	270	841	737	1578	......	......	......	904	133	541	....	58	412	175	55	17	322	37	262
1350	Julien, exc. of Dubuque	224	226	706	644	1350	......	......	......	718	267	365	....	42	336	143	28	26	300	30	194

DUBUQUE COUNTY.—Continued.

Total population.	Names of townships, towns, and cities.	No. dwelling houses.	No. of families.	White population. Male.	White population. Female.	White population. Total.	Colored pop'lation. Male.	Colored pop'lation. Female.	Colored pop'lation. Total.	Nativity of inhabitants. No. born in Iowa.	Nativity of inhabitants. No. born in U. S., but not in Iowa.	Nativity of inhabitants. No. born in foreign countries.	Nativity of inhabitants. Surplus or deficiency.	Between 5 and 21 years old. No. 5 years old and under 6.	Between 5 and 21 years old. No. 6 years old and under 16.	Between 5 and 21 years old. No. 16 years old and under 21.	No. births in 1874.	No. deaths in 1874.	No. of voters.	No. foreigners not naturalized.	No. of militia.
924	Liberty	148	148	493	431	924	......	......	......	550	25	349	......	64	256	94	35	14	171	20	109
667	Mosalem	120	120	360	307	667	......	......	......	304	40	323	......	17	106	62	16	6	156	20	126
1264	New Wine, exc. of Dyersville	206	206	699	565	1264	......	......	......	627	106	536	5	43	286	128	49	21	221	35	172
960	Peru	178	178	510	450	960	......	......	......	533	64	352	— 11	40	266	98	41	18	187	5	135
998	Prairie Creek	150	150	548	450	998	......	......	......	550	146	301	— 1	41	275	136	19	14	224	5	146
1453	Table Mound	210	210	744	708	1452	1	......	1	883	114	456	......	85	458	122	22	3	294	18	149
1833	Taylor	340	340	959	874	1833	......	......	......	803	671	359	......	96	449	159	52	30	423	10	275
1265	Vernon	191	191	703	562	1265	......	......	......	657	260	286	— 62	44	331	97	45	14	313	20	176
929	Washington	161	161	484	445	929	......	......	......	480	235	158	— 56	42	222	120	30	5	188	3	103
1067	Whitewater	245	245	546	520	1066	1	......	1	538	199	279	— 51	51	261	110	36	7	216	16	129
20240	Total	3531	3533	10666	9572	20238	2	......	2	10690	3189	6027	......	915	5179	2025	640	244	4205	312	2790
	Dubuque, city of, C. H.																				
5204	" First ward	850	895	2605	2583	5188	7	9	16	2501	1267	1436	......	375	1095	316	212	212	1090	42	786
2278	" Second ward	238	271	1299	939	2238	20	20	40	882	542	854	......	85	449	122	77	27	451	119	358
4829	" Third ward	771	937	2292	2469	4761	37	31	68	2181	1046	1602	......	372	995	235	231	48	979	115	693
5951	" Fourth ward	984	1085	2829	3096	5925	12	14	26	2714	2008	1229	......	222	1463	500	178	69	1194	73	793
5343	" Fifth ward	934	972	2672	2668	5340	2	1	3	2635	575	2133	......	236	1591	390	269	59	840	245	403
23605	Total of city	3769	4160	11697	11755	23452	78	75	153	10913	5438	7254	......	1290	5591	1563	967	258	4554	592	3033
43845	Total of county	7300	7693	22363	21327	43690	80	75	155	21603	8627	13281	......	2205	10770	3588	1607	502	8759	904	5823

EMMET COUNTY.

Total population.	Names of townships, towns, and cities.	No. dwelling houses.	No. of families.	White population. Male.	White population. Female.	White population. Total.	Colored pop'lation. Male.	Colored pop'lation. Female.	Colored pop'lation. Total.	Nativity of inhabitants. No. born in Iowa.	Nativity of inhabitants. No. born in U. S., but not in Iowa.	Nativity of inhabitants. No. born in foreign countries.	Nativity of inhabitants. Surplus or deficiency.	Between 5 and 21 years old. No. 5 years old and under 6.	Between 5 and 21 years old. No. 6 years old and under 16.	Between 5 and 21 years old. No. 16 years old and under 21.	No. births in 1874.	No. deaths in 1874.	No. of voters.	No. foreigners not naturalized.	No. of militia.
192	Armstrong Grove	38	38	113	79	192	......	......	......	46	73	73	......	8	53	17	5	1	40	45	30
115	Centre	20	20	60	55	115	......	......	......	39	19	49	— 8	11	30	5	2	......	24	1	15

62	Ellsworth	17	17	34	28	62	......	......	......	17	38	7	....	5	6	5	6	4	19	......	14
173	Emmet	32	32	98	75	173	......	......	......	53	88	32	....	8	47	17	7	1	42	1	33
381	Estherville—Estherville, C. H.	85	85	191	186	377	3	1	4	123	183	75	....	22	89	27	21	4	82	1	67
205	High Lake	31	31	113	92	205	......	......	......	62	64	86	7	18	55	16	3	......	33	10	20
45	Iowa Lake	9	9	29	16	45	......	......	......	......	45	....	....	2	14	8	......	......	15	......	4
216	Peterson	37	37	114	102	216	......	......	......	90	25	98	—3	26	48	15	8	1	32	2	21
47	Swan Lake	11	11	27	20	47	......	......	......	12	4	31	....	2	7	1	3	......	12	......	10
1436	Total	280	280	779	653	1432	3	1	4	442	539	451	....	102	349	111	55	11	299	60	214

FAYETTE COUNTY.

1103	Auburn	201	201	556	547	1103	......	......	......	460	548	103	8	42	211	157	16	3	228	......	136
277	Banks	55	55	153	124	277	......	......	......	92	121	63	—1	11	71	29	7	3	65	......	51
484	Bethel	100	100	272	212	484	......	......	......	280	282	10	88	23	119	33	17	2	110	......	76
560	Center	117	117	310	250	560	......	......	......	181	336	40	—3	13	96	25	4	2	127	......	107
1566	Clermont	293	293	787	779	1566	......	......	......	660	496	403	—7	66	413	153	56	6	318	......	166
1406	Dover	253	253	713	693	1406	......	......	......	711	361	364	30	58	392	116	61	21	220	56	120
1119	Eden	212	212	623	496	1119	......	......	......	452	506	150	—11	44	276	104	39	5	253	15	188
1253	Fairfield	250	250	646	607	1253	......	......	......	520	503	62	—168	52	325	73	66	16	289	3	122
868	Fayette, town of	174	206	419	449	868	......	......	......	258	556	59	5	22	203	68	22	7	234	6	145
575	Fremont	105	105	297	278	575	......	......	......	237	249	93	4	26	146	61	8	3	125	4	89
560	Harlan	115	115	294	266	560	......	......	......	163	298	57	—42	28	122	30	18	5	145	1	96
1010	Illyria	192	192	520	482	1002	4	4	8	461	405	132	—12	37	295	124	39	14	224	4	144
914	Jefferson	197	197	490	424	914	......	......	......	336	343	131	—104	39	202	67	39	18	207	......	114
776	Oran	148	148	402	374	776	......	......	......	314	347	102	—13	35	199	84	24	14	156	8	115
1704	Pleasant Valley	320	320	905	789	1694	5	5	10	758	613	351	18	77	418	37	80	21	470	32	235
737	Putnam	149	149	382	355	737	......	......	......	257	360	126	6	22	198	73	20	6	146	......	96
430	Scott	78	78	214	216	430	......	......	......	141	189	99	—1	11	102	52	10	5	89	15	65
769	Smithfield	141	106	402	364	766	1	1	2	244	456	74	5	21	197	95	18	10	189	4	95
1054	Westfield, exc. of Fayette	196	196	549	499	1048	5	1	6	421	506	100	—27	16	268	110	13	4	232	1	146
1083	West Union, exc. of town	220	220	542	541	1083	......	......	......	537	534	124	112	44	307	133	31	4	271	3	167
1388	West Union, town of, C. H.	244	244	670	718	1388	......	......	......	471	668	132	—117	49	220	93	36	8	327	......	193
883	Windsor	168	168	457	426	883	......	......	......	358	423	96	—6	27	254	75	29	10	202	4	115
20518	Total	3928	3925	10603	9889	20492	15	11	26	8312	9100	2871	....	763	5034	1792	653	187	4637	156	2781

FLOYD COUNTY.

496	Cedar	46	46	254	242	496	......	......	......	194	233	69	....	28	119	33	15	6	107	......	82
1125	Floyd	226	226	587	537	1124	1	......	1	357	674	94	....	39	253	126	41	15	284	14	177
769	Niles	70	71	393	376	769	......	......	......	269	306	194	....	55	208	57	26	8	158	5	94
742	Nora Springs, town of	143	147	388	354	742	......	......	......	199	448	95	....	52	127	52	32	17	187	9	129
581	Pleasant Grove	108	108	313	268	581	......	......	......	154	308	119	....	22	143	52	19	8	135	31	111

FLOYD COUNTY.—Continued.

Total population.	NAMES OF TOWNSHIPS, TOWNS, AND CITIES.	No. of dwelling houses.	Number of families.	WHITE POPULATION. Males.	Female.	Total.	COLORED POP'LATION Male.	Female.	Total.	NATIVITY OF INHABITANTS. No. born in Iowa.	No. born in U. S., but not in Iowa.	No. born in foreign countries.	Surplus or deficiency.	BETWEEN 5 AND 21 YEARS OLD. No. 5 years old and under 6.	No. 6 years old and under 16.	No. 16 years old and under 21.	No. births in 1874.	No. deaths in 1874.	No. of voters.	No. foreigners not naturalized.	No. of militia.
925	Riverton	164	164	464	461	925	......	......	......	331	489	105	......	36	219	72	20	8	188	15	128
1058	Rockford	202	207	541	517	1058	......	......	......	300	701	57	......	38	234	100	27	9	264	15	189
713	Rock Grove, exc. Nora Springs	128	128	380	333	713	......	......	......	280	359	74	......	35	174	68	29	15	159	9	101
590	Rudd	118	118	301	289	590	......	......	......	190	285	115	......	43	102	84	30	2	127	5	99
357	Scott	66	66	189	168	357	......	......	......	121	206	30	......	18	92	29	14	5	81	......	63
1490	St. Charles, exc. of City	270	274	783	706	1489	1	......	1	463	654	373	......	73	299	99	41	22	303	......	254
727	Ulster	159	159	399	328	727	......	......	......	207	306	214	......	37	170	42	37	6	131	32	99
1258	Union	230	238	652	606	1258	......	......	......	463	635	160	......	81	332	94	45	8	253	15	202
10831	Total	1930	1952	5644	5185	10829	2	......	2	3528	5605	1699	......	557	2472	908	376	129	2377	150	1728
	Charles City, C. H.																				
560	" First Ward	101	109	277	283	560	......	......	......	146	320	94	......	15	133	51	17	5	130	40	90
567	" Second Ward	112	121	286	281	567	......	......	......	162	323	82	......	15	133	47	11	1	136	20	91
539	" Third Ward	112	116	250	289	539	......	......	......	154	282	103	......	19	112	43	21	8	124	21	78
603	" Fourth Ward	121	126	304	299	603	......	......	......	188	290	125	......	14	161	54	20	3	117	51	79
2269	Total of city	446	472	1117	1152	2269	......	......	......	650	1215	404	......	63	539	195	69	17	507	132	338
13100	Total of county	2376	2424	6761	6337	13098	2	......	2	4178	6819	2103	......	620	3011	1103	445	146	2884	282	2066

FRANKLIN COUNTY.

Total population.	NAMES OF TOWNSHIPS, TOWNS, AND CITIES.	No. of dwelling houses.	Number of families.	Males.	Female.	Total.	Male.	Female.	Total.	No. born in Iowa.	No. born in U. S., but not in Iowa.	No. born in foreign countries.	Surplus or deficiency.	No. 5 years old and under 6.	No. 6 years old and under 16.	No. 16 years old and under 21.	No. births in 1874.	No. deaths in 1874.	No. of voters.	No. foreigners not naturalized.	No. of militia.
552	Clinton	107	107	302	250	552	......	......	......	144	271	109	— 28	24	118	58	15	1	135	14	73
669	Geneva	132	122	356	313	669	......	......	......	89	320	131	—129	30	230	61	25	9	126	21	95
273	Grant	55	55	163	110	273	......	......	......	90	164	24	5	28	64	25	9	1	62	......	43
183	Hamilton	36	36	97	86	183	......	......	......	68	69	42	— 4	34	46	17	8	5	39	1	31

1048	Hampton, town of, C. H.	224	224	522	526	1048	......	......	......	277	468	100	—203	35	202	100	43	13	262	11	218
456	Ingham	81	81	249	207	456	......	......	......	134	301	21	......	19	121	36	14	2	105	......	74
206	Lee	43	43	110	96	206	......	......	......	47	138	21	......	5	51	19	8	3	48	......	38
129	Marion	27	27	68	61	129	......	......	......	30	68	31	......	9	51	13	8	1	29	8	17
339	Morgan	64	64	186	153	339	......	......	......	102	144	92	— 1	17	86	27	14	5	62	55	41
429	Oakland	77	77	204	225	429	......	......	......	126	218	85	......	21	103	31	19	3	68	26	50
657	Osceola	132	132	330	327	657	......	......	......	214	247	75	9	33	172	64	18	10	102	9	85
588	Reeve	118	118	311	277	588	......	......	......	211	345	38	— 6	25	137	58	20	10	125	......	76
148	Richland	27	27	71	77	148	......	......	......	53	76	25	— 6	10	34	21	5	......	24	3	26
536	Washington, exc. of Hampton	98	98	277	259	536	......	......	......	135	226	151	24	24	41	31	23	11	109	5	95
345	West Fork	61	61	182	163	345	......	......	......	93	203	55	— 6	14	88	26	6	1	78	5	57
6558	Total	1272	1272	3428	3130	6558	......	......	......	1813	3258	1000	......	328	1544	587	235	75	1374	158	1019

FREMONT COUNTY.

106	Bartlett, town of	22	22	51	55	106	......	......	......	26	78	2	......	2	18	11	3	1	33	......	23
809	Benton, exc. of towns of East Port and Percival	152	152	419	386	805	2	2	4	263	495	51	......	30	186	45	11	1	192	......	138
134	East Port, town of	27	27	73	61	134	......	......	......	60	64	10	......	6	28	7	2	1	27	......	17
103	Farragut, town of	24	24	58	45	103	......	......	......	38	62	3	......	10	12	7	8	3	29	......	22
893	Fisher, exc. of Farragut	152	152	485	408	893	......	......	......	347	520	96	70	40	143	66	32	1	188	7	129
750	Franklin, exc. of Hamburg	139	139	379	371	750	......	......	......	352	309	89	......	41	160	51	34	8	148	12	115
189	Fremont City, town of	36	36	101	88	189	......	......	......	90	97	2	......	12	40	17	7	5	39	......	25
2058	Hamburg, city of	374	374	1062	984	2046	7	5	12	673	1242	143	......	106	296	150	55	35	437	25	366
389	Locust Grove	79	79	210	176	389	......	......	......	120	242	27	......	12	69	22	27	8	94	4	47
1026	Madison	171	171	555	470	1025	1	......	1	455	536	35	......	51	228	97	38	7	214	2	162
9	McPaul, town of	2	2	5	4	9	......	......	......	3	3	3	......	1	......	......	1	......	2	......	2
810	Monroe	150	150	453	356	809	1	......	1	273	493	44	......	36	199	54	25	6	191	......	142
55	Percival, town of	11	11	30	25	55	......	......	......	25	23	7	......	3	15	3	3	1	12	......	8
550	Prairie	98	98	286	264	550	......	......	......	214	327	9	......	39	54	31	5	4	117	......	89
298	Riverton, exc. of town	62	62	168	130	298	......	......	......	98	188	12	......	45	95	62	18	2	63	......	98
456	Riverton, town of	92	92	230	226	456	......	......	......	150	293	13	......	24	75	30	12	10	101	......	89
1068	Ross, exc. of Tabor	203	203	557	511	1068	......	......	......	491	541	36	......	95	275	88	15	16	248	1	171
1232	Scott, exc. of towns of McPaul, Bartlett, and Fremont City	239	239	611	621	1232	......	......	......	538	668	26	......	68	33	113	50	17	248	4	156
1310	Sidney, exc. of town	231	231	701	609	1310	......	......	......	585	708	17	......	87	352	131	43	15	279	2	206
822	Sidney, town of, C. H	151	151	430	390	820	......	2	2	318	491	13	......	45	203	73	31	2	198	1	130
298	Tabor, town of	56	56	147	148	295	2	1	3	102	181	15	......	5	61	31	4	6	52	......	42
354	Walnut	65	65	197	157	354	......	......	......	116	235	3	......	36	88	50	7	6	86	......	66
13719	Total	2436	2436	7208	6488	13696	13	10	23	5337	7796	556	......	794	2630	1139	431	155	2998	58	2243

GREENE COUNTY.

Total population.	NAMES OF TOWNSHIPS, TOWNS, AND CITIES.	No. of dwelling houses.	No. of families.	WHITE POPULATION. Male.	Female.	Total.	COLORED POP'LATION Male.	Female.	Total.	NATIVITY OF INHABITANTS. No. born in Iowa.	No. born in U. S., but not in Iowa.	No. born in foreign countries.	Surplus or deficiency.	BETWEEN 5 AND 21 YEARS OLD. No. 5 years old and under 6.	No. 6 years old and under 16.	No. 16 years old and under 21.	No. births in 1874.	No. deaths in 1874.	No. of voters.	No. foreigners not naturalized.	No. of militia.
514	Bristol	101	101	278	236	514	......	......	......	214	280	20	......	40	112	29	8	9	118	......	94
369	Cedar	69	69	189	180	369	......	......	......	137	142	90	......	17	96	38	15	14	75	......	67
31	Dawson	6	6	14	17	31	......	......	......	18	13	......	......	2	4	4	4	......	8	......	6
395	Franklin	70	70	211	184	395	......	......	......	127	105	30	−133	17	14	18	10	4	81	2	56
479	Grand Junction, town of	93	93	251	227	478	1	......	1	144	257	78	......	20	98	26	15	5	125	6	89
208	Greenbrier	47	47	108	100	208	......	......	......	39	153	16	......	13	60	11	10	1	47	11	31
293	Hardin	63	63	152	141	293	......	......	......	82	154	52	— 5	19	65	4	8	3	63	5	48
122	Highland	21	21	66	56	122	......	......	......	27	53	42	......	6	32	7	5	2	22	6	22
489	Jackson	95	95	253	236	489	......	......	......	193	296	......	......	22	101	27	21	9	116	......	85
802	Jefferson, exc. of town	148	148	424	387	802	......	......	......	310	429	26	— 37	22	223	61	27	9	172	8	166
895	Jefferson, town of, C. H.	186	186	446	449	895	......	......	......	291	547	57	......	42	233	75	22	14	211	......	156
469	Junction, exc. of Grand Junction	90	90	247	122	469	......	......	......	142	260	70	3	35	99	3	12	1	100	2	65
608	Kendrick	119	119	307	301	608	......	......	......	256	346	6	......	33	151	56	18	11	137	1	91
218	Scranton, exc. of town	40	40	120	98	218	......	......	......	51	128	39	......	11	51	23	4	1	48	4	42
234	Scranton, town of	43	43	126	108	234	......	......	......	60	142	32	......	8	49	11	7	4	68	......	55
775	Washington	140	140	417	358	775	......	......	......	323	389	63	......	22	212	56	18	6	198	......	143
127	Willow	28	28	68	59	127	......	......	......	27	74	26	......	3	19	7	5	1	33	8	28
7028	Total	1359	1359	3677	3259	7027	1		1	2441	3768	647		332	1619	456	209	94	1622	53	1244

GRUNDY COUNTY.

Total population.	NAMES OF TOWNSHIPS, TOWNS, AND CITIES.	No. of dwelling houses.	No. of families.	Male.	Female.	Total.	Male.	Female.	Total.	No. born in Iowa.	No. born in U. S., but not in Iowa.	No. born in foreign countries.	Surplus or deficiency.	No. 5 years old and under 6.	No. 6 years old and under 16.	No. 16 years old and under 21.	No. births in 1874.	No. deaths in 1874.	No. of voters.	No. foreigners not naturalized.	No. of militia.
503	Beaver	95	95	260	243	503	......	......	......	148	245	110	......	19	124	37	20	7	90	20	68
557	Blackhawk	83	83	314	241	555	2	......	2	160	243	154	......	23	116	44	24	5	122	2	101
492	Clay	91	91	258	234	492	......	......	......	121	335	36	......	11	122	42	22	8	122	8	98
522	Colfax	102	102	281	241	522	......	......	......	116	198	208	......	33	117	33	17	4	74	14	91
740	Fairfield	139	148	401	339	740	......	......	......	280	271	189	......	29	190	62	23	6	133	36	122

652	Felix	127	127	351	301	652	......	......	......	248	392	12	....	32	164	49	27	10	151	1	137
930	German	188	188	479	451	930	......	......	......	363	226	341	....	43	244	81	36	26	105	63	134
578	Grant	100	100	321	257	578	......	......	......	156	223	199	....	16	141	46	26	4	96	5	68
352	Lincoln	70	70	191	161	352	......	......	......	74	159	119	....	18	59	31	11	1	71	9	72
597	Melrose	113	113	314	283	597	......	......	......	183	354	60	....	20	161	56	15	15	137	1	119
962	Palermo, Grundy Center, C. H.	166	166	525	437	962	......	......	......	250	579	133	....	40	201	80	34	18	234	30	191
698	Pleasant Valley	132	137	388	310	698	......	......	......	154	200	344	....	25	149	40	41	18	101	72	67
551	Shiloh	102	102	299	252	551	......	......	......	177	174	200	....	18	112	56	31	12	89	36	89
8134	Total	1508	1522	4382	3750	8132	2	......	2	2430	3599	2105	....	327	1900	657	327	134	1525	297	1357

GUTHRIE COUNTY.

524	Bear Grove	97	97	281	243	524	......	......	......	198	282	16	— 28	15	110	30	13	3	113	......	68
539	Beaver	110	110	278	261	539	......	......	......	181	333	3	— 22	34	112	35	4	1	131	......	95
1191	Cass, exc. of Panora	222	222	624	567	1191	......	......	......	460	682	27	— 22	48	276	106	39	17	272	5	180
808	Center	193	193	418	390	808	......	......	......	300	477	31	....	28	177	66	41	21	199	......	152
204	Dodge	34	34	112	91	203	1	......	1	98	105	7	6	5	62	12	5	2	44	......	31
222	Grant	45	45	118	104	222	......	......	......	70	118	33	— 1	15	57	17	11	5	51	1	44
317	Highland	61	61	158	159	317	......	......	......	132	171	16	2	18	78	24	17	3	71	2	54
819	Jackson	149	151	425	394	819	......	......	......	336	459	24	....	32	213	77	32	9	181	......	143
278	Orange	47	47	147	131	278	......	......	......	123	149	3	— 3	9	78	23	12	5	60	......	38
526	Panora, town of, C. H.	104	104	264	262	526			......	193	301	5	— 24	22	116	33	17	12	115	......	96
1531	Penn	293	293	839	690	1529	1	1	2	514	845	143	— 29	61	294	126	72	20	406	9	359
473	Richland	81	81	260	213	473	......	......	......	101	319	57	4	20	123	48	16	5	124	3	104
755	Thompson	137	137	399	356	755	......	......	......	312	391	52	....	50	179	54	22	3	162	4	112
286	Union	47	47	154	132	286	......	......	......	116	152	12	— 6	16	63	38	12	3	65	1	57
578	Valley	101	101	301	277	578	......	......	......	247	304	19	— 8	30	168	51	23	7	120	......	94
587	Victory	106	106	307	280	587	......	......	......	273	267	42	— 5	29	160	52	26	12	125	......	89
9638	Total	1827	1829	5085	4550	9635	2	1	3	3657	5355	490	....	432	2266	792	362	128	2239	25	1716

HAMILTON COUNTY.

453	Blairsburg	85	85	235	218	453	......	......	......	138	224	87	— 4	28	115	19	23	4	91	4	....
2262	Boone, Webster City, C. H.	531	531	1150	1111	2261	......	1	1	683	1359	321	101	139	469	118	43	9	548	44	164
538	Cass	98	98	276	262	538	......	......	......	178	305	38	— 17	16	148	61	24	3	109	......	....
359	Clear Lake	59	59	189	170	359	......	......	......	109	97	153	....	18	61	33	22	5	41	39	57
418	Ellsworth	71	71	212	206	418	......	......	......	126	73	220	1	17	89	22	13	5	42	72	20
470	Fremont	93	93	253	216	469	1	......	1	158	216	62	— 34	18	117	....	17	4	81	......	26
730	Hamilton	113	113	384	346	730	......	......	......	309	356	65	....	33	197	65	32	5	101	......	95
275	Lyon	51	51	150	125	275	......	......	......	106	125	58	14	6	61	73	14	4	56	4	49
786	Marion	146	146	404	382	786	......	......	......	295	240	234	— 17	52	164	50	33	7	128	33	70
107	Rose Grove	25	25	58	49	107	......	......	......	35	68	4	....	5	25	14	.....	6	32	......	21

HAMILTON COUNTY.—Continued.

Total population.	Names of townships, towns, and cities.	No. of dwellings.	Number of families.	White population. Male.	White population. Female.	White population. Total.	Colored pop'lation. Male.	Colored pop'lation. Female.	Colored pop'lation. Total.	Nativity of inhabitants. No. born in Iowa.	No. born in U. S., but not in Iowa.	No. born in foreign countries.	Surp'us or deficiency.	Between 5 and 21 years old. No. 5 years old and under 6.	No. 6 years old and under 16.	No. 16 years old and under 21.	No. births in 1874.	No. deaths in 1874.	No. of voters.	No. foreigners not naturalized.	No. of militia.
485	Scott	88	88	249	236	485	......	......	......	127	107	242	— 9	25	111	25	25	5	59	62	40
818	Webster	159	160	426	392	818	......	......	......	341	431	22	— 24	18	214	80	11	1	167	6	127
7701	Total	1519	1520	3986	3713	7699	1	1	2	2605	3601	1506	......	375	1771	560	257	58	1455	264	669

HANCOCK COUNTY,

Total population.	Names of townships, towns, and cities.	No. of dwellings.	Number of families.	White population. Male.	White population. Female.	White population. Total.	Colored pop'lation. Male.	Colored pop'lation. Female.	Colored pop'lation. Total.	Nativity of inhabitants. No. born in Iowa.	No. born in U. S., but not in Iowa.	No. born in foreign countries.	Surp'us or deficiency.	Between 5 and 21 years old. No. 5 years old and under 6.	No. 6 years old and under 16.	No. 16 years old and under 21.	No. births in 1874.	No. deaths in 1874.	No. of voters.	No. foreigners not naturalized.	No. of militia.
200	Amsterdam	37	37	97	103	200	......	......	......	55	122	23	......	7	60	9	5	1	39	1	18
114	Avery	25	25	60	49	109	2	3	5	47	58	6	— 3	10	24	4	3	1	31	......	19
50	Britt	10	12	26	24	50	......	......	......	9	28	13	......	2	14	7	......	......	11	......	4
375	Concord, Concord, C. H.	66	66	188	187	375	......	......	......	113	194	68	......	13	95	17	6	......	77	......	59
83	Crystal	18	18	53	30	83	......	......	......	10	58	14	— 1	4	21	8	2	......	17	2	13
505	Ellington	107	109	262	243	505	......	......	......	188	195	68	— 54	9	114	23	20	4	102	6	88
155	Madison	28	28	82	73	155	......	......	......	69	61	3	— 22	10	39	24	......	......	26	......	26
1482	Total	291	295	768	709	1477	2	3	5	491	716	195	......	55	367	92	36	6	303	9	227

HARDIN COUNTY.

Total population.	Names of townships, towns, and cities.	No. of dwellings.	Number of families.	White population. Male.	White population. Female.	White population. Total.	Colored pop'lation. Male.	Colored pop'lation. Female.	Colored pop'lation. Total.	Nativity of inhabitants. No. born in Iowa.	No. born in U. S., but not in Iowa.	No. born in foreign countries.	Surp'us or deficiency.	Between 5 and 21 years old. No. 5 years old and under 6.	No. 6 years old and under 16.	No. 16 years old and under 21.	No. births in 1874.	No. deaths in 1874.	No. of voters.	No. foreigners not naturalized.	No. of militia.
1286	Ackley, town of	....	246	624	660	1284	2	......	2	373	495	418	......	47	285	81	61	30	250	54	166
862	Alden	165	165	445	417	862	......	......	......	276	477	109	......	33	200	63	29	9	177	......	124
215	Buckeye	44	44	113	102	215	......	......	......	70	123	12	— 10	15	46	11	15	3	44	......	32
1371	Clay	266	264	680	691	1371	......	......	......	523	635	201	— 12	57	358	107	47	13	281	111	217
93	Concord	19	19	49	44	93	......	......	......	22	48	23	......	6	19	7	7	1	22	6	22
765	Eldora, exc. of town	....	143	409	356	765	......	......	......	302	408	62	7	33	205	78	5	2	168	6	129

1494	Eldora, town of, C. H.		313	754	737	1491	2	1	3	511	817	166	*	56	326	114	41	11	366	21	256
498	Ellis		103	252	246	498				172	196	43	— 87	16	133	40	9	1	110	3	78
854	Etna, exc. of Ackley		183	442	412	854				299	342	147	— 66	57	152	53	24	16	153		109
274	Grant		54	145	129	274				164	89	21		10	83	12	14	3	47		34
919	Hardin, exc. of Iowa Falls		194	466	452	918	1		1	259	558	60	— 42	30	226	76	22	17	214	10	155
1074	Iowa Falls, town of		245	509	548	1057	6	11	17	264	719	63	— 28	50	230	95	6	6	261	10	191
866	Jackson		160	444	422	866				327	459	80		42	227	73	29	14	179	3	126
1100	Pleasant		152	646	439	1085	15		15	405	411	82	—202	50	220	87	25	12	199	7	144
1186	Providence		231	609	577	1186				521	571	16	— 78	53	259	123	34	18	268		215
150	Sherman		28	83	67	150				44	58	48		4	32	15	8	3	28	7	21
464	Tipton	88	89	238	226	464				193	231	38	— 2	21	126	44	19	8	102	4	73
1068	Union, exc. of town		209	551	517	1068				478	569	21		49	284	103	36	17	228	6	168
471	Union, town of		134	244	226	470	1		1	180	273	1	— 17	29	117	28	20	16	118		88
15029	Total	582	2976	7703	7268	14971	27	12	39	5383	7479	1611		658	3528	1210	451	200	3215	248	2343

HARRISON COUNTY.

90	Allen	23	23	47	43	90				30	60			12	31		4		25		20
674	Boyer	130	130	352	322	674				278	300	58	— 34	39	164	60	11	10	148	6	108
365	Calhoun	69	69	197	168	365				162	163	37	— 3	11	80	29	7	2	89	2	57
256	Cass	51	51	125	131	256				108	130	16	— 2	13	52	20	12	3	58		42
518	Cincinnati	101	101	246	272	518				214	295	28	19	22	91	34	18	6	111	2	83
641	Clay	114	114	325	316	641				275	349	17		36	175	59	23	7	122		67
305	Douglas	64	64	162	143	305				103	141	57	— 4	22	54	20	11	3	70	7	52
636	Dunlap, town of	140	140	324	312	636				185	371	76	— 4	40	123	37	24	4	150		112
375	Harrison, exc. of Dunlap	70	70	195	180	375				113	100	16	146	24	85	34	11	2	85	1	65
329	Jackson	60	60	150	179	329				150	159	20		31	75	39			56		50
1038	Jefferson	206	206	535	503	1038				395	591	52		37	236	90	45	15	251	8	175
331	Lagrange	69	69	183	148	331				127	106	28	— 70	12	77	31	8	1	78		44
123	Lincoln	22	22	67	56	123				31	70	19	— 3	4	28	14	8	2	30	1	20
780	Little Sioux	146	146	416	364	780				333	417	32	2	44	193	74	34	12	179	16	136
939	Magnolia, Magnolia, C. H.	172	172	501	438	939				391	453	87	— 8	39	248	58	22	8	204		155
948	Missouri Valley, town of	207	207	504	444	948				257	590	102	1	52	160	55	24	7	267	18	132
682	Morgan	129	130	374	308	682				263	367	41	— 11	22	159	60	31	10	151	9	124
375	Raglan	66	66	202	173	375				176	164	34	— 1	10	87	39	10	1	88	1	71
1210	St. John	201	201	643	567	1210				542	618	63	13	57	383	94	46	20	247	2	202
668	Taylor	78	78	365	303	668				321	277	55	— 15	40	166	64	21	10	133	2	118
371	Union	76	76	202	169	371				152	171	25	— 23	21	86	35	13	4	82	3	55
164	Washington	31	31	83	81	164				90	58	11	— 5	14	37	10	8	2	34	1	26
11818	Total	2225	2226	6198	5620	11818				4696	5950	874		602	2790	956	392	129	2658	79	1914

HENRY COUNTY.

Total population.	NAMES OF TOWNSHIPS, TOWNS, AND CITIES.	No. of dwelling houses.	Number of families.	WHITE POPULATION. Male.	WHITE POPULATION. Female.	WHITE POPULATION. Total.	COLORED POP'LATION Male.	COLORED POP'LATION Female.	COLORED POP'LATION Total.	NATIVITY OF INHABITANTS. No. born in Iowa.	No. born in U. S., but not in Iowa.	No. born in foreign countries.	Surplus or deficiency.	BETWEEN 5 AND 21 YEARS OLD. No. 5 years old and under 6.	No. 6 years old and under 16.	No. 16 years old and under 21.	No. births in 1874.	No. deaths in 1874.	No. of voters.	No. foreigners not naturalized.	No. of militia.
1172	Baltimore	223	223	575	562	1137	19	16	35	594	528	53	3	53	337	135	38	5	244	6	157
928	Canaan	163	163	485	443	928	......	......	......	458	388	72	— 10	9	240	79	41	12	202	2	135
1989	Center, exc. of Mt. Pleasant	278	263	1020	950	1970	10	9	19	666	655	168	—500	40	341	156	44	69	346	19	241
1149	Jackson	207	207	566	548	1114	21	14	35	623	455	71	....	34	339	128	35	19	248	4	155
1267	Jefferson	260	259	660	605	1265	2	......	2	647	75	8	—537	50	308	107	36	18	255	33	210
1264	Marion	223	223	609	642	1251	5	8	13	618	515	54	— 77	69	73	202	28	20	278	6	170
1254	New London, exc. of town	236	236	633	608	1241	7	6	13	675	527	63	11	51	309	113	32	10	287	2	215
553	New London, town of	129	129	268	282	550	1	2	3	255	278	17	— 3	14	116	62	14	6	136	......	85
364	Rome, town of	92	92	176	188	364	......	......	......	172	128	41	— 23	9	78	30	24	10	74	11	43
1262	Salem, exc. of town	239	239	659	593	1252	5	5	10	696	535	37	6	42	310	136	31	17	342	1	216
479	Salem, town of	112	112	233	246	479	......	......	......	240	216	23	....	15	101	56	14	11	112	......	....
1122	Scott	205	205	569	553	1122	......	......	......	475	575	17	— 55	43	297	103	29	11	253	2	154
1407	Tippecanoe, exc. of Rome	259	264	708	659	1367	20	20	40	787	1352	55	787	47	422	138	32	23	277	10	193
1457	Trenton	291	296	735	689	1424	20	13	33	865	499	63	— 30	52	362	129	51	35	304	6	207
1364	Wayne	263	263	740	624	1364	......	......	......	575	531	285	27	49	320	96	33	24	377	34	246
17031	Total	3180	3174	8636	8192	16828	110	93	203	8346	7257	1027	....	577	3953	1670	482	290	3635	136	2427
	Mt. Pleasant, city of, c. H.																				
1715	" First ward	350	350	754	794	1548	87	80	167	669	866	131	— 49	63	391	149	37	27	395	27	256
1180	" Second ward	200	245	526	566	1092	45	43	88	485	624	67	— 4	52	281	95	30	21	244	5	105
836	" Third ward	175	175	423	405	828	3	5	8	199	417	81	—139	37	192	82	10	9	188	4	56
832	" Fourth ward	175	175	398	429	827	1	4	5	334	409	89	....	30	219	88	17	2	179	8	42
4563	Total of city	900	945	2101	2194	4295	136	132	268	1687	2316	368	....	182	1083	414	94	59	1006	44	459
21594	Total of county	4080	4119	10737	10886	21123	246	225	471	10033	9573	1395	....	759	5036	2084	576	349	4641	180	2886

HOWARD COUNTY.

620	Albion	118	118	347	273	620	......	......	......	205	307	108	......	142	58	37	18	......	159	8	106
661	Alton	116	116	362	299	661	......	......	......	293	316	52	......	50	166	49	28	12	149	14	115
391	Chester	70	70	201	190	391	......	......	......	131	214	46	......	16	77	61	21	6	92	......	71
1201	Cresco, town of, C. H.	225	225	606	579	1185	10	6	16	393	569	232	— 7	175	184	50	38	8	286	2	210
941	Forest City	183	183	496	445	941	......	......	......	228	496	217	......	33	208	97	65	3	215	30	181
381	Howard	69	69	207	174	381	......	......	......	137	144	100	......	20	104	32	15	6	75	4	60
381	Howard Center	78	78	212	169	381	......	......	......	64	214	103	......	11	87	53	14	8	94	4	67
389	Jamestown	74	74	213	176	389	......	......	......	118	182	89	......	10	88	39	9	......	90	2	48
1153	New Oregon	216	216	620	533	1153	......	......	......	452	340	361	......	48	298	100	28	4	208	56	147
255	Oak Dale	45	45	128	127	255	......	......	......	78	141	36	......	14	73	24	5	1	50	......	43
571	Paris	98	98	311	258	569	2	......	2	324	201	46	......	29	151	37	20	4	106	1	63
179	Saratoga	36	34	107	72	179	......	......	......	59	77	43	......	5	41	8	10	3	43	2	28
752	Vernon Springs, exc. of Cresco	135	135	389	352	741	6	5	11	254	384	114	......	49	140	76	24	9	145	17	50
7875	Total	1463	1461	4199	3647	7846	18	11	29	2736	3585	1547	......	602	1675	663	295	64	1712	140	1189

HUMBOLDT COUNTY.

185	Avery	......	30	106	79	185	......	......	......	35	116	19	— 15	5	55	22	6	1	36	......	18
429	Dakota, Dakota City, C. H.	......	101	238	191	429	......	......	......	128	177	140	16	20	95	30	15	1	89	17	66
316	Delano	......	61	166	150	316	......	......	......	91	113	112	......	19	64	25	13	3	50	......	39
327	Grove	......	61	178	149	327	......	......	......	145	141	41	......	14	92	31	6	3	77	......	57
303	Humboldt	......	53	151	152	303	......	......	......	124	125	42	— 12	18	82	39	11	......	54	......	38
399	Humboldt, town of	......	80	200	199	399	......	......	......	114	257	22	— 6	19	91	23	16	2	101	1	80
66	Lake	......	11	32	34	66	......	......	......	26	29	9	— 2	3	13	7	2	......	14	......	9
290	Norway	......	59	145	145	290	......	......	......	95	46	142	— 7	12	45	11	15	8	38	23	43
266	Rutland	......	50	137	129	266	......	......	......	80	134	34	— 18	16	54	14	7	2	63	......	45
272	Springvale, exc. of Humboldt	......	49	138	134	272	......	......	......	68	139	71	6	24	81	38	3	1	50	1	49
341	Vernon	......	70	181	160	341	......	......	......	127	175	48	9	24	89	27	3	1	70	......	57
165	Wacousta	......	29	81	84	165	......	......	......	68	52	45	......	7	33	12	7	......	31	......	22
96	Weaver	......	20	54	42	96	......	......	......	15	61	20	......	4	25	9	1	1	22	......	15
3455	Total	......	674	1807	1648	3455	......	......	......	1116	1565	745	......	185	819	288	105	23	695	42	538

IDA COUNTY.

232	Corwin, Ida, C. H.	150	150	132	100	232	......	......	......	72	136	23	— 1	11	47	28	10	3	64	......	58
94	Douglas	22	22	47	47	94	......	......	......	50	35	9	......	7	25	6	3	......	26	......	16

IDA COUNTY.—Continued.

Total population.	Names of townships, towns, and cities.	No. of dwelling houses.	Number of families.	White population. Male.	White population. Female.	White population. Total.	Colored pop'lation. Male.	Colored pop'lation. Female.	Colored pop'lation. Total.	Nativity of inhabitants. No. born in Iowa.	No. born in U. S., but not in Iowa.	No. born in foreign countries.	Surplus or deficiency.	Between 5 and 21 years old. No. 5 years old and under 6.	No. 6 years old and under 16.	No. 16 years old and under 21.	No. births in 1874.	No. deaths in 1874.	No. of voters.	No. foreigners not naturalized.	No. of militia.
105	Silver Creek	18	18	60	45	105	......	......	......	39	59	9	2	3	26	4	......	......	26	......	23
363	Maple	50	50	144	219	363	......	......	......	76	176	45	— 66	10	61	27	17	1	56	3	44
794	Total	240	240	383	411	794	......	......	......	237	406	86	......	31	159	65	30	4	172	3	141

IOWA COUNTY.

Total population.	Names of townships, towns, and cities.	No. of dwelling houses.	Number of families.	White population. Male.	White population. Female.	White population. Total.	Colored pop'lation. Male.	Colored pop'lation. Female.	Colored pop'lation. Total.	Nativity of inhabitants. No. born in Iowa.	No. born in U. S., but not in Iowa.	No. born in foreign countries.	Surplus or deficiency.	Between 5 and 21 years old. No. 5 years old and under 6.	No. 6 years old and under 16.	No. 16 years old and under 21.	No. births in 1874.	No. deaths in 1874.	No. of voters.	No. foreigners not naturalized.	No. of militia.
1624	Amana	208	1	827	797	1624	......	......	......	303	161	1160	......	57	274	69	41	25	313	231	......
234	Cono	41	41	123	111	234	......	......	......	103	38	2	9	8	51	21	10	2	33	......	41
1065	Dayton	210	210	578	487	1065	......	......	......	533	436	85	— 11	42	319	93	43	23	212	10	165
1596	English	309	309	820	776	1596	......	......	......	816	685	115	20	68	431	158	39	18	330	1	224
1073	Fillmore	148	183	548	525	1073	......	......	......	510	401	167	5	41	295	123	31	21	212	2	116
920	Green	168	164	484	436	920	......	......	......	470	351	93	— 6	43	259	85	34	18	183	1	108
825	Hartford, exc. of Victor	170	170	423	402	825	......	......	......	328	409	60	72	28	203	79	29	14	184	5	118
749	Hilton	139	139	384	365	749	......	......	......	309	180	224	— 36	36	159	43	29	6	108	9	46
977	Honey Creek	194	195	533	444	977	......	......	......	413	531	48	15	46	198	107	32	13	229	2	179
890	Iowa	195	175	451	439	890	......	......	......	351	169	364	— 6	42	204	47	43	11	177	20	123
504	Lenox	91	92	256	248	504	......	......	......	237	117	147	— 3	18	122	62	16	16	104	14	70
550	Lincoln	98	98	285	265	550	......	......	......	241	187	116	— 6	22	126	37	30	2	110	19	81
669	Marengo, exc. of town	130	130	356	313	669	......	......	......	288	307	118	44	35	116	74	23	9	146	1	115
1650	Marengo, town of, C. H.	373	360	807	836	1643	5	2	7	676	833	165	24	88	359	130	52	23	387	8	224
720	Pilot	136	133	397	323	720	......	......	......	321	272	127	......	38	180	48	35	9	152	16	97
785	Sumner	152	152	410	375	785	......	......	......	315	246	113	—111	37	33	32	19	8	143	......	107
939	Troy	163	163	486	450	936	2	1	3	400	314	222	— 3	67	229	106	29	19	188	5	91
496	Victor	98	98	250	246	496	......	......	......	141	319	58	22	16	118	29	16	10	119	......	85
579	Washington	104	102	309	270	579	......	......	......	154	201	45	—179	27	115	51	33	2	116	7	50
611	York	112	112	330	281	611	......	......	......	254	217	140	......	32	169	61	13	12	130	17	79
17456	Total	3239	3027	9057	8389	17446	7	3	10	7163	6374	3569	......	791	3960	1455	597	261	3576	368	2119

JACKSON COUNTY.

264	Andrew, town of	....	57	145	119	264	......	......	......	124	107	34	1	20	59	29	......	......	57	4	44
1623	Bellevue City	....	301	789	832	1621	2	......	2	741	482	390	— 10	92	370	133	71	29	356	41	256
961	Bellevue, exc. of town	....	143	503	458	961	......	......	......	582	73	275	— 31	82	361	70	25	5	155	7	90
1101	Brandon	....	217	589	512	1101	......	......	......	625	407	10	— 59	42	282	105	43	19	265	......	174
817	Butler	....	153	435	382	817	......	......	......	508	23	236	— 40	40	157	138	20	16	200	11	128
794	Fairfield	....	144	432	362	794	......	......	......	372	216	206	....	44	195	64	35	5	162	4	82
1640	Farmer's Creek	....	313	867	773	1640	......	......	......	866	666	101	— 7	73	403	149	40	4	361	4	205
1163	Iowa	....	228	585	578	1163	......	......	......	505	257	390	— 11	35	247	87	22	13	228	48	143
945	Jackson	....	164	459	486	945	......	......	......	506	218	274	53	124	179	44	45	4	182	......	....
1069	Maquoketa	....	189	567	502	1069	......	......	......	508	431	108	— 22	44	275	97	41	16	221	......	....
1415	Monmouth	....	284	724	691	1415	......	......	......	708	460	248	1	62	340	106	69	23	213	9	207
886	Otter Creek	....	130	441	445	886	......	......	......	459	191	183	— 53	27	237	95	24	4	169	......	....
847	Perry, exc. of Andrew	....	154	473	374	847	......	......	......	412	317	111	— 7	33	207	74	23	10	183	......	....
1045	Prairie Spring	....	170	543	501	1044	......	1	1	608	73	364	....	70	310	79	33	25	207	24	120
876	Richland	....	140	463	413	876	......	......	......	482	209	185	....	30	253	82	20	11	180	......	....
1003	Sabula, town of	....	222	540	462	1002	1	......	1	364	398	241	....	39	216	58	37	7	226	......	....
925	South Fork, exc. of Maquoketa	....	187	498	427	925	......	......	......	406	450	60	— 9	33	189	89	17	5	263	......	127
979	Tete Des Morts	....	170	522	457	979	......	......	......	516	37	428	— 2	33	236	98	28	14	148	69	92
206	Union, exc. of Sabula	....	39	108	98	206	......	......	......	68	73	36	— 29	24	38	22	8	......	44	5	19
1325	Van Buren	....	243	696	623	1319	4	2	6	559	437	327	— 2	61	280	105	42	7	271	93	179
1064	Washington	....	190	575	489	1064	......	......	......	514	226	310	— 14	52	279	93	35	15	173	35	83
20950	Total	....	3738	10954	9984	20938	8	4	12	10433	5751	4517	....	1060	5113	1817	678	232	4364	354	1849
	Maquoketa City, C. H.																				
685	" First ward	....	146	332	353	685	......	......	......	241	356	88	....	31	133	58	16	2	167	5	93
599	" Second ward	....	125	298	301	599	......	......	......	213	256	130	....	24	138	57	10	6	158	1	87
390	" Third ward	....	86	195	195	390	......	......	......	164	167	59	....	11	79	30	15	5	91	1	65
438	" Fourth ward	....	101	216	222	438	......	......	......	137	232	69	....	15	90	38	6	3	121	......	69
2112	Total of city	....	458	1041	1071	2112	......	......	......	755	1011	346	....	81	440	183	47	16	537	7	314
23062	Total of county	....	4296	11995	11055	23050	8	4	12	11188	6762	4863	....	1141	5553	2000	725	248	4901	361	2263

JASPER COUNTY.

1024	Buena Vista	201	185	527	497	1024	......	......	......	498	492	34	....	48	261	88	32	21	223	6	181
1098	Clear Creek	202	198	574	524	1098	......	......	......	549	514	35	....	58	296	109	43	12	217	4	160
1496	Des Moines, exc. of Prairie City	279	279	774	720	1494	2	......	2	666	777	53	....	87	334	119	33	21	276	......	181
1367	Elk Creek	232	239	685	681	1366	1	......	1	624	628	115	....	54	378	117	48	13	300	17	211
1689	Fairview, exc. of Monroe	286	286	868	821	1689	......	......	......	701	800	188	....	58	445	195	52	18	366	6	274
487	Hickory Grove	86	86	264	223	487	......	......	......	157	326	4	....	23	109	11	30	2	100	3	71

JASPER COUNTY.—Continued.

Total population.	Names of townships, towns, and cities.	No. of dwelling houses.	Number of families.	White population. Male.	White population. Female.	White population. Total.	Colored pop'lation. Male.	Colored pop'lation. Female.	Colored pop'lation. Total.	Nativity of inhabitants. No. born in Iowa.	No. born in U. S., but not in Iowa.	No. born in foreign countries.	Surplus or deficiency.	Between 5 and 21 years old. No. 5 years old and under 6	No. 6 years old and under 16.	No. 16 years old and under 21.	No. births in 1874.	No. deaths in 1874.	No. of voters.	No. foreigners not naturalized.	No. of militia.
989	Independence	177	177	520	469	989	......	......	......	423	457	109	....	47	266	77	36	11	197	23	144
500	Jasper City, town of	119	119	256	244	500	......	......	......	166	214	120	....	20	90	23	32	11	103	3	79
827	Kellogg, exc. of Jasper City	160	160	436	391	827	......	......	......	352	433	42	....	43	240	68	19	22	170	3	129
1281	Lynn Grove	244	244	670	611	1281	......	......	......	596	655	30	....	60	331	95	48	12	286	......	134
1026	Malaka	178	178	557	469	1026	......	......	......	439	483	104	....	69	297	111	38	7	212	2	150
571	Mariposa	105	104	298	273	571	......	......	......	185	258	128	....	116	179	41	16	7	107	......	75
1328	Monroe, town of	274	274	664	663	1327	1	......	1	455	817	56	....	104	276	113	36	9	303	......	180
789	Mound Prairie	151	151	405	384	789	......	......	......	292	450	47	....	35	209	66	26	6	164	3	133
646	Newton, exc. of city	124	124	341	301	642	1	3	4	257	332	57	....	26	167	58	20	6	143	9	88
2354	Newton, city of, C. H	496	496	1116	1175	2291	31	32	63	890	1384	80	....	77	564	233	23	7	543	6	356
1274	Palo Alto	218	218	674	598	1272	1	1	2	459	617	198	....	66	294	68	49	18	268	10	145
1121	Poweshiek	217	216	590	531	1121	......	......	......	469	612	40	....	35	262	99	40	22	250	2	124
781	Prairie City, town of	201	201	385	394	779	1	1	2	228	542	11	....	24	142	49	28	4	188	......	144
952	Richland	178	185	502	430	952	......	......	......	378	524	50	....	50	233	83	32	21	220	6	145
576	Rock Creek,	107	109	314	262	576	......	......	......	237	307	32	....	29	150	47	35	4	128	2	84
997	Sherman	191	191	543	454	997	......	......	......	415	536	46	....	34	250	93	44	10	249	2	182
955	Washington	191	191	522	433	955	......	......	......	324	590	41	....	40	214	71	45	16	226	......	184
24128	Total	4617	4611	12485	11568	24053	38	37	75	9760	12748	1620	......	1203	5987	2034	805	280	5239	107	3554

JEFFERSON COUNTY.

Total population.	Names of townships, towns, and cities.	No. of dwelling houses.	Number of families.	White population. Male.	White population. Female.	White population. Total.	Colored pop'lation. Male.	Colored pop'lation. Female.	Colored pop'lation. Total.	Nativity of inhabitants. No. born in Iowa.	No. born in U. S., but not in Iowa.	No. born in foreign countries.	Surplus or deficiency.	Between 5 and 21 years old. No. 5 years old and under 6	No. 6 years old and under 16.	No. 16 years old and under 21.	No. births in 1874.	No. deaths in 1874.	No. of voters.	No. foreigners not naturalized.	No. of militia.
359	Batavia, town of	....	75	167	192	359	......	......	......	149	187	12	— 11	9	80	28	14	2	83	1	50
988	Black Hawk	....	182	513	475	988	......	......	......	503	441	45	1	52	254	105	35	14	213	36	156
1157	Buchanan	....	235	595	562	1157	......	......	......	644	443	76	6	75	307	120	35	11	255	8	177
757	Cedar	....	150	392	361	752	4	......	4	416	245	98	2	20	174	87	23	17	156	26	107
1202	Des Moines	....	218	603	599	1202	......	......	......	682	514	15	9	28	295	117	43	17	281	1	197
1544	Fairfield, exc. of city	....	304	781	756	1537	3	4	7	672	741	100	— 31	41	383	164	34	13	356	4	247

1071	Liberty	......	201	558	513	1071	......	......	......	568	497	21	15	55	227	79	33	17	244	......	185
1675	Lockridge	......	322	869	801	1670	2	3	5	826	278	557	— 14	66	412	164	53	18	277	86	192
1112	Locust Grove, exc. of Batavia	......	204	562	550	1112	......	......	......	603	583	33	57	57	289	131	48	15	246	......	166
1678	Penn	......	826	874	803	1677	......	1	1	886	622	124	— 46	53	450	154	40	25	322	14	255
1096	Polk	......	239	579	517	1096	......	......	......	562	494	40	......	47	259	98	......	......	256	3	209
1047	Round Prairie	......	214	522	525	1047	......	......	......	542	334	191	8	39	285	73	32	20	214	37	158
1076	Walnut	......	184	551	525	1076	15	7	22	652	243	189	8	39	284	113	37	15	228	......	145
14784	Total	......	2854	7566	7179	14745	24	15	39	7705	5612	1501	......	561	3699	1433	422	184	3131	216	2244
	Fairfield, City of, C. H.,																				
540	First Ward	......	118	258	271	529	3	8	11	219	292	29	..	20	118	49	17	4	145	......	91
676	" Second Ward	......	160	343	330	673	1	2	3	295	340	41	......	25	134	63	21	12	178	1	129
608	" Third Ward	......	133	285	306	591	10	7	17	250	329	29	......	19	128	58	26	11	150	2	125
519	" Fourth Ward	......	100	353	264	517	2	......	2	222	270	27	......	20	125	57	18	4	117	......	91
2343	Total of city	......	511	1139	1171	2310	16	17	33	986	1231	126	......	84	505	227	82	31	590	3	436
17127	Total of county	......	3365	8705	8350	17055	40	32	72	8691	6843	1627	......	645	4204	1660	504	215	3721	219	2680

JOHNSON COUNTY.

1311	Big Grove	234	234	692	619	1311	......	......	......	661	384	266	......	55	323	128	40	8	238	18	229
939	Cedar	167	167	480	459	939	......	......	......	468	222	239	— 10	41	258	75	40	17	189	32	137
754	Clear Creek	125	125	404	350	754	......	......	......	367	292	95	......	45	121	74	20	4	148	9	94
297	Coralville, town of	73	73	152	145	297	......	......	......	113	140	44	......	11	51	16	12	4	67	......	51
889	Fremont	137	137	450	439	889	......	......	......	462	397	30	......	20	109	73	11	3	197	8	132
880	Graham	154	154	447	432	879	1	......	1	424	285	171	......	26	252	111	25	6	191	16	135
764	Hardin	130	130	406	358	764	......	......	......	363	238	161	— 2	59	227	62	18	10	175	1	129
862	Jefferson	158	158	443	419	862	......	......	......	352	178	332	......	38	234	58	48	10	174	13	117
614	Liberty	97	97	338	276	614	......	......	......	227	226	161	......	20	199	85	10	3	112	6	77
568	Lincoln	103	103	295	273	568	......	......	......	215	224	129	......	23	142	63	18	3	125	8	86
1429	Lucas, exc. of Iowa City and addition, and Coralville	260	260	723	707	1429	......	......	......	663	487	379	100	80	357	148	39	8	307	11	187
(93	Madison	114	114	364	329	693	......	......	......	340	270	83	......	49	169	84	29	4	140	12	105
899	Monroe	158	158	445	454	899	......	......	......	399	169	331	......	34	264	78	29	13	128	253	102
746	Newport	132	132	379	367	746	......	......	......	416	110	220	......	59	227	125	20	5	135	5	74
1009	Oxford	182	182	516	493	1009	......	......	......	445	330	185	— 49	37	286	77	26	9	215	3	99
694	Penn	130	130	359	335	694	......	......	......	326	274	79	— 18	23	164	69	33	6	151	9	105
579	Pleasant Valley	111	111	311	268	579	......	......	......	252	272	55	......	19	140	23	15	4	128	......	118
854	Scott	154	154	443	409	852	2	......	2	361	302	191	......	33	196	87	21	7	196	1	129
1196	Sharon	201	201	637	559	1196	......	......	......	600	416	170	— 10	38	336	117	42	19	225	23	157
713	Union	122	122	368	323	709	2	2	4	303	214	196	......	31	220	66	20	13	140	13	68
809	Washington	163	163	430	379	809	......	......	......	440	341	28	......	68	200	89	35	5	169	......	103
17499	Total	3105	3105	9100	8392	17492	5	2	7	8194	5771	3545	......	809	4475	1703	551	161	3550	441	2434

JOHNSON COUNTY.—Continued.

Total population.	Names of townships, towns, and cities.	No. of dwelling houses.	Number of families.	White population. Male.	White population. Female.	White population. Total.	Colored pop'lation. Male.	Colored pop'lation. Female.	Colored pop'lation. Total.	Nativity of inhabitants. No. born in Iowa.	Nativity of inhabitants. No. born in U. S., but not in Iowa.	Nativity of inhabitants. No. born in foreign countries.	Nativity of inhabitants. Surplus or deficiency.	Between 5 and 21 years old. No. 5 years old and under 6.	Between 5 and 21 years old. No. 6 years old and under 16.	Between 5 and 21 years old. No. 16 years old and under 21.	No. births in 1874.	No. deaths in 1874.	No. of voters.	No. foreigners not naturalized.	No. of militia.
	Iowa City, C. H.																				
1478	" First ward	251	251	788	687	1475	2	1	3	566	697	233	18	61	403	201	20	10	436	23	358
1209	" Second ward	210	210	553	643	1196	5	8	13	507	254	178	270	58	236	128	34	6	297	9	226
2626	" Third ward	385	385	1041	973	2014	4	8	12	923	372	371	360	144	524	151	97	12	412	43	267
1658	" Fourth ward	282	282	823	814	1637	6	15	21	618	733	307	....	67	370	216	45	16	382	19	387
6371	Total of city	1128	1128	3205	3117	6322	17	32	49	2614	2056	1089	....	330	1533	696	196	44	1527	94	1235
784	Addition to Iowa City	170	170	375	365	740	25	19	44	314	134	336	....	39	209	64	20	12	148	10	93
24654	Total of county	4403	4403	12680	11874	24554	47	53	100	11122	7961	4970	....	1178	6217	2463	767	217	5225	545	3762

JONES COUNTY.

Total population.	Names of townships, towns, and cities.	No. of dwelling houses.	Number of families.	White population. Male.	White population. Female.	White population. Total.	Colored pop'lation. Male.	Colored pop'lation. Female.	Colored pop'lation. Total.	Nativity of inhabitants. No. born in Iowa.	Nativity of inhabitants. No. born in U. S., but not in Iowa.	Nativity of inhabitants. No. born in foreign countries.	Nativity of inhabitants. Surplus or deficiency.	Between 5 and 21 years old. No. 5 years old and under 6.	Between 5 and 21 years old. No. 6 years old and under 16.	Between 5 and 21 years old. No. 16 years old and under 21.	No. births in 1874.	No. deaths in 1874.	No. of voters.	No. foreigners not naturalized.	No. of militia.
775	Cass	....	166	394	378	772	3	......	3	364	448	51	88	74	214	86	32	10	190	......	86
707	Castle Grove	....	126	375	332	707	......	......	......	308	202	131	— 66	16	130	54	19	4	147	14	84
962	Clay	....	169	543	419	962	......	......	......	564	288	121	11	25	250	100	28	20	199	3	122
1173	Fairview, exc. of Anamosa	....	220	594	579	1173	......	......	......	554	528	104	13	40	309	119	43	7	258	2	160
1091	Greenfield	....	178	604	487	1091	......	......	......	502	543	63	17	31	324	130	26	11	235	18	183
988	Hale	....	187	528	460	988	......	......	......	503	456	31	2	48	288	102	30	8	201	......	145
800	Jackson	....	150	415	385	800	......	......	......	408	369	43	20	148	238	81	37	5	179	......	108
997	Madison	....	167	510	487	997	......	......	......	475	339	83	—100	24	219	58	22	9	153	3	94
909	Monticello, exc. of town	....	159	474	435	909	......	......	......	409	344	146	— 10	30	244	94	24	9	188	16	78
1587	Monticello, town of	....	332	760	825	1585	2	......	2	580	779	243	15	87	307	116	39	24	390	18	182
975	Oxford	....	201	506	468	974	1	......	1	417	305	253	....	35	231	72	33	14	206	23	125
740	Richland	....	134	387	353	740	......	......	......	367	166	178	— 29	32	196	97	20	20	160	2	80
1281	Rome	....	254	651	629	1280	1	......	1	537	711	34	1	65	306	94	24	14	316	4	199
821	Scotch Grove	....	137	421	400	821	......	......	......	388	289	135	— 9	40	216	79	20	......	166	14	72

130	Strawberry Hill, town of	......	30	59	66	125	1	4	5	38	91	9	8	8	31	6	......	......	31	......	......
787	Washington	......	140	422	365	787	......	......	......	443	421	227	304	54	221	115	2	......	173	16	90
1135	Wayne	......	210	581	554	1135	......	......	......	487	434	212	— 2	35	300	86	36	13	225	34	113
1014	Wyoming, exc. of town	......	181	504	510	1014	......	......	......	477	459	85	7	54	325	137	19	10	210	5	95
689	Wyoming, town of	......	157	331	358	689	......	......	......	251	366	57	— 15	21	143	51	14	5	158	......	98
17561	Total	......	3298	9059	8490	17549	8	4	12	8034	7347	2197	......	859	4461	1671	468	183	3654	172	2114
	Anamosa, town of, C. H.—																				
224	" First ward	......	57	101	116	217	4	3	7	70	114	33	— 7	8	59	15	5	4	63	......	35
582	" Second ward	......	124	312	270	582	......	......	......	238	305	35	— 4	32	151	54	11	......	141	......	74
467	" Third ward	......	105	240	227	467	......	......	......	173	250	33	— 11	20	105	39	9	4	121	4	28
332	" Fourth ward	......	70	161	171	332	......	......	......	136	164	22	— 6	9	83	26	12	......	70	......	58
1605	Total of town	......	356	814	784	1598	4	3	7	655	924	132	......	77	429	140	37	8	426	4	195
19166	Total of county	......	3654	9873	9274	19147	12	7	19	8689	8371	2329	......	936	4890	1811	505	191	4180	176	2309

KEOKUK COUNTY.

949	Adams	149	149	499	450	949	......	......	......	394	523	32	......	43	236	65	23	10	161	2	129
1199	Benton	220	224	606	593	1199	......	......	......	682	468	49	......	48	304	116	42	22	252	1	185
1270	Clear Creek	190	199	669	601	1270	......	......	......	592	411	267	......	41	290	40	42	14	242	14	143
1260	English River	228	228	654	606	1260	......	......	......	567	664	29	......	46	272	124	36	15	262	......	191
1532	German	261	272	784	748	1532	......	......	......	730	391	411	......	57	383	148	33	13	299	10	171
1467	Jackson	269	275	770	697	1467	......	......	......	827	626	14	......	78	394	123	50	22	289	......	213
1454	Lancaster	250	255	748	706	1454	......	......	......	810	579	65	......	39	361	137	59	19	281	12	228
1116	La Fayette, exc. of Keota	204	207	587	529	1116	......	......	......	499	443	174	......	68	282	101	27	18	220	16	171
646	Keota, town of	124	124	338	308	646	......	......	......	237	375	34	......	27	146	60	31	18	170	5	128
1080	Liberty	190	192	582	498	1080	......	......	......	478	558	44	......	59	338	85	48	22	228	......	154
926	Prairie	158	161	484	442	926	......	......	......	388	527	11	......	28	216	64	28	5	189	4	147
1050	Richland, exc. of town	194	200	547	503	1050	......	......	......	575	458	17	......	32	243	131	37	25	238	......	185
492	Richland, town of	98	98	239	253	492	......	......	......	227	261	4	......	16	118	......	9	10	119	2	72
948	Steady Run	190	193	469	479	948	......	......	......	474	444	30	......	48	193	195	3	1	203	......	168
733	Sigourney, exc. of town	140	143	385	348	733	......	......	......	370	297	66	......	27	181	72	25	11	170	2	113
1377	Sigourney, town of, C. H.	260	264	686	688	1374	2	1	3	592	687	98	......	77	275	120	32	10	311	2	230
1036	Van Buren	167	167	514	522	1036	......	......	......	540	388	108	......	45	294	122	15	3	199	18	92
707	Warren	144	148	362	345	707	......	......	......	397	305	5	......	31	158	58	19	5	135	......	102
1246	Washington	254	264	644	602	1246	......	......	......	588	623	35	......	123	308	139	28	24	234	4	123
20488	Total	3690	3763	10567	9918	20485	2	1	3	9967	9028	1493	......	933	4992	1900	587	267	4202	92	2945

KOSSUTH COUNTY.

Total Population.	NAMES OF TOWNSHIPS, TOWNS, AND CITIES.	No. of dwelling houses.	Number of families.	WHITE POPULATION. Male.	Female.	Total.	COLORED POP' LATION. Male.	Female.	Total.	NATIVITY OF INHABITANTS. No. born in Iowa.	No. born in U. S., but not in Iowa.	No. born in foreign countries.	Surplus or deficiency.	BETWEEN 5 AND 21 YEARS OLD. No 5 years old and under 6.	No. 6 years old and under 16.	No. 16 years old and under 21.	No. births in 1874.	No. deaths in 1874.	No. of voters.	No. foreigners not naturalized.	No. of militia.
417	Algona, exc. of town	....	....	217	200	417	.....	.....	.....	150	216	71	20	20	150	34	12	1	88	.....	55
989	Algona, town of, C. H.	....	....	496	493	989	.....	.....	.....	281	621	60	— 27	44	217	82	43	8	237	5	145
520	Cresco	....	....	261	259	520	.....	.....	.....	192	190	139	1	24	103	41	27	4	99	17	82
145	Fenton	....	....	74	71	145	.....	.....	.....	40	70	34	— 1	4	42	10	.....	.....	30	2	22
333	Greenwood	....	....	173	160	333	.....	.....	.....	86	103	142	— 2	17	76	28	17	3	43	27	19
460	Irvington	....	....	234	225	459	1	.....	1	185	213	61	— 1	12	141	28	3	3	90	5	58
186	Lotts Creek	....	....	97	89	186	.....	.....	.....	43	104	7	— 32	6	47	20	7	3	39	.....	29
469	Portland	....	....	251	216	467	1	1	2	139	260	36	— 34	22	77	33	6	5	93	5	56
246	Wesley	....	....	127	119	246	.....	.....	.....	63	133	41	— 9	8	43	13	11	2	54	3	44
3765	Total	....	....	1930	1832	3762	2	1	3	1179	1910	591	....	157	896	289	126	29	773	64	510

LEE COUNTY.

Total Population.	NAMES OF TOWNSHIPS, TOWNS, AND CITIES.	No. of dwelling houses.	Number of families.	WHITE POPULATION. Male.	Female.	Total.	COLORED POP' LATION. Male.	Female.	Total.	NATIVITY OF INHABITANTS. No. born in Iowa.	No. born in U. S., but not in Iowa.	No. born in foreign countries.	Surplus or deficiency.	BETWEEN 5 AND 21 YEARS OLD. No 5 years old and under 6.	No. 6 years old and under 16.	No. 16 years old and under 21.	No. births in 1874.	No. deaths in 1874.	No. of voters.	No. foreigners not naturalized.	No. of militia.
843	Cedar	178	178	401	438	839	2	2	4	566	344	53	120	44	238	76	29	10	208	2	148
1162	Charleston	225	225	593	560	1153	5	4	9	586	398	178	....	46	307	123	22	6	264	3	114
942	Denmark	179	188	444	456	900	21	21	42	435	415	57	— 35	29	232	121	18	8	207	2	136
1046	Des Moines	201	210	504	470	974	40	32	72	505	391	150	....	53	250	88	33	4	236	20	152
1747	Franklin	305	312	892	848	1740	2	5	7	953	241	541	— 12	74	479	187	56	26	362	10	206
631	Green Bay	101	109	351	280	631	.....	.....	.....	296	225	105	— 5	30	113	43	22	6	157	4	101
1017	Harrison	160	188	515	476	991	16	10	26	524	367	112	— 14	41	223	123	34	16	236	13	188
1052	Jackson, exc. of Keokuk	180	190	487	459	946	60	46	106	435	416	201	....	41	300	89	34	17	220	43	100
981	Jefferson,	184	190	509	461	970	4	7	11	572	274	131	— 4	35	229	94	27	11	240	1	177
225	Madison	36	36	115	110	225	.....	.....	.....	131	37	57	....	11	72	22	6	2	41	4	16
1298	Marion	247	247	691	605	1296	1	1	2	662	390	205	— 41	70	318	106	43	20	294	6	202
1551	Montrose, exc. of town	278	287	791	705	1496	26	29	55	661	504	387	1	77	313	140	49	19	277	60	166
782	Montrose, town of	166	163	368	409	777	2	3	5	374	326	22	— 60	38	179	53	9	6	181	.....	54
891	Pleasant Ridge	170	175	447	429	876	9	6	15	457	342	92	....	20	231	85	19	7	201	14	145

902	Van Buren	160	168	452	429	881	10	11	21	444	382	69	— 7	34	211	98	35	27	197	1	137
927	Washington, exc. Ft. Madison.	182	187	465	448	913	7	7	14	501	308	118	......	29	217	115	22	8	239	8	145
1062	West Point, exc. of town	178	189	544	518	1062	......	......	......	630	134	290	— 8	58	281	117	29	28	214	3	95
709	West Point, town of	128	140	352	357	709	......	......	......	395	179	161	26	28	176	61	25	3	148	4	85
17768	Total	3258	3382	8921	8458	17379	205	184	389	9127	5673	2929	......	758	4369	1741	512	224	3922	198	2367
	Fort Madison, city of, C. H.,																				
901	" First ward	110	118	541	322	863	28	10	38	309	232	360	......	35	144	52	30	11	139	1	66
1033	" Second ward	178	183	505	525	1030	2	1	3	515	337	181	......	38	221	126	29	9	244	6	131
1068	" Third ward	187	199	499	547	1046	13	9	22	543	285	240	......	61	280	102	41	9	234	9	106
1303	" Fourth ward	238	244	604	665	1269	21	13	34	708	223	372	......	90	368	134	57	24	239	......	84
4305	Total of city	713	744	2149	2059	4208	64	33	97	2075	1077	1153	......	224	1013	414	157	53	856	16	387
	Keokuk, city of, C. H.,																				
1776	" First ward	300	321	742	942	1684	54	38	92	594	1011	171	......	46	321	215	55	14	434	......	422
2721	" Second ward	470	519	1292	1284	2576	81	64	145	985	1102	634	......	122	655	248	116	37	651	......	714
2017	" Third ward	360	368	890	952	1842	88	87	175	764	920	333	......	74	479	214	79	21	422	......	412
2058	" Fourth ward	370	385	901	974	1875	88	95	183	847	838	373	......	109	627	222	76	27	510	......	502
1747	" Fifth ward	320	326	795	777	1572	87	88	175	667	727	353	......	94	455	168	44	32	332	......	327
1522	" Sixth ward	290	309	681	669	1350	74	98	172	597	451	474	......	59	389	164	45	22	382	......	290
11841	Total of city	2110	2228	5301	5598	10899	472	470	942	4454	5049	2338	......	504	2926	1231	415	153	2731	......	2667
33914	Total of county	6081	6354	16371	16115	32486	741	687	1428	15656	11799	6420	......	1486	8308	3386	1084	430	7509	214	5421

LINN COUNTY.

824	Bertram	156	156	467	357	824	......	......	......	424	347	53	......	35	210	86	34	11	194	7	166
893	Boulder	162	162	457	436	893	......	......	......	423	338	132	......	33	215	86	13	12	205	7	135
1327	Brown	274	274	668	659	1327	......	......	......	600	693	34	......	60	352	123	43	12	305	3	174
559	Buffalo	92	92	311	248	559	......	......	......	270	291	98	100	28	195	60	25	4	123	5	83
1042	Clinton	264	264	548	494	1042	......	......	......	447	468	127	......	36	311	87	28	5	225	5	148
920	College, exc. of Western	171	175	499	421	920	......	......	......	406	236	278	......	37	238	88	33	13	164	155	120
1120	Fairfax	202	201	590	530	1120	......	......	......	426	478	216	......	51	272	90	34	5	251	4	128
857	Fayette	171	171	465	392	857	......	......	......	394	417	46	......	44	200	77	14	10	216	4	132
997	Franklin, exc. of towns of Mt. Vernon and Lisbon	184	184	502	495	997	......	......	......	500	376	121	......	32	257	121	26	10	219	9	135
820	Grant	162	162	457	363	820	......	......	......	338	424	58	— 2	32	189	51	30	8	185	20	183
965	Jackson	185	185	500	465	965	......	......	......	445	445	75	......	42	270	80	31	12	223	5	123
925	Linn	194	194	478	447	925	......	......	......	495	401	29	......	31	227	76	26	9	226	2	165
561	Lisbon, town of	124	124	273	288	561	......	......	......	213	329	21	2	15	124	65	19	6	137	......	88
1315	Maine	270	270	668	647	1315	......	......	......	572	669	74	......	58	323	119	36	14	315	2	229
1954	Marion, exc. of city	381	381	1009	945	1954	......	......	......	885	992	77	......	59	451	191	15	7	468	......	299
1150	Monroe	226	226	568	582	1150	......	......	......	572	524	54	......	40	294	100	45	19	262	2	189
779	Mount Vernon, town of	167	167	364	403	767	7	5	12	292	449	38	......	29	161	77	9	3	186	3	129

LINN COUNTY.—Continued.

Total population.	Names of townships, towns, and cities.	No. of dwelling houses.	Number of families.	White population. Male.	White population. Female.	White population. Total.	Colored pop' lation. Male.	Colored pop' lation. Female.	Colored pop' lation. Total.	Nativity of inhabitants. No. born in Iowa.	Nativity of inhabitants. No. born in U. S., but not in Iowa.	Nativity of inhabitants. No. born in foreign countries.	Nativity of inhabitants. Surplus or deficiency.	Between 5 and 21 years old. No. 5 years old and under 6.	Between 5 and 21 years old. No. 6 years old and under 16.	Between 5 and 21 years old. No. 16 years old and under 21.	No. births in 1874.	No. deaths in 1874.	No. of voters.	No. foreigners not naturalized.	No. of militia.
798	Otter Creek	138	138	408	390	798	......	......	......	394	286	118	......	28	258	61	28	5	156	5	77
799	Putnam	138	140	427	371	798	......	1	1	370	163	266	......	40	221	72	39	10	148	35	99
1332	Rapids, exc. of Cedar Rapids	247	259	688	644	1332	......	......	......	569	543	220	......	53	306	140	44	14	305	9	207
927	Spring Grove	168	168	486	441	927	......	......	......	475	354	98	......	36	235	98	43	16	188	5	118
1487	Washington	285	285	791	696	1487	......	......	......	765	684	38	......	87	384	141	54	29	347	......	235
238	Western, town of	55	55	113	125	238	......	......	......	100	131	7	......	16	57	29	5	5	62	5	21
22589	Total	5416	4433	11737	10839	22576	7	6	13	10375	9938	2278	......	922	5750	2118	674	239	5110	292	3383
	Cedar Rapids, city of—																				
1881	" First ward	365	365	968	888	1856	14	11	25	529	909	443	......	43	330	222	79	16	541	44	429
1330	" Second ward	260	266	619	688	1307	14	9	23	447	661	222	......	42	249	170	51	14	336	16	235
2231	" Third ward	460	460	1091	1129	2220	7	4	11	766	669	796	......	89	523	152	149	33	440	83	325
1031	" Fourth ward	214	214	515	509	1024	3	4	7	371	516	144	......	39	226	93	55	14	232	14	175
706	" Fifth ward	146	146	341	359	700	2	4	6	228	298	180	......	27	150	59	38	13	152	17	122
7179	Total of city	1445	1451	3534	3573	7107	40	32	72	2341	3053	1785	......	240	1478	696	372	90	1701	174	1286
	Marion, city of, C. H.,																				
535	" First ward	106	108	241	279	520	9	6	15	207	297	31	......	15	111	47	13	2	119	......	66
411	" Second ward	82	83	207	199	406	2	3	5	126	277	8	......	16	82	35	6	1	100	......	51
588	" Third ward	119	119	280	307	587	......	1	1	194	365	29	......	15	110	31	8	2	142	......	67
513	" Fourth ward	98	98	227	286	513	......	......	......	182	278	53	......	25	121	28	......	1	102	......	63
2047	Total of city	405	408	955	1071	2026	11	10	21	709	1217	121	......	71	424	141	27	6	463	......	247
31815	Total of county	6266	6292	16226	15483	31709	58	48	106	13425	14208	4184	......	1233	7652	2955	1073	335	7274	466	4916

LOUISA COUNTY.

1416	Columbus City, exc. of Columbus City and Col. Junction	260	260	716	700	1416	......	......	......	712	548	161	5	67	343	142	46	25	312	14	173
605	Columbus City, town of	138	138	311	291	602	2	1	3	260	322	23	......	37	139	53	10	7	150	......	93
517	Columbus Junction, town of	95	95	278	234	512	2	3	5	205	284	26	— 2	22	85	42	16	11	145	......	122
637	Concord, exc. of Fredonia	106	106	330	307	637	......	......	......	353	214	33	— 37	29	172	62	19	7	137	4	90
398	Eliot	71	71	214	184	398	......	......	......	219	145	35	1	11	97	31	20	2	73	1	56
694	Elm Grove	122	122	373	320	693	1	......	1	225	331	28	—110	27	206	90	16	4	153	4	117
123	Fredonia, town of	27	27	61	62	123	......	......	......	61	51	......	— 11	6	34	8	3	2	26	......	17
1385	Grandview	267	267	704	668	1372	8	5	13	739	568	78	......	37	374	129	35	18	319	2	197
712	Jefferson	148	148	376	316	692	13	7	20	348	301	63	......	31	187	56	25	12	163	16	120
781	Marshall	153	153	392	389	781	......	......	......	405	357	22	3	50	171	78	21	8	194	......	120
730	Morning Sun, exc. of town	136	136	386	344	730	......	......	......	393	316	11	— 10	35	182	60	22	6	168	......	111
785	Morning Sun, town of	152	152	372	413	785	......	......	......	350	402	33	......	176	61	......	......	7	181	......	141
552	Oakland	96	96	289	263	552	......	......	......	301	235	23	7	29	161	55	17	5	131	2	92
721	Port Louisa	136	136	378	343	720	1	......	1	399	236	70	— 16	27	164	49	20	15	174	......	124
581	Union	76	76	310	271	581	......	......	......	304	266	11	......	20	130	65	16	3	142	1	136
959	Wapello, exc. of town	175	175	519	440	959	......	......	......	528	366	65	......	30	251	105	36	13	224	......	157
11596	Total	2158	2158	6009	5545	11553	27	16	43	5802	4942	682	......	634	2757	1025	322	145	2692	44	1866
	Wapello, town of, C. H.,																				
246	" First ward	54	54	114	131	246	......	......	......	118	98	28	— 2	7	66	20	7	......	57	1	39
319	" Second ward	70	70	172	146	318	1	......	1	156	118	45	......	8	77	29	11	4	78	3	53
338	" Third ward	70	70	177	161	338	......	......	......	175	127	34	— 2	18	85	29	8	1	72	6	49
933	Total of town	194	194	463	438	902	1	......	1	449	343	107	......	33	228	78	26	5	207	10	141
12499	Total of county	2352	2352	6472	5983	12455	28	16	44	6251	5285	789	......	667	2985	1103	348	150	2899	54	2007

LUCAS COUNTY.

703	Benton	....	135	379	324	703	......	......	......	281	387	35	......	27	180	83	23	8	151	......	48
755	Cedar	....	107	388	367	755	......	......	......	348	398	9	......	25	172	76	26	4	163	...	115
973	Chariton, exc. of city	....	173	487	486	973	......	......	......	389	465	119	......	35	238	112	36	7	186	24	131
833	English	....	151	422	411	833	......	......	......	371	397	65	......	26	242	107	34	16	162	13	124
598	Jackson	....	108	308	290	598	......	......	......	256	297	45	......	37	159	59	25	16	130	12	111
820	Liberty	....	144	431	389	820	......	......	......	395	377	48	......	35	236	82	30	14	163	......	134
710	Otter Creek	....	132	363	347	710	......	......	......	324	371	15	......	30	187	56	20	15	155	2	115
809	Pleasant	....	128	408	401	809	......	......	......	369	387	53	......	61	198	68	32	15	162	......	126
726	Union	....	155	375	351	726	......	......	......	314	389	23	......	26	193	81	30	17	154	......	130
957	Warren	....	173	506	451	957	......	......	......	411	507	39	......	39	257	100	42	11	187	4	147

LUCAS COUNTY.—CONTINUED.

Total Population.	NAMES OF TOWNSHIPS, TOWNS, AND CITIES.	No. of dwelling houses.	Number of families.	WHITE POPULATION.			COLORED POP'LATION			NATIVITY OF INHABITANTS.				BETWEEN 5 AND 21 YEARS OLD.			No. births in 1874.	No deaths in 1874.	No. of voters.	No. foreigners not naturalized.	No. of militia.
				Male.	Female.	Total.	Male.	Female.	Total.	No. born in Iowa.	No. born in U. S., but not in Iowa.	No. born in foreign countries.	Surplus or deficiency.	No. 5 years old and under 6.	No. 6 years old and under 16.	No. 16 years old and under 21.					
1001	Washington	....	175	507	494	1001	.....	.....	.....	405	542	54	....	44	262	91	44	13	221	9	180
666	White Breast	....	118	337	325	662	2	2	4	252	337	77	....	32	161	67	25	11	137	49	95
9551	Total	....	1699	4011	4636	9547	2	2	4	4115	4854	582	....	417	2485	982	367	147	1971	113	1456
	Chariton, city of, C. H.,																				
1293	" First ward	....	....	647	632	1279	8	6	14	490	716	87	....	62	232	69	53	27	288	42	200
881	" Second ward	....	....	452	423	875	4	2	6	304	535	42	....	38	179	65	40	19	238	9	154
2174	Total of city	....	....	1099	1055	2154	12	8	20	794	1251	129	....	100	411	134	93	46	526	51	354
11725	Total of county	....	1699	6010	5691	11701	14	10	24	4909	6105	711	....	517	2896	1116	460	193	2497	164	1810

LYON COUNTY.

Total Population.	NAMES OF TOWNSHIPS, TOWNS, AND CITIES.	No. of dwelling houses.	Number of families.	White Male.	White Female.	White Total.	Colored Male.	Colored Female.	Colored Total.	No. born in Iowa.	No. born in U. S., but not in Iowa.	No. born in foreign countries.	Surplus or deficiency.	No. 5 years old and under 6.	No. 6 years old and under 16.	No. 16 years old and under 21.	No. births in 1874.	No deaths in 1874.	No. of voters.	No. foreigners not naturalized.	No. of militia.
292	Dale	75	75	155	137	292	.....	.....	.....	80	208	15	11	....	....	....	......	......	79	......	51
170	Doon	40	40	101	69	170	.....	.....	.....	45	45	30	— 50	4	55	10	10	......	43	......	32
126	Grant	27	27	64	62	126	.....	.....	.....	41	70	15	....	11	29	....	......	7	27	......	25
97	Larchwood	25	25	47	50	97	.....	.....	.....	12	38	45	— 2	2	20	6	4	......	16	5	21
350	Lyon	76	76	183	167	350	.....	.....	.....	131	54	124	— 41	17	70	23	29	10	63	36	69
197	Rock, Rock Rapids, C. H.	54	54	123	74	197	.....	.....	.....	61	96	18	— 22	24	25	4	......	......	59	.....	44
1232	Total	297	297	673	559	1232	.....	.....	.....	370	511	247	....	58	199	43	43	17	287	41	242

MADISON COUNTY.

863	Crawford	174	174	434	428	862	1	......	1	422	350	91	......	38	211	69	28	9	183	2	111
972	Douglas	176	176	524	448	972	......	......	......	437	509	26	......	30	248	79	34	14	245	......	146
266	Earlham, town of	51	51	149	117	266	......	......	......	81	176	9	......	12	37	11	6	1	66	......	55
765	Grand River	143	143	405	359	764	1	......	1	341	410	14	......	25	210	83	31	13	181	......	127
670	Jackson	127	127	344	325	669	1	......	1	274	372	24	......	32	152	54	30	12	135	......	94
828	Jefferson	156	156	438	390	828	......	......	......	414	367	47	......	34	206	69	33	15	185	4	104
537	Lee	97	97	285	252	537	......	......	......	247	227	63	......	8	126	58	23	11	122	6	72
962	Lincoln	203	203	519	443	962	......	......	......	398	518	46	......	33	261	85	39	16	221	3	166
774	Madison, exc. of Earlham	148	148	395	379	774	......	......	......	300	421	53	......	29	193	95	19	4	172	6	116
619	Monroe	112	112	330	289	619	......	......	......	287	308	24	......	33	130	49	30	8	130	......	109
852	Ohio	146	146	446	406	852	......	......	......	452	389	11	......	42	263	86	35	8	224	......	150
769	Penn	132	132	403	365	768	1	......	1	263	480	26	......	65	179	53	22	7	177	33	120
1131	Scott	208	208	587	544	1131	......	......	......	561	564	6	......	67	287	106	47	27	246	......	132
1081	South	173	173	575	506	1081	......	......	......	520	548	13	......	51	292	111	41	12	224	......	150
1098	Union	200	200	584	514	1098	......	......	......	530	533	35	......	55	306	92	40	14	243	1	179
875	Walnut	146	146	485	390	875	......	......	......	432	437	6	......	41	256	91	23	8	179	......	143
625	Webster	111	111	328	297	625	......	......	......	306	291	28	......	30	180	50	29	11	131	......	86
13687	Total	2503	2503	7231	6452	13683	4	......	4	6265	6900	522	......	625	537	1242	510	190	3064	55	2060
	Winterset, city of, C. H.,																				
1128	" First ward	277	277	556	572	1128	......	......	......	466	628	34	......	50	232	84	22	10	263	......	181
1215	" Second ward	334	334	623	587	1210	2	3	5	458	716	41	......	56	237	78	24	9	305	1	218
2343	Total of city	611	611	1179	1159	2338	2	3	5	924	1344	75		106	3469	162	46	19	568	1	399
16030	Total of county	3114	3114	8410	7611	16021	6	3	9	7189	8244	597		731	4006	1404	556	209	3632	56	2459

MAHASKA COUNTY.

889	Adams	160	160	457	432	889	......	......	......	442	429	18	......	49	208	91	35	6	207	3	163
680	Beacon, town of	141	141	339	341	680	......	......	......	251	210	209	— 10	38	181	48	42	9	97	36	81
1056	Black Oak	182	181	560	494	1054	1	1	2	391	320	209	—136	46	243	108	13	14	231	25	176
1174	Cedar	206	206	591	580	1171	1	2	3	565	578	30	— 1	47	329	107	36	22	260	3	176
1295	Des Moines	234	234	684	611	1295	......	......	......	588	580	126	— 1	58	332	123	57	25	288	11	228
1249	Harrison	244	244	640	596	1236	7	6	13	596	555	98	......	46	335	109	50	13	281	12	208
1033	Jefferson	189	188	555	478	1033	......	......	......	505	497	31	......	33	263	122	39	28	228	8	183
902	Madison	161	149	476	418	894	3	5	8	457	437	8	......	27	249	121	30	14	201	1	155
1279	Monroe	240	240	661	618	1279	......	......	......	652	616	11	......	64	327	121	45	28	290	......	216
603	New Sharon, town of	143	143	296	296	592	4	7	11	198	380	25	......	20	123	36	18	4	156	......	116
2465	Oskaloosa, exc. of Oskaloosa and Beacon	452	452	1293	1156	2449	11	5	16	1061	1281	105	— 18	81	624	288	68	27	575	16	396
906	Pleasant Grove	159	162	470	436	906	....	......	......	468	412	26	......	40	262	73	39	9	191	......	130

MAHASKA COUNTY.—Continued.

Total population.	NAMES OF TOWNSHIPS, TOWNS, AND CITIES.	No. of dwelling houses.	Number of families.	WHITE POPULATION. Male.	WHITE POPULATION. Female.	WHITE POPULATION. Total.	COLORED POP'LATION Male.	COLORED POP'LATION Female.	COLORED POP'LATION Total.	NATIVITY OF INHABITANTS. No. born in Iowa.	NATIVITY OF INHABITANTS. No. born in U. S., but not in Iowa.	NATIVITY OF INHABITANTS. No. born in foreign countries.	NATIVITY OF INHABITANTS. Surplus or deficiency.	BETWEEN 5 AND 21 YEARS OLD. No. 5 years old and under 6.	BETWEEN 5 AND 21 YEARS OLD. No. 6 years old and under 16.	BETWEEN 5 AND 21 YEARS OLD. No. 16 years old and under 21.	No. births in 1874.	No. deaths in 1874.	No. of voters.	No. foreigners not naturalized.	No. of militia.
1110	Prairie, exc. of New Sharon	212	227	581	529	1110	......	......	......	458	567	85	....	40	306	100	37	11	234	8	172
1381	Richland	266	266	702	679	1381	......	......	......	677	566	138	....	72	367	107	46	13	271	20	224
1006	Scott	196	196	498	508	1006	......	......	......	483	479	44	....	38	252	88	34	16	226	4	176
1186	Union	194	194	618	562	1180	4	2	6	579	526	174	— 7	61	286	93	23	14	222	7	142
1241	White Oak	198	198	627	612	1239	2	......	2	663	564	7	— 7	72	340	136	42	17	274	2	200
19455	Total	3577	3581	10048	9346	19394	33	28	61	9034	8997	1344		832	5027	1871	684	270	4232	156	3142
	Oskaloosa, city of, C. H.,																				
1629	" First ward	335	335	734	741	1475	78	76	154	591	949	89	....	44	405	146	41	14	415	3	308
940	" Second ward	196	196	445	495	940	......	......	......	364	498	78	....	23	235	90	24	6	220	......	164
1054	" Third ward	215	215	498	526	1024	16	14	30	374	628	52	....	21	232	112	30	10	271	1	190
640	" Fourth ward	131	131	287	337	624	6	10	16	233	387	20	....	12	129	56	22	6	149	......	106
4263	Total of city	877	877	1964	2099	4063	100	100	200	1562	2462	239		100	1001	404	117	36	1055	4	768
23718	Total of county	4454	4458	12012	11445	23457	133	128	261	10596	11459	1583		932	6028	2275	801	306	5287	160	3910

MARION COUNTY.

Total population.	NAMES OF TOWNSHIPS, TOWNS, AND CITIES.	No. of dwelling houses.	Number of families.	WHITE POPULATION. Male.	WHITE POPULATION. Female.	WHITE POPULATION. Total.	COLORED POP'LATION Male.	COLORED POP'LATION Female.	COLORED POP'LATION Total.	NATIVITY OF INHABITANTS. No. born in Iowa.	NATIVITY OF INHABITANTS. No. born in U. S., but not in Iowa.	NATIVITY OF INHABITANTS. No. born in foreign countries.	NATIVITY OF INHABITANTS. Surplus or deficiency.	BETWEEN 5 AND 21 YEARS OLD. No. 5 years old and under 6.	BETWEEN 5 AND 21 YEARS OLD. No. 6 years old and under 16.	BETWEEN 5 AND 21 YEARS OLD. No. 16 years old and under 21.	No. births in 1874.	No. deaths in 1874.	No. of voters.	No. foreigners not naturalized.	No. of militia.
1197	Clay	200	200	618	579	1197	......	......	......	635	540	22	....	49	322	168	41	11	252	......	192
1036	Dallas	158	158	530	506	1036	......	......	...	449	468	119	....	44	259	119	39	18	237	7	173
879	Franklin	158	158	480	399	879	......	......	......	370	461	48	....	46	218	82	36	16	197	......	169
1303	Indiana	240	240	626	655	1281	14	8	22	696	599	9	1	68	348	108	47	28	315	1	212
2483	Knoxville, exc. of town	475	475	1384	1099	2483	......	......	......	1519	1041	12	79	289	288	354	5	18	499	2	421
2673	Lake Prairie, exc. of Pella	475	484	1407	1266	2673	......	......	......	1430	288	955	200	132	719	225	134	22	441	109	350

1574	Liberty	275	275	804	770	1574	......	......	......	812	712	11	— 39	78	399	191	49	27	362	......	225
1161	Pleasant Grove, exc. of Pleasantville	220	220	598	563	1161	......	......	......	550	590	21	......	58	333	79	33	15	256	1	197
337	Pleasantville, town of	76	76	169	168	337	......	......	......	136	196	5	......	20	73	28	11	3	88	2	76
491	Perry	94	94	248	243	491	......	......	......	236	238	17	......	27	119	40	22	9	109	1	70
879	Polk	166	166	475	404	879	......	......	......	462	338	59	— 20	45	235	45	11	10	180	7	119
1445	Red Rock	250	250	741	704	1445	......	......	......	730	685	30	......	81	382	140	56	18	298	1	222
1616	Summit	286	286	832	784	1616	......	......	......	801	576	234	— 5	77	424	191	76	27	275	36	203
883	Swan	156	156	425	408	883	......	......	......	445	393	10	— 35	66	256	71	20	10	176	......	129
700	Union	136	136	371	329	700	......	......	......	320	369	11	......	26	116	29	25	4	161	......	116
1252	Washington	229	229	615	631	1246	2	4	6	622	620	10	......	68	340	125	42	24	263	......	186
19857	Total	3594	3603	10323	9508	19831	16	12	28	10213	8114	1573	......	1174	4831	1995	646	260	4109	167	3060
	Knoxville, town of, C. H.																				
718	" First ward	151	151	355	363	718	......	......	......	300	403	15	......	33	153	71	15	6	183	......	99
250	" Second ward	53	53	126	124	250	......	......	......	103	139	8	......	11	66	13	7	2	59	......	39
731	" Third ward	146	146	357	374	731	......	......	......	342	378	10	1	33	176	54	20	3	178	......	107
1699	Total of town	350	350	838	861	1699	......	......	......	745	920	33	......	77	395	138	42	11	420	......	245
	Pella, city of.																				
715	" First ward	140	140	347	368	715	......	......	......	280	186	191	58	27	174	56	19	11	125	16	60
598	" Second ward	134	134	291	307	598	......	......	......	315	90	193	......	19	129	42	18	6	129	5	49
763	" Third ward	149	149	377	386	763	......	......	......	384	64	315	......	25	193	53	18	8	118	43	88
460	" Fourth ward	87	87	244	216	460	......	......	......	199	160	55	46	19	111	42	13	12	87	3	17
2536	Total of city	510	510	1259	1277	2536	......	......	......	1178	500	754	......	90	607	193	68	37	459	67	214
24094	Total of county	4454	4463	12420	11646	24066	16	12	28	12136	9534	2360	......	1341	5833	2326	757	308	4988	234	3519

MARSHALL COUNTY.

508	Albion, town of	145	......	237	263	503	1	4	5	176	327	5	......	22	109	45	13	3	138	......	78
844	Bangor	156	......	440	401	841	2	1	3	347	474	23	......	39	236	92	26	5	181	2	124
693	Eden	126	......	379	313	692	1	......	1	239	390	54	— 10	23	173	55	25	7	159	......	100
1153	Green Castle	210	......	622	525	1147	6	......	6	369	604	180	......	51	279	98	46	10	245	111	168
460	Iowa, exc. of Albion	90	......	233	227	460	......	......	......	212	239	9	......	20	125	54	11	2	95	......	52
759	Jefferson	145	......	410	349	759	......	......	......	267	389	103	......	34	194	70	29	7	153	3	124
1597	Le Grand	300	......	815	782	1597	......	......	......	575	722	300	......	89	405	131	51	14	312	52	273
756	Liberty	134	......	399	357	756	......	......	......	327	381	48	......	28	160	51	15	12	172	1	119
593	Liscomb, exc. of town	118	......	299	289	588	3	2	5	232	340	21	......	22	162	62	21	10	135	......	109
372	Liscomb, town of	82	......	203	169	372	......	......	......	120	245	7	......	26	85	23	13	......	97	4	64
433	Logan	88	......	233	199	432	1	......	1	137	216	80	......	23	98	32	18	6	85	9	88
916	Marietta	184	......	495	421	916	......	......	......	329	510	77	......	31	212	76	40	16	202	4	126
860	Marion	155	......	459	401	860	......	......	......	343	477	40	......	44	221	67	34	10	190	2	128
475	Marshall, exc. of Marshalltown	92	......	238	231	469	4	2	6	158	215	102	......	23	94	40	14	......	108	2	74

MARSHALL COUNTY.—Continued.

Total population.	Names of townships, towns, and cities.	No. of dwelling houses.	Number of families.	White population. Male.	White population. Female.	White population. Total.	Colored pop'lation. Male.	Colored pop'lation. Female.	Colored pop'lation. Total.	Nativity of inhabitants. No. born in Iowa.	Nativity of inhabitants. No. born in U. S., but not in Iowa.	Nativity of inhabitants. No. born in foreign countries.	Nativity of inhabitants. Surplus or deficiency.	Between 5 and 21 years old. No. 5 years old and under 6.	Between 5 and 21 years old. No. 6 years old and under 16.	Between 5 and 21 years old. No. 16 years old and under 21.	No. births in 1874.	No. deaths in 1874.	No. of voters.	No. foreigners not naturalized.	No. of militia.
696	Minerva	116	......	378	318	696	......	......	......	262	246	121	— 67	41	173	57	28	9	117	17	76
533	State Center, exc. of town	102	......	297	236	533	......	......	......	178	303	52	......	23	139	41	19	6	115	......	93
796	State Center, town of	151	......	413	383	796	......	......	......	185	486	125	......	29	155	59	29	14	203	13	155
487	Taylor	91	......	247	220	467	13	7	20	177	299	11	......	18	113	51	......	......	106	......	72
725	Timber Creek	133	......	373	348	721	......	4	4	263	399	63	......	30	197	60	14	5	163	5	100
744	Vienna	158	......	408	336	744	......	......	......	244	448	44	— 8	83	142	48	27	3	185	......	145
845	Washington	156	......	455	390	845	......	......	......	251	448	146	......	43	215	77	40	15	185	23	145
15245	Total	2932	......	8033	7161	15194	31	20	51	5391	8158	1611	......	742	3687	1289	513	154	3346	248	2413
	Marshalltown, city of, C. H.,																				
956	" First ward	177	194	473	476	949	3	4	7	247	525	185	1	29	173	65	25	13	224	50	173
901	" Second ward	163	185	439	460	899	1	1	2	285	504	112	......	22	174	77	33	10	219	42	151
1384	" Third ward	257	278	707	673	1380	2	2	4	367	734	283	......	40	255	116	49	24	328	139	247
1143	" Fourth ward	180	200	583	560	1143	......	......	......	327	630	186	......	24	199	94	33	14	328	58	250
4384	Total of city	777	857	2202	2169	4371	6	7	13	1226	2393	766	......	115	801	352	140	61	1099	289	821
19629	Total of county	3709	857	10235	9330	19565	37	27	64	6617	10551	2377	......	857	4488	1641	653	215	4445	537	3234

MILLS COUNTY.

Total population.	Names of townships, towns, and cities.	No. of dwelling houses.	Number of families.	White population. Male.	White population. Female.	White population. Total.	Colored pop'lation. Male.	Colored pop'lation. Female.	Colored pop'lation. Total.	Nativity of inhabitants. No. born in Iowa.	Nativity of inhabitants. No. born in U. S., but not in Iowa.	Nativity of inhabitants. No. born in foreign countries.	Nativity of inhabitants. Surplus or deficiency.	Between 5 and 21 years old. No. 5 years old and under 6.	Between 5 and 21 years old. No. 6 years old and under 16.	Between 5 and 21 years old. No. 16 years old and under 21.	No. births in 1874.	No. deaths in 1874.	No. of voters.	No. foreigners not naturalized.	No. of militia.
842	Anderson	145	150	455	387	842	......	......	......	329	448	65	......	36	216	70	39	15	193	4	160
698	Deer Creek	117	124	376	322	698	......	......	......	210	428	60	......	28	141	93	33	4	154	4	140
117	Emerson, town of	23	15	63	54	117	......	......	......	43	64	10	......	6	25	2	3	3	25	1	24
959	Glenwood, exc. of city	185	180	523	434	957	1	1	2	394	521	44	......	43	237	97	45	17	218	1	143
149	Hastings, town of	30	30	74	75	149	......	......	......	34	109	6	......	6	39	8	6	1	35	......	29

86	Hillsdale, town of	20	20	46	40	86	......	......	......	39	45	2	......	5	19	4	3	4	22	......	16
505	Indian Creek, exc. of Emerson and Hastings	103	103	280	225	505	......	......	......	200	270	35	......	16	149	23	16	10	126	6	99
504	Ingraham	105	96	245	258	503	1	......	1	185	268	51	......	30	113	35	13	5	107	1	34
796	Lyons	147	147	444	351	795	1	......	1	375	410	11	......	28	202	75	37	13	179	......	160
493	Malvern, town of	105	105	246	246	492	1	......	1	145	290	58	......	14	91	38	15	12	130	9	92
881	Oak	147	150	498	383	881	......	......	......	381	219	281	......	33	227	60	33	15	173	40	130
739	Platteville	147	147	387	352	739	......	......	......	272	432	35	......	43	170	70	27	13	151	10	93
819	Rawles	163	163	416	403	819	......	......	......	395	414	10	......	48	231	76	18	10	171	16	124
204	St. Mary	34	34	113	91	204	......	......	......	82	97	25	......	19	44	17	7	2	54	4	27
831	Silver Creek, exc. of Hillsdale and Malvern	155	155	420	411	831	......	......	......	352	434	45	......	44	221	75	41	17	189	9	100
621	White Cloud	105	105	334	286	620	1	......	1	254	316	51	......	22	172	71	19	9	146	1	123
9244	Total	1731	1724	4920	4318	9238	5	1	6	3690	4765	788	......	421	2297	814	355	150	2073	106	1497
	Glenwood, city of, C. H.—																				
489	" First ward	80	......	237	250	487	2	......	2	193	267	29	......	24	165	38	14	12	97	......	79
511	" Second ward	97	......	244	266	510	1	......	1	214	279	18	......	28	122	64	17	13	108	......	87
311	" Third ward	63	......	163	148	311	......	......	......	110	189	12	......	5	71	38	9	3	87	......	65
1311	Total of city	240	240	644	664	1308	3	......	3	517	735	59	......	57	358	140	40	28	292	......	231
10555	Total of county	1971	1964	5564	4982	10546	8	1	9	4207	5500	848	......	478	2655	954	395	178	2365	106	1728

MITCHELL COUNTY.

588	Burr Oak	123	123	314	274	588	......	......	......	161	348	79	......	27	85	36	9	2	158	......	......
934	Cedar	159	159	504	430	934	......	......	......	323	273	321	— 17	39	240	74	32	17	159	67	92
490	Douglas	80	80	248	242	490	......	......	......	134	239	114	— 3	12	124	48	18	6	91	1	73
672	Jenkins	131	132	357	315	672	......	......	......	266	316	87	— 3	37	153	42	13	2	140	......	100
305	Liberty	55	55	169	136	305	......	......	......	113	154	49	11	20	68	20	11	3	65	1	53
771	Lincoln	145	145	415	355	770	1	......	1	268	223	96	—184	55	179	91	17	8	183	4	132
1215	Mitchell	243	243	619	596	1215	......	......	......	313	699	178	— 25	36	269	135	29	3	279	5	85
782	Newburg	133	133	397	384	781	1	......	1	241	250	270	— 21	49	178	32	46	4	138	22	127
315	Osage, exc. of town	63	63	165	150	315	......	......	......	99	212	18	14	22	89	28	6	4	75	3	48
1488	Osage, town of, C. H.	330	330	747	741	1488	......	......	......	442	874	175	3	78	259	111	44	18	349	3	262
834	Otranto	126	140	437	397	834	......	......	......	271	209	363	9	32	199	69	36	5	102	80	68
628	Rock	108	108	349	279	628	......	......	......	142	206	283	3	64	142	66	24	6	114	25	92
971	St. Ansgar	176	176	525	446	971	......	......	......	282	328	358	— 3	40	188	82	36	6	190	138	121
580	Stacyville	101	109	309	271	580	......	......	......	152	255	173	1	26	125	46	22	10	123	24	86
578	Union	111	111	288	290	578	......	......	......	150	248	207	27	34	146	60	23	14	92	36	76
372	Wayne	68	68	206	166	372	......	......	......	148	152	71	— 1	8	111	40	16	3	80	1	46
11523	Total	2152	2175	6049	5472	11521	2	......	2	3505	4986	2763	......	579	2555	980	382	111	2338	410	1461

MONONA COUNTY.

Total population.	Names of townships, towns, and cities.	No. of dwelling houses.	Number of families.	White population. Male.	White population. Female.	White population. Total.	Colored pop'lation. Male.	Colored pop'lation. Female.	Colored pop'lation. Total.	Nativity of inhabitants. No. born in Iowa.	Nativity of inhabitants. No. born in U. S., but not in Iowa	Nativity of inhabitants. No. born in foreign countries.	Nativity of inhabitants. Surplus or deficiency.	Between 5 and 21 years old. No. 5 years old and under 6.	Between 5 and 21 years old. No. 6 years old and under 16.	Between 5 and 21 years old. No. 16 years old and under 21.	No. births in 1874.	No. deaths in 1874.	No. of voters.	No. foreigners not naturalized.	No. of militia.
129	Ashton	24	24	63	66	129	......	......	......	44	68	17	......	8	36	13	5	1	28	......	24
245	Belvidere	48	48	133	112	245	......	......	......	94	111	40	......	6	59	32	11	4	45	......	31
274	Center	49	49	151	123	274	......	......	......	146	125	3	......	13	71	21	17	6	58	......	55
404	Fairview	75	75	208	196	404	......	......	......	116	124	164	......	22	97	30	15	11	72	18	60
560	Franklin, exc. of Onawa	107	107	313	247	560	......	......	......	190	273	97	......	23	134	39	28	14	128	23	75
316	Grant	65	65	166	150	316	......	......	......	125	166	25	......	15	85	20	9	4	70	......	42
170	Jordan	34	34	69	64	133	16	21	37	74	87	9	......	7	31	6	11	4	42	......	23
445	Kennebec	81	84	241	204	445	......	......	......	201	212	32	......	14	104	37	16	7	104	......	67
199	Lake	35	35	109	90	199	......	......	......	67	120	12	......	14	53	31	......	......	47	......	35
687	Lincoln	165	165	367	320	687	......	......	......	202	442	43	......	42	140	55	22	8	166	1	157
631	Maple	132	132	306	325	631	......	......	......	296	309	26	......	30	165	41	31	10	129	......	59
719	Onawa, town of, C. H.	144	144	381	338	719	......	......	......	247	371	101	......	30	159	49	30	12	159	5	146
325	Sherman	65	65	169	151	320	3	2	5	116	168	41	......	12	91	24	13	......	72	......	47
189	Soldier	36	36	91	98	189	......	......	......	61	77	51	......	7	36	19	7	3	34	6	31
300	Spring Valley	52	52	159	141	300	......	......	......	121	134	45	......	14	70	25	15	7	66	4	51
191	St. Clair	34	34	92	99	191	......	......	......	105	84	2	......	17	44	13	10	5	34	......	29
89	West Fork	18	18	55	34	89	......	......	......	29	50	10	......	12	13	8	3	......	25	......	22
94	Willow	16	16	53	41	94	......	......	......	33	30	31	......	4	33	6	3	......	13	6	13
5967	Total	1180	1183	3126	2799	5925	19	23	42	2267	2951	749	......	290	1421	469	246	96	1292	63	967

MONROE COUNTY.

Total population.	Names of townships, towns, and cities.	No. of dwelling houses.	Number of families.	White population. Male.	White population. Female.	White population. Total.	Colored pop'lation. Male.	Colored pop'lation. Female.	Colored pop'lation. Total.	Nativity of inhabitants. No. born in Iowa.	Nativity of inhabitants. No. born in U. S., but not in Iowa	Nativity of inhabitants. No. born in foreign countries.	Nativity of inhabitants. Surplus or deficiency.	Between 5 and 21 years old. No. 5 years old and under 6.	Between 5 and 21 years old. No. 6 years old and under 16.	Between 5 and 21 years old. No. 16 years old and under 21.	No. births in 1874.	No. deaths in 1874.	No. of voters.	No. foreigners not naturalized.	No. of militia.
1993	Albia, city of, C. H.	365	371	926	901	1827	30	36	66	513	1003	314	—163	88	469	126	20	24	480	......	306
906	Bluff Creek	163	163	494	412	906	......	......	......	442	432	32	......	38	241	93	22	13	188	1	149
734	Cedar	138	139	398	336	734	......	......	......	388	368	26	48	77	160	65	25	8	153	41	106
681	Franklin	117	117	349	332	681	......	......	......	334	259	81	— 7	37	192	79	18	9	149	......	100
769	Guilford	135	135	404	365	769	......	......	......	293	202	191	— 83	33	210	71	8	11	153	1	98

843	Jackson	154	154	428	415	843	......	......	......	352	329	162	....	46	232	83	13	4	154	7	77
1208	Mantua	227	227	607	597	1204	2	2	4	637	484	155	68	44	355	49	45	25	260	25	178
774	Monroe	133	131	408	366	774	......	......	......	381	360	33	....	27	217	86	22	7	169	5	112
1301	Pleasant	235	235	686	615	1301	......	......	......	602	546	153	....	45	283	132	36	31	284	8	212
1057	Troy, exc. of Albia	204	208	529	498	1027	14	16	30	480	538	17	— 22	35	219	83	44	16	233	......	165
1084	Union	202	202	549	535	1084	......	......	......	580	451	50	— 3	49	296	133	47	23	249	2	160
817	Urbana	146	146	405	412	817	......	......	......	453	319	35	— 10	17	222	105	22	9	147	3	93
644	Wayne	107	107	341	303	644	......	......	......	326	239	93	14	41	173	96	14	7	124	......	92
12711	Total	2326	2335	6524	6087	12611	46	54	100	5781	5530	1342	....	577	3269	1201	336	187	2743	93	1848

CORRECTION.—The population of Albia is 1893.

MONTGOMERY COUNTY.

656	Douglas	120	124	361	295	656	......	......	......	214	431	11	....	13	160	58	35	17	151	5	118
527	Frankfort	101	101	287	240	527	......	......	......	174	519	128	294	19	128	50	25	......	103	31	92
852	Grant	....	....	446	405	851	1	......	1	240	414	198	....	40	176	60	38	5	177	81	169
789	Jackson, exc. of Villisca	....	137	424	365	789	......	......	......	284	400	9	— 96	19	240	70	16	7	173	......	126
541	Lincoln	....	105	290	251	541	......	......	......	149	246	146	....	19	100	44	24	6	114	65	74
677	Pilot Grove	....	128	359	318	677	......	......	......	234	425	18	....	41	160	36	28	5	151	3	150
838	Red Oak, exc. of town	....	173	422	416	838	......	......	......	315	468	60	5	35	203	75	29	17	190	163	35
1823	Red Oak Junction, town of, C. H.	....	384	887	908	1795	12	16	28	505	1161	157	....	49	364	102	70	18	485	......	410
502	Scott	....	....	239	263	502	......	......	......	140	172	136	— 54	34	80	7	19	6	77	32	66
684	Sherman	....	129	386	298	684	......	......	......	260	362	37	— 25	41	133	50	36	7	171	2	172
83[illegible]	Villisca, town of	164	172	433	403	836	......	......	......	236	538	62	....	40	183	37	38	14	223	1	131
654	Walnut	112	116	371	282	653	1	......	1	179	406	63	— 6	38	162	64	28	7	156	5	126
648	Washington	....	....	341	307	648	......	......	......	216	381	48	— 3	18	18	72	27	11	126	1	104
812	West	....	152	430	382	812	......	......	......	260	449	72	— 31	53	180	53	31	10	188	11	147
10839	Total	497	1721	5676	5133	10809	14	16	30	2406	6372	1145	....	459	2287	778	444	130	2485	400	1920

MUSCATINE COUNTY.

1156	Bloomington, exc. of Muscatine	225	225	610	543	1153	2	1	3	505	503	148	....	55	231	153	7	1	297	8	156
383	Cedar	67	67	190	193	383	......	......	......	198	160	25	....	8	108	36	13	3	141	2	25
1162	Fulton	189	189	624	538	1162	......	......	......	540	316	306	....	52	297	118	43	8	198	68	187
1235	Goshen	221	221	638	597	1235	......	......	......	555	566	114	....	34	316	124	40	12	283	......	188
762	Lake	133	131	413	349	762	......	......	......	375	249	138	....	26	206	80	22	9	169	11	103
794	Moscow	163	170	419	375	794	......	......	......	376	237	181	....	45	190	63	26	9	171	19	97
667	Montpelier	109	109	357	310	667	......	......	......	340	133	194	....	31	198	61	12	2	114	21	90
7537	Muscatine, city of, C. H.	1435	1495	3668	3739	7407	66	64	130	3408	2412	1717	....	....	....	....	232	69	1606	105	....
501	Orono	87	87	250	251	501	......	......	......	238	240	22	— 1	24	119	56	13	4	103	......	79
840	Pike	160	160	461	379	840	......	......	......	385	319	136	....	45	186	59	38	8	190	4	123

MUSCATINE COUNTY.—Continued.

Total population.	NAMES OF TOWNSHIPS, TOWNS, AND CITIES.	No. dwelling houses.	No. of families.	WHITE POPULATION. Male.	WHITE POPULATION. Female.	WHITE POPULATION. Total.	COLORED POP'LATION Male.	COLORED POP'LATION Female.	COLORED POP'LATION Total.	NATIVITY OF INHABITANTS. No. born in Iowa.	NATIVITY OF INHABITANTS. No. born in U. S., but not in Iowa.	NATIVITY OF INHABITANTS. No. born in foreign countries.	NATIVITY OF INHABITANTS. Surplus or deficiency.	BETWEEN 5 AND 21 YEARS OLD. No. 5 years old and under 6.	BETWEEN 5 AND 21 YEARS OLD. No. 6 years old and under 16.	BETWEEN 5 AND 21 YEARS OLD. No. 16 years old and under 21.	No. births in 1874.	No. deaths in 1874.	No. of voters.	No. foreigners not naturalized.	No. of militia.
849	Seventy-Six	147	147	431	418	849	......	......	......	573	258	18	....	26	221	86	25	15	177	7	96
1415	Sweetland	262	262	723	692	1415	......	......	......	661	534	220	....	....	353	135	42	14	295	126	....
987	Wapsinonoc, exc. of West Liberty	173	173	501	470	971	8	8	16	466	401	120	....	35	253	97	22	7	211	3	131
937	West Liberty, town of	202	202	453	480	933	1	3	4	373	503	61	....	38	210	73	11	......	2098	6	130
1047	Wilton, exc. of town	179	197	538	508	1046	1	......	1	456	358	233	....	45	248	130	50	9	199	11	149
1351	Wilton, town of	272	272	683	661	1344	2	5	7	503	635	213	....	43	246	110	29	24	336	30	216
21623	Total	4024	4107	10959	10503	21462	80	81	161	9952	7824	3846	....	507	3382	1381	625	194	6588	421	1770

O'BRIEN COUNTY.

Total population.	NAMES OF TOWNSHIPS, TOWNS, AND CITIES.	No. dwelling houses.	No. of families.	WHITE POPULATION. Male.	WHITE POPULATION. Female.	WHITE POPULATION. Total.	COLORED POP'LATION Male.	COLORED POP'LATION Female.	COLORED POP'LATION Total.	NATIVITY OF INHABITANTS. No. born in Iowa.	NATIVITY OF INHABITANTS. No. born in U. S., but not in Iowa.	NATIVITY OF INHABITANTS. No. born in foreign countries.	NATIVITY OF INHABITANTS. Surplus or deficiency.	BETWEEN 5 AND 21 YEARS OLD. No. 5 years old and under 6.	BETWEEN 5 AND 21 YEARS OLD. No. 6 years old and under 16.	BETWEEN 5 AND 21 YEARS OLD. No. 16 years old and under 21.	No. births in 1874.	No. deaths in 1874.	No. of voters.	No. foreigners not naturalized.	No. of militia.
199	Baker	51	51	112	87	199	......	......	......	65	115	19	....	9	41	17	13	2	49	6	36
176	Carroll	60	60	94	82	176	......	......	......	50	113	13	....	5	15	5	4	......	51	......	36
391	Center	80	90	196	195	391	......	......	......	107	274	10	....	22	73	13	24	3	108	......	65
399	Floyd	80	80	209	190	399	......	......	......	114	260	25	....	18	84	16	19	5	114	......	80
401	Grant	88	89	206	177	383	9	9	18	143	228	30	....	29	76	24	15	8	92	......	60
299	Highland	75	75	162	137	299	......	......	......	115	144	40	....	24	64	23	22	5	67	2	43
282	Liberty	70	71	147	135	282	......	......	......	106	162	14	....	17	39	19	9	3	71	......	52
74	Summit,—Primghar, C. H.	14	16	39	35	74	......	......	......	30	42	2	....	6	14	....	6	......	15	......	9
128	Waterman	31	31	65	63	128	......	......	......	44	74	10	....	....	13	6	4	......	28	......	19
2349	Total	549	563	1230	1101	2331	9	9	18	774	1412	163	....	130	419	123	116	26	595	8	400

OSCEOLA COUNTY.

63	Fairview	17	17	29	34	63	......	......	......	18	30	15	......	5	7	4	3	......	19	1	10
227	Gilman	71	71	126	101	227	......	......	......	57	147	28	5	14	39	7	19	3	71	......	57
395	Goewey	108	108	214	181	395	......	......	......	84	247	35	— 29	41	92	17	19	6	113	......	96
338	Holman, Sibley, C. H	123	123	278	260	538	......	......	......	130	332	75	— 1	18	87	30	33	5	154	......	97
89	Horton	20	20	44	45	89	......	......	......	30	48	4	— 10	......	16	3	3	......	19	......	18
175	Ocheyedan	43	43	98	77	175	......	......	......	53	104	18	......	10	30	13	6	......	47	......	25
150	Viola	53	53	79	71	150	......	......	......	42	92	14	— 2	5	25	3	5	......	44	......	39
141	Wilson	29	29	66	75	141	......	......	......	42	86	10	— 3	6	38	10	4	......	31	......	13
1778	Total	464	464	934	844	1778	......	......	......	456	1086	199	......	99	334	87	92	14	498	1	355

PAGE COUNTY.

1152	Amity	217	217	585	537	1122	10	20	30	376	682	94	......	51	283	59	46	16	248	......	179
907	Buchanan	155	155	469	438	907	......	......	......	405	496	6	......	43	246	107	28	17	214	......	168
1100	Clarinda, town of, C. H.	227	227	548	527	1075	11	14	25	392	659	49	......	62	236	85	35	18	270	2	190
519	Colfax	98	98	276	237	513	3	3	6	153	316	50	......	29	96	51	23	3	115	2	98
838	Douglas	147	147	445	393	838	......	......	......	295	372	171	......	28	202	66	42	12	177	40	112
909	East River	170	170	500	409	909	......	......	......	396	501	12	......	40	252	115	52	26	231	1	191
775	Fremont	140	140	407	368	775	......	......	......	193	235	347	......	35	173	53	25	13	118	66	96
540	Grant, exc. of Shenandoah	100	100	288	252	540	......	......	......	141	364	35	......	27	121	35	25	7	121	4	114
936	Harlan	174	174	486	427	913	15	8	23	387	469	80	......	41	232	73	30	5	190	7	138
745	Lincoln	105	105	410	334	744	1	......	1	250	435	60	......	39	230	62	20	6	162	12	132
382	Morton	82	82	203	179	382	......	......	......	65	317	......	......	13	63	44	17	3	93	......	60
699	Nebraska	136	136	345	335	680	9	10	19	254	434	11	......	45	189	46	28	9	160	......	113
1274	Nodaway, exc. of Clarinda	232	232	654	592	1246	16	12	28	464	777	33	......	75	347	103	53	17	283	15	202
750	Pierce	176	176	394	356	750	......	......	......	286	426	38	......	44	165	33	32	19	184	6	138
711	Shenandoah, town of	150	150	368	340	708	2	1	3	152	523	36	......	24	119	45	20	13	210	......	164
688	Tarkio	133	133	375	313	688	......	......	......	162	495	31	......	22	155	72	33	9	165	......	140
836	Valley	144	144	435	401	836	......	......	......	283	503	50	......	30	214	90	44	18	188	......	151
513	Washington	101	101	275	238	513	......	......	......	157	327	29	......	23	149	46	17	2	94	8	82
14274	Total	2687	2687	7463	6676	14139	67	68	135	4811	8331	1132	......	671	3472	1185	570	213	3223	163	2468

PALO ALTO COUNTY.

170	Ellington	35	35	106	64	170	......	......	......	64	64	51	9	6	31	15	9	1	36	3	28
402	Emmetsburg, Emmetsburg, C. H	79	79	206	196	402	......	......	......	120	207	75	......	73	115	47	11	3	85	9	52
92	Fairfield	16	16	52	40	92	......	......	......	25	50	15	— 2	7	23	7	5	1	17	......	12
121	Fern Valley	27	27	55	66	121	......	......	......	34	70	18	1	3	36	10	5	......	27	......	19

PALO ALTO COUNTY.—Continued.

Total population.	Names of townships, towns, and cities.	No. of dwelling houses.	No. of families.	White population. Male.	White population. Female.	White population. Total.	Colored pop'lation. Male.	Colored pop'lation. Female.	Colored pop'lation. Total.	Nativity of inhabitants. No. born in Iowa.	No. born in U. S., but not in Iowa.	No. born in foreign countries.	Surplus or deficiency.	Between 5 and 21 years old. No. 5 years old and under 6.	No. 6 years old and under 16.	No. 16 years old and under 21.	No. births in 1874.	No. deaths in 1874.	No. of voters.	No. foreigners not naturalized.	No. of militia.
300	Freedom	59	59	156	139	294	3	3	6	93	144	40	— 23	21	64	27	......	......	67	1	51
271	Great Oak	39	39	151	120	271	......	......	......	71	119	90	9	25	105	23	13	1	53	......	47
217	Highland	46	46	113	104	217	......	......	......	48	92	81	4	5	49	18	10	1	35	......	35
120	Lost Island	30	30	66	54	120	......	......	......	24	40	48	— 8	5	25	7	8	......	21	8	17
124	Nevada	18	18	64	66	124	......	......	......	48	40	36	....	6	38	10	4	......	23	2	16
163	Rush Lake	34	34	78	85	163	......	......	......	57	75	32	1	7	47	14	......	......	31	2	....
172	Silver Lake	35	35	91	81	172	......	......	......	38	72	41	— 21	8	38	17	......	6	40	2	21
147	Vernon	27	27	75	72	147	......	......	......	52	67	29	1	10	48	7	4	1	26	2	17
183	Walnut	35	35	98	85	183	......	......	......	64	51	57	— 11	21	44	9	9	1	37	5	14
246	West Bend	46	46	137	109	246	......	......	......	91	177	14	36	15	65	21	6	2	58	26	22
2728	Total	526	526	1448	1281	2722	3	3	6	829	1268	627	....	212	728	232	84	17	556	60	351

PLYMOUTH COUNTY.

Total population.	Names of townships, towns, and cities.	No. of dwelling houses.	No. of families.	White population. Male.	White population. Female.	White population. Total.	Colored pop'lation. Male.	Colored pop'lation. Female.	Colored pop'lation. Total.	Nativity of inhabitants. No. born in Iowa.	No. born in U. S., but not in Iowa.	No. born in foreign countries.	Surplus or deficiency.	Between 5 and 21 years old. No. 5 years old and under 6.	No. 6 years old and under 16.	No. 16 years old and under 21.	No. births in 1874.	No. deaths in 1874.	No. of voters.	No. foreigners not naturalized.	No. of militia.
1235	America, Le Mars, C. H.	244	244	621	614	1235	......	......	......	318	712	83	—122	86	224	69	48	18	297	3	253
207	Elgin	54	54	119	88	207	......	......	......	38	113	47	— 9	7	44	13	14	5	52	5	33
278	Fredonia	65	65	148	130	278	......	......	......	80	91	87	— 20	19	63	23	13	4	59	.....	48
276	Grant	68	68	140	136	276	......	......	......	72	96	93	— 17	19	51	8	16	1	58	14	43
410	Johnson	77	77	225	185	410	......	......	......	139	125	141	— 5	17	118	27	27	21	77	17	64
712	Lincoln	132	132	368	344	712	......	......	......	240	286	183	— 3	31	155	59	26	3	165	......	127
178	Marion	38	38	91	87	178	......	......	......	54	41	33	— 50	8	42	7	27	21	42	......	36
565	Perry	133	133	305	260	565	......	......	......	157	157	71	—180	23	128	44	25	15	100	......	84
275	Plymouth	58	58	148	127	275	......	......	......	89	94	81	— 11	22	73	14	13	6	51	6	35
249	Portland	57	57	140	109	249	......	......	......	69	116	75	11	7	53	17	12	6	50	8	55
246	Sioux	45	45	125	121	246	......	......	......	87	151	28	20	9	71	18	12	2	43	......	31
275	Stanton	62	62	140	135	275	......	......	......	73	107	86	— 9	10	49	18	14	6	71	......	89

145	Union	31	31	80	65	145	......	......	......	48	62	39	4	5	44	4	4	1	29	8	12
231	Washington	58	58	127	104	231	......	......	......	63	99	24	— 45	14	53	18	4	......	42	......	37
5282	Total	1122	1122	2777	2505	5282	......	......	......	1527	2250	1071	......	275	1168	339	255	109	1136	61	917

POCAHONTAS COUNTY.

282	Bellville	59	59	155	127	282	......	......	......	73	46	158	— 5	9	65	19	12	......	43	......	......
290	Cedar	62	62	151	139	290	......	......	......	95	145	41	— 9	12	54	21	11	7	70	28	30
100	Center	19	19	54	46	100	......	......	......	29	8	31	— 32	24	32	8	6	4	9	......	53
116	Clinton	27	27	67	49	116	......	......	......	44	60	25	13	5	27	7	6	1	29	7	......
240	Colfax	56	56	119	121	240	......	......	......	44	91	75	— 30	19	61	13	7	2	43	2	13
265	Des Moines, Rolfe, C. H.	56	56	141	124	265	......	......	......	50	37	27	—151	18	56	12	8	2	65	18	21
139	Dover	30	29	68	71	139	......	......	......	50	72	15	— 2	5	27	15	2	......	28	......	34
114	Grant	26	26	61	53	114	......	......	......	21	48	45	......	1	31	9	5	2	23	......	23
186	Jackson	38	38	97	89	186	......	......	......	38	149	28	29	4	53	18	5	2	40	5	17
85	Lincoln	17	17	43	42	85	......	......	......	23	34	22	— 6	9	23	5	6	......	16	......	18
496	Lizard	88	89	257	239	496	......	......	......	174	141	145	— 36	25	127	47	16	9	90	......	11
36	Swan Lake	7	7	21	15	36	......	......	......	9	27	......	......	......	......	......	......	......	8	7	58
2249	Total	485	485	1134	1115	2249	......	......	......	650	858	482	......	131	556	174	84	29	464	67	278

POLK COUNTY.

630	Allen	121	121	328	302	630	......	......	......	289	310	31	......	28	144	68	21	6	140	2	106
1692	Beaver	329	329	915	771	1686	1	5	6	573	1021	98	......	62	400	140	65	21	407	15	319
1309	Bloomfield	217	217	674	618	1292	9	8	17	481	662	166	......	50	344	119	38	6	232	......	222
1366	Camp	255	255	703	663	1366	......	......	......	746	597	23	......	50	344	118	63	23	305	3	218
1055	Crocker	176	176	558	497	1055	......	......	......	487	542	26	......	43	315	96	25	11	208	9	141
1012	Delaware	180	180	538	470	1008	2	2	4	411	545	56	......	39	224	72	25	11	235	2	139
680	Douglas	124	124	371	309	680	......	......	......	290	330	60	......	30	192	67	24	9	166	12	120
776	Elkhart	145	145	408	368	776	4	7	11	358	296	122	......	36	162	46	29	7	138	21	84
449	Four Mile	93	93	244	205	449	......	......	......	203	166	80	......	16	88	21	15	9	109	......	66
737	Franklin	134	134	387	339	726	4	7	11	304	397	36	......	21	196	69	35	10	168	4	130
400	Grant	68	68	203	197	400	......	......	......	203	180	17	......	17	104	35	14	7	91	4	75
903	Jefferson	161	161	470	425	895	4	4	8	438	440	25	......	51	219	47	42	10	177	8	127
1103	Lincoln	168	168	581	522	1103	......	......	......	439	245	419	......	54	343	84	50	14	138	54	33
1631	Madison	303	303	857	777	1631	......	......	......	803	789	39	......	91	435	129	55	12	339	1	265
691	Saylor	119	119	350	328	678	6	7	13	325	330	36	......	36	180	76	25	3	152	......	107
884	Valley	150	150	456	428	884	......	......	......	375	431	78	......	37	230	106	32	6	191	4	160

POLK COUNTY.—Continued.

Total population.	NAMES OF TOWNSHIPS, TOWNS, AND CITIES.	No. of dwelling houses.	Number of families.	WHITE POPULATION.			COLORED POP'LATION			NATIVITY OF INHABITANTS.				BETWEEN 5 AND 21 YEARS OLD.			No. births in 1874.	No. deaths in 1874.	No. of voters.	No. foreigners not naturalized.	No. of militia.
				Male.	Female.	Total.	Male.	Female.	Total.	No. born in Iowa.	No. born in U. S., but not in Iowa.	No. born in foreign countries.	Surplus or deficiency.	No. 5 years old and under 6.	No. 6 years old and under 16.	No. 16 years old and under 21.					
1008	Walnut	177	177	536	467	1003	5	......	5	440	464	104	....	84	248	96	29	12	218	3	170
789	Washington	150	150	406	383	789	......	......	......	416	261	112	....	34	191	71	33	8	165	4	114
17095	Total	3070	3070	8985	8066	17050	31	33	64	7581	8006	1528	....	779	4359	1460	620	185	3579	146	2596
	Des Moines, city of, C. H.,																				
1484	" First ward	257	283	791	671	1462	11	11	22	496	568	420	....	54	345	108	42	19	351	41	309
2267	" Second ward	398	418	1107	1103	2210	46	11	57	556	1332	379	....	17	451	76	39	15	596	25	388
2934	" Third ward	509	577	1358	1536	2894	18	22	40	849	1740	345	....	118	619	213	73	25	694	14	464
2073	" Fourth ward	397	416	1003	1068	2071	......	2	2	768	952	353	....	78	487	174	47	3	432	42	331
2207	" Fifth ward	456	475	1068	1061	2129	35	43	78	788	951	468	....	66	523	141	129	30	453	66	350
1737	" Sixth ward	296	338	866	856	1722	7	8	15	552	942	243	....	49	315	72	49	20	422	33	268
1741	" Seventh ward	343	370	854	790	1644	48	49	97	595	652	494	....	18	389	49	31	17	315	88	210
14443	Total of city	2656	2877	7047	7085	14132	165	146	311	4604	7137	2702	....	400	3129	833	410	129	3263	309	2320
31558	Total of county	5726	5947	16032	15151	31183	196	179	375	12185	15143	4230	....	1179	7488	2293	1030	314	6842	455	4916

Note by the Secretary of State.—An enumeration of the inhabitants of the city of Des Moines was taken by order of the city council on the 14th of September, 1875, the result of which is hereto annexed.

Total population.	Names	No. of dwelling houses.	Number of families.	Male.	Female.	Total.	Male.	Female.	Total.	No. born in Iowa.	No. born in U. S., but not in Iowa.	No. born in foreign countries.	Surplus or deficiency.	No. 5 years old and under 6.	No. 6 years old and under 16.	No. 16 years old and under 21.	No. births in 1874.	No. deaths in 1874.	No. of voters.	No. foreigners not naturalized.	No. of militia.
1575	First ward	....	....	878	672	1550	12	13	25	540	610	425	....	55	375	118	52	25	....	......	....
2542	Second ward	....	....	1321	1159	2480	60	9	69	644	1475	430	....	27	491	83	43	18	....	......	....
3660	Third ward	....	....	1746	1877	3623	17	20	37	1030	2088	542	....	128	680	253	91	30	....	......	....
2111	Fourth ward	....	....	1012	1098	2110	......	1	1	783	970	358	....	85	507	182	49	4	....	......	....
2348	Fifth ward	....	....	1149	1126	2275	37	36	73	853	1024	774	....	74	548	148	138	33	....	......	....
2011	Sixth ward	....	....	1061	930	1991	14	6	20	660	1072	279	....	53	360	85	55	25	....	......	....
1876	Seventh ward	....	....	921	832	1753	67	56	123	655	712	509	....	27	429	51	34	19	....	......	....
16130	Total	....	....	8088	7694	15782	207	141	343	5165	7951	3014	....	449	3390	920	462	154	....	......	....

POTTAWATTAMIE COUNTY.

846	Avoca, town of	200	200	429	414	843	1	2	3	217	401	146	— 82	23	116	49	39	15	207	32	180
188	Belknap	83	33	103	85	188	......	......	......	62	120	6	......	4	52	10	13	4	42	......	35
557	Boomer	102	102	289	286	557	......	......	......	244	186	117	— 10	22	164	42	16	3	103	......	49
836	Center	145	145	455	381	836	......	......	......	316	447	38	— 35	39	251	74	40	11	170	6	133
530	Crescent	110	110	295	235	530	......	......	......	216	248	101	35	27	135	43	18	14	110	......	79
507	Grove	126	126	264	243	507	......	......	......	211	269	44	17	36	192	53	15	3	159	......	137
250	Hardin	53	53	133	117	250	......	......	......	108	117	40	— 25	10	67	18	7	2	57	8	44
636	Hazel Dell	120	120	330	305	635	1	......	1	288	209	151	12	30	149	54	38	4	111	28	68
193	James	35	35	94	99	193	......	......	......	71	93	16	— 13	11	51	14	7	......	40	......	30
1122	Kane, exc. of Council Bluffs	187	187	605	515	1120	1	1	2	482	422	254	36	89	227	69	38	10	212	17	154
386	Keg Creek	50	50	251	135	386	......	......	......	104	25	4	—253	23	84	19	10	3	44	28	32
1340	Knox, exc. of Avoca	245	245	696	631	1327	8	5	13	491	693	141	— 15	53	314	121	56	13	315	28	272
1003	Layton	190	190	559	444	1003	......	......	......	321	456	194	— 32	35	210	35	51	11	233	37	159
451	Macedonia	96	96	251	200	451	......	......	......	192	250	13	4	20	106	44	19	6	106	6	93
359	Neola	61	61	199	160	359	......	......	......	164	77	108	— 10	27	74	29	13	1	75	21	63
289	Norwalk	54	54	158	131	289	......	......	......	134	104	63	12	14	68	20	16	6	52	18	55
484	Pleasant	82	82	257	227	484	......	......	......	154	199	118	— 13	19	99	34	14	4	110	19	89
911	Rockford	174	174	476	435	911	......	......	......	416	437	25	— 33	32	220	79	37	6	199	3	139
231	Silver Creek	48	48	134	97	231	......	......	......	60	138	24	— 9	3	45	14	8	4	50	2	44
216	Washington	33	33	130	86	216	......	......	......	73	119	24	......	13	67	18	6	4	44	3	37
465	Waveland	98	98	244	221	465	......	......	......	165	281	25	6	15	95	39	23	10	106	......	81
396	Wright	75	75	220	176	396	......	......	......	134	227	13	— 22	79	102	40	23	5	94	......	87
182	York	35	35	96	86	182	......	......	......	79	72	46	15	12	51	9	6	1	35	......	26
12378	Total	2352	2353	6668	5691	12359	11	8	19	4602	5589	1713	......	646	2939	927	514	147	2674	236	2113
	Council Bluffs, city of, C. H.,																				
1985	" First ward	399	391	1009	966	1975	3	7	10	692	873	420	......	115	406	142	64	31	394	82	229
2919	" Second ward	503	527	1583	1299	2882	19	18	37	798	1393	728	......	125	413	225	108	36	517	192	384
1796	" Third ward	357	357	884	909	1793	2	1	3	551	911	334	......	80	313	141	74	22	342	99	223
2587	" Fourth ward	446	461	1323	1242	2565	14	8	22	746	1347	494	......	105	451	203	121	25	465	140	313
9287	Total of city	1705	1736	4799	4416	9215	38	34	72	2787	4524	1976	......	425	1583	711	367	114	1718	513	1149
21665	Total of county	4057	4088	11467	10107	21574	49	42	91	7489	10113	3687	......	1066	4522	1638	876	261	4392	749	3235

POWESHIEK COUNTY.

670	Bear Creek, exc. of Brooklyn	121	121	364	306	670	......	......	......	232	402	28	— 8	26	168	74	22	5	148	6	146
1109	Brooklyn, town of	251	251	566	542	1108	1	......	1	380	606	21	—102	46	288	68	22	8	303	1	185
523	Chester	107	107	298	225	523	......	......	......	186	304	33	......	19	106	35	15	7	136	5	100
1055	Deep River	187	187	576	479	1055	......	......	......	401	612	42	......	45	289	100	40	13	232	3	190
883	Grinnell, exc. of town	171	171	461	422	883	......	......	......	306	493	41	— 43	28	201	116	29	8	185	5	142

POWESHIEK COUNTY.—Continued.

Total population.	Names of townships, towns, and cities.	No. of dwelling houses.	Number of families.	White population. Males.	White population. Female.	White population. Total.	Colored pop'lation. Male.	Colored pop'lation. Female.	Colored pop'lation. Total.	Nativity of inhabitants. No. born in Iowa.	Nativity of inhabitants. No. born in U. S., but not in Iowa.	Nativity of inhabitants. No. born in foreign countries.	Nativity of inhabitants. Surplus or deficiency.	Between 5 and 21 years old. No. 5 years old and under 6.	Between 5 and 21 years old. No. 6 years old and under 16.	Between 5 and 21 years old. No. 16 years old and under 21.	No. births in 1874.	No. deaths in 1874.	No. of voters.	No. foreigners not naturalized.	No. of militia.
1480	Grinnell, town of	295	295	719	736	1455	15	10	25	362	1002	86	— 30	44	261	114	25	11	356	9	278
1049	Jackson, exc. of Montezuma	203	203	557	487	1044	4	1	5	441	603	7	2	53	230	119	30	14	243	......	167
836	Jefferson	150	150	443	393	836	......	......	......	352	456	60	32	152	165	63	39	22	178	6	148
811	Lincoln	144	141	414	397	811	......	......	......	306	355	147	— 3	38	235	64	39	13	153	16	117
837	Madison	156	156	439	398	837	......	......	......	302	445	82	— 8	43	214	98	23	9	183	10	116
722	Malcom, exc. of town	99	99	475	245	720	2	......	2	124	290	97	—211	26	119	41	10	......	115	24	125
353	Malcom, town of	80	80	181	172	353	......	......	......	119	200	32	— 2	21	68	24	11	7	91	3	59
460	Montezuma, town of, C. H.	94	94	234	226	460	......	......	......	177	258	......	— 25	3	29	115	4	4	116	1	79
695	Pleasant	127	127	363	317	680	10	5	15	254	335	104	— 2	36	177	61	26	10	157	15	118
633	Scott	124	124	333	300	633	......	......	......	204	339	92	2	21	145	58	14	4	124	15	53
679	Sheridan	126	126	363	316	679	......	......	......	227	321	130	— 1	28	167	48	34	11	139	22	107
1070	Sugar Creek	102	102	566	504	1070	......	......	......	567	559	13	69	60	250	109	20	10	229	......	139
785	Union	153	153	395	389	784	1	......	1	406	358	15	— 6	31	206	86	42	13	160	......	115
1092	Warren	191	191	575	517	1092	......	......	......	447	536	64	— 45	53	252	110	46	9	229	......	152
740	Washington	133	133	384	356	740	......	......	......	328	344	67	— 1	29	201	72	25	8	157	8	119
16482	Total	3014	3011	8706	7727	16433	33	16	49	6121	8818	1161	......	802	3771	1585	516	186	3634	149	2655

RINGGOLD COUNTY.

Total population.	Names of townships, towns, and cities.	No. of dwelling houses.	Number of families.	White population. Males.	White population. Female.	White population. Total.	Colored pop'lation. Male.	Colored pop'lation. Female.	Colored pop'lation. Total.	Nativity of inhabitants. No. born in Iowa.	Nativity of inhabitants. No. born in U. S., but not in Iowa.	Nativity of inhabitants. No. born in foreign countries.	Nativity of inhabitants. Surplus or deficiency.	Between 5 and 21 years old. No. 5 years old and under 6.	Between 5 and 21 years old. No. 6 years old and under 16.	Between 5 and 21 years old. No. 16 years old and under 21.	No. births in 1874.	No. deaths in 1874.	No. of voters.	No. foreigners not naturalized.	No. of militia.
381	Athens	64	64	200	181	381	......	......	......	159	200	22	......	10	114	34	21	5	80	1	62
431	Benton	81	81	231	200	431	......	......	......	134	289	8	......	20	112	29	16	4	102	......	69
469	Clinton	80	80	238	231	469	......	......	......	244	222	3	......	20	135	43	21	6	92	......	56
470	Grant	72	74	245	225	470	......	......	......	192	258	20	......	21	141	47	18	5	44	......	81
592	Jefferson	107	107	307	285	592	......	......	......	254	314	24	......	21	181	59	12	8	140	......	106
395	Liberty	71	71	201	194	395	......	......	......	132	251	12	......	15	101	36	8	5	90	......	71
492	Lincoln	86	87	263	229	492	......	......	......	204	263	25	......	17	137	44	15	4	92	......	84
652	Lotts Creek	108	116	354	298	652	......	......	......	275	351	26	......	30	176	50	19	10	142	3	98

510	Middle Fork	83	83	251	259	510	......	......	......	228	276	6	......	21	154	46	28	10	93	......	77
383	Monroe	68	68	184	199	383	......	......	......	129	236	18	......	11	106	44	9	10	74	3	59
952	Mount Ayr, Mount Ayr, C. H.	168	169	480	469	949	2	1	3	396	512	44	......	35	229	81	22	6	193	2	116
422	Rice	80	80	218	204	422	......	......	......	174	210	38	......	15	114	39	29	13	85	1	52
320	Riley	60	60	164	156	320	......	......	......	159	155	6	......	12	86	26	16	7	69	......	54
203	Tingley	35	35	107	96	203	......	......	......	73	130	......	......	8	50	25	5	4	34	......	35
209	Union	41	40	108	92	200	5	4	9	91	112	6	......	6	37	47	3	2	44	......	25
665	Washington	124	124	345	320	665	......	......	......	321	321	23	......	25	164	148	30	10	122	2	95
7546	Total	1328	1339	3896	3638	7534	7	5	12	3165	4100	281	......	287	2037	798	272	109	1496	12	1140

SAC COUNTY.

234	Boyer Valley	48	50	127	107	234	......	......	......	56	167	14	3	6	53	6	9	......	62	......	52
155	Clinton	37	27	77	78	155	......	......	......	47	87	21	......	8	41	4	9	2	33	3	25
386	Douglas	78	78	194	192	386	......	......	......	103	198	61	— 24	14	59	61	11	2	82	......	44
173	Eden	34	36	99	74	173	......	......	......	73	59	12	— 29	19	49	6	5	......	40	......	35
811	Jackson, Sac City, C. H	167	171	429	382	811	......	......	......	255	511	45	......	41	173	66	27	2	212	......	156
297	Levey	60	53	170	127	297	......	......	......	79	150	68	......	14	63	16	10	6	55	13	38
473	Sac	89	91	245	228	473	......	......	......	125	256	92	......	22	128	29	25	21	104	1	65
344	Wall Lake	62	62	169	175	344	......	......	......	109	213	22	......	18	85	23	2	......	69	......	57
2873	Total	575	568	1510	1363	2873	......	......	......	847	1641	335	......	142	651	211	98	33	657	17	472

SCOTT COUNTY.

684	Allen's Grove	117	117	354	330	684	......	......	......	338	147	185	— 14	35	153	42	45	9	116	46	104
1389	Blue Grass	240	237	732	657	1389	......	......	......	698	128	563	......	56	354	134	56	16	200	108	131
1284	Buffalo, exc. of town	211	211	660	623	1283	......	1	1	594	394	203	— 93	......	1	......	40	11	260	17	165
453	Buffalo, town of	87	87	220	232	452	1	......	1	232	83	138	1	37	117	31	21	4	97	7	56
892	Butler	155	150	487	405	892	......	......	......	428	181	283	......	38	244	73	34	9	143	60	100
870	Cleona	143	143	496	374	870	......	......	......	346	76	448	......	41	197	69	42	13	101	136	201
8439	Davenport, exc. of city	600	600	1824	1606	3430	5	4	9	1504	592	1343	......	122	916	302	120	20	494	257	156
1196	Hickory Grove	200	201	645	551	1196	......	......	......	531	161	504	......	38	306	105	45	15	194	1130	249
764	LeClaire, exc. of town	149	149	394	370	764	......	......	......	335	313	114	— 2	21	184	90	19	4	171	11	94
1121	LeClaire, town of	259	259	586	532	1118	1	2	3	477	498	93	— 53	23	294	68	8	2	297	......	149
1043	Liberty	196	196	544	498	1042	......	1	1	430	274	325	— 14	33	265	81	8	3	177	......	108
992	Lincoln	160	160	534	458	992	......	......	......	480	211	299	— 2	41	216	103	33	5	180	60	207
737	Pleasant Valley	146	146	371	364	735	2	......	2	324	255	158	......	20	157	71	18	11	170	29	102
683	Princeton, exc. of town	102	105	367	316	683	......	......	......	324	372	80	93	41	144	57	19	3	147	16	107
445	Princeton, town of	103	102	223	222	445	......	......	......	194	208	45	2	21	99	41	9	6	105	......	63
318	Rockingham	55	56	168	150	318	......	......	......	146	48	124	......	12	72	31	10	......	58	19	32
1211	Sheridan	215	215	634	577	1211	......	......	......	551	165	497	2	60	250	112	48	10	191	102	116

SCOTT COUNTY.—Continued.

Total population.	Names of townships, towns, and cities.	No. of dwelling houses	No. of families.	White population. Male.	White population. Female.	White population. Total.	Colored pop'lation. Male.	Colored pop'lation. Female.	Colored pop'lation. Total.	Nativity of inhabitants. No. born in Iowa.	No. born in U. S., but not in Iowa.	No. born in foreign countries.	Surplus or deficiency.	Between 5 and 21 years old. No. 5 years old and under 6.	No. 6 years old and under 16.	No. 16 years old and under 21.	No. births in 1874.	No. deaths in 1874.	No. of voters.	No. foreigners not naturalized.	No. of militia.
981	Winfield	163	162	520	460	980	......	1	1	460	122	393	6	38	259	116	28	10	177	39	119
18502	Total	3301	3296	9759	8725	18484	9	9	18	8392	4128	5795	......	677	4228	1526	603	151	3278	2037	2259
	Davenport, city of, C. H.,																				
6317	" First ward	1162	1373	3163	3152	6315	1	1	2	2672	431	3214	......	155	1531	187	241	116	903	411	511
2938	" Second ward	465	626	1511	1426	2937	......	1	1	1242	253	1443	......	102	692	164	115	24	410	808	200
2551	" Third ward	446	524	1284	1251	2535	8	8	16	951	562	1038	......	64	571	184	85	7	473	115	337
3321	" Fourth ward	626	620	1561	1693	3254	27	40	67	1090	1507	724	......	173	587	235	58	28	475	6	599
3218	" Fifth ward	609	659	1496	1663	3159	25	34	59	1150	1420	648	......	151	606	263	62	23	693	78	551
2889	" Sixth ward	596	578	1399	1456	2855	18	16	34	1148	1054	687	......	112	540	211	66	11	607	45	362
21234	Total of city	3904	4380	10414	10641	21055	79	100	179	8253	5227	7754	......	757	4527	1244	627	214	3831	1463	2560
39736	Total of county	7205	7676	20173	19366	39539	88	109	197	16645	9455	13549	......	1434	8755	2770	1230	365	7109	3500	4819

SHELBY COUNTY.

Total population.	Names of townships, towns, and cities.	No. of dwelling houses	No. of families.	White Male.	White Female.	White Total.	Colored Male.	Colored Female.	Colored Total.	No. born in Iowa.	No. born in U. S., but not in Iowa.	No. born in foreign countries.	Surplus or deficiency.	No. 5 years old and under 6.	No. 6 years old and under 16.	No. 16 years old and under 21.	No. births in 1874.	No. deaths in 1874.	No. of voters.	No. foreigners not naturalized.	No. of militia.
116	Cass	20	20	53	58	116	......	......	......	44	58	14	......	4	36	10	5	1	22	2	15
287	Clay	57	57	146	141	287	......	......	......	85	179	23	......	5	54	16	15	9	50	14	25
319	Douglas	57	57	169	146	315	3	1	4	116	194	9	......	15	76	30	13	4	49	1	48
740	Fairview	160	160	390	350	740	......	......	......	294	275	171	......	24	149	46	33	16	144	24	135
653	Grove	110	110	338	310	648	1	4	5	298	292	63	......	29	176	66	18	7	123	41	90
77	Greeley	15	15	43	34	77	......	......	......	17	60	......	......	3	22	7	2	2	14	......	7
927	Harlan, Harlan, C. H.	171	171	509	418	927	......	......	......	224	569	34	......	33	191	61	28	20	221	......	187
271	Jackson	52	52	141	130	271	......	......	......	115	87	69	......	11	55	17	16	7	37	27	32
114	Jefferson	20	20	64	50	114	......	......	......	29	81	4	......	4	32	9	7	3	27	......	19
343	Lincoln	82	82	179	164	343	......	......	......	131	169	43	......	16	57	22	23	4	82	2	79

660	Monroe	138	138	353	307	660	......	......	......	188	247	225	....	43	154	25	28	6	72	......	....
181	Polk	32	32	92	89	181	......	......	......	85	94	2	....	10	53	14	3	......	34	......	28
390	Shelby	75	81	239	151	390	......	......	......	174	189	27	....	12	78	17	16	4	102	2	97
183	Union	32	32	102	81	183	......	......	......	61	93	29	....	7	43	17	14	2	37	6	34
196	Washington	35	35	103	93	196	......	......	......	80	105	11	....	4	51	19	6	1	46	1	39
207	Westphalia	31	37	109	98	207	......	......	......	31	45	131	....	11	55	17	16	7	24	89	24
5664	Total of county	1087	1099	3035	2620	5655	4	5	9	272	2737	855	....	231	1282	396	243	93	1084	209	859

SIOUX COUNTY.

201	Buncombe	47	47	106	95	201	......	......	......	66	114	18	....	10	40	16	11	1	51	1	38
246	Floyd	51	51	138	108	246	......	......	......	77	21	63	....	9	51	18	13	5	38	21	42
226	Grant	55	55	116	110	226	......	......	......	87	100	28	....	9	27	11	12	3	53	......	48
1021	Holland, Orange City, C. H.	187	187	540	481	1021	......	......	......	410	109	399	....	59	268	92	57	12	159	69	128
227	Lincoln	59	59	123	104	227	......	......	......	66	127	30	....	31	43	16	9	2	54	4	53
568	Nassau	125	125	360	208	568	......	......	......	198	114	187	....	28	114	37	33	7	116	37	83
288	Reading	60	27	163	123	286	......	......	......	85	152	48	....	16	80	16	6	2	60	......	43
88	Rock	27	27	49	39	88	......	......	......	23	51	14	....	1	18	8	3	......	30	......	23
119	Settler	33	28	67	52	119	......	......	......	42	45	32	....	3	25	11	8	3	23	11	11
238	Sheridan	56	56	120	118	238	......	......	......	90	90	58	....	14	44	8	14	3	53	8	45
3220	Total	700	698	1782	1438	3220	......	......	......	1144	923	877	....	180	710	233	166	38	637	151	514

STORY COUNTY.

820	Ames, town of	210	210	413	407	820	......	......	......	233	517	70	....	33	145	50	29	8	211	6	156
754	Collins	139	139	397	357	754	......	......	......	335	392	27	....	35	221	94	30	6	151	2	117
959	Franklin	172	172	482	477	959	......	......	......	399	481	79	....	30	261	81	44	14	182	13	140
534	Grant	102	102	288	246	534	......	......	......	172	312	50	....	27	117	34	19	17	119	......	71
1143	Howard	198	198	581	562	1143	......	......	......	426	177	540	....	43	317	79	41	......	129	79	49
1022	Indian Creek	184	184	520	502	1022	......	......	......	439	534	49	....	149	266	144	25	17	211	2	147
743	Lafayette	137	137	404	339	743	......	......	......	231	152	360	....	30	192	66	38	13	89	67	66
292	Lincoln	52	52	157	135	292	......	......	......	85	165	42	....	14	83	34	12	5	60	15	30
636	Milford	104	104	340	296	636	......	......	......	255	280	101	....	22	153	57	18	8	127	8	96
786	Nevada, exc. of town	135	135	405	381	786	......	......	......	348	404	34	....	31	204	68	33	7	168	......	121
1105	Nevada, town of, C. H.	216	219	528	577	1105	......	......	......	355	577	173	....	42	267	74	35	13	243	17	153
827	New Albany	172	172	413	414	827	......	......	......	248	494	85	....	35	189	74	31	1	179	5	132
898	Palestine	162	162	459	438	897	1	......	1	365	206	327	....	44	234	106	35	22	122	37	67
453	Richland	75	75	236	217	453	......	......	......	160	264	29	....	10	112	60	10	3	94	2	54
261	Sherman	48	47	142	119	261	......	......	......	62	140	59	....	8	65	26	9	7	59	4	49
1119	Union	207	207	582	537	1119	......	......	......	477	505	137	....	40	307	84	49	14	219	16	182
132	Warren	27	27	73	59	132	......	......	......	39	56	37	....	8	29	12	7	2	19	9	16
827	Washington, exc. of Ames	150	150	419	408	827	......	......	......	263	462	102	....	35	167	44	22	2	192	......	113
13311	Total	2490	2492	6839	6471	13310	1	......	1	4892	6118	2301	....	636	3329	1187	487	159	2574	282	1759

TAMA COUNTY.

Total population.	NAMES OF TOWNSHIPS, TOWNS, AND CITIES.	No. of dwelling houses.	No. of families.	WHITE POPULATION. Male.	Female.	Total.	COLORED POP'LATION Male.	Female.	Total.	NATIVITY OF INHABITANTS. No. born in Iowa.	No. born in U. S., but not in Iowa.	No. born in foreign countries.	Surplus or deficiency.	BETWEEN 5 AND 21 YEARS OLD. No. 5 years old and under 6.	No. 6 years old and under 16.	No. 16 years old and under 21.	No. births in 1874.	No. deaths in 1874.	No. of voters.	No. foreigners not naturalized.	No. of militia.
668	Buckingham	114	114	349	319	668	......	......	......	227	325	116	....	37	154	40	24	8	150	21	90
844	Carlton	148	148	456	388	844	......	......	......	212	338	19	10	26	137	46	11	2	176	14	135
575	Carroll	98	98	318	257	575	......	......	......	227	202	146	....	17	161	69	17	9	103	26	86
711	Clark	130	130	389	322	711	......	......	......	233	379	129	11	12	178	63	39	9	137	77	96
776	Columbia	144	146	388	388	776	......	......	......	289	344	103	— 40	25	181	70	39	9	153	13	94
616	Crystal	107	107	342	274	616	......	......	......	206	235	175	....	47	139	45	24	5	120	35	143
569	Geneseo	102	102	316	253	569	......	......	......	212	338	19	....	26	137	46	11	2	122	......	148
343	Grant	64	64	181	162	343	......	......	......	121	97	139	14	20	87	20	11	......	50	32	31
593	Highland	112	112	314	279	593	......	......	......	180	351	61	— 1	25	144	40	22	6	127	27	96
902	Howard	167	167	473	429	902	......	......	......	371	477	54	....	29	230	84	35	2	196	5	144
1059	Indian Village, exc. of Montour	197	197	553	506	1059	......	......	......	453	545	53	— 8	42	264	110	35	10	188	......	150
389	Lincoln	86	86	210	179	389	......	......	......	107	107	178	3	23	61	21	10	3	59	47	33
514	Montour, town of	110	112	268	245	513	1	......	1	157	229	27	—101	20	114	27	16	10	123	11	89
790	Oneida	139	139	440	350	790	......	......	......	258	306	230	4	30	195	63	36	12	143	52	187
1043	Otter Creek	187	178	578	465	1043	......	......	......	428	330	275	— 10	56	244	80	50	9	190	42	113
778	Perry, exc. of Traer	148	148	416	362	778	......	......	......	273	360	116	— 29	26	190	61	31	7	171	16	89
870	Richland	168	168	462	408	870	......	......	......	386	437	86	39	29	224	88	30	15	191	7	140
1062	Salt Creek	197	197	546	516	1062	......	......	......	412	402	161	— 87	39	269	90	43	9	220	2	122
713	Spring Creek	140	140	388	324	712	1	......	1	257	280	167	— 9	36	158	39	33	11	179	7	141
222	Tama, exc. of Tama City	41	41	122	100	222	......	......	......	86	106	11	— 19	8	64	18	2	1	41	2	27
1197	Tama City, town of	246	246	600	597	1197	......	......	......	443	661	111	18	42	250	83	32	10	280	3	183
655	Toledo, exc. of town	132	132	332	316	648	5	2	7	286	340	29	....	41	180	62	23	6	141	4	74
1022	Toledo, town of, C. H	216	216	466	523	989	14	19	33	356	574	92	....	33	210	106	34	18	255	4	151
740	Traer, town of	148	148	413	327	740	......	......	......	199	414	123	— 4	30	202	34	34	4	214	9	147
1120	York	196	196	602	518	1120	......	......	......	418	223	479	....	54	273	88	51	13	182	51	200
18771	Total	3537	3532	9922	8807	18729	21	21	42	6938	8505	3138	....	795	4523	1528	706	192	3911	507	2909

TAYLOR COUNTY.

861	Bedford, town of, C. H.	202	202	426	425	851	5	5	10	294	539	28	......	74	169	52	14	5	215	1	184
659	Benton, exc. of town	140	140	339	318	657	1	1	2	238	417	4	......	64	176	57	12	3	143	......	102
624	Clayton	113	113	324	300	624	......	......	......	234	371	19	......	26	163	39	32	6	131	1	110
927	Dallas	149	149	488	439	927	......	......	......	393	229	5	—300	51	260	71	33	22	183	......	155
346	Gay	72	72	191	155	346	......	......	......	129	209	8	......	14	89	40	12	4	74	......	59
371	Grant	69	69	205	166	371	......	......	......	105	254	12	......	15	76	43	15	1	78	......	57
212	Grove	53	53	113	99	212	......	......	......	58	141	13	......	13	29	14	7	4	62	......	49
796	Holt	142	142	405	380	785	7	4	11	283	445	68	......	35	226	58	34	6	155	7	67
421	Jackson	74	74	210	211	421	......	......	......	200	218	3	......	14	104	37	19	9	81	......	55
639	Jefferson	119	119	336	302	638	1	......	1	256	383	......	......	53	172	39	24	12	125	......	100
710	Mason	124	124	360	350	710	......	......	......	243	444	23	......	71	149	51	20	7	147	......	111
485	Marshall	103	103	251	229	480	2	3	5	178	286	21	......	18	104	29	23	10	107	2	85
613	Nodaway	110	110	327	286	613	......	......	......	221	358	34	......	27	185	41	16	5	134	2	87
665	Platte	130	130	366	299	665	......	......	......	210	401	54	......	33	155	55	25	7	176	1	146
893	Polk	168	168	470	423	893	......	......	......	374	514	5	......	43	232	74	30	18	200	......	154
626	Ross	117	117	308	318	626	......	......	......	278	338	10	......	26	180	60	32	12	136	......	93
570	Washington	110	110	299	271	570	......	......	......	215	346	9	......	22	141	54	31	13	135	2	103
10418	Total	1995	1995	5418	4971	10389	16	13	29	3909	5893	316	......	599	2610	814	379	144	2282	16	1717

UNION COUNTY.

1123	Afton, town of, C. H.	175	175	562	561	1123	......	......	......	391	653	22	— 57	46	212	78	37	11	268	......	206
1819	Creston, town of	245	245	1035	778	1813	2	4	6	707	941	183	12	8	65	167	13	8	470	18	436
299	Dodge	46	46	154	145	299	......	......	......	112	186	......	— 1	15	86	37	5	7	54	......	55
586	Douglas, exc. of Creston	128	128	317	269	586	......	......	......	138	384	68	4	35	115	40	6	1	137	2	124
262	Grant	50	50	143	119	262	......	......	......	100	154	8	......	16	61	18	8	1	59	......	50
563	Highland	105	105	295	268	563	......	......	......	152	309	60	— 42	9	54	21	20	18	98	......	77
880	Jones	147	147	460	419	879	1	......	1	251	415	52	—162	25	236	73	39	7	165	......	120
448	Lincoln	80	80	238	210	448	......	......	......	183	237	31	3	25	128	46	22	4	91	......	60
321	New Hope	56	58	169	152	321	......	......	......	125	179	17	......	16	87	29	13	5	74	......	61
735	Platte	127	127	369	366	735	......	......	......	323	402	10	......	45	201	80	28	8	145	......	96
541	Pleasant	106	106	291	250	541	......	......	......	244	287	15	4	27	131	43	21	5	110	......	78
402	Sand Creek	69	69	194	188	382	13	7	20	197	191	15	1	20	124	31	8	6	75	......	54
231	Spaulding	39	39	121	110	231	......	......	......	89	127	15	......	58	54	20	7	1	53	......	57
617	Union, exc. of Afton	114	114	335	282	617	......	......	......	230	351	36	......	22	176	57	19	10	125	10	78
8827	Total	1487	1489	4683	4117	8800	16	11	27	3242	4816	532	......	367	1730	740	246	92	1924	30	1554

VAN BUREN COUNTY.

Total population.	NAMES OF TOWNSHIPS, TOWNS, AND CITIES.	No. of dwelling houses.	Number of families.	WHITE POPULATION. Male.	WHITE POPULATION. Female.	WHITE POPULATION. Total.	COLORED POP'LATION Male.	COLORED POP'LATION Female.	COLORED POP'LATION Total.	NATIVITY OF INHABITANTS. No. born in Iowa.	NATIVITY OF INHABITANTS. No. born in U. S., but not in Iowa.	NATIVITY OF INHABITANTS. No. born in foreign countries.	NATIVITY OF INHABITANTS. Surplus or deficiency.	BETWEEN 5 AND 21 YEARS OLD. No. 5 years old and under 6.	BETWEEN 5 AND 21 YEARS OLD. No. 6 years old and under 16.	BETWEEN 5 AND 21 YEARS OLD. No. 16 years old and under 21.	No. births in 1874.	No. deaths in 1874.	No. of voters.	No. foreigners not naturalized.	No. of militia.
338	Bentonsport, town of	80	80	159	175	334	......	4	4	131	176	31	....	10	76	36	13	5	85	......	41
595	Birmingham, town of	130	130	296	291	587	1	7	8	279	293	23	....	25	172	58	19	14	120	1	69
1349	Bonaparte	270	270	668	671	1339	3	7	10	687	529	133	....	37	271	128	32	7	309	32	213
187	Cantril, town of	50	50	94	93	187	......	......	......	72	104	11	....	9	41	10	......	......	50	......	38
917	Cedar	173	173	490	427	917	......	......	......	529	373	15	....	33	265	90	28	7	200	......	147
996	Chequest	198	198	516	480	996	......	......	......	502	455	39	....	30	254	94	38	14	222	14	148
1063	Des Moines	207	207	561	502	1063	......	......	......	549	468	46	....	40	272	92	37	7	245	1	200
842	Farmington, exc. of town	170	170	425	413	838	2	2	4	460	296	86	....	26	213	106	26	10	180	9	100
679	Farmington, town of	179	179	345	331	676	2	1	3	301	297	81	....	24	150	61	12	2	149	2	84
955	Harrisburg	179	179	482	473	955	......	......	......	525	397	33	....	38	198	81	49	8	228	1	119
639	Henry	134	134	310	329	639	......	......	......	371	245	23	....	19	146	60	25	5	161	1	106
1633	Jackson, exc. of Cantril	324	324	845	787	1632	......	1	1	797	814	22	....	37	361	135	46	20	403	......	262
788	Keosauqua, town of, C. H	177	177	341	374	715	41	32	73	400	350	38	....	33	191	73	20	17	172	2	110
954	Lick Creek	188	188	503	450	953	1	......	1	566	370	18	....	29	257	118	26	15	225	......	156
892	Union, exc. of Birmingham	172	172	459	423	882	5	5	10	482	379	31	1	36	238	95	27	26	214	......	156
1431	Van Buren, exc. of Keosauqua	264	264	726	702	1428	1	2	3	756	605	70	....	55	355	149	37	30	316	......	218
822	Vernon	188	188	432	390	822	......	......	......	413	361	48	....	30	170	90	36	10	194	7	154
1444	Village	280	280	734	705	1439	4	1	5	834	553	57	....	63	333	122	51	16	323	......	218
456	Washington, exc. Bentonsport	90	90	242	214	456	......	......	......	261	181	14	....	18	84	27	21	2	97	......	74
16980	Total	3453	3453	8628	8230	16858	60	62	122	8909	7246	819	....	592	4047	1625	543	215	3893	70	2613

WAPELLO COUNTY.

Total population.	NAMES OF TOWNSHIPS, TOWNS, AND CITIES.	No. of dwelling houses.	Number of families.	WHITE POPULATION. Male.	WHITE POPULATION. Female.	WHITE POPULATION. Total.	COLORED POP'LATION Male.	COLORED POP'LATION Female.	COLORED POP'LATION Total.	NATIVITY OF INHABITANTS. No. born in Iowa.	NATIVITY OF INHABITANTS. No. born in U. S., but not in Iowa.	NATIVITY OF INHABITANTS. No. born in foreign countries.	NATIVITY OF INHABITANTS. Surplus or deficiency.	BETWEEN 5 AND 21 YEARS OLD. No. 5 years old and under 6.	BETWEEN 5 AND 21 YEARS OLD. No. 6 years old and under 16.	BETWEEN 5 AND 21 YEARS OLD. No. 16 years old and under 21.	No. births in 1874.	No. deaths in 1874.	No. of voters.	No. foreigners not naturalized.	No. of militia.
1321	Adams	224	225	696	625	1321	......	......	......	734	543	44	....	55	368	148	51	5	260	13	172
564	Agency, exc. of town	117	117	287	263	550	7	7	14	300	236	28	....	28	134	63	24	6	112	......	83
658	Agency City, town of	148	148	330	327	657	1	......	1	299	338	21	....	25	161	40	19	7	157	......	107
787	Cass	131	131	386	401	787	......	......	......	386	297	104	....	32	191	77	40	16	185	16	71

2970	Center, exc. of Ottumwa	568	568	1486	1446	2932	24	14	38	1301	1269	400	......	118	842	268	108	46	644	47	460
908	Columbia, exc. of Eddyville	163	163	479	429	908	......	......	......	476	367	65	......	25	255	53	27	11	189	20	140
929	Competine	173	173	467	462	929	......	......	......	440	458	31	......	38	224	85	45	11	201	1	142
589	Dahlonega	118	118	295	290	585	1	3	4	271	308	10	......	21	148	60	14	6	128	......	95
427	Eldon, town of	98	98	217	209	426	1	......	1	178	192	57	......	24	77	23	15	10	101	13	87
1215	Green	219	219	633	580	1213	1	1	2	638	512	65	......	45	353	127	48	12	254	16	178
913	Highland	169	169	492	421	913	......	......	......	439	442	32	......	36	257	94	35	11	194	1	156
577	Keokuk	104	104	309	266	575	1	1	2	300	244	33	......	26	121	99	21	7	166	......	77
1124	Pleasant	209	216	571	553	1124	......	......	......	593	508	23	......	54	243	121	45	21	257	......	170
998	Polk	192	192	524	474	998	......	......	......	489	279	230	......	36	271	95	20	13	193	26	125
1411	Richland	273	273	721	676	1397	7	7	14	655	748	8	......	91	362	126	20	2	321	2	208
898	Washington, exc. of Eldon	163	163	452	446	898	......	......	......	510	377	11	......	39	218	171	30	19	178	......	86
16289	Total	3069	3069	8345	7868	16213	43	33	76	8009	7118	1162	......	693	747	1650	562	103	3440	155	2357
	Eddyville, town of,																				
717	" First ward	150	150	354	363	717	......	......	......	311	347	59	......	......	21	6	......	......	165	......	12
533	" Second ward	110	110	270	255	525	3	5	8	202	301	30	......	17	130	43	16	2	116	15	91
1250	Total of town	260	260	624	618	1242	3	5	8	513	648	89	......	17	151	49	16	2	281	15	103
	Ottumwa, city of, C. H.,																				
2538	" First ward	393	393	1389	1037	2426	50	62	112	915	1144	479	......	607	479	205	93	30	678	38	616
1020	" Second ward	182	182	484	487	971	23	26	49	401	469	150	......	47	192	86	43	15	240	5	202
1403	" Third ward	179	179	751	611	1362	17	24	41	492	677	234	......	55	227	99	42	8	312	10	272
1365	" Fourth ward	274	274	622	711	1333	15	17	32	538	654	173	......	71	319	126	62	13	295	15	223
6326	Total of city	1028	1028	3246	2846	6092	105	129	234	2346	2944	1036	......	780	1217	516	240	66	1525	68	1313
1175	Addition to Ottumwa	......	......	563	577	1140	22	13	35	......	......	......	......	......	......	......	......	......	......	......	......
23865	Total of county	4357	4365	12215	11332	23547	151	167	318	10868	10710	2287	......	1490	5593	2215	818	271	5346	238	3773

WARREN COUNTY.

869	Allen	158	161	447	418	865	2	2	4	432	396	42	1	33	254	75	33	10	200	3	136
1145	Belmont	218	218	589	556	1145	......	......	......	458	645	42	......	44	274	94	38	6	254	2	166
1399	Greenfield	255	255	724	660	1384	11	4	15	661	657	81	......	52	340	155	65	14	304	6	195
1884	Indianola, town of, C. H.	391	391	909	948	1857	10	17	27	741	1085	52	— 6	36	422	181	70	30	427	12	221
832	Jackson	142	142	431	401	832	......	......	......	383	415	9	— 25	45	224	90	42	7	148	......	92
930	Jefferson	170	170	483	447	930	......	......	......	423	506	136	135	54	224	82	36	9	179	......	139
1031	Liberty	191	191	535	496	1031	......	......	......	473	542	16	......	46	303	89	47	25	205	1	128
958	Linn	176	176	524	434	958	......	......	......	440	453	69	4	48	286	109	32	111	198	3	152
909	Otter	154	154	489	414	903	5	1	6	409	483	16	— 1	33	240	106	36	12	195	4	142
1118	Palmyra	218	218	565	553	1118	......	......	......	565	421	2	—130	55	317	122	21	......	227	2	150
1210	Richland	239	239	609	601	1210	......	......	......	649	550	14	3	57	287	89	56	40	260	......	181

WARREN COUNTY.—CONTINUED.

Total population.	NAMES OF TOWNSHIPS, TOWNS, AND CITIES.	No. of dwelling houses.	Number of families.	WHITE POPULATION. Male.	WHITE POPULATION. Female.	WHITE POPULATION. Total.	COLORED POP' LATION Male.	COLORED POP' LATION Female.	COLORED POP' LATION Total.	NATIVITY OF INHABITANTS. No. born in Iowa.	NATIVITY OF INHABITANTS. No. born in U. S., but not in Iowa.	NATIVITY OF INHABITANTS. No born in foreign countries.	NATIVITY OF INHABITANTS. Surplus or deficiency.	BETWEEN 5 AND 21 YEARS OLD. No. 5 years old and under 6.	BETWEEN 5 AND 21 YEARS OLD. No. 6 years old and under 16.	BETWEEN 5 AND 21 YEARS OLD. No. 16 years old and under 21.	No. births in 1874.	No. deaths in 1874.	No. of voters.	No. foreigners not naturalized.	No. of militia.
764	Squaw	151	151	389	375	764	......	......	......	347	407	10	......	32	194	57	40	10	166	......	104
695	Union	137	133	357	333	695	......	......	......	375	294	3	— 23	36	213	68	18	7	149	......	104
913	Virginia	124	124	575	338	913	......	......	......	268	436	16	—193	44	185	58	35	15	155	2	118
2143	Washington, exc. of Indianola	386	386	1145	996	2141	2	......	2	887	1201	65	10	74	504	203	81	34	512	......	383
1069	White Breast	188	188	532	529	1069	......	......	......	407	462	61	—139	52	297	82	38	15	202	5	150
672	White Oak	121	121	352	320	672	......	......	......	277	384	17	6	28	191	64	29	13	142	1	123
18541	Total	3419	3418	9655	8819	18487	30	24	54	8195	9337	651	......	769	4755	1724	717	358	3923	41	2684

WAYNE COUNTY.

Total population.	NAMES OF TOWNSHIPS, TOWNS, AND CITIES.	No. of dwelling houses.	Number of families.	WHITE POPULATION. Male.	WHITE POPULATION. Female.	WHITE POPULATION. Total.	COLORED POP' LATION Male.	COLORED POP' LATION Female.	COLORED POP' LATION Total.	NATIVITY OF INHABITANTS. No. born in Iowa.	NATIVITY OF INHABITANTS. No. born in U. S., but not in Iowa.	NATIVITY OF INHABITANTS. No born in foreign countries.	NATIVITY OF INHABITANTS. Surplus or deficiency.	BETWEEN 5 AND 21 YEARS OLD. No. 5 years old and under 6.	BETWEEN 5 AND 21 YEARS OLD. No. 6 years old and under 16.	BETWEEN 5 AND 21 YEARS OLD. No. 16 years old and under 21.	No. births in 1874.	No. deaths in 1874.	No. of voters.	No. foreigners not naturalized.	No. of militia.
571	Allenton, town of	119	119	307	264	571	......	......	......	164	338	13	— 56	27	93	30	24	14	154	......	129
892	Benton	151	151	460	431	891	....	1	1	436	446	10	......	30	274	89	25	14	176		96
634	Clay	126	126	327	307	634	......	......	......	307	297	36	6	43	167	41	31	7	115	......	94
679	Clinton	116	116	350	329	679	......	......	......	240	248	6	—185	37	195	66	28	19	140	......	122
762	Corydon, exc. of town	121	121	405	356	761	......	1	1	306	406	48	— 2	27	220	87	31	8	152	2	115
672	Corydon, town of, C. H.	......	135	342	330	672	......	......	......	238	396	32	— 6	23	149	59	23	15	172	1	116
611	Grand River, exc. of Lineville	121	121	305	306	611	......	......	......	339	232	13	— 27	36	164	75	27	3	106	......	168
626	Howard	109	109	330	295	625	1	......	1	211	402	13	......	35	185	48	18	8	130	5	88
490	Jackson	96	96	258	232	490	......	......	......	206	270	......	— 14	28	123	37	12	3	114	......	73
745	Jefferson	141	141	387	358	745	......	......	......	311	421	13	......	32	186	33	35	16	149	......	107
465	Lineville, town of	89	89	225	240	465	......	......	......	174	288	13	10	23	124	54	17	19	97	......	61
640	Monroe	110	110	325	315	640	......	......	......	345	284	1	— 10	25	181	71	27	21	127	......	102
545	Richman	109	109	289	256	545	......	......	......	165	365	10	— 5	28	139	42	24	7	125	......	82
408	Seymour, town of	91	91	209	195	404	2	2	4	139	256	15	2	14	83	24	19	18	122	......	......
810	South Fork	156	156	440	369	809	1	......	1	365	443	12	10	49	193	52	43	21	167	......	120
1101	Union	199	199	551	549	1100	1	......	1	495	601	5	......	44	314	119	48	18	217	......	164
782	Walnut, exc. of Seymour	145	145	397	385	782	......	......	......	309	427	46	......	30	248	79	24	16	164	......	107

654	Warren, exc. of Allerton	113	113	346	308	654	......	......	......	277	394	8	25	27	181	82	32	10	127	......	115
802	Washington	143	144	394	408	802	......	......	......	311	287	18	—186	69	122	35	25	17	168	......	121
1089	Wright	196	196	559	530	1089	......	......	......	437	623	19	— 10	41	313	105	47	14	225	2	166
13978	Total	2451	2587	7206	6763	13969	5	4	9	5775	7424	331	....	668	3654	1228	560	268	2947	10	2146

WASHINGTON COUNTY.

596	Brighton, exc. of town	110	110	309	287	596	......	......	......	321	264	11	....	20	161	65	17	4	123	......	86
634	Brighton, town of	145	145	317	315	632	2	......	2	289	325	17	— 3	16	126	72	11	8	158	1	84
883	Cedar	162	162	449	434	883	......	......	......	414	431	3	— 35	37	187	99	7	2	191	......	142
690	Clay	134	134	360	323	683	2	5	7	343	333	14	....	13	157	79	9	24	172	1	106
1241	Crawford	248	248	641	600	1241	......	......	......	610	581	75	25	53	298	109	47	13	282	13	168
1185	Dutch Creek	211	212	617	567	1184	......	1	1	571	484	76	— 54	41	324	113	28	15	264	4	171
1431	English River	246	246	718	713	1431	......	......	......	740	429	252	— 10	57	431	133	52	7	298	5	187
741	Franklin	128	128	390	351	741	......	......	......	360	358	13	— 10	79	183	64	4	2	162	......	96
787	Highland	146	146	396	391	787	......	......	......	353	357	81	4	67	182	40	21	7	143	43	113
1422	Iowa	254	254	733	689	1422	......	......	......	760	430	255	23	87	368	120	56	17	294	19	139
971	Jackson	161	161	486	481	967	4	......	4	403	415	153	....	32	259	109	19	12	196	2	124
1383	Lime Creek	248	248	681	702	1383	......	......	......	783	525	125	50	48	366	133	49	14	274	19	131
1082	Marion	185	185	571	511	1082	......	......	......	580	374	85	— 43	32	318	112	34	5	222	16	173
1309	Oregon	273	273	661	648	1309	......	......	......	624	631	54	....	58	325	108	31	13	279	3	192
914	Seventy-Six	159	159	492	422	914	......	......	......	373	495	56	10	39	274	65	47	12	207	6	156
1811	Washington, exc. of city,	348	348	904	883	1787	17	7	24	842	846	123	....	66	397	224	32	49	409	3	270
17080	Total	3158	3159	8725	8317	16988	25	13	38	8366	7278	1393	....	745	4356	1645	461	204	3674	135	2338
	Washington, city of, C. H.,																				
573	" First ward	125	125	252	321	573	......	......	......	229	306	36	— 2	33	136	45	21	6	133	......	71
446	" Second ward	92	103	214	228	442	2	2	4	162	236	58	10	18	91	24	20	8	117	7	55
507	" Third ward	103	104	235	267	502	2	3	5	213	260	34	....	28	123	45	18	3	85	3	54
663	" Fourth ward	142	144	293	341	634	13	16	29	263	378	22	....	26	150	67	33	13	159	......	75
2189	Total of city	462	476	994	1157	2151	17	21	38	867	1180	150	....	105	500	181	92	30	494	10	255
19269	Total of county	3620	3635	9719	9474	19139	42	34	76	9233	8458	1543	....	850	4856	1826	556	234	4168	145	2593

WEBSTER COUNTY.

479	Badger	76	78	274	205	479	......	......	......	162	138	179	....	14	150	37	......	1	73	6	21
156	Clay	30	30	82	74	156	......	......	......	51	71	34	....	17	40	5	7	1	24	6	20
179	Colfax	31	31	89	90	179	......	......	......	62	91	26	....	7	53	21	2	......	35	......	24
1283	Dayton	251	251	702	581	1283	......	......	......	377	328	578	....	57	311	107	65	11	249	74	244
301	Deer Creek	55	55	162	139	301	......	......	......	121	100	80	....	19	70	11	7	2	61	8	35

WEBSTER COUNTY.—CONTINUED.

Total population.	NAMES OF TOWNSHIPS, TOWNS, AND CITIES.	No. of dwelling houses.	Number of families.	WHITE POPULATION.			COLORED POP'LATION			NATIVITY OF INHABITANTS.				BETWEEN 5 AND 21 YEARS OLD.			No. births in 1874.	No. deaths in 1874.	No. of voters.	No. foreigners not naturalized.	No. of militia.
				Male.	Female.	Total.	Male.	Female.	Total.	No. born in Iowa.	No. born in U. S., but not in Iowa.	No. born in foreign countries.	Surplus or deficiency.	No. 5 years old and under 6	No. 6 years old and under 16.	No. 16 years old and under 21.					
510	Douglas	98	98	268	242	510	......	......	......	180	251	79	......	15	123	38	4	3	128	5	72
441	Elkhorn	79	79	229	212	441	......	......	......	281	101	59	......	19	113	19	19	4	71	13	32
208	Fulton	36	36	107	101	208	......	......	......	30	80	98	......	4	53	22	8	1	35	11	41
157	Gowrie	34	36	77	80	157	......	......	......	52	79	26	......	14	29	6	......	......	37	......	23
396	Hardin	75	75	213	183	396	......	......	......	145	38	213	......	17	67	40	12	4	50	38	33
438	Jackson	70	70	250	188	438	......	......	......	223	109	106	......	76	73	28	14	4	75	2	43
435	Johnson	74	74	235	200	435	......	......	......	173	194	68	......	20	121	38	25	4	90	1	60
315	Lost Grove	64	64	177	138	315	......	......	......	68	61	186	......	9	77	19	13	7	43	35	56
116	Newark	23	23	63	53	116	......	......	......	47	48	21	......	4	22	16	7	1	20	......	14
479	Otho	85	85	244	235	479	......	......	......	172	238	69	......	22	97	35	9	12	113	......	95
882	Pleasant Valley	146	146	489	393	882	......	......	......	266	311	305	......	57	186	67	37	13	228	15	199
730	Sumner	127	127	396	334	730	......	......	......	303	340	87	......	44	178	51	28	8	159	3	128
414	Wahkonsa, exc. of Fort Dodge	70	70	195	219	414	......	......	......	196	145	73	......	44	131	58	1	1	75	2	56
813	Washington	161	161	424	389	813	......	......	......	321	367	125	......	53	213	81	16	3	158	4	90
544	Webster	104	104	294	250	544	......	......	......	212	287	45	......	26	143	64	26	5	128	7	94
301	Yell	56	56	163	138	301	......	......	......	151	145	5	......	55	98	4	18	3	56	......	35
9577	Total	1745	1739	5133	4444	9577	......	......	......	3593	3522	2462	......	593	2348	767	318	83	1608	230	1415
	Fort Dodge, city of, C. H.,																				
842	" First ward	147	157	432	410	842	......	......	......	253	310	279	......	18	232	45	35	12	178	17	113
759	" Second ward	143	150	363	396	759	......	......	......	224	418	117	......	22	182	38	23	2	170	5	120
772	" Third ward	143	152	379	393	772	......	......	......	219	435	118	......	15	197	46	25	5	172	4	117
1164	" Fourth ward	203	230	603	561	1164	......	......	......	308	568	288	......	17	212	65	43	4	319	17	241
3537	Total of city	636	689	1777	1760	3537	......	......	......	1004	1731	802	......	72	822	194	126	23	839	43	591
13114	Total of county	2381	2438	6910	6204	13114	......	......	......	4597	5253	3264	......	665	3170	961	444	106	2747	273	2006

WINNEBAGO COUNTY

652	Center	....	121	353	299	652	......	......	......	210	118	178	—146	30	107	28	29	6	85	54	105
590	Forest, Forest City, C. H.	....	118	316	274	590	......	......	......	170	253	167	....	39	139	36	21	8	101	39	71
832	Iowa	....	149	436	396	832	......	......	......	222	180	425	— 5	17	225	55	20	33	91	37	27
391	Norway	....	80	203	189	391	......	......	......	111	93	257	70	13	103	30	18	10	39	5	9
521	Pleasant	....	99	273	248	521	......	......	......	150	180	191	....	34	102	40	38	21	90	31	60
2986	Total	....	567	1581	1406	2986	......	......	......	863	824	1218	....	133	676	189	126	78	406	166	272

WINNESHIEK COUNTY.

1188	Bloomfield	210	220	628	560	1188	......	......	......	417	523	128	—120	52	305	731	23	18	259	14	163
870	Bluffton	161	161	468	402	870	......	......	......	391	245	256	22	133	258	113	19	2	163	......	92
946	Burr Oak	184	184	492	454	946	......	......	......	295	436	171	— 44	30	204	82	35	12	212	73	138
1760	Calmar	338	340	886	873	1759	1	......	1	748	216	838	42	93	419	215	92	21	272	5	166
883	Canoe	158	158	457	426	883	......	......	......	360	249	274	....	33	226	87	44	1	141	43	151
1521	Decorah, exc. of city	250	275	890	631	1521	......	......	......	559	481	471	— 10	50	291	118	32	20	238	126	120
2596	Decorah, city of, C. H.	472	570	1303	1291	2594	1	1	2	946	937	713	....	109	515	173	......	......	564	......	....
952	Frankville	180	181	518	434	952	......	......	......	412	300	227	— 13	37	232	112	22	7	196	......	30
692	Fremont	121	122	362	330	692	......	......	......	274	265	155	2	22	175	70	19	5	129	11	86
1253	Glenwood	211	211	641	612	1253	......	......	......	522	71	660	....	44	316	140	30	8	157	91	76
1025	Hesper	188	188	525	500	1025	......	......	......	376	350	294	— 5	32	237	102	28	16	198	53	178
852	Highland	141	141	446	406	852	......	......	......	355	76	412	— 9	27	232	102	34	18	102	77	69
820	Jackson	140	141	420	400	820	......	......	......	294	145	381	....	38	202	75	38	11	103	69	64
1107	Lincoln	204	220	593	514	1107	......	......	......	400	152	494	— 61	45	218	100	48	18	154	67	89
968	Madison	151	160	535	433	968	......	......	......	343	90	527	— 8	24	219	104	42	20	126	145	175
1539	Military	275	273	794	744	1538	1	......	1	674	267	588	— 10	53	390	140	63	12	269	69	155
681	Orleans	123	123	364	317	681	......	......	......	261	261	160	1	34	167	65	21	12	146	53	89
1026	Pleasant	159	160	542	484	1026	......	......	......	495	99	407	— 25	48	293	128	45	15	139	77	84
1123	Springfield	170	170	592	531	1123	......	......	......	504	58	581	20	28	305	116	33	6	141	51	85
949	Sumner	167	166	484	465	949	......	......	......	421	37	483	— 8	50	272	76	8	1	116	302	132
1482	Washington	257	257	772	710	1482	......	......	......	631	311	540	....	83	367	137	64	34	292	60	221
24233	Total	4260	4421	12712	11517	24229	3	1	4	9678	5569	8760	....	1065	5903	2986	740	257	4117	1386	2363

WOODBURY COUNTY.

77	Arlington	....	18	45	32	77	......	......	......	......	......	......	......	10	29	7	......	......	22	......	14
280	Concord	....	48	137	143	280	......	......	......	89	170	16	— 5	14	60	28	12	7	69	......	36
60	Floyd	....	11	35	25	60	......	......	......	15	41	4	....	1	14	5	5	......	11	......	16
335	Grant	....	68	181	154	335	......	......	......	191	125	23	4	18	90	27	11	4	71	1	58

WOODBURY COUNTY.—CONTINUED.

Total population.	NAMES OF TOWNSHIPS, TOWNS, AND CITIES.	No. of dwelling houses.	Number of families.	WHITE POPULATION.			COLORED POP'LATION.			NATIVITY OF INHABITANTS.				BETWEEN 5 AND 21 YEARS OLD.			No. births in 1874.	No. deaths in 1874.	No. of voters.	No. foreigners not naturalized.	No. of militia.
				Male.	Female.	Total.	Male.	Female.	Total.	No. born in Iowa.	No. born in U. S., but not in Iowa.	No. born in foreign countries.	Surplus or deficiency.	No. 5 years old and under 6.	No. 6 years old and under 16.	No. 16 years old and under 21.					
262	Kedron	....	57	133	129	262	.....	.....	.....	111	140	....	— 11	14	59	21	14	6	60	.....	45
293	Lakeport	....	50	150	143	293	.....	.....	.....	60	186	62	— 15	27	45	29	7	3	64	20	50
374	Liberty	....	65	217	157	374	.....	.....	.....	116	193	65	....	13	71	7	10	4	97	3	77
142	Liston	....	32	84	58	142	.....	.....	.....	10	13	17	—102	....	9	1	3	.....	9	2	4
576	Little Sioux	....	109	310	266	576	.....	.....	.....	218	307	47	— 4	23	140	30	13	9	144	1	104
41	Moville	....	11	22	19	41	.....	.....	.....	10	13	17	— 1	....	9	1	3	.....	9	2	4
84	Rock	....	23	41	43	84	.....	.....	.....	31	42	11	....	2	17	5	3	.....	17	1	15
75	Rutland	....	17	41	34	75	.....	.....	.....	39	26	10	....	2	21	10	3	3	17	.....	....
271	Sioux City, exc. of city	....	62	138	133	271	.....	.....	.....	92	112	67	....	28	55	11	14	.....	81	.....	70
444	Union	....	92	238	206	444	.....	.....	.....	169	249	21	— 5	26	107	35	22	10	105	.....	70
326	West Fork	....	63	166	160	326	.....	.....	.....	64	167	13	— 82	23	65	21	18	1	71	.....	47
287	Wolf Creek	....	54	146	141	287	.....	.....	.....	149	127	10	— 1	11	85	26	6	6	31	.....	49
351	Woodbury	....	77	202	149	351	.....	.....	.....	94	196	63	2	13	55	21	13	7	91	13	72
4278	Total	....	857	2286	1992	4278	.....	.....	.....	1458	2107	446	....	225	931	285	157	60	969	43	731
	Sioux City, city of, C. H.,																				
885	" First ward	....	200	443	442	885	.....	.....	.....	345	212	212	—116	46	152	....	40	21	149	10	92
1141	" Second ward	....	175	657	462	1119	13	9	22	209	433	184	—315	36	102	27	26	9	190	2	113
1092	" Third ward	....	217	530	537	1067	16	9	25	234	529	285	— 44	34	147	26	47	11	188	.....	96
1172	" Fourth ward	....	212	558	611	1169	1	2	3	301	584	195	— 47	40	183	40	44	14	280	.....	172
4290	Total of city	....	804	2188	2052	4240	30	20	50	1089	1758	876	....	156	574	93	157	55	807	12	473
8568	Total of county	....	1661	4474	4044	8518	30	20	50	2547	3865	1322	....	381	1505	378	314	115	1776	55	1204

WORTH COUNTY.

650	Bristol	117	117	338	311	649	1	......	1	191	192	267	....	30	160	58	25	5	100	33	57
448	Brookfield	83	80	236	212	448	......	......	......	140	94	214	....	29	108	6	18	20	46	33	72
199	Danville	36	36	110	85	195	2	2	4	47	110	42	....	4	44	15	14	2	30	19	37
342	Deer Creek	68	67	168	174	342	......	......	......	119	77	146	....	10	63	14	18	......	48	17	47
497	Fertile	93	93	246	251	497	......	......	......	122	176	199	....	17	108	32	24	6	56	43	40
631	Hartland	104	104	311	320	631	......	......	......	237	104	290	....	31	182	40	17	10	80	12	66
292	Kensett	54	54	160	132	292	......	......	......	102	111	79	....	29	93	8	4	2	45	15	31
1000	Northwood, Northwood, C. H.	190	193	527	472	999	1	......	1	297	452	251	....	37	213	77	55	19	226	37	215
463	Silver Lake	81	82	233	230	463	......	......	......	207	52	204	....	17	131	50	21	5	47	34	30
386	Union	79	79	215	171	386	......	......	......	100	149	137	....	15	63	19	24	2	85	8	71
4908	Total	905	905	2545	2358	4902	4	2	6	1562	1517	1829	....	219	1165	319	220	71	763	251	660

WRIGHT COUNTY.

399	Belmont	73	73	215	183	398	1	......	1	128	224	46	— 1	16	95	41	11	1	90	6	68
178	Boone	30	30	94	84	178	......	......	......	76	96	5	— 1	10	45	18	8	......	30	......	18
261	Clarion, Clarion, C. H.	54	54	138	123	261	......	......	......	85	158	18	....	12	54	18	11	2	65	......	44
279	Eagle Grove	49	49	153	126	279	......	......	......	98	129	52	....	5	73	19	10	......	51	12	37
288	Iowa	56	56	157	131	288	......	......	......	92	166	30	....	16	63	31	6	1	71	2	50
304	Liberty	67	67	152	152	304	......	......	......	89	202	18	5	11	58	26	1	1	83	......	43
446	Pleasant	87	88	233	213	446	......	......	......	168	241	37	....	32	104	34	17	5	94	1	62
406	Troy	66	66	221	185	406	......	......	.....	148	216	42	....	23	98	32	14	......	85	5	65
237	Vernon	43	43	133	104	237	......	......	......	48	132	57	....	11	62	27	10	1	46	6	29
230	Wall Lake	51	51	117	113	230	......	......	......	69	119	41	— 1	18	58	24	8	1	45	......	26
216	Woodstock	40	40	117	99	216	......	......	......	57	115	44	....	12	39	....	4	4	34	6	33
3244	Total	616	617	1730	1513	3243	1	......	1	1058	1798	390	....	166	749	270	100	16	694	38	475

LANDS AND FIELD CROPS.

ADAIR COUNTY.

NAMES OF TOWNSHIPS, TOWNS, AND CITIES.	No. of acres of improved land.	No. of acres of unimprovod land.	No. of rods of fence.	No. of acres in cultivation in 1874.	SPRING WHEAT. Number of acres.	SPRING WHEAT. Number of bushels harvested.	WINTER WHEAT. Number of acres.	WINTER WHEAT. Number of bushels harvested.	INDIAN CORN. Number of acres.	INDIAN CORN. Number of bushels harvested.	RYE. Number of acres.	RYE. Number of bushels harvested.	OATS. Number of acres.	OATS. Number of bushels harvested.	BARLEY. Number of acres.	BARLEY. Number of bushels harvested.	BUCKWHEAT. Number of acres.	BUCKWHEAT. Number of bushels harvested.
Eureka	1426	1541	18388	1303	627	8672	....	....	663	27820	....	....	128	5155	468	10797	1	17
Fontanelle, town of	1105	1254	4687	992	393	8168	....	....	450	19415	....	....	61	3959	10	250	....	....
Grand River	3101	2761	15744	2767	827	12983	....	....	1431	53735	....	....	225	6814	5	150	....	5
Greenfield	3591	3179	3005	3933	1452	20904	....	....	1862	69430	4	65	277	9550	39	1185	6	60
Grove	2491	1757	3466	2738	1208	17766	....	....	1194	39570	11	225	131	4711	61	1449	6	55
Harrison	7182	3722	23495	6144	2699	48587	70	3500	2856	123993	6	105	337	11250	70	2334	4	46
Jackson	4949	3144	13270	3964	1512	23470	....	....	2013	82515	....	....	301	9896	22	616	1	
Jefferson	13413	4113	5648	10258	4741	81835	....	....	436½	200580	10	150	450	17551	45	902	....	....
Lincoln	14325	1902	28760	11709	4664	76245	....	....	4484	219071	....	....	498	17821	88	2920	2	25
Orient	3179	14600	2000	3015	974	5796	....	....	1596	190720	....	....	330	12842	42	882	1	14
Prussia	902	3112	536	574	805	11015	....	....	655	12110	1	8	95	3545	26	704	....	....
Richland	5163	3900	7620	4193	1768	30636	....	....	2445	94964	....	....	428	16280	89	1803	....	....
Summerset	7912	2483	3035	2631	1081	18214	....	....	1187	49015	....	....	213	8053	30	698	....	....
Summit	1225	414	260	906	429	6073	....	....	871	15540	....	....	64	2360	....	....	....	....
Union	3605	2139	7457	3174	1008	14702	....	....	1511	56475	....	....	308	9507	75	2410	1	22
Walnut	2983	1823	1726	2107	958	14588	....	....	698	22830	6	160	149	5487	....	....	....	....
Washington	6630	3836	27551	5857	2404	35360	....	....	2580	124645	....	....	460	14958	93	2062	1	24
Total	83182	55680	166648	66265	27550	435014	70	3500	30860	1402428	38	713	4455	159739	1163	29162	28	271

ADAMS COUNTY.

Carl	4299	2622	19491	3645	1435	21341	....	....	1772	74640	....	....	273	8568	34	951	2	20
Colony	3037	3290	1290	2981	986	15439	....	....	1456	58080	....	....	287	9284	75	1563	....	....
Douglas	6464	5670	35597	5994	2024	30224	....	....	3258	113280	10	220	445	14605	99	2227	6	38
Grant	5414	3351	42300	4046	1190	20664	....	....	1847	77355	....	....	277	10545	3	56	....	....
Jasper	8845	3009	30200	5946	1628	26351	....	....	2480	82431	30	470	574	21197	173	3441	2	12
Lincoln	7597	2185	24720	5520	2082	33100	....	....	1992	86160	13	390	244	8255	190	4458	1	8
Mercer	4528	3409	19806	3928	1151	20318	....	....	1647	63125	....	....	247	9179	86	2294	4	52
Nodaway	7393	6004	47556	6666	1870	31660	7	174	3604	123126	4	35	579	23243	9	210	2	22
Prescott	3842	4402	20535	3243	990	15269	....	....	1692	61600	3	61	174	5473	56	822	10	130
Quincy, exc. of town	4075	4586	27701	3211	1302	19739	....	....	1985	70030	6	60	256	10316	88	1831	10	91
Quincy town of	4	....	94	22	10	148	....	....	8	200	....	....	3	55	....	....	....	....
Union	3507	2527	17950	3280	1020	15961	....	....	1366	58960	....	....	198	8023	65	1469	....	....
Washington	6454	2680	35946	5870	2259	31162	....	....	2367	100790	....	....	394	12550	104	2052	1	19
Total	65459	43735	323186	54352	17947	281376	7	174	25474	969777	66	1236	3951	141293	982	21374	38	392

ALLAMAKEE COUNTY.

Center	8816	11405	78330	7486	5219	84882	20	185	1034	34385	4	107	767	26268	11	175	5	100
Fairview	2305	6930	24520	1580	596	8799	8	52	699	22530	2	17	130	3749	3	45	....	....
Franklin	5743	7729	49590	3771	1574	23177	25	410	1267	45465	....	....	440	13707	5	121	32	704
French Creek	6968	10205	49858	5406	3412	57067	2	29	1327	43770	4	70	637	19213	19	625	2	26
Hanover	4247	9712	32975	4247	2353	20206	....	....	1159	40040	....	....	505	16645	10	350	....	....
Iowa	2414	5338	17821	2369	992	13189	....	....	887	37860	56	853	110	3129	....	....	13	117
Jefferson	10244	8123	65920	6149	3842	60438	5	100	1713	59227	....	....	1122	39492	109	2443	21	398
Lafayette	9361	13300	74222	9194	4750	73395	3	36	1823	62022	....	....	636	20800	14	340	3	45
Lansing	6771	9586	45982	5748	3582	63693	8	120	1153	50094	17	170	690	24795	18	570	1	44
Linton	4602	7420	43700	4491	1425	22024	35	682	1020	36765	31	495	430	13333	4	60	13	311
Ludlow	14783	5319	71208	14578	6375	85515	....	....	2416	90792	....	....	1827	65571	318	7072	4	53
Makee	9320	7268	39285	9001	5078	85475	....	....	1444	54360	....	....	1016	36457	83	2283	18	228
Paint Creek	9670	12903	71700	7733	4540	69756	23	330	1405	50186	23	238	1031	36728	41	1237	8	135
Post	10184	7022	65141	7600	2899	44922	2	20	1804	74569	....	....	761	27823	37	981	17	235
Postville, town of	29	15	140	29	9	180	....	....	26	870	....	....	....	....	....	....	....	....
Taylor	6911	12537	55080	6758	3646	52112	50	....	1303	44829	27	350	614	21335	7	130	10	100
Union City	4734	6867	33690	4545	2929	35565	....	....	1185	55490	....	....	347	11948	....	....	3	30
Union Prairie	10744	7227	63440	8430	4704	74420	....	....	1743	56380	....	....	1159	39904	117	4141	4	75
Waterloo	6921	7915	49281	273	3955	62824	....	....	917	46286	....	....	554	21927	80	1742	....	4
Waukon	206	120	680	80	52	1100	....	....	19	700	....	....	10	300	....	....	....	....
Total	124973	156941	932563	109468	61932	938734	181	1964	24344	906620	164	2300	12786	443129	876	22315	154	2605

APPANOOSE COUNTY.

NAMES OF TOWNSHIPS, TOWNS, AND CITIES.	No. of acres of improved land.	No. of acres of unimproved land.	No. of rods of fence.	No. of acres in cultivation in 1874.	SPRING WHEAT.		WINTER WHEAT.		INDIAN CORN.		RYE.		OATS.		BARLEY.		BUCK-WHEAT.	
					Number of acres.	Number of bushels harvested.	Number of acres.	Number of bushels harvested.	Number of acres.	Number of bushels harvested.	Number of acres.	Number of bushels harvested.	Number of acres.	Number of bushels harvested.	Number of acres.	Number of bushels harvested.	Number of acres.	Number of bushels harvested.
Bellair	8892	5442	48574	8560	402	3371	....	....	3877	150255	14	144	815	25487	....	....	15	242
Caldwell	8217	17249	72982	6589	392	2284	128	1030	4301	133555	129	1214	768	18943	25	10	47	674
Center, exc. of Centerville	7048	9173	38190	6634	469	3166	30	475	3195	114205	27	319	733	23253	....	....	24	356
Centerville, town of	62	....	....	....	....	....	....	....	....	....	....	....	....	....	....	....	....	....
Chariton	10847	8044	55976	8896	960	9673	15	63	4150	177585	22	321	930	28538	....	....	21	320
Douglas	6560	6968	39257	4903	400	3236	48	437	2787	95530	20	161	652	15640	....	....	6	73
Franklin	11206	10488	49646	10485	451	3143	3	62	4731	163200	82	1024	927	29765	....	....	13	211
Independence	12189	10266	56920	9113	999	9773	18	120	4389	182890	13	133	875	26530	....	....	8	111
Johns	15648	1379	55175	12085	1095	8598	3	12	5962	233790	23	198	1417	41827	....	....	32	295
Lincoln	8449	6603	40497	7279	448	3409	25	275	3380	133669	6	48	620	19480	....	....	10	141
Moulton, town of	194	160	2259	197	26	185	....	13	218	7240	8	80	64	1800	....	....	....	....
Pleasant	8817	15201	62537	7836	385	2061	48	390	4175	129935	53	354	763	21651	....	....	1	35
Sharon	6858	8332	41096	5012	263	2027	58	564	2375	85574	28	210	461	11845	....	....	13	117
Taylor	11665	6696	56792	6397	1056	9715	34	226	3710	133630	35	358	1226	28820	....	....	36	466
Udell	7318	10006	4848	4988	551	4204	124	1163	3128	118185	44	277	617	17905	....	....	20	210
Union	4305	11853	29887	3132	203	1543	96	852	1821	60550	51	436	330	5466	....	....	12	140
Walnut	7383	7981	41139	6216	650	5076	34	237	3671	155230	31	312	757	21669	3	25	7	98
Washington, exc. of Moulton	12465	10079	73526	8834	609	4501	98	1066	5399	196860	22	171	1251	34289	....	....	20	299
Wells	12936	9113	62933	8032	247	1833	287	3853	3602	113360	58	551	550	14438	....	....	8	73
Total	161059	161083	832234	125188	9606	77798	1049	10838	64871	2385243	666	6311	13756	387346	28	35	293	3861

AUDUBON COUNTY.

NAMES OF TOWNSHIPS, TOWNS, AND CITIES.	No. of acres of improved land.	No. of acres of unimproved land.	No. of rods of fence.	No. of acres in cultivation in 1874.	Spring wheat: Number of acres.	Spring wheat: Number of bushels harvested.	Winter wheat: Number of acres.	Winter wheat: Number of bushels harvested.	Indian corn: Number of acres.	Indian corn: Number of bushels harvested.	Rye: Number of acres.	Rye: Number of bushels harvested.	Oats: Number of acres.	Oats: Number of bushels harvested.	Barley: Number of acres.	Barley: Number of bushels harvested.	Buckwheat: Number of acres.	Buckwheat: Number of bushels harvested.
Audubon	2051	1523	9140	1619	699	9710	....	....	696	31265	6	100	94	3032	32	715	3	29
Douglas	808	490	....	667	181	2563	10	97	361	17200	....	....	38	1260	....	....	....	....
Exira	5085	7527	27592	3947	1345	21684	....	....	2352	105520	....	....	169	6773	16	366	....	....
Greeley	1116	4462	392	783	501	6828	....	....	546	20378	....	....	30	1024	....	....	....	....

Hamlin	3319	1743	10413	1906	590	9245	...	...	1186	51645	...	...	90	3622	...	...	1	25
Leroy	1130	721	3444	1013	386	5575	...	...	635	26443	...	...	51	1984	4	88	...	...
Melville	817	480	686	817	379	3853	...	...	363	10850	...	...	26	697	...	...	...	...
Oakfield	3993	3848	11379	2507	1720	23888	...	...	2010	89610	...	...	176	10576	...	...	...	...
Viola	2727	3025	830	2727	1075	5889	...	...	1076	41744	...	...	114	4235	32	582	...	...
Total	21046	23819	63876	15986	6876	89235	10	97	9225	394655	6	100	788	33233	84	1751	4	54

NOTE.—Non-resident lands not returned by townships, 233549 acres.

BENTON COUNTY.

Belle Plaine, town of	60	37	...	...	...	...	...	...	...	...	...	...	...	...	...	...	...	...
Benton	4063	4128	28565	3244	777	9090	...	...	1560	57345	4	40	347	7778	5	80	58	728
Big Grove	18615	1482	68712	12507	5298	73663	...	...	4639	190852	...	...	875	28040	698	13444	...	...
Bruce	12224	4637	41636	12827	6343	99760	...	...	3375	132720	...	...	871	27768	254	6036	17	243
Canton, exc. of Shellsburg	18689	2237	84867	13109	3574	38246	...	...	5489	223525	39	298	788	20982	145	2601	15	167
Cedar	21945	1061	56060	14463	6228	85616	...	...	5583	229885	108	2027	1195	34331	239	6185	47	703
Eden	17413	1194	60720	14853	5422	65740	...	...	5196	179035	3	47	803	21464	979	18713	5	75
Eldorado	16508	3496	45872	15511	7326	97552	...	...	3993	146570	...	...	976	23180	1254	24034	1	...
Florence	16887	3802	71177	12751	4802	70300	...	...	5959	254990	...	...	857	25601	173	3399	2	20
Fremont	16212	190	42177	23056	4254	68719	...	...	4933	205895	1	16	734	22577	357	6925	2	20
Harrison	8646	2662	34503	4253	1410	18219	...	...	2614	88046	...	...	624	16542	...	...	1	5
Homer	16137	120	23501	14067	7641	92682	...	...	3244	130350	...	...	815	25738	1465	29943	1	36
Iowa, exc. of Belle Plaine	11186	4745	42756	11186	4457	61086	...	...	3973	166497	10	120	677	17652	861	8976	11	122
Jackson	19108	1055	67007	12447	6609	80719	7	280	5198	204174	20	200	635	24691	93	2131	5	79
Kane	16843	3452	41300	7374	6824	89420	...	...	3651	129650	...	...	938	27390	1772	34407	...	...
Leroy	15230	1885	60520	12059	6045	88340	...	...	3741	156535	6	128	675	15663	676	13553	33	407
Monroe	13733	2513	38180	13445	5949	86967	...	...	3639	152880	...	...	596	21136	286	5954	...	...
Polk	18977	4049	87970	12890	4117	51668	...	...	5529	223107	40	330	1256	35531	112	1911	10	109
Shellsburg, town of	240	...	...	150	82	680	...	...	120	3100	27	600	...	120	5	50	...	...
St. Clair	14731	5881	55984	9974	4589	67036	...	...	4295	178335	25	328	606	17206	240	5614	5	79
Taylor	7715	2648	28771	5568	1892	23926	...	...	2561	128630	...	...	522	16043	76	1435	13	88
Union	12356	2637	45587	13674	5767	74237	...	...	3952	146800	...	...	700	15637	1479	28480	3	32
Total	297518	53911	1025865	239408	99406	1343666	7	280	83244	3328921	283	4134	15490	445070	11169	213871	229	2913

BLACK HAWK COUNTY.

Barclay	19572	3306	53108	11890	5790	68122	...	...	3436	119805	...	...	1091	32676	22	371	3	44
Bennington	9280	13425	40865	10134	4853	55609	...	...	3071	122785	25	355	1134	34467	101	2054	41	146
Big Creek, exc. of town of Laporte	11319	1262	31325	9276	5838	73858	...	...	2588	97195	10	142	755	25687	88	1195	35	481
Black Hawk	14676	7502	33072	12375	7792	106630	...	...	3055	110750	...	...	1466	53847	227	4604	8	146

BLACK HAWK COUNTY.—Continued.

NAMES OF TOWNSHIPS, TOWNS, AND CITIES.	No. of acres of improved land.	No. of acres of unimproved land.	No. of rods of fence.	No. of acres in cultivation in 1874.	SPRING WHEAT. Number of acres.	SPRING WHEAT. Number of bushels harvested.	WINTER WHEAT. Number of acres.	WINTER WHEAT. Number of bushels harvested.	INDIAN CORN. Number of acres.	INDIAN CORN. Number of bushels harvested.	RYE. Number of acres.	RYE. Number of bushels harvested.	OATS. Number of acres.	OATS. Number of bushels harvested.	BARLEY. Number of acres.	BARLEY. Number of bushels harvested.	BUCK-WHEAT. Number of acres.	BUCK-WHEAT. Number of bushels harvested.
Cedar	11008	7553	28820	10329	5881	77314	....	....	3345	108270	....	....	821	26110	80	1330	14	164
Cedar Falls, exc. of city of Cedar Falls	14235	8192	43689	13651	5436	61083	....	....	4087	155078	44	177	1247	44134	146	2863	14	303
Eagle	11937	11687	13090	11825	7028	91406	....	....	3512	109165	....	....	1030	31517	379	8548	1	27
East Waterloo, exc. of city of Waterloo	17106	4465	48761	10544	5265	50137	....	....	4501	118030	65	648	939	21456	136	1962	28	167
Fox	8989	12169	37934	9792	5626	61690	....	....	3762	120231	14	170	916	31057	43	849	25	290
Lester	13348	9621	49989	7755	3325	46749	....	....	2463	99040	....	....	968	31508	25	521	14	173
Lincoln	11348	11366	10687	11924	6200	77742	....	....	3275	123430	2	35	1005	36443	348	7169	....	....
Mt. Vernon	12976	9668	65471	11265	5889	67475	....	....	4011	137197	32	296	983	31681	16	260	6	88
Orange	18214	4248	60161	12951	7550	103717	....	....	4058	139695	40	660	1582	54308	42	754	11	110
Poyner	14441	18468	61742	18817	5636	79906	....	....	4047	136099	41	411	991	30856	49	737	14	147
Spring Creek	9196	8748	41790	7265	2531	29376	....	....	2470	83485	....	....	625	18231	....	....	9	127
Union	3700	7614	15885	2737	1025	12392	....	....	1410	49600	12	326	396	11100	6	74	25	235
Washington	5395	5998	31250	4680	2016	23769	....	....	1952	57720	174	2434	345	8683	21	444	10	82
Waterloo, exc. of city of Waterloo	6062	5177	30424	3823	1674	20989	....	....	1476	48315	10	127	504	14255	18	395	10	105
Cedar Falls, city of	223	112	3745	223	6	60	....	....	73	3700	....	....	6	180	....	....	....	....
Total	213025	150881	701808	181256	89361	1108024	....	....	56592	1939590	469	5781	16804	538196	1747	34130	268	2835

BOONE COUNTY.

NAMES OF TOWNSHIPS, TOWNS, AND CITIES.	No. of acres of improved land.	No. of acres of unimproved land.	No. of rods of fence.	No. of acres in cultivation in 1874.	SPRING WHEAT. Number of acres.	SPRING WHEAT. Number of bushels harvested.	WINTER WHEAT. Number of acres.	WINTER WHEAT. Number of bushels harvested.	INDIAN CORN. Number of acres.	INDIAN CORN. Number of bushels harvested.	RYE. Number of acres.	RYE. Number of bushels harvested.	OATS. Number of acres.	OATS. Number of bushels harvested.	BARLEY. Number of acres.	BARLEY. Number of bushels harvested.	BUCK-WHEAT. Number of acres.	BUCK-WHEAT. Number of bushels harvested.
Amaqua	10520	285	28063	13275	3721	35995	....	....	2282	64305	7	130	743	115724	484	9734	....	....
Beaver	3346	1637	11120	3000	1135	14562	....	....	1312	39350	5	48	320	9423	67	1500	....	....
Boonsboro, town of	240	116	1195	179	176	850	....	....	78	3250	....	....	33	1405	10	200	....	....
Cass	7662	4722	24188	9420	1267	18614	....	....	3854	101090	24	418	581	20374	....	....	8	120

Colfax	5438	4281	31260	5848	1476	20886	....	....	2851	80825	....	....	785	24968	101	2850	10	163
Des Moines, exc. of Boone and Boonsboro	7662	6717	56558	6942	1785	25669	....	....	3954	138560	....	....	809	26570	129	2950	10	67
Dodge	15881	4033	65640	11255	4096	45285	....	....	5162	200180	4	74	805	25002	10	350	....	....
Douglas	5822	5459	34966	2868	621	8199	....	....	1049	80425	14	151	330	10142	24	360	1	37
Garden	8086	1627	133816	6723	1696	24985	....	....	3318	109030	16	351	722	2173	34	493	10	120
Grant	4243	2868	18474	3928	2162	15095	....	....	1229	37002	....	45	209	7244	75	4118	....	....
Harrison	5781	3071	30637	4482	1377	20128	....	....	2111	66295	....	....	618	16993	98	2578	....	8
Jackson	10942	853	34260	6928	1820	21687	....	....	2501	111625	....	....	876	25631	28	1692	2	48
Marcy	6855	8298	26862	6321	1974	28315	7	60	3004	107125	....	....	751	23562	43	997	5	58
Peoples	7888	6086	32795	6948	1972	26608	....	....	3346	93960	4	70	850	27322	22	373	2	63
Pilot Mound	4506	3834	22590	4400	2081	28649	....	....	1766	58285	8	97	268	9115	122	2980	....	....
Union	5221	5436	54215	4629	1215	37047	4	24	2484	95105	30	496	428	15855	10	245	....	3
Worth	9530	7605	43584	5680	1293	19016	....	....	3544	134300	....	....	668	24734	12	327	5	104
Yell	7694	4882	37529	5816	2638	37667	....	....	2306	75050	....	....	605	18383	312	6987	1	43
Total	156987	71810	687752	108642	32505	429257	11	84	46151	1595752	112	1880	10401	404620	1581	38734	55	839

BREMER COUNTY.

Dayton	6517	3950	35200	6172	2768	39292	....	....	1208	35470	....	....	908	29476	46	913	1	9
Douglas	8759	5403	37036	7740	3800	51336	....	....	2184	73300	....	....	1180	45066	120	2300	5	59
Franklin	12602	2365	48081	8297	4242	55225	....	....	1963	73725	9	43	998	42023	62	1239	3	55
Frederika	3545	2820	23200	2104	770	12594	....	....	776	26270	....	....	352	13223	2	76	9	70
Fremont	14103	4127	51342	8683	3821	50545	....	....	2204	72170	....	....	1702	60564	91	1598	3	35
Jackson	9492	2539	49120	6520	2689	33930	....	....	2974	103815	38	460	664	19734	7	62	29	203
Jefferson	10581	....	44423	5671	2664	34733	....	....	1842	81205	7	80	690	26696	70	1602	....	....
La Fayette	8842	4725	47810	8344	4184	51528	....	....	3010	89570	....	....	1166	38573	28	482	14	176
Le Roy	3293	3027	24686	2744	1090	15731	....	....	1167	34930	2	36	548	21405	24	513	1	8
Maxfield	17348	1708	64277	8898	5075	64871	....	....	1651	80876	3	79	1275	48828	172	3789	8	191
Polk	16323	1172	68679	10456	4631	61450	....	....	3269	96410	....	....	1190	37796	43	838	5	54
Sumner	7914	4842	47089	7543	3454	52163	....	....	1474	53905	4	24	1351	50275	56	1102	4	36
Warren	11340	9101	67859	10771	5085	60001	....	....	2508	109615	....	....	1464	58243	124	2601	13	72
Washington, exc. of Waverly	13166	1103	53385	9463	3718	49701	....	....	2212	83535	29	295	680	23196	29	585	....	15
Waverly, city of	2142	118	10750	1404	907	11695	....	....	311	11845	10	200	90	3500	14	300	....	....
Total	145967	47000	672937	104810	48898	644795	....	....	28753	1026641	102	1217	14259	518571	888	18000	95	983

BUCHANAN COUNTY.

Buffalo	9726	7418	47175	9730	3549	42425	....	....	2972	88906	....	....	1420	43888	50	740	8	99
Byron	12389	3865	62116	23571	5018	74316	....	....	3228	119830	6	150	1194	41728	41	945	9	182
Cono	5475	5298	32823	6805	2821	23065	....	....	2655	96435	....	....	854	22288	....	....	22	225
Fairbank	14595	2570	61880	7812	4109	66961	....	....	2894	111070	6	100	810	37297	3	72	4	58

BUCHANAN COUNTY.—Continued.

NAMES OF TOWNSHIPS, TOWNS, AND CITIES.	No. of acres of improved land.	No. of acres of unimproved land.	No. of rods of fence.	No. of acres in cultivation in 1874.	SPRING WHEAT. Number of acres.	SPRING WHEAT. Number of bushels harvested.	WINTER WHEAT. Number of acres.	WINTER WHEAT. Number of bushels harvested.	INDIAN CORN. Number of acres.	INDIAN CORN. Number of bushels harvested.	RYE. Number of acres.	RYE. Number of bushels harvested.	OATS. Number of acres.	OATS. Number of bushels harvested.	BARLEY. Number of acres.	BARLEY. Number of bushels harvested.	BUCK-WHEAT. Number of acres.	BUCK-WHEAT. Number of bushels harvested.
Fremont	14023	2503	46332	11520	4394	50759	....	....	2400	87125	3	50	979	30501	45	965	9	125
Hazleton	9088	10041	54317	8550	3792	52869	....	....	2832	91117	....	....	1252	32598	73	1556	8	49
Homer	8571	3540	34391	8005	3652	46785	....	....	3184	119715	....	....	906	27749	68	971	9	108
Jefferson	12620	6989	53820	11589	4755	61450	....	....	4104	143158	25	340	1211	37771	....	....	5	60
Liberty	8450	3406	57690	6048	3149	42169	....	....	2906	107806	3	31	769	26301	18	315	16	225
Madison	12565	2750	50850	8837	4406	38468	....	....	3134	97990	....	....	1578	45477	40	733	13	146
Middlefield	15909	265	55089	10589	5164	62888	....	....	2435	115605	....	....	1135	38786	61	987	11	171
Newton	16985	1649	65136	10545	4976	59238	....	....	3907	119998	....	....	1172	31118	69	1513	6	81
Perry	14249	4745	61068	10398	4270	54038	....	....	3594	128945	17	240	1030	32211	61	544	19	230
Sumner	5438	3318	24820	4718	2216	29363	....	....	2382	80065	....	....	828	24980	12	155	1	25
Washington	17008	4057	70750	10811	4320	58299	....	....	3327	113025	....	....	1117	40626	57	408	18	184
Westburg	13460	9000	46010	7711	3700	49269	....	....	2876	91360	....	....	1176	42890	....	942	23	317
Total	190551	71414	824267	157239	64291	812342	....	....	48830	1811250	60	911	17431	556209	598	10846	181	2285

BUENA VISTA COUNTY.

NAMES OF TOWNSHIPS, TOWNS, AND CITIES.	No. of acres of improved land.	No. of acres of unimproved land.	No. of rods of fence.	No. of acres in cultivation in 1874.	SPRING WHEAT. Number of acres.	SPRING WHEAT. Number of bushels harvested.	WINTER WHEAT. Number of acres.	WINTER WHEAT. Number of bushels harvested.	INDIAN CORN. Number of acres.	INDIAN CORN. Number of bushels harvested.	RYE. Number of acres.	RYE. Number of bushels harvested.	OATS. Number of acres.	OATS. Number of bushels harvested.	BARLEY. Number of acres.	BARLEY. Number of bushels harvested.	BUCK-WHEAT. Number of acres.	BUCK-WHEAT. Number of bushels harvested.
Barnes	2251	3974	2960	2069	1375	13880	....	....	386	13700	....	40	243	7381	66	986	1	6
Brookes	1091	1846	170	1000	460	6326	....	....	151	4700	....	....	107	3118	5	135	1	14
Coon	2253	3438	....	2099	908	6488	....	....	570	15411	....	....	190	3232	....	....	3	3
Elk	4577	2940	40	2820	1906	24549	....	....	1033	33455	....	....	277	9498	12	254	5	59
Fairfield	1010	2459	....	660	347	3073	....	....	161	4174	3	50	104	1970	15	254	1	6
Grant	1129	1501	402	1105	620	3985	....	....	404	12290	2	14	99	1860	12	184	2	15
Lee	2349	3913	5729	2157	1045	10411	....	....	503	15170		15	378	8283	150	1290	....	....
Lincoln	828	1542	....	634	546	2323	....	....	171	3065	....	....	85	1640	7	57	....	....
Maple Valley	3898	2786	4723	3081	1659	22251	....	....	857	26048	....	....	201	5143	1	36	....	....
Newell	1835	2157	530	1462	895	4528	....	....	610	15957	....	....	242	3956	3	....	12	86
Nokomis	5689	3483	280	4152	2753	35642	....	....	925	28072	27	205	334	10661	....	....	....	....

DRYNESS:

—*Throat* (with): Alum. kal-ch. *lact. merc.* petr. phytol. puls. rhus. squill. *sulph.*

DUST (as from having inspired): *Am-c.* bell. calc. cin. dros.

EATING (after): Æth. agar. am-m. anac. *bry.* calc. carb-v. chin. dig. ferr. kal-bich. lach. *nux-v.* op. puls. sang. sil. staph. sulph. tart.

EATING (when): Calc. *op.* phos. puls.

EMACIATION (with): Hep. iod. lyc. stann.

EVENING (in the): Acon. amb. am-c. am-m. anac. *ars.* bar-c. bell. bov. calc. caps. *carb-an. carb-v.* caus. coff. cham. chin. cin. *con.* crot. dros. eug. eup. fer-acet. *hep.* ign. ind. iod. ipec. kal. kal-hyd. kreos. *lach.* lyc. *mag.* magn-m. magn-s. *merc.* mez. natr. *natr-m.* nic. nitr-ac. nux-v. ol-an. par. petr. *puls.* rhod. rhus. rhus-r. ruta. sang. *sep. sil.* squill. *stann.* staph. *sulph. verat.* zinc.

EXPIRATION (during): *Carb-v.* caus. dros. lach.

FEVER (with): *Acon. con.* hep. iod. kreos. *lyc.* samb. sulph.

HEADACHE (with): Amb. *am-c. bell. bry.* caps. carb-v. caus. con. hep. lach. lyc. *merc. natr-m.* nitr. *nux-v. phos. ph-ac. puls.* rhus. sabad. squill. *sulph.* verat. Compare: PAINS in the HEAD.

HEAT (with general): *Acon. ars.* kreos. lach. natr.

HEAVINESS in the Chest (with): Am-c. calad. kal-bich.

INSPIRATION (during): Con. hep. kal-bich. men. op. *squill.* sulph.

INSPIRATION DEEP (when taking a): Am-m. bell. brom. *chin.* con. cupr. dulc. graph. ipec. *lyc. natr-m.* nitr-ac. *squill.*

IRRITATION in the Chest (from): Acon. *bell.* carb-an. dros. eug. euphorb. mag-arc. *merc.* petr. *phos.* rhus-r. spong. stann.

—*Larynx* (in the): Acon. asar. bry. calad. calc. canth. cocc. coloc. dros. hep. ign. kal-ch. merc. mez. par. phos. stront.

—*Pit of the Stomach* (in the): *Bry.* guaj. lach. natr-m.

—*Stomach* (in the): Bell. *bry. merc.* puls. *sep.* tart.

—*Throat*, or *Trachea* (in the): Acon. amb. asa. bry. calad. carb-an. carb-v. chin. chin-s. cocc. coff. coloc. croc. dros. hep. kal-hyd. *merc.* par. petr. spig. stront. tab.
Compare: ROUGHNESS, and TICKLING.

ITCHING in the Chest (from): Magn-m. phos. puls.

—*Larynx* (in the): *Bell.* lyc. nux-v. puls.

—*Throat* (in the): *Con.* mang. *nux-v. sil.*

CARROLL COUNTY.

NAMES OF TOWNSHIPS, TOWNS, AND CITIES.	No. of acres of improved land.	No. of acres of unimproved land.	No. of rods of fence.	No. of acres in cultivation in 1874.	SPRING WHEAT.		WINTER WHEAT.		INDIAN CORN.		RYE.		OATS.		BARLEY.		BUCK-WHEAT.	
					Number of acres.	Number of bushels harvested.	Number of acres.	Number of bushels harvested.	Number of acres.	Number of bushels harvested.	Number of acres.	Number of bushels harvested.	Number of acres.	Number of bushels harvested.	Number of acres.	Number of bushels harvested.	Number of acres.	Number of bushels harvested.
Arcadia	5558	17742	400	3756	2354	29241	....	....	1068	31715	....	....	257	6000	5	70	2	21
Carroll, exc. of town	3342	18413	....	2251	1395	17098	....	....	667	20750	....	....	138	4415	9	180	....	....
Carroll, town of	1025	4318	2220	850	275	4327	....	....	90	3750	....	....	8	400	....	....	....	....
Eden	2567	44031	330	2530	1467	18640	....	....	831	30216	....	....	110	3732	18	409	....	....
Glidden	2480	20718	7500	2390	1334	18000	....	....	1500	50500	....	....	125	7297	....	....	....	....
Grant	2124	19250	1280	1617	1027	9805	....	....	502	12185	1	....	157	3555	17	360	....	....
Jasper	2413	20389	5466	2205	750	9286	....	....	1410	47618	3	20	116	3511	....	....	....	10
Kniest	7285	15679	6662	1616	4134	48892	....	....	1882	57470	....	....	594	19403	139	2651	....	....
Newton	3757	19658	9385	3350	1768	22347	....	....	1340	54885	....	....	190	6391	5	204	....	....
Pleasant Valley	2666	19013	2312	1666	1419	18574	....	....	820	31530	....	....	153	4748	17	412	5	40
Richland	2526	19911	2793	1842	813	10577	....	....	721	23875	....	....	115	3136	....	....	....	....
Roselle	4792	18029	....	2888	2095	31879	....	....	888	43650	....	....	231	9440	43	805	....	....
Sheridan	5823	16603	1675	4715	2353	27315	3	20	1566	54320	....	....	451	13596	71	1349	....	....
Union	3612	19653	4884	2123	1520	19384	....	....	1545	48067	....	....	236	8424	8	563	....	....
Washington	2762	19964	340	1747	1382	20028	....	....	467	15440	5	60	150	5255	57	1642	....	....
Wheatland	5333	16368	525	3613	2670	34768	....	....	717	24070	....	....	207	8274	25	670	....	....
Total	58065	309744	45772	39159	26756	340161	3	20	16014	550041	9	80	3238	107577	414	9315	7	71

CASS COUNTY.

NAMES OF TOWNSHIPS, TOWNS, AND CITIES.	No. of acres of improved land.	No. of acres of unimproved land.	No. of rods of fence.	No. of acres in cultivation in 1874.	Spring wheat, number of acres.	Spring wheat, number of bushels harvested.	Winter wheat, number of acres.	Winter wheat, number of bushels harvested.	Indian corn, number of acres.	Indian corn, number of bushels harvested.	Rye, number of acres.	Rye, number of bushels harvested.	Oats, number of acres.	Oats, number of bushels harvested.	Barley, number of acres.	Barley, number of bushels harvested.	Buckwheat, number of acres.	Buckwheat, number of bushels harvested.
Atlantic, exc. of town	9623	2761	40144	6941	3060	49485	....	....	4140	220780	....	....	456	23468	6	340	....	....
Atlantic, town of	913	451	1024	260	50	600	....	....	170	6700	....	....	....	....	....	....	....	....
Bear Grove	7378	1991	21280	6160	2915	49116	....	....	2823	127965	....	....	207	9239	37	900	..	....
Benton	5814	3268	25790	5177	2068	34124	....	....	2193	104335	....	....	192	7310	140	4342	4	31
Brighton	9011	2780	18375	9:83	3110	50780	....	....	3003	142550	....	....	339	13186	162	4432	....	....
Cass	11577	2621	37085	8168	3458	57592	....	....	3899	191747	....	....	351	14247	62	1386	....	....
Edna	4141	3691	12855	3581	1535	21767	....	....	1573	7350	....	....	153	4817	68	1400	1	7

Franklin	6388	2396	34765	5686	2803	58455			2669	127960			281	12052	14	370		
Grant	4074	1573	4238	3061	1644	25764			1399	58970			168	5019	15	460		
Lincoln	4784	1908	12770	4042	1853	30497			1260	66315			199	6565	77	1891		
Massena	2555	1670	3255	2598	952	13955			915	42240			110	4095			2	23
Noble	8099	4965	20390	7278	2099	53720			2412	111535			280	9843	48	1331	4	43
Pleasant	7576	2386	23412	5717	3110	56504			3240	136600			350	12766	250	6529	3	28
Pymosa	11348	3703	48730	10218	4352	67318			4352	230979			5061	21389	91	2665	2	19
Union	3298	2437	8855	2706	1501	24531			1242	54154			134	7583	3	110		
Victoria	4479	3390	9770	3385	1816	28631			1053	48590			349	7089	37	825		
Washington	9806	3313	36220	8224	3797	53370			4239	222292			449	17420	65	1718		
Total	110864	45304	358959	92785	40123	676209			40582	1901062			9079	176088	1075	28699	16	151

CEDAR COUNTY.

Cass	9717	1184	46978	6470	1297	19934			3474	134915	49	697	1132	39570			2	26
Center, exc. of Tipton	24228	9967	118094	15096	2675	40084			8136	294265	2	40	2210	77833	294	6622	26	401
Dayton, exc. of Clarence	19594		79496	12054	3315	49801			6264	222387	20	200	1298	42421	1053	26624	6	113
Fairfield	16874	528	60287	11339	2064	55899			5852	234860			1208	42278	1079	23064	6	83
Farmington, exc. of Durant	13288	251	46980	11603	4061	67340			4814	163675	63	425	1361	49393	2448	57105	5	75
Fremont	18974	1935	77742	11131	2848	43110			6184	251597	37	599	1156	36557	231	5482	8	119
Gower	13614	3554	170384	11458	1868	30508			3700	121220	5	75	892	27581	31	658	5	50
Inland	16109	852	55035	10875	3372	58128			3995	176840			1349	47666	1673	32316	3	27
Iowa	15088	1908	91329	13350	1514	22680	9	110	4526	146637	202	2940	1757	58963	113	2276	20	303
Linn	8158	425	42935	5325	1321	8935			3232	120830			923	28689				9
Louden, town of	244		1200	100					100	4000								
Massillon	16642	880	61526	10681	3454	47526			4788	152755	1	20	1227	35761	1000	21184	212	471
Pioneer, exc. of Mechanicsville	15051	4484	690[illegible]	10454	3013	44604			5567	187675	14	157	1211	39185	31	560	2	57
Red Oak	9929	2094	54549	7481	1296	18461	7	113	3118	140221	14	265	776	25686	95	2198	1	14
Rochester	8245	3780	52062	6044	1043	25949			2757	91535	28	339	649	21193	12	250	22	365
Springdale	13660	2690	74489	6115	1538	29594			4 11	149930	42	708	1084	38525	47	841	4	20
Springfield, exc. of Louden	17890	2191	59386	11323	4003	48494		12	4585	146695	4	120	1188	33228	881	18406	8	55
Sugar Creek	11388	4694	48980	5586	1785	29597	10	60	2821	105884			822	31208	234	3451	7	196
Total	248693	41417	1210531	166485	40467	640544	26	295	78224	2845921	481	6585	20243	675837	9122	201037	337	2384

CERRO GORDO COUNTY.

Clear Lake, exc. of town	2237	48430	16464	2167	1264	23227			470	12250	1	10	327	10626	23	550	2	30
Daugherty	2905	20154	4030	2488	1229	16387			768	21700			314	9499	81	2843		
Falls	7822	16497	31300	7142	4523	74935			1184	33302			1063	40447	51	1430		
Geneseo	5140	36944	6880	4851	2770	37299			1195	26180			729	20232	49	1145		
Grant	1443	21254	9140	1251	820	11006			137	9170			259	7377			4	56
Lake	3223	25822	12590	3011	1766	25566			460	11885			490	15136	110	2389	7	86

CERRO GORDO COUNTY.—Continued.

NAMES OF TOWNSHIPS, TOWNS, AND CITIES.	No. of acres of improved land.	No. of acres of unimproved land.	No of rods of fence.	No. of acres in cultivation in 1874.	SPRING WHEAT.		WINTER WHEAT.		INDIAN CORN		RYE.		OATS.		BARLEY.		BUCK-WHEAT.	
					Number of acres.	Number of bushels harvested.	Number of acres.	Number of bushels harvested.	Number of acres.	Number of bushels harvested.	Number of acres.	Number of bushels harvested.	Number of acres.	Number of bushels harvested.	Number of acres.	Number of bushels harvested.	Number of acres.	Number of bushels harvested.
Lime Creek	6265	16412	24790	6003	3367	53792	....	....	1110	31805	18	284	838	19220	138	2861	15	143
Lincoln	4670	18473	20140	4456	2552	35220	....	....	955	26663	....	....	679	18156	102	2550	....	....
Mason, exc. of Mason City	7313	66504	21643	6977	3624	51240	....	....	1445	40303	11	155	1056	34058	228	4728	15	124
Owen	5347	23312	10122	4340	2617	39606	....	....	803	18545	....	....	589	21580	96	1818	....	....
Portland	6615	16093	21036	5962	3667	47185	....	....	985	33640	....	....	855	31766	149	3394	3	43
Total	52980	309895	178135	48648	28199	415463	....	....	9512	265443	30	449	7199	228097	1027	23708	46	482

CHEROKEE COUNTY.

NAMES OF TOWNSHIPS, TOWNS, AND CITIES.	No. of acres of improved land.	No. of acres of unimproved land.	No of rods of fence.	No. of acres in cultivation in 1874.	Spring wheat, number of acres.	Spring wheat, number of bushels harvested.	Winter wheat, number of acres.	Winter wheat, number of bushels harvested.	Indian corn, number of acres.	Indian corn, number of bushels harvested.	Rye, number of acres.	Rye, number of bushels harvested.	Oats, number of acres.	Oats, number of bushels harvested.	Barley, number of acres.	Barley, number of bushels harvested.	Buckwheat, number of acres.	Buckwheat, number of bushels harvested.
Afton	8522	14218	1681	7456	4760	53939	....	....	2053	56746	....	....	536	18220	53	1099	....	....
Amherst	2292	20748	....	2135	1224	13478	....	....	397	4020	2	35	156	2661	4	60	....	....
Cedar	5191	17849	520	5010	3538	38653	....	....	954	26565	3	55	386	11374	14	594	....	....
Cherokee, exc. of town	4803	18237	2770	4335	2954	41882	....	....	859	33060	7	95	356	12973	73	1479	....	....
Cherokee, town of	1555	21485	1092	868	540	7354	....	....	183	5260	....	....	74	2221	....	400	....	....
Diamond	1785	21255	110	1774	1380	10299	....	....	292	7410	....	....	116	3857	12	335	....	....
Liberty	2531	20509	....	2150	1539	19004	....	....	364	10740	....	....	160	5410	....	....	....	....
Marcus	620	21498	....	588	353	2505	....	....	102	230	....	....	43	270	....	....	....	....
Pilot	6548	16492	3120	3934	3970	51171	....	....	484	46283	....	....	383	12627	37	537	2	....
Pitcher	5639	17401	581	4720	3121	38841	....	....	853	31320	....	....	343	12646	50	600	8	56
Sheridan	4291	18749	80	3633	2757	41597	....	....	747	24152	....	....	292	11523	....	....	....	....
Silver	3428	19612	1000	3236	1751	25644	....	....	512	14245	....	....	190	5894	53	567	....	....
Spring	1207	21833	950	722	560	9771	....	....	252	8310	....	....	67	2101	15	445	....	....
Tilden	3138	19902	666	2369	1730	20807	....	....	535	17910	....	....	210	7220	9	299	5	50
Willow	3088	19952	2417	2482	1578	26562	....	....	872	28964	....	....	233	6598	22	515	....	....
Total	54638	289740	14987	45412	31693	401507	....	....	9459	315215	12	185	3545	115595	342	6930	15	106

CHICKASAW COUNTY.

Bradford, exc. of Nashua	10197	7467	48759	4587	4661	62306	....	....	2116	53450	15	370	1085	39076	75	1764	15	208
Chickasaw	9348	11899	54937	5251	2805	43045	....	....	1649	45185	8	116	863	31131	27	484	23	297
Dayton	7643	5889	35830	5342	2349	35809	....	....	1180	35200	13	296	727	28930	149	3038	3	37
Deerfield	8293	8751	46565	6467	4293	69810	....	....	1640	56350	....	....	1162	46148	96	2790	4	110
Dresden	5556	4612	33944	4647	1727	27589	....	....	1197	37934	9	122	878	30596	69	1502	17	189
Fredricksburg	6377	3508	32771	5178	1206	36732	....	....	1280	41005	5	80	815	33446	69	1859	42	448
Jacksonville	12972	7040	46940	8237	4661	69177	....	....	1437	43627	....	....	1211	46541	73	2021	1	....
Nashua, town of	657	254	3270	657	....	....	....	....	195	5250	....	....	46	2050	12	280	6	60
New Hampton, exc. of town	4060	4804	22845	3336	2021	32645	....	....	866	24417	4	100	663	24248	42	1014	5	36
New Hampton, town of	227	1	770	221	28	640	3	63	....	....	....	....	4	350	4	100	....	....
Richland	5638	7537	39535	5137	2123	33491	....	....	1381	44040	11	99	1008	36601	20	518	23	234
Stapleton	9082	10065	54542	9014	5618	90152	....	....	1311	40165	1	32	1195	44625	45	1167	3	35
Utica	9421	13212	56875	8997	4904	79053	....	....	1297	34286	2	30	1070	40348	73	1690	8	122
Washington	7033	9733	52792	7033	3766	63070	....	....	1272	53370	....	....	1017	42230	65	1562	6	222
Total	96504	94772	530375	74104	40162	643519	3	63	16821	514279	68	1245	11744	446300	819	19789	156	1998

CLARKE COUNTY.

Doyle, exc. of Hopeville	7291	3952	42609	5443	3900	43549	7	55	3281	108407	52	895	921	28513	4	151	....	47
Franklin	9431	4524	44016	6787	704	7855	....	....	3790	156195	29	422	1117	33170	8	60	....	....
Fremont	6392	6247	29984	5287	1253	16517	....	....	3177	118791	....	....	476	15685	1	46	....	....
Green Bay	10504	3707	38537	7590	1239	12959	....	....	2159	126348	100	1111	1261	36243	24	427	5	9
Hopeville, town of	1952	576	12803	1317	293	3405	....	....	954	34045	....	....	308	10767	....	....	2	78
Jackson	8295	4933	25702	8316	1658	19407	....	....	3604	107505	7	136	1051	27095	28	860	1	14
Knox	11408	3772	46985	7934	1662	20758	....	....	3975	161082	47	700	1684	54996	243	5904	6	35
Liberty	9704	3349	42005	6667	1616	21313	....	....	3602	128293	5	64	707	19570	51	860	5	63
Madison	5328	3255	28594	4936	1035	12563	....	....	2716	114220	10	162	643	18352	17	342	3	81
Osceola, exc. of town	4567	2037	20030	4400	1227	14928	....	....	2061	118699	4	36	684	23243	70	1432	....	54
Osceola, town of	4154	2092	17103	3594	944	10600	....	....	1410	47568	1	10	705	20217	52	1022	3	5
Troy	4505	2671	26169	5250	776	10296	....	....	2518	118740	50	696	1107	26128	44	1595	....	41
Ward	7596	4196	30938	5151	661	9705	....	....	2 66	112380	4	76	812	29314	62	1163	2	44
Washington	7565	5175	26598	6131	999	13235	....	....	2852	127987	5	37	859	24350	22	525	....	75
Total	98694	50486	432073	78803	17968	217090	7	55	39065	1580260	314	4345	12336	367643	626	14387	27	546

CLAY COUNTY.

Bridgewater	3665	4470	100	3376	1704	13017	....	....	890	16164	....	....	613	11792	12	93	....	....
Clay	7070	7811	4500	7165	3831	40672	....	....	1737	35017	44	493	815	20960	47	673	13	79

CLAY COUNTY—Continued.

Names of townships, towns, and cities.	No. of acres of improved land.	No. of acres of unimproved land.	No. of rods of fence.	No. of acres in cultivation in 1874.	Spring wheat.		Winter wheat.		Indian corn.		Rye.		Oats.		Barley.		Buckwheat.	
					Number of acres.	Number of bushels harvested.	Number of acres.	Number of bushels harvested.	Number of acres.	Number of bushels harvested.	Number of acres.	Number of bushels harvested.	Number of acres.	Number of bushels harvested.	Number of acres.	Number of bushels harvested.	Number of acres.	Number of bushels harvested.
Douglas	4268	4186	4222	3620	2002	23424	......	......	945	27695	......	......	580	17253	63	1477	1	11
Gillett's Grove	2677	3213	630	2449	992	8181	......	......	696	16495	......	......	289	6715	15	182	2	14
Herdland	1261	1638	627	1272	681	6086	......	......	335	7320	......	......	160	2854	......	......	1	12
Lincoln	3518	4315	......	2876	1508	14332	......	......	819	16620	30	214	363	8207	16	366	1	11
Riverton	3468	2394	......	3127	1617	17046	......	......	707	15135	......	......	422	10547	23	398	......	......
Spencer	6871	7337	320	6208	2953	14362	......	......	1847	31289	......	......	872	13560	40	393	......	......
Summit	4261	4555	......	3282	2193	16039	......	......	821	14385	3	8	322	6878	16	234	......	......
Total	37059	39919	10399	33375	17481	153149	......	......	8797	180120	77	715	4436	98766	232	3816	18	127

CLAYTON COUNTY.

Names of townships, towns, and cities.	No. of acres of improved land.	No. of acres of unimproved land.	No. of rods of fence.	No. of acres in cultivation in 1874.	Spring wheat, acres.	Spring wheat, bushels.	Winter wheat, acres.	Winter wheat, bushels.	Indian corn, acres.	Indian corn, bushels.	Rye, acres.	Rye, bushels.	Oats, acres.	Oats, bushels.	Barley, acres.	Barley, bushels.	Buckwheat, acres.	Buckwheat, bushels.
Boardman	11196	6037	41561	10036	6072	90855	......	......	2027	78075	4	40	1286	37207	99	2338	2	10
Buena Vista	1681	2625	10223	1265	669	15459	......	......	358	11340	......	......	127	2854	2	46	3	40
Cass	8683	6560	40763	5316	2159	26837	......	......	1823	61020	......	......	1076	27724	44	903	10	203
Clayton	4623	7685	30602	3861	1778	26481	16	350	902	39726	10	149	505	16752	58	1355	22	374
Cox Creek	9393	10897	74446	8020	4521	45620	......	......	2100	52595	8	59	953	18138	71	1695	19	76
Elk	4554	6396	50055	3417	1348	15689	247	3984	1455	61584	16	157	231	5877	4	85	32	368
Farmersburg	19766	2252	70840	23838	6906	111723	......	......	2685	116985	......	......	1573	58948	360	8891	......	......
Garnavillo	12214	10059	70150	8789	5079	78341	......	......	2176	101830	9	164	1193	48468	265	6734	1	10
Girard	8366	1824	61624	6637	4253	58102	......	......	1825	78948	......	......	1160	45544	67	1643	3	50
Grand Meadow	17750	1723	67573	10491	6646	1075[illegible]1	......	......	2230	87730	......	......	1403	51581	164	3400	11	245
Guttenberg, town of	176	135	......	157	49	519	......	......	32	1570	......	......	10	222	......	......	......	......
Highland	10669	7835	55913	9440	5151	84662	......	......	1853	54350	......	......	1007	34772	21	700	5	130
Jefferson, exc. of Guttenberg	12172	14866	101370	12103	6834	92509	64	832	2073	99570	30	395	1288	39619	58	1558	3	48
Lodomillo	8870	6227	73126	4093	1941	22727	23	304	1945	74570	......	......	646	26225	17	430	53	754
Mallory	6775	9312	72005	5373	1632	19579	898	13848	1854	54078	18	169	430	12675	16	299	27	659

Marion	10653	8566	69036	9653	6044	106082	....	....	1443	48744	....	....	1149	40817	....	1730	....	....
Mendon, exc. of McGregor and North McGregor	2267	6836	32820	1989	489	7083	8	120	568	20250	20	302	209	6097	15	360	16	210
Millville	3517	6574	45510	3269	874	11205	83	1582	1384	55945	1	34	203	5127	6	187	6	96
Monona	16692	4100	81013	13182	8689	126121	....	....	1971	81295	....	....	1483	58673	133	3001	7	148
Read	8815	6223	55457	7233	3921	58795	1	10	1732	81134	1	9	973	34658	209	4891	....	....
Sperry	13754	9422	79894	8148	3605	56354	....	....	2347	87014	....	....	1072	28541	48	1181	12	143
Volga	8377	10095	72[illegible]23	7466	4326	54863	7	....	1722	63985	38	612	849	22143	82	1932	1	20
Wagner	11328	5659	20917	9846	3897	87938	....	....	1443	58925	....	....	1198	47223	79	2032	....	....
Total	212291	151908	1277821	173622	86883	1305125	1347	21030	37948	1471263	155	2090	20024	669895	1818	45391	233	3584

CLINTON COUNTY.

Berlin	16186	414	50878	16332	3507	50796	....	....	4543	180395	25	318	969	27332	1179	14793	5	140
Bloomfield	18973	2257	98128	9245	4163	66073	....	....	5478	192870	2	30	1516	41519	265	3871	11	154
Brookfield	19511	400	95270	13614	3306	50175	....	....	5312	179563	5	35	1073	28808	165	3420	8	94
Camanche, exc. of town	7866	1863	25395	4456	970	16092	....	....	3001	118075	67	839	968	297[illegible]0	235	6501	7	77
Camanche, town of	677	30	3916	497	48	745	....	....	300	9900	52	1023	33	837	....	....	3	65
Center	22340	511	88413	15423	5138	82242	....	....	6320	243548	34	546	1754	54486	1302	37918	6	75
Clinton, exc. of town	2188	643	15782	1375	202	23044	....	....	619	25750	....	....	190	5740	....	250	....	25
Deep Creek	13106	2399	60918	12798	3127	47469	....	....	4231	148970	....	....	1255	35935	726	15864	1	34
De Witt, exc. of town	21760	6986	96270	14678	7581	70408	....	....	6617	222210	4	30	1983	65189	590	13248	31	538
De Witt, town of	3656	666	11022	2299	229	4391	....	....	280	1[illegible]870	....	....	62	2207	66	1783	....	....
Eden	14112	4524	74928	9386	1968	34168	....	....	4898	187100	6	150	1763	51061	486	13334	34	694
Elk River	22181	3453	94928	12953	3870	62142	9	315	6200	214940	13	312	1730	53036	1411	30026	9	110
Hampshire	15232	2692	60551	10821	4322	67928	....	....	3945	110700	....	....	1155	36831	986	23668	1	20
Liberty	9836	5228	43721	7927	2101	27629	....	....	3848	121335	....	....	841	22485	518	9863	5	110
Lincoln	6343	1099	33338	4069	1089	17807	....	....	2216	89176	8	144	652	21472	176	3330	3	22
Lyons, exc. of city	2175	1542	10064	1253	541	8168	3	113	888	19610	6	174	112	5188	54	918	5	80
Lyons, city of	130	....	....	104	....	....	....	....	....	4400	....	....	....	500	....	100	....	....
Olive	22215	1049	67078	13797	3899	51865	....	....	6567	207835	15	217	1493	45824	1149	24312	18	306
Orange	11046	3106	56509	8637	3288	47273	....	....	3659	123454	16	114	1009	32000	631	13661	9	187
Sharon	14079	5293	79263	9559	3480	47367	....	....	5505	163585	4	100	1270	30346	278	4867	20	219
Spring Rock, exc. of/Wheatland	9814	5354	50655	7660	2555	35706	....	....	3183	97405	4	60	819	23337	626	11993	18	208
Washington	16042	1882	41785	57487	4253	64210	....	....	3660	124150	....	....	673	20407	500	11588	....	....
Waterford	13220	4549	49953	11671	4750	69411	....	....	3721	113381	5	46	1285	33893	849	8249	5	73
Welton	17028	1397	55370	11167	4255	64828	....	....	4268	151126	....	....	1086	33571	620	15181	4	30
Wheatland, town of	139	....	370	105	41	408	....	....	38	990	....	....	13	325	....	....	....	....
Total	299855	57337	264505	257313	68683	1010345	12	428	89297	3061338	266	4138	23704	702059	12812	268738	203	3261

CRAWFORD COUNTY.

NAMES OF TOWNSHIPS, TOWNS, AND CITIES.	No. of acres of improved land.	No. of acres of unimproved land.	No. of rods of fence.	No. of acres in cultivation in 1874.	SPRING WHEAT.		WINTER WHEAT.		INDIAN CORN.		RYE.		OATS.		BARLEY.		BUCK-WHEAT.	
					Number of acres.	Number of bushels harvested.	Number of acres.	Number of bushels harvested.	Number of acres.	Number of bushels harvested.	Number of acres.	Number of bushels harvested.	Number of acres.	Number of bushels harvested.	Number of acres.	Number of bushels harvested.	Number of acres.	Number of bushels harvested.
Boyer	2676	20364	13918	2272	984	11560	....	....	1057	50510	29	342	173	6450	25	350	3	10
Charter Oak	1000	22040	660	1092	678	6580	....	....	365	18050	....	....	40	1261	9	195	....	....
Denison	3094	19940	14096	2987	1402	22048	....	....	1531	68240	20	470	230	9221	23	373	9	165
East Boyer	5045	17995	21230	3680	1907	27956	....	....	1531	58840	....	....	157	7268	....	....	9	74
Goodrich	2532	20508	10702	2124	969	18050	....	....	972	40075	12	300	131	4599	10	250	....	....
Hanover	300	22740	....	79	26	600	....	....	53	1800	....	....	....	14	....	....	....	....
Hays	5130	17910	3844	4345	2233	29834	....	....	1624	40307	2	45	253	7754	167	3758	....	6
Iowa	1630	21410	940	1630	918	9081	....	....	611	16920	....	....	76	2316	20	500	....	....
Jackson	4194	18846	1930	3099	1581	21276	....	....	883	29100	....	....	238	6248	70	1247	4	27
Milford	6270	17770	24560	4638	2424	35376	....	....	1907	61710	2	15	197	6872	....	30	5	51
Morgan	1570	21470	160	985	582	9193	....	....	271	10310	....	....	83	2494	40	500	....	....
Nishnabotany	1341	21699	2250	909	427	6487	....	....	368	11990	....	....	84	2752	12	276	....	15
Otter Creek	5785	17255	9243	4294	2223	33784	....	....	1680	61880	....	....	283	8468	53	1340	2	....
Paradise	3388	20652	8348	1245	718	9965	....	....	423	18250	....	....	78	2900	....	....	....	....
Soldier	439	22601	800	439	290	4686	....	....	179	8010	....	....	48	1508	....	....	....	....
Stockholm	3118	19925	13170	2779	1874	28864	....	....	731	35832	....	....	130	4460	....	....	....	....
Union	3916	19124	22204	3916	1682	12229	....	....	1727	47105	7	120	298	5326	55	809	5	75
Washington	1703	21337	7970	1703	839	9927	....	....	860	22795	....	....	76	2688	26	423	2	40
West Side	4037	19003	6460	3371	1918	22290	....	....	918	35094	....	....	270	8398	74	1535	11	8
Willow	890	825	1570	675	325	5108	....	....	266	12040	....	....	56	161	....	....	....	....
Total	58058	383414	164055	45262	24000	324894	....	....	17957	648858	72	1292	1901	99158	584	11586	50	471

DALLAS COUNTY.

NAMES OF TOWNSHIPS, TOWNS, AND CITIES.	No. of acres of improved land.	No. of acres of unimproved land.	No. of rods of fence.	No. of acres in cultivation in 1874.	Spring wheat, number of acres.	Spring wheat, number of bushels harvested.	Winter wheat, number of acres.	Winter wheat, number of bushels harvested.	Indian corn, number of acres.	Indian corn, number of bushels harvested.	Rye, number of acres.	Rye, number of bushels harvested.	Oats, number of acres.	Oats, number of bushels harvested.	Barley, number of acres.	Barley, number of bushels harvested.	Buckwheat, number of acres.	Buckwheat, number of bushels harvested.
Adams	10351	5260	70230	10235	2348	44755	....	....	3951	230090	3	40	650	22467	....	....	2	41
Adel, exc. of town	13244	3108	54204	9320	1877	25539	....	....	5678	238080	25	525	701	23312	9	200	9	132
Beaver	3752	2710	19995	3606	1157	23928	....	....	1864	69501	9	188	420	12091	60	1331	....	....

Boone	11628	2058	51150	8010	2455	42923	....	....	4737	230870	80	900	712	25860	226	6426	1	10
Colfax	11617	1011	44755	7538	2282	30058	....	....	3901	153790	39	565	904	29864	30	585	....	....
Dallas	4458	4524	23550	4967	1345	20047	....	....	2582	109600	8	216	510	19579	19	430	....	....
Des Moines	7486	4644	36220	5493	1140	13026	7	166	2941	105855	21	362	641	19025	....	....	8	11
Grant	6507	2409	32064	5992	1453	25445	....	....	3320	135825	....	....	760	21690	128	2674	....	13
Lincoln	5101	5298	11759	11951	1342	18821	....	....	1845	74875	1	25	354	13834	66	1304	2	24
Linn	9669	3721	50320	7500	2472	33436	....	....	4108	176720	14	188	679	21950	43	1168	....	19
Spring Valley	5876	6544	33713	5645	1374	19430	1	20	3750	144550	31	583	447	17408	9	150	....	....
Sugar Grove	7064	3381	30495	6064	1093	14375	....	....	2987	125250	12	276	684	24383	17	359	....	....
Union, exc. of Dexter	10214	1809	33053	7057	2450	34706	....	....	4433	199050	24	620	667	24800	19	454	1	35
Van Meter	9724	5182	64678	9185	2418	37036	....	....	4537	201202	54	1400	640	18943	12	390	....	....
Walnut	8179	5894	36464	6997	2586	41155	....	....	4219	185180	6	110	782	25821	30	684	2	35
Washington	7565	2212	32149	5065	1464	21168	....	....	2899	104460	17	157	386	14097	12	224	....	....
Total	132435	57765	624799	114625	29256	445848	8	186	57652	2484898	344	6155	9937	335124	680	16379	25	320

DAVIS COUNTY.

Bloomfield, exc. of town	14638	6415	93001	13616	473	2811	281	2342	7052	254277	35	329	1510	43936	....	....	11	145
Drakeville, exc. of town	4291	3991	30187	3965	250	1513	40	452	1524	53772	9	50	381	8623	....	8	7	96
Drakeville, town of	198	166	1777	181	10	50	21	230	233	7385	....	....	44	1145	....	....	....	....
Fabius	10967	9203	90271	7350	306	1769	139	1278	4707	136445	26	231	930	23681	....	....	10	139
Fox River	8458	6347	48795	5095	305	2018	183	1621	2716	74770	46	385	638	13618	....	....	12	171
Grove	13632	8262	70162	15175	277	1240	517	6105	4880	191387	79	698	1616	45066	....	....	18	188
Lick Creek	8132	8803	63965	6306	385	2412	515	4552	4339	142252	221	2160	671	13600	....	....	18	217
Marion	8050	7737	66550	7731	334	2452	611	6482	3874	119385	183	1536	555	10555	....	....	3	91
Perry	11340	5829	53657	7871	354	1875	199	1748	3612	141047	23	263	720	18052	....	....	10	179
Prairie	7113	10758	31152	7481	289	1620	191	2382	3276	131315	60	520	804	24448	....	....	15	308
Roscoe	8752	4435	34435	8303	285	697	311	3183	3418	118440	30	213	748	21108	....	....	17	189
Salt Creek	8108	9240	89200	6909	687	4320	701	6740	3317	134665	166	1436	430	11556	....	....	21	370
Soap Creek	9869	13140	77289	7991	253	1017	531	5830	3514	118325	51	462	602	13350	....	....	9	129
Union	8466	8536	83583	8907	383	2711	914	11006	3984	119571	113	1134	978	22659	....	....	85	561
West Grove	10803	8475	83672	13541	473	2383	71	770	5466	189593	12	94	1315	32719	....	....	11	114
Wyacondah	18121	4666	92537	11175	314	1605	154	1684	6215	182940	22	194	1701	41591	....	....	7	55
Total	150938	116003	1010234	131597	5378	30993	5379	56405	62127	2115569	1076	9705	13643	345707	....	8	254	2952

DECATUR COUNTY.

Bloomington	4417	2704	21409	3417	284	3067	58	866	2034	55197	61	907	487	16490	1	18	15	234
Burrell	6282	7064	46215	5475	585	6781	47	574	2808	85840	36	429	553	16298	....	....	11	207
Center, exc. of Leon	9502	4263	56790	9012	693	7295	14	272	4473	167700	25	415	733	24427	....	....	4	76
Decatur	9756	3268	53500	7220	886	8027	85	1446	4929	147840	73	981	845	28927	5	50	10	169
Eden	7643	8000	68462	4421	463	3436	76	1027	2541	75096	138	687	377	10583	....	....	9	205

DECATUR COUNTY.—Continued.

Names of townships, towns, and cities.	No. of acres of improved land.	No. of acres of unimproved land.	No. of rods of fence.	No. of acres in cultivation in 1874.	Spring wheat. Number of acres.	Spring wheat. Number of bushels harvested.	Winter wheat. Number of acres.	Winter wheat. Number of bushels harvested.	Indian corn. Number of acres.	Indian corn. Number of bushels harvested.	Rye. Number of acres.	Rye. Number of bushels harvested.	Oats. Number of acres.	Oats. Number of bushels harvested.	Barley. Number of acres.	Barley. Number of bushels harvested.	Buckwheat. Number of acres.	Buckwheat. Number of bushels harvested.
Fayette	3662	2497	28181	3501	245	2325	2	18	2051	42955	25	391	659	26417	....	....	3	24
Franklin	10295	7092	42718	9593	762	8700	32	550	4898	196458	147	890	1591	54843	6	142	4	73
Garden Grove	16637	5564	82679	11289	845	9261	....	....	5489	259866	99	1282	1516	53030	19	403	24	265
Grand River	3419	3233	21410	2538	436	4126	38	789	2090	75420	70	1202	343	10095	....	....	1	8
Hamilton	4021	4966	27420	3749	346	3136	21	179	1807	47980	96	798	284	6808	....	....	10	150
High Point	7924	7978	50611	7556	467	3459	6	66	3998	140984	94	1022	640	21184	2	20	17	226
Long Creek	6400	5844	41225	6431	620	6118	47	1236	3598	137569	66	706	867	29568	....	....	....	....
Morgan	4308	6082	41625	3192	203	1309	136	1543	1517	39005	136	1703	280	6421	....	....	9	167
New Buda	5986	4805	31210	4905	285	2725	42	596	2648	70475	56	591	477	13474	....	....	6	96
Richland	6420	6687	44395	6312	615	4854	146	2341	3398	124365	92	441	548	15256	3	12	3	18
Woodland	9079	7125	77541	6664	478	2550	67	736	3005	96390	151	1854	355	10730	3	80	11	175
Total	115751	87172	735391	95275	8211	77169	817	12239	50484	1763140	1365	17299	10355	344551	39	725	137	2093

DELAWARE COUNTY.

Names of townships, towns, and cities.	No. of acres of improved land.	No. of acres of unimproved land.	No. of rods of fence.	No. of acres in cultivation in 1874.	Spring wheat. Number of acres.	Spring wheat. Number of bushels harvested.	Winter wheat. Number of acres.	Winter wheat. Number of bushels harvested.	Indian corn. Number of acres.	Indian corn. Number of bushels harvested.	Rye. Number of acres.	Rye. Number of bushels harvested.	Oats. Number of acres.	Oats. Number of bushels harvested.	Barley. Number of acres.	Barley. Number of bushels harvested.	Buckwheat. Number of acres.	Buckwheat. Number of bushels harvested.
Adams	16104	1466	54504	10923	3705	52091	....	....	4090	131084	6	70	1141	36054	21	346	5	81
Bremer	14996	7642	49353	8540	4321	59264	....	....	3738	117625	5	62	1089	37665	209	5878	....	....
Coffin's Grove	13139	1944	43713	13886	4299	49555	....	....	2939	89985	10	150	1236	42788	166	2881	19	219
Colony	259301	6762	89093	18187	4997	68031	5	50	4882	162715	39	....	1320	48852	322	7693	11	209
Delaware, exc. of Manchester	10370	6937	54379	8332	2723	37834	....	....	2844	85455	....	....	1209	39379	75	2069	6	53
Delhi	12564	4174	53094	7173	2655	32063	....	....	2842	88265	....	....	1005	26108	25	1452	39	545
Elk	10243	4949	49940	7673	3473	37035	....	....	2698	94285	....	....	1201	37846	49	1416	17	235
Hazel Green	10759	6036	58777	7826	3620	43509	....	....	3969	40410	....	....	1499	38665	61	1205	4	50
Honey Creek	18949	726	89300	12395	4510	53318	....	....	4211	148495	1	18	1794	55873	60	1181	19	270
Manchester, town of	8151	6720	35749	7400	2637	37294	....	....	2121	74997	26	500	505	35978	97	2241	21	198
Milo	14617	1938	58454	10747	4333	36625	....	....	2544	90593	11	88	1240	31762	43	850	18	221
North Fork	15556	1577	70485	8516	3215	37160	....	....	3570	104370	25	318	872	22286	31	504	11	166

Oneida	17533	636	51879	10823	4043	60166	....	....	3838	119220	11	170	1996	55202	108	2012	15	81
Prairie	11133	....	33532	7958	3907	55860	....	....	2724	106195	....	....	920	32815	64	1512	9	130
Richland	11943	3132	47215	12252	2432	31162	....	....	2348	73805	5	100	1046	30082	16	327	12	130
South Fork, exc. of Hopkinton	15449	....	55856	8051	2725	29757	....	....	3954	93991	80	118	1366	37233	....	....	7	194
Union	10922	7666	39633	675	2806	21004	....	....	2838	68845	....	....	1137	23575	6	156	6	58
Total	472029	62305	934956	161357	60401	741728	5	50	56150	1690335	219	1594	20577	632113	1353	31723	219	2840

DES MOINES COUNTY.

Augusta	3953	3065	37185	2963	70	303	664	10445	1456	62440	2	30	248	5619	12	161	5	93
Benton	8967	7640	81233	8694	697	4554	1084	10115	3748	139766	77	637	641	16249	8	79	7	97
Burlington, exc. of city	7361	6152	55690	6696	189	1308	542	7190	2544	99461	42	326	498	9984	47	906	9	93
Danville	18788	2565	128131	9870	717	7198	1767	27168	6041	264111	58	639	1644	54333	12	219	17	278
Flint River	12501	4831	97679	6765	415	3226	844	12996	4680	165630	36	412	840	19237	8	119	24	414
Franklin	10521	5347	7849	7810	2237	20674	731	7216	5166	238570	13	159	....	21374	91	1599	44	871
Huron	8650	9229	68930	7166	721	5836	641	8748	3880	170329	28	351	361	7498	....	....	18	340
Jackson	1247	1862	6155	1101	60	633	11	139	818	30400	10	55	116	2461	....	....	1	11
Pleasant Grove	15458	7876	97095	8049	786	7522	742	8814	4327	170903	40	438	1252	39739	....	....	1	15
Union	14947	4949	103845	7323	806	6965	1440	22368	8477	195925	155	1477	854	22642	....	....	1	18
Washington	17810	715	71781	16410	2148	31724	25	213	7513	319638	9	90	1233	41697	14	215	3	112
Yellow Springs	23462	3937	134985	14771	1769	23453	197	1898	54274	450765	69	885	1555	46559	4	102	27	501
Total	143665	53168	890558	97618	10615	113396	8638	117310	802924	2307938	539	5499	9242	287392	196	3400	157	2843

DICKINSON COUNTY.

Center Grove	6292	5465	15883	3730	1749	7235	....	....	823	12250	....	....	744	11504	16	12	12	....
Diamond Lake	597	1727	90	539	281	1273	....	....	87	925	....	10	106	875	....	....	....	....
Excelsior	968	2842	226	856	348	961	....	....	249	2411	....	....	127	994	....	....	10	....
Lakeville	623	1848	1000	520	210	1362	....	....	132	1610	....	....	107	2429	....	....	3	20
Lloyd	1107	3322	30	1000	251	2090	....	....	312	3456	....	....	133	2637	....	....	....	....
Milford	1162	2371	....	1017	484	3834	....	....	325	6110	....	....	205	4568	4	64	1	14
Okoboji	885	3401	2134	1620	801	3565	....	....	361	6515	....	....	394	5796	14	90	....	....
Richland	686	1993	....	537	228	684	....	....	173	1640	....	....	70	890	2	....	9	....
Silver Lake	371	630	....	149	149	816	....	....	87	497	....	....	62	591	....	....	....	....
Spirit Lake	2357	4223	5095	1883	1080	3618	....	....	589	8555	....	....	431	6499	11	68	4	18
Superior	722	2028	60	110	120	384	....	....	45	486	....	....	24	499	....	....	....	....
Total	15770	29850	24518	11961	5701	25822	....	....	3183	44455	....	10	2403	37282	47	234	39	52

DUBUQUE COUNTY.

NAMES OF TOWNSHIPS, TOWNS, AND CITIES.	No. of acres of improved land.	No. of acres of unimproved land.	No. of rods of fence.	No. of acres in cultivation in 1874.	SPRING WHEAT. Number of acres.	SPRING WHEAT. Number of bushels harvested.	WINTER WHEAT. Number of acres.	WINTER WHEAT. Number of bushels harvested.	INDIAN CORN. Number of acres.	INDIAN CORN. Number of bushels harvested.	RYE. Number of acres.	RYE. Number of bushels harvested.	OATS. Number of acres.	OATS. Number of bushels harvested.	BARLEY. Number of acres.	BARLEY. Number of bushels harvested.	BUCKWHEAT. Number of acres.	BUCKWHEAT. Number of bushels harvested.
Cascade	8995	6631	64000	7643	2405	30860			3193	98075	12	141	1217	32659	28	485	15	241
Center	7436	7875	63997	5912	1550	22507			2147	70758	39	507	1046	22505	41	939	3	37
Concord	8972	8582	65105	8722	3557	47401	9	148	2444	87420	4	40	1223	34907	90	2094	9	131
Dodge	10704	1759	48434	9610	4190	47536		2	3094	90170			1950	52032				
Dubuque, city of	867	532	11727	326	65	820			161	6570			23	730	4	40		
Dyersville, town of	160	12	1644	171	63	921			62	2575			79	1058	40	1200		
Iowa	7607	7444	137760	6181	2246	28162			2434	67240			766	22249	44	1320	5	45
Jefferson	12526	9780	97381	8402	3727	52148	65	1425	2589	95475	21	310	1574	39636	152	3566	5	115
Julien, exc. of Dubuque	9343	1947	48137	5653	1049	18276			1999	56415	7	120	644	15343	21	325	5	55
Liberty	11895	5948	46054	11140	5347	60251			3853	95593			1659	37842	188	5110	1	6
Mosalem	5439		32885	5439	2196	29909			1017	41362			1046	21157	70	900		
New Wine, exc. of Dyersville	13972	5556	77662	7440	4650	68117			4728	150758	3	51	1526	47640	246	6074		
Peru	7800	4871	74864	6251	2394	28328	9	125	952	37265	48	594	1002	27139	103	2015	7	124
Prairie Creek	14722	4870	81810	10268	2774	34965			5917	174480			2610	51050	73	1337		
Table Mound	9834	13493	51970	9497	1570	18580			3382	98010			1955	53980	35	695	1	20
Taylor	19052	2633	90349	11164	3132	42329	1	20	5237	128955	1	12	2286	61695	207	4562	4	43
Vernon	16725	3818	83529	11288	2927	37122			4874	158640			1808	49086	255	5575	6	67
Washington	13410	5479	63380	14311	3415	41311			14841	224825			1939	46705	88	1446	9	67
Whitewater	9272	8330	59108	6826	1983	24592			4190	117705			762	25909	4	110	8	30
Total	187831	98560	1199796	146244	49240	634135	84	1720	67114	1802291	135	1775	25115	643322	1689	37793	78	981

EMMET COUNTY.

NAMES OF TOWNSHIPS, TOWNS, AND CITIES.	No. of acres of improved land.	No. of acres of unimproved land.	No. of rods of fence.	No. of acres in cultivation in 1874.	SPRING WHEAT. Number of acres.	SPRING WHEAT. Number of bushels harvested.	WINTER WHEAT. Number of acres.	WINTER WHEAT. Number of bushels harvested.	INDIAN CORN. Number of acres.	INDIAN CORN. Number of bushels harvested.	RYE. Number of acres.	RYE. Number of bushels harvested.	OATS. Number of acres.	OATS. Number of bushels harvested.	BARLEY. Number of acres.	BARLEY. Number of bushels harvested.	BUCKWHEAT. Number of acres.	BUCKWHEAT. Number of bushels harvested.
Armstrong Grove	1264	5387	1750	1057	320	239			448	4535			129	320	2		4	50
Center	608	1964	1140	408	226				77	233			130					
Ellsworth	799	1192	570	486	252	4			155	1204			78	390			4	
Emmet	1672	3204	4120	1540	700	135			410	2800			361	1152	36	8	2	

Estherville	2587	4501	8160	2151	823	40	...	...	494	1345	...	...	470	594	5	...	4	35
High Lake	1337	3063	6900	1310	748	117	...	...	307	2437	...	...	185	...	17	...	...	...
Iowa Lake	312	1029	375	162	21	...	...	...	129	350	...	...	...	...	...	...	...	...
Peterson	1178	4006	4630	1041	665	895	...	...	167	1324	10	...	177	775	23	124	...	...
Swan Lake	232	1240	...	232	156	80	...	...	10	45	10	60	19	10	...	...	...	...
Total	9989	25586	27645	8387	3911	1510	...	...	2197	14273	20	60	1549	3241	93	132	14	85

FAYETTE COUNTY.

Auburn	7029	3798	40780	4904	2017	29980	...	...	1083	35365	5	40	749	23366	58	1348	13	233
Banks	3240	3490	16722	3072	1297	18545	...	...	722	17380	...	...	601	20997	55	903	...	...
Bethel	8730	1703	33990	5324	2749	32427	...	...	1047	28397	4	89	728	26519	24	542	8	40
Center	6702	4502	29675	4669	2373	34148	...	...	1393	51735	...	...	998	30831	108	1967	1	10
Clermont	9478	9113	74250	8929	5635	89829	...	...	...	...	...	...	...	...	...	...	...	...
Dover	13891	2125	93460	7068	3227	66246	4	78	1616	61002	...	...	814	30595	68	1563	12	299
Eden	8744	9544	63156	7418	3722	58054	...	...	1996	57643	...	...	1061	32011	149	2288	24	310
Fairfield	10701	5692	66263	6893	2152	28787	15	450	2256	68570	...	...	1299	41453	102	1907	...	...
Fayette, town of	...	...	...	...	...	...	...	...	16	880	...	...	...	...	...	...	...	...
Fremont	7894	3627	33257	3802	3587	40355	...	...	1563	56405	...	...	769	23799	52	748	4	34
Harlan	6337	4277	32295	5246	2548	33854	...	...	1907	49630	...	...	844	27662	17	328	11	117
Illyria	8881	6880	67510	7333	2408	41260	18	277	2336	93035	4	20	798	30194	85	2158	3	70
Jefferson	11741	2937	45490	8329	3406	41434	...	...	2360	88850	...	...	1151	40614	132	3059	2	21
Oran	13112	948	47497	8348	3583	51843	...	...	2078	80793	...	...	1129	31030	56	1258	7	131
Pleasant Valley	3554	7995	55866	5286	2058	30339	...	...	1633	59138	...	...	654	19853	10	244	23	250
Putnam	10285	6331	61219	8144	3277	36163	...	...	2890	86441	...	...	2112	65623	63	1272	17	266
Scott	5744	4378	30460	5068	2388	31821	...	...	1501	53105	...	...	938	33290	57	1089	6	122
Smithfield	10181	8550	46465	8829	3586	48162	...	...	2443	82355	...	...	1683	63015	109	2179	16	132
Westfield	10950	2461	38020	6174	1988	28002	...	...	1211	84975	14	155	889	33960	36	832	31	357
West Union	10783	8085	68659	7784	3866	54755	2	...	2887	108727	...	...	984	35852	79	1584	10	184
West Union, town of	1466	416	10542	1056	387	8351	...	...	196	7220	...	...	76	3085	6	200	...	...
Windsor	10061	1304	57385	10082	4525	59319	7	163	2370	60920	...	...	1510	53698	114	2074	14	198
Total	179504	98156	1032961	133758	60779	863670	46	968	37091	1296480	27	304	20770	704407	1400	28127	224	3060

FLOYD COUNTY.

Cedar	5349	5273	32188	4685	2704	46581	...	...	1037	34963	3	45	705	26853	40	1328	9	127
Charles City	297	62	2838	187	53	753	...	...	77	1740	...	...	33	925	...	...	...	...
Floyd	13949	5112	55006	10021	4971	79224	...	...	1844	48912	8	144	1417	44602	267	5294	7	96
Niles	9673	3460	44574	5634	3312	60420	...	...	1261	39106	4	60	868	25324	31	840	30	326
Nora Springs, town of	3620	695	15055	1776	1251	21209	...	...	232	6660	...	...	283	12025	...	...	1	5
Pleasant Grove	13026	2031	47341	10731	6267	93849	...	...	1815	43345	4	35	2285	21910	206	4243	...	...

FLOYD COUNTY.—Continued.

Names of townships, towns, and cities.	No. of acres of improved land.	No. of acres of unimproved land.	No. of rods of fence.	No. of acres in cultivation in 1874.	Spring wheat		Winter wheat.		Indian corn.		Rye.		Oats.		Barley.		Buckwheat.	
					Number of acres.	Number of bushels harvested.	Number of acres.	Number of bushels harvested.	Number of acres.	Number of bushels harvested.	Number of acres.	Number of bushels harvested.	Number of acres.	Number of bushels harvested.	Number of acres.	Number of bushels harvested.	Number of acres.	Number of bushels harvested.
Riverton	17548	1447	107644	11150	5388	82105	....	....	2637	78165	18	130	1616	56299	267	5297	7	68
Rockford	14363	3421	44855	9106	5240	81487	....	....	2349	59355	....	....	1284	38295	142	2562	7	92
Rock Grove, exc. Nora Springs	11098	3816	42145	6691	4350	75999	....	....	1228	39445	....	....	863	34522	137	2766	13	130
Rudd	10403	1330	32608	6565	3860	62129	....	....	1029	30490	....	....	945	24975	183	3496	....	....
Scott	5916	2639	14555	5100	3117	41957	....	....	1628	40170	....	....	830	25141	158	2926	4	36
St. Charles, exc. of city	20170	12833	113356	19326	10067	139251	....	....	7174	112630	29	607	1938	105095	159	3597	13	122
Ulster	8264	5601	34571	7911	4617	68316	....	....	1514	38642	....	....	1030	34935	174	3384	7	30
Union	13422	4410	55326	11826	6870	88159	....	....	2637	68825	4	48	1364	36828	165	3484	25	260
Total	147098	52130	642062	110708	62067	941439	....	....	26462	642448	70	1069	15461	487729	1929	39217	123	1292

FRANKLIN COUNTY.

Names of townships, towns, and cities.	No. of acres of improved land.	No. of acres of unimproved land.	No. of rods of fence.	No. of acres in cultivation in 1874.	Spring wheat: Number of acres.	Spring wheat: Number of bushels harvested.	Winter wheat: Number of acres.	Winter wheat: Number of bushels harvested.	Indian corn: Number of acres.	Indian corn: Number of bushels harvested.	Rye: Number of acres.	Rye: Number of bushels harvested.	Oats: Number of acres.	Oats: Number of bushels harvested.	Barley: Number of acres.	Barley: Number of bushels harvested.	Buckwheat: Number of acres.	Buckwheat: Number of bushels harvested.
Clinton	6510	2550	20130	6903	3140	45710	....	....	2429	85815	....	....	1158	41263	164	3163	2	24
Geneva	8278	3079	14472	7857	3737	54303	....	....	2506	77450	....	....	1011	37991	320	8055	3	42
Grant	3193	2236	1980	2976	1679	23013	....	....	957	21828	....	....	329	10462	....	....	....	....
Hamilton	2543	2440	7813	2969	1251	18136	....	....	876	22600	....	....	512	13792	61	1050	7	66
Hampton, town of	83	24	900	133	8	144	....	....	65	2155	....	....	28	1040	....	....	....	....
Ingham	6585	5024	15484	5304	2392	32104	....	....	3049	85240	....	....	620	21596	119	2286	5	176
Lee	1346	1542	4970	1863	950	13295	....	....	728	11240	....	....	374	11865	4	70	4	30
Marion	1293	1282	1125	1127	606	7553	....	....	292	7125	....	....	168	4393	26	676	16	86
Morgan	3476	2798	11190	2608	1057	15067	....	....	794	26130	....	....	443	16177	42	760	....	....
Oakland	3682	4266	8840	3136	1317	22275	....	....	1094	35825	13	245	517	19206	19	610	2	126
Osceola	12515	4304	24539	10392	5455	89003	....	....	3711	135690	....	....	1022	42391	448	8986	9	113
Reeve	7775	5408	25844	7119	3658	47504	....	....	2679	95950	....	....	1074	35772	107	2210	19	489
Richland	2394	1948	7735	2349	849	14089	....	....	717	22320	....	....	489	14222	3	120	....	....

Washington, exc. of Hampton	6532	3600	21665	8563	3455	52974			2997	93570			1303	41656	242	5616	21	346
West Fork	3654	2545	5497	2281	1542	20730			1172	36045			484	16853	45	943	7	42
Total	69859	43046	172184	65580	31096	455909			24066	758983	13	245	9532	328679	1600	34545	95	1540

FREMONT COUNTY.

Benton, exc. of towns	6806	16885	32158	6169	393	5819	72	851	5156	170585	21	350	141	5423	195	3590		
Fisher, exc of Farragut	11700	12132	25716	10510	1546	19534	287	5729	6344	121840	30	451	690	20946	210	2862		
Franklin, exc. of Hamburg	12960	18974	35391	6528	816	12217	34	370	9138	143101	12	165	317	8474	811	14534		
Locust Grove	5184	14417	18745	6443	595	9645	32	604	2885	52431	8	102	314	8896	112	2760		
Madison	15474	8776	58100	10415	1329	21259	131	2146	9368	235385	183	1090	754	25932	309	9102		16
Monroe	10285	27466	31213	8894	2350	36622			6250	130726	13	176	807	25712	332	10582	2	
Prairie	6535	12900	20590	6075	850	15759	22	118	3604	104160			288	9250	501	13813	5	56
Riverton, exc. of town	6597	11619	25179	5847	788	15367	165	3251	3706	93275	45	506	235	8546	148	5109	3	40
Ross, exc. of Tabor	11661	17787	53401	19259	1458	23778			8210	210170			961	33157	217	5283		
Scott, exc. of towns	10074	15545	51421	6619	771	13284	60	3000	6296	177354	650	196	266	9794	6	60		
Sidney, exc. of town	12655	31557	61843	11832	1727	27488	14	196	8241	193360	44	195	442	18630	317	6915		
Sidney, town of	209	160	1880	196	13	232			51	1000								
Tabor, town of	475		2890	321	24	370	12	120	225	7155	8		23	620				
Walnut	5292	10614	24496	3931	569	7527	12	240	4371	63443			181	4265	72	1137	2	
Total	115907	198832	443023	103030	13229	206901	841	16625	73845	1703985	1014	3231	5419	179645	3230	75747	12	112

GREENE COUNTY.

Bristol	6943	3813	27012	5606	1898	30682	1	29	1661	94730	5	89	452	14006	54	1395	15	180
Cedar	5333	3077	25270	3406	1372	17875			1733	65250			285	7196	32	558		
Dawson	377	2213	170	341	108	1082			156	5239	1	20	33	701				
Franklin	3984	3238	16090	3692	1352	15001	1	15	1868	66555	4	63	340	9832	75	1801		
Grand Junction, town of	1228	4308	4200	900	146	1671			166	5390			50	895				
Greenbrier	1835	2916	1520	1479	870	10727			774	18985			132	4071	13	176		6
Hardin	5100	3138	14834	4481	1910	20273			1491	52395	44	509	316	7339	162	3727	2	14
Highland	1619	902	6516	1461	592	6686			534	19465	10	100	134	3303	11	225		
Jackson	5133	3432	18350	3604	1984	23800			2051	66547			317	7789	29	1491	5	47
Jefferson, exc. of town	6652	6167	40526	6135	1962	24457			3109	107690	3	60	588	17015	82	2183	4	14
Jefferson, town of	350	275	1520	290	149	2008			180	5930			10	600				
Junction, exc. of Grand Junction	3905	3625	5985	4923	853	24299			1886	61158	47	841	471	14711	99	4732	4	50
Kendrick	7931	4170	37560	5920	2264	30853			2660	84290	1	16	439	11772	20	491	6	103
Scranton, exc. of town	434	1813	5391	1724	766	9945			593	18350			113	3563	21	515		
Scranton, town of	100	60	300	100	70	1016			6	18			8	440				

GREENE COUNTY—CONTINUED.

NAMES OF TOWNSHIPS, TOWNS, AND CITIES.	No. of acres of improved land.	No. of acres of unimproved land.	No. of rods of fence.	No. of acres in cultivation in 1874.	SPRING WHEAT.		WINTER WHEAT.		INDIAN CORN.		RYE.		OATS.		BARLEY.		BUCKWHEAT.	
					Number of acres.	Number of bushels harvested.	Number of acres.	Number of bushels harvested.	Number of acres.	Number of bushels harvested.	Number of acres.	Number of bushels harvested.	Number of acres.	Number of bushels harvested.	Number of acres.	Number of bushels harvested.	Number of acres.	Number of bushels harvested.
Washington	7134	5508	37932	7117	2521	29874	....	....	3181	103235	2	47	500	16597	50	1161	3	15
Willow	1882	1183	385	1144	574	7511	....	....	264	7810	3	30	39	1118	7	95	....	....
Total	59940	49838	243561	52323	19391	257760	2	44	22313	783037	120	1775	4227	120948	655	18550	39	429

GRUNDY COUNTY.

NAMES OF TOWNSHIPS, TOWNS, AND CITIES.	No. of acres of improved land.	No. of acres of unimproved land.	No. of rods of fence.	No. of acres in cultivation in 1874.	Spring wheat: Number of acres.	Spring wheat: Number of bushels harvested.	Winter wheat: Number of acres.	Winter wheat: Number of bushels harvested.	Indian corn: Number of acres.	Indian corn: Number of bushels harvested.	Rye: Number of acres.	Rye: Number of bushels harvested.	Oats: Number of acres.	Oats: Number of bushels harvested.	Barley: Number of acres.	Barley: Number of bushels harvested.	Buckwheat: Number of acres.	Buckwheat: Number of bushels harvested.
Beaver	7040	3409	9318	6326	3680	46277	....	....	2242	77475	18	145	720	23003	389	6810	31	389
Black Hawk	10149	3871	5290	9601	4664	74256	....	....	1952	69600	15	265	627	24035	1057	15630	4	50
Clay	11295	3523	16956	10310	4231	63492	....	....	3085	123530	2	44	798	26731	250	6307	12	142
Colfax	7159	2191	3060	7139	3509	60549	....	....	2476	83770	....	....	527	22936	646	16787	....	....
Fairfield	15851	640	23705	15705	4580	61146	....	....	3411	123455	....	....	1047	34432	297	5226	10	124
Felix	11003	3616	20239	9756	5210	72674	....	....	3655	134920	32	444	654	22594	265	5311	4	53
German	12334	5217	19777	11209	5786	86701	....	....	3162	107590	15	150	1070	39550	952	20982	....	....
Grant	10260	4349	3610	10288	6315	78877	....	....	2622	99682	....	....	964	37542	368	7707	4	60
Lincoln	6071	1835	1935	4388	3164	45802	....	....	1901	72835	....	....	701	22992	477	8508	....	....
Melrose	12287	1505	20262	9870	5235	69532	....	....	4051	161110	135	1930	1047	34908	376	8041	18	139
Palermo	19013	7346	22163	19668	8690	129690	....	....	5336	193516	....	....	1814	59070	539	10373	13	127
Pleasant Valley	13739	3356	7530	10884	6356	92455	....	....	2578	89290	....	....	933	30740	1207	25104	2	24
Shiloh	9888	7068	6685	9964	5964	95156	....	....	3704	145809	....	....	884	23415	1022	15376	....	....
Total	146089	47926	160530	135108	67384	976607	....	....	40175	1482582	217	2978	11786	401948	7845	152162	98	1108

GUTHRIE COUNTY.

Bear Grove	6759	3171	24665	4590	1354	18951	20	350	2321	91280			247	7747	4	127		13
Beaver	6669	2561	24806	5962	2494	41077			3318	194540	4	81	219	8764	9	200		
Cass, exc. of Panora	12599	7933	46816	12200	3851	52444	2	10	5721	229710	19	277	336	26251	99	2312	13	197
Center	6923	3504	26681	6657	2361	30373			3349	141440			363	11640	54	1468		
Dodge	2266	1711	5950	1901	749	11274			864	32315	2	22	148	5292	56	1680		
Grant	2746	1858	7850	2916	1640	20275			1172	39375			155	4465	9	261		7
Highland	2986	2840	11690	2882	1316	16827			1456	57025			182	6216			2	36
Jackson	7662	6791	46236	7277	2536	35851			3902	177644			345	11847	6	150	6	136
Orange	3092	1149	13250	3416	1098	17370			1373	48440			125	3869				7
Panora, town of	927	359	44	872	133	1707			178	5335			18	371				
Penn	5223	3476	24220	5318	1970	31821			2837	133480			315	10582	25	781	6	67
Richland	6196	4306	12600	5019	1243	17204			2600	92185	11	162	456	15108	1119	2437	2	17
Thompson	5776	2029	10880	3178	1621	25298			2057	83705	12	260	311	10710	20	560	1	2
Union	4156	2591	45800	3647	1106	15322			2323	106340			194	7314	4	70		6
Valley	6649	3841	31760	5582	1947	29887			2851	136425			332	11509	12	300		
Victory	6630	2250	27914	5475	2070	28393			2580	105895			399	11820	81	1458	2	
Total	87259	47220	331162	76892	27489	393574	22	360	38902	1669134	48	802	4145	153505	498	11804	32	488

HAMILTON COUNTY.

Blairsburg	2835	3560	2320	3463	1519	20536			1310	41325	32	412	481	14598	62	1290	4	25
Boone	12597	4290	42038	8702	3241	52371			3294	111996	8	133	892	33682	158	1668	52	310
Cass	8966	1367	30998	5752	2404	35418			2244	72055	4	65	626	19363	71	1377	4	34
Clear Lake	2895	2094	9410	2162	1200	16574			802	24560			241	7839	49	1063		
Ellsworth	3557	3303	14826	2147	931	13264			1045	37750			236	7728	27	557	1	13
Fremont	3999	3243	14200	704	1888	26606			1595	57270			435	14984	15	358	1	20
Hamilton	5192	3942	32310	4592	1868	26648			1668	65845			472	14050	46	885	8	102
Lyon	3912	1556	8310	3697	1070	16121			1278	41065			359	9977	73	1477	4	40
Marion	6535	7336	40390	6500	2512	34376			3065	107445	7	140	399	14464	93	2053		
Rose Grove	1850	3246	2130	1595	317	3828			733	22070			163	4544	16	420		
Scott	5989	703	19945	7666	1485	13682			1400	24350			296	10898	50	678		
Webster	5639	5295	33129	5070	2241	35258			2007	65000	1	41	508	16135	42	966	5	65
Total	63966	39935	250006	52050	20676	294682			20441	670731	52	791	5108	168262	702	12792	79	609

HANCOCK COUNTY.

Amsterdam	1317	72552	6760	1254	662	8536			315	8300			235	8687	37	434	2	29
Avery	1317	44497	8115	1047	684	12091			429	12642			235	8414	1	18	2	17

HANCOCK COUNTY.—Continued.

Names of townships, towns, and cities.	No. of acres of improved land.	No. of acres of unimproved land.	No. of rods of fence.	No. of acres in cultivation in 1874.	Spring Wheat. Number of acres.	Spring Wheat. Number of bushels harvested.	Winter Wheat. Number of acres.	Winter Wheat. Number of bushels harvested.	Indian Corn. Number of acres.	Indian Corn. Number of bushels harvested.	Rye. Number of acres.	Rye. Number of bushels harvested.	Oats. Number of acres.	Oats. Number of bushels harvested.	Barley. Number of acres.	Barley. Number of bushels harvested.	Buckwheat. Number of acres.	Buckwheat. Number of bushels harvested.
Britt	573	42000	140	257	180	2248	....	....	40	1450	....	....	42	1157	....	....	2	18
Concord	1625	47166	1450	1557	612	7686	....	....	219	5945	....	....	163	5457	22	539	3	60
Crystal	734	36792	3055	621	301	2514	....	....	191	4000	....	....	68	1301	10	110	....	....
Ellington	3939	45711	27208	3421	1995	30455	....	....	653	19347	....	....	430	19030	22	463	15	116
Madison	957	52897	160	848	455	6476	....	....	220	6215	....	....	180	4770	....	....	....	....
Total	10462	341615	46888	9005	4889	70006	....	....	2067	57899	....	....	1353	48816	92	1564	24	240

HARDIN COUNTY.

Names of townships, towns, and cities.	No. of acres of improved land.	No. of acres of unimproved land.	No. of rods of fence.	No. of acres in cultivation in 1874.	Spring Wheat. Number of acres.	Spring Wheat. Number of bushels harvested.	Winter Wheat. Number of acres.	Winter Wheat. Number of bushels harvested.	Indian Corn. Number of acres.	Indian Corn. Number of bushels harvested.	Rye. Number of acres.	Rye. Number of bushels harvested.	Oats. Number of acres.	Oats. Number of bushels harvested.	Barley. Number of acres.	Barley. Number of bushels harvested.	Buckwheat. Number of acres.	Buckwheat. Number of bushels harvested.
Alden	6653	3442	21880	4419	2084	30426	....	....	1648	43586	....	....	707	26978	71	1296	1	10
Buckeye	2263	2235	8632	2278	661	8141	....	....	1045	28550	....	....	501	13619	34	562	3	28
Clay	10605	2429	38180	9372	3665	50268	....	....	3558	133916	4	80	766	27975	461	7346	4	31
Concord	1139	734	80	933	484	5315	....	....	334	9751	....	....	62	1365	33	420	....	....
Eldora, exc. of town	11368	4728	45001	7286	3496	39082	....	....	3793	142060	37	702	780	24786	97	1261	....	....
Eldora, town of	1105	519	5700	892	327	4669	....	....	351	13360	....	....	115	3561	20	500	2	15
Ellis	7541	469	25983	4259	1780	24102	....	....	1823	44945	2	30	704	19060	128	2622	13	186
Etna, exc. of Ackley	12935	2841	35240	9789	4148	44028	....	....	3054	94612	....	....	1011	40047	256	3776	1	22
Grant	2668	1701	3546	2534	1362	16286	....	....	1171	29400	2	15	269	7550	21	224	9	100
Hardin, exc. of Iowa Falls	12272	1211	50345	7474	3214	48889	....	....	3373	114185	25	461	1127	38887	131	2208	7	98
Jackson	14118	1303	50840	8863	2706	33269	....	....	3657	130795	3	40	1319	43117	198	3397	9	159
Pleasant	13790	4026	63360	9861	3168	41058	....	....	4060	123386	9	180	1084	32693	111	2141	4	63
Providence	14858	4240	65474	13007	4929	69278	....	....	6334	235570	26	255	1071	36337	29	387	2	30
Sherman	1779	1276	1172	1836	863	9195	....	....	567	13270	....	....	275	5991	18	320	1	8
Tipton	4378	3571	25925	4284	1467	17698	....	....	1769	46460	24	406	517	13250	125	1999	34	802
Union, exc. of town	11267	5182	57234	10574	4077	55087	....	....	4758	175675	21	276	674	22629	52	1187	14	137

Union, town of	92	23	1670	104	33	460	....	....	9	450	....	....	....	....	....	....	....	....
Total	128831	39030	500262	97765	38454	497251	....	....	41304	157996	147	2445	10982	556945	1785	29646	104	1689

HARRISON COUNTY.

Allen	532	22532	1890	464	239	3463	....	....	340	9950	....	....	15	526	....	....	....	....
Boyer	4552	19198	28957	3567	953	5945	30	1000	2333	112230	....	....	94	2548	....	....	10	110
Calhoun	3978	8443	18341	2420	1027	3275	....	....	1879	75185	....	....	121	1307	....	....	9	110
Cass	2444	20595	13910	1737	518	3876	....	....	905	34385	5	5	200	5685	16	500	1	....
Cincinnati	3937	16264	20370	2442	1322	13438	....	....	2724	102955	....	....	146	4510	1	12	7	70
Clay	2925	14592	16525	2057	542	8517	20	200	1579	55504	....	....	72	1943	....	....	....	....
Douglas	3133	20045	17235	3282	1010	6399	....	....	1565	47367	10	28	178	3377	46	134	11	75
Harrison	4496	18225	25971	4680	2077	12343	....	....	1875	66405	6	120	219	5407	10	50	....	....
Jackson	3995	16736	17955	2249	682	3118	30	....	1339	39325	....	....	49	1079	....	....	9	76
Jefferson	10855	15713	60124	9602	3816	2120	....	....	5815	136290	37	82	562	2857	....	....	50	473
La Grange	3511	17842	23417	2813	1035	4307	4	....	2103	81340	....	....	355	4769	....	108	9	47
Lincoln	1476	19860	6210	1393	454	4701	....	....	704	31550	....	....	92	2912	....	....	2	15
Little Sioux	5203	16684	27367	3681	1157	6656	....	....	2281	72985	4	63	156	3262	....	....	1	9
Magnolia	6899	23429	41605	6202	1254	10426	....	....	3290	163385	....	5	217	3618	....	42	....	664
Morgan	5648	6978	20927	4007	933	8602	....	....	2336	86095	20	185	105	1898	....	....	....	....
Raglan	4355	11433	23506	2621	601	6294	....	....	2082	86121	2	29	66	2049	....	....	....	....
St. John	12269	12173	57632	8975	1841	12229	....	....	5294	226830	10	200	274	6922	3	50	....	....
Taylor	9412	11461	33390	5913	1860	18696	....	....	2835	123710	2	25	180	5834	4	160	....	....
Union	4032	21145	16871	3077	2024	5824	....	....	1902	46875	....	....	281	6882	....	....	....	....
Washington	1193	24107	3898	1105	603	3472	....	....	539	21755	....	....	80	1760	....	....	....	....
Total	94848	337451	473101	72287	23948	143701	84	1200	44720	1620192	96	742	3462	69140	80	1056	109	1649

HENRY COUNTY.

Baltimore	10754	6447	38142	5917	131	782	1065	12926	2166	84020	20	250	357	7060	....	....	12	153
Canaan	15509	2545	57080	2406	2184	30562	106	1630	7228	316560	136	1655	1248	43732	39	970	20	505
Center, exc. of Mt. Pleasant	17224	3088	119602	6712	963	10015	853	11855	4655	179070	213	2383	832	25464	....	....	11	209
Jackson	11611	8345	103688	8120	873	6452	1154	15785	4317	172325	148	1310	743	21122	8	76	27	498
Jefferson	17653	5030	56473	10498	1205	12432	1204	12124	4196	135063	8	43	891	26496	28	458	11	98
Marion	17801	1811	73144	12915	1283	16413	608	7941	5551	204787	57	773	889	30308	....	817	19	356
Mt. Pleasant, city of	853	....	18539	60	19	165	20	310	19	2334	....	....	33	550	....	....	....	....
New London, exc. of town	19869	2033	104868	18676	2074	23298	463	5443	6945	289059	89	1294	1794	59005	....	....	8	98
New London, town of	....	....	....	....	19	138	....	....	29	1625	4	35	23	760	....	....	....	....
Rome, town of	397	472	1890	367	....	....	....	442	275	10940	28	120	29	429	....	....	....	....
Salem, exc. of town	12299	4120	72654	6634	889	6904	437	3879	4219	157120	115	1210	860	22450	....	....	30	500
Scott	13929	2265	64603	8704	1935	28958	56	834	6056	267270	135	1687	2998	34845	63	1428	38	553

HENRY COUNTY.—Continued.

Names of townships, towns, and cities.	No. of acres of improved land.	No. of acres of unimproved land.	No. of rods of fence.	No. of acres in cultivation in 1874.	Spring wheat. Number of acres.	Spring wheat. Number of bushels harvested.	Winter wheat. Number of acres.	Winter wheat. Number of bushels harvested.	Indian corn. Number of acres.	Indian corn. Number of bushels harvested.	Rye. Number of acres.	Rye. Number of bushels harvested	Oats. Number of acres.	Oats. Number of bushels harvested.	Barley. Number of acres.	Barley. Number of bushels harvested.	Buck-wheat. Number of acres.	Buck-wheat. Number of bushels harvested.
Tippecanoe, exc. of Rome	10522	7778	92499	7397	435	6534	1048	13561	3187	125584	127	1678	626	14554	....	....	8	227
Trenton	13682	6040	94097	9022	286	2449	1967	25942	6280	109618	50	582	819	21821	10	139	8	217
Wayne	19977	275	93841	13403	2713	35127	60	558	7549	360295	54	715	1351	49625	29	640	22	250
Total	182080	50249	992030	110831	15026	180229	9041	113203	62672	2415670	1184	13735	13393	358221	177	4528	214	3664

HOWARD COUNTY.

Names of townships, towns, and cities.	No. of acres of improved land.	No. of acres of unimproved land.	No. of rods of fence.	No. of acres in cultivation in 1874.	Spring wheat. Number of acres.	Spring wheat. Number of bushels harvested.	Winter wheat. Number of acres.	Winter wheat. Number of bushels harvested.	Indian corn. Number of acres.	Indian corn. Number of bushels harvested.	Rye. Number of acres.	Rye. Number of bushels harvested	Oats. Number of acres.	Oats. Number of bushels harvested.	Barley. Number of acres.	Barley. Number of bushels harvested.	Buck-wheat. Number of acres.	Buck-wheat. Number of bushels harvested.
Albion	11026	7676	38930	9745	5324	95984	....	....	1058	37476	....	....	959	33670	93	2119	18	371
Afton	15376	18575	39765	6718	3905	66777	....	....	2490	56482	....	....	1444	48614	105	8701	....	....
Chester	8717	10117	11540	2942	1643	26200	....	....	421	14850	....	....	589	18521	84	1508	20	217
Forest City	12228	5763	26800	7181	4751	71560	....	....	658	24455	4	100	965	33543	170	3795	6	95
Howard	5209	28637	20355	3688	2205	35688	....	....	532	18691	....	....	583	22407	8	151	2	10
Howard Center	8683	12920	2275	4804	3190	43878	....	....	688	24730	....	....	907	26722	133	2128	10	164
Jamestown	6797	15833	13698	3251	1781	29803	....	....	483	17860	....	....	680	25642	289	7988	....	....
New Oregon	18060	15749	43510	8185	3972	62102	....	....	1517	37820	....	....	1251	44093	119	3592	11	47
Oak Dale	6071	12525	15264	2785	1804	27753	....	....	337	10238	....	....	448	18270	39	737	15	236
Paris	9019	13471	24000	5363	3303	54569	....	....	762	29065	....	....	1028	27976	86	1641	4	42
Saratoga	5618	16310	8697	1846	934	13920	....	....	208	7180	....	....	328	12834	48	1032	1	15
Vernon Springs, exc. of Cresco	9019	13471	24000	5363	3303	54569	....	....	762	29065	....	....	1028	27976	31	655	5	54
Total	115823	171048	278844	61871	36115	582803	....	....	9916	307912	4	100	10210	340268	1205	34047	92	1251

13

HUMBOLDT COUNTY.

Avery	1961	2500	1127	1838	784	1628	....	....	787	21690	4	27	226	3652	....	....	....	....
Dakota	2574	2231	6045	2355	1010	13404	....	....	742	23751	2	35	258	7486	72	1329	6	38
Delano	2805	3252	250	2691	1439	7954	....	....	838	23470	....	....	335	5450	....	....	....	....
Grove	3878	4752	7585	3779	1447	12017	....	....	1523	51160	....	....	588	14925	13	280	....	....
Humboldt	3463	4955	7460	3036	1568	9295	....	....	1074	29185	....	....	459	10054	25	374	....	....
Humboldt, town of	632	469	296	465	322	1698	....	....	371	12285	....	....	105	1698	....	....	....	....
Lake	765	1015	940	725	274	2807	....	....	264	7300	....	....	125	2620	....	....	....	....
Norway	735	3348	....	1559	729	14744	....	....	286	8300	....	....	121	4202	6	150	....	....
Rutland	2585	2478	1274	2307	939	34616	....	....	922	27845	10	80	393	5630	23	323	76	466
Springvale	2665	3619	10590	2494	1161	5723	....	....	957	28770	2	18	426	7144	21	58	....	8
Vernon	4579	4842	4614	3688	1588	11873	....	....	1223	32160	....	....	647	10756	60	477	....	....
Wac usta	1231	2159	1360	1188	349	1227	....	....	653	18965	....	....	164	4617	....	....	....	....
Weaver	1241	1286	....	887	436	3916	....	....	358	12500	....	....	127	2710	....	....	....	....
Total	29114	36906	41541	27012	12046	120902	....	....	9998	297381	18	160	3974	90944	220	2991	82	512

IDA COUNTY.

Corwin	2196	3221	320	1610	812	14944	....	....	565	17250			163	6700	24	511	....	....
Douglas	1139	1510	1033	1090	515	6331	....	....	410	11415			50	1369	2	20	1	5
Maple	3101	3017	1866	3101	1384	21133	....	....	1036	71600			213	4975	44	1039	12	25
Silver Creek	856	1746	....	713	397	6407	....	....	290	8200			29	1016	13	155	....	....
Total	7292	9494	3219	6514	3108	48815	....	....	2301	108465			455	14060	83	1725	13	30

IOWA COUNTY.

Amana	4883	13619	30430	3070	647	12400	....	....	615	29525	138	3890	737	26900	415	11890	....	....
Cono	2926	1487	13209	5237	680	9499	....	....	1271	63800	....	....	185	5234	....	150	1	12
Dayton	13671	9345	61373	9265	2714	35428	....	....	4588	215276	21	210	887	26421	316	6016	31	362
English	10530	8865	66349	8234	1866	23414	2	20	4405	185915	47	473	838	25850	....	....	38	713
Fillmore	12371	5667	64441	10511	2553	37439	....	....	4226	158397	20	344	705	18280	85	1894	14	170
Greene	14232	1712	58537	10239	1686	32657	....	....	5118	201350	43	290	751	21610	116	2074	32	442
Hartford, exc. of Victor	11818	3582	49491	11198	4376	35354	....	....	4900	211268	2	18	733	14560	237	3707	6	53
Hilton	14552	1886	48760	10088	4098	65732	....	....	3302	176222	....	....	519	15662	510	10587	....	....
Honey Creek	14923	8981	48925	12758	4945	53133	....	....	4906	165705	12	147	906	18167	201	3538	5	29
Iowa	11410	4943	51545	9784	3383	56493	7	60	2543	158697	47	937	889	21694	199	6932	10	161
Lenox	7193	5768	37940	5719	2450	37729	....	....	2545	104730	14	180	501	13775	88	2031	4	49
Lincoln	8952	2139	32720	4824	1984	23779	....	....	2698	110970	5	45	440	9694	191	2931	4	48
Marengo, exc. of town	10112	4932	52387	7135	2735	44579	....	....	3779	171410	8	68	706	17643	109	3418	12	184

IOWA COUNTY.—Continued.

Names of townships, towns, and cities.	No. of acres of improved land.	No. of acres of unimproved land.	No. of rods of fence.	No. of acres in cultivation in 1874.	Spring Wheat.		Winter Wheat.		Indian Corn.		Rye.		Oats.		Barley.		Buck-Wheat.	
					Number of acres.	Number of bushels harvested.	Number of acres.	Number of bushels harvested.	Number of acres.	Number of bushels harvested.	Number of acres.	Number of bushels harvested.	Number of acres.	Number of bushels harvested.	Number of acres.	Number of bushels harvested.	Number of acres.	Number of bushels harvested.
Marengo, town of	120	70	470	112	151	660	27	1000	57	3450	....	....	4	45	10	100	....	....
Pilot	10076	4079	41095	8613	2855	40013	....	....	3540	146990	10	123	787	20737	296	4655	17	238
Sumner	11726	2596	49588	14790	3275	50206	....	....	3568	150415	30	333	619	19465	520	11693	19	288
Troy	13214	4142	51549	12977	3204	47981	....	....	4723	208380	....	....	706	19371	52	1434	3	35
Victor, town of	395	305	1860	395	130	1535	....	....	168	5450	....	....	34	770	....	....	....	....
Washington	5477	3903	32476	4227	2293	25549	....	....	2207	100000	4	187	276	10496	33	816	15	162
York	12460	1335	42022	9312	2385	36667	....	....	3359	145880	38	452	533	12697	72	1466	6	721
Total	191041	89357	835167	158488	48410	670247	36	1080	62518	2713830	439	7697	11756	319071	3450	75332	217	3018

JACKSON COUNTY.

Names of townships, towns, and cities.	No. of acres of improved land.	No. of acres of unimproved land.	No. of rods of fence.	No. of acres in cultivation in 1874.	Spring Wheat: Number of acres.	Spring Wheat: Number of bushels harvested.	Winter Wheat: Number of acres.	Winter Wheat: Number of bushels harvested.	Indian Corn: Number of acres.	Indian Corn: Number of bushels harvested.	Rye: Number of acres.	Rye: Number of bushels harvested.	Oats: Number of acres.	Oats: Number of bushels harvested.	Barley: Number of acres.	Barley: Number of bushels harvested.	Buckwheat: Number of acres.	Buckwheat: Number of bushels harvested.
Andrew, town of	18	....	1305	....	....	....	....	....	3	160	....	....	6	180	....	....	....	....
Bellevue, exc. of town	9221	12663	94530	8941	3238	42850	....	....	2361	91145	5	95	1629	35484	6	85	6	110
Brandon	5401	12326	60334	4839	715	7985	180	2667	1542	51645	28	207	514	10333	....	....	54	733
Butler	10323	8987	72755	6663	1587	22230	....	....	3482	87195	....	....	1718	30233	3	62	....	....
Fairfield	16825	2007	72132	7133	3276	45946	6	100	3726	111655	4	65	1432	28757	110	2569	65	1009
Farmer's Creek	10730	12000	101266	7453	1613	21779	181	3016	3271	86610	54	621	854	18850	3	50	46	484
Iowa	14044	7728	91637	10264	3313	50670	....	....	4588	175084	1	15	1505	42994	242	5604	63	828
Jackson	11100	7585	68737	10062	3861	33433	....	....	4138	87095	2	15	1899	39092	....	....	49	557
Maquoketa, exc. of city	10399	6995	62932	10399	2281	29796	55	936	3177	97627	56	796	894	20853	58	1257	38	554
Maquoketa, city of	977	446	7368	726	63	701	25	600	241	9115	....	....	28	775	....	....	17	142
Monmouth	13062	4683	73050	6384	1841	21721	....	....	3231	95110	31	372	1099	23831	69	871	20	261
Otter Creek	15116	6799	85067	7401	2342	28358	4	63	2381	89576	6	20	1677	32285	18	292	1	42
Perry, exc. of Andrew	9129	9141	75984	5565	1850	26502	11	231	3013	108725	22	264	1279	32608	4	116	115	1918
Prairie Spring	12507	10121	67285	9408	4607	49843	....	....	2612	76090	....	....	1975	35921	122	1820	2	30
Richland	13124	7043	69654	13124	2956	35985	....	....	3398	86480	....	....	1863	41325	94	1450	6	98
Sabula, town of	7	15	200	7	....	....	....	....	....	5	....	....	....	....	....	....	....	....

South Fork, exc. of Maquoketa	7807	1662	61333	4203	974	10806	18	199	2569	78306	11	136	727	17764	35	656	21	181
Tete Des Morts	9276	10541	81717	8079	3653	45067	....	....	2084	80300	4	49	1801	39580	5	117	3	25
Union, exc. of Sabula	2539	2591	20600	2508	553	10149	....	....	729	24255	40	550	151	6333	11	310	5	110
Van Buren	14102	5924	88069	12673	2500	37544	....	....	4856	165905	....	....	1637	44968	202	3684	27	330
Washington	7583	13144	45147	6569	2292	28635	11	130	2560	63435	8	49	964	18990	48	788	....	....
Total	193290	142401	1301102	142401	43515	550000	491	7942	53962	1665518	272	3254	23652	521156	1030	19731	538	7412

JASPER COUNTY.

Buena Vista	18975	4049	71900	14364	4922	73229	....	....	5718	265663	7	90	838	25294	280	5471	14	195
Clear Creek	14576	8464	69053	9322	2905	38448	....	....	4728	203628	19	357	722	27351	29	794	7	103
Des Moines, exc. of Prairie City	20501	10219	78479	19418	5959	82188	....	....	8018	378030	31	685	1226	48962	132	3090	14	241
Elk Creek	17247	7713	70616	11631	8435	49779	....	....	6963	322195	41	762	951	32683	9	275	5	58
Fairview, exc. of Monroe	23347	10338	121735	17626	6460	95455	....	....	9493	441855	63	1501	1282	46802	72	2205	18	328
Hickory Grove	8629	14000	20688	9547	8908	57561	....	....	2982	117878	6	175	458	17396	100	4504	....	....
Independence	12596	10444	57493	9338	4031	57491	....	....	4132	175220	13	196	745	25806	165	2898	13	173
Jasper City, town of	....	....	....	....	55	725	....	....	50	2650	....	....	11	1000	....	....	....	....
Kellogg, exc. of Jasper City	13951	8449	37979	9872	3850	40718	....	....	4770	211950	7	90	744	24266	116	2202	20	339
Lynn Grove	17909	5831	51465	14931	3244	44996	....	....	6249	289455	66	1297	987	32385	6	132	12	153
Malaka	20835	9000	61185	16428	5715	86859	....	....	6129	301660	....	....	1076	41329	442	11908	5	85
Mariposa	12042	11000	14303	9063	5882	76232	....	....	2010	161750	....	....	718	24217	452	10085	1	18
Monroe, town of	47	8	320	7	5	60	....	....	41	1700	....	....	1	50	....	....	....	....
Mound Prairie	12948	5612	37050	9571	3078	42883	....	....	4908	214880	58	1000	887	31270	219	4551	10	124
Newton, exc. of city	7890	8923	31532	6311	2745	41872	....	....	3196	144855	....	....	464	13944	159	2240	3	34
Palo Alto	13251	9149	54137	10117	3095	44362	....	....	5194	238200	11	250	636	20534	61	1379	....	11
Poweshiek	13547	9493	62852	10617	5194	46894	....	....	5455	207880	29	610	901	29478	28	664	11	152
Richland	12324	10916	47087	9752	3954	57615	....	....	5346	242975	....	....	781	24285	386	8970	8	121
Rock Creek	9450	13500	33362	6861	2939	45694	....	....	2909	118095	14	280	509	15566	75	1604	4	113
Sherman	14958	12562	56856	11430	4725	64339	....	....	5868	217595	12	150	623	21003	172	4923	27	425
Washington	13858	10082	40115	10743	4225	59770	....	....	6058	267775	33	698	707	28618	86	2325	7	138
Total	278881	179752	1018207	216949	79926	1107170	....	....	100217	4525889	411	8141	15267	532239	2989	70220	179	2811

JEFFERSON COUNTY.

Batavia, town of	5	....	112	1	2	....	....	....	....	....	....	....	....	....	....	....	....	....
Black Hawk	18018	1884	68565	14810	1929	21244	56	546	5522	26802	220	2869	1881	65588	....	....	43	812
Buchanan	16872	5504	110465	14605	1246	11303	496	4545	5441	180415	89	861	1704	55310	....	....	41	648
Cedar	12103	10398	73630	4915	755	6704	391	4801	2933	88335	147	1967	784	19904	15	250	20	372
Des Moines	14697	3040	106958	9712	1936	22257	107	1158	5725	187095	196	2143	1577	58274	....	....	41	640
Fairfield, exc. of city	18039	3956	105034	10584	1026	11225	151	3071	4591	162095	208	2631	1330	45356	22	340	28	635
Liberty	11650	3601	79809	6842	1498	14985	316	3195	4046	147855	124	1640	935	30030	....	....	42	465
Lockridge	12473	7197	112435	7644	907	7866	1518	16316	4773	177500	369	6828	929	24920	8	222	15	409

JEFFERSON COUNTY—Continued.

Names of townships, towns, and cities.	No. of acres of improved land.	No. of acres of unimproved land.	No. of rods of fence.	No. of acres in cultivation in 1874.	Spring wheat: Number of acres.	Spring wheat: Number of bushels harvested.	Winter wheat: Number of acres.	Winter wheat: Number of bushels harvested.	Indian corn: Number of acres.	Indian corn: Number of bushels harvested.	Rye: Number of acres.	Rye: Number of bushels harvested.	Oats: Number of acres.	Oats: Number of bushels harvested.	Barley: Number of acres.	Barley: Number of bushels harvested.	Buckwheat: Number of acres.	Buckwheat: Number of bushels harvested.
Locust Grove	11991	7184	113345	10874	1185	12226	177	2008	4401	157565	93	939	944	30138	....	....	15	243
Penn	15397	4008	105022	12179	1628	18070	1118	9478	3933	132661	47	435	935	27520	5	64	32	584
Polk	16091	3003	75333	14997	1968	20815	10	164	5762	204626	142	1178	1401	45412	9	203	11	189
Round Prairie	9716	7784	80363	10296	1058	8393	538	6457	4058	136996	313	3906	844	24292	10	264	23	553
Walnut, exc. of Batavia	10337	9420	99513	8131	1099	9716	1314	15000	3876	93565	212	1935	741	19384	11	208	32	571
Total	167389	66979	1130584	125590	16237	164904	6192	66739	55061	1695510	2160	27332	14005	446128	80	1551	343	6121

JOHNSON COUNTY.

Names of townships, towns, and cities.	No. of acres of improved land.	No. of acres of unimproved land.	No. of rods of fence.	No. of acres in cultivation in 1874.	Spring wheat: Number of acres.	Spring wheat: Number of bushels harvested.	Winter wheat: Number of acres.	Winter wheat: Number of bushels harvested.	Indian corn: Number of acres.	Indian corn: Number of bushels harvested.	Rye: Number of acres.	Rye: Number of bushels harvested.	Oats: Number of acres.	Oats: Number of bushels harvested.	Barley: Number of acres.	Barley: Number of bushels harvested.	Buckwheat: Number of acres.	Buckwheat: Number of bushels harvested.
Additions to Iowa City	181	13	4314	32	7	110	....	....	24	1040	5	60	6	165	....	....	....	....
Big Grove	15155	1762	69862	7380	1994	29522	21	279	4072	155105	56	690	1303	37251	11	210	13	195
Cedar	14350	2648	87973	9363	2354	33608	15	58	4879	175388	72	2117	963	31934	10	41	42	328
Clear Creek	10062	4618	47702	7045	1470	29692	....	....	3677	153471	11	118	500	16565	5	100	2	31
Coralville, town of	248	....	960	40	....	....	....	....	10	800	2	120	....	....	....	....	....	....
Fremont	13564	8131	41902	12125	3067	48776	....	....	5126	201030	217	2085	1298	37393	681	14300	7	173
Graham	15392	1770	84657	13527	2221	36047	....	....	4311	171212	21	274	914	29849	75	1459	7	174
Hardin	14467	2822	47258	10199	2384	36491	10	175	4138	187295	47	410	597	16815	8	200	4	73
Jefferson	8375	3157	40333	6819	3183	39122	....	....	2508	90666	154	1818	607	13266	....	....	2	19
Liberty	9964	3248	44911	7592	2132	27348	....	....	3766	119315	92	907	947	22940	183	3736	4	80
Lincoln	11392	2283	42329	12043	2250	36880	....	....	2606	139635	122	1412	848	27664	810	17468	8	124
Lucas, exc. of Iowa City and additions, and Coralville	12893	7387	82839	6709	1442	23176	8	100	3759	145515	97	1268	869	27221	24	550	3	50
Madison	11501	1618	47600	14327	2150	31760	3	55	3853	183250	83	1801	804	23827	7	145	1	24
Monroe	10765	2228	61326	8144	4016	35765	....	....	3489	140660	94	1309	714	19386	38	1093	2	23
Newport	3585	2717	39465	2923	801	12270	....	....	1309	51706	44	620	400	9637	3	100	....	115
Oxford	12889	7741	65418	12415	3724	61853	....	....	5022	197683	38	619	887	23021	43	871	4	116
Penn	6207	1143	39043	6167	1209	14352	....	....	2296	103561	30	166	628	18377	....	....	9	85

Pleasant Valley	10730	934	40294	6832	949	14885	....	....	3240	151662	50	589	1041	29347	93	1916	2	21
Scott	15289	4334	81400	13725	2568	35050	....	....	5178	217915	44	567	1443	39079	227	4862	11	118
Sharon	15421	5955	105997	15481	2899	43369	29	450	5034	206019	154	1924	1192	40266	213	5029	4	65
Union	14699	2861	76608	7173	2407	37913	....	....	4485	171530	17	136	815	26599	129	3270	1	10
Washington	13892	3887	65560	12958	2079	38790	14	157	4360	193720	56	737	984	31592	63	1330	22	315
Total	241021	71257	1217751	193019	45306	666779	100	1274	77142	3158178	1506	19747	17760	522197	2623	56680	148	2139

JONES COUNTY.

Cass	14914	3264	62872	9857	3625	42739	20	241	4348	110103	4	39	1183	25982	44	885	22	237
Castle Grove	16461	857	47090	6766	2359	27855	....	....	3341	98995	....	....	1478	37184	42	757	....	....
Clay	9734	5642	63833	5716	1041	14299	....	....	3353	100020	11	141	852	21965	6	142	2	38
Fairview	8999	2452	62902	5013	722	10408	1	18	3300	116025	....	....	812	21933	....	....	19	172
Greenfield	19351	252	105105	16656	2632	37051	....	....	6120	241360	29	526	1463	45366	1	12	13	240
Hale	15350	3900	58302	10173	3013	38899	....	....	5256	155335	15	133	1125	30090	252	5661	36	432
Jackson	12489	3260	47825	9312	2660	31381	....	....	2646	131966	....	....	1133	26496	25	628	66	167
Madison	12316	1642	43327	6585	1797	28514	....	....	3546	115900	7	116	759	22943	100	2682	12	183
Monticello, exc. of town	11801	5206	75964	7392	1940	21318	....	....	3788	89986	10	117	1308	27069	8	117	4	56
Monticello, town of	116	25	1090	191	237	2520	....	....	60	1650	....	....	41	1141	10	260	....	....
Oxford	13668	4882	63059	8935	3033	33622	....	....	4733	111130	24	303	945	23040	82	1740	16	210
Richland	8973	7491	67437	8558	1495	21040	....	....	2881	81855	....	....	1079	27038	4	100	....	....
Rome	13808	2933	50547	9436	1913	27031	....	....	4659	173560	21	390	1131	28772	96	2130	19	362
Scotch Grove	14962	4148	82864	7780	1951	25192	10	150	4203	20833	4	40	1281	37510	24	274	10	118
Washington	11332	9011	67390	11131	1731	20299	....	....	4480	131920	....	....	1267	24933	....	....	....	....
Wayne	17937	3831	89677	10352	4413	63154	....	....	4716	112251	9	214	1396	41717	46	709	8	216
Wyoming	6696	4502	71611	6831	1528	17156	....	....	3993	116645	13	183	1007	21645	57	1139	94	530
Total	208907	63298	1060896	140684	36090	462478	31	409	65423	1909534	147	2202	18260	464824	797	17236	321	2961

KEOKUK COUNTY.

Adams	12727	2855	55967	8322	2400	35134	....	....	4955	220375	25	260	1073	32393	235	4962	20	286
Benton	15876	6107	67137	4677	1926	19710	2	16	5747	248070	143	1315	1273	34509	10	300	10	195
Clear Creek	12974	8476	63871	12555	2331	25126	....	....	5114	182980	94	944	1054	30119	67	1518	8	190
English River	10680	5105	58286	7326	1571	17835	2	20	4064	164400	35	530	1083	30413	31	438	29	509
German	17535	11265	99953	10800	3631	25144	....	....	6374	257375	118	1349	1343	34104	101	1555	14	319
Jackson	12120	2363	56730	8345	1744	16550	40	402	4555	325820	105	1273	957	17624	17	140	20	420
Keota, town of	38	....	140	38	....	....	....	....	8	480	....	....	....	....	....	....	....	....
Lafayette, exc. of Keota	16078	6251	41806	16065	2839	39799	14	152	5860	266962	54	684	1194	43103	466	9060	14	333
Lancaster	20280	5849	88605	12667	2537	27843	16	113	5646	260390	111	1015	1165	31795	22	167	31	704
Liberty	14997	3989	60535	10674	3435	44222	....	....	4943	219888	31	309	945	30618	85	1351	33	400
Prairie	13166	3286	34819	10585	2276	28602	....	....	4715	218392	50	582	1030	29957	154	2884	25	306
Richland, exc. of town	9239	6788	77926	6999	1268	14363	64	559	3848	132880	48	555	660	20116	13	257	6	83

KEOKUK COUNTY.—Continued.

NAMES OF TOWNSHIPS, TOWNS, AND CITIES.	No. of acres of improved land.	No. of acres of unimproved land.	No. of rods of fence.	No. of acres in cultivation in 1874.	SPRING WHEAT.		WINTER WHEAT.		INDIAN CORN.		RYE.		OATS.		BARLEY.		BUCK-WHEAT.	
					Number of acres.	Number of bushels harvested.	Number of acres.	Number of bushels harvested.	Number of acres.	Number of bushels harvested.	Number of acres.	Number of bushels harvested.	Number of acres.	Number of bushels harvested.	Number of acres.	Number of bushels harvested.	Number of acres.	Number of bushels harvested.
Richland, town of	1187	712	14681	995	148	1635	2	14	492	18125	....	....	94	3009	....	....	1	7
Sigourney, exc. of town	7105	2950	41810	4967	830	7046	....	....	1784	85915	22	315	432	10714	1	27	7	128
Steady Run	14039	6196	45547	13159	1500	16912	5	66	4584	193510	44	424	1175	33822	72	1113	6	142
Van Buren	9239	7491	52211	7858	1478	12776	....	....	3919	176330	23	297	860	22397	44	570	6	96
Warren	8430	11547	38525	5891	1536	15364	3	21	4577	180420	44	573	477	18733	....	....	12	165
Washington	12415	7769	51685	7758	1828	20467	....	....	4512	174970	77	720	777	24177	62	1132	4	115
Total	208125	98999	950234	149672	33278	368528	148	1363	75697	3327282	1024	11145	15582	447603	1380	25474	246	4398

KOSSUTH COUNTY.

NAMES OF TOWNSHIPS, TOWNS, AND CITIES.	No. of acres of improved land.	No. of acres of unimproved land.	No. of rods of fence.	No. of acres in cultivation in 1874.	Spring wheat: Number of acres.	Spring wheat: Number of bushels harvested.	Winter wheat: Number of acres.	Winter wheat: Number of bushels harvested.	Indian corn: Number of acres.	Indian corn: Number of bushels harvested.	Rye: Number of acres.	Rye: Number of bushels harvested.	Oats: Number of acres.	Oats: Number of bushels harvested.	Barley: Number of acres.	Barley: Number of bushels harvested.	Buckwheat: Number of acres.	Buckwheat: Number of bushels harvested.
Algona, exc of town	4779	7803	8510	4347	2030	735	....	....	1355	14126	....	....	1033	4863	25	....	33	401
Algona, town of	3479	9439	5476	2397	973	355	140	....	856	10785	....	....	450	1311	35	....	52	566
Cresco	5474	5447	4510	5789	2742	4871	....	....	1684	26120	20	13	881	8110	11	....	27	361
Fenton	1167	1477	260	1097	469	....	....	....	606	1502	....	....	220	25	3	....	7	10
Greenwood	1878	5394	816	1633	565	57	....	....	715	5416	....	....	300	653	....	....	23	127
Irvington	5288	7663	12310	3990	2288	5234	....	....	1837	33610	5	25	738	5822	14	....	10	78
Lotts Creek	1866	1330	730	1452	498	217	....	....	653	5022	....	....	476	1237	30	14	24	212
Portland	5771	7637	9517	6490	464	502	....	....	1559	15451	....	....	826	3655	10	75	....	....
Wesley	1848	2605	380	1639	768	1168	....	....	516	7745	....	....	219	2181	....	....	....	....
Total	31550	48793	42509	28834	10796	13138	140	....	9780	119777	25	38	5141	27857	158	89	176	1745

LEE COUNTY.

Cedar	18161	1788	56557	16344	1345	11536	720	15231	6642	265265	115	2043	1332	38337	77	873	11	131
Charleston	9468	7765	64928	8464	666	3122	1172	14252	3557	115038	452	4794	985	21742	80	1179	6	75
Denmark	6973	4710	17012	5333	390	2780	776	10968	2056	81692	26	453	407	10522	20	400	18	159
Des Moines	14499	6689	75843	8961	93	488	550	8304	4040	129885	309	2712	799	10674	......	......	29	299
Franklin	14639	1214	23720	11917	1300	8334	1985	27027	4819	166600	453	5743	1281	30590	422	6717	2	37
Green Bay	7197	6532	49915	6953	471	4068	678	11226	3308	156490	155	2124	386	9551	......	......	11	126
Harrison	19088	4187	76075	12222	937	5775	591	9165	4441	157007	288	3767	940	25237	94	1390	34	632
Jackson, exc. of Keokuk	5682	5402	29452	3865	41	100	602	6967	2605	91075	206	1479	341	4682	......	......	8	142
Jefferson	11061	5659	59102	9779	537	2319	2070	20954	4260	135419	542	4947	484	7668	8	76	20	337
Keokuk, city of	431	177	2180	161	20	......	10	83	124	4290	7	70	48	1430	......	......	......	......
Madison, exc. of Fort Madison	1652	392	11875	1540	84	574	214	3204	619	22090	60	550	29	401	......	......	9	174
Marion	17042	4183	63191	9047	1672	14441	697	7883	5893	307035	158	1522	1013	32555	56	1010	9	165
Montrose, exc. of town	12842	4859	59937	9472	598	1500	1479	16272	3629	112390	137	1804	579	9682	17	1?7	41	9
Pleasant Ridge	14934	4860	38220	7562	1053	7964	1005	13678	4258	141410	64	750	1046	32038	25	490	18	271
Van Buren	8469	4164	46355	4590	208	907	456	5094	2509	75000	272	2950	604	14593	......	......	32	497
Washington	13212	9319	91014	7452	618	3743	1209	14572	3966	139640	207	2120	857	18268	2	20	25	320
West Point, exc. of town	8482	6750	63855	9877	821	4813	1186	15527	3104	89450	454	4522	682	10999	42	336	32	434
West Point, town of	......	42	......	41	......	160	......	......	33	630	3	50	4	100	......	......	......	......
Total	183832	78692	829231	133580	10854	72624	15400	200407	59863	2190306	3908	42400	11817	279069	843	12628	305	3808

LINN COUNTY.

Bertram	6636	6832	49646	4256	1096	13562	......	......	2894	94658	38	321	437	9026	......	......	10	88
Boulder	15749	2381	64449	11033	3928	48232	......	......	4211	121843	3	32	1294	32153	174	3104	20	210
Brown	16107	2761	81882	11658	1261	14642	......	......	4408	192205	22	8	2021	38345	18	336	22	268
Buffalo	4577	1152	42838	4214	1270	16263	......	......	2358	80085	1	10	425	9000	28	625	9	93
Cedar Rapids, city of	......	......	......	......	......	......	......	......	8	356	......	......	......	......	......	......	......	......
Clinton	15766	1393	68447	10360	3978	50003	......	......	7272	202795	4	42	1127	28717	91	1591	11	55
College, exc. of Western	15034	457	79992	11049	4495	60394	......	......	4889	192980	94	1122	1173	32014	103	1938	3	33
Fairfax	20482	866	79067	10664	4401	63042	......	......	6363	270059	87	575	1350	38634	9	145	2	44
Fayette	9627	632	36603	6739	2089	25306	......	......	3341	130635	2	20	454	11750	9	130	25	234
Franklin, exc. of towns of Mount Vernon and Lisbon	15114	3912	87869	7770	1995	29037	9	131	4511	163565	109	1135	1147	34516	16	200	9	161
Grant	14377	602	57105	8749	3343	41069	......	......	3714	124678	37	522	1174	26168	122	2460	44	495
Jackson	11873	793	63632	7073	2033	24180	......	......	3593	203395	......	......	1193	37189	6	140	22	222
Linn	18082	4693	90281	8519	1738	22568	......	......	5202	213280	54	553	1338	37375	......	......	6	79
Lisbon, town of	175	110	610	35	20	250	......	......	40	1500	......	......	8	250	......	......	......	......
Maine	20352	5525	87727	10924	2864	36388	......	......	6002	211055	......	......	1803	48196	168	3047	22	379
Marion, exc. of city	32659	1471	176889	19166	4735	61736	......	......	11491	430408	......	......	2556	61023	215	4735	35	545
Marion, city of	59	25	380	40	......		......	......	22	1150	......	......	......	......	......	......	......	......
Monroe	10538	4574	59655	5406	1495	17826	......	......	3383	125605	4	30	540	13103	1	8	6	98
Mount Vernon, town of	753	190	5435	426	88	1325	......	......	213	8593	7	70	63	1155	20	600	1	18

LINN COUNTY.—Continued.

Names of townships, towns, and cities.	No. of acres of improved land.	No. of acres of unimproved land.	No. of rods of fence.	No. of acres in cultivation in 1874.	Spring Wheat. Number of acres.	Spring Wheat. Number of bushels harvested.	Winter Wheat. Number of acres.	Winter Wheat. Number of bushels harvested.	Indian Corn. Number of acres.	Indian Corn. Number of bushels harvested.	Rye. Number of acres.	Rye. Number of bushels harvested.	Oats. Number of acres.	Oats. Number of bushels harvested.	Barley. Number of acres.	Barley. Number of bushels harvested.	Buckwheat. Number of acres.	Buckwheat. Number of bushels harvested.
Otter Creek	10732	5524	70436	9994	3140	42176	....	....	4584	172283	29	437	1009	32262	84	1873	21	341
Putnam	10829	6858	54803	7220	2443	23772	....	4	2983	109850	86	1000	1117	29210	7	117	5	69
Rapids, exc. of Cedar Rapids	8303	5956	62984	4779	742	8440	3	25	2651	106865	72	1238	674	16860	....	....	36	447
Spring Grove	10619	1300	36370	7640	3150	32976	....	....	3273	111105	....	....	851	23360	104	1702	10	94
Washington	11276	4049	53306	6703	1605	19658	....	....	3808	149605	49	1038	795	22020	5	112	39	631
Western, town of	1414	584	8976	1238	269	3752	....	....	559	21370	5	60	121	3302	2	20	....	8
Total	281118	62649	1419383	175655	52178	656597	12	160	91773	3439923	703	8213	22670	585648	1182	22883	358	4612

LOUISA COUNTY.

Names of townships, towns, and cities.	No. of acres of improved land.	No. of acres of unimproved land.	No. of rods of fence.	No. of acres in cultivation in 1874.	Spring Wheat. Number of acres.	Spring Wheat. Number of bushels harvested.	Winter Wheat. Number of acres.	Winter Wheat. Number of bushels harvested.	Indian Corn. Number of acres.	Indian Corn. Number of bushels harvested.	Rye. Number of acres.	Rye. Number of bushels harvested.	Oats. Number of acres.	Oats. Number of bushels harvested.	Barley. Number of acres.	Barley. Number of bushels harvested.	Buckwheat. Number of acres.	Buckwheat. Number of bushels harvested.
Columbus City, exc. of Columbus City and Columbus Junction	22627	1584	116779	11610	2493	23147	24	199	7609	276585	39	293	1651	37300	3	35	15	336
Columbus City, town of	275	58	900	235	37	249	....	....	173	6925	....	....	57	1270	....	....	....	....
Columbus Junction, town of	100	170	1090	97	4185	....	....	....	84	....	....	....	....	....	....	....	....	....
Concord, exc. of Fredonia	10569	2115	58831	6120	1146	11996	....	....	3744	131023	365	2952	325	7816	....	....	7	124
Eliot	4783	2214	14743	2803	258	2276	250	3242	2036	87735	6	67	154	3259	....	....	6	35
Elm Grove	12087	1580	21645	6560	667	20479	....	4	785	230675	....	....	654	19819	27	683	10	122
Fredonia, town of	771	108	3635	615	77	690	....	....	386	11760	62	920	7	110	....	....	....	....
Grandview	16011	6017	87774	12671	1882	21847	72	421	4674	179606	41	420	514	13284	....	....	9	160
Jefferson	5449	16697	33540	5141	599	8289	565	7778	2999	128785	....	....	243	6026	....	....	5	65
Marshall	12149	449	58236	6215	1475	20137	....	....	3129	178995	44	422	587	18915	14	275	14	233
Morning Sun, exc. of town	13244	4279	63570	11349	1892	25350	35	325	5557	253555	17	255	850	26555	13	375	29	343
Oakland	9184	2521	27602	6580	1364	14098	....	....	4228	141635	513	4851	397	7079	....	....	8	111
Port Louisa	7636	5884	38766	5756	697	11794	261	2457	2943	107795	243	2330	296	7939	....	....	41	505
Union	11089	3223	49547	9844	1351	11596	6	30	3613	122285	65	450	553	11562	3	43	46	171
Wapello, exc. of town	23483	5799	97442	12820	1533	16599	175	1811	6833	308658	71	626	484	14651	....	....	19	264

Wapello, town of	1550	223	6408	1649	108	1392	....	....	848	18641	....	....	20	170	....	....	....	....
Total	151007	52921	680508	100065	19764	189939	1388	16267	49641	2184658	1466	14586	6792	175755	60	1411	209	2469

LUCAS COUNTY.

Benton	8673	4551	41435	7203	885	9873	....	....	4860	188200	28	334	1370	34881	....	....	22	529
Cedar	7921	4482	46861	6778	921	7697	3	20	3310	156563	46	362	1276	32123	8	140	21	276
Chariton, exc. of city	13335	2920	48190	7971	1020	12418	....	....	4141	160230	46	934	1092	27711	47	450	18	289
English	12447	3957	44987	10865	2057	20803	....	....	4768	190480	10	92	954	21975	22	240	8	114
Jackson	4282	4257	27472	4140	819	11436	....	....	2251	91170	9	123	515	14801	5	125	2	58
Liberty	5963	4389	38470	5574	1115	11065	....	....	3185	119775	....	....	635	18652	86	1342	7	167
Otter Creek	7205	3183	36259	5610	1887	22074	....	....	3460	123930	14	137	783	22125	8	75	3	45
Pleasant	5917	4812	45223	5691	1256	13762	11	83	3003	120370	....	....	484	11011	25	715	21	387
Union	9559	5533	94262	8348	865	8972	12	140	3533	138315	85	1218	1536	44007	21	465	3	72
Warren	14885	4907	55870	10314	1398	14455	5	86	6606	286083	107	1193	1567	51353	13	215	16	255
Washington	8275	12552	37660	8276	978	10977	....	....	4532	188659	34	520	1304	38923	....	....	20	307
White Breast	10490	4214	46538	8087	953	10055	....	....	3373	138755	19	219	858	24602	....	....	9	175
Total	108952	59757	563227	88857	13954	153587	31	329	47022	1902530	398	5132	12374	342164	235	3767	150	2674

LYON COUNTY.

Dale	3533	47814	....	3021	1830	14387	....	....	746	1523	....	....	187	2151	15	287	1	35
Doon	2789	77793	890	2150	1092	11008	....	54	846	3422	....	....	2193	349	72	1370	2	....
Grant	1060	51121	....	1060	628	4669	....	....	233	796	....	....	40	125	38	500	....	....
Larchwood	1050	50397	200	787	517	6094	....	....	118	886	....	....	114	2891	6	180	....	....
Lyon	5440	45703	2420	3880	3030	30234	....	....	602	2269	....	....	939	7392	19	329	3	....
Rock	2000	46013	40	1868	1035	10350	....	....	100	1500	....	....	54	1006	....	....	....	....
Total	15872	318841	3550	12766	8132	76742	....	54	2645	10396	....	....	3477	13114	150	2666	6	35

MADISON COUNTY.

Crawford	6986	14364	64065	7520	2199	59525	....	....	4449	181695	....	....	462	14506	8	200	6	103
Douglas	12925	9519	60106	11812	3357	53187	....	....	5870	260660	....	....	664	24415	32	800	3	24
Grand River	7883	9248	46229	6350	1983	29702	....	....	3465	150790	16	292	519	18084	23	561	1	9
Jackson	10383	10907	34127	8740	3364	44994	....	....	4089	181730	....	....	489	16952	197	5080	1	21
Jefferson	15543	7172	60107	10630	3843	62159	....	....	4973	225376	9	146	563	19658	83	2365	4	49
Lee	7355	13737	35882	6450	2293	34905	....	....	3433	112660	....	....	249	7376	22	620	2	39
Lincoln	12413	10285	57555	10304	2237	33885	2	30	4656	210370	....	....	646	21419	....	....	7	75

MADISON COUNTY.—Continued.

NAMES OF TOWNSHIPS, TOWNS, AND CITIES.	No. of acres of improved land.	No. of acres of unimproved land.	No of rods of fence.	No. of acres in cultivation in 1874.	SPRING WHEAT.		WINTER WHEAT.		INDIAN CORN		RYE.		OATS.		BARLEY.		BUCK-WHEAT.	
					Number of acres.	Number of bushels harvested.	Number of acres.	Number of bushels harvested.	Number of acres.	Number of bushels harvested.	Number of acres.	Number of bushels harvested.	Number of acres.	Number of bushels harvested.	Number of acres.	Number of bushels harvested.	Number of acres.	Number of bushels harvested.
Madison, exc. of Earlham	13566	8965	53306	10724	3119	56596	......	......	5409	249471	......	......	606	18589	101	2891	1	11
Monroe	6555	16389	37482	6299	1496	23413	......	......	3468	142870	2	21	550	15651	......	......	......	......
Ohio	9058	12650	45355	6755	1509	25335	7	100	3704	149050	20	414	693	22324	105	2423	16	173
Penn	14761	6948	43177	15385	3182	76688	......	......	6476	263243	78	1728	591	24341	288	9301	3	30
Scott	11561	11367	68117	9999	2537	39312	10	176	5484	253818	......	......	674	22586	5	150	4	33
South	7356	14014	52190	6430	1483	18134	......	......	3451	141180	......	......	539	15646	......	......	1	16
Union	9290	13532	66740	8783	2092	27951	6	178	4707	187465	9	137	567	18054	6	84	8	148
Walnut	9732	13296	29157	5560	1063	15852	......	......	3454	117397	......	......	505	10179	13	244	2	43
Webster	6546	16316	28950	6173	1785	26521	......	......	2390	124957	8	156	416	14898	63	1232	1	12
Winterset, city of	105	......	860	65	11	155	......	......	16	900	......	......	10	425	......	......	......	......
Total	161198	188709	783405	137979	37553	628314	25	484	69494	2953630	142	2894	8743	285103	946	25951	60	786

MAHASKA COUNTY.

NAMES OF TOWNSHIPS, TOWNS, AND CITIES.	No. of acres of improved land.	No. of acres of unimproved land.	No of rods of fence.	No. of acres in cultivation in 1874.	Spring wheat: Number of acres.	Spring wheat: Number of bushels harvested.	Winter wheat: Number of acres.	Winter wheat: Number of bushels harvested.	Indian corn: Number of acres.	Indian corn: Number of bushels harvested.	Rye: Number of acres.	Rye: Number of bushels harvested.	Oats: Number of acres.	Oats: Number of bushels harvested.	Barley: Number of acres.	Barley: Number of bushels harvested.	Buckwheat: Number of acres.	Buckwheat: Number of bushels harvested.
Adams	13546	8708	119270	9743	2958	38552	......	......	5698	255250	13	155	963	30834	1	10	9	135
Beacon, town of	88	61	890	10	5	46	......	......	38	1385	......	......	7	155	......	......	......	......
Black Oak	14208	8307	46516	10003	2148	26807	1	3	5844	272910	15	167	1676	41994	3	48	19	301
Cedar	15288	7596	69972	14931	2197	25194	......	......	6130	266935	7	147	1454	40668	3	57	15	260
Des Moines	12874	8895	63228	6992	1438	14140	8	62	4535	204461	33	442	788	18806	16	290	16	302
Harrison	17130	5152	88840	8120	1929	26195	......	......	5610	258010	......	......	1076	27750	32	480	22	388
Jefferson	20464	5539	87790	15489	2810	25321	16	75	6547	295490	64	720	1112	24495	......	......	8	108
Madison	13130	9300	64755	10971	1592	19680	8	46	5790	242685	48	648	1078	35103	14	260	2	53
Monroe	14019	9021	75625	10955	1979	24400	......	......	5177	235565	27	322	1139	32604	20	270	18	295
New Sharon, town of	363	......	1104	204	64	1502	......	......	123	6706	......	......	32	1020	......	......	......	......
Oskaloosa, exc. of Oskaloosa and Beacon	33257	8856	176819	13957	2848	31263	71	1228	8930	400627	75	1029	1969	56465	10	222	29	351
Oskaloosa, city of	55	......	......	55	......	......	......	......	8	400	......	......	......	......	......	......	......	......
Pleasant Grove	10211	11830	38183	6074	2098	24407	......	......	3635	149775	32	416	576	17507	151	2585	22	253

Prairie, exc. of New Sharon	14307	7342	64449	13870	3375	43340	....	....	5870	284725	38	449	1147	37376	31	760	26	219
Richland	14008	8372	77974	....	2423	30804	18	255	5468	243705	38	796	931	24421	....	....	7	86
Scott	14642	4477	71696	10433	1500	17735	22	280	4201	188737	15	169	1072	64327	7	110	14	207
Union	13860	8927	56140	11696	3352	31498	2	17	5092	204736	13	193	874	23127	15	400	16	188
White Oak	10948	10097	77476	7365	1646	14652	59	731	5079	256107	36	334	752	19596	30	325	12	129
Total	232398	122490	1180727	150368	34362	395532	205	2697	83775	3768209	454	5987	16646	496248	333	5817	235	3275
MARION COUNTY.																		
Clay	10907	4431	76443	10727	3118	34797	6	75	5389	242947	29	465	659	17127	19	271	11	171
Dallas	18029	3484	57724	10431	2551	30917	19	92	5172	185815	26	313	896	26928	161	3380	9	197
Franklin	11861	4984	50180	8975	3131	47798	....	....	5310	273575	7	35	660	22182	119	3198	11	144
Indiana	15856	7026	79318	10763	2214	23920	17	129	5233	233248	37	334	1007	27559	116	2294	11	126
Knoxville, exc. of town	28600	9456	107469	18665	7053	92519	....	....	11812	619944	29	606	1548	54320	10	146	24	499
Knoxville, town of	1255	83	9266	760	137	2131	....	....	2334	18640	3	53	72	2594	....	....	....	....
Lake Prairie, exc. of Pella	21747	15400	87490	19885	5223	84495	....	....	11776	546915	39	590	2097	56220	89	1915	13	160
Liberty	7821	6559	68946	7451	1701	20003	110	1203	4049	155194	84	1094	737	13765	1	12	25	397
Perry	2641	2513	23210	2499	860	11877	1	27	1471	63820	13	50	113	3284	....	....	3	54
Pleasant Grove, exc. of Pleasantville	14234	3074	78615	9231	3349	36524	....	....	5808	303500	4	69	294	11011	34	780	....	....
Polk	7388	1572	33977	6064	1765	20794	....	....	3127	139310	2	30	217	6914	....	....	7	75
Red Rock	12922	5752	71243	9353	2987	47592	6	73	3887	162725	14	278	323	9988	10	193	....	....
Summit	15017	5782	88127	14581	3548	54443	....	....	6832	283220	....	....	923	31756	14	249	11	131
Swan	7166	4906	3542	5327	2388	31127	22	533	2813	160610	5	50	212	6069	36	878	1	36
Union	10325	3736	49975	8107	2500	30347	8	80	3871	199660	31	499	318	11989	39	925	1	25
Washington	13900	4021	63205	11395	2605	29379	....	....	5746	245940	33	390	861	22040	58	1209	4	71
Total	199669	82779	948730	153214	45136	598663	189	2212	84630	3835063	356	4856	10937	335746	706	15450	131	2086
MARSHALL COUNTY.																		
Albion, town of	184	49	522	183	70	798	....	....	73	3130	....	....	....	....	....	....	1	6
Bangor	7590	2766	40001	6796	2201	28960	....	....	2820	116619	....	....	518	16302	....	....	2	20
Eden	9836	4046	31030	9293	3375	49870	....	....	3741	152630	61	1100	704	23195	369	7410	7	89
Greencastle	15457	2601	24362	10953	6571	100185	....	....	4471	186125	20	250	1038	36621	191	3939	15	281
Iowa, exc. of Albion	8561	1404	43018	4421	1731	22992	....	....	2209	96090	....	....	401	12538	....	....	....	....
Jefferson	14070	2584	28695	13255	5851	88082	....	....	4174	161712	....	....	1087	34730	227	5823	2	39
Le Grand	16980	3125	63110	11446	5839	93845	....	....	4916	187120	....	....	843	32578	193	4735	5	85
Liberty	13463	1141	39812	12995	3613	48443	....	....	4090	172325	18	205	720	26086	42	1090	16	130
Liscomb, exc. of town	10812	6749	38942	7345	3521	50687	....	....	3143	134615	....	....	609	20978	63	1425	8	61
Liscomb, town of	401	46	2260	370	116	1958	....	....	219	10580	....	....	33	300	25	500	....	....
Logan	9887	3657	13652	8981	4031	60852	10	80	3161	133000	5	89	594	22574	412	9718	1	26
Marietta	17010	2298	55443	10866	4678	65125	....	....	4914	208785	30	572	985	30492	96	1784	25	459
Marion	13376	3347	52231	11959	6196	89898	....	....	4097	162455	....	....	723	25257	119	2373	27	429

MARSHALL COUNTY.—Continued.

NAMES OF TOWNSHIPS, TOWNS, AND CITIES.	No. of acres of improved land.	No. of acres of unimproved land.	No. of rods of fence.	No. of acres in cultivation in 1874.	SPRING WHEAT.		WINTER WHEAT.		INDIAN CORN.		RYE.		OATS.		BARLEY.		BUCK-WHEAT.	
					Number of acres.	Number of bushels harvested.	Number of acres.	Number of bushels harvested.	Number of acres.	Number of bushels harvested.	Number of acres.	Number of bushels harvested.	Number of acres.	Number of bushels harvested.	Number of acres.	Number of bushels harvested.	Number of acres.	Number of bushels harvested.
Marshall, exc. of city	4864	1474	16173	3563	1260	21438	....	....	1471	61890	19	363	432	13851	37	905	1	29
Marshalltown, city of	2360	1985	9571	1826	428	5845	....	....	259	10620	....	....	61	1870	....	....	....	....
Minerva	11951	3411	41695	10150	3809	56197	10	100	4317	198155	....	....	583	22715	39	662	6	80
State Center, exc. of town	10475	2527	29953	10388	3207	43964	....	....	4351	183955	9	80	705	25414	281	5432	9	98
State Center, town of	9	....	2192	263	459	5813	....	....	400	16105	....	....	43	1591	32	800	10	80
Taylor	8918	362	36760	7485	3218	46079	1	20	2864	122925	....	....	655	18961	26	452	9	150
Timber Creek	12994	1806	41431	9647	4154	67943	....	....	3352	131390	12	210	904	28988	133	3030	5	73
Vienna	17770	350	27335	11930	....	87278	....	....	4161	157070	2	35	1055	37959	421	7748	16	319
Washington	16767	1824	42042	12988	5867	88830	....	....	4496	200960	27	304	918	32245	488	9325	22	107
Total	223735	47552	680230	177303	69895	112582	21	200	67699	2808256	203	3208	13611	465245	3194	67151	187	2561

MILLS COUNTY.

NAMES OF TOWNSHIPS, TOWNS, AND CITIES.	No. of acres of improved land.	No. of acres of unimproved land.	No. of rods of fence.	No. of acres in cultivation in 1874.	Spring wheat: Number of acres.	Spring wheat: Number of bushels harvested.	Winter wheat: Number of acres.	Winter wheat: Number of bushels harvested.	Indian corn: Number of acres.	Indian corn: Number of bushels harvested.	Rye: Number of acres.	Rye: Number of bushels harvested.	Oats: Number of acres.	Oats: Number of bushels harvested.	Barley: Number of acres.	Barley: Number of bushels harvested.	Buckwheat: Number of acres.	Buckwheat: Number of bushels harvested.
Anderson	14970	8239	50485	12348	4263	60764	....	....	6234	175308	28	560	544	16509	602	11618	3	25
Deer Creek	13267	2810	26346	8779	2779	40756	....	....	5010	80630	10	....	473	13929	63	1789	....	....
Emerson, town of	457	104	1330	384	127	1141	....	....	187	2650	....	....	22	250	....	....	....	....
Glenwood, exc. of town	12329	5243	44671	7114	1051	14136	....	....	5771	141879	36	433	601	12631	15	350	....	....
Hastings, town of	755	141	2940	685	240	3500	....	....	150	2250	....	....	....	....	120	4000	....	....
Hillsdale, town of	....	....	....	40	....	....	....	....	40	1200	....	....	....	....	....	....	....	....
Indian Creek, exc. of Emerson and Hastings	12729	8438	39022	10104	3318	43588	2	30	5755	139095	....	....	413	55008	561	11298	....	....
Ingraham	9809	2536	41072	7609	2151	28763	....	....	4075	111470	10	200	526	15756	551	11111	2	18
Lyons	5378	6426	42353	4138	450	7333	2	40	5057	161126	5	100	174	4940	....	....	....	....
Malvern, town of	260	....	560	....	....	....	....	....	3	120	....	....	....	....	....	....	....	....
Oak	14192	8135	64446	12659	3108	41359	....	....	3847	157875	52	761	1122	34065	840	17404	....	....
Platteville	1830	2367	15430	2677	158	2654	....	....	2356	76355	2	15	205	4430	10	280	....	....
Rawles	14462	1812	61349	9952	1803	27667	2	13	6118	135220	10	61	786	23550	11	230	....	....

St. Mary	1917	1748	11470	1917	369	6968			1096	27975	5	50	152	4288	46	1733	2	36
Silver Creek, exc. of Hillsdale and Malvern	27736	736	57006	11651	3015	36388	10	170	7528	193293	3	12	888	24382	139	2985	6	
White Cloud	11421	4869	34702	9780	1553	27944	16	290	6316	127530			622	22901	10	140		
Total	141512	53604	493482	99837	24385	342961	39	543	59543	1533976	161	2192	6528	232639	2968	62938	13	79

MITCHELL COUNTY.

Burr Oak	8749	2836	23842		4394	71912			1116	37921			993	41445	150	4270		30
Cedar	11033	5735	49097	9072	5648	103705		12	1327	47519			1346	51035	160	4597	1	20
Douglas	7999	2822	23470	4704	2920	48255			517	20575			693	28310	83	2074		
Jenkins	9248	5522	33055	5093	3825	61765			930	40820			1119	42705	247	6636		20
Liberty	3727	2014	14430	3115	2184	36443			348	14845			392	18347	134	3578		
Lincoln	11826	5141	25141	8151	4342	72446			1153	44650	2	6	829	25798	294	8103		
Mitchell	9443	2468	30184	7624	4804	75176			1110	40210	2		1157	43906	230	7815	27	265
Newburg	9221	4117	31270	8510	5642	98536			420	15030	7	128	1148	44680	123	3045	5	25
Osage, exc. of town	3173	1713	20251	2735	1471	21407			544	19690	2	16	412	16895	93	3226	46	402
Osage, town of	515	68	953	416	527	5984			199	7905		6	348	5265	46	821		
Otranto	9311	5876	40235	7611	5490	94950			407	14131	4	96	944	33133	99	2028		
Rock	10833	2114	24760	8640	6587	100068			649	22415			1066	44193	349	8459	2	22
St. Ansgar	12510	5008	46090	11982	5901	113620			997	28530			1289	62154	323	8320		
Stacyville	3939	15564	13323	2832	1986	33266			280	11390			473	18044	83	2153		
Union	10909	2957	32694	9723	6595	109668			847	32780			1218	39480	388	9221		8
Wayne	3945	6221	20895	3915	3218	37610			430	13550			651	27272	169	3778	1	21
Total	126384	70176	429690	94132	65534	1083811		12	11274	411961	17	252	14078	542662	2971	78124	85	813

MONONA COUNTY.

Ashton	2006	965	12930	1612	328	4798			1116	55260	10	200	138	5888			10	75
Belvidere	2084	2165	9660	1643	440	1575			1108	34400			80	353				
Center	2778	1628	13253	2189	968	9986			1048	50610			146	4495			4	27
Fairview	3650	3260	27616	3100	1576	16172			1282	29923			206	6944	10	180		
Franklin, exc. of Onawa	6962	2606	20468	4756	1345	15771			3106	127090			236	6973	2	60		
Grant	2807	5388	16275	2693	1117	16270			1393	60170			114	2394	5	150		
Jordan	630	850	1940	619	181	3017			402	13565			21	582				
Kennebec	5884	5255	22668	3138	990	7163			1982	73630			141	2755	6	180		
Lake	1848	2723	11840	1788	639	9482			1068	35000			67	2436				
Lincoln	3969	11604	28175	3334	636	10285			2477	97180			185	6813				
Maple	5874	6363	20950	5168	2957	35146			1674	55700			455	10786	16	424	3	36
Onawa, town of	10		200	10					10	950								
Sherman	2789	4118	17442	2336	902	10209			1301	44605			103	2216				
Soldier	1819	1003	5290	1639	921	10544			534	19430	6	130	106	3956	61	1547		

MONONA COUNTY—CONTINUED.

Names of townships, towns, and cities.	No. of acres of improved land.	No. of acres of unimproved land.	No. of rods of fence.	No. of acres in cultivation in 1874.	Spring Wheat. Number of acres.	Spring Wheat. Number of bushels harvested.	Winter Wheat. Number of acres.	Winter Wheat. Number of bushels harvested.	Indian Corn. Number of acres.	Indian Corn. Number of bushels harvested.	Rye. Number of acres.	Rye. Number of bushels harvested.	Oats. Number of acres.	Oats. Number of bushels harvested.	Barley. Number of acres.	Barley. Number of bushels harvested.	Buckwheat. Number of acres.	Buckwheat. Number of bushels harvested.
Spring Valley	5179	2025	18169	2489	1029	14345	....	....	1291	54600	....	....	130	3801	10	290	4	35
St Clair	1360	1549	3534	1280	682	8790	....	....	522	11455	....	....	60	1528	4	94	....	....
West Fork	1845	4980	6745	1384	284	5308	....	....	1018	42800	....	....	60	2575	....	....	....	....
Willow	748	796	2750	666	339	4950	....	....	245	12020	....	....	56	1980	13	200	....	....
Total	52242	57278	239905	39844	15334	183811	....	....	21577	818388	16	330	2304	66475	127	3125	21	173

MONROE COUNTY.

Names of townships, towns, and cities.	No. of acres of improved land.	No. of acres of unimproved land.	No. of rods of fence.	No. of acres in cultivation in 1874.	Spring Wheat. Number of acres.	Spring Wheat. Number of bushels harvested.	Winter Wheat. Number of acres.	Winter Wheat. Number of bushels harvested.	Indian Corn. Number of acres.	Indian Corn. Number of bushels harvested.	Rye. Number of acres.	Rye. Number of bushels harvested.	Oats. Number of acres.	Oats. Number of bushels harvested.	Barley. Number of acres.	Barley. Number of bushels harvested.	Buckwheat. Number of acres.	Buckwheat. Number of bushels harvested.
Bluff Creek	14276	3544	69397	13813	1701	19012	12	73	5861	229215	16	196	1348	36853	....	....	88	503
Cedar	6263	4732	37934	5885	1429	8712	12	33	4111	161665	31	305	705	14326	....	....	4	78
Franklin	5721	6190	42160	5626	777	6434	....	....	5240	101160	2	21	537	12368	....	....	22	139
Guilford	6768	10876	51181	6118	689	6858	17	137	3233	148270	67	556	748	20109	....	....	3	86
Jackson	6955	5345	35405	5668	695	7822	....	....	3691	153650	3	32	840	21785	....	....	97	270
Mantua	8832	8139	84752	10862	854	6243	59	3447	3567	133880	151	1015	766	5962	....	....	48	545
Monroe	10795	5828	61723	6150	866	8584	21	305	3806	150105	32	321	1443	32443	....	....	17	241
Pleasant	10079	7706	48310	10371	1237	11574	4	....	4042	142585	....	....	878	18093	15	130	3	69
Troy, exc. of Albia	9129	5113	35569	8720	748	6968	56	566	3336	141685	11	166	902	24347	....	....	21	360
Union	8223	7998	71284	8571	1423	9845	38	410	3872	166115	11	130	1877	28132	....	....	8	221
Urbana	10783	6814	62510	6599	639	4419	44	613	2962	104300	73	694	683	16103	....	....	19	308
Wayne	4391	5921	28106	3346	580	4942	....	....	1853	106286	12	100	784	10560	....	....	15	252
Total	102215	78206	628331	91729	11638	101413	263	5584	45574	1738916	409	3536	11511	241081	15	130	345	3072

MONTGOMERY COUNTY.

Douglas	7877	6657	16407	5895	2131	36168	....	....	3092	115812	30	400	385	12340	50	1250	....	12
Frankfort	7962	2878	28588	7124	2452	42099	....	....	2814	100170	....	....	329	12675	25	799	....	....
Grant	11645	4788	32240	10876	3536	83605	....	....	3820	154530	5	131	565	20650	24	660	....	15
Jackson, exc. of Villisca	5312	5312	36980	6497	1658	24881	2	46	3688	120400	18	304	387	13789	....	....	....	....
Lincoln	10753	3805	16288	7392	3209	54128	6	120	2682	83540	6	162	355	11544	51	1701	....	....
Pilot Grove	10118	3932	30757	8758	3164	53200	....	....	3546	133005	2	40	565	19854	25	834	....	....
Red Oak, exc. of town	7903	3374	26509	7956	2855	37403	....	....	4535	166710	3	30	456	15722	5	175	....	13
Scott	4286	2025	11521	3313	1416	24741	....	....	1747	51955	....	....	230	7276	9	300	....	....
Sherman	8150	3616	33055	7444	2647	51270	....	....	2794	155340	12	120	442	17705	....	....	....	....
Villisca, town of	....	....	....	....	22	300	....	....	220	6400	....	....	12	270	....	....	....	....
Walnut	14821	3589	25240	12092	3982	69264	....	....	4112	156625	....	....	510	19756	33	1195	....	86
Washington	4684	4819	25750	....	1458	24200	....	....	2652	99130	2	32	458	27149	82	712	....	74
West	11122	5812	22232	8679	2851	50280	....	....	3549	97850	9	170	628	22905	206	5510	....	14
Total	104633	50607	303567	86026	31381	551539	8	166	39251	1441467	87	1389	5322	201635	510	13136	....	214

MUSCATINE COUNTY.

Bloomington, exc. of Muscatine	19294	1271	79443	10111	1799	23131	12	80	4861	116154	481	5667	764	22215	298	940	116	1358
Cedar	5002	5867	30525	2242	445	4259	....	....	1692	43280	45	412	212	13292	....	....	3	25
Fulton	16757	2283	85067	19672	5097	75681	....	....	4398	182520	23	353	1527	68712	....	....	....	....
Goshen	23700	3176	86457	16574	2520	35858	1	11	6221	214101	168	2499	2401	76360	45	945	31	562
Lake	16318	1289	68258	7951	2026	23867	2	39	3205	129895	161	1706	681	16083	16	288	7	180
Moscow	8635	4663	44958	7362	2604	31602	....	....	2944	75970	314	3708	749	20070	36	11020	6	93
Montpelier	7486	4550	4854	7886	2187	32133	5	25	2401	69815	12	194	608	16045	347	11020	2	40
Muscatine, city of	1760	1250	6100	2400	....	....	....	....	870	7900	....	....	5	200	....	....	....	....
Orono	8110	735	31161	6092	1060	12461	....	....	3021	108775	553	5546	334	9292	11	280	5	93
Pike	10338	7298	90655	12352	2930	40907	27	350	4988	166420	534	5462	1048	25365	323	7552	30	486
Seventy-Six	9860	6003	50066	8663	1498	16359	8	40	4009	116870	70	721	883	18751	....	....	4	64
Sweetland	13776	6294	55182	8532	2461	36098	....	....	4725	119248	88	1409	983	30782	290	5939	8	168
Wapsinonoc, exc. of West Liberty	16872	2646	65664	8172	2238	34447	2	28	5141	200125	18	160	1333	45350	306	6833	5	104
Wilton, exc. of town	20129	1315	58144	11475	3248	46448	6	56	5789	150655	69	1547	1604	49208	676	14110	13	222
Wilton, town of	908	192	2516	215	2262	3220	....	....	495	14245	5	70	155	3837	10	200	2	50
Total	178945	48832	759050	129699	32375	416471	63	629	54760	1715973	2541	29455	13287	405562	2358	59127	232	3445

O'BRIEN COUNTY.

Baker	2957	42800	....	2319	1509	14513	....	....	341	3860	....	....	170	3128	48	715	....	....
Carroll	3993	18905	40	3481	1164	19932	....	....	647	7564	....	....	283	4265	148	2043	....	....

O'BRIEN COUNTY.—Continued.

NAMES OF TOWNSHIPS, TOWNS, AND CITIES.	No. of acres of improved land.	No. of acres of unimproved land.	No. of rods of fence.	No. of acres in cultivation in 1874.	SPRING WHEAT. Number of acres.	SPRING WHEAT. Number of bushels harvested.	WINTER WHEAT. Number of acres.	WINTER WHEAT. Number of bushels harvested.	INDIAN CORN. Number of acres.	INDIAN CORN. Number of bushels harvested.	RYE. Number of acres.	RYE. Number of bushels harvested.	OATS. Number of acres.	OATS. Number of bushels harvested.	BARLEY. Number of acres.	BARLEY. Number of bushels harvested.	BUCKWHEAT. Number of acres.	BUCKWHEAT. Number of bushels harvested.
Center	3840	41874	100	2111	1970	13741			764	7600	20	315	301	9845	78	1362		
Floyd	4127	41663	120	2823	1931	19917			532	6299			273	4038	21	336		8
Grant	4699	63502	1020	4027	2210	21277			1126	22039	48	535	303	7350	36	624		66
Highland	4770	41343	537	3937	2211	26613			902	23060	29	291	343	11353	51	1004	6	98
Liberty	4390	41383	116	2963	1827	26448			765	23310	8	140	272	8367	48	928	24	
Summit	452	22344	116	376	220	2625			90	900			49	1139	16	338	6	28
Waterman	4398	18250	120	4297	1862	12460			1212	11720			1113	4446	5	38		
Total	33626	332070	2175	26434	14904	157526			6379	106052	105	1281	3107	53931	451	7388	36	200

OSCEOLA COUNTY.

NAMES OF TOWNSHIPS, TOWNS, AND CITIES.	No. of acres of improved land.	No. of acres of unimproved land.	No. of rods of fence.	No. of acres in cultivation in 1874.	SPRING WHEAT. Number of acres.	SPRING WHEAT. Number of bushels harvested.	WINTER WHEAT. Number of acres.	WINTER WHEAT. Number of bushels harvested.	INDIAN CORN. Number of acres.	INDIAN CORN. Number of bushels harvested.	RYE. Number of acres.	RYE. Number of bushels harvested.	OATS. Number of acres.	OATS. Number of bushels harvested.	BARLEY. Number of acres.	BARLEY. Number of bushels harvested.	BUCKWHEAT. Number of acres.	BUCKWHEAT. Number of bushels harvested.
Fairview	485			318	407	1429			48	206			68	1641	1	20		
Gilman	3517	3946		3938	2224	21208			298	2995			209	3235	13	138	24	59
Goewey	5275	8855		3491	2404	24532			730	6356			335	9160				
Holman	4110	8812	14	2982	1700	12423		6	760	3366			292	5435	1	20	1	1
Horton	558	2401		326	163	1410			71	740			44	881				
Ocheyedan	1224	135		1000	534	3728			147	1666			194	3040	6	51		
Viola	2275	4459		1669	1009	7653			315	940			169	2265				
Wilson	1046	2798		927	328	2374		20	141	1010			79	1172				
Total	18490	31406	14	14651	8769	74757		26	2510	17279			1390	26829	21	229	25	60

PAGE COUNTY

Amity	9932	9068	57170	8782	1320	19065	65	1604	4101	136215	64	1111	657	28544	116	3556		
Buchanan	10110	9453	72744	9000	843	11601	118	1711	4739	264005	107	1473	743	23105	71	2122	......	29
Clarinda, town of	......	......	4206	......	......	......	......	......	......	......	......	......	......	......	......	......	......	......
Colfax	6234	12958	31328	5446	1073	14800	56	866	4137	81650	28	275	506	17383	26	424	3	5
Douglas	12478	6422	40557	9357	2454	33031	......	......	6056	233400	36	433	850	28000	157	3664	3	14
East River	15545	4159	48800	6623	1139	14761	73	838	5254	142863	16	200	667	22147	42	923	......	......
Fremont	13268	9594	29590	7952	2510	47876	......	......	3767	123440	4	45	317	12012	......	......	......	......
Grant, exc. of Shenandoah	10436	11443	18838	7984	1568	28725	153	2620	5475	173872	5	163	425	18121	60	1280	2	22
Harlan	10504	9188	62616	8966	1437	20026	165	3091	6114	147335	218	3116	955	34178	56	1351	1	37
Lincoln	9313	9880	40061	8026	1418	22223	85	1132	4895	109100	100	1595	824	33214	119	3421	......	5
Morton	6882	12207	11540	4407	1308	23829	112	2217	2795	60740	48	1177	360	14036	107	2336	......	......
Nebraska	3726	6552	21569	2472	484	5744	13	168	2194	64890	44	944	273	7779	......	......	3	33
Nedaway, exc. of Clarinda	14434	20781	54535	12091	1666	25255	202	3147	7754	250571	211	3240	1232	39796	152	3617	3	28
Pierce	7533	15303	19337	5129	1242	23242	......	......	2385	73740	4	50	243	10559	55	1375	1	20
Shenandoah, town of	72	......	320	69	69	2370	......	......	......	......	......	......	......	......	......	......	......	......
Tarkio	10557	12382	25622	6220	1576	25652	152	2547	4211	113358	11	148	632	23226	36	785	......	......
Valley	9178	13260	33350	8094	1578	21276	10	50	5154	184880	21	290	678	19898	37	759	8	70
Washington	6580	12821	12930	4866	1004	16316	16	244	2355	78984	33	549	396	14509	44	1698	......	......
Total	156782	175471	585113	115484	22689	355792	1220	20235	71386	2239043	950	14809	9758	346507	1078	27311	24	263

PALO ALTO COUNTY.

Ellington	1337	2938	5	1348	400	1382	......	......	637	14958	......	......	227	3629	2	6	3	11
Emmetsburg	2351	2984	4772	1792	628	1515	......	......	648	13195	......	......	305	3590	4	......	......	......
Fairfield	781	889	3	746	290	100	6	......	360	1493	......	......	103	66	......	......	9	21
Fern Valley	922	1821	926	817	284	713	......	......	419	8080	......	......	130	1004	......	......	......	......
Freedom	2023	2487	1050	1388	680	1030	......	......	656	10060	......	......	355	4009	......	......	7	42
Great Oak	1853	3577	2630	1739	514	4483	......	......	645	17890	......	......	281	6590	......	......	......	......
Highland	1720	2591	......	1520	684	5338	......	......	95	5858	......	......	255	4434	2	10	4	......
Lost Island	784	1970	420	820	287	1715	......	......	209	2373	......	......	102	1800	3	7	......	......
Nevada	926	3009	5020	906	218	614	......	......	391	10165	......	......	215	4882	2	6	......	......
Rush Lake	1187	1880	......	1187	309	2474	......	......	488	11225	......	......	192	3068	......	......	......	......
Silver Lake	336	1624	5	223	453	2614	......	......	396	7820	......	......	233	4109	......	......	18	119
Vernon	913	1129	191	837	312	216	......	......	385	3500	......	......	198	1680	......	......	18	......
Walnut	1063	3023	1740	1124	3141	632	319	......	......	7710	444	......	......	2901	271	4	2	2
West Bend	2321	3203	4845	2232	406	382	......	......	1312	28630	9	......	383	5097	3	......	5	33
Total	18517	32225	21607	16679	8606	23208	325	......	6641	142957	453	......	2979	46859	287	33	66	228

PLYMOUTH COUNTY.

NAMES OF TOWNSHIPS, TOWNS, AND CITIES.	No. of acres of improved land.	No. of acres of unimproved land.	No. of rods of fence.	No. of acres in cultivation in 1874.	SPRING WHEAT		WINTER WHEAT.		INDIAN CORN.		RYE.		OATS.		BARLEY.		BUCK-WHEAT.	
					Number of acres.	Number of bushels harvested.	Number of acres.	Number of bushels harvested.	Number of acres.	Number of bushels harvested.	Number of acres.	Number of bushels harvested.	Number of acres.	Number of bushels harvested.	Number of acres.	Number of bushels harvested.	Number of acres.	Number of bushels harvested.
America	5072	3463	300	1569	3443	45270			508	9705			331	8816	30	541		
Elgin	3011	1349	1000	2747	1949	28705			439	10312			191	4875	74	1795		
Fredonia	4777	3879		4004	3004	40888			601	12660			283	6180	31	593		
Grant	4594	3495	540	3582	2422	29072			596	1790	5	51	281	6237	5	100	10	
Johnson	6301	5869		5044	2322	43036			1096	5357			458	11884	60	1682		
Lincoln	7234	7822	10875	7484	4712	59545			1892	39207			729	26294				
Marion	2511	2292	160	2288	1726	25382			343	8030			147	3701	28	506		
Perry	6947	7159	5175	5963	3944	46519			1516	20924	1	4	564	14015	70	806	4	
Plymouth	2936	3381	5875	2248	2225	30201			790	15190			354	11739	2	86		
Portland	4179	3160		525	2167	13893			10	300			109	2417	12	200		
Sioux	1024	4291	2404	435	437	4262	10	160	501	2735			47	329			6	16
Stanton	4366	3419		4449	2501	39526			852	26420			353	12835				
Union	1988	1518	30	1705	940	14793			464	17520			63	6268		17		
Washington	3293	815		2336	1836	21614			489	5628			251	4844	19	266		
Total	58233	51912	26359	44379	33628	442736	10	160	10097	175778	6	55	4161	120437	331	6592	20	16

POCAHONTAS COUNTY.

NAMES OF TOWNSHIPS, TOWNS, AND CITIES.	No. of acres of improved land.	No. of acres of unimproved land.	No. of rods of fence.	No. of acres in cultivation in 1874.	Spring wheat: Number of acres.	Spring wheat: Number of bushels harvested.	Winter wheat: Number of acres.	Winter wheat: Number of bushels harvested.	Indian corn: Number of acres.	Indian corn: Number of bushels harvested.	Rye: Number of acres.	Rye: Number of bushels harvested.	Oats: Number of acres.	Oats: Number of bushels harvested.	Barley: Number of acres.	Barley: Number of bushels harvested.	Buckwheat: Number of acres.	Buckwheat: Number of bushels harvested.
Bellville	2607	4103		2155	937	2490			791	14980			243	2841	6	71	4	66
Cedar	2376	2651		2381	884	4317			800	23155			344	3928	2	35		
Center	587	1997		191	289	1525			110	2365			46	1457	2		2	10
Clinton	1100	940	1975	1003	382	2002			635	19775			130	3330	4	150		
Colfax	2455	3844	418	2246	874	3194			890	19208			241	2710	6	30	32	38
Des Moines	2689	5920	8510	2380	529	1285			1608	42500	40	600	238	3951				
Dover	1150	2699		900	546	3882			398	8940			147	2454				
Grant	1032	1952	160	795	340	2132			370	6740			90	786			10	68
Jackson	1474	3817	160	1289	298	2205			756	25775			225	4415				

Lincoln	537	788	552	498	199	1005	....	....	208	4570	....	....	74	1225	....	....	....	....
Lizard	5744	6210	4406	5214	2141	6546	....	....	2303	58655	18	47	763	13399	80	545	5	160
Swan Lake	177	651	....	167	15	191	....	....	112	2600	....	....	....	....	....	....	....	....
Total	21928	35572	16181	19219	7434	30774	....	....	8981	229263	58	647	2541	40494	100	831	53	342

POLK COUNTY.

Allen	7518	2149	17550	5497	1275	17379	....	....	2530	120750	10	102	307	8688	15	500	....	20
Beaver	19619	4528	78353	13407	5036	76220	....	....	7495	309290	9	145	884	34485	377	8695	16	204
Bloomfield	13172	1429	61572	8734	3392	49328	....	....	5686	281650	13	176	554	21001	81	1754	13	155
Camp	17954	7125	86926	12995	4176	54396	5	86	6667	289990	22	299	759	22887	50	1169	....	....
Crocker	14179	2390	60181	9683	1769	26518	....	....	4986	169530	11	210	1177	46203	50	1037	2	20
Delaware	15533	152	57939	7037	2844	43611	....	....	5931	208597	37	542	848	31655	280	6045	1	24
Des Moines, city of	222	140	1330	222	10	120	....	....	27	5165	....	....	11	200	....	....	....	....
Douglas	15300	373	51340	9490	1451	23392	....	....	4982	199800	....	....	640	25935	13	185	....	....
Elkhart	7726	2272	25242	5478	805	14280	....	....	2098	116115	8	144	544	17320	....	1	2	34
Four Mile	2068	1882	17670	3472	1099	13719	....	....	1710	69080	....	....	174	6069	13	175	2	30
Franklin	11491	12518	56160	8039	2407	33085	....	....	4001	185410	....	....	471	18098	65	1579	4	100
Grant	4514	665	22677	3376	701	10328	....	....	1917	83780	....	....	222	6915	....	....	1	12
Jefferson	10740	3253	29243	7967	1756	26798	6	105	4868	183263	37	769	868	30192	60	2994	....	....
Lincoln	12409	1168	48473	6836	1876	28152	....	....	3352	127030	33	500	896	31183	26	628	....	....
Madison	12664	4908	56644	7941	1700	25123	....	....	4270	160690	15	245	1000	29745	....	....	7	51
Taylor	5374	3002	26617	4865	848	13901	....	....	3373	156960	58	830	718	30215	12	400	2	12
Valley	6057	1889	34836	4263	782	12940	10	203	2215	99925	18	286	355	10415	....	....	3	45
Walnut	19089	4379	64593	11687	3149	51413	....	....	7416	350890	22	400	1314	43093	211	4580	8	99
Washington	12060	2599	44840	9461	2610	42686	....	....	3973	154125	47	862	446	17542	52	1079	4	50
Total	207689	56821	842186	140450	37686	563389	21	394	77497	3272040	335	5510	12188	431841	1305	30821	65	856

POTTAWATTAMIE COUNTY.

Avoca, town of	419	272	1780	290	144	2420	6	....	105	5600	....	....	....	....	....	....	....	....
Belknap	2358	1408	9168	1452	837	11840	....	22	1039	44750	....	....	108	5605	31	599	....	....
Boomer	3944	3476	23810	3578	557	1026	....	....	2332	62950	....	....	87	1950	10	156	12	272
Center	9754	7190	2065	8813	639	67826	12	130	2767	126870	....	....	553	15362	159	3651	....	....
Council Bluffs, city of	1353	718	7677	1004	20	200	....	....	726	29115	....	....	27	800	....	....	....	....
Crescent	2178	3329	17153	2155	401	3966	7	39	1882	54500	....	....	43	1705	6	100	....	....
Grove	7866	5132	36790	501	317	53939	....	....	2674	90247	....	....	220	8691	12	194	....	....
Harden	3867	2520	16522	2997	1059	7534	....	....	2132	67900	....	....	264	6040	20	525	16	190
Hazel Dell	6179	3445	32732	4321	774	6115	....	....	2524	87800	34	360	97	4339	2	40	....	22
James	12022	1298	4815	1781	1038	13322	....	....	803	34950	....	....	51	1957	25	600	6	392
Kane, exc. of Council Bluffs	0559	14240	65280	9953	2266	26590	28	134	5216	186835	18	546	786	20658	245	4264	....	....
Keg Creek	3972	3445	30505	3039	1548	23862	....	....	1783	95550	....	....	283	8905	167	4183	....	....

POTTAWATTAMIE COUNTY.—Continued.

NAMES OF TOWNSHIPS, TOWNS, AND CITIES.	No. of acres of improved land.	No. of acres of unimproved land.	No. of rods of fence.	No. of acres in cultivation in 1874.	SPRING WHEAT.		WINTER WHEAT.		INDIAN CORN.		RYE.		OATS.		BARLEY.		BUCK-WHEAT.	
					Number of acres.	Number of bushels harvested.	Number of acres.	Number of bushels harvested.	Number of acres.	Number of bushels harvested.	Number of acres.	Number of bushels harvested.	Number of acres.	Number of bushels harvested.	Number of acres.	Number of bushels harvested.	Number of acres.	Number of bushels harvested.
Knox, exc. of Avoca	14172	7810	53000	11481	5039	90534	......	......	3904	183595	......	......	514	19526	300	4343	......	......
Layton	10362	4354	22520	6078	3237	78809	......	......	2450	109880	......	......	431	17345	225	5857	1	36
Macedonia	4811	3159	18524	3780	2132	27865	......	......	2542	49340	......	......	210	5159	30	480	......	......
Neola	1749	2179	8882	1564	527	7126	......	......	834	32425	......	......	95	2979	15	500	......	......
Norwalk	3068	1130	13770	3440	1324	8145	10	150	1431	50150	2	10	152	4200	87	4168	1	9
Pleasant	5423	5763	5580	2910	2470	39269	......	......	1399	54400	......	......	196	6830	156	......	......	......
Rockford	5308	10422	31150	4933	1180	4194	......	......	3765	122967	21	517	274	2358	76	2819	9	39
Silver Creek	3066	1180	9527	2744	985	14298	......	......	1440	39095	18	376	178	5604	136	275	......	......
Washington	1525	1595	4736	1397	697	9925	......	......	675	18720	......	......	119	2720	12	350	......	......
Waveland	6275	5207	20596	5016	2330	37528	......	......	1973	84579	......	......	213	8879	20	1040	......	......
Wright	6638	3507	19225	5410	2983	46980	......	......	1912	94225	......	......	279	14309	21	457	......	......
York	7762	6710	8128	2042	865	6158	......	......	950	23595	......	......	98	2160	54	442	......	......
Total	124630	119439	463935	90679	33369	588971	63	475	47258	1750038	93	1809	5278	168081	1809	35043	45	960

POWESHIEK COUNTY.

NAMES OF TOWNSHIPS, TOWNS, AND CITIES.	No. of acres of improved land.	No. of acres of unimproved land.	No. of rods of fence.	No. of acres in cultivation in 1874.	Spring wheat: Number of acres.	Spring wheat: Number of bushels harvested.	Winter wheat: Number of acres.	Winter wheat: Number of bushels harvested.	Indian corn: Number of acres.	Indian corn: Number of bushels harvested.	Rye: Number of acres.	Rye: Number of bushels harvested.	Oats: Number of acres.	Oats: Number of bushels harvested.	Barley: Number of acres.	Barley: Number of bushels harvested.	Buckwheat: Number of acres.	Buckwheat: Number of bushels harvested.
Bear Creek, exc. of Brooklyn	13461	2500	52707	9305	4138	56595	......	......	4731	250525	22	280	597	18946	425	5882	1	10
Brooklyn, town of	36	......	......	......	......	......	......	......	......	400	......	......	......	......	......	......	......	......
Chester	16626	735	48550	14312	3381	46385	......	......	5046	219095	12	105	804	27065	402	8552	8	105
Deep River	14431	1601	57544	9503	3229	41789	......	......	5207	223350	63	800	1070	30274	1161	10261	1	27
Grinnell, exc. of town	12788	3406	56131	10606	2440	35694	......	......	5095	236470	10	148	1003	36158	398	8674	......	5
Grinnell, town of	......	......	......	......	......	......	......	......	8	425	......	......	......	......	......	......	......	......
Jackson, exc. of Montezuma	17706	2877	61027	14823	3872	47804	......	......	17153	287212	4	50	973	29185	632	4939	104	408
Jefferson	11711	4008	67074	11509	5260	62160	......	......	4875	394026	......	......	770	17149	210	4249	3	34
Lincoln	16406	5824	50286	11666	3885	48607	......	......	4573	207875	......	......	528	15766	276	4655	7	120
Madison	14169	1387	50913	10240	3684	57542	......	......	5069	190367	31	377	593	12818	374	6543	4	69
Malcom, exc. of town	12700	1318	35207	11996	3710	51933	......	......	5061	215950	......	......	671	20021	691	15129	......	......

Malcom, town of	440	....	200	245	114	1433	....	....	201	7150	....	....	25	440	....	....	....	....
Pleasant	14356	691	36997	11307	4122	52640	....	....	5294	242340	4	60	560	16802	377	8710	6	111
Scott	10356	710	28565	10042	3009	45500	....	....	4494	199800	....	....	505	17703	207	3868	....	....
Sheridan	14616	1839	41264	11941	4189	63342	....	....	4617	193285	5	20	686	21579	940	17645	12	94
Sugar Creek	9897	6773	51421	8342	2891	29404	....	....	4302	206360	....	....	773	21453	12	208	31	595
Union	6381	4674	45828	5161	1438	16586	....	....	2590	119360	8	116	466	10405	17	346	16	137
Warren	11744	4086	46277	10369	4177	53128	....	....	4306	184520	....	....	597	14329	198	3305	35	502
Washington	11165	6268	53646	10221	3773	52284	....	....	4126	192595	4	50	795	23472	291	6173	9	115
Total	208989	48697	783637	171588	57312	762826	....	....	86748	3571105	163	2006	11416	333565	6611	109139	237	2332

RINGGOLD COUNTY.

Athens	3339	2164	19900	2997	292	2668	2	30	1932	55175	48	632	391	14858	....	....	5	57
Benton	4775	5197	25785	1649	493	6594	....	....	3242	142750	19	244	532	21188	3	81	3	47
Clinton	4075	2778	24000	3003	307	3427	26	456	1771	48655	67	928	412	15751	....	....	....	....
Grant	5900	1814	28619	4390	620	10017	....	....	2643	83430	9	125	530	18906	29	460	1	21
Jefferson	5638	4555	29363	5023	686	9249	....	....	3179	131145	43	560	766	27190	....	....	2	40
Liberty	3076	3809	23162	2598	264	3151	7	78	2095	77060	32	250	473	16137	....	....	3	36
Lincoln	4793	3380	28656	3870	953	12313	....	....	2435	82653	....	....	438	13530	....	....	3	22
Lotts Creek	4176	4641	33992	3539	307	2610	20	426	2096	34428	41	831	552	17091	....	....	2	12
Middle Fork	4540	3240	25329	3568	297	3057	7	132	2472	67900	17	167	462	15857	....	....	....	....
Monroe	4242	2398	18926	3769	305	3886	8	100	1988	68330	40	384	353	11839	4	111	10	119
Mount Ayr	7680	6902	48510	5951	453	4130	25	107	3964	116521	46	797	831	25122	1	32	8	81
Rice	2708	5741	15460	2385	204	2572	....	....	1626	41985	10	155	182	5182	....	....	1	28
Riley	3463	2884	19190	388	192	1644	15	298	1422	23800	36	529	313	11804	....	....	4	44
Tingley	2050	2090	8640	1065	231	3318	....	....	868	37800	....	....	317	11970	....	....	....	15
Union	1789	2670	11600	1617	290	3378	13	115	1136	42190	21	543	1915	7670	14	321	3	28
Washington	6156	4566	34402	5061	5032	6837	2	20	2744	92115	90	1018	651	20912	4	40	3	22
Total	18400	58829	395534	50873	10926	78851	125	1762	35613	1145937	519	7163	9118	255007	55	1045	48	572

SAC COUNTY.

Boyer Valley	4511	4873	....	2703	1450	16765	....	....	711	11230	....	....	355	7478	....	....	....	....
Clinton	1571	3960	260	393	263	3074	....	....	158	4450	....	....	16	466	10	125	5	58
Douglas	4587	6515	2040	3847	1506	13951	....	....	1199	36456	....	....	582	11729	32	680	2	23
Eden	3142	4702	871	2179	1181	12941	....	....	650	18640	....	....	279	7083	60	1318	5	55
Jackson	7798	11418	8037	6712	2918	16387	....	10	2519	76580	20	190	934	14867	48	200	14	78
Levey	3875	9269	1910	2318	1083	15531	....	....	843	33735	1	25	180	6012	8	123	10	56
Sac	2953	3740	7375	3587	1557	18777	....	....	1494	58880	....	....	451	11516	22	485	4	36
Wall Lake	2899	2724	2573	2440	1098	12668	....	....	1088	39745	7	70	238	6845	....	....	....	....
Total	31336	47201	23066	24179	11056	110094	....	10	8662	279716	28	285	3035	65996	180	2931	40	306

SCOTT COUNTY.

NAMES OF TOWNSHIPS, TOWNS, AND CITIES.	No. of acres of improved land.	No. of acres of unimproved land.	No. of rods of fence.	No. of acres in cultivation in 1874.	SPRING WHEAT. Number of acres.	SPRING WHEAT. Number of bushels harvested.	WINTER WHEAT. Number of acres.	WINTER WHEAT. Number of bushels harvested.	INDIAN CORN. Number of acres.	INDIAN CORN. Number of bushels harvested.	RYE. Number of acres.	RYE. Number of bushels harvested.	OATS. Number of acres.	OATS. Number of bushels harvested.	BARLEY. Number of acres.	BARLEY. Number of bushels harvested.	BUCKWHEAT. Number of acres.	BUCKWHEAT. Number of bushels harvested.
Allen's Grove	10696	2540	35116	10434	2065	32196			3040	117753	16	175	896	31706	1334	29647	4	90
Blue Grass	22448		68567	16078	5178	85107			5161	197895			1510	53870	4019	92795	3	46
Buffalo, exc. of town	7078	4049	51343	5242	1444	23453			2399	80770	3	45	501	13674	251	5691		
Butler	16603	4680	51959	12215	3915	58574			5516	166830	34	325	1398	36368	2123	45386	2	74
Cleona	20446		42000	15000	4589	78020			4184	137610			1253	45750	4287	97110	1	24
Davenport, exc. of city	23450	110	61280	13504	2979	48075			5277	201475			1155	38740	2703	59890		
Davenport, city of	177	6	2216	700	33	600			31	1459					8	400		
Hickory Grove	21932		44435	16163	4063	69360			5243	220590			1502	55092	4400	99290		
Le Claire, exc. of town	11974	2986	50085	7993	2493	35728	8	150	3757	147740			868	26679	281	6734	10	194
Liberty	15757	1706	46247	10302	3645	54741			4467	144505			1313	42158	2274	51373	8	124
Lincoln	19263		73100	19263	4784	78989			4646	189275			1237	46885	2906	67308		
Pleasant Valley	8679	2230	39822	5533	1099	16788	30	450	2865	107725			609	19440	431	9173	1	5
Princeton, exc. of town	13356	90	49072	8554	2583	37328	2	18	4167	149960	6	60	947	27802	438	8988		
Rockingham	3969	312	19455	1550	264	3340			592	16540	4	45	189	5025	224	4205	3	75
Sheridan	22449	49	60039	22402	4839	81586			4843	204805			1453	52103	3500	73786		
Winfield	17238	365	60156	20809	3725	58430			2853	141416	8	76	1084	33576	1724	40879	2	35
Total	235515	19123	754912	185742	47698	762315	40	618	59071	2226346	71	726	15915	528868	30903	692655	34	667

SHELBY COUNTY.

NAMES OF TOWNSHIPS, TOWNS, AND CITIES.	No. of acres of improved land.	No. of acres of unimproved land.	No. of rods of fence.	No. of acres in cultivation in 1874.	SPRING WHEAT. Number of acres.	SPRING WHEAT. Number of bushels harvested.	WINTER WHEAT. Number of acres.	WINTER WHEAT. Number of bushels harvested.	INDIAN CORN. Number of acres.	INDIAN CORN. Number of bushels harvested.	RYE. Number of acres.	RYE. Number of bushels harvested.	OATS. Number of acres.	OATS. Number of bushels harvested.	BARLEY. Number of acres.	BARLEY. Number of bushels harvested.	BUCKWHEAT. Number of acres.	BUCKWHEAT. Number of bushels harvested.
Cass	865	1600	2729	725	172	315			477	3554			38	260	9	161		
Clay	2370	2458	5611	2159	1091	15644			864	36180			127	4669	26	680		
Douglas	3734	2086	9035	2960	1430	22533			1268	57524			141	4495	20	200	1	25
Fairview	10902	8055	33294	9137	3453	63464			2833	126600			430	14738	346	7708		
Greeley	706	443	1120	623	255	3347			291	10705			53	1665				
Grove	4656	4884	33855	4610	2141	16250			2186	55780			170	2233	5	156	7	35
Harlan	6328	3097	25074	5754	2742	43401			2257	116417			321	12967				

Jackson	2434	909	7710	2227	893	11962	....	....	947	38700	5	80	98	2831	....	....	....	....
Jefferson	1084	3980	210	840	435	6021	....	....	315	10885	....	....	47	1651	....	....	....	....
Lincoln	4026	1642	1940	2671	793	26365	....	....	1415	54510	....	....	181	6241	15	275	1	29
Monroe	6496	2980	8852	5320	3784	41827	....	....	1207	48131	....	....	280	8444	138	3337	....	....
Polk	1709	616	3410	1610	849	11187	....	....	567	21750	....	....	33	1638	....	....	....	....
Shelby	5090	2227	8775	4387	2042	31030	....	....	1597	64465	12	200	181	5634	93	2456	....	....
Union	1200	746	1860	1895	776	12453	....	....	518	20770	....	....	103	2990	1[illegible]	105	....	....
Washington	1840	870	4195	1562	694	5357	....	....	734	16920	....	....	31	550	....	....	....	....
Westphalia	1740	2733	767	750	479	6788	....	....	198	5665	....	....	20	670	....	....	....	....
Total	55180	39326	148137	47230	22029	317944	....	....	17674	689556	17	280	2254	71676	667	15078	9	89

SIOUX COUNTY.

Buncombe	2839	57584	....	2186	1311	15628	....	....	533	1200	....	....	146	2287	35	405	....	....
Floyd	1640	28743	....	1586	1416	18955	....	....	312	2302	....	....	198	3023	....	....	....	7
Grant	2734	23957	....	1662	900	12504	....	....	543	4220	....	....	1466	2861	19	351	4	....
Holland	11563	43108	100	9371	6957	76050	....	....	1823	9280	5	9	871	10715	5	87	....	....
Lincoln	2790	26331	....	2436	1609	10431	....	....	624	275	....	....	325	3820	21	374	....	....
Nassau	7498	48406	....	7451	5133	59661	....	....	1135	9373	28	186	584	6645	42	692	....	....
Reading	4089	33149	....	3476	2532	27355	....	....	742	1862	....	....	223	4350	27	434	....	....
Rock	1503	34408	....	1358	827	7061	....	....	233	530	....	....	185	2867	....	....	....	....
Settler	2203	49923	840	1664	1145	11854	....	....	286	2612	....	....	284	5485	3	30	....	....
Sheridan	2965	21785	....	2325	1369	11787	....	....	549	384	....	....	309	3043	36	560	7	7
Total	39824	367394	940	33515	22996	251286	....	....	6780	32038	33	195	4591	45096	188	2933	11	14

STORY COUNTY.

Ames, town of	193	123	4781	119	43	494	....	....	241	21535	....	....	43	1095	....	....	5	34
Collins	8961	6045	36501	7486	2778	38094	....	....	3364	124325	19	286	632	23351	36	552	3	25
Franklin	10769	3440	48530	7326	1450	18213	....	....	4223	135333	35	497	1072	31718	32	470	12	148
Grant	8568	1849	14041	5730	1124	14858	....	....	2586	93380	6	60	637	18970	26	432	10	89
Howard	14634	....	51755	7734	2232	28371	....	....	4723	131335	....	....	838	25274	29	434	....	....
Indian Creek	14214	2785	60846	9492	2838	32248	....	....	4878	180000	80	1117	1026	29913	20	700	2	40
LaFayette	6761	2837	24272	4003	1121	15357	....	....	2247	69955	....	....	473	13511	43	1490	7	54
Lincoln	4163	2421	12694	3866	1519	21485	....	....	1323	43845	....	....	355	10418	40	498	4	30
Milford	10752	2152	34998	6516	1385	17237	8	20	3724	152055	....	....	883	24770	22	485	24	319
Nevada, exc. of town	12412	2258	48068	7375	1661	19004	....	....	3426	122155	....	....	731	22866	23	417	18	312
Nevada, town of	364	319	5511	262	45	566	....	....	150	5505	....	....	39	1403	....	....	2	20
New Albany	10964	1355	23705	7070	2049	23611	....	....	2889	97520	17	178	802	24490	61	1110	7	135
Palestine	10092	5053	35875	5034	1535	12627	....	....	3449	121150	10	156	675	21715	8	160	3	18
Richland	4708	5513	22690	5949	1283	13411	....	....	2486	73280	7	93	790	18582	8	178	7	54
Sherman	3394	2870	11310	2751	1394	15690	....	....	1074	33832	10	160	301	9965	30	426	6	52

STORY COUNTY.—Continued.

Names of townships, towns, and cities.	No. of acres of improved land.	No. of acres of unimproved land.	No. of rods of fence.	No. of acres in cultivation in 1874.	Spring wheat. Number of acres.	Spring wheat. Number of bushels harvested.	Winter wheat. Number of acres.	Winter wheat. Number of bushels harvested.	Indian corn. Number of acres.	Indian corn. Number of bushels harvested.	Rye. Number of acres.	Rye. Number of bushels harvested.	Oats. Number of acres.	Oats. Number of bushels harvested.	Barley. Number of acres.	Barley. Number of bushels harvested.	Buckwheat. Number of acres.	Buckwheat. Number of bushels harvested.
Union	13410	2949	65935	9901	2124	32029			4692	208645	20	90	887	30837	68	1315		
Warren	1107	1048	1560	814	430	4879			333	8645			87	1929			6	48
Washington, exc. of Ames	13183	857	51131	7959	1647	22723			5465	160982	27	253	1002	32458	15	203	22	646
Total	148649	43874	554233	99387	26658	330897	8	20	51273	1783477	231	2890	11273	343265	461	8870	138	2024

TAMA COUNTY.

Names of townships, towns, and cities.	No. of acres of improved land.	No. of acres of unimproved land.	No. of rods of fence.	No. of acres in cultivation in 1874.	Spring wheat. Number of acres.	Spring wheat. Number of bushels harvested.	Winter wheat. Number of acres.	Winter wheat. Number of bushels harvested.	Indian corn. Number of acres.	Indian corn. Number of bushels harvested.	Rye. Number of acres.	Rye. Number of bushels harvested.	Oats. Number of acres.	Oats. Number of bushels harvested.	Barley. Number of acres.	Barley. Number of bushels harvested.	Buckwheat. Number of acres.	Buckwheat. Number of bushels harvested.
Buckingham	13200	9807	36160	13200	4501	76399			4266	163855			736	16372	194	4314	4	92
Carlton	10079	5169	42980	9158	3929	57111			3424	123704	2	42	677	22133	257	5118	6	112
Carroll	7880	4659	22380	6237	3787	58234			2571	99725	5	85	413	10468	206	4423	2	32
Clark	12210	11010	20260	10423	5280	70768			3078	104660			652	17504	603	8795	6	90
Columbia	14889	4722	41832	9907	4833	71967			3806	156214	1	20	557	13582	376	6798	18	170
Crystal	10739	1729	31075	9419	5276	75580			3271	106200			742	22045	669	13020		
Geneseo	13984	3507	15590	11352	7105	86231			3584	126480			684	15601	40	904		
Grant	8242	14798	45306	6799	2983	45105			2387	278940		10	479	12451	430	7694	4	30
Highland	9515	1573	24340	9427	4336	64899			3630	123345	8	56	516	16419	147	2416		
Howard	17403	5586	50360	11759	5807	75040			4758	173775			993	29925	265	4780		
Indian Village, exc. of Montour	9128	6212	57552	9013	3580	49269			3602	122001	10	50	605	17233	59	1126	17	134
Lincoln	7593	1835	1510	8352	2932	58269			2391	97320			663	23527	1182	25459		
Montour, town of	70		610	56	8	80			5	150			1	65				
Oneida	15002	1818	22730	12609	5580	90560			4016	156870			725	21330	891	16866	8	110
Otter Creek	17508	2688	58545	11297	5858	91327			4434	159756	9	115	615	16388	172	3021	3	42
Perry, exc. of Traer	15811	2671	43656	12788	5215	80978			4427	157784			683	22965	115	2140	2	45
Richland	11718	2965	51355	11230	4545	64303			4042	157990	5	63	573	15741	124	2322	2	45
Salt Creek	19117	6376	41820	17261	3568	55320			3375	129830			419	10731	11	228	11	146
Spring Creek	10587	3727	19730	10204	5829	88456			3271	116545	1	12	1170	36632	1161	25612	27	384
Tama, exc. of Tama City	2120	1925	11141	1631	747	10588			727	24340	8	200	106	2948	7	125		

Tama City, town of	272	165	736	249	54	1093	....	....	156	5370	....	....	....	....	....	....	....	....
Toledo, exc. of town	8424	3582	41723	5132	2142	26149	....	....	2144	70506	2	35	331	9476	20	320	8	108
Toledo, town of	6725	8653	20713	5676	2409	36337	....	....	2001	45250	....	....	472	12643	220	4465	3	50
Traer, town of	315	40	760	255	55	440	....	....	125	4050	....	....	28	900	....	....	....	....
York	12653	5005	46394	11507	6654	103304	....	....	3757	138199	58	800	734	17390	156	2816	9	96
Total	255182	90222	743258	214941	97013	1437807	....	....	73251	2842859	110	1488	13574	384469	7305	142765	120	1686

16

TAYLOR COUNTY.

Benton, exc. of Bedford	5214	4192	33474	5193	1256	14222	37	330	3963	81020	25	325	608	20414	17	310	5	45
Clayton	6499	5095	39444	4676	847	11281	19	296	3885	80112	30	389	760	25586	46	935	2	21
Dallas	9436	3894	34454	6947	1708	14784	....	....	4646	145300	48	631	576	15899	154	1470	8	71
Gay	3990	4746	18884	3558	413	5701	....	....	2267	62370	52	92	492	17869	....	....	1	38
Grant	4743	1988	13277	4222	579	10125	....	....	2329	61610	39	728	487	19325	74	1628	2	50
Grove	3045	1894	3140	2670	804	10977	....	....	1220	35845	6	180	183	5137	118	2966	2	50
Holt	9508	5307	36055	7882	1818	30351	....	....	3027	102215	15	310	453	16911	150	3027	4	70
Jackson	4052	4676	20894	3801	365	4459	22	348	2230	73670	26	437	517	14636	34	618	7	88
Jefferson	6598	5223	23690	4246	327	3478	17	345	3298	104133	46	693	1113	21140	....	....	1	24
Marshall	4374	3641	18492	3934	596	8724	....	....	2048	52280	....	....	375	13759	114	2002	5	43
Mason	10205	4568	37645	6577	1418	21132	13	218	4062	115635	7	79	640	19727	15	341	2	19
Nodaway	6067	5506	30320	4672	1319	18672	50	680	3198	94950	25	481	464	13827	50	1016	16	312
Platte	5247	3788	17747	4005	675	10240	....	....	2572	92800	21	270	243	9431	26	600	38	446
Polk	10274	5087	44436	7186	1297	17502	73	776	4358	134465	105	1266	653	22061	12	254	2	28
Ross	6966	4049	22286	4784	968	11008	13	75	3171	96350	44	630	586	17641	45	1210	5	10
Washington	6643	3164	29628	5089	1056	14162	....	....	2986	86925	13	147	568	16294	81	966	1	15
Total	102861	235515	423866	79442	15446	206818	244	3068	48260	1419680	502	6658	8718	269657	936	17343	103	1330

NOTE.—Non-resident lands not reported by townships, 168,742 acres.

UNION COUNTY.

Dodge	3124	1882	16102	2744	454	7341	....	....	1653	61250	12	130	301	7820	20	390	2	35
Douglas, exc. of Creston	3981	1786	14048	3117	1508	12620	5	50	1582	64640	15	265	223	8501	33	920	....	....
Grant	3233	1249	13745	2246	321	4775	....	....	1291	53770	2	40	257	7816	22	385	1	10
Highland	5853	1815	19600	4093	532	9095	....	....	1966	94878	10	153	525	17651	51	1023	8	89
Jones	6841	2702	41200	3922	1062	14564	10	151	2581	108520	40	547	638	20794	27	397	8	101
Lincoln	4209	686	15450	2493	1086	14500	....	....	1924	38115	8	145	444	15031	115	2590	....	....
New Hope	4942	3242	24965	4497	622	9064	....	....	2335	102550	10	139	510	18138	62	1340	1	9
Platte	6528	5177	43002	6528	1553	23069	....	....	2720	129685	....	....	641	20426	46	920	2	45
Pleasant	4882	4552	32870	4499	1069	12018	18	219	2246	182860	26	390	456	16487	37	844	6	43
Sand Creek	4666	3082	20016	3507	610	9111	10	240	1654	66280	49	592	424	14244	58	1834	2	42

UNION COUNTY.—Continued.

Names of townships, towns, and cities.	No. of acres of improved land.	No. of acres of unimproved land.	No. of rods of fence.	No. of acres in cultivation in 1874.	Spring wheat. Number of acres.	Spring wheat. Number of bushels harvested.	Winter wheat. Number of acres.	Winter wheat. Number of bushels harvested.	Indian corn. Number of acres.	Indian corn. Number of bushels harvested.	Rye. Number of acres.	Rye. Number of bushels harvested	Oats. Number of acres.	Oats. Number of bushels harvested.	Barley. Number of acres.	Barley. Number of bushels harvested.	Buckwheat. Number of acres.	Buckwheat. Number of bushels harvested.
Spaulding	3295	2053	2000	2794	875	12790	....	....	1387	59280	9	171	270	9154	33	451	1	12
Union, exc. of Afton	5451	4990	23403	5386	894	12240	10	300	2724	109102	68	515	1438	31686	60	1172	5	78
Total	57005	33216	266401	45826	16586	141187	53	960	24063	1130930	249	3087	6127	187748	564	12275	36	464

VAN BUREN COUNTY.

Names of townships, towns, and cities.	No. of acres of improved land.	No. of acres of unimproved land.	No. of rods of fence.	No. of acres in cultivation in 1874.	Spring wheat. Number of acres.	Spring wheat. Number of bushels harvested.	Winter wheat. Number of acres.	Winter wheat. Number of bushels harvested.	Indian corn. Number of acres.	Indian corn. Number of bushels harvested.	Rye. Number of acres.	Rye. Number of bushels harvested	Oats. Number of acres.	Oats. Number of bushels harvested.	Barley. Number of acres.	Barley. Number of bushels harvested.	Buckwheat. Number of acres.	Buckwheat. Number of bushels harvested.
Bentonsport, town of	248	26	1520	137	6	9	4	45	40	2080	8	70	13	330	....	....	15	76
Birmingham, town of	14	100	14	....	40	447	10	126	173	6420	16	155	43	938	5	100	3	50
Bonaparte	4687	5710	39546	2579	252	1488	512	7130	1535	58555	103	855	339	8112	....	....	12	241
Cantril, town of	....	....	577	....	....	....	....	....	....	....	....	....	....	....	....	....	....	....
Cedar	15776	4474	280742	11457	1176	10884	181	1673	4973	197750	101	672	1632	48240	4	38	53	834
Chequest	8380	9539	69552	7628	389	2391	1195	12331	2661	118635	125	1106	564	12415	....	....	35	563
Des Moines	14231	11638	115847	8072	340	1357	917	8166	4854	181132	154	919	1338	33298	8	39	59	1079
Farmington, exc. of town	5833	8136	60312	3754	112	679	905	11030	1855	70560	115	761	347	6931	2	47	19	236
Harrisburg	14918	565	68881	8411	1254	11501	315	3023	5181	197851	192	1646	1411	42447	2	35	46	948
Henry	3430	4585	49131	3387	179	594	739	8404	2196	88690	31	275	492	13807	....	....	12	145
Jackson, exc. of Cantril	17940	9158	107135	17881	570	2461	492	4588	6951	253540	109	511	2062	48368	32	164	73	1022
Keosauqua, town of	550	433	7078	372	7	27	92	1164	251	7500	....	....	44	940	....	....	....	....
Lick Creek	10744	10034	103612	10515	555	5333	1091	13523	2845	105000	195	2189	690	16273	....	....	33	624
Union, exc. of Birmingham	17187	4799	83339	14118	1062	10265	296	4724	5023	183162	100	912	642	46484	....	....	39	846
Van Buren, exc. of Keosauqua	12891	9653	126860	7155	439	3024	2071	23310	3823	155043	73	732	1096	24087	....	....	43	748
Vernon	9974	8997	74831	6792	120	650	706	7303	3269	120255	91	1413	892	24917	1	8	13	340
Village	8320	7547	79078	8499	605	5060	1128	12260	2859	108619	72	938	535	12720	1	26	26	485
Washington, exc. of Bentonsport	6551	4134	53800	2506	349	2638	274	3054	1722	68830	24	309	456	13391	....	....	16	281
Total	153674	99528	1321855	113263	7455	58808	10928	121854	50211	1923622	1509	13466	12596	353698	55	457	487	8518

WAPELLO COUNTY.

Adams	11272	8354	98820	11892	1211	9272	146	1905	4763	161745	180	1116	1263	24105	6	52	23	345
Agency, exc. of town	5490	1920	30996	6000	426	4173	22	198	2181	74678	29	177	341	7932	2	59	13	186
Agency City, town of	...	...	...	81	8	55	...	...	65	2100	1	12	2	30	...	...	1	16
Cass	3774	2581	32418	3492	405	3270	132	1642	1535	62145	33	348	220	3413	...	...	3	56
Center, exc. of Ottumwa	12994	4891	92453	11448	1002	8644	161	1724	4800	188642	148	1698	726	15225	...	...	28	294
Columbia, exc. of Eddyville	11951	5000	77400	9045	1175	12045	105	1310	3925	167360	74	975	655	16225	23	450	18	336
Competine	16904	3126	54111	12882	1721	22715	10	152	5205	260460	51	711	1223	40335	92	1855	21	588
Dahlonega	8798	1680	39943	9806	2700	8193	22	213	2927	116688	13	154	522	15314	...	...	7	98
Eddyville, town of	90	25	560	302	30	400	...	...	251	9475	...	...	35	780	...	...	...	...
Greene	11132	6940	87925	7395	576	3969	373	3331	3346	114212	301	3180	706	11671	...	...	34	643
Highland	13367	3895	56176	12815	1751	21315	14	174	6523	276065	23	191	1511	47619	39	752	18	359
Keokuk	4255	3328	33079	2369	267	1805	204	1607	1199	65695	104	1024	183	3239	...	...	9	130
Pleasant	13308	6220	78635	15271	1754	20847	57	818	5903	194905	68	920	1343	39548	31	795	30	689
Polk	9065	6358	65612	8150	1037	6974	211	1686	3539	136017	211	2328	894	15061	...	...	13	144
Richland	14073	4876	53758	14333	2129	23695	68	509	6520	191704	43	456	1325	36400	57	622	5	136
Washington, exc. of Eldon	13736	4297	75086	9892	1176	10163	92	1090	4343	121900	117	840	621	16643	4	116	13	264
Total	150209	63491	876972	135173	17368	157535	1617	16159	57035	2143791	1396	14130	11570	293540	254	4701	236	4284

WARREN COUNTY.

Allen	7299	3673	45072	5346	1517	24434	22	346	3032	141240	32	484	335	12489	1	50	1	27
Belmont	18980	3943	51939	14659	4505	60678	...	...	6616	310020	10	84	611	18766	429	9532	7	121
Greenfield	21588	4489	91737	14034	4745	69242	...	...	7385	342250	9	102	760	26525	15	393	3	76
Indianola, town of	162	610	1640	99	20	335	...	...	23	1150	7	200	...	...	...	...	...	...
Jackson	7424	15512	31360	7581	2855	40446	...	...	4121	156635	...	...	370	13150	198	4194	3	59
Jefferson	10946	11996	45437	8130	3020	44063	...	...	4674	187929	...	...	482	25547	94	3184	9	117
Liberty	11610	11293	32301	9647	2611	37513	2	26	4246	208280	72	1087	647	22303	203	4728	18	210
Linn	18417	4760	78678	12940	4021	55330	2	44	6774	304735	...	...	503	22960	20	440	2	18
Otter	9789	13208	55340	8751	2032	26842	4	40	4660	225180	18	180	543	16653	30	500	4	74
Palmyra	9354	7059	52390	9303	2481	38338	...	...	4470	216950	16	380	404	12792	10	285	1	16
Richland	8171	8712	49368	8171	1744	24597	23	364	3371	131483	14	200	315	10032	8	100	...	8
Squaw	6949	15833	42586	6855	1980	25498	...	...	4065	171760	...	...	526	12062	49	1251	7	121
Union	8686	9532	48121	7348	2946	36811	...	...	4059	194078	...	...	216	5997	...	...	7	116
Virginia	6442	16493	40856	5517	1841	25200	8	90	3371	137470	13	145	424	13922	70	1159	9	88
Washington, exc. of Indianola	30077	12497	125109	24116	5899	83510	...	...	10624	485180	65	925	1133	35319	113	3137	17	270
White Breast	10376	12648	47235	8882	2453	31020	...	...	4248	160335	13	149	624	18258	508	10505	19	241
White Oak	8005	14920	46017	7358	2457	30822	...	...	4541	186690	25	200	498	14735	34	1360	3	32
Total	194265	167178	885186	158737	47157	651679	61	910	80280	3561365	294	4136	8391	281510	1782	40818	110	1594

WASHINGTON COUNTY.

NAMES OF TOWNSHIPS, TOWNS, AND CITIES.	No. of acres of improved land.	No. of acres of unimproved land.	No. of rods of fence.	No. of acres in cultivation in 1874.	SPRING WHEAT.		WINTER WHEAT.		INDIAN CORN.		RYE.		OATS.		BARLEY.		BUCK-WHEAT.	
					Number of acres.	Number of bushels harvested.	Number of acres.	Number of bushels harvested.	Number of acres.	Number of bushels harvested.	Number of acres.	Number of bushels harvested.	Number of acres.	Number of bushels harvested.	Number of acres.	Number of bushels harvested.	Number of acres.	Number of bushels harvested.
Brighton, exc. of town	7122	6237	46935	5486	1383	11156	17	145	2427	78265	64	574	441	7646	....	....	14	236
Brighton, town of	819	550	4550	513	102	822	14	245	259	7425	12	156	41	895	....	....	....	....
Cedar	13274	974	42442	10700	2773	15045	....	....	5684	234010	13	161	1328	34841	7	182	2	24
Clay	8671	4915	57205	5936	1000	9789	314	1588	2502	84185	93	755	439	10792	....	....	5	111
Crawford	17029	122	77509	7885	2456	27543	182	1863	3040	226865	15	136	1077	34174	24	383	29	422
Dutch Creek	15822	6278	58847	15228	3188	35328	22	293	5662	165874	182	1830	1291	33323	26	610	31	506
English River	17728	4570	98267	11985	3151	40543	162	2381	4700	202350	165	2189	1074	32906	57	1017	7	62
Franklin	14865	1830	49398	13686	2302	28610	....	....	5076	193550	33	554	1015	31235	....	....	7	112
Highland	14049	1588	41329	8106	3147	32497	....	....	4737	181715	51	668	940	22228	27	359	5	40
Iowa	17237	4596	82555	9572	3314	38850	....	....	4875	164870	129	2614	1119	31215	154	3727	10	237
Jackson	17284	1208	56658	14914	3288	42121	....	....	5897	230233	40	452	1327	43963	128	2299	7	285
Lime Creek	13346	4007	58060	9761	3208	40582	6	80	4969	177117	53	548	916	28276	15	348	17	284
Marion	11133	6657	64246	7999	1401	12822	674	7274	3770	137205	10	45	944	25496	21	478	17	238
Oregon	15795	3266	53854	10266	2722	38966	4	41	5015	208813	35	322	1095	31513	54	1186	20	250
Seventy-Six	17151	1597	57858	12663	4739	58859	....	....	6185	250964	72	899	1199	37818	35	804	24	446
Washington, exc. of city	21291	3518	128542	12464	3371	35101	28	239	7449	281500	142	2085	1439	45364	82	1546	49	648
Washington, city of	2560	3739	9146	720	101	1245	16	44	1018	7300	13	400	16	635	....	....	....	....
Total	225176	55652	987401	157884	41646	469868	1439	14193	73265	2832241	1122	14388	15701	452320	630	12939	244	3901

WAYNE COUNTY.

Allerton, town of	....	....	....	....	....	....	....	....	....	....	....	....	....	....	8	108	40	491
Benton	9983	5938	53480	7040	765	5353	....	....	5177	181345	15	257	946	25830	....	....	6	197
Clay	9679	6050	3783	8266	734	6314	5	76	4182	144965	75	941	604	21182	....	....	23	303
Clinton	2621	2701	30708	4914	186	1749	8	46	2696	75235	123	970	505	10462	....	....	27	367
Corydon, exc. of town	8163	4626	33473	6475	386	2339	20	86	3201	132728	49	399	773	29272	23	224	13	159
Corydon, town of	1230	663	5776	1092	31	141	....	....	536	19380	5	130	70	1589	....	....	....	....
Grand River, exc. of Lineville	9539	5386	44053	11599	487	2443	60	451	3062	85675	143	257	1023	17209	....	....	14	249

Howard	8256	2376	29188	4258	286	1327	5	100	2430	68760	53	536	493	13191			11	139
Jackson	4752	3182	16318	4350	339	2684			2893	96095	21	195	412	15269			10	132
Jefferson	5357	7372	44060	5151	360	2400	14	194	3510	100180	167	1629	571	12357			14	269
Monroe	5891	3548	27355	4756	403	2874	8	86	2469	82765	20	167	499	15676			12	129
Richman	10334	4552	31647	7860	770	8309			3906	149596	14	221	1044	35759	47	891	2	37
Seymour, town of									13	600								
South Fork	8657	5098	25319	595	1003	4022			4526	176255	1	20	805	19975	15	320	13	194
Union	14628	3228	45539	10842	934	9162			5654	212650	38	500	1182	36172			29	264
Walnut, exc. of Seymour	12411	3896	48240	11025	965	8398	9	76	5719	237183	70	627	991	31711	6	80	16	243
Warren, exc. of Allerton	10709	415	44341	540	602	4196	14	121	4318	147748	49	582	818	22877	8	108	40	491
Washington	9820	3175	33948	28820	1266	7868			5754	275132	8	80	1106	27773			13	137
Wright	12742	4589	31630	10106	858	6767			5580	217895	23	190	1399	40092			10	172
Total	147766	66795	548855	117689	10375	76346	143	1236	65625	2405187	874	7701	13242	367396	99	1623	255	3496

WEBSTER COUNTY.

Badger	4701	4855	30255	4882	2784	28531			1295	43455	2	32	453	14060	14	500		
Clay	1621	168	4646	833	455	6168			279	8705			94	2730	16	290		
Colfax	1041	2361	1235	1041	528	6913			274	7208			134	3906	6	80		
Dayton	17923	4703	60295	10952	4755	76584			4610	173725			876	33322	28	736		
Deer Creek	4099	2184	9978	4574	1222	6460			1069	34460			451	5945				
Douglas	9560	5773	39269	5955	2284	25780			2798	93932	6	100	610	15064	71	794	29	523
Elkhorn	5172	1916	18932	3047	1770	21261			1245	33460			318	10260	61	1905		
Fulton	1058	1412		973	454	6026			466	13170			58	1672	6	100		
Gowrie	379	1626	2580	644	424	3826			173	3350			87	1231				
Hardin	2676	2973	27890	2672	866	15819			1244	42395	21	391	147	2793	55	1668		
Jackson	4357	3952	15888	4354	1574	10011			1849	36540			490	10578	31	290	3	30
Johnson	5677	4912	11060	3996	1695	15072			1961	50960	14	26	660	11679	33	359		
Lost Grove	3593	2231	10882	2942	1679	23343			1125	35220			190	4677	14	430		
Newark	1016	1974	2405	950	468	7015			221	7899			116	4466	7	175	1	10
Otho	3386	3212	17313	2973	1211	16160			1345	40150			366	11839	25	659	9	147
Pleasant Valley	1591	1559	9904	1575	641	8535	5		747	24595	8	71	138	4384	2	25		
Sumner	13472	1719	8728	4160	1341	34255			1635	57422			418	13175	55	1106	2	9
Wahkonsa, exc. of Ft. Dodge	4107	3505	16996	3727	1304	13319			1534	46650	40	380	597	15992	21	345		4
Washington	3342	3849	25389	4825	2341	34117			2162	60270	11	130	698	21630	11	331	8	111
Webster	5439	4350	30049	3286	1025	16343			1616	62815	5	83	330	11536	27	621	12	116
Yell	3028	2510	23843	2539	1733	15513			1065	41530	3	40	260	6554	42	860		
Total	97238	61744	367537	70910	30554	391051	5		28713	917911	110	1253	7491	207493	525	11274	64	950

WINNEBAGO COUNTY.

Names of townships, towns, and cities.	No. of acres of improved land.	No. of acres of unimproved land.	No. of rods of fence.	No. of acres in cultivation in 1874.	Spring wheat. Number of acres.	Spring wheat. Number of bushels harvested.	Winter wheat. Number of acres.	Winter wheat. Number of bushels harvested.	Indian corn. Number of acres.	Indian corn. Number of bushels harvested.	Rye. Number of acres.	Rye. Number of bushels harvested.	Oats. Number of acres.	Oats. Number of bushels harvested.	Barley. Number of acres.	Barley. Number of bushels harvested.	Buckwheat. Number of acres.	Buckwheat. Number of bushels harvested.
Center	3864	5073	26620	3202	2186	34404	....	....	528	17575	5	66	268	9311	22	502	2	30
Forest	2201	7112	13638	1447	931	14080	....	....	214	10400	....	....	225	7135	38	646	9	127
Iowa	4331	7169	28895	3421	2787	60335	....	....	248	11335	....	....	327	12503	4	123		
Norway	2430	5894	8325	1930	1484	27018	11	270	139	4509	....	....	231	7150	13	243	....	....
Pleasant	4763	5377	19861	2421	1550	26444	....	....	248	8606	....	....	276	9010	11	241	1	16
Total	17589	39625	97339	12421	8938	162281	11	270	1378	52425	5	66	1327	45109	88	1755	12	173

WINNESHIEK COUNTY.

Names of townships, towns, and cities.	No. of acres of improved land.	No. of acres of unimproved land.	No. of rods of fence.	No. of acres in cultivation in 1874.	Spring wheat. Number of acres.	Spring wheat. Number of bushels harvested.	Winter wheat. Number of acres.	Winter wheat. Number of bushels harvested.	Indian corn. Number of acres.	Indian corn. Number of bushels harvested.	Rye. Number of acres.	Rye. Number of bushels harvested.	Oats. Number of acres.	Oats. Number of bushels harvested.	Barley. Number of acres.	Barley. Number of bushels harvested.	Buckwheat. Number of acres.	Buckwheat. Number of bushels harvested.
Bloomfield	21251	7120	108219	86287	5796	86287	....	....	1974	82145	1	24	1381	49754	158	2951	....	6
Bluffton	7600	8174	48091	7564	3893	63719	....	....	1870	57702	....	....	1057	36907	85	1397	6	120
Burr Oak	11172	3639	47914	9683	5457	95308	....	....	1202	40910	2	54	1348	36394	265	7218	7	45
Calmar	9245	7265	43231	8400	6326	92640	....	....	818	6740	8	128	976	32925	15	451	....	....
Canoe	7852	7507	55040	7095	3466	54986	....	....	1471	49165	....	....	766	26803	80	3333	15	85
Decorah, exc. of city	7339	5019	52325	7807	3113	58387	....	....	1058	42923	....	....	860	26777	122	2985	4	50
Frankville	19676	2502	81866	11128	6687	98658	....	....	2402	88[illegible]73	....	....	1869	66157	422	8248	....	....
Fremont	8490	5270	39815	7027	4564	73275	....	....	1156	40425	....	....	1146	38672	111	2205	....	....
Glenwood	6825	9555	53654	6603	4855	74212	....	....	1148	42225	1	10	1027	24072	98	3253	....	....
Hesper	10225	7372	69314	8488	5374	86078	....	....	1408	56345	4	30	952	38711	134	2648	12	214
Highland	9380	8405	60100	7627	5157	79250	....	....	1088	44710	7	107	1020	38064	221	4998	....	....
Jackson	12398	7322	42039	8121	5322	80361	....	....	1158	36612	....	....	996	33245	71	1456	....	....
Lincoln	11466	5544	45311	7425	5635	90195	....	....	809	54060	....	....	974	33472	22	626	....	....
Madison	16919	2716	60925	9277	7057	113284	....	....	1229	46262	....	....	1255	45164	121	2760	10	274
Military	16423	6038	87390	13032	8100	132715	....	....	2000	76800	....	....	1688	55848	166	3674	....	....
Orleans	18023	1850	61583	11766	7332	115596	....	....	1491	61220	....	....	1871	64670	364	8279	36	463
Pleasant	9707	10311	59053	7725	4472	88838	....	....	831	33180	2	20	1005	32138	147	3484	1	4
Springfield	10768	8693	68326	10713	7757	127601	....	....	1044	37900	16	219	1383	50182	98	1694	....	....
Sumner	10827	10648	54139	10224	5455	106400	....	....	1203	38589	43	599	1417	46672	70	1478	....	....

Washington	20554	6220	62238	13477	6357	95675	....	....	1785	40530	....	....	1316	39881	83	1602	4	67
Total	246140	131670	1200575	259469	112175	1813465	....	....	27145	977316	85	1191	24307	826508	2853	64740	97	1328

WOODBURY COUNTY.

Arlington	673	602	40	701	464	5156	....	....	220	5120	....	....	98	1032	....	....	....	....
Concord	2216	2181	6950	2150	1226	12543	....	....	646	12592	....	....	135	2597	....	....	....	....
Floyd	467	851	940	419	125	1432	....	....	187	7500	....	....	42	1165	....	....	....	....
Grant	3364	5644	16174	2866	1[illegible]97	18905	....	....	1375	47244	2	50	276	7345	....	....	....	....
Kedron	2105	2723	6550	1939	746	10837	....	....	846	28910	....	....	214	5523	....	....	....	....
Lakeport	2116	6002	12130	1593	789	8852	....	....	1080	34615	....	....	29	3856	....	....	....	....
Liberty	6102	2433	32736	4033	1873	42711	....	....	1595	66315	....	....	279	11582	2	50	....	....
Liston	1283	1393	4037	1030	821	13602	....	....	323	15300	....	....	....	....	64	155	....	....
Little Sioux	3832	7809	27090	2786	1434	22744	....	....	1851	78195	....	....	431	13384	38	928	....	....
Moville	368	710	1620	171	177	2367	....	....	110	3280	....	....	34	988	17	170	....	....
Rock	775	544	2450	774	309	3801	....	....	253	7130	....	....	51	1675	....	....	....	....
Rutland	735	870	440	711	414	3274	....	....	320	8425	....	....	67	2342	....	....	....	....
Sioux City, exc. of city	1751	3490	10941	1741	743	9512	....	....	668	13350	....	....	256	5572	....	....	....	....
Sioux City, city of	80	....	500	50	10	145	....	....	20	500	....	....	15	359	....	....	....	....
Union	4979	5064	5476	4523	1898	25494	....	....	1617	53100	....	205	493	16371	....	....	2	2
West Fork	3311	4193	9014	1895	827	10563	....	....	1012	27350	....	....	130	2730	14	200	8	26
Wolf Creek	3376	4713	4015	3263	1281	16319	....	....	1[illegible]53	39360	4	40	257	7750	....	....	....	....
Woodbury	3446	2875	18973	2452	799	11618	....	....	1191	42085	....	5	265	7376	....	....	....	....
Total	41179	57097	160076	33097	15243	218875	....	....	14667	490371	6	300	3072	91647	135	1503	10	28

WORTH COUNTY.

Bristol	8221	4923	25976	4686	2596	40449	....	....	678	24894	....	....	613	21306	56	1352	....	....
Brookfield	3806	6342	17449	3092	2415	33761	....	....	282	8167	....	....	395	12464	37	538	....	....
Danville	2639	1220	7910	1977	1319	19262	....	....	261	9485	....	....	278	12112	29	649	2	38
Deer Creek	4899	3517	15130	2785	2182	37520	....	....	153	6920	....	....	348	14858	82	2192	3	35
Fertile	2809	4146	12865	2142	1571	26775	....	....	290	9654	....	....	346	12931	7	204	2	55
Hartland	5175	6884	24285	2909	2099	32696	....	....	315	11533	....	....	387	12359	9	195	2	12
Kensett	3081	3365	4060	2789	2076	37601	....	....	291	9920	....	....	358	12110	43	1129	....	....
Northwood	6050	8734	30809	5181	3407	60428	....	....	508	17451	....	....	757	26780	38	640	5	100
Silver Lake	6605	3333	24873	2765	1998	35984	....	....	191	5745	....	....	316	9970	20	403	....	....
Union	5642	3493	8225	4831	3429	86211	....	....	561	18522	....	....	647	26667	108	2324	....	....
Total	48927	45957	171082	33157	23092	410487	....	....	3530	122291	....	....	4445	161557	429	9626	14	240

WRIGHT COUNTY.

NAMES OF TOWNSHIPS, TOWNS, AND CITIES.	No. of acres of improved land.	No. of acres of unimproved land.	No. of rods of fence.	No. of acres in cultivation in 1874.	SPRING WHEAT.		WINTER WHEAT.		INDIAN CORN.		RYE.		OATS.		BARLEY.		BUCK-WHEAT.	
					Number of acres.	Number of bushels harvested.	Number of acres.	Number of bushels harvested.	Number of acres.	Number of bushels harvested.	Number of acres.	Number of bushels harvested.	Number of acres.	Number of bushels harvested.	Number of acres.	Number of bushels harvested.	Number of acres.	Number of bushels harvested.
Belmond	6188	1690	20194	4829	2123	33585	....	....	1303	36355	5	83	667	20203	177	3071	1	13
Boone	1068	1186	6745	749	573	6250	....	....	408	10576	....	....	148	3085	....	....	....	....
Clarion	2166	3704	1175	1788	792	11697	....	....	664	10735	....	....	242	7525	28	456	5	19
Eagle Grove	2363	3058	15908	1851	797	13536	....	....	643	25080	....	....	256	10556	11	386	2	21
Iowa	4352	3147	15560	2540	1155	14359	....	....	923	30010	....	....	474	16279	124	2366	3	11
Liberty	2496	3474	14474	1925	975	9766	....	....	818	27301	5	35	305	8515	42	510	2	30
Pleasant	2817	2342	13370	2605	1031	15926	....	....	994	28505	....	....	410	12871	18	373	3	25
Troy	4764	4472	24167	4567	2072	28082	....	....	1955	55650	29	324	563	20490	14	302	2	65
Vernon	2840	3883	10500	2663	1252	20149	....	....	777	22920	....	....	443	13387	12	357	1	10
Wall Lake	3600	4086	....	2784	1253	22254	....	....	839	24020	....	....	345	12580	7	250	....	....
Woolstock	2862	1345	9810	2656	1606	20562	....	....	765	10669	....	....	281	9685	12	360	3	28
Total	35516	32387	136903	28957	13629	196166	....	....	10089	281821	39	442	4134	135176	445	8431	22	222

FLAX, SORGHUM, GRASSES, POTATOES, TURNIPS, ONIONS, PEAS AND BEANS.

ADAIR COUNTY.

NAMES OF TOWNSHIPS, TOWNS, AND CITIES.	FLAX.		SORGHUM.		Number of acres of blue grass for pasture.	Number of acres of tame grass.	Number of tons of hay from same	Number of tons of hay from wild grass.	Number of bushels of grass seed.	HUNGARIAN GRASS.		POTATOES.		SWEET POTATOES.		ONIONS.		Number of bushels of turnips.	Number of bushels of beets.	Number of bushels of peas and beans.
	Number of acres in flax seed.	Number of bushels harvested.	Number of acres in sorghum.	Number of gallons of syrup from sorghum.						Number of acres.	Number of tons of hay.	Number of acres.	Number of bushels.	Number of acres.	Number of bushels.	Number of acres.	Number of bushels.			
Eureka	....	....	1	80	....	....	....	497	....	....	....	11	785	....	....	....	2	120	30	7
Fontanelle, town of	....	....	....	....	....	8	21	247	....	....	....	10	1001	....	34	....	19	90	165	25
Grand River	12	61	6	711	20	118	76	967	....	23	46	20	1824	....	18	....	18	39	17	24
Greenfield	....	....	5	1642	....	21	45	1004	....	3	7	21	2125	....	....	....	....	....	....	....
Grove	....	2	3	310	....	20	25	581	....	....	....	14	1100	....	8	....	39	279	15	30
Harrison	2	10	2	293	10	137	124	623	3	....	....	41	3375	....	31	....	67	824	94	72
Jackson	....	....	3	278	2	38	53	1391	....	....	....	25	2319	....	2	....	68	555	146	74
Jefferson	1	15	5	634	....	313	126	2097	80	3	6	51	4258	....	54	....	58	772	127	29
Lincoln	5	9	....	53	65	254	200	1254	....	16	41	50	5767	....	95	....	162	366	114	67
Orient	41	270	....	....	....	313	186	472	....	40	100	24	2111	....	....	....	....	....	50	250
Prussia	....	....	....	....	....	....	....	509	....	....	....	12	545	....	40	5	237	50	43	17
Richland	44	417	8	406	....	109	52	1303	50	....	....	41	3507	....	7	....	46	79	84	91
Summerset, exc. of Fontanelle	....	....	1	73	....	13	22	796	....	....	....	30	1363	....	11	....	9	234	23	46
Summit	....	....	....	....	....	10	....	160	....	....	....	4	330	....	13	....	40	....	8	....
Union	....	....	2	295	4	41	29	583	....	18	31	21	1932	....	2	....	25	40	164	78
Walnut	16	184	....	....	....	20	15	627	16	1	2	18	1300	....	....	5	439	416	2	9
Washington	81	306	8	....	30	233	257	1927	70	....	....	41	4096	....	11	5	181	524	131	95
Total	202	1274	44	4775	131	1648	1231	15038	219	104	233	434	37738	....	326	15	1410	4388	1213	914

ADAMS COUNTY.

NAMES OF TOWNSHIPS, TOWNS, AND CITIES.	FLAX.		SORGHUM.		Number of acres of blue grass for pasture.	Number of acres of tame grass.	Number of tons of hay from same.	Number of tons of hay from wild grass.	Number of bushels of grass seed.	HUNGARIAN GRASS.		POTATOES.		SWEET POTATOES.		ONIONS.		Number of bushels of turnips.	Number of bushels of beets.	Number of bushels of peas and beans.
	Number of acres in flax seed.	Number of bushels harvested.	Number of acres in sorghum.	Number of gallons of syrup from sorghum.						Number of acres.	Number of tons of hay.	Number of acres.	Number of bushels.	Number of acres.	Number of bushels.	Number of acres.	Number of bushels.			
Carl	29	281	2	339	....	1	2	956	....	....	....	10	1032	....	....	....	....	....	....	....
Colony	6	65	5	536	4	41	29	851	....	6	5	36	2481	....	85	....	....	160	....	....
Douglas	35	187	12	1412	35	183	207	1714	45	9	12	40	3435	....	23	....	145	128	105	49
Grant	....	....	3	474	....	25	42	1030	....	....	....	9	1112	....	58	....	93	34	....	6
Jasper	487	4083	2	263	....	122	108	1611	8	7	2	45	2462	....	37	....	10	39	70	5
Lincoln	433	3800	7	510	....	14	....	1278	....	14	20	26	1815	....	....	....	....	....	....	....
Mercer	328	2977	7	290	....	34	27	845	....	13	38	22	935	....	....	....	....	50	....	....
Nodaway	24	80	10	1132	2	258	250	1617	14	22	46	73	4531	....	125	....	88	120	95	18
Prescott	23	251	8	420	2	67	18	1322	6	15	25	35	2067	....	93	....	77	163	38	69
Quincy, exc. of towns	88	631	26	1126	....	73	116	1426	....	7	20	65	2206	....	....	3	165	95	40	73
Union	85	400	2	220	....	99	180	960	....	4	8	19	840	....	50	2	215	83	8	6
Washington	25	180	18	1882	....	101	186	1009	9	25	108	29	2452	1	81	....	57	331	50	29
Total	1563	12935	102	8604	43	1018	1165	14619	82	122	284	409	25378	1	552	5	850	1203	406	255

ALLAMAKEE COUNTY.

NAMES OF TOWNSHIPS, TOWNS, AND CITIES.	Number of acres in flax seed.	Number of bushels harvested.	Number of acres in sorghum.	Number of gallons of syrup from sorghum.	Number of acres of blue grass for pasture.	Number of acres of tame grass.	Number of tons of hay from same.	Number of tons of hay from wild grass.	Number of bushels of grass seed.	Hungarian grass: Number of acres.	Hungarian grass: Number of tons of hay.	Potatoes: Number of acres.	Potatoes: Number of bushels.	Sweet potatoes: Number of acres.	Sweet potatoes: Number of bushels.	Onions: Number of acres.	Onions: Number of bushels.	Number of bushels of turnips.	Number of bushels of beets.	Number of bushels of peas and beans.
Center	....	....	13	1256	....	1372	1521	25	....	....	....	158	6663	....	....	....	20	6262	18	37
Fairview	....	....	....	....	....	486	409	....	....	....	....	59	6977	....	....	....	....	....	....	....
Franklin	....	....	12	1111	151	742	732	235	3	4	8	69	7885	....	10	....	20	1403	57	139
French Creek	....	....	....	....	8	745	588	34	....	....	....	66	5699	....	....	....	....	700	....	....
Howard	....	....	....	....	....	140	91	723	....	....	....	40	4540	....	....	....	....	....	....	....
Iowa	....	....	....	....	....	116	194	1510	....	....	....	31	3620	....	....	....	13	75	23	25
Jefferson	....	....	....	19	....	1976	1212	35	6	....	....	70	7590	....	....	....	33	1502	142	278
Lafayette	....	....	9	890	....	729	796	240	....	....	....	92	8723	....	....	....	14	3918	19	46
Lansing, exc. of city	....	....	....	....	23	872	869	70	....	4	7	76	8202	....	....	....	181	3835	33	47
Linton	....	....	10	674	....	647	1503	9	13	2	3	105	12494	....	....	....	22	1816	19	34
Ludlow	....	....	1	127	922	1095	1087	191	417	3	3	79	7293	....	....	....	29	1308	191	132

Makee, exc. of Waukon	....	....	3	237	....	1379	1725	71	143	....	....	99	9364	....	....	....	90	....	....	35
Paint Creek	....	....	4	787	565	1253	1077	462	28	3	8	90	10604	....	....	....	75	1791	156	56
Post, exc. of Postville	....	....	3	389	2326	1616	2142	436	56	....	....	62	7271	....	....	....	106	1544	145	171
Postville, town of	....	....	....	....	....	....	....	3	....	....	....	....	40	....	....	....	....	....	....	....
Taylor	....	....	....	....	42	562	712	221	22	....	....	86	8797	....	....	....	....	350	....	....
Union City	....	....	....	....	97	351	571	50	....	....	....	35	3830	....	....	....	....	....	....	....
Union Prairie	....	....	1	72	....	989	778	....	....	....	....	86	9539	....	....	....	100	700	140	3
Waterloo	....	....	1	40	91	494	706	455	4	1	1	22	4928	....	....	....	52	631	16	30
Waukon, town of	....	....	....	....	50	44	81	....	....	....	....	1	60	....	....	....	....	....	....	....
Total	....	....	57	5602	4275	1568	16794	4770	692	17	30	1326	134119	....	10	....	755	25835	959	1033

APPANOOSE COUNTY.

Bellair	27	275	12	995	261	1985	1573	93	1093	371	500	37	3855	2	244	....	112	638	31	62
Caldwell	....	....	28	3925	45	1410	1226	303	254	295	369	60	6120	....	415	....	148	1715	102	159
Center, exc. Centerville	25	244	81	961	292	1589	1363	55	322	305	389	56	5819	4	525	....	15	179	9	29
Chariton	89	727	24	3042	530	1776	1163	158	1048	291	578	27	3071	1	136	12	22	305	23	86
Douglas	4	28	23	2436	120	906	806	118	283	186	263	18	1698	....	....	....	7	368	16	77
Franklin	88	474	15	793	....	1813	1470	533	1488	216	303	57	3141	1	66	....	3	30	....	31
Independence	115	590	27	3121	340	1687	1303	183	1036	374	745	41	4155	....	87	....	74	491	22	105
Johns	40	325	15	1099	326	3282	2183	436	2191	514	788	53	4572	....	156	....	71	163	77	142
Lincoln	14	124	20	1338	479	1834	1515	108	2040	450	694	25	2758	1	100	5	66	165	71	52
Moulton, town of	....	....	2	195	....	15	....	35	47	16	29	5	470	1	32	6	....	20	6	8
Pleasant	18	229	39	3029	1743	2351	2228	24	1064	242	331	48	4824	1	303	....	55	764	39	51
Sharon	....	....	23	2036	44	941	733	350	226	259	309	57	4637	3	116	4	130	171	43	129
Taylor	12	63	35	3311	1	1680	1114	....	....	180	311	47	4346	1	326	....	....	50	....	11
Udel	4	6	20	3148	1044	1412	1252	9	88	133	179	10	3450	....	297	....	32	123	7	5
Union	....	....	38	3905	158	375	420	130	....	81	92	33	3138	1	79	....	33	289	9	72
Walnut	....	....	8	1542	1007	1302	1060	22	758	351	577	5	1536	....	30	....	18	185	4	72
Washington, exc. Moult'n	....	....	68	6562	1633	2474	1792	341	433	638	937	128	10351	....	340	2	1147	686	43	102
Wells	....	....	31	2891	298	1522	1485	672	143	339	428	57	4535	....	144	4	585	447	6	122
Total	436	3085	436	44329	8321	28354	22686	3570	12514	5241	7822	764	72456	16	3396	33	2518	6789	508	1315

AUDUBON COUNTY.

Audubon	....	....	2	310	....	1	3	74	....	....	....	12	1328	....	22	1	178	168	10	18
Douglas	23	90	4	290	....	....	....	502	....	....	....	....	432	....	....	....	5	....	10	3
Exira	....	....	6	838	....	32	50	2110	....	16	35	20	2224	....	72	....	10	141	62	16
Greeley	....	....	1	112	....	....	....	692	....	....	....	3	347	....	50	....	6	63	7	4
Hamlin	....	....	5	440	....	5	10	953	....	2	5	8	959	2	217	....	57	371	67	20
Leroy	....	....	....	....	....	3	1	268	....	....	....	3	386	....	....	....	2	20	5	13
Melville	....	....	1	104	....	....	....	188	....	....	....	2	275	....	....	....	5	50	....	5

AUDUBON COUNTY.—Continued.

NAMES OF TOWNSHIPS, TOWNS, AND CITIES.	FLAX.		SORGHUM.		Number of acres of blue grass for pasture.	Number of acres of tame grass.	Number of tons of hay from same.	Number of tons of hay from wild grass.	Number of bushels of grass seed.	HUNGARIAN GRASS.		POTATOES.		SWEET POTATOES.		ONIONS.		Number of bushels of turnips.	Number of bushels of beets.	Number of bushels of peas and beans.
	Number of acres in flax seed.	Number of bushels harvested.	Number of acres in sorghum.	Number of gallons of syrup from sorghum.						Number of acres.	Number of tons of hay.	Number of acres.	Number of bushels.	Number of acres.	Number of bushels.	Number of acres.	Number of bushels.			
Oakfield	......	......	5	646	......	......	......	1564	......	35	61	16	2263	......	3	36	83	134	482	86
Viola	......	......	1	120	......	......	......	......	......	......	......	14	1151	......	......	......	39	686	46	24
Total	23	90	25	2860	......	41	64	6351	......	53	101	78	9365	2	364	37	385	1633	689	189

BENTON COUNTY.

NAMES OF TOWNSHIPS, TOWNS, AND CITIES.	Number of acres in flax seed.	Number of bushels harvested.	Number of acres in sorghum.	Number of gallons of syrup from sorghum.	Number of acres of blue grass for pasture.	Number of acres of tame grass.	Number of tons of hay from same.	Number of tons of hay from wild grass.	Number of bushels of grass seed.	Hungarian grass: Number of acres.	Hungarian grass: Number of tons of hay.	Potatoes: Number of acres.	Potatoes: Number of bushels.	Sweet potatoes: Number of acres.	Sweet potatoes: Number of bushels.	Onions: Number of acres.	Onions: Number of bushels.	Number of bushels of turnips.	Number of bushels of beets.	Number of bushels of peas and beans.
Benton	......	......	28	2821	147	335	386	598	37	2	6	67	6108	......	38	......	100	286	68	103
Big Grove	333	2817	4	425	241	1512	610	1416	106	......	......	44	4070	......	46	......	39	141	77	41
Bruce	90	654	3	145	1	828	410	1470	258	5	8	128	5779	......	15	1	83	645	218	282
Canton, exc. of Shellsburg	86	677	19	1735	740	1610	1673	877	50	......	......	71	6179	......	12	......	......	14	6	23
Cedar	63	495	3	1779	30	1919	1305	2160	662	5	12	4	8426	......	60	......	34	949	1550	270
Eden	532	6566	8	531	185	1794	635	7861	321	......	......	100	5736	2	57	1	47	432	8	13
Eldorado	187	1488	5	393	16	345	166	1714	145	......	......	78	6630	......	6	1	42	74	9	29
Florence	10	110	5	357	41	3156	1404	1560	1430	......	......	89	7430	......	4	1	53	126	112	40
Fremont	41	336	10	1036	......	1567	775	1519	25	......	......	81	9023	......	12	......	40	79	100	74
Harrison	5	25	21	1568	405	360	337	1013	3	14	34	35	3185	1	126	......	33	71	51	69
Homer	157	1353	......	35	220	208	110	1550	36	3	6	60	6060	......	7	......	......	69	......	......
Iowa, exc. of Belle Plaine	......	......	4	374	12	1504	649	1189	13	1	2	69	6288	......	14	......	......	4	204	......
Jackson	74	455	5	251	26	1550	816	1490	54	1	1	25	6594	......	37	......	27	466	226	50
Kane	......	......	......	......	......	1027	122	1261	72	......	......	75	7902	......	10	......	......	25	......	......
Leroy, exc. of Blairstown	......	......	12	1391	......	744	491	1509	217	......	......	74	6952	......	55	2	80	897	38	39
Monroe	274	2899	......	......	25	330	294	1877	......	......	......	73	7241	......	......	......	......	145	......	......
Polk	23	35	44	332	1980	649	434	3042	20	19	26	83	8934	......	75	2	107	1408	117	199

St. Clair	98	561	......	......	......	1402	672	1455	1005	3	5	70	5454	......	......	1	200	250	......	9
Taylor, exc. of Vinton	23	180	7	349	353	1064	1008	686	317	......	......	52	4014	4	562	......	2	......	10	......
Union	1	5	5	282	......	755	92	1564	122	......	......	96	7873	......	10	......	2	98	22	3
Total	1997	18656	183	13804	4422	22659	8389	35811	4893	53	100	1374	129878	7	1146	9	889	6179	2816	1244

BLACK HAWK COUNTY.

Barclay	13	56	6	487	200	850	673	1795	152	39	72	71	6495	......	14	......	75	262	12	21
Bennington	3	30	17	1357	......	766	676	2034	195	......	......	83	8166	4	1	......	41	203	97	83
Big Creek, exc. La Porte	......	......	9	819	20	886	585	851	69	9	20	80	5940	......	53	......	33	151	200	87
Black Hawk	......	......	......	25	......	1090	811	2104	2	8	17	107	8326	......	......	......	142	551	206	46
Cedar	......	......	5	383	......	458	338	1315	68	......	......	62	4815	......	10	......	15	265	21	37
Cedar Falls, exc. of city	177	1346	10	1925	17	1487	821	1844	285	8	11	130	10368	......	2	......	7	587	202	25
Cedar Falls, city of	......	......	......	......	3	38	38	5	......	38	5	17	1590	......	14	......	......	25	21	......
Eagle	......	......	......	10	......	719	257	1469	......	......	......	80	7575	......	......	2	80	7	4	......
East Waterloo, exc. of Waterloo	10	48	8	792	14	960	542	1476	83	5	10	93	6217	......	71	......	42	185	261	48
Fox	30	352	14	1066	......	1065	513	1580	417	54	103	60	5840	......	11	......	40	170	29	18
Lester	......	......	......	......	63	466	517	2156	93	1	2	83	8564	......	6	......	57	403	17	123
Lincoln	1	10	10	......	......	806	381	1476	97	4	6	60	5360	......	......	......	6	321	90	66
Mt. Vernon	......	......	......	60	......	1127	657	988	10	......	......	71	4455	......	......	......	......	......	......	......
Orange	......	......	......	31	1494	836	940	2053	45	......	......	187	8241	......	33	......	11	177	60	28
Poyner	19	65	64	2899	290	835	545	1132	20	2	4	61	6062	......	18	......	78	310	86	62
Spring Creek	......	......	12	903	163	785	499	845	444	11	18	38	2420	......	19	......	12	363	......	69
Union	......	......	19	1818	......	116	117	687	......	3	7	30	2220	......	......	......	8	239	6	39
Washington	......	......	8	263	123	257	127	218	16	14	34	45	2186	......	17	......	1	333	46	......
Waterloo, exc. of city	......	......	4	325	......	554	657	498	......	......	......	127	9234	......	9	......	77	315	20	18
Total	253	1907	186	13163	2387	14101	9694	24526	1996	196	309	1485	114086	4	278	2	725	4867	1378	770

BOONE COUNTY.

Amaqua	5	60	......	......	......	10	10	1641	......	......	......	46	2336	......	......	......	......	......	......	......
Beaver	37	236	......	......	......	10	10	955	......	......	......	31	2345	......	......	......	......	......	......	......
Boonsboro, town of	......	......	......	......	......	18	28	47	......	......	......	3	88	......	3	......	......	......	......	......
Cass	......	......	12	948	188	286	364	806	......	4	12	41	3523	2	108	40	32	230	74	11
Colfax	265	2030	9	957	......	56	61	1773	......	......	......	50	3891	......	......	......	......	101	10	15
Des Moines, exc. of Boone and Boonsboro	......	......	6	910	5	598	2087	2087	9	4	15	161	6991	1	183	......	60	371	44	25
Dodge	......	......	28	3674	159	433	543	2768	35	......	4	89	7316	......	67	......	32	316	10	21
Douglas	72	299	11	1662	98	132	220	707	......	53	115	53	2704	......	30	......	6	86	2	27
Garden	551	4083	14	1585	34	94	198	2203	......	......	......	34	3381	......	14	......	18	377	......	97
Grant	......	......	2	171	......	8	13	1125	......	......	......	22	4492	......	......	......	......	......	......	......

BOONE COUNTY.—Continued.

Names of townships, towns, and cities.	Flax. Number of acres in flax seed.	Flax. Number of bushels harvested.	Sorghum. Number of acres in sorghum.	Sorghum. Number of gallons of syrup from sorghum.	Number of acres of blue grass for pasture.	Number of acres of tame grass.	Number of tons of hay from same.	Number of tons of hay from wild grass.	Number of bushels of grass seed.	Hungarian grass. Number of acres.	Hungarian grass. Number of tons of hay	Potatoes. Number of acres.	Potatoes. Number of bushels.	Sweet potatoes. Number of acres.	Sweet potatoes. Number of bushels.	Onions. Number of acres.	Onions. Number of bushels.	Number of bushels of turnips.	Number of bushels of beets.	Number of bushels of peas and beans.
Harrison	......	......	2	316	......	......	......	1398	7	......	......	38	2667	......	26	......	10	82	8	18
Jackson	91	304	4	564	10	265	177	2383	......	......	......	51	4285	......	......	......	......	......	......	......
Marcy	......	......	6	371	......	14	183	1767	......	11	28	28	3963	......	30	......	......	......	......	......
Peoples	......	......	7	791	6	48	30	2132	......	......	......	41	3061	6	405	......	41	282	40	73
Pilot Mound	......	......	6	885	......	71	49	753	4	2	10	4	1960	......	......	......	......	......	......	......
Union	......	......	8	607	10	41	78	1708	......	14	85	49	3049	......	......	......	155	120	4	29
Worth	86	399	......	1267	199	338	235	1082	11	1	2	59	4884	......	......	......	12	......	92	......
Yell	......	......	15	1313	3	112	98	1385	22	15	41	60	4848	......	19	......	159	618	83	49
Total	1107	7411	120	16031	712	2534	4384	26720	88	104	312	860	65784	9	885	40	525	2583	367	360

BREMER COUNTY.

Names of townships, towns, and cities.	Flax. Number of acres in flax seed.	Flax. Number of bushels harvested.	Sorghum. Number of acres in sorghum.	Sorghum. Number of gallons of syrup from sorghum.	Number of acres of blue grass for pasture.	Number of acres of tame grass.	Number of tons of hay from same.	Number of tons of hay from wild grass.	Number of bushels of grass seed.	Hungarian grass. Number of acres.	Hungarian grass. Number of tons of hay	Potatoes. Number of acres.	Potatoes. Number of bushels.	Sweet potatoes. Number of acres.	Sweet potatoes. Number of bushels.	Onions. Number of acres.	Onions. Number of bushels.	Number of bushels of turnips.	Number of bushels of beets.	Number of bushels of peas and beans.
Dayton	79	637	12	846	......	127	113	1356	16	......	......	52	3187	......	......	......	18	145	16	15
Douglas	4	49	20	1229	35	310	224	1626	38	2	3	75	5467	......	1	......	1	60	11	19
Franklin	34	282	7	648	......	468	474	1922	121	1	3	53	4482	......	......	......	......	......	......	......
Frederika	......	......	3	301	......	147	160	1028	143	2	......	39	2488	......	......	......	4	35	3	18
Fremont	......	......	23	1411	10	536	562	3089	279	3	14	88	7011	......	......	......	40	117	26	32
Jackson	......	......	13	1200	172	595	433	238	6	30	60	68	4360	......	......	......	4	150	79	45
Jefferson	......	......	3	624	2150	419	395	1304	......	......	......	56	6524	......	......	......	213	194	265	98
La Fayette	......	......	7	562	559	751	666	1223	......	11	22	65	6070	......	......	......	17	256	30	36
Le Roy	......	......	9	840	......	188	208	1566	90	2	2	37	2980	......	......	......	20	......	......	......
Maxfield	10	61	18	1485	......	321	98	2689	75	2	6	113	9765	......	......	......	32	553	17	44
Polk	......	......	9	788	12	814	434	1503	107	107	152	72	5300	......	......	......	35	185	17	21
Sumner	......	......	15	974	......	364	468	1645	50	......	......	57	3334	......	10	......	......	175	......	......
Warren	......	......	20	1974	......	416	289	2526	91	3	11	138	13335	......	......	......	20	555	151	19
Washington, exc. of Waverly	......	......	7	804	536	510	480	740	60	7	10	85	6122	......	......	2	542	438	21	48

Waverly, city of	....	....	....	....	5	231	214	38	....	7	7	17	1990	....	....	....	20	50	450	....
Total	127	1029	166	13686	3479	6200	5218	22493	1076	177	290	1015	82415	....	11	2	966	2913	1086	395

BUCHANAN COUNTY.

Buffalo	8	55	5	40	611	749	899	2712	25	14	43	48	3590	....	....	....	40	184	71	44
Byron	....	....	16	1951	80	1857	1641	1509	30	24	47	56	7990	....	27	18	113	465	250	108
Cono	....	....	9	773	....	227	230	1165	....	....	....	39	3953	....	....	....	....	....	....	....
Fairbank	....	....	17	1582	....	809	860	1334	23	5	10	65	6146	....	24	....	7	130	....	7
Fremont	....	....	5	523	....	581	576	2217	50	9	10	66	6584	....	....	....	12	867	28	23
Hazelton	....	....	....	....	34	509	617	1454	4	....	....	95	4285	....	....	....	....	1162	65	96
Homer	....	....	18	1612	....	210	209	1378	....	....	....	....	....	....	....	....	....	520	....	....
Jefferson	....	....	24	2083	90	643	861	1424	6	32	65	110	5246	....	5	....	....	70	....	....
Liberty	....	....	17	1654	14	824	990	328	75	....	2	60	6890	1	56	....	16	413	11	13
Madison	....	....	12	706	....	830	787	2283	509	11	26	57	4292	....	....	....	7	320	26	41
Middlefield	....	....	11	1221	375	689	226	1720	700	34	80	73	6087	....	12	....	40	886	81	33
Newton	....	5	22	1981	183	853	549	2462	372	....	....	77	6466	1	63	....	3	619	84	57
Perry	16	220	23	1998	419	938	993	1661	160	226	72	79	7817	....	81	6	353	235	24	63
Sumner	10	70	....	120	193	570	641	1049	70	....	....	21	2205	....	....	....	....	....	....	....
Washington, exc. of Independence	....	....	16	1443	....	1610	1859	1827	....	....	....	115	9161	....	80	....	215	362	91	83
Westburg	51	515	15	1784	....	716	839	1402	245	....	....	53	5510	....	....	....	....	....	....	88
Total	85	865	210	19471	1999	12615	12777	25925	2270	355	355	1014	86222	2	348	24	856	6233	731	656

BUENA VISTA COUNTY.

Barnes	....	....	6	467	....	4	13	1104	....	....	....	9	986	....	....	....	....	40	....	....
Brookes	1	10	2	224	....	....	....	345	....	....	....	6	330	....	....	....	....	65	5	3
Coon	....	....	1	63	....	....	....	133	....	....	....	28	1326	....	....	....	....	....	....	....
Elk	....	....	....	44	....	....	....	743	....	....	....	16	1681	....	....	....	....	57	48	29
Fairfield	....	....	2	93	....	....	....	636	....	....	....	18	1000	....	....	....	....	110	17	9
Grant	....	....	2	42	....	....	....	323	....	....	....	12	907	....	....	....	3	80	71	7
Lee	....	....	....	....	....	....	....	933	....	....	....	21	1544	....	....	....	21	152	45	33
Lincoln	....	....	3	58	....	....	....	205	....	....	....	4	192	....	....	....	....	60	....	....
Maple Valley	....	7	....	....	....	9	1	811	....	....	....	23	1520	....	2	....	7	626	28	23
Newell	....	....	1	116	....	....	....	1150	....	1	4	27	1328	....	....	....	....	616	....	336
Nokomis	....	....	1	106	....	10	3	1310	....	....	....	23	2490	....	....	....	10	144	7	20
Poland	....	....	....	....	....	....	....	415	....	....	....	10	488	....	....	....	....	25	....	....
Providence	....	....	....	....	....	....	....	577	....	....	....	19	1041	....	....	....	2	216	222	5
Scott	....	....	....	....	....	....	....	351	....	....	....	12	640	....	....	1	15	145	34	29
Storm Lake, exc. of town	....	....	....	....	....	....	....	873	....	....	....	28	1829	....	12	....	39	817	586	51

BUENA VISTA COUNTY.—Continued.

Names of townships, towns, and cities.	Flax.		Sorghum.		Number of acres of blue grass for pasture.	Number of acres of tame grass.	Number of tons of hay from same.	Number of tons of hay from wild grass.	Number of bushels of grass seed.	Hungarian grass.		Potatoes.		Sweet potatoes.		Onions.		Number of bushels of turnips.	Number of bushels of beets.	Number of bushels of peas and beans.
	Number of acres in flax seed.	Number of bushels harvested.	Number of acres in sorghum.	Number of gallons of syrup from sorghum.						Number of acres.	Number of tons of hay.	Number of acres.	Number of bushels.	Number of acres.	Number of bushels.	Number of acres.	Number of bushels.			
Storm Lake, town of	....	....	....	....	....	....	....	....	....	....	....	....	541	....	35	....	9	97	65	....
Total	1	17	18	1213	....	23	17	9909	....	1	4	256	17843	....	49	1	106	3250	1128	546

BUTLER COUNTY.

Names of townships, towns, and cities.	Number of acres in flax seed.	Number of bushels harvested.	Number of acres in sorghum.	Number of gallons of syrup from sorghum.	Number of acres of blue grass for pasture.	Number of acres of tame grass.	Number of tons of hay from same.	Number of tons of hay from wild grass.	Number of bushels of grass seed.	Hungarian grass: Number of acres.	Hungarian grass: Number of tons of hay.	Potatoes: Number of acres.	Potatoes: Number of bushels.	Sweet potatoes: Number of acres.	Sweet potatoes: Number of bushels.	Onions: Number of acres.	Onions: Number of bushels.	Number of bushels of turnips.	Number of bushels of beets.	Number of bushels of peas and beans.
Albion	120	701	7	336	....	482	320	1371	64	11	21	93	7290	....	....	2	306	180	....	53
Beaver	4	27	19	910	5	545	415	1536	93	16	22	102	6862	....	18	1	114	827	125	231
Bennezett	....	....	2	138	....	261	210	552	49	....	....	17	2770	....	....	....	9	405	32	27
Butler, exc. of Clarksville	....	....	8	802	180	1158	769	667	10	5	10	59	4929	....	13	1	71	334	55	48
Clarksville, town of	....	....	....	....	....	....	....	....	....	....	....	....	....	....	8	....	....	....	....	....
Cold Water	....	....	8	411	....	287	234	650	85	37	69	54	3662	....	13	1	7	400	35	35
Dayton	....	....	6	426	59	201	96	945	103	23	36	33	2768	....	....	....	33	197	50	23
Fremont	21	180	7	446	1	619	358	628	50	36	49	56	3959	....	....	....	101	630	91	81
Jackson	46	328	5	345	....	279	201	1108	12	28	37	55	3444	....	....	....	10	....	....	5
Jefferson	....	....	7	632	5	3891	237	1503	....	4	10	48	4285	....	....	1	54	768	91	100
Madison	244	1794	3	159	....	18	26	990	....	....	....	38	3426	....	....	....	....	202	64	36
Monroe	979	6531	6	504	172	388	401	1403	....	....	....	54	4891	....	....	....	18	7	....	45
Pittsford	969	516	5	52067	....	341	164	1563	52	....	....	33	2538	....	3	....	17	304	32	43
Ripley	276	1904	3	266	....	163	190	1364	....	....	....	20	1898	....	....	....	....	335	....	6
Shell Rock	25	201	6	4911	85	747	845	1591	216	7	10	59	6548	1	40	....	30	1010	26	113
Washington	1056	11104	....	22	....	180	48	905	32	....	....	39	3473	....	....	1	65	450	35	50
West Point	....	....	3	211	60	622	....	782	64	....	....	30	2522	....	....	....	....	271	29	58
Total	2848	23296	95	6365	567	6680	4514	17558	830	167	264	790	65265	1	82	5	828	6320	655	954

CALHOUN COUNTY.

Butler	76	538				10	10	1494				34	2671					1006		3
Calhoun			4	967		10	10	2303		1		48	2863		20		34	2509	608	90
Center				28				357				10	618					720		
Greenfield	5	45	6	508		6	6	917				30	1927					610		
Jackson	26	125	30	3425		89	98	2364		1	1	49	3783		9		26	1577	99	110
Lincoln				987		188	3	1743	35			65	4746				2	723		30
Sherman			8	328		188		1643				50	3569					505	5	13
Williams								795				20	966					110	30	2
Total	107	704	48	6243		491	127	11616	35	2	1	307	21143		29		62	7760	742	248

18

CARROLL COUNTY.

Arcadia	83	560						1158				17	2110		75					
Carroll, exc. of town	59	381		8				428				13	1040				8	15	2	
Carroll, town of													1281		32			220	20	25
Eden			1	32		1	1	630				17	946				8	240	40	10
Glidden								950				10	1020				12	275	6	5
Grant			6	244				934				18	451			1	7		2	6
Jasper			4	475		20	2	632				12	681			6	87	138	4	17
Kniest	64	390	14	1012		20	33	1360				81	3751			4	24	1040	66	24
Newton			7	216				1288				18	1020		4		63	220	74	101
Pleasant Valley	12	43	1	66	53	12	2	873				21	1091				30	255	2	15
Richland						47	47	503				1	120							
Roselle	19	111						1118				12	939					485	2	13
Sheridan	42	218	22	1690				1077				49	2243				4	663	45	68
Union								735				14	1190							
Washington	10	17					12	618				14	1490					85	110	4
Wheatland			1	69				858				25	1738				7	174	4	17
Total	289	1720	56	3812	53	112	85	13162				322	21111		111	11	250	3810	377	305

CASS COUNTY.

Atlantic, exc, of town			1	135		135	92	1748	4	49	114	75	6018	4	535		6	25	60	102
Atlantic, town of												2	40							
Bear Grove			3	393		3	5	1323		3	8	26	1575		26		7	296	10	18
Benton			12	1140		7	8	1032		11	30	33	3363		16		21	225	18	19
Brighton				40		29	8	1541		25	70	49	5384	2	178		11	238	119	70
Cass			1	150	100	194	182	1388	3	13	30	42	2522		52		6	186	19	3

CASS COUNTY.—Continued.

Names of townships, towns, and cities.	Flax.		Sorghum.		Number of acres of blue grass for pasture.	Number of acres of tame grass.	Number of tons of hay from same.	Number of tons of hay from wild grass.	Number of bushels of grass seed.	Hungarian grass.		Potatoes.		Sweet potatoes.		Onions.		Number of bushels of turnips.	Number of bushels of beets.	Number of bushels of peas and beans.
	Number of acres in flax seed.	Number of bushels harvested.	Number of acres in sorghum.	Number of gallons of syrup from sorghum.						Number of acres.	Number of tons of hay.	Number of acres.	Number of bushels.	Number of acres.	Number of bushels.	Number of acres.	Number of bushels.			
Edna	25	250	6	345	......	......	......	947	......	......	......	12	565	......	5	......	15	45	3	6
Franklin	......	......	......	......	......	22	......	1295	......	25	47	31	3085	......	8	......	20	1315	80	36
Grant	......	......	2	140	......	32	9	750	......	21	42	32	3925	2	118	4	500	289	......	......
Lincoln	30	240	1	115	......	32	30	745	......	......	......	21	2271	......	25	......	40	163	34	11
Massena	......	......	......	......	......	......	......	564	......	......	......	14	1098	......	......	1	50	153	12	15
Noble	......	......	3	390	......	19	15	1361	2	1	2	34	3130	......	......	1	10	115	......	......
Pleasant	85	150	3	300	......	35	35	970	6	16	47	30	2492	......	2	......	1	127	......	5
Pymosa	......	......	7	517	......	144	106	984	26	85	108	92	7927	......	348	2	677	180	80	51
Union	......	......	4	526	......	8	......	983	......	2	15	17	1592	......	......	......	......	330	70	20
Victoria	......	......	8	825	25	......	......	852	......	......	......	21	1398	......	9	......	27	126	40	10
Washington	......	......	......	......	......	67	87	661	......	......	......	23	3277	......	......	......	......	......	......	......
Total	140	640	51	5016	125	727	577	17144	41	251	513	554	49662	8	1322	8	1391	3813	545	366

CEDAR COUNTY.

Names of townships, towns, and cities.	Number of acres in flax seed.	Number of bushels harvested.	Number of acres in sorghum.	Number of gallons of syrup from sorghum.	Number of acres of blue grass for pasture.	Number of acres of tame grass.	Number of tons of hay from same.	Number of tons of hay from wild grass.	Number of bushels of grass seed.	Hungarian grass: Number of acres.	Hungarian grass: Number of tons of hay.	Potatoes: Number of acres.	Potatoes: Number of bushels.	Sweet potatoes: Number of acres.	Sweet potatoes: Number of bushels.	Onions: Number of acres.	Onions: Number of bushels.	Number of bushels of turnips.	Number of bushels of beets.	Number of bushels of peas and beans.
Cass	75	571	12	805	1910	1010	761	578	230	18	27	35	3942	......	55	......	6	57	22	32
Center, exc. of Tipton	2	12	21	1021	5080	3883	5331	1073	809	61	50	122	11918	3	175	5	98	364	1377	71
Dayton, exc. of Clarence	......	......	7	604	65	3267	1476	1024	612	......	......	144	9595	......	......	......	200	83	6	5
Fairfield	......	......	......	......	615	2815	1989	895	398	14	39	77	8389	......	......	......	126	297	108	38
Farmington, exc. Durant	28	280	4	325	506	2258	1508	879	296	15	26	103	14072	......	107	6	882	126	30	9
Fremont	......	......	5	415	3558	1696	2524	1075	210	6	13	50	4988	......	4	......	75	120	......	......
Gower	1090	8527	36	2429	940	3123	1807	176	9999	8	14	58	6311	......	198	......	40	70	70	52
Inland	......	......	1	67	2564	1304	1546	472	28	14	25	80	6171	......	1	......	2	13	37	8
Iowa	346	3404	10	1103	1095	3141	2613	157	3410	5	20	64	5887	......	93	......	10	220	82	2
Linn	......	......	5	540	479	1630	1005	158	117	12	14	30	3030	2	59	......	10	39	20	9
Louden, town of	......	......	......	......	60	65	30	40	......	......	......	......	297	......	2	......	16	30	7	......
Massillon	......	......	8	788	3189	868	952	1699	1785	......	......	59	5502	......	49	......	15	105	103	33

Pioneer			13	1199	2170	2126	297	56		6	12	47	5090		58		29	122	45	33
Red Oak			2	211	1197	1827	1635	599	240	22	40	34	4467		47		29	527	6	23
Rochester			12	714	513	1189	1430	203	22	10	17	51	4941		1			113	2	2
Springdale	867	7283	30	2620	1965	4185	2683	350	7286	8	8	76	6463	1	43	8	427	163	248	29
Springfield, exc. of Louden			5	429	867	1325	1004	1108	113	18	37	68	6000		89		6	130	24	24
Sugar Creek	37	323	3	265	1677	1248	1498	75	49	10	7	68	4341	7	67		21	19	25	8
Tipton, town of													1431				8			
Total	2445	20400	174	13535	28450	36960	30089	10316	25604	227	349	1166	112835	13	1048	19	2000	2598	2212	378

CERRO GORDO COUNTY.

Clear Lake, exc. of town			2	87		10	18	1784				39	3185			5	11	631	5	73
Daugherty						50	65	443		10	15	17	1350				5	150	3	6
Falls			2	100		233	244	1620				40	4045				10	250		78
Geneseo					40	8	10	1087	16			38	2429				13	167	9	18
Grant			1	40		2	2	1124				17	1172		5		15	114	177	17
Lake			4	446	10	90	110	1955	20		10	26	1249		5	2	366	520		31
Lime Creek	42	295	2	166	7	338	373	1037	154	1	2	63	5606		2	1	81	2129	678	78
Lincoln						100	38	121				28	2497					2065		22
Mason, exc. of Mason City	124	50		45		356	217	1607	80	5	18	78	4732			3	68	1427	537	45
Owen	20	100			122	58		1878				21	1860			8	470	470	2	15
Portland	4	40			5	141	157	1661				64	3785				15	1059	150	27
Total	190	485	11	884	184	1386	1234	14317	270	26	35	431	31910		12	19	1054	8982	1561	410

CHEROKEE COUNTY.

Afton						39	12	1653	6			35	2804				12	80	26	60
Amherst						5	5	466				7	229				2		32	
Cedar								835				30	1317					115		10
Cherokee, exc. of town	2	10						1434				12	1477							7
Cherokee, town of				60		26	5	140				5	315				2	10	8	5
Diamond								369				12	579							
Liberty	52	219						392				10	668				4	45	43	1
Marcus								248				4	54					12	4	
Pilot	10	15	1	114		25	5	823	1	8	8	14	2634		5		13	64	24	38
Pitcher				45				1160				29	2112				30			3
Sheridan	100	631						1047				32	2092							
Silver					40	2		499				8	617				3	154	33	7
Spring								404				3	197							

CHEROKEE COUNTY.—Continued.

NAMES OF TOWNSHIPS, TOWNS, AND CITIES.	FLAX. Number of acres in flax seed.	FLAX. Number of bushels harvested.	SORGHUM. Number of acres in sorghum.	SORGHUM. Number of gallons of syrup from sorghum.	Number of acres of blue grass for pasture.	Number of acres of tame grass.	Number of tons of hay from same.	Number of tons of hay from wild grass.	Number of bushels of grass seed.	HUNGARIAN GRASS. Number of acres.	HUNGARIAN GRASS. Number of tons of hay.	POTATOES. Number of acres.	POTATOES. Number of bushels.	SWEET POTATOES. Number of acres.	SWEET POTATOES. Number of bushels.	ONIONS. Number of acres.	ONIONS. Number of bushels.	Number of bushels of turnips.	Number of bushels of beets.	Number of bushels of peas and beans.
Tilden	8	....	....	....	....	....	....	537	....	....	....	6	392	....	....	....	....	38	....	....
Willow	....	....	3	200	....	....	....	779	....	....	....	17	838	....	....	....	....	81	63	12
Total	172	875	4	419	40	97	27	10786	7	8	8	224	16325	....	5	....	66	599	238	143

CHICKASAW COUNTY.

NAMES OF TOWNSHIPS, TOWNS, AND CITIES.	FLAX. Number of acres in flax seed.	FLAX. Number of bushels harvested.	SORGHUM. Number of acres in sorghum.	SORGHUM. Number of gallons of syrup from sorghum.	Number of acres of blue grass for pasture.	Number of acres of tame grass.	Number of tons of hay from same.	Number of tons of hay from wild grass.	Number of bushels of grass seed.	HUNGARIAN GRASS. Number of acres.	HUNGARIAN GRASS. Number of tons of hay.	POTATOES. Number of acres.	POTATOES. Number of bushels.	SWEET POTATOES. Number of acres.	SWEET POTATOES. Number of bushels.	ONIONS. Number of acres.	ONIONS. Number of bushels.	Number of bushels of turnips.	Number of bushels of beets.	Number of bushels of peas and beans.
Bradford, exc. of Nashua	....	....	12	811	126	719	646	1018	140	4	4	66	6225	....	....	....	40	....	....	....
Chickasaw	....	....	25	2578	....	333	392	1998	13	9	13	79	7165	....	....	....	29	590	94	44
Dayton	....	....	16	1526	....	205	212	2095	35	....	....	90	4528	....	....	....	....	850	61	2
Deerfield	....	....	9	706	160	220	268	2404	....	4	5	49	4729	....	....	....	26	386	47	38
Dresden	....	....	13	1332	....	620	495	1679	1074	6	12	44	3744	....	....	....	....	125	25	39
Fredericksburgh	....	....	6	370	18	741	317	1626	1426	....	....	47	3455	....	....	....	33	135	35	94
Jacksonville	....	....	1	52	11	282	561	4672	189	....	....	87	7464	....	....	....	17	848	15	27
Nashua, town of	....	....	....	....	....	6	6	26	....	....	....	5	408	....	....	....	....	....	....	....
New Hampton, exc. town	....	....	3	162	....	161	87	1691	323	....	....	62	4740	....	....	....	5	33	19	14
New Hampton, town of	....	....	....	....	65	42	40	3	200	....	....	....	....	....	....	....	....	....	....	....
Richland	38	495	19	2091	77	694	782	2134	898	....	....	41	4900	....	....	....	26	1205	398	35
Stapleton	2	15	4	132	166	465	869	3405	2060	....	....	150	10199	....	....	....	23	583	19	81
Utica	....	....	5	233	....	357	171	5119	580	....	....	92	8122	....	....	....	1	40	2	....
Washington	....	....	13	1251	....	48	59	2271	....	....	....	80	6385	....	....	6	300	310	....	11
Total	40	510	126	11244	623	4893	4905	30141	6938	23	34	892	72064	....	....	6	500	5105	715	385

CLARKE COUNTY.

Doyle, exc. of Hopeville	8	40	76	2771	91	4790	896	101	214	96	197	16	3774		82	13	117	153	53	467
Franklin			20	1783	123	1586	1334	537	629	97	149	26	2232		75		50	82	51	56
Fremont			9	1226		536	622	723	69	15	20	28	1668	1	84			378	49	29
Green Bay			13		235	1073	1017	424	83	84	150	48	3596	1	162	1	46	641	25	76
Hopeville, town of	18	151	26	264	30	308	308	83		32	57	9	816		11	34	21	89	8	
Jackson			20	1937		948	849	836	102	33	55	24	1393		5		5	221		15
Knox			31	2963	80	1063	1025	1083	454	85	127	50	5343		189		156	1277	180	204
Liberty			11	979	12	560	571	638	72	3	3	20	1287	7	58	1	119	129	44	86
Madison	30	33	21	2389	3	490	275	591		4	4	37	3205		5		12	91		2
Osceola, exc. of town			8	634	35	627	558	246	38	23	32	25	1464		115		5	97	5	21
Osceola, town of			1	80	4	626	678	282	1			33	2749	2	312	2	8	445	15	12
Troy	112	1037	24	568		539	630	973	386	26	57	276	2220		28		2	45	962	12
Ward			2	916	127	665	748	1041		25	39	4	2088			6	177			35
Washington			17	1826	669	650	867	19		11	14	30	1331		8			155	5	2
Total	168	1261	283	18336	1409	14462	10378	7576	2048	534	904	626	33166	11	1134	57	718	3803	1397	1017

CLAY COUNTY.

Bridgewater						4		1602				42	2393				15	133	48	44
Clay	105	415	2	83		23		2104				24	1361							
Douglas			7	383	1	6	7	1267				28	1920				7	125	44	
Gillett's Grove			3	167		9		945				19	1154				5	175	5	13
Herdland			3	317				584				15	1170				19	427	87	18
Lincoln			12	422				806				30	1687		10					4
Riverton												7	1112				4	5		2
Spencer						8		2576	12			62	2867							
Summit	100	400						1049				33	1874				2	5	4	33
Total	205	815	27	1372	1	50	7	10933	12			260	15538		10		52	870	188	114

CLAYTON COUNTY.

Boardman					952	389	511	1147	12			114	8574				24	1229	10	28
Buena Vista						87	98	20		12	16	36	2354							
Cass			5	443	384	1157	1028	886	425	10	29	54	4221				15	335	1	73
Clayton			8	193	426	519	741	76	29	4	8	92	7946	1	72	1	63	1267	226	168
Cox Creek			12	1331	25	430	529	479	9	1	2	110	8843				68	1214	47	87
Elk			17	1018	125	426	526			36	65	67	7355		6		72	783	50	125
Farmersburg			2	215	153	1222	1510	368	41			92	8562					217	175	24

CLAYTON COUNTY.—Continued.

Names of townships, towns, and cities.	Flax. Number of acres in flax seed.	Flax. Number of bushels harvested.	Sorghum. Number of acres in sorghum.	Sorghum. Number of gallons of syrup from sorghum.	Number of acres of blue grass for pasture.	Number of acres of tame grass.	Number of tons of hay from same.	Number of tons of hay from wild grass.	Number of bushels of grass seed.	Hungarian grass. Number of acres.	Hungarian grass. Number of tons of hay.	Potatoes. Number of acres.	Potatoes. Number of bushels.	Sweet potatoes. Number of acres.	Sweet potatoes. Number of bushels.	Onions. Number of acres.	Onions. Number of bushels.	Number of bushels of turnips.	Number of bushels of beets.	Number of bushels of peas and beans.
Garnavillo	....	....	....	....	1434	685	915	674	20	....	....	91	8445	....	20	....	131	795	116	54
Girard	....	....	....	....	630	1146	1468	....	2	....	....	129	12982	....	....	1	32	486	37	44
Grand Meadow	....	....	5	375	....	1665	1006	1584	371	....	....	82	9845	....	....	....	99	322	105	100
Guttenberg town of	....	....	1	90	....	24	44	180	....	....	....	5	487	....	....	....	....	220	20	....
Highland	....	....	4	333	104	784	980	596	32	....	....	66	6186	....	....	....	50	300	....	15
Jefferson, exc. of Guttenberg	....	....	16	1994	406	1070	1232	218	....	....	....	142	14805	....	....	....	....	....	....	....
Ledomillo	....	....	11	1333	1094	996	1721	694	66	....	....	77	10689	....	....	6	226	1155	314	136
Mallory	....	....	18	1611	2327	856	630	....	....	....	....	82	7805	....	54	....	84	1119	143	234
Marion	....	....	10	564	546	829	924	1541	44	....	....	50	4279	....	....	....	....	405	....	6
Mendon, exc. of McGregor and North McGregor	....	....	7	50	78	38	496	488	4	4	4	54	11399	....	....	1	161	777	368	123
Millville	....	....	10	825	18	490	316	136	2	....	....	56	5573	....	....	6	58	271	145	65
Monona	....	....	1	80	....	1292	1668	581	34	....	....	94	12259	....	....	....	47	754	324	126
Read	....	....	5	235	799	814	1000	61	25	....	....	99	9235	....	....	....	12	720	42	57
Sperry	....	....	20	2297	....	849	862	1111	120	....	....	84	7378	....	....	....	63	845	158	111
Volga	....	....	2	307	131	643	648	41	....	6	12	79	8832	....	....	....	....	....	....	....
Wagner	....	....	1	93	53	1146	1162	424	29	....	....	60	7350	....	....	....	....	....	....	....
Total	....	....	155	13387	9685	17557	20015	11305	1265	73	136	1815	185504	1	152	15	1205	13214	2281	1576

CLINTON COUNTY.

Names of townships, towns, and cities.	Flax. Number of acres in flax seed.	Flax. Number of bushels harvested.	Sorghum. Number of acres in sorghum.	Sorghum. Number of gallons of syrup from sorghum.	Number of acres of blue grass for pasture.	Number of acres of tame grass.	Number of tons of hay from same.	Number of tons of hay from wild grass.	Number of bushels of grass seed.	Hungarian grass. Number of acres.	Hungarian grass. Number of tons of hay.	Potatoes. Number of acres.	Potatoes. Number of bushels.	Sweet potatoes. Number of acres.	Sweet potatoes. Number of bushels.	Onions. Number of acres.	Onions. Number of bushels.	Number of bushels of turnips.	Number of bushels of beets.	Number of bushels of peas and beans.
Berlin	89	1467	2	277	2134	598	554	1720	....	32	3	58	5327	....	....	....	....	....	....	....
Bloomfield	....	....	7	596	1144	3044	2740	710	58	17	35	78	7069	....	75	1	155	214	80	112
Brookfield	....	....	5	465	3487	1960	2027	525	4	54	99	57	4220	....	....	....	200	348	16	157
Camanche, exc. of town	....	....	....	....	53	976	1267	776	22	9	15	31	2513	....	48	....	99	310	4	81
Camanche, town of	....	....	....	....	....	....	....	....	....	....	....	2	150	....	....	....	....	....	....	....

Center					60	2957	2340	1097	118	11	21	116	11397		10			100		
Clinton, exc. of city					405	527	670	42	8	13	28	30	4072	2	404	1	208	102	252	350
Deep Creek	50	513	1	120		4415	3260	404	75	19	25	63	4962				35	65	20	17
De Witt, exc. of town			11	990	3551	2568	2300	1880	54	59	131	108	9877		46	1	254	317	89	144
De Witt, town of					440	186	120	100		5	6	5	2858		90		18	77	138	140
Eden				40	1048	3417	3596	1155	1415	105	102	79	5286							
Elk River			2	344	4451	1544	1922	828	4	32	69	72	6607					193	34	14
Hampshire					2013	810	995	467	45	5	14	129	11667							
Liberty			13	812		918	694	1522	65	3	6	49	4469					50	4	5
Lincoln					1220	971	1247	166	20	18	38	57	5456			7	1050	100	1025	5
Lyons, exc. of city					112	269	352	380	11	5	9	28	2740	1	98		38	45	48	24
Lyons, city of									150											
Olive	407	4139	2	339	2977	943	1003	2123	23	43	56	93	7441		3		9	87	9	48
Orange	92	1518	2	110	299	1673	1312	982	428	13	28	.102	7528	1	108		9	197	64	76
Sharon			8	596		2650	2750	1365	14	7	8	85	5321		8	1	51	90	64	28
Spring Rock, exc. of Wheatland			7	328	2166	754	1043	1254		14	24	67	5385		12			300		
Washington						2345	2752	1054				92	8691					50		
Waterford			2	107	195	1229	1048	414	2	6	20	87	6397			1	99	317	58	27
Welton	48	504	7	270	1156	569	588	1060	14	32	67	91	8818			3	670			
Wheatland, town of				24	10	20		20				2	110		10					
Total	686	8161	69	5418	26921	35343	34580	20044	2530	505	804	1581	1318361	4	912	15	2895	2962	1905	1228

CRAWFORD COUNTY.

Boyer				16		4	8	1208		86	206	38	2689				4	909	2	1
Charter Oak								480				1	15							
Denison				168		9	2	1552		57	167	28	3607		70		218	726	12	43
East Boyer			2	366		2	4	1781		3	4	39	3040		1			25		65
Goodrich						4	6	819		2	8	23	2203							
Hanover								125					180				1	50	6	3
Hays	40	30						1064				25	2460							1
Iowa								592				30	799		10		10	540	24	8
Jackson	220	651					12	1260		3	5	33	2331				2	101	260	12
Milford			1	20	31	14	5	1502	11	12	21	44	2293		3		22	556	47	56
Morgan						40		291				8	383					14		1
Nishnabotany	3	16	2	86				612				11	918				40			
Otter Creek			6	358			1	1249		10	27	33	2161			3	83	105	43	65
Paradise						1	2	716		6	10	18	1726	1	125		29	80		3
Soldier			1	206				400				9	740							
Stockholm	13	64	8	650				1030		7	30	16	1330							
Union			1	160		3		2676		61	32	75	5204		38		2	400		3
Washington			1	148				718				11	1518				3	5	6	33
West Side	141	652	2	70		53		1749				37	4433		2		71	240	624	6

CRAWFORD COUNTY.—CONTINUED.

NAMES OF TOWNSHIPS, TOWNS, AND CITIES.	FLAX. Number of acres in flax seed.	FLAX. Number of bushels harvested.	SORGHUM. Number of acres in sorghum.	SORGHUM. Number of gallons of syrup from sorghum.	Number of acres of blue grass for pasture.	Number of acres of tame grass.	Number of tons of hay from same.	Number of tons of hay from wild grass.	Number of bushels of grass seed.	HUNGARIAN GRASS. Number of acres.	HUNGARIAN GRASS. Number of tons of hay.	POTATOES. Number of acres.	POTATOES. Number of bushels.	SWEET POTATOES. Number of acres.	SWEET POTATOES. Number of bushels.	ONIONS. Number of acres.	ONIONS. Number of bushels.	Number of bushels of turnips.	Number of bushels of beets.	Number of bushels of peas and beans.
Willow	....	....	....	....	....	....	....	669	....	....	....	5	451	....	....	....	....	200	....	....
Total	417	1413	24	2248	31	131	42	20493	11	247	510	484	38476	1	249	3	485	3951	1024	300

DALLAS COUNTY.

NAMES OF TOWNSHIPS, TOWNS, AND CITIES.	FLAX. Number of acres in flax seed.	FLAX. Number of bushels harvested.	SORGHUM. Number of acres in sorghum.	SORGHUM. Number of gallons of syrup from sorghum.	Number of acres of blue grass for pasture.	Number of acres of tame grass.	Number of tons of hay from same.	Number of tons of hay from wild grass.	Number of bushels of grass seed.	HUNGARIAN GRASS. Number of acres.	HUNGARIAN GRASS. Number of tons of hay.	POTATOES. Number of acres.	POTATOES. Number of bushels.	SWEET POTATOES. Number of acres.	SWEET POTATOES. Number of bushels.	ONIONS. Number of acres.	ONIONS. Number of bushels.	Number of bushels of turnips.	Number of bushels of beets.	Number of bushels of peas and beans.
Adams	....	....	26	3695	....	397	508	770	....	29	39	23	6635	1	172	....	16	7070	11	25
Adel, exc. of town	....	....	23	2319	....	300	342	1149	5	....	2	76	5021	....	13	....	....	....	20	7
Adel, town of	....	....	....	....	....	....	....	841	....	....	....	....	....	....	....	....	....	....	....	....
Beaver	50	320	3	291	....	....	....	1194	....	....	....	12	1728	....	19	....	21	3	....	5
Boone	....	....	12	1373	....	283	426	446	....	....	....	60	8075	....	50	2	50	....	2	....
Colfax	....	....	12	1702	10	198	169	2338	51	1	1	43	3846	....	59	1	24	503	69	109
Dallas	20	150	13	1537	....	12	16	1574	9	....	....	36	2920	....	....	....	....	....	....	....
Des Moines	26	231	7	799	34	292	358	1039	....	3	5	17	2156	....	....	....	8	32	4	23
Grant	30	308	7	673	....	125	67	1806	....	....	....	42	3949	....	20	....	....	494	135	55
Lincoln	185	1644	13	1473	....	14	....	1271	40	1	2	33	2647	....	74	....	....	561	72	56
Linn	22	180	27	2838	15	125	169	1454	....	5	12	31	3168	....	24	....	....	141	9	10
Spring Valley	....	....	11	744	....	47	45	2542	....	8	10	42	3209	....	....	....	....	....	....	....
Sugar Grove	16	180	7	570	7	112	177	1667	....	21	37	45	5481	....	100	1	22	244	24	58
Union, exc. of Dexter	6	48	15	1891	107	311	336	795	....	....	....	39	5083	....	192	1	24	885	77	49
Vanmeter	20	144	14	1425	530	406	512	389	22	....	....	45	6354	3	501	1	102	297	104	57
Walnut	67	614	13	643	8	130	190	1288	....	2	3	51	5650	2	155	1	125	280	10	8
Washington	6	48	10	1048	....	36	43	1649	50	....	....	20	1988	....	....	....	....	221	....	7
Total	448	3867	214	23021	711	2788	3358	22212	177	8	136	615	67910	6	1379	7	392	4731	537	459

DAVIS COUNTY.

Bloomfield, exc. of town	18	140	22	2618	2279	2954	2695	152	1504	457	781	62	9028	3	522	....	118	1456	95	279
Bloomfield, town of	....	....	....	....	....	....	....	....	....	....	....	6	500	1	25	....	7	5	6	2
Drakeville, exc. of town	....	....	8	531	431	758	552	133	101	29	23	22	1690	....	....	....	23	118	26	48
Drakeville, town of	....	....	....	....	57	96	99	4	....	....	....	1	544	....	214	....	....	....	....	....
Fabius	....	....	24	3275	1571	2619	1523	59	1073	209	208	16	2792	....	244	....	15	460	....	48
Fox River	....	....	30	3091	437	788	636	29	142	226	306	32	3671	....	286	....	87	332	51	92
Grove	....	....	38	5639	2043	4354	2229	102	7425	409	512	54	5340	....	32	....	....	247	128	114
Lick Creek	....	....	46	4245	365	1336	923	32	141	227	244	72	6217	1	29	1	128	947	42	129
Marion	....	....	11	3860	89	1203	1022	87	64	86	117	19	4540	....	148	....	5	1070	....	20
Perry	....	....	23	2323	1255	1943	1510	97	534	220	331	37	3471	9	131	....	14	486	14	43
Prairie	....	....	24	1791	....	2165	1843	131	3825	174	233	13	2540	....	129	....	....	108	20	202
Roscoe	38	309	26	2866	468	2261	1359	141	3733	255	265	31	3537	....	34	....	44	170	17	858
Salt Creek	....	....	42	2731	416	1108	1090	....	22	63	83	44	4257	1	127	....	6	413	1	119
Soap Creek	....	....	30	3489	551	1384	1117	....	36	50	62	64	5483	....	417	....	14	819	8	39
Union	....	....	39	3425	1087	2207	2322	....	418	129	160	59	4786	....	46	....	85	135	....	6
West Grove	....	....	21	2325	1812	3672	2241	206	1807	438	499	42	3649	1	329	....	24	412	42	103
Wyacondah	....	....	30	4087	1582	1783	1297	120	....	430	326	30	3695	....	211	....	....	159	....	35
Total	56	449	414	46296	14443	30631	22458	1293	20825	3402	4150	604	65740	16	2924	1	570	7337	450	2137

DECATUR COUNTY.

Bloomington	....	....	17	1174	....	311	346	470	59	35	45	23	1609	....	24	....	11	22	16	1
Burrell	7	85	40	2750	42	601	579	629	55	135	164	59	3505	1	77	....	105	993	22	37
Center, exc. of Leon	....	....	11	1441	74	1589	1657	455	380	137	204	24	3018	1	240	....	14	240	12	27
Decatur	....	....	33	2756	654	1318	1403	374	45	224	359	43	4084	....	252	....	146	343	81	112
Eden	....	....	35	3189	704	1372	1096	50	10	214	211	50	4728	1	288	....	102	1932	73	1[illegible]2
Fayette	....	....	6	433	4	417	473	875	440	96	131	31	1987	....	2	2	21	9	12	3
Franklin	....	....	21	2714	88	1493	2694	1001	65	47	123	47	4712	1	111	....	77	389	79	150
Garden Grove	....	....	17	1329	699	1883	2013	868	323	103	179	76	7309	....	2	....	5	415	96	103
Grand River	....	....	11	1471	....	156	267	16	....	....	....	21	2493	....	21	....	13	37	9	22
Hamilton	1	45	20	1214	207	605	607	243	1	72	72	31	2250	....	36	....	4	273	10	18
High Point	30	270	31	2896	211	1231	1128	369	35	284	464	43	3562	....	65	....	76	253	10	50
Long Creek	....	....	22	1789	175	922	1318	401	8	14	38	24	3459	2	174	....	79	566	39	41
Morgan	....	1	23	1945	225	1005	918	431	26	64	92	28	2018	....	35	....	33	470	8	6
New Buda	....	....	9	1336	101	489	683	1090	8	164	172	30	2508	....	14	....	54	95	8	16
Richland	....	....	33	3661	2	375	437	1307	6	17	14	38	3753	....	87	1	180	300	99	133
Woodland	....	....	30	3585	122	1177	1197	488	43	234	323	45	3390	2	270	....	126	1469	21	59
Total	38	401	369	33683	3398	14944	16816	9061	1504	1840	2591	613	54385	8	1698	3	1046	7806	595	900

DELAWARE COUNTY.

NAMES OF TOWNSHIPS, TOWNS, AND CITIES.	FLAX.		SORGHUM.		Number of acres of blue grass for pasture.	Number of acres of tame grass.	Number of tons of hay from same.	Number of tons of hay from wild grass.	Number of bushels of grass seed.	HUNGARIAN GRASS		POTATOES.		SWEET POTATOES.		ONIONS.		Number of bushels of turnips.	Number of bushels of beets.	Number of bushels of peas and beans.
	Number of acres in flax seed.	Number of bushels harvested.	Number of acres in sorghum.	Number of gallons of syrup from sorghum.						Number of acres.	Number of tons of hay.	Number of acres.	Number of bushels.	Number of acres.	Number of bushels.	Number of acres.	Number of bushels.			
Adams	1	....	5	657	....	1040	1042	3214	14	5	6	84	7117	....	13	....	25	268	17	31
Bremen	....	....	4	344	1831	21	191	1186	84	....	....	54	3578	....	....	1	18	784	35	20
Coffin's Grove	....	2	10	488	54	965	920	1386	29	29	46	76	6548	....	1	....	95	933	230	59
Colony	....	....	3	170	2691	873	1290	100	34	2	4	72	6347	2	....	....	18	187	500	48
Delaware, exc. of Manchester	....	....	4	332	....	1420	1822	1039	96	15	22	83	6689	....	....	....	426	26	11	23
Delhi	....	2	10	647	199	1173	1330	1303	2	....	....	61	6821	....	....	....	21	975	51	99
Elk	....	....	7	823	....	920	1108	631	150	....	....	63	6501	....	....	....	....	258	63	....
Hazel Green	14	110	11	573	1834	....	1302	2238	25	....	....	67	6153	....	....	....	33	248	84	172
Honey Creek	....	....	8	742	845	1244	1358	2484	50	4	8	84	8158	1	128	....	149	1040	145	168
Manchester, town of	....	....	5	218	290	880	862	882	61	5	7	52	6571	....	33	....	45	407	107	77
Milo	....	3	5	501	791	881	1018	2091	169	14	20	81	6638	....	25	....	44	1285	45	66
North Fork	....	....	4	316	367	877	966	1619	....	8	9	82	7138	....	....	....	....	....	....	28
Oneida	....	....	5	418	273	1168	1283	1845	25	....	....	67	6356	....	1	3	173	707	4	61
Prairie	....	....	4	190	197	450	380	2789	....	....	....	76	7962	....	....	....	12	4	549	15
Richland	....	....	3	377	52	347	438	1581	93	2	4	36	4271	....	....	....	121	565	9	45
South Fork, exc. of Hopkinton	....	1	6	697	3805	1750	1821	1542	52	....	....	17	6704	10	8	....	68	85	2	7
Union	....	....	9	591	250	779	946	653	22	3	4	70	6215	....	37	....	66	260	118	60
Total	15	118	103	8084	13478	14788	18077	26583	906	87	130	1125	109767	13	246	4	1314	8032	1970	979

DES MOINES COUNTY.

NAMES OF TOWNSHIPS, TOWNS, AND CITIES.	Number of acres in flax seed.	Number of bushels harvested.	Number of acres in sorghum.	Number of gallons of syrup from sorghum.	Number of acres of blue grass for pasture.	Number of acres of tame grass.	Number of tons of hay from same.	Number of tons of hay from wild grass.	Number of bushels of grass seed.	Hungarian grass: Number of acres.	Hungarian grass: Number of tons of hay.	Potatoes: Number of acres.	Potatoes: Number of bushels.	Sweet potatoes: Number of acres.	Sweet potatoes: Number of bushels.	Onions: Number of acres.	Onions: Number of bushels.	Number of bushels of turnips.	Number of bushels of beets.	Number of bushels of peas and beans.
Augusta	....	....	682	322	503	642	717	1	90	....	....	70	6504	....	98	....	151	135	21	23
Benton	....	....	24	2681	560	1217	1032	320	28	3	3	186	17608	....	29	....	87	352	57	75
Burlington, exc. of city	....	....	5	206	24	1475	1453	32	....	....	....	275	22339	16	1412	3	221	268	202	3
Danville	....	....	8	710	4402	3274	374	....	1152	....	....	112	11230	2	499	2	54	394	42	78

Flint River	8	26	23	1779	542	2017	2135	....	30	2	3	258	25650	11	875	....	150	230	243	95
Franklin	....	....	21	2762	....	1740	1974	....	....	....	....	105	13635	....	....	....	....	395	....	....
Huron	....	....	23	1403	1624	1211	1152	1484	71	5	6	122	10743	....	....	....	....	....	....	....
Jackson	....	....	2	161	....	85	72	716	....	....	....	7	526	....	5	....	....	23	....	....
Pleasant Grove	....	....	16	1492	884	2992	1116	....	532	....	....	64	6070	....	93	....	106	156	61	115
Union	....	....	7	619	2703	1908	2112	28	58	....	....	212	24861	4	379	2	5	906	195	2
Washington	....	....	6	573	407	1832	1475	27	902	....	....	85	7739	....	6	....	3	190	....	25
Yellow Springs	25	....	12	1527	1066	4924	2871	49	164	8	12	151	13330	3	274	18	29	535	33	46
Total	33	26	829	14235	12715	23317	16484	2653	3027	18	24	1647	160235	36	3670	25	806	3584	854	462

DICKINSON COUNTY.

Center Grove	....	....	13	813	....	40	....	933	....	....	....	62	2216	....	....	....	17	40	50	11
Diamond Lake	....	....	....	....	....	....	....	385	....	....	....	4	270	....	....	....	25	....	10	....
Excelsior	10	....	....	....	....	....	....	439	....	....	....	17	255	....	....	....	....	3	25	1
Lakeville	....	....	....	....	....	....	....	425	....	....	....	11	302	....	....	....	4	102	47	5
Lloyd	....	....	1	61	....	....	....	521	....	....	....	19	1195	....	....	....	6	50	14	5
Milford	....	....	....	....	....	....	....	414	....	....	....	14	834	....	....	....	8	6	6	18
Okoboji	....	....	1	72	....	....	....	1057	....	....	....	30	549	....	....	....	....	....	34	....
Richland	....	....	5	122	....	....	....	235	....	....	....	10	405	....	....	....	4	80	22	3
Silver Lake	....	....	....	....	....	....	....	202	....	....	....	7	156	....	....	....	....	....	3	16
Spirit Lake	60	....	....	....	....	24	....	1937	....	....	....	36	1311	....	....	....	3	19	18	3
Superior	....	....	....	....	....	....	....	....	....	....	....	....	110	....	....	....	....	....	....	....
Total	70	....	20	1068	....	64	....	6548	....	....	....	210	7603	....	....	....	67	300	229	63

DUBUQUE COUNTY.

Cascade	....	....	19	1874	476	895	846	662	31	6	10	60	5591	....	26	....	19	137	....	12
Center	....	....	6	309	365	1164	1426	115	1	2	3	147	8639	....	....	....	....	1464	6	45
Concord	....	....	14	1376	....	666	598	1091	....	1	1	101	9028	....	....	....	....	....	....	....
Dodge	....	....	2	80	....	1206	967	305	....	....	....	52	5066	....	....	....	....	....	3	2
Dubuque, city of	....	....	....	....	72	49	49	....	....	....	....	12	600	....	....	....	....	....	....	....
Dyersville, town of	....	....	....	....	....	2	8	8	....	....	....	4	355	....	....	....	....	3	5	....
Iowa	....	....	2	113	224	1322	871	323	....	....	....	108	9770	....	....	....	121	534	7	727
Jefferson	....	....	24	1816	1022	1804	2025	214	....	....	....	248	23985	....	....	....	13	1640	80	103
Julien, exc. of Dubuque	....	....	2	150	1235	2110	2311	286	1	2	3	160	9360	....	15	3	830	3780	273	47
Liberty	....	....	16	240	2562	177	121	1113	2	....	....	75	5390	....	....	....	....	798	....	5
Mosalem	....	....	....	....	....	998	1107	....	....	....	....	116	5320	....	....	....	....	....	....	....
New Wine, exc. of Dyersville	....	....	5	411	811	710	850	1215	....	....	....	78	6265	....	....	....	....	....	....	....
Peru	....	....	17	1125	....	1103	1226	183	....	....	....	231	17859	....	....	2	57	1750	250	58
Prairie Creek	....	....	1	11	1942	2650	15227	472	....	....	....	116	10874	....	15	....	....	20	400	....

DUBUQUE COUNTY.—Continued.

NAMES OF TOWNSHIPS, TOWNS, AND CITIES.	FLAX. Number of acres in flax seed.	FLAX. Number of bushels harvested.	SORGHUM. Number of acres in sorghum.	SORGHUM. Number of gallons of syrup from sorghum.	Number of acres of blue grass for pasture.	Number of acres of tame grass.	Number of tons of hay from same.	Number of tons of hay from wild grass.	Number of bushels of grass seed.	HUNGARIAN GRASS. Number of acres.	HUNGARIAN GRASS. Number of tons of hay.	POTATOES. Number of acres.	POTATOES. Number of bushels.	SWEET POTATOES. Number of acres.	SWEET POTATOES. Number of bushels.	ONIONS. Number of acres.	ONIONS. Number of bushels.	Number of bushels of turnips.	Number of bushels of beets.	Number of bushels of peas and beans.
Table Mound						1895	1455					69	5120							
Taylor			12	684	1759	1326	1227	1066	105	4	6	135	10138				29	529	91	34
Vernon			5	225	1082	2424	9660	429	35			134	12592				64	1652	55	77
Washington,			1	177	1200	1915	1585	212	28			89	7303			1	23	114		57
Whitewater			15	820		616	770	1031		22	35	88	7974				16	440	28	26
Total			42	9411	12750	23032	35339	8725	203	37	58	2024	161229		56	6	1175	12863	1194	1193

EMMET COUNTY.

NAMES OF TOWNSHIPS, TOWNS, AND CITIES.	FLAX. Number of acres in flax seed.	FLAX. Number of bushels harvested.	SORGHUM. Number of acres in sorghum.	SORGHUM. Number of gallons of syrup from sorghum.	Number of acres of blue grass for pasture.	Number of acres of tame grass.	Number of tons of hay from same.	Number of tons of hay from wild grass.	Number of bushels of grass seed.	HUNGARIAN GRASS. Number of acres.	HUNGARIAN GRASS. Number of tons of hay.	POTATOES. Number of acres.	POTATOES. Number of bushels.	SWEET POTATOES. Number of acres.	SWEET POTATOES. Number of bushels.	ONIONS. Number of acres.	ONIONS. Number of bushels.	Number of bushels of turnips.	Number of bushels of beets.	Number of bushels of peas and beans.
Armstrong Grove			2	125				1217				31	1840					471		5
Center			7	185				946				18	459							
Ellsworth								406				16	657							
Emmet			9	180		14		1255	1			28	1146						2	2
Estherville						4		2016				34	1102					8	6	6
High Lake			3	23				2496				24	675							3
Iowa Lake								500		10		4	265			3				
Preston			6	130				1695				25	598							
Swan Lake								305				3	105							
Total			37	643		18		10836	1	10		183	6847			3		479	8	16

FAYETTE COUNTY.

NAMES OF TOWNSHIPS, TOWNS, AND CITIES.	FLAX. Number of acres in flax seed.	FLAX. Number of bushels harvested.	SORGHUM. Number of acres in sorghum.	SORGHUM. Number of gallons of syrup from sorghum.	Number of acres of blue grass for pasture.	Number of acres of tame grass.	Number of tons of hay from same.	Number of tons of hay from wild grass.	Number of bushels of grass seed.	HUNGARIAN GRASS. Number of acres.	HUNGARIAN GRASS. Number of tons of hay.	POTATOES. Number of acres.	POTATOES. Number of bushels.	SWEET POTATOES. Number of acres.	SWEET POTATOES. Number of bushels.	ONIONS. Number of acres.	ONIONS. Number of bushels.	Number of bushels of turnips.	Number of bushels of beets.	Number of bushels of peas and beans.
Auburn			9	496		433	529	1220	396			45	5016							2

Banks	9	87	....	....	....	147	107	1068	113	....	....	11	1422	....	....	....	....	....	....	7
Bethel	....	....	....	....	....	646	531	1643	1707	....	....	43	2811	....	....	....	19	820	....	13
Center	....	....	15	935	....	692	524	1396	311	....	....	52	3900	....	....	....	....	....	....	56
Clermont	....	....	....	45	47	298	414	1079	450	....	....	87	12354	....	....	....	....	....	....	....
Dover	....	....	13	806	194	656	964	930	1	....	....	81	7376	....	21	....	372	369	36	18
Eden	....	....	4	214	10	670	394	2653	891	....	....	105	9321	....	....	....	13	899	50	52
Fairfield	....	....	15	2224	121	977	1046	....	1473	....	....	71	8257	....	....	8	296	....	....	29
Fayette, town of	....	....	....	....	....	....	....	....	....	....	....	....	187	....	....	....	....	....	....	....
Fremont	16	155	11	1093	....	152	161	1693	....	8	12	58	2929	....	....	....	48	610	38	87
Harlan	....	....	12	2837	....	503	357	1038	39	....	....	46	3400	....	....	....	6	885	31	96
Illyria	....	....	19	3368	342	777	1037	790	6	7	15	58	7522	....	....	....	324	645	215	78
Jefferson	9	113	16	1137	10	283	323	1658	....	2	10	51	4355	....	....	....	4	....	2	71
Oran	121	1087	17	1540	30	340	299	1848	45	....	....	66	5386	....	1	....	42	247	48	85
Pleasant Valley	....	....	6	416	....	593	847	832	20	1	4	59	4081	....	....	....	54	....	3	13
Putnam	....	....	11	642	....	1110	1084	2545	153	....	....	75	6242	....	1	....	126	881	70	80
Scott	....	....	7	555	....	91	87	1346	....	....	1	37	3550	....	....	....	7	260	15	26
Smithfield	25	330	10	2037	....	919	735	2889	119	....	....	85	7621	....	....	....	185	542	50	74
Westfield, exc. of Fayette	....	....	12	1254	....	1397	1682	313	193	....	....	40	5476	....	....	....	40	2285	....	20
West Union, exc. of town	....	....	4	212	43	1450	1694	706	92	....	....	74	7943	....	4	....	143	547	55	80
West Union, town of	....	....	....	....	....	271	236	92	....	....	....	12	1116	....	....	....	26	82	106	11
Windsor	....	....	14	664	....	1276	973	2285	806	....	....	80	11779	....	....	2	165	222	289	62
Total	180	1672	204	20475	797	13681	14124	28024	6815	18	42	1236	122044	....	27	10	1870	9294	1008	960

FLOYD COUNTY.

Cedar	....	....	7	608	14	154	154	1601	52	1	1	69	7563	....	....	1	100	929	31	49
Charles City, city of	....	....	....	....	....	23	25	6	....	2	2	7	535	....	....	....	....	50	50	....
Floyd	....	....	1	56	203	713	710	1581	13	55	67	139	10429	....	....	1	138	853	45	85
Niles	60	540	14	981	72	152	676	1366	....	3	3	89	7328	....	....	....	15	472	28	79
Nora Springs, town of	....	....	....	....	....	48	66	593	4	....	....	20	1711	....	....	....	25	76	55	22
Pleasant Grove	21	160	....	....	....	20	36	678	....	6	6	40	2616	....	....	3	278	24	29	24
Riverton	....	....	14	636	....	631	1016	1379	178	55	116	75	5973	....	....	1	290	107	5	....
Rockford	....	....	6	444	....	501	507	1495	5	2	4	72	5729	....	....	....	4	1466	54	79
Rock Grove, exc. of Nora Springs	....	....	....	250	....	148	161	953	3	11	7	130	4936	....	1	....	221	212	53	63
Rudd	....	....	7	....	....	205	208	8	....	2	4	56	5384	....	....	....	5	525	....	17
St. Charles, exc. of city	2	12	6	597	14	1336	1127	2833	62	8	13	202	13339	....	4	....	146	520	204	76
Scott	28	64	1	57	....	167	11	607	142	29	46	47	2335	....	....	....	4	357	53	48
Ulster	....	....	6	148	....	101	113	1327	....	5	7	77	5307	....	....	....	....	22	30	130
Union	42	351	6	395	....	561	357	760	....	17	23	106	7968	....	....	....	104	586	117	92
Total	153	1127	68	4172	303	4734	5167	15187	459	196	299	1129	81153	....	5	6	1330	6199	754	764

FRANKLIN COUNTY.

NAMES OF TOWNSHIPS, TOWNS, AND CITIES.	FLAX.		SORGHUM.		Number of acres of blue grass for pasture.	Number of acres of tame grass.	Number of tons of hay from same.	Number of tons of hay from wild grass.	Number of bushels of grass seed.	HUNGARIAN GRASS.		POTATOES.		SWEET POTATOES.		ONIONS.		Number of bushels of turnips.	Number of bushels of beets.	Number of bushels of peas and beans.
	Number of acres in flax seed.	Number of bushels harvested.	Number of acres in sorghum.	Number of gallons of syrup from sorghum.						Number of acres.	Number of tons of hay.	Number of acres.	Number of bushels.	Number of acres.	Number of bushels.	Number of acres.	Number of bushels.			
Clinton	1	8	3	267	10	23	12	2003	....	....	....	53	5174	1	50	....	18	905	8	111
Geneva	....	....	51	....	103	250	221	1284	....	30	49	75	5994	....	12	....	6	300	5	....
Grant	....	....	2	285	....	2	25	1108	498	....	....	21	2245	....	....	....	....	40	....	....
Hamilton	30	292	....	....	40	21	11	775	....	....	....	26	2023	....	4	....	13	88	12	24
Hampton, town of	....	....	....	....	....	16	23	....	....	....	....	2	125	....	....	....	....	100	....	....
Ingham	....	....	1	30	....	184	44	2048	....	4	71	10	3452	....	....	....	....	390	....	19
Lee	....	....	....	....	....	8	....	771	....	....	....	26	2405	....	....	....	4	665	98	26
Marion	....	....	....	....	....	3	....	313	....	....	....	14	1021	....	....	....	5	245	62	15
Morgan	1	2	2	100	....	....	....	1504	....	....	....	28	2081	....	....	....	17	571	101	23
Oakland	....	....	....	....	....	122	82	1950	....	8	20	35	2208	....	....	....	....	300	....	20
Osceola	203	1673	2	92	233	252	311	1551	139	....	....	143	11474	....	39	1	119	373	....	134
Reeve	13	125	6	402	4	171	116	1420	104	8	10	62	5707	....	....	3	254	800	....	82
Richland	40	485	....	....	....	28	11	570	....	....	....	15	1065	....	....	....	....	132	4	11
Washington, exc. of Hampton	....	....	5	130	65	685	400	1556	341	....	....	78	5918	....	8	1	30	450	14	75
West Fork	....	....	1	40	....	95	75	325	....	15	35	34	1995	....	....	....	6	171	23	65
Total	288	2385	73	1346	455	1860	1332	17178	1082	65	185	622	52887	1	113	5	472	5530	327	605

FREMONT COUNTY.

NAMES OF TOWNSHIPS, TOWNS, AND CITIES.	Number of acres in flax seed.	Number of bushels harvested.	Number of acres in sorghum.	Number of gallons of syrup from sorghum.	Number of acres of blue grass for pasture.	Number of acres of tame grass.	Number of tons of hay from same.	Number of tons of hay from wild grass.	Number of bushels of grass seed.	Hungarian grass: Number of acres.	Hungarian grass: Number of tons of hay.	Potatoes: Number of acres.	Potatoes: Number of bushels.	Sweet potatoes: Number of acres.	Sweet potatoes: Number of bushels.	Onions: Number of acres.	Onions: Number of bushels.	Number of bushels of turnips.	Number of bushels of beets.	Number of bushels of peas and beans.
Benton, exc. of East Port and Percival	....	....	....	....	....	20	10	4472	....	26	55	66	6405	....	96	....	28	....	91	1
Fisher, exc. of Farragut	34	425	2	100	4	313	237	1558	8	61	120	88	2060	....	27	....	10	205	125	....
Franklin, exc. of Hamburg	....	....	....	40	....	60	143	2672	....	12	21	41	2753	2	160	....	20	1	5	....
Locust Grove	....	....	1	40	....	....	24	24	515	12	12	15	884	....	....	....	....	....	....	....
Madison	....	....	10	787	....	191	143	578	34	12	25	52	2332	2	82	5	63	....	14	16
Monroe	262	2469	2	250	....	42	63	1485	197	52	115	36	1942	....	2	....	....	55	37	....
Prairie	53	460	5	236	26	207	264	229	304	36	99	16	1144	....	....	....	....	....	5	....

Riverton, exc. of town	...	...	2	130	...	54	183	603	28	4	5	32	1453	...	37	...	...	...	...	...
Ross, exc. of Tabor	35	300	23	2069	6	376	348	1433	101	76	117	79	4912	1	63	30	22	...	6	...
Scott	...	...	8	887	264	78	37	1722	4	50	99	33	2407	3	155	8	169	115	107	18
Sidney, exc. of town	...	...	7	701	33	189	145	2861	22	60	91	62	3750	9	551	9	41	...	18	...
Sidney, town of	...	...	...	...	...	...	...	...	...	...	...	1	556	2	75	...	17	2	12	...
Tabor, town of	...	...	...	...	...	71	33	25	...	24	40	13	359	...	23	...	33	...	4	...
Walnut	273	1681	...	...	...	3	3	1121	...	13	26	19	745	...	...	...	...	...	...	...
Total	657	5333	69	5240	333	1628	1733	19274	708	438	825	53	31732	19	12715	25	403	378	428	35

GREENE COUNTY.

Bristol	...	...	3	409	2	19	48	2251	8	...	...	30	2500	3	365	...	54	560	5	20
Cedar	...	2	13	1170	...	13	8	1319	...	...	...	33	3549	...	11	...	30	1340	144	39
Dawson	...	...	...	10	...	...	...	110	...	...	...	3	235	...	10	...	2	190	1	3
Franklin	8	1	12	732	...	60	44	1044	6	...	...	36	2115	...	14	...	31	338	69	137
Grand Junction, town of	...	...	...	...	...	9	2	410	...	...	...	...	60	...	...	...	...	...	...	...
Greenbrier	15	88	18	465	...	16	13	722	...	...	...	12	1007	...	...	...	1	97	54	38
Hardin	...	...	...	29	3	66	35	1464	15	1	2	9	610	...	...	...	...	40	...	...
Highland	...	...	...	...	...	76	50	437	15	...	...	6	588	...	...	...	...	...	...	...
Jackson	...	...	13	925	...	...	10	1796	...	...	...	18	2323	...	99	...	83	148	7	42
Jefferson, exc. of town	28	131	15	1768	...	158	103	2507	...	10	19	82	3944	...	37	...	18	510	86	23
Jefferson, town of	...	...	1	106	...	8	11	...	...	...	...	1	140	...	...	...	4	...	...	...
Junction, exc. of Grand Junction	...	...	8	500	...	13	18	1673	1	...	...	48	3273	...	40	...	9	20	3	74
Hendricks	...	...	6	625	...	65	63	1561	...	...	...	33	2380	3	225	...	...	374	14	69
Scranton, exc. of town	...	...	2	129	...	...	...	605	...	...	...	17	995	...	...	...	...	25	...	3
Scranton, town of	...	...	...	...	...	...	...	10	...	...	...	...	20	...	...	...	...	...	...	...
Washington	...	...	10	1180	64	77	109	1612	5	...	4	14	7120	18	42	...	58	82	92	82
Willow	...	...	4	301	...	...	...	341	...	...	...	8	356	...	...	...	...	...	...	...
Total	51	222	107	8349	69	581	514	17862	50	11	25	350	31215	24	842	...	290	3614	475	530

GRUNDY COUNTY.

Beaver	104	750	3	191	...	168	73	765	139	3	5	92	7168	...	...	1	54	145	122	19
Blackhawk	13	75	10	...	42	738	622	1215	1165	...	...	48	3521	...	...	...	70	111	49	64
Clay	494	3406	1	40	...	906	680	1323	845	...	...	47	3535	...	4	...	1	958	63	37
Colfax	15	173	...	...	...	75	...	...	...	...	...	48	4492	...	...	...	...	...	...	...
Fairfield	90	430	...	...	...	306	358	2188	15	...	...	97	7692	...	10	...	...	10	10	1
Felix	81	555	2	411	...	727	537	1436	24	...	...	74	6973	...	26	2	327	1372	56	75
German	43	498	15	1058	4	841	84	1176	9	2	7	79	6339	...	...	...	3	275	29	36
Grant	...	...	...	...	33	376	223	1441	...	...	...	67	7380	...	...	...	26	452	90	17
Lincoln	16	168	...	...	3	107	21	934	...	...	...	34	3319	...	...	...	16	167	10	...

GRUNDY COUNTY.—Continued.

Names of townships, towns, and cities.	Flax. Number of acres in flax seed.	Flax. Number of bushels harvested.	Sorghum. Number of acres in sorghum.	Sorghum. Number of gallons of syrup from sorghum.	Number of acres of blue grass for pasture.	Number of acres of tame grass.	Number of tons of hay from same.	Number of tons of hay from wild grass.	Number of bushels of grass seed.	Hungarian grass. Number of acres.	Hungarian grass. Number of tons of hay.	Potatoes. Number of acres.	Potatoes. Number of bushels.	Sweet potatoes. Number of acres.	Sweet potatoes. Number of bushels.	Onions. Number of acres.	Onions. Number of bushels.	Number of bushels of turnips.	Number of bushels of beets.	Number of bushels of peas and beans.
Melrose	37	270	4	506	142	632	204	1556	181	....	5	74	8249	....	14	....	310	473	76	33
Palermo	52	414	....	....	17	972	586	2525	101	8	15	69	7578	....	31	1	209	858	20	23
Pleasant Valley	211	1420	8	437	....	63	52	923	4	....	....	82	6022	....	....	2	464	131	....	5
Shiloh	....	....	1	40	4	2630	1803	568	....	....	....	60	5434	....	....	....	....	....	....	....
Total	1156	8159	44	2683	245	8541	5243	16050	2483	18	27	871	77702	....	85	6	1480	4952	526	310

GUTHRIE COUNTY.

Names of townships, towns, and cities.	Flax. Number of acres in flax seed.	Flax. Number of bushels harvested.	Sorghum. Number of acres in sorghum.	Sorghum. Number of gallons of syrup from sorghum.	Number of acres of blue grass for pasture.	Number of acres of tame grass.	Number of tons of hay from same.	Number of tons of hay from wild grass.	Number of bushels of grass seed.	Hungarian grass. Number of acres.	Hungarian grass. Number of tons of hay.	Potatoes. Number of acres.	Potatoes. Number of bushels.	Sweet potatoes. Number of acres.	Sweet potatoes. Number of bushels.	Onions. Number of acres.	Onions. Number of bushels.	Number of bushels of turnips.	Number of bushels of beets.	Number of bushels of peas and beans.
Bear Grove	....	....	14	1308	....	7	12	669	....	....	....	36	3475	....	....	1	235	63	14	16
Beaver	....	....	....	....	....	....	....	....	....	....	....	13	1978	....	....	....	....	....	....	....
Cass, exc. of Panora	582	4159	42	3262	....	282	264	2360	58	21	38	55	4594	2	339	1	286	206	30	33
Center	2	11	13	1181	....	75	96	354	2	2	2	36	3397	....	13	....	40	273	56	3
Dodge	300	1974	4	380	....	1	....	557	....	....	....	12	1225	....	15	....	23	37	52	36
Grant	18	113	4	331	....	....	....	513	....	....	....	10	713	....	....	....	....	20	....	4
Highland	....	....	9	757	25	11	4	766	....	....	....	15	1319	....	....	....	....	....	....	20
Jackson	31	188	18	2599	150	175	147	828	49	32	65	29	3782	....	36	....	3	....	9	5
Orange	....	....	8	637	3	6	....	663	....	....	....	14	1262	....	1	....	20	170	66	95
Panora, town of	15	71	....	60	....	11	30	116	....	2	3	5	574	....	15	....	14	25	7	1
Penn	....	....	8	986	....	54	57	933	....	7	14	33	3531	1	138	1	78	824	107	45
Richland	601	3817	6	535	5	44	12	1572	11	....	....	21	1958	....	141	....	11	381	25	38
Thompson	75	723	3	265	....	62	7	1074	....	....	....	27	1928	....	15	15	2182	303	....	....
Union	15	100	5	442	....	27	22	1432	....	....	....	21	1930	....	....	....	10	175	....	89
Valley	....	....	8	1182	3	152	176	1247	....	38	80	24	2881	....	27	....	14	111	8	39
Victory	....	....	12	1215	....	9	7	1319	21	15	20	26	2671	1	30	3	80	263	89	86
Total	1639	11156	146	15140	186	916	834	14403	141	117	222	387	37218	4	770	20	2996	2851	463	510

HAMILTON COUNTY.

Blairsburg	14	114	14	1168	...	23	1	1290	11	1	3	54	3792	...	5	...	49	110	104	17
Boone	87	388	15	1060	10	51	37	4234	...	...	15	105	6551	...	30	...	59	238	111	86
Cass	17	129	3	250	5	136	152	2307	13	8	10	81	3145	...	...	...	...	...	...	...
Clear Lake	...	...	2	183	...	1	2	1146	...	...	...	20	1524	...	...	...	...	...	...	4
Ellsworth	...	...	3	297	...	33	43	2410	...	...	...	24	1598	...	2	...	9	112	11	20
Fremont	...	...	8	405	...	69	84	1099	...	...	...	44	4215	...	...	...	...	60	...	...
Hamilton	...	...	11	1170	5	12	12	2731	...	...	...	48	3982	...	...	...	...	...	...	...
Lyon	...	...	4	399	1	18	9	1632	5	...	...	23	1156	...	10	...	40	140	5	...
Marion	...	...	23	2071	28	9	13	3296	...	9	17	50	4106	...	18	...	60	56	91	35
Rose Grove	...	...	4	285	...	10	10	617	...	...	...	10	985	...	...	...	...	...	...	78
Scott	...	...	1	165	...	10	...	2767	55	...	...	23	1217	...	...	...	...	100	4	...
Webster	...	...	15	1695	3	55	68	1685	2	9	20	37	3475	...	...	...	9	206	47	59
Total	118	631	103	9148	52	427	431	25214	86	27	65	519	35746	...	65	...	226	1022	373	299

HANCOCK COUNTY.

Amsterdam	...	...	...	...	...	10	15	1060	6	...	...	8	935	...	...	...	18	30	13	6
Avery	...	...	1	59	...	30	38	513	...	...	...	7	600	...	...	...	22	5	12	6
Britt	...	...	...	...	...	...	...	450	...	...	...	2	270	...	...	...	...	...	10	1
Concord	...	...	...	...	...	...	...	624	...	...	...	11	950	...	5	...	...	100	10	30
Crystal	...	...	...	...	...	20	30	521	...	...	...	7	254	...	...	...	...	355	...	15
Ellington	...	...	...	...	...	22	22	1851	...	...	...	37	3735	...	...	...	6	787	151	42
Madison	...	...	3	216	...	...	...	625	...	...	...	9	57	...	...	...	15	155	9	...
Total	...	...	4	275	...	82	105	5644	6	...	...	82	6801	...	5	...	61	1432	205	100

HARDIN COUNTY.

Alden	10	105	9	969	...	60	65	1686	...	...	...	111	7749	...	...	4	166	7	16	...
Buckeye	1	10	7	488	...	19	19	323	...	19	38	46	2182	...	...	2	200	...	70	...
Clay	10	75	8	579	385	527	682	1459	...	...	...	88	9236	...	23	...	35	370	49	43
Concord	20	160	1	60	...	...	...	256	...	...	...	2	148	...	...	...	...	45	...	3
Eldora, exc. of town	68	245	6	400	69	898	945	1289	131	21	22	90	8760	...	5	...	140	357	45	21
Eldora, town of	...	...	1	150	3	37	37	196	...	...	...	7	705	...	...	...	...	...	...	...
Ellis	104	876	16	1286	22	65	28	1263	...	5	12	59	2474	1	9	3	205	148	...	48
Etna, exc. of Ackley	22	244	...	...	16	189	264	1952	...	...	...	121	10800	...	...	...	...	1014	31	32
Grant	...	...	9	289	...	...	...	796	...	...	...	17	990	...	40	...	13	191	30	12
Hardin, exc. Iowa Falls	87	768	15	1419	197	324	272	2433	185	22	31	118	8642	...	...	...	4	200	...	...
Jackson	78	523	6	634	...	321	297	2180	...	1	2	74	5609	...	10	...	58	714	3	22

20

HARDIN COUNTY.—Continued.

NAMES OF TOWNSHIPS, TOWNS, AND CITIES.	FLAX.		SORGHUM.		Number of acres of blue grass for pasture.	Number of acres of tame grass.	Number of tons of hay from same.	Number of tons of hay from wild grass.	Number of bushels of grass seed.	HUNGARIAN GRASS.		POTATOES.		SWEET POTATOES.		ONIONS.		Number of bushels of turnips.	Number of bushels of beets.	Number of bushels of peas and beans.
	Number of acres in flax seed.	Number of bushels harvested.	Number of acres in sorghum.	Number of gallons of syrup from sorghum.						Number of acres.	Number of tons of hay.	Number of acres.	Number of bushels.	Number of acres.	Number of bushels.	Number of acres.	Number of bushels.			
Pleasant	...	...	32	2423	...	453	397	2033	100	...	...	68	5124	2	167	...	93	1744	75	79
Providence	...	...	42	6910	1014	734	848	1687	127	15	28	53	5288	...	65	...	44	550	195	78
Sherman	13	60	4	248	...	20	30	525	...	...	...	12	696	...	...	...	7	311	22	13
Tipton	1	3	26	1872	29	231	87	1200	47	11	21	51	2428	...	...	1	127	282	57	40
Union, exc. of town	...	...	20	2050	54	1319	927	1488	605	11	15	59	4579	...	58	...	52	479	71	72
Union, town of	...	...	...	...	...	19	20	...	...	...	...	...	...	...	...	...	...	...	...	...
Total	414	3069	204	19774	1789	5216	4918	20766	1195	135	169	976	75410	3	377	10	1144	6412	654	463

HARRISON COUNTY.

NAMES OF TOWNSHIPS, TOWNS, AND CITIES.	Number of acres in flax seed.	Number of bushels harvested.	Number of acres in sorghum.	Number of gallons of syrup from sorghum.	Number of acres of blue grass for pasture.	Number of acres of tame grass.	Number of tons of hay from same.	Number of tons of hay from wild grass.	Number of bushels of grass seed.	Hungarian grass: Number of acres.	Hungarian grass: Number of tons of hay.	Potatoes: Number of acres.	Potatoes: Number of bushels.	Sweet potatoes: Number of acres.	Sweet potatoes: Number of bushels.	Onions: Number of acres.	Onions: Number of bushels.	Number of bushels of turnips.	Number of bushels of beets.	Number of bushels of peas and beans.
Allen	...	...	1	149	...	...	...	726	...	...	...	4	396	...	35	...	...	26	...	...
Boyer	...	...	7	480	33	51	...	2139	...	42	60	55	3740	1	250	...	3	255	...	100
Calhoun	...	...	...	40	...	...	...	1865	...	66	100	9	712	1	108	...	50	1090	...	6
Cass	...	...	3	325	...	1	...	...	...	28	42	23	1592	...	20	...	130	650	3	3
Cincinnati	...	...	27	925	...	...	...	2624	...	...	...	29	2461	1	115	1	...	...	33	25
Clay	...	...	5	407	...	14	92	413	...	52	160	28	1764	...	...	1	...	214	7	...
Douglas	10	...	3	170	8	7	5	1912	...	93	143	41	3333	1	23	...	...	510	...	...
Harrison, exc. of Dunlap	20	250	...	...	...	...	...	575	...	77	183	56	3940	...	...	...	...	...	...	...
Jackson	...	...	8	924	...	...	...	2034	...	63	127	19	948	...	...	...	180	...	...	4
Jefferson	...	...	17	1129	10	46	...	3285	...	193	294	47	1446	...	112	...	8	5785	8	13
Lagrange	...	...	3	135	14	...	...	1326	...	88	140	12	766	...	10	...	...	413	...	2
Lincoln	52	290	2	128	...	...	...	819	...	6	15	55	3175	...	...	...	...	1000	...	...
Little Sioux	...	...	6	809	26	1	1	2771	1	5	9	9	1643	...	118	...	6	565	105	4
Magnolia	...	...	17	1549	...	...	...	2986	...	65	152	47	3316	2	341	...	12	1268	400	20
Morgan	...	...	15	1668	1	5	7	2546	...	...	...	27	2621	4	430	...	25	208	28	7
Raglan	...	...	13	1289	...	9	20	2234	...	20	45	12	1389	2	140	...	...	1102	...	3

St. John, exc. of Missouri Valley	....	....	18	2576	....	33	10	3574	....	33	79	27	2350	....	....	....	3	2147	5	7
Taylor	....	....	14	1474	....	....	....	2437	....	11	23	46	2639	1	51	....	50	447	72	3
Union	....	....	8	620	....	....	....	1389	....	20	29	27	1469	....	....	....	....	40	....	....
Washington	....	....	1	165	....	....	....	673	....	3	3	15	645	....	6	....	20	419	1	6
Total	82	540	168	14962	92	157	135	36328	1	865	1604	588	40345	13	1759	2	487	16139	662	203

HENRY COUNTY.

Baltimore	....	....	32	2657	198	780	820	2	431	....	....	105	9866	2	236	....	93	565	65	173
Canaan	....	....	....	2585	224	1946	1373	291	505	2	2	19	5506	....	....	....	....	113	40	....
Center, exc. Mt. Pleasant	....	....	13	1107	5100	2726	3432	61	1158	4	6	150	17458	3	503	....	331	839	516	383
Jackson	....	....	39	3810	2681	2528	2122	30	1780	9	10	39	9390	....	401	....	76	559	84	171
Jefferson	....	....	24	1703	1848	1276	1523	7	89	....	....	116	6607	5	1457	2	222	489	103	198
Marion	....	....	....	4812	2509	1967	2869	57	756	3	5	....	7613	....	259	....	62	438	12	18
Mt. Pleasant, city of	....	....	....	....	25	114	76	80	....	....	....	2	127	....	5	....	10	10	100	....
New London, exc. town	....	....	12	1525	1445	4751	2705	3	1881	4	4	81	9745	....	121	....	52	120	54	126
Rome, town of	....	....	....	53	141	81	71	....	55	15	7	....	1301	....	62	....	42	74	28	8
Salem, exc. of town	....	....	43	3754	1729	2540	2316	14	2668	7	9	59	86187	5	2556	2	14	612	56	104
Scott	....	....	15	1165	637	4207	2667	140	443	11	19	70	7231	....	47	....	1	8	....	....
Tippecanoe, exc. of Rome	....	....	45	4429	1643	1919	1799	....	312	11	7	40	8313	2	728	....	44	235	24	171
Trenton	....	....	35	2243	1728	1761	1571	....	63	26	13	67	4630	....	197	....	64	205	26	22
Wayne	....	....	28	4126	3076	1951	1971	272	184	2	2	68	17000	....	86	....	56	34	9	6
Total	....	....	286	33969	22784	28547	25315	957	10325	94	84	816	190974	17	6708	4	1067	4301	1117	1380

HOWARD COUNTY.

Afton	....	....	2	206	....	88	83	3429	....	....	....	53	8110	....	....	....	20	575	....	23
Albion	....	....	....	....	....	500	566	144	7	....	....	53	7601	....	....	....	....	....	....	....
Chester	....	....	....	....	....	121	110	1313	....	....	....	38	4202	....	....	....	427	1840	152	20
Forest City	....	....	....	....	....	361	370	953	7	4	6	34	4794	....	....	....	3	1185	60	13
Howard	....	....	....	....	....	49	54	1408	....	....	....	15	3650	....	....	....	365	20	....	42
Howard Center	....	....	....	....	....	107	89	1206	56	10	60	36	3809	....	....	....	41	654	23	33
Jamestown	....	....	....	....	....	230	193	1526	296	....	....	42	4815	....	....	....	....	1600	....	....
New Oregon	....	....	....	....	....	214	208	3511	3	....	....	86	7562	....	....	....	1	495	5	100
Oak Dale	....	....	....	....	....	45	75	1169	....	....	....	35	5007	....	....	....	16	3080	....	36
Paris	....	....	....	....	....	139	123	3076	....	4	25	70	6490	....	....	....	....	4	150	....
Saratoga	....	....	....	....	....	37	47	836	....	....	....	17	1902	....	....	....	....	675	....	3
Vernon Springs, exc. of Cresco	....	6	....	....	40	638	616	800	....	....	....	39	4530	....	....	....	....	1601	55	15
Total	....	6	2	206	40	2529	2534	19371	369	18	91	518	62472	....	....	....	873	11729	445	285

HUMBOLDT COUNTY.

NAMES OF TOWNSHIPS, TOWNS, AND CITIES.	FLAX. Number of acres in flax seed.	FLAX. Number of bushels harvested.	SORGHUM. Number of acres in sorghum.	SORGHUM. Number of gallons of syrup from sorghum.	Number of acres of blue grass for pasture.	Number of acres of tame grass.	Number of tons of hay from same.	Number of tons of hay from wild grass.	Number of bushels of grass seed.	HUNGARIAN GRASS. Number of acres.	HUNGARIAN GRASS. Number of tons of hay.	POTATOES. Number of acres.	POTATOES. Number of bushels.	SWEET POTATOES. Number of acres.	SWEET POTATOES. Number of bushels.	ONIONS. Number of acres.	ONIONS. Number of bushels.	Number of bushels of turnips.	Number of bushels of beets.	Number of bushels of peas and beans.
Avery			2	140				651				20	1361							
Dakota			4	421		3	4	743				12	1261	9	635					
Delana			10	940				1301				22	1471				3	415		17
Grove				29		17	11	2041				37	3000					73	5	15
Humboldt			7	480	8	2	2	1927				29	1909							
Humboldt, town of								40				5	593				5		150	
Lake												5	450							
Norway			129	210				1506				7	1317						10	8
Rutland			2	174		3		1007				29	1701					90		12
Springvale, exc. of Humboldt			6	493		105	20	943				3	3157					265		
Vernon			18	232		74	17	1446	97			32	2100				75			11
Wacousta								898				16	1271					145		5
Weaver			5	382				249				10	1165							
Total			183	3501	8	204	54	12752	97			257	20756	9	635		83	988	165	68

IDA COUNTY.

NAMES OF TOWNSHIPS, TOWNS, AND CITIES.	FLAX. Number of acres in flax seed.	FLAX. Number of bushels harvested.	SORGHUM. Number of acres in sorghum.	SORGHUM. Number of gallons of syrup from sorghum.	Number of acres of blue grass for pasture.	Number of acres of tame grass.	Number of tons of hay from same.	Number of tons of hay from wild grass.	Number of bushels of grass seed.	HUNGARIAN GRASS. Number of acres.	HUNGARIAN GRASS. Number of tons of hay.	POTATOES. Number of acres.	POTATOES. Number of bushels.	SWEET POTATOES. Number of acres.	SWEET POTATOES. Number of bushels.	ONIONS. Number of acres.	ONIONS. Number of bushels.	Number of bushels of turnips.	Number of bushels of beets.	Number of bushels of peas and beans.
Corwin								1411				10	1203					710	10	15
Douglas				20				576				4	165				3	19	10	16
Maple						6	8	1188				17	1517				19	206	42	36
Silver Creek								313				7	425				33	10	4	9
Total				20		6	8	3508				38	3310				55	945	66	76

IOWA COUNTY.

Amana			6	550		1613	2320	330	247			192	20578					4100	9200	
Cono			2	252	25	205	251	190				12	1477	1	72	7	32	177	425	18
Dayton	264	2011	27	2827	196	926	990	2182	392			83	8613	1	65		16	127	14	134
English	97	732	34	4060	48	1583	1443	2005	224	4	14	82	9240	2	185		134	416	53	203
Fillmore	855	5691	11	1237		1117	676	2107	225			107	9802	1	47		10	144	16	89
Green	1454	9597	19	2218		1422	1205	2281	992			79	10256		4		5	196	20	11
Hartford, exc. of Victor	243	2818	9	714		757	651	1222	105	17	28	76	6945	1	320			110	125	68
Hilton	206	1846	9	611		984	671	1537				78	3404					676	29	6
Honey Creek	317	1874	20	1849	217	1683	1409	960	87	30	35	78	3847				15	280	17	14
Iowa	153	1542	15	1128		1221	1163	1277	145			36	10883				150	1800		50
Lenox			3	437		1048	759	597	62	5	8	40	3280				3	80		9
Lincoln	433	1987	9	666	61	401	322	1181	350	4	10	65	6006		11		101	248	90	34
Marengo, exc. of town	50	400	7	655	556	1206	1349	1275	603	26	65	77	7027		36		60	96	80	8
Marengo, town of			1	40	6	10														
Pilot	368	2557	16	1907	30	451	353	2135	323			64	6247		24		89	95	324	141
Sumner	266	2879	3	618	6	744	634	705	405	29	21	62	7903		10		60	10	150	
Troy	480	4681	8	471		858	728	2632	158			89	9160					25		
Victor, town of			5	500		4		13	35											
Washington	5	32	12	1093	127	327	123	987				50	4068		23		16	370	130	26
York	1573	9611	5	334		466	193	1580	128	2	3	75	8517		25		7	74	18	67
Total	6864	48258	221	22167	1272	17026	15240	25216	4481	117	184	1345	137253	6	822	7	698	9024	10691	878

JACKSON COUNTY

Andrew, town of												1	324						5	
Bellevue, exc. of town			4	235		1945		1763		3	5	94	7042			1	110			
Brandon			7	369	21	873	712		17	21	25	55	4228							
Butler					1875	1414	1326	391				150	10795			18	32	646		
Fairfield			1	128		1941	1204	211	10	5	13	68	6424				7	195	3	33
Farmer's Creek			27	1878	380	1641	1400	38	16	37	74	79	6954				6	202	8	106
Iowa			4	434	158	3533	1616	1021	117	20	51	76	15065				68	200	82	141
Jackson			27	1904	1032	1057	633	27	2	4	4	86	6175		10		230			46
Maquoketa, exc. of city			10	555	300	2026	1418	114	24	12	16	79	5313		38		31	1434	72	171
Maquoketa, city of					86	316	341	12	50	29	55	9	813	1	50	2	308	33	127	29
Monmouth			18	1492	288	2208	1726	145	37	55	122	64	5402		11			190		41
Otter Creek			5	316	301	1632	1018	68		2	3	78	6957		10		5	160		7
Perry, exc. of Andrew			8	941	668	1585	1922		57	27	40	64	7143	2			45	493	48	162
Prairie Spring			4	240	982	2117	1535		116			92	7412				50	200		
Richland			2	247	50	1949	1500	65	89			99	9075				1	15		
Sabula, town of												1	125				10	10	14	23
South Fork, exc. of Maquoketa			12	1079		1555	1688	239	8	76	162	44	3342							38

JACKSON COUNTY.—Continued.

Names of townships, towns, and cities.	Flax.		Sorghum.		Number of acres of blue grass for pasture.	Number of acres of tame grass.	Number of tons of hay from same.	Number of tons of hay from wild grass.	Number of bushels of grass seed.	Hungarian grass.		Potatoes.		Sweet potatoes.		Onions.		Number of bushels of turnips.	Number of bushels of beets.	Number of bushels of peas and beans.
	Number of acres in flax seed.	Number of bushels harvested.	Number of acres in sorghum.	Number of gallons of syrup from sorghum.						Number of acres.	Number of tons of hay.	Number of acres.	Number of bushels.	Number of acres.	Number of bushels.	Number of acres.	Number of bushels.			
Tete Des Morts	....	....	....	....	2024	1179	1112	....	7	....	....	83	4508	....	....	....	16	490	....	14
Union, exc. of Sabula	....	....	....	....	176	273	463	310	....	....	....	134	770	....	....	....	....	....	....	....
Van Buren	....	....	6	520	407	1976	2040	615	20	16	52	76	5465	....	7	2	45	119	72	57
Washington	....	....	9	679	359	790	507	1785	4	....	....	84	4449	....	....	1	14	254	102	53
Total	....	....	144	11017	9107	30010	22141	6804	574	307	622	1516	117781	3	126	24	978	4641	533	921

JASPER COUNTY.

Names of townships, towns, and cities.	Number of acres in flax seed.	Number of bushels harvested.	Number of acres in sorghum.	Number of gallons of syrup from sorghum.	Number of acres of blue grass for pasture.	Number of acres of tame grass.	Number of tons of hay from same.	Number of tons of hay from wild grass.	Number of bushels of grass seed.	Hungarian grass: Number of acres.	Hungarian grass: Number of tons of hay.	Potatoes: Number of acres.	Potatoes: Number of bushels.	Sweet potatoes: Number of acres.	Sweet potatoes: Number of bushels.	Onions: Number of acres.	Onions: Number of bushels.	Number of bushels of turnips.	Number of bushels of beets.	Number of bushels of peas and beans.
Buena Vista	27	166	39	4525	321	1229	1157	889	138	6	15	58	6909	....	40	....	16	870	124	78
Clear Creek	279	2830	38	3595	77	477	350	1539	45	....	....	61	5843	....	145	....	156	349	82	178
Des Moines, exc. of Prairie City	71	370	20	2786	56	1138	787	451	119	....	....	609	57313	....	3	....	....	....	....	....
Elk Creek	....	....	43	5375	....	1011	599	987	53	2	3	72	7484	....	20	1	308	195	....	30
Fairview, exc of Monroe	....	....	41	3751	131	3866	2208	927	384	2	5	196	23521	....	31	....	10	142	....	31
Hickory Grove	747	6313	....	....	....	126	134	909	....	2	2	11	3282	....	32	....	....	32	....	35
Independence	....	....	22	1958	69	284	484	1453	45	16	45	78	7092	3	246	....	143	971	4034	92
Jasper City, town of	30	75	1	104	....	....	....	....	....	....	....	....	....	....	....	....	....	....	....	....
Kellogg, exc. of Jasper City	44	339	23	1700	157	1403	797	714	27	18	46	37	5599	3	106	....	138	409	121	50
Lynn Grove	8	112	45	6776	....	2712	1181	242	....	....	....	33	4436	1	197	....	5	1068	....	16
Malaka	21	196	31	2088	569	1112	969	1734	....	5	10	136	12185	....	1	1	267	702	110	172
Mariposa	8	77	9	980	....	169	124	1153	....	6	22	57	6445	....	....	1	674	864	5	7
Monroe, town of	....	....	....	....	8	63	40	30	....	....	....	20	1337	....	71	....	....	....	1	....
Mound Prairie	....	....	16	2315	12	659	627	727	....	2	3	706	38368	....	15	....	28	10	10	....
Newton, exc. of city	10	53	3	297	310	356	345	1088	....	5	5	106	12541	....	46	1	210	654	229	104
Palo Alto	47	351	9	1247	12	745	720	754	216	....	....	23	6739	....	10	....	4	130	25	1
Poweshiek	40	420	26	3401	183	847	798	330	44	2	6	52	6935	....	167	....	30	125	24	31

Richland	113	905	33	3365	340	390	324	1193	63	...	...	49	4515	...	131	1	261	795	7	40
Rock Creek	161	1066	...	735	...	203	181	1339	6	8	12	31	7525	...	116	2	1418	296	19	65
Sherman	...	...	6	648	147	494	355	1499	14	...	...	74	7950	...	72	3	457	712	171	13
Washington	109	1141	2	84	614	376	821	11	...	...	...	256	12955	...	...	...	1	10	4	...
Total	1715	14414	407	45940	3006	17660	13001	18969	1154	74	174	2665	238974	7	1449	10	4126	8334	4966	943

JEFFERSON COUNTY.

Batavia, town of	...	...	...	...	...	...	...	...	...	...	...	...	20	...	6	...	2	3	3	...
Black Hawk	...	...	32	3522	2276	2696	1958	230	4110	40	45	62	6508	7	773	...	6	212	18	56
Buchanan	...	...	25	2051	3391	3542	1970	51	3368	19	21	76	5604	2	215	...	6	70	...	7
Cedar	...	...	9	766	1435	2506	2021	1	2701	16	20	62	6048	...	105	...	64	112	10	12
Des Moines	...	...	37	4344	2541	2961	1452	24	3455	32	39	79	6708	...	222	...	177	232	171	104
Fairfield, exc. of city	...	...	9	1049	4420	4133	3089	19	5741	38	60	97	8854	9	730	...	...	611	70	32
Fairfield, city of	...	...	...	...	...	...	...	...	...	...	...	...	2922	...	371	...	85	139	156	153
Liberty	...	...	22	1941	223	2759	2905	50	1823	54	59	59	5311	11	265	...	46	204	19	32
Lockridge	...	...	36	6117	1181	2219	2074	65	1445	1	1	45	8329	...	181	2	91	386	95	67
Locust Grove, exc. of Batavia	...	...	22	2870	1947	2844	2373	146	4296	45	90	41	4277	1	156	...	35	79	5	45
Penn	...	...	70	3764	910	2505	1582	16	1438	21	25	1	9000	4	853	...	69	296	79	64
Polk	...	...	15	1587	1485	3687	1376	...	5242	13	6	39	3312	...	4	...	...	6	...	...
Round Prairie	...	...	30	3460	814	2486	1860	30	3449	2	4	39	5862	...	297	...	56	542	66	80
Walnut	...	...	32	3007	1185	1436	1483	...	149	1	1	68	6824	...	34	...	10	540	1	60
Total	...	...	339	34478	21808	33774	24143	632	37217	282	371	668	79579	34	4212	2	647	3432	693	662

JOHNSON COUNTY.

Big Grove	9	72	20	1064	408	2377	1675	838	18	4	11	63	9076	...	12	...	68	334	56	22
Cedar	82	723	23	1885	1093	1593	1998	1101	414	25	62	48	7670	...	13	2	327	327	92	45
Clear Creek	84	768	8	1076	1483	1385	1640	357	54	18	25	72	9457	...	41	...	92	888	99	135
Coralville, town of	...	...	...	...	201	...	...	...	...	10	30	19	852	...	2	2	101	105	55	5
Fremont	183	1451	17	772	80	868	709	1068	564	83	242	147	6745	...	19	...	...	3	...	3
Graham	325	2826	17	2587	90	4001	1946	715	11710	6	7	114	14554	...	76	...	30	298	27	53
Hardin	524	4620	4	344	143	1023	1178	1438	199	...	...	71	10117	...	...	1	100	...	...	...
Iowa City, additions to	...	...	...	...	...	5	11	...	...	1	2	6	495	...	...	...	89	37	140	45
Jefferson	...	...	27	3130	387	909	501	549	24	...	...	43	3749	...	85	...	2	2	...	7
Liberty	...	...	15	1040	68	915	982	521	57	21	16	63	4009	...	...	...	2	94	58	...
Lincoln	156	1498	11	810	1940	1149	918	770	1490	1	2	141	12360	...	35	30	4906	17	5	3
Lucas, exc. of Iowa City and additions and Coralville	129	1050	4	325	1436	2631	3231	469	874	50	96	134	13325	3	205	...	85	394	889	182

JOHNSON COUNTY.—Continued.

Names of townships, towns, and cities.	Flax.		Sorghum.		Number of acres of blue grass for pasture.	Number of acres of tame grass.	Number of tons of hay from same.	Number of tons of hay from wild grass.	Number of bushels of grass seed.	Hungarian grass.		Potatoes.		Sweet potatoes.		Onions.		Number of bushels of turnips.	Number of bushels of beets.	Number of bushels of peas and beans.
	Number of acres in flax seed.	Number of bushels harvested.	Number of acres in sorghum.	Number of gallons of syrup from sorghum.						Number of acres.	Number of tons of hay.	Number of acres.	Number of bushels.	Number of acres.	Number of bushels.	Number of acres.	Number of bushels.			
Madison	62	597	60	1475	1570	1683	1364	495	258	50	76	44	4216	1	40	....	67	7256	61	92
Monroe	....	....	11	957	40	820	618	740	....	2	4	51	4227				5	363		
Newport	....	....	4	887	887	242	379	497	27	....	....	90	8675	....	....	....	105	....	....	....
Oxford	151	481	14	1104	467	785	1005	382	77	13	23	76	1167	....	7	5	12	....	6	4
Penn	....	....	16	1310	....	788	968	314	18	12	30	53	7060	1	24	....	....	61	23	....
Pleasant Valley	296	2525	5	421	895	1464	1428	299	1350	39	74	39	3276	....	....	....	....	....	....	....
Scott	438	3799	8	789	155	3517	2449	1449	4938	4	6	76	11789	....	10	2	100	50	10	5
Sharon	9	84	37	4317	96	3397	2442	731	175	8	13	72	8234	1	106	....	34	176	55	58
Union	87	1327	4	839	1826	1874	2035	960	328	1	1	58	7011	....	8	....	11	71	6	3
Washington	161	1120	32	2333	277	3078	2478	650	445	4	8	50	6204	2	141	16	640	96	40	20
Total	2696	22941	337	27465	13542	34504	29955	14343	23120	352	728	1530	154268	9	824	59	6776	10572	1622	682

JONES COUNTY.

Names of townships, towns, and cities.	Number of acres in flax seed.	Number of bushels harvested.	Number of acres in sorghum.	Number of gallons of syrup from sorghum.	Number of acres of blue grass for pasture.	Number of acres of tame grass.	Number of tons of hay from same.	Number of tons of hay from wild grass.	Number of bushels of grass seed.	Hungarian grass: Number of acres.	Hungarian grass: Number of tons of hay.	Potatoes: Number of acres.	Potatoes: Number of bushels.	Sweet potatoes: Number of acres.	Sweet potatoes: Number of bushels.	Onions: Number of acres.	Onions: Number of bushels.	Number of bushels of turnips.	Number of bushels of beets.	Number of bushels of peas and beans.
Cass	25	181	2	237	1235	1599	1435	1561	19	8	2	78	5932	....	....	....	....	....	....	....
Castle Grove	....	....	6	373	370	2031	1229	1419	14	....	14	71	6188	....	....	....	....	....	....	....
Clay	....	....	13	1553	1921	1314	1183	343	27	61	109	53	4886	....	9	3	131	253	24	30
Fairview, exc. Anamosa	....	....	6	399	1027	1582	i779	307	33	2	4	61	6142	....	60	....	7	146	51	124
Greenfield	....	....	9	1188	3129	1183	1547	1424	90	....	....	46	5950	....	94	....	60	157	91	49
Hale	....	....	10	774	1068	316	1082	597	39	73	111	64	6164	....	10	1	85	531	....	27
Jackson	....	....	6	397	414	966	827	1229	28	2	3	54	4324	....	13	....	5	125	273	70
Madison	....	....	1	50	110	1331	1338	1129	20	25	49	17	1615	....	....	....	....	40	....	40
Monticello, exc. of town	....	....	20	180	....	2899	1964	681	5	19	22	87	6232	....	10	....	52	3217	105	60
Monticello, town of	....	....	....	30	....	....	2	11	....	....	....	2	68	....	....	....	....	....	....	....
Oxford	2	20	8	761	20	3217	1950	608	118	11	12	44	3427	1	10	....	165	40	61	3
Richland	....	....	4	299	....	1423	1588	398	10	....	....	38	5085	....	....	....	....	171	61	2

Rome	....	....	13	325	899	1479	1552	590	18	26	47	44	4080	....	....	....	....	....	....	5
Scotch Grove	....	....	11	763	3270	1620	1932	790	86	31	43	34	3430	1	77	8	20	40	20	32
Washington	....	....	8	671	190	1621	1649	489	....	....	....	82	6115	....	....	....	....	....	....	....
Wayne	....	....	4	345	....	3460	2389	1976	248	....	....	64	5942	....	....	....	14	55	4	24
Wyoming, exc. of town	....	....	18	1276	517	2653	2322	164	57	1[illegible]3	282	60	4347	....	....	7	45	364	84	46
Total	27	201	139	9621	13970	28694	25768	13709	812	411	698	899	80227	2	283	19	584	5139	777	512

KEOKUK COUNTY.

Adams	....	....	15	1430	333	2207	2130	943	985	....	....	72	6798	4	92	9	547	565	67	109
Benton	....	....	38	4584	1085	1725	1142	182	433	22	43	86	9511	....	194	....	33	779	19	67
Clear Creek	25	118	37	3616	1910	1545	1545	158	166	....	....	69	6718	....	13	....	....	27	....	14
English River	....	....	26	2403	115	2518	2354	1294	310	2	4	56	5948	....	191	1	174	265	117	122
German	....	....	48	5084	....	2073	1920	1043	217	....	....	111	9617	....	8	....	9	109	104	3
Jackson	....	....	....	2427	370	1757	1445	266	2008	18	21	....	3200	2	701	....	47	345	6	5
LaFayette exc. of Keota	120	1078	7	2272	30	2211	1296	984	1524	....	....	....	6900	....	143	....	29	295	31	31
Lancaster	....	....	54	6128	1352	1852	1847	1270	476	51	83	79	7975	6	283	....	110	798	150	156
Liberty	165	1403	28	2879	1204	1311	1921	1649	188	....	....	81	7003	9	518	....	31	337	80	44
Prairie	164	1198	15	675	39	1206	1045	1015	1058	....	....	52	5006	3	275	2	140	....	10	7
Richland, exc of town	....	....	30	3108	2194	1365	1435	11	404	....	....	42	4933	12	1422	....	32	190	38	35
Richland, town of	....	....	5	513	232	71	256	1	53	....	....	19	1222	8	1193	....	4	68	34	23
Sigourney, exc. of town	....	....	9	666	1231	1273	1414	336	30	15	104	47	5656	1	268	....	33	163	26	63
Steady Run	....	....	27	3198	1268	1851	1130	160	782	2	13	50	4243	1	183	37	1240	194	15	36
Van Buren	....	....	25	2628	202	1684	1759	685	283	1	1	66	7931	1	138	....	26	852	32	94
Warren	....	....	27	2785	460	1018	953	492	53	....	....	33	3524	1	63	1	61	98	28	64
Washington	10	....	30	2170	150	1746	1644	1019	210	6	12	36	4734	....	67	....	....	87	....	....
Total	484	3797	421	46566	12175	27413	25236	11508	9180	117	281	899	100919	49	5752	50	2516	5172	757	873

KOSSUTH COUNTY.

Algona, exc, of town	201	107	2	159	....	43	....	3892	....	....	....	86	3282	....	....	....	....	725	5	....
Algona, town of	108	....	1	33	330	10	....	685	....	....	....	49	2249	....	....	....	....	1985	....	1
Cresco	32	13	5	205	5	93	....	3329	....	....	....	70	2842	....	....	....	1	847	8	1
Fenton	43	....	....	21	....	....	....	755	....	....	....	35	753	....	....	....	....	411	....	....
Greenwood	68	15	5	155	....	5	....	666	....	....	....	47	2058	....	....	....	....	384	....	14
Irvington	....	....	5	450	....	246	60	3079	....	....	....	42	2434	....	....	....	....	615	....	....
Lott's Creek	85	....	4	101	....	17	....	1016	....	....	....	28	1333	....	....	....	....	317	5	....
Portland	118	....	6	435	....	10	....	4366	....	....	....	58	865	....	....	....	....	....	1	....
Wesley	107	112	....	....	....	....	....	891	....	....	....	24	1087	....	....	....	....	70	....	8
Total	762	247	28	1559	335	424	60	18679	....	....	....	439	16906	....	....	....	1	5354	19	24

LEE COUNTY.

NAMES OF TOWNSHIPS, TOWNS, AND CITIES.	FLAX. Number of acres in flax seed.	FLAX. Number of bushels harvested.	SORGHUM. Number of acres in sorghum.	SORGHUM. Number of gallons of syrup from sorghum.	Number of acres of blue grass for pasture.	Number of acres of tame grass.	Number of tons of hay from same.	Number of tons of hay from wild grass.	Number of bushels of grass seed.	HUNGARIAN GRASS. Number of acres.	HUNGARIAN GRASS. Number of tons of hay	POTATOES. Number of acres.	POTATOES. Number of bushels.	SWEET POTATOES. Number of acres.	SWEET POTATOES. Number of bushels.	ONIONS. Number of acres.	ONIONS. Number of bushels.	Number of bushels of turnips.	Number of bushels of beets.	Number of bushels of peas and beans.
Cedar	......	......	18	2693	2269	5556	3055	615	11267	27	27	57	5413	......	58	2	108	118	165	114
Charleston	......	......	42	4009	591	1677	1268	11	1134	28	22	174	16174	......	51	......	7	19	3	73
Denmark	......	......	18	1603	1696	1459	1666	15	1090	36	42	68	7737	......	88	......	6	123	15	113
Des Moines	......	......	31	2272	1222	2439	1884	889	950	35	59	248	9008	......	24	......	1	440	15	120
Franklin	......	2	37	2998	1023	2784	2232	......	3471	18	28	167	172650	1	80	......	8	153	......	43
Green Bay	......	......	3	534	......	760	824	458	40	......	6	32	3735	......	60	......	76	155	130	......
Harrison	......	......	21	2375	3466	3133	2695	2	4210	46	38	79	6567	1	196	......	......	276	39	159
Jackson, exc. of Keokuk	......	......	25	2064	282	1074	986	13	5	50	37	104	8010	7	543	......	24	475	430	334
Jefferson	......	......	68	5312	578	753	727	73	138	154	94	322	28894	27	2422	......	39	218	38	131
Keokuk, city of	......	......	......	......	......	......	......	......	......	......	......	29	850	......	......	......	......	......	......	......
Madison, exc. of Fort Madison	......	......	8	680	91	125	151	2	......	14	18	37	3085	1	105	4	506	75	40	460
Marion	......	......	32	2532	1446	3615	1972	......	7701	13	10	81	6800	......	81	......	8	171	......	16
Montrose, exc. of town	......	......	41	3125	1822	1754	1300	28	428	......	......	293	27029	14	923	......	32	841	89	111
Pleasant Ridge	......	......	20	2271	3057	3284	2940	......	6428	6	......	84	9553	4	335	......	10	172	1	71
Van Buren	......	......	57	3050	2297	935	696	3	925	49	50	70	7845	......	......	......	35	......	97	......
Washington, exc. of Fort Madison	......	......	11	592	2793	3839	2867	41	2101	7	7	111	10467	......	153	......	97	253	12	95
West Point, exc. of town	......	......	32	2291	373	1565	1087	79	1098	3	6	125	11242	1	65	......	4	36	2	99
West Point, town of	......	......	......	27	......	......	......	......	......	......	......	2	130	......	......	......	......	......	......	......
Total	......	2	464	38428	23006	34752	26350	2229	40986	486	444	2083	335189	56	5184	6	961	3525	1076	1939

LINN COUNTY.

NAMES OF TOWNSHIPS, TOWNS, AND CITIES.	FLAX. Number of acres in flax seed.	FLAX. Number of bushels harvested.	SORGHUM. Number of acres in sorghum.	SORGHUM. Number of gallons of syrup from sorghum.	Number of acres of blue grass for pasture.	Number of acres of tame grass.	Number of tons of hay from same.	Number of tons of hay from wild grass.	Number of bushels of grass seed.	HUNGARIAN GRASS. Number of acres.	HUNGARIAN GRASS. Number of tons of hay	POTATOES. Number of acres.	POTATOES. Number of bushels.	SWEET POTATOES. Number of acres.	SWEET POTATOES. Number of bushels.	ONIONS. Number of acres.	ONIONS. Number of bushels.	Number of bushels of turnips.	Number of bushels of beets.	Number of bushels of peas and beans.
Bertram	......	......	13	1158	1799	828	1138	287	10	11	20	51	4885	......	1	......	8	339	57	22
Boulder	......	......	8	531	......	532	291	2060	31	......	......	32	3554	......	......	......	2	169	42	27
Brown	45	213	25	1550	2001	2295	1054	620	64	......	......	44	4564	2	387	......	9	279	359	76
Buffalo	......	......	5	1125	46	476	446	894	......	6	13	7	2710	......	6	......	44	63	17	49

Cedar Rapids, city of	......	......	......	......	......	8	3	......	......	......	......	......	135	......	63	......	18	35	26	52
Clinton	225	1176	18	2140	1342	1373	1304	1703	80	8	11	109	11599	......	3	......	1	1155	110	......
College, exc. of Western	14	40	9	1075	1321	826	1052	1758	15	......	......	88	6918	......	......	......	......	486	94	75
Fairfax	8	80	32	3862	......	2282	1560	1398	405	......	......	100	9792	......	5	......	157	219	150	48
Fayette	1	28	24	3284	821	804	926	474	......	......	......	47	3883	......	7	......	14	129	47	119
Franklin, exc. of Mt. Vernon and Lisbon	......	......	26	2676	2313	2236	2937	262	126	28	44	63	6142	......	72	......	10	70	220	20
Grant	437	4036	23	2089	1179	477	484	1550	197	11	31	43	4715	......	22	......	36	268	28	85
Jackson	......	......	33	9495	1344	1148	1248	2218	216	......	......	60	4702	......	10	......	49	765	10	76
Linn	36	315	3	304	451	3601	2085	735	115	2	1	54	4952	......	93	......	79	235	43	23
Lisbon, town of	......	......	......	......	21	30	30	......	......	......	......	3	307	......	11	......	......	......	......	......
Maine	65	559	27	3049	......	1445	1410	2497	173	48	46	65	5663	2	384	......	230	......	......	115
Marion, exc. of city	159	1270	52	5808	5713	5053	4713	2477	8	10	12	132	12700	4	959	......	......	257	134	......
Marion, city of	......	......	......	......	......	7	15	......	......	......	......	5	275	1	40	1	55	......	90	30
Monroe	......	......	39	5640	715	1009	1379	521	......	......	......	60	5854	......	97	......	87	655	23	42
Mount Vernon, town of	......	......	......	......	157	88	115	6	8	......	......	5	832	......	54	......	9	68	214	1
Otter Creek	87	794	32	3310	411	1211	1411	1363	6	6	8	62	7186	......	65	......	59	541	69	142
Putnam	......	......	20	1539	766	644	725	664	40	5	10	53	4850	......	......	......	......	62	......	44
Rapids, exc. Cedar Rapids	......	......	16	3006	1034	1438	1611	756	37	......	......	133	13160	6	795	......	82	1400	729	380
Spring Grove	223	1890	32	3294	32	262	244	1372	5	9	14	41	3853	......	3	......	47	385	59	76
Washington	85	696	29	2203	174	1230	1307	1304	......	14	29	38	4120	......	30	......	......	......	......	42
Western, town of	43	335	......	......	70	83	107	41	......	......	......	4	270	......	......	......	......	......	......	......
Total	1428	11432	466	50138	21710	29386	28495	24957	1536	158	239	1299	127621	15	3107	1	996	7580	2521	1544

LOUISA COUNTY.

Columbus City, exc. Columbus City and Columbus Junction	......	......	23	2122	2110	5820	2710	92	223	40	35	67	9928	......	400	......	83	747	234	269
Columbus City, town of	......	......	......	......	65	64	70	......	10	......	......	......	1129	1	......	14	......	......	......	......
Columbus Junction, town of	......	......	......	......	......	11	7	8	......	......	......	2	396	......	24	......	1	10	4	9
Concord, exc. of Fredonia	......	......	137	3013	1014	1842	887	347	22	35	46	45	5516	......	169	......	94	393	121	20
Eliot	6	......	17	1679	568	843	461	241	24	......	......	22	3022	1	156	......	......	111	6	35
Elm Grove	......	......	15	1356	......	1429	1406	129	66	16	53	50	5372	1	35	......	22	64	33	43
Fredonia, town of	......	......	......	15	53	40	18	54	......	1	2	4	310	......	98	......	17	30	8	9
Grandview	......	......	18	1671	4592	2202	1266	145	11	5	8	134	14081	......	16	......	16	325	6	40
Jefferson	......	......	16	1397	15	545	732	832	75	3	9	85	8773	......	32	......	21	152	......	51
Marshal	10	......	14	1393	1943	1812	1301	85	525	29	47	68	6307	1	76	......	15	156	19	96
Morning Sun, exc. town	13	......	6	423	729	3140	1632	30	751	2	8	50	6101	......	206	......	37	117	40	30
Oakland	......	......	17	1422	602	565	471	657	20	79	67	88	3197	......	81	......	39	56	42	70
Port Louisa	......	......	21	2031	......	895	747	850	......	2	4	196	13880	27	1683	......	58	18	15	21
Union	......	......	25	1584	......	2575	877	161	19	16	37	55	4304	2	242	......	12	81	1	9

LOUISA COUNTY.—Continued.

NAMES OF TOWNSHIPS, TOWNS, AND CITIES.	FLAX. Number of acres in flax seed.	FLAX. Number of bushels harvested.	SORGHUM. Number of acres in sorghum.	SORGHUM. Number of gallons of syrup from sorghum.	Number of acres of blue grass for pasture.	Number of acres of tame grass.	Number of tons of hay from same.	Number of tons of hay from wild grass.	Number of bushels of grass seed.	HUNGARIAN GRASS. Number of acres.	HUNGARIAN GRASS. Number of tons of hay.	POTATOES. Number of acres.	POTATOES. Number of bushels.	SWEET POTATOES. Number of acres.	SWEET POTATOES. Number of bushels.	ONIONS. Number of acres.	ONIONS. Number of bushels.	Number of bushels of turnips.	Number of bushels of beets.	Number of bushels of peas and beans.
Wapello, exc. of town	....	....	23	2594	4701	3348	1948	269	147	87	135	68	7391	....	....	1	230	43	47	23
Wapello, town of	....	....	1	60	250	100	139	31	....	7	8	23	1486	....	....	....	....	....	....	....
Total	29	....	333	207060	16642	25231	14672	3931	1893	322	459	957	91193	34	3218	15	645	2303	576	725

LUCAS COUNTY.

NAMES OF TOWNSHIPS, TOWNS, AND CITIES.	FLAX. Number of acres in flax seed.	FLAX. Number of bushels harvested.	SORGHUM. Number of acres in sorghum.	SORGHUM. Number of gallons of syrup from sorghum.	Number of acres of blue grass for pasture.	Number of acres of tame grass.	Number of tons of hay from same.	Number of tons of hay from wild grass.	Number of bushels of grass seed.	HUNGARIAN GRASS. Number of acres.	HUNGARIAN GRASS. Number of tons of hay.	POTATOES. Number of acres.	POTATOES. Number of bushels.	SWEET POTATOES. Number of acres.	SWEET POTATOES. Number of bushels.	ONIONS. Number of acres.	ONIONS. Number of bushels.	Number of bushels of turnips.	Number of bushels of beets.	Number of bushels of peas and beans.
Benton	....	....	21	2588	181	1650	1468	98	268	125	232	28	2844	....	....	....	....	....	....	....
Cedar	....	....	15	1637	255	1328	941	197	171	106	200	45	3353	1	175	....	33	523	44	98
Chariton, exc. of city	....	....	12	2369	44	1506	1388	491	548	93	137	25	5173	1	95	1	180	647	256	7
English	....	....	23	2760	....	1017	779	369	54	101	155	45	4525	1	114	....	....	370	13	15
Jackson	....	....	15	1622	....	462	538	879	9	137	431	29	3179	....	69	....	87	385	75	113
Liberty	....	....	17	1972	40	573	695	839	67	123	192	21	2944	....	30	....	17	340	....	....
Otter Creek	....	....	11	1301	....	897	1017	214	146	44	96	10	684	....	....	....	6	3	4	4
Pleasant	....	....	20	2860	....	378	289	206	....	54	111	30	2665	....	9	....	19	600	2	49
Union	....	....	13	1229	138	1787	1353	391	1174	54	117	28	2110	....	18	....	....	175	....	4
Warren	....	....	26	1856	175	3439	2925	660	686	174	189	69	4842	1	47	....	14	194	87	101
Washington	5	24	26	3871	132	766	539	602	120	110	182	26	4264	....	181	....	78	436	147	193
White Breast	....	....	6	1203	378	1775	1452	406	473	217	405	61	5570	1	90	....	35	631	57	54
Total	5	24	205	25268	1343	15579	13384	5352	3716	1338	2447	417	42153	5	828	1	469	4304	685	638

LYON COUNTY.

NAMES OF TOWNSHIPS, TOWNS, AND CITIES.	FLAX. Number of acres in flax seed.	FLAX. Number of bushels harvested.	SORGHUM. Number of acres in sorghum.	SORGHUM. Number of gallons of syrup from sorghum.	Number of acres of blue grass for pasture.	Number of acres of tame grass.	Number of tons of hay from same.	Number of tons of hay from wild grass.	Number of bushels of grass seed.	HUNGARIAN GRASS. Number of acres.	HUNGARIAN GRASS. Number of tons of hay.	POTATOES. Number of acres.	POTATOES. Number of bushels.	SWEET POTATOES. Number of acres.	SWEET POTATOES. Number of bushels.	ONIONS. Number of acres.	ONIONS. Number of bushels.	Number of bushels of turnips.	Number of bushels of beets.	Number of bushels of peas and beans.
Dale	74	....	2	71	....	....	....	950	....	....	....	54	1039	....	....	....	....	....	....	....

Doon	....	....	1	107	....	....	....	975	....	....	....	34	855	....	....	....	5	5	6	123
Grant	30	50	....	....	....	....	....	214	....	....	....	20	606	....	....	....	....	....	....	....
Larchwood	50	292	....	....	....	....	....	362	....	....	....	5	303	....	....	....	....	150	3	....
Lyon	75	136	....	....	....	13	5	1350	....	....	....	159	492	....	....	....	....	13	3	3
Rock	....	....	....	....	....	....	....	359	....	....	....	12	600	....	....	....	....	....	31	....
Total	229	480	3	178	....	13	5	4210	....	....	....	284	3895	....	....	....	5	168	43	126

MADISON COUNTY.

Crawford	18	300	26	2308	....	289	221	1320	....	....	....	55	7030	....	54	4	18	3	2	1
Douglas	6	48	5	592	464	1064	1115	716	....	12	18	52	6255	1	50	....	....	135	5	4
Grand River	54	427	13	1019	10	210	275	994	7	....	....	39	3658	....	230	....	107	395	132	96
Jackson	....	....	9	967	10	518	361	731	18	....	....	34	5515	1	105	....	53	771	40	42
Jefferson	452	1760	11	828	79	530	536	1293	99	4	5	77	7791	....	147	....	114	203	224	77
Lee	88	860	5	276	26	219	264	906	....	10	30	51	7090	....	....	....	....	....	....	....
Lincoln	28	211	10	1216	127	794	952	600	171	12	21	71	5484	1	362	....	54	607	52	52
Madison, exc. of Earlham	....	....	7	599	88	388	480	574	34	17	13	40	6823	....	260	10	33	332	34	51
Monroe	156	1122	8	848	....	177	150	319	....	4	6	22	3019	....	10	....	22	....	....	....
Ohio	37	120	22	1196	70	375	447	865	....	17	30	30	5248	1	129	1	203	236	103	139
Penn, exc. of Earlham	29	228	2	415	97	971	728	757	60	....	....	69	7576	8	207	3	124	824	50	71
Scott	....	....	25	1912	314	834	1123	394	10	35	43	70	4457	2	267	....	97	205	26	12
South	10	75	24	2563	....	850	1002	269	68	23	41	42	4632	....	25	1	59	407	2	56
Union	10	80	41	3660	302	904	940	719	39	57	98	76	7090	1	147	1	36	862	190	88
Walnut	....	....	23	1752	15	433	446	296	47	6	11	32	2844	....	73	2	56	36	45	23
Webster	12	120	11	1435	....	117	139	998	4	3	5	30	3111	1	187	....	118	531	79	67
Winterset, city of	....	....	....	....	10	18	20	....	....	....	....	1	50	....	....	....	....	....	....	....
Total	900	5351	242	21586	1612	8691	9199	11751	557	200	321	791	87693	16	2253	22	1094	5547	984	779

MAHASKA COUNTY.

Adams	....	....	12	1640	1969	1592	1507	796	10	....	....	46	7070	....	33	....	....	67	18	56
Beacon, town of	....	....	....	85	5	19	21	....	....	....	....	....	95	....	....	....	....	5	....	....
Black Oak	....	....	34	3987	643	1329	774	943	6	....	....	172	20241	....	13	....	44	400	16	37
Cedar	....	....	42	5081	409	2590	1930	467	274	59	84	84	9698	....	97	....	85	227	24	62
Des Moines	....	....	23	3010	1146	1634	1407	179	48	40	64	77	9018	....	....	....	....	....	....	....
Harrison	....	....	24	2763	1686	4376	2940	311	31	6	12	68	8657	1	60	....	....	220	....	97
Jefferson	....	....	40	4930	143	2830	1511	132	37	54	90	55	6368	....	110	....	82	289	40	70
Madison	....	....	31	4274	102	1756	1528	1350	40	....	....	57	6948	....	177	....	62	728	30	56
Monroe	4	60	33	3634	1290	1607	1760	773	65	6	11	62	6672	1	79	3	125	285	44	93
New Sharon, town of	....	....	....	....	....	85	77	19	1	....	....	5	578	....	....	....	....	....	70	....
Oskaloosa, exc. of Oskaloosa and Beacon	....	....	57	9186	5247	5406	4921	1120	134	26	52	118	18386	5	1503	....	265	944	531	173

MAHASKA COUNTY.—Continued.

Names of townships, towns, and cities.	Flax.		Sorghum.		Number of acres of blue grass for pasture.	Number of acres of tame grass.	Number of tons of hay from same.	Number of tons of hay from wild grass.	Number of bushels of grass seed.	Hungarian grass.		Potatoes.		Sweet potatoes.		Onions.		Number of bushels of turnips.	Number of bushels of beets.	Number of bushels of peas and beans.
	Number of acres in flax seed.	Number of bushels harvested.	Number of acres in sorghum.	Number of gallons of syrup from sorghum.						Number of acres.	Number of tons of hay.	Number of acres.	Number of bushels.	Number of acres.	Number of bushels.	Number of acres.	Number of bushels.			
Oskaloosa, city of	....	....	1	130	20	26	36	....	....	....	....	....	....	....	....	....	....	....	....	....
Pleasant Grove	....	....	31	3456	72	809	668	940	187	2	1	48	4414	1	185	2	211	279	80	221
Prairie, exc. New Sharon	17	100	28	4121	54	2567	1473	1184	810	....	....	84	9160	....	92	....	....	344	100	10
Richland	....	....	35	4584	578	1885	1512	477	224	1	2	101	10807	....	114	....	77	87	6	42
Scott	15	....	25	2795	2199	1219	1340	418	16	....	....	64	8377	....	5	....	22	43	12	23
Union	30	300	31	200	873	939	903	792	39	....	....	65	5687	2	220	....	40	....	....	10
White Oak	....	....	66	6410	658	1363	1128	416	79	13	21	124	7722	....	207	....	34	896	37	147
Total	66	460	513	60286	17094	32032	25436	10317	2001	207	337	1230	139898	10	2895	5	1047	4814	1008	1097

MARION COUNTY.

Names of townships, towns, and cities.	Number of acres in flax seed.	Number of bushels harvested.	Number of acres in sorghum.	Number of gallons of syrup from sorghum.	Number of acres of blue grass for pasture.	Number of acres of tame grass.	Number of tons of hay from same.	Number of tons of hay from wild grass.	Number of bushels of grass seed.	Hungarian grass: Number of acres.	Hungarian grass: Number of tons of hay.	Potatoes: Number of acres.	Potatoes: Number of bushels.	Sweet potatoes: Number of acres.	Sweet potatoes: Number of bushels.	Onions: Number of acres.	Onions: Number of bushels.	Number of bushels of turnips.	Number of bushels of beets.	Number of bushels of peas and beans.
Clay	....	....	63	6223	957	1353	1598	19	120	....	....	59	6721	....	132	....	59	362	11	49
Dallas	1	4	8	660	106	1311	1083	401	137	44	85	18	6730	....	214	....	107	583	117	106
Franklin	....	....	13	1797	129	658	752	947	50	14	35	45	6017	....	68	....	67	315	50	59
Indiana	....	....	53	4750	1543	1400	1167	27	22	26	30	33	4423	3	326	....	86	275	41	55
Knoxville, exc. of town	....	....	63	8338	....	2290	3258	323	....	11	22	152	28700	2	73	....	20	....	....	....
Knoxville, town of	....	....	7	100	8	344	232	....	....	....	2	2	100	....	....	....	....	....	....	....
Lake Prairie, exc. of Pella	....	....	124	10540	376	1485	1162	1379	12	....	....	524	50770	....	....	....	33	235	12	5
Liberty	....	....	34	4424	....	1652	1137	9	10	20	36	35	5242	1	142	....	....	362	....	81
Perry	....	....	24	2591	....	85	116	118	43	2	4	41	4643	....	3	....	44	64	7	15
Pleasant Grove, exc. of Pleasantville	12	121	24	2798	1742	1268	1393	245	51	9	17	32	6189	1	299	....	15	22	61	17
Polk	....	....	37	3603	54	290	294	....	3	5	10	48	4578	1	52	1	238	217	32	14
Red Rock	....	....	54	6051	474	862	1018	361	144	....	....	81	11774	1	172	1	326	570	149	88
Summit	....	....	50	6508	415	1052	1066	951	41	....	....	471	39109	....	150	....	91	874	85	102
Swan	....	....	63	1485	338	633	743	269	....	7	18	51	3245	....	....	....	18	159	51	17

Union	119	739	8	1066		883	736	218	15		2	23	3108	1	39	2	66	67	64	70
Washington	5	50	43	4316	356	1907	1313	173	31	46	82	48	5229		141		63	260	57	83
Total	137	913	668	65250	6498	17473	17068	5440	679	184	343	1663	186478	10	1811	4	1233	4365	737	761

MARSHALL COUNTY.

Albion, town of				43		20	16	30				7	926	1	81		17	33	99	10
Bangor	124	811	19	1839	103	1015	876	615	161			35	3597	5	617		18	442	79	77
Eden	243	1965		30	146	363	298	978	144	5	10	61	5768	1	30		85	161	158	84
Green Castle	70	466	4	381	126	486	431	1058	190	3	6	63	5955					2362	30	71
Iowa, exc. of Albion	30	350	10	934	81	1512	1188	694	38	7	13	37	2894		19		31	150	53	7
Jefferson	267	2115	1	115		582	312	1204		2	3	70	6270		60	2	406	1186	156	79
Le Grand	46	321	10	1016	140	1470	999	1602	150			180	13135		20	1	165	466	51	44
Liberty	68	607	8	703	953	725	1291	1104	83			46	6359		31		4	830	42	53
Liscomb, exc. of town	93	740	11	1046	215	1305	723	1168	506			58	5374		51		31	837	51	54
Liscomb, town of						39	25	180	60			11	828	1	48		8	24	26	
Logan	142	1309		25		175	169	955	164		3	43	5244				24	25	7	40
Marietta	554	4414	6	429		1769	1470	1092	287	30	76	77	7866					20	120	
Marion	47	410	5	425	21	1243	613	1263	358	11	29	218	19836		38		87	683	21	49
Marshall, exc. of Marshalltown	2	16	2	204	150	967	817	776	5	2	3	183	10380				4	232	685	256
Marshalltown, city of					7	675	203	254		10	5	134	9659	1	268	2	458	697	906	482
Minerva	531	4039				1599	595	2028	641			63	7095		2		45	504	53	6
State Center, exc. of town	307	2912				1028	414	1805	979			109	9861					726	60	69
State Center, town of	48	408				40		93	425			2	1696		110		60	307	125	61
Taylor	69	541	2	223	3	1194	841	813	70	4		85	6288							
Timber Creek	286	2061	112	100	70	1125	809	1191	5	1	11	212	16801		76		65	815		11
Vienna	705	6261	9	142	64	332	193	1199	359			99	8434		32		63	99	13	36
Washington	628	5046		54		1705	823	1468	797	11	15	113	11645		4		22	35	218	18
Total	4260	34792	199	7709	2079	19369	13106	21570	5422	86	174	1906	166211	9	1487	5	1593	10634	2953	1507

MILLS COUNTY.

Anderson	83	435				47	24	1675		97	92	44	3000	1	232		106	101	128	28
Deer Creek	436	3643	4	270		82	47	978		3	7	41	3056	2	86		51	50	6	1
Emerson, town of						3	2	98												
Glenwood, exc. of town			9	611	57	76	50	1138	25	123	216	189	9707	10	1109		38	85	32	11
Glenwood, town of												1	75	3	300					
Hastings, town of	155	975						22		13	25	2	80							
Hillsdale, town of												1	40							
Indian Creek, exc. of Emerson and Hastings	166	901			80	128	73	1334		65	117	39	2164							

MILLS COUNTY.—CONTINUED.

NAMES OF TOWNSHIPS, TOWNS, AND CITIES.	FLAX. Number of acres in flax seed.	FLAX. Number of bushels harvested.	SORGHUM. Number of acres in sorghum.	SORGHUM. Number of gallons of syrup from sorghum.	Number of acres of blue grass for pasture.	Number of acres of tame grass.	Number of tons of hay from same.	Number of tons of hay from wild grass.	Number of bushels of grass seed.	HUNGARIAN GRASS. Number of acres.	HUNGARIAN GRASS. Number of tons of hay.	POTATOES. Number of acres.	POTATOES. Number of bushels.	SWEET POTATOES. Number of acres.	SWEET POTATOES. Number of bushels.	ONIONS. Number of acres.	ONIONS. Number of bushels.	Number of bushels of turnips.	Number of bushels of beets.	Number of bushels of peas and beans.
Ingraham	79	305	......	......	......	128	80	1288	50	10	22	44	2655	1	48	16	29	40	32	3
Lyons	......	......	18	343	......	......	......	1988	......	59	89	33	2304	1	150	2	281	10	40	29
Malvern, town of	......	......	......	......	......	......	......	120	......	......	......	2	255	......	......	......	......	......	......	......
Oak	......	......	5	367	......	16	18	2391	......	73	160	125	7650	......	......	......	15	......	......	......
Platteville	......	......	1	150	......	6	10	2378	......	12	25	195	10075	18	355	29	4680	12	62	......
Rawles	......	......	4	387	36	91	69	1173	......	96	162	64	5144	......	107	......	192	48	61	4
St. Mary	......	......	2	70	......	......	......	1190	......	4	8	23	1277	2	105	......	10	60	15	......
Silver Creek, exc. of Hillsdale and Malvern	......	......	2	163	12	826	167	1185	......	171	265	68	3915	......	......	1	2	51	......	......
White Cloud	......	......	3	350	2	698	212	2143	114	90	171	61	4696	......	......	......	......	......	......	......
Total	919	6259	48	2711	187	2101	752	19101	189	816	1359	932	56093	38	2492	48	5404	457	376	76

MITCHELL COUNTY.

NAMES OF TOWNSHIPS, TOWNS, AND CITIES.	FLAX. Number of acres in flax seed.	FLAX. Number of bushels harvested.	SORGHUM. Number of acres in sorghum.	SORGHUM. Number of gallons of syrup from sorghum.	Number of acres of blue grass for pasture.	Number of acres of tame grass.	Number of tons of hay from same.	Number of tons of hay from wild grass.	Number of bushels of grass seed.	HUNGARIAN GRASS. Number of acres.	HUNGARIAN GRASS. Number of tons of hay.	POTATOES. Number of acres.	POTATOES. Number of bushels.	SWEET POTATOES. Number of acres.	SWEET POTATOES. Number of bushels.	ONIONS. Number of acres.	ONIONS. Number of bushels.	Number of bushels of turnips.	Number of bushels of beets.	Number of bushels of peas and beans.
Burr Oak	......	......	......	......	......	355	456	1043	100	8	18	49	5936	......	......	......	......	......	......	......
Cedar	......	......	4	440	......	763	823	1277	446	59	98	56	5913	......	......	1	142	721	328	78
Douglas	......	......	3	378	......	62	102	1604	......	......	......	50	6016	......	......	......	5	555	7	14
Jenkins	......	......	......	30	......	216	236	2041	18	......	......	58	7540	......	......	......	......	200	......	......
Liberty	......	......	1	50	104	132	157	523	......	15	35	24	4165	......	......	......	......	108	15	13
Lincoln	......	......	......	24	32	595	704	1098	608	10	27	60	7226	......	......	......	80	340	117	29
Mitchell	......	......	......	......	......	971	733	814	260	33	66	84	10594	......	......	......	159	592	89	23
Newberg	......	......	......	......	......	327	237	......	15	6	20	45	4497	......	......	......	......	......	......	3
Osage, exc. of town	......	......	......	20	18	599	562	170	38	37	58	30	4285	......	1	......	14	127	52	11
Osage, town of	......	......	......	......	......	36	60	62	......	7	7	26	3380	......	......	......	......	110	......	2
Otranto	......	......	......	......	......	248	286	1244	4	41	87	48	4316	......	......	......	12	260	10	21
Rock	......	......	......	300	......	360	379	1226	8	8	12	52	5012	......	......	......	29	280	128	32
St. Ansgar	......	......	......	......	......	493	769	567	35	33	64	61	7435	......	......	......	......	70	......	......

Stacyville	.....	.....	.....	.....	.....	99	111	657	.....	12	19	23	2860	.....	.....	.....	.....	.....	200	.....
Union	.....	.....	.....	.....	.....	415	387	575	5	28	54	63	8120	.....	.....	.....	.....	18	100	.....
Wayne	.....	.....	.....	54	44	103	132	1742	.....	.....	.....	44	5987	.....	.....	.....	19	933	42	30
Total	.....	.....	8	1296	198	5774	6134	14643	1537	297	565	773	93282	.....	1	1	460	4314	1088	256

MONONA COUNTY.

Ashton	.....	.....	1	28	.....	.....	.....	2234	.....	.....	.....	9	854	.....	.....	.....	.....	170	225	.....
Belvidere	.....	.....	7	673	.....	.....	.....	2483	.....	.....	.....	8	532	.....	.....	.....	.....	200	.....	40
Center	.....	.....	8	757	.....	.....	.....	1315	.....	.....	.....	15	1646	.....	.....	.....	12	18	22	18
Fairview	.....	.....	3	263	.....	.....	.....	1927	.....	4	5	18	1436	1	45	.....	.....	.....	.....	.....
Franklin, exc. of Onawa	.....	.....	2	228	.....	45	.....	4437	.....	.....	.....	20	2004	.....	15	.....	5	214	32	39
Grant	.....	.....	14	1497	.....	.....	.....	2136	.....	.....	.....	7	661	3	250	.....	.....	237	55	21
Jordan	.....	.....	6	241	.....	.....	.....	662	.....	.....	.....	9	570	.....	.....	.....	15	.....	2	1
Kennebec	.....	.....	12	1211	.....	.....	.....	4157	.....	.....	.....	7	773	.....	.....	.....	4	115	.....	5
Lake	.....	.....	5	344	.....	.....	.....	1206	.....	.....	.....	9	1140	.....	.....	.....	.....	.....	.....	.....
Lincoln	.....	.....	5	535	.....	.....	.....	3223	.....	.....	.....	29	2873	2	496	.....	11	149	17	38
Maple	.....	.....	24	1658	.....	.....	.....	2074	.....	.....	.....	39	2735	.....	.....	.....	39	1147	210	75
St. Clair	.....	.....	5	516	.....	.....	.....	608	.....	.....	.....	7	594	.....	.....	.....	.....	125	.....	.....
Sherman	.....	.....	7	825	.....	.....	.....	2057	.....	.....	.....	23	1401	.....	8	.....	32	16	123	26
Soldier	.....	.....	2	214	.....	.....	.....	1004	.....	.....	.....	9	512	.....	10	.....	.....	.....	7	1
Spring Valley	.....	.....	12	720	.....	.....	.....	2481	.....	.....	.....	13	1244	.....	25	.....	2	380	64	18
West Fork	.....	.....	.....	.....	.....	15	.....	1058	30	.....	.....	7	850	.....	15	.....	12	7	.....	.....
Willow	.....	.....	2	158	.....	.....	.....	750	.....	.....	.....	11	665	.....	7	.....	5	120	13	11
Total	.....	.....	115	9868	.....	60	.....	33812	30	4	5	240	20490	6	871	.....	137	2898	770	293

MONROE COUNTY.

Bluff Creek	18	97	30	3218	1993	2628	2735	45	329	131	279	53	6780	.....	50	.....	115	898	16	309
Cedar	.....	8	26	3508	84	597	393	750	7	40	49	28	3791	.....	1	.....	112	217	54	159
Franklin	118	118	14	1498	.....	961	835	658	73	211	439	47	4223	.....	.....	.....	.....	172	.....	.....
Guilford	.....	.....	22	1984	10	919	786	887	.....	71	118	68	7884	.....	.....	.....	12	38	.....	.....
Jackson	.....	.....	3	281	70	728	553	271	21	248	513	24	2030	.....	.....	.....	.....	.....	.....	.....
Mantua	6	20	94	4249	1668	4189	10304	101	69	52	62	92	8527	2	1423	.....	62	1133	284	94
Monroe	60	385	32	3263	163	2048	1749	106	330	161	236	47	5703	.....	38	.....	9	296	3	98
Pleasant	.....	.....	31	3579	1788	2264	2001	31	148	23	.....	87	7855	1	36	11	710	30	.....	46
Troy, exc. of Albia	5	50	14	1548	1570	1862	1771	87	.....	170	239	59	6598	.....	103	.....	1	684	56	125
Union	.....	3	26	4790	144	1426	1294	167	79	132	259	92	6334	.....	10	.....	71	831	131	156
Urbana	.....	.....	.....	3738	600	1498	978	.....	48	45	72	1	4296	.....	.....	.....	.....	.....	.....	.....
Wayne	.....	.....	16	1932	4	321	312	550	.....	143	275	32	3355	.....	16	.....	15	8	.....	12
Total	205	681	308	33593	8094	19441	23711	3653	1104	1427	2541	630	67376	3	1677	11	1107	4307	544	999

MONTGOMERY COUNTY.

NAMES OF TOWNSHIPS, TOWNS, AND CITIES.	FLAX. Number of acres in flax seed.	FLAX. Number of bushels harvested.	SORGHUM. Number of acres in sorghum.	SORGHUM. Number of gallons of syrup from sorghum.	Number of acres of blue grass for pasture.	Number of acres of tame grass.	Number of tons of hay from same.	Number of tons of hay from wild grass.	Number of bushels of grass seed.	HUNGARIAN GRASS. Number of acres.	HUNGARIAN GRASS. Number of tons of hay.	POTATOES. Number of acres.	POTATOES. Number of bushels.	SWEET POTATOES. Number of acres.	SWEET POTATOES. Number of bushels.	ONIONS. Number of acres.	ONIONS. Number of bushels.	Number of bushels of turnips.	Number of bushels of beets.	Number of bushels of peas and beans.
Douglas	93	550	1	60	7	24	......	1011	4	32	56	29	1793	......	10	......	16	26	24	......
Frankfort	196	2192	1	110	......	132	118	1385	......	35	37	24	1645	......	......	......	......	......	......	......
Grant	1088	11575	12	672	37	78	78	903	24	......	......	57	3396	......	10	......	......	55	......	......
Jackson, exc. of Villisca	......	......	8	1372	3	167	253	1763	......	24	44	14	3644	2	81	......	18	126	......	2
Lincoln	569	4722	......	......	......	10	15	940	......	......	......	31	2226	......	......	......	......	......	......	......
Pilot Grove	263	1978	......	275	16	89	61	1403	......	24	30	32	2619	......	......	......	......	......	......	34
Red Oak, exc. of town	847	5333	......	187	50	86	127	961	39	84	170	85	5939	3	433	......	30	265	25	10
Scott	76	782	......	235	......	......	......	571	......	......	......	26	1720	......	......	......	......	......	......	......
Sherman	599	5236	......	140	16	84	90	854	......	37	71	65	3799	......	......	......	......	25	40	......
Villisca, town of	......	......	......	......	......	......	42	......	......	......	......	14	479	2	243	1	55	41	67	12
Walnut	1993	16477	......	95	......	9	......	1547	......	19	44	123	9918	......	10	1	106	......	......	......
Washington	94	820	......	1401	......	40	53	996	......	22	43	42	3162	......	25	......	......	......	......	6
West	1392	11997	......	66	33	49	37	1442	......	23	76	84	4442	......	15	1	34	12	4	21
Total	7210	61662	22	4913	132	768	874	13776	67	300	571	626	44782	7	827	3	259	550	160	85

MUSCATINE COUNTY.

NAMES OF TOWNSHIPS, TOWNS, AND CITIES.	FLAX. Number of acres in flax seed.	FLAX. Number of bushels harvested.	SORGHUM. Number of acres in sorghum.	SORGHUM. Number of gallons of syrup from sorghum.	Number of acres of blue grass for pasture.	Number of acres of tame grass.	Number of tons of hay from same.	Number of tons of hay from wild grass.	Number of bushels of grass seed.	HUNGARIAN GRASS. Number of acres.	HUNGARIAN GRASS. Number of tons of hay.	POTATOES. Number of acres.	POTATOES. Number of bushels.	SWEET POTATOES. Number of acres.	SWEET POTATOES. Number of bushels.	ONIONS. Number of acres.	ONIONS. Number of bushels.	Number of bushels of turnips.	Number of bushels of beets.	Number of bushels of peas and beans.
Bloomington, ex. of Muscatine	1	3	20	726	1698	2316	2570	1177	56	6	12	452	32105	162	11536	......	20	384	882	......
Cedar	......	......	14	1405	206	1415	890	161	11	30	33	53	7343	......	......	1	47	38	1	16
Fulton	......	......	1	68	3655	1129	1524	863	......	2	5	194	13419	......	74	2	298	170	221	6
Goshen	25	349	29	2441	2321	4182	2984	633	2600	79	133	128	11610	1	220	5	534	20	250	6
Lake	......	......	14	1360	2573	1671	1672	539	241	55	82	269	23605	2	287	......	633	94	......	75
Montpelier	......	......	9	1000	456	527	532	271	10	14	22	98	9858	1	20	2	103	187	2	12
Moscow	12	98	21	1247	941	841	1012	230	61	16	28	69	6152	1	172	......	15	88	13	31
Muscatine, city of	......	......	......	......	......	265	130	......	......	......	......	6	300	26	400	......	......	......	......	......
Orono	45	......	19	1616	160	114	108	785	2	86	211	18	1500	1	200	......	......	......	......	......

Pike	152	850	7	462	112	545	394	897	205	25	49	73	6998	1	42	1	105	70	10	19
Seventy-Six	…	…	18	1587	274	2656	1339	529	85	8	18	224	27627	1	173			28	2	
Sweetland	24	200	38	2378	2489	2720	3171	25	137	3	5	182	18241	2	101	…	…	30	…	…
Wapsinonoc, exc. of West Liberty	143	1295	19	2067	1711	3502	2114	478	2921	28	62	102	10880	2	131	4	534	189	570	25
Wilton, exc. of town	10	80	12	122	100	6759	3253	237	65	7	12	150	12628	…	…	1	35	…	200	…
Wilton, town of	35	280	1	28	230	251	309	10	…	2	3	12	850	1	16	…	…	53	53	171
Total	447	3155	222	16507	16926	28893	22002	6838	6394	361	675	2030	183116	201	13672	16	2324	1281	2204	361

O'BRIEN COUNTY.

Baker	110	216	…	…	…	…	…	486	…	…	…	11	882	…	…	…	…	36	…	17
Carroll	103	226	…	…	…	…	…	595	…	…	…	19	1376	…	…	2	60	373	…	3
Center	180	599	…	…	…	1	1	675	…	…	…	48	2289	1	4	2	63	74	121	107
Floyd	85	161	…	10	…	…	…	1051	…	…	…	27	1513	…	…	1	6	85	81	9
Grant	20	59	7	227	…	…	…	1103	…	…	…	38	2111	…	…	…	…	124	1100	12
Highland	7	30	…	…	…	7	7	995	…	…	…	42	3092	1	57	1	36	430	70	82
Liberty	…	…	…	…	…	23	25	529	…	…	…	33	1739	…	…	…	15	…	11	18
Summit	…	…	…	…	…	…	…	133	…	…	…	2	239	…	…	…	187	…	16	28
Waterman	48	…	5	65	…	…	…	950	…	…	…	16	1465	…	…	…	16	112	44	21
Total	553	1291	12	302	…	31	33	6517	…	…	…	236	14706	2	61	6	383	1234	1443	297

OSCEOLA COUNTY.

Fairview	…	…	…	…	…	…	…	211	…	…	…	9	376	…	…	…	…	102	8	7
Gilman	39	120	…	…	…	…	…	…	…	…	…	13	785	…	…	…	…	…	30	17
Goewey	63	244	…	30	…	…	…	1108	…	…	…	13	3137	…	…	…	…	120	40	10
Holman	25	30	…	…	…	…	…	1546	…	…	…	59	2979	…	…	…	11	101	105	14
Horton	7	20	…	…	…	…	…	339	1	…	…	6	510	…	…	…	3	158	112	2
Ocheyedan	…	…	…	…	…	…	…	798	…	…	…	…	962	…	…	…	3	168	…	30
Viola	…	…	…	…	…	…	…	645	…	…	…	29	1098	…	…	…	…	4	31	…
Wilson	1	4	…	…	…	…	…	579	…	…	…	24	1675	…	…	…	32	509	84	14
Total	135	418	…	30	…	…	…	5226	1	…	…	153	11522	…	…	…	49	1162	410	94

PAGE COUNTY.

Amity	42	133	11	1199	10	310	320	1040	108	31	71	35	2706	2	200	…	13	16	115	…
Buchanan	19	95	11	1288	121	488	764	787	5	29	46	140	2585	…	55	1	142	22	10	5

PAGE COUNTY.—CONTINUED.

NAMES OF TOWNSHIPS, TOWNS, AND CITIES.	FLAX. Number of acres in flax seed.	FLAX. Number of bushels harvested.	SORGHUM. Number of acres in sorghum.	SORGHUM. Number of gallons of syrup from sorghum.	Number of acres of blue grass for pasture.	Number of acres of tame grass.	Number of tons of hay from same.	Number of tons of hay from wild grass.	Number of bushels of grass seed.	HUNGARIAN GRASS. Number of acres.	HUNGARIAN GRASS. Number of tons of hay.	POTATOES. Number of acres.	POTATOES. Number of bushels.	SWEET POTATOES. Number of acres.	SWEET POTATOES. Number of bushels.	ONIONS. Number of acres.	ONIONS. Number of bushels.	Number of bushels of turnips.	Number of bushels of beets.	Number of bushels of peas and beans.
Clarinda, town of	....	....	....	....	....	....	....	....	....	....	....	....	1063	2	279	....	....	2	....	....
Colfax	....	....	7	478	15	132	56	1353	55	26	66	31	2163	....	....	....	9	42	52	5
Douglas	....	....	9	1190	10	153	172	1573	273	13	27	43	3844	....	....	....	21	....	....	....
East River	....	....	86	955	111	212	212	949	8	53	74	51	2487	1	81	1	121	18	59	48
Fremont	638	6776	6	480	....	1	1	1145	....	16	19	69	4960	2	52	....	10	....	68	16
Grant, exc. Shenandoah	653	5706	....	30	....	288	118	1737	13	29	47	44	3637	3	129	2	210	39	23	7
Harlan	35	370	23	850	272	596	482	1354	112	44	28	16	3625	1	85	....	29	7	7	....
Lincoln	23	237	6	548	15	255	204	1309	257	4	7	36	2490	....	2	....	34	23	73	6
Morton	149	1952	1	100	....	32	40	70	....	....	....	66	3743	....	3	7	935	....	....	....
Nebraska	....	....	14	1732	32	210	256	494	....	36	62	67	1853	1	57	....	23	84	7	2
Nodaway, exc. Clarinda	76	911	14	1198	247	717	848	3498	24	56	81	68	5144	2	78	....	....	1	75	....
Pierce	704	6778	....	96	....	30	35	374	116	....	....	36	2865	2	132	....	....	....	....	....
Shenandoah, town of	....	....	....	....	....	....	....	25	....	....	....	2	150	3	500	....	....	....	....	....
Tarkio	636	6940	5	818	10	85	60	1017	....	3	6	9	1731	1	52	....	12	6	77	1
Valley	71	743	16	1556	109	184	226	1832	....	....	....	41	3751	1	168	1	106	166	74	29
Washington	3	36	7	554	....	2	3	414	....	....	....	39	2300	....	....	....	3	....	....	....
Total	3049	30677	216	13072	952	3695	3733	18971	971	340	534	4793	51098	21	1873	11	1668	426	640	119

PALO ALTO COUNTY.

NAMES OF TOWNSHIPS, TOWNS, AND CITIES.	FLAX. Number of acres in flax seed.	FLAX. Number of bushels harvested.	SORGHUM. Number of acres in sorghum.	SORGHUM. Number of gallons of syrup from sorghum.	Number of acres of blue grass for pasture.	Number of acres of tame grass.	Number of tons of hay from same.	Number of tons of hay from wild grass.	Number of bushels of grass seed.	HUNGARIAN GRASS. Number of acres.	HUNGARIAN GRASS. Number of tons of hay.	POTATOES. Number of acres.	POTATOES. Number of bushels.	SWEET POTATOES. Number of acres.	SWEET POTATOES. Number of bushels.	ONIONS. Number of acres.	ONIONS. Number of bushels.	Number of bushels of turnips.	Number of bushels of beets.	Number of bushels of peas and beans.
Ellington	....	....	14	507	....	....	....	854	....	6	9	39	1998	....	....	1	2	923	13	57
Emmetsburg	....	....	4	146	....	....	....	2912	....	....	....	59	2351	....	....	....	....	5	9	1
Fairfield	13	....	....	....	....	....	....	593	....	....	....	16	475	....	....	....	....	....	....	....
Fern Valley	....	....	2	93	....	6	1	1109	....	....	....	15	825	....	....	....	10	99	4	....
Freedom	....	....	....	....	....	....	....	1994	....	....	....	29	2402	....	....	....	....	95	10	6
Great Oak	....	....	2	95	....	....	....	2123	....	....	....	46	3452	....	....	....	....	315	....	10

Highland			1	42				1023				34	1651				5	189	24	13
Lost Island								525				11	425				2	238	24	3
Nevada								2332				24	1245					378		12
Rush Lake			8	548				651				20	1628					743	18	19
Silver Lake			2	41				707				29	1458				9	1848	26	8
Vernon								1003				27	1157					455	2	1
Walnut			1	58				2330					1146	33				65		1
West Bend			11	589				2097				34	1500				5	557	2	
Total	13		45	2119		6	1	20253		6	9	383	21713	33		1	33	5910	132	131

PLYMOUTH COUNTY.

America					80	2	4	2456		6	12	6	895	12	805			400	450	
Elgin	10	55						451		9	30	13	747							
Fredonia	91	111						1065				29	1208							
Grant	196	876						812		5	7	27	590			4			80	
Johnson	10	23	1	41				1383				53	1283							
Lincoln	20	50	8	396		1		3961				76	3324		2	1	13	133	167	37
Marion	10	60						709				12	688				2	50	15	
Perry	15	75	2	175				3073		37	145	74	2457		1		27	56	466	135
Plymouth			1	131				1564				42	2166			1	43	66	719	7
Portland	62	194																		
Sioux								1224				10	412		2				10	
Stanton	9	44						1149				27	2715							
Union	9	67				1		552	6	4	9	16	1498				20	48	90	2
Washington								376				27	658						5	
Total	432	1555	12	743	80	4	4	18775	6	61	203	412	18341	12	810	6	105	753	2002	181

POCAHONTAS COUNTY.

Bellville	9		5	205				889				54	3661				8	127		15
Cedar			3	118		1		1534				41	2588				4	1100		6
Center	7	7	7	386								10	543							
Clinton			1	3				659				16	1067					252	5	17
Colfax								1445				50	3590					1339		
Des Moines			7	386		72		2732				27	1604					1290		27
Dover								632				8	914					60		25
Grant								531				16	914					385		19
Jackson	1	5	3	286				1176				20	1303							
Lincoln			5	64				323				14	882				128		6	10

POCAHONTAS COUNTY.—Continued.

Names of townships, towns, and cities.	Flax. Number of acres in flax seed.	Flax. Number of bushels harvested.	Sorghum. Number of acres in sorghum.	Sorghum. Number of gallons of syrup from sorghum.	Number of acres of blue grass for pasture.	Number of acres of tame grass.	Number of tons of hay from same	Number of tons of hay from wild grass.	Number of bushels of grass seed.	Hungarian grass. Number of acres.	Hungarian grass. Number of tons of hay.	Potatoes. Number of acres.	Potatoes. Number of bushels.	Sweet potatoes. Number of acres.	Sweet potatoes. Number of bushels.	Onions. Number of acres.	Onions. Number of bushels.	Number of bushels of turnips.	Number of bushels of beets.	Number of bushels of peas and beans.
Lizard	....	....	18	1020	....	....	....	2814	....	....	....	72	4411	....	....	....	....	980	....	66
Swan Lake	....	....	3	....	....	....	....	249	....	....	....	5	235	....	....	....	10	470	47	20
Total	17	12	52	2468	....	73	....	12984	....	....	....	333	21712	....	....	....	150	6003	58	205

POLK COUNTY.

Names of townships, towns, and cities.	Flax. Number of acres in flax seed.	Flax. Number of bushels harvested.	Sorghum. Number of acres in sorghum.	Sorghum. Number of gallons of syrup from sorghum.	Number of acres of blue grass for pasture.	Number of acres of tame grass.	Number of tons of hay from same	Number of tons of hay from wild grass.	Number of bushels of grass seed.	Hungarian grass. Number of acres.	Hungarian grass. Number of tons of hay.	Potatoes. Number of acres.	Potatoes. Number of bushels.	Sweet potatoes. Number of acres.	Sweet potatoes. Number of bushels.	Onions. Number of acres.	Onions. Number of bushels.	Number of bushels of turnips.	Number of bushels of beets.	Number of bushels of peas and beans.
Allen	....	....	12	1167	958	602	479	125	8	15	29	62	7989	1	146	15	134	310	98	27
Beaver	89	802	14	1074	184	622	658	1552	....	28	51	173	17200	7	675	3	335	1795	6	30
Bloomfield	32	246	4	472	....	998	1283	724	25	15	33	325	31991	17	2311	4	670	1395	756	265
Camp	10	60	39	3691	343	710	573	330	....	6	8	100	12138	....	33	....	....	....	....	2
Crocker	85	573	15	1415	195	420	566	2116	....	18	32	100	13475	....	....	....	....	256	20	4
Delaware	9	150	10	1023	235	785	919	1470	19	39	73	150	10808	24	2868	1	301	730	20	33
Des Moines, city of	....	....	....	....	....	....	....	....	....	....	....	13	1645	1	240	....	20	13	254	11
Douglas	750	6414	15	1603	169	344	494	2646	....	19	49	54	6530	....	105	....	5	30	28	4
Elkhart	761	4767	8	874	....	102	84	2319	....	6	10	35	3784	....	17	....	....	125	....	10
Four Mile	....	....	11	1012	243	96	211	102	7	10	16	30	3754	....	....	....	30	....	3	2
Franklin	37	256	29	2149	35	167	343	2267	21	21	42	38	4324	....	123	....	61	189	20	42
Grant	....	....	7	924	389	158	219	264	....	32	55	88	9672	25	3169	1	291	200	66	41
Jefferson	10	57	3	410	16	101	117	2195	....	46	100	19	5457	....	60	....	....	....	....	....
Lincoln	64	555	13	1573	....	29	39	3843	10	....	....	58	6930	....	13	....	13	104	4	35
Madison	863	5837	26	2739	47	155	291	2139	....	34	68	47	4652	1	94	....	102	26	51	8
Saylor	....	....	15	819	160	308	424	1897	....	40	79	75	5444	3	576	....	2	300	....	....
Valley	....	....	7	508	141	286	296	336	....	....	....	117	10996	7	892	....	274	965	448	74
Walnut	67	638	17	2085	122	583	590	1827	....	13	35	113	12805	1	83	....	30	365	321	39
Washington	1045	8078	18	2011	35	396	512	2198	....	21	36	44	5614	1	74	....	30	237	16	70
Total	3822	28433	263	25549	3272	6862	8098	28350	90	364	718	1641	175208	88	11479	24	2298	7040	2111	697

POTTAWATTAMIE COUNTY.

Avoca, town of	....	....	....	....	....	....	....	....	53	....	....	1	66	....	25	....	....	....	....	....
Belknap	....	....	3	640	....	12	102	813	....	15	24	13	813	1	86	....	25	5	52	1
Boomer	....	....	2	160	....	....	....	1534	....	81	116	72	6855	....	....	....	1200	....	....	40
Center	....	....	6	807	....	24	15	1861	....	28	37	57	3029	....	25	3	273	589	73	72
Council Bluffs, city of	....	....	....	....	82	8	16	100	....	39	8	46	3900	25	2960	1	316	215	265	297
Crescent	....	....	1	30	....	....	....	1918	....	28	44	52	2210	5	195	....	....	80	....	....
Grove	138	1246	5	411	....	7	16	1424	....	6	17	32	1859	....	....	1	25	40	....	....
Harden	....	....	2	80	....	....	....	1914	....	35	70	44	3060	....	....	....	....	....	....	....
Hazel Dell	....	2	1	186	....	14	16	1965	....	99	177	125	7910	....	26	....	4	470	3	8
James	....	....	2	160	....	10	....	742	....	....	....	22	1260	1	65	....	7	145	6	8
Kane, exc. Council Bluffs	....	....	4	253	....	20	14	3560	....	16	234	234	15814	13	2320	5	1050	900	....	....
Keg Creek	12	130	7	264	....	....	....	1504	....	9	40	33	2433	1	33	....	8	....	2	5
Knox, exc. of Avoca	....	....	5	750	24	51	40	2423	40	12	26	94	8362	3	758	1	195	432	238	79
Layton	104	1247	1	29	....	....	....	....	....	....	....	49	5264	....	....	....	....	....	....	....
Macedonia	10	....	....	....	2	20	43	1282	....	4	10	27	1647	....	10	....	....	....	....	....
Neola	....	....	....	40	....	....	....	1325	....	2	4	35	1429	....	....	1	8	182	2	....
Norwalk	....	....	....	....	....	....	....	1352	....	37	55	56	3141	....	....	....	....	....	....	....
Pleasant	....	....	1	80	....	21	20	1233	....	....	....	29	1776	....	75	....	....	45	1	3
Rockford	....	....	8	794	....	....	....	2359	....	131	197	39	1257	....	25	....	....	2036	....	7
Silver Creek	20	....	....	....	....	....	....	703	....	....	....	16	967	....	23	....	2	2	4	....
Washington	....	....	1	347	....	....	....	813	....	....	....	24	1076	1	31	....	4	199	14	7
Waveland	374	....	....	142	....	37	37	1094	5	3	11	13	2271	....	65	....	21	....	21	61
Wright	32	410	4	683	4	27	1	1110	....	2	3	14	2518	....	....	....	9	114	10	5
York	....	....	1	120	....	....	....	588	....	....	....	30	1850	....	....	....	....	140	3	3
Total	690	3035	54	5976	112	251	320	1614	98	547	1073	1157	80767	50	6722	12	3147	5594	694	596

POWESHIEK COUNTY.

Bear Creek, exc. Brooklyn	18	137	5	452	669	1334	986	1583	383	19	42	70	8600	3	49	9	133	228	35	69
Chester	1447	11997	....	79	....	1759	1033	1569	513	17	18	97	10415	....	33	....	40	180	12	63
Deep River	33	202	11	1089	....	1453	905	1694	692	....	....	53	6450	....	147	....	136	270	26	129
Grinnell, exc. of town	997	9016	....	20	346	1409	1088	1553	....	38	97	99	11201	....	24	17	444	....	467	11
Grinnell, town of	....	....	....	....	....	....	....	....	....	....	....	....	40	....	....	....	....	....	....	....
Jackson, exc. of Montezuma	....	....	9	3988	87	347	1680	1404	399	....	....	35	7456	....	139	....	12	671	....	89
Jefferson	....	....	39	1150	391	1198	391	876	4	1	2	77	7360	....	54	....	44	337	27	35
Lincoln	....	....	12	1221	....	1104	618	1678	247	2	4	74	8049	....	13	1	4	325	....	69
Madison	20	180	1	134	254	1335	1150	730	211	22	57	108	10605	....	13	4	726	241	2	71
Malcom, exc. of town	313	2487	....	40	....	800	765	1778	414	....	....	49	5920	....	....	10	1520	115	8	22
Malcom town of	....	....	....	....	....	1013	84	45	....	....	....	6	735	....	....	2	400	110	60	....
Pleasant	39	303	19	2195	85	538	392	1323	507	....	....	55	6416	1	28	28	1501	284	6	19

POWESHIEK COUNTY.—Continued.

NAMES OF TOWNSHIPS, TOWNS, AND CITIES.	FLAX.		SORGHUM.		Number of acres of blue grass for pasture.	Number of acres of tame grass.	Number of tons of hay from same.	Number of tons of hay from wild grass.	Number of bushels of grass seed.	HUNGARIAN GRASS.		POTATOES.		SWEET POTATOES.		ONIONS.		Number of bushels of turnips.	Number of bushels of beets.	Number of bushels of peas and beans.
	Number of acres in flax seed.	Number of bushels harvested.	Number of acres in sorghum.	Number of gallons of syrup from sorghum.						Number of acres.	Number of tons of hay.	Number of acres.	Number of bushels.	Number of acres.	Number of bushels.	Number of acres.	Number of bushels.			
Scott	44	270	2	171	....	498	452	1357	....	....	....	79	8065	....	....	....	....	....	....	....
Sheridan	103	1064	3	263	88	756	615	1423	....	2	5	95	9870	....	20	1	444	666	130	224
Sugar Creek	52	402	36	4484	....	1816	768	1148	161	....	....	57	5178	18	254	20	330	....	20	33
Union	6	29	25	2535	158	1042	1031	417	2	....	....	27	2824	1	32	....	....	123	8	23
Warren	....	....	22	2679	122	479	397	1258	101	2	4	91	8202	....	83	3	607	978	119	86
Washington	79	362	24	2284	88	1014	677	1178	19	7	13	66	8107	....	65	60	16007	793	110	71
Total	3151	26449	200	22784	2288	17895	13032	21014	3653	110	242	1138	125493	23	954	154	22348	5321	1030	1014

RINGGOLD COUNTY.

NAMES OF TOWNSHIPS, TOWNS, AND CITIES.	Acres in flax seed	Bushels flax harvested	Acres in sorghum	Gallons of syrup	Acres blue grass	Acres tame grass	Tons hay from same	Tons hay wild grass	Bushels grass seed	Hungarian acres	Hungarian tons	Potatoes acres	Potatoes bushels	Sweet potatoes acres	Sweet potatoes bushels	Onions acres	Onions bushels	Turnips	Beets	Peas and beans
Athens	146	1291	10	884	49	197	290	1116	76	12	22	22	1969	....	42	....	77	195	47	71
Benton	....	....	17	2098	....	103	402	1833	18	16	8	22	1588	....	50	....	70	42	21	8
Clinton	....	....	16	1508	40	80	129	1204	14	....	....	25	1448	....	....	2	67	67	38	38
Grant	....	....	14	1356	....	213	143	1663	7	....	....	23	1620	1	90	....	31	70	11	18
Jefferson	61	643	17	2310	1	509	584	1373	117	35	127	24	2323	1	20	....	103	235	39	74
Liberty	141	810	11	716	15	273	272	1634	76	1	3	25	1774	....	....	....	10	130	604	41
Lincoln	41	411	12	1277	....	8	20	1391	....	....	....	20	1822	....	14	3	4	57	43	14
Lot's Creek	84	158	24	1456	....	211	257	1222	18	26	43	29	1162	1	36	5	120	10	21	14
Middle Fork	....	....	12	1218	1	304	333	1291	24	....	....	24	1626	2	83	....	73	127	38	18
Monroe	696	5680	5	381	....	251	341	808	16	3	1	16	1355	....	7	....	1	....	....	42
Mount Ayr	285	2256	5	276	....	942	1111	1978	21	38	81	24	1225	....	....	....	24	104	69	59
Rice	5	52	1	334	....	142	138	1097	....	....	....	2	1629	....	21	....	18	15	14	3
Riley	42	257	2	110	10	294	367	1670	142	18	15	2	70	....	....	....	....	....	....	....
Tingley	76	1062	2	288	....	32	48	718	....	....	....	1	910	....	....	....	....	....	....	....

Union	68	496	1	180	....	103	173	8010	17	....	....	9	872	....	2	....	36	50	13	9
Washington	86	648	24	2195	....	225	258	1749	38	....	....	32	2283	....	5	....	41	313	40	22
Total	1731	13764	173	16587	116	3887	4866	28770	587	149	300	300	23676	5	370	10	675	1415	998	431

SAC COUNTY.

Boyer	....	....	....	....	....	....	....	1067	....	....	....	17	1739	....	....	....	....	215	....	38
Clinton	....	....	6	464	....	....	....	726	....	....	....	8	845	....	....	....	....	400	4	7
Douglas	....	....	....	....	....	....	....	1958	....	....	....	43	2578	....	....	....	19	....	....	....
Eden	....	....	....	....	....	....	....	735	....	....	....	16	1007	....	....	....	17	175	91	3
Jackson	42	342	9	1311	....	14	82	1596	40	3	6	38	2263	....	....	2	82	1226	533	67
Levey	117	760	....	16	....	167	72	1523	....	....	....	22	2085	....	....	....	33	402	12	33
Sac	10	60	7	529	87	7	33	1432	40	....	....	35	2644	....	....	....	....	448	115	17
Wall Lake	....	....	7	569	....	7	4	736	....	....	....	11	2008	....	16	....	112	405	31	35
Total	169	1162	29	2889	87	195	191	9773	80	3	6	191	15169	....	16	2	263	3271	486	201

SCOTT COUNTY.

Allen's Grove	....	....	1	50	1050	937	811	925	20	....	....	81	7856	....	....	1	250	....	....	....
Blue Grass	....	....	....	40	2624	978	1330	687	27	18	23	196	12944	1	49	6	800	280	80	35
Buffalo, exc. of town	....	....	1	40	2793	1243	1563	69	29	25	46	247	11620	1	54	5	280	350	....	....
Butler	....	....	1	32	2363	1495	1773	338	148	....	....	95	7640	....	....	2	282	105	....	5
Cleona	....	....	....	....	2364	494	656	1263	....	10	10	212	13950	....	....	1	120	....	....	....
Davenport, exc. of city	....	....	21	2010	3889	1936	2588	739	11	48	95	665	42405	11	1170	106	16330	720	3273	76
Davenport, city of	....	....	....	....	13	7	57	60	....	....	6	16	1035	5	1100	....	....	....	....	....
Hickory Grove	....	....	....	....	2708	612	846	1675	63	4	11	353	24822	....	....	2	195	34	60	8
Le Claire, exc. of town	....	....	1	65	1264	1534	1655	243	14	25	47	77	7974	....	....	2	329	342	177	64
Liberty	....	....	1	20	605	2431	1851	435	38	25	26	75	6269	....	....	....	....	40	....	....
Lincoln	....	....	....	....	2621	740	903	841	30	22	72	301	25095	....	....	8	1260	30	140	2
Pleasant Valley	....	....	1	87	1192	161	2105	226	10	102	164	205	17529	6	825	101	15748	340	2892	132
Princeton, exc. of town	....	....	4	770	1702	1333	772	1443	34	10	12	45	3952	....	10	5	770	....	200	....
Rockingham	....	....	1	20	687	609	681	304	....	11	13	50	2690	4	600	2	110	271	166	22
Sheridan	....	....	....	....	3173	2278	1935	599	15	5	8	405	33355	....	....	1	185	375	....	....
Winfield	....	....	1	34	2084	747	887	1338	....	13	38	199	15700	....	....	2	145	50	....	....
Total	....	....	33	3168	31132	17535	20413	11185	439	318	571	3222	234836	28	3808	244	36804	2937	6988	344

SHELBY COUNTY.

NAMES OF TOWNSHIPS, TOWNS, AND CITIES.	FLAX.		SORGHUM.		Number of acres of blue grass for pasture.	Number of acres of tame grass.	Number of tons of hay from same.	Number of tons of hay from wild grass.	Number of bushels of grass seed.	HUNGARIAN GRASS.		POTATOES.		SWEET POTATOES.		ONIONS.		Number of bushels of turnips.	Number of bushels of beets.	Number of bushels of peas and beans.
	Number of acres in flax seed.	Number of bushels harvested.	Number of acres in sorghum.	Number of gallons of syrup from sorghum.						Number of acres.	Number of tons of hay.	Number of acres.	Number of bushels.	Number of acres.	Number of bushels.	Number of acres.	Number of bushels.			
Cass								704				18	182		10		10	295	14	
Clay						2	5	1058		5	12	16	1238		35		30	128	14	8
Douglas				50		5	10	1183	16	4	10	16	1519				20			
Fairview			7	593		32	34	1783	23	4	11	29	3361		19		104	335	21	26
Greeley			1	110		15	5	300		8	20	4	437		13		28	82	12	7
Grove			10	1026				3142		158	306	49	3778					989		6
Harlan			17	900		12	24	1626		8	50	91	2688	1	81		75	890	101	54
Jackson			3	270				681				10	816						4	15
Jefferson	2	15						567				7	781		21		22	568	69	16
Lincoln								1038				25	2290							48
Monroe	82	723	1	119				376		5	7	21	1745		17		165			
Polk								259				6	550				20			
Shelby						25	231	1065				19	2706		38	1	160	70		104
Union								652				11	1200		6			84		43
Washington								1102		12	35		144							
Westphalia								740				10	708							
Total	84	738	39	3086		91	309	16276	39	204	451	332	24203	1	240	1	634	3441	235	327

SIOUX COUNTY.

NAMES OF TOWNSHIPS, TOWNS, AND CITIES.	Number of acres in flax seed.	Number of bushels harvested.	Number of acres in sorghum.	Number of gallons of syrup from sorghum.	Number of acres of blue grass for pasture.	Number of acres of tame grass.	Number of tons of hay from same.	Number of tons of hay from wild grass.	Number of bushels of grass seed.	Hungarian grass: Number of acres.	Hungarian grass: Number of tons of hay.	Potatoes: Number of acres.	Potatoes: Number of bushels.	Sweet potatoes: Number of acres.	Sweet potatoes: Number of bushels.	Onions: Number of acres.	Onions: Number of bushels.	Number of bushels of turnips.	Number of bushels of beets.	Number of bushels of peas and beans.
Buncombe	45	95	2	115				260				14	166						6	
Floyd	5	30						456				21	735					1	17	1
Grant	73	105	3	107				852		3	7	40	770					35	89	
Holland	178	393	10	266		10	20	2360		1	3	122	2708			7		22		25
Lincoln	37	46						880				40	149							
Nassau	66	182	2	97				1701				59	1678	3	139			1	15	13
Reading	82	358	1	1				889				2.	925						14	

Rock	30	85	....	....	....	....	....	479	....	....	....	2	75	....	....	....	....	124	20	3
Settler	5	18	....	....	....	8	....	696	....	....	....	7	214	....	3	....	7	160	3	1
Sheridan	120	378	....	....	....	....	....	704	....	....	....	39	300	....	....	....	....	....	....	....
Total	641	1690	18	586	....	18	20	9277	....	4	10	372	7720	3	142	7	7	343	164	43

STORY COUNTY.

Ames, town of	....	....	1	83	....	3	6	12	....	....	....	2	439	....	27	....	....	....	....	6
Collins	425	3700	23	2169	20	148	96	1888	....	....	....	32	2475	1	272	1	69	241	79	91
Franklin	37	168	26	1852	80	946	351	1947	175	4	4	59	3882	....	....	1	60	175	40	35
Grant	576	4680	7	424	....	81	52	2575	....	22	46	62	3901	....	103	....	33	47	170	67
Howard	....	....	17	1089	....	280	71	4395	87	5	16	50	3604	....	....	....	....	....	....	....
Indian Creek	481	4152	20	1415	44	609	578	2467	28	....	....	52	3533	3	99	3	72	293	99	84
La Fayette	....	....	4	446	....	115	93	3021	113	....	....	34	1813	....	4	....	38	....	10	7
Lincoln	178	1047	3	162	12	57	30	1030	....	3	9	29	1217	....	....	....	29	242	46	25
Milford	179	1353	10	455	8	213	177	3804	....	....	....	72	3473	....	65	....	60	697	70	88
Nevada, exc. of town	278	2212	13	1059	63	220	303	2462	20	23	57	65	4924	....	127	....	36	539	145	107
Nevada, town of	....	....	....	....	....	18	24	317	....	2	3	17	1650	2	137	....	....	162	114	6
New Albany	231	1912	9	348	5	186	147	2083	78	18	41	50	4286	....	....	1	131	145	....	4
Palestine	351	2956	19	1566	....	93	90	3507	30	....	....	61	4545	....	....	....	17	210	86	36
Richland	97	630	7	211	5	23	16	1863	....	28	48	81	2395	....	72	....	5	50	802	252
Sherman	82	766	11	838	....	62	4	1011	28	10	20	25	1829	....	11	1	23	109	....	22
Union	1239	9155	15	948	....	131	60	3894	29	20	40	63	5194	1	35	....	5	118	430	64
Warren	16	96	1	32	....	....	....	435	....	....	....	7	310	....	9	....	....	....	48	20
Washington, exc. Ames.	116	884	16	1441	54	424	272	2848	45	2	5	73	6412	....	18	2	112	184	307	142
Total	4286	33717	202	14538	291	3609	2370	39554	633	137	289	834	55882	7	980	9	690	3212	2446	1056

TAMA COUNTY.

Buckingham	....	....	2	180	....	1230	1238	1597	105	....	....	40	4451	....	6	....	62	736	1280	66
Carlton	353	2608	19	947	214	549	678	1486	675	24	31	80	6510	1	53	1	59	501	43	41
Carroll	....	....	6	664	28	94	64	995	....	....	....	47	3296	....	9	....	31	451	96	31
Clark	18	123	1	50	....	632	322	1400	312	2	3	47	3864	....	29	....	21	128	166	18
Columbia	96	694	9	1160	....	548	357	774	10	....	....	74	5282	....	35	....	25	....	....	39
Crystal	12	100	1	219	....	603	363	1285	165	....	....	36	3950	....	....	....	....	390	450	....
Geneseo	....	....	....	....	56	1084	778	1266	468	....	....	49	4838	....	....	....	3	....	....	....
Grant	12	150	....	....	....	209	139	910	42	....	....	30	2855	....	....	....	6	150	....	....
Highland	232	2356	1	145	....	623	439	1388	45	....	....	45	4025	....	....	....	5	423	21	23
Howard	58	405	5	474	218	805	753	1353	112	20	41	121	7200	....	....	....	....	187	....	56
Indian Village, exc. of Montour	10	70	11	851	....	794	722	1460	11	2	4	100	7191	....	....	....	....	817	2	81
Lincoln	92	850	....	....	....	58	19	868	15	23	45	28	3315	....	....	....	....	....	400	....

TAMA COUNTY.—Continued.

NAMES OF TOWNSHIPS, TOWNS, AND CITIES.	FLAX. Number of acres in flax seed.	FLAX. Number of bushels harvested.	SORGHUM. Number of acres in sorghum.	SORGHUM. Number of gallons of syrup from sorghum.	Number of acres of blue grass for pasture.	Number of acres of tame grass.	Number of tons of hay from same.	Number of tons of hay from wild grass.	Number of bushels of grass seed.	HUNGARIAN GRASS. Number of acres.	HUNGARIAN GRASS. Number of tons of hay.	POTATOES. Number of acres.	POTATOES. Number of bushels.	SWEET POTATOES. Number of acres.	SWEET POTATOES. Number of bushels.	ONIONS. Number of acres.	ONIONS. Number of bushels.	Number of bushels of turnips.	Number of bushels of beets.	Number of bushels of peas and beans.
Montour, town of	......	......	......	......	......	30	40	......	......	......	......	......	......	......	......	......	......	15	2	......
Oneida	39	405	2	189	......	260	311	1509	......	......	......	55	5485	......	......	......	21	75	11	41
Otter Creek	......	......	4	469	5	632	283	1694	47	7	14	48	4909	......	25	......	7	314	6	29
Perry, exc. of Traer	124	1151	1	110	5	1698	488	1916	307	......	......	52	5824	......	10	......	15	195	805	16
Richland	......	......	2	224	......	439	450	995	......	......	2	63	4657	......	54	......	13	59	......	72
Salt Creek	......	......	8	704	......	682	612	1093	20	60	......	48	3966	1	80	......	......	......	40	......
Spring Creek	341	3307	4	295	14	656	219	1727	303	......	......	58	5651	......	......	......	12	48	72	7
Tama, exc. of Tama City	......	......	......	20	80	88	248	293	5	4	12	5	680	......	......	......	......	......	......	......
Tama City, town of	......	......	......	......	114	114	......	......	......	......	......	1	155	......	......	......	......	......	......	......
Toledo, exc. of town	......	......	1	150	377	3133	876	922	23	......	......	66	2067	......	71	......	......	741	35	46
Toledo, town of	28	200	......	80	10	273	297	1025	......	......	......	9	927	......	......	......	......	......	30	18
Traer, town of	......	......	......	......	......	8	......	60	......	2	4	1	100	......	......	......	......	......	......	......
York	8	110	49	2125	468	402	443	1601	59	4	10	8	3835	......	......	......	......	......	......	......
Total	1423	12529	132	9047	1589	15644	10169	27667	2724	148	166	1189	95041	2	372	1	280	5231	3459	585

TAYLOR COUNTY.

NAMES OF TOWNSHIPS, TOWNS, AND CITIES.	FLAX. Number of acres in flax seed.	FLAX. Number of bushels harvested.	SORGHUM. Number of acres in sorghum.	SORGHUM. Number of gallons of syrup from sorghum.	Number of acres of blue grass for pasture.	Number of acres of tame grass.	Number of tons of hay from same.	Number of tons of hay from wild grass.	Number of bushels of grass seed.	HUNGARIAN GRASS. Number of acres.	HUNGARIAN GRASS. Number of tons of hay.	POTATOES. Number of acres.	POTATOES. Number of bushels.	SWEET POTATOES. Number of acres.	SWEET POTATOES. Number of bushels.	ONIONS. Number of acres.	ONIONS. Number of bushels.	Number of bushels of turnips.	Number of bushels of beets.	Number of bushels of peas and beans.
Bedford, town of	......	......	......	......	......	......	......	......	......	......	......	......	......	......	......	......	......	......	......	......
Benton, exc. of Bedford	......	......	5	475	30	212	229	1161	18	......	......	38	2318	......	15	......	......	......	......	......
Clayton	33	215	9	809	......	463	462	1302	39	49	52	37	3958	......	147	......	80	98	47	12
Dallas	66	527	15	1313	40	136	131	1688	......	12	19	30	3203	1	148	......	73	192	85	37
Gray	1	14	6	518	......	252	180	642	3	48	63	20	1140	......	......	......	12	......	......	......
Grant	42	455	4	398	9	28	36	792	25	......	......	31	2027	......	......	......	......	......	......	......
Grove	66	452	......	115	......	64	55	522	10	......	......	15	1293	......	23	2	173	60	8	3
Holt	900	8865	5	591	......	178	109	1230	......	6	5	40	3782	......	......	......	45	......	2	13
Jackson	13	40	3	291	40	681	672	870	10	51	84	26	1762	......	......	......	......	......	......	......
Jefferson	......	......	7	702	25	272	347	739	134	......	......	18	1336	......	......	1	40	32	100	......

Marshall	4	....	4	548	....	147	171	1102	....	17	13	20	1990	....	102	....	40	12	....	....
Mason	27	267	20	1209	106	104	131	1535	10	40	53	39	3281	....	117	....	132	36	115	9
Nodaway	6	60	5	713	24	219	116	1484	4	19	57	25	3465	....	50	1	96	109	95	21
Platte	44	415	9	637	....	128	188	864	15	4	12	15	2369	....	85	6	465	341	324	41
Polk	20	218	6	471	20	58	73	1330	....	34	55	43	3336	....	186	....	121	71	35	5
Ross	5	64	9	816	21	211	275	1307	47	33	36	50	3502	3	240	....	42	75	53	14
Washington	52	569	6	416	....	161	220	1139	34	46	86	40	2617	....	61	....	41	15	25	19
Total	1279	12161	114	10022	315	3314	3395	17707	349	359	535	487	41379	4	1174	10	1360	1041	889	174

UNION COUNTY.

Dodge	334	1820	6	668	....	189	201	582	....	....	....	20	1791	....	19	....	10	38	24	4
Douglas, exc. of Creston	20	98	....	....	....	....	....	....	....	....	....	14	875	....	....	7	....	775	90	50
Grant	16	100	1	100	....	95	91	352	....	....	....	31	2120	....	....	....	....	285	....	....
Highland	90	1114	1	158	....	393	479	1704	81	25	65	28	2402	....	....	....	....	200	....	30
Jones	12	104	12	1861	14	871	844	960	1082	83	169	40	3374	....	....	....	16	219	23	15
Lincoln	257	2098	2	200	....	87	116	161	....	4	5	40	5162	....	....	....	40	....	5	20
New Hope	282	2631	8	555	....	326	435	574	50	5	5	23	1572	....	20	....	17	294	21	34
Platte	32	160	2	1381	119	609	509	1242	451	21	38	14	2439	....	112	....	65	110	....	8
Pleasant	144	1271	10	1115	....	418	435	708	450	90	178	14	2665	....	6	....	58	198	35	36
Sand Creek	461	2772	10	961	....	104	83	1012	117	....	....	41	4110	....	....	....	44	228	3	33
Spaulding	52	161	....	....	....	44	55	726	30	....	....	25	1748	1	125	5	1093	250	84	46
Union, exc. of Afton	528	2166	9	820	....	643	763	1530	76	59	139	62	5291	1	94	....	8	134	27	16
Total	2222	14495	61	7819	133	3779	4011	9551	2337	287	599	352	33549	2	376	12	2126	2046	272	242

VAN BUREN COUNTY.

Bentonsport, town of	....	....	....	....	....	31	28	....	....	....	....	3	195	....	6	....	4	85	2	2
Birmingham, town of	....	....	....	40	....	135	61	33	....	....	....	4	777	....	31	1	8	22	13	3
Bonaparte	....	....	....	1326	1637	872	719	6	711	32	28	24	4769	2	269	....	25	144	4	22
Cantril, town of	....	....	....	....	....	....	....	....	....	....	....	....	70	....	....	....	....	....	....	....
Cedar	....	....	34	2947	2795	2777	1542	8	4982	54	57	54	4695	....	114	....	11	211	10	79
Chequest	....	....	36	4506	1295	1169	1156	....	233	95	124	49	5317	....	221	10	119	557	60	285
Des Moines	....	....	28	3160	3517	3237	3044	154	1216	131	166	68	5901	4	91	....	16	309	26	272
Farmington, exc. of town	....	....	18	1776	771	1169	1068	....	223	60	86	113	12873	1	292	....	30	274	4	243
Harrisburg	....	....	16	1477	1315	5529	2814	....	9713	15	25	63	4792	1	60	....	....	56	....	48
Henry	....	....	6	546	897	1429	1145	....	?59	4	4	29	2732	....	30	....	....	187	12	123
Jackson, exc. of Cantril	70	415	32	3073	2753	4118	3131	139	3923	334	401	47	4643	2	92	....	44	227	2	848
Keosauqua, town of	....	....	....	....	....	....	....	....	....	....	....	2	225	....	....	....	....	....	....	....
Lick Creek	....	....	34	2168	497	2663	1670	48	112	1	2	78	6910	1	203	....	40	580	56	194
Union, exc. Birmingham	....	....	11	867	4193	2793	2500	....	3657	16	22	46	4679	7	129	....	2	152	16	45
VanBuren, ex. Keosa'qua	....	....	23	2585	4226	2265	2116	30	798	57	61	100	9564	....	356	....	90	378	66	263

VAN BUREN COUNTY.—CONTINUED.

NAMES OF TOWNSHIPS, TOWNS, AND CITIES.	FLAX.		SORGHUM.		Number of acres of blue grass for pasture.	Number of acres of tame grass.	Number of tons of hay from same.	Number of tons of hay from wild grass.	Number of bushels of grass seed.	HUNGARIAN GRASS.		POTATOES.		SWEET POTATOES.		ONIONS.		Number of bushels of turnips.	Number of bushels of beets.	Number of bushels of peas and beans.
	Number of acres in flax seed.	Number of bushels harvested.	Number of acres in sorghum.	Number of gallons of syrup from sorghum.						Number of acres.	Number of tons of hay.	Number of acres.	Number of bushels.	Number of acres.	Number of bushels.	Number of acres.	Number of bushels.			
Vernon	....	....	20	2261	1656	2095	1642	171	1008	62	125	41	4655	1	106	....	37	142	11	35
Village	....	....	22	3155	829	1646	1519	3	470	16	6	62	7281	1	69	....	50	642	....	66
Washington, exc. of Bentonsport	....	....	2	138	150	956	1054	....	1173	11	13	23	1650	....	75	12	2	13	4	....
Total	70	415	282	30005	26531	32884	25209	592	28578	888	1120	806	81728	20	2144	23	498	3979	286	2528

WAPELLO COUNTY.

NAMES OF TOWNSHIPS, TOWNS, AND CITIES.	Number of acres in flax seed.	Number of bushels harvested.	Number of acres in sorghum.	Number of gallons of syrup from sorghum.	Number of acres of blue grass for pasture.	Number of acres of tame grass.	Number of tons of hay from same.	Number of tons of hay from wild grass.	Number of bushels of grass seed.	Hungarian grass: Number of acres.	Hungarian grass: Number of tons of hay.	Potatoes: Number of acres.	Potatoes: Number of bushels.	Sweet potatoes: Number of acres.	Sweet potatoes: Number of bushels.	Onions: Number of acres.	Onions: Number of bushels.	Number of bushels of turnips.	Number of bushels of beets.	Number of bushels of peas and beans.
Adams	....	....	46	4429	1387	2658	1140	1	38	117	181	92	9320	....	363	....	110	1238	27	99
Agency, exc. of town	....	....	3	491	1018	890	504	6	126	19	26	56	5137	....	142	....	44	423	61	49
Agency City, town of	....	....	....	....	....	....	....	....	....	....	....	4	666	....	118	....	3	244	1	10
Cass	....	....	14	934	145	920	421	10	1	....	....	46	3686	1	22	....	7	28	....	29
Center, exc. of Ottumwa	....	....	26	3412	1773	2400	1704	186	212	46	59	325	35832	10	1539	3	248	2224	810	349
Columbia, exc. of Eddyville	....	....	27	2836	519	2467	1251	46	30	5	6	51	7305	....	38	....	4	107	....	14
Competine	....	....	12	1415	1317	3142	1873	66	2632	30	60	58	5590	....	....	....	....	339	....	....
Dahlonega	....	....	5	352	2219	1313	1006	....	273	9	13	68	6969	....	....	....	....	....	....	....
Eddyville, town of	....	....	....	100	....	....	....	....	....	....	....	5	736	....	94	....	8	70	1	....
Green	....	....	41	4704	609	1222	1023	12	22	61	93	126	13380	....	42	....	....	1655	25	74
Highland	....	....	22	2399	650	2148	1445	227	91	5	9	110	12081	....	30	....	6	180	....	5
Keokuk	....	....	24	1324	244	....	373	111	27	28	42	106	10011	....	37	....	....	382	....	15
Pleasant	....	....	26	2847	3797	2146	1162	170	1242	53	48	59	6743	....	131	4	19	275	8	42
Polk	....	....	30	3038	315	1784	951	6	17	32	32	83	7876	....	43	....	19	216	1	71
Richland	....	....	21	2158	211	3716	2493	397	181	4	4	234	25311	....	30	....	....	140	....	....
Washington, ex. of Eldon	....	....	24	2321	1054	2332	1299	202	643	71	150	42	3780	....	32	....	60	....	122	12
Total	....	....	321	32760	15258	27138	16645	1440	5535	480	723	1465	15447	11	2661	7	528	7521	1056	814

Allen	....	....	10	1030	110	782	633	386	9	4	9	60	8567	....	114	....	107	377	1031	13
Belmont	22	150	20	2426	523	1069	899	527	82	....	....	48	5174	....	84	....	66	208	8	29
Greenfield	23	207	28	2756	148	1324	972	1202	77	5	14	146	24240	....	251	....	133	196	114	30
Indianola, town of	....	....	....	....	....	70	127	....	2	3	8	....	45	....	....	....	....	....	5	....
Jackson	269	2205	17	1559	....	509	847	766	....	5	14	43	4880	....	8	....	....	208	....	4
Jefferson	....	....	20	1868	30	580	576	908	6	....	....	27	5213	....	79	....	50	28	38	12
Liberty	72	591	20	1859	7	730	687	404	119	5	9	57	4457	....	114	....	115	368	55	79
Linn	....	....	12	1255	669	564	1107	1502	5	....	....	102	11955	....	....	....	....	67	....	107
Otter	20	170	13	1889	153	754	896	521	6	10	32	35	3495	....	18	....	6	450	14	4
Palmyra	....	....	8	916	244	636	729	299	....	....	....	76	8958	....	314	....	169	114	118	141
Richland	10	60	16	1394	159	523	731	49	15	51	45	58	6261	2	18)	....	19	....	....	1
Squaw	....	....	23	1945	22	384	381	755	....	....	....	50	2504	....	30	....	203	137	123	106
Union	....	....	28	2108	884	1111	1146	245	....	....	....	36	3508	3	48	....	4	59	1	29
Virginia	....	2	19	1895	1	520	453	1043	....	4	8	36	3288	2	149	....	92	322	59	57
Washington, exc. of Indianola	41	485	28	3469	1445	2742	3252	1943	64	25	40	119	20873	....	480	....	421	2005	272	144
White Breast	91	697	18	3958	....	743	727	239	409	11	22	16	3003	....	121	....	79	40	16	17
White Oak	114	1014	9	870	62	608	600	542	....	23	30	46	4094	....	59	....	1	241	2	19
Total	662	581	280	31197	4457	13649	14763	11331	794	146	231	957	120515	7	2049	....	1465	4820	1856	793

WASHINGTON COUNTY.

Brighton, exc. of town	....	....	10	1027	633	1096	952	275	145	4	7	26	3064	....	39	....	....	25	3	9
Brighton, town of	....	....	1	95	117	185	163	20	38	....	....	6	622	....	....	....	....	3	....	6
Cedar	20	240	14	1637	45	3464	1743	429	360	....	....	46	5664	....	80	....	4	83	33	55
Clay	....	....	26	2674	1821	1605	1433	22	439	2	2	39	5032	....	326	....	17	176	18	45
Crawford	....	....	34	4004	223	3012	190	222	138	6	10	81	8415	2	317	....	18	137	37	44
Dutch Creek	....	....	95	3814	1506	2202	1837	71	595	....	....	75	8930	....	....	....	....	80	2	....
English River	68	552	12	3375	3455	1728	2050	417	132	....	4	46	5518	....	122	1	77	293	35	67
Franklin	....	....	3	375	2825	2968	2421	733	391	....	....	52	4903	....	4	....	....	....	....	6
Highland	43	380	23	2407	734	2760	1895	395	430	10	20	49	4986	....	25	....	....	....	....	3
Iowa	....	....	29	2625	991	1677	1728	623	85	16	24	73	6747	....	....	....	4	202	204	24
Jackson	....	....	4	1589	2147	2014	2136	701	495	11	57	51	8199	....	18	....	5	51	17	27
Lime Creek	362	2593	39	3407	....	2314	1770	347	234	....	....	68	5798	....	3	....	....	7	....	89
Marion	....	....	36	3955	1102	1904	2162	38	222	32	48	53	7674	....	133	....	39	163	17	46
Oregon	132	1412	30	3082	772	3540	2126	375	584	10	25	70	7130	10	581	....	13	14	....	27
Seventy-Six	30	169	20	2602	682	1935	1435	769	222	....	....	70	5789	....	88	1	110	174	6	71
Washington, exc. of city	5	50	38	3869	2328	3055	2991	9615	518	4	5	123	13290	4	469	4	197	429	324	256
Washington, city of	....	....	....	....	....	85	110	....	....	1	....	3	280	....	....	....	....	....	....	....
Total	660	5396	414	40537	19381	35544	27142	15052	5028	96	202	931	102041	16	2205	6	484	1837	696	775

WAYNE COUNTY.

NAMES OF TOWNSHIPS, TOWNS, AND CITIES.	FLAX.		SORGHUM.		Number of acres of blue grass for pasture.	Number of acres of tame grass.	Number of tons of hay from same.	Number of tons of hay from wild grass.	Number of bushels of grass seed.	HUNGARIAN GRASS.		POTATOES.		SWEET POTATOES.		ONIONS.		Number of bushels of turnips.	Number of bushels of beets.	Number of bushels of peas and beans.
	Number of acres in flax seed.	Number of bushels harvested.	Number of acres in sorghum.	Number of gallons of syrup from sorghum.						Number of acres.	Number of tons of hay.	Number of acres.	Number of bushels.	Number of acres.	Number of bushels.	Number of acres.	Number of bushels.			
Benton	....	2	18	2088	97	2621	1819	771	396	310	477	24	3439	....	84	....	15	187	5	206
Clay	72	573	17	1906	48	983	758	716	161	301	408	41	3026	....	35	3	103	173	12	131
Clinton	....	....	36	2463	86	432	327	564	122	181	187	40	2868	....	12	2	38	466	3	37
Corydon, exc. of town	44	140	25	2086	200	375	91	113	10	231	377	50	4211	....	90	3	6	400	17	86
Corydon, town of	....	....	....	....	13	1226	712	908	422	....	....	10	1232	....	82	....	11	67	50	41
Grand River, exc. of Lineville	4	17	19	1191	....	712	917	219	....	253	244	28	2285	1	23	20	50	447	5	74
Howard	10	60	17	1496	81	546	411	525	330	51	56	22	1422	....	20	....	....	301	....	23
Jackson	90	920	8	655	....	570	578	695	286	254	374	26	1122	....	46	1	28	476	80	65
Jefferson	....	....	24	1740	10	684	689	623	....	238	302	36	3657	....	150	....	95	924	28	51
Monroe	7	79	7	895	4	1097	650	545	825	100	117	14	1519	....	2	....	13	195	75	40
Richman	....	....	9	581	....	1188	1095	422	67	9	27	28	1817	....	....	....	....	25	....	....
Seymour, town of	....	....	....	....	....	....	....	17	....	2	4	1	90	....	....	....	....	....	....	....
South Fork	65	420	19	1586	55	1492	1256	487	2310	383	421	32	3332	....	53	....	48	90	18	58
Union	....	....	15	1568	125	2233	1623	714	674	214	281	36	3583	....	31	....	32	432	32	112
Walnut, exc. of Seymour	70	725	21	756	90	2227	1972	790	2980	301	656	46	4416	....	73	....	221	316	16	57
Warren, exc. of Allerton	5	40	9	823	....	1175	807	565	62	350	650	2	5194	....	54	....	5	210	10	58
Washington	....	....	16	1945	....	2443	1222	895	461	219	359	33	2554	....	84	1	67	294	45	76
Wright	....	....	28	2020	246	1285	1870	360	14	429	759	36	4550	1	115	....	3	965	99	135
Total	367	2976	288	24729	1055	21289	16797	9929	9120	3828	5699	508	50317	2	954	30	735	6068	495	1252

WEBSTER COUNTY.

NAMES OF TOWNSHIPS, TOWNS, AND CITIES.	Number of acres in flax seed.	Number of bushels harvested.	Number of acres in sorghum.	Number of gallons of syrup from sorghum.	Number of acres of blue grass for pasture.	Number of acres of tame grass.	Number of tons of hay from same.	Number of tons of hay from wild grass.	Number of bushels of grass seed.	Hungarian grass: Number of acres.	Hungarian grass: Number of tons of hay.	Potatoes: Number of acres.	Potatoes: Number of bushels.	Sweet potatoes: Number of acres.	Sweet potatoes: Number of bushels.	Onions: Number of acres.	Onions: Number of bushels.	Number of bushels of turnips.	Number of bushels of beets.	Number of bushels of peas and beans.
Badger	....	....	....	....	....	....	....	....	....	....	....	35	4907	....	....	....	....	....	....	....
Clay	....	....	1	81	....	....	....	732	....	....	....	4	430	....	....	....	....	62	....	8
Colfax	....	....	9	548	....	....	....	1008	....	....	....	20	1210	....	....	....	....	....	....	....
Dayton	....	....	37	3469	....	73	64	5301	....	2	4	73	7315	....	....	....	....	405	....	15

Deer Creek												57	4372							
Douglas			2	100		22	11	3094				108	9864					1001		22
Elkhorn			8	708				2131				36	2661		1		5	272	2	10
Fulton			1	136				725				15	1130							
Gowrie								421				2	158							
Hardin			13	1506	9	16		1401				20	2180							
Jackson			9	466		12	4	966				75	6198					500		50
Johnson			6	309		5	6	3176				66	5769				3	875	10	13
Lost Grove	10	100	7	227				994				10	947							2
Newark			2	261		2		428				10	755					27	29	8
Otho			6	466		25	12	1200				29	1904		6		15	105	2	6
Pleasant Valley			2	286		6	6	1604				35	1990				20	195	11	26
Sumner	16	74	11	1056	3	20	14	2010				45	3490		21		23	339	53	54
Wahkonsa, exc. of Ft. Dodge	107				30	30	40	1065	2			95	4173				29	420	27	40
Washington			16	1651			570	2320				34	4559		5					25
Webster			35	2850	2	39	50	1209		11	18	39	2911				40	174	82	74
Yell			8	762			5	875		10	28	3	500							
Total	133	174	173	14882	44	250	782	30660	2	28	50	811	67423		33		135	4375	216	353

24

WINNEBAGO COUNTY.

Center			2	240				2629				36	2455				70	455		
Forest						21	41	1389				30	2062		2		6	80	32	5
Iowa								2885				23	1623							
Norway						6	16	2071				12	887							
Pleasant						10	16	1700				33	2364				11	32	30	35
Total			2	240		37	73	10674				134	9391		2		87	567	62	67

WINNESHIEK COUNTY.

Bloomfield			5	381	2558	1993	1091	740	5			109	13851			1	181	1681	600	181
Bluffton						560	399	1125				272	12555				314	75		
Burr Oak						1085	1200	378	195			61	8195				26	615	4	25
Calmar						221	262	1583				26	4202		9			219	33	12
Canoe						998	1166	562				140	7027				11	463	4	8
Decorah, exc. of city					129	1123	1341	802				40	5226	28	210		75	2261	357	45
Frankville						1493	1942	668	2359			60	6032					250	1605	7
Fremont						671	505	335				52	5535				11	120	237	20
Glenwood						810	826	282	30	1		49	4113			1		378	23	7
Hesper			5	495		1345	1772	500	941			47	6030		25		16	651	1471	220
Highland			2	163		1086	1241	703	254	13	23	29	3534				39	239	19	10

WINNESHIEK COUNTY.—Continued.

NAMES OF TOWNSHIPS, TOWNS, AND CITIES.	FLAX. Number of acres in flax seed.	FLAX. Number of bushels harvested.	SORGHUM. Number of acres in sorghum.	SORGHUM. Number of gallons of syrup from sorghum.	Number of acres of blue grass for pasture.	Number of acres of tame grass.	Number of tons of hay from same.	Number of tons of hay from wild grass.	Number of bushels of grass seed.	HUNGARIAN GRASS. Number of acres.	HUNGARIAN GRASS. Number of tons of hay.	POTATOES. Number of acres.	POTATOES. Number of bushels.	SWEET POTATOES. Number of acres.	SWEET POTATOES. Number of bushels.	ONIONS. Number of acres.	ONIONS. Number of bushels.	Number of bushels of turnips.	Number of bushels of beets.	Number of bushels of peas and beans.
Jackson	....	....	....	7	....	177	108	2294	214	....	....	72	6060	....	....	....	....	363	6	20
Lincoln	....	....	....	....	....	148	122	2070	....	....	....	46	4556	....	....	....	....	200	....	....
Madison	....	....	....	....	....	780	589	2317	6	....	....	77	2725	....	....	....	....	312	....	30
Military	....	....	....	36	2203	934	691	1942	123	....	....	120	10428	....	....	....	....	445	550	....
Orleans	....	....	....	....	....	909	934	1737	604	....	....	57	6551	3	....	....	18	1145	23	19
Pleasant	....	....	3	293	....	888	954	919	25	1	3	51	5254	....	....	....	....	600	42	6
Springfield	....	....	....	....	....	263	264	1818	....	....	....	53	3727	....	....	....	....	185	....	....
Sumner	....	....	....	....	....	106	66	3228	....	....	....	88	4899	....	....	....	....	....	....	....
Washington	....	....	....	....	....	254	258	1564	....	....	....	118	9214	....	....	....	....	....	....	....
Total	....	....	15	1375	6890	15844	15726	25567	4756	15	26	1567	100314	31	244	2	691	10202	4984	610

WOODBURY COUNTY.

NAMES OF TOWNSHIPS, TOWNS, AND CITIES.	FLAX. Number of acres in flax seed.	FLAX. Number of bushels harvested.	SORGHUM. Number of acres in sorghum.	SORGHUM. Number of gallons of syrup from sorghum.	Number of acres of blue grass for pasture.	Number of acres of tame grass.	Number of tons of hay from same.	Number of tons of hay from wild grass.	Number of bushels of grass seed.	HUNGARIAN GRASS. Number of acres.	HUNGARIAN GRASS. Number of tons of hay.	POTATOES. Number of acres.	POTATOES. Number of bushels.	SWEET POTATOES. Number of acres.	SWEET POTATOES. Number of bushels.	ONIONS. Number of acres.	ONIONS. Number of bushels.	Number of bushels of turnips.	Number of bushels of beets.	Number of bushels of peas and beans.
Arlington	....	....	....	....	....	....	....	....	....	1	4	4	175	....	....	....	....	....	....	....
Concord	....	....	....	30	....	....	....	1163	....	....	....	12	540	....	....	....	....	70	....	55
Floyd	....	....	....	....	....	....	....	782	....	....	....	4	155	....	....	....	1	2	10	....
Grant	....	....	....	40	....	....	....	2170	....	....	....	27	1205	....	....	1	66	115	82	....
Kedron	....	....	....	....	....	....	....	....	....	....	....	9	679	....	....	....	....	....	....	....
Lakeport	....	....	....	....	....	....	....	1302	....	....	....	14	890	1	75	....	....	26	63	4
Liberty	....	....	2	105	....	24	12	....	....	....	....	44	2206	1	100	1	175	230	644	55
Liston	....	....	....	....	....	....	....	....	....	....	....	9	818	....	....	....	....	....	....	....
Little Sioux	....	....	....	....	....	....	....	4059	....	....	....	22	1807	....	....	....	....	80	....	....
Moville	....	....	....	....	....	....	....	316	....	....	....	3	98	....	....	....	....	20	1	2
Rock	....	....	....	....	....	....	....	460	....	....	....	4	281	....	....	....	....	100	....	....
Rutland	....	....	....	....	....	....	....	227	....	....	....	1	185	....	....	....	....	....	....	....
Sioux City, exc. of city	....	....	....	....	....	....	....	1550	....	10	35	6	210	....	....	....	....	....	....	....
Sioux City, city of	....	....	....	....	....	....	....	....	....	3	6	....	....	....	....	....	....	2	....	....

Union	....	....	....	....	....	....	....	1501	....	....	3	30	1580	....	....	....	19	160	51	60
West Fork	....	....	2	281	....	....	....	2236	....	....	....	28	798	....	....	2	259	218	105	34
Wolf Creek	....	....	1	36	....	....	....	715	....	....	2	18	775	....	....	....	4	....	18	14
Woodbury	....	....	....	....	....	....	....	2092	....	9	20	49	4910	1	150	3	192	75	795	85
Total	....	....	5	492	....	24	12	18573	....	24	70	285	17812	3	325	7	716	1098	1769	309

WORTH COUNTY.

Bristol	....	....	4	322	....	33	30	2706	....	22	44	38	3327	....	....	....	17	349	12	32
Brookfield	....	....	....	31	....	....	....	2096	....	....	....	15	809	....	....	....	2	282	....	6
Danville	....	....	....	....	....	5	5	794	....	....	....	12	1477	....	25	....	30	188	42	35
Deer Creek	....	....	....	20	....	16	26	658	7	10	15	17	1955	....	....	....	2	428	24	6
Fertile	....	....	....	....	....	3	3	1643	....	....	....	17	1786	....	....	....	142	192	419	14
Hartland	....	....	1	50	....	12	13	3354	....	....	....	30	2440	....	....	....	20	....	....	....
Kensett	....	....	1	101	....	7	8	990	....	3	6	21	1579	....	....	....	6	205	5	13
Northwood	....	....	....	8	....	173	233	2522	128	1	1	56	3311	....	....	....	30	558	33	38
Silver Lake	....	....	4	195	....	....	....	2639	....	....	....	24	1505	....	....	....	2	100	....	3
Union	....	....	....	....	....	67	90	1069	....	....	....	29	3020	....	....	....	3	202	17	11
Total	....	....	10	727	....	316	408	18471	135	36	66	259	21209	....	25	....	256	2804	552	158

WRIGHT COUNTY.

Belmond	....	....	2	172	20	134	100	1622	....	....	....	38	2145	....	....	....	....	135	4	4
Boone	....	....	1	193	....	....	....	542	....	....	....	8	541	....	....	....	....	....	....	....
Clarion	....	....	....	....	....	32	21	764	....	....	....	20	1008	....	....	....	....	241	35	13
Eagle Grove	....	....	8	646	45	78	44	1616	....	....	....	16	2192	....	....	....	15	523	36	101
Iowa	....	....	....	....	....	....	....	1348	....	....	....	27	2264	....	....	....	....	475	43	15
Liberty	1	2	4	481	....	66	82	1502	....	....	....	14	1323	....	3	....	250	506	62	18
Pleasant	....	3	1	20	....	31	50	1486	....	....	....	28	1790	....	....	1	88	286	32	20
Troy	43	395	13	1109	....	21	....	2336	....	45	80	50	3062	....	....	....	21	633	79	77
Vernon	....	....	8	658	....	36	15	1033	16	....	....	27	1890	....	....	....	12	722	20	108
Wall Lake	69	618	2	96	....	14	....	1219	....	....	....	17	1098	....	....	....	....	....	....	....
Total	113	1018	39	3375	65	412	312	13468	16	45	80	245	17313	....	3	1	386	3521	311	356

ACRES OF TIMBER, RODS OF HEDGE, AND STATISTICS OF THE ORCHARD AND VINE.

ADAIR COUNTY.

NAMES OF TOWNSHIPS, TOWNS AND CITIES.	Acres of natural timber.	Acres of planted timber.	Rods of hedge.	APPLES.		PEARS.		PEACHES		PLUMS.		CHERRIES.		Number of other fruit trees in bearing.	Number of fruit trees not in bearing.	GRAPES IN VINEYARD.			GRAPES NOT IN VINEYARD.		
				Number of trees in bearing.	Bushels gathered in 1874.	Number of trees in bearing.	Bushels gathered in 1874.	Number of trees in bearing.	Bushels gathered in 1874.	Number of trees in bearing.	Bushels gathered in 1874.	Number of trees in bearing.	Bushels gathered in 1874.			Number of acres.	Pounds of grapes gathered.	Gallons of wine made.	Number of vines.	Pounds of grapes gathered.	Gallons of wine made.
Eureka	1	16	600												1555				131	110	
Fontanelle, town of		18	1021	207						49	9	166	16	321	2584		30		619	895	
Grand River	576	67	1623	487	261			6				80	5	2	2574				1099	2065	21
Greenfield	148	43	3550	5					20	6	42				6108				1354	530	
Grove	126	38	1384					4				11			1896				573		
Harrison	1075	21	2370	381	350	2		4		1	2	124	8		6752				1462	4085	107
Jackson	708	18	1396									44	6	35	5897		400		939	135	
Jefferson	776	63	4072	829	755	10		4		16		32	20	1352	7181				1968	760	4
Lincoln	49	6	9970	86								80			8035				1609	620	
Orient		52	2510												5999				907		
Prussia	29	10													2794				365		
Richland	556	121	4405	50	8							99	25	15	7746				1081	550	132
Summerset, exc. of Fontanelle.	191	25	2215	6	4					3		42	1	32	2845				432	23	
Summit		13													837				80		
Union	381	34	1680	94	70							7	2	20	2238	1	4		126		
Walnut	97	14	1190																		
Washington	2248	11	3205	156	228			12	1			30	6	14	6080				685	1465	4
Total	6961	570	41191	2301	1676	12		30	21	75	53	705	89	1791	71121	1	434		13430	11238	268

ADAMS COUNTY.

Carl	377	21	2614	106	61					1		14		8	4350				689	1294	
Colony	84	79	2380	105	106	5				60	53	32	2	12	4538		4200	3	484	450	
Corning, town of																					
Douglas	1468	17	1999	194	101	4	1			209	9	67	2	26	3407	2	3600	350	973	826	4
Grant	140	62	5454	26	10					155	2	11			3974				553	25	
Jasper	780	8	4500	214	100	2	5	20	1			75	6	3	4996				1193	2125	1
Lincoln	359	32	4985									62			6302				639	185	
Mercer		14	2100	60	30					14	3	24	1		3040	1			172		
Nodaway	2184	33	4339	310	610	4	1	14	2			115	4	31	8174		500		1082	2510	1
Prescott	784	20	3330	135	227			1				49	2	10	3516	2	4500	200	310	1750	125
Quincy, exc. of town	907	12	2290	249	92	4	1	9				71			2555				478	230	20
Quincy, town of			12									9	2		400				250		2
Union	147	24	3050	2		1						17		16	4273				766	365	
Washington	1457	89	4350	528	360	7	1			164	108	67	7	55	9205				1625	4825	2
Total	8687	411	41403	1929	1698	27	90	48	3	603	175	613	26	161	58730	5	12800	553	9214	14585	155

ALLAMAKEE COUNTY.

Center	1269			983	438	3								6	2693				213	303	48
Fairview	6128			1253	277																
Franklin	7680			1358	720			12			6	46	3	8	2309				503	870	
French Creek	618			848	287										2628				331	315	
Hanover	70			20	10																
Iowa	1508	300		118	72							10		49	264						
Jefferson	6914			1295	586	13	3			4		15		235	6406				368	1189	
Lalayette	5439			1255	472	3				51	58	16	2		3963		10		692	263	5
Lansing, exc. of city	5707			2334	756	2				4		33			5288				8	200	10
Lansing, city of					20	2				9		1					200		40	200	
Linton	3968			625	409	10								30	1426				344	802	
Ludlow	2525		30	1356	563							15		34	8164				25	70	
Makee, exc. of Waukon	315			1247	1174									18	4962				89		
Paint Creek	7728		40	585	419					2	2	6		145	1807		10	8	107	35	5
Post, exc. of Postville	4503	6	180	1427	853							26	1		5564				129	167	
Postville, town of																					
Taylor	1756	20		558	235									119	2807						
Union City	1806																				
Union Prairie	1329			434	283					8	4	10	2	50	2779						
Waterloo	2663			1349	66					134	27	1		95	82		77	35	4		9
Waukon, town of				2104	602					8	16	40	4		1765				160	1350	90
Total	61956	326	250	19149	8242	33	3	12		220	113	219	13	789	52907		297	43	3013	5764	167

APPANOOSE COUNTY.

NAMES OF TOWNSHIPS, TOWNS, AND CITIES.	Acres of natural timber.	Acres of planted timber.	Rods of hedge.	APPLES.		PEARS.		PEACHES		PLUMS.		CHERRIES.		Number of other fruit trees in bearing.	Number of fruit trees not in bearing.	GRAPES IN VINEYARD.			GRAPES NOT IN VINEYARD.		
				Number of trees in bearing.	Bushels gathered in 1874.	Number of trees in bearing.	Bushels gathered in 1874.	Number of trees in bearing.	Bushels gathered in 1874.	Number of trees in bearing.	Bushels gathered in 1874.	Number of trees in bearing.	Bushels gathered in 1874.			Number of acres.	Pounds of grapes gathered.	Gallons of wine made.	Number of vines.	Pounds of grapes gathered.	Gallons of wine made.
Bellair	3605	5	12017	1855	1377	11	8	523	25	44	27	969	307	....	7200	......	....	......	824	5153	68
Caldwell	7568	2	2196	3993	2364	21	....	809	607	100	408	1635	142	122	12012	......	50	......	2387	7814	105
Center, exc. of Centerville	1958	2	6643	2173	1448	10	12	57	20	26	21	792	326	....	13707	6	10000	245	2047	7370	223
Centerville, town of	....	....	200	1389	203	147	25	520	76	142	34	1027	367	....	1720	......	....	......	2311	21940	125
Chariton	3258	9	9005	1520	781	29	17	39	2	51	1	606	100	....	4658	......	....	......	1517	3140	135
Douglas	2891	....	4503	1816	537	30	12	201	96	8	3	524	94	18	4508	......	....	......	420	1835	......
Franklin	2246	2	13770	2624	1760	6	1	101	28	17	5	1962	316	2	8684	1	6000	185	1304	3522	3
Independence	3310	85	10021	1951	702	20	6	193	11	37	4	684	68	17	5098	......	....	......	1096	1210	......
Johns	2360	19	25170	1742	1435	10	8	26	....	42	8	631	97	2	8210	......	....	......	717	2309	......
Lincoln	2473	....	11713	2465	1294	19	22	338	26	118	23	709	101	120	4945	......	....	......	628	1642	......
Moulton, town of	....	....	112	90	6	11	....	5	6	4	....	172	25	5	1435	......	....	......	1172	3230	......
Pleasant	5074	....	8739	5415	2758	26	24	1061	151	7	1	1910	475	257	7540	3	1860	30	1096	1302	64
Taylor	4621	3	10706	2152	1325	52	58	40	6	28	10	880	169	....	9461	......	....	......	1229	4045	2
Sharon	3092	2	2102	809	908	...	....	4	3	100	10	170	28	....	4476	......	1200	......	545	1412	10
Udell	4586	2	10009	4128	2025	57	25	224	39	116	61	1194	409	5	5635	1	1200	......	1598	11365	......
Union	3099	....	215	711	329	9	1	12	2	492	49	353	14	15	2242	......	200	......	272	474	......
Walnut	3020	2	9087	1500	969	17	3	186	2	47	1	617	119	45	5211	......	....	......	833	2690	......
Washington, exc. of Moulton	4749	5	13140	4251	3252	20	3	258	72	15	5	825	226	....	12331	......	....	......	2072	9128	1
Wells	4127	2	2898	2422	1736	10	5	22	31	17	14	315	90	....	6012	5	3620	55	2417	3676	72
Total	62037	141	152246	43006	25204	505	230	4619	1203	1411	685	75975	3473	608	125085	16	24130	515	24485	95257	808

AUDUBON COUNTY.

NAMES OF TOWNSHIPS, TOWNS, AND CITIES.	Acres of natural timber.	Acres of planted timber.	Rods of hedge.	Apples: Number of trees in bearing.	Apples: Bushels gathered in 1874.	Pears: Number of trees in bearing.	Pears: Bushels gathered in 1874.	Peaches: Number of trees in bearing.	Peaches: Bushels gathered in 1874.	Plums: Number of trees in bearing.	Plums: Bushels gathered in 1874.	Cherries: Number of trees in bearing.	Cherries: Bushels gathered in 1874.	Number of other fruit trees in bearing.	Number of fruit trees not in bearing.	Grapes in vineyard: Number of acres.	Grapes in vineyard: Pounds of grapes gathered.	Grapes in vineyard: Gallons of wine made.	Grapes not in vineyard: Number of vines.	Grapes not in vineyard: Pounds of grapes gathered.	Grapes not in vineyard: Gallons of wine made.
Audubon	55	16	1035	119	55	......	....	......	....	......	....	....	......	....	1366	......	....	......	169	50	......
Douglas	30	11	1105	....	....	......	....	......	....	......	....	3	......	....	55	......	....	......	....	....	......
Exira	1062	12	590	563	125	......	....	......	....	......	....	5	3	....	4582	......	....	......	587	977	......
Greeley	50	14	850	....	....	......	....	......	....	......	....	11	......	....	458	......	....	......	50	....	......

Hamlin	563	12	210	7	5	.....	....	.....	.....	....	....	25	.....	1	931	.....	....	.....	245	150	.....
Leroy	102	5	486	....	....	.....	....	.....	.....	....	....	....	.....	....	414	.....	....	.....	....	....	.....
Melville	....	3	86	....	....	.....	....	.....	.....	....	....	....	.....	....	....	.....	....	.....	....	....	.....
Oakfield	968	17	248	382	118	1	1	1	1	....	....	62	7	152	2798	.....	....	.....	232	263	6
Viola	13	26	1139	....	....	.....	....	.....	.....	....	....	....	.....	3	662	.....	....	.....	342	....	.....
Total	2843	116	5749	1071	303	1	1	1	1	....	....	106	10	156	11266	.....	....	.....	1625	1440	6

BENTON COUNTY.

Belle Plaine, town of	....	....	....	....	....	.....	....	.....	.....	....	....	....	.....	....	....	.....	....	.....	....	....	.....
Benton	1733	7	130	1579	811	2	....	.....	.....	65	18	103	10	18	13294	7	7750	78	900	3220	40
Big Grove	709	289	11740	3049	1158	.....	....	.....	.....	....	....	200	10	2	10867	1	....	.....	1265	4360	38
Blairstown, town of	....	8	....	25	30	.....	....	.....	.....	65	13	7	5	....	100	.....	....	.....	140	1000	.....
Bruce	713	120	5740	933	525	1	....	5	.....	91	7	203	6	801	13560	.....	....	.....	939	3701	20
Canton, exc. of Shellsburg	1887	92	4235	7489	1027	.....	....	.....	.....	....	....	302	22	....	18187	.....	....	.....	2543	11267	10
Cedar	1503	169	4569	2182	348	4	....	7	2	106	17	478	19	....	14172	.....	....	.....	1322	2470	8
Eden	....	225	8767	1180	400	1	....	.....	.....	337	52	201	17	56	11105	2	800	3	973	3514	15
Eldorado	5	220	9792	632	228	1	....	.....	.....	38	1	139	2	559	8200	.....	....	.....	1670	440	49
Florence	561	207	10398	1494	877	8	7	.....	.....	15	2	97	22	212	7716	.....	....	.....	1259	4390	53
Fremont	173	510	10684	2017	896	.....	....	.....	.....	18	....	78	.....	24	9489	1	8000	140	1098	3124	108
Harrison	2663	37	277	1185	527	.....	....	.....	.....	7	....	145	5	23	5606	.....	....	.....	555	2224	4
Homer	....	553	5680	184	26	.....	....	.....	.....	20	2	24	.....	3	4768	.....	....	.....	435	622	.....
Iowa, exc. of Belle Plaine	1726	29	2862	13738	1410	76	....	2	.....	31	1	230	10	209	12778	7	9100	804	1149	....	.....
Jackson	913	292	4389	9164	500	12	....	.....	.....	479	98	246	6	17	9084	.....	....	.....	992	3589	8
Kane	....	160	10535	950	505	3	....	.....	.....	....	....	....	.....	....	9016	.....	....	.....	1296	2225	40
Leroy, exc. of Blairstown	633	103	3200	4835	1033	10	3	.....	.....	66	16	323	59	....	13051	1	1200	.....	919	4020	20
Monroe	198	164	9270	808	358	.....	....	.....	.....	4	1	59	18	40	8827	.....	....	.....	1018	3205	.....
Polk	3662	80	326	1714	588	.....	....	.....	.....	69	20	373	8	12	16635	.....	100	.....	1182	2248	.....
St. Clair	229	151	10130	3998	1727	5	....	2	.....	240	35	486	85	26	8586	.....	....	.....	1561	8235	81
Shellsburg, town of	....	....	....	....	....	.....	....	.....	.....	....	....	....	.....	....	....	.....	....	.....	....	....	.....
Taylor, exc. of Vinton	608	38	2545	3029	1036	104	....	10	1	213	8	549	33	50	10781	2	2800	.....	2658	7665	.....
Union	100	149	6786	437	79	1	....	1	.....	78	13	61	11	24	4928	.....	....	.....	591	473	.....
Vinton, city of	....	....	....	120	50	.....	....	.....	.....	....	....	150	20	....	300	.....	....	.....	400	1000	35
Total	18016	3603	122055	60742	14139	228	10	27	3	1942	304	4454	369	2076	211050	21	29750	1025	24865	72992	529

BLACK HAWK COUNTY.

Barclay	171	78	3175	812	408	.....	....	.....	....	1902	291	119	9	52	5171	.....	....	.....	819	381	.....
Bennington	212	103	1925	673	122	.....	....	.....	....	40	1	190	2	1387	5829	.....	....	.....	689	771	.....
Big Creek, exc. of La Porte	902	130	1025	2020	1426	17	....	.....	....	157	103	495	45	237	13472	.....	....	.....	458	1735	12
Black Hawk	672	108	4120	2348	922	7	....	.....	....	505	105	532	81	119	10308	.....	....	.....	1291	1856	.....
Cedar	667	31	570	353	374	.....	....	.....	....	.....	....	44	4	....	5825	.....	....	.....	510	1520	1

BLACK HAWK COUNTY.—Continued.

NAMES OF TOWNSHIPS, TOWNS, AND CITIES.	Acres of natural timber.	Acres of planted timber.	Rods of hedge.	APPLES.		PEARS.		PEACHES		PLUMS.		CHERRIES.		Number of other fruit trees in bearing.	Number of fruit trees not in bearing.	GRAPES IN VINEYARD.			GRAPES NOT IN VINEYARD.		
				Number of trees in bearing.	Bushels gathered in 1874.	Number of trees in bearing.	Bushels gathered in 1874.	Number of trees in bearing.	Bushels gathered in 1874.	Number of trees in bearing.	Bushels gathered in 1874.	Number of trees in bearing.	Bushels gathered in 1874.			Number of acres.	Pounds of grapes gathered.	Gallons of wine made.	Number of vines.	Pounds of grapes gathered.	Gallons of wine made.
Cedar Falls, exc. of city	1302	203	120	1239	819									13	8360				1239	6296	5
Cedar Falls, city of	14	41	16	1365	896	9	6			235	112	226	124	201	119180	3	2000	100	7439	56547	60
Eagle		159	720	61	20																
East Waterloo, exc. Waterloo	573	141	388	2151	407	4				1474	177	204	15	169	11765				637	875	
Fox	235	119	278	926	329		1			34	8	245	23	1070	5156	1	10		1069	1806	
La Porte, town of																					
Lester	1724	30	210	634	440	1		2		257	149	74	6	37	3067				383	1133	2
Lincoln	35	190	3230	666	239	5				66	7	113	9		12321				601	200	
Mt. Vernon	756	103	1417	483	270					1344	238	116	10		7472				193	660	
Orange	229	189	3649	3649	807	20	2		53	202	37	910	46	857	14013				2052	587	204
Poyner	1358	98	1260	1368	555	4	2			195	58	323	9	1228	8338		525		2905	834	
Spring Creek	3356	30	520	2316	1043					2		199	4		4581				858	725	
Union	1244	12	50	43	58														12		
Washington	1420	25	315	501	241					19	1	47		80	3296				295	728	
Waterloo, exc. of city	964	22	263	1668	345	8	3			92	26	99	12		10864	5	5850		1308	3250	
Waterloo, city of																			1300	2700	
Total	15834	1812	23251	23276	9721	75	14	2	53	6524	1313	3936	399	5450	249028	9	8385	100	24358	82804	284

BOONE COUNTY.

NAMES OF TOWNSHIPS, TOWNS, AND CITIES.	Acres of natural timber.	Acres of planted timber.	Rods of hedge.	Apples: Number of trees in bearing.	Apples: Bushels gathered in 1874.	Pears: Number of trees in bearing.	Pears: Bushels gathered in 1874.	Peaches: Number of trees in bearing.	Peaches: Bushels gathered in 1874.	Plums: Number of trees in bearing.	Plums: Bushels gathered in 1874.	Cherries: Number of trees in bearing.	Cherries: Bushels gathered in 1874.	Number of other fruit trees in bearing.	Number of fruit trees not in bearing.	Grapes in vineyard: Number of acres.	Grapes in vineyard: Pounds of grapes gathered.	Grapes in vineyard: Gallons of wine made.	Grapes not in vineyard: Number of vines.	Grapes not in vineyard: Pounds of grapes gathered.	Grapes not in vineyard: Gallons of wine made.
Amaqua	264	43	3130																341	100	
Beaver	15	27		62	10										2710				83		
Boone, city of																					
Boonsboro, town of	8		10	1053	606	44	8			433	111	504	120	212	3353		500	7	2751	12073	11
Cass	2152	15	1340	1286	307					14		87			4158				561	1300	

Colfax	429	34	2070	208	111	...	...	...	...	20	10	50	3	...	5735	...	...	...	204	50	...
Des Moines, exc. of Boone and Boonsboro	3291	28	1621	2928	995	16	1	...	...	477	93	354	90	432	13051	7	3150	...	3937	10513	60
Dodge	2569	35	3506	1014	414	2	...	...	...	28	5	81	20	22	5927	...	...	...	2204	3516	97
Douglas	3610	8	725	895	728	...	...	...	...	1	...	97	16	48	2383	...	3000	...	784	3010	...
Garden	97	8	1180	354	174	2	1	...	...	97	21	68	4	49	5760	...	...	...	728	2275	...
Grant	36	9	3990	2	10	...	...	...	...	...	...	...	...	...	1910	...	...	...	111	130	...
Harrison	486	23	635	564	8	...	...	...	...	27	6	84	1	279	2786	...	...	...	401	59	20
Jackson	280	11	2430	87	70	...	...	...	...	...	...	2	...	...	35	...	...	...	339	700	...
Marcy	2125	30	1534	809	68	7	2	...	...	109	17	50	5	20	6328	...	...	...	1454	2010	...
Peoples	528	58	4629	883	107	...	...	...	...	6	1	49	3	17	9076	...	...	...	736	530	...
Pilot Mound	705	7	580	200	155	...	...	...	...	...	...	...	...	...	700	...	...	...	40	200	...
Union	919	28	3185	588	117	2	...	...	...	20	1	32	3	...	6041	...	...	...	1007	620	...
Worth	3775	6	460	2533	317	11	...	...	...	3	...	124	18	12	5595	...	...	...	2747	8870	...
Yell	2261	10	1087	318	79	...	...	...	...	28	...	50	...	160	3517	...	...	...	951	715	...
Total	27550	380	32112	13784	3876	84	12	...	...	1263	265	1632	283	1251	78965	7	6650	7	19379	46671	188

BREMER COUNTY.

Dayton	702	...	...	23	1	...	...	...	...	1	...	11	...	...	...	...	...	...	4	25	...
Douglas	1023	34	3239	193	34	...	...	...	...	20	5	28	2	...	2767	...	...	...	36	10	...
Franklin	1634	2	140	107	34	...	...	...	...	60	100	...	...	30	2455	...	...	...	176	151	2
Frederika	1211	3	194	213	74	...	...	...	...	...	...	...	...	...	2273	...	...	...	154	290	...
Fremont	2014	16	845	598	83	...	...	15	2	43	11	146	16	...	4744	...	...	...	386	52	8
Jackson	2220	85	...	753	287	...	...	...	...	10	...	75	1	36	8642	1	3657	19	1639	2309	2
Jefferson	2140	2	...	938	590	...	...	...	...	13	3	42	2	...	3161	...	...	...	304	785	...
La Fayette	1664	35	1174	482	135	...	...	...	...	...	...	41	1	72	5760	...	...	...	932	786	...
Leroy	502	1	...	...	...	...	...	...	...	...	...	...	...	...	...	...	...	...	...	...	...
Maxfield	1393	7	4954	583	76	25	...	1	...	76	5	128	2	...	3366	...	...	...	459	97	7
Polk	3299	14	275	447	195	...	...	...	...	...	...	103	6	...	4465	...	...	...	465	570	...
Sumner	105	75	3160	383	123	...	...	...	...	...	...	...	...	100	9345	...	...	...	...	...	...
Warren	1152	39	1928	382	163	1	...	...	...	...	...	24	3	...	5043	...	...	...	568	596	...
Washington, exc. of Waverly	1810	56	190	697	384	...	...	...	...	6	...	57	6	57	7281	1	460	42	1328	1173	85
Waverly, city of	221	10	425	1355	52	...	...	...	...	2	...	51	5	406	530	3	8500	66	1130	895	...
Total	21090	379	16521	7154	2231	26	...	16	2	231	124	706	44	701	59832	5	12617	127	7580	7739	104

BUCHANAN COUNTY.

Buffalo	1240	65	3123	467	230	...	...	...	...	...	...	37	6	...	2508	...	...	...	9	42	...
Byron	992	48	10710	820	418	3	...	1	5	25	25	82	10	80	7498	...	...	...	548	2510	8
Cono	117	16	326	411	166	...	...	...	...	...	...	15	...	13	3201	...	...	...	...	...	...
Fairbank	2311	3	1668	996	438	...	...	...	...	...	...	16	3	...	...	...	...	...	22	120	...

BUCHANAN COUNTY.—Continued.

Names of townships, towns, and cities.	Acres of natural timber.	Acres of planted timber.	Rods of hedge.	Apples. Number of trees in bearing.	Apples. Bushels gathered in 1874.	Pears. Number of trees in bearing.	Pears. Bushels gathered in 1874.	Peaches. Number of trees in bearing.	Peaches. Bushels gathered in 1874.	Plums. Number of trees in bearing.	Plums. Bushels gathered in 1874.	Cherries. Number of trees in bearing.	Cherries. Bushels gathered in 1874.	Number of other fruit trees in bearing.	Number of fruit trees not in bearing.	Grapes in vineyard. Number of acres.	Grapes in vineyard. Pounds of grapes gathered.	Grapes in vineyard. Gallons of wine made.	Grapes not in vineyard. Number of vines.	Grapes not in vineyard. Pounds of grapes gathered.	Grapes not in vineyard. Gallons of wine made.
Fremont	5	23	6472	750	380					177	50	84	6	247	2452				188	205	10
Hazelton	2475	10	431	35	37							6	1	464	2906				141	175	
Homer	220	30		249	134									249	5967						
Independence, city of																					
Jefferson	2021	16	850	2130	1168			1		5		51		13	7366				429	1665	2
Liberty	2914	5	1318	3403	1171					4	1	80	2	60	5425				621	2604	8
Madison	533	80	2740	1290	211					3		89	9	13	2796				94	55	
Middlefield	681	22	1698	1223	514					78	14	34	3	240	8323				416	745	
Newton	726	4	1527	1967	762	1				8		123	2	13	7488				477	1102	
Perry	2465	58	3092	2349	391	90				749	163	533	52	576	9495				1626	3650	12
Sumner	597	18	595	1274	570										4314						
Washington, ex. Independence	2879	23	630	2033	604	5				48	3	499	10	157	6005				1481	365	
Westburg	583	27	6160	810	362										4463				357	702	
Total	20759	448	41350	20207	7556	99		2	5	1097	256	1649	104	2125	80107				6409	13740	40

BUENA VISTA COUNTY.

Names of townships, towns, and cities.	Acres of natural timber.	Acres of planted timber.	Rods of hedge.	Apples. Number of trees in bearing.	Apples. Bushels gathered in 1874.	Pears. Number of trees in bearing.	Pears. Bushels gathered in 1874.	Peaches. Number of trees in bearing.	Peaches. Bushels gathered in 1874.	Plums. Number of trees in bearing.	Plums. Bushels gathered in 1874.	Cherries. Number of trees in bearing.	Cherries. Bushels gathered in 1874.	Number of other fruit trees in bearing.	Number of fruit trees not in bearing.	Grapes in vineyard. Number of acres.	Grapes in vineyard. Pounds of grapes gathered.	Grapes in vineyard. Gallons of wine made.	Grapes not in vineyard. Number of vines.	Grapes not in vineyard. Pounds of grapes gathered.	Grapes not in vineyard. Gallons of wine made.
Barnes	543	34	100							13	8				1150						
Brookes	187	15	280																		
Coon		54	3365																		
Elk		85	2837							30					2002				248	5	
Fairfield		12	610												154				39		
Grant		19	392									3			50				18		
Lee	117	67	440	16	5									62	799				22	3	
Lincoln		8	520												127						
Maple Valley		30	1905	30	1					35	12				449				139	100	
Newell		90	3615							54	1			200	1650				92		

Nokomis	....	93	3920	....	....	....	....	.....	....	49	9	....	.....	....	1183	.....	....	.....	181	....	.....
Poland	....	34	755	....	....	....	....	.....	....	.....	....	....	.....	2	397	.....	....	.....	....	....	.....
Providence	....	22	2300	....	....	....	....	.....	....	.....	....	....	.....	....	433	.....	....	.....	19	....	.....
Scott	....	22	923	....	....	....	....	.....	....	.....	....	....	.....	....	354	.....	....	.....	169	....	.....
Storm Lake, exc. of town	....	57	1930	....	....	....	....	.....	....	13	1	6	.....	....	1782	.....	....	.....	322	....	.....
Storm Lake, town of	....	....	....	20	....	1	....	.....	....	.....	....	43	.....	13	342	.....	....	.....	79	....	.....
Total	847	642	23892	66	6	1	....	.....	....	194	31	52	.....	277	10872	.....	....	.....	1328	108	.....

BUTLER COUNTY.

Albion	378	72	2600	653	270	.....	....	.....	....	.....	....	10	.....	....	8297	.....	....	.....	353	1090	.....
Beaver	1985	55	1488	582	251	.....	....	.....	....	76	60	350	33	397	5542	.....	....	.....	911	1172	.....
Bennezett	126	98	4640	79	....	.....	....	.....	....	.....	....	24	.....	....	2616	.....	....	.....	52	....	.....
Butler, exc. of Clarksville	1969	97	3034	1334	493	.....	....	.....	....	20	....	202	2	....	5872	.....	....	.....	354	815	.....
Clarksville, town of	....	....	....	3	....	.....	....	.....	....	.....	....	12	.....	....	35	.....	....	.....	6	3	.....
Cold Water	799	35	2089	363	107	1	3	.....	....	.....	6	3	4	....	105747	5	....	.....	....	....	.....
Dayton	1141	61	1028	339	40	.....	....	.....	....	59	....	53	1	....	2342	.....	....	.....	252	243	.....
Fremont	557	940	1707	80	21	7	....	.....	....	357	54	53	2	146	5318	.....	....	.....	296	427	.....
Jackson	510	81	547	150	19	.....	....	.....	....	.....	....	....	6	....	....	.....	....	.....	....	....	.....
Jefferson	1446	689	241	475	160	.....	....	.....	....	118	15	44	5	33	5800	.....	....	.....	498	1350	2
Madison	372	21	160	40	15	.....	....	.....	....	.....	....	4	.....	....	1823	.....	....	.....	133	40	.....
Monroe	130	67	1240	179	120	4	....	.....	....	352	94	32	6	....	....	.....	....	.....	145	116	.....
Pittsford	1186	54	3851	263	64	.....	....	.....	....	318	61	58	3	223	4712	1	100	.....	901	125	.....
Ripley	450	31	1340	....	....	.....	....	.....	....	.....	....	....	.....	....	....	.....	....	.....	....	....	.....
Shell Rock	1255	1144	1090	485	270	.....	....	.....	....	.....	....	248	4	219	10048	.....	....	.....	459	1050	.....
Washington	127	25	1940	56	7	.....	....	.....	....	157	38	21	2	6	3091	.....	....	.....	146	30	.....
West Point	413	26	2719	96	24	.....	....	.....	....	411	70	....	.....	16	2933	.....	....	.....	189	200	.....
Total	12844	3496	29714	5177	1861	12	3	.....	....	1868	398	1120	62	1040	164176	6	100	.....	4695	6761	2

CALHOUN COUNTY.

Butler	....	56	2065	204	12	.....	....	.....	....	7	3	....	.....	....	2380	.....	....	.....	....	....	.....
Calhoun	461	126	1000	....	....	.....	....	.....	....	.....	....	....	74	....	3554	.....	140	.....	21	51	.....
Center	....	10	1480	....	....	.....	....	.....	....	.....	....	....	.....	....	....	.....	....	.....	....	....	.....
Greenfield	....	44	1720	6	....	.....	....	.....	....	6	....	....	5	....	269	.....	....	.....	19	....	.....
Jackson	829	89	4020	95	....	.....	....	.....	....	.....	....	....	267	....	5955	.....	60	.....	388	172	.....
Lincoln	....	94	8980	5	1	.....	....	.....	....	149	9	....	76	....	3797	.....	....	.....	92	95	2
Sherman	....	76	3285	570	....	.....	....	.....	....	125	10	....	.....	....	1267	.....	....	.....	34	....	.....
Williams	....	23	1150	....	....	.....	....	.....	....	.....	....	....	.....	....	....	.....	....	.....	....	....	.....
Total	1290	520	23700	880	13	.....	....	.....	....	287	22	....	422	....	17222	.....	200	.....	554	318	2

CARROLL COUNTY.

NAMES OF TOWNSHIPS, TOWNS, AND CITIES.	Acres of natural timber.	Acres of planted timber.	Rods of hedge.	APPLES. Number of trees in bearing.	APPLES. Bushels gathered in 1874.	PEARS. Number of trees in bearing.	PEARS. Bushels gathered in 1874.	PEACHES. Number of trees in bearing.	PEACHES. Bushels gathered in 1874.	PLUMS. Number of trees in bearing.	PLUMS. Bushels gathered in 1874.	CHERRIES. Number of trees in bearing.	CHERRIES. Bushels gathered in 1874.	Number of other fruit trees in bearing.	Number of fruit trees not in bearing.	GRAPES IN VINEYARD. Number of acres.	GRAPES IN VINEYARD. Pounds of grapes gathered.	GRAPES IN VINEYARD. Gallons of wine made.	GRAPES NOT IN VINEYARD. Number of vines.	GRAPES NOT IN VINEYARD. Pounds of grapes gathered.	GRAPES NOT IN VINEYARD. Gallons of wine made.
Arcadia		53	6191												1094				352		
Carroll, exc. of town	27														2						
Carroll, town of	130	31	700							11		54		56	2182				450	380	
Eden		51	1710								10		24		1005				19		
Glidden		15	360																		
Grant	550	40	200	1220	162					50	13	134	4	30	3000				234		
Jasper	642	29	1613	27	7							6			305				48	60	
Kniest		165	2538	31	1	5				129	17	48	2		3809	3	700		743	40	
Newton	664	34	1320	170	72							24	1	8	1950				393	85	
Pleasant Valley	1000	50	900									4	1						113	195	3
Richland	25	34	395																		
Roselle		56	2510			1						2			1585						
Sheridan	154	74	2190							8		30			3043				195		
Union	717	25	3040		20			12	1			6					300				
Washington		11	1600												627					125	
Wheatland	3	17	520												100						
Total	3912	685	25787	1448	262	6		12	1	198	40	308	32	94	18702	3	1000		2672	760	3

CASS COUNTY.

NAMES OF TOWNSHIPS, TOWNS, AND CITIES.	Acres of natural timber.	Acres of planted timber.	Rods of hedge.	APPLES. Number of trees in bearing.	APPLES. Bushels gathered in 1874.	PEARS. Number of trees in bearing.	PEARS. Bushels gathered in 1874.	PEACHES. Number of trees in bearing.	PEACHES. Bushels gathered in 1874.	PLUMS. Number of trees in bearing.	PLUMS. Bushels gathered in 1874.	CHERRIES. Number of trees in bearing.	CHERRIES. Bushels gathered in 1874.	Number of other fruit trees in bearing.	Number of fruit trees not in bearing.	GRAPES IN VINEYARD. Number of acres.	GRAPES IN VINEYARD. Pounds of grapes gathered.	GRAPES IN VINEYARD. Gallons of wine made.	GRAPES NOT IN VINEYARD. Number of vines.	GRAPES NOT IN VINEYARD. Pounds of grapes gathered.	GRAPES NOT IN VINEYARD. Gallons of wine made.
Atlantic, exc. of town	915	45	4277	58	115					18	20	461	41		8599				2737	5050	88
Atlantic, town of	45	1	160	9		1						30			400			49	50		
Bear Grove	83	54	2349	30	30					22	12	50	1		4237				668	599	
Benton	994	31	1090	207	129			5		3		68	2	9	4503	1			586	388	
Brighton	291	18	1566									1			2992				367		
Cass	889	21	2580	550	424	13	4			51	15	386	64	168	10677	2	3300	120	2395	4945	
Edna	852	14	810	13	3					4		13			650				235		

Franklin	165	52	2710	224	65	3	1			15	4	81	3	136	5044				1164	100	
Grant	165	25	520	25								5		40	6930				394	5	
Lincoln		22	360									6			2685				441		
Massena		31	680												2973				341		
Noble	4	3	5876	14	10																
Pleasant	27	95	7865	79	26							32	12		4300				696	200	16
Pymosa	536	64	1530	234	94					134	8	144	10	3643	4912				2056	3925	2
Union	266	45	1040							29		22			2540				337		
Victoria		4	715												1650				71		
Washington	628	206	910	85	80							58	22		1000				874	325	
Total	5860	731	35038	1528	976	17	5	5		276	59	1359	155	3996	64092	3	3300	169	13412	15537	106

CEDAR COUNTY.

Cass	2958	7	2287	3500	1366					9		291	51	201	3668		200		415	2111	
Center, exc. of Tipton	7017	44	20308	19088	4877	69	13	20	12	34	3	1324	246	180	9023	1	8000		4692	23870	11
Clarence, town of				575	35	2						196	50	5	258				641	4630	
Dayton, exc. of Clarence	379	188	20680	1243	813					3		234	25	20	8695				1351	5450	
Durant, town of				123	30	1		18	4	1	2	160	43		115		2100		473	4610	40
Fairfield	416	95	16731	2190	538	17		1		35	7	471	153	69	9824				967	8547	14
Farmington, exc. of Durant	701	105	21955	5651	1739	4	2			22	2	221	54	46	4099				1299	6140	12
Fremont	380	92	14768	4168	792	45	8			122	53	506	65	66	9361		500		3079	16818	77
Gower	1738	84	4493	4946	3519	6		16	1	27	3	666	87	2	6299	2	7000	12	1003	6415	5
Inland	1081	79	25543	1427	897	7	1	4		62	17	172	29	114	5142		10		801	6835	22
Iowa	3589	44	14111	5342	2636	63	2	2		14	68	745	126	43	6057		4000	2	2232	16443	323
Linn	2942	8	4728	817	224							192	38	10	4100				1205	8687	
Louden, town of				93	23	30	1			51	9	236	18	2	641				336	1707	20
Massillon	831	48	9690	1521	485	11		1		9	2	566	119	111	5773	3	6		958	3322	17
Mechanicsville, town of																					
Pioneer, exc. of Mechanicsville	4293	8	5655	1970	456	5	1			64	15	880	231	367	4545	4	66200	458	2256	7322	
Red Oak	1629	8	2137	3409	817	35	7			22	4	349	49	298	3378		3000	30	1125	7822	18
Rochester	3147		4355	2818	1320	31	9	49	8	4		596	149	68	1236		50		626	2790	4
Springdale	1305	108	20748	7405	2729	48	4	7	2	75	4	1193	224	151	14154	1	6950		3892	22585	5
Springfield, exc. of Louden	1786	81	14403	2584	744	15		2	35	191	92	594	181	570	5178		4000	100	1001	7912	49
Sugar Creek	1908	11	8397	4430	1666	7	1	24	4	21		711	77		2879				1049	10295	
Tipton, town of				853	350	88	9	10	1	235	79	770	376	169	99				996	11565	60
Total	36100	1010	210989	74335	25056	484	58	154	67	1001	361	11023	2367	2492	104524	14	102016	602	29397	185876	677

CERRO GORDO COUNTY.

Clear Lake, exc. of town	552	24	2292	68	14					78	10	5	2		148				81	143	
Clear Lake, town of																					

CERRO GORDO COUNTY.—Continued.

Names of townships, towns, and cities.	Acres of natural timber.	Acres of planted timber.	Rods of hedge.	Apples. Number of trees in bearing.	Apples. Bushels gathered in 1874.	Pears. Number of trees in bearing.	Pears. Bushels gathered in 1874.	Peaches. Number of trees in bearing.	Peaches. Bushels gathered in 1874.	Plums. Number of trees in bearing.	Plums. Bushels gathered in 1874.	Cherries. Number of trees in bearing.	Cherries. Bushels gathered in 1874.	Number of other fruit trees in bearing.	Number of fruit trees not in bearing.	Grapes in vineyard. Number of acres.	Grapes in vineyard. Pounds of grapes gathered.	Grapes in vineyard. Gallons of wine made.	Grapes not in vineyard. Number of vines.	Grapes not in vineyard. Pounds of grapes gathered.	Grapes not in vineyard. Gallons of wine made.
Daugherty		19	680	8	1										1300						
Falls	798	46	161	66	35	1	1					2	2		4687						
Geneseo	371	22	1160																		
Grant	192	11	220	43	4					15	2	1		9					30	10	
Lake	87	36	3612	25	4										212				6		
Lime Creek	1388	63	2072	117	4					1		27		25	5166				343	6	
Lincoln	841	38	1713	57	11					20	15				800				121	6	
Mason, exc. of Mason City	261	32	2989	113	11										3585				310	200	
Mason City, town of																					
Owen		6	1046	52	12							7		3	698				6		
Portland	396	89	5285	226	29					12	5				5245				399	170	
Total	4886	386	21230	775	125	1	1			126	32	42	4	37	21839				1296	535	

CHEROKEE COUNTY.

Names of townships, towns, and cities.	Acres of natural timber.	Acres of planted timber.	Rods of hedge.	Apples. Number of trees in bearing.	Apples. Bushels gathered in 1874.	Pears. Number of trees in bearing.	Pears. Bushels gathered in 1874.	Peaches. Number of trees in bearing.	Peaches. Bushels gathered in 1874.	Plums. Number of trees in bearing.	Plums. Bushels gathered in 1874.	Cherries. Number of trees in bearing.	Cherries. Bushels gathered in 1874.	Number of other fruit trees in bearing.	Number of fruit trees not in bearing.	Grapes in vineyard. Number of acres.	Grapes in vineyard. Pounds of grapes gathered.	Grapes in vineyard. Gallons of wine made.	Grapes not in vineyard. Number of vines.	Grapes not in vineyard. Pounds of grapes gathered.	Grapes not in vineyard. Gallons of wine made.
Afton	142	73	6075	61	2							6			3274				453		
Amherst		30	730							8	3	3			1529				39	5	
Cedar	71	40	3580																		
Cherokee, exc. of town	232	59	1560											4	2204				120		
Cherokee, town of																					
Diamond		25	390												595						
Liberty		50													578						
Marcus		3													224						
Pilot	345	124	2336							60	2		6	19	2224				67	10	1
Pitcher															549						
Sheridan	4	71	1797																		
Silver	3	36	540																		

Spring	45	14	11	2																	
Tilden		26	130												18						
Willow	243	19	1535	7											573						
Total	1085	570	19684	70	2					68	5	9	6	23	11768				679	15	1

CHICKASAW COUNTY.

Bradford, exc. of Nashua	2039	22	675	596	52					1	2				5707		400		373	670	26
Chickasaw	2631	1	220	252	56							5		47	2824				150	514	2
Dayton	304	2	200	100	12										1377						
Deerfield	1634	12	1236	79	17					6		17	1	6	2354				143	255	
Dresden	1241	14	40	98	19									17	3480	9			22	4	
Fredericksburgh	300	128		319	67					6		37	1		5553				38	160	
Jacksonville	1658	89	35	239	44					1		55	3	21	2958				155	4	
Nashua, town of																					
New Hampton, exc. of town	737	15		194	67							3			968				70	210	
New Hampton, town of																					
Richland	1008	46	624	404	71					106	91		8	10	2084			2			
Stapleton	1938	72	1684	813	154					22	3	46	28	3					24		
Utica	2109	52	40	301	60	2						20			3329				232	953	
Washington	1775	30	205	162	47							15	5	10	372				1	20	
Total	17374	483	4959	3557	666	2				142	96	198	46	114	31006	9	400	2	1208	2790	28

CLARKE COUNTY.

Doyle, exc. of Hopeville	1891	38	4265	1352	2400	6		192		1	22	7638	59	3172	588				1040	1498	
Franklin	2940	9	4135	1780	1132					53	5	256	37		4147		100		1045	2755	3
Fremont	1540		2555	1479	872	4		63	11	8		109	19		4696	75	50		1721	7885	6
Green Bay	2687	8	5177	1243	895	7	1	6		8		271	18	60	7334				2333	2980	5
Hopeville, town of	556	4	1132	554	284	6	6	24	5	2		305	66		1317				406	2298	25
Jackson	453	9	5444	1797	665	4	1			5		417	34	66	11095				1270	1341	
Knox	1825	45	6110	1978	2058	4		9		125	11	422	18	9	8906	1	75		1942	1829	
Liberty	1711	7	6606	1204	611	7		19		2		228	6	10	5541	1	3650		867	1408	
Madison	1233	14	11178	789	244	4	2	10	2	200	20	1	1		6027		600	40	2008	2557	
Osceola, exc. of town	1110	10	5000	470	364	3		4	25	167	39	192	17	24	16191				1014	2015	
Osceola, town of	910	10	1861	1883	466	77	11	31	3	243	42	1160	251	92	9210	2	121000		4642	10284	79
Troy	482	11	10571	89	20										4048				249		
Ward	2198	8	7151	529	233	9	2	8		5	1	95	8	9	5065				1056	2338	
Washington	2067	18	7455	1876	1711	8	4			12		160	15	54	3322				1781	5937	
Total	21573	191	78640	17023	11955	139	27	366	46	831	140	11254	549	3496	87487	79	125475	40	21374	45125	118

CLAY COUNTY.

NAMES OF TOWNSHIPS, TOWNS, AND CITIES.	Acres of natural timber.	Acres of planted timber.	Rods of hedge.	APPLES. Number of trees in bearing.	APPLES. Bushels gathered in 1874.	PEARS. Number of trees in bearing.	PEARS. Bushels gathered in 1874.	PEACHES Number of trees in bearing.	PEACHES Bushels gathered in 1874.	PLUMS. Number of trees in bearing.	PLUMS. Bushels gathered in 1874.	CHERRIES. Number of trees in bearing.	CHERRIES. Bushels gathered in 1874.	Number of other fruit trees in bearing.	Number of fruit trees not in bearing.	GRAPES IN VINEYARD. Number of acres.	GRAPES IN VINEYARD. Pounds of grapes gathered.	GRAPES IN VINEYARD. Gallons of wine made.	GRAPES NOT IN VINEYARD. Number of vines.	GRAPES NOT IN VINEYARD. Pounds of grapes gathered.	GRAPES NOT IN VINEYARD. Gallons of wine made.
Bridgewater		59	1247							150	10				1288				44		
Clay	255	229	2160	34	7										2055				45		
Douglas	312	91	684	5	1					470	26	25			505				11		
Gillett's Grove	107	80	2008					6	1			21		13	1552				73		
Herdland	52	40	960							262	10				108						
Lincoln		74	5120									10				1			168		
Riverton		60	1460																		
Spencer	3	178	2800											3	2133				262		
Summit		32	540											50	585				90		
Total	729	843	16979	39	8			6	1	882	46	56		66	8226	1			693		

CLAYTON COUNTY.

NAMES OF TOWNSHIPS, TOWNS, AND CITIES.	Acres of natural timber.	Acres of planted timber.	Rods of hedge.	APPLES. Number of trees in bearing.	APPLES. Bushels gathered in 1874.	PEARS. Number of trees in bearing.	PEARS. Bushels gathered in 1874.	PEACHES Number of trees in bearing.	PEACHES Bushels gathered in 1874.	PLUMS. Number of trees in bearing.	PLUMS. Bushels gathered in 1874.	CHERRIES. Number of trees in bearing.	CHERRIES. Bushels gathered in 1874.	Number of other fruit trees in bearing.	Number of fruit trees not in bearing.	GRAPES IN VINEYARD. Number of acres.	GRAPES IN VINEYARD. Pounds of grapes gathered.	GRAPES IN VINEYARD. Gallons of wine made.	GRAPES NOT IN VINEYARD. Number of vines.	GRAPES NOT IN VINEYARD. Pounds of grapes gathered.	GRAPES NOT IN VINEYARD. Gallons of wine made.
Boardman	1857	2	60	730	690	4	3			25	24	36	10		25		600	23	40		15
Buena Vista	2084			330	78	1	1			5	1	6	3	48	284				193	725	
Cass	3323		112	1435	758					18	5	173	18		3555				185	526	1
Clayton	4688			1758	1097	17				23	5	4	1	76	4223	30	100		45	410	20
Cox Creek	5672			730	295	8	1			7		24	3	56	3076				846	1386	47
Elk	4962			1916	1330					181	77	40	4	12	5291				252	746	
Farmersburg	5148			1033	496	4				54	56	24	3						293	734	138
Garnavillo	8229	4		3453	1908	5				67	43	48	11		7130	2	3850	20	728	3973	94
Girard	5588	1		1539	592												54		169	359	3
Grand Meadow	2758	4		2742	820	2						88	71	435	6272				261	707	
Guttenberg, town of	314			185	193	8	1								864	3	7500	520	45	134	2
Highland	2050		180	1102	860							27	3		3809	1	3990	40	259	615	40
Jefferson, exc. of Guttenberg	10035			2365	1298	3	1					55	14	35	4974				100	324	8
Lodomillo	5063	33	500	5524	2313	3				2		239	9	50	4834		20		942	847	

McGregor, town of	......	......	......	......	......	......	......	......	......	......	......	......	......	......	......	......	......	......	......	......	......
Mallory	8771	......	......	3263	2313	......	......	......	......	821	324	178	12	......	6443	......	......	......	215	1186	......
Marion	1657	1	120	887	517	......	......	......	......	66	26	57	1	111	4196	1	225	65	150	263	790
Mendon, exc. of McGregor and North McGregor	5980	......	100	3112	1738	......	......	......	......	129	47	23	6	......	7223	2	6920	46	1112	8193	50
Millville	3642	20	......	742	483	1	......	......	......	59	21	17	2	14	1065	......	......	......	197	770	21
Monona	2732	29	160	2338	1221	......	......	......	......	......	......	......	......	......	22011	......	......	......	1221	12703	68
North McGregor, town of	......	......	......	......	......	......	......	......	......	......	......	......	......	......	......	......	......	......	......	......	......
Read	5845	......	......	1387	519	......	......	......	......	14	4	10	2	33	1531	......	......	......	318	337	13
Sperry	4591	......	......	1547	423	......	......	......	......	2	......	52	......	......	4711	......	......	......	759	772	47
Volga	......	......	......	227	198	......	......	......	......	......	......	8	1	......	......	12	16	2	19	29	......
Wagner	4233	......	......	687	184	......	......	......	......	......	......	12	......	30	1777	......	......	......	......	......	......
Total	99222	94	1232	39032	20324	56	7	......	......	1473	633	1121	174	900	93294	51	23275	716	8349	35739	1357

CLINTON COUNTY.

Berlin	48	23	4888	1777	432	14	1	6	......	318	78	340	26	1	3916	1	775	87	439	1285	95
Bloomfield	167	......	6525	4086	2077	......	......	......	......	508	348	358	168	4850	10569	......	......	80	1232	1460	......
Brookfield	77	102	2293	3097	1805	6	1	......	......	564	448	605	120	......	11587	......	......	......	......	1147	1821
Camanche, exc. of town	854	1	5079	4300	4907	14	3	......	......	6	1	486	91	......	4766	......	......	......	1002	3935	......
Camanche, town of	103	2	40	......	......	......	......	......	......	......	......	......	......	......	720	......	......	......	......	......	......
Center	683	11	12039	2764	1816	1	......	......	......	130	26	409	61	59	4060	......	......	......	535	1464	......
Clinton, exc. of city	266	......	23158	3336	1633	63	7	29	3	30	2	530	114	33	5930	1	12380	......	2295	11021	54
Clinton, city of	......	......	......	......	......	......	......	......	......	......	......	......	......	......	......	......	......	......	......	......	......
Deep River	1452	3	5857	1584	898	6	4	1	......	53	11	195	41	......	4006	......	......	......	332	1730	44
De Witt, exc. of town	3084	16	6356	4829	1727	17	2	11	1	186	102	1395	360	182	7338	2	1159	......	774	3260	3
De Witt, town of	......	1	320	945	759	31	14	3	......	149	60	929	345	21	1672	......	......	1	543	8155	147
Eden	952	19	13392	4685	2083	12	7	2	13	40	34	509	66	435	4644	1	8500	30	963	6210	38
Elk River	3027	24	10265	3628	1561	......	......	......	......	......	......	338	45	......	6227	......	......	......	1103	4660	30
Hampshire	1371	1	5115	6313	1983	7	3	6	1	15	......	417	95	8	2494	1	1000	60	894	2521	160
Liberty	1282	21	1925	723	377	2	1	......	......	......	......	364	78	31	1677	......	......	......	476	3260	20
Lincoln	245	5	3284	4751	2530	1	1	......	......	......	......	85	26	......	4042	......	......	......	982	3585	......
Lyons, exc. of city	1116	8	1427	5264	2352	25	7	1	......	15	2	812	97	260	5499	21	31694	1413	1233	871	40
Lyons, city of	......	......	......	......	......	......	......	......	......	......	......	......	......	......	......	......	......	......	......	......	......
Olive	1688	16	16224	1793	793	30	......	29	21	26	2	301	35	1	5163	......	......	......	1606	4500	218
Orange	1504	24	11233	1496	537	8	1	83	23	65	1	804	97	210	4363	......	800	......	646	4372	2
Sharon	847	57	3005	2823	820	1	......	......	......	90	35	421	48	6	808	......	......	......	2060	8603	250
Spring Rock, exc. of Wheatland	1760	23	5685	1660	435	10	2	......	......	2	......	131	20	......	4892	2	600	4	......	......	......
Washington	676	8	9620	689	211	3	......	......	......	35	3	25	......	......	4299	......	......	......	160	650	15
Waterford	1564	2	1654	965	379	2	......	1	......	71	24	138	44	275	1717	......	......	......	1321	3204	125
Welton	146	54	4410	1205	716	2	......	......	......	9	2	233	31	185	4560	2	520	46	335	1378	......
Wheatland, town of	......	1	62	130	81	7	......	......	......	......	......	6	8	9	100	......	......	......	210	2000	30
Total	22912	422	153906	62843	30912	262	54	172	62	2312	1179	9831	2016	6566	105554	31	57428	1721	19141	79301	3092

CRAWFORD COUNTY.

NAMES OF TOWNSHIPS, TOWNS, AND CITIES.	Acres of natural timber.	Acres of planted timber.	Rods of hedge,	APPLES.		PEARS.		PEACHES		PLUMS.		CHERRIES.		Number of other fruit trees in bearing.	Number of fruit trees not in bearing.	GRAPES IN VINEYARD.			GRAPES NOT IN VINEYARD.		
				Number of trees in bearing.	Bushels gathered in 1874.	Number of trees in bearing.	Bushels gathered in 1874.	Number of trees in bearing.	Bushels gathered in 1874.	Number of trees in bearing.	Bushels gathered in 1874.	Number of trees in bearing.	Bushels gathered in 1874.			Number of acres.	Pounds of grapes gathered.	Gallons of wine made.	Number of vines.	Pounds of grapes gathered.	Gallons of wine made.
Boyer	512	30	264	420	10							40			825						
Charter Oak																					
Denison	572	59	908	42	2			1		206	20	118	22	33	6039	1	300		1056	205	158
East Boyer	277	54	5247	159	50	2				202	100	80	6	62	3183		700		681		
Goodrich	398	16																			
Hanover															1						
Hays		52	3449												1263				258		
Iowa		19	940												329				287		
Jackson		17	520												989						
Milford	1610	57	1600	146	95					105	57	53	11	62	3027		2000	10	495	200	
Morgan	10	3													85				45		
Nishnabotany	3	17	1650																		
Otter Creek	145	15	400	5								5			886				126		
Paradise	56	21	326	10				12	1			5		4	994				269		
Soldier		15	350																		
Stockholm	193	9	760	12						50	2				567				60		
Union	1331	33	1280	278	21	4	1			20		38			2170		200		202	150	
Washington	244	6	561												20		50	2	142		
West Side	25	8	620												1421				290		
Willow		2	1040												230						
Total	5376	433	19915	1072	178	6	1	13	1	583	179	339	39	161	22029	1	3250	12	3911	555	158

DALLAS COUNTY.

NAMES OF TOWNSHIPS, TOWNS, AND CITIES.	Acres of natural timber.	Acres of planted timber.	Rods of hedge,	Apples: Number of trees in bearing.	Apples: Bushels gathered in 1874.	Pears: Number of trees in bearing.	Pears: Bushels gathered in 1874.	Peaches: Number of trees in bearing.	Peaches: Bushels gathered in 1874.	Plums: Number of trees in bearing.	Plums: Bushels gathered in 1874.	Cherries: Number of trees in bearing.	Cherries: Bushels gathered in 1874.	Number of other fruit trees in bearing.	Number of fruit trees not in bearing.	Vineyard: Number of acres.	Vineyard: Pounds of grapes gathered.	Vineyard: Gallons of wine made.	Not in vineyard: Number of vines.	Not in vineyard: Pounds of grapes gathered.	Not in vineyard: Gallons of wine made.
Adams	3412	37		3598	2407			29	4			406	103	20	15191				4757	23990	12
Adel, exc. of town	2328	20	1025	6174	3935	2	2			17	2	45	9		9729	4	11200	100	3396	10635	50
Adel, town of																					

Beaver	389	17	1039	....	....	......	....	......	....	......	....	19	2	....	3216	......	....	......	293	464	....
Boone	1809	15	2385	1576	651	2	2	......	....	4	....	187	35	10	6465	......	....	......	2311	6870	......
Colfax	1166	51	4578	1218	646	......	....	11	3	6	2	144	9	....	15723	......	....	......	2892	8435	......
Dallas	725	27	515	78	57	......	....	......	....	......	....	8	2	....	6883	......	....	......	653	3000	......
Des Moines	2533	17	1781	1501	1213	7	1	......	....	126	24	171	12	8	4104	......	....	......	841	3014	......
Dexter, town of	....	....	....	....	....	......	....	......	....	......	....	....	......	....	....	......	....	......	....	....	......
Grant	133	96	4475	496	94	4	2	......	....	8	1	199	......	....	4372	......	....	......	1047	2828	......
Lincoln	127	49	2945	145	63	......	....	......	....	8	1	17	1	....	7861	......	....	......	627	260	......
Linn	2311	25	9183	3453	3005	2	1	15	3	20	5	169	35	....	15939	......	....	.....	2461	10328	......
Spring Valley	1148	20	1477	353	192	2	5	......	....	20	15	140	17	....	11424	......	....	......	1619	2505	20
Sugar Grove	1126	112	1265	1162	295	......	....	......	....	191	3	113	3	131	8570	3	700	......	978	3581	......
Union, exc. of Dexter	2326	55	2457	1985	1694	5	....	41	1	38	32	189	67	....	11909	......	....	......	2753	6020	......
Vanmeter	3641	57	3384	2429	1451	......	....	......	....	13	2	208	23	26	8657	4	14300	48	2069	6653	54
Walnut	28	115	3045	572	45	......	....	......	....	......	....	112	42	....	9151	......	....	......	2189	5375	......
Washington	1449	29	2035	580	198	......	....	......	....	......	....	78	2	....	5826	......	....	......	1322	1125	......
Total	24651	742	41589	25320	15946	24	13	96	11	451	87	2205	363	195	145020	11	26200	148	30008	95083	136

DAVIS COUNTY.

Bloomfield, exc. of town	4509	8	21461	6655	5085	276	93	1080	412	92	41	2341	672	....	13812	6	40000	1593	3355	17960	......
Bloomfield, town of	....	2	60	710	331	230	72	118	80	60	9	629	240	....	633	......	....	......	3536	7330	......
Drakeville, exc. of town	2046	3	3675	2142	1523	10	2	93	7	4	....	389	48	21	874	......	....	.. ...	430	2645	2
Drakeville, town of	198	....	....	425	264	11	10	47	13	19	9	211	72	2	1216	......	....	......	174	2327	......
Fabius	5738	160	930	2487	2226	21	....	188	84	83	5	438	39	....	7325	1	600	......	1308	1861	......
Fox River	3400	....	2790	2274	1761	38	25	88	34	23	2	297	42	5	4285	......	250	6	394	1327	......
Grove	4979	4	31307	3009	2955	543	8	379	295	129	22	648	115	2	7998	6	13200	455	2272	8672	......
Lick Creek	6229	....	2693	2302	1979	18	7	195	192	93	34	258	58	....	8713	......	....	......	1540	5746	30
Marion	7237	....	650	2346	1592	7	20	25	....	24	....	221	11	15	3500	......	....	......	315	810	......
Perry	6206	....	8206	4039	2833	73	12	391	99	53	6	711	73	....	3622	......	2000	200	944	3848	......
Prairie	1817	....	10130	3898	2168	47	3	171	18	4	....	697	4	27	40	......	....	......	2181	6550	57
Roscoe	1188	....	22084	2338	1782	7	1	387	759	16	2	807	230	....	10083	......	115	......	3038	5399	30
Salt Creek	9946	....	1145	3360	2361	80	9	263	98	58	13	540	75	83	....	......	....	......	732	2931	......
Soap Creek	7199	....	5289	4008	2014	56	46	56	47	1	....	706	199	200	5630	......	200	......	828	10227	......
Union	8264	....	9653	10698	3212	138	12	643	15	265	30	1471	158	....	5614	......	13936	......	5645	....	246
West Grove	6048	5	19352	2763	2466	31	14	232	60	31	2	838	163	75	7525	......	1200	......	921	4992	6
Wyacondah	6768	....	9615	3317	3795	34	8	119	23	20	12	139	37	....	6673	......	....	....	541	2921	......
Total	81772	182	149040	56771	38347	1580	342	4575	1636	975	188	11341	2236	430	87553	13	71501	2254	28154	35546	371

DECATUR COUNTY.

Bloomington	1211	14	3115	230	50	12	1	146	22	......	....	32	......	210	2789	......	50	......	745	50	......
Burrell	2592	6	1214	1087	864	4	....	61	14	7	2	289	19	30	5357	2	360	14	793	695	1

DECATUR COUNTY.—CONTINUED.

NAMES OF TOWNSHIPS, TOWNS, AND CITIES.	Acres of natural timber.	Acres of planted timber.	Rods of hedge.	APPLES. Number of trees in bearing.	APPLES. Bushels gathered in 1874.	PEARS. Number of trees in bearing.	PEARS. Bushels gathered in 1874.	PEACHES. Number of trees in bearing.	PEACHES. Bushels gathered in 1874.	PLUMS. Number of trees in bearing.	PLUMS. Bushels gathered in 1874.	CHERRIES. Number of trees in bearing.	CHERRIES. Bushels gathered in 1874.	Number of other fruit trees in bearing.	Number of fruit trees not in bearing.	GRAPES IN VINEYARD. Number of acres.	GRAPES IN VINEYARD. Pounds of grapes gathered.	GRAPES IN VINEYARD. Gallons of wine made.	GRAPES NOT IN VINEYARD. Number of vines.	GRAPES NOT IN VINEYARD. Pounds of grapes gathered.	GRAPES NOT IN VINEYARD. Gallons of wine made.
Center, exc. of Leon	3240		7546	3876	2305	48	8	20	1			684	264	10	11154	3	8000	93	2095	10560	470
Decatur	3861	30	3053	3628	3145	25		47	2	45	18	782	59	25	10247		6950	20	1422	6770	24
Eden	4920		2470	3492	1697	11	1	369	39	109	24	784	95	20	8267	6	8240	60	698	1236	30
Fayette	647	49	9350	360	182	1		86	12	3		218	12		4516				982	1313	10
Franklin	950	29	5893	1216	1036	1				124	14	587	49	23	8299				1232	1896	
Garden Grove	2609	14	15585	4643	1730	431	28	54		66	151	1578	122	47	15874	5	400	32	1399	1792	
Grand River	1081	49	245	404	168			24	2	2		54	5		3403		250				
Hamilton	2555		4	1168	462	2	7	178	95	6	2	450	41		5558		250		743	275	
High Point	1889	6	5455	3171	1074	14	2	160	18	33	1	591	43	26	5895				471	2747	
Leon, town of				304	45	46	4	78	9	65	1	808	172	58	1319				1189	3765	5
Long Creek	3103	5	6599	1311	1278	2	1			15	27	81	24		4642				799	1496	180
Morgan	2900		583	842	460	3		159	39	6		308	21	41	5300	1	540		325	265	
New Buda	1914	3	1642	876	1877	1	5	25	94	5	32	174	79	83	545				466	279	9
Richland	2828	4	2326	615	170			84	5	330	33	275	17	102	4959		500		445	430	
Woodland	5741		287	2149	1170	9	4	230	57	19	3	414	52		7668		500	13	613	637	
Total	43041	200	75367	29372	17713	610	61	1721	409	835	311	8109	1074	675	105792	17	26040	232	14417	34196	729

DELAWARE COUNTY.

NAMES OF TOWNSHIPS, TOWNS, AND CITIES.	Acres of natural timber.	Acres of planted timber.	Rods of hedge.	APPLES. Number of trees in bearing.	APPLES. Bushels gathered in 1874.	PEARS. Number of trees in bearing.	PEARS. Bushels gathered in 1874.	PEACHES. Number of trees in bearing.	PEACHES. Bushels gathered in 1874.	PLUMS. Number of trees in bearing.	PLUMS. Bushels gathered in 1874.	CHERRIES. Number of trees in bearing.	CHERRIES. Bushels gathered in 1874.	Number of other fruit trees in bearing.	Number of fruit trees not in bearing.	GRAPES IN VINEYARD. Number of acres.	GRAPES IN VINEYARD. Pounds of grapes gathered.	GRAPES IN VINEYARD. Gallons of wine made.	GRAPES NOT IN VINEYARD. Number of vines.	GRAPES NOT IN VINEYARD. Pounds of grapes gathered.	GRAPES NOT IN VINEYARD. Gallons of wine made.
Adams	1442	13	3150	1064	348					312	123	142	10	30	4165				317	979	
Bremer	674			946	182	91		1				54		20	1712		10				
Coffin's Grove	1549	44	2525	1166	468	5				52	10	103		114	4487	2	6000	500	1079	1550	60
Colony	6982	50		2889	1423	2				9	1	40	2	39	4732	2	1250		353	1752	210
Delaware, exc. of Manchester	2447	39	223	1725	958							26	3	290	5429				685	251	
Delhi	4917	13	100	8532	1529	13	11	2		16	2	311	43	250	3016	4	4000	250	1083	1593	17
Elk	8268			2077	881														49	320	
Hazel Green	38	232	3528	645	295					4	1	41	1		3971				479		

Honey Creek	2483	52	985	5026	1998	8		4		70	23	375	25	85	12940	1	500		852	1594	12
Hopkinton, town of					9		2										150	30	300		
Manchester, town of	2185	10	320	1217	375	1				32	6	77		3	3277				1104	1980	4
Milo	1593	13	625	1389	388	10	1	5		18	4	108	9	58	5306	2	4100		672	653	
North Fork	3243	1		784	292							153	3	21	3555				432	377	
Oneida	889	136	3812	4199	1322							109	6	63	3711				504	3380	
Prairie	59	9	1051	1491	186	2				58	6	195	17	374	6680				547		150
Richland	3103	9		691	346										2423				60	93	11
South Fork, exc. of Hopkinton	3539	1	724	1314	444					4	5	53	16	249	1424			6	738	1655	2
Union	6770	27	448	1669	996					17		52		76	3458	1	300		681	352	3
Total	45181	652	17491	36824	12440	132	14	12		592	181	1839	135	1672	70286	12	16310	786	9935	16529	469

DES MOINES COUNTY.

Augusta	2428		1686	5147	4016	45	55	215	112	116	17	931	300	3	2632				5623	16309	618
Benton	7204		4502	7033	6850	44	41	353	157	8	2	1316	396	881	6416	3401	17540	1581	2824	8889	118
Burlington, exc. of city	4626		5544	17825	26764	430	325	1487	1256	51	2	2171	1373	60	18463	140	345400	25152	13484	32815	1786
Burlington, city of																					
Danville	1356	17	16844	15080	17640	249	121	950	418	365	88	3874	1049	24	10419	1	5500	150	3353	29690	8
Flint River	5931	6	4644	12431	11511	321	143	611	469	14	3	2521	660	57	8625	15	36725	146	4317	8098	231
Franklin	3956		9633	7836	8001	50	40	119	53	20	5	406	288	60	859	1	3500	80	1746	5034	934
Huron	4865	8	6125	9982	8395	154	17	337	252	18	1	1148	328	280	6007				3190	15261	
Jackson	751		160	335	63	2		10	4			136	35		258				24		
Pleasant Grove	8464		7156	7017	3860	51	6	908	224	104	14	1013	157	9	6632				2076	13400	
Union	5011	13	8810	24650	28587	99	100	687	380	109	13	3408	1519		13443	52	405900	14968	10006	51720	775
Washington	130	10	29145	6931	2668	30	9	564	63	85	32	1182	88	10	7886				764	5037	
Yellow Springs	2254	6	32584	18290	11641	86	33	760	156	7		3137	774	692	7956	836	475		2207	15872	
Total	46976	60	126833	132557	129996	1561	890	7001	3545	897	177	21243	6967	2076	89596	4446	815040	42077	49614	202125	4470

DICKINSON COUNTY.

Center Grove	680	83	2280	13										3	1031				126	20	
Diamond Lake		7	120																		
Excelsior		56	1420							3					949				63		
Lakeville	54	32	700												260				134		
Lloyd	64	17	160							5				12	25				220	20	
Milford		24	1163												53						
Okoboji	215	25	80	1																	
Richland		39	120	55						112	5								9		
Silver Lake	16	9								65	11										

DICKINSON COUNTY.—Continued.

NAMES OF TOWNSHIPS, TOWNS, AND CITIES.	Acres of natural timber.	Acres of planted timber.	Rods of hedge.	APPLES. Number of trees in bearing.	APPLES. Bushels gathered in 1874.	PEARS. Number of trees in bearing.	PEARS. Bushels gathered in 1874.	PEACHES. Number of trees in bearing.	PEACHES. Bushels gathered in 1874.	PLUMS. Number of trees in bearing.	PLUMS. Bushels gathered in 1874.	CHERRIES. Number of trees in bearing.	CHERRIES. Bushels gathered in 1874.	Number of other fruit trees in bearing.	Number of fruit trees not in bearing.	GRAPES IN VINEYARD. Number of acres.	GRAPES IN VINEYARD. Pounds of grapes gathered.	GRAPES IN VINEYARD. Gallons of wine made.	GRAPES NOT IN VINEYARD. Number of vines.	GRAPES NOT IN VINEYARD. Pounds of grapes gathered.	GRAPES NOT IN VINEYARD. Gallons of wine made.
Spirit Lake	160	85	1460	23	....	....	....	....	....	....	....	....	....	2	364	....	....	....	18	....	....
Superior	5	2	160	....	....	....	....	....	....	....	....	....	....	....	....	....	....	....	....	....	....
Total	1194	379	7663	92	....	....	....	....	....	185	16	....	....	17	2682	....	....	....	570	40	....

DUBUQUE COUNTY.

NAMES OF TOWNSHIPS, TOWNS, AND CITIES.	Acres of natural timber.	Acres of planted timber.	Rods of hedge.	APPLES. Number of trees in bearing.	APPLES. Bushels gathered in 1874.	PEARS. Number of trees in bearing.	PEARS. Bushels gathered in 1874.	PEACHES. Number of trees in bearing.	PEACHES. Bushels gathered in 1874.	PLUMS. Number of trees in bearing.	PLUMS. Bushels gathered in 1874.	CHERRIES. Number of trees in bearing.	CHERRIES. Bushels gathered in 1874.	Number of other fruit trees in bearing.	Number of fruit trees not in bearing.	GRAPES IN VINEYARD. Number of acres.	GRAPES IN VINEYARD. Pounds of grapes gathered.	GRAPES IN VINEYARD. Gallons of wine made.	GRAPES NOT IN VINEYARD. Number of vines.	GRAPES NOT IN VINEYARD. Pounds of grapes gathered.	GRAPES NOT IN VINEYARD. Gallons of wine made.
Cascade	3549	....	....	1768	758	2	....	6	....	2	....	20	....	7	9256	4	....	....	336	354	10
Center	5914	....	....	2565	919	12	1	....	....	10	20	8	4	....	4998	....	....	....	2192	582	98
Concord	6028	....	100	1351	618	1	....	....	....	28	2	10	....	....	1631	....	...	....	493	2020	180
Dodge	602	31	272	451	211	....	....	....	....	....	....	25	13	1100	100	....	....	....	....	....	6
Dubuque, city of	92	1	....	4721	545	325	13	28	....	2626	220	2512	399	22882	26210	6	300	510	3593	2400	340
Dyersville, town of	40	....	....	134	2	....	....	....	....	1	....	9	....	....	590	2	200	....	228	70	....
Iowa	8187	....	10	431	163	....	....	....	....	....	....	10	....	139	2265	3	3016	600	254	110	3
Jefferson	6775	....	....	8080	3266	14	....	....	....	56	26	161	7	....	7911	1	4000	200	2722	5174	305
Julien, exc. of Dubuque	1000	6	60	4295	1413	4	1	....	....	205	65	435	240	180	9475	36	5330	135	1454	115	....
Liberty	3588	....	....	1016	90	14	1	....	....	13	4	24	2	....	....	....	....	25	25	135	....
Mosalem	3336	....	....	8292	10000	....	....	....	....	....	....	60	83	7337	....	6	1950	....	....	....	....
New Wine, exc. of Dyersville	2751	....	300	619	89	....	1	....	....	6	1	28	2	....	2206	....	....	....	255	310	....
Peru	7124	....	....	4018	1601	28	....	....	....	56	40	88	4	57	5663	6	4350	150	2811	1145	22
Prairie Creek	1923	4	105	887	99	....	....	....	....	45	4	9	....	6	2360	....	....	....	823	480	20
Table Mound	5655	....	....	2370	1010	....	....	....	....	....	....	....	....	375	....	2	500	100	....	....	....
Taylor	2585	17	510	2054	800	4	1	....	....	326	171	128	75	138	6455	....	....	....	968	3172	7
Vernon	3833	15	....	3412	906	....	....	....	....	22	16	176	5	129	2708	1	5258	341	7	600	141
Washington	3805	33	....	1554	347	....	....	....	....	254	43	26	21	10	2584	6	40	....	206	73	....
Whitewater	2986	....	....	438	240	....	....	....	....	....	....	....	....	4	1404	....	....	....	....	....	....
Total	69773	107	1357	48456	23077	404	18	34	....	3650	612	3729	855	32364	85816	73	24944	2061	16367	16740	1132

EMMET COUNTY.

Armstrong Grove	67	27	740																		
Center	64	9																			
Ellsworth	42	29	185												56						
Emmet	267	57	160	18	1					122	9	1			1160						
Estherville	376	40	960	11						10	2			6	1176				10	20	
High Lake	146	9																			
Iowa Lake	96	12	170	11		1						2			25				6		
Peterson	168	7		30	1										98						
Swan Lake	8	5																			
Total	1234	193	2215	70	2	1				132	11	3		6	2515				16	20	

FAYETTE COUNTY.

Auburn	2523			328	136									40	1459				20	55	
Banks	559	35	3	132	32							3			2197				52	100	
Bethel	300	110	2053	175	50	40	3								2887				32	135	
Center	396	3	80	339	42					24	3	79		67	2393				98	46	
Clermont	52	3	50	835	327											1	200				
Dover	3561	100	40	600	521							7	4	108	7009		9	12	147	290	4
Eden	2675	16	350	403	151	1				12	3	186		281	2424	1		30	246		
Fairfield	4226	44	12	1098	366	3				2		299	36		5266				518	862	
Fayette, town of																			20	400	
Fremont	828	20	2371	219	50					48	12	31	3	250	2060				254	248	
Harlan	423	52	2855	208	29				12			79			2360				163	178	10
Illyria	3671		21	1169	629							81	8		300				231	545	248
Jefferson	1310	31	9624	686	247	1	1			49	31	119	11								
Oran	2435	62	2300	549	69	2				28	8	121	2	30	148		80		286	498	17
Pleasant Valley	5893	6	290	885	593									25	2596				345	846	433
Putnam	465	172	2068	1132	393							174	3	336	3722				507	540	3
Scott	360	34	2875	84	2					1		49			1953				70		
Smithfield	336	50	600	526	270					100	10	10	1	187	5384				95		
Westfield, exc. of Fayette	1402	110	100	662	164										4557						
West Union, exc. of town	3769	20	215	1765	628	20						29		40	6052		500		408	1222	27
West Union, town of	800	2		360	180	1						110	8		20				309	3028	
Windsor	2555	107	3540	601	243					925	371	109	2	5	33624				224	490	6
Total	38539	977	29447	12756	5122	68	4		12	1189	438	1486	78	1369	86411	2	789	42	4025	9483	748

FLOYD COUNTY.

NAMES OF TOWNSHIPS, TOWNS, AND CITIES.	Acres of natural timber.	Acres of planted timber.	Rods of hedge.	APPLES. Number of trees in bearing.	APPLES. Bushels gathered in 1874.	PEARS. Number of trees in bearing.	PEARS. Bushels gathered in 1874.	PEACHES. Number of trees in bearing.	PEACHES. Bushels gathered in 1874.	PLUMS. Number of trees in bearing.	PLUMS. Bushels gathered in 1874.	CHERRIES. Number of trees in bearing.	CHERRIES. Bushels gathered in 1874.	Number of other fruit trees in bearing.	Number of fruit trees not in bearing.	GRAPES IN VINEYARD. Number of acres.	GRAPES IN VINEYARD. Pounds of grapes gathered.	GRAPES IN VINEYARD. Gallons of wine made.	GRAPES NOT IN VINEYARD. Number of vines.	GRAPES NOT IN VINEYARD. Pounds of grapes gathered.	GRAPES NOT IN VINEYARD. Gallons of wine made.
Cedar	464	22	296	455	68										2466				30	35	
Charles City, city of			42	20						20	5				735				433	275	
Floyd	2612	80	3600	684	139					456	171	441		679	4825				321	605	4
Niles	2188	12	731	87	14										6				8	80	
Nora Springs, town of	519	22	480	501	43							20		421	8260				178	201	2
Pleasant Grove	716	22	2810								15				8382				121		
Riverton	2423	47	1962	501	74					4	1	27	2	254	8503	1	500		373	204	2
Rockford	1351	45	1415	56	31							8	1						472	269	10
Rock Grove, exc. Nora Springs	1249	71	680	1043	357							48		1428	3502				380	427	
Rudd	342	28	100	288	48							15		40	1763				159	324	
St. Charles, exc. of city	3093	60	1393	1025	338	2	1			135	26	100			8044				1708	150	
Scott	180	50	1529	18	1					1		3			3310				93		
Ulster	844	16		103	19										2469				399		
Union	1313	53	4935	281	26					54	39	47	1	205	743		200		1475	41	8
Total	17294	528	19973	5062	1158	2	1			670	257	709	4	3027	53008	1	700		6150	2611	26

FRANKLIN COUNTY.

NAMES OF TOWNSHIPS, TOWNS, AND CITIES.	Acres of natural timber.	Acres of planted timber.	Rods of hedge.	APPLES. Number of trees in bearing.	APPLES. Bushels gathered in 1874.	PEARS. Number of trees in bearing.	PEARS. Bushels gathered in 1874.	PEACHES. Number of trees in bearing.	PEACHES. Bushels gathered in 1874.	PLUMS. Number of trees in bearing.	PLUMS. Bushels gathered in 1874.	CHERRIES. Number of trees in bearing.	CHERRIES. Bushels gathered in 1874.	Number of other fruit trees in bearing.	Number of fruit trees not in bearing.	GRAPES IN VINEYARD. Number of acres.	GRAPES IN VINEYARD. Pounds of grapes gathered.	GRAPES IN VINEYARD. Gallons of wine made.	GRAPES NOT IN VINEYARD. Number of vines.	GRAPES NOT IN VINEYARD. Pounds of grapes gathered.	GRAPES NOT IN VINEYARD. Gallons of wine made.
Clinton	337	49	2066	64	2							1		56	3144					965	49
Geneva	20	70	3742	172	11	60				130	8	124			2635		50		346	154	
Grant	10	45	2975											81	1950						
Hamilton		40	2203	46	46					209	52	21	1		666				54	50	
Hampton, town of		5		62	15					6		43	6	12	227				75	155	
Ingham	483	80	1945	123	11							6			2579				316		
Lee	10	49	1985	14						6	1	2		10	58						
Marion	41	13		1						2					180				10		

Morgan	531	36	1156							22	61			110	2039				12	20	
Oakland	466	35	1315	156						28		34		36	2244				63		
Osceola	73	196	870	242	50					100	20	96		273	8569		30		551	230	2
Reeve	1779	85	190	660	119	1				48	5	42	1	36	3109				516	1586	
Richland	139	12	847	91	9							8			1613				20	25	
Washington, exc. of Hampton	91	38	40	143	16					41	5	23		73	3022				26	181	
West Fork	205	62	5100	135	24					440	88	13	3		2597						
Total	4185	815	24434	1909	303	61				1032	240	413	11	687	34662		80		2225	3366	51

FREMONT COUNTY.

Bartlett, town of																					
Benton, exc. of Eastport and Percival	1272	1	2530	906	542	8	4	12		12	8	37	37	2	4014				2105	2425	
Eastport, town of																					
Farragut, town of																					
Fisher, exc. of Farragut	292	42	26427	344	160	117	1	117	55			152	5	1498	10783	2	2000		1587	950	
Franklin, exc. of Hamburg	2167		4571	1737	1737	8	3	772	848	31		191	17	204	2142	4	900		604	1332	30
Fremont City, town of																					
Hamburg, town of																					
Locust Grove		47	6339					17	4			12		54	5105				971		
McPaul, town of																					
Madison	3211	39	12518	1661	1966	15	45	1366	857	82	40	414	189	2	1830	9	7143		300	8	
Monroe	567	27	12085	143	88	1		63	26	50	9	15	...	2	7886				1739		
Percival, town of																					
Prairie	463	28	7340	225	186	2	1	162	90				...	10	4760				727	230	
Riverton, exc. of town	618	14	3250	179	137	8	2	760	274			240	12		10879	2	4000	60	760	650	1
Riverton, town of																					
Ross, exc. of Tabor	3989	95	19290	1607	1103	103	17	1286	4326	340	56	296	60		11404	2	4000	50	1910	4460	2
Scott, exc. of Fremont City, Bartlett, and McPaul	4225	10	3470	1216	1043	46	23	284	152	27	3	543	57	45	5133				1037	732	
Sidney, exc. of town	6456	2	14717	5544	4103	298	240	4911	3812	4	2	687	100	6	15013	1	2650		2503	1979	
Sidney, town of			242	1170	504	85	12	571	423	61	37	409	120		4997	4	1500	500	1431	5300	
Tabor, town of		2	475	451	267	11		112	80	16	8	50	5	100	414		100	135	441	1850	
Walnut	664	34	8415	260	69			35	5			16			2919				410		
Total	23924	341	121669	15443	11905	702	348	10468	10952	623	163	3062	602	1923	87279	24	22293	745	16525	19916	33

GREENE COUNTY.

Bristol	1299		1156	245	119	8	2					23	10		2590				840	425	
Cedar	882	15	1840	54	9							66	1		2616				248	158	
Dawson		6	760	9								6			120				37		

GREENE COUNTY.—Continued.

Names of townships, towns, and cities.	Acres of natural timber.	Acres of planted timber.	Rods of hedge.	Apples. Number of trees in bearing.	Apples. Bushels gathered in 1874.	Pears. Number of trees in bearing.	Pears. Bushels gathered in 1874.	Peaches. Number of trees in bearing.	Peaches. Bushels gathered in 1874.	Plums. Number of trees in bearing.	Plums. Bushels gathered in 1874.	Cherries. Number of trees in bearing.	Cherries. Bushels gathered in 1874.	Number of other fruit trees in bearing.	Number of fruit trees not in bearing.	Grapes in vineyard. Number of acres.	Grapes in vineyard. Pounds of grapes gathered.	Grapes in vineyard. Gallons of wine made.	Grapes not in vineyard. Number of vines.	Grapes not in vineyard. Pounds of grapes gathered.	Grapes not in vineyard. Gallons of wine made.
Franklin	298	21	2068	161	...	...	...	1	...	3	1	52	...	18	3737	...	...	...	426	555	...
Grand Junction, town of	129	15	...	...	...	...	...	...	...	...	...	...	...	...	...	...	...	...	75	...	...
Greenbrier	24	13	2340	...	...	...	...	...	...	50	5	18	3	6	2537	...	...	...	376	100	...
Hardin	198	17	4185	65	...	...	...	...	...	...	...	67	...	...	2726	...	...	...	...	...	...
Highland	58	10	510	...	...	...	...	...	...	...	...	14	1	3	343	...	...	...	50	400	...
Jackson	1485	4	1217	159	58	7	1	...	...	2	...	47	...	10	4540	...	500	46	862	473	4
Jefferson, exc. of town	2114	17	3004	576	214	...	...	...	...	213	22	62	6	36	8065	1	100	...	1238	1897	1
Jefferson, town of	...	...	...	314	35	11	10	...	...	245	42	162	4	45	8794	...	...	...	2897	2088	...
Junction, exc. Grand Junction	1	13	3541	24	4	...	...	...	...	...	...	13	2	107	937	...	10	6	138	186	...
Kendrick	1540	...	3460	1157	77	20	...	1	...	...	...	39	2	...	3859	...	...	...	899	2470	...
Scranton, exc. of town	...	36	2134	...	...	...	...	...	...	...	...	6	...	...	2387	...	...	...	259	30	...
Scranton, town of	...	8	...	...	...	...	...	...	...	...	...	...	...	...	400	...	...	...	4	...	...
Washington	1382	50	21674	540	95	...	...	...	...	65	11	61	6	60	8269	2	75	...	911	130	...
Willow	...	5	220	...	...	...	...	...	...	...	...	...	...	...	...	...	...	...	...	...	...
Total	9410	230	48109	3304	611	46	13	2	...	578	81	636	36	285	51920	3	685	52	9260	8912	5

GRUNDY COUNTY.

Names of townships, towns, and cities.	Acres of natural timber.	Acres of planted timber.	Rods of hedge.	Apples. Number of trees in bearing.	Apples. Bushels gathered in 1874.	Pears. Number of trees in bearing.	Pears. Bushels gathered in 1874.	Peaches. Number of trees in bearing.	Peaches. Bushels gathered in 1874.	Plums. Number of trees in bearing.	Plums. Bushels gathered in 1874.	Cherries. Number of trees in bearing.	Cherries. Bushels gathered in 1874.	Number of other fruit trees in bearing.	Number of fruit trees not in bearing.	Grapes in vineyard. Number of acres.	Grapes in vineyard. Pounds of grapes gathered.	Grapes in vineyard. Gallons of wine made.	Grapes not in vineyard. Number of vines.	Grapes not in vineyard. Pounds of grapes gathered.	Grapes not in vineyard. Gallons of wine made.
Beaver	1	78	3895	584	264	2	...	...	...	127	21	15	1	...	6914	...	...	...	636	580	...
Black Hawk	315	225	2755	87	24	...	...	...	...	...	...	10	1	...	4962	...	600	...	12	...	...
Clay	207	99	7020	209	94	...	...	...	...	...	...	58	4	...	5043	...	...	...	985	1230	8
Colfax	60	57	140	212	...	1	1	...	...	...	...	109	...	...	...	...	500	5	...	...	...
Fairfield	...	198	2650	1182	527	...	...	...	...	14	11	101	...	39	7783	...	...	...	...	...	...
Felix	...	118	8353	946	164	...	...	...	...	93	15	128	13	...	7239	...	...	...	1260	857	...
German	...	66	3577	338	25	...	...	...	...	412	53	77	4	852	4559	...	...	...	347	24	1
Grant	...	5	480	74	5	...	...	...	...	212	16	27	...	...	...	...	...	...	...	...	...
Lincoln	...	52	1680	46	3	...	...	...	...	64	...	8	...	...	1979	...	...	...	39	11	...

Melrose		109	10818	1337	132					47	21	152	13	197	10373				1814	5194	50
Palermo	217	251	12485	174	108					13	73	45	13	31	16170				858	646	
Pleasant Valley	66	90	3760	75	13										5689				466	415	
Shiloh		72	101	15	5							13			5866						
Total	866	1420	57714	5279	1364	3	1			982	210	743	49	1119	76577		1100	5	6417	8957	59

GUTHRIE COUNTY.

Bear Grove	921	6		845	193					50	4	98	1		60		100		457	1295	
Beaver	238	83	940																2922	12191	
Cass, exc. of Panora	2368	187	13585	3911	1044	10		5		119	14	236	22	9	19626	2	6000		379	582	
Center	703	132	350	408	74							94	5	17	7273				137	100	
Dodge	225	24	460	34	14					10		1			1718				32		
Grant	175	14	462							50	2	21			1443				129		
Highland	873	24	1000	116								10	1		1850				1645	6000	
Jackson	3518	1	4494	1958	661	2		1		11	1	97	3		11872				305	410	
Orange	103	13	1535	455	130							32	4	9	1553				1230	2250	
Panora, town of	228	5	768	1027	202	7				25	3	75	4	8	1563				950	1330	1
Penn	781	29	898	717	381					12	7	44	6		5921				597	100	
Richland	151	86	7277	32	10					1		63	5	5	4688	2	300		959	710	
Thompson	398	24	1372	50	25					55	4	77			9942		200		181	20	
Union	479	11	180	115	101							7			3083				1463	848	
Valley	959	51	3695	1092	368	1				108	35	78	4		10155				800	1094	
Victory	2060	57	4100	1569	430	4				1		95		278	6357						
Total	14180	747	41116	12329	3633	24		6		442	70	1028	55	326	87104	4	6600		2186	26930	1

HAMILTON COUNTY.

Blairsburg		52	3532							286	7	348	33		2232				181		
Boone	1371	380	1255	272	47					165	13	23	4	328	7879		100		636	514	
Cass	1227	76		25	9																
Clear Lake	51	13	1492	23								25			425				41		
Ellsworth	242	18	2512	167	17					122	5	15	4	54	2172				70	12	1
Fremont	420	93		67								12		2	490						
Hamilton	1356	32	1542	123											3725				391		
Lyon	246	21	1490	99	2					70	7				25		50	6	14	20	
Marion	1647	21	3781	467	370	4	6			768	38	92	3	1317	10126		60		375	915	
Rose Grove	140	118	2160	40								75	12		2375		300		202	100	
Scott		21	4089	28	13										991						
Webster	1472	31	1313	471	87							102	3		2485				349	1510	
Total	8172	876	23166	1782	545	4	6			1411	70	692	59	1701	32925		510	6	2259	3071	1

HANCOCK COUNTY.

NAMES OF TOWNSHIPS, TOWNS, AND CITIES.	Acres of natural timber.	Acres of planted timber.	Rods of hedge.	APPLES. Number of trees in bearing.	APPLES. Bushels gathered in 1874.	PEARS. Number of trees in bearing.	PEARS. Bushels gathered in 1874.	PEACHES. Number of trees in bearing.	PEACHES. Bushels gathered in 1874.	PLUMS. Number of trees in bearing.	PLUMS. Bushels gathered in 1874.	CHERRIES. Number of trees in bearing.	CHERRIES. Bushels gathered in 1874.	Number of other fruit trees in bearing.	Number of fruit trees not in bearing.	GRAPES IN VINEYARD. Number of acres.	GRAPES IN VINEYARD. Pounds of grapes gathered.	GRAPES IN VINEYARD. Gallons of wine made.	GRAPES NOT IN VINEYARD. Number of vines.	GRAPES NOT IN VINEYARD. Pounds of grapes gathered.	GRAPES NOT IN VINEYARD. Gallons of wine made.
Amsterdam	241	33	3610	38	1							16		50	100				20	10	
Avery	354	38	3380	85	8					6	2	20	2		270				7	12	
Britt	150	1																			
Concord		14	1920	7	1							5			560				50	50	
Crystal	38	8	765							90	32				111						
Ellington	8970	6	728	21															73		
Madison	247	14	1516	1	2																
Total	10000	114	11919	152	12					96	34	41	2	50	1041				150	72	

HARDIN COUNTY.

NAMES OF TOWNSHIPS, TOWNS, AND CITIES.	Acres of natural timber.	Acres of planted timber.	Rods of hedge.	APPLES. Number of trees in bearing.	APPLES. Bushels gathered in 1874.	PEARS. Number of trees in bearing.	PEARS. Bushels gathered in 1874.	PEACHES. Number of trees in bearing.	PEACHES. Bushels gathered in 1874.	PLUMS. Number of trees in bearing.	PLUMS. Bushels gathered in 1874.	CHERRIES. Number of trees in bearing.	CHERRIES. Bushels gathered in 1874.	Number of other fruit trees in bearing.	Number of fruit trees not in bearing.	GRAPES IN VINEYARD. Number of acres.	GRAPES IN VINEYARD. Pounds of grapes gathered.	GRAPES IN VINEYARD. Gallons of wine made.	GRAPES NOT IN VINEYARD. Number of vines.	GRAPES NOT IN VINEYARD. Pounds of grapes gathered.	GRAPES NOT IN VINEYARD. Gallons of wine made.
Ackley, town of																					
Alden	896	37	2952												3892						
Buckeye	152	39	2695																		
Clay	2019	27	690	960	442	2				2	5	24	2		4960				271	2170	
Concord		3	480												243						
Eldora, exc. of town	4027	71	3830	1617	654	4	1			249		252	63		3614				713	2465	
Eldora, town of	671	24	210	415	76	7	3			13		106	1	20	1188				708	1156	17
Ellis	559	64	4630	444	78					178	69	46			3638				101	118	
Etna, exc. of Ackley		236		1020	167							373	1						829	368	1
Grant	20	15	1485	28	11					166	56	62			1680				85	40	
Hardin, exc. of Iowa Falls	1116	68	2845	1510	187					545	99	203	46		10509	1			462	110	
Iowa Falls, town of																					
Jackson	1746	79	5250	434	84					81	11	9	5	2	8872				534	597	
Pleasant	1847	8	4226	759	239					2	1	138	30	4	5633				630	330	
Providence	1536	174	13626	3525	1521	10	2			838	174	710	214	45	9673				1123	4314	
Sherman	54	10	1390							10	2				2731				40		

Tipton	1008	22	6426	266	98	1	......	......	......	143	57	179	10	39	3816	......	......	......	445	440	19
Union, exc. of town	2455	84	5903	2137	506	2	1	......	......	159	7	411	61	146	8279	1	3500	15	969	2097	......
Union, town of	......	......	......	......	......	......	......	......	......	......	......	......	......	......	......	......	......	......	......	......	......
Total	18106	961	46638	13115	4063	26	7	......	......	2391	481	2513	433	256	68728	2	3500	15	6910	14205	37

HARRISON COUNTY.

Allen	60	......	......	50	3	......	......	......	......	......	4	8	......	......	......	......	......	......	......	......	......
Boyer	1042	248	170	163	208	......	......	9	......	100	17	254	7	100	170	......	......	......	496	......	5
Calhoun	881	4	130	117	4	2	......	......	......	64	5	57	3	27	1336	1	200	......	158	260	......
Cass	811	4	90	146	136	......	......	3	......	66	20	36	1	......	1955	......	......	......	278	353	......
Cincinnati	1070	15	407	109	22	......	......	......	......	51	14	30	......	40	1729	......	......	......	129	152	......
Clay	2160	2	......	2	1	......	......	......	......	......	......	25	1	302	802	1	......	......	90	12	......
Douglas	861	27	762	152	26	2	......	......	......	32	14	130	4	143	4669	1	40	......	266	200	......
Dunlap, town of	......	......	......	......	......	......	......	......	......	......	......	......	......	......	......	......	......	......	......	......	......
Harrison, exc. of Dunlap	......	75	......	6	......	......	......	......	......	......	......	9	......	......	1509	......	......	......	......	......	......
Jackson	821	......	......	24	2	......	......	......	......	......	......	20	10	48	1558	......	......	......	141	......	......
Jefferson	2994	39	578	841	231	14	......	1	......	8	......	244	......	5	4885	......	......	......	501	40	......
Lagrange	1702	3	10	251	341	4	1	2	......	8	1	89	2	12	2386	......	......	......	202	......	......
Lincoln	73	12	......	114	3	......	......	......	......	......	......	......	......	......	136	......	......	......	......	......	......
Little Sioux	1081	1	......	33	12	......	......	......	......	1	1	17	2	24	2964	......	......	......	303	215	3
Magnolia	3292	11	48	288	26	63	......	9	......	20	2	210	45	18	8478	......	......	......	641	32	......
Missouri Valley, town of	......	......	......	......	......	......	......	......	......	......	......	......	......	......	......	......	......	......	......	......	......
Morgan	1191	3	60	57	12	......	......	......	......	41	3	33	7	2	2222	......	......	......	325	611	......
Raglan	1303	2	71	151	18	8	3	......	......	......	......	35	3	......	2236	......	......	......	218	35	......
St. John, exc. of Missouri Valley	1823	39	440	538	......	......	......	......	......	4	4	77	6	14	2984	......	......	......	433	20	......
Taylor	1616	29	372	71	7	2	......	2	......	......	......	30	5	......	1675	......	......	......	368	95	......
Union	497	......	......	305	65	......	......	......	......	......	......	......	......	......	1700	......	......	......	12	100	......
Washington	214	14	......	......	......	......	......	......	......	......	......	......	......	......	679	......	......	......	248	......	......
Total	23497	528	3138	3418	1117	95	4	26	......	395	85	1304	96	735	43073	3	240	......	4809	2125	8

HENRY COUNTY.

Baltimore	6363	......	2822	4785	4177	41	40	326	114	34	10	1346	382	9	9529	2	4520	35	997	4665	......
Canaan	3	50	25821	9394	3954	28	1	640	127	36	1	894	78	100	16559	......	......	......	1939	13580	15
Center, exc. of Mt. Pleasant	4052	18	14895	16136	8360	200	48	1874	906	298	84	2929	992	26	14174	17	43628	507	2063	15823	344
Jackson	6705	14	15393	12662	7418	63	300	1475	571	107	28	3109	2015	......	11602	......	8000	32	1441	9329	2
Jefferson	3503	9	5073	7218	5101	80	3	116	51	23	7	350	86	301	1782	......	5160	80	644	4003	33
Marian	1269	137	34119	17021	19259	780	107	2561	552	96	33	2616	523	42	9311	42	12000	330	2756	24230	1682
Mt. Pleasant, city of	......	......	49	7103	6453	1331	475	1107	495	212	190	5573	4346	904	3868	3	3511	......	4965	153402	266
New London, exc. of town	2426	27	27895	15834	10979	213	40	1575	515	179	40	3246	907	......	8214	......	1250	20	2569	36204	53

HENRY COUNTY.—Continued.

NAMES OF TOWNSHIPS, TOWNS, AND CITIES.	Acres of natural timber.	Acres of planted timber.	Rods of hedge.	APPLES.		PEARS.		PEACHES		PLUMS.		CHERRIES.		Number of other fruit trees in bearing.	Number of fruit trees not in bearing.	GRAPES IN VINEYARD.			GRAPES NOT IN VINEYARD.		
				Number of trees in bearing.	Bushels gathered in 1874.	Number of trees in bearing	Bushels gathered in 1874.	Number of trees in bearing.	Bushels gathered in 1874	Number of trees in bearing.	Bushels gathered in 1874.	Number of trees in bearing.	Bushels gathered in 1874.			Number of acres.	Pounds of grapes gathered.	Gallons of wine made.	Number of vines.	Pounds of grapes gathered.	Gallons of wine made.
New London, town of			40	1402	1108	28	13	317	159	48	18	649	350	1	556				301	2968	5
Rome, town of	265			250	64	10		25		13		162	41		625			3	189	840	
Salem, exc. of town	7586	20	19876	12414	10927	510	466	1172	511	169	37	3965	1794	20	13377	32	1400	1	1323	7705	
Salem, town of				735	723	68	90	200	145	101	58	863	836	25	897				302	8865	148
Scott	1473	37	36470	7345	3742	25	4	63	12	32	6	1389	507		8725	2	15750	95	1283	6959	
Tippecanoe, exc. of Rome	5264		5953	6015	4256	100	50	368	179	42	13	2119	362	30	9503				1756	9095	130
Trenton	5269		1090	7748	4935	115	31	717	134	36	8	1277	251		4651	3	900	60	1563	5392	178
Wayne			29502	5811	7694	37	5	205	29	25	5	784	184	47	12491		4000	84	2779	16647	150
Total	44178	312	218998	131873	99150	3629	1673	12741	4500	1451	538	31274	13654	1505	125864	102	100119	1249	26870	319707	3006

HOWARD COUNTY.

NAMES OF TOWNSHIPS, TOWNS, AND CITIES.	Acres of natural timber.	Acres of planted timber.	Rods of hedge.	APPLES. Number of trees in bearing.	APPLES. Bushels gathered in 1874.	PEARS. Number of trees in bearing	PEARS. Bushels gathered in 1874.	PEACHES. Number of trees in bearing.	PEACHES. Bushels gathered in 1874	PLUMS. Number of trees in bearing.	PLUMS. Bushels gathered in 1874.	CHERRIES. Number of trees in bearing.	CHERRIES. Bushels gathered in 1874.	Number of other fruit trees in bearing.	Number of fruit trees not in bearing.	GRAPES IN VINEYARD. Number of acres.	GRAPES IN VINEYARD. Pounds of grapes gathered.	GRAPES IN VINEYARD. Gallons of wine made.	GRAPES NOT IN VINEYARD. Number of vines.	GRAPES NOT IN VINEYARD. Pounds of grapes gathered.	GRAPES NOT IN VINEYARD. Gallons of wine made.
Afton	1529	45	1123	47	57					84	75				1808						
Albion	1353	66	2682	234	104	12				43	10	5	5		170				201	205	
Chester	841	6		332	1							6		75	495				168	33	20
Cresco, town of																					
Forest City	888	15	658	245	35	30				24	3	13			653				54	4	
Howard	843	7	42	11	4														58	30	
Howard Center	294	108	305	482	131					167	62	6	2	2	150				152	150	
Jamestown	1021	28	278	47										14	2599				9	90	
New Oregon	1216	111	160	588	160										1909				5	150	
Oak Dale	474	29	1310	40	10										622				26		
Paris	898	58	761	24	3																
Saratoga	308	24	552											65	345						
Vernon Springs, exc. of Cresco	828	37	228	347	142					63	17	18	5	24	100				100		
Total	10493	534	8189	2397	647	42				381	167	48	12	180	8851				773	662	20

HUMBOLDT COUNTY.

Avery	113	35	895	5	...	...	...	...	...	9	...	...	...	...	811	...	...	...	...	...	...
Dakota	74	16	245	82	13	1	...	...	...	61	5	64	1	5	1099	...	...	...	123	382	40
Delana	79	40	...	5	1	...	...	...	...	...	...	...	...	...	...	...	...	...	...	...	...
Grove	447	28	1960	240	32	...	...	...	...	...	...	7	...	10	2070	...	...	168	150	...	...
Humboldt	488	32	1720	65	12	...	...	...	...	...	...	...	...	...	1390	...	...	14	50	...	...
Humboldt, town of	5	...	...	...	...	...	...	...	...	...	...	...	...	...	...	...	...	...	8	...	4
Lake	30	20	...	...	...	...	...	...	...	...	...	...	...	...	...	...	...	...	...	...	...
Norway	1	7	1514	...	...	...	...	...	...	...	...	...	...	...	...	...	...	...	...	...	...
Rutland	31	49	1400	21	3	...	...	...	...	475	22	30	1	...	1179	...	...	...	12	...	...
Springvale, exc. of Humboldt	310	41	258	48	3	...	...	...	...	25	...	...	...	...	880	...	...	37	44	...	1
Vernon	172	...	4054	5	...	...	...	...	...	2	...	...	...	...	...	...	...	...	...	...	...
Wacousta	128	31	160	43	...	...	...	...	...	...	...	...	...	...	111	...	...	...	...	...	...
Weaver	...	10	600	...	...	...	...	...	...	...	...	...	...	...	198	...	...	...	...	...	...
Total	1878	309	12806	514	64	1	...	...	...	572	27	101	2	15	7738	...	...	219	387	382	45

IDA COUNTY.

Corwin	420	26	...	...	...	...	...	...	...	...	...	...	...	...	...	...	...	...	...	...	...
Douglas	50	12	240	...	...	...	...	...	...	...	...	...	...	...	453	...	...	...	17	5	...
Maple	193	15	680	50	2	...	...	...	...	...	...	...	...	27	200	...	...	...	...	...	...
Silver Creek	40	3	230	...	...	...	...	...	...	...	...	...	1	...	179	...	...	...	9	...	...
Total	703	56	1150	50	2	...	...	...	...	...	...	...	1	27	832	...	...	...	26	5	...

IOWA COUNTY.

Amana	3150	47	6600	2200	1120	...	...	...	...	...	...	340	220	...	3500	10	28800	4000	3000	8000	1000
Cono	963	...	250	489	444	1	...	...	...	14	...	71	23	3	2299	...	...	...	194	648	...
Dayton	1298	...	18681	1477	961	2	2	...	...	3	1	200	84	...	7930	...	...	...	1345	4233	...
English	3743	...	16184	2842	672	13	2	3	4	65	1	764	154	28	11958	...	2000	6	4099	7558	80
Fillmore	1905	7	9001	2231	1618		...	3	...	25	4	205	12	39	5756	...	...	...	716	1513	...
Green	2150	24	10333	1108	636	...	...	...	...	...	...	47	11	...	6271	...	...	...	928	4927	...
Hartford, exc. of Victor	467	28	13335	983	334	...	...	3	...	8	1	229	31	...	9667	...	650	200	1731	4634	5
Hilton	170	53	6051	383	82	...	...	...	...	52	7	33	5	...	7562	...	...	...	919	1395	...
Honey Creek	2726	43	13363	2555	893	8	...	...	...	167	48	672	37	22	9692	...	...	...	1510	4691	96
Iowa	1015	72	2717	728	505	35	...	10	...	17	...	179	46	17	2283	472	14295	1500	2365	7926	1163
Lenox	400	36	861	1592	1220	3	1	...	...	...	...	43	6	10	25659	...	...	...	305	2975	289
Lincoln	426	25	5545	216	111	2	...	...	...	...	...	64	14	32	4749	...	...	...	1106	4565	30
Marengo, exc. of town	1765	21	7475	1677	869	10	1	16	3	88	36	275	50	60	8555	1	2000	20	2197	9947	406

IOWA COUNTY.—CONTINUED.

NAMES OF TOWNSHIPS, TOWNS, AND CITIES.	Acres of natural timber.	Acres of planted timber.	Rods of hedge.	APPLES. Number of trees in bearing.	APPLES. Bushels gathered in 1874.	PEARS. Number of trees in bearing.	PEARS. Bushels gathered in 1874.	PEACHES. Number of trees in bearing.	PEACHES. Bushels gathered in 1874.	PLUMS. Number of trees in bearing.	PLUMS. Bushels gathered in 1874.	CHERRIES. Number of trees in bearing.	CHERRIES. Bushels gathered in 1874.	Number of other fruit trees in bearing.	Number of fruit trees not in bearing.	GRAPES IN VINEYARD. Number of acres.	GRAPES IN VINEYARD. Pounds of grapes gathered.	GRAPES IN VINEYARD. Gallons of wine made.	GRAPES NOT IN VINEYARD. Number of vines.	GRAPES NOT IN VINEYARD. Pounds of grapes gathered.	GRAPES NOT IN VINEYARD. Gallons of wine made.
Marengo, town of	12	2	420	132	52	1	......	......	......	13	3	45	6	25	77	......	......	......	33	300	5
Pilot	92	18	7790	442	223	......	......	......	......	......	......	......	......	......	8380	......	......	......	1640	3446	95
Sumner	901	35	8822	713	269	150	......	......	......	1	2	211	50	3	3379	18	3025	310	1087	2705	......
Troy	765	27	7902	529	162	......	......	......	......	5	2	114	......	20	9099	4	3700	......	1419	1015	......
Victor, town of	......	......	......	......	......	......	......	......	......	......	......	9	4	......	120	......	......	......	46	250	18
Washington	631	4	120	2858	727	......	......	3	6	8	6	120	10	30	6096	5	1650	4821	......	2327	326
York	394	64	6815	1339	594	......	......	......	......	94	5	194	43	20	6442	2	12000	25	2149	10746	......
Total	22973	506	142265	24494	11492	225	6	38	13	560	116	3815	806	309	139474	512	68120	10882	26789	83800	3513

JACKSON COUNTY.

NAMES OF TOWNSHIPS, TOWNS, AND CITIES.	Acres of natural timber.	Acres of planted timber.	Rods of hedge.	APPLES. Number of trees in bearing.	APPLES. Bushels gathered in 1874.	PEARS. Number of trees in bearing.	PEARS. Bushels gathered in 1874.	PEACHES. Number of trees in bearing.	PEACHES. Bushels gathered in 1874.	PLUMS. Number of trees in bearing.	PLUMS. Bushels gathered in 1874.	CHERRIES. Number of trees in bearing.	CHERRIES. Bushels gathered in 1874.	Number of other fruit trees in bearing.	Number of fruit trees not in bearing.	GRAPES IN VINEYARD. Number of acres.	GRAPES IN VINEYARD. Pounds of grapes gathered.	GRAPES IN VINEYARD. Gallons of wine made.	GRAPES NOT IN VINEYARD. Number of vines.	GRAPES NOT IN VINEYARD. Pounds of grapes gathered.	GRAPES NOT IN VINEYARD. Gallons of wine made.
Andrew, town of	......	......	......	334	176	7	11	......	......	23	23	......	......	......	60	......	1	2120	293	1280	......
Bellevue, exc. of town	4187	......	60	3112	1694	15	2	4	1	......	......	80	......	......	3941	1	......	100	296	558	......
Bellevue, town of	......	......	......	......	......	......	......	......	......	......	......	......	......	......	......	......	......	......	......	......	......
Brandon	8682	......	......	2527	2512	4	1	......	......	25	11	157	39	......	3125	......	480	......	177	427	......
Butler	6777	......	......	569	625	......	......	......	......	8	12	......	......	......	......	......	......	......	......	......	......
Fairfield	3295	......	1291	1804	782	5	1	......	......	19	9	64	12	68	4029	......	......	......	426	2196	20
Farmers' Creek	5347	1	40	6385	3791	3	1	......	......	80	56	34	11	300	2353	......	......	......	239	1188	9
Iowa	3050	......	9367	6775	3854	7	2	39	5	555	182	542	98	......	2293	......	......	......	354	2315	......
Jackson	5147	......	125	2592	1103	......	......	......	......	24	......	44	......	22	3840	......	60	......	261	963	10
Maquoketa, exc. of city	4062	1	1360	2879	1966	5	7	......	......	184	81	100	21	75	5934	1	2500	100	1535	7727	14
Maquoketa, city of	318	......	180	833	792	6	4	......	......	189	63	257	52	823	2423	1	3500	30	965	3799	7
Monmouth	4971	......	......	3397	613	......	......	14	1	46	14	222	14	158	15246	......	......	......	939	2775	41
Otter Creek	4505	1	20	1168	176	......	......	......	......	5	10	77	......	2	928	......	......	......	192	590	......
Perry, exc of Andrew	3835	......	90	4053	2130	20	4	6	......	73	52	175	32	6	7815	1	2500	......	700	5682	65
Prairie Spring	5418	8	......	642	540	1	1	......	......	22	20	23	19	......	4023	......	......	......	260	524	......
Richland	5237	3	965	2995	595	2	......	......	......	......	......	33	1	......	3696	......	......	......	50	......	......

Sabula, town of	....	....	....	276	268	9	1	2	....	32	3	469	118	13	621	1	1200	....	367	685	....
South Fork, exc. of Maquoketa	12069	5	80	5204	1593	6	2	1	1	210	89	421	79	78	4622	....	....	....	388	1055	....
Tete Des Morts	7092	....	....	3378	1748	12	1	....	....	6	....	....	....	....	3727	2	5150	182	33	366	10
Union, exc. of Sabula	886	....	620	1278	920	....	....	....	....	....	....	62	30	180	250	....	....	....	....	....	....
Van Buren	1896	8	4575	4237	2096	8	6	9	....	146	68	659	160	29	3649	1	20	....	377	2295	....
Washington	8386	....	200	3084	1069	3	2	....	....	28	9	190	33	162	1830	....	....	....	1660	520	36
Total	95160	27	18973	57522	29043	113	46	75	8	1675	702	3609	719	1916	74405	8	15411	532	9512	34945	212

28

JASPER COUNTY.

Buena Vista	1881	43	11063	1881	1347	31	12	1	....	16	5	983	1292	377	10495	....	....	....	1730	5534	2
Clear Creek	4399	9	4176	1890	813	9	2	....	....	19	....	260	19	98	5730	....	....	....	1136	3357	....
Des Moines, exc. of Prairie City	2522	109	11052	2959	2586	6	....	....	....	40	5	134	17	2	12250	....	....	....	3364	22926	30
Elk Creek	1097	5	3810	1795	600	5	....	....	....	....	....	346	109	....	11403	....	....	....	1371	10120	....
Fairview, exc. of Monroe	3744	71	11350	3119	1517	15	8	4	....	21	4	466	149	7	12785	2	2600	....	3331	15275	77
Hickory Grove	154	88	9967	60	1	....	....	....	....	....	....	51	3	....	2986	....	....	....	452	207	....
Independence	2570	19	4608	3078	945	6	....	....	....	8	5	340	95	9	7041	....	....	....	1630	3301	30
Jasper City, town of	....	....	....	....	....	....	....	....	....	....	....	....	....	....	....	....	....	....	....	....	....
Kellogg, exc. of Jasper City	1411	111	7169	2993	991	15	2	5	....	12	....	463	138	64	9863	....	50	....	1345	2560	167
Lynn Grove	1823	47	13037	2595	908	22	2	....	....	68	15	617	113	....	5189	....	....	....	1376	8050	37
Malaka	706	389	22090	955	717	13	2	....	....	278	97	201	44	142	13421	2	500	....	2088	5017	8
Mariposa	....	63	9495	185	118	....	....	....	....	....	....	9	7	....	4170	....	....	....	1556	434	50
Monroe, town of	....	1	70	438	36	40	20	12	....	15	....	310	7	8	2064	....	....	....	2476	9734	25
Mound Prairie	568	11	14145	1330	432	....	....	....	....	....	....	130	....	....	8801	1	2000	....	3655	9500	....
Newton, ex. of city	855	23	4374	4311	589	5	2	....	....	112	23	306	45	18	11502	....	....	....	3466	14237	107
Newton, city of	....	....	....	....	....	....	....	....	....	....	....	....	....	....	....	....	....	....	6099	30605	....
Palo Alto	973	50	3910	3435	600	11	4	....	....	22	5	292	50	68	7560	....	....	....	1757	4252	....
Poweshiek	2742	11	1031	3204	974	13	100	1	....	11	....	166	19	1	9832	2	6550	15	2123	4985	....
Prairie City, town of	....	....	....	58	43	....	....	....	....	16	9	121	20	68	376	....	....	....	410	9430	100
Richland	751	11	6965	1555	739	2	....	3	....	63	....	481	34	....	5649	....	....	....	753	3184	....
Rock Creek	1150	26	3175	747	99	....	....	....	....	30	8	213	1	34	345[illegible]	....	....	....	1427	2900	20
Sherman	1330	67	11880	1163	756	5	3	....	....	26	1	290	63	69	7449	....	....	....	1926	7570	17
Washington	544	58	5556	273	246	....	....	....	....	3	....	68	7	....	6942	....	....	....	686	7250	....
Total	29223	1212	158923	38024	15057	198	157	29	....	760	177	6247	2232	965	158585	7	11700	15	44157	180489	670

JEFFERSON COUNTY.

Batavia, town of	....	....	....	99	18	18	9	3	....	13	3	145	23	....	684	....	....	....	793	3750	....
Black Hawk	2820	37	13881	2875	2297	9	2	10	1	11	2	1250	785	1	13934	1	8000	....	1840	9798	....
Buchanan	3244	15	14742	10956	5601	213	46	399	84	76	14	1367	286	62	10735	1	12000	300	3949	25055	50
Cedar	7672	....	5660	7144	6817	53	12	197	69	80	15	907	139	1	6014	....	8000	100	1457	6880	....
Des Moines	6221	....	15339	8923	11598	67	12	192	23	77	10	2763	945	96	10025	....	....	....	1678	13102	11

JEFFERSON COUNTY.—Continued.

NAMES OF TOWNSHIPS, TOWNS, AND CITIES.	Acres of natural timber.	Acres of planted timber.	Rods of hedge.	APPLES. Number of trees in bearing.	APPLES. Bushels gathered in 1874.	PEARS. Number of trees in bearing.	PEARS. Bushels gathered in 1874.	PEACHES. Number of trees in bearing.	PEACHES. Bushels gathered in 1874.	PLUMS. Number of trees in bearing.	PLUMS. Bushels gathered in 1874.	CHERRIES. Number of trees in bearing.	CHERRIES. Bushels gathered in 1874.	Number of other fruit trees in bearing.	Number of fruit trees not in bearing.	GRAPES IN VINEYARD. Number of acres.	GRAPES IN VINEYARD. Pounds of grapes gathered.	GRAPES IN VINEYARD. Gallons of wine made.	GRAPES NOT IN VINEYARD. Number of vines.	GRAPES NOT IN VINEYARD. Pounds of grapes gathered.	GRAPES NOT IN VINEYARD. Gallons of wine made.
Fairfield, exc. of city	4398	2	3500	9536	4926	122	46	250	31	55	11	1785	507	284	9500	1	7000	…	4918	44538	146
Fairfield, city of	…	…	…	1789	774	278	82	299	98	430	188	2276	1071	79	3524	…	…	…	3608	36355	110
Liberty	3423	7	11960	6774	7239	232	33	253	39	139	14	2281	390	89	5267	1	3450	230	1731	13155	10
Lockridge	3717	…	6353	9275	6231	92	13	617	173	162	45	1120	251	21	7426	3	9000	20	4802	25635	583
Locust Grove, exc. of Batavia	5932	4	7685	6231	6300	80	69	187	38	74	23	1058	288	22	6591	3	14340	100	1492	18383	362
Penn	5173	18	11128	11640	8578	85	44	152	20	75	1	2458	294	1	7415	6	12600	60	2924	12292	40
Polk	1742	11	15379	4860	3221	49	20	…	…	…	…	535	79	…	3975	5	11200	…	1454	11200	…
Round Prairie	6893	4	12572	7726	5706	91	42	641	100	32	33	999	248	45	6306	4	4680	158	1191	4875	16
Walnut	4243	…	463	5643	3484	57	14	97	39	35	6	642	130	…	5897	6	5620	553	1192	3503	67
Total	55478	99	118662	93471	72790	1446	444	3297	715	1259	365	19586	5436	701	97343	32	95890	1521	33029	228521	1395

JOHNSON COUNTY.

NAMES OF TOWNSHIPS, TOWNS, AND CITIES.	Acres of natural timber.	Acres of planted timber.	Rods of hedge.	APPLES. Number of trees in bearing.	APPLES. Bushels gathered in 1874.	PEARS. Number of trees in bearing.	PEARS. Bushels gathered in 1874.	PEACHES. Number of trees in bearing.	PEACHES. Bushels gathered in 1874.	PLUMS. Number of trees in bearing.	PLUMS. Bushels gathered in 1874.	CHERRIES. Number of trees in bearing.	CHERRIES. Bushels gathered in 1874.	Number of other fruit trees in bearing.	Number of fruit trees not in bearing.	GRAPES IN VINEYARD. Number of acres.	GRAPES IN VINEYARD. Pounds of grapes gathered.	GRAPES IN VINEYARD. Gallons of wine made.	GRAPES NOT IN VINEYARD. Number of vines.	GRAPES NOT IN VINEYARD. Pounds of grapes gathered.	GRAPES NOT IN VINEYARD. Gallons of wine made.
Big Grove	3393	12	5945	4219	1279	4	…	…	…	6	…	81	19	…	1517	…	50	…	2166	8490	411
Cedar	3351	74	8981	4580	1738	10	…	12	1	35	15	428	152	3	4044	…	…	…	1886	10766	234
Clear Creek	754	14	3740	2254	1391	22	2	18	4	115	…	414	73	20	5624	1	6000	2	1228	15250	56
Coralville, town of	…	…	20	212	32	…	…	…	…	…	…	10	8	5	3[illegible]0	…	600	…	100	1075	120
Fremont	1008	13	7031	1312	1518	59	…	7	2	…	…	219	27	…	300	…	…	…	383	1665	…
Graham	2723	18	11625	5559	1632	15	1	42	4	91	10	450	75	5	6479	12	14500	…	2399	6713	718
Hardin	857	24	2275	228	117	…	…	…	…	…	6	6	…	80	3094	…	…	…	1023	2510	…
Iowa City	…	…	…	1668	753	112	25	4	1	153	55	784	446	16	16	12	16000	4050	3218	24965	22
Iowa City, additions to	3	…	…	198	240	…	…	…	…	…	…	29	31	…	1555	2	5000	…	2707	9540	355
Jefferson	1687	7	3230	2167	940	…	…	…	…	140	37	143	29	…	3399	…	6000	80	1417	2050	40
Liberty	2684	…	4535	2479	741	20	…	29	2	20	2	195	30	3	2920	1	3000	160	1927	3259	270
Lincoln	4	41	18219	650	115	2	…	…	…	41	2	211	…	7	5827	1	…	…	2085	289	…
Lucas	3628	3	6074	11174	6561	102	37	7	…	73	27	743	383	169	21390	49	16400	550	11750	53185	420
Madison	2097	66	8074	1473	751	4	…	1	…	304	61	486	124	7	5726	…	…	…	1088	11942	34

Monroe	2368	2	1337	1652	1104	13	......	......	......	3	......	186	10	17	2957	......	......	......	335	2090	34
Newport	1570	......	280	5963	1921	......	......	......	......	137	36	130	30	......	2237	......	......	......	1585	1165	......
Oxford	1759	89	2598	1034	430	9	......	......	......	6	10	35	6	......	4206	4	8900	55	1922	5417	......
Penn	2166	4	995	4273	2283	12	......	1	......	3	3	458	1008	18	1268	......	......	......	1038	1925	......
Pleasant Valley	686	11	7558	2026	1837	12	1	4	......	......	......	270	15	......	2577	......	......	......	696	1867	......
Scott	1830	78	8705	5046	1966	121	......	......	......	44	11	222	32	5	4372	4	6600	......	1137	6769	......
Sharon	3099	10	13331	4670	1344	37	11	6	......	35	3	311	22	3	6468	3	8200	982	3330	6218	132
Union	1772	6	5212	1088	350	......	......	......	......	61	16	127	16	127	4511	2	1920	157	1163	4240	......
Washington	2532	150	16027	3821	1260	31	2	1	......	32	10	455	71	35	945	......	650	150	3135	13802	185
Total	39971	622	135792	67748	30303	585	80	132	14	1304	304	6393	2607	520	91732	91	93820	6186	47718	195192	3031

JONES COUNTY.

Anamosa, town of	......	......	......	87	34	......	......	......	......	7	......	61	11	......	133	......	......	......	429	3455	4
Cass	2168	44	8962	1605	470	38	......	......	......	45	......	161	2	114	3282	......	881	......	1792	2216	......
Castle Grove	1487	......	1922	3445	1285	......	......	......	......	......	4	......	......	......	3116	......	200	......	41	10	12
Clay	4780	8	670	1144	597	......	......	1	......	1	......	15	3	......	9502	......	600	30	437	3166	......
Fairview, exc. of Anamosa and Strawberry Hill	3344	......	3648	2071	1000	......	......	......	......	35	14	715	134	188	5419	......	......	......	1795	7707	......
Greenfield	2056	67	7248	1992	564	......	......	......	......	......	......	733	165	269	7409	......	......	......	1259	4460	4
Hale	2487	74	8442	1950	446	5	......	......	......	7	......	397	23	95	6775	1	2000	......	806	5418	......
Jackson	9193	13	4363	1570	388	......	......	......	......	135	56	218	16	51	4100	......	......	......	361	1875	......
Madison	718	22	3146	1867	445	......	......	......	......	......	......	82	......	......	5358	......	......	......	296	2000	......
Monticello, exc. of town	3270	23	787	973	286	2	......	......	......	47	20	83	6	300	5239	3	2600	12	1064	3893	70
Monticello, town of	......	......	100	152	12	......	......	......	......	27	......	24	......	......	1524	2	1250	......	496	2180	......
Oxford	1155	37	6670	3006	657	......	......	......	......	12	7	372	47	45	6048	......	515	10	918	2321	5
Richland	4440	......	80	1167	697	......	......	......	......	......	......	......	......	......	2039	......	......	......	677	1582	58
Rome	2939	25	4982	3587	1105	6	1	......	......	46	7	458	66	110	1292	......	......	......	1078	6520	......
Scotch Grove	3857	8	991	1687	789	......	......	......	......	4	1	176	33	127	4629	......	50	......	185	904	3359
Strawberry Hill, town of	......	......	......	25	6	......	......	......	......	7	......	23	2	12	113	......	......	......	82	......	......
Washington	7743	......	......	52	70	......	......	......	......	......	......	......	......	......	......	......	......	......	......	......	......
Wayne	561	135	3402	3866	718	15	......	1	......	32	1	312	66	311	5498	......	......	......	1754	4756	60
Wyoming, exc. of town	2348	16	1580	3493	1139	10	1	1	......	93	20	245	46	......	9897	......	2640	......	973	4809	25
Wyoming, town of	......	......	......	467	138	1	......	......	......	52	20	208	49	30	1537	......	......	......	1251	10195	......
Total	52546	473	56903	34183	10840	77	2	3	......	543	150	4260	667	1640	82797	6	10736	52	14612	67067	3597

KEOKUK COUNTY.

Adams	852	31	22359	2633	1442	4	4	......	......	3	4	274	38	......	7375	......	......	......	753	5562	......
Benton	3712	......	24814	3156	2020	7	2	14	2	14	4	462	67	......	7288	......	......	......	1236	4139	20
Clear Creek	3366	......	8841	2378	22[illegible]9	5	1	3	3	7	2	166	36	163	5696	3	1000	50	521	2910	25
English River	1767	25	26063	2434	2015	14	2	......	......	6	2	152	80	......	10483	......	300	......	1237	9993	24

KEOKUK COUNTY.—Continued.

NAMES OF TOWNSHIPS, TOWNS, AND CITIES.	Acres of natural timber.	Acres of planted timber.	Rods of hedge.	APPLES.		PEARS.		PEACHES		PLUMS.		CHERRIES.		Number of other fruit trees in bearing.	Number of fruit trees not in bearing.	GRAPES IN VINEYARD.			GRAPES NOT IN VINEYARD.		
				Number of trees in bearing.	Bushels gathered in 1874.	Number of trees in bearing.	Bushels gathered in 1874.	Number of trees in bearing.	Bushels gathered in 1874.	Number of trees in bearing.	Bushels gathered in 1874.	Number of trees in bearing.	Bushels gathered in 1874.			Number of acres.	Pounds of grapes gathered.	Gallons of wine made.	Number of vines.	Pounds of grapes gathered.	Gallons of wine made.
German	6467	....	12144	2852	1121	....	....	....	....	30	19	114	23	75	10453	....	....	....	3667	21400	399
Jackson	2990	7	12540	4520	2451	23	7	....	....	8	2	426	127	....	6001	....	....	....	1727	7320	....
Keota, town of	....	....	....	....	....	....	....	....	....	....	....	....	....	....	....	....	....	....	....	....	....
LaFayette, exc. of Keota	203	108	34592	1519	378	10	....	6	....	394	59	412	30	....	13034	1	2000	6	2034	6925	61
Lancaster	3840	2	11545	5217	2847	11	3	331	35	45	21	868	81	68	7366	1	800	160	1227	5920	22
Liberty	1385	108	23660	2870	1183	17	1	17	....	185	30	530	115	36	12108	....	....	....	1833	9781	63
Prairie	32	69	8363	2095	188	....	....	....	....	....	....	48	7	40	7367	....	....	....	2775	5119	....
Richland, exc. of town	5004	4	4222	4558	2405	12	2	68	10	5	1	406	159	....	6235	....	....	....	2619	25299	163
Richland, town of	799	20	924	1549	1353	57	45	45	15	101	44	574	158	29	3091	3	16000	522	1335	7311	4
Sigourney, exc. of town	2195	1	715	3426	2302	8	1	63	7	207	161	595	163	3	7228	4	25000	530	1291	9680	71
Sigourney, town of	....	....	....	798	2046	129	33	77	1	362	89	956	629	34	1853	....	....	....	1175	32042	16
Steady Run	3438	6	23729	3792	2010	24	10	64	31	308	138	892	233	140	3833	1	3450	....	1435	4985	3
Van Buren	3540	....	7992	4066	1819	....	....	36	6	49	19	220	34	130	2020	....	....	....	774	5876	....
Warren	2805	1	3817	1913	785	2	....	12	....	25	2	118	20	10	5043	1	2000	....	384	3620	....
Washington	2605	18	12430	2649	839	....	....	350	52	100	2	71	16	....	....	....	....	....	617	2133	280
Total	45000	400	238750	52425	29473	323	111	1086	162	1849	599	7284	2016	728	116474	14	50550	1268	26640	170015	1151

KOSSUTH COUNTY.

NAMES OF TOWNSHIPS, TOWNS, AND CITIES.	Acres of natural timber.	Acres of planted timber.	Rods of hedge.	Apples: Number of trees in bearing.	Apples: Bushels gathered in 1874.	Pears: Number of trees in bearing.	Pears: Bushels gathered in 1874.	Peaches: Number of trees in bearing.	Peaches: Bushels gathered in 1874.	Plums: Number of trees in bearing.	Plums: Bushels gathered in 1874.	Cherries: Number of trees in bearing.	Cherries: Bushels gathered in 1874.	Number of other fruit trees in bearing.	Number of fruit trees not in bearing.	Vineyard: Number of acres.	Vineyard: Pounds of grapes gathered.	Vineyard: Gallons of wine made.	Not in vineyard: Number of vines.	Not in vineyard: Pounds of grapes gathered.	Not in vineyard: Gallons of wine made.
Algona, exc. of town	382	107	....	31	2	....	....	....	....	225	87	....	....	....	....	....	....	....	26	140	....
Algona, town of	538	61	640	20	....	....	....	....	....	10	2	1	....	....	9	....	....	....	13	10	....
Cresco	349	66	753	67	2	....	....	....	....	....	....	....	....	....	509	....	....	....	25	....	54
Fenton	....	26	494	....	....	....	....	....	....	26	....	10	....	....	232	....	....	....	23	1	....
Greenwood	150	33	1700	14	....	....	....	....	....	609	36	....	....	....	579	....	....	....	12	....	....
Irvington	584	74	4585	61	....	....	....	....	....	....	....	....	....	....	369	....	....	....	11	....	....
Lotts Creek	1	63	480	4	....	....	....	....	....	333	3	8	....	33	243	....	....	....	134	60	2

Portland	339	103	630	......	......	......	......	......	......	70	8	......	......	......	......	......	......	......	......	......	......
Wesley	......	50	533	3	......	......	......	......	......	51	2	......	......	......	934	......	......	......	24	......	......
Total	2344	583	9815	200	4	......	......	......	......	1324	138	19	......	33	2875	......	......	......	268	210	56

LEE COUNTY.

Cedar	1466	29	51950	10202	9748	268	132	1967	611	368	106	2916	920	106	11882	......	......	......	2358	9557	27
Charleston	7464	......	13222	8990	7074	59	67	1625	1031	14	3	1589	587	......	6604	3	9720	720	1786	6864	159
Denmark	3495	......	16848	10729	11217	244	71	577	93	2	20	981	417	372	1806	46	5300	20	1467	6410	......
Des Moines	6291	......	9440	9007	5194	159	32	2349	1414	20	2	1392	311	16	9522	1	9600	510	2106	9813	......
Fort Madison, city of	......	......	......	2163	2526	432	139	1912	1538	85	28	1657	956	3	4390	9	7700	390	29029	78330	3570
Franklin	4604	......	24229	10102	8169	176	146	1223	889	60	10	1739	943	......	7047	20	1500	8005	6282	4045	1495
Green Bay	4348	......	3670	4571	4555	12	3	142	30	5	......	233	241	147	924	15	12775	2990	583	80	......
Harrison	4603	8	26889	10358	6807	241	148	1773	968	64	15	1950	736	......	4651	1	2100	75	1120	6911	75
Jackson, exc. of Keokuk	3599	......	810	4665	5730	125	32	2961	1517	14	2	732	318	......	13019	78	31900	47270	3519	3722	140
Jefferson	3677	......	4957	6105	5666	67	18	718	476	22	2	1182	381	3	11939	5	9240	1210	1536	4325	147
Keokuk, city of	25	......	50	1797	955	167	52	743	630	32	5	703	257	......	......	16	41600	535	......	......	......
Madison, exc. of Fort Madison	214	......	2090	1086	1348	117	14	306	235	......	......	289	106	......	1525	8	18000	1280	2835	9650	380
Marion	3273	31	41505	9689	7187	68	74	1266	702	63	23	1971	511	70	8880	3	200	890	1309	6440	30
Montrose, exc. of town	4079	......	14608	11776	11920	616	312	4041	2791	19	7	1770	910	32	17403	9	2540	100	1452	3150	55
Montrose, town of	......	......	......	376	307	24	......	105	126	......	......	130	35	......	......	......	......	......	......	......	......
Pleasant Ridge	4188	4	37835	11822	12233	72	56	1428	463	18	14	1653	733	37	7170	2	4500	......	3535	22332	295
Van Buren	5060	1	7305	2602	2538	20	11	466	234	28	5	484	143	12	4058	1	1400	290	808	3172	35
Washington	6133	7	22477	21312	16370	521	330	3752	2015	158	13	3299	777	5	11051	37	78229	6735	2086	7610	40
West Point, exc. of town	6197	......	14250	8839	7655	109	65	1926	1057	6	2	1297	325	5	11627	14	37080	2339	6799	6711	813
West Point, town of	......	......	......	691	1063	22	15	343	204	7	5	661	246	......	......	9	10400	1960	1578	7770	451
Total	68716	80	292035	146882	128262	3519	1717	29523	17024	985	262	26628	9853	808	133498	277	283784	75319	70188	196897	7712

LINN COUNTY.

Bertram	4431	......	......	937	250	1	......	......	......	......	......	65	......	54	1642	......	......	......	784	1918	......
Boulder	1583	19	1200	617	256	......	......	......	......	......	......	55	2	48	4168	......	......	......	367	533	......
Brown	2695	118	7120	2687	1737	8	......	1	......	39	26	845	118	519	7037	2	3600	......	1363	8939	2
Buffalo	3748	7	100	313	125	......	......	......	......	20	40	10	2	13	1704	......	......	......	235	293	......
Cedar Rapids, city of	......	......	......	20	25	......	......	......	......	20	8	15	2	......	......	1	2000	70	921	13170	320
Clinton	1363	47	4355	2623	526	13	......	24	......	26	1	296	6	12	9690	......	......	......	3618	6240	......
College, exc. of Western	2371	48	4385	1043	453	2	1	......	......	3	1	188	28	34	6808	4	3000	......	713	1827	22
Fairfax	509	62	5450	3107	377	5	......	......	......	6	......	546	34	37	11533	......	......	......	1702	4570	......
Fayette	1157	11	175	2481	373	4	8	......	......	49	42	89	12	107	7106	6	1600	5	736	2954	5
Franklin, exc. of Mt. Vernon and Lisbon	4380	8	4937	5763	825	50	......	2	......	38	18	737	178	428	1250	3	21500	92	2017	13356	41
Grant	382	87	2672	665	260	1	......	......	......	13	8	28	12	......	6467	......	......	......	968	1536	7
Jackson	4269	21	868	1212	491	......	......	......	......	......	......	60	41	122	9467	......	......	......	627	1672	......

LINN COUNTY.—CONTINUED.

NAMES OF TOWNSHIPS, TOWNS AND CITIES.	Acres of natural timber.	Acres of planted timber.	Rods of hedge.	APPLES. Number of trees in bearing.	APPLES. Bushels gathered in 1874.	PEARS. Number of trees in bearing.	PEARS. Bushels gathered in 1874.	PEACHES. Number of trees in bearing.	PEACHES. Bushels gathered in 1874.	PLUMS. Number of trees in bearing.	PLUMS. Bushels gathered in 1874.	CHERRIES. Number of trees in bearing.	CHERRIES. Bushels gathered in 1874.	Number of other fruit trees in bearing.	Number of fruit trees not in bearing.	GRAPES IN VINEYARD. Number of acres.	GRAPES IN VINEYARD. Pounds of grapes gathered.	GRAPES IN VINEYARD. Gallons of wine made.	GRAPES NOT IN VINEYARD. Number of vines.	GRAPES NOT IN VINEYARD. Pounds of grapes gathered.	GRAPES NOT IN VINEYARD. Gallons of wine made.
Linn	5057	54	7270	3113	1221	18	....	2	....	174	17	501	34	116	5662	......	....	......	1048	6175	9
Lisbon, town of	13	....	20	25	36	......	....	......	....	......	....	57	22	....	....	6	....	......	179	2030	8
Maine	3420	137	7284	525	145	......	....	......	....	......	....	99	39	....	8414	1	2500	......	1325	3195	......
Marion, exc. of city	5392	107	9328	6402	1823	......	....	......	....	1711	514	225	13	....	12162	1	5200	......	3349	13339	15
Marion, city of	....	....	....	....	....	......	....	......	....	......	....	20	15	....	....	......	....	......	50	100	20
Monroe	4475	4	30	1937	524	......	....	......	....	41	10	89	10	31	4430	......	1200	......	742	1587	......
Mount Vernon, town of	....	....	....	674	239	......	....	......	....	32	10	513	282	18	1134	6	12600	......	943	9870	12
Otter Creek	1487	27	3328	1224	384	4	3	......	....	32	7	251	23	623	7282	......	....	......	1246	7351	19
Putnam	6712	1	1420	722	265	......	....	......	....	2	....	155	27	9	2873	......	....	......	1054	3000	13
Rapids, exc. of Cedar Rapids	5200	2	262	5124	514	37	....	33	....	219	35	1583	105	433	8923	15	16890	45	3189	7810	......
Spring Grove	1545	7	2340	381	94	......	....	......	....	20	6	68	6	38	4851	......	....	......	663	625	......
Washington	2929	37	1024	332	....	......	....	......	....	......	....	10	......	....	4930	......	....	......	586	1345	9
Western, town of	235	11	660	863	314	2	1	......	....	30	9	118	24	....	895	3	17150	70	1312	1920	......
Total	63383	815	64228	42790	11257	145	13	62	....	2475	752	6623	1035	2642	128428	49	87240	282	29767	115355	502

LOUISA COUNTY.

NAMES OF TOWNSHIPS, TOWNS AND CITIES.	Acres of natural timber.	Acres of planted timber.	Rods of hedge.	APPLES. Number of trees in bearing.	APPLES. Bushels gathered in 1874.	PEARS. Number of trees in bearing.	PEARS. Bushels gathered in 1874.	PEACHES. Number of trees in bearing.	PEACHES. Bushels gathered in 1874.	PLUMS. Number of trees in bearing.	PLUMS. Bushels gathered in 1874.	CHERRIES. Number of trees in bearing.	CHERRIES. Bushels gathered in 1874.	Number of other fruit trees in bearing.	Number of fruit trees not in bearing.	GRAPES IN VINEYARD. Number of acres.	GRAPES IN VINEYARD. Pounds of grapes gathered.	GRAPES IN VINEYARD. Gallons of wine made.	GRAPES NOT IN VINEYARD. Number of vines.	GRAPES NOT IN VINEYARD. Pounds of grapes gathered.	GRAPES NOT IN VINEYARD. Gallons of wine made.
Columbus City, exc. of Columbus City and Colun bus Junc.	4052	....	22057	12917	6354	92	39	229	16	349	44	1974	233	89	6125	1552	30000	489	3371	10960	7
Columbus City, town of	45	....	175	2147	810	21	1	......	....	12	7	141	44	....	150	2	16500	1000	290	8230	......
Columbus Junction, town of	2	....	....	15	6	......	....	......	....	......	....	2	......	....	15	......	....	......	2	2	......
Concord, exc. of Fredonia	1419	2	7889	2767	1475	20	....	27	6	3	1	689	84	15	3970	......	....	......	1921	10002	49
Eliot	1937	63	4140	2587	1222	13	1	89	16	17	16	323	94	2	3270	......	500	......	638	1165	......
Elm Grove	1192	14	16060	4949	2441	18	8	78	16	26	....	1599	172	48	3881	......	75	4	1182	6340	......
Fredonia, town of	179	....	200	183	27	1	....	3	....	12	1	101	17	14	283	......	....	......	42	15	......
Grandview	4879	4	6114	7630	3372	11	6	1047	36	58	4	1465	396	576	3490	5	29300	6156	1678	15946	230
Jefferson	3672	....	1241	3238	2768	32	11	186	57	5	1	649	196	....	9109	......	....	......	1983	27710	49

Marshall	2692	17	8608	6172	3031	30	16	141	41	29	11	1873	250	116	5172	2	2500	200	1126	6719	......
Morning Sun, exc. of town	3133	66	25917	7643	3790	78	14	726	164	158	18	1532	269	450	11227	550	3300	......	994	5373	......
Morning Sun, town of	....	....	....	....	....	......	....	......	....	......	....	....	......	....	....	....	....	......	....	....	......
Oakland	1704	9	7850	1228	552	8	2	5	2	6	1	258	46	....	2815	....	....	......	213	973	......
Port Louisa	3321	....	640	2478	1467	6	1	90	53	7	2	533	82	60	5375	1	450	80	803	1410	......
Union	2409	3	11517	2674	1774	3	4	47	13	......	....	51	8	8	3443	....	....	......	935	2695	......
Wapello, exc. of town	6181	....	9717	7573	4355	49	10	639	224	16	2	1678	443	2	6307	....	....	......	1027	7397	17
Wapello, town of	482	....	440	889	590	43	19	130	28	54	5	998	276	9	817	....	....	......	223	612	4
Total	37299	178	122565	65090	34034	425	133	3437	672	752	113	13866	2710	1389	65549	*2113	82625	7929	16428	105549	356

* NOTE BY COUNTY AUDITOR.—Vines and acres are evidently badly mixed.

LUCAS COUNTY.

Benton	1949	27	17347	1955	650	8	1	3	....	22	5	184	24	37	3854	....	....	......	722	1987	15
Cedar	2523	3	11145	1324	936	3	1	53	19	4	2	115	21	620	3948	....	....	......	9267	9155	......
Chariton, exc. of city	1258	3	14205	2958	1642	81	28	......	....	58	9	704	254	....	14684	5	7100	140	1917	8680	......
Chariton, city of	....	....	....	650	771	79	15	26	10	134	23	662	328	428	2745	....	....	......	2996	16980	5
English	2225	17	14222	994	337	8	1	22	1	10	5	159	43	....	7587	....	....	......	1080	2776	......
Jackson	1473	5	5045	455	451	1	....	1	....	2	....	163	54	6	1640	....	....	......	823	5682	......
Liberty	1544	2	8014	597	659	6	2	5	5	...	....	204	45	....	4278	....	....	......	521	2675	...
Otter Creek	2180	9	13470	742	923	2	1	......	....	......	....	20	3	52	2735	....	....	......	686	2510	......
Pleasant	1346	25	6353	913	546	16	3	12	....	62	25	249	17	27	3734	50	....	......	730	2157	......
Union	2124	11	16680	574	357	......	2	1	....	10	5	111	58	47	7016	....	....	......	702	2255	5
Warren	2004	41	30858	2262	844	20	1	32	....	182	28	970	86	38	11952	2	360	......	1616	3445	22
Washington	2224	5	13236	706	255	2	....	30	....	75	6	255	13	14	4521	....	....	......	729	798	......
White Breast	2034	2	14440	875	867	4	5	......	....	......	....	305	48	....	6174	1	2500	......	602	5592	......
Total	22884	150	165015	15005	9238	230	60	185	35	559	108	4101	994	1269	74868	58	9960	140	22391	64692	47

LYON COUNTY.

Dale	....	41	....	....	....	......	....	......	....	......	....	....	......	....	....	....	....	......	....	....	......
Doon	50	....	1130	....	....	......	....	......	....	......	....	....	......	....	....	....	....	......	....	....	......
Grant	....	4	380	....	....	......	....	......	....	......	....	....	......	....	365	....	....	......	104	....	32
Larchwood	54	23	270	....	....	......	....	......	....	......	....	....	......	....	300	....	....	......	300	....	......
Lyon	587	52	575	....	....	......	....	......	....	......	....	....	......	....	1441	....	....	56	....	....	......
Rock	....	25	580	....	....	......	....	......	....	......	....	....	......	....	....	....	....	......	....	....	......
Total	691	145	2935	....	....	......	....	......	....	......	....	....	......	....	2106	....	....	56	404	....	32

MADISON COUNTY.

NAMES OF TOWNSHIPS, TOWNS, AND CITIES.	Acres of natural timber.	Acres of planted timber.	Rods of hedge.	APPLES. Number of trees in bearing.	APPLES. Bushels gathered in 1874.	PEARS. Number of trees in bearing.	PEARS. Bushels gathered in 1874.	PEACHES. Number of trees in bearing.	PEACHES. Bushels gathered in 1874.	PLUMS. Number of trees in bearing.	PLUMS. Bushels gathered in 1874.	CHERRIES. Number of trees in bearing.	CHERRIES. Bushels gathered in 1874.	Number of other fruit trees in bearing.	Number of fruit trees not in bearing.	GRAPES IN VINEYARD. Number of acres.	GRAPES IN VINEYARD. Pounds of grapes gathered.	GRAPES IN VINEYARD. Gallons of wine made.	GRAPES NOT IN VINEYARD. Number of vines.	GRAPES NOT IN VINEYARD. Pounds of grapes gathered.	GRAPES NOT IN VINEYARD. Gallons of wine made.
Crawford	1812	3	4428	1914	1181	...	...	5	1	5	...	81	...	4	7102	...	601	...	1866	220	25
Douglas	4800	24	5875	2517	1544	3	...	...	...	...	...	150	38	...	13612	10	35400	433	2300	7551	20
Earlham, town of	...	...	...	...	...	...	...	...	...	...	...	...	...	...	...	...	...	...	...	...	...
Grand River	1365	57	10225	1173	766	3	...	2	...	79	5	95	5	17	7428	1	1500	10	1477	2056	1
Jackson	828	40	7452	539	388	4	1	18	...	...	...	56	9	20	8132	1	150	...	1310	5257	...
Jefferson	1550	64	8313	1890	1041	9	...	58	13	9	2	266	27	78	15660	1	400	...	3798	6175	...
Lee	1058	268	5955	670	285	4	...	...	...	...	...	...	...	4	4699	1	30	...	1159	200	...
Lincoln	3985	12	6544	2028	1220	2	...	1	1	...	...	152	10	...	9274	...	...	...	3124	19720	...
Madison, exc. of Earlham	1129	124	10568	1763	725	19	100	49	1	2	...	524	87	10	11907	...	...	...	1841	8441	...
Monroe	423	4	6540	851	625	...	...	1	...	...	...	58	...	...	5377	...	...	...	1367	2580	43
Ohio	742	35	6010	630	379	1	...	1	...	45	23	27	10	13	7959	...	...	...	1284	8291	...
Penn, exc. of Earlham	253	240	20326	1112	308	1	...	...	...	64	4	652	59	6	15607	1	208	...	4495	4848	...
Scott	3919	5	8165	3515	1354	22	5	38	...	32	...	134	6	27	7898	...	...	...	2304	6365	15
South	4636	4	2815	1715	1097	19	3	8	2	1	...	35	7	8	8411	4	2100	...	1954	7272	63
Union	4046	4	3376	4613	2116	26	5	30	10	18	5	322	39	6	12497	8	9500	...	2292	9851	...
Walnut	2527	7	4516	1759	697	23	...	33	...	70	40	180	7	256	4873	2	1150	...	1530	3152	...
Webster	1353	18	5870	786	398	19	...	121	2	91	94	98	6	100	6235	...	200	...	832	1620	...
Winterset, city of	...	1	180	1916	1016	96	56	28	6	384	195	756	298	101	5866	6	10000	...	4991	55053	870
Total	34426	910	117158	29391	15140	251	170	414	36	800	368	3586	608	650	152637	35	61239	443	37924	148652	1037

MAHASKA COUNTY.

NAMES OF TOWNSHIPS, TOWNS, AND CITIES.	Acres of natural timber.	Acres of planted timber.	Rods of hedge.	APPLES. Number of trees in bearing.	APPLES. Bushels gathered in 1874.	PEARS. Number of trees in bearing.	PEARS. Bushels gathered in 1874.	PEACHES. Number of trees in bearing.	PEACHES. Bushels gathered in 1874.	PLUMS. Number of trees in bearing.	PLUMS. Bushels gathered in 1874.	CHERRIES. Number of trees in bearing.	CHERRIES. Bushels gathered in 1874.	Number of other fruit trees in bearing.	Number of fruit trees not in bearing.	GRAPES IN VINEYARD. Number of acres.	GRAPES IN VINEYARD. Pounds of grapes gathered.	GRAPES IN VINEYARD. Gallons of wine made.	GRAPES NOT IN VINEYARD. Number of vines.	GRAPES NOT IN VINEYARD. Pounds of grapes gathered.	GRAPES NOT IN VINEYARD. Gallons of wine made.
Adams	2091	12	11842	1892	1031	6	...	...	...	...	...	366	70	...	4888	...	...	...	1086	10010	...
Beacon, town of	27	...	...	...	...	...	...	...	...	...	...	...	...	...	75	...	...	...	100	1600	...
Black Oak	1362	39	10112	3180	1068	8	2	20	...	4	...	450	157	842	4216	2	1600	65	972	7401	26
Cedar	1462	...	21098	4345	3627	1	2	...	...	1	1	492	234	...	7305	...	...	...	1005	6012	11
Des Moines	2455	...	3842	1750	620	15	8	52	16	27	18	375	42	4	8065	...	...	...	3097	16525	170

Harrison	2178	5	13195	4266	3020	31	15	20	10	25	10	233	144	19	8066	1	2000	......	1378	27825	40
Jefferson	5220	11	7410	2638	1225	9	3	67	19	64	25	319	93	......	7204	......	......	......	881	10495	4
Madison	2566	28	11198	3818	674	13	3	1	......	16	3	520	123	96	6324	......	......	......	1959	12189	......
Monroe	6302	1	7260	2144	2103	11	8	4	......	110	55	230	70	42	9341	2	1500	......	916	5965	80
New Sharon, town of	......	......	280	667	504	6	2	......	......	24	6	143	57	74	1443	......	......	......	190	1093	......
Oskaloosa, exc. of city and Beacon	5598	......	17166	18562	11756	108	14	63	6	190	17	1759	457	59	30574	......	......	......	7130	55099	5
Oskaloosa, city of	......	......	......	800	625	10	1	......	......	......	......	170	88	375	355	3	11400	......	544	5600	......
Pleasant Grove	845	6	7883	1922	720	4	......	......	......	1	......	169	19	8	6190	1	4250	100	650	1688	......
Prairie, exc. of New Sharon	550	44	30517	3399	1364	22	3	13	......	16	1	1386	323	263	17147	......	1500	......	2692	11865	......
Richland	3115	17	7760	3824	1827	8	6	......	......	......	......	239	70	......	6963	......	......	......	1997	9618	15
Scott	5477	39	5110	3407	708	15	1	60	6	247	35	745	94	2	5465	......	......	......	2568	23680	87
Union	2124	332	8956	2011	1244	......	......	......	......	178	100	137	24	82	8620	......	......	......	793	5838	......
White Oak	4760	10	3560	3770	3069	12	6	13	6	6	6	237	59	89	7170	......	......	......	972	6965	11
Total	46132	544	167189	62395	35185	279	75	313	63	909	278	7970	2124	1955	137411	10	22250	165	28940	219468	449

MARION COUNTY.

Clay	3564	......	3478	4352	1534	30	9	112	......	44	9	338	24	......	......	......	......	......	1068	15387	......
Dallas	2645	7	10334	2518	1254	22	14	14	......	43	......	275	57	17	7783	851	17490	575	2822	6888	33
Franklin	853	30	14670	10[illegible]3	873	4	1	......	......	......	......	164	24	10	9528	......	......	......	3454	14018	......
Indiana	4017	......	6932	4066	1281	35	3	24	4	69	13	742	191	135	6105	......	......	......	1213	9188	2
Knoxville, exc. of town	6042	116	7271	11210	4029	23	7	14	3	116	30	1381	196	......	12120	......	......	......	4363	25651	30
Knoxville, town of	......	......	160	3559	785	60	14	4	......	425	63	1424	625	......	5574	......	......	......	4430	36865	216
Lake Prairie, exc. of Pella	6185	9	7281	5782	2952	......	......	......	......	49	11	488	156	......	8048	2	6000	......	1710	10166	285
Liberty	3548	7	4006	3120	1235	8	5	19	16	101	89	479	219	160	6182	......	......	......	1311	15895	......
Pella, city of	......	......	......	1028	189	36	......	24	12	164	66	340	144	......	1706	4	5700	......	1890	21580	199
Perry	1433	......	100	1584	584	1	......	......	......	10	2	188	17	3	1985	......	......	......	370	1926	3
Pleasant Grove, exc. of Pleasantville	3154	15	9108	2357	1698	10	......	8	......	220	102	257	31	90	7677	......	......	......	3627	14975	171
Pleasantville, town of	......	......	......	......	......	......	......	......	......	......	......	......	......	......	......	......	......	......	......	......	......
Polk	1907	......	160	1342	915	......	......	......	......	44	10	172	17	89	2486	......	......	......	498	2902	......
Red Rock	6154	......	2150	3079	1611	2	1	40	......	36	7	379	24	10	6429	2	4040	70	929	1260	......
Summit	2411	27	5388	3275	2757	......	......	3	......	28	22	549	83	6	7676	......	......	......	1199	7527	21
Swan	2931	......	1400	3250	2947	65	17	37	......	......	18	282	27	55	3958	......	......	......	1052	4076	65
Union	2149	......	2972	853	584	2	......	......	......	7	4	148	66	......	2592	......	......	......	596	3140	......
Washington	2188	10	4923	2383	1102	15	......	......	......	......	9	387	84	32	5437	1	1000	......	1131	6595	1
Total	49181	221	80333	55061	26330	313	71	289	35	1256	445	7993	1985	607	95186	860	34230	645	31663	198030	1026

MARSHALL COUNTY.

Albion, town of	10	5	120	1073	224	9	......	......	......	715	211	644	259	68	3890	4	7000	......	2735	10985	15
Bangor	1384	97	10452	4105	671	27	3	......	......	1165	182	868	262	101	7416	1	100	......	1781	1983	220

MARSHALL COUNTY.—Continued.

Names of townships, towns, and cities.	Acres of natural timber.	Acres of planted timber.	Rods of hedge.	Apples. Number of trees in bearing.	Apples. Bushels gathered in 1874.	Pears. Number of trees in bearing.	Pears. Bushels gathered in 1874.	Peaches. Number of trees in bearing.	Peaches. Bushels gathered in 1874.	Plums. Number of trees in bearing.	Plums. Bushels gathered in 1874.	Cherries. Number of trees in bearing.	Cherries. Bushels gathered in 1874.	Number of other fruit trees in bearing.	Number of fruit trees not in bearing.	Grapes in vineyard. Number of acres.	Grapes in vineyard. Pounds of grapes gathered.	Grapes in vineyard. Gallons of wine made.	Grapes not in vineyard. Number of vines.	Grapes not in vineyard. Pounds of grapes gathered.	Grapes not in vineyard. Gallons of wine made.
Eden	1517	100	14925	952	246	8	4	......	......	58	24	93	18	......	4484	......	......	......	790	2965	24
Greencastle	111	173	16958	414	65	......	......	......	......	......	......	50	6	......	8717	......	......	......	2204	2297	......
Iowa, exc. of Albion	1346	35	4783	2022	440	15	3	......	......	1	......	640	119	172	9416	7	1900	6	2048	4857	13
Jefferson	118	114	11850	159	23	3	3	......	......	1	......	144	8	32	9712	......	......	......	1206	1470	......
Le Grand	1706	157	12793	2419	1270	9	2	......	......	304	97	642	191	219	14036	......	......	......	2170	10808	......
Liberty	827	159	14623	966	779	4	1	......	......	322	104	239	58	11	11326	......	......	......	1046	1925	......
Liscomb, exc. of town	913	125	12280	1025	276	......	......	......	......	413	62	738	65	177	7478	5	7500	......	2403	2413	......
Liscomb, town of	......	6	679	174	62	......	......	......	......	16	3	105	11	2	665	......	200	......	452	865	......
Logan	45	69	9555	4	......	......	......	......	......	20	......	28	......	28	3827	......	......	......	1450	110	......
Marietta	868	116	5070	1387	479	12	1	4	1	420	175	531	153	41	8163	4	5958	......	1573	3290	......
Marion	2348	61	9340	2355	719	33	1	......	......	163	118	319	15	1076	7134	1	1300	......	2897	4755	3
Marshall, exc. of Marshalltown	613	32	1741	632	242	60	6	......	......	242	28	577	222	15	6481	2	1500	......	1193	8850	6
Marshalltown, city of	304	19	830	2256	414	128	27	......	......	838	283	2505	772	712	18906	9	17650	31	20125	61526	339
Minerva	666	55	5850	363	209	13	6	......	......	1	......	302	6	36	4227	......	......	......	629	775	......
State Center, exc. of town	353	3527	6885	391	62	1	......	......	......	15	1	158	19	12	6429	......	......	......	1185	2748	40
State Center, town of	......	5	195	260	24	1	......	1	......	......	......	732	100	......	2905	......	......	......	969	3030	100
Taylor	691	127	8906	2597	492	37	1	......	......	15	......	527	41	6	8413	......	500	5	1741	7170	......
Timber Creek	1385	48	5305	1092	234	......	......	......	......	8	3	621	85	......	9129	3	3500	......	3036	7435	......
Vienna	135	215	4107	592	175	2	......	......	......	655	85	121	53	......	8988	......	......	......	1581	1239	......
Washington	347	281	18600	572	109	2	......	......	......	126	13	141	21	6	9012	......	......	......	2381	4401	9
Total	15687	5526	175847	25810	7215	364	58	5	1	5498	1389	10725	2484	2718	170754	36	47108	42	56595	145897	869

MILLS COUNTY.

Names of townships, towns, and cities.	Acres of natural timber.	Acres of planted timber.	Rods of hedge.	Apples. Number of trees in bearing.	Apples. Bushels gathered in 1874.	Pears. Number of trees in bearing.	Pears. Bushels gathered in 1874.	Peaches. Number of trees in bearing.	Peaches. Bushels gathered in 1874.	Plums. Number of trees in bearing.	Plums. Bushels gathered in 1874.	Cherries. Number of trees in bearing.	Cherries. Bushels gathered in 1874.	Number of other fruit trees in bearing.	Number of fruit trees not in bearing.	Grapes in vineyard. Number of acres.	Grapes in vineyard. Pounds of grapes gathered.	Grapes in vineyard. Gallons of wine made.	Grapes not in vineyard. Number of vines.	Grapes not in vineyard. Pounds of grapes gathered.	Grapes not in vineyard. Gallons of wine made.
Anderson	1695	35	7735	281	78	3	......	35	7	2	......	50	5	5	5814	......	1300	......	466	432	......
Deer Creek	163	70	23262	338	70	......	4	10	4	......	......	59	24	164	6160	......	......	......	598	......	......
Emerson, town of	79	......	40	......	......	......	......	......	......	......	......	......	......	......	190	65	......	......	......	......	......

Glenwood, exc. of town	...	...	...	1655	1280	31	4	640	112	10	...	403	36	54	22198	3	4200	...	3056	5755	...
Glenwood, town of	33	...	...	400	530	...	20	...	...	...	...	5	1	5	400	...	...	...	...	...	...
Hastings, town of	40	...	...	...	...	...	...	...	...	...	...	...		...	712	...	...	...	...	...	...
Hillsdale, town of	...	...	...	...	...	...	...	...	...	...	...	...	...	...	...	...	...	...	...	...	...
Indian Creek, exc. of Emerson and Hastings	1023	38	8049	18	15	2	1	5	...	...	...	63	1	...	3858	...	...	...	675	150	...
Ingraham	1001	54	5493	619	177	12	...	176	58	85	8	167	9	1231	5227	...	...	...	729	235	...
Lyons	3116	3	2009	720	1270	7	1	173	29	1	2	46	5	...	...	...	1000	...	810	653	...
Malvern, town of	3	240	...	...	...	...	...	...	...	...	...	...	...	...	142	...	...	...	2	...	...
Oak	4289	19	2111	1881	3166	3	...	50	7	29	7	190	25	45	9314	3	50	...	1626	1655	20
Platteville	479	12	470	16	3	...	...	...	...	4	1	54	...	2	2090	...	100	...	607	1015	...
Rawles	1570	95	15268	3869	4591	48	8	466	278	5	3	289	49	50	10424	...	1000	...	2535	2068	...
St. Mary	1055	...	80	196	675	6	...	2	1	1	...	71	18	...	1191	12	...		...	...	...
Silver Creek, exc. of Hillsdale and Malvern	2933	115	15095	2822	3145	...	...	201	90	95	15	232	86	4	14575	1503	10000	190	3099	2129	450
White Cloud	1023	68	17266	141	43	...	...	125	24	20	7	32	4	12	4463	...	...	...	558	3460	25
Total	18502	749	96869	12956	15043	112	38	1883	610	252	43	1661	263	1572	86758	1588	17650	190	14761	17552	495

MITCHELL COUNTY.

Burr Oak	297	39	175	165	23	...	...	...	...	...	...	...	...	...	...	...	...	...	...	...	...
Cedar	1186	78	...	63	9	...	...	...	...	...	...	42	2	...	1968	...	...	...	646	780	300
Douglas	288	27	270	116	27	...	...	...	...	37	9	12	...	...	...	...	...	...	42	27	...
Jenkins	1130	43	630	96	7	...	...	...	...	12	...	...	...	...	2308	...	...	...	...	...	...
Liberty	521	6	1420	70	4	...	...	...	...	...	...	...	...	...	...	...	...	...	...	...	...
Lincoln	2201	344	280	587	144	...	...	...	...	150	35	...	...	...	128	...	...	...	...	...	...
Mitchell	363	20	...	121	52	...	...	...	...	...	...	...	...	...	...	...	...	...	...	...	...
Newburg	1471	1	...	...	...	...	...	...	...	...	...	...	...	...	...	...	...	...	...	...	...
Osage, exc. of town	919	4	533	195	16	3	...	...	...	1	...	132	...	87	1649	...	255	...	87	15	...
Osage, town of	122	2	180	246	50	1	...	85	...	255	171	23	...	178	1502	...	...	...	482	826	2
Otranto	1329	18	85	28	8	...	...	...	...	6	1	...	...	13	1125	...	...	...	130	170	4
Rock	10	53	1925	27	2	...	...	...	...	28	...	9	1	12	1796	...	...	...	...	...	...
St. Ansgar	694	56	1220	348	13	...	...	...	...	120	...	250	1	...	...	...	...	...	41	...	...
Stacyville	...	...	...	...	...	...	...	...	...	...	...	...	...	...	...	...	...	...	...	...	...
Union	79	54	3121	80	10	...	...	...	...	...	...	1	...	...	661	...	...	...	54	...	...
Wayne	1578	65	1875	41	11	...	...	...	...	...	...	...	...	37	1360	...	...	...	89	100	...
Total	12188	810	11714	2183	376	4	...	85	...	609	216	469	4	327	12497	...	255	...	1571	1918	306

MONONA COUNTY.

Ashton	40	22	...	32	10	...	...	...	...	751	88	8	...	...	450	...	...	...	119	60	...
Belvidere	377	8	...	11	5	...	...	...	...	...	...	11	...	...	684	...	...	...	110	100	...

MONONA COUNTY.—Continued.

Names of townships, towns, and cities.	Acres of natural timber.	Acres of planted timber.	Rods of hedge.	Apples. Number of trees in bearing.	Apples. Bushels gathered in 1874.	Pears. Number of trees in bearing.	Pears. Bushels gathered in 1874.	Peaches. Number of trees in bearing.	Peaches. Bushels gathered in 1874.	Plums. Number of trees in bearing.	Plums. Bushels gathered in 1874.	Cherries. Number of trees in bearing.	Cherries. Bushels gathered in 1874.	Number of other fruit trees in bearing.	Number of fruit trees not in bearing.	Grapes in vineyard. Number of acres.	Grapes in vineyard. Pounds of grapes gathered.	Grapes in vineyard. Gallons of wine made.	Grapes not in vineyard. Number of vines.	Grapes not in vineyard. Pounds of grapes gathered.	Grapes not in vineyard. Gallons of wine made.
Center	271	77	820	8								3			200				120		
Fairview	626	20										3	1								
Franklin, exc. of Onawa	992	77	1620	174	70					36	10	89	16		2787				807	412	
Grant	464	25		82	25							4	1		1674		500		202		10
Jordan	117	1	160	10	1																
Kennebec	1065	44	100	215	186					132	25				2383		100	5	84		
Lake	510	10		41						112	40										
Lincoln	1708	8		11	5					73	7				533				66	50	
Maple	593	129	720	27	1							18		4	1513				189		
Onawa, town of																					
St. Clair				35	11																
Sherman	977	1	388	112	11					212	13	13			793		36		134		
Soldier	85	21		4								13	1	25	659				104	236	
Spring Valley	622	22		2															26	25	
West Fork	220	71		400	57	15	20			350	275	25	5		518				18		
Willow	61																		3		
Total	8728	536	3808	1164	382	15	20			1666	458	187	24	29	12194		636	5	1982	883	10

MONROE COUNTY.

Names of townships, towns, and cities.	Acres of natural timber.	Acres of planted timber.	Rods of hedge.	Apples. Number of trees in bearing.	Apples. Bushels gathered in 1874.	Pears. Number of trees in bearing.	Pears. Bushels gathered in 1874.	Peaches. Number of trees in bearing.	Peaches. Bushels gathered in 1874.	Plums. Number of trees in bearing.	Plums. Bushels gathered in 1874.	Cherries. Number of trees in bearing.	Cherries. Bushels gathered in 1874.	Number of other fruit trees in bearing.	Number of fruit trees not in bearing.	Grapes in vineyard. Number of acres.	Grapes in vineyard. Pounds of grapes gathered.	Grapes in vineyard. Gallons of wine made.	Grapes not in vineyard. Number of vines.	Grapes not in vineyard. Pounds of grapes gathered.	Grapes not in vineyard. Gallons of wine made.
Albia, town of																					
Bluff Creek	2887	1	12666	4013	1189	83	1	447	41	272	20	1233	170	119	12470		2500		1405	9594	8
Cedar	1137		891	818	536	1		67	14	65	27	251	24		1734				585	1312	
Franklin	1322		3954	881	194	3	10	6		20		218	90	12	2607				112		
Guilford	4501		2972	351	201	2		11				65	13	3	234	2	900	50	151	246	8
Jackson	320		5800	597	272	5		25		7		120		60	3012		600		757	3400	
Mantua	3834		3979	3090	1012	36	17	119	9	57	7	1217	181	36	6092	2	2250	860	1563	6045	105

Monroe	2895	9	7537	4064	1264	45	27	148	2	185	74	684	90	3	8146				1023	11873	3
Pleasant	4216	4	10268	3513	820	47	7	109	12	168	48	400	57	41	6955				934	7820	28
Troy, exc. of Albia	4234	1	4738	5421	2195	41	13	57	10	102	26	1285	321	252	4952	2	18000	280	2326	15150	
Union	7142		2950	2141	1228	8	8	28	7	138	91	426	195		6977		100		1018	3918	1
Urbana	2254	4	1755	3156	973							230	33		4472				635	4560	90
Wayne	1655	19	3221	700	301	5	6			803	8	126	5								
Total	36397	38	60731	28745	10185	276	89	1017	95	1817	301	6255	1179	526	57651	6	24350	1190	10509	63918	243

MONTGOMERY COUNTY.

Douglas	1248	10	7085	16	5						12	3		365	315				39	70	
Frankfort	20	27	9135	120	7	4		3		1	1	79	1	4	4824		200	20	580	600	4
Grant	960	21	20409	82	156							42	5	6	7354				403	480	
Jackson exc. of Villisca	1137	4	3736	587	941	15		21	2			104	4		4772				513	2352	15
Lincoln			4020																		
Pilot Grove	634	80	9183	73	18	10		39	10	8		92	3	2	5592				739	1077	
Red Oak, exc. of town	820	33	8270	75	43			251	6	125	35	215	45	30	9251	3			1603	1505	
Red Oak Junction, town of																					
Scott	49		3215												782						
Sherman	870	16	5730	43	5							12			3700				300		
Villisca, town of						1				12	1	96	15	27	334				287	150	
Walnut	300	37	12970					5				112	6	17	7344				368	90	
Washington	809	5	2380																		
West	398	87	20285	111	106			21	10			134	23	22	5010		500		648	65	
Total	7445	320	106418	1107	1281	30		340	28	146	49	889	102	473	49278	3	700	20	5480	6389	19

MUSCATINE COUNTY.

Bloomington, exc. Muscatine	2182	23	15304	15083	6696	129	23		2	10	8	3273	801	124	12153	107	20400	1200	11230	38085	493
Cedar	3245		5540	2048	1851	11	2	7	2	8	3	290	70	30	1239				1240	6319	10
Fulton	485	272	29470	5091	2460	388	81	640	233	313	15	1538	430	107	8027				1321	18580	204
Goshen	2618	43	13975	4469	1613	40	1	18		69	3	1276	181		20149	4	25800	40	4449	31925	7
Lake	2405	9	14885	10889	6515	458	428	133	4	60	2	1997	542	41	7302				7527	37237	45
Montpelier	4390		5765	3850	2873	1	1	64	23			451	165		3191	5	150	883	366	651	9
Moscow	2661		8074	2057	1213	17	1	33		8	1	323	50	25	1097				493	842	
Muscatine, city of	100			4160	4150		52					82	18			6	20000		150	1000	
Orono	1369	4	7090	1546	515	27	5					161	17	200	799	517	3200		439	1205	
Pike	1653	3681	9350	1315	467			5	1	28	8	164	10	45	3039				626	660	
Seventy Six	3806		9924	5186	4269	43	15	56	16	26	2	718	156	16	2220				1155	11160	
Sweetland	4792	230	30824	11994	6278	270	2	32	6			1897	420	144	1773	1004	9300	2080	5161	20313	203
Wapsinonoc, exc. of West Liberty	1769	60	31845	3148	1447	10	1	28	1	17	2	655	102	547	6468	2	26000	1100	2885	22480	30

MUSCATINE COUNTY.—Continued.

Names of townships, towns, and cities.	Acres of natural timber.	Acres of planted timber.	Rods of hedge.	Apples. Number of trees in bearing.	Apples. Bushels gathered in 1874.	Pears. Number of trees in bearing.	Pears. Bushels gathered in 1874.	Peaches. Number of trees in bearing.	Peaches. Bushels gathered in 1874.	Plums. Number of trees in bearing.	Plums. Bushels gathered in 1874.	Cherries. Number of trees in bearing.	Cherries. Bushels gathered in 1874.	Number of other fruit trees in bearing.	Number of fruit trees not in bearing.	Grapes in vineyard. Number of acres.	Grapes in vineyard. Pounds of grapes gathered.	Grapes in vineyard. Gallons of wine made.	Grapes not in vineyard. Number of vines.	Grapes not in vineyard. Pounds of grapes gathered.	Grapes not in vineyard. Gallons of wine made.
West Liberty, town of	...	...	...	347	184	6	...	...	...	10	3	360	120	16	1676	1	2000	...	777	6930	...
Wilton, exc. of town	544	46	44075	3135	1289	19	3	22	1	26	5	966	167	3	7177	2	2900	...	2301	12685	1
Wilton, town of	58	5	500	505	274	27	5	5	2	8	2	622	308	...	2086	...	...	...	1824	1750	44
Total	32077	4373	226621	74823	42094	1446	620	1043	291	583	54	14773	3557	1298	78396	1648	109750	5303	41944	211822	1046

O'BRIEN COUNTY.

Names of townships, towns, and cities.	Acres of natural timber.	Acres of planted timber.	Rods of hedge.	Apples. Number of trees in bearing.	Apples. Bushels gathered in 1874.	Pears. Number of trees in bearing.	Pears. Bushels gathered in 1874.	Peaches. Number of trees in bearing.	Peaches. Bushels gathered in 1874.	Plums. Number of trees in bearing.	Plums. Bushels gathered in 1874.	Cherries. Number of trees in bearing.	Cherries. Bushels gathered in 1874.	Number of other fruit trees in bearing.	Number of fruit trees not in bearing.	Grapes in vineyard. Number of acres.	Grapes in vineyard. Pounds of grapes gathered.	Grapes in vineyard. Gallons of wine made.	Grapes not in vineyard. Number of vines.	Grapes not in vineyard. Pounds of grapes gathered.	Grapes not in vineyard. Gallons of wine made.
Baker	...	41	1165	...	...	...	...	...	...	...	...	...	...	...	1585	...	...	...	...	...	...
Carroll	...	47	1175	...	...	...	...	...	...	...	...	...	...	...	587	...	...	...	32	...	...
Center	...	71	...	...	...	...	...	...	...	...	...	...	...	...	670	...	...	...	...	...	...
Floyd	...	33	1947	...	...	...	...	...	...	...	...	...	...	...	824	...	...	...	23	...	...
Grant	148	87	255	...	...	...	...	...	...	...	...	...	...	...	1638	...	...	...	150	...	...
Highland	...	107	8432	...	...	...	...	...		...	...	...	...	...	1480	...	...	...	92	...	...
Liberty	1	72	3195	...	...	...	...	...		...	...	...	...	...	1848	...	...	...	319	...	...
Summit	...	...	850	...	...	...	...	...	...	...	...	...	...	...	...	...	...	...	...	...	...
Waterman	58	26	1170	...	...	...	...	...	...	6	2	...	...	...	...	...	...	...	...	...	...
Total	207	484	18189	...	...	...	...	...	...	6	2	...	...	...	8632	...	...	...	616	...	...

OSCEOLA COUNTY.

Names of townships, towns, and cities.	Acres of natural timber.	Acres of planted timber.	Rods of hedge.	Apples. Number of trees in bearing.	Apples. Bushels gathered in 1874.	Pears. Number of trees in bearing.	Pears. Bushels gathered in 1874.	Peaches. Number of trees in bearing.	Peaches. Bushels gathered in 1874.	Plums. Number of trees in bearing.	Plums. Bushels gathered in 1874.	Cherries. Number of trees in bearing.	Cherries. Bushels gathered in 1874.	Number of other fruit trees in bearing.	Number of fruit trees not in bearing.	Grapes in vineyard. Number of acres.	Grapes in vineyard. Pounds of grapes gathered.	Grapes in vineyard. Gallons of wine made.	Grapes not in vineyard. Number of vines.	Grapes not in vineyard. Pounds of grapes gathered.	Grapes not in vineyard. Gallons of wine made.
Fairview	...	3	160	...	...	...	...	...	...	...	...	...	...	...	...	...	...	...	...	...	...
Gilman	...	5	1130	...	...	...	...	...	...	...	...	...	...	...	...	...	...	...	...	...	...
Goewey	...	26	1304	...	...	...	...	...	...	...	...	...	...	...	...	...	...	...	...	...	...

Holman	......	48	3599	......	......	......	......	......	......	......	......	......	......	......	......	......	......	......	......	......	......
Horton	......	3	490	......	......	......	......	......	......	......	......	......	......	......	162	......	......	......	58	......	......
Ocheyedan	......	14	1990	......	......	......	......	......	......	......	......	......	......	......	......	......	......	......	......	......	......
Viola	......	18	2491	4	......	......	......	......	......	4	......	......	......	......	1010	......	......	......	14	......	......
Wilson	......	5	1620	......	......	......	......	......	......	......	......	4	......	......	518	......	......	......	50	2	......
Total	......	122	12784	4	......	......	......	......	......	4	......	4	......	......	1690	......	......	......	122	2	......

PAGE COUNTY.

Amity	687	179	17508	5421	3820	58	15	431	156	321	83	310	67	......	14998	1	3000	12	3198	13739	......
Buchanan	3149	9	11746	1886	2727	1	6	933	631	......	......	431	26	180	6411	......	1000	......	1563	3145	13
Clarinda, town of	......	......	406	1030	499	90	10	11	......	382	20	256	39	104	1803	......	500	......	8575	30660	220
Colfax	643	119	9810	111	538	......	......	132	50	......	......	106	7	27	6091	......	200	......	661	800	......
Douglas	628	547	35582	177	25	20	12	152	15	......	......	94	9	36	5704	......	......	......	1054	1520	......
East River	3446	3	9377	1309	1197	303	1	196	56	38	22	214	43	......	8961	10	10610	60	1790	19801	4
Fremont	678	61	23805	171	179	3	......	17	2	......	......	68	4	11	6783	......	......	......	404	176	......
Grant, exc. of Shenandoah	124	90	28527	37	6	10	......	25	1	254	22	145	3	......	9462	......	......	......	1089	762	......
Harlan	815	27	26734	2165	1124	3	1	247	45	1	1	96	......	......	8120	1	600	......	1493	540	......
Lincoln	106	88	23906	449	249	1	......	113	12	9	......	66	2	67	6517	......	500	......	1419	855	......
Morton	70	73	17600	102	10	......	......	100	50	......	......	162	......	......	8029	2	2797	......	808	......	......
Nebraska	2231	2	2003	647	746	5	3	16	4	1	2	57	9	......	2727	......	......	......	441	815	4
Nodaway, exc. of Clarinda	1509	91	39837	3804	3148	48	20	627	131	22	8	852	79	97	15029	5	5315	40	4786	6772	5
Pierce	456	43	5905	65	195	......	......	......	......	......	......	13	2	......	4541	......	......	......	1406	1400	......
Shenandoah, town of	......	......	140	......	......	......	......	......	......	......	......	......	......	......	......	......	......	......	......	......	......
Tarkio	628	80	21859	330	89	1	......	232	33	......	......	63	5	2	5537	......	......	......	1034	532	......
Valley	1514	22	13446	535	530	......	......	144	9	11	3	55	5	144	7576	......	......	......	450	939	7
Washington	72	68	16143	286	46	6	......	20	20	......	......	......	......	......	6999	......	......	......	851	201	......
Total	16756	1502	304334	18525	15128	549	68	3396	1215	1039	161	2988	300	668	125288	19	24522	112	31022	82657	254

PALO ALTO COUNTY.

Ellington	14	16	300	......	......	......	......	......	......	12	......	......	......	......	144	......	......	......	......	......	......
Emmetsburg	287	35	740	46	......	......	......	......	......	68	10	14	......	2	305	......	......	......	100	20	29
Fairfield	......	12	510	......	......	......	......	......	......	......	......	......	......	......	......	......	......	......	......	......	......
Fern Valley	156	11	......	......	6	......	......	......	......	25	3	......	......	......	......	......	......	......	......	......	......
Freedom	11	65	......	......	......	......	......	......	......	......	......	......	......	......	......	......	......	......	......	......	......
Great Oak	110	53	1080	......	......	......	......	......	......	20	1	......	......	......	54	......	......	......	100	300	20
Highland	1	9	120	......	......	......	......	......	......	31	2	......	......	......	129	......	......	......	......	......	......
Lost Island	8	4	......	......	......	......	......	......	......	......	......	......	......	......	22	......	......	......	......	......	......
Nevada	227	8	20	......	......	......	......	......	......	......	......	......	......	......	12	......	......	......	......	......	......
Rush Lake	......	30	1498	......	......	......	......	......	......	9	2	......	......	......	......	......	......	......	......	......	......
Silver Lake	......	23	527	......	......	......	......	......	......	......	......	......	......	......	......	......	......	......	......	......	......

PALO ALTO COUNTY—Continued.

Names of townships, towns, and cities.	Acres of natural timber.	Acres of planted timber.	Rods of hedge.	Apples. Number of trees in bearing.	Apples. Bushels gathered in 1874.	Pears. Number of trees in bearing.	Pears. Bushels gathered in 1874.	Peaches. Number of trees in bearing.	Peaches. Bushels gathered in 1874.	Plums. Number of trees in bearing.	Plums. Bushels gathered in 1874.	Cherries. Number of trees in bearing.	Cherries. Bushels gathered in 1874.	Number of other fruit trees in bearing.	Number of fruit trees not in bearing.	Grapes in vineyard. Number of acres.	Grapes in vineyard. Pounds of grapes gathered.	Grapes in vineyard. Gallons of wine made.	Grapes not in vineyard. Number of vines.	Grapes not in vineyard. Pounds of grapes gathered.	Grapes not in vineyard. Gallons of wine made.
Vernon		27	320												113				79		
Walnut	201	16	300	2											50						
West Bend	309	55	862							1062	79	10			125						75
Total	1324	364	6277	48	6					1227	97	24		2	954				279	320	124

PLYMOUTH COUNTY.

Names of townships, towns, and cities.	Acres of natural timber.	Acres of planted timber.	Rods of hedge.	Apples. Number of trees in bearing.	Apples. Bushels gathered in 1874.	Pears. Number of trees in bearing.	Pears. Bushels gathered in 1874.	Peaches. Number of trees in bearing.	Peaches. Bushels gathered in 1874.	Plums. Number of trees in bearing.	Plums. Bushels gathered in 1874.	Cherries. Number of trees in bearing.	Cherries. Bushels gathered in 1874.	Number of other fruit trees in bearing.	Number of fruit trees not in bearing.	Grapes in vineyard. Number of acres.	Grapes in vineyard. Pounds of grapes gathered.	Grapes in vineyard. Gallons of wine made.	Grapes not in vineyard. Number of vines.	Grapes not in vineyard. Pounds of grapes gathered.	Grapes not in vineyard. Gallons of wine made.
America	16	71	184												1226						
Elgin	25	66	2728												2658						
Fredonia		80																			
Grant		24	202												86						
Johnson		52	100												485						
Lincoln	117	173	1000	5						150	15	9		8	2459				64		
Marion		14	246																		
Perry	14	102	160	41				2		50	6	46		261	809				83		
Plymouth	60	62	100									8			585	2			122		
Portland	18		80																		
Sioux	328	19																			
Stanton		138	1620												908				19		
Union		65	340							118	2	6			559				23		
Washington		51	445												50						
Total	578	917	7205	46				2		318	23	69		269	9825	2			311		

POCAHONTAS COUNTY.

Bellville		29	80												791				15		
Cedar		83	1140	2						12		22			764				9		
Center		1	55												30						
Clinton	45	15	1080	8	2							6			60				30		
Colfax		51	1462	26		3		2		2		17		25	860				12		
Des Moines	416	70	911	194	28	2				56	34			70							
Dover		21																			
Grant		19	668												796						
Jackson		58	1245									4		100							
Lincoln		10	235							18	2								18		
Lizard	180	57	1355	10						16		5									
Swan Lake	10	6	100																		
Total	651	420	8331	240	30	5		2		104	36	54		195	2601				84		

30

POLK COUNTY.

Allen	1270	1	4900	2317	1922	8	1	10	1	4		212	11	8	9935	3	14700	40	3547	25185	120
Beaver	954	75	9935	1794	1279					37	14	576	108		19652	2	4150		5981	21175	8
Bloomfield	1303	65	4928	11025	5215	67	12			226	33	1130	407	9	16227	35	71300	160	7909	42900	34
Camp	6233	10	1796	3142	1707	5	1			11	1	86	26		14503	1	6000		3086	23480	30
Crocker	3135	13	2562	3031	1895	12				23	7	263	43	14	9344	2	3760	12	2061	15481	105
Delaware	1576	12	2496	3530	1584	8		12	1	107	12	253	72	60	16599	3	14000	80	5768	16476	
Des Moines, city of	300		20	2480	156	343	28	13	3	185	29	1552	227	87	2335	29	35750	354	10461	33719	520
Douglas	929	48	4390	1838	1082					6	2	52	6	10	11282				2231	1170	
Elkhart	1166	361	2019	2139	1086	2				14	6	89	7	33	5421				1555	3930	32
Four Mile	1449	2	592	1240	1350	7	1			6	4	98	11	67	2510	1	2000		994	10834	19
Franklin	1922	14	2843	1502	546	1				2	3	130	9	8	5065				2142	6715	
Grant	972	1	580	1346	832	10	1			12	1	205	33	31	6412				2776	14287	70
Jefferson	6090	4	240	422	192							14		268	4599	1		264			
Lincoln		2	5187	409	278				12	1		20	10		4370						
Madison	4395	5	998	1800	688					5	1	89	21		9512	2	13000	30	2002	13715	10
Saylor	1278	5	330	2133	798	54	12	11		17	2	299	109	6	9344				5384	26190	241
Valley	2068	6	1330	9431	2927	140	26			6		1139	394		20551	9	92200	270	14546	133690	20
Walnut	2792	5	2655	1834	834	41	6			17	1	815	190		17098				3981	15805	16
Washington	786	76	4976	469	114	7				20	3	55	5	47	8990				1829	650	70
Total	38623	705	52771	51882	24485	705	88	46	17	699	119	7077	1689	648	193749	88	256860	1210	76253	405402	1295

POTTAWATTAMIE COUNTY.

NAMES OF TOWNSHIPS, TOWNS, AND CITIES.	Acres of natural timber.	Acres of planted timber.	Rods of hedge.	APPLES. Number of trees in bearing.	APPLES. Bushels gathered in 1874.	PEARS. Number of trees in bearing.	PEARS. Bushels gathered in 1874.	PEACHES Number of trees in bearing.	PEACHES Bushels gathered in 1874.	PLUMS. Number of trees in bearing.	PLUMS. Bushels gathered in 1874.	CHERRIES. Number of trees in bearing.	CHERRIES. Bushels gathered in 1874.	Number of other fruit trees in bearing.	Number of fruit trees not in bearing.	GRAPES IN VINEYARD. Number of acres.	GRAPES IN VINEYARD. Pounds of grapes gathered.	GRAPES IN VINEYARD. Gallons of wine made.	GRAPES NOT IN VINEYARD. Number of vines.	GRAPES NOT IN VINEYARD. Pounds of grapes gathered.	GRAPES NOT IN VINEYARD. Gallons of wine made.
Avoca, town of	23	5	400	...	...	...	...	...	...	...	...	12	...	258	...	...	...	...	298	105	...
Belknap	399	14	720	108	14	...	...	2	...	...	...	27	2	...	900	...	...	...	403	100	...
Boomer	761	5	...	5	15	...	...	...	...	...	...	...	...	...	1585	...	...	...	72	...	...
Center	985	110	4005	1657	1832	26	14	21	14	601	144	638	33	3245	7493	3	10600	...	1687	1286	...
Council Bluffs, city of	649	...	...	2720	1539	316	90	108	34	693	328	1043	293	466	14003	455	54600	15	6166	26745	118
Crescent	1044	13	217	454	87	9	1	114	114	316	86	337	84	127	5272	2	400	...	246	140	...
Grove	1248	13	865	30	46	...	...	5	1	...	...	54	2	...	1998	...	...	...	226	17	...
Harden	150	25	...	15	...	...	...	...	...	15	...	6	...	...	45	...	...	...	...	...	...
Hazel Dell	1739	5	...	430	151	10	...	14	...	581	5	83	...	214	4252	...	...	...	753	200	...
James	14	11	738	...	...	...	...	...	...	...	...	20	2	...	139	...	...	...	397	...	...
Kane, exc. of Council Bluffs	4214	65	580	993	640	...	...	147	3	580	225	1105	204	170	19600	1	400	...	5088	5750	...
Keg Creek	302	21	835	117	1	...	...	...	...	101	200	49	5	214	1165	3	50	...	50	...	...
Knox, exc. of Avoca	1139	54	4080	154	68	...	...	2	2	5	...	163	3	83	12405	2	105	...	2530	1081	6
Layton	...	10	2676	...	...	...	...	...	...	...	...	25	...	...	3374	...	6	...	813	...	...
Macedonia	683	12	830	135	10	2	2	30	1	7	...	57	3	2	2358	...	6	...	355	220	...
Neola	79	35	90	5	...	...	...	...	...	...	...	7	...	...	593	...	...	...	...	...	...
Norwalk	590	21	420	...	...	...	...	...	...	10	1	16	3	...	1570	...	...	...	488	4	...
Pleasant	...	10	560	...	...	1	...	...	...	260	30	53	...	...	50	...	...	...	308	...	...
Rockford	5152	20	...	416	260	3	...	10	2	94	8	52	1	1953	1349	...	50	...	124	2550	4
Silver Creek	52	29	590	20	...	...	...	...	...	2	...	20	...	5	1253	...	...	...	282	150	...
Washington	220	28	...	161	13	2	1	...	2	4	...	23	1	7	1121	...	...	...	236	25	...
Waveland	533	41	2290	89	212	...	...	...	...	...	...	69	27	...	2003	...	...	...	316	40	...
Wright	296	44	4340	75	8	...	...	7	2	...	...	26	4	2	1087	1	300	...	327	450	...
York	211	9	...	...	...	...	...	...	...	...	...	5	...	40	356	1	...	...	133	20	...
Total	20483	600	24236	7584	4896	369	108	460	175	3269	1027	3890	667	6786	83971	468	66517	15	21298	38883	128

POWESHIEK COUNTY.

Bear Creek, exc. of Brooklyn	451	63	16140	1047	604	14	1	...	...	4	2	400	46	140	17718	5	2230	...	2405	9960	...
Brooklyn, town of	...	...	...	...	...	...	...	...	...	...	...	14	7	...	...	...	...	...	1300	410	4600
Chester	25	203	20855	676	188	...	...	...	...	39	3	280	50	9	10745	...	...	...	2310	6518	49
Deep River	1230	2	22533	1255	1764	...	...	...	...	233	77	382	48	9	10241	...	...	...	1117	4555	46
Grinnell, exc. of town	365	43	11610	1056	480	2	...	...	...	...	...	851	132	25	10242	1	...	...	2849	6370	...
Grinnell, town of	...	...	...	10	5	...	...	32	12	...	...	14	3	24	...	3	600	...	40	...	...
Jackson, exc. of Montezuma	918	37	26273	1300	972	2	...	...	...	17	6	291	43	148	6003	...	...	...	1470	2259	...
Jefferson	1416	43	8774	3061	1105	15	1	...	...	64	20	345	7	79	7165	...	2000	...	1118	2989	4
Lincoln	853	15	17531	367	119	4	1	...	...	48	32	94	13	...	5134	...	...	...	631	2665	...
Madison	866	158	15891	1266	521	9	...	2	...	7	...	247	7	...	10054	1	500	...	1319	4923	...
Malcom, exc. of town	53	18	10954	1264	787	...	...	...	...	...	...	84	18	...	4637	...	...	...	389	1640	...
Malcom, town of	...	...	145	...	...	...	...	...	...	...	...	25	...	...	160	...	...	...	95	...	...
Montezuma, town of	...	...	11	309	87	...	20	1	...	61	16	164	11	...	...	...	...	...	156	1565	...
Pleasant	32	32	17362	2621	368	...	...	...	...	10	...	219	17	...	8127	...	...	...	872	4011	3
Scott	214	34	17180	620	34	5	...	...	...	17	...	142	...	...	8560	3	2000	...	462	...	...
Sheridan	20	86	16660	430	33	...	...	...	...	16	...	185	9	14	7348	...	...	...	996	1416	5
Sugar Creek	1681	6	2892	1549	547	12	...	...	...	...	...	296	23	...	6656	...	...	...	637	1888	...
Union	1422	8	4500	1555	613	22	4	3	...	50	17	247	49	32	4708	...	1000	...	1104	4836	55
Warren	1415	16	7987	2330	671	6	...	...	...	9	1	250	58	...	8716	5	10300	...	2595	6320	2
Washi:.gton	1236	13	6769	1398	564	20	...	...	...	...	...	115	30	...	7675	350	...	...	922	2642	...
Total	12197	777	224067	22114	9462	111	27	38	12	575	174	4645	571	480	133889	368	27630	...	22785	64967	4758

RINGGOLD COUNTY.

Athens	687	19	7000	533	326	...	...	120	23	...	...	131	18	24	7738	1	200	...	1228	508	...
Benton	1913	...	8288	507	272	4	...	43	1	...	...	93	2	12	3389	...	40	...	435	30	...
Clinton	1147	2	2793	148	377	...	...	58	41	5	4	101	37	243	3710	1	1000	...	462	595	...
Grant	1033	15	10914	159	225	2	1	153	39	123	44	72	6	2	3618	...	...	...	365	2144	...
Jefferson	1908	34	14524	204	397	3	...	50	7	9	...	348	56	2	5877	...	...	...	478	1225	...
Liberty	1118	16	8016	254	121	...	...	50	...	...	...	90	7	...	6788	...	...	...	1402	390	...
Lincoln	793	18	9305	322	186	...	...	70	8	184	25	102	5	3	707	...	...	...	424	682	...
Lots Creek	1652	4	2510	461	205	10	6	6117	75	10	6	116	46	5	5722	...	...	...	604	445	...
Middle Fork	986	7	5807	342	222	...	...	164	54	11	...	149	14	11	6083	3	50	...	761	861	...
Monroe	624	29	9312	274	188	...	...	12	6	5	...	89	...	...	5998	...	50	...	413	65	...
Mount Ayr	2248	57	17495	642	566	13	9	434	38	3	1	192	79	16	12341	...	...	...	776	7024	...
Rice	661	...	3300	12	10	...	...	...	...	...	...	...	...	...	200	...	...	...	24	...	...
Riley	940	8	3650	215	146	1	...	40	7	...	...	89	6	15	2820	...	...	...	216	505	...
Tingley	265	...	1120	...	...	...	...	...	...	...	...	...	...	...	...	...	...	...	...	...	...
Union	480	6	1981	182	141	...	...	64	2	50	10	77	5	80	1629	...	...	...	200	375	...
Washington	1794	11	7093	316	233	18	1	64	12	10	1	170	11	4	5809	1	150	...	670	564	...
Total	18149	226	113108	4571	3615	51	17	1439	313	410	91	1819	292	417	72429	6	1490	...	8558	15323	...

SAC COUNTY.

NAMES OF TOWNSHIPS, TOWNS, AND CITIES.	Acres of natural timber.	Acres of planted timber.	Rods of hedge.	APPLES. Number of trees in bearing.	APPLES. Bushels gathered in 1874.	PEARS. Number of trees in bearing.	PEARS. Bushels gathered in 1874.	PEACHES. Number of trees in bearing.	PEACHES. Bushels gathered in 1874.	PLUMS. Number of trees in bearing.	PLUMS. Bushels gathered in 1874.	CHERRIES. Number of trees in bearing.	CHERRIES. Bushels gathered in 1874.	Number of other fruit trees in bearing.	Number of fruit trees not in bearing.	GRAPES IN VINEYARD. Number of acres.	GRAPES IN VINEYARD. Pounds of grapes gathered.	GRAPES IN VINEYARD. Gallons of wine made.	GRAPES NOT IN VINEYARD. Number of vines.	GRAPES NOT IN VINEYARD. Pounds of grapes gathered.	GRAPES NOT IN VINEYARD. Gallons of wine made.
Boyer Vallley	...	47	4706	...	...	...	...	...	...	20	2	...	...	...	1872	...	...	...	...	...	...
Clinton	...	8	120	...	...	...	...	...	...	...	...	...	...	...	960	...	...	...	17	...	...
Douglas	333	135	7088	...	...	...	...	...	...	14	...	...	...	...	3354	...	...	...	...	...	...
Eden	...	79	3229	2	...	...	...	...	...	...	...	...	...	...	1889	...	...	...	82	...	...
Jackson	1319	203	2615	149	31	...	...	5	...	79	17	104	5	14	37250	113	...	...	5245	...	...
Levey	...	24	1600	...	...	...	...	...	...	...	...	34	...	...	14451	...	...	...	48	350	...
Sac	742	80	603	5	...	...	...	...	...	...	...	10	1	...	...	200	...	...	20	...	...
Wall Lake	268	49	1410	288	30	...	...	...	...	...	...	3	...	...	2297	...	...	...	243	...	...
Total	2662	624	21371	444	61	...	...	5	...	113	19	151	6	14	62073	313	...	...	5655	350	...
SCOTT COUNTY.																					
Allen's Grove	1624	...	5690	1822	992	8	2	5	...	2	1	305	35	...	...	1	4500	40	183	1210	...
Blue Grass	335	50	23991	7281	13073	34	11	907	349	155	17	162	19	...	4198	14	36000	2260	3551	10085	520
Buffalo, exc. of town	3024	...	1870	113296	6031	96	6	1097	199	112	3	653	104	214	3075	3	1600	250	3094	5544	168
Buffalo, town of	...	...		346	27	15	1	17	4	47	5	56	12	...	147	...	...	...	9367	12635	967
Butler	978	8	14336	940	1593	28	5	108	23	347	75	775	129	18	6665	...	...	...	865	5063	85
Cleona	...	...	22110	744	410	...	...	...	...	...	...	...	...	...	5777	...	...	...	419	1630	25
Davenport, exc. of city	465	10	18540	17543	11331	258	96	784	282	39	6	1634	464	20	17354	49	190900	8155	13958	54685	1001
Davenport, city of	...	...	164	3497	2422	933	206	278	101	248	41	989	326	213	3017	11	8600	80	19042	118740	2224
Hickory Grove	349	12	26141	3974	1829	25	2	15	1	21	1	335	61	37	3027	1	200	...	1767	4733	331
Le Claire, exc. of town	2654	22	15185	11023	12627	136	22	191	35	14	3	834	234	5	3858	...	...	...	900	12865	77
Le Claire, town of	...	...	...	432	272	22	2	13	8	5	...	201	29	1	...	4	4400	1090	408	6040	...
Liberty	712	11	15505	2050	609	16	...	45	3	...	...	87	12	152	1935	...	...	...	991	4591	22
Lincoln	...	...	22480	4885	3726	18	4	...	...	...	...	480	141	...	7230	...	...	...	1415	3800	159
Pleasant Valley	1668	3	15855	7669	10502	667	79	311	105	421	77	1165	272	104	8989	22	81200	151	1255	9965	30
Princeton, exc. of town	1209	...	10796	5626	3505	3	1	2	...	5	2	631	133	...	4125	...	...	...	511	2900	25

Princeton, town of																					
Rockingham	1051		1100	4871	3683	553	32	159	46	8	1	326	91	10	3315	17	87500	7980	1313	3095	41
Sheridan	50	63	19336	3897	3313	4	1				2	130	17		5220	450	800	109	915	2115	95
Winfield	1345	49	10509	2549	1363	6	2			4	1	405	98	15	3498				346	1897	1
Total	15464	228	223608	92445	77308	2822	472	3932	1156	1428	235	9168	2177	789	81430	572	415700	20115	60270	261593	5771

SHELBY COUNTY.

Cass	115	2	85																		
Clay	170	27	450	14	1							16	1		675	1			172		
Douglas	165	32	1270	110	100							7	1		2910						
Fairview	683	56	410	20	3	1				12	2	1			3765				986	120	
Greeley	12	4	590												205				6		
Grove	3045	7		132	95					6	2	36	5	136	1795				448	20	
Harlan	753	45	3139	363	583							105	10		9038				996	1645	
Jackson	304	7	1289	354	159							53	3	174	735				319	206	
Jefferson	60	4	255												244				43		
Lincoln		25	700		12			2		62	12	3			3909		200		68		
Monroe	160	4	1000									5	1				80		25		
Polk	146	8	275																		
Shelby	5	65	530									2	1		3106				513	161	
Union	14	14	245																		
Washington		2													140						
Westphalia		41													130						
Total	5632	343	10238	993	953	1		2		80	16	228	22	310	26652	1	280		3576	2152	

SIOUX COUNTY.

Buncombe		24	280												352				49		
Floyd		9	440																		
Grant		62	953									6			25				8		
Holland		47	100									6			336				12		
Lincoln	2	43	552											25	1092						
Nassau	1	26										1									
Reading		24	240																		
Rock	40	19	270												798				63		
Settler	175	4													193				10		
Sheridan		18	4450																		
Total	218	276	7285									13		25	2796				142		

STORY COUNTY.

NAMES OF TOWNSHIPS, TOWNS, AND CITIES.	Acres of natural timber.	Acres of planted timber.	Rods of hedge.	APPLES.		PEARS.		PEACHES		PLUMS.		CHERRIES.		Number of other fruit trees in bearing.	Number of fruit trees not in bearing.	GRAPES IN VINEYARD.			GRAPES NOT IN VINEYARD.		
				Number of trees in bearing.	Bushels gathered in 1874.	Number of trees in bearing.	Bushels gathered in 1874.	Number of trees in bearing.	Bushels gathered in 1874.	Number of trees in bearing.	Bushels gathered in 1874.	Number of trees in bearing.	Bushels gathered in 1874.			Number of acres.	Pounds of grapes gathered.	Gallons of wine made.	Number of vines.	Pounds of grapes gathered.	Gallons of wine made.
Ames, town of	30	....	16	174	30	1	....	....	....	....	9	430	41	144	1762	24	42	12	264	91	10
Collins	1210	53	7818	430	307	8	2	....	....	5	1	71	4	3	6107	....	....	....	920	2120	....
Franklin	1821	115	6724	1452	496	24	....	....	....	....	....	196	9	....	8730	....	....	....	708	2424	....
Grant	399	101	5365	682	82	5	....	....	....	644	60	314	6	142	6915	1	50	....	562	655	....
Howard	664	1	17075	109	25	....	....	....	....	3	....	16	....	....	4198	....	50	....	468	197	18
Indian Creek	2180	20	10029	1617	463	3	....	....	....	159	45	297	26	108	6338	....	....	....	1363	2681	106
La Fayette	370	17	5446	49	3	3	....	....	....	....	....	4	1	....	1990	....	....	....	....	99	....
Lincoln	30	98	8246	432	138	....	....	....	....	202	....	121	16	....	4626	1	120	....	327	22	....
Milford	976	59	17870	1205	290	7	1	....	....	258	62	123	12	40	8032	....	....	....	623	453	....
Nevada, exc. of town	2300	43	8792	2463	1097	12	3	....	....	46	16	312	32	111	8805	....	....	....	1982	7480	5
Nevada, town of	8	13	25	468	51	7	2	....	....	167	44	499	72	3	5224	1	3000	....	2940	9473	40
New Albany	127	51	3220	110	65	....	....	....	....	....	....	....	....	....	5426	....	....	....	10	100	....
Palestine	794	12	7350	1099	326	16	1	....	....	47	3	110	4	163	4325	....	....	....	1092	2350	20
Richland	570	52	9265	565	91	1	....	....	....	20	....	324	....	....	2799	....	....	....	57	....	....
Sherman	72	33	2146	....	....	....	....	....	....	....	....	....	....	....	1368	....	....	....	297	....	....
Union	1157	57	10642	3449	897	3	....	....	....	15	4	151	28	56	4558	2	310	8	1398	8316	80
Warren	....	9	690	....	....	....	....	....	....	12	1	32	1	46	712	....	....	....	98	....	....
Washington, exc. of Ames	1457	44	5635	2235	430	8	1	....	....	32	5	327	24	1944	19639	....	....	....	1792	1884	35
Total	14165	778	126354	16539	4781	98	10	....	....	1610	250	3327	276	2760	101554	29	3572	20	14901	38332	314

TAMA COUNTY.

NAMES OF TOWNSHIPS, TOWNS, AND CITIES.	Acres of natural timber.	Acres of planted timber.	Rods of hedge.	Apples: Number of trees in bearing.	Apples: Bushels gathered in 1874.	Pears: Number of trees in bearing.	Pears: Bushels gathered in 1874.	Peaches: Number of trees in bearing.	Peaches: Bushels gathered in 1874.	Plums: Number of trees in bearing.	Plums: Bushels gathered in 1874.	Cherries: Number of trees in bearing.	Cherries: Bushels gathered in 1874.	Number of other fruit trees in bearing.	Number of fruit trees not in bearing.	Vineyard: Number of acres.	Vineyard: Pounds of grapes gathered.	Vineyard: Gallons of wine made.	Not in vineyard: Number of vines.	Not in vineyard: Pounds of grapes gathered.	Not in vineyard: Gallons of wine made.
Buckingham	736	244	9846	2220	876	12	3	....	....	9	1	220	17	178	9610	....	....	....	704	2540	....
Carlton	2365	74	6222	1625	501	27	....	....	....	176	5	132	12	504	6442	....	10	....	839	2392	....
Carroll	1146	35	3535	[illegible]	182	....	....	....	....	41	7	74	....	99	4826	....	....	....	831	635	....
Clark	....	134	3386	98	21	....	....	....	....	8	2	30	6	27	6795	....	....	....	519	780	....
Columbia	1120	10	4697	410	158	12	....	....	2	....	....	23	3	5	6418	....	....	....	875	2065	....

Crystal	218	117	6415	514	275							4	1		3927				628	360	
Geneseo	718	147	1200	1446	129					500	10	250			10078						
Grant	15	52	2110	3											4351				355		
Highland	53	25	4438	210	84					50	5	62	7		4996				815		
Howard	104	81	10895	1474	529					18	4	113	11	8	8248				1273	3200	28
Indian Village, exc. of Montour	1522	18	1321	2638	1545	2				31	5	416	29		7541				730	2767	
Lincoln	18	3	440									19			1052						
Montour, town of				160	94	2				8		67	8	20	687				144	860	
Oneida	201	191	12720	43	43										7957				358	950	
Otter Creek	933	9	1516	2030	473	12	1	2		13		191	21	73	10012				699	1664	
Perry, exc. of Traer	565	179	8780	1309	591	1	1					45	16	1	11270				1104	3365	40
Richland	1409	47	3456	1744	215	1		3		20	5	106	10		400		3300		1409	5863	111
Salt Creek	1844	12	1607	2384	946	6	4			29	6	75	6		15490		2000		3791	8745	75
Spring Creek	91	112	8900	2208	383	6				21	1	116	6	12	9541	3	1000		1340	1430	
Tama, exc. of Tama City	804		100	575	147	12				20	5	12	1	8	1436	2	4000	200	140	810	
Tama City, town of	72		60	508	88					27	9	92	12	29	1408	1	2000		962	1915	
Toledo, exc. of town	2870	47	1138	4485	918	42	2	4	1	92	4	221	20	105	7328		200	5	1213	4566	36
Toledo, town of	575	14	1165	591	298	5	2			125	45	84	21	1762	3955				1823	6830	84
Traer, town of	17	5	130	5											550				112		
York	886	33	4758	1148	711	9	2			10	3	52	6	15	9317	1	850		777	1370	
Total	18282	1589	98835	28464	9207	149	15	9	3	1198	117	2404	213	2846	153635	7	13360	205	21441	53107	374

TAYLOR COUNTY.

Bedford, town of																					
Benton, exc. of Bedford	857	24	12321	696	586	83	2	41		11	2	99	23		1811				330	925	10
Clayton	1698	21	14032	1143	821	6	3	157	63	4	1	259	17	8	6376				1115	1953	11
Dallas	1969	15	13210	1018	394			175	72			91	13		5057				826	1566	14
Gay	521	26	6791	290	202			54	24	10	2	111	16		2273				216	586	
Grant	2	29	7597	455	75	6	2	24	3	26	10	94		10	1958				675	500	3
Grove	79	32	7370							5		24			1910				253	300	
Holt	1531	7	3311	138	134	2	4	31	1	4		136	6		7120				704	813	
Jackson	1647	83	7230	1131	688			20	42			9			3347				635	225	
Jefferson	2132	25	6982	1019	669	3	3	123	272	62	61	162	75	3	4951	1	1000		860	319	
Marshall	627	26	7597	388	380	2		24	4	42	8	25	1		4165	2	100		454	425	
Mason	2429	38	9847	906	1018	4		141	46	2		534	28		5612				961	2755	18
Nodaway	1172	21	1945	402	382	16	2	2				38			5756				783	1575	
Platte	3	66	12340	125	115			9	5	145	30	19	2	433	5169				1015	85	
Polk	1613	4	17378	2042	1815	1	1	264	321	10	10	296	57		14090				96	1060	
Ross	1556	7	8176	832	639	2		192	54	6	2	253	23		5705	1	700		1081	834	
Washington	1203	76	11821	2696	981	19		280	2	31	17	228	128		5821				515	1760	
Total	19039	500	147948	13281	8899	134	17	1537	908	358	143	2378	389	454	81121	4	1800		10519	15681	56

UNION COUNTY.

NAMES OF TOWNSHIPS, TOWNS, AND CITIES.	Acres of natural timber.	Acres of planted timber.	Rods of hedge.	APPLES.		PEARS.		PEACHES		PLUMS.		CHERRIES		Number of other fruit trees in bearing.	Number of fruit trees not in bearing.	GRAPES IN VINEYARD.			GRAPES NOT IN VINEYARD.		
				Number of trees in bearing.	Bushels gathered in 1874.	Number of trees in bearing.	Bushels gathered in 1874.	Number of trees in bearing.	Bushels gathered in 1874.	Number of trees in bearing.	Bushels gathered in 1874.	Number of trees in bearing.	Bushels gathered in 1874.			Number of acres.	Pounds of grapes gathered.	Gallons of wine made.	Number of vines.	Pounds of grapes gathered.	Gallons of wine made.
Afton, town of				330	90	16		4		29	18	160	22	12	652				534	2770	
Creston, town of			175																		
Dodge	851	4	2005	281	178			25	2			100			3125				302	530	
Douglas, exc. of Creston	154	7	2790																		
Grant	105	41	1530	210	45							50			2600				500	50	
Highland	369	20	3745	707	312			50		4	4	175	4		620				164		
Jones	2189	16	8405	515	425	3		12	6	18	8	21	7		6065				700	1248	
Lincoln	306	261	5880	60	55	1	9			5	2	122	29		3343	6	400				
New Hope	1028	54	4457	499	370	1		14	2	36	5	80	13		5398				199	364	
Platte	1201	64	16800	1670	650	7	2	27	4	23	5	265	33	5	9533	1	200	6	1105	1295	
Pleasant	1446	11	2312	735	319	10	2	60	15	43	4	41			2472				219	925	
Sand Creek	361	45	9605	359	195							90	7		6793		500	50	870	745	
Spaulding		49	5790	2				10				19			2908	2	300		215		
Union, exc. of Afton	1193	51	6485	555	464	5	2	24		57	10	128	18		9779		800		2757	635	
Total	9203	623	69979	5923	3103	43	15	226	29	215	56	1251	133	17	53288	9	2200	56	7665	8562	

VAN BUREN COUNTY.

NAMES OF TOWNSHIPS, TOWNS, AND CITIES.	Acres of natural timber.	Acres of planted timber.	Rods of hedge.	Apples: Number of trees in bearing.	Apples: Bushels gathered in 1874.	Pears: Number of trees in bearing.	Pears: Bushels gathered in 1874.	Peaches: Number of trees in bearing.	Peaches: Bushels gathered in 1874.	Plums: Number of trees in bearing.	Plums: Bushels gathered in 1874.	Cherries: Number of trees in bearing.	Cherries: Bushels gathered in 1874.	Number of other fruit trees in bearing.	Number of fruit trees not in bearing.	Grapes in vineyard: Number of acres.	Grapes in vineyard: Pounds of grapes gathered.	Grapes in vineyard: Gallons of wine made.	Grapes not in vineyard: Number of vines.	Grapes not in vineyard: Pounds of grapes gathered.	Grapes not in vineyard: Gallons of wine made.
Bentonsport, town of	3		101	703	1274	100	84	152	96	37	22	398	231	1	1529	1	6000	20	1180	10774	37
Birmingham, town of				786	433	37	8	118	25	68	15	553	200		735	1	8100		434	2850	
Bonaparte	4091		13771	5179	4213	211	84	766	277	110	54	1376	608		5798	5	10000	630	2262	8037	97
Cantril, town of																					
Cedar	4169	12	28759	8081	5444	87	48	1043	65	86	14	1916	390	2	7622				1362	6916	26
Chequest	9951		7518	2508	2778	328	21	273	74	56	26	364	100	57	6847	1	500		914	3312	33
Des Moines	5968		11119	6534	4939	104	41	1727	325	143	38	1410	385	13	9676				961	4566	129
Farmington, exc. of town	6148		1030	5207	4962	54	44	531	267	26	3	898	233	19	7372	1	5200		1858	5967	62
Farmington, town of																					

Harrisburg	4038	....	37241	8620	6797	185	98	868	158	62	5	1791	629	20	8423	......	50	......	1428	6226	34
Henry	3713	....	3035	3540	3337	71	39	303	165	40	13	734	289	7	3486	......	3500	310	883	5140	......
Jackson, exc. of Cantril	3779	....	30710	6727	4954	97	34	428	225	42	12	789	526	....	11798	......	....	......	797	2960	2
Keosauqua, town of	348	....	205	2472	2199	192	95	136	78	127	32	915	400	20	1169	......	....	......	3687	24320	610
Lick Creek	8964	1	2835	8033	10855	77	42	334	141	147	41	1545	340	34	7367	6	25600	70	2182	11177	12
Union, exc. of Birmingham	5822	....	18457	11223	9956	60	36	824	130	146	37	2161	514	70	7628	6	20570	195	810	4456	10
Van Buren, exc. of Keosauqua	9692	1	8445	13392	11488	174	62	1255	255	228	64	1752	507	82	11554	1	7500	160	1261	9994	63
Vernon	3358	360	13964	3189	3527	53	25	329	175	65	19	420	120	27	10229	1	10000	......	988	5055	22
Village	5818	....	6070	3843	5121	25	8	93	26	6	3	95	34	407	9681	......	....	......	1765	6239	18
Washington, exc. of Bentonsport	2462	....	2845	3738	3397	78	30	267	129	19	11	592	250	14	3701	......	....	......	335	1600	30
Total	78324	384	186105	93775	85674	1933	799	9447	2611	1408	409	17709	5756	773	114615	23	97020	1385	23107	118689	1185

WAPELLO COUNTY.

Adams	5694	4	2820	3471	1504	55	10	92	4	41	5	1039	143	....	7695	......	400	8	895	4310	......
Agency, exc. of town	1906	2	4252	6033	2921	73	9	406	132	87	22	985	196	16	4132	5	8300	170	1423	6668	28
Agency City, town of	....	....	30	833	405	52	7	99	71	65	19	567	229	4	290	......	1100	......	441	4546	778
Cass	1918	....	535	850	660	2	1	......	....	7	1	69	8	30	1700	......	200	1	434	1420	......
Center, exc. of Ottumwa	4300	....	5603	6069	3209	190	50	49	28	......	....	1879	528	14	25413	19	74100	2086	17768	36868	63
Columbia, exc. of Eddyville	3474	10	2230	2403	1878	1	2	63	13	35	15	205	89	85	2353	......	3000	......	470	4170	......
Competine	2410	10	26869	2162	1766	5	2	12	6	24	5	616	62	....	6804	......	....	......	1746	3695	78
Dahlonega	2575	12	8267	2822	1980	17	10	58	8	......	....	549	86	133	4332	......	....	......	2188	7150	......
Eddyville, town of	70	....	....	439	347	27	12	......	....	68	32	273	116	76	675	......	....	......	542	4065	......
Eldon, town of	....	....	....	....	....	......	......	......	....	......	....	....	......	....	....	......	....	......	....	....	......
Green	7126	....	520	3188	815	33	2	334	26	26	1	584	41	2	7654	......	700	......	1260	5106	10
Highland	1176	15	34680	2324	2098	25	13	......	....	26	10	700	93	3429	7342	......	....	......	830	6216	4
Keokuk	12219	....	....	1506	1079	4	10	151	53	13	1	230	31	458	3820	......	....	......	1257	....	......
Ottumwa, city of	....	....	....	730	612	407	159	141	125	248	147	1516	958	....	2292	......	....	......	4531	58696	292
Pleasant	4032	5	18725	6090	3802	29	22	150	19	34	7	926	151	....	5482	......	....	......	971	5023	15
Polk	3444	1	2067	2177	574	33	12	41	9	107	13	316	25	21	6182	......	200	......	942	2184	5
Richland	2981	9	24598	5675	3321	8	22	20	1	15	5	585	137	11	5423	1	4000	......	897	8985	3
Washington, exc. of Eldon	4658	8	6050	6496	5393	71	11	201	20	36	6	1038	181	2	14732	......	....	......	1431	9981	......
Total	57983	76	137246	53268	32364	1032	354	1817	515	832	289	12077	3074	4281	106321	28	92000	2265	37026	169083	1276

WARREN COUNTY.

Allen	1824	2	2109	2420	1554	11	4	......	....	17	6	102	37	2	13481	......	....	......	2888	21765	263
Belmont	1115	75	27840	2278	1453	......	....	......	....	......	....	133	9	....	20123	......	1000	......	2923	9390	15
Greenfield	3117	28	12976	4539	2198	32	1	5	....	9	2	692	99	120	18974	......	....	......	6506	39125	15
Indianola, town of	....	....	....	....	....	......	....	......	....	......	....	....	......	....	....	......	....	......	....	....	......

WARREN COUNTY—Continued.

Names of townships, towns and cities.	Acres of natural timber.	Acres of planted timber.	Rods of hedge.	Apples. Number of trees in bearing.	Apples. Bushels gathered in 1874.	Pears. Number of trees in bearing.	Pears. Bushels gathered in 1874.	Peaches. Number of trees in bearing.	Peaches. Bushels gathered in 1874.	Plums. Number of trees in bearing.	Plums. Bushels gathered in 1874.	Cherries. Number of trees in bearing.	Cherries. Bushels gathered in 1874.	Number of other fruit trees in bearing.	Number of fruit trees not in bearing.	Grapes in vineyard. Number of acres.	Grapes in vineyard. Pounds of grapes gathered.	Grapes in vineyard. Gallons of wine made.	Grapes not in vineyard. Number of vines.	Grapes not in vineyard. Pounds of grapes gathered.	Grapes not in vineyard. Gallons of wine made.
Jackson	340	23	2759	1027	1418	...	...	...	...	...	...	7	...	...	7246	...	300	...	1987	5325	30
Jefferson	1951	2	9568	2587	1199	...	...	...	...	...	...	206	10	205	4057	...	...	1	3870	12563	130
Liberty	1454	48	21380	1953	1412	18	...	36	1	67	10	530	46	8	14454	1	14000	...	1954	11336	7
Linn	1572	68	11197	3609	3813	5	...	...	...	8	...	163	16	22	11214	...	300	...	4316	14552	...
Otter	2442	12	6020	1500	2020	...	...	...	...	...	...	88	34	40	8340	...	...	...	1280	5115	15
Palmyra	1784	81	5630	5030	3667	7	3	135	15	105	10	189	102	47	5866	1	5000	...	2528	19983	...
Richland	4595	5	485	3227	2844	42	10	10	...	26	16	200	56	...	9424	2	4500	8	2060	20240	...
Squaw	1691	29	10707	934	894	3	...	34	3	75	8	95	9	4	10285	...	...	...	1114	1885	2
Union	1782	13	3848	2429	2089	1	1	...	...	...	25	6	88	21	5679	1	1500	...	2127	15510	21
Virginia	1765	6	11221	218	297	3	...	2	...	...	...	36	2	20	7988	...	...	...	1618	1920	3
Washington, exc. of Indianola	5271	112	34546	7571	6711	35	1	70	...	35	4	728	83	662	26296	9	32400	...	6508	21005	49
White Breast	2755	...	9893	1173	1041	8	3	...	...	...	...	141	13	...	6255	...	400	20	1812	6355	...
White Oak	1260	46	12517	1576	950	4	...	11	2	4	...	55	2	8	8857	...	...	...	1252	1809	...
Total	34718	550	182696	42071	33560	169	23	303	21	346	81	3371	606	1159	178539	14	59400	29	44743	207878	550

WASHINGTON COUNTY.

Names of townships, towns and cities.	Acres of natural timber.	Acres of planted timber.	Rods of hedge.	Apples. Number of trees in bearing.	Apples. Bushels gathered in 1874.	Pears. Number of trees in bearing.	Pears. Bushels gathered in 1874.	Peaches. Number of trees in bearing.	Peaches. Bushels gathered in 1874.	Plums. Number of trees in bearing.	Plums. Bushels gathered in 1874.	Cherries. Number of trees in bearing.	Cherries. Bushels gathered in 1874.	Number of other fruit trees in bearing.	Number of fruit trees not in bearing.	Grapes in vineyard. Number of acres.	Grapes in vineyard. Pounds of grapes gathered.	Grapes in vineyard. Gallons of wine made.	Grapes not in vineyard. Number of vines.	Grapes not in vineyard. Pounds of grapes gathered.	Grapes not in vineyard. Gallons of wine made.
Brighton, exc. of town	2860	2	1998	4019	3675	54	13	41	4	33	3	573	68	...	4025	2	6500	...	670	4249	...
Brighton, town of	349	...	188	1409	653	69	35	58	10	102	23	564	238	...	1924	2	1100	12	533	5307	210
Cedar	937	39	24635	6241	3090	7	...	...	...	74	6	859	75	53	5352	...	6810	320	561	3287	...
Clay	3100	11	6903	7384	4086	66	20	107	26	23	6	942	272	7	6840	4	20900	...	2536	15185	1
Crawford	3198	34	20082	6893	3865	41	6	212	20	61	12	1519	272	72	1067	5	24000	947	3573	44290	100
Dutch Creek	2707	4	25578	5588	3986	30	11	30	7	24	7	1380	187	3	4996	...	700	...	805	3260	6
English River	4643	...	9579	4709	3606	29	2	42	...	10	66	297	135	449	8185	1	500	100	5487	11275	681
Franklin	1695	36	27004	3093	2987	14	4	34	4	58	47	533	165	20	5185	1	1500	...	277	4700	...

Highland	434	55	28608	943	430	6	3	....	....	....	2	209	36	91	10751	....	....	....	498	3340	2
Iowa	4126	1146	10884	4126	2132	5	28	10	1	105	7	828	98	33	7333	3	3700	178	1782	3672	....
Jackson	54	124	29772	2440	1793	....	....	....	....	....	....	635	87	....	13427	....	2800	....	2298	17795	....
Lime Creek	2796	21	23460	3272	1363	....	....	25	....	63	13	950	193	62	10636	2	1800	....	3090	9714	151
Marion	4133	2	8615	6030	4353	22	33	50	21	65	36	734	251	3	10090	2	6200	408	1898	11302	210
Oregon	1888	25	38250	4973	2700	29	2	55	....	55	5	787	87	37	12680	....	....	....	2801	15431	57
Seventy-Six	972	151	42532	2543	2730	....	....	....	....	18	7	99	44	200	11540	17	2600	....	1018	7720	....
Washington, exc. of city	3521	104	10229	8914	6361	78	23	161	7	73	3	1980	353	967	14893	10	28000	705	3207	8401	37
Washington, city of	937	5	1510	1925	886	146	51	17	1	111	20	1232	442	12	1055	2	12800	....	1620	23072	795
Total	38350	1759	309827	74502	48696	596	231	842	101	875	263	14121	3003	2009	129979	51	119910	2670	32654	192000	2250

WAYNE COUNTY.

Allerton, town of	....	....	....	....	....	....	....	....	....	....	....	....	....	....	....	....	....	....	....	....	....
Benton	2025	13	11865	1731	978	11	1	137	8	54	18	448	56	10	9733	1	2500	....	1203	1795	....
Clay	791	6	11503	817	405	6	....	64	6	....	....	251	5	327	7171	1	4020	56	712	717	....
Clinton	1130	4	1500	707	160	7	....	81	28	....	....	226	29	....	4510	....	150	....	784	1222	....
Corydon, exc. of town	2169	9	9195	1051	445	2	....	154	46	2	1	351	83	17	8928	4	3275	196	1595	2475	15
Corydon, town of	....	....	....	354	75	26	4	75	28	37	2	434	157	51	2337	....	....	....	1029	4842	15
Grand River, exc. of Lineville	4082	2	4330	1206	394	8	....	521	13	....	....	86	8	....	5395	....	....	....	705	630	....
Howard	1574	4	2486	1497	1159	40	6	157	117	104	104	85	29	2	5272	....	....	....	541	4930	....
Jackson	1047	....	3130	1299	815	11	1	167	23	16	....	335	34	28	7133	2	1020	10	476	464	....
Jefferson	1541	4	3452	914	450	1	4	58	52	....	....	384	77	....	5698	2	3000	....	968	2814	....
Lineville, town of	....	....	....	....	....	....	....	....	....	....	....	....	....	....	....	....	....	....	....	....	....
Monroe	2014	....	6067	1539	690	5	4	75	7	3	....	443	73	2	3152	....	100	....	539	2292	....
Richman	245	2	17197	1043	255	47	25	1	....	23	2	234	7	....	6605	....	....	....	417	800	....
Seymour, town of	....	....	....	....	....	....	....	....	....	....	....	41	....	....	6941	....	30	....	74	30	....
South Fork	1310	....	15194	779	533	3	1	4	....	173	29	20	4	....	9821	....	....	....	1136	1447	5
Union	1422	80	27930	2545	1031	18	11	19	....	42	4	616	86	71	11969	....	300	....	1345	6526	....
Walnut, exc. of Seymour	558	5	15723	2776	1796	21	19	54	12	7	....	794	121	46	11968	2	16300	200	1216	1745	10
Warren, exc. of Allerton	47	27	7670	1871	351	....	....	152	32	11	....	264	40	70	13122	1	24000	....	1697	2220	....
Washington	1720	6	62338	1437	3660	4	....	64	....	....	....	232	48	14	6082	....	....	....	1016	2685	4
Wright	2539	9	11300	1458	491	3	1	20	....	....	....	295	108	6	6921	3	160	....	926	8107	15
Total	24214	171	210880	23024	13688	213	77	1803	372	472	160	5539	1005	644	132758	15	54855	462	16379	47741	64

WEBSTER COUNTY.

Badger	629	137	2	20	....	....	....	....	....	....	....	....	....	....	....	....	....	....	....	....	....
Clay	....	6	205	....	....	....	....	....	....	....	....	....	....	....	577	....	....	....	50	65	....

WEBSTER COUNTY.—Continued.

Names of townships, towns, and cities.	Acres of natural timber.	Acres of planted timber.	Rods of hedge.	Apples. Number of trees in bearing.	Apples. Bushels gathered in 1874.	Pears. Number of trees in bearing.	Pears. Bushels gathered in 1874.	Peaches. Number of trees in bearing.	Peaches. Bushels gathered in 1874.	Plums. Number of trees in bearing.	Plums. Bushels gathered in 1874.	Cherries. Number of trees in bearing.	Cherries. Bushels gathered in 1874.	Number of other fruit trees in bearing.	Number of fruit trees not in bearing.	Grapes in vineyard. Number of acres.	Grapes in vineyard. Pounds of grapes gathered.	Grapes in vineyard. Gallons of wine made.	Grapes not in vineyard. Number of vines.	Grapes not in vineyard. Pounds of grapes gathered.	Grapes not in vineyard. Gallons of wine made.
Colfax			530																		
Dayton	1735	60	4890	860	145							11			8617				736	10	
Deer Creek	34	46	524	75	41									25	325					6	
Douglas	319	27	1823	499	19							15			2378				77		
Elkhorn	30	28	2204	355	53					299	5	49	1	18	1287				104		
Fort Dodge, city of																					
Fulton		19													246						
Gowrie			170	250																	
Hardin	1933		1575	128	138										1229				153	85	
Jackson	259	147	1877												2210				100	50	
Johnson	287	62	2245	101	28	2				114	17	41	1	12	1787				96	45	
Lost Grove			4320												1085						
Newark		6	412	4								2			475				19		
Otho	1016	1	209	278	79							91	7		2361				163	206	
Pleasant Valley	760	1	180	394	123					150	15	13	1	4	671				18	235	1
Sumner	740	76	805	362	120	1						20	1		4021				345		
Wahkonsa, exc. of Fort Dodge	295	25	690	2198	296	25				2		226	14		6827				1225	2200	8
Washington	374	7	815	700	288										1000	2	205		134	20	
Webster	2558	4	520	1353	146	1				18		83	2	35	2895	1	1600	63	161	100	
Yell	361			50	24									30	70						
Total	11330	652	23996	7627	1500	29				583	37	551	27	124	38061	3	1805	63	3381	3016	9

WINNEBAGO COUNTY.

Names of townships, towns, and cities.	Acres of natural timber.	Acres of planted timber.	Rods of hedge.	Apples. Number of trees in bearing.	Apples. Bushels gathered in 1874.	Pears. Number of trees in bearing.	Pears. Bushels gathered in 1874.	Peaches. Number of trees in bearing.	Peaches. Bushels gathered in 1874.	Plums. Number of trees in bearing.	Plums. Bushels gathered in 1874.	Cherries. Number of trees in bearing.	Cherries. Bushels gathered in 1874.	Number of other fruit trees in bearing.	Number of fruit trees not in bearing.	Grapes in vineyard. Number of acres.	Grapes in vineyard. Pounds of grapes gathered.	Grapes in vineyard. Gallons of wine made.	Grapes not in vineyard. Number of vines.	Grapes not in vineyard. Pounds of grapes gathered.	Grapes not in vineyard. Gallons of wine made.
Center	709	38		11						20	10										
Forest	671	22	83	40	12						22		1		550						

Iowa	573			8																	
Norway	349		130	132	45																
Pleasant	677	32	601											20	1366				52	20	
Total	2779	92	814	191	57					20	32		1	20	1916				52	20	

WINNESHIEK COUNTY.

Bloomfield	3934	19	430	964	608					6	2	10	2	117	9248				700	2020	2
Bluffton	954	4	160	296	157					200	40				2885				39	25	
Burr Oak	1223	4	225	767	166					15	9	3			5600				523	285	130
Calmar	1058	5		109	94										885						130
Canoe	2020			713	173							10			4994				338	695	2
Decorah, exc. of city	2140	9		339	175									206	3332	4	900	150	338		5
Decorah, city of																					
Frankville	4025	9	670	1857	929							12	2	50	5132				1009	17210	5
Fremont	1539	6	731	288	92					50	20	1			3649				598	130	6
Glenwood	1622		90	579	111										1071		20			363	140
Hesper	3203	22	470	1714	506					51	26	13			6276				449	3604	
Highland	1747		958	313	89										1582				4	75	
Jackson	705	63	100	152	43										6370				87	113	
Lincoln	1492	12		33	6									60	1244						
Madison	2385	10	25	455	45					110	21	1	1	343	543						
Military	2061	13	240	360	160					10	10	10	1	25	4220				25	70	6
Orleans	1381	49	400	489	93					2		8			3816				177	170	
Pleasant	3244		120	483	359									121	3681				368	860	88
Springfield	2485	1		133	86							3	1	6	3541				283	70	14
Sumner	1567	55		16	6																
Washington	1059	3	240	284	102										4927				1		
Total	39844	284	5059	10344	4000					444	128	71	7	928	72796	4	920	150	4939	25690	528

WOODBURY COUNTY.

Arlington	12	16							60					75	100						
Concord	74	31										3		42	886				27		
Floyd	20	10	40	4						18											
Grant	1030	34	111							20	10	16	5		528						
Kedron	661	16	135																		
Lakeport	846	10																			
Liberty	650	218	880			2				72	8				1895						
Liston	101	26	820	27	1					180	10										

WOODBURY COUNTY.—Continued.

NAMES OF TOWNSHIPS, TOWNS, AND CITIES.	Acres of natural timber.	Acres of planted timber.	Rods of hedge.	APPLES. Number of trees in bearing.	APPLES. Bushels gathered in 1874.	PEARS. Number of trees in bearing.	PEARS. Bushels gathered in 1874.	PEACHES Number of trees in bearing.	PEACHES Bushels gathered in 1874.	PLUMS. Number of trees in bearing.	PLUMS. Bushels gathered in 1874.	CHERRIES. Number of trees in bearing.	CHERRIES. Bushels gathered in 1874.	Number of other fruit trees in bearing.	Number of fruit trees not in bearing.	GRAPES IN VINEYARD Number of acres.	GRAPES IN VINEYARD Pounds of grapes gathered.	GRAPES IN VINEYARD Gallons of wine made.	GRAPES NOT IN VINEYARD. Number of vines.	GRAPES NOT IN VINEYARD. Pounds of grapes gathered.	GRAPES NOT IN VINEYARD. Gallons of wine made.
Little Sioux	2320	20	80	40	87							10		60	1796						
Moville	17	4													66						
Rock	142	6																			
Rutland	15	8	84												50						
Sioux City, exc. of city	256	16													577				530		
Sioux City, city of		2	160	12	2							12	2		200	2					
Union	340	73	1775									6			1672				169		
West Fork	70	32	40																	115	
Wolf Creek	2	78	2405							50					1170				127		
Woodbury	648	93	110	18						334	52	53			3696						
Total	7204	503	7640	101	90	2			60	674	80	100	7	177	12636	2			853	115	

WORTH COUNTY.

NAMES OF TOWNSHIPS, TOWNS, AND CITIES.	Acres of natural timber.	Acres of planted timber.	Rods of hedge.	APPLES. Number of trees in bearing.	APPLES. Bushels gathered in 1874.	PEARS. Number of trees in bearing.	PEARS. Bushels gathered in 1874.	PEACHES Number of trees in bearing.	PEACHES Bushels gathered in 1874.	PLUMS. Number of trees in bearing.	PLUMS. Bushels gathered in 1874.	CHERRIES. Number of trees in bearing.	CHERRIES. Bushels gathered in 1874.	Number of other fruit trees in bearing.	Number of fruit trees not in bearing.	GRAPES IN VINEYARD Number of acres.	GRAPES IN VINEYARD Pounds of grapes gathered.	GRAPES IN VINEYARD Gallons of wine made.	GRAPES NOT IN VINEYARD. Number of vines.	GRAPES NOT IN VINEYARD. Pounds of grapes gathered.	GRAPES NOT IN VINEYARD. Gallons of wine made.
Bristol	1383	29	1110	233	14							6			1000						
Brookfield	420	2	355	18	3					31	9	3		7	184	1			14	25	9
Danville	10	26	1267												724				133		
Deer Creek	75	17		12		2				5					539						
Fertile	344	17	335	20	2										5						
Hartland	1724	8		103	14																
Kensett	53	19	1900	8		25						1		139	633				57		
Northwood	1009	38	610	280	30	1				2		50		13	2109				135	207	8
Silver Lake	270	3	85	14	2					11	2			50	492		1			136	23
Union	140	2	220	10	2									55	704						
Total	5428	161	5882	698	67	28				49	11	60		264	6390	1	1		339	368	40

WRIGHT COUNTY.

Belmond	388	103	7660	86	2	...	...	...	...	...	...	84	5	...	998	...	...	...	221	435	8
Boone	64	19	1742	...	...	...	...	...	...	...	...	...	...	...	...	...	...	...	...	...	...
Clarion	30	57	2129	8	...	...	...	...	...	...	...	40	1	...	350	...	...	...	76	25	...
Eagle Grove	481	25	1270	107	10	...	...	...	...	165	24	27	...	...	1713	2	150	5	117	20	...
Iowa	353	52	575	558	16	...	...	...	...	...	...	25	1	...	638	...	...	...	...	...	...
Liberty	503	13	1959	214	36	1	...	...	...	...	...	4	...	31	537	...	...	...	283	95	...
Pleasant	441	58	3266	86	12	...	...	...	...	...	...	337	14	...	400	...	...	...	...	...	...
Troy	499	61	2175	380	98	...	...	...	...	...	...	5	...	17	3320	...	...	...	488	500	86
Vernon	206	80	2890	13	2	...	...	...	...	...	...	...	...	...	3237	...	...	...	110	130	...
Wall Lake	...	82	...	...	...	...	...	...	...	...	...	...	...	...	...	...	...	...	...	...	...
Woolstock	267	24	475	...	...	...	...	...	...	...	...	...	...	...	...	...	...	...	...	...	...
Total	3232	574	24141	1452	176	1	...	...	...	165	24	522	21	48	11193	2	150	5	1245	1205	94

STATISTICS OF THE HERD, AND NUMBER OF DOGS.

ADAIR COUNTY.

NAMES OF TOWNSHIPS, TOWNS, AND CITIES.	Number of horses of all ages.	Number of horses sold for export in 1874.	Number of mules and asses.	Number of same sold for export in 1874.	Number of milch cows.	Number of pounds of butter made in 1874.	Number of pounds of cheese made in 1874 not in factory.	Number of gallons of milk sold in 1874.	Number of work oxen.	Number of all other cattle.	No. of cattle slaughtered and sold for slaughter in 1874.	Number of thorough-bred short-horns.	HOGS. Number on hand.	HOGS. Number of Berk-shires.	HOGS. Number of Poland-China.	HOGS. No. slaughtered or sold for slaughter in 1874.	SHEEP. Number on hand.	SHEEP. Number of pounds of wool obtained in 1874.	SHEEP. No. slaughtered or sold for slaughter in 1874.	SHEEP. Number killed by dogs in 1874.	Number of dogs.
Eureka	89	...	...	...	78	3464	...	...	...	214	425	...	428	3	554	313	...	...	...	...	91
Fontanelle, town of	121	16	7	...	112	4818	...	490	2	58	73	...	258	5	34	293	...	...	...	...	146
Grand River	235	8	6	...	253	10060	110	...	16	426	66	1	1120	...	286	692	631	4480	17	...	78
Greenfield	244	37	7	7	157	9715	3000	...	...	371	42	1	926	235	...	961	478	2415	15	1	39
Grove	181	2	9	...	143	8272	...	...	...	252	5	...	557	133	20	522	6	...	...	...	57
Harrison	264	9	17	2	313	24760	275	...	...	685	85	2	2450	9	165	1391	312	1216	23	19	135
Jackson	362	7	20	...	235	9124	...	...	4	700	67	...	1400	9	8	1146	139	991	1	...	19
Jefferson	509	16	38	...	366	26725	80	...	...	1236	10	...	2287	403	...	2240	386	1564	3	46	118
Lincoln	447	5	47	2	305	14125	...	...	...	972	...	1	3179	16	74	1761	...	200	4	4	94
Orient	149	23	10	...	72	5630	...	...	...	551	255	4	1253	...	701	788	...	...	...	...	49
Prussia	123	...	10	...	106	4670	...	...	...	111	365	...	208	...	3	173	...	...	...	...	53
Richland	296	3	33	1	269	15400	...	...	4	376	17	...	1562	5	218	1087	177	804	12	4	105
Summerset, exc. of Fontanelle	172	7	13	...	166	8095	...	...	50	281	30	1	647	...	27	724	26	...	...	...	155
Summit	73	...	...	...	55	2250	...	...	4	110	...	2	280	...	2	87	240	...	...	...	32
Union	199	21	17	...	208	9347	2321	...	...	458	234	3	1785	24	3	855	158	660	51	4	57
Walnut	...	...	...	...	...	...	...	...	...	...	...	...	...	40	...	...	...	...	...	...	...
Washington	453	...	42	...	346	21185	90	...	31	1157	299	6	2054	66	61	2154	564	2359	22	41	168
Total	3917	154	276	12	3184	177640	5876	490	111	7958	1973	21	20394	948	2156	15187	3117	14689	148	119	1396

ADAMS COUNTY.

Carl	324	...	18	...	312	15145	500	...	2	580	11	...	1110	24	46	860	159	1046	...	...	108
Colony	232	...	10	...	248	9820	2000	...	...	341	5	...	1554	16	47	1037	...	...	...	...	75
Corning, town of	172	...	9	...	131	...	...	...	...	98	...	...	263	...	...	...	...	...	...	...	117
Douglas	464	16	52	5	422	20676	275	...	20	1113	198	2	3601	45	400	1861	734	3919	131	88	143
Grant	272	...	21	...	295	13767	...	...	...	527	...	...	1758	...	...	893	...	...	...	...	79
Jasper	377	1	43	...	332	16610	...	150	4	909	57	2	1619	5	87	1302	1	1000	60	...	158
Lincoln	315	...	33	2	260	11950	...	...	8	836	45	...	1145	20	17	1108	...	...	...	...	101
Mercer	234	2	11	2	203	10435	...	...	2	910	136	...	1174	8	16	855	113	580	6	1	77
Nodaway	528	19	18	...	569	21170	440	...	2	1151	445	5	2278	8	192	2259	183	1856	99	40	188
Prescott	246	...	14	...	262	16686	600	75	14	719	56	2	848	5	115	1128	570	2725	16	1	85
Quincy, exc. of towns	297	12	19	1	285	13600	...	10010	...	477	51	20	1894	208	71	819	1233	424	16	...	111
Quincy, town of	73	...	7	...	69	4200	...	...	...	33	1	...	104	5	...	142	1	...	...	...	45
Union	243	...	15	1	228	14050	4108	...	10	755	177	4	1228	236	585	...	...	...	...	...	85
Washington	484	...	10	...	439	21277	90	...	14	823	89	...	2426	1	16	1129	557	2274	36	61	162
Total	4261	50	280	11	4055	189386	8013	10235	76	9272	1271	35	21002	581	1592	13393	3560	13824	364	191	1534

ALLAMAKEE COUNTY.

Center	422	2	21	...	547	27997	1407	26	42	1001	210	...	786	...	...	673	279	1130	110	43	194
Fairview	180	...	...	...	168	10057	...	...	8	312	24	...	259	...	...	347	49	125	...	3	94
Franklin	372	2	11	...	358	28690	1400	...	8	510	136	...	811	5	2	716	204	860	44	29	153
French Creek	432	...	...	...	390	14735	...	...	6	901	195	...	1341	...	...	1434	241	942	...	12	186
Hanover	206	...	4	...	279	13720	...	...	8	407	14	...	428	...	...	518	174	551	...	...	113
Iowa	277	2	2	...	274	12900	...	...	18	605	179	...	438	...	...	586	384	1816	35	17	111
Jefferson	558	...	4	...	414	43770	815	...	6	518	271	4	1142	23	34	1492	434	2323	86	15	130
La Fayette	518	6	4	...	415	19482	...	167	38	708	188	...	1333	...	13	1210	917	611	41	30	221
Lansing, exc. of city	349	26	6	...	438	22536	1820	...	30	680	174	1	907	5	43	942	166	720	38	26	136
Lansing, city of	165	2	2	...	125	...	...	...	...	...	...	...	13	...	...	26	16	...	...	...	109
Linton	299	15	6	...	280	14066	...	...	26	768	126	1	771	1	11	769	542	1066	70	40	178
Ludlow	823	33	2	...	537	37750	716	...	8	904	179	...	2032	10	50	1988	431	2500	161	40	177
Makee, exc. of Waukon	489	...	...	...	480	27565	1500	40	19	411	126	...	1134	25	90	1310	478	2271	34	10	139
Paint Creek	401	42	5	2	539	23425	160	...	64	1121	211	1	2106	...	1	1200	837	2703	228	131	187
Post, exc. of Postville	564	40	8	...	453	33513	376	375	8	1047	498	1	1563	22	197	1685	191	1293	122	7	131
Postville, town of	41	...	1	...	43	2868	...	14010	...	...	...	...	...	...	...	...	...	...	...	...	37
Taylor	323	11	...	...	369	13540	...	...	31	642	146	1	1010	...	...	670	363	1177	52	9	160
Union City	244	...	...	...	255	15530	...	...	...	577	50	...	998	...	...	715	191	1036	...	12	113
Union Prairie	430	21	...	...	406	21353	...	...	11	435	153	...	1531	...	...	1172	1079	927	61	33	171
Waterloo	354	16	8	...	435	15225	...	...	6	468	62	...	1135	...	...	824	396	1758	15	71	164
Waukon, town of	163	...	2	...	80	1840	...	55	...	6	...	...	32	6	...	57	...	...	...	...	33
Total	7610	218	86	2	7294	400562	8194	14673	337	12021	2942	9	19770	97	441	18334	7372	23809	1097	528	2937

APPANOOSE COUNTY.

NAMES OF TOWNSHIPS, TOWNS AND CITIES	Number of horses of all ages.	Number of horses sold for export in 1874.	Number of mules and asses.	Number of same sold for export in 1874.	Number of milch cows.	Number of pounds of butter made in 1874.	Number of pounds of cheese made in 1874 not in factory.	Number of gallons of milk sold in 1874.	Number of work oxen.	Number of all other cattle.	No. of cattle slaughtered or sold for slaughter in 1874.	Number of thorough-bred short-horns.	HOGS. Number on hand.	HOGS. Number of Berk-shires.	HOGS. Number of Poland-China.	HOGS. No. slaughtered or sold for slaughter in 1874.	SHEEP. Number on hand.	SHEEP. Number of pounds of wool obtained in 1874.	SHEEP. No. slaughtered or sold for slaughter in 1874.	SHEEP. Number killed by dogs in 1874.	Number of dogs.
Bellair	434	29	49	......	403	25531	....	7725	......	1260	253	3	2648	26	21	3056	877	5803	887	19	90
Caldwell	685	12	52	1	568	40290	....	192	......	1132	146	5	3037	28	11	2089	1443	4945	245	145	217
Center, exc. of Centerville	502	10	12	......	356	29753	....	3285	......	904	345	9	2137	9	114	2324	637	1670	25	3	144
Centerville, town of	66	......	10	......	71	....	....	....	......	12	235	......	175	....	....	375	....	....	....	....	50
Chariton	560	14	78	......	465	34191	....	....	2	1124	160	......	3804	10	27	2736	664	3928	574	80	154
Douglas	365	4	32	......	289	23307	49	....	17	640	67	1	3651	14	5	1842	710	2080	100	19	110
Franklin	613	37	23	......	2434	32933	13	20	......	1455	432	......	2716	....	....	3502	761	2504	574	39	150
Independence	621	19	37	2	498	23855	....	....	6	1254	146	10	3174	13	56	2680	1553	4227	398	12	153
Johns	729	18	24	3	586	42792	....	....	......	2848	517	...	7474	15	18	5333	1175	4754	138	52	150
Lincoln	406	27	11	......	376	30180	240	....	......	1161	327	4	2230	120	197	2340	677	2861	168	22	120
Moulton, town of	130	16	9	4	129	10554	....	250	2	179	23	......	745	40	68	309	230	....	....	....	84
Pleasant	656	25	37	4	532	35647	420	56	4	1496	346	6	4284	93	....	2787	799	3109	312	74	182
Taylor	501	27	46	10	481	35668	5200	900	2	1001	152	......	2563	12	207	2620	1234	4169	197	58	171
Sharon	357	26	18	3	337	23190	....	....	37	776	187	1	2073	1	3	1394	885	2795	116	38	120
Udell	483	29	39	6	378	36112	....	330	......	907	81	......	4800	153	756	2164	1942	5117	289	87	132
Union	283	14	15	1	215	16771	....	20	......	322	83	......	900	30	74	899	595	1955	592	43	146
Walnut	461	9	54	......	380	21985	35	....	4	1139	230	24	3359	123	242	2750	726	2257	125	14	145
Washington, exc. of Moulton	688	5	106	2	555	40540	500	....	4	1506	420	4	5294	74	206	2767	3003	7471	644	57	194
Wells	569	......	50	......	512	30816	200	45	4	1553	155	......	2382	18	11	2027	1779	3840	60	33	181
Total	9109	321	702	36	9565	534115	6657	12833	82	20669	4305	67	57446	779	2016	43994	19690	63485	5444	795	2693

AUDUBON COUNTY.

NAMES OF TOWNSHIPS, TOWNS AND CITIES	Number of horses of all ages.	Number of horses sold for export in 1874.	Number of mules and asses.	Number of same sold for export in 1874.	Number of milch cows.	Number of pounds of butter made in 1874.	Number of pounds of cheese made in 1874 not in factory.	Number of gallons of milk sold in 1874.	Number of work oxen.	Number of all other cattle.	No. of cattle slaughtered or sold for slaughter in 1874.	Number of thorough-bred short-horns.	HOGS. Number on hand.	HOGS. Number of Berk-shires.	HOGS. Number of Poland-China.	HOGS. No. slaughtered or sold for slaughter in 1874.	SHEEP. Number on hand.	SHEEP. Number of pounds of wool obtained in 1874.	SHEEP. No. slaughtered or sold for slaughter in 1874.	SHEEP. Number killed by dogs in 1874.	Number of dogs.
Audubon	211	9	13	......	147	7635	....	....	......	277	24	3	727	26	14	501	....	....	....	....	69
Douglas	5[illegible]	......	6	......	46	1570	147	....	2	114	....	......	164	....	1	....	....	....	....	....	26
Exira	418	......	42	......	354	12957	130	660	......	968	321	9	2514	23	162	1577	29	156	....	....	141
Greeley	92	4	13	......	144	4397	....	....	......	281	23	......	68	1	....	94	....	....	....	....	38

Hamlin	214	1	25	......	122	6165	25	5	7	534	149	4	1364	34	5	733	......	100	2	......	55
Leroy	97	......	16	......	136	2250	150	......	......	229	4	2	362	......	1	222	......	......	......	......	33
Melville	48	3	1	2	47	1105	......	......	......	78	4	......	132	1	2	91	......	......	......	......	21
Oakfield	297	......	30	......	373	17280	......	......	......	509	100	......	1464	7	12	1061	12	674	25	5	117
Viola	126	......	19	2	111	6360	......	......	13	287	9	......	582	23	18	306	......	......	......	......	54
Total	1554	17	165	4	1480	59719	452	665	22	3277	634	18	7377	115	215	4585	41	930	27	5	554

BENTON COUNTY.

Belle Plaine, town of	......	......	......	......	......	......	......	......	......	......	......	......	......	......	......	......	......	......	......	......	......
Benton	355	7	25	4	328	19420	......	......	2	399	79	1	954	3	41	767	125	500	15	16	147
Big Grove	762	8	38	......	501	43041	100	......	......	1430	156	7	3350	32	286	2987	233	1129	17	......	159
Blairstown, town of	122	......	......	......	97	100	......	......	......	2	......	......	5	......	......	......	......	......	......	......	......
Bruce	634	7	14	......	450	43995	80	......	4	1009	176	3	3880	41	393	1710	20	144	2	3	120
Canton, exc. of Shellsburg	734	26	30		562	47540	150	......	......	1527	467	2	3179	15	44	2958	523	2579	150	24	185
Cedar	872	11	32	......	969	73315	30	......	8	1747	218	18	4041	35	52	3477	41	118	10	2	201
Eden	570	36	28	2	483	41180	460	35	......	1181	199	4	3255	21	89	2454	39	150	7	5	164
Eldorado	666	......	21	......	534	35160	214	......	......	983	99	1	3619	......	8	1978	19	76	......	......	166
Florence	670	24	12	11	705	54265	2700	......	......	1648	261	2	3523	3	130	3578	192	739	20	......	147
Fremont	648	8	20	2	479	43469	200	......	......	1204	130	3	3327	12	45	2327	87	373	16	2	183
Harrison	414	28	22	8	354	28750	430	......	......	787	161	12	1510	75	78	1461	299	1490	98	19	91
Homer	550	3	43	......	389	22678	......	......	......	754	110	......	2114	15	19	1292	35	147	3	3	130
Iowa, exc. of Belle Plaine	890	19	7	......	592	28940	2602	2125	2	974	294	......	2971	43	127	2162	192	1147	46	1	128
Jackson	740	9	31	......	563	35067	500	5	......	1341	194	9	3008	17	67	2600	34	52	4	......	181
Kane	468	2	39	......	449	30800	......	......	8	1283	244	......	2432	7	4	1677	......	......	......	......	172
Leroy, exc. of Blairstown	705	6	46	......	550	40695	......	775	2	892	228	4	2182	27	59	2087	81	......	......	......	181
Monroe	668	1	40	......	489	44353	......	......	......	814	52	1	2649	3	44	1571	......	......	......	......	159
Polk	888	24	71	......	889	50112	5280	70	4	1458	160	1	3325	72	30	2938	617	2803	142	52	257
St. Clair	618	8	19	......	575	33848	100	......	......	1098	168	23	3285	34	500	2940	204	1075	35	20	142
Shellsburg, town of	58	30	13	2	69	3240	......	445	20	2	150	......	65	......	......	4	......	......	......	......	31
Taylor, exc. of Vinton	440	19	33	1	422	26175	......	7240	......	771	190	13	2376	73	315	624	171	638	14	19	104
Union	644	39	25	......	497	26305	......	......	......	1069	172	......	2555	15	52	1668	19	82	7	......	188
Vinton, city of	356	16	15	......	206	4000	......	10000	......	308	......	......	342	20	40	200	......	......	......	......	300
Total	13472	331	624	30	11152	776448	12846	20695	50	22681	3908	104	57947	563	2423	43460	2932	13242	586	166	3536

BLACK HAWK COUNTY.

Barclay	565	21	27	......	647	43743	......	......	6	1081	108	3	2054	45	27	1494	35	133	4	9	137
Bennington	569	15	22	......	500	38240	......	......	2	964	268	11	1384	131	29	1309	87	983	198	2	121
Big Creek, exc. of La Porte	498	50	11	3	395	23795	......	......	......	781	308	16	1754	21	46	1684	87	275	35	......	126
Black Hawk	633	31	22	1	460	45850	110	......	2	1057	122	1	2016	48	280	1481	49	216	12	1	158
Cedar	458	1	7	......	393	36300	600	75	6	655	96	......	1836	28	36	1646	40	130	3	1	121

BLACK HAWK COUNTY.—Continued.

NAMES OF TOWNSHIPS, TOWNS, AND CITIES.	Number of horses of all ages.	Number of horses sold for export in 1874.	Number of mules and asses.	Number of same sold for export in 1874.	Number of milch cows.	Number of pounds of butter made in 1874.	Number of pounds of cheese made in 1874 not in factory.	Number of gallons of milk sold in 1874.	Number of work oxen.	Number of all other cattle.	No. of cattle slaughtered or sold for slaughter in 1874.	Number of thorough-bred short-horns.	HOGS. Number on hand.	HOGS. Number of Berk-shires.	HOGS. Number of Poland-China.	HOGS. No. slaughtered or sold for slaughter in 1874.	SHEEP. Number on hand.	SHEEP. Number of pounds of wool obtained in 1874.	SHEEP. No. slaughtered or sold for slaughter in 1874.	SHEEP. Number killed by dogs in 1874.	Number of dogs.
Cedar Falls, exc. of city	676	9	28	.....	541	44765	.....	18280	2	1092	174	3	2180	86	1459	633	276	880	20	.....	144
Cedar Falls, city of	379	87	8	.....	287	27325	8	7631	.....	220	775	2	501	95	196	3115	.....	.....	70	.....	222
Eagle	507	...	9	.....	357	24515	.....	.....	.....	600	140	.....	1978	10	80	1707	9	.....	.....	.....	113
East Waterloo, exc. of city	607	11	26	5	562	47507	100	14684	6	1006	265	6	3347	47	100	1809	308	1747	172	2	155
Fox	600	144	28	.....	448	33836	9780	.....	4	1165	121	.....	4019	15	.....	2025	186	1600	40	.....	112
LaPorte City, town of	128	81	7	2	106	6663	.....	1930	.....	.....	191	.....	184	30	13	1032	.....	.....	.....	.....	19
Lester	532	2	39	.....	578	43268	.....	20	15	1129	126	2	1578	8	3	1304	254	1958	206	7	170
Lincoln	592	15	11	1	350	24925	300	.....	5	689	92	3	2282	5	28	1799	9	80	.....	.....	119
Mt. Vernon	622	8	27	.....	503	35720	.....	.....	.....	800	143	.....	1844	9	19	1692	40	200	5	.....	88
Orange	736	12	18	.....	647	44032	.....	35339	.....	1231	188	13	3013	271	406	2427	.....	56	.....	.....	138
Poyner	697	12	15	.....	628	53694	2295	533	.....	906	159	6	3913	16	28	2422	50	235	20	1	160
Spring Creek	448	5	24	.....	421	25037	405	.....	3	915	155	1	2772	27	100	1290	.....	600	54	10	131
Union	228	10	9	.....	190	8424	.....	.....	2	337	71	.....	678	58	334	530	.....	.....	.....	.....	62
Washington	319	17	15	.....	290	32605	250	150	.....	432	72	1	1110	25	27	944	92	474	7	56	71
Waterloo, exc. of city	272	5	.....	10	277	23456	.....	2000	1	467	71	4	889	34	73	922	869	4869	66	.....	65
Waterloo, city of	561	.....	16	.....	389	.....	.....	.....	.....	.....	.....	.....	.....	.....	.....	.....	.....	.....	.....	.....	158
Total	10627	536	369	22	8969	663700	13848	80642	54	15527	3445	72	39332	1009	3284	31265	2391	14436	912	89	2590

BOONE COUNTY.

NAMES OF TOWNSHIPS, TOWNS, AND CITIES.	Number of horses of all ages.	Number of horses sold for export in 1874.	Number of mules and asses.	Number of same sold for export in 1874.	Number of milch cows.	Number of pounds of butter made in 1874.	Number of pounds of cheese made in 1874 not in factory.	Number of gallons of milk sold in 1874.	Number of work oxen.	Number of all other cattle.	No. of cattle slaughtered or sold for slaughter in 1874.	Number of thorough-bred short-horns.	HOGS. Number on hand.	HOGS. Number of Berk-shires.	HOGS. Number of Poland-China.	HOGS. No. slaughtered or sold for slaughter in 1874.	SHEEP. Number on hand.	SHEEP. Number of pounds of wool obtained in 1874.	SHEEP. No. slaughtered or sold for slaughter in 1874.	SHEEP. Number killed by dogs in 1874.	Number of dogs.
Amaqua	368	.....	21	.....	663	30640	.....	.....	.....	699	12	.....	1624	11	8	1209	928	.....	.....	.....	105
Beaver	152	.....	.....	.....	176	8350	.....	.....	.....	243	45	.....	810	9	107	694	.....	184	.....	.....	144
Boone, city of	.....	.....	.....	.....	.....	.....	.....	.....	.....	.....	.....	.....	.....	.....	.....	.....	.....	.....	.....	.....	.....
Boonsboro, town of	335	89	35	16	296	14982	.....	3194	10	328	189	1	1027	299	330	800	329	.....	.....	.....	.....
Cass	370	4	54	.....	449	22245	.....	.....	.....	1116	338	9	3578	121	64	2341	1032	3898	100	87	134

Colfax	402	......	6	.....	390	18695	....	....	......	1124	146	......	189	....	....	1222	352	637	29	7	89
Des Moines, exc. of Boone and Boonsboro	522	40	54	12	679	45755	880	18770	2	1299	473	1	3397	22	352	2334	230	1662	202	34	237
Dodge	765	6	30	30	657	35927	338	62	......	1848	422	....	3853	64	381	3776	858	2228	158	29	201
Douglas	393	......	28	......	233	18062	316	....	2	658	72	......	4421	3	64	1538	669	2411	89	65	144
Garden	453	......	43	......	201	30455	....	....	5	1365	163	4	1843	6	89	1777	303	1204	26	38	144
Grant	272	4	2	......	243	10675	527	....	8	250	11	......	679	....	4	643	140	118	10	4	100
Harrison	282	3	11	......	334	14325	....	1188	2	767	1609	......	1060	98	164	1108	625	2212	....	....	87
Jackson	459	3	4	......	496	27920	6180	....	4	1580	74	......	2361	....	450	1463	76	185	....	5	124
Marcy	648	......	34	......	707	35100	....	1614	12	836	243	2	2756	30	112	2038	275	964	39	31	316
Peoples	488	....	39	......	492	38125	145	....	6	1210	50	2	2062	60	154	1667	95	77	1	2	131
Pilot Mound	334	......	23	......	299	15225	....	....	......	731	12	....	1113	....	52	986	165	555	....	....	65
Union	372	......	36	......	442	30870	844	....	......	1086	170	1	1475	15	142	1408	269	977	17	10	88
Worth	500	16	30	4	361	25083	120	....	2	1440	333	......	4908	46	144	2417	2539	1655	119	84	135
Yell	665	2	40	......	480	33034	5000	215	49	855	73	......	2934	42	143	1477	237	865	51	22	254
Total	7780	167	490	32	7538	455458	14350	25043	102	17438	4435	20	37090	826	2760	28898	9122	19832	841	418	2498

BREMER COUNTY.

Dayton	345	......	......	......	473	32520	2400	....	2	550	47	......	892	24	27	476	16	57	....	1	120
Douglas	479	......	12	......	512	39431	5164	....	12	969	94	5	1806	21	2	1209	106	421	30	3	120
Franklin	516	35	7	......	595	44353	....	....	......	1256	123	......	1138	6	9	951	72	223	12	4	142
Frederika	231	3	4	......	289	21740	150	....	4	567	110	2	473	37	5	485	57	351	26	7	86
Fremont	596	43	3	......	825	65940	586	50	......	1958	343	......	2710	5	....	1546	178	866	53	15	141
Jackson	534	6	17	......	443	37100	610	12173	2	690	159	......	2034	43	20	2011	585	2433	141	19	108
Jefferson	502	11	4	......	552	30230	....	....	......	1026	239	......	1648	18	4	1294	198	489	....	....	178
La Fayette	543	10	7	2	515	38855	50	....	8	1291	177	2	3421	65	32	1743	162	1643	225	119	111
Le Roy	260	1	......	......	380	27250	....	....	4	793	43	......	616	1	1	654	237	972	21	6	71
Maxfield	555	36	6	2	751	44395	20	900	......	1573	335	......	2914	2	....	1561	137	600	22	2	205
Polk	674	19	12	......	643	44336	282	....	8	930	270	1	1984	161	82	2193	264	1706	....	23	150
Sumner	453	7	2	......	497	45271	....	....	11	896	30	1	1007	1	2	1071	276	1305	113	1	151
Warren	686	40	4	2	779	60210	....	....	2	1561	175	1	3341	5	2	1735	169	703	35	4	178
Washington, exc. of Waverly	456	7	13	......	417	41955	2550	2160	2	595	141	1	1264	14	5	1112	47	163	17	4	131
Waverly, city of	355	180	7	......	246	24605	....	3125	......	131	14	......	4	12	....	75	....	200	50	....	96
Total	7185	398	98	6	7917	508191	11812	18408	55	14786	2300	13	25252	415	191	18116	2504	12132	745	208	1988

BUCHANAN COUNTY.

Buffalo	544	6	24	....	476	43085	410	4175	......	1335	275	45	1347	27	16	1254	576	2750	40	15	100
Byron	682	52	27	12	761	68320	3775	1265	......	1329	255	12	1884	138	450	1782	272	1849	35	16	149

BUCHANAN COUNTY.—Continued.

Names of townships, towns, and cities.	Number of horses of all ages.	Number of horses sold for export in 1874.	Number of mules and asses.	Number of same sold for export in 1874.	Number of milch cows.	Number of pounds of butter made in 1874.	Number of pounds of cheese made in 1874 not in factory.	Number of gallons of milk sold in 1874.	Number of work oxen.	Number of all other cattle.	No. of cattle slaughtered or sold for slaughter in 1874.	Number of thorough-bred short-horns.	HOGS. Number on hand.	HOGS. Number of Berkshires.	HOGS. Number of Poland-China.	HOGS. No. slaughtered or sold for slaughter in 1874.	SHEEP. Number on hand.	SHEEP. Number of pounds of wool obtained in 1874.	SHEEP. No. slaughtered or sold for slaughter in 1874.	SHEEP. Number killed by dogs in 1874.	Number of dogs.
Cono	346	......	22	......	470	31890	....	....	8	825	34	......	1570	19	7	1213	10	70	12	5	78
Fairbank	602	8	29	......	726	52425	2550	....	......	1129	65	......	2045	....	33	1199	393	799	28	9	125
Fremont	497	......	8	......	425	55095	50	2137	4	1104	113	1	1441	2	6	1299	83	415	23	15	120
Hazleton	526	26	23	......	530	32898	....	....	20	1138	452	1	1419	30	85	1027	307	2578	44	18	129
Homer	502	11	......	......	439	43580	50	....	......	917	29	......	2400	....	....	1388	75	....	....	....	139
Independence, city of	....	......	......	......	......	....	....	....	......	....	....	......	....	....	....	....	....	....	....	....	....
Jefferson	73	17	31	......	603	52925	....	....	4	1133	133	4	2253	9	178	2344	211	1289	100	19	162
Liberty	651	2	14	......	622	31218	1600	....	......	1050	378	111	3193	12	317	2702	98	441	15	7	155
Madison	536	4	20	7	798	58766	....	6375	......	1071	95	11	1728	11	22	1244	312	1210	90	19	102
Middlefield	602	17	11	......	628	40810	181	....	4	1252	106	......	1920	18	22	1812	607	2620	....	37	136
Newton	657	23	22	......	727	48420	30	50	6	1288	165	......	2550	81	104	2526	936	4487	329	56	201
Perry	750	......	23	4	716	54550	150	1870	10	1465	641	5	2599	44	42	2002	272	515	98	....	218
Sumner	381	7	10	......	351	31200	....	....	2	791	....	......	1334	17	34	912	1334	60	....	....	110
Washington, exc. of Independence	627	1	16	......	694	39502	250	8141	12	1727	280	7	2145	44	35	2803	384	872	271	7	202
Westburg	474	......	20	......	441	34580	400	....	......	1136	78	23	1617	11	9	1477	8	117	7	....	108
Total	8450	174	300	23	9407	719264	9446	24013	70	18690	3099	220	31445	473	1360	26984	5878	20072	1092	223	2234

BUENA VISTA COUNTY.

Names of townships, towns, and cities.	Number of horses of all ages.	Number of horses sold for export in 1874.	Number of mules and asses.	Number of same sold for export in 1874.	Number of milch cows.	Number of pounds of butter made in 1874.	Number of pounds of cheese made in 1874 not in factory.	Number of gallons of milk sold in 1874.	Number of work oxen.	Number of all other cattle.	No. of cattle slaughtered or sold for slaughter in 1874.	Number of thorough-bred short-horns.	HOGS. Number on hand.	HOGS. Number of Berkshires.	HOGS. Number of Poland-China.	HOGS. No. slaughtered or sold for slaughter in 1874.	SHEEP. Number on hand.	SHEEP. Number of pounds of wool obtained in 1874.	SHEEP. No. slaughtered or sold for slaughter in 1874.	SHEEP. Number killed by dogs in 1874.	Number of dogs.
Barnes	109	......	......	......	114	7990	....	....	33	296	40	......	212	12	18	140	183	722	16	....	41
Brookes	53	......	......	......	38	1710	300	....	2	82	5	......	175	5	4	6	6	11	....	....	17
Coon	118	......	2	......	75	4065	....	....	18	117	....	......	126	....	....	118	....	....	....	....	....
Elk	133	......	4	......	86	5475	....	....	32	114	3	......	528	20	15	271	276	678	12	....	49
Fairfield	31	......	4	......	58	3400	217	....	24	137	15	......	63	1	....	23	10	37	....	1	15
Grant	32	2	2	......	35	2250	130	....	8	74	6	......	86	....	....	25	....	....	....	....	18

Lee	156	......	2	......	126	9255	125	205	42	212	31	......	417	9	12	248	11	49	1	......	46
Lincoln	30	......	......	......	27	2660	......	......	8	19	8	......	61	......	......	18	......	......	......	......	16
Maple Valley	152	......	8	......	114	4040	100	......	57	298	28	......	407	25	......	207	244	35	2	......	45
Newell	104	20	3	......	118	4061	250	95	15	165	45	......	213	54	40	386	......	......	......	......	66
Nokomis	201	......	18	......	129	7011	......	30	34	170	6	......	454	20	5	232	18	......	......	......	70
Poland	49	......	1	......	45	3485	......	......	8	103	7	......	50	......	......	66	......	......	......	......	20
Providence	50	2	9	......	61	3070	......	......	18	100	3	......	192	3	11	72	......	......	......	......	47
Scott	55	......	5	......	50	4524	135	......	......	3	......	......	73	7	29	40	......	......	......	......	12
Storm Lake, exc. of town	138	1	6	......	94	5872	120	141	24	123	34	1	333	27	28	192	......	......	......	......	37
Storm Lake, town of	84	......	2	......	38	985	......	690	3	3	2	......	24	......	......	......	......	......	......	......	95
Total	1495	25	66	......	1208	69853	1377	1161	326	2016	233	1	3414	183	162	2044	748	1532	31	1	524

BUTLER COUNTY.

Albion	485	......	6	......	441	33955	8000	......	2	657	85	25	1658	175	85	1299	29	65	......	......	135
Beaver	593	68	16	8	524	50650	255	241	2	1195	197	3	2175	36	125	2012	116	481	15	4	174
Bennezett	200	15	2	......	197	16335	600	......	......	262	29	......	1016	......	......	535	34	163	......	......	52
Butler, exc. of Clarksville	609	4	6	......	485	37560	284	......	2	1212	297	14	2224	81	228	2199	512	1967	44	4	153
Clarksville, town of	167	24	2	......	118	6730	......	......	......	366	......	......	1319	29	17	766	702	......	......	......	49
Cold Water	398	31	13	......	300	16225	......	2101	......	490	45	......	1120	8	8	834	761	284	16	8	123
Dayton	326	1	16	......	231	15248	......	......	10	657	66	......	1116	9	10	843	39	608	13	12	87
Fremont	527	33	16	......	385	25445	......	......	10	633	95	2	1172	36	144	1099	223	996	59	16	122
Jackson	375	3	1	......	471	28405	31975	......	......	988	112	1	1406	85	44	1281	137	......	......	......	103
Jefferson	445	2	2	......	532	32195	150	......	......	984	134	......	1466	18	21	1263	63	424	4	22	116
Madison	324	......	2	......	226	14485	......	......	......	401	36	......	598	1	2	475	510	144	2	8	90
Monroe	448	13	11	3	405	34100	......	1800	4	858	204	......	1308	122	259	926	1140	314	55	......	93
Pittsford	439	1	8	......	323	17980	400	......	4	853	54	......	2004	5	5	1021	91	523	6	4	108
Ripley	282	2	3	......	252	24540	......	......	......	477	......	......	931	1	7	701	473	658	16	1	88
Shell Rock	689	9	18	......	522	45425	1770	2378	4	1015	115	......	3594	49	2	1777	201	1080	41	7	152
Washington	364	22	......	......	279	20075	......	......	7	201	38	1	1629	5	5	934	1229	281	13	......	122
West Point	333	5	4	......	245	14080	120	30	......	546	90	......	1124	83	36	678	949	440	12	6	73
Total	7004	233	126	11	5936	433463	43554	6550	45	11795	1597	46	25860	743	998	18643	6909	8228	296	92	1840

CALHOUN COUNTY.

Butler	101	......	17	......	104	8425	......	130	46	212	8	......	415	......	......	223	209	......	......	......	56
Calhoun	291	1	14	......	307	30930	200	......	16	776	27	......	1521	175	146	851	25	......	......	......	115
Center	57	......	9	......	59	2075	250	......	14	76	......	......	105	......	......	62	96	......	......	......	30
Greenfield	82	......	7	......	[illegible]	5636	......	......	20	195	7	......	89	6	4	79	......	......	......	......	50

CALHOUN COUNTY.—CONTINUED.

NAMES OF TOWNSHIPS, TOWNS, AND CITIES.	Number of horses of all ages.	Number of horses sold for export in 1874.	Number of mules and asses.	Number of same sold for export in 1874.	Number of milch cows.	Number of pounds of butter made in 1874.	Number of pounds of cheese made in 1874 not in factory.	Number of gallons of milk sold in 1874.	Number of work oxen.	Number of all other cattle.	No. of cattle slaughtered or sold for slaughter in 1874.	Number of thorough-bred short-horns.	HOGS. Number on hand.	HOGS. Number of Berk-shires.	HOGS. Number of Poland-China.	HOGS. No. slaughtered or sold for slaughter in 1874.	SHEEP. Number on hand.	SHEEP. Number of pounds of wool obtained in 1874.	SHEEP. No. slaughtered or sold for slaughter in 1874.	SHEEP. Number killed by dogs in 1874.	Number of dogs.
Jackson	439	11	17	......	370	22150	245	....	19	817	74	2	2632	....	2	1190	394	1512	24	14	107
Lincoln	228	......	13	15	232	21422	310	283	16	315	27	......	718	3	52	458	296	121	1	....	81
Sherman	151	......	11	......	246	18985	....	....	7	324	12	......	386	20	5	317	....	....	....	....	86
Williams	62	2	2	......	66	5235	....	....	......	156	....	......	117	....	....	....	....	....	....	....	141
Total	1411	14	90	15	1471	114858	1005	413	138	2871	155	2	5983	204	209	3180	1020	1633	25	14	666

CARROLL COUNTY.

NAMES OF TOWNSHIPS, TOWNS, AND CITIES.	Number of horses of all ages.	Number of horses sold for export in 1874.	Number of mules and asses.	Number of same sold for export in 1874.	Number of milch cows.	Number of pounds of butter made in 1874.	Number of pounds of cheese made in 1874 not in factory.	Number of gallons of milk sold in 1874.	Number of work oxen.	Number of all other cattle.	No. of cattle slaughtered or sold for slaughter in 1874.	Number of thorough-bred short-horns.	HOGS. Number on hand.	HOGS. Number of Berk-shires.	HOGS. Number of Poland-China.	HOGS. No. slaughtered or sold for slaughter in 1874.	SHEEP. Number on hand.	SHEEP. Number of pounds of wool obtained in 1874.	SHEEP. No. slaughtered or sold for slaughter in 1874.	SHEEP. Number killed by dogs in 1874.	Number of dogs.
Arcadia	216	......	17	2	141	4475	....	250	25	253	54	......	417	5	4	250	10	50	....	....	76
Carroll, exc. of town	133	......	2	......	53	1745	....	....	......	79	8	......	422	....	....	86	403	....	....	....	36
Carroll, town of...	177	......	14	......	158	1717	....	1631	6	239	....	......	532	8	20	....	....	....	....	....	53
Eden	108	......	15	......	97	5205	210	....	4	221	14	......	667	....	....	270	446	....	....	....	36
Glidden	210	......	14	......	148	15500	....	....	......	550	8	......	1650	4	5	1200	750	3560	6	....	45
Grant	103	2	4	......	65	3725	....	....	1	65	17	......	247	54	39	236	....	....	....	....	44
Jasper	122	2	7	......	107	6251	....	....	......	204	22	......	897	25	4	728	....	....	....	....	39
Kniest	372	3	14	......	234	9720	40	150	22	538	32	5	1249	100	96	1193	62	391	13	....	127
Newton	165	......	23	......	200	9260	....	10	......	245	85	......	881	31	2	947	....	....	....	....	124
Pleasant Valley	157	7	6	......	116	2075	180	....	22	291	15	......	717	6	15	438	70	156	....	....	58
Richland	81	......	7	......	68	3125	....	....	......	168	....	......	318	....	....	228	....	....	....	....	....
Roselle	181	......	8	......	107	3770	....	....	16	133	10	......	379	....	....	330	....	....	....	....	88
Sheridan	271	9	18	......	186	13429	204	....	16	245	13	......	807	64	7	859	....	....	....	....	91
Union	171	4	21	20	143	1378	....	....	......	155	....	2	820	13	81	1187	62	....	....	....	86
Washington	117	......	5	......	79	5725	....	....	......	121	....	......	266	....	....	136	160	1240	4	....	44
Wheatland	224	......	17	71	73	6320	....	1	2	97	12	1	369	53	25	193	1	4	....	....	87
Total	2808	27	192	93	1975	93120	634	2042	117	3604	290	8	10638	363	298	8281	1964	5341	23	....	1034

CASS COUNTY.

Atlantic, exc. of town	502	16	23	4	444	24458	100	......	......	1127	271	2	2679	16	81	3049	......	......	......	......	112
Atlantic, town of	102	......	2	......	142	......	......	4810	......	23	......	11	181	28	49	20	......	......	......	......	53
Bear Grove	324	......	23	......	284	16550	300	......	......	702	25	......	1063	24	18	910	10	675	6	10	42
Benton	450	3	32	......	228	11485	40	......	......	792	155	3	1543	10	34	1050	......	......	......	......	117
Brighton	408	......	79	......	331	28975	......	......	......	774	26	3	1383	55	56	362	18	70	4	......	138
Cass	613	......	46	......	459	19780	260	240	3	1463	460	......	3043	8	355	2891	600	2000	100	2	188
Edna	264	60	60	23	190	9900	......	......	45	435	74	......	1574	9	17	901	57	247	10	......	190
Franklin	452	42	27	2	319	26276	......	......	......	662	218	3	3306	431	1422	1756	......	......	......	......	140
Grant	243	1	13	2	211	10075	......	350	2	435	55	......	886	7	7	421	17	......	......	......	160
Lincoln	234	......	25	......	128	8193	32	......	......	278	60	......	768	1	96	477	......	......	......	......	68
Massena	212	......	8	1	86	2170	......	......	14	409	46	......	875	74	139	362	......	......	......	......	35
Noble	457	......	32	......	274	16165	......	......	......	534	6	1	1928	603	973	1355	1	2	......	......	129
Pleasant	408	11	24	......	394	9040	......	......	2	602	108	1	2488	3	9	1161	......	......	......	......	119
Pymosa	560	6	21	......	517	23030	75	......	10	935	306	3	1206	8	62	2322	54	116	3	......	183
Union	210	......	13	......	163	10920	......	......	10	334	41	......	924	......	11	510	24	58	5	4	167
Victoria	263	......	24	....	175	8095	......	......	......	......	33	......	925	12	46	507	649	150	23	......	66
Washington	504	......	39	......	461	17488	......	......	4	1042	823	1	2229	158	412	1857	......	......	......	......	125
Total	6206	139	491	32	4806	242600	807	5400	90	10547	2707	28	27001	1447	3787	19911	1430	3318	151	16	2033

CEDAR COUNTY.

Cass	515	26	21	6	432	24147	......	86	......	1348	181	9	2443	6	2	1777	157	622	21	20	121
Center, exc of Tipton	1374	120	82	14	1045	50944	......	14135	......	3978	1491	348	6441	291	143	8100	440	1690	486	29	270
Clarence, town of	337	14	7	......	145	7316	......	1500	......	151	17	14	817	235	233	260	......	......	......	......	41
Dayton, exc. of Clarence	618	47	17	......	576	58270	186	......	......	1455	461	12	4231	2012	2157	3816	147	620	12	3	111
Durant, town of	81	4	4	......	93	2990	......	2360	......	......	41	......	143	......	......	202	......	......	......	......	44
Fairfield	628	32	64	6	463	39178	310	......	......	1482	406	16	7968	25	80	4542	3704	2628	18	6	128
Farmington, exc. of Durant	620	11	117	1	549	28199	150	290	......	1837	252	21	2910	127	293	2973	84	325	11	10	123
Fremont	772	22	27	5	656	43270	16012	4000	......	1427	578	29	5433	100	75	5155	8	28	......	......	131
Gower	714	21	25	1	495	45850	1320	2866	......	1467	271	2	2719	19	123	2364	2845	1260	12	14	174
Inland	662	10	65	2	638	38234	445	......	......	1570	318	2	4099	204	301	4475	148	628	14	......	157
Iowa	816	53	40	......	770	58253	470	700	......	1796	366	7	3266	175	183	3794	2782	10157	106	48	182
Linn	393	16	6	......	385	17380	......	......	......	1268	162	......	5106	36	5	2453	379	1137	16	11	81
Louden, town of	33	4	......	......	68	2800	......	815	......	139	......	......	229	......	......	10	......	......	......	......	37
Massillon	690	42	43	......	605	46405	370	15	6	1175	384	3	2987	2	124	2888	68	873	11	......	155
Mechanicsville, town of	96	......	9	......	49	......	......	......	......	......	......	......	......	......	......	......	......	......	......	......	11
Pioneer, exc. Mechanicsville	625	19	21	2	640	40292	......	75	4	1628	248	......	4467	1462	1191	3003	1037	4818	272	55	150
Red Oak	555	22	12	......	482	32105	400	10	2	1463	353	3	3239	60	7	2542	572	4195	312	41	88
Rochester	515	5	37	......	479	16990	......	......	......	1206	88	......	1897	84	50	1641	230	1266	29	12	121
Springdale	969	109	40	12	1072	53361	433	36358	......	2050	579	35	7186	380	768	4291	557	2436	30	35	151
Springfield, exc. of Louden	690	10	38	2	615	41743	......	......	9	1193	370	6	3453	195	570	3001	126	1215	28	3	161

CEDAR COUNTY.—Continued.

Names of townships, towns, and cities.	Number of horses of all ages.	Number of horses sold for export in 1874.	Number of mules and asses.	Number of same sold for export in 1874.	Number of milch cows.	Number of pounds of butter made in 1874.	Number of pounds of cheese made in 1874 not in factory.	Number of gallons of milk sold in 1874.	Number of work oxen.	Number of all other cattle.	No. of cattle slaughtered and sold for slaughter in 1874.	Number of thorough-bred short-horns.	Hogs. Number on hand.	Hogs. Number of Berk-shires.	Hogs. Number of Poland-China.	Hogs. No. slaughtered or sold for slaughter in 1874.	Sheep. Number on hand.	Sheep. Number of pounds of wool obtained in 1874.	Sheep. No. slaughtered or sold for slaughter in 1874.	Sheep. Number killed by dogs in 1874.	Number of dogs.
Sugar Creek	449	15	42	2	624	22248	....	960	.....	925	160	5	1843	48	64	2011	44	54	....	....	127
Tipton, town of	151	8	.....	.....	128	13846	....	3017	.....	7	....	.....	382	....	....	355	....	....	....	....	45
Total	12303	610	717	53	11009	683821	20096	67187	21	27565	6726	512	71259	5456	6369	59653	13328	33952	1378	287	2609

CERRO GORDO COUNTY.

Names of townships, towns, and cities.	Number of horses of all ages.	Number of horses sold for export in 1874.	Number of mules and asses.	Number of same sold for export in 1874.	Number of milch cows.	Number of pounds of butter made in 1874.	Number of pounds of cheese made in 1874 not in factory.	Number of gallons of milk sold in 1874.	Number of work oxen.	Number of all other cattle.	No. of cattle slaughtered and sold for slaughter in 1874.	Number of thorough-bred short-horns.	Hogs. Number on hand.	Hogs. Number of Berk-shires.	Hogs. Number of Poland-China.	Hogs. No. slaughtered or sold for slaughter in 1874.	Sheep. Number on hand.	Sheep. Number of pounds of wool obtained in 1874.	Sheep. No. slaughtered or sold for slaughter in 1874.	Sheep. Number killed by dogs in 1874.	Number of dogs.
Clear Lake, exc. of town	209	9	8	.....	233	20170	7150	140	43	336	55	.....	403	....	....	232	109	75	15	....	88
Clear Lake, town of	....	.....	.....	.....	....	....	....	....	.....	....	....	.....	....	....	....	....	....	....	....	....	....
Daugherty	123	1	.....	.....	76	6440	....	....	12	220	29	.....	475	2	6	192	99	455	20	....	24
Falls	416	.....	11	.....	304	27538	....	....	.....	414	120	1	235	25	....	538	257	1160	22	13	99
Geneseo	248	18	17	.....	147	10175	....	91	4	289	27	.....	438	2	34	306	644	767	9	....	69
Grant	120	7	4	.....	103	8006	....	....	14	233	45	.....	88	....	....	130	102	167	35	....	25
Lake	199	12	7	3	269	8280	....	....	18	388	12	.....	130	12	2	222	105	305	5	....	60
Lime Creek	362	5	5	.....	289	19325	5200	....	11	507	116	3	359	59	2	399	196	566	5	4	78
Lincoln	253	3	2	.....	244	11430	....	....	8	384	22	.....	384	1	....	493	195	770	19	20	75
Mason, exc. of Mason City	310	27	5	.....	326	20285	....	7300	16	527	633	9	687	101	2	507	42	94	....	4	78
Mason City, town of	244	.....	.....	.....	204	....	....	....	.....	....	....	.....	....	....	....	....	....	....	....	....	110
Owen	275	.....	4	.....	216	17225	150	....	7	510	64	.....	515	5	....	335	246	755	27	2	47
Portland	354	.....	5	.....	282	19622	....	....	6	559	63	2	351	20	2	382	117	265	5	2	68
Total	3113	82	68	3	2693	168496	12500	7531	139	4367	1186	15	4015	227	48	3736	2112	5379	162	45	821

CHEROKEE COUNTY.

Afton	327	......	29	......	182	13533	....	2	12	297	36	......	560	15	....	1416	....	....	....	....	95
Amherst	95	......	2	......	42	1883	....	....	6	62	12	......	135	....	....	55	....	....	....	....	25
Cedar	206	......	......	......	115	5555	....	....	10	169	....	......	576	....	....	345	334	....	....	....	62
Cherokee, exc. of town	205	......	5	......	131	11867	....	....	10	389	9	1	492	....	21	346	40	114	....	2	53
Cherokee, town of	112	14	2	2	96	1154	140	3700	8	23	25	......	215	13	....	239	....	....	....	....	37
Diamond	64	......	......	......	33	1435	....	....	6	28	....	......	110	2	....	69	....	....	....	....	19
Liberty	74	......	5	......	53	600	150	....	23	63	....	......	43	....	....	19	....	....	....	....	34
Marcus	17	......	2	......	12	490	....	20	33	5	2	......	39	8	....	20	....	....	....	....	5
Pilot	255	......	9	......	6275	8634	1	....	43	98	17	......	604	8	1	471	7	16	....	....	94
Pitcher	166	......	16	......	145	18285	....	....	20	211	29	......	537	193	120	191	....	....	....	....	85
Sheridan	151	......	7	......	126	2559	....	....	40	133	15	......	561	....	....	291	....	....	....	....	74
Silver	119	......	7	......	74	5431	....	....	13	113	....	......	228	....	....	239	....	....	....	....	36
Spring	32	......	4	......	44	5348	....	....	28	57	9	......	122	....	20	90	....	....	....	....	20
Tilden	91	2	13	......	66	4280	....	....	......	145	9	......	222	....	5	150	....	....	....	....	40
Willow	160	28	15	7	110	6450	....	....	17	148	66	......	689	....	....	450	337	....	....	....	41
Total	2074	44	116	9	7504	87504	291	3722	264	1941	220	1	5133	239	167	4391	718	130	....	2	720

CHICKASAW COUNTY.

Bradford, exc. of Nashua	575	......	17	......	526	38870	430	100	8	743	144	1	1526	18	207	1281	542	2290	63	46	141
Chickasaw	471	4	14	......	455	37160	200	25	18	929	83	2	954	3	6	867	682	1747	46	14	163
Dayton	360	16	16	......	431	34070	475	....	10	557	85	......	875	....	....	624	231	760	12	10	114
Deerfield	463	22	8	......	490	43950	....	....	8	1127	208	......	968	15	62	1038	958	867	24	14	131
Dresden	320	......	......	......	435	34043	800	....	4	712	81	1	818	3	9	752	195	964	8	18	87
Fredericksburgh	439	54	6	......	419	34110	....	60	......	673	39	13	484	35	28	547	504	2770	31	3	91
Jacksonville	597	25	13	......	857	67895	130	....	59	1651	....	......	1405	5	6	997	151	396	23	....	217
Nashua, town of	76	......	2	......	74	450	....	....	......	53	....	......	44	....	....	33	....	....	....	....	3
New Hampton, exc. of town	340	4	7	3	95	29446	150	....	2	603	63	1	471	....	5	389	237	811	55	16	106
New Hampton, town of	....	......	......	......	....	....	....	....	......	....	....	......	....	....	....	....	....	....	....	....	32
Richland	359	38	6	......	539	37695	600	....	6	778	115	2	795	60	9	704	275	1877	26	23	98
Stapleton	577	87	10	2	661	55170	6000	603	38	1189	44	2	1229	4	2	882	243	840	50	2	197
Utica	531	44	5	1	767	55097	....	....	37	1767	276	......	874	....	....	941	255	717	31	53	208
Washington	492	29	16	......	529	27540	20	....	16	1512	129	......	1469	....	53	981	108	580	3	10	135
Total	5600	323	120	6	6278	495496	8805	788	206	12294	1267	22	11912	143	387	10036	4381	14619	372	209	1723

CLARKE COUNTY.

NAMES OF TOWNSHIPS, TOWNS, AND CITIES.	Number of horses of all ages	Number of horses sold for export in 1874.	Number of mules and asses.	Number of same sold for export in 1874.	Number of milch cows.	Number of pounds of butter made in 1874.	Number of pounds of cheese made in 1874 not in factory.	Number of gallons of milk sold in 1874.	Number of work oxen.	Number of all other cattle.	No. of cattle slaughtered or sold for slaughter in 1874.	Number of thorough-bred short-horns.	HOGS. Number on hand.	HOGS. Number of Berk-shires.	HOGS. Number of Poland-China.	HOGS. No. slaughtered or sold for slaughter in 1874.	SHEEP. Number on hand.	SHEEP. Number of pounds of wool obtained in 1874.	SHEEP. No. slaughtered or sold for slaughter in 1874.	SHEEP. Number killed by dogs in 1874.	Number of dogs.
Doyle, exc. of Hopeville	497	26	22	.....	644	35660	....	....	......	1429	125	1	35721	115	1024	659	699	1083	35	41	133
Franklin	507	4	15	......	461	21135	48	....	......	1356	150	28	3973	52	709	2130	2192	3823	166	66	111
Fremont	466	10	31	.....	469	24481	95	60	...	11690	365	1	1918	29	137	1802	164	636	45	27	125
Green Bay	470	16	37	3	341	21980	200	6	2	1402	255	1	2190	41	201	1818	20425	936	137	36	91
Hopeville, town of	184	27	24	4	189	10466	....	8	......	314	482	... ..	1155	109	169	210	79	211	....	6	51
Jackson	553	53	74	13	458	29107	....	8	2	1456	358	8	3049	35	219	2116	1074	4312	238	30	163
Knox	627	4	47	......	607	42316	250	....	2	1470	105	2	2704	118	191	2011	702	2983	186	60	141
Liberty	573	2	27	......	415	24556	936	....	6	975	192	3	12262	20	11	1896	679	2394	48	19	215
Madison	399	5	22	......	381	22851	100	....	......	1128	....	......	4979	79	379	1894	437	988	52	9	112
Osceola, exc. of town	321	......	29	.....	274	14270	....	25	......	558	68	...	2333	....	22	1450	472	1062	88	33	87
Osceola, town of	421	2	55	19	406	17099	....	1475	......	540	117	2	2303	91	134	1047	1787	4477	284	118	173
Troy	301	12	17	......	389	15822	60	325	......	1518	121	135	1683	2	34	1589	3096	10265	779	....	68
Ward	329	2	42	3	435	20146	50	....	2	1755	310	2	1552	53	24	1351	1090	2202	21	11	93
Washington	399	21	21	.....	425	22260	....	....	......	1097	396	1	1943	2	27	2381	714	1305	11	18	188
Total	6047	184	463	42	5894	322149	1739	1907	14	26688	3044	184	45616	746	3281	22354	33610	36617	2090	474	1751

CLAY COUNTY.

NAMES OF TOWNSHIPS, TOWNS, AND CITIES.	Number of horses of all ages	Number of horses sold for export in 1874.	Number of mules and asses.	Number of same sold for export in 1874.	Number of milch cows.	Number of pounds of butter made in 1874.	Number of pounds of cheese made in 1874 not in factory.	Number of gallons of milk sold in 1874.	Number of work oxen.	Number of all other cattle.	No. of cattle slaughtered or sold for slaughter in 1874.	Number of thorough-bred short-horns.	HOGS. Number on hand.	HOGS. Number of Berk-shires.	HOGS. Number of Poland-China.	HOGS. No. slaughtered or sold for slaughter in 1874.	SHEEP. Number on hand.	SHEEP. Number of pounds of wool obtained in 1874.	SHEEP. No. slaughtered or sold for slaughter in 1874.	SHEEP. Number killed by dogs in 1874.	Number of dogs.
Bridgewater	176	5	12	......	171	13090	....	....	60	251	11	......	210	9	2	282	....	....	....	....	80
Clay	340	6	18	......	210	16810	....	....	52	200	70	......	609	....	....	465	85	100	6	12	112
Douglas	211	18	4	......	193	14555	200	....	27	221	21	1	333	....	2	159	....	....	....	....	64
Gillett's Grove	124	6	9	......	83	7690	....	....	25	170	12	......	307	2	3	188	....	....	....	....	39
Herdland	67	3	6	2	80	4256	20	....	18	143	6	2	127	....	....	72	....	....	....	....	26
Lincoln	126	5	20	......	114	....	....	....	36	69	....	......	167	15	16	185	3	....	....	....	51
Riverton	141	10	4	......	103	5995	....	....	16	146	13	......	227	2	....	221	....	....	....	....	59

Spencer	282	...	14	...	279	20980	...	...	50	271	...	...	501	...	5	...	...	...	...	...	105
Summit	113	...	4	...	109	8860	25	...	29	158	14	...	227	...	...	144	...	...	...	...	48
Total	1580	53	91	2	1342	92236	245	...	313	1629	147	3	2708	28	28	1666	88	100	6	12	584

CLAYTON COUNTY.

Boardman	715	145	33	12	530	28554	700	...	10	1807	653	...	3746	...	...	2999	603	2253	421	45	243
Buena Vista	75	2	8	1	101	2945	...	185	...	144	31	...	185	...	...	259	4	95	...	4	68
Cass	553	56	13	6	673	36825	...	...	16	1178	602	3	687	4	96	1410	403	2384	170	7	167
Clayton	262	19	18	...	318	22025	35	2045	10	307	92	2	1216	17	19	967	241	1145	54	7	183
Cox Creek	539	21	11	...	482	18070	50	...	16	887	138	1	1372	11	141	1529	314	1199	136	30	242
Elk	362	1	26	...	366	24430	...	...	20	554	82	1	1148	...	7	1045	222	920	74	26	200
Farmersburg	649	...	89	...	623	39190	340	190	8	861	103	...	2716	...	9	3145	409	1777	66	17	195
Garnavillo	503	19	75	5	635	50320	650	407	4	876	259	17	4317	10	88	2537	571	2612	166	51	245
Girard	523	2	18	...	421	43575	150	10	14	504	164	...	2612	22	...	1527	386	1797	132	16	262
Grand Meadow	635	7	36	...	569	43857	840	20	5	865	180	...	1730	218	24	1716	435	2741	61	24	175
Guttenburg, town of	77	5	4	6	126	7206	2670	2333	...	46	37	1	207	1	1	347	22	115	5	5	80
Highland	534	...	11	...	511	23900	...	...	...	892	162	...	950	...	2	1238	913	158	4	2	146
Jefferson, exc. of Guttenburg	578	10	32	1	630	37058	525	...	6	702	239	...	3839	...	...	1943	454	2055	84	6	254
Lodomillo	508	41	12	...	544	42600	200	12	6	956	119	30	2161	175	705	1573	526	1503	95	49	126
McGregor, town of	155	...	6	...	82	...	...	500	...	14	...	...	23	...	...	...	...	...	...	...	127
Mallory	481	40	22	1	488	24152	12	3270	14	789	321	...	2772	50	...	1844	320	1862	49	21	269
Marion	557	68	14	...	640	26799	984	...	10	798	237	...	1373	...	82	917	399	1296	98	9	144
Mendon, exc. of McGregor and North McGregor	246	33	24	...	325	15439	130	4300	4	253	80	...	436	5	...	280	251	124	8	...	191
Millville	256	17	26	2	240	9392	10	50	4	292	144	1	409	30	3	1098	402	569	16	14	171
Monona	803	92	32	...	617	57680	7200	400	4	675	219	9	1477	...	1	1551	249	1105	162	26	166
North McGregor, town of	...	...	...	...	...	...	...	...	...	...	52	...	...	...	...	27	...	...	...	...	...
Read	350	1	54	2	477	31990	...	...	10	568	200	6	2611	15	92	1873	375	1415	101	7	199
Sperry	629	...	26	...	733	54067	108	495	10	1390	214	4	1584	1	72	1643	323	2132	136	17	221
Volga	457	40	16	...	494	14390	50	20	9	478	39	3	1311	1	3	1500	338	1312	19	21	218
Wagner	594	12	14	...	471	30104	225	...	2	524	182	...	2175	...	...	1043	1135	1380	91	1	157
Total	11041	631	620	36	11096	684568	14879	14237	182	16360	4549	78	41057	560	1345	34011	9295	31949	2148	405	4449

CLINTON COUNTY.

Berlin	500	6	13	...	517	46125	...	...	...	1567	169	...	2862	2	32	2698	293	428	1638	2	137
Bloomfield	842	34	15	...	918	97502	60[illegible]	1980	...	2244	328	...	6665	...	...	4492	283	1241	36	4	146
Brookfield	855	81	12	7	755	60716	700	90	...	2225	681	25	7020	98	184	4291	564	2724	96	4	166
Camanche, exc. of town	441	12	4	...	426	40260	200	...	...	1148	345	2	2110	64	85	2570	210	640	43	6	96
Camanche, town of	139	...	2	...	91	9685	...	...	...	73	...	...	163	...	30	179	...	...	...	...	37
Center	883	69	34	7	1071	70870	...	...	2	2723	810	2	9008	...	...	4625	250	1481	125	33	282

CLINTON COUNTY.—Continued.

Names of townships, towns, and cities.	Number of horses of all ages.	Number of horses sold for export in 1874.	Number of mules and asses.	Number of same sold for export in 1874.	Number of milch cows.	Number of pounds of butter made in 1874.	Number of pounds of cheese made in 1874 not at factory.	Number of gallons of milk sold in 1874.	Number of work oxen.	Number of all other cattle.	No. of cattle slaughtered and sold for slaughter in 1874.	Number of thorough-bred short-horns.	Hogs. Number on hand.	Hogs. Number of Berk-shires.	Hogs. Number of Poland-China.	Hogs. No. slaughtered or sold for slaughter in 1874.	Sheep. Number on hand.	Sheep. Number of pounds of wool obtained in 1874.	Sheep. No. slaughtered or sold for slaughter in 1874.	Sheep. Number killed by dogs in 1874.	Number of dogs.
Clinton, exc. of city	250	3	3	......	251	12175	....	24525	......	104	160	......	448	97	79	839	....	144	2	....	166
Clinton, city of	....	......	......	......	....	....	....	....	......	....	....	......	....	....	....	....	....	....	....	....	415
Deep Creek	693	59	43	......	851	58971	620	....	......	2020	784	35	4327	118	179	4496	498	2840	310	30	143
De Witt, exc. of town	930	31	30	6	978	86475	410	2700	......	2055	377	18	4122	5	553	4592	597	3268	441	91	204
De Witt, town of	194	21	3	1	149	12640	....	1141	......	226	258	......	447	....	74	757	....	....	....	....	103
Eden	676	81	11	3	680	73890	....	....	......	1996	896	2	3497	220	592	3248	420	2030	74	54	186
Elk River	962	33	12	4	969	56420	....	....	......	2305	643	......	4792	28	7	4824	420	1679	135	10	236
Hampshire	594	8	21	......	624	38385	....	....	......	941	239	......	2962	16	....	3102	93	490	54	6	231
Liberty	577	4	32	......	599	44966	....	....	......	1443	229	11	3061	7	145	2308	60	326	10	11	183
Lincoln	280	7	3	......	375	23700	....	7752	......	957	271	13	1375	12	66	1487	165	510	51	2	54
Lyons, exc. of city	186	20	2	......	195	16040	....	6715	......	108	38	......	354	1	....	543	89	261	506	5	91
Lyons, city of	....	......	......	......	....	....	....	....	......	....	....	......	....	....	....	....	....	....	....	....	326
Olive	967	69	26	2	932	42526	....	....	......	2694	470	3	3410	129	2	3284	270	901	70	3	246
Orange	884	16	22	......	602	57570	140	34	......	1248	129	4	3603	....	161	2051	200	647	18	4	178
Sharon	743	41	30	2	853	64967	732	392	......	1441	454	16	3283	12	401	3720	121	813	110	13	185
Spring Rock	509	52	15	4	623	33020	710	....	......	1435	501	......	2275	....	24	2597	75	292	1	....	157
Washington	589	11	4	......	522	26209	....	....	......	1018	229	......	1908	....	....	2242	1905	820	53	10	176
Waterford	593	28	11	2	706	27880	....	335	......	510	205	1	2609	220	429	2742	2055	748	30	....	184
Welton	628	38	16	......	591	29850	90	....	......	1248	194	2	2685	14	6	2967	228	640	....	10	138
Wheatland	13	......	......	......	17	600	....	....	......	39	11	......	110	....	70	70	....	32	2	....	3
Total	12928	724	364	38	14295	1031442	4202	45664	2	31768	8421	134	73096	1044	3119	64724	8796	22955	3805	298	4469

CRAWFORD COUNTY.

Names of townships, towns, and cities.	Number of horses of all ages.	Number of horses sold for export in 1874.	Number of mules and asses.	Number of same sold for export in 1874.	Number of milch cows.	Number of pounds of butter made in 1874.	Number of pounds of cheese made in 1874 not at factory.	Number of gallons of milk sold in 1874.	Number of work oxen.	Number of all other cattle.	No. of cattle slaughtered and sold for slaughter in 1874.	Number of thorough-bred short-horns.	Hogs. Number on hand.	Hogs. Number of Berk-shires.	Hogs. Number of Poland-China.	Hogs. No. slaughtered or sold for slaughter in 1874.	Sheep. Number on hand.	Sheep. Number of pounds of wool obtained in 1874.	Sheep. No. slaughtered or sold for slaughter in 1874.	Sheep. Number killed by dogs in 1874.	Number of dogs.
Boyer	145	......	4	......	209	7085	180	....	......	786	282	14	736	....	74	600	53	265	1	....	40
Charter Oak	51	......	2	......	51	800	....	....	......	45	181	1	51	....	....	195	227	1550	....	....	2
Denison	501	171	23	13	563	21170	20000	19392	22	1340	727	8	3415	32	56	2536	1017	....	25	....	117

East Boyer	241	4	4		243	8520			12	563	37	1	745	68	240	622					63
Goodrich	146	3	10	4	139	11296			16	235	87		366	1	34	327	273	1110	180	5	52
Hanover	24	2	4		48	1200				13	15		44			30	53				13
Hays	226		24		174	5120			2	273	2		576			239	14	51			104
Iowa	108	2	10		107	3710			6	256	65	2	217		1	138	41	126	5		39
Jackson	190		15		135	6576			7	132	50	1	401	11	47	276	3	14			74
Milford	398	24	9		321	18425			14	522	254		1277	54	10	868	125	2063	557	44	92
Morgan	62		10		55	2155	100			49	3		178	1	16	107					17
Nishnabotany	74	2	4		86	4890			8	220	37		351			146					25
Otter Creek	224		34		219	6602	100		4	243	51		909	2	12	639	1359	4011	164	8	93
Paradise	107		19		115	1960		5845	2	285	27		178	1	11	145					26
Soldier	57		4	11	53	800			5	447	3		100	23		43					21
Stockholm	233	2			122	10690	925			244	4		429			335	98	418	6		39
Union	247	32	11	4	449	11145		7691	12	931	245	8	999	35	108	427	836	3930	25	41	86
Washington	114		4		149	9755	69623		17	314	59	2	389	40	20	217	264		3		51
West Side	274		15		195	8220		220		473	101		852	90	107	536					99
Willow	50		2		78	475	162				10		181			169	4	28			17
Total	3472	242	208	32	3511	140694	91090	37122	127	7371	2240	37	12394	358	736	8595	4367	13566	966	98	1070

DALLAS COUNTY.

Adams	606	53	62	6	499	34500		1300		750	28		3498		11	3173	525	2115	9	26	137
Adel, exc. of town	606	5	58		554	35225	200	150	3	1315	198	10	3102	3	62	3046	411	1753	129	12	170
Adel, town of	235	51	25	4	168	9049		2081	4	153	70	1	710	7	27	732					56
Beaver	298	2	21		317	16920		1		378	457	123	1881		40	1092	87	216	3		76
Boone	511	15	27		496	21200				966	182	60	3294			2068	110	440	23	1	114
Colfax	527		30		484	59090			8	2214	118		4275	5	61	2169	175	973	24		125
Dallas	311	24	36	3	319	13475			24	697	161		1126	25	210	1382	84	360	1		73
Des Moines	498	4	16	2	452	22049	25		8	1502	126	1	2862	18	30	1485	349	1343	10	52	157
Dexter, town of																					
Grant	243	34	35	6	364	22110	1000		8	1152	176	8	2827	109	621	1249	17	54			123
Lincoln	299	4	38	2	276	19938	80		7	415	52	2	971	12	61	1027	450	892	3	1	114
Linn	551		52		438	33000				1728	225	2	2879	1	1	3117	788	3413	52	105	158
Spring Valley	498		25		542	31075	100		10	1021	79	14	4120		29	1969	2469	5152	31	30	202
Sugar Grove	444	52	37	10	502	22086		140	2	1019	136	9	1674	72	308	1517	250	1048	14	28	147
Union, exc. of Dexter	600		82		441	27017	321			1099	324	3	3968	72	20	3721	653	2925	209	67	165
Van Meter	613		73		613	35213	70	321	16	1483	373	9	3884	232	707	3508	3509	2780	123	86	200
Walnut	465	1	16		324	21970	100	250		1407	155	1	2567		13	1059	8	32			75
Washington	402		46		460	29650				990	71		2052	2	11	1598	204	724	10	8	127
Total	7707	245	679	33	7249	453567	1896	4243	90	18289	2931	243	44690	658	2212	33912	10089	24220	640	417	2219

DAVIS COUNTY.

NAMES OF TOWNSHIPS, TOWNS AND CITIES.	Number of horses of all ages.	Number of horses sold for export in 1874.	Number of mules and asses.	Number of same sold for export in 1874.	Number of milch cows.	Number of pounds of butter made in 1874.	Number of pounds of cheese made in 1874 not in factory.	Number of gallons of milk sold in 1874.	Number of work oxen.	Number of all other cattle.	No. of cattle slaughtered or sold for slaughter in 1874.	Number of thorough-bred short-horns.	HOGS. Number on hand.	HOGS. Number of Berk-shires.	HOGS. Number of Poland-China.	HOGS. No. slaughtered or sold for slaughter in 1874.	SHEEP. Number on hand.	SHEEP. Number of pounds of wool obtained in 1874.	SHEEP. No. slaughtered or sold for slaughter in 1874.	SHEEP. Number killed by dogs.	Number of dogs.
Bloomfield, exc. of town	823	39	124	24	612	47040	400	1056	......	2201	524	19	5011	101	96	4394	1457	4570	531	29	185
Bloomfield, town of	149	21	8	......	76	800	....	325	......	2	....	......	261	41	23	....	....	....	....	....	68
Drakeville, exc. of town	165	24	2	2	158	7882	341	....	......	259	127	......	798	23	83	1035	261	1163	215	76	65
Drakeville, town of	53	3	......	......	56	4110	....	100	......	6	19	......	432	2	44	497	....	....	....	....	22
Fabius	634	7	120	......	579	27764	....	....	8	2130	243	......	2873	63	73	3343	4153	13594	276	84	195
Fox River	429	40	24	2	340	14920	....	....	2	821	65	......	1474	62	211	1575	1523	7423	192	174	123
Grove	860	46	42	2	727	40584	403	....	......	1586	310	4	3730	146	18	3390	1872	5776	304	40	170
Lick Creek	679	16	62	3	492	40283	237	82	......	1010	471	1	4645	189	415	5145	948	3700	166	49	248
Marion	556	62	17	......	502	26930	8050	....	2	755	110	4	2595	47	39	2469	892	3426	324	72	188
Perry	526	66	62	20	371	34272	120	....	......	1336	290	27	3626	415	316	2094	152	566	9	....	20
Prairie	395	56	78	11	384	21185	....	50	......	988	344	......	1599	34	10	1787	720	2899	881	22	113
Roscoe	504	30	61	6	284	32070	500	....	......	1600	280	2	3216	34	96	1897	1770	3140	301	36	120
Salt Creek	590	65	38	9	419	21230	30	....	2	864	105	......	3244	43	3	2289	1401	4533	916	10	132
Soap Creek	597	40	31	1	443	24820	18	50	......	718	169	17	2508	112	125	2387	920	4237	427	88	187
Union	740	96	37	11	553	28456	....	....	.....	1795	675	27	6377	5	10	3267	3111	7115	252	23	186
West Grove	686	71	94	14	581	36486	125	....	2	728	208	5	4233	135	7	2990	3278	7558	630	53	134
Wyacondah	768	9	285	......	615	42232	200	....	......	1880	731	......	3954	16	4	5768	2686	9289	174	80	200
Total	9154	692	1035	105	7192	450954	10424	1663	16	18679	4671	116	50576	1468	1573	44337	25144	78944	5602	836	2356

DECATUR COUNTY.

NAMES OF TOWNSHIPS, TOWNS AND CITIES.	Number of horses of all ages.	Number of horses sold for export in 1874.	Number of mules and asses.	Number of same sold for export in 1874.	Number of milch cows.	Number of pounds of butter made in 1874.	Number of pounds of cheese made in 1874 not in factory.	Number of gallons of milk sold in 1874.	Number of work oxen.	Number of all other cattle.	No. of cattle slaughtered or sold for slaughter in 1874.	Number of thorough-bred short-horns.	HOGS. Number on hand.	HOGS. Number of Berk-shires.	HOGS. Number of Poland-China.	HOGS. No. slaughtered or sold for slaughter in 1874.	SHEEP. Number on hand.	SHEEP. Number of pounds of wool obtained in 1874.	SHEEP. No. slaughtered or sold for slaughter in 1874.	SHEEP. Number killed by dogs.	Number of dogs.
Bloomington	280	14	27	......	339	11200	....	....	.. ...	939	123	......	690	1	3	1018	709	994	30	22	72
Burrell	562	33	46	......	521	26125	....	12	......	1255	244	2	2072	32	57	1448	669	2226	167	19	166
Center, exc. of Leon	544	45	28	.....	607	34336	....	....	......	1453	304	1	2221	6	6	2794	1019	2997	142	59	155
Decatur	619	13	49	2	573	36450	180	. ...	3	1478	724	3	2455	39	23	1849	832	2655	272	64	200
Eden	543	22	32	......	503	32057	500	....	6	784	128	9	1797	145	160	1457	1404	2624	223	72	211

Fayette	274	7	36	2	342	12395	416	....	......	841	177	......	911	2	....	1212	1141	5215	391	28	59
Franklin	533	2	23	......	580	27989	....	....	2	1522	460	15	3669	229	541	2656	859	3296	63	48	119
Garden Grove	759	83	37	11	595	43929	1606	873	2	1773	437	34	6625	275	698	3658	3711	10330	1602	32	153
Grand River	296	4	16	4	533	19595	1010	....	......	727	8	1	793	7	6	610	125	200	52	....	96
Hamilton	375	31	32	9	379	15577	....	....	10	557	146	......	2041	27	227	1049	983	2455	190	42	111
High Point	622	12	34	1	498	26960	316	....	......	1202	195	5	2485	115	13	1713	716	2282	92	81	126
Leon, town of	91	15	3	......	102	4955	....	312	......	....	....	......	173	....	21	101	....	....	....	....	36
Long Creek	528	7	25	......	460	18199	3040	....	......	1453	214	4	2866	22	148	1561	2536	5706	164	41	159
Morgan	308	2	37	......	290	14193	....	....	6	1033	131	6	1321	22	17	947	679	1844	26	16	99
New Buda	337	44	41	6	360	14910	....	....	2	760	170	11	1424	20	11	1794	694	1436	16	45	112
Richland	528	1	55	......	545	28888	240	....	6	1377	194	1	2663	61	117	1944	1215	2913	761	31	189
Woodland	609	115	60	22	621	28505	65	....	16	1431	184	2	3199	4	20	1762	4070	8127	1602	60	186
Total	7808	440	581	57	7848	396243	7373	1197	53	18575	3839	94	37405	1007	2068	27573	21362	55300	5793	660	2249

DELAWARE COUNTY.

Adams	562	22	13	......	625	35175	200	....	......	1606	459	......	4378	....	....	2572	117	814	85	14	150
Bremen	506	17	6	......	638	22254	1100	4702	......	9093	61	......	....	....	....	2798	2930	690	35	11	160
Coffin's Grove	687	37	11	......	741	60300	150	5466	......	1167	117	4	2281	32	106	1620	61	140	1	....	157
Colony	791	23	47	......	735	37834	....	11016	......	1117	175	1	8425	11	2	3692	4108	3003	125	23	162
Delaware, exc. Manchester	580	20	11	......	804	52030	1650	69848	2	1157	177	6	236	47	181	1656	343	1281	10	8	128
Delhi	636	13	25	......	651	43955	150	450	......	1252	181	3	2157	13	8	1971	132	466	76	14	163
Elk	712	13	12	3	556	38602	1500	....	4	778	140	......	2084	31	28	2150	253	1309	106	5	155
Hazel Green	614	27	10	......	590	44250	360	14350	......	1454	149	1	3570	190	22	1731	1479	5441	376	43	160
Honey Creek	759	18	18	......	736	54565	1240	....	6	1436	200	3	2213	17	3	2367	630	2344	76	46	154
Hopkinton, town of	126	......	9	3	104	....	....	....	......	23	200	......	205	12	12	175	....	....	100	....	38
Manchester, town of	472	73	12	3	283	9840	....	11098	......	483	363	23	1215	318	274	927	13	5	200	4	132
Milo	506	43	6	2	810	47621	200	27074	......	1061	223	10	1357	47	13	2001	141	667	31	....	117
North Fork	636	35	5	2	777	44580	1400	....	2	1458	210	3	2381	22	202	....	246	672	87	31	192
Oneida	738	6	23	......	916	70600	7500	4840	4	1654	170	1	3596	8	34	2329	50	128	4	1	121
Prairie	457	15	4	......	638	49870	200	9400	4	1039	187	5	1366	37	153	1680	457	2861	96	20	87
Richland	546	3	12	......	657	37345	....	53900	2	843	58	1	1360	20	7	1384	30	136	12	....	155
South Fork, exc. Hopkinton	690	204	48	35	1079	58121	48552	39137	2	1390	290	2	2405	5	37	2771	321	1462	142	43	198
Union	443	53	38	5	460	31263	....	50	......	1109	162	1	1586	22	111	1855	374	1895	160	41	153
Total	10461	622	310	52	11800	738205	64202	251331	26	28120	3522	65	40815	832	1193	33679	11685	23314	1722	304	2582

DES MOINES COUNTY.

Augusta	190	1	17	......	228	12950	3227	....	......	420	179	3	946	10	54	935	552	2392	85	32	108
Benton	621	14	48	5	665	36431	....	18	......	1970	345	21	2054	6	31	2542	419	1608	80	3	281
Burlington, exc. of city	545	7	23	......	543	26079	....	47629	43	473	179	20	1502	1	94	1401	92	463	36	24	422

DES MOINES COUNTY.—Continued.

NAMES OF TOWNSHIPS, TOWNS, AND CITIES.	Number of horses of all ages.	Number of horses sold for export in 1874.	Number of mules and asses.	Number of same sold for export in 1874.	Number of milch cows	Number of pounds of butter made in 1874.	Number of pounds of cheese made in 1874 not in factory.	Number of gallons of milk sold in 1874.	Number of work oxen.	Number of all other cattle.	No. of cattle slaughtered or sold for slaughter in 1874.	Number of thorough-bred short-horns.	HOGS. Number on hand.	HOGS. Number of Berk-shires.	HOGS. Number of Poland-China.	HOGS. No. slaughtered or sold for slaughter in 1874.	SHEEP. Number on hand.	SHEEP. Number of pounds of wool obtained in 1874.	SHEEP. No. slaughtered or sold for slaughter in 1874.	SHEEP. Number killed by dogs in 1874.	Number of dogs.
Burlington, city of																					
Danville	1193	103	114	23	857	78574	1120	74290		1796	858	3	3656	6	186	3810	3545	16356	1240	144	270
Flint River	761	3	57		745	31017		66000	2	927	332	3	3035	34	26	1858					
Franklin	753	9	12		639	55252				957	127		3440			2982	743	2604		13	293
Huron	397	60	28		611	28530				1731	385	2	3017	6	10	2417	513	2159	159	58	166
Jackson	113		13		142	2595				550	15		597	7	2	479	34	72			37
Pleasant Grove	740	46	42		564	35570		10177	4	1749	321		4679	11	74	2937	935	3911	204	97	246
Union	775	68	109	14	649	51555		21210		1065	223		2804		37	2730	401	1423	156	52	346
Washington	861	64	61	2	679	35483				2139	566	1	4875	114	188	3094	264	983	29	33	178
Yellow Springs	1149	96	74	4	1087	70447	50	20	3	2923	481	2	9373	2282	5788	5655	630	1559	130	13	257
Total	8098	471	603	48	7409	464483	4397	219344	52	16700	4011	55	39978	2477	6490	31740	8128	33530	2119	469	2604

DICKINSON COUNTY.

NAMES OF TOWNSHIPS, TOWNS, AND CITIES.	Number of horses of all ages.	Number of horses sold for export in 1874.	Number of mules and asses.	Number of same sold for export in 1874.	Number of milch cows	Number of pounds of butter made in 1874.	Number of pounds of cheese made in 1874 not in factory.	Number of gallons of milk sold in 1874.	Number of work oxen.	Number of all other cattle.	No. of cattle slaughtered or sold for slaughter in 1874.	Number of thorough-bred short-horns.	HOGS. Number on hand.	HOGS. Number of Berk-shires.	HOGS. Number of Poland-China.	HOGS. No. slaughtered or sold for slaughter in 1874.	SHEEP. Number on hand.	SHEEP. Number of pounds of wool obtained in 1874.	SHEEP. No. slaughtered or sold for slaughter in 1874.	SHEEP. Number killed by dogs in 1874.	Number of dogs.
Center Grove	241	9	6		289	20445	350	67	20	308	44		342			277	147	596	4	20	99
Diamond Lake	38				6	500			4	15	1		6				29				
Excelsior	47	10	8		42	10815			11	60	17		28	2	2	51	3	7			21
Lakeville	51	1	1		49	5089	150		16	127	3	1	83		2	48	115	357	4	12	19
Lloyd	50	2	2		79	6995	650		12	132	29	6	42		10	59	36	78	5	4	29
Milford	52		7		51	5301	230	25	24	49	10		51			100	45	225		3	26
Okoboji	97				86	5030	724		20	249	38		135		2	125	27	114	3		31
Richland	25				33	2465			6	59			34			14					13
Silver Lake	14				19	2070			14	31			31		2	19					9
Spirit Lake	130	13	7		173	12210	120		36	9	5		167			178	4	10	1		57
Superior	21				24	30			3	10			15			1					
Total	766	35	31		851	70950	2224	92	166	1049	147	7	934	2	18	897	406	1387	17	39	304

DUBUQUE COUNTY.

Cascade	546	24	31	4	599	23672	80	415	1	1173	171	......	3510	17	2	2617	2521	2110	93	12	178
Center	550	10	26	2	596	25981	440	50	4	1105	357	2	2513	236	292	1774	324	1152	131	22	351
Concord	544	49	8	......	557	22425	....	....	2	1400	149	2	1876	4	6	2471	787	2875	170	131	202
Dodge	478	......	7	3	446	20920	....	....	8	567	118	2	2262	6	18	2150	71	271	....	41	158
Dubuque, city of	1013	1	15	......	1110	79145	750	25100	......	....	....	......	505	....	....	407	....	40	....	....	1948
Dyersville, town of	160	2	6	......	191	6245	75	1746	......	28	35	......	241	....	....	447	10	35	....	....	92
Iowa	440	30	41	......	534	17046	....	....	10	489	202	......	3975	41	6	2186	433	1611	191	35	208
Jefferson	678	28	52	2	943	46210	1200	....	8	1173	472	2	3298	50	1	2379	453	2444	349	11	394
Julien, exc. of Dubuque	637	14	7	4	790	38240	1590	69965	3	1162	195	7	1734	46	45	1821	582	2210	259	10	268
Liberty	562	53	44	2	673	12345	....	....	......	580	197	8	3605	9	....	2800	2173	1932	187	56	161
Mosalem	485	43	2	1	468	16820	....	....	......	919	187	......	778	....	....	998	182	813	18	53	163
New Wine, exc. of Dyersville	652	13	73	......	864	31620	250	440	......	974	247	......	3878	....	....	4357	442	1638	153	14	269
Peru	432	1	11	......	562	23980	390	91	8	593	114	......	734	....	....	705	35	174	4	2	220
Prairie Creek	784	33	35	......	582	25870	....	....	......	1636	348	......	4097	9	34	3719	1850	4282	211	91	224
Table Mound	520	......	10	......	738	32350	1400	....	......	1202	....	......	2024	....	....	1957	230	910	....	22	154
Taylor	872	102	49	12	955	43107	360	11922	6	1624	545	7	4697	61	8	3389	335	1490	159	31	183
Vernon	875	44	35	4	795	132432	....	6006	10	2171	398	85	3826	112	44	3979	839	3938	324	39	261
Washington	642	60	44	......	633	32940	....	....	......	1192	269	1	5776	329	3	3395	384	1949	114	87	211
Whitewater	693	13	27	4	581	18108	....	132	......	916	150	1	3012	3	2	2659	566	1728	105	26	209
Total	11563	520	523	38	12617	649056	6535	115867	60	18904	4154	117	52341	923	461	44210	12217	31602	2468	683	5854

EMMET COUNTY.

Armstrong Grove	74	......	......	......	107	8060	264	....	15	220	3	1	87	....	2	77	....	....	....	....	33
Center	57	5	......	......	85	7700	112	....	6	188	20	......	23	....	3	24	142	165	10	3	20
Ellsworth	31	......	......	......	40	4100	....	....	2	76	....	......	26	....	2	23	5	....	....	....	11
Emmet	86	2	9	......	139	12455	100	....	24	210	8	......	97	2	....	88	66	260	15	5	31
Estherville	183	......	12	......	241	18600	....	....	38	366	124	......	165	....	....	129	121	336	25	8	59
High Lake	107	3	......	......	179	12550	250	....	8	500	62	2	97	....	....	80	452	1151	82	17	40
Iowa Lake	15	1	......	......	56	2350	5000	....	10	139	22	......	....	....	....	11	19	114	....	....	....
Peterson	83	8	......	......	193	15000	767	....	32	544	49	3	62	....	....	87	269	859	53	18	32
Swan Lake	13	......	......	......	33	2400	....	....	16	103	13	......	....	....	....	....	81	335	12	....	11
Total	649	19	21	......	1073	83215	6493	....	151	2346	301	6	557	2	7	519	1155	3220	197	51	237

FAYETTE COUNTY.—Continued.

NAMES OF TOWNSHIPS, TOWNS, AND CITIES.	Number of horses of all ages.	Number of horses sold for export in 1874.	Number of mules and asses.	Number of same sold for export in 1874.	Number of milch cows.	Number of pounds of butter made in 1874.	Number of pounds of cheese made in 1874 not in factory.	Number of gallons of milk sold in 1874.	Number of work oxen.	Number of all other cattle.	No. of cattle slaughtered or sold for slaughter in 1874.	Number of thorough-bred short horns.	HOGS. Number on hand.	HOGS. Number of Berk-shires.	HOGS. Number of Poland-China.	HOGS. No. slaughtered or sold for slaughter in 1874.	SHEEP. Number on hand.	SHEEP. Number of pounds of wool obtained in 1874.	SHEEP. No. slaughtered or sold for slaughter in 1874.	SHEEP. Number killed by dogs in 1874.	Number of dogs.
Auburn	391	13	13	......	474	39000	150	....	4	955	84	......	711	....	....	952	279	1208	....	4	115
Banks	224	......	6	......	235	15282	....	....	......	499	80	1	191	8	....	368	147	480	4	....	57
Bethel	333	......	23	......	346	28198	1000	....	10	605	90	......	564	....	....	885	435	2174	191	1	89
Center	351	......	14	......	392	29649	7830	....	......	657	84	......	698	....	....	649	376	1484	39	6	95
Clermont	496	31	6	......	522	34310	....	....	2	582	221	......	1179	....	....	841	964	293	16	13	207
Dover	458	70	47	......	747	42601	....	86	20	983	217	......	1152	5	3	1248	1494	6699	143	11	223
Eden	540	11	21	6	541	57505	1378	80	51	1820	270	......	885	4	9	1112	421	1422	79	12	157
Fairfield	583	31	12	......	548	46930	1500	360	6	1842	557	7	228	1	40	1576	1109	2381	137	42	153
Fayette, town of	....	......	......	......	....	....	....	....	......	....	....	......	....	....	....	....	....	....	....	....	....
Fremont	405	8	14	......	482	37930	....	....	......	988	165	1	1258	17	2	761	90	286	8	1	121
Harlan	359	9	20	2	339	27915	200	....	12	686	144	1	1409	3	10	757	549	1960	90	1	102
Illyria	520	11	43	......	508	46880	5000	....	......	883	45	1	2826	2	22	1659	700	2324	71	31	210
Jefferson	514	5	8	......	489	31635	....	515	8	1016	141	......	1046	39	34	1325	272	754	6	2	130
Oran	520	16	13	......	636	48605	140	....	16	1254	136	3	1946	74	3	1069	90	323	7	5	151
Pleasant Valley	530	19	10	......	478	37475	....	....	14	504	156	......	878	....	....	1105	362	2142	59	....	181
Putnam	520	14	10	......	699	60120	575	....	8	1558	145	4	1678	47	5	1107	304	1044	54	24	130
Scott	343	1	11	......	334	30200	723	....	......	639	62	......	681	....	....	662	97	576	4	2	87
Smithfield	754	......	27	......	564	47672	200	....	......	1025	....	1	1047	10	2	974	247	1107	....	13	115
Westfield, exc. of Fayette	505	......	26	......	474	36214	....	....	2	1045	210	......	1576	73	12	1588	770	3009	49	....	140
West Union, exc. of town	576	68	22	7	516	43750	....	400	10	1028	262	1	2662	....	4	2203	1549	7198	179	25	127
West Union, town of	228	9	8	4	130	12320	....	1350	......	62	9	......	206	15	40	267	117	200	....	2	99
Windsor	602	2	9	2	700	52250	3580	8395	20	1144	172	5	2158	5	21	1271	981	4591	171	76	162
Total	9752	318	363	21	10554	806441	22276	11186	183	19775	3250	25	24979	303	207	21879	11353	41655	1307	271	2851

FLOYD COUNTY.

Cedar	378	32	…	…	242	32710	300	…	14	741	151	4	791	8	20	593	542	710	32	42	86
Charles City, exc. of city	378	…	5	…	247	10064	1586	4769	8	101	119	49	149	…	…	335	…	135	…	4	134
Floyd	718	2	7	…	633	41198	…	182	4	1970	172	5	1528	42	42	953	890	4729	246	19	178
Niles	439	37	2	…	429	37147	…	…	30	884	135	…	816	30	3	690	349	1006	50	18	119
Nora Springs, town of	200	…	2	…	148	11940	…	1457	…	152	28	1	109	1	8	173	100	660	18	29	50
Pleasant Grove	406	2	15	…	363	29050	…	…	5	534	42	1	809	2	20	829	69	…	…	…	111
Riverton	566	4	3	…	508	33408	720	50	…	1444	92	1	1479	16	296	1521	615	2433	19	13	153
Rockford	553	9	4	2	459	60175	5700	2890	8	1356	284	…	1761	1	8	1122	758	2974	81	43	135
Rock Grove, exc. of Nora Springs	488	…	4	…	370	37000	…	…	7	776	147	3	506	2	29	530	195	705	25	16	100
Rudd	524	12	…	…	307	25118	…	…	…	497	117	…	682	86	259	433	4	…	…	…	86
St. Charles, exc. of city	985	50	13	…	949	77715	…	6120	41	1507	147	3	2012	106	75	2132	205	723	63	7	242
Scott	317	13	4	…	297	21558	…	…	12	564	123	3	1191	5	18	637	219	1193	26	29	71
Ulster	477	15	9	…	432	42250	…	…	22	800	119	…	868	86	32	882	277	1244	45	25	113
Union	639	1	14	1	474	40320	…	…	4	1007	171	…	1613	67	101	1497	579	2943	36	6	189
Total	7067	177	82	3	5858	499739	8306	15478	155	12333	1847	70	14314	452	911	12327	4802	19455	641	251	1767

FRANKLIN COUNTY.

Clinton	404	1	26	…	336	24080	510	6805	4	950	276	…	1999	88	40	1362	49	264	…	2	98
Geneva	416	33	8	…	339	24100	400	…	8	797	119	5	1273	197	220	1196	127	…	…	…	118
Grant	176	…	2	…	132	6590	…	…	4	264	…	…	307	…	…	374	320	…	…	…	53
Hamilton	104	12	8	…	118	9890	100	…	2	184	11	…	358	9	8	342	…	…	…	…	28
Hampton, town of	161	11	2	…	100	3925	…	290	…	38	18	…	144	31	…	164	…	…	…	…	26
Ingham	418	…	2	…	257	13220	…	…	16	986	…	…	1492	…	…	1912	545	2700	25	40	41
Lee	121	…	…	…	141	9025	…	…	6	264	19	…	330	87	241	156	…	…	…	…	44
Marion	67	…	4	…	56	3038	…	…	7	101	4	…	142	9	1	121	5	9	…	…	24
Morgan	187	3	2	…	185	14870	…	…	12	495	23	…	908	28	78	449	273	780	…	…	70
Oakland	251	3	…	…	303	17760	…	…	18	812	317	…	657	113	13	522	316	1663	48	12	74
Osceola	504	30	13	…	352	26900	100	…	…	890	80	5	2405	6	32	1702	6	42	…	…	119
Reeve	367	11	11	7	312	28968	…	…	8	683	45	1	1611	6	21	1367	9	14	…	3	106
Richland	136	5	5	…	87	5875	…	…	…	254	29	5	322	17	60	221	2	15	…	…	27
Washington, exc. of Hampton	371	13	14	3	298	22275	400	1600	10	979	304	13	2708	40	29	2039	3	32	1	…	112
Total	3973	122	104	10	3208	222366	2470	8695	97	7907	1270	29	15244	635	745	12280	1693	5682	74	57	1007

FREMONT COUNTY.

Names of townships, towns and cities.	Number of horses of all ages.	Number of horses sold for export in 1874.	Number of mules and asses.	Number of same sold for export in 1874.	Number of milch cows.	Number of pounds of butter made in 1874.	Number of pounds of cheese made in 1874 not in factory.	Number of gallons of milk sold.	Number of work oxen.	Number of all other cattle.	No. of cattle slaughtered or sold for slaughter in 1874.	Number of thoroughbred short-horns.	Hogs: Number on hand.	Hogs: Number of Berkshires.	Hogs: Number of Poland-China.	Hogs: No. slaughtered or sold for slaughter in 1874.	Sheep: Number on hand.	Sheep: Number of pounds of wool obtained in 1874.	Sheep: No. slaughtered or sold for slaughter in 1874.	Sheep: Number killed by dogs in 1874.	Number of dogs.
Bartlett, town of																					
Benton, exc. of Eastport and Percival	320	1	47		501	18190		50		1336	300		2687		187	1855	139	875	20		103
Eastport, town of																					
Farragut, town of																					
Fisher, exc. of Farragut	627		71	2	541	19550			18	2189	897	3	5266	6	3544	4028	30	130			143
Franklin, exc. of Hamburg	403	99	85	39	367	20118		3127	10	1700	855		3129	101	182	3925					133
Fremont City, town of																					
Hamburg, town of	248		23		139	8350		1000		30			251			115					254
Locust Grove	240	16	52	2	251	9667	1450	1000	1	492	77	4	1165	1	89	876					91
McPaul, town of																					
Madison	695	4	184		627	29755			1	2030	108	5	4496	99	279	3680	650	2096	131	20	200
Monroe	507	1	29		471	20290	325		8	2706	2024		3575	140	594	3253	800				209
Percival, town of																					
Prairie	378	11	41	1	296	10150				1122	223	7	1519	28	55	1776	290	1279	20	23	106
Riverton, exc. of town	238		40		345	11485		40		916	29	3	1866	509	1077	946	146	543		22	44
Riverton, town of													8240	22	1743	5460	5508	7683	3	3	182
Ross, exc. of Tabor	761	24	97	3	727	99752	100		9	1486	849	4	500	5	3	105					6
Scott, exc. of Fremont City, Bartlett and McPaul	733		135		1000	25385	50	625	14	2529	544	7	5576	27	78	3403	767	2950	214	55	249
Sidney, exc. of town	769	2	164		935	27521	110		22	2336	336	4	4238	110	137	1863	927	3172	457	53	281
Sidney, town of	60		5		69	1594		370	12	16			213	13	25	183	226				22
Tabor, town of	91		6		79	3710	1050	3600		67	333										
Walnut	308	21	30	1	436	11270	60		8	1155	1456	13	2036	7	159	3505	392	535	23		79
Total	6378	179	1009	48	6784	316787	3145	9812	103	20110	8031	69	44757	1068	8152	34973	9875	19263	868	176	1102

GREENE COUNTY.

Bristol	311	45	33	32	384	34525	1710	....	2	1402	103	1	2302	105	440	1893	1326	330	2	....	137
Cedar	243	15	18	......	340	18205	....	....	2	610	91	1	2135	13	18	1111	993	....	....	....	95
Dawson	20	1	......	......	13	610	....	....	4	39	1	......	164	5	1	75	....	....	....	....	9
Franklin	245	......	19	......	236	17665	200	....	12	537	78	2	1053	171	28	1147	152	1289	....	7	94
Grand Junction, town of	92	1	7	......	85	2414	....	1690	4	150	9	......	387	7	31	209	....	....	....	....	58
Greenbrier	128	7	14	2	85	4537	....	....	3	363	32	1	551	29	39	351	102	1086	....	....	56
Hardin	216	......	17	......	319	10736	....	....	14	414	85	2	957	46	37	928	105	400	26	....	68
Highland	41	......	31	......	85	5080	....	....	......	210	44	3	317	56	8	369	200	600	....	2	28
Jackson	276	27	48	......	340	15611	....	25	......	1113	37	......	1336	239	591	1351	465	770	6	7	121
Jefferson, exc. of town	325	......	29	......	427	33525	440	....	14	889	241	7	2377	1339	435	2313	1215	3020	38	11	174
Jefferson, town of	91	......	8	......	127	5927	....	....	......	84	....	......	161	....	13	359	....	....	....	....	67
Junction, exc. Grand Junction	272	3	5	......	254	23160	....	....	4	404	14	......	1081	12	17	603	....	....	....	....	67
Kendrick	400	......	41	......	421	29352	75	....	18	975	170	1	3395	84	571	1867	760	1830	70	11	129
Scranton, exc. of town	202	......	......	......	104	5075	....	....	4	108	5	......	562	69	108	295	266	....	....	....	55
Scranton, town of	36	......	1	......	26	1405	....	2	......	5	....	......	187	....	17	68	41	....	....	....	15
Washington	325	13	29	......	390	27715	30	....	28	822	182	......	3035	95	75	1043	695	2727	281	47	173
Willow	88	......	5	......	58	3100	....	....	4	80	12	......	187	4	....	116	200	500	....	12	27
Total	3311	112	305	34	3694	238642	2455	1717	113	8205	1104	18	20187	2274	2429	14098	6520	12552	323	97	1373

GRUNDY COUNTY.

Beaver	352	......	8	......	292	14778	11385	50	......	386	33	......	880	....	12	597	21	15	2	....	101
Black Hawk	395	4	19	1	226	19099	....	1200	7	356	21	......	749	73	211	914	306	952	27	....	108
Clay	496	2	18	......	349	19650	8000	....	......	885	153	......	2091	449	931	1229	898	4050	150	....	107
Colfax	484	......	16	......	269	12375	....	....	2	639	....	......	1976	....	....	938	....	....	....	....	....
Fairfield	605	6	2	......	522	26230	450	....	2	1071	223	2	1992	2	....	1676	593	220	12	2	149
Felix	579	......	30	......	398	27216	....	....	......	782	121	......	2880	9	44	1473	7	28	....	....	123
German	438	24	8	2	589	23192	545	....	2	963	106	......	3572	11	7	1829	63	266	3	3	198
Grant	442	......	17	......	305	20562	9050	....	4	632	293	......	1839	....	....	1205	41	304	22	2	105
Lincoln	323	2	......	1	162	12475	....	....	......	290	....	......	1263	....	508	801	205	1635	....	....	66
Melrose	580	......	31	6	372	32275	240	....	2	950	84	3	3155	56	73	2102	16	50	....	3	116
Palermo	766	26	58	......	551	34753	....	595	4	846	150	6	4235	317	1721	7104	375	1200	8	....	166
Pleasant Valley	572	4	12	......	340	18813	....	100	2	544	44	......	2644	1	3	1133	52	187	12	....	133
Shiloh	430	......	16	......	352	19290	....	....	16	1077	443	26	2687	....	....	2938	18	....	....	....	104
Total	6402	68	235	10	4727	280708	29670	1945	41	9431	1671	37	29963	918	3510	23939	2595	8907	236	10	1476

GUTHRIE COUNTY.

NAMES OF TOWNSHIPS, TOWNS AND CITIES.	Number of horses of all ages.	Number of horses sold for export in 1874.	Number of mules and asses.	Number of same sold for export in 1874.	Number of milch cows.	Number of pounds of butter made in 1874.	Number of pounds of cheese made in 1874 not in factory.	Number of gallons of milk sold in 1874.	Number of work oxen.	Number of all other cattle.	No. of cattle slaughtered or sold for slaughter in 1874.	Number of thorough-bred short-horns.	HOGS. Number on hand.	HOGS. Number of Berk-shires.	HOGS. Number of Poland China.	HOGS. No. slaughtered or sold for slaughter in 1874.	SHEEP. Number on hand.	SHEEP. Number of pounds of wool obtained in 1874.	SHEEP. No. slaughtered or sold for slaughter in 1874.	SHEEP. Number killed by dogs in 1874.	Number of dogs.
Bear Grove	340	2	8	......	381	12443	......	......	......	1103	......	......	1832	3	......	1450	101	427	......	5	122
Beaver	329	......	13	......	286	17402	......	305	2	1008	324	......	1324	219	786	1327	40	......	......	......	74
Cass, exc. of Panora	821	42	30	......	764	33610	15	70	......	1023	237	11	3343	42	48	2659	657	2754	46	40	226
Center	491	1	15	......	367	23400	410	348	......	1287	275	......	1939	7	76	1883	843	3675	97	......	144
Dodge	128	2	15	......	116	2050	......	......	......	253	9	......	929	1	54	582	6	28	......	......	48
Grant	151	......	8	......	145	8200	......	......	11	198	30	......	535	......	3	316	30	125	......	1	53
Highland	205	1	7	......	160	8995	......	......	......	410	20	1	1135	4	6	880	105	511	......	3	118
Jackson	552	2	23	......	474	32719	......	......	......	1281	695	2	2935	7	36	4358	750	4692	209	12	177
Orange	185	11	21	......	171	14370	......	......	2	365	14	......	1194	24	9	1638	727	200	2	16	70
Panora, town of	150	4	4	......	96	2900	10	302	......	23	8	......	220	1	1	230	......	......	......	......	32
Penn	498	16	28	......	452	37695	......	6500	2	906	108	2	2547	104	65	1661	236	1218	2	44	206
Richland	329	......	10	......	226	21565	......	......	4	689	181	......	2142	10	96	2019	......	......	......	......	97
Thompson	293	......	11	......	305	......	......	......	......	439	......	......	673	2	......	......	......	......	......	......	......
Union	265	......	7	......	231	12175	......	......	......	728	158	2	1705	38	89	1372	......	......	...	......	67
Valley	429	......	9	......	470	27900	......	......	2	1058	340	2	1596	33	16	2452	611	3056	208	8	129
Victory	421	47	15	9	340	22945	40	......	2	1104	327	2	1691	1	......	1921	221	1624	82	70	131
Total	5587	128	224	9	4984	278369	475	7525	25	11875	2726	22	25740	496	1285	24748	4327	18310	646	199	1693

HAMILTON COUNTY.

NAMES OF TOWNSHIPS, TOWNS AND CITIES.	Number of horses of all ages.	Number of horses sold for export in 1874.	Number of mules and asses.	Number of same sold for export in 1874.	Number of milch cows.	Number of pounds of butter made in 1874.	Number of pounds of cheese made in 1874 not in factory.	Number of gallons of milk sold in 1874.	Number of work oxen.	Number of all other cattle.	No. of cattle slaughtered or sold for slaughter in 1874.	Number of thorough-bred short-horns.	HOGS. Number on hand.	HOGS. Number of Berk-shires.	HOGS. Number of Poland China.	HOGS. No. slaughtered or sold for slaughter in 1874.	SHEEP. Number on hand.	SHEEP. Number of pounds of wool obtained in 1874.	SHEEP. No. slaughtered or sold for slaughter in 1874.	SHEEP. Number killed by dogs in 1874.	Number of dogs.
Blairsburg	236	9	5	......	208	14841	......	......	6	323	7	1	417	24	60	316	......	......	......	......	104
Boone	802	93	35	10	739	47155	800	6970	20	3498	1795	1	4440	23	405	3430	148	532	37	......	174
Cass	374	......	16	......	386	30620	100	......	12	872	21	......	1013	82	503	1031	7	12	1	2	114
Clear Lake	159	5	......	......	225	14616	100	......	15	590	......	13	585	20	63	350	25	20	5	......	65
Ellsworth	209	1	......	......	368	28600	40	......	......	597	8	......	387	2	3	369	69	234	......	3	82
Fremont	238	......	4	......	304	16241	......	......	10	658	......	......	539	......	......	......	12	......	......	......	94

Hamilton	403	....	55	....	479	36415	....	....	37	928	....	....	1243	7	23	978	60	82	....	....	125
Lyon	188	11	7	....	162	11950	....	....	14	461	137	1	363	29	20	459	17	37	6	3	66
Marion	522	2	14	2	555	26959	1747	....	4	1102	38	....	2207	40	75	1395	326	813	15	38	128
Rose Grove	86	5	....	....	107	5800	....	....	....	254	86	....	455	....	....	239	29	....	....	....	30
Scott	250	....	2	....	457	31012	....	....	....	795	46	....	684	....	....	703	58	195	....	....	64
Webster	399	17	24	....	365	25835	....	....	8	773	40	....	1621	....	....	1084	82	185	....	....	119
Total	3866	143	162	12	4355	290044	2787	6970	126	10851	2178	16	13954	227	1152	10354	833	2110	64	46	1165

HANCOCK COUNTY.

Amsterdam	86	3	11	....	125	5250	8390	....	8	270	18	1	74	2	7	140	27	144	....	....	47
Avery	71	....	6	....	81	5602	....	....	11	162	17	1	107	1	1	164	22	78	....	2	27
Britt	13	....	....	....	55	1300	....	....	4	48	4	1	27	....	....	....	....	....	....	....	5
Concord	69	....	2	2	103	4550	....	....	6	158	11	1	76	....	....	43	31	150	....	....	30
Crystal	41	....	....	....	53	4100	....	....	16	82	1	....	55	....	10	....	10	60	....	....	14
Ellington	221	1	14	4	309	13697	8000	....	28	516	69	....	150	....	8	217	66	325	12	15	91
Madison	63	....	....	....	79	5435	....	....	2	131	3	....	46	....	....	96	52	208	....	....	21
Total	564	4	33	6	805	39934	16390	....	75	1367	123	4	535	3	26	660	208	965	12	17	235

HARDIN COUNTY.

Ackley, town of	198	9	2	....	148	7405	....	....	....	34	....	....	63	....	....	6	....	....	....	....	67
Alden	421	....	12	....	481	28603	....	20170	8	696	14	2	1502	48	71	968	694	....	....	....	144
Buckeye	137	15	3	....	179	7745	950	1000	4	242	20	5	420	27	52	460	1264	5000	510	....	49
Clay	649	25	27	1	483	39045	....	550	2	712	117	35	3481	690	1593	2113	100	431	176	41	182
Concord	64	2	10	2	60	3345	....	....	....	104	3	....	156	....	....	88	....	....	....	....	20
Eldora, exc. of town	524	70	8	1	410	37555	....	7152	....	880	314	1	3689	1270	2559	1990	247	70	232	1	118
Eldora, town of	240	54	8	....	169	9570	....	3250	....	74	21	....	787	6	15	396	12	75	....	4	82
Ellis	302	....	3	....	317	20495	6800	82495	10	584	49	3	848	58	76	756	557	2700	16	7	83
Etna, exc. of Ackley	598	20	11	4	284	23409	990	....	....	907	37	....	2252	70	75	770	4	10	....	....	172
Grant	157	15	16	....	129	8600	....	....	....	251	5	....	885	413	183	382	92	210	16	....	49
Hardin, exc. of Iowa Falls	515	....	6	....	673	42932	1250	47675	4	1033	61	....	1876	223	103	1498	169	1117	26	....	128
Iowa Falls, town of	....	....	....	....	....	....	....	....	....	....	....	....	....	....	....	....	....	....	....	....	....
Jackson	500	10	28	....	470	58300	200	760	6	1125	148	7	2577	562	141	1791	90	300	6	12	121
Pleasant	656	65	34	....	617	33873	150	15247	12	1241	205	3	4249	36	107	1828	389	1427	93	45	169
Providence	715	54	30	20	578	34187	330	14053	6	998	481	18	4553	155	19	4139	180	2007	84	1	182
Sherman	92	3	3	....	87	5698	....	....	....	186	23	1	256	32	103	184	85	290	12	....	42
Tipton	309	6	15	....	254	25690	10	....	4	496	59	6	1038	61	65	642	93	279	3	6	87
Union, exc. of town	610	....	13	....	497	37301	40	880	4	1030	201	1	3300	31	10	3127	155	635	20	....	193
Union, town of	91	8	3	....	56	2074	....	1323	....	56	25	....	317	3	....	273	....	....	....	....	39
Total	6778	356	232	28	5892	425827	10720	194555	60	10649	1783	82	32249	3685	5172	21411	4131	14551	1194	117	1927

HARRISON COUNTY.

NAMES OF TOWNSHIPS, TOWNS, AND CITIES.	Number of horses of all ages.	Number of horses sold for export in 1874.	Number of mules and asses.	Number of same sold for export in 1874.	Number of milch cows.	Number of pounds of butter made in 1874.	Number of pounds of cheese made in 1874 not in factory.	Number of gallons of milk sold in 1874.	Number of work oxen.	Number of all other cattle.	No. of cattle slaughtered or sold for slaughter in 1874.	Number of thorough-bred short-horns.	HOGS.				SHEEP.				Number of dogs.
													Number on hand.	Number of Berk-shires.	Number of Poland-China.	No. slaughtered or sold for slaughter in 1874.	Number on hand.	Number of pounds of wool obtained in 1874.	No. slaughtered or sold for slaughter in 1874.	Number killed by dogs in 1874.	
Allen	44	2	3	......	67	2367	......	......	2	241	41	......	171	......	1	133	......	......	......	......	18
Boyer	398	2	9	1	395	15853	1330	......	......	1037	717	3	1618	42	201	3093	143	528	55	7	103
Calhoun	283	10	11	2	346	15125	200	......	......	780	216	......	1052	1	3	912	40	180	3	15	78
Cass	199	3	......	......	184	14670	......	......	2	287	68	......	730	......	1	475	46	320	2	7	66
Cincinnati	328	5	18	......	395	17099	100	50	2	1389	246	2	1340	4	21	1018	195	......	......	......	132
Clay	316	36	26	3	253	4711	......	......	12	621	256	......	1711	2	27	1380	......	18	2	......	120
Douglas	105	3	6	......	140	6487	......	......	2	486	79	11	713	1	53	520	......	......	......	......	71
Dunlap, town of	117	......	8	......	70	......	......	......	......	108	......	......	......	......	......	......	......	......	......	......	......
Harrison, exc. of Dunlap	255	......	11	......	317	19600	500	......	......	732	307	25	696	23	57	930	3	......	10	......	81
Jackson	211	7	4	......	395	11214	1726	......	......	496	169	......	728	5	143	955	......	......	......	......	74
Jefferson	667	4	30	......	647	31032	900	......	2	1611	638	6	3561	13	217	4063	167	815	94	......	174
Lagrange	238	20	14	......	285	12495	......	......	......	503	119	......	1926	25	259	1343	184	865	46	52	76
Lincoln	100	......	......	......	131	4791	......	......	......	433	54	......	476	9	2	556	......	......	......	......	34
Little Sioux	429	3	19	......	404	18251	......	......	19	1172	234	......	1642	1	33	1422	140	648	52	38	133
Magnolia	581	10	9	......	677	26345	4200	368	2	1118	105	5	2228	10	125	2022	138	502	1	......	140
Missouri Valley, town of	97	......	......	......	74	......	......	......	......	......	......	......	......	......	......	......	......	......	......	......	65
Morgan	366	2	45	......	306	16132	......	335	4	832	180	3	2748	61	53	1748	132	395	9	7	144
Raglan	295	......	11	......	321	12702	385	200	8	959	257	1	1147	14	44	1941	145	625	8	1	94
St. John, ex Missouri Valley	710	......	33	......	742	45470	......	4520	7	1677	530	1	3127	......	24	2942	148	1395	181	23	214
Taylor	336	13	28	3	409	22870	566	......	......	1002	216	2	1847	6	33	1624	124	372	3	3	113
Union	294	......	......	......	277	11725	......	......	......	482	57	......	1231	......	......	1001	......	......	......	......	73
Washington	170	......	......	......	143	6793	......	......	2	261	45	......	673	......	11	418	......	......	......	......	46
Total	6539	120	285	9	6978	315732	9907	5473	64	16227	4534	59	29365	217	1314	28496	1605	6663	466	153	2049

HENRY COUNTY.

Baltimore	517	47	57	9	650	21425	....	....	10	645	173	3	5564	23	1001	3092	889	2667	333	102	238
Canaan	795	4	55	......	675	33415	....	....	......	1974	378	1	4758	47	462	2845	250	1464	44	8	194
Center, exc. of Mt. Pleasant	847	15	81	2	806	50522	200	16914	4	1552	2499	2	3043	1	30	13199	3849	15014	1824	157	321
Jackson	753	33	54	10	622	43242	2818	....	......	1588	418	5	3192	218	624	3255	3378	9893	522	129	215
Jefferson	835	66	12	5	628	39480	....	....	2	1883	656	8	3672	227	1050	4049	815	3994	156	98	144
Marion	799	84	75	11	663	49579	1295	....	6	2490	1839	16	4964	89	2005	5423	84	5643	921	153	198
Mt. Pleasant, city of	308	18	23	1	257	350	....	100	......	7	1	......	189	4	....	620	....	....	....	....	345
New London, exc. of town	1039	104	88	21	694	64622	....	....	2	2639	707	11	4302	316	2705	4997	1786	6565	320	40	235
New London, town of	62	......	10	......	40	2845	....	....	......	7	....	......	32	....	....	....	....	....	....	....	34
Rome, town of	67	7	......	......	55	3297	....	230	4	26	27	......	340	....	4	863	....	....	2	....	29
Salem, exc. of town	717	34	85	23	520	42281	235	551	4	1407	212	2	5037	16	167	3165	2337	10215	624	71	215
Salem, town of	82	27	10	8	52	4320	....	175	......	3	89	......	95	....	11	118	....	....	18	....	41
Scott	812	19	49	......	930	66907	....	....	......	2227	892	37	4472	47	156	4686	198	3265	199	61	157
Tippecanoe, exc. of Rome	699	17	57	......	535	38452	....	20	......	1002	407	2	2218	60	66	2085	1390	5196	1271	50	265
Trenton	825	46	40	2	618	44680	25	....	18	1249	229	......	4782	1	9	2741	1079	4128	137	156	269
Wayne	767	28	41	......	807	41101	1008	....	6	1562	398	1	9664	180	1240	5969	751	2397	42	25	223
Total	9924	549	737	92	8552	546518	5581	17990	56	20261	8925	88	56324	1229	9530	57107	16806	70451	6413	1051	3123

HOWARD COUNTY.

Afton	473	5	5	......	514	44260	....	....	10	1058	151	7	844	....	3	889	248	1021	110	5	169
Albion	440	5	......	......	305	20957	....	....	8	418	104	......	502	....	....	421	....	....	....	....	77
Chester	270	......	5	......	312	29535	....	15	51	561	53	......	292	1	16	188	121	477	23	....	62
Cresco, town of	124	......	......	......	....	....	....	....	......	....	....	......	....	....	....	....	....	....	....	....	....
Forest City	383	14	7	......	356	34270	3400	40	28	458	30	......	430	89	20	275	21	....	....	5	68
Howard	233	3	6	......	263	21200	50	....	10	840	10	1	309	6	58	337	2	7	....	1	76
Howard Center	306	1	20	......	255	21485	154	....	6	487	32	......	447	20	15	270	246	28	1	....	82
Jamestown	260	......	......	......	324	17310	600	....	28	547	125	......	259	....	9	334	244	1056	20	25	77
New Oregon	117	9	4	......	832	41775	30	200	35	1180	144	......	1023	1	9	890	180	664	114	18	218
Oak Dale	....	208	......	2	233	18290	....	....	12	418	52	......	210	....	3	191	18	100	1	3	53
Paris	448	16	2	4	483	37960	....	....	38	1026	88	......	968	....	2	555	571	144	22	5	140
Saratoga	136	5	6	......	157	14125	....	....	31	377	21	......	149	20	10	118	11	50	2	....	60
Vernon Springs, exc. of Cresco	243	12	3	......	324	21950	12437	5177	22	648	66	8	344	34	18	370	210	....	....	....	52
Total	3433	278	58	6	4358	323116	16671	5432	279	8018	876	16	5777	171	163	4838	1872	3547	293	62	1134

HUMBOLDT COUNTY.

NAMES OF TOWNSHIPS, TOWNS, AND CITIES.	Number of horses of all ages.	Number of horses sold for export in 1874.	Number of mules and asses.	Number of same sold for export in 1874.	Number of milch cows.	Number of pounds of butter made in 1874.	Number of pounds of cheese made in 1874 not in factory.	Number of gallons of milk sold in 1874.	Number of work oxen.	Number of all other cattle.	No. of cattle slaughtered or sold for slaughter in 1874.	Number of thorough-bred short-horns.	HOGS. Number on hand.	HOGS. Number of Berk-shires.	HOGS. Number of Poland-China.	HOGS. No. slaughtered or sold for slaughter in 1874.	SHEEP. Number on hand.	SHEEP. Number of pounds of wool obtained in 1874.	SHEEP. No. slaughtered or sold for slaughter in 1874.	SHEEP. Number killed by dogs in 1874.	Number of dogs.
Avery	85	......	4	......	196	7930	......	...	......	430	......	......	455	......	1	316	267	1426	17	......	46
Dakota	182	......	4	......	343	13755	......	......	22	368	23	......	464	42	5	709	......	8	......	1	88
Delana	160	......	3	......	173	10025	......	......	21	274	21	......	333	13	1	315	15	62	2	......	61
Grove	233	......	7	......	176	10790	......	......	6	604	39	......	864	7	5	814	......	......	......	......	84
Humboldt	197	21	7	......	182	14645	1100	......	22	395	10	4	647	20	23	359	175	822	14	1	60
Humboldt, town of	47	49	......	......	29	1928	350	......	5	7	8	......	45	25	6	123	......	......	......	......	46
Lake	51	......	......	......	71	7500	1650	......	......	140	......	......	80	......	......	104	10	90	......	......	16
Norway	46	......	2	......	187	11890	......	......	24	167	......	......	45	2	......	9	25	86	......	......	49
Rutland	154	5	......	......	190	10235	200	430	6	337	34	......	519	18	10	229	48	320	15	4	46
Springvale, exc of Humboldt	185	11	13	......	282	17485	550	......	4	360	15	31	515	......	......	......	......	......	......	......	30
Vernon	235	12	16	......	257	15773	1515	......	29	233	13	......	295	5	9	185	255	779	45	......	72
Wacousta	67	......	......	......	121	7850	......	......	13	345	......	......	302	1	3	198	......	......	......	......	......
Weaver	60	......	1	......	61	5260	......	......	6	41	10	......	134	......	......	106	......	......	......	......	23
Total	1702	98	57	......	2268	135066	5365	430	158	3701	173	35	4698	133	63	3467	795	3593	93	6	621

IDA COUNTY.

NAMES OF TOWNSHIPS, TOWNS, AND CITIES.	Number of horses of all ages.	Number of horses sold for export in 1874.	Number of mules and asses.	Number of same sold for export in 1874.	Number of milch cows.	Number of pounds of butter made in 1874.	Number of pounds of cheese made in 1874 not in factory.	Number of gallons of milk sold in 1874.	Number of work oxen.	Number of all other cattle.	No. of cattle slaughtered or sold for slaughter in 1874.	Number of thorough-bred short-horns.	HOGS. Number on hand.	HOGS. Number of Berk-shires.	HOGS. Number of Poland-China.	HOGS. No. slaughtered or sold for slaughter in 1874.	SHEEP. Number on hand.	SHEEP. Number of pounds of wool obtained in 1874.	SHEEP. No. slaughtered or sold for slaughter in 1874.	SHEEP. Number killed by dogs in 1874.	Number of dogs.
Corwin	126	......	4	......	157	6400	......	......	22	491	29	......	541	1	2	299	......	......	......	......	31
Douglas	71	......	3	......	46	2862	......	......	4	176	35	......	271	......	2	240	......	......	......	......	20
Maple	173	10	4	......	136	10068	......	......	19	222	30	2	820	14	49	532	91	900	6	4	46
Silver Creek	61	......	2	1	60	1505	......	......	21	91	13	1	201	27	2	88	......	......	......	......	68
Total	431	10	13	1	399	20835	......	......	66	980	107	3	1833	42	55	1159	91	900	6	4	165

IOWA COUNTY.

Amana	176	....	4	....	389	....	....	....	127	672	250	7	1234	....	....	920	2775	169470	450	....	48
Cono	189	10	....	....	147	6116	....	1370	...	263	103	16	846	77	97	686	117	850	115	1	45
Dayton	656	15	34	2	754	43390	590	....	22	1881	245	19	3039	....	109	2672	226	1544	27	14	220
English	849	35	48	6	876	48581	238	6	....	2205	201	....	5087	119	699	2979	1223	3688	302	99	305
Fillmore	640	38	45	6	665	37180	80	....	....	2410	195	1	4302	4	507	2504	318	1314	64	81	194
Green	712	34	29	1	542	32985	210	....	....	1928	363	....	3563	9	8	3484	478	2376	97	....	215
Hartford, exc. of Victor	566	69	45	10	509	35822	60	137	....	1093	420	13	2172	110	6	2503	21	284	25	....	145
Hilton	586	10	31	....	583	28430	....	....	....	1104	337	....	2583	....	....	2141	....	45	....	....	136
Honey Creek	727	31	45	6	650	30335	942	1600	2	1600	365	3	3087	237	925	2287	290	1548	70	60	179
Iowa	446	34	....	....	479	31528	2400	....	358	1004	401	2	2377	....	....	1887	....	....	4	....	111
Lenox	442	8	5	381	27975	....	....	....	....	878	148	....	1788	3	37	1678	55	275	....	....	126
Lincoln	361	4	33	....	361	27723	200	....	....	1353	123	10	1630	37	20	1406	82	368	3	1	124
Marengo, exc. of town	496	39	8	2	457	31900	....	5160	....	1275	281	....	2561	492	....	2511	60	369	50	8	122
Marengo, town of	249	8	10	1	223	400	....	....	....	2	....	....	19	1	....	10	....	....	....	....	139
Pilot	494	14	31	589	32175	10356	....	....	....	1943	337	9	2015	6	22	1783	541	1975	69	....	166
Sumner	491	23	36	....	518	32636	300	....	....	783	147	20	1920	14	38	905	59	357	....	1	....
Troy	625	14	39	2	509	35805	170	....	....	1863	392	8	4556	35	117	2378	602	2455	43	3	162
Victor, town of	18	2	1	2	23	240	....	376	....	1	1	....	31	2	....	27	....	....	....	....	25
Washington	429	8	12	69	285	18845	....	....	....	899	167	6	1645	28	108	....	1240	....	....	....	143
York	450	5	19	....	358	19690	2000	....	....	1671	180	3	2070	4	8	1992	112	1416	4	8	159
Total	9602	393	475	1077	68478	471962	7190	8649	509	24828	4656	117	46475	1178	2701	34753	8199	188334	1323	276	2764

JACKSON COUNTY.

Andrew, town of	34	8	....	....	34	940	....	....	....	5	1	....	62	....	....	54	....	....	....	....	29
Bellevue, exc. of town	580	3	12	....	691	26335	....	2400	....	1175	375	....	1262	1	....	2267	211	638	64	32	230
Bellevue, town of	61	18	9	....	134	....	....	2500	....	....	140	....	2	....	....	70	....	20	50	....	76
Brandon	507	29	33	....	410	28359	....	....	10	619	84	2	1156	2	6	768	301	1253	27	69	216
Butler	625	57	29	5	444	8601	....	....	....	1194	153	....	3366	....	....	3026	966	3438	163	83	225
Fairfield	698	11	16	....	627	31185	510	....	....	1659	202	7	5260	42	7	3037	270	1442	127	10	185
Farmer's Creek	880	....	53	....	589	28705	....	....	....	1295	71	1	1941	63	87	2121	478	2324	93	50	194
Iowa	862	67	13	....	781	45774	....	....	....	2469	850	....	3824	45	113	4246	765	3670	119	70	217
Jackson	576	35	28	....	626	24541	275	10	4	1122	215	3	3063	1	....	2772	2228	1097	4	29	237
Maquoketa, exc. of city	609	86	10	7	747	49210	40	95	....	2116	417	6	4283	10	59	2497	475	2224	94	20	204
Maquoketa, city of	217	8	4	....	222	12378	....	4960	....	103	22	....	237	3	24	145	237	....	....	....	38
Monmouth	704	91	54	12	606	49480	....	20	....	1326	906	5	2411	32	220	2958	259	1282	47	41	184
Otter Creek	510	41	26	2	519	26606	....	....	....	3756	238	9	6562	52	74	8727	436	1881	176	74	237
Perry, exc. of Andrew	850	43	5	6	563	42355	330	....	....	1150	369	....	2710	2	7	1913	338	1497	98	33	140
Prairie Spring	588	....	20	....	710	25875	150	....	....	670	146	1	1728	....	7	2453	201	1211	31	22	187
Richland	635	39	28	3	757	17805	....	....	....	1088	304	....	4749	7	41	2713	138	662	....	13	162
Sabula, town of	144	33	14	3	117	2685	....	3430	....	39	17	....	132	....	8	99	34	....	....	....	82
South Fork, exc. Maquoketa	454	43	17	3	545	48291	151	5310	....	1130	439	2	1373	38	77	1978	523	3059	80	40	119

JACKSON COUNTY.—Continued.

NAMES OF TOWNSHIPS, TOWNS AND CITIES.	Number of horses of all ages.	Number of horses sold for export in 1874.	Number of mules and asses.	Number of same sold for export in 1874.	Number of milch cows.	Number of pounds of butter made in 1874.	Number of pounds of cheese made in 1874 not in factory.	Number of gallons of milk sold in 1874.	Number of work oxen.	Number of all other cattle.	No. of cattle slaughtered or sold for slaughter in 1874.	Number of thorough-bred short-horns.	HOGS. Number on hand.	HOGS. Number of Berk-shires.	HOGS. Number of Poland-China.	HOGS. No. slaughtered or sold for slaughter in 1874.	SHEEP. Number on hand.	SHEEP. Number of pounds of wool obtained in 1874.	SHEEP. No. slaughtered or sold for slaughter in 1874.	SHEEP. Number killed by dogs in 1874.	Number of dogs.
Tete Des Morts	588	28	12	......	664	25185	....	11169	......	1080	339	......	1675	33	30	2219	399	1757	100	5	185
Union, exc. of Sabula	174	24	5	2	145	1100	....	....	......	278	81	5	176	....	....	380	96	130	5	1	39
Van Buren	748	79	2	......	956	60526	13742	550	......	2929	821	1	130	22	15	4221	441	2496	129	19	196
Washington	507	31	14	1	607	20525	50	....	4	1302	347	......	1510	....	7	1785	238	2364	75	34	188
Total	11551	774	404	44	11503	576161	15248	30444	18	26505	6537	42	47612	353	782	50449	9031	32445	1482	645	3570

JASPER COUNTY.

NAMES OF TOWNSHIPS, TOWNS AND CITIES.	Number of horses of all ages.	Number of horses sold for export in 1874.	Number of mules and asses.	Number of same sold for export in 1874.	Number of milch cows.	Number of pounds of butter made in 1874.	Number of pounds of cheese made in 1874 not in factory.	Number of gallons of milk sold in 1874.	Number of work oxen.	Number of all other cattle.	No. of cattle slaughtered or sold for slaughter in 1874.	Number of thorough-bred short-horns.	HOGS. Number on hand.	HOGS. Number of Berk-shires.	HOGS. Number of Poland-China.	HOGS. No. slaughtered or sold for slaughter in 1874.	SHEEP. Number on hand.	SHEEP. Number of pounds of wool obtained in 1874.	SHEEP. No. slaughtered or sold for slaughter in 1874.	SHEEP. Number killed by dogs in 1874.	Number of dogs.
Buena Vista	775	16	59	......	585	40330	375	....	......	2351	449	2	3950	36	40	4447	3745	2376	178	38	208
Clear Creek	728	5	39	2	577	39013	60	15	......	1416	127	......	6411	26	53	3128	3476	2120	100	47	197
Des Moines, exc. of Prairie City	924	3	101	......	621	45205	....	....	......	1123	147	......	6449	103	710	3752	1166	3972	....	103	256
Elk Creek	849	3	62	......	816	55220	120	....	......	1983	340	1	4489	7	66	4182	585	3127	390	51	213
Fairview, exc. of Monroe	998	2	198	2	948	69294	....	....	8	3204	1037	146	6726	9	50	6004	778	3076	108	23	344
Hickory Grove	400	1	32	......	225	25873	....	....	......	680	20	......	2099	2	1	774	1	....	....	....	106
Independence	649	......	24	......	563	33045	1110	1253	22	2206	136	2	4058	32	96	3050	328	803	94	28	211
Jasper City, town of	13	1	......	......	35	2000	....	140	......	7	108	......	81	2	....	276	....	....	....	....	8
Kellogg, exc. of Jasper City	1207	58	36	8	500	34053	2340	....	......	1490	318	176	3045	391	256	3151	91	474	281	34	172
Lynn Grove	665	7	123	......	486	27770	....	....	11	2760	854	2	4182	550	65	4983	263	1873	58	95	176
Malaka	770	64	64	1	736	48582	300	....	4	2243	463	1	5522	115	184	3461	996	2274	140	1	228
Mariposa	408	12	10	6	348	28550	....	....	......	1132	120	......	1737	1	1	1136	306	1554	90	....	129
Monroe, town of	182	5	13	14	115	8240	80	4825	......	38	4	......	724	192	427	485	90	300	....	....	34
Mound Prairie	607	......	44	......	386	25517	....	....	8	610	....	......	2350	2	23	1833	124	414	2	16	145
Newton, exc. of city	421	35	35	13	378	25925	1150	580	......	562	236	......	1555	16	80	1613	137	600	2	35	133
Newton, city of	182	......	17	......	93	....	....	2560	......	....	....	......	304	3	....	....	....	....	....	....	79
Palo Alto	609	16	15	3	598	38206	....	....	......	1453	413	......	2772	51	57	2612	244	943	1	5	190
Poweshiek	860	133	34	6	616	21209	....	100	2	1630	391	4	5136	6	318	3313	465	1781	174	14	183

	1	2	3	4	5	6	7	8	9	10	11	12	13	14	15	16	17	18	19	20	21
Prairie City, town of	27	7	2	2	......	37	......	200	.....	......	......	.....	5	......	......	......	......	......	......	......	56
Richland	591	3	51	.....	473	35055	......	......	.....	1018	246	28	3308	105	195	2823	394	991	18	35	195
Rock Creek	471	4	19	.....	402	26650	110	......	.....	893	170	.....	2640	7	37	1608	231	715	6	20	139
Sherman	788	15	45	2	651	64665	1909	......	18	1501	472	1	3481	2	15	3527	193	1032	21	24	222
Washington	544	2	17	.....	298	27930	......	......	.....	781	89	.....	4489	......	......	2868	1699	101	5	......	155
Total	13668	392	1040	49	10450	722369	7554	9673	73	29081	6140	363	75513	1658	2674	59026	15312	28526	1668	569	3779

JEFFERSON COUNTY.

	1	2	3	4	5	6	7	8	9	10	11	12	13	14	15	16	17	18	19	20	21
Batavia, town of	53	.....	2	1	39	325	......	......	.....	......	4	.....	370	......	......	209	......	......	......	......	31
Black Hawk	821	32	33	.....	617	54853	200	......	.....	1796	681	9	10480	226	58	4982	610	2405	95	49	174
Buchanan	898	67	53	8	660	42210	458	1200	.....	1705	689	17	3230	66	225	3464	2313	11952	1020	113	203
Cedar	637	18	29	4	478	23880	120	15000	10	1323	312	.....	1871	11	176	2447	1019	4913	243	55	195
Des Moines	873	90	73	10	644	72808	240	......	.....	2018	337	.....	9773	......	......	4964	4809	7404	757	58	245
Fairfield, exc. of city	757	99	33	13	710	56960	40	3995	.....	1456	463	2	2898	119	278	3491	1605	7735	246	53	233
Fairfield, city of	230	330	8	9	151	13675	......	11004	.....	7	919	.....	335	112	15	802	9	46	300	7	229
Liberty	735	56	43	5	546	48870	86	128	.....	1266	303	8	3788	568	176	3259	3159	6504	137	128	161
Lockridge	779	40	62	1	763	31252	2268	146	6	1603	402	6	3107	16	120	3896	1791	6248	457	222	290
Locust Grove, exc. of Batavia	689	96	67	21	505	44690	100	......	.....	1585	328	3	3312	116	221	4671	1950	9294	809	126	209
Penn	905	25	40	.....	699	43571	495	613	4	1166	206	2	3243	22	24	3857	1987	9263	219	44	244
Polk	739	41	112	12	531	42039	......	......	.....	1433	509	17	7125	75	......	4253	......	5555	481	7	146
Round Prairie	700	71	61	7	527	28351	176	375	.....	1756	263	6	3538	75	189	2505	1853	6275	328	164	193
Walnut	632	29	17	.....	558	19777	50	......	.....	1212	290	2	3013	13	37	3489	711	2378	136	104	209
Total	9448	994	633	91	7428	523261	4233	32461	20	18326	5706	72	59083	1418	1519	46289	21816	79972	5228	1130	2762

JOHNSON COUNTY.

	1	2	3	4	5	6	7	8	9	10	11	12	13	14	15	16	17	18	19	20	21
Big Grove	514	26	67	4	532	27110	......	56	.....	1999	145	2	2455	2	4	1623	510	2304	68	16	187
Cedar	649	25	62	3	707	27720	2640	......	5	2345	795	4	3538	23	18	3060	2994	7320	225	114	225
Clear Creek	456	4	34	.....	447	26369	10300	......	.....	1284	271	7	3095	2	53	2481	144	668	15	7	152
Coralville, town of	56	9	27	11	176	2525	......	120	.....	206	502	.....	512	52	......	300	90	400	90	6	43
Fremont	763	37	34	.....	650	39797	100	......	.....	2141	104	18	3374	1	24	2732	3151	5000	18	2	59
Graham	693	39	47	6	575	39200	215	90	6	1848	385	5	5936	8	87	3099	3205	1021	50	7	176
Hardin	583	27	63	4	586	27770	5	......	.....	1620	406	.....	3173	5	30	2816	157	405	9	10	181
Iowa City, city of	412	34	77	16	282	3700	......	4005	.....	27	......	.....	876	7	3	886	......	......	......	......	285
Iowa City, additions to	41	.....	9	.....	68	5315	......	905	.....	8	3	.....	117	15	45	82	......	......	......	......	125
Jefferson	408	18	40	2	412	9720	......	......	2	825	88	.....	1676	57	207	1036	460	2505	50	15	209
Liberty	583	10	22	.....	431	18063	471	......	.....	1062	127	6	2400	3	28	1766	704	1965	83	53	158
Lincoln	441	22	39	2	429	23509	......	......	.....	931	148	6	2495	11	399	1945	562	2430	77	......	127
Lucas exc. of Iowa City, additions, and Coralville	702	18	63	5	716	42527	2550	36715	3	1160	283	22	3057	168	679	1804	81	408	21	20	294

JOHNSON COUNTY.—Continued.

Names of townships, towns, and cities.	Number of horses of all ages.	Number of horses sold for export in 1874.	Number of mules and asses.	Number of same sold for export in 1874.	Number of milch cows.	Number of pounds of butter made in 1874.	Number of pounds of cheese made in 1874 not in factory.	Number of gallons of milk sold in 1874.	Number of work oxen.	Number of all other cattle.	No. of cattle slaughtered or sold for slaughter in 1874.	Number of thorough-bred short-horns.	HOGS.				SHEEP.				Number of dogs.
													Number on hand.	Number of Berkshires.	Number of Poland-China.	No. slaughtered or sold for slaughter in 1874.	Number on hand.	Number of pounds of wool obtained in 1874.	No. slaughtered or sold for slaughter in 1874.	Number killed by dogs in 1874.	
Madison	472	20	49	3	308	23665	224	....	......	1485	270	20	4477	13	39	2464	289	2774	44	40	157
Monroe	542	2	55	......	503	29070	450	....	......	1051	221	1	3662	4	2	2329	350	1459	22	56	230
Newport	302	......	19	......	353	21770	....	....	......	1649	48	......	834	....	....	552	58	515	....	....	108
Oxford	599	11	33	......	649	31110	300	115	......	1234	293	1	2442	52	....	2330	90	252	2	1	201
Penn	338	19	31	5	388	17590	....	....	......	735	88	3	2053	59	140	1166	181	815	....	1	141
Pleasant Valley	432	......	51	......	359	21617	1700	....	......	820	148	......	2382	5	70	1948	152	620	25	8	124
Scott	715	21	35	2	479	47230	160	....	......	1435	350	2	3238	66	725	3157	3245	3858	158	....	137
Sharon	878	79	36	4	839	54690	660	....	......	1761	551	......	5725	46	43	4115	2744	10337	458	119	231
Union	593	25	67	2	650	39325	....	....	......	1830	558	20	3845	15	51	3034	371	2991	115	32	140
Washington	714	60	16	3	798	35225	245	....	......	1918	262	18	4332	508	1700	3137	2079	8676	260	81	178
Total	11886	506	976	72	11337	614617	20520	42006	16	28374	6046	135	66594	1122	4347	47862	21617	56523	1790	588	3868

JONES COUNTY.

Names of townships, towns, and cities.	Number of horses of all ages.	Number of horses sold for export in 1874.	Number of mules and asses.	Number of same sold for export in 1874.	Number of milch cows.	Number of pounds of butter made in 1874.	Number of pounds of cheese made in 1874 not in factory.	Number of gallons of milk sold in 1874.	Number of work oxen.	Number of all other cattle.	No. of cattle slaughtered or sold for slaughter in 1874.	Number of thorough-bred short-horns.	Hogs: Number on hand.	Hogs: Number of Berkshires.	Hogs: Number of Poland-China.	Hogs: No. slaughtered or sold for slaughter in 1874.	Sheep: Number on hand.	Sheep: Number of pounds of wool obtained in 1874.	Sheep: No. slaughtered or sold for slaughter in 1874.	Sheep: Number killed by dogs in 1874.	Number of dogs.
Anamosa, town of	167	......	9	......	....	....	....	....	......	....	....	......	....	....	....	....	....	....	....	....	....
Cass	637	50	35	3	739	53905	2025	7910	8	1155	283	5	2655	180	166	2908	68	294	46	....	355
Castle Grove	603	15	13	......	742	32145	....	33870	......	1314	....	1	4864	....	2	2378	915	2084	3	....	133
Clay	574	10	34	......	656	31154	....	5815	2	1298	364	......	2574	66	109	2358	1053	3616	226	18	175
Fairview, exc. of Anamosa and Strawberry Hill	561	9	26	2	592	39611	745	54	......	1389	212	31	4962	69	97	2698	603	2693	59	38	189
Greenfield	967	89	38	4	838	76110	....	....	......	....	....	......	8723	6552	1449	4960	626	2483	237	35	169
Hale	752	18	31	2	778	48570	....	9632	......	1224	284	16	4910	1	140	2847	258	1198	43	28	132
Jackson	603	4	8	......	798	43173	....	....	......	1061	197	......	3284	25	54	2205	152	1189	35	5	125
Madison	506	10	30	......	656	25565	....	21006	......	817	399	1	2158	5	59	2258	336	596	14	4	103
Monticello, exc. of town	721	67	8	......	915	46592	13256	88597	......	2047	254	......	4198	50	15	2418	313	1255	81	9	174
Monticello, town of	222	94	1	1	141	10790	....	3095	......	34	505	......	223	52	2	617	14	....	25	1	90
Oxford	647	39	32	14	679	47453	....	....	7	1606	523	31	3685	44	173	3728	151	270	5	5	170

Richland	526	36	29	.....	645	18825	400	32767	.....	1644	175	8	2305	98	28	....	186	848	9	20	136
Rome	591	7	32	1	720	47667	....	2782	.....	1211	68	7	2967	427	493	3139	500	1710	21	5	107
Scotch Grove	537	76	32	3	605	37115	....	24060	.....	1359	541	.....	4068	8	65	3060	157	1588	193	19	142
Strawberry Hill, town of	....	.....	.....	.....	17	830	....	100	.....	1856	473	1	13	....	....	4	....	....	....	....	9
Washington	555	2	19	.....	432	16869	....	....	1378	25	....	.....	3030	....	....	3230	678	2144	....	284	174
Wayne	761	28	11	.....	1078	59876	12900	34109	.....	1774	248	1	3129	20	24	3447	1320	5599	8	....	198
Wyoming, exc. of town	554	53	43	23	737	39571	100	23746	.....	1071	873	9	3104	29	65	3151	413	1488	27	24	170
Wyoming, town of	121	5	4	.....	96	6365	....	2165	.....	....	....	.....	211	27	44	92	....	....	....	....	....
Total	10605	612	435	53	11864	682177	29426	289708	1395	20885	5399	111	61050	7653	2985	43403	7743	29055	1032	495	2751

KEOKUK COUNTY.

Adams	648	45	43	3	584	49622	896	....	.....	1991	279	19	2663	221	596	2556	196	1084	91	9	156
Benton	779	.....	84	.....	624	31900	425	....	.....	1530	385	3	3320	94	448	2827	892	3974	83	99	232
Clear Creek	704	15	29	4	518	28435	....	....	2	1621	184	1	5508	....	1772	3381	488	1313	31	9	193
English River	647	86	57	30	737	55782	1750	338	5	1727	285	5	3225	71	173	3403	408	1532	339	32	149
German	931	38	20	.....	777	44569	400	....	.....	2324	534	.....	4608	60	174	4143	811	2407	242	108	306
Jackson	786	7	50	.....	543	35930	30	....	.....	982	126	.....	3730	....	....	2889	2671	2350	119	78	279
Keota, town of	85	.....	6	16	99	536	....	270	.....	....	17	.....	131	....	1	380	....	....	....	....	....
Lafayette, exc. of Keota	721	34	48	3	571	38330	1710	1951	6	1592	226	31	4146	357	1503	3078	70	220	88	13	158
Lancaster	841	25	58	5	647	39030	570	....	4	1156	248	2	3506	90	365	3206	721	2673	104	53	241
Liberty	779	80	43	11	722	46005	35	....	8	1690	358	13	3044	309	2396	2799	579	2443	294	68	211
Prairie	446	63	32	6	499	35575	100	....	.....	847	63	.....	2620	22	1	1988	2719	11312	128	23	185
Richland, exc. of town	695	21	26	.....	516	31782	....	....	.....	1575	193	.....	4689	66	4	3470	1129	3582	104	38	205
Richland, town of	176	8	12	5	112	7325	....	614	.....	178	72	2	655	190	16	648	441	131	34	....	36
Sigourney, exc. of town	317	17	18	.....	451	30822	530	12239	.....	759	497	.....	1640	27	46	1462	150	793	30	17	116
Sigourney, town of	205	2	2	.....	152	7301	....	2435	.....	125	88	.....	219	2	....	1087	....	....	....	....	104
Steady Run	599	.....	55	1	506	31567	83	35	4	1649	505	4	4273	76	785	2551	1311	3476	239	120	142
Van Buren	582	50	24	2	658	54270	....	....	.....	1843	221	.....	2784	26	229	3051	346	1448	....	22	203
Warren	397	9	30	.....	417	25379	....	....	.....	1083	301	1	1975	107	240	1694	498	1480	83	13	104
Washington	623	64	12	.....	600	50305	100	7150	8	903	264	.....	2390	....	62	2103	802	287[illegible]	92	31	194
Total	10961	564	649	86	9733	644465	6629	25032	37	23575	4846	81	55126	1718	8801	46716	14232	43091	2101	732	3214

KOSSUTH COUNTY.

Algona, exc. of town	269	.....	7	.....	371	25715	400	....	11	680	59	4	237	1	33	322	108	....	....	....	71
Algona, town of	199	.....	6	.....	157	1100	....	....	16	41	92	.....	404	....	12	162	134	....	....	....	96
Cresco	301	.....	7	.....	352	22555	1350	....	40	761	430	5	658	....	....	476	44	150	....	8	110
Fenton	79	.....	.....	.....	79	6220	....	....	15	122	4	2	46	....	....	67	58	137	2	3	30
Greenwood	90	.....	.....	.....	207	16150	290	....	57	325	25	.....	115	1	....	91	40	138	4	....	49
Irvington	288	2	2	.....	313	17400	810	....	28	813	98	.....	268	39	10	306	223	970	....	7	76
Lotts Creek	106	.....	8	.....	133	8850	150	....	7	122	4	.....	88	1	1	125	90	210	7	....	43

KOSSUTH COUNTY.—Continued.

NAMES OF TOWNSHIPS, TOWNS, AND CITIES.	Number of horses of all ages.	Number of horses sold for export in 1874.	Number of mules and asses.	Number of same sold for export in 1874.	Number of milch cows.	Number of pounds of butter made in 1874.	Number of pounds of cheese made in 1874 not in factory.	Number of gallons of milk sold in 1874.	Number of work oxen.	Number of all other cattle.	No. of cattle slaughtered or sold for slaughter in 1874.	Number of thorough-bred short-horns.	HOGS.				SHEEP.				Number of dogs.
													Number on hand.	Number of Berk-shires.	Number of Poland-China.	No. slaughtered or sold for slaughter in 1874.	Number on hand.	Number of pounds of wool obtained in 1874.	No. slaughtered or sold for slaughter in 1874.	Number killed by dogs in 1874.	
Portland	327	4	9	......	371	21320	....	....	17	698	58	......	233	....	2	291	....	....	....	....	77
Wesley	89	1	8	......	125	9200	....	....	39	226	27	1	108	2	....	90	....	....	....	....	48
Total	1748	7	47	......	2108	128510	3000	....	234	3788	797	12	2157	44	58	1930	697	1605	13	18	600

LEE COUNTY.

NAMES OF TOWNSHIPS, TOWNS, AND CITIES.	Number of horses of all ages.	Number of horses sold for export in 1874.	Number of mules and asses.	Number of same sold for export in 1874.	Number of milch cows.	Number of pounds of butter made in 1874.	Number of pounds of cheese made in 1874 not in factory.	Number of gallons of milk sold in 1874.	Number of work oxen.	Number of all other cattle.	No. of cattle slaughtered or sold for slaughter in 1874.	Number of thorough-bred short-horns.	Hogs: Number on hand.	Hogs: Number of Berk-shires.	Hogs: Number of Poland-China.	Hogs: No. slaughtered or sold for slaughter in 1874.	Sheep: Number on hand.	Sheep: Number of pounds of wool obtained in 1874.	Sheep: No. slaughtered or sold for slaughter in 1874.	Sheep: Number killed by dogs in 1874.	Number of dogs.
Cedar	856	72	157	39	587	40425	....	10	......	1230	311	15	6553	76	76	5150	3258	12084	1203	29	188
Charleston	672	8	59	......	576	37730	....	....	2	1260	124	2	1775	88	2	1567	587	1951	52	83	275
Denmark	518	14	19	......	552	30950	60950	27810	......	786	310	12	1617	30	321	1156	1164	2755	110	99	117
Des Moines	652	10	106	1	559	31610	40	400	......	1433	385	46	3073	232	13	1985	896	3310	566	133	229
Fort Madison, city of	202	......	15	......	213	....	....	3640	......	....	735	......	709	5	1	2856	....	....	....	....	388
Franklin	808	83	41	19	726	40055	1522	365	......	2146	324	......	2772	25	....	3060	776	2703	150	93	339
Green Bay	424	2	81	......	538	19320	6040	....	2	1957	200	1	1616	43	16	875	185	265	18	26	138
Harrison	660	71	71	27	590	34403	406	100	......	1657	750	7	3603	146	19	3699	3034	12892	975	137	193
Jackson, exc. of Keokuk	453	9	51	......	459	21128	150	235	3	784	182	15	1154	75	70	1323	218	1156	116	71	245
Jefferson	662	50	69	11	516	23990	....	....	......	1402	402	2	2535	19	22	1565	1093	1005	154	67	239
Keokuk, city of	811	......	71	......	709	25	....	43400	......	194	65	......	943	....	....	35	164	....	....	....	903
Madison, exc. of Fort Madison	87	6	8	2	65	5230	....	125	......	39	11	......	360	1	51	996	....	....	....	....	46
Marion	931	82	44	7	757	34565	20	....	......	1691	384	2	4854	....	3	3941	1929	9101	729	147	234
Montrose, exc. of town	638	49	71	16	493	41143	....	37	......	1228	537	8	1876	49	522	1675	103	451	7	30	208
Montrose, town of	44	......	4	......	37	....	....	....	......	7	....	......	67	....	....	42	....	....	....	....	37
Pleasant Ridge	691	48	46	5	646	37480	6100	690	......	1424	240	5	3565	131	114	2239	1958	6999	245	71	180
Van Buren	458	14	52	4	372	22050	50	....	......	930	110	2	1461	12	1	1379	929	3055	200	77	226
Washington	704	54	57	3	656	47443	23230	7037	2	1544	389	1	3972	148	231	2238	2196	3654	156	91	178
West Point, exc. of town	484	9	44	......	532	26892	....	30	......	860	221	9	1375	53	20	1731	369	1372	62	53	207

West Point, town of	89	13	7	2	68	2280	....	255	......	20	....	......	119	....	....	137	....	....	....	....	72
Total	10844	594	1073	136	9651	496719	98508	84134	9	20592	5680	127	43999	1133	1482	37729	18859	62753	4743	1207	4640

LINN COUNTY.

Bertram	475	14	41	3	368	17779	....	34	......	1421	461	......	4073	18	30	2307	331	1177	53	62	162
Boulder	644	15	17	1	641	28935	2460	185	2	863	212	16	2506	86	108	2036	178	521	4	15	171
Brown	780	24	27	2	664	51337	4635	145	2	1759	367	12	6122	104	129	3759	731	3615	193	65	167
Buffalo	389	2	17	......	405	33824	60	....	6	873	222	......	1855	36	2	1832	65	189	....	1	121
Cedar Rapids, city of	461	12	30	......	403	16320	....	19726	......	21	10	......	156	....	....	250	10	....	....	....	348
Clinton	658	9	35	......	803	57812	....	19136	......	2415	179	......	3643	7	24	2632	22	162	....	4	195
College, exc. of Western	684	5	55	......	565	37064	....	42	......	1509	428	24	4251	7	59	2117	28	133	50	8	208
Fairfax	744	......	41	......	735	52872	5172	90	......	1353	366	2	4311	21	7	2587	129	417	6	....	131
Fayette	450	12	17	9	436	40875	70	....	......	571	223	2	6473	48	136	1915	334	1919	71	45	75
Franklin, exc. of Mt. Vernon and Lisbon	687	6	29	......	802	67170	150	....	......	1816	351	2	3821	73	30	3361	1983	7914	214	48	247
Grant	553	34	20	4	367	51814	350	....	......	1106	276	2	1836	5	104	1772	112	442	13	6	135
Jackson	687	11	20	......	780	36520	630	....	......	1570	147	6	4814	....	18	2912	346	1122	26	3	200
Linn	779	17	9	......	821	58876	250	5	......	2075	434	20	7415	....	43	3418	796	3965	154	85	177
Lisbon, town of	60	1	......	......	69	6200	....	....	......	3	1	......	139	....	....	258	4	20	....	....	44
Maine	939	9	49	......	904	94070	1150	....	......	1807	366	17	4494	8	134	3850	58	143	....	2	232
Marion, exc. of city	1338	68	61	9	1463	115055	3204	1200	......	1834	640	1	5051	....	162	6090	834	3236	12	7	41
Marion, city of	151	......	26	......	152	550	100	....	......	....	....	......	42	....	....	11	....	....	....	....	41
Monroe	695	24	24	2	658	36634	50	....	......	1109	406	...	2061	28	22	2474	403	1426	92	42	218
Mt. Vernon, town of	138	17	7	......	124	10075	....	3500	......	77	61	......	343	....	....	310	30	....	....	....	37
Otter Creek	669	28	26	3	531	56645	200	....	2	1246	344	2	2776	44	274	2637	413	2296	318	24	175
Putnam	431	13	45	2	382	19836	....	....	......	1003	137	1	2007	46	43	1432	221	1240	53	21	147
Rapids, exc. of C. Rapids	576	70	39	4	576	44587	110	37785	10	926	574	8	1741	113	218	1615	200	2186	181	35	212
Spring Grove	516	16	48	......	541	39764	120	....	......	1040	81	10	1769	18	62	1632	138	762	4	26	171
Washington	629	21	55	9	512	31945	....	....	4	1267	400	......	2665	5	11	2481	597	2656	173	61	177
Western, town of	107	32	14	6	74	5310	....	770	......	121	....	......	621	....	2	394	....	....	....	....	18
Total	14240	460	752	54	13776	1011869	18711	82618	26	27785	6686	125	74985	667	1618	54082	7963	35541	1617	560	3850

LOUISA COUNTY.

Columbus City, exc. of Columbus City and Columbus Junction	1013	133	30	6	1020	53683	172	....	......	3085	1057	15	6292	44	248	6052	956	4361	264	48	230
Columbus City, town of	4	6	......	......	14	1200	....	....	......	17	13	6	246	93	27	91	....	....	....	....	35
Columbus Junction, town of	100	32	2	......	92	3400	....	2130	......	34	7	......	337	....	1	136	....	....	....	....	31
Concord, exc. of Fredonia	488	46	52	10	407	24770	20	....	......	1358	502	12	2196	83	749	2578	284	1734	128	57	135
Eliot	286	18	9	2	258	12420	30	....	2	797	432	9	1619	18	425	981	134	514	115	9	78

LOUISA COUNTY.—Continued.

Names of townships, towns, and cities.	Number of horses of all ages.	Number of horses sold for export in 1874.	Number of mules and asses.	Number of same sold for export in 1874.	Number of milch cows.	Number of pounds of butter made in 1874.	Number of pounds of cheese made in 1874 not in factory.	Number of gallons of milk sold in 1874.	Number of work oxen.	Number of all other cattle.	No. of cattle slaughtered or sold for slaughter in 1874.	Number of thorough-bred short-horns.	Hogs.				Sheep.				Number of dogs.
													Number on hand.	Number of Berk-shires.	Number of Poland-China.	No. slaughtered or sold for slaughter in 1874.	Number on hand.	Number of pounds of wool obtained in 1874.	No. slaughtered or sold for slaughter in 1874.	Number killed by dogs in 1874.	
Elm Grove	513	13	39	......	460	32750	30	90	......	1857	338	......	2555	25	213	3675	168	640	17	24	103
Fredonia, town of	43	10	3	7	37	1850	....	....	......	30	3	......	85	3	46	106	25	100	5	3	20
Grandview	886	44	63	......	668	31313	15	622	2	1627	1479	......	3672	....	69	3632	148	570	25	10	196
Jefferson	549	15	36	2	454	16932	100	....	......	2013	142	1	3273	1218	8	1684	287	1195	34	1	154
Marshall	582	24	25	56	427	26376	....	....	......	1368	353	7	5186	90	239	3007	154	834	52	41	163
Morning Sun, exc. of town	732	57	30	12	483	39099	....	720	......	1664	831	1	4545	1447	1713	3704	780	1799	196	36	137
Morning Sun, town of	....	......	......	......	....	....	....	....	......	....	....	......	....	....	....	....	......	....	....	....	....
Oakland	454	54	14	......	289	13719	....	....	......	1629	189	1	3670	20	475	2148	287	1152	34	65	124
Port Louisa	488	23	36	......	475	16720	250	....	......	1234	233	2	1379	15	2	1951	235	840	52	2	147
Union	451	26	23	1	416	20775	....	....	......	1962	445	......	3676	5	125	2098	45	112	....	2	103
Wapello, exc. of town	797	3	30	578	....	47675	295	100	......	2724	2091	36	3646	12	109	3660	426	2146	89	48	196
Wapello, town of	171	8	11	4	156	5092	25	1609	4	298	160	......	1056	39	17	376	57	439	12	15	61
Total	7557	513	403	678	5656	347774	937	5271	8	21697	3275	90	43433	3112	4466	35882	3986	16436	1023	361	1913

LUCAS COUNTY.

Names of townships, towns, and cities.	Number of horses of all ages.	Number of horses sold for export in 1874.	Number of mules and asses.	Number of same sold for export in 1874.	Number of milch cows.	Number of pounds of butter made in 1874.	Number of pounds of cheese made in 1874 not in factory.	Number of gallons of milk sold in 1874.	Number of work oxen.	Number of all other cattle.	No. of cattle slaughtered or sold for slaughter in 1874.	Number of thorough-bred short-horns.	Hogs: Number on hand.	Hogs: Number of Berk-shires.	Hogs: Number of Poland-China.	Hogs: No. slaughtered or sold for slaughter in 1874.	Sheep: Number on hand.	Sheep: Number of pounds of wool obtained in 1874.	Sheep: No. slaughtered or sold for slaughter in 1874.	Sheep: Number killed by dogs in 1874.	Number of dogs.
Benton	487	37	36	......	446	47680	4372	....	......	795	181	......	3742	3	101	2754	652	3609	108	86	113
Cedar	488	28	59	4	544	26063	5053	325	8	1970	496	2	4077	130	592	2411	1496	4588	29	56	162
Chariton, exc. of city	573	16	37	......	580	39870	814	3561	2	1207	211	8	3955	49	115	2204	720	3431	39	22	162
Chariton, city of	278	5	22	1	196	12450	190	2885	......	21	80	......	435	23	5	467	....	....	....	....	111
English	427	9	46	......	534	26046	310	....	4	1531	225	......	2606	3	82	2858	437	2538	192	14	159
Jackson	388	......	36	......	405	25015	....	....	6	1053	199	1	3247	108	215	2564	603	1792	390	61	130
Liberty	490	9	20	......	443	27455	....	....	......	1173	227	1	2644	2	9	1700	456	2592	119	60	140
Otter Creek	534	45	32	6	386	23602	221	....	......	1186	222	......	2965	....	....	1965	849	3135	72	27	148
Pleasant	435	35	58	8	389	26350	25	....	......	812	110	1	1878	69	215	1657	485	1312	79	29	134
Union	495	2	35	......	556	31779	250	20	......	1463	109	4	3439	38	....	2445	730	2269	608	62	118
Warren	686	20	65	4	637	41082	3010	60	1	1661	914	1	4820	237	96	3640	475	297	553	8	174

Washington	622	12	41	......	580	39365	200	125	......	1308	137	......	6100	....	130	2947	569	1564	42	19	162
White Breast	472	2	37	......	407	35540	200	....	4	1268	358	22	2068	36	3	2130	397	1256	69	13	123
Total	6375	220	524	23	6103	402297	14645	6976	25	15448	3469	40	41976	698	1564	29742	7869	28383	2300	457	1836

LYON COUNTY.

Dale	102	......	6	......	108	3725	......	....	49	96	11	......	83	....	....	176	....	....	....	....	25
Doon	85	1	3	......	70	5235	400	....	34	143	14	1	98	20	1	196	50	450	5	....	31
Grant	37	......	1	......	37	....	....	....	22	48	....	......	31	....	....	26	....	....	....	....	23
Larchwood	44	......	......	......	43	....	....	....	22	34	5	......	47	....	....	46	7	15	....	....	18
Lyon	138	50	8	9	189	10520	452	243	63	80	229	......	202	....	....	209	129	345	30	....	60
Rock	70	5	2	......	61	1850	....	....	21	43	13	......	48	....	18	46	....	....	....	....	25
Total	476	56	20	9	508	21330	852	243	211	444	272	1	509	20	19	699	186	810	35	....	182

MADISON COUNTY.

Crawford	524	3	65	2	533	22904	....	....	......	1542	177	......	2898	5	35	2208	467	1442	30	28	172
Douglas	720	......	119	......	425	22485	....	....	4	1524	301	2	2462	2	2	2752	130	1589	17	18	178
Earlham, town of	....	......	......	......	....	....	....	....	......	....	....	......	....	....	....	....	....	....	....	....	....
Grand River	519	3	22	......	518	26580	123	....	......	1146	251	1	2157	269	965	2171	645	2806	110	26	126
Jackson	449	12	37	2	373	16850	....	....	6	1301	406	......	4451	2	205	3413	337	1935	10	41	117
Jefferson	599	1	28	......	489	41596	722	....	2	1064	95	......	5668	6	....	2419	512	1863	272	14	174
Lee	388	13	7	4	355	14670	....	....	......	1003	188	......	1963	....	10	1923	802	2505	1790	24	89
Lincoln	618	6	50	......	508	38833	50	....	2	1581	280	7	5572	77	290	2700	2621	9458	620	37	173
Madison, exc. of Earlham	570	2	59	......	471	18218	....	....	......	1155	284	5	6414	72	272	2681	534	2207	20	60	127
Monroe	399	21	61	3	402	17610	4400	....	4	1171	199	5	4684	....	....	3062	681	2631	6	30	114
Ohio	506	40	23	17	507	33385	....	....	2	1023	356	......	2746	39	32	2211	594	1485	59	10	152
Penn, exc. of Earlham	547	11	33	......	380	23870	400	200	7	2057	834	2	8401	117	103	5677	3051	10145	3078	215	120
Scott	579	8	72	......	560	39758	....	....	4	1757	483	47	3537	6	107	2627	615	1897	18	24	189
South	477	......	51	......	411	21450	....	....	......	1811	278	3	3155	30	2	2737	856	2715	14	7	136
Union	609	20	46	5	444	25227	125	10965	6	963	311	8	3277	71	192	4754	799	4564	75	108	203
Walnut	423	......	16	......	431	22251	....	....	9	957	378	1	3664	....	216	2586	365	914	14	11	125
Webster	432	11	18	2	407	18929	210	....	6	968	160	......	1424	....	....	1812	194	1671	111	23	124
Winterset, city of	358	......	21	......	210	21461	....	2163	2	3	5	1	362	....	30	10004	14	....	....	....	92
Total	8717	151	728	35	7424	426077	6030	13328	54	21025	4986	82	62835	696	2461	55717	13237	49827	6244	676	2411

MAHASKA COUNTY.

NAMES OF TOWNSHIPS, TOWNS AND CITIES	Number of horses of all ages.	Number of horses sold for export in 1874.	Number of mules and asses.	Number of same sold for export in 1874.	Number of milch cows.	Number of pounds of butter made in 1874.	Number of pounds of cheese made in 1874 not in factory.	Number of gallons of milk sold in 1874.	Number of work oxen.	Number of all other cattle.	No. of cattle slaughtered or sold for slaughter in 1874.	Number of thorough-bred short horns.	HOGS.				SHEEP.				Number of dogs.
													Number on hand.	Number of Berk-shires.	Number of Poland-China.	No. slaughtered or sold for slaughter in 1874.	Number on hand.	Number of pounds of wool obtained in 1874.	No. slaughtered or sold for slaughter in 1874.	Number killed by dogs in 1874.	
Adams	637	45	43	3	515	30960	....	25	....	1198	467	6	3727	37	83	3814	1041	5149	7	44	133
Beacon, town of	50	....	18	....	59	4740	....	....	....	9	5	....	105	4	....	40	....	....	....	....	71
Black Oak	608	2	44	....	474	32545	330	....	....	1572	407	3	4015	79	259	2674	477	2245	24	59	173
Cedar	789	7	83	....	581	45350	....	6209	....	1891	257	10	3160	44	34	2987	4345	13831	930	98	207
Des Moines	690	164	44	2	526	38685	....	400	4	1600	651	8	6994	19	13	3563	3454	5220	724	103	217
Harrison	745	19	56	....	603	43215	....	277	....	1642	398	1	5140	5	100	3800	3909	15647	1036	155	236
Jefferson	745	11	91	....	670	38485	40	500	4	2238	434	5	5808	39	68	5171	1444	3524	92	35	212
Madison	590	20	53	2	568	36447	40	6484	....	1853	439	4	8073	7	3	4152	4148	4662	47	88	194
Monroe	816	81	43	2	732	56075	250	6194	7	2582	701	2	12326	22	235	8563	3924	6138	623	52	251
New Sharon, town of	118	23	6	2	73	6673	....	740	....	43	6	15	146	....	....	170	....	....	....	....	26
Oskaloosa, exc. of Oskaloosa and Beacon	1592	53	60	....	1442	121444	190	92324	....	3148	937	90	9386	580	432	7613	6033	21757	953	201	346
Oskaloosa, city of	412	25	30	....	335	22885	....	9965	....	22	7	....	680	....	....	612	....	....	....	....	250
Pleasant Grove	564	6	30	1	427	30670	....	6575	2	868	137	....	2140	....	15	1930	802	3216	19	21	136
Prairie, exc. of New Sharon.	738	46	62	....	1165	63852	50	4808	....	1753	666	7	3639	73	42	5044	903	5745	137	51	177
Richland	720	22	44	....	605	38615	175	....	....	1591	403	3	5202	131	184	3141	3203	3998	229	81	186
Scott	730	26	28	2	473	39420	40	....	4	1549	159	3	4499	22	33	2240	1159	4213	145	73	173
Union	634	13	59	4	605	38362	....	10314	....	1007	124	13	2582	65	526	2374	431	1498	24	83	156
White Oak	694	42	22	7	636	37911	....	6581	2	1494	312	5	3497	63	555	2865	2965	6541	165	84	264
Total	11874	605	816	25	10489	726334	1115	151396	23	26060	6510	175	81120	1190	2582	60753	38238	109384	5155	1228	3408

MARION COUNTY.

Clay	653	48	55	3	553	39615	225	....	2	1540	226	2	7554	196	176	3921	2547	15594	....	....	....
Dallas	580	....	57	....	477	20221	176	65	7	1254	197	1	3954	83	58	6808	1089	3636	....	....	....
Franklin	645	71	64	6	589	34926	300	....	13	1687	378	15	3413	63	111	3067	701	3697	....	....	....
Indiana	723	24	49	....	575	35405	....	....	....	1283	220	2	4352	4	25	3661	2528	....	....	....	....

Knoxville, exc. of town	2163	2	103	.....	1133	79943	....	1000	.....	3563	50	8	10910	31	26	5781	3817	....	....	....	....
Knoxville, town of	293	.....	33	.....	185	15570	....	3555	.....	105	....	.....	727	....	87	772	9	47	....	....	128
Lake Prairie, exc. of Pella	1354	41	99	.....	902	80135	5370	2000	.....	2481	1167	.....	8764	57	96	7455	197	2885	211	14	522
Liberty	748	3	79	.....	526	39221	....	....	.....	876	53	.....	3502	....	22	4140	1035	3461	....	....	....
Pella, city of	189	.....	15	.....	189	7223	....	4930	.....	....	....	.....	477	....	....	3229	217	625	....	....	217
Perry	237	.....	22	.....	182	9925	....	....	.....	417	25	.....	1135	2	26	893	515	1946	33	41	98
Pleasant Grove, exc. of Pleasantville	901	40	47	.....	664	52525	....	....	2	2169	383	.....	5262	7	59	....	....	....	....	....	....
Pleasantville, town of	....	.....	.....	.....	....	....	....	....	.....	....	....	.....	....	....	....	....	....	....	....	....	....
Polk	452	.....	52	.....	319	14555	100	....	3	582	121	2	4540	....	....	1905	2987	3206	316	26	140
Red Rock	635	3	44	2	411	29045	....	15	2	769	70	.....	4000	320	116	2496	1619	6173	836	190	235
Summit	812	20	39	3	549	36780	325	354	.....	1792	754	1	4946	94	63	4485	609	3451	465	33	257
Swan	801	17	23	.....	360	15325	105	....	2	902	303	1	3333	93	447	1838	2554	5114	553	72	139
Union	458	2	19	.....	305	20725	100	....	.....	1230	227	.....	2933	2	60	2628	916	4044	83	41	128
Washington	684	13	70	.....	566	35911	....	....	.....	1905	639	16	3900	106	402	4597	1364	5712	912	59	184
Total	12328	284	870	14	8485	567050	6701	11984	31	22555	4813	48	73702	1058	1774	57676	22704	59591	3409	472	2048

MARSHALL COUNTY.

Albion, town of	135	8	4	.....	96	6576	75	440	.....	48	84	.....	465	57	60	269	....	....	6	....	37
Bangor	494	6	28	.....	348	21995	498	....	4	742	146	7	4108	65	10	1976	351	949	26	3	120
Eden	421	.....	32	.....	353	27950	50	....	.....	574	74	1	4419	24	225	2114	2395	10	....	2	117
Green Castle	622	.....	58	.....	467	35940	....	830	.....	1097	178	4	2206	23	70	2125	237	927	45	6	114
Iowa, exc. of Albion	409	6	4	.....	254	19125	....	50	2	884	197	6	3497	14	227	1975	420	1591	113	3	78
Jefferson	624	59	13	4	451	28580	573	....	4	982	113	1	3275	14	83	2144	....	59	2	6	170
LeGrand	759	8	23	.....	597	60950	500	....	.....	959	252	.....	3606	155	10	2727	690	3000	500	100	172
Liberty	525	41	33	2	423	39450	1425	....	.....	1067	158	5	3043	....	....	2016	277	1130	72	5	104
Liscomb, exc. of town	514	26	15	.....	373	28676	310	380	.....	805	183	.....	1981	18	82	1528	129	344	13	4	111
Liscomb, town of	112	.....	.....	.....	68	4970	....	270	.....	50	57	.....	268	13	....	179	....	....	....	....	21
Logan	375	1	14	.....	293	17675	....	....	.....	710	41	.....	2557	9	523	1291	....	....	....	....	88
Marietta	657	6	24	.....	518	45450	200	....	6	1574	215	25	3449	10	17	2783	385	565	5	....	146
Marion	587	59	10	.....	528	34612	352	1757	.....	1194	200	.....	2865	227	315	2073	127	596	18	6	130
Marshall, exc. of Marshalltown	293	32	2	.....	235	16699	....	19963	2	738	5414	5	5793	1588	537	5192	1344	760	50	3	64
Marshalltown, city of	512	76	32	3	326	17299	....	18728	.....	109	130	6	750	45	81	1128	20	100	1	15	247
Minerva	314	154	8	6	546	53850	....	....	2	1387	267	1	2644	1	21	2826	458	2265	38	....	140
State Center, exc. of town	501	19	27	.....	455	33580	....	65	.....	1181	334	3	2414	152	740	1821	55	....	....	....	101
State Center, town of	154	5	2	21	72	3240	....	2825	.....	10	17	.....	222	13	16	304	....	....	....	....	67
Taylor	408	20	14	2	371	19554	....	21003	4	663	249	6	1816	22	29	1338	....	....	....	....	107
Timber Creek	561	25	7	.....	389	37035	100	....	.....	810	148	.....	2107	14	24	1641	135	670	41	1	104
Vienna	668	39	14	.....	464	32655	300	....	4	770	136	3	2282	73	140	1589	....	....	....	....	162
Washington	637	18	48	3	508	38957	700	....	2	1213	356	28	2786	55	108	2470	39	283	10	....	102
Total	10282	608	412	41	8135	625418	5083	66311	30	17567	8949	101	56553	2592	3318	41509	7062	13249	940	154	2502

MILLS COUNTY.

NAMES OF TOWNSHIPS, TOWNS, AND CITIES.	Number of horses of all ages.	Number of horses sold for export in 1874.	Number of mules and asses.	Number of same sold for export in 1874.	Number of milch cows.	Number of pounds of butter made in 1874.	Number of pounds of cheese made in 1874 not in factory.	Number of gallons of milk sold in 1874.	Number of work oxen.	Number of all other cattle.	No. of cattle slaughtered or sold for slaughter in 1874.	Number of thorough-bred short-horns.	HOGS. Number on hand.	HOGS. Number of Berkshires.	HOGS. Number of Poland-China.	HOGS. No. slaughtered or sold for slaughter in 1874.	SHEEP. Number on hand.	SHEEP. Number of pounds of wool obtained in 1874.	SHEEP. No. slaughtered or sold for slaughter in 1874.	SHEEP. Number killed by dogs in 1874.	Number of dogs.
Anderson	744	11	53	5	409	27735	......	......	6	1605	435	3	3801	189	998	3681	36	......	......	......	193
Deer Creek	508	......	71	......	489	12387	......	180	......	975	439	......	1831	3	198	1964	12	100	15	1	134
Emerson, town of	56	3	1	......	41	1500	......	......	......	32	23	......	115	......	......	94	50	150	11	......	20
Glenwood, exc. of town	649	......	58	......	434	25930	50	6610	2	2384	971	7	4664	16	52	3306	67	335	12	3	187
Glenwood, town of	118	......	14	......	80	4700	25	875	......	......	......	......	14	......	8	......	......	......	......	......	74
Hastings, town of	42	3	10	1	18	600	......	175	2	103	1	......	326	5	......	226	......	......	......	......	......
Hillsdale, town of	23	......	......	......	12	249	......	208	......	6	......		177	......	......	163	......	......	......	......	6
Indian Creek, exc. of Emerson and Hastings	531	53	53	2	297	17215	......	......	......	1815	699	1	5132	9	38	3172	191	......	......	......	125
Ingraham	426	55	29	5	452	29171	82	60	10	1197	489	27	2948	15	243	2313	19	1005	120	......	134
Lyons	476	1	56	......	452	23246	......	......	......	1193	467	......	3685	......	......	2070	203	719	69	......	193
Malvern, town of	74	2	3	......	33	1280	......	1405	......	31	71	......	170	......	11	102	1	......	......	......	38
Oak	777	66	41	2	783	56165	1610	......	4	2078	237	1	2882	10	224	2382	246	550	83	......	246
Platteville	382	11	46	......	180	8490	150	400	4	1144	91	1	1258	4	59	1581	......	......	......	......	115
Rawles	761	54	42	8	555	25867	175	495	......	1255	243	14	7307	56	184	4432	91	981	......	......	188
St. Mary	161	8	4	......	158	5640	350	......	......	389	121	......	321	20	15	209	24	100	2	......	68
Silver Creek, exc. of Hillsdale and Malvern	730	......	73	......	495	27273	......	20	......	2688	1788	5	12737	154	852	6722	......	......	......	......	173
White Cloud	538	......	53	......	453	21329	4000	......	2	1855	834	1	2412	146	2135	3348	1	......	......	......	114
Total	6996	267	607	23	5341	288776	6442	10428	30	18750	6909	60	49780	627	5017	35765	941	3940	312	4	2008

MITCHELL COUNTY.

NAMES OF TOWNSHIPS, TOWNS, AND CITIES.	Number of horses of all ages.	Number of horses sold for export in 1874.	Number of mules and asses.	Number of same sold for export in 1874.	Number of milch cows.	Number of pounds of butter made in 1874.	Number of pounds of cheese made in 1874 not in factory.	Number of gallons of milk sold in 1874.	Number of work oxen.	Number of all other cattle.	No. of cattle slaughtered or sold for slaughter in 1874.	Number of thorough-bred short-horns.	HOGS. Number on hand.	HOGS. Number of Berkshires.	HOGS. Number of Poland-China.	HOGS. No. slaughtered or sold for slaughter in 1874.	SHEEP. Number on hand.	SHEEP. Number of pounds of wool obtained in 1874.	SHEEP. No. slaughtered or sold for slaughter in 1874.	SHEEP. Number killed by dogs in 1874.	Number of dogs.
Burr Oak	466	......	10	......	359	18525	......	......	6	618	......	......	518	......	......	455	189	815	......	......	57
Cedar	538	3	9	......	553	38160	240	......	20	1066	230	......	534	1	11	595	421	1536	89	11	131
Douglas	290	......	6	......	319	21220	2700	......	20	421	100	......	338	......	70	365	41	369	41	2	81
Jenkins	446	2	4	......	409	28150	350	......	18	770	98	......	537	......	......	667	55	251	......	8	114

Liberty	197	....	9	....	139	9825	....	3200	4	134	....	....	132	....	1	146	321	2140	52	17	51
Lincoln	382	....	4	....	469	28996	....	....	8	808	152	7	565	32	10	626	143	726	8	2	105
Mitchell	604	6	6	....	420	35965	700	900	14	393	156	3	647	8	9	578	459	1365	35	9	131
Newburg	455	....	4	....	362	23765	200	....	20	328	66	2	385	1	1	311	123	553	....	4	129
Osage, exc. of town	174	17	....	....	133	10605	400	4662	4	257	59	22	349	6	96	231	245	487	17	13	51
Osage, town of	320	33	1	....	178	6461	....	3280	....	7	329	....	189	20	8	333	....	....	120	....	86
Otranto	397	....	14	....	409	26093	290	496	56	434	378	3	358	10	....	257	238	917	74	13	110
Rock	410	7	3	....	296	19710	700	....	6	886	65	3	462	....	....	332	353	409	28	....	109
St. Ansgar	484	5	6	....	384	45950	....	200	6	365	85	3	551	....	....	423	339	1685	49	2	110
Stacyville	279	....	2	....	216	13805	....	....	4	321	73	....	254	15	3	309	58	260	7	....	73
Union	407	21	4	....	303	17915	....	....	12	299	62	3	409	....	5	307	76	315	6	2	78
Wayne	273	2	4	....	263	19375	690	....	18	752	45	2	366	2	4	250	17	....	2	3	72
Total	6122	95	86	....	5212	364520	6270	12738	216	7859	1898	48	6594	95	218	6185	3078	11828	528	86	1488

MONONA COUNTY.

Ashton	122	....	....	....	271	4115	....	....	6	773	13	13	742	....	476	479	....	....	....	....	27
Belvidere	164	15	13	4	172	4100	200	....	14	1062	303	....	846	....	202	490	90	500	4	1	53
Center	177	8	10	....	111	9345	....	....	....	515	39	1	566	8	1	340	542	....	....	....	41
Fairview	203	2	....	....	267	13405	....	....	17	908	64	2	570	12	8	422	60	257	....	....	61
Franklin, exc. of Onawa	341	....	16	....	293	12245	200	1025	18	1908	329	1	1542	5	58	1321	550	1415	....	3	132
Grant	217	....	8	....	243	1660	800	....	....	740	....	....	872	3	20	658	569	2880	....	....	72
Jordan	102	2	1	....	93	1550	....	....	4	113	17	....	162	....	64	128	467	3007	....	....	39
Kennebec	305	....	20	....	553	18087	500	....	6	1173	193	10	939	....	....	706	675	2900	108	20	76
Lake	155	....	....	....	214	....	200	....	2	377	21	....	671	21	2	392	11	39	....	....	52
Lincoln	386	....	16	....	425	14001	....	....	50	1183	30	....	2655	....	....	1385	36	102	1	....	116
Maple	379	1	33	....	296	15878	....	....	24	891	118	2	1098	1	17	637	50	384	1	....	131
Onawa, town of	172	....	....	....	192	....	....	....	....	247	358	....	246	7	45	1541	13	115	70	....	70
St. Clair	98	....	8	....	142	5165	....	....	....	286	27	....	358	....	2	145	....	....	....	....	45
Sherman	278	....	15	....	270	4618	....	....	4	393	86	....	768	....	7	816	....	....	....	....	77
Soldier	134	11	1	....	178	6775	40	....	8	288	14	....	406	....	4	311	198	1860	80	2	43
Spring Valley	219	....	16	....	208	10674	400	....	8	1203	266	....	1538	37	55	666	133	661	30	2	68
West Fork	65	....	10	....	46	3700	....	....	6	619	78	1	681	26	16	437	2	15	....	....	15
Willow	54	....	5	6	59	4500	....	....	2	212	35	10	170	....	91	151	43	152	3	....	23
Total	3571	39	172	10	4033	129818	2340	1025	169	12891	1991	40	14830	120	1068	11025	3439	14287	297	28	1141

MONROE COUNTY.

Albia	149	....	....	....	116	....	....	....	....	18	....	....	....	....	....	....	....	....	....	....	85
Bluff Creek	652	69	50	8	585	38050	50	33540	....	1927	578	9	3461	23	69	3343	1675	5278	660	79	165

MONROE COUNTY.—Continued.

Names of townships, towns, and cities.	Number of horses of all ages.	Number of horses sold for export in 1874.	Number of mules and asses.	Number of same sold for export in 1874.	Number of milch cows.	Number of pounds of butter made in 1874.	Number of pounds of cheese made in 1874 not in factory.	Number of gallons of milk sold in 1874.	Number of work oxen.	Number of all other cattle	No. of cattle slaughtered or sold for slaughter in 1874.	Number of thorough-bred short-horns.	Hogs: Number on hand.	Hogs: Number of Berk-shires.	Hogs: Number of Poland-China.	Hogs: No. slaughtered or sold for slaughter in 1874.	Sheep: Number on hand.	Sheep: Number of pounds of wool obtained in 1874.	Sheep: No. slaughtered or sold for slaughter in 1874.	Sheep: Number killed by dogs in 1874.	Number of dogs.
Cedar	440	29	43	4	424	18447	......	......	......	884	54	......	2908	28	6	2687	1136	3035	72	116	156
Franklin	507	5	38	......	499	21170	800	......	......	1593	65	......	1801	......	1	1577	2353	2721	646	13	162
Guilford	524	26	33	4	540	23909	......	......	......	1441	284	......	3068	9	9	2258	2196	2323	1550	117	178
Jackson	395	12	24	4	527	24200	......	170	2	1111	344	......	1868	1	9	2133	580	2225	......	......	110
Mantua	568	21	42	7	486	36883	1915	1318	19	987	250	5	4005	......	89	2371	1927	6664	239	108	182
Monroe	559	22	47	......	545	35818	160	2403	......	1611	238	......	2241	10	13	2721	821	2300	170	58	165
Pleasant	454	7	29	1	526	70225	......	......	11	1333	319	57	3135	18	11	3042	1683	6645	97	72	215
Troy, exc. of Albia	510	123	34	2	440	31985	......	18620	2	826	223	14	2015	138	154	2032	961	4185	27	38	203
Union	696	69	67	18	556	39075	250	24	......	1839	140	25	3518	39	174	3325	294	2875	175	91	210
Urbana	489	7	15	......	435	21705	......	......	......	1326	786	1	2855	1	54	2171	868	2464	5	26	139
Wayne	353	9	19	......	396	14050	......	......	......	1575	1	......	2059	242	95	......	545	1375	......	23	130
Total	6296	399	441	48	6075	375517	3175	56075	34	16471	3282	111	32934	509	684	27660	15039	42090	3641	741	2100

MONTGOMERY COUNTY.

Names of townships, towns, and cities.	Number of horses of all ages.	Number of horses sold for export in 1874.	Number of mules and asses.	Number of same sold for export in 1874.	Number of milch cows.	Number of pounds of butter made in 1874.	Number of pounds of cheese made in 1874 not in factory.	Number of gallons of milk sold in 1874.	Number of work oxen.	Number of all other cattle	No. of cattle slaughtered or sold for slaughter in 1874.	Number of thorough-bred short-horns.	Hogs: Number on hand.	Hogs: Number of Berk-shires.	Hogs: Number of Poland-China.	Hogs: No. slaughtered or sold for slaughter in 1874.	Sheep: Number on hand.	Sheep: Number of pounds of wool obtained in 1874.	Sheep: No. slaughtered or sold for slaughter in 1874.	Sheep: Number killed by dogs in 1874.	Number of dogs.
Douglas	468	68	24	17	401	25937	......	50	16	1432	299	21	1581	22	18	2063	67	397	......	......	131
Frankfort	294	2	50	......	414	7606	......	......	......	415	190	......	1722	......	102	1207	35	182	2	......	186
Grant	574	......	47	......	294	20975	......	420	......	770	86	1	5500	84	198	2591	42	150	12	2	183
Jackson, exc. of Villisca	312	......	42	......	475	20552	40	......	......	1086	94	......	2394	29	11	1638	259	1079	......	14	120
Lincoln	403	......	35	......	273	12290	......	......	......	405	10	......	1516	......	......	1092	25	100	......	......	133
Pilot Grove	441	8	31	2	382	17262	......	......	18	716	50	1	2754	53	72	1769	167	770	......	15	166
Red Oak, exc. of town	557	......	33	......	468	17285	6500	1650	43	1734	104	82	3250	81	388	2933	46	313	31	15	173
Red Oak Junction, town of	229	......	......	......	......	......	......	......	......	......	......	......	......	......	......	......	......	......	......	......	101
Scott	229	......	13	......	181	8418	......	......	......	264	......	1	1179	......	......	683	......	......	......	......	89
Sherman	468	6	58	......	347	1997	......	......	......	908	214	1	2683	283	361	2222	3	......	......	5	203
Villisca, town of	123	7	12	......	109	2682	......	2555	......	23	10	......	58	......	......	402	1	......	......	1	46

Walnut	425	40	37	4	311	17365	1000	......	......	2074	458	......	5939	......	304	3071	......	......	......	......	128
Washington	348	......	18	......	396	18410	......	......	2	833	130	1	1835	......	2	1401	56	200	......	5	141
West	499	3	30	......	356	27255	100	......	14	719	97	1	2324	182	888	1688	......	......	......	......	172
Total	53170	134	430	23	4407	208034	7640	4675	93	11379	1742	109	32736	734	2359	22760	701	3191	45	57	1972

MUSCATINE COUNTY.

Bloomington, exc. of Muscatine	1055	60	80	......	1017	66076	......	14490	2	1492	689	2	1848	135	597	2031	86	682	51	......	232
Cedar	364	15	41	......	246	16005	......	......	......	898	395	......	1572	......	......	1439	302	1580	135	43	72
Fulton	880	12	85	......	775	70107	1208	800	......	1903	443	2	8142	15	117	4753	88	351	23	13	217
Goshen	857	29	30	......	613	55715	......	......	......	1951	555	106	4446	133	210	3159	2667	10476	603	59	178
Lake	737	14	43	5	619	41974	186	......	......	1790	722	8	2062	46	216	2125	128	1297	133	19	140
Montpelier	435	19	14	2	428	26803	340	......	......	728	210	1	3143	22	22	2223	80	469	61	6	146
Mocsow	447	43	24	3	397	15087	......	......	......	1152	219	......	1394	67	173	1526	99	388	26	7	175
Muscatine, city of	403	......	73	......	342	......	......	......	......	......	......	......	226	......	......	......	......	......	......	......	639
Orono	311	11	27	1	307	11405	100	......	......	957	62	38	915	15	96	678	7	28	3	4	61
Pike	698	14	33	2	571	28360	......	......	......	1181	166	......	2514	626	1377	1760	94	262	12	1	186
Seventy Six	483	37	64	......	472	32503	70	......	......	1909	1877	13	2336	26	67	2237	527	1788	172	152	175
Sweetland	1628	25	13	2	797	41199	1450	......	......	1497	425	8	3240	31	171	3117	29	168	......	......	226
Wapsinonoc, exc. of West Liberty	718	71	27	......	539	41270	350	5	......	1908	726	69	4441	633	1204	4059	254	2012	55	20	104
West Liberty, town of	111	3	2	......	95	5235	......	896	......	23	14	......	204	6	......	201	......	......	......	......	25
Wilton, exc. of town	847	32	64	8	712	41005	......	11864	......	1631	817	43	3465	77	296	4577	181	816	44	45	186
Wilton, town of	128	9	7	4	147	6224	......	3975	......	132	127	......	221	14	......	533	10	......	......	......	103
Total	10102	394	627	27	8077	498968	3704	32030	2	19152	7447	290	40169	1846	4546	34418	4550	20317	1318	369	2865

O'BRIEN COUNTY.

Baker	75	......	6	......	64	5565	......	......	28	62	1	......	140	......	11	93	......	......	......	......	41
Carroll	92	......	19	......	70	3901	......	......	35	98	......	......	245	......	......	99	......	......	......	......	28
Center	191	......	......	......	106	11575	......	......	14	99	20	......	217	......	......	162	3	15	......	......	54
Floyd	156	......	22	......	110	7695	30	320	48	106	12	......	148	......	......	......	12	90	8	2	49
Grant	198	......	8	......	135	13144	200	......	24	172	17	......	231	81	51	305	10	......	......	1	63
Highland	89	28	9	......	100	9990	180	......	37	163	13	......	444	......	......	255	......	......	......	......	43
Liberty	129	3	6	2	84	5496	......	......	27	103	14	1	336	4	78	54	......	......	......	......	30
Summit	28	......	4	......	17	691	......	......	9	89	......	......	93	6	18	40	......	......	......	......	13
Waterman	56	......	7	......	56	190	......	......	9	48	......	......	137	......	......	105	......	......	......	......	30
Total	1014	31	81	2	742	58146	410	320	231	940	77	1	1991	91	158	1113	25	105	8	3	351

OSCEOLA COUNTY.

Names of townships, towns, and cities.	Number of horses of all ages.	Number of horses sold for export in 1874.	Number of mules and asses.	Number of same sold for export in 1874.	Number of milch cows.	Number of pounds of butter made in 1874.	Number of pounds of cheese made in 1874 not in factory.	Number of gallons of milk sold in 1874.	Number of work oxen.	Number of all other cattle.	No. of cattle slaughtered and sold for slaughter in 1874.	Number of thorough-bred short-horns.	Hogs. Number on hand.	Hogs. Number of Berk-shires.	Hogs. Number of Poland-China.	Hogs. No. slaughtered or sold for slaughter in 1874.	Sheep. Number on hand.	Sheep. Number of pounds of wool obtained in 1874.	Sheep. No. slaughtered or sold for slaughter in 1874.	Sheep. Number killed by dogs in 1874.	Number of dogs.
Fairview	15	...	4	...	19	1080	...	...	15	25	3	...	16	...	...	13	...	...	...	...	12
Gilman	97	...	8	...	66	...	...	...	52	39	...	...	50	...	...	...	...	...	...	...	28
Goewey	145	...	12	...	110	9490	...	...	60	41	5	...	50	2	3	38	...	...	...	...	48
Holman	163	...	6	...	117	12325	...	260	61	162	145	...	88	...	8	144	180	300	...	...	73
Horton	33	...	2	...	39	2350	...	...	12	21	...	...	16	...	...	14	...	...	...	...	16
Ocheyedan	65	...	3	...	55	3867	...	...	24	57	8	...	36	...	3	42	...	...	...	...	27
Viola	71	...	3	...	48	2628	650	25	44	73	13	...	57	...	27	37	...	...	...	...	22
Wilson	42	2	2	2	55	4405	50	11	26	66	1	...	34	...	...	38	...	...	...	...	33
Total	631	2	40	2	539	36145	700	296	294	484	175	...	348	2	241	326	180	300	...	...	249

PAGE COUNTY.

Names of townships, towns, and cities.	Number of horses of all ages.	Number of horses sold for export in 1874.	Number of mules and asses.	Number of same sold for export in 1874.	Number of milch cows.	Number of pounds of butter made in 1874.	Number of pounds of cheese made in 1874 not in factory.	Number of gallons of milk sold in 1874.	Number of work oxen.	Number of all other cattle.	No. of cattle slaughtered and sold for slaughter in 1874.	Number of thorough-bred short-horns.	Hogs. Number on hand.	Hogs. Number of Berk-shires.	Hogs. Number of Poland-China.	Hogs. No. slaughtered or sold for slaughter in 1874.	Sheep. Number on hand.	Sheep. Number of pounds of wool obtained in 1874.	Sheep. No. slaughtered or sold for slaughter in 1874.	Sheep. Number killed by dogs in 1874.	Number of dogs.
Amity	722	...	64	...	533	34411	300	50	...	1512	356	8	5421	2	631	4044	90	300	...	...	320
Buchanan	1277	2	104	...	618	29245	...	10	4	6528	408	...	3506	10	5	11991	1026	2918	137	49	239
Clarinda, town of	149	...	14	...	124	3240	...	290	...	...	100	...	580	72	76	4496	...	...	...	...	85
Colfax	384	25	38	2	345	19085	290	...	...	1097	291	3	6553	...	1546	4263	2253	...	...	...	139
Douglas	612	...	41	...	501	21302	200	...	...	1842	691	1	3179	24	22	4707	3283	400	115	...	165
East River	676	47	55	5	491	36476	...	...	10	1365	441	5	5396	45	115	2995	432	1287	156	26	161
Fremont	506	...	73	...	370	14500	620	...	15	748	108	...	2330	1	62	2203	30	251	...	1	160
Grant, exc. of Shenandoah	464	1	56	...	214	15329	...	90	...	2744	1963	1	4167	39	384	2663	78	104	48	...	92
Harlan	561	58	97	6	591	27050	110	...	9	1926	801	2	4084	1	...	3912	54	417	2	24	191
Lincoln	554	23	61	...	376	26295	...	...	6	1127	338	8	3678	3	971	3583	425	2345	61	23	167
Morton	285	...	60	...	204	10569	...	...	...	524	177	6	3219	24	61	1490	...	...	...	...	66
Nebraska	358	20	24	10	232	17110	120	...	...	645	246	...	1782	9	2	1531	1253	3969	43	12	157
Nodaway, exc. of Clarinda	1064	15	41	2	712	40395	...	150	...	2065	1237	12	3671	78	1072	7110	1121	3428	30	30	321
Pierce	482	32	34	5	349	20575	...	...	10	704	402	4	1395	166	322	2423	716	3450	9	14	160

Shenandoah, town of	123	12	4	...	93	350	...	10	...	46	1	...	124	17	29	479	2	...	...	...	28
Tarkio	464	...	52	...	304	11991	400	...	4	874	311	3	1999	37	448	2330	53	111	...	15	172
Valley	582	4	53	3	490	2000	625	...	5	1152	112	12	2673	21	118	2147	758	3317	21	74	180
Washington	339	2	51	...	229	13184	500	...	...	1231	120	21	4292	1274	2498	5151	...	...	...	...	104
Total	9602	241	922	33	6776	343107	3165	600	63	26130	8103	86	58049	1823	8362	67818	11574	22297	622	268	2907

PALO ALTO COUNTY.

Ellington	74	2	5	...	140	7270	...	...	20	166	10	2	184	...	1	132	...	...	...	...	35
Emmetsburg	64	...	1	...	179	19496	84	200	14	754	103	...	240	...	...	231	20	64	4	...	66
Fairfield	28	2	...	...	90	3950	790	...	2	110	3	...	20	...	...	21	...	...	...	...	18
Fern Valley	50	4	8	...	75	3465	...	3	14	206	32	...	73	23	2	88	6	7	1	...	21
Freedom	79	...	10	9	204	7810	...	...	19	452	...	3	74	...	...	...	...	...	...	...	41
Great Oak	88	1	5	...	219	25085	...	...	7	743	...	...	149	...	...	181	...	...	...	...	60
Highland	82	...	...	...	132	6451	700	...	33	145	1	...	92	...	2	81	8	12	...	...	40
Lost Island	57	...	...	...	59	2990	...	10	9	117	1	...	18	...	...	38	...	...	...	...	20
Nevada	73	2	...	...	121	10825	...	...	2	684	90	...	184	...	...	131	128	6	...	...	28
Rush Lake	62	...	4	...	60	1210	...	...	8	102	3	...	86	...	...	85	...	...	...	...	39
Silver Lake	67	...	2	...	82	4150	...	...	18	114	1	...	50	...	...	105	1	4	...	1	27
Vernon	53	...	5	...	114	8580	2125	...	12	149	7	1	99	...	...	75	...	...	...	...	23
Walnut	96	...	6	...	179	13035	...	...	16	569	214	...	141	26	...	127	74	127	...	...	39
West Bend	143	...	6	...	260	16983	452	...	22	773	121	2	699	39	12	375	350	285	...	...	47
Total	1016	11	52	9	1914	134200	4151	213	196	5084	586	8	2109	88	17	1670	587	505	5	1	504

PLYMOUTH COUNTY.

America	222	5	10	...	167	...	...	...	69	2	100	...	185	4	8	460	117	150	6	...	98
Elgin	112	4	4	...	70	3575	...	...	4	42	9	...	172	...	34	119	...	...	...	...	25
Fredonia	130	...	8	...	81	7153	...	...	22	121	...	...	108	59	26	124	47	...	...	...	49
Grant	143	...	6	...	97	6262	...	...	6	117	...	...	111	3	4	116	...	...	...	...	35
Johnson	205	...	8	...	168	9603	100	...	30	216	51	...	470	1	...	313	3	17	...	...	83
Lincoln	407	59	45	4	330	19950	280	35	28	726	207	...	840	...	...	575	6	15	1	...	126
Marion	78	...	2	...	54	1845	...	...	20	96	4	...	88	...	8	69	3	40	2	...	36
Perry	275	13	14	...	216	16770	...	...	78	490	59	4	553	23	58	474	263	204	...	...	143
Plymouth	169	11	2	3	172	6395	10	4	33	404	88	...	174	7	7	230	157	10	...	...	75
Portland	153	2	2	...	81	3400	...	...	12	48	22	...	154	...	...	110	57	...	...	...	42
Sioux	117	...	11	...	106	200	...	...	20	234	16	...	89	...	12	189	5	...	...	...	32
Stanton	167	4	13	...	122	4420	...	...	32	216	24	...	335	8	13	172	22	...	...	...	40
Union	79	13	5	...	56	3158	20	...	19	81	12	...	137	7	1	104	...	...	...	...	30
Washington	110	...	13	...	110	6115	...	3650	19	83	15	...	143	...	4	124	...	...	...	...	51
Total	2367	111	143	7	1830	88846	410	3689	392	2876	607	4	3559	112	175	3179	680	436	9	...	865

POCAHONTAS COUNTY.

NAMES OF TOWNSHIPS, TOWNS AND CITIES.	Number of horses of all ages.	Number of horses sold for export in 1874.	Number of mules and asses.	Number of same sold for export in 1874.	Number of milch cows.	Number of pounds of butter made in 1874.	Number of pounds of cheese made in 1874 not in factory.	Number of gallons of milk sold in 1874.	Number of work oxen.	Number of all other cattle.	No. of cattle slaughtered or sold for slaughter in 1874.	Number of thorough-bred short-horns.	HOGS. Number on hand.	HOGS. Number of Berkshires.	HOGS. Number of Poland-China.	HOGS. No. slaughtered or sold for slaughter in 1874.	SHEEP. Number on hand.	SHEEP. Number of pounds of wool obtained in 1874.	SHEEP. No. slaughtered or sold for slaughter in 1874.	SHEEP. Number killed by dogs in 1874.	Number of dogs.
Bellville	70	......	2	......	109	8000	......	......	39	105	......	......	173	12	16	107	14	23	3	1	52
Cedar	138	2	......	......	174	1100	6000	......	19	245	......	......	244	8	19	206	20	50	......	......	59
Center	20	......	6	......	47	1130	......	......	22	40	......	......	16	......	......	1	1	1	......	......	18
Clinton	69	1	......	......	78	4455	......	......	6	218	......	......	243	......	44	193	......	......	......	......	21
Colfax	105	......	6	......	165	9140	100	......	31	487	......	......	325	4	153	312	......	......	......	......	45
Des Moines	256	......	1	......	263	19690	1772	......	7	800	......	......	394	27	133	461	......	......	......	......	56
Dover	66	......	1	......	76	4880	......	......	2	79	......	......	65	1	......	1	......	......	......	......	30
Grant	48	......	6	......	50	3000	......	......	12	158	......	......	52	2	1	11	......	......	......	......	24
Jackson	76	......	......	......	134	9915	......	......	10	307	......	......	256	1	8	130	72	......	......	......	36
Lincoln	31	......	......	......	51	2755	......	......	4	81	......	......	55	3	8	45	1	6	......	......	112
Lizard	227	2	9	......	296	19317	......	......	59	618	......	......	745	3	2	459	536	46	3	......	105
Swan Lake	14	......	......	......	40	2900	......	......	4	92	......	......	40	......	......	18	......	......	......	......	12
Total	1120	5	31	......	1483	86172	7872	......	215	3230	......	......	2608	61	384	1947	644	126	6	1	470

POLK COUNTY.

NAMES OF TOWNSHIPS, TOWNS AND CITIES.	Number of horses of all ages.	Number of horses sold for export in 1874.	Number of mules and asses.	Number of same sold for export in 1874.	Number of milch cows.	Number of pounds of butter made in 1874.	Number of pounds of cheese made in 1874 not in factory.	Number of gallons of milk sold in 1874.	Number of work oxen.	Number of all other cattle.	No. of cattle slaughtered or sold for slaughter in 1874.	Number of thorough-bred short-horns.	HOGS. Number on hand.	HOGS. Number of Berkshires.	HOGS. Number of Poland-China.	HOGS. No. slaughtered or sold for slaughter in 1874.	SHEEP. Number on hand.	SHEEP. Number of pounds of wool obtained in 1874.	SHEEP. No. slaughtered or sold for slaughter in 1874.	SHEEP. Number killed by dogs in 1874.	Number of dogs.
Allen	357	5	22	......	289	16548	......	......	......	588	178	8	2123	5	142	2095	345	873	64	56	78
Beaver	917	30	26	......	554	40810	100	802	2	1264	294	3	6106	26	236	2983	3170	336	7	1	200
Bloomfield	735	26	43	......	760	47197	5250	3160	4	1243	396	137	3898	207	324	2766	561	2250	420	4	156
Camp	856	......	93	2	499	27728	20	......	......	1749	438	1	5325	14	39	3750	870	2659	274	23	269
Crocker	684	31	10	......	618	49505	136	......	2	1195	170	......	3888	83	209	2358	336	929	33	25	182
Delaware	697	......	39	......	491	36468	......	......	......	1326	458	2	5742	......	......	3664	106	375	4	......	147
Des Moines, city of	1147	2	66	......	940	46508	......	29091	......	97	53	......	1006	36	25	405	......	......	......	......	381
Douglas	528	......	31	......	624	31695	......	......	2	1581	246	2	3603	4	1	3422	748	3403	108	2	110
Elkhart	392	3	36	......	508	41737	50	......	7	1200	68	......	1951	37	115	1832	20	64	......	......	111
Four Mile	213	5	17	2	128	5805	......	......	......	317	32	9	1013	26	27	690	228	210	......	2	47
Franklin	516	......	26	......	439	36296	176	......	11	1440	275	2	4532	......	37	2247	351	1785	44	51	131

Grant	124	18	7	......	230	14101	....	4536	......	683	139	2	1262	15	56	857	198	869	15	6	61
Jefferson	580	5	26	......	624	29810	....	....	4	1202	564	......	2758	5	....	1935	88	300	5	....	141
Lincoln	545	14	8	......	826	43438	2150	....	8	1050	84	......	2200	....	....	1802	220	917	19	13	157
Madison	646	3	35	......	631	26520	40	....	14	1172	130	1	4252	3	12	2238	509	1731	72	27	195
Saylor	414	21	50	......	420	22420	....	25550	......	1010	245	1	2453	12	71	1897	234	655	6	26	151
Valley	393	29	12	4	447	20111	10000	62220	......	547	92	13	2861	44	122	1541	99	450	29	3	111
Walnut	689	47	66	......	613	37041	33	262	......	2206	679	26	4387	78	120	3737	460	3972	114	26	211
Washington	494	......	33	......	953	33227	252	....	......	1316	202	2	2958	8	77	2610	296	1687	297	26	126
Total	10927	239	646	8	10594	606965	18207	125621	54	21186	4743	209	62318	603	1613	42829	8830	23465	1511	291	2965

POTTAWATTAMIE COUNTY.

Avoca, town of	129	......	9	......	89	1755	....	554	......	94	2	......	218	5	11	137	28	140	150	1	72
Belknap	155	......	6	......	129	6725	90	....	13	551	223	10	1151	5	62	778	14	....	....	....	46
Boomer	367	12	2	......	369	22560	....	....	......	739	238	......	997	4	2	1099	162	620	20	....	154
Center	524	3	20	......	414	21360	3760	25	10	760	154	1	1511	2	42	1168	....	....	....	....	180
Council Bluffs, city of	713	195	32	54	770	51155	18850	103275	14	95	53	2	195	57	88	3659	4	....	....	....	778
Crescent	310	......	21	2	329	16055	1600	20	1	770	128	1	643	15	....	934	47	65	....	....	154
Grove	484	......	19	......	332	23140	....	....	2	596	23	......	2060	....	22	1944	....	....	....	....	194
Harden	279	......	15	......	412	22700	....	....	......	759	109	3	782	36	206	890	15	....	....	....	72
Hazel Dell	493	4	1	2	570	28965	250	....	......	1030	33	......	910	23	6	561	100	10	....	....	157
James	128	21	10	......	120	8410	....	32	......	316	174	4	356	5	68	215	....	....	....	1	50
Kane, exc. of Council Bluffs	830	2	21	......	898	40074	....	....	......	2228	....	......	1994	1	3	2040	30	200	2	1	270
Keg Creek	232	5	2	3	310	13154	....	....	......	690	162	17	869	15	3	439	....	....	....	......	81
Knox, exc. of Avoca	807	3	55	......	596	33006	380	1890	10	1498	275	4	2806	28	161	1994	337	1204	53	48	297
Layton	587	......	56	......	345	225	....	....	4	710	87	1	1286	26	24	289	....	....	....	....	226
Macedonia	316	10	44	2	228	7083	....	....	......	668	54	......	1282	32	393	662	31	....	....	....	105
Neola	196	14	9	......	217	10167	23	50	4	508	125	......	1644	9	47	1020	133	....	....	....	86
Norwalk	246	......	6	......	280	14200	....	....	......	959	71	......	672	12	19	876	166	1000	100	....	50
Pleasant	325	......	24	......	289	9560	100	....	......	470	41	......	789	111	335	349	140	324	11	1	157
Rockford	592	19	30	1	599	32385	240	....	18	1211	258	1	3787	13	59	2109	40	820	29	4	173
Silver Creek	177	......	12	......	116	6215	....	....	2	690	132	3	1124	8	4	939	....	....	....	....	34
Washington	158	......	9	......	124	8455	400	....	1	386	27	1	297	15	27	330	....	....	....	....	62
Waveland	343	......	32	......	221	33175	340	540	......	663	57	......	1319	10	64	1085	302	2464	159	20	113
Wright	265	30	15	......	230	11100	....	....	2	160	94	6	1325	....	9	705	....	....	....	....	79
York	149	......	5	......	166	10935	....	....	2	328	31	......	609	....	11	391	387	....	....	....	50
Total	8805	318	455	64	8180	432559	26033	106386	83	16869	2551	54	28626	431	1666	24513	1936	6847	524	76	3640

POWESHIEK COUNTY.

Bear Creek, ex. of Brooklyn	646	52	18	......	531	34650	4225	....	......	1268	51	3152	3152	408	771	2597	....	800	....	....	115
Brooklyn, town of	113	......	2	......	77	3383	....	36055	......	....	....	......	6	....	....	....	....	....	....	....	50

POWESHIEK COUNTY.—Continued.

NAMES OF TOWNSHIPS, TOWNS, AND CITIES.	Number of horses of all ages.	Number of horses sold for export in 1874.	Number of mules and asses.	Number of same sold for export in 1874.	Number of milch cows.	Number of pounds of butter made in 1874.	Number of pounds of cheese made in 1874 not in factory.	Number of gallons of milk sold in 1874.	Number of work oxen.	Number of all other cattle.	No. of cattle slaughtered or sold for slaughter in 1874.	Number of thorough-bred short-horns.	HOGS. Number on hand.	HOGS. Number of Berk-shires.	HOGS. Number of Poland-China.	HOGS. No slaughtered or sold for slaughter in 1874.	SHEEP. Number on hand.	SHEEP. Number of pounds of wool obtained in 1874.	SHEEP. No. slaughtered or sold for slaughter in 1874.	SHEEP. Number killed by dogs in 1874.	Number of dogs.
Chester	579	2	35	4	527	32090	1600	6	......	1955	319	14	2798	123	98	2032	......	......	......	......	70
Deep River	724	15	43	......	514	38300	340	277	8	1436	630	1	2959	17	83	3191	572	3139	232	......	210
Grinnell, exc. of town	706	190	27	......	599	34935	1406	4000	......	1818	720	9	2816	12	48	2858	402	3575	55	30	119
Grinnell, town of	195	......	4	......	141	1150	......	......	......	5	360	......	319	13	7	8650	......	......	......	130	41
Jackson, exc. of Montezuma	839	7	90	......	726	41881	......	......	......	1840	46	1	5775	1	58	3865	647	2341	8	1	219
Jefferson	675	5	44	......	520	55775	......	......	2	1235	167	2	3215	23	1279	2243	20	225	18	12	12
Lincoln	645	8	26	......	614	29750	......	......	11	1373	190	7	2794	18	......	2324	386	2512	49	4	148
Madison	646	36	22	......	509	57980	200	......	......	1487	388	......	3289	723	2626	2144	......	......	11	1	143
Malcom, exc. of town	476	......	89	......	454	21000	1200	......	......	1446	281	......	2254	9	1531	2261	87	855	18	8	100
Malcom, town of	76	2	5	......	54	2815	......	275	......	32	168	......	172	4	14	217	......	......	10	......	14
Montezuma, town of	105	......	4	......	65	3607	......	117	2	......	......	......	227	458	......	103	......	......	......	......	38
Pleasant	681	40	35	5	503	23760	70	......	......	2245	534	22	4998	......	101	2734	225	729	18	34	133
Scott	444	......	27	......	518	28040	......	......	......	828	......	2	1662	49	51	1856	221	667	......	5	136
Sheridan	590	21	32	......	468	43426	180	......	4	1520	294	32	2836	......	834	2109	50	255	10	6	144
Sugar Creek	587	17	42	......	614	28585	......	......	......	1272	75	......	2224	5	137	2180	412	1834	9	33	168
Union	476	11	26	4	417	20470	......	......	......	707	96	8	1783	345	87	1858	671	1342	23	132	161
Warren	636	158	37	2	547	40116	25	130	......	1722	301	4	2302	131	382	1976	333	1760	17	19	200
Washington	572	44	19	2	475	28115	176	......	4	1040	189	3	2271	......	115	1999	521	879	47	25	154
Total	10411	608	627	17	8873	568668	9422	40860	31	23229	4809	3257	47852	2339	8222	47197	4547	20913	525	440	2375

RINGGOLD COUNTY.

NAMES OF TOWNSHIPS, TOWNS, AND CITIES.	Number of horses of all ages.	Number of horses sold for export in 1874.	Number of mules and asses.	Number of same sold for export in 1874.	Number of milch cows.	Number of pounds of butter made in 1874.	Number of pounds of cheese made in 1874 not in factory.	Number of gallons of milk sold in 1874.	Number of work oxen.	Number of all other cattle.	No. of cattle slaughtered or sold for slaughter in 1874.	Number of thorough-bred short-horns.	HOGS. Number on hand.	HOGS. Number of Berk-shires.	HOGS. Number of Poland-China.	HOGS. No slaughtered or sold for slaughter in 1874.	SHEEP. Number on hand.	SHEEP. Number of pounds of wool obtained in 1874.	SHEEP. No. slaughtered or sold for slaughter in 1874.	SHEEP. Number killed by dogs in 1874.	Number of dogs.
Athens	240	19	34	1	252	15490	100	......	......	623	117	......	946	3	1	1019	59	513	178	22	92
Benton	241	33	47	11	343	16635	230	......	......	2024	220	5	2223	17	315	2306	168	331	1	1	95
Clinton	297	3	36	13	278	17235	150	......	......	767	158	2	2781	1	5	1700	1152	4234	129	13	79
Grant	321	18	45	......	328	17137	......	......	25	1019	83	3	2079	15	702	1514	449	873	37	......	102

	1	2	3	4	5	6	7	8	9	10	11	12	13	14	15	16	17	18	19	20	21
Jefferson	434	57	14	11	412	19170	247	....	8	1304	370	1	1923	452	416	1915	292	942	18	21	143
Liberty	241	18	12	......	304	11798	....	....	2	974	172	15	1167	18	41	1235	223	2099	413	3	92
Lincoln	318	13	23	12	294	15631	720	....	2	1020	155	6	1899	20	99	1542	77	278	15	2	108
Lots Creek	441	20	30	2	347	14989	....	....	......	723	218	1	1196	2	....	1502	274	913	189	11	110
Middle Fork	305	31	20	3	304	19957	36	....	2	929	147	......	1691	14	104	1430	536	1676	94	16	70
Monroe	281	8	26	......	324	11270	575	....	......	872	144	......	1012	....	....	1390	405	2099	1	46	48
Mount Ayr	468	77	67	......	433	17251	45	1145	4	1755	544	1	2989	1	....	2315	25	....	....	....	116
Rice	251	......	12	......	264	10915	....	....	......	733	140	......	939	....	....	654	120	398	3	5	86
Riley	224	13	18	......	196	10343	....	....	2	689	54	......	1678	1	....	1088	184	594	13	17	71
Tingley	128	6	8	2	141	9305	....	....	......	312	8	......	565	....	....	601	....	....	....	....	37
Union	137	6	16	......	190	14705	100	....	8	547	19	......	689	....	....	825	516	248	8	1	44
Washington	409	36	23	4	454	16913	390	....	11	1008	198	2	1685	4	25	1521	1639	1488	72	17	127
Total	4736	358	431	59	4864	238744	2593	1145	64	15299	2747	36	25462	548	1708	22557	6119	16686	1171	175	1420

38

SAC COUNTY.

	1	2	3	4	5	6	7	8	9	10	11	12	13	14	15	16	17	18	19	20	21
Boyer Valley	144	......	2	......	114	2200	....	....	4	456	....	......	349	3	15	174	....	....	....	....	14
Clinton	100	......	3	......	70	3450	....	....	4	107	6	2	75	....	13	186	604	40	....	....	15
Douglas	233	14	14	......	210	16730	....	....	48	775	....	......	618	1	1	235	....	30	1	....	86
Eden	124	......	3	......	91	5250	....	8	11	178	5	3	344	2	3	196	10	85	12	....	35
Jackson	318	12	41		256	12708	....	447	24	317	216	1	916	5	22	1759	29	9	....	....	121
Levey	201	......	18	......	101	9915	400	....	18	559	184	......	631	....	3	484	179	2000	5	....	52
Sac	217	2	17	......	251	21150	....	....	13	498	59	2	1068	663	368	745	426	45	....	....	106
Wall Lake	137	15	14	1	149	13550	45	....	6	181	40	......	538	41	51	413	....	....	....	....	60
Total	1474	43	112	1	1242	84953	445	455	128	3071	510	8	4539	715	476	4192	1248	2209	18	....	489

SCOTT COUNTY.

	1	2	3	4	5	6	7	8	9	10	11	12	13	14	15	16	17	18	19	20	21
Allen's Grove	408	......	46	......	489	20620	5100	....	......	918	125	3	2882	2	281	1994	2148	142	7	1	137
Blue Grass	842	7	68	......	900	57714	2405	....	......	1801	308	......	8497	....	166	4514	164	927	50	29	303
Buffalo, exc. of town	617	63	23	3	421	30369	....	200	......	681	159	1	2568	....	242	1957	202	1203	26	21	137
Buffalo, town of	56	......	2	......	45	2642	910	....	......	....	....	......	58	....	8	101	....	....	....	....	64
Butler	664	1	43	......	639	45140	50	....	......	1196	435	40	2925	24	178	2634	1445	3630	601	3	205
Cleona	576	1	126	......	742	40450	....	800	......	1336	179	27	3392	1	91	2707	97	685	12	1	217
Davenport, exc. of city	1099	18	57	1	1515	100010	120	180700	......	901	298	......	2983	27	101	1991	60	503	79	....	621
Davenport, city of	874	5	67	2	524	19090	150	80429	......	26	9	......	239	9	....	162	....	25	2	3	1959
Hickory Grove	780	8	109	......	867	53770	7945	....	......	1481	243	1	4121	....	20	3463	102	261	6	2	282
LeClaire, exc, of town	590	8	12	......	561	53945	....	4434	......	956	268	......	3106	45	8	3353	543	2010	92	23	179
LeClaire, town of	25	......	4	......	27	....	....	....	......	....	....	......	63	3	....	....	....	....	....	....	....
Liberty	621	26	82	12	769	37334	3000	....	......	1460	486	5	3793	3	275	3086	2916	1412	304	....	173
Lincoln	821	54	45	1	697	59520	....	....	......	986	253	......	4076	8	62	3439	129	355	60	3	231

SCOTT COUNTY.—Continued.

Names of townships, towns, and cities.	Number of horses of all ages.	Number of horses sold for export in 1874.	Number of mules and asses.	Number of same sold for export in 1874.	Number of milch cows.	Number of pounds of butter made in 1874.	Number of pounds of cheese made in 1874 not in factory.	Number of gallons of milk sold in 1874.	Number of work oxen.	Number of all other cattle.	No. of cattle slaughtered and sold for slaughter in 1874.	Number of thorough-bred short-horns.	Hogs: Number on hand.	Hogs: Number of Berkshires.	Hogs: Number of Poland-China.	Hogs: No. slaughtered or sold for slaughter in 1874.	Sheep: Number on hand.	Sheep: Number of pounds of wool obtained in 1874.	Sheep: No. slaughtered or sold for slaughter in 1874.	Sheep: Number killed by dogs in 1874.	Number of dogs.
Pleasant Valley	459	23	31	5	427	39930		250		745	272	20	2131	58	105	2320	150	1932	164	25	130
Princeton, exc. of town	640		25		492	31185				1128	393		2942			2756	378	19	56	3	151
Princeton, town of																					
Rockingham	171		3		192	12751		10200		155			297		15	312	35	105	2	5	86
Sheridan	840	18	52	3	680	60245				1171	262		3753			3167	3	15			284
Winfield	748	20	29		709	45588				938	215		3199	4	84	2574	34	150	4	3	239
Total	10831	252	824	27	10696	710303	19680	277013		15929	3905	97	51025	184	1636	40530	8406	13874	1465	122	5398

SHELBY COUNTY.

Names of townships, towns, and cities.	Number of horses of all ages.	Number of horses sold for export in 1874.	Number of mules and asses.	Number of same sold for export in 1874.	Number of milch cows.	Number of pounds of butter made in 1874.	Number of pounds of cheese made in 1874 not in factory.	Number of gallons of milk sold in 1874.	Number of work oxen.	Number of all other cattle.	No. of cattle slaughtered and sold for slaughter in 1874.	Number of thorough-bred short-horns.	Hogs: Number on hand.	Hogs: Number of Berkshires.	Hogs: Number of Poland-China.	Hogs: No. slaughtered or sold for slaughter in 1874.	Sheep: Number on hand.	Sheep: Number of pounds of wool obtained in 1874.	Sheep: No. slaughtered or sold for slaughter in 1874.	Sheep: Number killed by dogs in 1874.	Number of dogs.
Cass	90	1	2		89	2820			2	515	47		840			375					31
Clay	167	2	19		156	14725	200			573	11	2	666	22	2	363					74
Douglas	259		15		216	10500				504	69		893	14	1	437					60
Fairview	535		21		391	19270	60	5		739	65		2767	9	106	1394	137	559	19	19	215
Greeley	43	12			48	5490	100			109	50		150		1	190	84	375	2		13
Grove	457	8	16		492	25469	200		2	1431	207	2	1000	1	47	950	565	2413	70	17	134
Harlan	383	22	13	4	505	72946		85		675	402	1	2872	25	425	1145	21	98	419		116
Jackson	201		12		157	7080	230			387	25		1118	23	4	653					73
Jefferson	69	5	5		64	4995		15	4	71	9	2	188	6	14	140	20	77	4	3	30
Lincoln	234	10	8		207	6370	800			234		2	596	95	150	467					47
Monroe	411		22		306	2955				316			703	2	1	189					123
Polk	120		10		86	1525				145	12		568	1		238	1	8			53
Shelby	210		19		149	8535		25	2	700	151	5	1138	85	61	734					69
Union	131		14		111	6775			10	143	16		163			146					11
Washington	131		12		142	7450				465	151		700	2	12	508					37

Westphalia	88	......	4	......	57	3400	....	....	......	130	6	3	94	....	8	49	....	....	....	....	35
Total	3529	60	192	4	3176	200305	1590	130	20	7137	1221	17	14456	288	832	7984	828	3530	514	39	1121

SIOUX COUNTY.

Buncombe	122	16	1	......	76	4860	144	....	24	86	24	......	177	2	....	148	....	....	....	....	28
Floyd	67	1	7	......	86	4400	....	....	34	103	17	......	104	....	....	59	....	....	....	....	51
Grant	93	2	22	......	75	7969	....	....	21	93	20	......	212	....	....	147	....	....	....	....	41
Holland	372	......	20	......	213	15690	300	175	88	235	14	......	288	29	33	508	39	286	....	....	203
Lincoln	89	......	20	......	88	4787	240	....	55	160	25	2	171	....	6	150	7	24	....	....	50
Nassau	246	7	26	......	170	10209	382	....	43	152	25	2	462	....	....	241	6	15	2	....	125
Reading	125	......	6	......	96	7600	....	....	18	63	1	......	65	....	....	31	....	....	....	....	32
Rock	48	......	6	......	32	1585	....	....	38	76	5	......	181	27	11	65	....	....	....	....	24
Settler	70	......	4	......	71	4330	....	....	14	101	22	1	42	1	....	91	13	38	2	....	24
Sheridan	111	......	12	......	90	5475	....	....	21	108	10	......	55	....	....	170	24	75	....	....	51
Total	1343	26	124	......	997	66905	1066	175	356	1177	163	5	1757	59	50	1610	89	438	4	....	629

STORY COUNTY.

Ames, town of	104	2	5	8	84	4623	....	1900	2	58	215	1	222	10	9	1638	....	2300	20	4	36
Collins	483	31	50	1	449	33977	600	....	......	987	409	3	1905	3	10	2510	22	94	....	....	144
Franklin	531	12	26	2	639	49495	18325	4613	2	1412	116	5	3101	22	207	2191	1094	4615	64	42	69
Grant	376	......	28	......	498	35914	....	8610	2	1145	90	4	2796	34	154	1209	....	....	....	....	112
Howard	622	......	2	......	1125	92250	....	....	......	1747	214	1	4200	....	40	2323	243	497	....	....	135
Indian Creek	651	75	58	4	718	125270	9	....	......	1132	207	8	2576	393	616	3273	92	755	101	23	198
La Fayette	317	20	19	......	588	29835	390	....	......	1229	304	1	1156	....	1	2510	76	173	10	1	149
Lincoln	208	8	......	......	178	13720	....	....	6	346	41	......	692	12	135	544	....	....	....	....	61
Milford	374	42	48	3	574	45575	....	5600	......	1825	261	......	3362	635	2846	2191	159	166	33	2	119
Nevada, exc. of town	470	......	50	......	559	54670	....	1500	......	1074	48	25	2107	13	44	2220	259	1307	51	30	136
Nevada, town of	228	7	9	......	442	3565	500	7645	......	138	54	3	372	35	37	654	....	....	....	....	57
New Albany	221	16	27	......	505	28175	505	....	4	1464	85	......	2005	1	....	1196	2	21	....	....	111
Palestine	460	24	12	......	740	47690	....	78	12	2135	123	1	2124	15	44	1858	177	589	19	5	151
Richland	302	6	16	......	388	33515	60	1721	......	773	97	......	1720	10	12	1135	6	20	1	2	88
Sherman	190	......	9	......	213	22293	....	....	2	384	42	1	447	4	40	501	2	....	....	....	58
Union	590	75	38	5	748	66080	....	100	6	1652	549	1	6682	1023	5236	3397	3274	4809	140	19	193
Warren	75	5	......	......	75	3116	....	....	2	114	15	......	128	....	59	118	....	....	....	....	36
Washington, exc. of Ames	513	21	33	......	637	55335	200	4740	10	1321	241	1	2799	340	1049	2229	84	290	5	7	117
Total	6715	344	430	23	9160	765098	20589	36507	48	18936	3111	55	38394	2550	10569	31697	5490	15636	444	135	1970

TAMA COUNTY.

NAMES OF TOWNSHIPS, TOWNS, AND CITIES.	Number of horses of all ages.	Number of horses sold for export in 1874.	Number of mules and asses.	Number of same sold for export in 1874.	Number of milch cows.	Number of pounds of butter made in 1874.	Number of pounds of cheese made in 1874 not in factory.	Number of gallons of milk sold in 1874.	Number of work oxen.	Number of all other cattle.	No. of cattle slaughtered or sold for slaughter in 1874.	Number of thorough-bred short horns.	HOGS. Number on hand.	HOGS. Number of Berk-shires.	HOGS. Number of Poland-China.	HOGS. No. slaughtered or sold for slaughter in 1874.	SHEEP. Number on hand.	SHEEP. Number of pounds of wool obtained in 1874.	SHEEP. No. slaughtered or sold for slaughter in 1874.	SHEEP. Number killed by dogs in 1874.	Number of dogs.
Buckingham	612	43	15	2	359	25370		20		1079	305		3836	33	92	3018					109
Carlton	590	44	33	2	475	32205			2	1038	151	3	2052	646	194	1578	191	1155	21	9	157
Carroll	431	37	11	3	284	19706	195	10	9	548	121	2	1704	9	·7	1216					117
Clark	465		21		348	22435	750	290		589	77		1385	18	3	800	65	365	27		105
Columbia	117	2	16		444	42970	228			976	45		2419			1252					122
Crystal	508	36	38		391	27490	425			755	162	12	2224			1440	18				119
Geneseo	532	29	13		410	26080				572	71		2731		5	1754	41	200			100
Grant	281		23		229	4635	170			623	25		1437	2	15	1023	93	203	6	1	62
Highland	432	2	18		386	27724				978	147	1	2016	20	1	1845	9				143
Howard	764	7	23		526	42155	175			1205	162		2803			2086	238	1410	55		162
Indian Village, exc. of Montour	613	26	29		570	34722	150	40	4	1575	278	27	3989	15	58	2037	2132	1882	79	27	190
Lincoln	356	5	37		261	15280	522			436	3	2	1203	1	2	161	2	8			108
Montour, town of	96		3	18	54	3140	150	1100	2	101	13		306			215	10	65	1		22
Oneida	598	6	46		399	25560	400			696	151	1	2152	4		1360					136
Otter Creek	731	3	27	2	557	27549	30		12	1292	260	2	2018	12		1732	122	1041	97		168
Perry, exc. of Traer	639	2	17		487	35808	9300			1235	339	3	2979	20	10	2611					129
Richland	53	325	12		496	32385			2	727	35	2	2074	14	47	2352	40	204	4		189
Salt Creek	553		13		517	30250		4000	2	1353	380		2040	3	169	1860	79	325	40	10	164
Spring Creek	472		28		334	31560	1000			536	56		1062			1495	400	2708	30	2	152
Tama, exc. of Tama City	28	6	7		110	5545				379	89	1	693	54	281	384	11	80	3		35
Tama City, town of	248	6	10		138	5850		1595		128	223	5	295	3	2	831					110
Toledo, exc. of town	357	6	14		335	22262		1895	6	761	.127	2	2294	91	251	1266	400	1228	86	22	129
Toledo, town of	209	41	4	2	114	6618		30780	2	106	51		473	2		321					90
Traer, town of	87				46	900		840		18	3		115			63					36
York	647	9	21		536	26799			2	1034	377	1	2079	8	5	1518					238
Total	10419	635	479	29	8806	574998	13495	40570	43	18740	3654	64	16379	966	1260	34218	3851	10874	449	71	3092

TAYLOR COUNTY.

Bedford, town of	112	1	7	......	61	800	....	....	2	99	....	......	87	5	10	55	....	....	....	....	19
Benton, exc. of Bedford	425	22	16	......	435	25250	1000	....	......	1255	284	4	2228	....	62	3025	279	710	31	22	56
Clayton	503	8	33	......	378	19636	643	34	20	1558	351	4	4303	37	339	2734	189	822	34	5	125
Dallas	537	10	19	4	380	22940	300	....	4	859	269	1	2131	17	72	1962	352	1986	16	37	203
Gay	262	3	41	2	274	11125	40	....	......	634	311	1	875	3	12	1203	1691	4317	56	21	67
Grant	248	17	26	......	232	14295	....	12	14	840	10	6	1368	2	134	786	13	78	....	....	71
Grove	164	......	6	......	116	3785	....	....	......	347	89	......	728	31	36	510	....	....	....	....	71
Holt	491	7	16	......	474	20595	....	....	......	796	33	......	2655	....	....	1508	130	465	....	4	164
Jackson	376	16	17	1	308	12134	....	....	......	1156	411	......	2592	7	81	1277	858	3549	83	7	105
Jefferson	369	4	86	......	322	18975	....	....	6	1340	326	2	3454	....	5	1739	155	490	8	3	101
Marshall	281	5	11	......	292	22400	....	....	......	661	43	......	1068	2	220	951	128	250	213	14	96
Mason	495	18	38	1	601	25860	175	40	16	1182	248	1	1989	10	146	3411	671	1286	48	28	168
Nodaway	435	57	38	1	385	15695	180	....	......	1250	206	7	1992	10	376	1730	207	950	7	17	147
Platte	375	......	17	......	265	8065	....	235	2	641	220	......	1412	12	....	1201	15	104	3	....	113
Polk	555	11	70	......	603	30680	356	....	......	1396	199	......	2234	....	8	2381	427	1548	13	39	156
Ross	437	7	20	......	412	19275	840	....	......	984	330	5	1935	32	169	2255	275	1136	38	42	118
Washington	398	5	26	6	312	19443	....	....	2	896	265	2	2020	23	110	1779	150	1096	16	15	124
Total	6463	191	487	15	5850	290953	3534	321	66	15894	3595	33	33071	191	1780	28507	5550	18787	566	254	1904

UNION COUNTY.

Afton, town of	123	......	12	......	140	7035	....	1328	......	....	309	......	51	1	29	340	....	....	....	....	30
Creston, town of	87	1	5	......	111	625	....	2337	......	....	10	......	130	....	....	....	....	....	....	....	75
Dodge	197	10	13	......	194	12025	....	....	2	471	50	......	1141	....	261	1050	977	693	25	....	62
Douglas, exc. of Creston	266	......	31	......	263	540	....	....	......	277	220	......	893	31	245	737	....	....	....	....	75
Grant	199	3	13	......	237	6880	....	....	......	487	156	23	1151	10	5	960	....	....	....	....	56
Highland	269	12	20	2	222	12854	125	3650	......	935	98	5	860	15	407	723	....	....	....	....	75
Jones	458	25	37	......	518	34038	....	35	2	1325	249	......	2794	....	....	1551	351	820	28	7	149
Lincoln	380	2	10	......	273	17470	9417	148	......	1103	7	......	1133	2	....	941	78	126	....	....	99
New Hope	262	2	25	......	244	12800	....	....	8	949	305	4	1397	....	317	886	53	263	361	2	71
Platte	470	3	45	......	498	29618	300	....	4	1396	692	3	3028	2	39	2783	244	636	16	....	155
Pleasant	311	40	39	2	480	17663	450	....	4	740	178	......	1052	226	....	1060	392	1353	157	4	111
Sand Creek	277	2	21	2	265	8015	90	....	......	770	135	19	921	7	131	785	374	151	3	6	75
Spaulding	145	......	11	......	106	4720	....	....	......	249	47	......	1149	27	98	592	500	2500	20	20	42
Union, exc. of Afton	436	82	23	6	436	30968	....	....	16	1441	499	2	1651	161	626	1743	453	1260	106	21	118
Total	3880	182	305	12	3987	195251	10382	7498	36	10143	2955	56	17351	482	2158	14161	3422	7802	716	60	1193

VAN BUREN COUNTY.

NAMES OF TOWNSHIPS, TOWNS, AND CITIES.	Number of horses of all ages.	Number of horses sold for export in 1874.	Number of mules and asses.	Number of same sold for export in 1874.	Number of milch cows.	Number of pounds of butter made in 1874.	Number of pounds of cheese made in 1874 not in factory.	Number of gallons of milk sold in 1874.	Number of work oxen.	Number of all other cattle.	No. of cattle slaughtered or sold for slaughter in 1874.	Number of thorough-bred short-horns.	HOGS. Number on hand.	HOGS. Number of Berk-shires.	HOGS. Number of Poland-China.	HOGS. No. slaughtered or sold for slaughter in 1874.	SHEEP. Number on hand.	SHEEP. Number of pounds of wool obtained in 1874.	SHEEP. No. slaughtered or sold for slaughter in 1874.	SHEEP. Number killed by dogs.	Number of dogs.
Bentonsport, town of	74	19	2	2	45	5895	....	435	....	2	11	......	340	....	....	153	5	20	....	....	25
Birmingham, town of	113	15	......	......	73	5635	80200	744	......	42	9	1	329	....	....	231	....	10	....	....	25
Bonaparte	322	11	64	......	374	24460	....	1422	......	415	84	......	2494	38	2	1359	3402	13113	115	118	193
Cantril, town of	29	......	9	......	24	....	....	....	......	....	....	......	17	....	....	....	....	....	....	....	....
Cedar	704	52	70	12	524	43071	30	....	......	1757	453	36	3599	119	197	3483	1816	7878	741	69	190
Chequest	538	55	46	2	483	31844	240	....	2	1229	233	1	4897	214	278	1998	2751	8985	264	172	213
Des Moines	848	67	36	6	646	35257	599	22	......	1539	1013	6	4805	326	27	3341	5122	15434	1279	149	175
Farmington, exc. of town	381	8	54	12	339	16096	....	220	......	916	131	......	1341	37	17	1153	2203	10855	346	60	176
Farmington, town of	....	......	......	......	....	....	....	....	......	....	....	......	....	....	....	....	....	....	....	....	....
Harrisburg	653	30	105	3	571	64789	375	....	......	1824	261	1	4453	28	58	3575	2902	10481	211	52	186
Henry	317	8	26	......	258	20409	1505	160	......	790	88	10	3489	67	8	1651	2037	7360	332	36	94
Jackson, exc. of Cantril	950	48	112	9	915	54880	8700	....	......	2732	637	2	4042	37	36	4081	579	11629	544	136	258
Keosauqua, town of	115	10	9	3	65	4810	....	1315	......	14	9	......	227	4	2	298	56	168	4	16	57
Lick Creek	595	61	14	8	521	30775	60	9120	2	896	143	2	1934	33	3	1927	1910	7005	425	71	178
Union, exc. of Birmingham	707	35	66	......	528	37209	....	12250	......	1435	288	6	3766	6	....	3477	2167	9519	330	78	157
Van Buren, exc. Keosauqua	739	80	33	2	589	52840	....	886	4	2064	226	4	5035	66	221	3368	4959	20134	584	169	194
Vernon	545	18	33	......	618	31615	1708	....	......	1370	265	......	4082	4	....	2201	1797	7500	341	40	136
Village	623	50	27	2	502	29652	....	....	14	7773	229	8	3464	25	23	2282	1313	4763	137	64	145
Washington, exc. of Bentonsport	275	3	14	3	256	15325	....	....	......	514	13	......	2276	1	16	1138	854	3410	168	79	58
Total	8528	570	720	64	7324	504562	93417	27574	22	18312	4093	77	50590	1005	888	35716	33873	138264	5821	1309	2460

WAPELLO COUNTY.

NAMES OF TOWNSHIPS, TOWNS, AND CITIES.	Number of horses of all ages.	Number of horses sold for export in 1874.	Number of mules and asses.	Number of same sold for export in 1874.	Number of milch cows.	Number of pounds of butter made in 1874.	Number of pounds of cheese made in 1874 not in factory.	Number of gallons of milk sold in 1874.	Number of work oxen.	Number of all other cattle.	No. of cattle slaughtered or sold for slaughter in 1874.	Number of thorough-bred short-horns.	HOGS. Number on hand.	HOGS. Number of Berk-shires.	HOGS. Number of Poland-China.	HOGS. No. slaughtered or sold for slaughter in 1874.	SHEEP. Number on hand.	SHEEP. Number of pounds of wool obtained in 1874.	SHEEP. No. slaughtered or sold for slaughter in 1874.	SHEEP. Number killed by dogs.	Number of dogs.
Adams	796	45	16	......	579	25855	350	....	10	1471	126	7	4592	7	145	2673	1694	5730	461	159	200
Agency, exc. of Agency City	296	25	33	2	222	12520	300	25	......	659	87	3	1923	13	4	1608	591	2676	41	80	113
Agency City, town of	63	21	6	......	65	5080	....	777	......	18	9	......	299	14	2	272	....	....	....	....	35

Cass	260	81	8	.....	262	15124	75	195	4	530	142	11	1115	15	94	1019	439	1044	63	23	155
Center, exc. of Ottumwa	963	96	64	5	842	73865	320	30152	.....	1285	882	12	2789	200	20	3363	613	2423	392	120	420
Columbia, exc. of Eddyville	542	51	9	3	438	20395	.....	750	2	1421	401	2	3877	95	283	2504	2064	7634	340	202	152
Competine	679	32	92	8	549	40803	.....	.....	.....	8121	533	7	4035	185	531	3753	2305	8921	429	89	202
Dahlonega	394	44	30	5	269	15759	420	.....	.....	903	402	.....	3010	87	405	2120	741	2328	99	28	99
Eddyville, town of	93	19	6	.....	69	3225	.....	900	1	56	60	1	384	.....	.....	266	20	.....	1	.....	77
Eldon, town of	36	.....	2	.....	42	1020	.....	.....	.....	.....	.....	.....	54	.....	.....	.....	.....	.....	.....	.....	41
Greene	658	9	50	.....	494	37045	.....	.....	2	1327	137	4	2438	52	88	1757	1044	3065	299	18	285
Highland	727	17	56	7	577	40258	.....	.....	7	1701	410	1	3911	125	826	4198	538	2894	315	104	176
Keokuk	274	5	19	.....	299	15230	.....	.....	.....	512	.....	.....	1767	.....	.....	739	457	1542	.....	30	80
Ottumwa, city of	261	136	22	16	166	14690	.....	4780	.....	23	601	.....	237	11	17	22715	.....	.....	589	5	377
Pleasant	776	33	159	14	630	29890	205	.....	.....	1482	286	6	7246	18	218	4551	2256	8020	293	112	211
Polk	548	71	19	4	464	22684	402	15	6	859	183	.....	3158	4	148	1718	1500	3702	238	126	174
Richland	823	54	44	9	638	48078	50	40630	.....	1989	153	.....	5212	42	55	3147	1820	5443	86	208	201
Washington, exc. of Eldon	576	26	56	2	468	38366	100	357	2	1083	154	6	2662	39	.....	3291	2708	7873	422	417	124
Total	8765	765	691	75	7073	469887	2222	78581	34	23440	4566	60	48709	907	2836	59694	18790	63225	4068	1721	3102

WARREN COUNTY.

Allen	405	17	33	5	305	19682	75	640	.....	608	146	11	3892	3	23	2845	1423	4489	689	3	109
Belmont	809	2	47	.....	519	27127	50	.....	.....	1637	450	1	4256	19	8	3948	374	1463	51	59	175
Greenfield	852	5	40	2	663	39886	160	.....	.....	1695	431	1	5294	57	627	4125	1101	3800	151	21	212
Indianola, town of	266	8	19	.....	205	14820	.....	1845	.....	79	1	.....	613	33	39	.....	.....	.....	.....	.....	.....
Jackson	525	3	29	.....	507	20878	.....	.....	2	1730	44	6	2985	22	67	2157	698	2589	175	41	157
Jefferson	635	2	33	2	836	20359	400	.....	.....	1037	105	.....	3418	1	49	2770	1389	1979	58	29	158
Liberty	671	8	34	1	472	32811	500	.....	.....	1475	293	2	3778	24	22	3806	639	3314	79	9	179
Linn	803	10	41	.....	807	40615	367	.....	.....	2410	632	1	4484	3	9	4058	328	1722	64	61	172
Otter	672	1	37	.....	344	26850	.....	.....	10	1531	301	3	6980	52	38	3481	750	2980	210	79	145
Palmyra	684	1	28	.....	359	22209	.....	.....	.....	975	2	.....	3552	123	16	4383	189	743	44	16	215
Richland	603	3	33	.....	429	62790	.....	30	6	584	308	4	3717	28	156	3454	881	3945	46	130	108
Squaw	537	9	46	2	504	23931	2682	.....	4	1074	96	2	5500	7	79	2713	1434	3599	106	30	133
Union	416	2	13	.....	386	30660	342	.....	.....	1281	1995	.....	3266	4	55	24127	793	3890	29	99	124
Virginia	357	35	19	1	398	25355	55	.....	3	1176	332	1	2321	5	96	2433	454	1490	1	14	130
Washington, ex. of Indianola	1374	84	110	13	1085	57528	424	11450	.....	2971	1617	35	7647	181	550	9078	1243	5379	781	132	340
White Breast	576	.....	25	.....	302	24904	.....	150	.....	937	178	6	2857	99	28	2448	598	1490	.....	.....	198
White Oak	581	5	23	.....	408	25495	.....	.....	10	1270	453	3	3545	9	184	3109	787	2485	91	11	110
Total	10766	195	610	26	8529	515910	5055	14115	35	22470	7384	76	68105	670	2046	78935	13081	45357	2575	734	2665

WASHINGTON COUNTY.

Brighton, exc. of town	391	19	21	.....	409	24653	900	280	1	1165	261	1	3439	40	136	2187	598	2320	26	36	124
Brighton, town of	64	15	8	2	74	4316	.....	1748	.....	71	5	.....	394	.....	1	199	4	20	.....	.....	43

WASHINGTON COUNTY.—Continued.

Names of townships, towns, and cities.	Number of horses of all ages.	Number of horses sold for export in 1874.	Number of mules and asses.	Number of same sold for export in 1874.	Number of milch cows.	Number of pounds of butter made in 1874.	Number of pounds of cheese made in 1874 not in factory.	Number of gallons of milk sold.	Number of work oxen.	Number of all other cattle.	No. of cattle slaughtered or sold for slaughter in 1874.	Number of thorough-bred short-horns.	Hogs. Number on hand.	Hogs. Number of Berk-shires.	Hogs. Number of Poland-China.	Hogs. No. slaughtered or sold for slaughter in 1874.	Sheep. Number on hand.	Sheep. Number of pounds of wool obtained in 1874.	Sheep. No. slaughtered or sold for slaughter in 1874.	Sheep. Number killed by dogs in 1874.	Number of dogs.
Cedar	508	23	42	2	501	35927	500	.....	.....	1260	209	1	8642	297	975	3840	619	1888	504	46	163
Clay	511	34	12	.....	445	33228	3250	.....	.....	1442	232	3	3377	5	9	2354	2086	8506	668	63	147
Crawford	810	22	53	.....	873	62710	9890	15	2	1977	332	.....	4436	12	5	4262	590	2438	192	28	172
Dutch Creek	811	49	62	.....	730	49060	1245	.....	.....	1864	339	1	4453	.....	92	4221	333	980	92	44	221
English River	873	48	42	26	734	38625	800	.....	3	2019	540	33	4996	146	568	3761	183	2819	364	30	234
Franklin	586	43	79	23	441	34325	1400	.....	.....	1908	433	3	3462	253	82	3166	750	2626	44	42	105
Highland	589	16	33	.....	543	33855	.....	.....	.....	2205	307	1	3035	.....	.....	1972	625	1721	201	9	157
Iowa	793	51	36	5	794	34155	340	95	.....	1451	283	3	3635	10	51	2882	554	1697	89	43	274
Jackson	729	27	64	9	690	35194	160	.....	.....	1583	497	4	5363	45	89	3579	437	1843	156	10	176
Lime Creek	828	10	47	.....	703	37900	3000	.....	.....	1315	166	1	3823	1	19	3299	698	3190	35	82	225
Marion	566	14	32	.....	617	36181	420	36	2	1644	178	4	1892	97	93	3060	909	1982	145	40	158
Oregon	844	73	103	35	830	52990	.....	.....	.....	2083	532	13	6851	15	40	4717	491	1921	158	47	185
Seventy Six	667	16	47	2	491	47720	.....	.....	12	2607	544	5	4370	11	44	3664	705	2787	12	29	152
Washington, exc. of city	1077	50	88	10	1000	56886	131	4348	8	1846	398	23	4752	290	296	4460	1091	3796	98	39	294
Washington, city of	140	13	23	.....	172	11322	.....	6916	.....	12	82	.....	156	92	32	650	.....	.....	.....	.....	105
Total	10787	523	792	114	10047	629047	22036	13438	28	26452	5338	96	67076	1314	2532	52273	10673	40534	2784	588	2935

WAYNE COUNTY.

Names of townships, towns, and cities.	Number of horses of all ages.	Number of horses sold for export in 1874.	Number of mules and asses.	Number of same sold for export in 1874.	Number of milch cows.	Number of pounds of butter made in 1874.	Number of pounds of cheese made in 1874 not in factory.	Number of gallons of milk sold.	Number of work oxen.	Number of all other cattle.	No. of cattle slaughtered or sold for slaughter in 1874.	Number of thorough-bred short-horns.	Hogs. Number on hand.	Hogs. Number of Berk-shires.	Hogs. Number of Poland-China.	Hogs. No. slaughtered or sold for slaughter in 1874.	Sheep. Number on hand.	Sheep. Number of pounds of wool obtained in 1874.	Sheep. No. slaughtered or sold for slaughter in 1874.	Sheep. Number killed by dogs in 1874.	Number of dogs.
Allerton, town of	58	1	3	.....	42	2160	.....	270	.....	15	2	.....	203	.....	.....	283	.....	.....	.....	.....	14
Benton	630	24	51	10	566	35995	.....	.....	.....	1739	376	2	2160	50	95	3247	1122	2334	224	66	142
Clay	506	8	20	.....	372	27710	100	.....	.....	1403	498	.....	2702	51	45	2607	1133	4669	204	7	127
Clinton	421	44	25	8	401	21407	1550	.....	6	864	268	.....	2650	8	264	1531	576	1569	297	26	135
Corydon, exc. of town	170	48	52	29	372	28880	.....	.....	2	1238	395	17	3614	14	23	2096	1749	863	3	6	143
Corydon, town of	195	63	13	3	152	9437	.....	598	5	431	145	.....	1085	55	5	749	352	.....	.....	.....	108
Grand River, exc. Lineville	462	6	26	2	360	18510	1000	.....	2	1029	182	.....	2553	17	80	1658	1144	8189	270	39	130

Howard	445	4	18	.....	338	1665	....	....	.....	820	67	1	1102	22	35	998	1027	2895	44	9	117
Jackson	332	21	17	5	280	14768	36	....	4	1030	127	2	1749	248	429	1781	1392	2828	....	....	83
Jefferson	450	24	30	9	502	34172	100	....	2	1079	170	.....	1605	33	128	1834	926	3477	188	46	143
Lineville, town of	....	.....	.....	.....	....	....	....	....	.....	....	....	.....	....	....	....	....	....	....	....	....	....
Monroe	304	24	23	.....	266	13470	140	....	.....	823	178	.....	1413	19	84	1092	746	2557	142	31	88
Richman	....	.....	10	.....	451	28720	....	....	.....	1190	132	.....	2121	59	75	1700	300	1380	178	3	111
Seymour, town of	69	12	4	.....	50	1555	....	1254	.....	40	4	.....	297	....	....	194	....	....	....	....	33
South Fork	553	59	30	12	451	24398	....	....	10	1719	349	1	2966	14	27	3631	373	1114	....	27	132
Union	704	3	62	.....	584	39430	....	....	2	1437	475	8	4868	1133	221	3249	3747	2437	103	43	142
Walnut, exc. of Seymour	638	33	37	.....	496	23565	30	30	4	1992	440	6	5809	19	43	4209	469	2001	175	22	161
Warren, exc. of Allerton	542	18	16	3	527	19807	....	....	.....	1521	183	10	2157	100	98	1896	107	505	44	11	90
Washington	451	10	51	.....	445	22353	145	....	6	1252	403	7	2486	74	41	15579	538	1886	126	37	125
Wright	675	5	66	5	545	34040	2399	....	2	1352	470	4	3537	120	114	4203	1261	4500	276	60	199
Total	7605	407	554	86	7200	402042	5500	2152	45	20974	4864	58	45077	2036	1807	52537	16862	43204	2274	433	2223

WEBSTER COUNTY.

Badger	251	.....	.....	.....	345	22275	....	....	10	1172	2	.....	736	....	....	515	22	110	2	....	75
Clay	94	.....	62	2	91	5550	100	....	20	165	9	.....	110	....	....	80	54	1861	57	4	39
Colfax	64	.....	3	.....	105	5620	200	....	.....	100	21	.....	33	....	....	97	....	....	....	....	38
Dayton	867	.....	35	.....	822	53950	800	....	10	2000	510	.....	2576	2	....	2753	347	1365	42	22	215
Deer Creek	170	1	13	.....	262	14995	....	....	17	255	45	.....	471	4	4	381	62	246	40	....	84
Douglas	287	27	48	5	573	37465	8200	....	18	1225	425	3	1704	5	11	1124	....	....	....	....	134
Elkhorn	203	.....	3	.....	281	9815	....	....	19	303	19	2	228	2	1	16	8	85	....	6	....
Fort Dodge, city of	369	.....	18	.....	423	....	....	....	.....	201	8	.....	375	....	9	187	....	....	....	....	64
Fulton	73	4	17	2	131	10750	....	....	6	246	....	.....	324	....	....	156	23	131	3	....	40
Gowrie	23	.....	.....	.....	30	2150	....	....	.....	69	7	.....	92	....	....	....	....	....	....	....	....
Hardin	257	.....	3	.....	253	6960	1542	....	.....	490	30	.....	785	....	....	529	785	1762	139	32	57
Jackson	219	8	13	.....	376	22195	....	....	4	738	20	.....	608	7	9	663	....	....	....	....	93
Johnson	197	12	28	2	340	27543	....	....	36	510	57	.....	726	5	1	456	27	....	5	7	110
Lost Grove	182	.....	6	.....	174	13074	620	....	.....	298	28	.....	355	....	20	392	16	50	7	....	49
Newark	72	2	2	2	70	5355	....	....	.....	187	16	.....	156	2	1	114	....	41	....	....	25
Otho	244	40	14	7	248	11557	....	....	.....	770	127	2	1249	2	163	961	310	630	20	....	69
Pleasant Valley	163	5	11	.....	213	14335	....	747	.....	393	102	17	337	5	34	252	....	....	....	....	116
Sumner	396	.....	15	.....	892	27675	1800	120	6	649	25	1	751	....	4	933	140	431	5	3	137
Wahkonsa, exc. Fort Dodge	154	.....	7	.....	320	15110	400	4450	8	600	54	6	256	23	56	167	14	33	....	....	89
Washington	446	8	11	.....	490	25325	....	60	20	720	110	.....	733	....	....	808	100	299	11	....	185
Webster	309	2	15	.....	295	23980	100	....	18	534	116	.....	1014	6	90	994	174	640	31	30	114
Yell	201	21	21	.....	140	10625	....	....	1	443	59	.....	572	....	....	499	224	290	133	8	40
Total	5241	130	345	20	6874	366304	13762	5377	193	12068	1784	31	14191	63	403	12077	2306	7974	495	112	1773

WINNEBAGO COUNTY.

NAMES OF TOWNSHIPS, TOWNS, AND CITIES.	Number of horses of all ages.	Number of horses sold for export in 1874.	Number of mules and asses.	Number of same sold for export in 1874.	Number of milch cows.	Number of pounds of butter made in 1874.	Number of pounds of cheese made in 1874 not in factory.	Number of gallons of milk sold in 1874.	Number of work oxen.	Number of all other cattle.	No. of cattle slaughtered or sold for slaughter in 1874.	Number of thorough-bred short-horns.	HOGS. Number on hand.	HOGS. Number of Berk-shires.	HOGS. Number of Poland-China.	HOGS. No. slaughtered or sold for slaughter in 1874.	SHEEP. Number on hand.	SHEEP. Number of pounds of wool obtained in 1874.	SHEEP. No. slaughtered or sold for slaughter in 1874.	SHEEP. Number killed by dogs in 1874.	Number of dogs.
Center	204	3	7	......	305	23615	....	....	111	266	42	......	171	....	....	226	172	571	....	....	99
Forest	137	......	2	......	194	18030	....	318	48	275	50	......	124	13	7	126	98	166	2	1	74
Iowa	229	......	6	......	420	22550	....	....	107	1260	48	......	251	....	....	263	294	964	92	28	89
Norway	133	3	......	......	278	18142	....	....	81	810	57	2	95	....	....	140	....	1014	107	40	71
Pleasant	165	22	22	2	301	18575	....	....	67	315	156	......	197	....	1	169	186	716	52	24	83
Total	868	28	37	2	1498	100912	....	318	414	2926	353	2	838	13	8	924	750	3431	253	93	416

WINNESHIEK COUNTY.

NAMES OF TOWNSHIPS, TOWNS, AND CITIES.	Number of horses of all ages.	Number of horses sold for export in 1874.	Number of mules and asses.	Number of same sold for export in 1874.	Number of milch cows.	Number of pounds of butter made in 1874.	Number of pounds of cheese made in 1874 not in factory.	Number of gallons of milk sold in 1874.	Number of work oxen.	Number of all other cattle.	No. of cattle slaughtered or sold for slaughter in 1874.	Number of thorough-bred short-horns.	HOGS. Number on hand.	HOGS. Number of Berk-shires.	HOGS. Number of Poland-China.	HOGS. No. slaughtered or sold for slaughter in 1874.	SHEEP. Number on hand.	SHEEP. Number of pounds of wool obtained in 1874.	SHEEP. No. slaughtered or sold for slaughter in 1874.	SHEEP. Number killed by dogs in 1874.	Number of dogs.
Bloomfield	745	78	18	......	767	79600	6740	3977	12	1323	249	2	2281	21	....	211	769	3571	261	7	147
Bluffton	512	37	1	......	427	21505	....	8344	21	669	183	......	998	1	1	1071	118	301	10	....	181
Burr Oak	569	19	4	......	391	22040	200	12132	20	538	212	......	674	10	5	643	257	1423	92	21	92
Calmar	474	3	2	......	632	35820	....	750	48	466	....	......	509	....	....	582	257	886	46	22	115
Canoe	489	......	......	......	443	28372	500	....	6	708	164	......	741	17	....	834	459	2802	149	24	77
Decorah, exc. of city	487	57	4	......	400	25995	150	6200	7	559	234	7	812	14	31	853	610	2676	198	7	69
Decorah, city of	304	......	......	......	269	....	....	....	......	....	....	......	....	....	....	....	....	....	....	....	....
Frankville	757	......	22	......	539	37555	....	7500	2	1167	67	1	1562	107	....	1920	313	1400	100	8	146
Fremont	434	22	2	......	390	23045	100	....	33	624	133	......	706	10	8	820	111	332	19	19	92
Glenwood	432	31	6	4	545	22050	370	....	24	632	....	......	972	....	....	961	504	2062	68	31	137
Hesper	641	......	4	......	469	32480	1320	4887	8	723	184	2	966	4	....	904	953	2453	155	16	135
Highland	463	......	4	......	486	31075	640	....	14	458	149	......	906	....	....	867	614	1357	160	33	140
Jackson	425	......	8	......	484	35675	200	....	66	854	111	......	633	....	....	791	310	1744	28	14	165
Lincoln	494	10	2	......	682	33865	2500	....	14	867	108	......	560	....	....	397	244	915	88	4	99
Madison	638	20	4	......	661	44400	5000	....	8	874	264	......	385	44	....	962	549	1359	159	6	158
Military	718	49	25	1	789	58140	200	5266	22	1243	328	4	2618	4	....	2093	1537	2401	139	31	206
Orleans	584	......	......	......	529	31280	....	16128	2	882	231	1	614	35	1	595	265	1218	32	28	94
Pleasant	470	15	2	......	552	29227	....	....	22	657	99	......	1211	16	65	746	896	3179	198	85	149

Springfield	640	15	......	......	690	37538	1200	145000	6	699	315	......	858	......	7	556	709	1883	180	39	76
Sumner	570	......	......	......	686	38030	......	......	39	1132	317	......	803	6	......	484	785	5148	140	27	161
Washington	628	63	......	......	798	68927	900	......	20	1091	246	......	1845	......	1	1344	367	1505	88	16	256
Total	11473	419	108	5	11629	736619	20020	210178	394	16116	3594	17	21104	316	119	17537	10627	38865	2310	429	2695

WOODBURY COUNTY.

Arlington	47	......	6	......	70	3125	......	......	4	156	2	......	141	......	......	54	......	......	......	......	23
Concord	142	......	16	......	152	11055	......	......	4	197	21	......	326	1	......	207	......	......	......	......	74
Floyd	51	2	......	......	59	2660	......	......	......	170	37	1	67	5	......	75	225	835	28	25	13
Grant	278	......	6	......	276	10305	......	......	20	640	100	......	569	6	38	695	150	430	43	7	89
Kedron	167	2	5	......	152	8380	300	......	10	359	42	6	570	2	47	296	328	......	......	......	64
Lakeport	162	......	4	2	173	2174	......	......	39	726	116	1	773	12	9	825	21	50	3	......	47
Liberty	325	......	21	......	281	18050	......	......	4	1143	419	......	604	84	6	1437	103	800	50	3	79
Liston	96	5	2	......	67	4817	......	......	10	88	4	......	221	7	......	88	......	......	......	......	36
Little Sioux	395	12	7	......	440	20920	......	......	......	962	105	6	2067	19	339	1090	84	190	29	13	119
Moville	32	2	2	......	40	1175	100	......	......	93	......	......	105	......	......	68	......	......	......	......	13
Rock	54	......	......	......	65	1540	......	......	......	81	4	......	118	......	......	75	24	110	8	10	22
Rutland	44	......	......	......	36	2735	......	......	4	91	......	......	170	......	4	141	160	......	......	......	26
Sioux City, exc. of city	183	......	22	......	130	8540	......	3672	80	211	21	......	86	25	4	131	28	......	......	......	61
Sioux City, city of	296	13	12	......	303	875	......	700	3	87	......	2	42	1	......	13	......	......	......	......	206
Union	228	1	19	1	213	15350	......	20	30	317	20	......	1038	......	......	686	......	......	......	......	97
West Fork	149	......	10	......	209	3710	300	......	12	621	184	1	310	23	77	293	70	......	......	......	176
Wolf Creek	474	10	4	......	151	15660	275	......	14	213	19	......	953	......	......	528	......	......	......	......	75
Woodbury	252	......	12	......	285	12434	16282	25150	8	1112	416	5	1196	74	162	610	65	......	......	......	49
Total	3375	47	148	3	3102	143505	17257	29542	242	7262	1510	22	9356	259	686	5812	1258	2415	151	58	1269

WORTH COUNTY.

Bristol	299	......	4	......	458	32870	......	......	73	609	178	2	286	......	......	274	176	622	18	6	102
Brookfield	169	5	2	1	306	23580	20	30	52	1461	94	1	157	......	......	201	142	448	44	8	73
Danville	124	......	4	......	120	11870	100	......	4	287	28	......	138	1	1	114	12	126	50	......	46
Deer Creek	213	......	6	......	164	13050	......	......	22	254	58	......	108	......	......	118	69	163	3	2	82
Fertile	143	42	7	......	334	21649	9056	1826	74	509	72	......	261	3	......	182	123	296	19	6	66
Hartland	243	......	4	......	494	36900	70	......	88	871	127	......	466	......	......	259	231	955	80	16	93
Kensett	162	......	6	......	189	11855	......	......	8	323	2	......	132	7	......	43	......	......	......	......	55
Northwood	442	......	10	......	479	36530	340	799	56	803	127	2	528	......	2	340	127	490	32	......	121
Silver Lake	180	......	......	......	292	20932	256	......	52	334	44	1	83	......	......	173	216	735	84	36	64
Union	273	......	3	......	203	17745	20	......	16	285	39	......	660	2	2	627	976	757	23	9	72
Total	2248	47	46	1	3039	226481	9862	2655	440	5736	769	6	2819	23	5	2331	2072	4592	353	83	774

WRIGHT COUNTY.

NAMES OF TOWNSHIPS, TOWNS, AND CITIES.	Number of horses of all ages.	Number of horses sold for export in 1874.	Number of mules and asses.	Number of same sold for export in 1874.	Number of milch cows.	Number of pounds of butter made in 1874.	Number of pounds of cheese made in 1874 not in factory.	Number of gallons of milk sold in 1874.	Number of work oxen.	Number of all other cattle.	No. of cattle slaughtered or sold for slaughter in 1874.	Number of thorough-bred short-horns.	HOGS.				SHEEP.				Number of dogs.
													Number on hand.	Number of Berk-shires.	Number of Poland-China.	No. slaughtered or sold for slaughter in 1874.	Number on hand.	Number of pounds of wool obtained in 1874.	No. slaughtered or sold for slaughter in 1874.	Number killed by dogs in 1874.	
Belmond	231	4	18	......	276	23560	......	......	28	445	53	1	295	25	5	480	......	......	......	......	68
Boone	88	11	6	......	92	6125	1470	......	12	123	......	......	109	......	......	115	73	150	1	4	32
Clarion	117	......	6	......	110	7000	55	......	4	186	15	......	404	......	6	243	......	......	......	......	52
Eagle Grove	150	5	6	......	207	12975	110	......	14	752	33	1	542	35	102	237	......	......	......	......	63
Iowa	206	5	12	......	202	23250	......	......	4	359	52	5	467	13	14	485	67	212	......	......	57
Liberty	204	12	2	......	209	9025	......	......	2	417	73	1	400	10	134	325	68	228	......	11	58
Pleasant	185	2	......	......	233	12870	......	110	6	339	95	......	283	......	......	440	......	......	......	......	57
Troy	220	18	19	......	318	29230	......	......	32	714	254	......	757	67	8	1073	70	285	......	......	82
Vernon	158	7	6	......	183	16100	2860	......	8	357	31	1	392	177	206	353	62	208	18	......	53
Wall Lake	155	2	2	......	184	......	......	......	......	222	......	......	275	......	......	359	......	......	......	......	55
Woolstock	173	......	4	......	178	8905	......	......	12	464	......	2	357	......	......	305	......	......	......	......	59
Total	1887	66	81	......	2192	149040	4495	110	122	4378	606	11	4281	327	475	4415	340	1083	19	15	636

STATISTICS OF BEES, AND VALUES OF PRODUCTS, IN 1874.

ADAIR COUNTY.

NAMES OF TOWNSHIPS, TOWNS, AND CITIES.	Number of stands of bees.	Number of pounds of honey and beeswax in 1874.	Value of products of farm.	Value of market garden produce.	Value of products of the orchard.	Value of small fruit.	Value of products of the herd.	Value of products of the dairy.	Value of products of the forest.
Eureka	......	......	$ 18177	$ 336	$	$ 5	$ 5060	$ 284	$ ......
Fontanelle, town of	......	......	7102	915	61	156	150	......	......
Grand River	17	245	33405	......	324	419	12543	1826	......
Greenfield	......	......	42248	......	......	......	14051	543	......
Grove	......	......	24422	......	......	......	4142	1947	......
Harrison	44	660	66178	231	791	108	17418	662	100
Jackson	40	350	36395	100	10	30	17063	......	1850
Jefferson	4	......	145240	40	......	......	33452	3002	2371
Lincoln	......	......	161205	1227	......	7	29718	2803	......
Orient	......	......	49177	......	......	......	29416	1045	......
Prussia	......	......	12170	......	......	......	2304	658	......
Richland	21	230	60960	54	......	17	11740	3063	......
Summerset, exc. of Fontanelle	......	......	30190	1148	5	39	......	50	......
Summit	......	......	7925	......	......	......	145	......	......
Union	10	86	32835	758	82	25	6181	3958	......
Walnut	......	......	29228	......	......	......	......	1513	......
Washington	72	912	71314	1891	264	195	38679	3562	4920
Total	208	2483	828171	6700	1537	1001	222062	24916	9241

ADAMS COUNTY.

NAMES OF TOWNSHIPS, TOWNS, AND CITIES.	Number of stands of bees.	Number of pounds of honey and beeswax in 1874.	Value of products of farm.	Value of market garden produce.	Value of products of the orchard.	Value of small fruit.	Value of products of the herd.	Value of products of the dairy.	Value of products of the forest.
Carl	......	......	44947	......	79	18	8064	3041	2471
Colony	7	10	36010	......	95	210	11387	2270	......
Corning, town of	......	......	......	......	......	......	......	......	......
Douglas	49	1075	69977	698	26	650	32026	3226	5713
Grant	......	......	58298	......	......	......	9861	2029	......
Jasper	49	515	57682	40	12	108	15593	3466	1215
Lincoln	6	20	70051	1780	......	10	14735	3610	......
Mercer	......	......	49569	......	......	......	18745	1780	......
Nodaway	61	907	82032	116	952	382	19092	5809	1074
Prescott	7	90	41391	988	354	32	13864	3903	2267
Quincy, exc. of town	42	170	74404	27	70	46	13641	2070	2996
Quincy, town of	2	......	187	......	......	......	......	......	......
Union	......	......	56893	185	......	......	22359	1885	750
Washington	51	534	53877	20	920	275	13819	2579	125
Total	274	3321	695318	3854	2508	1731	193186	35668	16611

ALLAMAKEE COUNTY.

NAMES OF TOWNSHIPS, TOWNS, AND CITIES.	Number of stands of bees.	Number of pounds of honey and beeswax in 1874.	Value of products of farm.	Value of market garden produce.	Value of products of the orchard.	Value of small fruit.	Value of products of the herd.	Value of products of the dairy.	Value of products of the forest.
Center	......	......	104278	577	398	50	13852	......	......
Fairview	......	......	23383	......	......	......	5573	......	......
Franklin	53	805	49728	1808	755	......	14941	5591	3990
French Creek	......	......	67420	35	224	......	5817	2165	......

ALLAMAKEE COUNTY.—Continued.

NAMES OF TOWNSHIPS, TOWNS, AND CITIES.	Number of stands of bees.	Number of pounds of honey and beeswax in 1874.	Value of products of farm.	Value of market garden products.	Value of products of the orchard.	Value of small fruit.	Value of products of the herd.	Value of products of the dairy.	Value of products of the forest.
Hanover	...	...	$ 47616	$	$	$	$ 650	$	$
Iowa	1	...	27725	...	...	...	19614	2709	530
Jefferson	16	300	99985	490	646	60	28093	7739	7530
La Fayette	43	150	111283	25	295	77	4695	2518	4114
Lansing, exc. of city	20	30	78228	90	317	45	18497	16	3398
Lansing, city of	...	...	...	...	...	...	...	...	...
Linton	5	100	45718	18	484	25	8837	2563	1306
Ludlow	1	...	160902	...	...	...	...	5628	183
Makee, exc. of Waukon	...	...	95840	...	25	...	...	4549	...
Paint Creek	1	...	127856	28	147	129	19500	3414	1105
Post, exc. of Postville.	26	335	103408	2377	795	207	30976	5934	7084
Postville, town of	...	...	...	...	...	...	...	2269	...
Taylor	6	5	46195	...	...	...	11554	...	...
Union City	20	225	58480	...	...	...	23070	...	...
Union Prairie	...	...	80145	...	...	...	26041	...	...
Waterloo	...	...	86279	1782	27	...	15736	...	...
Waukon, town of	...	...	1300	...	...	...	...	...	...
Total	192	1950	1415769	7230	4113	593	247446	45095	29240

APPANOOSE COUNTY.

NAMES OF TOWNSHIPS, TOWNS, AND CITIES.	Number of stands of bees.	Number of pounds of honey and beeswax in 1874.	Value of products of farm.	Value of market garden products.	Value of products of the orchard.	Value of small fruit.	Value of products of the herd.	Value of products of the dairy.	Value of products of the forest.
Bellair	124	740	105831	472	1311	954	65213	6928	...
Caldwell	197	1864	92067	2703	3145	942	22360	10416	2653
Center, exc. of Centerville	163	936	65202	742	989	1216	40537	5032	3194
Centerville, town of	26	...	...	50	135	250	6900	...	...
Chariton	141	361	102554	261	613	450	44963	7628	3678
Douglas	101	309	53827	997	777	291	23056	3933	3598
Franklin	134	721	108655	1851	2635	1578	69280	6237	2771
Independence	244	1475	107883	453	731	155	42143	4678	...
Johns	152	977	198053	811	895	742	96674	14215	...
Lincoln	97	807	97086	1036	1188	415	47911	2454	50
Moulton, town of	6	49	626	995	31	133	3280	944	...
Pleasant	221	1403	82866	876	2254	858	43721	5558	4142
Taylor	267	625	86264	2184	1426	600	33015	8865	3370
Sharon	143	626	57726	1058	758	260	23941	3426	4868
Udell	127	591	79769	3628	2124	1378	23637	6953	4222
Union	103	306	37869	936	389	128	15264	3371	7556
Walnut	140	258	86900	3045	787	345	39895	7235	1086
Washington, exc. of town of Moulton	207	1481	156530	354	2639	927	42476	8306	4881
Wells	179	1420	92229	60	1607	485	28363	6118	7676
Total	2772	14949	1611937	22512	24434	12107	712629	112297	53745

AUDUBON COUNTY.

NAMES OF TOWNSHIPS, TOWNS, AND CITIES.	Number of stands of bees.	Number of pounds of honey and beeswax in 1874.	Value of products of farm.	Value of market garden products.	Value of products of the orchard.	Value of small fruit.	Value of products of the herd.	Value of products of the dairy.	Value of products of the forest.
Audubon	3	...	21439	...	69	5	...	1425	...
Douglas	...	...	5087	...	...	...	1052	10	...
Exira	29	508	56182	56	60	53	36559	4581	595
Greeley	...	...	3183	...	...	...	...	...	...
Hamlin	18	158	27094	828	10	58	15503	2085	1581
Leroy	4	25	9417	...	...	...	1880	60	...
Melville	...	...	6190	...	...	...	1770	221	...
Oakfield	67	735	33935	1386	928	1715	240	7854	300
Viola	3	...	21650	...	...	...	3240	1539	...
Total	124	1426	184153	2270	1067	1831	60244	17775	2476

BENTON COUNTY.

NAMES OF TOWNSHIPS, TOWNS, AND CITIES.	Number of stands of bees.	Number of pounds of honey and beeswax in 1874.	Value of products of farm.	Value of market garden produce.	Value of products of the orchard.	Value of small fruit.	Value of products of the herd.	Value of products of the dairy.	Value of products of the forest.
Belle Plaine, town of	....	....	$........	$........	$........	$........	$........	$........	$........
Benton	169	1440	52280	497	1185	530	11975	5965	1160
Big Grove	12	....	164473	....	1115	....	50970	8359	730
Blairstown, town of	....	....	....	....	....	100	....	....	....
Bruce	3	....	189862	13	1428	1261	29581	8863	755
Canton, exc. of Shellsburg	35	140	102035	300	638	87	55530	9157	6223
Cedar	113	1135	201165	....	570	538	56051	13721	6164
Eden	10	4	169551	46	440	318	36376	9276	....
Eldorado	13	20	168790	....	334	323	24316	7098	....
Florence	44	188	162234	....	535	....	56882	12064	....
Fremont	11	100	189791	60	700	190	36345	6178	....
Harrison	51	427	48202	40	508	5	26607	4379	4380
Homer	....	....	151485	....	....	....	21127	4067	....
Iowa, exc of Belle Plaine	59	82	112886	100	584	....	41684	5394	2789
Jackson	48	203	141878	132	680	311	42429	5037	....
Kane	....	....	94900	....	....	....	15842	....	....
Leroy, exc. of Blairstown	10	....	167834	....	1466	538	27815	6635	6560
Monroe	....	....	113491	....	65	175	17888	7137	70
Polk	123	4318	145001	7474	891	1188	40647	11315	10907
St. Clair	7	150	148668	....	1747	375	38900	5554	....
Shellsburg, town of	....	....	....	....	....	....	10	....	....
Taylor, exc. of Vinton	95	740	75452	50	1295	587	20015	6527	....
Union	....	....	65017	....	....	....	27389	2857	....
Vinton, town of	93	600	....	2500	....	....	....	2000	....
Total	896	9547	2664995	11212	14181	6526	678379	141583	39738

BLACK HAWK COUNTY.

NAMES OF TOWNSHIPS, TOWNS, AND CITIES.	Number of stands of bees.	Number of pounds of honey and beeswax in 1874.	Value of products of farm.	Value of market garden produce.	Value of products of the orchard.	Value of small fruit.	Value of products of the herd.	Value of products of the dairy.	Value of products of the forest.
Barclay	16	260	115214	....	....	....	17416	897	50
Bennington	9	42	137267	172	83	44	20136	7654	855
Big Creek, exc. of La Porte	220	1565	100425	....	451	75	32454	3695	80
Black Hawk	26	185	150385	1015	1088	540	22389	11470	1550
Cedar	56	360	99430	231	326	82	20106	7004	2635
Cedar Falls, exc. of city	61	650	176726	439	422	2600	37937	7467	3580
Cedar Falls, city of	88	615	2165	135	997	3201	66400	7378	390
Eagle	....	....	121625	....	....	....	25110	6775	....
East Waterloo, exc. of Waterloo	11	50	103269	437	702	816	29153	12615	1250
Fox	24	360	108615	697	128	212	27001	7740	1693
La Porte City, town of	1	....	....	....	....	....	20	980	....
Lester	69	225	84264	....	509	132	3067	9492	....
Lincoln	....	....	129607	....	106	138	27670	6407	165
Mt. Vernon	....	....	109673	....	95	20	23974	6075	3685
Orange	65	443	158649	1438	969	390	37996	13462	....
Poyner	31	83	125592	24	755	115	29318	7903	5335
Spring Creek	110	825	64258	....	679	4	15129	4553	1440
Union	22	300	22400	....	....	....	2600	1691	2775
Washington	49	95	40716	....	249	30	12944	6479	4715
Waterloo, exc. of city	33	290	48144	445	293	1283	15504	7557	9202
Waterloo, city of	20	....	....	....	....	....	....	....	....
Total	911	6348	1898424	5033	7852	9682	466324	137294	39400

BOONE COUNTY.

NAMES OF TOWNSHIPS, TOWNS, AND CITIES	Number of stands of bees.	Number of pounds of honey and beeswax in 1874.	Value of products of farm.	Value of market garden produce.	Value of products of the orchard.	Value of small fruit.	Value of products of the herd.	Value of products of the dairy.	Value of products of the forest.
Amaqua	....	....	$ 54777	$ 347	$........	$........	$ 15369	$ 9884	$........
Beaver	....	....	25060	....	....	....	10350	1635	....
Boone, city of	....	....	....	....	....	....	....	....	....
Boonsboro, town of	56	25	2075	295	1171	1714	8000	....	....
Cass	69	840	57996	....	254	20	23551	3049	1701
Colfax	....	....	45728	....	....	....	19573	2615	....
Des Moines, exc. of Boone and Boonsboro	78	330	97435	2817	1612	1994	39476	12842	1868
Dodge	96	888	116176	20	468	446	53802	5647	5222
Douglas	642	....	46604	....	959	508	21912	3750	6585
Garden	10	....	88761	....	179	154	28908	6052	2155
Grant	....	....	35318	12	....	....	875	....	....
Harrison	5	21	38237	....	5	....	74930	....	....
Jackson	4	....	94078	....	....	....	8830	3441	....
Marcy	131	725	....	30	200	1040	32581	4614	....
Peoples	55	105	71629	28	135	30	23450	7790	1685
Pilot Mound	4	80	45599	....	125	25	9845	2147	....
Union	....	....	33777	....	225	200	22694	6810	3665
Worth	71	598	88727	....	1408	473	45782	5067	11003
Yell	74	540	76476	84	122	299	22332	7569	11430
Total	1295	4152	1018453	3633	6863	6903	462260	82512	45314

BREMER COUNTY.

NAMES OF TOWNSHIPS, TOWNS, AND CITIES	Number of stands of bees.	Number of pounds of honey and beeswax in 1874.	Value of products of farm.	Value of market garden produce.	Value of products of the orchard.	Value of small fruit.	Value of products of the herd.	Value of products of the dairy.	Value of products of the forest.
Dayton	....	....	42846	....	....	....	7342	5926	....
Douglas	3	....	86324	....	38	....	15015	8485	2338
Franklin	9	211	108999	....	....	....	6965	8606	5212
Frederika	52	650	25254	....	10	....	8974	4588	1494
Fremont	22	57	94190	29	....	15	38545	13494	326
Jackson	123	955	69887	55	287	276	31507	8070	5248
Jefferson	80	1145	59836	1336	570	229	17582	10158	6406
Lafayette	60	760	104253	205	180	213	28212	7403	6405
Leroy	7	....	48586	....	....	....	6673	....	....
Maxfield	23	450	91371	480	79	....	27910	7218	5862
Polk	23	534	109075	100	496	63	30154	7694	9568
Sumner	....	....	97900	....	143	....	....	2678	9633
Warren	43	750	107664	....	130	....	30172	12130	1071
Washington, exc. Waverly	23	237	84250	2750	555	922	20359	10347	9250
Waverly, city of	30	420	14185	200	6	735	20770	6105	....
Total	498	6169	1144620	5155	2494	2453	290180	112632	62813

BUCHANAN COUNTY.

NAMES OF TOWNSHIPS, TOWNS, AND CITIES	Number of stands of bees.	Number of pounds of honey and beeswax in 1874.	Value of products of farm.	Value of market garden produce.	Value of products of the orchard.	Value of small fruit.	Value of products of the herd.	Value of products of the dairy.	Value of products of the forest.
Buffalo	68	20	194641	50	168	78	29648	9171	1790
Byron	59	205	115467	1340	697	370	27774	1743	220
Cono	8	40	245809	....	184	....	14202	7316	....
Fairbank	52	200	98401	....	25	....	20392	5672	250
Fremont	8	50	92502	....	243	23	16720	12636	....
Hazleton	50	301	87711	27	5	3	20714	7517	3909
Homer	....	....	120293	....	134	....	....	6338	4528
Independence, city of	....	....	....	....	....	....	....	....	....
Jefferson	91	1010	128700	....	635	15	4030	7640	2310
Liberty	37	210	878634	....	513	131	25965	5375	2135
Madison	33	190	90606	20	493	610	13758	16468	....
Middleton	5	25	105235	200	326	646	22675	9889	....

BUCHANAN COUNTY.—Continued.

Names of townships, towns, and cities.	Number of stands of bees.	Number of pounds of honey and beeswax in 1874.	Value of products of farm.	Value of market garden produce.	Value of products of the orchard.	Value of small fruit.	Value of products of the herd.	Value of products of the dairy.	Value of products of the forest.
Newton	57	321	$ 111141	$ 1205	$ 750	$ 197	$ 36328	$ 13645	$ 622
Perry	93	231	81708	245	544	120	59238	11399	3580
Sumner	2		41753		212		6060	2415	
Washington, exc of Independence	37	58	121948	221	404	25	44006	9362	5453
Westburg			101400		345		23516	7165	2600
Total	600	2861	2615949	3308	5678	2218	365027	149439	27397

BUENA VISTA COUNTY.

Names of townships, towns, and cities.	Number of stands of bees.	Number of pounds of honey and beeswax in 1874.	Value of products of farm.	Value of market garden produce.	Value of products of the orchard.	Value of small fruit.	Value of products of the herd.	Value of products of the dairy.	Value of products of the forest.
Barnes			18830	392			2919	1132	
Brookes			5609				972	197	340
Coon			11080				804		
Elk			34169					811	
Fairfield			6413				600	721	
Grant	1	20	5815				267	567	
Lee			12600	75			2377	1615	1120
Lincoln			2833				470	399	
Maple Valley			23736	71				608	
Newell			9961				6738	341	
Nokomis	1		33319				2500	146	
Poland			5273					637	
Providence			7032	20			55	583	
Scott			6820				290	858	
Storm Lake, exc. of town			23473	290		32	2703	1045	
Storm Lake, town of	1		865					440	
Total	3	20	207828	848		32	20695	10100	1460

BUTLER COUNTY.

Names of townships, towns, and cities.	Number of stands of bees.	Number of pounds of honey and beeswax in 1874.	Value of products of farm.	Value of market garden produce.	Value of products of the orchard.	Value of small fruit.	Value of products of the herd.	Value of products of the dairy.	Value of products of the forest.
Albion	92	770	65750		400		15329	6927	8350
Beaver	89	915	101955	5	379	357	10431	14007	1675
Bennezett	1	150	36382				3197	2091	1147
Butler, exc. of Clarksville	21	140	119771	420	712	74	34437	5949	7910
Clarksville, town of									
Cold Water	8		60702	45	165		9635	4762	880
Dayton	8	133	81173	20	2	30	16133	2515	3399
Fremont	7	40	102275	17	57		14924	3690	2273
Jackson			77666		30		19126	4009	
Jefferson	22	369	90682	453	201	148	19355	6465	4321
Madison	4	60	62089		30		9016	3044	950
Monroe	54	632	76992	30			10099	8070	
Pittsford	60	880	56047	15	95	80	10280	3426	6110
Ripley	6		34010				28775	6443	
Shell Rock	15		123646	132	395	5	20931	10071	4104
Washington	10	166	69133	378	6	5	10784	3745	158
West Point	1		51512				12727	2766	4242
Total	398	4255	1209785	1515	2472	699	245159	87980	45519

CALHOUN COUNTY.

NAMES OF TOWNSHIPS, TOWNS, AND CITIES.	Number of stands of bees.	Number of pounds of honey and beeswax in 1874.	Value of products of farm.	Value of market garden produce.	Value of produce of the orchard.	Value of small fruit.	Value of products of the herd.	Value of products of the dairy.	Value of products of the forest.
Butler			$ 11538	$	$	$	$ 1184	$ 1147	$
Calhoun			39404				9209		
Center			7467				715	419	
Greenfield			11898				726		
Jackson	43	370	93370				15407	2490	
Lincoln			25350	3			10125	2834	
Sherman			24399					3366	
Williams			8187					1305	
Total	43	370	221613	3			37366	11561	

CARROLL COUNTY.

NAMES OF TOWNSHIPS, TOWNS, AND CITIES.	Number of stands of bees.	Number of pounds of honey and beeswax in 1874.	Value of products of farm.	Value of market garden produce.	Value of produce of the orchard.	Value of small fruit.	Value of products of the herd.	Value of products of the dairy.	Value of products of the forest.
Arcadia			38075				4271	1290	
Carroll, exc. of town			12940				20779		
Carroll, town of									
Eden			26591				2876		
Glidden			26000	1200	400	100	2000	3100	6250
Grant			14562				2335		
Jasper			27174				7886		
Kniest			90621	66	80	40	11619	1602	
Newton	3	10	29321		50		6516		2643
Pleasant Valley			40987				3009	2994	706
Richland									
Roselle			23964						
Sheridan			48108				865		2589
Union			18135		40		10162	970	295
Washington			19702				1849	1056	
Wheatland			35185					1022	
Total	3	10	451365	1266	570	140	74170	12034	12483

CASS COUNTY.

NAMES OF TOWNSHIPS, TOWNS, AND CITIES.	Number of stands of bees.	Number of pounds of honey and beeswax in 1874.	Value of products of farm.	Value of market garden produce.	Value of produce of the orchard.	Value of small fruit.	Value of products of the herd.	Value of products of the dairy.	Value of products of the forest.
Atlantic, exc. of town			141382		540	45	66174	4700	2133
Atlantic, town of	1		1000						
Bear Grove			22820			20	3406	1140	
Benton	28	155	53517	13	162	28	25227	1392	2335
Brighton	11	252	104690	110			28936	3350	2675
Cass	45	1260	111386	66	809	635	52122	3933	1206
Edna	12	345	55525	1195			10937	1535	2675
Franklin			104390				16835	3932	3669
Grant	12	410	43138	25	10		4069	1568	
Lincoln			49410	70			8646	1209	
Massena			26020	435			6099		
Noble			86879		14		12980	3231	
Pleasant			96857		25	15	18475	300	
Pymosa	35	575	161143	1660	113	277	40047	4600	1197
Union	2	60	40726				6777	2239	671
Victoria			42252				1266	1267	2118
Washington	15	206	143764				61966	3155	
Total	161	3263	1284899	3574	1673	1020	163962	37551	18679

CEDAR COUNTY.

NAMES OF TOWNSHIPS, TOWNS, AND CITIES.	Number of stands of bees.	Number of pounds of honey and beeswax in 1874.	Value of products of farm.	Value of market garden products.	Value of products of the orchard.	Value of small fruit.	Value of products of the herd.	Value of products of the dairy.	Value of products of the forest.
Cass	33	95	$ 101840	$ 1690	$ 1044	$ 299	$ 31596	$ 4899	$ 3655
Center, exc. of Tipton	94	235	240589	110	4330	1447	171753	10591	14367
Clarence, town of	......	......	......	......	......	......	......	......	......
Dayton, exc. of Clarence	8	50	201885	150	393	329	70496	11584	......
Durant, town of	10	50	......	35	10	216	......	......	......
Fairfield	70	455	218782	142	497	943	84270	8792	1069
Farmington, exc. of Durant	27	8	221389	1950	2715	477	93927	6747	1275
Fremont	30	370	179632	400	165	170	96796	......	......
Gower	35	187	139095	20	2940	572	46871	8780	4422
Inland	44	725	128794	144	245	260	31632	492	1625
Iowa	74	470	224010	95	2421	1070	69290	13525	5792
Linn	45	150	78205	51	258	570	43665	3398	3656
Louden, town of	4	100	1970	391	......	97	......	......	......
Massillon	68	500	155928	5	441	779	56231	29081	1825
Mechanicsville, town of	11	......	......	......	......	......	......	......	......
Pioneer, exc. of Mechanicsville	25	45	129182	159	380	866	50990	8634	7657
Red Oak	36	315	98723	939	688	689	51090	6999	4944
Rochester	21	200	64792	......	......	......	24047	......	5242
Springdale	68	872	176255	237	3117	2302	59684	20662	4370
Springfield, exc. of Louden	72	491	161672	502	653	567	46329	8205	4341
Sugar Creek	5	100	83406	134	762	656	15295	4362	3538
Tipton, town of	3	......	......	......	......	1780	......	2622	......
Total	783	5418	2606149	7154	21059	14089	1043962	149373	67778

CERRO GORDO COUNTY.

Clear Lake, exc. of town	......	......	27291	655	18	47	......	4189	5205
Clear Lake, town of	......	......	......	......	......	......	......	......	......
Daugherty	......	27	24820	......	......	......	......	253	......
Falls	......	......	93519	......	66	......	10582	5116	2397
Geneseo	......	......	48713	99	......	......	6159	1848	4050
Grant	31	245	13790	155	......	5	1046	1276	136
Lake	11	......	29133	......	......	......	380	6385	......
Lime Creek	50	290	73696	771	14	65	8515	2011	3603
Lincoln	......	......	60411	26	......	......	9725	......	1541
Mason, exc. of Mason City	12	142	101266	......	......	......	11437	5430	1820
Mason City, town of	......	......	......	......	......	......	......	......	......
Owen	......	......	47331	......	55	......	5298	3475	420
Portland	10	125	71647	60	......	......	6146	1630	178
Total	114	829	591617	1766	153	117	59288	31613	19350

CHEROKEE COUNTY.

Afton	......	......	59858	17	......	65	1407	9396	12
Amhurst	......	......	10801	121	......	......	653	560	......
Cedar	......	......	17425	......	......	......	......	......	......
Cherokee, exc. of town	......	......	43774	......	......	......	7830	2592	......
Cherokee, town of	......	......	5410	50	......	......	2068	1227	828
Diamond	......	......	14767	......	......	......	20	351	......
Liberty	......	......	15004	......	......	......	245	90	......
Marcus	......	......	10205	......	......	......	......	......	......
Pilot	2	5	51190	103	......	......	9502	2276	925
Pitcher	......	......	47550	......	......	......	......	4777	......
Sheridan	......	......	......	......	......	......	......	......	......

CHEROKEE COUNTY.—Continued.

Names of townships, towns, and cities.	Number of stands of bees.	Number of pounds of honey and beeswax in 1874.	Value of products of farm.	Value of market garden produce.	Value of products of the orchard.	Value of small fruit.	Value of products of the herd.	Value of products of the dairy.	Value of products of the forest.
Silver	....	....	$ 21765	$ 15	$........	$........	$ 193	$ 1029	$........
Spring	....	....	5475	....	....	....	....	....	550
Tilden	....	....	21532	....	....	....	1790	675	....
Willow	....	....	25441	....	....	....	5341	839	....
Total	2	5	350197	306	....	65	29049	23812	2315

CHICKASAW COUNTY.

Names of townships, towns, and cities.	Number of stands of bees.	Number of pounds of honey and beeswax in 1874.	Value of products of farm.	Value of market garden produce.	Value of products of the orchard.	Value of small fruit.	Value of products of the herd.	Value of products of the dairy.	Value of products of the forest.
Bradford, exc of Nashua	133	2640	91557	210	....	200	21607	7846	10254
Chickasaw	30	614	71040	....	38	....	13216	6235	1987
Dayton	....	....	25456	....	....	....	2957	5517	....
Deerfield	51	125	92360	....	....	....	21790	8215	5705
Dresden	....	....	58839	104	4	3	13438	5125	815
Fredricksburgh	13	37	68570	110	238	26	4900	6161	145
Jacksonville	47	55	89791	15	33	....	18070	12277	....
Nashua, town of	....	....	4400	....	....	....	500	....	....
New Hampton, exc. of town	5	40	35781	....	72	49	6030	6861	570
New Hampton, town of	....	....	....	....	....	....	....	....	....
Richland	36	670	60620	....	72	....	5225	9389	2680
Stapleton	7	20	80765	5	....	25	22711	12634	....
Utica	30	350	132197	....	112	96	20297	13453	....
Washington	4	10	83270	....	....	....	14674	3566	40
Total	356	4561	894656	444	569	399	165415	97279	22196

CLARKE COUNTY.

Names of townships, towns, and cities.	Number of stands of bees.	Number of pounds of honey and beeswax in 1874.	Value of products of farm.	Value of market garden produce.	Value of products of the orchard.	Value of small fruit.	Value of products of the herd.	Value of products of the dairy.	Value of products of the forest.
Doyle, exc. of Hopeville	45	195	5696348	29	550	50	468975	823718	162248
Franklin	45	520	78506	....	1330	309	33862	4137	4407
Fremont	54	542	70984	....	955	555	38951	5650	6425
Green Bay	62	651	94347	1924	937	2154	19099	3232	4375
Hopeville, town of	24	165	270490	16	....	....	16715	447	....
Jackson	35	175	57204	293	612	227	42175	5306	....
Knox	55	470	115353	156	1825	463	28083	7936	....
Liberty	57	516	84286	1248	687	474	41427	3135	7502
Madison	36	240	63902	....	....	70	158041	1871	5734
Osceola, exc. of town	29	210	48200	12	476	242	20102	3054	1163
Osceola, town of	27	130	35180	484	1183	1295	4872	4458	735
Troy	6	....	308513	....	....	....	31817	408	....
Ward	42	179	70233	953	325	198	34086	3371	2715
Washington	33	93	61441	155	1576	25	25491	2731	115
Total	550	4086	7054987	5270	10455	6062	964896	869454	195414

CLAY COUNTY.

Names of townships, towns, and cities.	Number of stands of bees.	Number of pounds of honey and beeswax in 1874.	Value of products of farm.	Value of market garden produce.	Value of products of the orchard.	Value of small fruit.	Value of products of the herd.	Value of products of the dairy.	Value of products of the forest.
Bridgewater	....	....	15665	34	....	....	2075	2590	....
Clay	....	....	39950	....	....	....	770	....	475
Douglas	....	....	12490	....	....	....	2846	2531	3868
Gillett's Grove	....	....	13757	....	....	....	2159	769	3738
Herdland	....	....	6756	758	....	....	1373	424	270
Lincoln	....	....	....	....	....	....	....	....	....

CLAY COUNTY.—Continued.

Names of townships, towns, and cities.	Number of stands of bees.	Number of pounds of honey and beeswax in 1874.	Value of products of farm.	Value of market garden produce.	Value of products of the orchard.	Value of small fruit.	Value of products of the herd.	Value of products of the dairy.	Value of products of the forest.
Riverton	....	....	$ 17780	$	$	$	$ 3720	$ 920	$ ......
Spencer	....	....	....	....	....	....	....	....	....
Summit	....	....	16945	....	....	10	2214	1368	....
Total	....	....	123343	792	....	10	15157	8602	8351

CLAYTON COUNTY.

Names of townships, towns, and cities.	Number of stands of bees.	Number of pounds of honey and beeswax in 1874.	Value of products of farm.	Value of market garden produce.	Value of products of the orchard.	Value of small fruit.	Value of products of the herd.	Value of products of the dairy.	Value of products of the forest.
Boardman	....	....	135219	129	1335	....	63465	4985	....
Buena Vista	....	....	8275	....	43	3	20	....	....
Cass	33	....	63688	165	798	113	32178	9997	1525
Clayton	3	320	62248	615	1189	410	14767	4276	4410
Cox Creek	....	....	66456	98	220	70	23153	2836	3076
Elk	29	665	49830	2132	1461	101	15666	6278	11092
Farmersburg	4	....	190172	....	510	30	59526	7926	5079
Garnavillo	49	220	136897	5883	1875	760	51237	15820	10646
Giard	31	350	134076	....	764	171	30462	16038	4487
Grand Meadow	11	215	157235	56	830	69	32569	8551	1482
Guttenberg, town of	11	260	1722	1396	210	43	5099	4936	491
Highland	1	....	99350	....	675	200	3827	3520	4215
Jefferson, exc. Guttenberg	13	175	162905	5445	1184	265	31675	18659	9075
Lodomillo	75	930	68407	2870	2653	551	24335	7442	11037
McGregor, town of	....	....	....	....	....	....	....	....	....
Mallory	63	780	67422	....	2321	11	27747	4247	15012
Marion	....	....	91996	45	46	15	18082	2916	90
Mendon, exc. of McGregor and North McGregor	21	375	24330	3854	1338	1255	4200	4293	2260
Millville	6	82	43857	135	599	44	3561	1401	4336
Monona	13	50	184491	....	1037	....	23850	12890	....
North McGregor, town of	....	....	....	....	....	....	....	....	....
Read	5	....	81415	3072	500	317	33653	4741	4764
Sperry	23	222	103510	....	423	75	30335	10934	....
Volga	....	....	....	....	....	....	....	....	....
Wagner	....	....	148292	....	89	....	17444	4687	....
Total	391	4644	2081793	25895	20100	4503	546851	157373	93077

CLINTON COUNTY.

Names of townships, towns, and cities.	Number of stands of bees.	Number of pounds of honey and beeswax in 1874.	Value of products of farm.	Value of market garden produce.	Value of products of the orchard.	Value of small fruit.	Value of products of the herd.	Value of products of the dairy.	Value of products of the forest.
Berlin	10	175	162157	....	1791	65	50903	10426	5
Bloomfield	7	75	180884	3409	1573	1661	60054	16143	....
Brookfield	....	....	198974	1764	1184	1515	86577	14956	....
Camanche, exc. of town	4	100	98995	800	4332	290	26098	9627	75
Camanche, town of	....	....	6968	....	....	....	2687	1674	....
Center	1	....	249652	....	1114	87	185540	17648	....
Clinton, exc. of city	64	822	20185	2623	849	2760	5566	3420	53
Clinton, city of	....	....	....	....	....	....	....	....	....
Deep Creek	1	82	198661	6	721	26	95673	14052	....
De Witt, exc. of town	131	1470	225073	102	1296	1220	82876	18393	350
De Witt, town of	19	325	8305	585	2736	1089	21754	2699	....
Eden	....	....	286947	1440	1366	697	40091	16871	939
Elk River	72	430	214221	....	791	....	100900	10726	6539
Hampshire	104	1620	112707	....	1277	55	56117	7116	500
Liberty	33	245	128817	....	344	279	34026	10028	2795
Lincoln	....	....	65056	150	1595	137	42361	6716	....
Lyons exc. of city	29	1300	32796	102	1458	1489	4959	4004	1316
Lyons, city of	....	....	....	....	....	....	....	....	....
Olive	40	360	208555	2097	165	110	54936	8109	540

CLINTON COUNTY.—CONTINUED.

NAMES OF TOWNSHIPS, TOWNS, AND CITIES.	Number of stands of bees.	Number of pounds of honey and beeswax in 1874.	Value of products of farm.	Value of market garden produce.	Value of products of the orchard.	Value of small fruit.	Value of products of the herd.	Value of products of the dairy.	Value of products of the forest.
Orange	70	459	$ 132329	$ 27	$ 561	$ 633	$ 23134	$ 11587	$ 771
Sharon	27	400	136161	17	1096	17	67393	15686	10
Spring Rock, exc. of Wheatland	25	300	37081	....	....	....	46116	4909	620
Washington	....	....	160490	....	....	....	35119	5680	....
Waterford	13	50	98376	200	64	31	29998	2716	....
Welton	6	30	135004	....	245	5	8811	5996	....
Wheatland, town of	1	30	625	....	25	20	600	....	....
Total	657	8273	3049019	13322	24583	12186	1162289	219182	14513

CRAWFORD COUNTY.

NAMES OF TOWNSHIPS, TOWNS, AND CITIES.	Number of stands of bees.	Number of pounds of honey and beeswax in 1874.	Value of products of farm.	Value of market garden produce.	Value of products of the orchard.	Value of small fruit.	Value of products of the herd.	Value of products of the dairy.	Value of products of the forest.
Boyer	16	100	30274	....	....	....	17758	....	....
Charter Oak	....	....	14605	....	....	....	5860	....	....
Denison	37	595	40686	902	65	255	64108	18875	2340
East Boyer	....	....	43709	....	....	....	11499	....	....
Goodrich	7	200	34175	....	....	....	6605	2369	....
Hanover	....	....	1110	....	....	....	300	....	....
Hays	....	...	24735	....	....	....	3029	346	....
Iowa	....	....	7687	....	....	....	980	1874	....
Jackson	....	....	27501	....	....	....	....	1501	....
Milford	8	100	44394	110	240	305	15422	2743	4618
Morgan	....	....	9200	....	....	....	105	196	176
Nishnabotany	....	....	4857	....	....	....	2406	495	....
Otter Creek	....	....	38905	....	....	....	2300	446	1125
Paradise	5	50	22824	5	....	....	2030	595	....
Soldier	....	....	4302	....	....	....	474	86	....
Stockholm	....	....	25295	....	....	....	10218	....	....
Union	30	182	50653	76	18	500	16552	1807	600
Washington	6	75	20146	....	....	....	4012	....	....
West Side	....	....	32418	45	....	....	12909	1227	....
Willow	....	......	5861	....	....	....	2899	15	....
Total	109	1302	483337	1138	323	1060	179516	32575	8859

DALLAS COUNTY.

NAMES OF TOWNSHIPS, TOWNS, AND CITIES.	Number of stands of bees.	Number of pounds of honey and beeswax in 1874.	Value of products of farm.	Value of market garden produce.	Value of products of the orchard.	Value of small fruit.	Value of products of the herd.	Value of products of the dairy.	Value of products of the forest.
Adams	106	565	112625	1415	1953	160	35554	5175	....
Adel, exc. of town	46	675	129366	60	4353	620	51708	6995	3754
Adel, town of	19	285	....	....	60	....	16004	2106	....
Beaver	8	40	43709	....	25	....	27555	2538	....
Boone	45	415	131612	....	260	200	47650	3180	2867
Colfax	24	187	111514	75	350	85	64593	10285	2214
Dallas	24	66	63195	....	....	....	23487	2021	....
Des Moines	44	175	61507	4	1238	170	31522	4206	3569
Dexter, town of	....	....	....	....	....	....	....	....	....
Grant	....	....	86844	14	130	142	29809	4779	....
Lincoln	1	40	57673	5	10	....	10630	2088	....
Linn	48	248	118869	....	5509	310	44167	17460	....
Spring Valley	12	160	82786	90	210	151	26358	4006	1607
Sugar Grove	49	290	82334	289	3172	273	14534	1375	1689
Union, exc. of Dexter	80	540	109666	1171	2562	523	61639	5642	194
Vanmeter	165	1166	115044	889	1782	1341	54570	5544	4469
Walnut	....	....	128563	1170	....	505	19098	4171	465
Washington	27	485	63740	40	305	12	26108	6220	3935
Total	698	5337	1502047	5222	21919	4492	584986	87791	24763

DAVIS COUNTY.

NAMES OF TOWNSHIPS, TOWNS, AND CITIES.	Number of stands of bees.	Number of pounds of honey and beeswax in 1874.	Value of products of farm.	Value of market garden produce.	Value of products of the orchard.	Value of small fruit.	Value of products of the herd.	Value of products of the dairy.	Value of products of the forest.
Bloomfield, exc. of town	178	628	$ 201872	$ 6124	$ 7437	$ 2045	$ 84014	$ 24870	$ 5186
Bloomfield, town of	29	210	20	50	240	175	28	....	....
Drakeville, exc. of town	25	136	149939	397	1397	137	42998	1640	1203
Drakeville, town of	13	40	4917	773	188	359	6281	1365	....
Fabius	172	1977	77798	772	1809	155	87438	5127	....
Fox River	107	346	35035	934	1141	382	25532	3112	3075
Grove	307	3480	221332	....	2985	1354	55976	6487	....
Lick Creek	100	843	99195	14	2288	532	72244	7814	9442
Marion	109	655	75660	1165	670	115	35738	5610	5080
Perry	32	105	44850	....	444	79	17825	1797	638
Prairie	121	591	77790	815	2111	10	31105	340	....
Roscoe	147	668	75901	1220	2470	1043	39392	9035	....
Salt Creek	81	334	87385	377	1578	252	42387	5214	16351
Soap Greek	133	453	82312	169	1679	576	37585	3468	5617
Union	234	1705	98023	2450	3215	1033	68002	6353	563
West Grove	197	1572	139068	281	2198	289	68921	13223	5314
Wyacondah	177	842	131993	....	2300	....	118948	....	....
Total	2162	14585	1603090	15541	34150	8536	834414	95455	52469

DECATUR COUNTY.

NAMES OF TOWNSHIPS, TOWNS, AND CITIES.	Number of stands of bees.	Number of pounds of honey and beeswax in 1874.	Value of products of farm.	Value of market garden produce.	Value of products of the orchard.	Value of small fruit.	Value of products of the herd.	Value of products of the dairy.	Value of products of the forest.
Bloomington	14	155	50356	40	....	....	13606	1884	2416
Burrell	86	396	55065	1846	860	84	25582	3676	786
Center, exc. of Leon	47	335	80203	610	1140	207	58671	2888	25
Decatur	66	385	80909	1827	2994	532	67152	4898	6480
Eden	82	1163	49842	1038	1463	383	21015	4414	7095
Fayette	16	202	39055	....	186	131	19354	5396	....
Franklin	56	690	115205	2753	1488	341	69088	5146	1226
Garden Grove	157	1479	130418	330	1640	894	87353	7242	4307
Grand River	19	37	39555	....	100	10	8372	1538	1865
Hamilton	88	462	29262	....	412	15	16455	1998	6592
High Point	73	675	73302	1574	1177	367	28079	6932	5418
Leon, town of	....	....	....	....	....	....	....	....	....
Long Creek	59	121	68150	1898	820	10	26833	3261	....
Morgan	47	135	38244	316	432	150	4905	2220	952
New Buda	39	102	41371	102	740	....	26891	1945	2400
Richland	51	292	71694	560	510	193	21218	3676	1995
Woodland	133	647	61910	1470	1275	165	44337	5675	180
Total	1033	7276	1024541	14364	15237	3482	538911	62789	41737

DELAWARE COUNTY.

NAMES OF TOWNSHIPS, TOWNS, AND CITIES.	Number of stands of bees.	Number of pounds of honey and beeswax in 1874.	Value of products of farm.	Value of market garden produce.	Value of products of the orchard.	Value of small fruit.	Value of products of the herd.	Value of products of the dairy.	Value of products of the forest.
Adams	12	12	118868	10	554	147	49521	12209	5649
Bremen	17	19	57277	....	....	....	22458	....	....
Coffin's Grove	63	372	96780	523	504	318	32823	14159	6915
Colony	32	105	159331	162	1707	23	74849	8130	4233
Delaware, exc. of Manchester	71	593	88513	1760	993	146	25315	17066	1155
Delhi	53	606	83375	3017	1534	1045	32367	9243	8817
Elk	9	45	91771	....	....	....	30330	9272	....
Hazel Green	32	129	75405	25	256	68	32975	12069	2753
Honey Creek	126	2070	144767	975	2029	654	41518	12166	3759
Hopkinton, town of	4	....	....	....	....	....	7950	....	....
Manchester, town of	37	800	77491	267	315	61	26106	2720	100
Milo	17	50	100255	170	260	449	25392	15839	3315
North Fork	21	131	72323	....	145	10	42338	9311	....

DECATUR COUNTY.—Continued.

NAMES OF TOWNSHIPS, TOWNS, AND CITIES.	Number of stands of bees.	Number of pounds of honey and beeswax in 1874.	Value of products of farm.	Value of market garden produce.	Value of products of the orchard.	Value of small fruit.	Value of products of the herd.	Value of products of the dairy.	Value of products of the forest.
Oneida	32	340	$ 128530	$ 320	$ 1098	$ 225	$ 38076	$ 17489	$14851
Prairie	17	15	89494	....	250	....	27263	10136	....
Richland	88	455	66530	874	347	192	17360	9812	2585
South Fork, exc. of Hopkinton	53	329	177302	2153	152	237	45509	21257	6123
Union	95	1113	61802	2728	72175	67	32885	6425	5293
Total	729	7184	1690314	12984	82319	3642	605035	187303	65548

DES MOINES COUNTY.

NAMES OF TOWNSHIPS, TOWNS, AND CITIES.	Number of stands of bees.	Number of pounds of honey and beeswax in 1874.	Value of products of farm.	Value of market garden produce.	Value of products of the orchard.	Value of small fruit.	Value of products of the herd.	Value of products of the dairy.	Value of products of the forest.
Augusta	63	74	43065	80	1955	518	18445	3672	3973
Benton	83	505	146487	2496	3264	492	21161	13082	10280
Burlington, exc. of city	160	591	87780	6983	11702	2716	9652	12350	7693
Burlington, city of	....	....	....	....	....	....	....	....	....
Danville	106	291	221192	3172	7365	2747	84556	27117	7359
Flint River	34	171	132561	2065	6041	2479	31884	17189	8655
Franklin	74	392	187730	....	3915	....	54015	11230	1915
Huron	111	30[illegible]	103590	....	3530	100	49662	5539	....
Jackson	12	80	30526	....	....	....	25797	....	....
Pleasant Grove	24	112	104803	....	3664	106	66082	12545	1641
Union	73	71	186340	8015	15725	7213	38245	11560	15110
Washington	29	30	272667	15	1544	247	88980	7005	4145
Yellow Springs	81	421	256251	638	5253	2097	136460	181836	51853
Total	850	3038	1772992	23464	63958	18710	624939	303125	112624

DICKINSON COUNTY.

NAMES OF TOWNSHIPS, TOWNS, AND CITIES.	Number of stands of bees.	Number of pounds of honey and beeswax in 1874.	Value of products of farm.	Value of market garden produce.	Value of products of the orchard.	Value of small fruit.	Value of products of the herd.	Value of products of the dairy.	Value of products of the forest.
Center Grove	....	....	16756	334	....	....	4719	3219	3193
Diamond Lake	....	....	....	....	....	....	....	....	....
Excelsior	....	....	2011	49	....	5	1513	....	....
Lakeville	....	....	4005	....	....	3	322	994	804
Lloyd	....	....	4902	38	....	....	926	1191	....
Milford	....	....	6719	....	....	....	1114	790	....
Okoboji	....	....	7902	....	....	....	1824	816	1101
Richland	....	....	1739	17	....	....	611	415	....
Silver Lake	....	....	1300	....	....	....	....	....	....
Spirit Lake	....	....	....	....	....	....	2116	60	....
Superior	....	....	....	....	....	....	....	....	....
Total	....	....	45334	438	....	8	13145	7485	5098

DUBUQUE COUNTY.

NAMES OF TOWNSHIPS, TOWNS, AND CITIES.	Number of stands of bees.	Number of pounds of honey and beeswax in 1874.	Value of products of farm.	Value of market garden produce.	Value of products of the orchard.	Value of small fruit.	Value of products of the herd.	Value of products of the dairy.	Value of products of the forest.
Cascade	23	195	68766	223	443	5	4969	4045	923
Center	52	3805	57361	167	1109	28	24972	5623	75658
Concord	....	....	95882	....	343	110	36907	4501	....
Dodge	2	....	83460	....	120	....	245	5646	....
Dubuque, city of	....	....	3400	14100	150	300	....	....	....
Dyersville, town of	49	150	3500	10	2	2	5766	2268	120
Iowa	10	50	62831	105	39	65	36609	40	6205
Jefferson	23	294	99465	....	2511	480	47386	9018	6465
Julien, exc. of Dubuque	16	85	89920	8525	1420	1585	31775	21985	565
Liberty	....	....	33943	....	....	....	33045	....	....

DUBUQUE COUNTY.—Continued.

NAMES OF TOWNSHIPS, TOWNS, AND CITIES.	Number of stands of bees.	Number of pounds of honey and beeswax in 1874.	Value of products of farm.	Value of market garden produce.	Value of products of the orchard.	Value of small fruit.	Value of products of the herd.	Value of products of the dairy.	Value of products of the forest.
Mosalem	....	....	$ 54680	$........	$........	$........	$........	$........	$ 4264
New Wine, exc. of Dyersville	....	....	153250	....	61	12	73003	17565	1960
Peru	6	30	71085	1830	970	335	8701	8240	6026
Prairie Creek	2	....	134435	....	....	....	70504	5092	....
Table Mound	....	....	88470	....	190	....	37800	5051	....
Taylor	122	5030	109590	30	517	426	56425	7010	16430
Vernon	25	125	155569	200	594	22	79058	11887	6505
Washington	13	50	172734	50	155	70	56663	6550	....
Whitewater	6	....	97791	....	168	10	45577	3384	2379
Total	349	9814	1636132	25240	8792	3450	646405	117905	127500

EMMET COUNTY.

NAMES OF TOWNSHIPS, TOWNS, AND CITIES.	Number of stands of bees.	Number of pounds of honey and beeswax in 1874.	Value of products of farm.	Value of market garden produce.	Value of products of the orchard.	Value of small fruit.	Value of products of the herd.	Value of products of the dairy.	Value of products of the forest.
Armstrong Grove	2	....	3027	....	....	....	945	1614	275
Center	....	....	370	....	....	....	1155	752	600
Ellsworth	....	....	781	....	....	....	....	810	....
Emmet	5	....	1377	17	....	....	751	1868	760
Estherville	37	303	7110	....	....	4	4869	3578	878
High Lake	....	....	1063	5	....	....	1904	1880	180
Iowa Lake	....	....	....	....	....	....	480	855	....
Peterson	18	....	1516	3	....	....	2193	2250	....
Swan Lake	....	....	....	....	....	....	200	350	....
Total	62	303	15244	25	....	4	12497	13957	2693

FAYETTE COUNTY.

NAMES OF TOWNSHIPS, TOWNS, AND CITIES.	Number of stands of bees.	Number of pounds of honey and beeswax in 1874.	Value of products of farm.	Value of market garden produce.	Value of products of the orchard.	Value of small fruit.	Value of products of the herd.	Value of products of the dairy.	Value of products of the forest.
Auburn	63	575	64985	....	....	....	3345	4746	....
Banks	....	....	27972	....	....	....	6440	2633	....
Bethel	3	10	49188	267	66	15	8137	5197	3631
Center	5	....	54361	....	....	....	14430	5141	3051
Clermont	....	....	128718	....	450	....	15274	5239	....
Dover	33	321	97481	224	814	119	23479	8608	7803
Eden	108	776	87080	....	46	100	16808	11387	....
Fairfield	31	330	93483	....	190	5	20643	8425	645
Fayette, town of	154	1636	....	....	....	....	....	....	....
Fremont	19	33	56107	....	24	....	12709	8240	3109
Harlan	3	505	63226	....	110	....	16452	5465	4872
Illyria	14	400	87351	....	456	10	26281	7148	7270
Jefferson	....	....	70116	....	....	....	....	....	....
Oran	21	100	88123	....	....	28	16986	9931	4740
Pleasant Valley	26	350	64720	150	438	81	15397	....	18506
Putnam	26	85	69140	70	419	62	18446	12529	3886
Scott	....	....	58895	....	....	....	8405	6170	3300
Smithfield	26	158	119663	38	571	....	13674	8105	364
Westfield, exc. of Fayette	38	473	3527	....	30	....	1320	785	3565
West Union, exc. of town	68	1690	115260	330	621	270	44471	9420	6908
West Union, town of	....	....	12254	....	30	967	4145	750	1860
Windsor	82	346	91477	216	205	10	22880	11627	380
Total	720	7788	1503127	1295	4470	1667	309722	131546	73890

FLOYD COUNTY.

NAMES OF TOWNSHIPS, TOWNS, AND CITIES.	Number of stands of bees.	Number of pounds of honey and beeswax in 1874.	Value of products of farm.	Value of market garden produce.	Value of products of the orchard.	Value of small fruit.	Value of products of the herd.	Value of products of the dairy.	Value of products of the forest.
Cedar	94	639	$ 6337	$ 593	$ 85	$ 10	$ 13828	$ 3570	$
Charles City, city of	26	91	3043	130	20	125	7208	7804	100
Floyd	77	100	106003	2301	411	521	10675	12449	7678
Niles	29	220	70884		5		4106	6880	3208
Nora Springs, town of	27	3	27518		81	182	2880	2766	2691
Pleasant Grove			95566	1062			11188	6091	4461
Riverton	35	255	132168	1532	2690	883	20062	4555	6555
Rockford	47	139	112295	100	48	589	19527	13051	6690
Rock Grove, exc. of Nora Springs	43		91138		811	417	8822	7295	5011
Rudd			75126			38	6485	4520	356
St. Charles, exc. of Charles City	89	263	324464	592	241	54	78892	13909	18714
Scott	5	50	78882				6098	5851	1090
Ulster	29	210	99145				13753	6872	4447
Union	21	43	87808	17		206	26603	7044	5609
Total	522	2013	1367377	6327	4392	3025	230127	102657	66610

FRANKLIN COUNTY.

NAMES OF TOWNSHIPS, TOWNS, AND CITIES.	Number of stands of bees.	Number of pounds of honey and beeswax in 1874.	Value of products of farm.	Value of market garden produce.	Value of products of the orchard.	Value of small fruit.	Value of products of the herd.	Value of products of the dairy.	Value of products of the forest.
Clinton	14	775	81713	245	12	104	26284	8314	209
Geneva	3		90061		8	72	12552	5246	
Grant			26900						
Hamilton	1		24532	3			4956	1853	
Hampton, town of	45	300	1317		70	40	3405	792	
Ingham			6552				37575		
Lee			18750					3315	
Marion			11574	4			1808	41585	1235
Morgan			37024	2355			2598		
Oakland	11		38495				15312	3705	350
Osceola			177103		20	155	21222		5180
Reeve	4	50	89380	450			15475	5733	429
Richland			40288		6	2	12939		
Washington	24	150	101891	15		4	36416	3593	392
West Fork			31526				3732	280	
Total	102	1275	777106	3072	116	377	194274	74416	7795

FREMONT COUNTY.

NAMES OF TOWNSHIPS, TOWNS, AND CITIES.	Number of stands of bees.	Number of pounds of honey and beeswax in 1874.	Value of products of farm.	Value of market garden produce.	Value of products of the orchard.	Value of small fruit.	Value of products of the herd.	Value of products of the dairy.	Value of products of the forest.
Bartlett									
Benton, exc. of Eastport and Percival	12	20	106035	300		110	33107	3960	2350
Eastport, town of									
Farragut, town of									
Fisher, exc. of Farragut	10	20	75198	75	20	130	93401	3922	30
Franklin, exc. of Hamburg	81	249	115469	380	2856		82211	54	1937
Fremont City, town of									
Hamburg, city of									
Locust Grove			36798	350	520		2267		
McPaul, town of									
Madison	81	640	103582	644	2236	209	97932	8480	4660
Monroe	11	130	97382	35	176	20	82547	4710	
Percival, town of									
Prairie	7		70543		165		31593	1529	
Riverton, exc. of town	42	684	6772		10		29403	760	
Riverton, town of									

FREMONT COUNTY.—Continued.

Names of townships, towns, and cities.	Number of stands of bees.	Number of pounds of honey and beeswax in 1874.	Value of products of farm.	Value of market garden produce.	Value of produce of the orchard.	Value of small fruit.	Value of products of the herd.	Value of products of the dairy.	Value of products of the forest.
Ross, exc. of Tabor	100	1030	$ 142292	$ 8	$ 1484	$ 481	$ 120975	$ 4442	$ 4380
Scott, exc. of McPaul, Bartlett, and Fremont City	144	1056	86146	......	950	529	70833	3793	12836
Sidney, exc. of town	228	4324	154398	2744	8847	1917	65972	6991	8308
Sidney, town of	17	200	....	10	565	265	....	....	....
Tabor, town of	4	20	2891	270	267	321	25204	410	....
Walnut	15	30	48560	....	65	7	57323	3262	....
Total	752	8403	1046066	4816	18161	3989	792768	42313	33901

GREENE COUNTY.

Names of townships, towns, and cities.	Number of stands of bees.	Number of pounds of honey and beeswax in 1874.	Value of products of farm.	Value of market garden produce.	Value of produce of the orchard.	Value of small fruit.	Value of products of the herd.	Value of products of the dairy.	Value of products of the forest.
Bristol	....	....	70400	....	350	....	33436	7522	4245
Cedar	2	22	27685	....	....	....	18335	2710	3367
Dawson	....	....	3100	300	....	....	645	465	....
Franklin	18	111	40892	16	80	15	14784	3520	1050
Grand Junction, town of	....	....	5002	....	....	....	2783	747	310
Greenbrier	....	....	73208	....	....	25	257	....	25
Hardin	....	....	42027	....	....	....	11257	2023	....
Highland	....	....	14048	....	....	....	2190	....	....
Jackson	19	85	31164	115	....	....	8571	1149	....
Jefferson, exc. of town	108	778	114032	640	389	258	38956	6009	7881
Jefferson, town of	30	271	....	....	....	305	....	....	....
Junction, exc. of Grand Junction	....	....	56938	....	....	....	9741	3527	575
Kendrick	25	....	59544	....	135	72	27112	4134	5674
Scranton, exc. of town	....	....	14235	....	....	....	3184	115	....
Scranton, town of	....	....	600	....	....	....	320	251	....
Washington	7	....	60100	2446	....	....	24198	11000	4576
Willow	....	....	7930	....	....	....	1812	681	....
Total	209	1267	620905	3517	954	675	197581	43853	27703

GRUNDY COUNTY.

Names of townships, towns, and cities.	Number of stands of bees.	Number of pounds of honey and beeswax in 1874.	Value of products of farm.	Value of market garden produce.	Value of produce of the orchard.	Value of small fruit.	Value of products of the herd.	Value of products of the dairy.	Value of products of the forest.
Beaver	10	97	69489	47	....	....	6255	4569	....
Black Hawk	....	....	123362	2943	....	....	30898	....	....
Clay	12	400	118044	....	20	....	23306	6775	....
Colfax	....	....	120017	....	....	....	21683	....	....
Fairfield	32	475	95450	....	....	....	25749	4594	....
Felix	....	....	117072	225	119	....	22136	5181	....
German	....	....	118081	1859	240	....	21158	4740	....
Grant	....	....	104170	....	....	41	15477	5860	....
Lincoln	10	....	78709	....	....	....	960	....	....
Melrose	....	....	134106	1790	119	253	34765	5547	....
Palermo	....	....	250254	....	30	8	40535	5514	....
Pleasant Valley	....	....	114225	....	....	10	14182	3020	....
Shiloh	....	....	150998	....	....	....	57406	6911	....
Total	64	972	1593977	6864	528	312	314510	52711	....

GUTHRIE COUNTY.

Names of townships, towns, and cities.	Number of stands of bees.	Number of pounds of honey and beeswax in 1874.	Value of products of farm.	Value of market garden produce.	Value of products of the orchard.	Value of small fruit.	Value of products of the herd.	Value of products of the dairy.	Value of products of the forest.
Bear Creek	21	320	$ 55920	$ 10	$......	$ 10	$ 28201	$ 1278	$ 120
Beaver	......	......	......	......	......	......	23956	......	......
Cass, exc. of Panora	71	280	116697	......	1325	40	52496	5115	950
Center	29	211	71228	40	155	92	23758	3443	2249
Dodge	......	......	12671	655	24	10	7291	1413	890
Grant	1	20	27335	50	......	......	640	415	700
Highland	15	143	27285	......	......	......	10782	1799	......
Jackson	20	195	91691	14	976	185	92090	6641	4006
Orange	4	50	16852	985	302	16	9352	3827	2959
Panora, town of	......	......	3365	......	150	32	3423	387	......
Penn	35	276	82288	225	190	103	24238	8396	......
Richland	......	......	63516	474	10	55	34368	4106	205
Thompson	3	40	61109	200	10	103	10049	140	45
Union	......	......	42534	......	......	......	20492	2030	2605
Valley	11	169	65318	......	356	170	46279	4722	10
Victory	30	111	54652	20	767	65	34051	3775	458
Total	240	1815	792461	2673	4265	881	421466	47487	15197

HAMILTON COUNTY.

Names of townships, towns, and cities.	Number of stands of bees.	Number of pounds of honey and beeswax in 1874.	Value of products of farm.	Value of market garden produce.	Value of products of the orchard.	Value of small fruit.	Value of products of the herd.	Value of products of the dairy.	Value of products of the forest.
Blairsburg	......	......	37765	......	......	5	14803	4813	......
Boone	28	180	89584	222	602	25	106657	16478	940
Cass	1	40	56340	......	......	......	10835	5584	......
Clear Lake	......	......	24395	346	......	5	6733	2780	......
Ellsworth	......	......	26675	......	28	15	6658	5752	......
Fremont	......	......	33462	......	......	......	......	......	......
Hamilton	67	486	37615	......	......	......	......	7488	......
Lyon	3	100	34185	......	......	......	9804	80	......
Marion	11	175	111444	43	797	935	20252	3983	7817
Rose Grove	......	......	13400	50	75	50	6355	1340	......
Scott	......	......	18637	......	......	......	9537	......	......
Webster	2	25	44170	367	146	70	10376	4785	1254
Total	112	1006	527672	1028	1648	1105	202010	53083	10011

HANCOCK COUNTY.

Names of townships, towns, and cities.	Number of stands of bees.	Number of pounds of honey and beeswax in 1874.	Value of products of farm.	Value of market garden produce.	Value of products of the orchard.	Value of small fruit.	Value of products of the herd.	Value of products of the dairy.	Value of products of the forest.
Amsterdam	13	100	10348	75	......	......	897	1217	1495
Avery	......	......	11744	65	......	......	4000	577	1862
Britt	......	......	1790	......	......	......	120	760	......
Concord	1	20	3360	20	......	20	240	645	1080
Crystal	......	......	3784	......	......	......	135	639	......
Ellington	14	400	50279	......	......	......	......	2054	2554
Madison	......	......	8100	......	......	......	......	1400	......
Total	28	520	89405	160	......	20	5392	7292	6991

HARDIN COUNTY.

Names of townships, towns, and cities.	Number of stands of bees.	Number of pounds of honey and beeswax in 1874.	Value of products of farm.	Value of market garden produce.	Value of products of the orchard.	Value of small fruit.	Value of products of the herd.	Value of products of the dairy.	Value of products of the forest.
Ackley, town of	......	......	......	......	......	......	......	1110	......
Alden	33	80	60380	......	23	......	10878	7261	......
Buckeye	23	295	25119	......	......	......	6296	1742	656
Clay	12	487	135029	65	485	......	38125	6880	3272
Concord	......	......	9418	......	......	......	1054	530	......

HARDIN COUNTY.—Continued.

NAMES OF TOWNSHIPS, TOWNS, AND CITIES.	Number of stands of bees.	Number of pounds of honey and beeswax in 1874.	Value of products of farm.	Value of market garden produce.	Value of products of the orchard.	Value of small fruit.	Value of products of the herd.	Value of products of the dairy.	Value of products of the forest.
Eldora, exc of town	19	135	$ 107497	580	$ 784	$ 618	$ 40898	$ 7844	$ 6150
Eldora, town of	......	......	10295	50	100	50	6800	2135	845
Ellis	5	35	37169	......	......	......	10270	4695	1185
Etna, exc. of Ackley	......	......	73837	......	......	......	10783	......	......
Grant	......	......	25529	567	100	......	4033	1720	......
Hardin, exc. of Iowa Falls	44	190	92908	......	91	20	22404	11750	250
Iowa Falls, town of	......	......	......	......	......	......	......	......	......
Jackson	65	1470	105823	......	71	61	28702	10579	10030
Pleasant	31	85	88402	1371	326	125	33003	11619	8639
Providence	38	139	123859	126	3091	1062	85996	7658	8581
Sherman	......	......	11095	......	4	......	3218	1089	......
Tipton	31	160	39986	318	110	103	9528	4609	738
Union, exc. of town	44	200	120281	5	468	381	47883	5276	495
Union, town of	......	......	......	......	......	......	......	......	......
Total	345	3276	1066627	3082	5653	2320	359871	86497	40841

HARRISON COUNTY.

NAMES OF TOWNSHIPS, TOWNS, AND CITIES.	Number of stands of bees.	Number of pounds of honey and beeswax in 1874.	Value of products of farm.	Value of market garden produce.	Value of products of the orchard.	Value of small fruit.	Value of products of the herd.	Value of products of the dairy.	Value of products of the forest.
Allen	......	......	7614	......	......	......	1175	355	......
Boyer	100	6110	51370	......	300	5	54990	3490	3243
Calhoun	30	410	28181	......	10	70	19796	3159	90
Cass	......	......	19600	150	140	......	7010	2730	......
Cincinnati	43	705	58305	80	18	15	13618	3260	561
Clay	144	1510	23350	......	......	25	11509	105	1441
Douglas	21	330	34414	......	10	44	5053	836	1894
Dunlap, town of	......	......	......	......	......	......	......	......	......
Harrison, exc. of Dunlap	......	......	44561	......	......	......	18183	2807	......
Jackson	18	90	15287	......	......	......	10727	2194	20
Jefferson	84	1527	54616	30	575	20	70523	5404	6256
Lagrange	16	230	33361	27	530	......	19320	759	......
Lincoln	......	......	23111	......	......	......	6887	946	......
Little Sioux	132	1850	33400	230	17	37	24589	2685	4007
Magnolia	8	200	77154	110	20	100	34782	5985	641
Missouri Valley, town of	......	......		......	......	......	......	......	......
Morgan	76	1533	48776	90	24	127	26653	2722	9329
Raglan	16	250	32314	......	......	5	19613	2057	2930
St. John, exc. of Missouri Valley	34	740	104055	10	30	......	54549	10009	1571
Taylor	16	150	63825	......	......	......	27209	7531	2449
Union	......	......	21777	......	......	......	......	......	3425
Washington	......	......	11606	......	......	......	5880	1098	1575
Total	738	15635	786677	727	1674	448	432066	58132	39402

HENRY COUNTY.

NAMES OF TOWNSHIPS, TOWNS, AND CITIES.	Number of stands of bees.	Number of pounds of honey and beeswax in 1874.	Value of products of farm.	Value of market garden produce.	Value of products of the orchard.	Value of small fruit.	Value of products of the herd.	Value of products of the dairy.	Value of products of the forest.
Baltimore	23	38	68340	2490	2207	847	29511	11015	6923
Canaan	38	169	197822	......	2171	......	54881	6681	......
Center, exc. of Mt. Pleasant	20	123	158092	6220	7600	2635	347548	32178	10578
Jackson	70	505	100080	1214	7249	840	64221	7117	4781
Jefferson	28	175	106994	45	2371	157	54225	7141	3386
Marion	119	372	185190	987	5123	1592	185065	7388	1264
Mt. Pleasant, city of	20	......	1202	......	2712	4663	415	60	......
New London, exc. of town	81	272	242392	3963	10560	2095	104150	11838	3920
New London, town of	......	......	1319	746	225	288	......	516	......
Rome, town of	1	......	7153	712	5	......	15277	389	5823

HENRY COUNTY.—Continued.

Names of townships, towns, and cities.	Number of stands of bees.	Number of pounds of honey and beeswax in 1874.	Value of products of farm.	Value of market garden produce.	Value of products of the orchard.	Value of small fruit.	Value of products of the herd.	Value of products of the dairy.	Value of products of the forest.
Salem, exc. of town	74	1835	$ 122347	$ 905	$ 5513	$ 2023	$ 52401	$ 7026	$ 4563
Salem, town of	....	....	....	....	1825	674	5409	970	....
Scott	102	640	143232	....	3087	26	101410	9405	310
Tippecanoe, exc. of Rome	39	55	103422	1610	2583	626	45871	6986	7967
Trenton	50	174	104638	14	3210	....	47820	8777	9488
Wayne	64	125	223447	395	1793	625	105214	....	....
Total	729	4483	1765670	19301	58234	17091	1213418	117487	59003

HOWARD COUNTY.

Names of townships, towns, and cities.	Number of stands of bees.	Number of pounds of honey and beeswax in 1874.	Value of products of farm.	Value of market garden produce.	Value of products of the orchard.	Value of small fruit.	Value of products of the herd.	Value of products of the dairy.	Value of products of the forest.
Afton	....	....	89209	15	....	....	7788	7587	608
Albion	....	....	102218	....	33	5	6025	4284	1682
Chester	39	371	34948	....	....	....	4915	6251	130
Cresco, town of	....	....	....	....	....	....	....	....	....
Forest City	36	627	77397	1550	....	....	6741	6390	....
Howard	....	....	51391	....	10	....	4823	4385	125
Howard Center	8	375	68573	9	102	105	4282	4120	1366
Jamestown	12	95	53328	....	....	....	5149	422	2317
New Oregon	24	200	86755	....	....	....	14867	9861	1020
Oak Dale	5	50	35429	....	12	30	4232	3710	1295
Paris	5	10	63886	....	....	....	8286	9027	....
Saratoga	....	....	19850	....	....	....	1655	3260	1878
Vernon Springs, exc. of Cresco	3	....	51424	430	7	....	3945	4680	....
Total	132	1728	734409	2004	164	140	72708	58777	10421

HUMBOLDT COUNTY.

Names of townships, towns, and cities.	Number of stands of bees.	Number of pounds of honey and beeswax in 1874.	Value of products of farm.	Value of market garden produce.	Value of products of the orchard.	Value of small fruit.	Value of products of the herd.	Value of products of the dairy.	Value of products of the forest.
Avery	....	....	13457	....	....	....	4410	4323	....
Dakota	20	80	14825	....	....	1	2497	1	1509
Delana	....	....	13865	....	1	....	8997	1326	2493
Grove	....	....	30461	....	....	....	9001	....	2127
Humboldt	....	....	23445	....	....	....	8050	3008	1495
Humboldt, town of	....	....	5183	58	....	16	1209	377	225
Lake	....	....	4156	....	....	....	....	1628	1175
Norway	....	....	11714	....	....	....	....	2270	....
Rutland	26	25	14313	....	10	50	1843	2311	25
Springvale, exc. Humboldt	5	12	18936	....	....	....	11798	6144	2249
Vernon	....	....	30645	....	....	....	4496	2152	....
Wacousta	35	....	10902	....	....	....	3815	1650	....
Weaver	....	....	8099	....	....	....	2312	....	....
Total	86	117	200001	58	11	67	53428	25190	11298

IDA CONNTY.

Names of townships, towns, and cities.	Number of stands of bees.	Number of pounds of honey and beeswax in 1874.	Value of products of farm.	Value of market garden produce.	Value of products of the orchard.	Value of small fruit.	Value of products of the herd.	Value of products of the dairy.	Value of products of the forest.
Corwin	....	....	22088	....	....	....	1494	1600	77
Douglas	....	....	7930	27	....	....	4897	429	....
Maple	....	....	35927	....	....	....	2298	2095	2139
Silver Creek	....	....	8876	....	....	....	....	289	....
Total	....	....	74821	27	....	....	8689	4413	2216

IOWA COUNTY.

NAMES OF TOWNSHIPS, TOWNS, AND CITIES.	Number of stands of bees.	Number of pounds of honey and beeswax in 1874.	Value of products of farm.	Value of market garden produce.	Value of products of the orchard.	Value of small fruit.	Value of products of the herd.	Value of products of the dairy.	Value of products of the forest.
Amana	45	260	$	$	$	$	$	$	$ ......
Cono	35	45	39776	22052	16010	352	8116	1115	1148
Dayton	99	581	115780	19	696	125	34789	3880	259
English	191	1559	119693	1033	255	438	43651	5860	562
Fillmore	52	268	95459	10	1329	317	43246	6926	896
Greene	66	125	165109	20	661	188	57401	3981	5261
Hartford, exc. of Victor	42	105	212627	......	......	......	......	......	......
Hilton	......	......	139166	......	......	......	43180	......	......
Honey Creek	171	329	126229	4390	946	638	37733	8397	6590
Iowa	20	100	91147	250	55	......	67586	2500	2000
Lenox	5	......	93235	......	721	70	8630	4100	510
Lincoln	22	125	92950	......	183	226	19993	4988	1720
Marengo, exc. of town	207	440	138687	2005	812	1571	11451	4300	1070
Marengo, town of	1	30	1100	100	1550	20	......	......	......
Pilot	33	137	117655	238	238	......	30110	6687	......
Sumner	24	94	93125	......	100	22	13228	7656	20
Troy	103	1270	145280	......	311	20	47330	5199	......
Victor, town of	10	105	3830	......	......	128	......	......	......
Washington	2	......	76428	115	300	109	......	......	......
York	16	65	137773	......	541	966	5560	2525	4861
Total	1144	5638	2005049	30232	24708	5190	472004	68114	24897

JACKSON COUNTY.

NAMES OF TOWNSHIPS, TOWNS, AND CITIES.	Number of stands of bees.	Number of pounds of honey and beeswax in 1874.	Value of products of farm.	Value of market garden produce.	Value of products of the orchard.	Value of small fruit.	Value of products of the herd.	Value of products of the dairy.	Value of products of the forest.
Andrew, town of	......	......	132	......	136	69	221	......	......
Bellevue, exc. of town	......	......	100650	......	......	......	31212	2967	828
Bellevue, town of	......	......	......	......	......	......	......	......	......
Brandon	18	125	......	1684	......	......	10753	......	6156
Butler	......	......	60515	......	388	......	49357	2020	3994
Fairfield	27	342	122156	30	668	125	52534	6397	7087
Farmer's Creek	7	54	88447	......	2339	......	36386	5173	4730
Iowa	57	811	177592	50	4328	234	98844	10367	3564
Jackson	5	......	84646	......	705	......	44253	3877	754
Maquoketa, exc. of city	29	280	77186	226	560	311	43735	10244	1081
Maquoketa, city of	10	50	8647	1191	515	350	2534	2844	100
Monmouth	25	965	96305	2850	598	224	70097	12236	7931
Otter Creek	6	11	96769	......	206	20	40189	4945	3356
Perry, exc. of Andrew	13	150	131172	5	1851	......	39032	7700	3535
Prairie Spring	......	......	110246	562	465	......	33453	4470	3472
Richland	......	......	112627	......	595	......	52657	3611	4530
Sabula, town of	34	200	......	40	255	65	3425	......	......
South Fork, exc. Maquoketa	154	1597	78417	1435	1423	813	45621	12350	6803
Tete Des Morts	1	......	112912	20	1480	110	40568	6765	5993
Union, exc. of Sabula	11	......	25630	......	30	......	3136	......	......
Van Buren	62	1130	186173	457	1996	680	82905	14890	9351
Washington	58	1460	79869	35	1012	70	32902	4098	5207
Total	517	7175	1750091	8585	19550	3067	813814	114954	78472

JASPER COUNTY.

NAMES OF TOWNSHIPS, TOWNS, AND CITIES.	Number of stands of bees.	Number of pounds of honey and beeswax in 1874.	Value of products of farm.	Value of market garden produce.	Value of products of the orchard.	Value of small fruit.	Value of products of the herd.	Value of products of the dairy.	Value of products of the forest.
Buena Vista	117	998	182150	1910	1168	605	80411	5291	4456
Clear Creek	154	785	119721	2398	1020	512	54117	7783	7784
Des Moines, exc. of Prairie City	117	1010	244310	8	1755	97	60813	9190	369
Elk Creek	190	2030	167081	......	550	630	66160	10923	2385

JASPER COUNTY.—Continued.

NAMES OF TOWNSHIPS, TOWNS, AND CITIES.	Number of stands of bees.	Number of pounds of honey and beeswax in 1874.	Value of products of farm.	Value of market garden produce.	Value of products of the orchard.	Value of small fruit.	Value of products of the herd.	Value of products of the herd.	Value of products of the forest.
Fairview, exc. of Monroe	282	1535	$ 305984	$........	$ 2213	$ 574	$ 130955	$ 13756	$........
Hickory Grove	....	....	113646	....	....	....	18349	30	....
Independence	165	776	119933	1328	1193	423	38232	6188	4440
Jasper City, town of	....	....	2080	....	....	....	1310	160	....
Kellogg, exc. of Jasper City	98	520	133497	138	559	330	76645	6035	4822
Linn Grove	265	4650	132244	....	1970	283	87032	....	2919
Malaka	50	943	200265	422	785	182	71820	10615	....
Mariposa	2	....	48499	....	....	....	17416	....	....
Monroe, town of	6	10	216	25	....	45	....	3785	....
Mound Prairie	87	1130	133839	75	220	159	27924	5190	....
Newton, exc. of city	85	495	96444	585	475	884	26058	14266	150
Newton, city of	....	....	....	....	....	....	....	....	....
Palo Alto	102	1655	105957	100	653	207	45378	3787	3392
Poweshiek	244	935	121370	13	1027	485	47818	3778	120
Prairie City, town of	....	....	....	....	....	20	....	....	....
Richland	63	304	143769	2899	964	227	45135	7397	1555
Rock Creek	19	20	103077	50	147	217	24415	....	....
Sherman	288	5821	235444	147	793	548	77841	14023	....
Washington	21	150	207312	....	115	54	....	3940	....
Total	2355	23767	2916838	10098	15607	6482	997329	126137	32390

JEFFERSON COUNTY.

NAMES OF TOWNSHIPS, TOWNS, AND CITIES.	Number of stands of bees.	Number of pounds of honey and beeswax in 1874.	Value of products of farm.	Value of market garden produce.	Value of products of the orchard.	Value of small fruit.	Value of products of the herd.	Value of products of the herd.	Value of products of the forest.
Batavia, town of	3	20	....	....	31	33	1664	915	....
Black Hawk	79	243	196037	16	1813	938	91580	10403	3874
Buchanan	83	475	146963	3381	3173	1286	84829	7869	5365
Cedar	41	620	71370	1170	3830	691	42183	5040	3780
Des Moines	92	318	141003	3392	6915	2857	81966	14559	5343
Fairfield, exc. of city	86	145	140577	1043	3081	2795	73955	13186	7427
Fairfield, city of	152	300	....	5101	2619	1012	85820	8040	....
Liberty	69	85	153567	1499	6017	1830	51274	2607	4656
Lockridge	23	106	131264	2814	3538	2163	110402	5945	5960
Locust Grove, exc. of Batavia	133	1025	138559	52	3817	1646	82164	25055	4773
Penn	68	246	116782	1589	4568	1489	40155	5856	2515
Polk	49	95	106798	....	2026	205	55888	....	....
Round Prairie	51	120	108013	780	3363	263	50490	5945	100
Walnut	89	619	79207	477	2121	240	60327	2798	1604
Total	1018	4417	1530140	21314	46912	17448	912657	108218	45397

JOHNSON COUNTY.

NAMES OF TOWNSHIPS, TOWNS, AND CITIES.	Number of stands of bees.	Number of pounds of honey and beeswax in 1874.	Value of products of farm.	Value of market garden produce.	Value of products of the orchard.	Value of small fruit.	Value of products of the herd.	Value of products of the herd.	Value of products of the forest.
Big Grove	31	90	118253	....	664	38	39246	5423	5067
Cedar	87	547	158536	13	1678	296	73369	4068	4375
Clear Creek	73	325	107829	417	1416	863	48251	6249	40
Coralville, town of	....	....	1250	....	20	35	10000	....	....
Fremont	8	100	162354	....	205	....	20696	6350	40
Graham	51	361	174659	81	1388	566	57621	6357	507
Hardin	11	....	107681	....	30	....	51920	4296	70
Iowa City, city of	....	....	....	75	....	530	....	30	24000
Iowa City, additions to	....	....	925	1253	770	1395	979	1695	....
Jefferson	76	....	80972	3	3806	....	18100	2666	3931
Liberty	60	79	100686	764	693	262	13693	3180	1766
Lincoln	40	21	138349	....	113	1450	36608	4457	1105
Lucas, exc of Iowa City, additions, and Coralville	53	60	130432	2705	6350	6442	35725	19765	9007

JOHNSON COUNTY.—Continued.

NAMES OF TOWNSHIPS, TOWNS, AND CITIES.	Number of stands of bees.	Number of pounds of honey and beeswax in 1874.	Value of products of farm.	Value of market garden produce.	Value of products of the orchard.	Value of small fruit.	Value of products of the herd.	Value of products of the dairy.	Value of products of the forest.
Madison	66	253	$ 125220	$ 36	$ 2847	$ 469	$ 24794	$ 7879	$ 4184
Monroe	49	575	105130	....	765	17	34479	4441	6051
Newport	....	....	38395	....	1975	....	11093	4329	920
Oxford	104	320	140245	210	60	37	32563	4622	1740
Penn	17	....	61525	....	1965	257	13836	4101	3108
Pleasant Valley	14	142	140103	....	2000	....	40750	4669	3500
Scott	64	390	182971	....	1493	25	64264	7667	1387
Sharon	78	565	161105	45	1134	323	91886	9096	....
Union	89	190	103852	....	35	16	72353	4423	1467
Washington	131	420	107403	....	1200	300	61258	6042	3500
Total	1102	4438	2447875	5602	30607	13321	853484	121805	75765

JONES COUNTY.

NAMES OF TOWNSHIPS, TOWNS, AND CITIES.	Number of stands of bees.	Number of pounds of honey and beeswax in 1874.	Value of products of farm.	Value of market garden produce.	Value of products of the orchard.	Value of small fruit.	Value of products of the herd.	Value of products of the dairy.	Value of products of the forest.
Anamosa, town of	....	....	....	....	....	....	....	....	....
Cass	20	362	277462	....	368	67	42315	10860	....
Castle Grove	....	....	93615	....	306	116	45493	9725	....
Clay	34	277	85169	80	614	219	39812	6459	2876
Fairview, exc. of Anamosa and Strawberry Hill	74	377	81760	....	777	1063	51689	6848	5155
Greenfield	26	510	191131	7	1600	1239	87719	16530	7787
Hale	70	405	130331	34	259	275	49228	10243	....
Jackson	28	489	89250	27	....	100	35060	6030	1213
Madison	29	....	78813	150	140	20	40503	4667	265
Monticello, exc. of town	10	15	89588	233	744	580	50495	21017	6256
Monticello, town of	19	69	7625	50	10	426	10161	2288	655
Oxford	41	560	123565	....	75	84	64963	2250	186
Richland	....	....	62680	20	60	....	34003	6320	3388
Rome	30	1131	130617	....	....	....	61108	9395	....
Scotch Grove	33	500	119197	23	740	301	59017	12224	10415
Strawberry Hill, town of	....	....	....	....	10	....	....	....	....
Washington	....	....	95580	....	....	....	51895	....	....
Wayne	38	195	150105	152	1224	531	54744	18601	7694
Wyoming, exc. of town	28	172	89929	174	934	325	42884	7588	8486
Wyoming, town of	....	....	....	....	....	....	....	....	....
Total	480	5062	1896416	950	7861	5396	812089	151037	54376

KEOKUK COUNTY.

NAMES OF TOWNSHIPS, TOWNS, AND CITIES.	Number of stands of bees.	Number of pounds of honey and beeswax in 1874.	Value of products of farm.	Value of market garden produce.	Value of products of the orchard.	Value of small fruit.	Value of products of the herd.	Value of products of the dairy.	Value of products of the forest.
Adams	37	90	133580	37	1213	502	32816	7144	2749
Benton	12	170	143018	1029	1564	464	49935	6957	3100
Clear Creek	7	....	119449	29	1975	408	47714	4141	....
English River	138	646	124338	1683	1820	1331	63194	12551	2432
German	2	....	177651	....	1089	236	74272	9292	7432
Jackson	45	200	64620	15	1596	351	37715	5288	3335
Keota, town of	....	....	....	....	....	....	....	....	....
Lafayette, exc. of Keota	24	170	183288	17	450	145	57827	6280	....
Lancaster	143	614	167820	1004	3946	873	48756	6486	6245
Liberty	154	821	158760	2401	1718	779	47867	10501	....
Prairie	138	500	119775	....	495	210	39418	....	....
Richland, exc. of town	46	170	108511	....	812	....	64853	5520	8827
Richland, town of	2	....	12485	63	971	1151	8940	1882	1534
Sigourney, exc. of town	57	539	81089	2022	2313	2368	35129	14908	3290
Sigourney, town of	3	....	....	....	3629	785	....	....	....
Steady Run	41	357	116747	224	1569	585	67762	5468	4079
Van Buren	27	260	96221	750	1875	....	59815	11735	7230

KEOKUK COUNTY.—Continued.

Names of townships, towns, and cities.	Number of stands of bees.	Number of pounds of honey and beeswax in 1874.	Value of products of farm.	Value of market garden produce.	Value of products of the orchard.	Value of small fruit.	Value of products of the herd.	Value of products of the dairy.	Value of products of the forest.
Warren	13	21	$ 87549	$ 75	$ 805	$ 78	$ 28980	$ 3344	90
Washington	60	333	24827	81	10	....	25474	391	292
Total	949	4891	1919728	9430	27850	10266	790467	111888	50635

KOSSUTH COUNTY.

Names of townships, towns, and cities.	Number of stands of bees.	Number of pounds of honey and beeswax in 1874.	Value of products of farm.	Value of market garden produce.	Value of products of the orchard.	Value of small fruit.	Value of products of the herd.	Value of products of the dairy.	Value of products of the forest.
Algona, exc. of town	....	....	19585	....	....	40	5202	4715	70
Algona, town of	15	240	15	....	....	....	....	....	....
Cresco	8	18	19479	79	6	....	19012	3537	1574
Fenton	....	....	3529	....	....	....	....	891	....
Greenwood	....	....	4885	....	....	15	1141	2728	546
Irvington	84	130	20010	....	....	....	4411	3045	....
Lott's Creek	....	....	4269	....	....	....	53	1763	....
Portland	....	2	8173	....	....	....	5655	3730	100
Wesley	....	....	5360	10	....	....	1169	2154	....
Total	107	388	105306	89	6	55	36643	22563	2310

LEE COUNTY.

Names of townships, towns, and cities.	Number of stands of bees.	Number of pounds of honey and beeswax in 1874.	Value of products of farm.	Value of market garden produce.	Value of products of the orchard.	Value of small fruit.	Value of products of the herd.	Value of products of the dairy.	Value of products of the forest.
Cedar	133	228	208339	415	4641	1022	146126	6242	10929
Charleston	30	93	104025	5	3443	662	23202	7156	3200
Denmark	52	207	60566	....	4486	711	25208	16320	4578
Des Moines	71	61	94894	1628	2721	621	28135	7179	5891
Fort Madison, city of	....	....	....	4420	2880	2965	....	730	....
Franklin	50	202	145540	....	4256	....	49460	....	4200
Green Bay	183	65	86900	1115	415	....	11593	4206	1150
Harrison	90	247	104731	81	3600	1604	86104	6701	2064
Jackson, exc. of Keokuk	163	613	65405	5580	3034	4257	20058	4347	5867
Jefferson	75	352	124826	5180	4924	471	33146	5701	3403
Keokuk, city of	15	185	....	....	800	540	....	....	....
Madison, exc. of Fort Madison	39	240	18125	2880	485	305	200	1470	300
Marion	119	70	139675	....	1350	....	56936	570	....
Montrose, exc. of town	60	474	95104	4051	7878	1894	44440	9995	12177
Montrose, town of	....	....	....	....	....	....	....	....	....
Pleasant Ridge	57	95	120414	40	5975	1085	40632	10659	643
Van Buren	102	515	60345	300	1110	205	28527	4250	1745
Washington	105	375	128564	926	10392	194	38221	14280	7976
West Point, exc. of town	35	57	73570	195	5554	....	32187	3976	3945
West Point, town of	38	200	495	....	418	15	235	....	....
Total	1418	4279	1631518	26816	68362	16551	664410	103782	68068

LINN COUNTY.

Names of townships, towns, and cities.	Number of stands of bees.	Number of pounds of honey and beeswax in 1874.	Value of products of farm.	Value of market garden produce.	Value of products of the orchard.	Value of small fruit.	Value of products of the herd.	Value of products of the dairy.	Value of products of the forest.
Bertram	17	95	64735	1136	215	78	43488	4460	24454
Boulder	16	120	119349	....	70	28	28708	17885	213
Brown	141	948	84536	150	965	481	66726	6903	4083
Buffalo	132	1180	54720	....	89	8	25892	7180	1117
Cedar Rapids, city of	21	515	165	1298	....	153	3183	8252	....
Clinton	63	....	168482	140	531	268	45569	14338	....
College, exc. of Western	21	71	166892	400	586	324	45060	7505	6171
Fairfax	25	....	203151	....	149	280	54558	9796	....

LINN COUNTY.—Continued.

NAMES OF TOWNSHIPS, TOWNS, AND CITIES.	Number of stands of bees.	Number of pounds of honey and beeswax in 1874.	Value of products of farm.	Value of market garden produce.	Value of products of the orchard.	Value of small fruit.	Value of products of the herd.	Value of products of the dairy.	Value of products of the forest.
Fayette	56	481	$ 86744	$ 2354	$ 1235	$ 209	$ 29529	$ 8210	$ 6719
Franklin, exc. of Mt. Vernon and Lisbon	54	465	151785	7	791	411	13199	6548	11630
Grant	63	191	102520	2502	291	56	28842	8305	5183
Jackson	55	325	108880	....	452	19	31148	20125	5413
Linn	70	181	139610	30	1144	329	62268	11814	5973
Lisbon, town of	1	....	720	....	....	18	....	515	200
Maine	14	....	140808	....	65	301	65149	19137	25
Marion, exc. of city	150	1975	366785	....	1803	1282	118327	23764	1845
Marion, city of	....	....	....	1000	20	....	....	....	....
Monroe	87	642	116805	426	453	221	38455	5575	11850
Mt. Vernon, town of	18	325	6546	275	740	787	5880	2017	1050
Otter Creek	85	700	140082	173	814	443	35167	....	....
Putnam	54	450	98927	5	448	354	22539	4028	6451
Rapids, exc. Cedar Rapids	118	565	72997	9445	1090	1956	38215	17437	14875
Spring Grove	8	....	85628	5	33	28	19614	8037	2084
Washington	126	2705	89565	50	125	10	5121	....	6830
Western, town of	22	100	13620	205	150	....	5750	428	....
Total	1417	12034	2590052	19601	12259	8044	832387	212259	116166

LOUISA COUNTY.

Columbus City, exc. of Columbus City and Columbus Junction	52	129	201304	2203	4700	2266	138380	10576	12740
Columbus City, town of	....	30	4175	....	300	2352	2295	245	....
Columbus Junct'n, town of	10	1	....	....	....	....	....	....	....
Concord, exc. of Fredonia	66	196	88596	1253	973	777	62105	4558	4085
Eliot	30	215	61872	28	459	95	40265	1818	5519
Elm Grove	23	5	132463	8	1671	112	98881	6403	2898
Fredonia, town of	1	....	7617	240	19	83	1089	364	1014
Grandview	67	2602	104102	912	1337	635	87314	8652	6779
Jefferson	63	155	87839	30	1580	547	29849	4880	6497
Marshall	54	2	123924	....	2829	711	35209	5113	425
Morning Sun, exc. of town	24	340	153640	1547	2431	668	97719	3917	....
Morning Sun, town of	....	....	....	....	....	....	....	....	....
Oakland	50	70	364815	12	318	131	181330	7860	3642
Port Louisa	82	246	75520	100	945	59	31798	5085	4420
Union	35	....	58704	70	1596	384	52733	3146	847
Wapello, exc. of town	121	407	183357	....	4159	1609	143754	9590	10641
Wapello, town of	15	....	18811	156	868	134	4297	1298	7199
Total	693	4398	1665739	6559	24085	10563	1007018	73505	66706

LUCAS COUNTY.

Benton	51	402	116514	....	....	....	63428	9986	....
Cedar	77	775	68648	843	962	464	37882	6268	....
Chariton, exc. of city	100	330	88590	565	1575	921	39248	9074	4304
Chariton, city of	6	....	....	118	851	1271	8419	2952	2230
English	78	340	96651	20	416	109	44532	5054	1116
Jackson	97	796	64538	54	300	137	31371	2712	11556
Liberty	70	255	59661	....	407	64	14915	5510	....
Otter Creek	27	155	73617	9	600	....	33405	....	....
Pleasant	45	585	58514	107	2	1	8314	1405	....
Union	70	520	88537	....	1532	289	36837	7263	1893
Warren	97	598	136602	672	871	427	119448	8505	2555

LUCAS COUNTY.—Continued.

Names of townships, towns, and cities.	Number of stands of bees.	Number of pounds of honey and beeswax in 1874.	Value of products of farm.	Value of market garden produce.	Value of products of the orchard.	Value of small fruit.	Value of products of the herd.	Value of products of the dairy.	Value of products of the forest.
Washington	53	258	$ 115638	$ 15	$ 259	$ 350	$ 37108	$ 7577	$ 5031
White Breast	55	513	63044	1601	898	442	41068	6338	3032
Total	826	5527	1030554	4004	8673	4475	515975	72644	31717

LYON COUNTY.

Names of townships, towns, and cities.	Number of stands of bees.	Number of pounds of honey and beeswax in 1874.	Value of products of farm.	Value of market garden produce.	Value of products of the orchard.	Value of small fruit.	Value of products of the herd.	Value of products of the dairy.	Value of products of the forest.
Dale	....	....	....	....	....	....	....	140	....
Doon	....	....	11199	....	....	....	1348	1095	....
Grant	....	....	....	....	....	....	....	140	....
Larchwood	....	....	5440	60	....	....	569	....	....
Lyon	....	....	16012	10	....	....	10047	1695	260
Rock	....	....	....	3	....	1	280	23	....
Total	....	....	32651	73	....	1	12244	3093	260

MADISON COUNTY.

Names of townships, towns, and cities.	Number of stands of bees.	Number of pounds of honey and beeswax in 1874.	Value of products of farm.	Value of market garden produce.	Value of products of the orchard.	Value of small fruit.	Value of products of the herd.	Value of products of the dairy.	Value of products of the forest.
Crawford	23	50	92081	....	....	30	29835	1354	237
Douglas	231	3945	146705	3305	1386	1697	57913	....	....
Earlham, town of	....	....	....	....	....	....	....	....	....
Grand River	30	470	95236	1686	960	527	35766	7844	5275
Jackson	18	360	106867	1307	398	73	82208	3121	277
Jefferson	81	525	111135	90	1154	443	35786	7818	2029
Lee	12	100	77065	....	....	....	30478	1439	....
Lincoln	79	403	93234	98	1783	1109	48533	5963	5385
Madison, exc. of Earlham	42	450	122401	....	486	431	61606	3721	5132
Monroe	6	20	84366	....	....	....	44008	....	....
Ohio	55	360	108692	2735	1721	1103	31253	5920	3099
Penn, exc. of Earlham	25	220	216883	88	567	179	146594	4787	....
Scott	46	527	141745	2537	1374	250	86590	15871	....
South	77	370	77145	112	1622	....	37477	8151	....
Union	139	938	96647	398	2236	1316	44462	6757	12594
Walnut	46	313	65461	45	900	215	41068	3575	2709
Webster	28	48	72787	43	32	....	27627	3947	....
Winterset, city of	....	....	580	....	1349	2450	150092	4557	....
Total	638	9099	1709030	12344	15968	9824	991296	79825	36737

MAHASKA COUNTY.

Names of townships, towns, and cities.	Number of stands of bees.	Number of pounds of honey and beeswax in 1874.	Value of products of farm.	Value of market garden produce.	Value of products of the orchard.	Value of small fruit.	Value of products of the herd.	Value of products of the dairy.	Value of products of the forest.
Adams	105	312	152176	....	952	60	63386	....	5375
Beacon, town of	....	....	861	38	....	20	636	850	3378
Black Oak	61	424	157404	3	1204	514	71932	4494	....
Cedar	104	307	169314	97	3793	648	57614	9004	2778
Des Moines	84	347	119464	4575	658	904	78413	7334	3586
Harrison	87	500	161039	....	1800	865	80111	9416	2435
Jefferson	177	340	133281	50	1197	661	88472	8602	50
Madison	161	....	144970	....	1166	314	81504	13443	2053
Monroe	73	175	140024	790	1450	795	131513	12530	....
New Sharon, town of	16	175	1386	....	651	18	3558	1487	35
Oskaloosa, exc. of Oskaloosa and Beacon	449	6038	264470	10534	10707	2783	156342	33118	18990
Oskaloosa, city of	....	....	540	2000	760	995	8592	7032	....
Pleasant Grove	92	219	94966	2887	798	632	32621	5409	2069

MAHASKA COUNTY.—Continued.

NAMES OF TOWNSHIPS, TOWNS, AND CITIES.	Number of stands of bees.	Number of pounds of honey and beeswax in 1874.	Value of products of farm.	Value of market garden produce.	Value of products of the orchard.	Value of small fruit.	Value of products of the herd.	Value of products of the dairy.	Value of products of the forest.
Prairie exc. of New Sharon	201	984	$ 165993	$ 2427	$ 1546	$ 1950	$ 102756	$ 16722	$ 6371
Richland	310	1980	136910	60	1820	776	53771	7937	278
Scott	61	494	115597	2920	729	1179	39911	7719	3434
Union	103	736	120865	29	1326	167	35593	6768	3339
White Oak	217	1234	116534	361	1496	2127	61242	4018	2395
Total	2301	14262	2195785	26771	32053	15408	1147967	155883	56566

MARION COUNTY.

NAMES OF TOWNSHIPS, TOWNS, AND CITIES.	Number of stands of bees.	Number of pounds of honey and beeswax in 1874.	Value of products of farm.	Value of market garden produce.	Value of products of the orchard.	Value of small fruit.	Value of products of the herd.	Value of products of the dairy.	Value of products of the forest.
Clay	139	675	146982	....	1253	626	61957	6367	334
Dallas	91	436	80109	2456	1163	776	55748	4042	9644
Franklin	36	430	137779	....	583	447	53435	10920	608
Indiana	62	152	98419	1922	1416	111	41827	4801	....
Knoxville, exc. of town	33	595	351526	586	3487	953	50804	11641	3774
Knoxville, town of	4	....	7525	....	1135	1603	13453	3785	....
Lake Prairie, exc. of Pella	120	4020	410300	230	3870	555	177160	18000	4935
Liberty	19	115	84709	213	809	735	46359	....	....
Pella, city of	....	....	....	....	....	....	....	....	....
Perry	61	153	26967	101	568	203	8739	3297	1265
Pleasant Grove, exc. of Pleasantville	45	543	163790	....	2028	406	69516	9470	387
Pleasantville, town of	....	....	....	....	....	....	....	....	....
Polk	32	352	78434	139	699	24	22206	2013	....
Red Rock	122	1236	118385	2700	1791	545	30851	4918	7189
Summit	74	658	199011	11	2659	855	88652	11915	3987
Swan	91	537	65175	130	2095	381	29927	2311	....
Union	38	310	95315	209	574	218	44679	2998	6270
Washington	58	708	116920	25	932	352	74301	6524	2922
Total	1025	10920	2181346	8722	25062	8790	869614	103102	41315

MARSHALL COUNTY.

NAMES OF TOWNSHIPS, TOWNS, AND CITIES.	Number of stands of bees.	Number of pounds of honey and beeswax in 1874.	Value of products of farm.	Value of market garden produce.	Value of products of the orchard.	Value of small fruit.	Value of products of the herd.	Value of products of the dairy.	Value of products of the forest.
Albion, town of	38	20	1677	1378	1308	381	5764	1200	3760
Bangor	61	340	77948	....	1321	953	23976	2403	6186
Eden	47	270	114895	100	106	130	3814	5231	....
Green Castle	....	....	215458	....	150	188	40360	6706	....
Iowa, exc. of Albion	13	15	74585	170	790	1361	40301	....	....
Jefferson	....	....	161150	35	....	17	40127	5965	....
Le Grand	7	....	180741	100	2301	1230	48060	10812	8160
Liberty	33	200	155633	....	80	35	....	7716	....
Liscomb, exc. of town	18	190	105795	128	379	406	29708	5718	3142
Liscomb, town of	1	....	....	....	75	10	300	....	....
Logan	....	....	122178	....	....	41	18005	3905	....
Marietta	33	390	160936	50	1002	1002	43869	6557	1058
Marion	21	80	153146	1558	1812	1082	42632	8127	3732
Marshall, ex. Marshalltown	9	....	59652	655	444	1302	31112	4626	2758
Marshalltown, city of	274	1832	17941	12021	3832	7708	25502	28578	3665
Minerva	12	150	103000	262	60	44	46810	8085	....
State Center, exc. of town	3	....	110593	1018	24	203	52436	6564	400
State Center, town of	14	30	12838	1455	20	933	3765	1319	....
Taylor	1	....	97047	....	167	69	30215	6257	165
Timber Creek	33	510	125001	130	831	915	13487	7817	660
Vienna	....	20	120991	22	127	136	3073	6463	467
Washington	....	....	197073	70	270	382	47387	7896	....
Total	608	4047	2368678	19152	15099	18528	590713	141945	34153

MILLS COUNTY.

NAMES OF TOWNSHIPS, TOWNS, AND CITIES.	Number of stands of bees.	Number of pounds of honey and beeswax in 1874.	Value of products of farm.	Value of market garden produce.	Value of products of the orchard.	Value of small fruit.	Value of products of the herd.	Value of products of the dairy.	Value of products of the forest.
Anderson	25	99	$ 133153	$ 175	$ 17	$ 138	$ 64559	$ 5721	$ 8314
Deer Creek	....	4	27658	13	56	....	20780	....	....
Emerson, town of	....	....	625	1031	....	....	925	....	260
Glenwood, exc. of city	105	398	93547	710	1530	877	83417	6627	8776
Glenwood, city of	....	....	....	....	....	....	....	....	....
Hastings, town of	....	....	8710	....	....	....	2660	....	1259
Hillsdale, town of	....	....	540	24	....	....	1016	81	....
Indian Creek, exc. of Emerson and Hastings	....	....	115327	....	....	....	98190	....	5200
Ingraham	15	285	84249	2123	329	333	43922	5487	....
Lyons	95	868	142586	....	1548	180	26646	3655	2838
Malvern, town of	51	200	52	120	....	....	4904	449	60
Oak	70	280	131554	39	3628	346	44641	9700	4211
Platteville	65	139	33210	350	10	1399	....	....	....
Rawles	....	625	106197	1825	4844	1215	58210	5324	4400
St. Mary	32	320	23304	25	825	....	3499	750	....
Silver Creek, exc. of Hillsdale and Malvern	....	....	102585	1073	3383	1238	188918	4805	8783
White Cloud	15	....	80212	....	....	....	74665	3607	....
Total	473	3218	1083509	7520	16170	5726	716952	46206	44101

MITCHELL COUNTY.

NAMES OF TOWNSHIPS, TOWNS, AND CITIES.	Number of stands of bees.	Number of pounds of honey and beeswax in 1874.	Value of products of farm.	Value of market garden produce.	Value of products of the orchard.	Value of small fruit.	Value of products of the herd.	Value of products of the dairy.	Value of products of the forest.
Burr Oak	70	100	110163	23	....	....	....	3705	....
Cedar	63	140	121481	530	214	129	14683	6593	7227
Douglas	1	50	56744	....	....	....	4993	3673	6575
Jenkins	41	105	107075	....	....	....	9845	6283	100
Liberty	11	75	321012	....	....	....	1731	1850	....
Lincoln	82	5078	115349	100	33	....	....	6354	4980
Mitchell	65	1050	89044	200	....	....	8598	2288	....
Newburg	50	450	56839	....	....	....	1961	385	....
Osage, exc. of town	42	650	36543	480	39	255	2847	3265	937
Osage, town of	14	245	12954	25	8	539	12584	1990	2765
Otranto	18	400	77036	70	154	55	11143	4794	6248
Rock	1	78	98297	191	....	....	4346	3891	....
St. Ansgar	1	....	119700	....	....	....	6818	8607	1005
Stacyville	....	....	101396	....	....	....	4870	2008	....
Union	2	15	120541	....	....	....	4796	3785	....
Wayne	20	254	56104	....	....	60	5773	4703	985
Total	491	8690	1591878	1628	448	1038	94988	64174	30822

MONONA COUNTY.

NAMES OF TOWNSHIPS, TOWNS, AND CITIES.	Number of stands of bees.	Number of pounds of honey and beeswax in 1874.	Value of products of farm.	Value of market garden produce.	Value of products of the orchard.	Value of small fruit.	Value of products of the herd.	Value of products of the dairy.	Value of products of the forest.
Ashton	2	85	29367	....	33	27	3936	795	....
Belvidere	79	1500	13403	....	....	8	16269	....	....
Center	....	....	22282	68	....	....	5605	1559	1075
Fairview	176	6585	22017	....	....	....	5264	1417	100
Franklin, exc. of Onawa	31	176	40105	....	86	257	29985	2660	3112
Grant	25	250	6000	....	....	....	18942	100	....
Jordan	....	....	12576	....	....	....	1855	311	....
Kennebec	32	440	41284	....	265	20	18358	2773	1706
Lake	....	....	30225	....	....	....	5951	....	....
Lincoln	77	695	25004	....	....	....	18678	3049	6650
Maple	7	45	92140	2499	2	30	15410	7054	610
Onawa, town of	....	....	....	....	....	....	24866	....	66

MONONA COUNTY.—Continued.

Names of townships, towns, and cities.	Number of stands of bees.	Number of pounds of honey and beeswax in 1874.	Value of products of farm.	Value of market garden produce.	Value of products of the orchard.	Value of small fruit.	Value of products of the herd.	Value of products of the dairy.	Value of products of the forest.
St. Clair	....	....	$ 13107	$	$	$	$ 2020	$ 987	$ ......
Sherman	23	350	27862	....	....	....	15462	992	1585
Soldier	21	200	17651	....	....	....	3545	1308	....
Spring Valley	22	225	22486	378	....	7	22610	2970	2178
West Fork	9	300	22212	20	275	20	11626	800	....
Willow	....	....	9944	7	....	....	2008	668	640
Total	504	10851	447665	2972	661	369	223424	27443	17722

MONROE COUNTY.

Names of townships, towns, and cities.	Number of stands of bees.	Number of pounds of honey and beeswax in 1874.	Value of products of farm.	Value of market garden produce.	Value of products of the orchard.	Value of small fruit.	Value of products of the herd.	Value of products of the dairy.	Value of products of the forest.
Albia City	....	....	....	....	....	....	....	....	....
Bluff Creek	131	698	173100	26	2965	10	66580	10278	....
Cedar	56	393	60836	405	505	116	27312	811	....
Franklin	59	196	5710	20	60	....	7335	805	240
Guilford	25	65	82922	271	167	64	39115	3869	....
Jackson	22	100	54970	....	....	....	....	....	....
Mantua	101	184	82099	1124	1451	1647	44824	11926	4544
Monroe	214	1567	110228	2108	1541	555	48595	7445	4200
Pleasant	66	63	105482	2058	3720	505	54674	7557	5220
Troy, exc. of Albia	107	1052	91100	2185	1965	2395	32001	7238	1076
Union	154	1465	85240	1505	1365	1005	56942	....	4826
Urbana	72	844	51470	....	75	23	57134	4869	5429
Wayne	22	240	35205	....	....	....	....	....	....
Total	1029	6867	938362	9702	13814	6320	434462	54798	25535

MONTGOMERY COUNTY.

Names of townships, towns, and cities.	Number of stands of bees.	Number of pounds of honey and beeswax in 1874.	Value of products of farm.	Value of market garden produce.	Value of products of the orchard.	Value of small fruit.	Value of products of the herd.	Value of products of the dairy.	Value of products of the forest.
Douglas	38	....	80887	65	....	....	33482	....	....
Frankfort	1	....	76520	....	....	10	24154	981	....
Grant	41	....	149227	50	382	83	32176	4295	2292
Jackson, exc. of Villisca	100	....	38882	....	1795	133	18465	3807	40
Lincoln	....	....	78401	....	....	....	5604	2133	....
Pilot Grove	3	....	82400	100	....	50	18311	3519	2379
Red Oak, exc. of town	108	....	102638	70	34	236	46019	4767	234
Red Oak, town of	....	....	....	....	....	....	....	....	....
Scott	1	....	42367	....	....	....	18865	....	....
Sherman	....	....	102901	....	....	....	24914	....	440
Villisca, town of	....	....	2970	502	7	49	1546	926	....
Walnut	....	....	141722	20	40	45	42952	3499	....
Washington	13	....	77278	20	....	5	17345	6766	1297
West	....	....	95934	....	146	72	20958	5758	5722
Total	305	....	1072127	817	2404	683	304791	36453	12403

MUSCATINE COUNTY.

Names of townships, towns, and cities.	Number of stands of bees.	Number of pounds of honey and beeswax in 1874.	Value of products of farm.	Value of market garden produce.	Value of products of the orchard.	Value of small fruit.	Value of products of the herd.	Value of products of the dairy.	Value of products of the forest.
Bloomington, exc. of Muscatine	100	361	190154	3257	2920	1478	44366	14396	286
Cedar	25	....	42195	....	1547	288	37537	2630	1153
Fulton	34	103	304652	128	2437	849	67460	14252	....
Goshen	56	355	189547	....	1380	1706	87314	9065	7120
Lake	61	29	118956	299	4181	1747	52112	8447	2995
Montpelier	19	30	72601	....	1216	91	28537	4040	2907

MUSCATINE COUNTY.—Continued.

Names of townships, towns, and cities.	Number of stands of bees.	Number of pounds of honey and beeswax in 1874.	Value of products of farm.	Value of market garden produce.	Value of products of the orchard.	Value of small fruits.	Value of products of the herd.	Value of products of the dairy.	Value of products of the forest.
Moscow	32	60	$ 59822	$ 1154	$ 711	$ 230	$ 33660	$ 2065	$ 3676
Muscatine, city of									
Orono	66	300	76106		785	28	13948	2293	300
Pike	90	325	123645	170		5	27619	5127	
Seventy-Six	27	21	90677		2041	633	56410	5119	4123
Sweetland	2		121144		3061	2656	54305	820	
Wapsinonoc, exc of West Liberty	71	360	179296	4510	1200	1778	92331	6594	8843
West Liberty	9			198	480	496	2786	1310	
Wilton, exc. of town	23	23	177689	75	713	677	92878	10751	10
Wilton, town of	1		1422	4		2450	3115		
Total	616	1967	1747906	9795	22672	15112	694378	88909	31413

O'BRIEN COUNTY.

Names of townships, towns, and cities.	Number of stands of bees.	Number of pounds of honey and beeswax in 1874.	Value of products of farm.	Value of market garden produce.	Value of products of the orchard.	Value of small fruits.	Value of products of the herd.	Value of products of the dairy.	Value of products of the forest.
Baker			11340	461			1533	761	
Carrol			21616				3068	410	
Center			27019				1984	2315	
Floyd			20977	6564			6276	6452	
Grant			29149				5390	1328	
Highland			36880	3416			1861	2172	
Liberty	1		29398	10			162	672	39
Summit			3324	100			4	50	
Waterman			11839					56	
Total	1		191542	10551			20278	13216	39

OSCEOLA COUNTY.

Names of townships, towns, and cities.	Number of stands of bees.	Number of pounds of honey and beeswax in 1874.	Value of products of farm.	Value of market garden produce.	Value of products of the orchard.	Value of small fruits.	Value of products of the herd.	Value of products of the dairy.	Value of products of the forest.
Fairview			1677				40	213	
Gilman			14275						
Goewey			20510				588	950	
Holman			12697	100			198	2020	
Horton			1665				25	436	
Ocheyedan			6375						
Viola			8054				584	787	
Wilson			4328	15				876	
Total			69581	115			1435	5291	

PAGE COUNTY.

Names of townships, towns, and cities.	Number of stands of bees.	Number of pounds of honey and beeswax in 1874.	Value of products of farm.	Value of market garden produce.	Value of products of the orchard.	Value of small fruits.	Value of products of the herd.	Value of products of the dairy.	Value of products of the forest.
Amity	102	110	93541		3939	1334	53729	65	
Buchanan	154	1011	110400		2166	1220	57263	6841	
Clarinda, town of	83	45		2075	770	1459	14013	3125	
Colfax	4		42772		340	110	25606		
Douglas	4	10	16670			23	21853	235	2890
East River	127	392	64631		2272	1310	39778	7355	8907
Fremont			115235	290	30	10	26142	3583	1225
Grant, exc. of Shenandoah	6	27	122095	94	2	1	90506	2719	
Harlan	50		109552	50	2814		76161	4640	4737
Lincoln	7	10	77332	1040	275	209	63754	7335	1940
Morton	6		51684				24447	1481	
Nebraska	93	824	32553	20	1062		24759	2563	2962

PAGE COUNTY.—CONTINUED.

NAMES OF TOWNSHIPS, TOWNS, AND CITIES.	Number of stands of bees.	Number of pounds of honey and beeswax in 1874.	Value of products of the farm.	Value of market garden produce.	Value of products of the orchard.	Value of small fruit.	Value of products of the herd.	Value of products of the dairy.	Value of products of the forest.
Nodaway, exc. of Clarinda..	78	875	160079	30	3371	379	71126	4080	....
Pierce	35	50	74514	115	200	95	33001	4315	364
Shenandoah	....	....	2200	....	....	....	....	....	....
Tarkio	7	75	75445	8	107	30	33307	3325	154
Valley	49	395	91937	499	529	103	30482	3146	4433
Washington	....	....	52823	....	....	....	28665	....	....
Total	805	3825	1293463	4221	17877	6283	714592	54708	27612

PALO ALTO COUNTY.

NAMES OF TOWNSHIPS, TOWNS, AND CITIES.	Number of stands of bees.	Number of pounds of honey and beeswax in 1874.	Value of products of the farm.	Value of market garden produce.	Value of products of the orchard.	Value of small fruit.	Value of products of the herd.	Value of products of the dairy.	Value of products of the forest.
Ellington	....	....	8189	63	....	2	1608	1326	....
Emmetsburg	....	....	9166	10	....	10	....	3995	....
Fairfield	....	....	310	....	....	....	30	220	....
Fern Valley	1	30	3831	....	....	....	2213	620	57
Freedom	....	....	7989	....	....	....	....	1981	....
Great Oak	....	....	12570	....	....	....	1814	3106	100
Highland	....	....	7336	....	....	....	461	1180	....
Lost Island	....	....	2802	....	....	....	....	487	1245
Nevada	....	....	9448	....	....	....	8078	....	....
Rush Lake	....	....	7930	50	....	1	419	678	....
Silver Lake	....	....	6441	33	....	....	....	....	....
Vernon	....	....	2298	....	....	....	902	1993	....
Walnut	....	....	2799	....	....	....	....	5348	....
West Bend	....	....	15507	....	....	....	633	1928	241
Total	1	30	96616	156	....	13	16158	22862	1643

PLYMOUTH COUNTY.

NAMES OF TOWNSHIPS, TOWNS, AND CITIES.	Number of stands of bees.	Number of pounds of honey and beeswax in 1874.	Value of products of the farm.	Value of market garden produce.	Value of products of the orchard.	Value of small fruit.	Value of products of the herd.	Value of products of the dairy.	Value of products of the forest.
America	....	....	32350	....	....	....	....	....	....
Elgin	....	....	27134	....	....	....	324	705	....
Fredonia	....	....	42986	....	....	....	76	1404	1439
Grant	....	....	21901	....	....	....	....	....	....
Johnson	....	....	42698	....	....	....	2987	1405	....
Lincoln	....	....	79194	880	25	33	15246	2734	276
Marion	....	....	12799	....	....	....	1459	....	....
Perry	....	....	48761	70	....	....	3860	3254	....
Plymouth	....	....	27258	239	....	....	2867	....	....
Portland	....	....	10490	....	....	....	....	....	....
Sioux	....	....	4429	....	....	....	986	80	340
Stanton	....	....	43775	....	....	....	3396	837	....
Union	....	....	23726	84	....	....	2736	561	....
Washington	....	....	16622	....	....	....	....	2028	....
Total	....	....	434123	1273	25	33	33937	13008	2055

POCAHONTAS COUNTY.

NAMES OF TOWNSHIPS, TOWNS, AND CITIES.	Number of stands of bees.	Number of pounds of honey and beeswax in 1874.	Value of products of the farm.	Value of market garden produce.	Value of products of the orchard.	Value of small fruit.	Value of products of the herd.	Value of products of the dairy.	Value of products of the forest.
Bellville	....	....	9069	....	....	....	50	1671	....
Cedar	....	....	12812	....	....	....	....	2006	....
Center	....	....	1595	....	....	....	....	....	....
Clinton	....	....	7036	....	....	....	1254	870	....
Colfax	....	....	10385	....	....	....	200	1945	....

POCAHONTAS COUNTY.—Continued.

Names of townships, towns, and cities.	Number of stands of bees.	Number of pounds of honey and beeswax in 1874.	Value of products of farm.	Value of market garden produce.	Value of products of the orchard.	Value of small fruit.	Value of products of the herd.	Value of products of the dairy.	Value of products of the forest.
Des Moines			$ 20025	$	$	$	$ 18024	$ 4807	
Dover			5454				82		
Grant			5702						
Jackson			8941				590	1775	
Lincoln			1770						
Lizard			29877	12			1677	2114	
Swan Lake									
Total			112666	12			21877	15188	

POLK COUNTY.

Names of townships, towns, and cities.	Number of stands of bees.	Number of pounds of honey and beeswax in 1874.	Value of products of farm.	Value of market garden produce.	Value of products of the orchard.	Value of small fruit.	Value of products of the herd.	Value of products of the dairy.	Value of products of the forest.
Allen	32	243	49983	1653	1745	1238	11868	2088	3466
Beaver	127	910	215386	30	1174	1561	43354	8505	535
Bloomfield	51	661	161186	3104	4708	2350	60649	11194	
Camp	73	794	139724		1380		65285	3149	
Crocker	133	843	107573		645	441	48942	4905	5412
Delaware	61	555	177891	6668	390	1203	61606	5744	4032
Des Moines, city of							818		
Douglas	25	340	126295	30	710	375	59290	6950	2600
Elkhart	88	402	58675	2237	823	850	21998	7814	2963
Four Mile	12	120	69131	300	616	300	6720		1525
Franklin	131	465	117882		441	224	39573	7167	1578
Grant	32	157	84244	975	642	551	12190	1117	1337
Jefferson	25		110676				29129	5698	1750
Lincoln			64585					7449	
Madison	220	706	143625		116	158	11659	3633	
Saylor	98	952	97015	425	1345	498	29145	4076	22105
Valley	67	495	58618	6135	2963	6564	24988	16576	790
Walnut	110	251	239687	41	933	486	101964	6085	1670
Washington	14	50	117847	1289	295	282	44833	7453	1371
Total	1299	7944	2140023	22887	18926	17081	674011	109603	51134

POTTAWATTAMIE COUNTY.

Names of townships, towns, and cities.	Number of stands of bees.	Number of pounds of honey and beeswax in 1874.	Value of products of farm.	Value of market garden produce.	Value of products of the orchard.	Value of small fruit.	Value of products of the herd.	Value of products of the dairy.	Value of products of the forest.
Avoca, town of	15	475	4429				1585	332	60
Belknap	8	20	24910			15	18937	1147	275
Boomer	1		30856				15014	4410	
Center	20	14	97963	245	2495	412	3955	4009	3765
Council Bluffs, city of	22	565	19245	11940	5571	8965	63340	44195	4590
Crescent	20	395	37737	1995	5		7767	3564	836
Grove	6	200	92566	12			18718	2816	
Harden	3	100	54800					5475	
Hazel Dell	27	115	49419	45		147	7760	4688	
James	7		32224	464			8086	3325	150
Kane, exc. of Council Bluffs	3	23	90704	2110	1410	1071		9055	
Keg Creek			63933	151	66		11024	801	115
Knox, exc. of Avoca	5	25	152331		53	3	31868	6528	90286
Layton	1		99454		1534		3200		
Macedonia			37910		160		7631		
Neola			13840				14877	1279	24
Norwalk			21175				9305	1622	
Pleasant			41470	50			1926	1247	20
Rockford	94	385	72540	10	544	151	30317	6291	5837
Silver Creek			28602		40		32618	1158	
Washington	1		18468	290	35	28	2123	1637	990

POTTAWATTAMIE COUNTY.—Continued.

Names of townships, towns, and cities.	Number of stands of bees.	Number of pounds of honey and beeswax in 1874.	Value of products of farm.	Value of market garden produce.	Value of products of the orchard.	Value of small fruit.	Value of products of the herd.	Value of products of the dairy.	Value of products of the forest.
Waveland	23	311	$ 73418	$........	$ 270	$........	$ 13110	$ 8119	$ 204
Wright	26	....	71448	....	....	32	12533	3084	700
York	5	150	23187	....	....	5	4142	1654	....
Total	287	2778	1252629	17312	12183	10829	319836	116536	107852

POWESHIEK COUNTY.

Names of townships, towns, and cities.	Number of stands of bees.	Number of pounds of honey and beeswax in 1874.	Value of products of farm.	Value of market garden produce.	Value of products of the orchard.	Value of small fruit.	Value of products of the herd.	Value of products of the dairy.	Value of products of the forest.
Bear Creek, exc. Brooklyn	24	65	182965	100	695	858	74115	7678	365
Brooklyn, town of	....	....	....	....	....	....	....	....	....
Chester	18	270	186185	....	310	461	45907	6470	10
Deep River	47	422	104427	39	1549	449	70790	7312	2872
Grinnell, exc. of town	....	....	180793	270	482	662	75629	7438	....
Grinnell, town of	....	....	....	....	....	....	182400	....	....
Jackson, exc. Montezuma	99	....	170133	752	2124	142	27732	8009	....
Jefferson	3	....	161159	....	200	100	27286	10255	....
Lincoln	16	126	134230	....	92	133	37276	6161	1185
Madison	....	....	194997	....	....	....	10072	11247	....
Malcom, exc. of town	....	....	149300	10	1013	....	17025	3538	....
Malcom, town of	2	....	3380	....	....	....	11318	454	....
Montezuma, town of	....	....	....	1076	....	227	....	1432	....
Pleasant	16	147	151063	63	508	314	88094	4016	....
Scott	....	....	144540	....	....	....	24564	5345	....
Sheridan	9	10	169262	1130	76	288	37637	14779	....
Sugar Creek	122	955	113887	....	40	....	27068	3806	22
Union	86	311	63492	....	539	209	4648	4049	....
Warren	44	352	135480	102	121	903	23850	7039	9214
Washington	80	355	147729	....	214	44	33506	5608	....
Total	566	3013	2393022	3542	7963	4790	818917	114636	13668

RINGGOLD COUNTY.

Names of townships, towns, and cities.	Number of stands of bees.	Number of pounds of honey and beeswax in 1874.	Value of products of farm.	Value of market garden produce.	Value of products of the orchard.	Value of small fruit.	Value of products of the herd.	Value of products of the dairy.	Value of products of the forest.
Athens	11	124	40000	2574	475	214	19294	3020	5289
Benton	44	410	74317	....	20	40	30996	690	....
Clinton	16	289	31628	....	385	215	24248	1195	2316
Grant	33	132	57694	3	312	168	26105	5789	2089
Jefferson	46	700	69756	293	623	196	31985	2967	6011
Liberty	21	405	48130	25	112	160	22228	2094	....
Lincoln	21	50	57004	10	80	40	30707	....	3620
Lot's Creek	19	138	28836	68	255	41	18842	2238	5667
Middle Fork	11	57	46681	20	321	165	25647	3054	3612
Monroe	12	139	40660	86	35	70	21422	....	796
Mount Ayr	4	75	452138	2517	590	717	43474	10676	9625
Rice	3	....	22507	....	....	....	....	1642	....
Riley	11	10	15805	1062	134	149	15658	3541	2824
Tingley	....	....	46483	....	....	....	....	1418	....
Union	6	58	34000	....	265	20	6012	....	1226
Washington	30	278	50143	9750	....	150	22620	1930	48
Total	288	2865	1115782	16408	3607	2345	339238	40254	43123

SAC COUNTY.

NAMES OF TOWNSHIPS, TOWNS, AND CITIES.	Number of stands of bees.	Number of pounds of honey and beeswax in 1874.	Value of products of farm.	Value of market garden produce.	Value of products of the orchard.	Value of small fruit.	Value of products of the herd.	Value of products of the dairy.	Value of products of the forest.
Boyer Valley	...	...	$ 23684	$...	$...	$...	$ 4367	$ 2756	$...
Clinton	...	...	4181	...	...	...	...	2725	...
Douglas	8	125	29030	...	...	...	398	2764	...
Eden	...	...	22267	...	...	...	...	887	...
Jackson	19	90	47785	...	50	30	21222	470	920
Levey	...	...	33499	...	4	2	9901	7727	...
Sac	...	...	52406	142	...	...	52406	4697	3625
Wall Lake	...	...	26028	...	35	...	22631	...	1807
Total	27	215	238880	142	89	32	110926	22026	6352

SCOTT COUNTY.

NAMES OF TOWNSHIPS, TOWNS, AND CITIES.	Number of stands of bees.	Number of pounds of honey and beeswax in 1874.	Value of products of farm.	Value of market garden produce.	Value of products of the orchard.	Value of small fruit.	Value of products of the herd.	Value of products of the dairy.	Value of products of the forest.
Allen's Grove	3	10	149827	...	324	...	35041	7684	3375
Blue Grass	16	180	300930	396	2382	1280	78036	11181	...
Buffalo, exc. of town	16	60	98335	...	1387	327	29054	4813	3067
Buffalo, town of	...	...	...	...	...	...	...	...	...
Butler	22	215	212576	1678	1525	635	60163	14198	515
Cleona	6	30	258683	...	383	54	35045	6311	...
Davenport, exc. of city	12	75	265635	6700	8560	10355	54040	51395	...
Davenport, city of	9	315	2900	3075	965	3271	190	8430	110
Hickory Grove	...	...	294323	5	945	83	58845	13813	438
LeClaire, exc, of town	20	100	130931	1502	6110	1849	56364	11215	1765
LeClaire, town of	...	...	...	...	...	...	...	...	...
Liberty	31	...	156113	25	279	146	39072	5675	100
Lincoln	2	...	298512	...	3749	124	66735	14629	...
Pleasant Valley	8	45	130660	905	8137	3616	45032	9992	3132
Princeton, exc. of town	100	440	144526	...	2003	20	61577	5797	...
Princeton, town of	...	...	...	...	...	...	...	...	...
Rockingham	...	...	28326	924	2395	537	4786	5237	4815
Sheridan	...	...	399286	...	1052	...	62035	12651	...
Winfield	3	3	170310	3	841	25	45377	9756	65
Total	248	1473	3041873	15213	41037	22322	731742	192777	17382

SHELBY COUNTY.

NAMES OF TOWNSHIPS, TOWNS, AND CITIES.	Number of stands of bees.	Number of pounds of honey and beeswax in 1874.	Value of products of farm.	Value of market garden produce.	Value of products of the orchard.	Value of small fruit.	Value of products of the herd.	Value of products of the dairy.	Value of products of the forest.
Cass	...	...	...	...	...	...	5245	438	...
Clay	...	...	28081	...	...	...	6150	1152	...
Douglas	...	...	36616	30	...	...	3432	...	...
Fairview	...	...	104642	52	...	...	20194	2306	4082
Greeley	...	...	6264	101	...	...	4916	966	...
Grove	35	170	27782	64	...	...	18193	3772	2193
Harlan	9	250	168491	2760	...	406	10326	9876	5664
Jackson	52	2200	22921	...	...	...	301	717	354
Jefferson	...	...	9213	183	...	...	1977	1373	300
Lincoln	...	...	43807	...	...	...	5260	1535	...
Monroe	...	...	...	...	...	...	...	...	...
Polk	...	...	14235	14	...	...	...	...	...
Shelby	...	...	91951	15	...	...	14401	2240	50
Union	...	...	11267	128	...	...	1525	507	479
Washington	...	...	7776	...	...	...	...	771	...
Westphalia	...	...	...	...	...	...	...	...	...
Total	96	2620	573046	3347	...	406	91920	25653	13122

SIOUX COUNTY.

NAMES OF TOWNSHIPS, TOWNS, AND CITIES.	Number of stands of bees.	Number of pounds of honey and beeswax in 1874.	Value of products of farm.	Value of market garden produce.	Value of products of the orchard.	Value of small fruit.	Value of products of the herd.	Value of products of the dairy.	Value of products of the forest.
Buncombe	....	....	9807	....	....	....	2217	606	....
Floyd	....	....	13929	....	....	....	751	653	....
Grant	....	....	12280	....	....	....	93	2682	....
Holland	....	....	46817	....	....	....	....	1508	....
Lincoln	....	....	6995	....	....	....	651	622	....
Nassau	....	....	35918	....	....	....	160	1000	....
Reading	....	....	19160	....	....	....	95	1211	....
Rock	....	....	5528	12	....	....	697	301	....
Settler	....	....	9502	....	....	....	1084	746	....
Sheridan	....	....	7044	....	....	....	....	606	....
Total	....	....	166980	12	....	....	5756	9935	....

STORY COUNTY.

NAMES OF TOWNSHIPS, TOWNS, AND CITIES.	Number of stands of bees.	Number of pounds of honey and beeswax in 1874.	Value of products of farm.	Value of market garden produce.	Value of products of the orchard.	Value of small fruit.	Value of products of the herd.	Value of products of the dairy.	Value of products of the forest.
Ames, town of	91	40	5109	43	....	960	1041	360	32
Collins	152	400	89189	1230	562	252	34459	5637	3637
Franklin	51	40	86685	48	579	25	31698	9958	5013
Grant	11	43	44762	735	198	327	21180	7810	3396
Howard	....	....	87045	....	....	....	40759	....	....
Indian Creek	161	351	11443	50	564	452	46351	10743	7800
Lafayette	7	105	36670	....	....	....	13186	2415	1165
Lincoln	....	....	36307	355	189	95	6515	2113	15
Milford	12	265	65573	937	477	533	44415	13306	3498
Nevada, exc. of town	145	845	99043	519	1194	914	4803	12225	535
Nevada, town of	60	255	3636	20	349	1558	8618	6409	....
New Albany	23	75	20397	....	8	10	11193	2479	100
Palestine	3	10	74885	61	401	87	3830	9070	4158
Richland	4	....	57942	....	264	67	3353	8392	....
Sherman	....	....	30079	....	....	....	6767	3920	....
Union	154	1249	134265	2733	2077	1770	52082	14894	8095
Warren	....	....	7972	115	1	5	1894	777	....
Washington, exc. of Ames	137	1038	142741	95	577	88	4571	14830	3676
Total	1011	4716	1033743	6941	7440	7143	336715	125338	41126

TAMA COUNTY.

NAMES OF TOWNSHIPS, TOWNS, AND CITIES.	Number of stands of bees.	Number of pounds of honey and beeswax in 1874.	Value of products of farm.	Value of market garden produce.	Value of products of the orchard.	Value of small fruit.	Value of products of the herd.	Value of products of the dairy.	Value of products of the forest.
Buckingham	9	120	153335	75	873	402	60585	5035	5425
Carlton	7	6	106734	553	596	308	26643	8844	1527
Carroll	13	....	86920	63	315	110	5638	5596	1260
Clark	2	....	108730	....	10	72	9365	3749	....
Columbia	19	165	113709	....	....	....	16414	7111	....
Crystal	4	75	89523	....	275	....	23500	5498	390
Geneseo	....	....	119910	....	....	....	29785	....	....
Grant	3	....	61233	....	....	....	12842	664	....
Highland	2	....	105106	....	....	....	25463	3773	1341
Howard	3	....	142825	....	811	237	31930	6605	295
Indian Village, ex. Montour	77	630	94925	....	970	166	27261	5509	7300
Lincoln	....	....	108698	....	....	....	5573	3415	....
Montour, town of	2	40	300	....	....	....	100	50	3200
Oneida	....	....	152530	....	....	22	19665	6044	....
Otter Creek	97	130	147436	25	565	158	37856	4996	4302
Perry, exc. of Traer	21	106	135576	51	1052	808	38463	14531	2248
Richland	51	295	110759	....	30	468	4865	5176	....
Salt Creek	18	....	97970	238	....	280	27243	363	....

TAMA COUNTY.—CONTINUED.

NAMES OF TOWNSHIPS, TOWNS, AND CITIES.	Number of stands of bees.	Number of pounds of honey and beeswax in 1874.	Value of products of farm.	Value of market garden produce.	Value of products of the orchard.	Value of small fruit.	Value of products of the herd.	Value of products of the dairy.	Value of products of the forest.
Spring Creek	5	50	$103675	$	$	$	$ 6439	$ 1530	$ ....
Tama, exc. of Tama City	16	....	19676	10	184	2	6876	668	715
Tama City, town of	132	....	150	150	40	90	....	....	....
Toledo, exc. of town	21	59	56511	1357	1211	392	23805	4175	8490
Toledo, town of	6	....	47980	1861	190	1059	6831	68060	597
Traer, town of	5	....	2184	....	....	....	845	348	25
York	29	119	150010	....	1341	568	30407	5288	170
Total	542	1795	2316405	4383	8463	5142	478394	167025	37285

TAYLOR COUNTY.

Bedford, town of	1	....	....	....	....	....	....	....	....
Benton, exc. of Bedford	16	....	85759	15	50	....	21439	1040	....
Clayton	43	147	52560	163	864	195	46445	3365	1476
Dallas	89	386	84596	229	420	145	25969	4780	1500
Gay	8	90	34233	....	126	41	28289	250	1200
Grant	11	10	28880	25	20	10	6691	290	65
Grove	3	....	23257	3	....	....	8096	103	600
Holt	48	....	71215	200	158	....	21255	....	....
Jackson	33	60	51878	....	....	....	10468	2174	1610
Jefferson	21	140	53881	108	860	....	34037	455	....
Marshall	14	140	23619	....	....	....	11826	3723	....
Mason	67	390	76204	85	1283	205	41097	7145	7355
Nodaway	74	587	60156	222	335	90	23360	2301	5880
Platte	12	25	52865	2369	175	16	23422	2453	....
Polk	16	20	71267	370	1128	70	69225	6395	....
Ross	27	40	56251	10	869	175	36730	3532	5114
Washington	73	985	51855	....	971	114	32920	3774	200
Total	556	3020	908476	3799	7259	1061	441269	41780	25000

UNION COUNTY.

Afton, town of	....	....	285	....	....	....	....	1412	....
Creston, town of	....	....	....	....	....	....	....	....	....
Dodge	17	312	26280	....	....	....	16735	2580	....
Douglas, exc. of Creston	3	20	37721	1000	....	....	5787	....	....
Grant	....	....	25403	....	....	....	2790	1165	....
Highland	31	218	50605	135	75	....	19202	310	650
Jones	83	380	78174	273	365	92	....	5991	1337
Lincoln	1	....	65770	....	....	....	....	....	....
New Hope	7	131	58474	717	561	137	28745	6725	3095
Platte	41	190	85090	135	1244	114	50067	5947	1220
Pleasant	49	420	36552	86	355	....	25640	....	....
Sand Creek	12	50	45076	41	206	138	1584	1637	....
Spaulding	....	....	33801	1945	....	....	8282	864	....
Union, exc. of Afton	17	34	71029	645	677	140	37496	3102	5149
Total	261	1755	624260	4977	3483	621	196328	29733	11451

VAN BUREN COUNTY.

NAMES OF TOWNSHIPS, TOWNS, AND CITIES.	Number of stands of bees.	Number of pounds of honey and beeswax in 1874.	Value of products of farm.	Value of market garden products.	Value of products of the orchard.	Value of small fruit.	Value of products of the herd.	Value of products of the dairy.	Value of products of the forest.
Bentonsport, town of	16	110	$ 1427	$ 170	$ 1415	$ 738	$ 3708	$ 1487	$ ......
Birmingham, town of	28	50	4160	347	210	775	2557	13050	....
Bonaparte	98	112	41575	3020	4216	726	22872	5142	1460
Cantril, town of	2	....	....	....	....	....	....	....	....
Cedar	122	457	153318	....	2713	300	72435	8402	2490
Chequest	85	367	80613	1692	2083	629	35594	6130	385
Des Moines	177	360	110956	1878	3942	876	121224	5484	2198
Farmington, exc. of town	60	199	65469	40	3138	120	22784	3148	3381
Farmington, town of	....	....	....	....	....	....	....	....	....
Harrisburg	107	62	158886	....	3478	74	57932	12724	....
Henry	62	200	52918	30	1927	478	33421	3051	874
Jackson, exc of Cantril	259	2308	172778	100	3458	1005	78224	10559	7480
Keosauqua, town of	13	100	4459	.....	1325	505	4135	906	1570
Lick Creek	62	378	80450	258	5488	1786	38337	10329	10303
Union, exc. of Birmingham	86	532	132358	....	4992	1123	56850	6563	2131
Van Buren, exc. Keosauqua	141	581	133455	6133	10082	673	50286	17532	5032
Vernon	150	366	94384	1295	1690	1048	40615	9306	5380
Village	99	396	106324	90	2130	30	30696	5113	10683
Washington, exc. of Bentonsport	41	224	46086	....	1502	55	17950	1350	515
Total	1608	6802	1439586	15053	53789	10941	689620	120276	53882

WAPELLO COUNTY.

Adams	107	481	86817	....	850	592	38302	5184	5660
Agency exc. of town	31	52	45962	327	2176	1040	19365	3566	1280
Agency City, town of	8	70	150	509	141	291	1903	80	15
Cass	44	251	33830	15	375	28	15745	2239	770
Center, exc. of Ottumwa	179	978	150470	8009	2035	3003	61247	28954	1784
Columbia, exc. of Eddyville	91	535	79810	325	1120	160	42330	4045	4475
Competine	69	395	126690	10	1275	135	87272	8061	2458
Dahlonega	30	79	84659	100	1798	344	48745	2875	3356
Eddyville, town of	14	160	5905	1810	700	717	5990	965	7825
Eldon, town of	....	....	....	....	....	....	....	....	....
Green	81	261	88201	1993	823	454	33738	7556	19662
Highland	70	744	153221	....	1083	973	84519	10064	....
Keokuk	6	20	34938	600	230	20	12113	3026	1102
Ottumwa, city of	10	40	....	2517	5467	1691	371251	14560	....
Pleasant	79	426	115195	94	2401	259	7605	15	4060
Polk	71	63	93068	71	580	357	29264	5349	1767
Richland	99	....	244082	....	638	170	47382	10679	645
Washington, exc. of Eldon.	88	390	112321	253	2974	805	38203	8505	35
Total	1077	4945	1455319	16633	24666	11039	944974	115723	54894

WARREN COUNTY.

Allen	107	750	75390	361	1376	738	48880	8771	3231
Belmont	21	500	156375	8	1389	521	68223	4148	....
Greenfield	197	1531	217738	198	2734	1267	70628	8787	10867
Indianola, town of	....	....	....	....	....	....	....	....	....
Jackson	54	545	135747	....	150	....	8703	528	....
Jefferson	76	770	205961	720	625	217	42285	9093	2936
Liberty	48	594	128193	10	1735	1491	79240	8298	5167
Linn	56	196	211827	....	3934	700	90714	7940	4426
Otter	98	905	119120	....	1895	423	55430	4440	75

WARREN COUNTY.—Continued.

Names of townships, towns, and cities.	Number of stands of bees.	Number of pounds of honey and beeswax in 1874.	Value of products of farm.	Value of market garden produce.	Value of products of the orchard.	Value of small fruit.	Value of products of the herd.	Value of products of the dairy.	Value of products of the forest.
Palmyra	6	25	$ 88955	$ 30	$ 900	$ 104	$ 535	$ 740	$.......
Richland	63	410	103130	92	2738	700	41471	13944	14000
Squaw	39	338	72094	440	757	197	42730	6794	1337
Union	142	1166	90600	5	740	104	....	100	2779
Virginia	49	428	75721	1491	435	257	44094	5129	5533
Washington, exc. of Indianola	161	1444	316168	14506	6890	3130	179443	11790	19540
White Breast	48	426	109446	....	616	33	44759	....	....
White Oak	48	385	101927	....	975	291	70926	890	122
Total	1213	10413	2208392	17861	27889	10173	888061	91392	70013

WASHINGTON COUNTY.

Names of townships, towns, and cities.	Number of stands of bees.	Number of pounds of honey and beeswax in 1874.	Value of products of farm.	Value of market garden produce.	Value of products of the orchard.	Value of small fruit.	Value of products of the herd.	Value of products of the dairy.	Value of products of the forest.
Brighton, exc. of town	125	1492	37421	16	2493	409	38104	5122	4530
Brighton, town of	3	6	3652	2	500	554	2738	1088	427
Cedar	87	152	187231	....	1537	487	18504	8349	2255
Clay	65	275	67994	5	1686	963	45573	7172	5199
Crawford	34	105	157611	1	2437	1803	62262	9649	6519
Dutch Creek	39	130	123225	....	1600	689	60569	18	5414
English River	70	180	42267	29	222	21	70240	2812	1342
Franklin	8	5	178225	....	1961	70	83994	....	4530
Highland	30	136	129112	20	446	292	40564	6128	....
Iowa	94	129	130748	2252	1353	1134	41582	6597	6980
Jackson	70	207	167447	....	400	218	64831	12680	....
Lime Creek	23	180	142508	65	1115	342	44284	6584	65
Marion	41	97	90920	2560	3015	408	48393	7058	7650
Oregon	139	290	166219	1890	24310	10435	83129	9025	....
Seventy Six	51	197	200526	252	2510	398	65378	8733	....
Washington, exc. of city	123	410	209857	452	5744	2662	80139	15086	17381
Washington, city of	14	72	300	....	2380	979	12222	7563	....
Total	1016	4063	2035264	7544	53709	21864	862506	113664	62292

WAYNE COUNTY.

Names of townships, towns, and cities.	Number of stands of bees.	Number of pounds of honey and beeswax in 1874.	Value of products of farm.	Value of market garden produce.	Value of products of the orchard.	Value of small fruit.	Value of products of the herd.	Value of products of the dairy.	Value of products of the forest.
Allerton, town of	....	....	....	....	....	....	....	....	....
Benton	119	980	113710	150	450	144	51646	3319	300
Clay	36	360	91635	....	467	4464	41814	3947	122
Clinton	43	469	52082	1142	179	231	23767	4551	2889
Corydon, exc. of town	51	536	65011	2449	571	739	51097	5656	371
Corydon, town of	90	272	12559	894	152	862	19284	1895	....
Grand River, ex. of Lineville	38	1250	46024	1517	288	97	32025	150	1540
Howard	45	824	36312	30	1470	240	17147	2488	1914
Jackson	82	231	53721	171	1154	316	36867	2370	2232
Jefferson	82	327	43372	87	2269	509	27793	9171	....
Lineville, town of	....	....	....	....	....	....	....	....	....
Monroe	39	415	43809	5	402	80	18409	....	....
Richman	16	145	83790	....	345	....	27314	5472	425
Seymour, town of	1	40	51	....	....	....	1492	382	499
South Fork	132	1364	104502	....	523	25	72156	3802	....
Union	92	681	116360	....	1147	827	62295	7871	....
Walnut, exc. of Seymour	135	1240	156529	....	1732	500	71860	1507	1698
Warren, exc. of Allerton	25	91	117464	175	300	770	30977	2430	....
Washington	71	727	111428	1726	890	377	51872	5411	1538
Wright	173	2443	113017	126	613	312	65197	4854	....
Total	1270	12395	1361376	8472	12952	10493	703012	65276	13528

WEBSTER COUNTY.

NAMES OF TOWNSHIPS, TOWNS, AND CITIES.	Number of stands of bees.	Number of pounds of honey and beeswax in 1874.	Value of products of farm.	Value of market garden produce.	Value of products of the orchard.	Value of small fruit.	Value of products of the herd.	Value of products of the dairy.	Value of products of the forest.
Badger			$ 9324	$	$	$	$	$ 2836	$
Clay			11501				469		
Colfax			8442			20		1148	
Dayton	67	660	137385		240	20	53247	10875	2645
Deer Creek	8	50	22104	20				2724	
Douglas	2		62866				28649	8433	
Elkhorn	3		12510			360	120	1042	
Ft. Dodge, city of	27	140							
Fulton			8676				2998	1682	
Gowrie									
Hardin			30291				10381		
Jackson			27114					3715	
Johnson	10	20	37113	60		157	2349	6803	
Lost Grove			26886				4697	1866	
Newark			7687				1465		
Otho	20	210	52396		22	20	24181	1866	2762
Pleasant Valley	14	121	18632		129	10	4218	2960	702
Sumner	13	70	109602		69		25720	4830	248
Wahkonsa, exc. Ft. Dodge	20		28005	1200	250	315	5585	6035	122
Washington	10	128	48420	65				5620	75
Webster	190	9511	38013		236	192	15902	5983	3672
Yell	124	684	36375				9123	4000	100
Total	508	11594	733342	1345	1036	1094	189104	72418	10326

WINNEBAGO COUNTY.

NAMES OF TOWNSHIPS, TOWNS, AND CITIES.	Number of stands of bees.	Number of pounds of honey and beeswax in 1874.	Value of products of farm.	Value of market garden produce.	Value of products of the orchard.	Value of small fruit.	Value of products of the herd.	Value of products of the dairy.	Value of products of the forest.
Center	3		30987	160			655	2812	
Forest	83	1535	15695	616	26	40		2770	
Iowa			43436				1156		
Norway			16173				1230		
Pleasant	38	430	33928	1143	58	76	5340	2791	
Total	124	1965	140219	1919	84	116	8381	8373	

WINNESHIEK COUNTY.

NAMES OF TOWNSHIPS, TOWNS, AND CITIES.	Number of stands of bees.	Number of pounds of honey and beeswax in 1874.	Value of products of farm.	Value of market garden produce.	Value of products of the orchard.	Value of small fruit.	Value of products of the herd.	Value of products of the dairy.	Value of products of the forest.
Bloomfield	15	124	153137	117	729	756	52293	17796	13708
Bluffton	21	210	66614					3763	1580
Burr Oak	11	70	111875	25	45	42	15247	5094	70
Calmar			115625	105	132		2875	4396	30
Canoe	31	555	84308	2740	205	40	17438	5072	5188
Decorah, exc. of city	8	15	117872	1580	177		18519	6645	4662
Decorah, city of									
Frankville	25	1000	158231		143	130	33975	7736	59806
Fremont			88566	110	90	35	15448	4501	
Glenwood	3	10	72320	11			16172	2743	3938
Hesper	6		115764	45	519	387	18613	6307	
Highland			98160		143		3778	3458	98
Jackson	2	1	94766		89	14	14077	5745	5275
Lincoln			64205				7015	3474	
Madison			130836				19055	7579	
Military	26	290	180130		20		43360	10235	20100
Orleans	34	125	163980		126	10	12724	8215	6897
Pleasant	17	186	109527	273	122	69	12601		
Springfield			85420	10	130		9061	488	
Sumner			140419				9921	5592	6313
Washington	15	42	113497		140	60	28426	9475	
Total	214	2628	2265252	5016	2810	1543	350598	118314	127665

WOODBURY COUNTY.

NAMES OF TOWNSHIPS, TOWNS, AND CITIES.	Number of stands of bees.	Number of pounds of honey and beeswax in 1874.	Value of products of farm.	Value of market garden produce.	Value of products of the orchard.	Value of small fruit.	Value of products of the herd.	Value of products of the dairy.	Value of products of the forest.
Arlington			6871				1697	325	
Concord			15060	60		20	1812	2266	1673
Floyd			6550				1898	550	825
Grant			24518	161			11261		
Kedron			14996				4315	1462	1245
Lakeport			14025	55			6367	175	2011
Liberty	23	200	47283	613			18505	2412	2286
Liston									
Little Sioux	7	100	40290	30					
Moville			2218				720	179	
Rock			4866				922		
Rutland			6980				194	570	490
Sioux City, exc. of city			13895	1389		75		2375	
Sioux City, city of			500				40	75	
Union			28936	881			9998		2634
West Fork			10150	2001			2325	2539	1838
Wolf Creek			27362				5710	2837	
Woodbury	65	700	33709	2244		50	20453	7463	780
Total	95	1000	298209	7434		145	86217	23233	13782

WORTH COUNTY.

NAMES OF TOWNSHIPS, TOWNS, AND CITIES.	Number of stands of bees.	Number of pounds of honey and beeswax in 1874.	Value of products of farm.	Value of market garden produce.	Value of products of the orchard.	Value of small fruit.	Value of products of the herd.	Value of products of the dairy.	Value of products of the forest.
Bristol	2	50	60264		10	15	9332	5718	217
Brookfield			19836				4244	3346	35
Danville			20289	77			1775	2274	
Deer Creek	2		37767	17			2990	2345	120
Fertile	10	100	25778	225			1972	5211	263
Hartland			42847				5442	4677	2110
Kensett			32839				390	2177	
Northwood	4	90	60400	70	52	85	17940	8854	1759
Silver Lake			29196				3087	2788	128
Union			67290				4448	3419	
Total	18	240	396506	389	62	100	51620	40809	4632

WRIGHT COUNTY.

NAMES OF TOWNSHIPS, TOWNS, AND CITIES.	Number of stands of bees.	Number of pounds of honey and beeswax in 1874.	Value of products of farm.	Value of market garden produce.	Value of products of the orchard.	Value of small fruit.	Value of products of the herd.	Value of products of the dairy.	Value of products of the forest.
Belmond			41867				5594	4373	
Boone									
Clarion			13906	25	8		2413	1850	
Eagle Grove	5	25	19144			122	7164	2596	1373
Iowa			60584				10131	6969	3517
Liberty	63	275	18705	30	10		6525	2002	255
Pleasant			24941				4500	1350	
Troy	19	116	60365	12	132	4	19426	7718	90
Vernon			21714				4559	2102	320
Wall Lake							5932		
Woolstock			27459				4394	1684	
Total	87	416	288685	67	150	126	70638	30644	5555

TABLE I.

Showing the Population by Counties, and the various classifications thereof; Number of Dwelling Houses and Families, Jan. 1st, 1875, Nativity of Inhabitants, Foreign Parentage, and Number of Persons between Five and Twenty-One Years of Age.

COUNTIES.	No. of dwelling houses.	Number of families.	WHITE POPULATION.			COLORED POP'LATION			Total population.	NATIVITY OF INHABITANTS.				FOREIGN PARENTAGE.			BETWEEN 5 AND 21 YEARS OLD.			
			Male.	Female.	Total.	Male.	Female.	Total.		No. born in Iowa.	No. born in U. S., but not in Iowa.	No. born in foreign countries.	Surplus or deficiency.	No. whose parents were both foreign born.	No. whose father only was born abroad.	No. whose mother only was foreign born.	No. 5 years old and under 6.	No. 6 years old and under 16.	No. 16 years old and under 21.	Whole number.
Adair	1335	1345	3771	3274	7045	......	......	......	7045	2332	4146	568	1	651	134	68	377	1683	567	2627
Adams	1512	1530	3991	3726	7716	25	31	56	7772	2732	4573	606	19	619	172	65	303	1781	570	2654
Allamakee	3339	3339	9929	9229	19158	6	4	10	19168	8654	4685	4959	—870	6548	306	120	961	4962	1782	7705
Appanoose	....	3186	8967	8410	17377	13	15	28	17405	8549	8510	346	....	279	143	77	710	4479	1692	6881
Audubon	....	475	1268	1102	2370	......	......	......	2370	954	1300	174	58	133	22	24	217	535	167	919
Benton	4295	4295	11865	10923	22788	12	7	19	22807	8842	9989	3403	—573	3539	427	170	1137	5598	1900	8635
Black Hawk	4226	4232	11809	11088	22897	12	4	16	22913	8068	11151	3691	— 3	3923	718	195	910	5724	2061	8695
Boone	3274	3276	9012	8328	17340	7	4	11	17351	6417	7931	3123	120	3279	299	99	1185	3868	1279	6332
Bremer	2539	2545	6853	6346	13199	10	11	21	13220	4687	5958	2575	....	2887	410	101	615	3326	1064	5005
Buchanan	3234	3231	8989	8315	17304	8	3	11	17315	6597	8017	2264	—437	2785	453	223	1058	3809	1456	6323
Buena Vista	738	734	1902	1659	3561	......	......	......	3561	1011	1760	799	9	673	79	42	160	793	234	1187
Butler	2265	2276	6214	5594	11718	9	7	16	11734	4142	5969	1555	— 68	1744	227	87	536	2787	948	4271
Calhoun	559	559	1691	1494	3185	......	......	......	3185	1000	1684	350	—151	204	47	46	156	717	207	1080
Carroll	1262	1175	3087	2671	5758	......	2	2	5760	1546	2446	1437	—331	770	66	25	304	1264	398	1966
Cass	1939	1992	5573	4967	10540	9	3	12	10552	2977	5688	1320	—567	1027	128	42	482	2095	817	3394
Cedar	3411	3428	9177	8643	17820	30	29	59	17879	8040	7959	1880	....	1676	288	130	771	4273	1645	6689
Cerro Cordo	1335	1344	3507	3161	6668	9	8	17	6685	1913	3693	1079	....	897	168	95	402	1385	514	2301
Cherokee	882	887	2284	1961	4245	......	......	......	4245	1266	2403	672	96	661	99	76	207	850	302	1359
Chickasaw	2149	2149	5927	5472	11399	1	......	1	11400	4267	5114	2126	107	2209	213	88	625	2565	1091	4281

TABLE I.—Continued.

COUNTIES.	No. of dwelling houses.	Number of families.	White Population: Male.	White Population: Female.	White Population: Total.	Colored Pop'lation: Male.	Colored Pop'lation: Female.	Colored Pop'lation: Total.	Total population.	Nativity of Inhabitants: No. born in Iowa.	Nativity of Inhabitants: No. born in U. S., but not in Iowa.	Nativity of Inhabitants: No. born in foreign countries.	Nativity of Inhabitants: Surplus or deficiency.	Foreign Parentage: No. whose parents were both foreign born.	Foreign Parentage: No. whose father only was born abroad.	Foreign Parentage: No. whose mother only was foreign born.	Between 5 and 21 years old: No. 5 years old and under 6.	Between 5 and 21 years old: No. 6 years old and under 16.	Between 5 and 21 years old: No. 16 years old and under 21.	Between 5 and 21 years old: Whole number.
Clarke	....	1855	5127	4952	10079	22	17	39	10118	4225	5276	457	—160	289	106	31	357	2427	918	3702
Clay	775	775	1894	1675	3569	......	......	......	3569	1099	1978	406	— 86	440	86	22	163	746	227	1136
Clayton	4579	5053	14132	13046	27178	3	3	6	27184	12233	7102	6931	—918	10355	785	264	1367	6675	2602	10644
Clinton	6427	6449	17561	16583	34144	66	85	151	34295	14050	11107	9138	....	5225	396	192	1790	6957	2870	11617
Crawford	1224	1240	3216	2814	6030	7	1	8	6038	1904	2674	1389	— 71	1064	113	30	300	1397	425	2122
Dallas	2628	2644	7508	6841	14349	19	18	37	14386	5619	7900	867	....	578	150	46	660	3231	1233	5124
Davis	2987	2987	7841	7877	15718	21	18	39	15757	8123	6987	550	— 97	262	109	99	532	4026	1594	6152
Decatur	2452	2452	6785	6398	13183	40	26	66	13249	5958	6921	370	....	453	163	62	673	3449	1289	5411
Delaware	....	3134	8717	8164	16881	7	2	9	16890	6709	7590	2644	53	2160	392	212	602	4093	1623	6318
Des Moines	5832	6094	17623	17136	34759	181	166	347	35106	15549	11979	7724	146	11419	1039	484	1373	7659	3192	12224
Dickinson	362	354	929	819	1748	......	......	......	1748	502	1000	262	16	191	20	32	111	441	148	700
Dubuque	7300	7693	22363	21327	43690	80	75	155	43845	21603	8627	13281	—334	16078	2051	902	2205	10770	3588	16563
Emmet	280	280	779	653	1432	3	1	4	1436	442	539	451	— 4	653	26	9	102	349	111	562
Fayette	3928	3925	10603	9889	20492	15	11	26	20518	8312	9100	2871	—235	3593	476	321	763	5034	1792	7589
Floyd	2376	2424	6761	6337	13098	2	......	2	13100	4178	6819	2103	....	2291	342	166	620	3011	1103	4734
Franklin	1272	1272	3428	3130	6558	......	......	......	6558	1813	3258	1000	—487	903	101	60	328	1544	587	2459
Fremont	2436	2436	7208	6488	13696	13	10	23	13719	5337	7796	556	— 30	353	118	56	794	2630	1139	4563
Greene	1359	1359	3677	3259	7027	1	......	1	7028	2441	3768	647	—172	791	143	27	332	1619	456	2407
Grundy	1508	1522	4382	3750	8132	2	......	2	8134	2430	3599	2105	....	1348	129	26	327	1900	657	2884
Guthrie	1827	1829	5085	4550	9635	2	1	3	9638	3657	5355	490	—136	477	142	24	432	2266	792	3490
Hamilton	1519	1520	3986	3713	7699	1	1	2	7701	2605	3601	1506	11	1053	86	35	375	1771	560	2706
Hancock	291	295	768	709	1477	2	3	5	1482	491	716	195	— 80	236	14	3	55	367	92	514
Hardin	582	2976	7703	7268	14971	27	12	39	15019	5383	7479	1611	—537	1858	270	104	658	3528	1210	5396
Harrison	2225	2226	6198	5620	11818	......	......	......	11818	4696	5950	874	—298	808	193	93	602	2790	956	4348
Henry	4080	4119	10737	10386	21123	246	225	471	21594	10033	9573	1395	—593	1780	253	94	759	5036	2084	7879
Howard	1463	1461	4199	3647	7846	18	11	29	7875	2736	3585	1547	— 7	1759	152	94	602	1675	663	2940

Humboldt	....	674	1807	1648	3455	......	......	......	3455	1116	1565	745	— 29	562	117	57	185	819	288	1292
Ida	240	240	383	411	794	......	......	......	794	237	406	86	— 65	79	152	68	31	159	65	255
Iowa	3239	3027	9057	8389	17446	7	3	10	17456	7163	6374	3569	—350	3404	448	336	791	3960	1455	6206
Jackson	....	4296	11995	11055	23050	8	4	12	23062	11188	6762	4863	—249	5534	768	186	1141	5553	2000	8694
Jasper	4617	4611	12485	11568	24053	38	37	75	24128	9760	12748	1620	....	1347	327	190	1203	5987	2034	9224
Jefferson	....	3365	8705	8350	17055	40	32	72	17127	8691	6843	1627	34	1648	323	136	645	4204	1660	6509
Johnson	4403	4403	12680	11874	24554	47	53	100	24654	11122	7961	4970	—601	6487	485	253	1178	6217	2463	9858
Jones	....	3654	9873	9274	19147	12	7	19	19166	8689	8371	2329	223	2417	346	134	936	4890	1811	7637
Keokuk	3690	3763	10567	9918	20485	2	1	3	20488	9967	9028	1493	....	1718	443	93	933	4992	1900	7825
Kossuth	....	....	1930	1832	3762	2	1	3	3765	1179	1910	591	— 85	911	106	42	157	903	289	1349
Lee	6081	6354	16371	16115	32486	741	687	1428	33914	15656	11799	6420	— 39	4019	454	209	1486	8308	3386	13180
Linn	6266	6292	16226	15483	31709	58	48	106	31815	13425	14208	4184	2	5474	677	219	1233	7652	2955	11840
Louisa	2352	2352	6472	5983	12455	28	16	44	12499	6251	5285	789	—174	983	253	114	667	2985	1103	4755
Lucas	....	1699	6010	5691	11701	14	10	24	11725	4909	6105	711	....	406	80	24	517	2896	1116	4529
Lyon	297	297	673	559	1232	......	......	......	1232	370	511	247	—104	203	14	9	58	199	43	300
Madison	3114	3114	8410	7611	16021	6	3	9	16030	7189	8244	597	....	591	190	77	731	4006	1404	6141
Mahaska	4454	4458	12012	11445	23457	133	128	261	23718	10596	11459	1583	— 80	1672	345	109	932	6028	2275	9235
Marion	4454	4463	12420	11646	24066	16	12	28	24094	12136	9534	2360	— 64	2147	267	81	1341	5833	2326	9500
Marshall	3709	857	10235	9330	19565	37	27	64	19629	7617	10551	2377	— 84	3168	374	175	857	4488	1641	6986
Mills	1971	1964	5564	4982	10546	8	1	9	10555	4207	5500	848	....	849	169	75	478	2655	954	4087
Mitchell	2152	2175	6049	5472	11521	2	......	2	11523	3505	4986	2763	—269	2605	167	110	579	2555	980	4114
Monona	1180	1183	3126	2799	5925	19	23	42	5967	2267	2951	749	....	622	80	63	290	1421	469	2180
Monroe	2326	2335	6524	6087	12611	46	54	100	12711	5781	5530	1342	— 58	1422	258	62	577	3269	1201	5047
Montgomery	497	1721	5676	5133	10809	14	16	30	10839	3406	6372	1145	84	1167	162	74	459	22·7	778	3524
Muscatine	4024	4107	10959	10503	21462	80	81	161	21623	9952	7824	3846	— 1	3867	572	204	507	3382	1381	5270
O'Brien	549	563	1230	1101	2331	9	9	18	2349	774	1412	163	....	134	15	11	130	419	123	672
Osceola	464	464	934	844	1778	......	......	......	1778	456	1086	199	— 37	124	35	25	99	334	87	520
Page	2687	2687	7463	6676	14139	67	68	135	14274	4811	8331	1132	....	1260	194	84	671	3472	1185	5328
Palo Alto	526	526	1448	1281	2729	3	3	6	2735	829	1268	627	— 11	861	155	106	212	728	232	1172
Plymouth	1122	1122	2777	2505	5282	......	......	......	5288	1527	2250	1071	—434	861	138	63	275	1168	339	1782
Pocahontas	485	485	1134	1115	2249	......	......	......	2249	650	858	482	—259	691	67	23	131	556	174	861
Polk	5726	5947	16032	15151	31183	196	179	375	31558	12185	15143	4230	....	3169	490	179	1179	7488	2293	10360
Pottawattamie	4057	4088	11467	10107	21574	49	42	91	21665	7489	10113	3687	—376	4398	455	170	1066	4522	1638	7226
Poweshiek	3014	3011	8706	7727	16433	33	16	49	16482	6121	8818	1161	—382	1090	282	118	802	3771	1585	6158
Ringgold	1328	1339	3896	3638	7534	7	5	12	7546	3165	4100	281	....	270	224	52	287	2037	798	3122
Sac	575	568	1510	1363	2873	......	......	......	2873	847	1641	335	— 50	336	56	20	142	651	211	1004
Scott	7205	7676	20173	19366	39539	88	109	197	39736	16645	9455	13549	— 87	22209	833	298	1434	8755	2770	12959
Shelby	1087	1099	3035	2620	5655	4	5	9	5664	2072	2737	855	....	527	82	53	231	1282	396	1909
Sioux	700	698	1782	1438	3220	......	......	......	3220	1144	923	877	—276	634	38	12	180	710	233	1123
Story	2490	2492	6839	6471	13810	1	......	1	13311	4892	6118	2301	....	2046	143	67	636	3329	1187	5152

TABLE I.—CONTINUED.

COUNTIES.	No. of dwellings.	No. of families.	WHITE POPULATION.			COLORED POP'LATION			Total population.	NATIVITY OF INHABITANTS.				FOREIGN PARENTAGE.			BETWEEN 5 AND 21 YEARS OLD.			
			Male.	Female.	Total.	Male.	Female.	Total.		No. born in Iowa.	No. born in U. S., but not in Iowa.	No. born in foreign countries.	Surplus or deficiency.	No. whose parents were both foreign born.	No. whose father only was born abroad.	No. whose mother only was foreign born.	No. 5 years old and under 16.	No. 6 years old and under 16.	No. 16 years old and under 21.	Whole number.
Tama	3537	3532	9922	8807	18729	21	21	42	18771	6938	8505	3138	—190	2457	478	197	795	4523	1528	6846
Taylor	1995	1995	5418	4971	10389	16	13	29	10418	3909	5893	316	—300	349	80	32	599	2610	814	4023
Union	1487	1489	4683	4117	8800	16	11	27	8827	3242	4816	532	—237	239	45	32	367	1730	740	2837
Van Buren	3453	3453	8628	8230	16858	60	62	122	16980	8909	7246	819	— 6	822	306	134	592	4047	1625	6264
Wapello	4357	4365	12215	11332	23547	151	167	318	23865	10868	10710	2287	....	1602	391	190	1490	5593	2215	9298
Warren	3419	3418	9655	8819	18474	30	24	54	18528	8195	9337	651	—345	862	316	65	769	4755	1724	7248
Washington	3620	3635	9719	9474	19193	42	34	76	19269	9233	8458	1543	— 35	1078	289	65	850	4856	1826	7532
Wayne	2451	2587	7206	6763	13969	5	4	9	13978	5775	7424	331	—448	323	135	56	668	3654	1228	5550
Webster	2381	2438	6910	6204	13114	......	......	......	13114	4597	5253	3264	....	4028	316	123	665	3170	961	4796
Winnebago	....	567	1581	1406	2987	......	......	......	2987	863	824	1218	— 82	1482	44	25	133	676	189	998
Winneshiek	4260	4421	12712	11517	24229	3	1	4	24233	9678	5569	8760	—226	8845	310	212	1065	5903	2986	9954
Woodbury	....	1661	4474	4044	8518	30	20	50	8568	2547	3865	1322	—834	405	74	17	381	1505	378	2264
Worth	905	905	2544	2358	4902	4	2	6	4908	1562	1517	1829	....	2364	144	95	219	1165	319	1703
Wright	616	617	1730	1513	3243	1	......	1	3244	1058	1798	390	2	470	46	42	166	749	270	1185
Total	221568	249624	697057	647420	1344568	3123	2853	5976	1350544	552482	581550	203501	....	318159	25962	10927	62144	317691	116636	496471

TABLE II.

Showing the number of Illiterate Persons, number of Deaf and Dumb not in State Institution, number of Blind not in the College for the Blind, number of Insane not in Hospitals, Births and Deaths in 1874, number of Voters and where Born, Foreigners and Militia.

COUNTIES.	ILLITERATE.										BIRTHPLACE OF VOTERS.															
	No. 16 and under 21 who cannot read.	No. over 21 who cannot read—male.	Same—female.	Whole number.	No. deaf and dumb not in State Institution.	Number blind not in College for the Blind.	Number insane not in hospitals.	Number of births in 1874.	Number deaths in 1874.	Number of voters.	Number born in United States.	Number born in British America.	No. born in England and Wales.	Number born in Ireland.	Number born in Scotland.	Number born in Germany.	No. born in Austria, Hungary, and Bohemia.	Number born in Holland.	Number born in Norway.	Number born in Sweden.	Number born in Denmark.	Number born in France.	Number born in all other countries.	Surplus or deficiency.	Number foreigners not naturalized.	Number of militia.
Adair	16	10	9	35	10	2	1	287	94	1616	1290	67	66	68	11	85	2	3	5	6	1	......	12	......	32	1244
Adams	25	22	20	67	1	2	3	319	78	1727	1421	19	72	45	6	26	7	1	17	......	8	31	36	— 38	56	1283
Allamakee	16	137	118	271	4	8	6	618	215	3653	1845	92	78	802	49	675	12	16	623	82	1	17	21	660	329	2366
Appanoose	52	80	64	196	16	7	7	650	304	3679	3426	16	57	88	7	64	......	1	......	10	1	8	1	......	26	2576
Audubon	11	6	3	20	......	1	1	92	39	527	1295	10	31	5	2	23	1	1	1	......	18	12	14	886	69	354
Benton	11	23	16	50	6	2	4	776	243	4770	4971	79	102	251	95	700	9	2	50	5	8	10	5	1517	244	3355
Black Hawk	24	29	22	75	9	3	3	801	240	4867	3641	124	198	265	49	489	5	5	3	14	20	23	31	......	329	2910
Boone	35	45	37	117	4	8	3	644	303	3515	6024	89	149	212	167	267	7	1	70	518	27	13	29	4058	488	2385
Bremer	4	14	11	29	3	2	2	452	126	2656	1842	42	138	85	19	483	......	......	1	4	4	9	29	......	370	1471
Buchanan	28	68	47	143	4	2	16	535	155	3890	5444	138	191	479	43	419	6	5	......	4	9	18	16	2882	108	2217
Buena Vista	9	5	5	19	......	......	1	141	35	817	578	30	30	23	9	27	1	1	72	23	7	3	10	— 3	98	563
Butler	25	10	8	43	1	2	1	373	128	2598	1861	116	105	200	31	189	20	9	6	3	4	5	3	— 46	168	1810
Calhoun	10	2	......	12	1	......	......	119	......	681	624	15	26	19	4	55	9	......	17	19	......	3	12	122	61	488
Carroll	3	7	1	11	1	1	3	257	104	1197	481	8	9	16	5	226	2	10	......	......	......	3	8	— 429	193	935
Cass	6	3	1	10	4	1	1	421	100	2422	2305	76	84	97	5	139	3	6	12	18	6	7	12	348	96	2181
Cedar	37	28	22	87	4	6	7	513	171	3934	3014	74	121	278	84	307	13	3	5	4	4	9	16	— 2	264	2600
Cerro Gordo	......	3	2	5	1	3	1	252	98	1526	1061	91	94	79	29	86	14	5	49	5	10	1	2	......	87	1129
Cherokee	5	13	13	31	......	......	......	189	53	1001	1293	34	59	51	20	73	......	6	19	13	3	5	3	578	73	736
Chickasaw	17	29	22	68	6	1	5	350	136	2392	2435	102	98	350	40	366	26	6	69	5	5	13	18	1141	133	1581

TABLE II.—CONTINUED.

COUNTIES.	ILLITERATE. No. 16 and under 21 who cannot read.	ILLITERATE. No over 21 who cannot read—male.	ILLITERATE. Same—female.	ILLITERATE. Whole number.	No. deaf and dumb not in State Institution.	Number blind not in College for the Blind.	Number insane not in hospitals.	Number of births in 1874.	Number deaths in 1874.	Number of voters.	BIRTHPLACE OF VOTERS. Number born in United States.	Number born in British America.	No. born in England and Wales.	Number born in Ireland.	Number born in Scotland.	Number born in Germany.	No. born in Austria, Hungary, and Bohemia.	Number born in Holland.	Number born in Norway.	Number born in Sweden.	Number born in Denmark.	Number born in France.	Number born in all other countries.	Surplus or deficiency.	Number foreigners not naturalized.	Number of militia.
Clarke	22	17	9	48	4	......	6	361	153	2213	2953	17	27	36	......	51	2	3	1	5	1	3	1	887	14	1523
Clay	......	1	......	1	1	1	......	157	37	868	634	39	51	28	3	31	....	......	34	22	46	1	7	28	8	627
Clayton	49	55	51	155	15	3	6	886	330	5272	7642	107	189	690	79	2298	26	3	764	57	5	18	68	6668	860	3289
Clinton	73	55	47	175	14	4	8	962	390	5569	4218	205	266	635	95	943	18	8	79	43	24	19	16	1000	1194	3644
Crawford	17	8	13	38	5	4	3	255	93	1254	1987	126	109	135	34	186	3	2	7	78	4	3	......	1420	149	852
Dallas	29	27	17	73	8	2	6	490	153	3170	2710	38	90	138	25	114	11	3	1	16	13	4	7	....	93	2285
Davis	36	69	65	170	7	9	12	569	211	3448	3057	53	33	41	36	148	3	......	......	2	......	55	20	....	58	2323
Decatur	33	38	24	95	12	5	7	455	176	2882	2655	20	68	53	12	44	8	......	4	5	2	2	9	....	16	2117
Delaware	21	14	13	48	7	6	9	499	183	3662	2364	112	261	299	67	494	23	2	2	4	......	14	3	—17	279	2353
Des Moines	55	59	67	181	11	8	19	1068	368	6654	4696	56	162	338	60	1575	25	9	24	168	18	23	27	527	611	4586
Dickinson	9	2	......	11	3	1	......	57	15	394	355	22	20	15	8	37	....	......	53	1	2	......	......	119	6	304
Dubuque	33	66	66	165	11	7	28	1607	502	8759	550	121	467	2117	71	2783	151	58	9	21	19	121	42	2727	904	5823
Emmet	5	......	......	5	......	......	......	55	11	299	156	14	8	16	5	4	2	......	94	......	......	......	......	....	60	214
Fayette	43	35	24	102	9	3	8	653	187	4637	3759	117	185	343	61	349	8	......	114	10	1	18	83	411	156	2781
Floyd	30	15	2	47	......	1	5	445	146	2884	2237	128	96	93	25	256	6	1	20	4	......	7	13	2	282	2066
Franklin	11	8	3	22	......	3	2	235	75	1374	2350	103	105	23	14	217	5	14	47	27	3	4	6	1644	158	1019
Fremont	33	20	12	65	2	8	8	431	155	2998	2670	31	76	67	16	94	2	1	3	11	10	7	8	— 2	58	2243
Greene	2	18	9	29	6	1	1	209	94	1622	1272	47	75	87	14	44	2	......	3	6	......	3	4	— 65	53	1244
Grundy	10	2	......	12	2	2	2	327	134	1525	1029	58	34	42	6	326	6	3	1	5	9	2	......	— 4	297	1357
Guthrie	12	14	16	42	1	2	2	362	128	2239	2554	22	81	78	8	74	12	......	......	8	15	1	10	624	25	1716
Hamilton	6	8	2	16	3	2	......	257	58	1455	1069	117	23	38	56	79	8	2	114	106	7	1	11	176	264	669
Hancock	12	4	......	16	1	......	......	36	6	303	145	14	4	14	6	27	....	1	......	2	5	2	......	— 83	9	227
Hardin	15	12	16	43	5	3	5	451	200	3215	2402	40	84	97	19	199	24	17	30	4	3	10	5	— 281	248	2343
Harrison	27	35	20	82	6	4	4	392	129	2658	2220	77	84	123	28	61	3	1	......	7	2	4	27	— 21	79	1914
Henry	58	49	45	152	8	6	5	576	349	4641	4023	28	159	152	14	206	5	6	1	164	4	33	25	179	180	2886
Howard	26	30	24	80	1	......	2	295	64	1712	958	111	167	203	59	121	14	16	41	16	5	5	11	15	140	1189

Humboldt	7	16	13	36	......	......	......	105	23	695	556	35	31	39	17	40	4	8	161	11	......	1	5	213	42	538
Ida	......	1	1	2	......	......	......	30	4	172	123	32	4	13	9	1	....	......	1	3	3	6	3	26	3	141
Iowa	94	67	54	215	......	49	9	597	261	3576	4019	94	200	394	77	687	23	......	107	29	4	51	45	2184	368	2119
Jackson	62	53	36	151	11	3	6	725	248	4901	7098	220	254	506	70	1452	66	12	3	21	35	20	30	4886	361	2263
Jasper	14	33	21	68	5	4	10	805	280	5239	4433	62	205	143	36	298	8	13	4	17	......	9	11	....	107	3554
Jefferson	17	30	25	72	5	11	18	504	215	3721	3175	21	101	93	40	210	5	......	2	125	4	30	15	100	219	2680
Johnson	101	65	30	196	10	10	19	767	217	5225	3238	43	179	422	64	631	563	3	7	13	13	24	25	....	543	3762
Jones	21	21	15	57	5	3	5	505	191	4180	6162	123	102	614	133	283	104	......	1	3	1	17	37	3400	176	2309
Keokuk	27	20	19	66	8	14	20	587	267	4202	2429	15	56	107	60	500	....	1	1	3	1	11	17	— 1	92	2945
Kossuth	7	5	6	18	1	1	......	126	29	773	1244	66	36	62	25	131	2	......	32	27	3	5	3	863	64	510
Lee	37	103	86	226	12	11	7	1084	430	7509	5755	58	139	529	42	1453	49	78	39	176	6	49	9	873	214	5421
Linn	21	29	44	94	9	9	12	1073	335	7274	5817	99	162	298	82	274	433	9	4	7	8	25	56	....	466	4916
Louisa	25	64	37	126	5	7	7	348	150	2899	2480	33	104	78	7	176	....	1	......	15	1	10	4	10	54	2007
Lucas	20	31	23	74	6	1	5	460	193	2497	1993	6	34	55	11	29	....	5	1	13	......	......	1	— 349	164	1810
Lyon	2	......	2	4	......	......	......	43	17	287	304	198	5	11	5	11	6	......	49	2	2	1	2	307	41	242
Madison	18	34	32	84	7	1	4	556	209	3632	3246	18	60	155	28	95	7	......	2	8	2	9	2	....	56	2459
Mahaska	40	90	62	192	3	6	8	801	306	5287	4557	17	125	79	14	88	5	79	14	6	1	2	5	— 295	160	3910
Marion	32	52	29	113	3	9	10	757	308	4988	3980	4	39	55	17	124	4	633	1	1	......	7	5	— 118	234	3519
Marshall	25	25	30	80	5	5	6	653	215	4445	3740	102	113	100	40	250	3	......	20	30	21	17	9	....	537	3234
Mills	18	22	21	61	3	2	16	395	178	2365	1923	23	119	70	11	173	7	8	2	9	6	7	7	....	106	1728
Mitchell	32	20	15	67	4	6	2	382	111	2338	2448	90	150	123	23	412	27	3	419	20	11	3	11	1402	410	1461
Monona	7	16	13	36	3	......	4	246	96	1292	1035	35	43	35	12	41	3	......	53	10	1	5	19	....	63	967
Monroe	56	44	42	142	11	4	5	336	187	2743	2226	30	119	249	25	50	1	......	1	9	5	6	6	16	93	1848
Montgomery	12	5	4	21	1	......	1	444	130	2485	2657	29	93	52	18	80	2	3	3	109	1	6	29	597	400	1920
Muscatine	71	93	75	239	11	9	41	625	194	6588	4286	43	134	336	102	813	5	14	2	5	......	11	62	775	421	1770
O'Brien	......	2	2	4	2	1	......	116	26	595	458	20	34	29	7	13	15	14	......	......	2	2	1	....	8	400
Osceola	......	1	......	1	......	2	......	92	14	498	472	10	25	11	3	47	....	2	5	3	1	......	6	87	1	355
Page	52	22	14	88	4	6	2	570	213	3223	2766	91	44	102	28	61	3	......	5	111	1	4	10	3	163	2468
Palo Alto	18	29	15	62	2	3	......	84	17	556	772	62	49	161	5	68	3	......	71	16	35	2	15	703	60	351
Plymouth	3	6	7	16	2	......	......	255	109	1136	842	85	94	88	37	285	10	19	7	12	16	1	31	391	61	917
Pocahontas	8	17	17	42	......	2	......	84	29	464	413	32	19	48	11	74	9	1	27	27	46	......	1	244	67	278
Polk	32	114	113	259	7	9	8	1030	314	6842	5529	45	186	393	78	360	13	5	101	94	9	16	13	....	455	4916
Pottawattamie	97	94	53	244	7	4	5	876	261	4392	4448	120	259	290	65	501	9	......	5	16	30	22	31	1404	749	3235
Poweshiek	47	32	30	109	9	5	8	516	186	3634	2867	99	119	209	80	165	18	4	39	7	8	14	31	26	149	2655
Ringgold	22	12	10	44	3	4	4	272	109	1496	3780	41	32	82	16	32	12	20	......	3	......	7	1	2530	12	1140
Sac	5	......	......	5	......	......	1	98	33	657	471	23	33	19	25	36	....	1	7	8	1	......	14	— 19	17	472
Scott	64	205	214	483	6	4	7	1230	365	7109	4414	94	255	654	116	2693	39	7	6	13	14	26	64	1286	3500	4819
Shelby	7	3	7	17	2	2	1	243	93	1084	821	35	59	30	14	50	7	2	......	26	21	......	19	....	209	859
Sioux	15	1	1	17	......	1	......	166	38	637	294	24	14	39	13	53	......	180	9	......	1	......	10	....	151	514
Story	75	74	60	209	10	2	......	487	159	2574	1902	44	67	127	27	63	3	5	267	16	50	9	1	7	282	1759

TABLE II.—CONTINUED.

COUNTIES.	ILLITERATE.				No. deaf and dumb not in State institution.	Number blind not in College for the blind.	Number insane not in hospital.	Number of births in 1874.	Number deaths in 1874.	Number of voters.	BIRTHPLACE OF VOTERS.														Number foreigners not naturalized.	Number of Militia.
	No. 16 and under 21 who cannot read.	No. over 21 who cannot read—male.	Same—female.	Whole number.							Number born in United States.	Number born in British America.	No. born in England and Wales.	Number born in Ireland.	Number born in Scotland.	Number born in Germany.	No. born in Austria Hungary and Bohemia.	Number born in Holland.	Number born in Norway.	Number born in Sweden.	Number born in Denmark.	Number born in France.	Number born in all other countries.	Surplus or deficiency.		
Tama	16	31	21	68	7	2	6	706	192	3911	4644	150	117	147	128	288	207	1	23	8	2	12	8	1824	507	2909
Taylor	22	38	14	74	......	3	2	379	144	2282	2045	15	93	46	26	26	7	.....	4	8	......	6	7	1	16	1717
Union	4	7	6	17	3	......	5	246	92	1924	1509	26	40	129	26	112	8	1	20	76	......	7	3	33	30	1554
Van Buren	35	65	71	171	11	4	11	543	215	3893	3466	23	108	110	19	154	3	......	......	12	......	6	3	11	70	2613
Wapello	44	85	50	179	13	8	15	818	271	5346	4482	19	133	322	27	221	7	19	3	94	1	5	13	....	238	3773
Warren	23	40	32	95	4	3	6	717	358	3923	3433	22	82	101	57	154	5	......	......	5	1	7	4	— 52	41	2684
Washington	44	32	20	96	7	6	7	556	234	4168	3598	41	50	122	28	186	103	2	......	3	2	60	26	63	145	2593
Wayne	41	37	29	107	5	5	4	560	268	2947	2963	8	44	39	4	73	10	......	2	10	1	3	4	214	10	2146
Webster	8	24	8	40	5	3	6	444	106	2747	1566	53	112	340	43	203	18	6	113	258	1	8	23	— 3	273	2006
Winnebago	......	1	2	3	......	......	......	126	78	406	464	4	14	13	4	5	......	......	270	72	10	1	1	452	166	272
Winneshiek	42	9	6	57	12	6	13	740	257	4117	6276	242	198	455	36	742	374	17	2085	53	23	27	34	6445	1386	2368
Woodbury	12	5	6	23	1	1	......	314	115	1776	1319	96	61	164	7	179	4	......	39	11	10	18	17	149	55	1204
Worth	10	3	......	13	......	......	2	220	71	763	331	15	22	28	6	43	2	......	194	8	3	1	30	— 80	251	660
Wright	......	1	2	3	......	2	1	100	16	694	538	31	18	39	3	37	1	......	5	3	6	8	......	— 5	38	475
Total	2513	3124	2511	8148	467	389	542	45421	16146	286282	257301	6117	9620	18369	3403	30696	2721	1407	6701	3164	758	1154	1520	....	23929	193918

TABLE III.

Showing number of Acres of Improved and Unimproved Land, Rods of Fence, Acres in Cultivation in 1874, *Acres and Bushels Harvested of Spring Wheat, Winter Wheat, Corn, Rye, Oats, Barley, and Buckwheat.*

COUNTIES.	Number of acres of improved land.	Number of acres of unimproved land.	Number of rods of fence.	Number of acres in cultivation in 1874.	SPRING WHEAT.		WINTER WHEAT.		INDIAN CORN.		RYE.		OATS.		BARLEY.		BUCKWHEAT.	
					Number of acres.	Number of bushels harvested.	Number of acres.	Number of bushels harvested.	Number of acres.	Number of bushels harvested.	Number of acres.	Number of bushels harvested.	Number of acres.	Number of bushels harvested.	Number of acres.	Number of bushels harvested.	Number of acres.	Number of bushels harvested.
Adair	83182	55680	166648	66265	27550	435014	70	3500	30860	1402428	38	713	4455	159739	1163	29162	23	271
Adams	65459	43735	323186	54352	17947	281376	7	174	25474	969777	66	1236	3951	141293	982	21374	38	392
Allamakee	134767	156821	931883	109388	61880	937639	181	1964	24325	905920	164	2300	12776	442829	876	22315	154	2605
Appanoose	161059	161083	832234	125188	9606	77798	1049	10838	64871	2385243	666	6311	13756	387346	28	35	293	3861
Audubon	21046	257368	63876	15986	6876	89235	10	97	9225	394655	6	100	788	33233	84	1751	4	54
Benton	297518	53911	1025865	239408	99406	1343666	7	280	83244	3328921	283	4134	15490	445070	11169	213871	229	2913
Black Hawk	213025	150881	701808	181256	89361	1108024	....	....	56592	1939590	469	5781	16804	538196	1747	34130	268	2835
Boone	156987	71810	687752	108642	32505	429257	11	84	46151	1595752	112	1880	10401	404620	1581	38734	54	839
Bremer	145967	47000	672937	104810	48898	644795	....	....	28753	1026641	102	1217	14259	518571	888	18000	95	983
Buchanan	190551	71414	824267	157239	64291	812342	....	....	48830	1811250	60	911	17431	556209	598	10846	181	2285
Buena Vista	33118	37034	15655	27010	15513	162737	....	....	7887	228231	39	358	2789	67069	307	3518	44	306
Butler	149498	58905	352296	124877	57907	779167	20	700	38685	1270878	353	4712	13827	421719	2489	53245	212	2454
Calhoun	26996	....	24520	26618	11040	109631	10	150	10656	351120	70	809	2993	73182	217	3251	13	167
Carroll	58065	309744	45772	39159	26756	340161	3	20	16014	550041	9	80	3238	107577	414	9315	7	71
Cass	110864	45304	358959	92785	40123	676209	....	....	40582	1901062	....	....	9079	176088	1075	28699	16	151
Cedar	248693	41417	1210531	166485	40467	640544	26	295	78224	2845921	481	6585	20243	675837	9122	201037	337	2384
Cerro Gordo	52890	309895	178135	48648	28199	415463	....	....	9512	265443	30	449	7199	228097	1027	23708	46	482
Cherokee	54638	289740	14987	45412	31693	411507	....	....	9459	315215	12	185	3545	115595	342	6930	15	106
Chickasaw	96504	94772	530375	74104	40162	643519	3	63	16821	514279	68	1245	11744	446300	819	19789	156	1998

TABLE III.—Continued.

COUNTIES.	Number of acres of improved land.	Number of acres of unimproved land.	Number of rods of fence.	Number of acres in cultivation.	SPRING WHEAT.		WINTER WHEAT.		INDIAN CORN.		RYE.		OATS		BARLEY.		BUCK-WHEAT.	
					Number of acres.	Number of bushels harvested.	Number of acres.	Number of bushels harvested.	Number of acres.	Number of bushels harvested.	Number of acres.	Number of bushels harvested.	Number of acres.	Number of bushels harvested.	Number of acres.	Number of bushels harvested.	Number of acres.	Number of bushels harvested.
Clarke	98694	50486	432073	78803	17967	217090	7	55	39065	1580260	314	4345	12335	367643	626	14387	27	546
Clay	37059	39919	10399	33375	17481	153149	....	....	8797	180120	77	715	4436	98766	232	3816	18	127
Clayton	212291	151908	1277821	173622	86883	1305125	1347	21030	37948	1471263	155	2090	20024	669895	1818	45391	233	3584
Clinton	299855	57337	264505	257313	68683	1010345	12	428	89297	3061338	266	4138	23704	702059	12812	268738	203	3261
Crawford	58058	383414	164055	45262	24000	324894	....	....	17957	648858	72	1292	2901	99158	584	11586	50	471
Dallas	132435	57765	624799	114625	29256	445848	8	186	57652	2484898	344	6155	9937	335124	680	16379	25	320
Davis	150938	116003	1010234	131597	5378	30993	5379	56405	62127	2115569	1076	9705	13643	345707	....	8	254	2952
Decatur	115751	87172	735391	95275	8211	77169	817	12239	50484	1763140	1365	17299	10555	344551	39	725	136	2093
Delaware	472029	62305	934956	161357	60401	741728	5	50	56150	1690335	219	1594	20577	632113	1353	31723	219	2840
Des Moines	143665	58168	890558	97618	10615	113396	8688	117310	102924	2307938	539	5499	9242	287392	196	3400	157	2843
Dickinson	15770	29850	24518	11961	5701	25822	....	....	3183	44455	....	10	2403	37282	47	234	39	52
Dubuque	187831	98565	1199796	146244	49240	634135	84	1720	67114	1802291	135	1775	25115	643322	1689	37793	78	981
Emmet	9989	25586	27645	8387	3911	1510	....	....	2197	14273	20	60	1549	3241	93	132	14	85
Fayette	179504	98156	1032961	133758	60779	863670	46	968	37091	1296480	27	304	20770	704407	1400	28127	224	3060
Floyd	147098	52130	642062	110708	62067	941439	....	....	26462	642448	70	1069	15461	487729	1929	39217	123	1292
Franklin	69859	43046	172184	65580	31096	455909	....	....	24066	758983	13	245	9532	328679	1600	34545	95	1540
Fremont	115907	198832	443023	103039	13229	206901	841	16625	73845	1703985	1014	3231	5419	179645	3230	75747	12	112
Greene	59940	49838	243561	52323	19391	257760	2	44	22313	783037	120	1775	4227	120948	655	18550	39	429
Grundy	146089	47926	160530	135108	67384	976607	....	....	40175	1482582	217	2978	11786	401948	7845	152162	98	1108
Guthrie	87259	47220	331162	76892	27489	393574	22	360	38902	1669134	48	802	4145	153505	498	11804	32	488
Hamilton	63966	39935	250006	52050	20676	294682	....	....	20441	670731	52	791	5108	168262	702	12792	79	609
Hancock	10462	341615	46888	9005	4889	70016	....	....	2067	57899	....	....	1353	48816	92	1564	24	240
Hardin	128831	39930	500262	97765	38464	497251	....	....	41304	1379961	147	2445	10982	356945	1785	29646	104	1689
Harrison	94848	337451	473101	72287	23948	143701	84	1200	44720	1620192	96	742	3462	69140	80	1056	109	1649
Henry	182080	50249	992020	110831	15026	180229	9041	113203	62672	2415670	1184	13735	13393	358221	177	4528	214	3664
Howard	115823	171048	278844	61871	36115	582808	....	....	9916	307912	4	100	10210	340268	1205	34047	92	1251

Humboldt	29114	36906	41541	27012	12046	120902	....	....	9998	297381	18	160	3974	90944	220	2991	82	512
Ida	7292	9494	3219	6514	3108	48815	....	....	2301	108465	....	....	455	14060	83	1725	13	30
Iowa	191041	89357	835167	158488	48410	670247	36	1080	62518	2713830	439	7697	11756	319071	3450	75332	217	3018
Jackson	193290	142401	1301102	142401	43515	550000	491	7942	53962	1665518	272	3254	23652	521156	1030	19731	538	7412
Jasper	278881	179752	1018207	216949	79926	1107170	....	....	100217	4525889	411	8141	15267	532239	2989	70220	179	2811
Jefferson	167389	66979	1130584	125590	16237	164904	6192	66739	55061	1695510	2160	27332	14005	446128	80	1551	343	6121
Johnson	241021	71257	1217751	193019	45306	666779	100	1274	77142	3158178	1506	19747	17760	522197	2623	56680	148	2139
Jones	208907	63298	1060896	140684	36090	462478	31	409	65423	1909534	147	2202	18260	464824	797	17236	321	2961
Keokuk	208125	98999	950234	149672	33278	368528	148	1363	75697	3327282	1024	11145	15582	447603	1380	25474	246	4398
Kossuth	31550	48793	42509	28835	10798	13139	140	....	9781	119777	25	38	5143	27857	159	89	177	1745
Lee	183832	78692	829231	133580	10854	72624	15400	200407	59863	2190306	3908	42400	11817	279069	843	12628	305	3808
Linn	281118	62649	1419382	175655	52178	656597	12	160	91773	3439923	703	8213	22670	585648	1182	22883	358	4612
Louisa	151007	52921	680508	100065	19764	189939	1388	16267	49642	2184658	1466	14586	6792	175755	60	1411	209	2469
Lucas	108952	59757	563227	88857	13954	153587	31	329	47022	1902530	398	5132	12374	342164	235	3767	150	2674
Lyon	15872	318841	3550	12766	8132	76742	....	54	2645	10396	....	....	3477	13114	150	2666	6	35
Madison	161998	188709	783405	137979	37553	628314	25	484	69494	2953630	142	2894	8743	285103	946	25951	60	786
Mahaska	232398	122490	1180727	150368	34362	395532	205	2697	83775	3768209	454	5987	16646	496248	333	5817	235	3275
Marion	199669	82779	948730	153214	45136	598663	189	2212	84630	3835063	356	4856	10937	335746	706	15450	131	2086
Marshall	223735	47552	680230	177303	69895	1125382	21	200	67679	2808256	203	3208	13611	465245	3194	67151	187	2561
Mills	141512	53604	493182	99837	24385	342961	32	543	39543	1533976	161	2192	6528	232639	2968	62938	13	79
Mitchell	126384	70176	429690	94132	65534	1083811	....	12	11274	411961	17	252	14078	542662	2971	78124	85	813
Monona	52242	57278	239905	39844	15334	183811	....	....	21577	818388	16	330	2304	66475	127	3125	21	173
Monroe	102215	78206	628331	91729	11638	101413	263	5584	45574	1738916	409	3536	11511	241081	15	130	345	3072
Montgomery	104633	50607	303567	86026	31381	551539	8	166	39251	1441467	87	1389	5322	201635	510	13136	....	214
Muscatine	178945	48832	759050	129699	32375	416471	63	629	54760	1715973	2541	29455	13287	405562	2358	59127	232	3445
O'Brien	33626	332070	2175	26434	14904	157526	....	....	6379	106052	105	1281	3107	53931	451	7388	36	200
Osceola	18490	31406	14	14651	8769	74757	....	26	2510	17279	....	....	1390	26329	21	229	25	60
Page	156782	175471	585113	115484	22689	355792	1220	20235	71386	2239043	950	14809	9758	346507	1078	27311	24	263
Palo Alto	18517	32225	21607	16679	8606	23208	325	....	6641	142957	453	....	2979	46859	287	33	66	228
Plymouth	58233	51912	26359	44379	33628	442736	10	160	10097	175778	6	55	4161	120437	331	6592	20	16
Pocahontas	21928	35572	16181	19219	7434	30774	....	....	8981	229263	58	647	2541	40494	100	831	53	342
Polk	207689	56821	842186	140450	37686	563389	21	394	77497	3272040	335	5510	12188	431841	1306	30821	65	856
Pottawattamie	124630	119489	463935	90679	33369	588971	63	475	47258	1750038	93	1809	5278	168081	1809	35043	45	960
Poweshiek	208989	48697	783637	171588	57312	762826	....	....	86748	3571105	163	2006	11416	333565	6611	109139	237	2332
Ringgold	68400	58829	395534	50873	10926	78851	125	1762	35613	1145937	519	7163	9118	255007	55	1045	48	572
Sac	31336	47201	23066	24179	11056	110094	....	10	8662	279716	28	285	3035	65996	180	2931	40	306
Scott	235515	19123	754912	185742	47698	762315	40	618	59071	2226346	71	726	15915	528868	30903	692655	34	667
Shelby	55180	39326	148437	47230	22029	317944	....	....	17674	689556	17	280	2254	71676	667	15078	9	89
Sioux	39824	367394	940	33515	22996	251286	....	....	6780	32038	33	195	4591	45096	188	2933	11	14
Story	148649	43874	544233	99387	26658	330897	8	20	51273	1783477	231	2890	11273	343265	461	8870	138	2024

TABLE III.—CONTINUED.

COUNTIES.	Number of acres of improved land.	Number of acres of unimproved land.	Number of rods of fence.	Number of acres in cultivation in 1874.	SPRING WHEAT.		WINTER WHEAT.		INDIAN CORN.		RYE.		OATS.		BARLEY.		BUCK-WHEAT.	
					Number of acres.	Number of bushels harvested.	Number of acres.	Number of bushels harvested.	Number of acres.	Number of bushels harvested.	Number of acres.	Number of bushels harvested.	Number of acres.	Number of bushels harvested.	Number of acres.	Number of bushels harvested.	Number of acres.	Number of bushels harvested.
Tama	255182	90222	743258	214941	97013	1437807	....	....	73251	2842859	109	1488	13574	384469	7305	142765	130	1686
Taylor	102861	235515	423866	79442	15446	206818	244	3068	48260	1419680	502	6658	8718	269657	936	17343	103	1330
Union	57005	83216	266401	45826	10586	141187	53	960	24063	1130930	249	3087	6127	187748	564	12275	36	464
Van Buren	153674	99528	1321855	113263	7455	58808	10928	121854	50211	1923622	1509	13466	12596	353698	55	459	487	8518
Wapello	150209	63491	876972	135173	17368	157535	1617	16159	57035	2143791	1396	14130	11570	293590	254	4701	236	4284
Warren	194265	167178	885186	158737	47157	654679	61	910	80280	3561365	294	4136	8391	281510	1782	40818	110	1594
Washington	225176	55652	987401	157884	41646	469879	1439	14193	73265	2832241	1122	14388	15701	452320	630	12939	244	3901
Wayne	147766	66795	548858	117689	10375	76346	143	1236	65625	2405187	874	7701	13242	367396	99	1623	255	3496
Webster	97238	61744	367537	70910	30554	391051	5	....	28713	917911	110	1253	7491	207493	525	11274	64	950
Winnebago	17589	30625	97339	12421	8938	162281	11	270	1378	52425	5	66	1327	45109	88	1755	12	173
Winneshiek	246140	131670	1200575	259469	112175	1813465	....	....	27145	977316	85	1191	24307	826508	2853	64740	96	1328
Woodbury	41179	57097	160076	33097	15243	218875	....	....	14667	490371	6	300	3072	91647	135	1503	10	28
Worth	48927	45957	171082	33137	23092	410487	....	....	3530	122291	....	....	4445	161557	429	9626	14	240
Wright	35516	32387	136903	28957	13629	196166	......	....	10089	281821	39	442	4134	135176	445	8431	22	222
Total	12658495	9803184	52164603	9645961	3176086	43280918	68868	850889	4019738	146993570	36827	432008	956687	29213891	166252	3534291	12154	160805

TABLE IV.

Showing number of acres and bushels of Flax Seed, acres of Sorghum and gallons of Syrup from same; gallons of Maple Syrup, pounds of Maple Sugar; acres of Blue Grass; of Tame Grass, and tons of hay from same; tons of Hay from wild grass; bushels of Grass Seed; of Clover Seed; acres of Hungarian Grass, tons of Hay and bushels of Seed from same; statistics of Hops, Tobacco, Broom Corn and Potatoes.

COUNTIES.	Number of acres in flax seed.	Number of bushels harvested.	SUGAR AND SYRUP. Number of acres in sorghum.	Number of gallons of syrup from sorghum.	Number of gallons of maple syrup.	Number of pounds of maple sugar.	Number of acres of blue grass for pasture.	Number of acres of tame grass.	Number of tons of hay from same.	Number of tons of hay from wild grass.	Number of bushels of grass seed.	Number of bushels of clover seed.	HUNGARIAN GRASS. Number of acres.	Number of tons of hay.	Number of bushels of seed.	HOPS. Number of acres.	Number of pounds.	TOBACCO. Number of acres.	Number of pounds of product.	BROOM CORN. Number of acres.	Number of tons.	POTATOES. Number of acres.	Number of bushels.
Adair	202	1274	44	4775	10	10	131	1648	1231	15038	219	......	104	233	......	......	3	......	447	8	3	434	37738
Adams	1563	12935	105	8604	......	1	43	1018	1165	14619	82	......	122	284	169	......	......	......	150	3	......	409	25378
Allamakee	......	......	57	5602	390	2504	4275	15608	16794	4770	692	134	17	30	......	11	8306	......	279	15	6	1326	134119
Appanoose	436	3085	436	44329	310	1263	8321	28354	22686	3570	12514	49	5241	7822	13457	......	16	4	5933	51	1	764	72456
Audubon	23	90	25	2860	......	......	......	41	64	6351	......	......	53	101	......	......	......	......	300	20	2	78	9365
Benton	1997	18656	183	13804	57	655	4422	22659	8389	35811	4893	122	53	100	30	6	2031	......	1154	6	2	1374	129878
Black Hawk	253	1907	186	13163	639	711	2387	14101	9694	24526	1996	344	196	309	27	10	410	......	668	57	15	1485	114086
Boone	1107	7411	120	16031	357	3619	712	2534	2925	26720	88	......	104	312	109	2	1805	......	387	2	......	860	65784
Bremer	127	1029	166	13686	247	812	3479	6200	5218	22493	1076	7	177	290	215	7	1200	......	310	6	5	1015	82415
Buchanan	85	865	210	19471	......	......	1999	12615	12777	25925	2269	25	355	355	79	......	5	......	142	12	402	1014	86222
Buena Vista	1	17	18	1213	......	......	......	23	17	9909	......	......	1	4	8	......	5	......	......	35	......	256	17843
Butler	2848	23296	95	6365	21	......	567	6680	4514	17558	830	1	167	264	245	......	......	1	264	20	8	790	65265
Calhoun	107	704	48	6243	......	......	......	491	127	11616	35	......	2	1	27	......	......	......	......	......	......	306	21143
Carroll	289	1720	56	3812	90)	......	53	112	85	13162	......	......	......	......	......	......	......	......	......	1	......	322	21111
Cass	140	640	51	5016	......	......	125	727	577	17144	41	54	251	513	20	......	......	......	125	......	......	554	49662
Cedar	2445	20400	174	13535	120	32	28450	36960	30089	10616	25604	303	227	349	122	......	11	......	770	75	13	1166	112835
Cerro Gordo	190	485	11	884	......	......	184	1386	1234	14317	270	5	26	35	28	......	......	......	......	2	2	431	31910
Cherokee	172	875	5	419	......	......	40	97	27	10786	7	......	8	8	129	......	......	......	......	......	......	224	16325

TABLE IV.—Continued.

COUNTIES.	Number of acres in flax seed.	Number of bushels harvested.	SUGAR AND SYRUP. Number of acres in sorghum.	Number of gallons syrup from sorghum.	Number of gallons of maple syrup.	Number of pounds of maple sugar.	Number of acres of blue grass for pasture.	Number of acres of tame grass.	Number of tons of hay from same.	Number of tons of hay from wild grass.	Number of bushels of grass seed.	Number of bushels of clover seed.	HUNGARIAN-GRASS. Number of acres.	Number of tons of hay.	Number of bushels of seed.	HOPS. Number of acres.	Number of pounds.	TOBACCO. Number of acres.	Number of pounds of product.	BROOM CORN. Number of acres.	Number of tons.	POTATOES. Number of acres.	Number of bushels.
Chickasaw	40	510	126	11244	131	8606	623	4898	4905	30141	6938	2	23	34	42	14	1773	...	583	7	3	892	72064
Clarke	168	1261	279	18336	20	5	1409	14462	10378	7576	2048	43	534	904	312	...	34	...	1184	...	39	626	33166
Clay	205	815	27	1372	...	...	1	50	7	10933	12	...	...	...	...	...	...	...	10	6	32	260	15538
Clayton	...	...	155	13387	3494	24005	9685	17557	20015	11305	1265	412	73	136	20	14	13440	3	2389	15	5	1815	185504
Clinton	686	8161	69	5418	20	405	26921	35343	34580	20044	2530	563	502	804	229	1	1311	...	672	214	43	1581	138361
Crawford	417	1413	24	2248	...	...	31	130	42	20493	11	...	247	510	152	...	...	...	30	10	6	483	38476
Dallas	448	3867	214	23021	64	...	711	2788	3358	22212	177	11	87	136	9	...	...	1	1407	13	3	615	67910
Davis	56	449	414	46296	52	1340	14443	30631	22458	1293	20825	719	3402	4150	5939	...	15	1	6746	6	5	604	65740
Decatur	38	401	369	33683	69	2294	3308	14944	16816	9061	1504	129	1840	2591	835	...	22	13	11908	27	11	613	54385
Delaware	15	118	103	8084	14	1210	13478	14788	18077	26583	906	60	87	130	2	32	12955	...	99	76	22	1125	109767
Des Moines	33	26	829	14235	426	997	12715	23317	16484	2653	3027	94	18	24	...	...	99	...	542	43	14	1647	160235
Dickinson	70	...	20	1068	...	...	...	64	...	6548	...	...	...	...	...	...	102	...	...	...	...	210	7603
Dubuque	...	...	141	9411	235	2912	12750	23032	35338	8725	203	10	37	58	...	2	1958	4	335	9	3	2023	161229
Emmet	...	...	27	643	...	...	...	18	...	10836	1	...	10	...	...	...	...	...	...	...	...	183	6847
Fayette	180	1672	204	20475	382	8765	797	13681	14124	28024	6815	119	18	42	4	50	23528	...	120	25	5	1236	122044
Floyd	153	1127	68	4172	363	2905	303	4734	5117	15187	459	56	196	299	92	1	541	...	205	14	7	1129	81153
Franklin	288	2585	73	1346	...	...	455	1860	1332	17178	1082	...	65	185	221	3	...	...	25	3	1700	622	52887
Fremont	657	5333	60	5240	53	...	333	1628	1733	19274	708	2	438	825	566	...	...	6	386	50	10	553	31732
Greene	51	222	105	8349	6	55	69	581	514	17862	50	...	11	25	8	...	39	...	...	7	2	350	31215
Grundy	1156	8159	44	2683	...	...	245	8541	5243	16050	2483	...	18	27	90	...	...	18	125	1	500	871	77702
Guthrie	1639	11156	154	15140	7	...	186	916	834	14403	141	...	117	222	15	...	...	...	545	16	8	387	37218
Hamilton	118	631	103	9148	5	610	52	427	431	25214	86	...	27	65	8	...	2	...	30	6	4	519	35746
Hancock	...	...	4	275	...	...	...	82	105	5644	6	...	...	...	...	...	...	...	...	...	...	81	6801
Hardin	414	3069	204	19774	17	420	1789	5216	4918	20766	1195	1	135	169	103	...	3	...	...	13	4	976	75410
Harrison	82	540	168	14962	...	9	92	157	135	36328	1	...	865	1604	242	...	...	...	75	...	...	588	40345
Henry	...	...	286	33969	1813	8057	22784	28547	25315	957	10325	861	94	84	30	4	2622	3	3283	79	42	816	110974

Howard		6	2	206			40	2529	2534	19371	369	50	18	91			2		254	6	22	518	62472
Humboldt			183	3501			8	204	54	12752	97									2	1	257	20756
Ida				20				6	8	3508												38	3310
Iowa	6864	48258	221	22167	6	3	1272	17026	15240	25216	4481	780	117	184	134		93	1	642	14	276	1345	137253
Jackson			144	11017	2324	36170	9107	30010	22141	6804	574	247	307	622	160	27	20750	2	648	1	350	1516	117781
Jasper	1715	14414	407	45940	187	1279	3006	17660	13001	18969	1154	27	74	174				1	1050	32	13	2665	238974
Jefferson			339	34478	219	544	21808	33774	24143	632	37217	704	282	371	1756		122	5	6390	20	966	668	79579
Johnson	2696	22941	337	27465		20	13542	34504	29955	74343	23120	975	352	728	653		101	1	1753	6	12	1530	154268
Jones	27	201	139	9621		1115	13970	28694	25768	13709	812	44	411	698	100	182	14968	1	466	12	3	899	80227
Keokuk	484	3797	421	46566	1259	5	12175	27413	25236	11508	9180	486	117	281	136		40	2	3255	6	18	899	100919
Kossuth	762	242	28	1559			335	424	60	18679												442	16906
Lee		2	464	38428	60	1756	23006	34753	26350	2229	40986	486	486	445	758	12	125	151	1170	45	24	2083	179589
Linn	1428	11432	466	50138	95	290	21710	29386	28495	24957	1536	731	158	239	92					4	1	1299	127621
Louisa	29	170	333	20760	40	1807	16642	25231	14672	3931	1893	75	322	459	169	19	73		893	42	12	957	91193
Lucas	5	24	205	25268			1343	15579	13384	5352	3716	489	1338	2447	285			2	1060	72	12	417	42153
Lyon	229	480	3	178				13	5	4210										2		284	3895
Madison	900	5351	242	21586	356	941	1612	8691	9199	11751	557	39	200	321			5	1	1140	16	43	791	87693
Mahaska	66	460	513	60286	8	4	17094	32032	25437	10317	2001	1085	207	337	57		86	2	3703	4	4	1230	139898
Marion	137	914	668	65250	157	1100	6498	17473	17068	5440	679	156	184	343	124		205	3	2867	19	51	1663	186478
Marshall	4260	34792	199	7709	25		2079	19369	13106	21570	5422	93	86	174	27		10		280	53	17	1906	166211
Mills	919	6259	48	2711			187	2101	752	19101	189	10	816	1359	211	15		1	878	8	2	932	56093
Mitchell			8	1296	300		198	5774	6134	14643	1537	24	297	565	138		402		6	11	3	773	93282
Monona			115	9868	70			60		33812	30		4	5	19				30	40	8	240	20490
Monroe	205	681	308	33593			8094	19441	23711	3653	1104	378	1427	2541	105		28	1	3499	11	4	630	67376
Montgomery	7210	61662	22	4913		2	132	768	874	13776	67	1	300	571	122			4	350	290	73	626	44782
Muscatine	447	3155	222	16507			16926	28893	22002	6838	6394	161	361	675	465	2	10	1	55	15		2030	183116
O'Brien	553	1291	12	302				31	33	6517										2	1	236	14706
Osceola	135	418		30						5226	1											153	11522
Page	3049	30677	216	13072	71	142	952	3695	3733	18971	971	21	340	534	386			19	3697	318	53	793	51098
Palo Alto	13		45	2119	87	62		6	1	20253			6	9		2			4	1	1	383	21713
Plymouth	432	1555	12	743			80	4	4	18775	6		61	203	84				50	12	3	412	18341
Pocahontas	17	12	52	2468				73		12980												333	21712
Polk	3822	28433	263	25549	15	40	3272	6862	8098	28350	90	12	364	718	246		12	3	4590	4	5	1641	175208
Pottawattamie	690	3035	54	5976		6	112	251	320	31614	98		547	1073	246	2		2	1100	2		1157	80767
Poweshiek	3151	26449	198	22784			2288	17895	13032	21014	3653	609	110	242	33		18	1	250	7	23	1138	125493
Ringgold	1731	13764	173	16587			116	3887	4866	28770	584	30	149	300	88		5	8	2927	3	2	300	23676
Sac	169	1162	29	2889		8	87	195	191	9773	80		3	6	10					1		190	15169
Scott			33	3168			31132	17535	20413	11185	439	30	318	571	100	3	2000	1	25	16	3	3222	234836
Shelby	84	738	39	3068				91	309	16276	39		204	451	19				1525			332	24203
Sioux	641	1690	18	586				18	20	9277			4	10	14					4		371	7720
Story	4286	33717	202	14538	1	104	291	3609	2370	39554	633	41	137	289	169		13			17	13	834	55882

46

TABLE IV.—Continued.

COUNTIES.	Number of acres in flax seed.	Number of bushels harvested.	SUGAR AND SYRUP.				Number of acres of blue grass for pasture.	Number of acres of tame grass.	Number of tons of hay from same.	Number of tons of hay from wild grass.	Number of bushels of grass seed.	Number of bushels of clover seed.	HUNGARIAN GRASS.			HOPS.		TOBACCO.		BROOM CORN.		POTATOES.	
			Number of acres in sorghum.	Number of gallons of syrup from sorghum.	Number of gallons of maple syrup.	Number of pounds of maple sugar.							Number of acres.	Number of tons of hay.	Number of bushels of seed.	Number of acres.	Number of pounds.	Number of acres.	Number of pounds of product.	Number of acres.	Number of tons.	Number of acres.	Number of bushels.
Tama	1423	12529	126	9047	......	....	1589	15644	10169	27667	2724	166	148	166	32	......	35	......	165	19	6	1184	95041
Taylor	1279	12161	113	10022	......	....	315	3314	3395	17707	349	7	359	535	82	......	....	......	....	6	2	487	41379
Union	2222	14495	61	7819	4	20	133	3779	4011	9551	2337	12	287	1599	2309	......	....	......	....	......	......	352	33549
Van Buren	70	415	282	30005	2588	8478	26531	32884	25209	592	28578	898	888	1120	2333	......	12	8	4851	33	11	806	81728
Wapello	....	....	320	32760	10	606	15258	27138	16645	1440	5535	331	480	723	374	1	465	......	3953	11	7	1465	154473
Warren	662	5581	279	31197	1117	348	4457	13649	14763	11331	794	460	146	231	37	......	194	......	3354	1	1	955	120515
Washington	660	5396	414	40537	181	457	19381	35544	27142	15052	5028	1404	96	202	189	......	7	......	1021	46	54	931	102041
Wayne	367	2976	288	24729	......	....	1055	21289	16797	9929	9120	73	3826	5699	10915	2	160	4	3028	2	2	503	50317
Webster	133	174	173	14882	149	95	44	250	782	30660	2	2	23	50	35	2	1100	......	....	6	2	811	67423
Winnebago	....	....	2	240	......	....	....	37	....	10674	....	....	......	....	......	......	....	......	....	......	......	134	9391
Winneshiek	....	....	13	1375	55	4600	6890	15844	15726	25567	4756	715	15	26	......	......	34	......	....	3	3	1567	100314
Woodbury	....	....	5	492	......	....	....	24	12	18573	....	....	23	70	10	......	....	......	....	5	2	284	17312
Worth	....	....	10	727	2	....	....	316	408	18471	135	....	36	66	......	......	3	......	90	......	......	259	21209
Wright	113	1018	39	3375	5	....	65	412	312	13468	16	....	45	80	......	......	....	......	135	......	......	245	17313
Total	72984	559836	15768	1386908	19613	132204	483200	1055730	908011	1506509	322497	15978	32427	51637	44800	426	113314	260	102782	2203	5036	81729	7289953

TABLE V.

Showing number of acres and bushels of Sweet Potatoes and Natural Timber, of Planted Timber, Rods of Hedge; Number Pears, Peaches, Plums and Cherries; other Fruit Trees in Bear- Pounds of Grapes gathered, Gallons of Wine made; Number not in Vineyard.

COUNTIES.	SWEET POTATOES		ONIONS.		Number of bushels of turnips.	Number of bushels of beets.	Number of bushels of peas and beans.	Acres of natural timber.	Acres of planted timber.	Rods of hedge.	APPLES.		Number of pear trees in bearing.
	Number of acres.	Number of bushels.	Number of acres.	Number of bushels.							Number of trees in bearing.	Bushels gathered in 1874.	
Adair....	......	326	15	1410	4388	1213	914	6961	570	41191	2301	1676	12
Adams	1	552	5	850	1203	406	255	8687	411	41403	1929	1697	27
Allamakee	......	10	......	755	25835	959	1033	61956	326	250	19149	8242	33
Appanoose	16	3396	33	2518	6789	508	1315	62037	140	152246	43006	25204	505
Audubon...	2	364	37	385	1633	689	189	2843	116	5749	1071	303	1
Benton......	7	1146	9	889	6179	2816	1244	18016	3603	122055	60742	14139	228
Bl'k Hawk	4	278	2	725	4867	1378	770	15834	1812	23251	23276	9721	75
Boone........	9	885	40	525	2583	367	360	27550	379	32112	13784	3876	84
Bremer......	......	11	2	966	2913	1086	395	21090	379	16524	7154	2232	26
Buchanan..	2	348	24	856	6233	731	656	20759	448	41350	20207	7556	99
Bu'na Vsta	......	49	1	106	3250	1128	545	847	642	23892	66	6	1
Butler........	1	82	6	828	6320	655	954	12844	3496	29714	5177	1861	12
Calhoun.....	......	29	......	62	7760	742	248	1290	518	23700	880	13	....
Carroll	......	111	11	250	3810	377	305	3912	685	25787	1448	262	6
Cass...........	8	1322	8	1391	3813	545	366	5830	731	35038	1528	976	17
Cedar.........	13	1048	19	2000	2598	2212	378	36100	1010	210989	74335	25056	484
Cerro Go'do	......	12	19	1054	8982	1561	410	4880	386	21230	775	125	1
Cherokee...	......	5	......	66	599	233	143	1085	570	19684	70	2	....
Chickasaw	......	....	6	500	5105	715	385	17374	483	4959	3557	666	2
Clarke........	11	1134	57	718	3803	1397	1017	21573	191	78640	17023	11955	139
Clay...........	......	10	......	52	870	188	114	729	843	16979	39	8	....
Clayton......	1	152	15	1205	13214	2281	1576	99222	94	1232	39032	20324	56
Clinton......	4	912	15	2895	2962	1905	1229	22912	422	153906	62843	30912	262
Crawford...	1	249	3	485	3951	1024	300	5376	434	19915	1072	178	6
Dallas........	6	1379	7	392	4731	537	459	24651	742	41589	25320	15946	24
Davis.........	16	2924	1	570	7337	450	2137	81772	182	149040	56771	38347	1580
Decatur......	8	1698	3	1046	7806	595	900	43041	200	75367	29372	17713	610
Delaware...	13	246	4	1314	8032	1970	979	45181	652	17491	36824	12440	132
Des Moin's	36	3670	25	806	3584	854	462	46976	60	126833	132557	129996	1561
Dickinson.	......	....	......	67	300	229	62	1194	379	7663	92	....	....
Dubuque....	......	56	6	1175	12863	1193	1193	69773	107	1357	48456	23077	404
Emmet......	......	....	3	....	479	8	16	1234	193	2215	70	2	1
Fayette......	......	27	10	1870	9294	1008	960	38539	977	29447	12756	5122	68
Floyd.........	......	5	6	1330	6199	754	764	17294	528	19973	5062	1158	2
Franklin...	1	113	5	472	5530	327	605	4185	815	24434	1909	303	61
Fremont....	19	1271	52	403	378	428	35	23924	341	121669	15443	11905	702
Greene	24	842	......	290	3614	475	530	9410	230	48109	3304	611	46
Grundy......	......	85	6	1480	4952	525	310	866	1420	57714	5279	1364	3
Guthrie.....	4	770	21	2996	2851	463	510	14180	747	41116	12329	3633	24

TABLE V.

Onions, bushels of Turnips, Beets, Peas and Beans; acres of of Trees in Bearing and Bushels gathered in 1874 *of Apples, ing and Fruit Trees not in Bearing; acres of Grapes in Vineyard, of Vines, Pounds gathered and Gallons of Wine made of Grapes*

Bushels of pears gathered in 1874.	PEACHES		PLUMS.		CHERRIES		Number of other fruit trees in bearing.	Number of fruit trees not in bearing.	GRAPES IN VINEYARD.			GRAPES NOT IN VINEYARD.		
	Number of trees in bearing.	Bushels gathered in 1874.	Number of trees in bearing.	Bushels gathered in 1874.	Number of trees in bearing.	Bushels gathered in 1874.			Number of acres.	Pounds of grapes gathered.	Gallons of wine made.	Number of vines.	Pounds of grapes gathered.	Gallons of wine made.
…	30	21	75	53	705	89	1791	71121	1	434	…	13430	11238	268
9	48	3	603	175	613	26	161	58730	5	12800	553	9214	14585	155
3	12	…	220	113	219	13	789	52907	…	297	43	3013	5764	167
230	4619	1203	1411	685	15975	3473	608	125085	16	24130	515	24485	93257	808
1	1	…	1	…	106	10	156	11266	…	…	…	1625	1440	6
10	27	3	1942	304	4451	369	2076	211050	21	29750	1025	24865	72992	529
14	2	53	6524	1313	3936	399	5450	249028	9	8385	100	24358	82804	284
12	…	…	1263	265	1632	283	1251	78965	7	6650	7	19379	46671	188
…	16	2	231	124	706	44	701	59832	5	12617	127	7580	7739	104
…	2	5	1097	256	1649	104	2125	80107	…	…	…	6409	13740	40
…	…	…	194	31	52	…	277	10872	…	…	…	1328	108	…
3	…	…	1868	398	1120	62	4040	164176	6	100	…	4695	6761	2
…	…	…	287	22	…	422	…	17222	…	200	…	554	318	2
…	12	1	198	40	308	32	94	18702	3	1000	…	2672	760	3
5	5	…	276	59	1357	155	3996	64092	3	3300	169	13412	15537	106
58	154	67	1001	360	11023	2367	2492	104524	11	102016	602	29397	185876	677
1	…	…	126	32	42	4	37	21839	…	…	…	1296	535	…
…	…	…	68	5	9	6	23	11768	…	…	…	679	15	1
…	…	…	142	96	198	46	114	31006	9	400	2	1208	2790	28
27	366	46	831	140	11254	549	3496	87487	79	125475	40	21374	45125	118
…	6	1	882	46	56	…	66	8226	1	…	…	693	…	…
7	…	…	1473	633	1121	174	900	93294	51	23275	716	8349	35739	1357
54	172	62	2312	1179	9831	2016	6566	105554	31	57428	1721	19141	79301	3092
1	13	1	583	179	339	39	161	22029	1	3250	12	3911	555	158
13	96	11	451	87	2205	363	195	145020	11	26200	148	30008	95083	136
342	4575	1636	975	187	11341	2236	430	87553	13	71501	2254	28154	85546	371
61	1721	409	835	311	8109	1074	675	105792	17	26040	232	14417	34196	729
14	12	…	592	181	1839	135	1672	70287	12	16310	786	9935	16529	469
890	7001	3545	897	177	21243	6967	2076	89596	4446	815040	42077	49614	202125	4470
…	…	…	185	16	…	…	17	2682	…	…	…	570	40	…
18	34	…	3650	6(2	3729	855	32364	85816	73	24944	2061	16367	16740	1132
…	…	…	132	11	3	…	6	2515	…	…	…	16	20	…
4	…	12	1189	438	1486	78	1369	86411	2	789	42	4025	9483	748
1	…	…	670	257	709	4	3027	53008	1	700	…	6150	2611	26
…	…	…	1032	240	413	11	687	34662	…	80	…	2225	3366	51
348	10468	10952	623	163	3062	602	1923	87279	24	22293	745	16525	19916	33
13	2	…	578	81	636	85	285	51920	3	685	52	9260	8912	5
1	…	…	982	210	743	49	1119	76577	…	1100	5	6417	8957	59
…	6	…	442	70	1028	55	326	87104	4	6600	…	12186	26930	1

TABLE V.—CONTINUED.

COUNTIES.	SWEET POTATOES		ONIONS.		Number of bushels of turnips.	Number of bushels of beets.	Number of bushels of peas and beans.	Acres of natural timber.	Acres of planted timber.	Rods of hedge.	APPLES.		Number of pear trees in bearing.
	Number of acres.	Number of bushels.	Number of acres.	Number of bushels.							Number of trees in bearing.	Bushels gathered in 1874.	
Hamilton	......	65	......	226	1022	373	299	8172	876	23166	1782	545	4
Hancock	......	5	......	61	1432	205	100	10000	114	11919	152	12	......
Hardin	3	377	10	1144	6412	664	463	18106	961	46638	13115	4063	26
Harrison	13	1759	2	487	16139	662	203	23497	528	3138	3418	1117	95
Henry	17	6708	4	1067	4301	1117	1380	44178	312	218998	131873	99150	3629
Howard	......	......	......	873	11729	445	285	10493	534	8189	2397	647	42
Humboldt	9	635	......	83	988	165	68	1878	309	12806	514	67	1
Ida	......	......	......	55	945	66	76	703	56	1150	50	2	......
Iowa	6	822	7	698	9024	10691	878	22973	506	142265	24494	11492	225
Jackson	3	126	24	978	4641	533	921	95160	27	18973	57522	29043	113
Jasper	7	1449	10	4126	8334	4966	943	29223	1213	158923	38024	15057	198
Jefferson	34	4212	2	647	3432	693	662	55478	98	118662	93471	72790	1446
Johnson	8	824	58	6776	10572	1622	682	39971	622	135792	67748	30303	385
Jones	2	283	19	584	5139	777	512	52546	472	56993	34183	10840	77
Keokuk	48	5752	50	2516	5172	757	873	45000	400	238750	52425	29473	323
Kossuth	......	......	......	2	5354	19	24	2343	578	9815	200	4	......
Lee	55	5184	6	961	3525	1076	1939	68716	80	292035	146882	128262	3519
Linn	15	3107	1	996	7580	2521	1544	63383	815	64228	42790	11257	145
Louisa	33	3218	15	645	2303	576	725	37299	178	122565	65090	34034	425
Lucas	5	828	1	469	4304	685	638	22884	150	165015	15005	9228	230
Lyon	......	......	......	5	168	43	126	691	145	2935	......	......	......
Madison	16	2253	22	1094	5547	984	779	34426	910	117158	29391	15140	251
Mahaska	10	2895	5	1047	4814	1008	1097	46132	544	167189	62395	35185	279
Marion	10	1811	4	1233	4365	737	761	49181	221	80333	55061	26330	313
Marshall	9	1487	5	1593	10634	2953	1507	15687	5526	175847	25810	7215	364
Mills	28	2492	48	5404	457	376	76	18502	749	96869	12956	15043	112
Mitchell	......	1	1	460	4314	1088	258	12188	810	11714	2183	376	4
Monona	6	871	......	137	2898	770	293	8728	536	3808	1164	382	15
Monroe	3	1677	11	1107	4307	544	999	36397	38	60731	28745	10185	276
Montg'm'y	7	827	3	259	550	160	85	7445	320	106418	1107	1281	30
Muscatine	201	13372	16	2324	1281	2204	361	32077	4373	226621	74823	42094	1446
O'Brien	2	61	6	383	1234	1443	297	201	484	18189	......	......	......
Osceola	......	......	......	49	1162	410	94	......	122	12784	4	......	......
Page	19	1873	11	1168	426	640	119	16756	1502	304334	18525	15128	549
Palo Alto	33	......	1	33	5910	132	131	1324	364	6277	48	6	......
Plymouth	12	810	6	105	753	2002	181	578	917	7205	46	......	......
Pocahont's	......	......	......	150	6003	58	205	651	420	8331	240	30	5
Polk	88	11479	24	2298	7040	2111	697	38623	705	52771	51882	24485	705
Pottawat'e	50	6722	12	3147	5594	694	596	20483	600	24236	7584	4896	369
Poweshiek	23	954	154	22348	5321	1030	1014	12197	777	224067	22114	9462	111
Ringgold	5	370	10	675	1415	998	431	18149	226	133108	4571	3615	51
Sac	......	16	2	263	3271	486	200	2662	626	21371	444	61	......
Scott	28	3808	244	36804	2937	6988	344	15464	228	223608	92445	77308	2822
Shelby	1	240	1	634	3441	235	327	5632	343	10238	993	953	1
Sioux	3	142	7	7	343	164	43	218	276	7285	......	......	......
Story	7	980	9	690	3212	2446	1056	14165	778	126354	16539	4781	98
Tama	2	372	1	280	5231	3459	584	18282	1589	98835	28464	9207	149
Taylor	4	1174	10	1360	1041	889	174	19039	500	147948	13281	8899	134
Union	2	376	12	2126	2046	272	242	9203	623	69979	5923	3103	43
Van Buren	20	2144	23	498	3979	286	2528	78324	384	186105	93775	85674	1933
Wapello	11	2661	7	528	7521	1056	814	57983	76	137246	53268	32364	1032
Warren	7	2049	......	1465	4820	1856	792	34718	550	182696	42071	33560	169

TABLE V.—Continued.

Bushels of pears gathered in 1874.	PEACHES. Number of trees in bearing.	PEACHES. Bushels gathered in 1874.	PLUMS. Number of trees in bearing.	PLUMS. Bushels gathered in 1874.	CHERRIES. Number of trees in bearing.	CHERRIES. Bushels gathered in 1874.	Number of other fruit trees in bearing.	Number of fruit trees not in bearing.	GRAPES IN VINEYARD. Number of acres.	GRAPES IN VINEYARD. Pounds of grapes gathered.	GRAPES IN VINEYARD. Gallons of wine made.	GRAPES NOT IN VINEYARD. Number of vines.	GRAPES NOT IN VINEYARD. Pounds of grapes gathered.	GRAPES NOT IN VINEYARD. Gallons of wine made
6	....	....	1411	70	692	59	1701	32925	....	510	6	2259	3071	1
....	....	....	96	34	41	2	50	1041	....	....	....	150	72	....
7	....	....	2391	481	2513	433	256	68728	2	3500	15	6910	14205	37
4	26	....	295	85	1304	96	735	43073	3	240	....	4809	2125	8
1673	12741	4500	1451	538	31274	13654	1505	125864	101	100119	1249	26870	19707	3006
....	....	....	381	167	48	12	180	8851	....	....	....	773	662	20
....	....	....	572	27	101	2	15	7738	....	....	219	387	382	45
....	....	....	....	....	....	1	27	832	....	....	....	26	5	....
6	38	13	560	116	3815	806	309	139474	512	68120	10882	26789	83801	3513
46	75	8	1675	702	3609	719	1916	74405	8	15411	532	9512	34945	212
157	29	....	760	177	6247	2232	965	158585	7	11700	15	44157	180489	670
444	3297	715	1259	365	19586	5436	701	97343	31	95890	1521	33029	228521	1395
80	132	14	1304	304	6393	2607	520	91732	91	93820	6186	47718	195192	3031
2	3	....	543	150	4260	667	1640	82797	6	10736	52	14612	67067	3597
111	1086	162	1849	599	7284	2016	728	116474	14	50550	1268	26640	170015	1151
....	....	....	1324	138	19	....	33	2875	....	....	....	268	210	56
1717	29523	17024	985	262	26628	9853	808	133498	275	283784	75319	70188	196897	7712
13	62	....	2475	752	6623	1035	2642	128428	48	87240	282	29767	115355	502
132	3437	672	752	113	13816	2710	1389	65549	2112	82625	7929	16428	105549	356
60	185	35	559	108	4101	994	1269	74568	58	9960	140	22391	64692	47
....	....	....	....	....	....	....	....	2106	....	....	56	404	....	32
170	414	36	800	368	3586	608	650	152637	35	61239	443	37924	148652	1037
75	313	63	909	278	7970	2124	1955	137411	9	22250	165	28940	219468	449
71	289	35	1256	445	7993	1985	607	95186	860	34230	645	31663	198030	1026
58	5	1	5498	1389	10725	2484	2718	170754	36	47108	42	56595	145897	869
38	1883	610	252	43	1661	263	1572	86758	1586	17650	190	14761	17552	495
....	85	....	609	216	469	4	327	12497	....	255	....	1571	1918	306
20	....	....	1666	458	187	24	29	12194	....	636	5	1982	883	10
89	1017	95	1817	301	6255	1169	526	57651	6	24350	1190	10509	63918	243
....	340	28	146	49	889	102	473	49278	3	700	20	5480	6389	19
620	1043	291	583	54	14773	3557	1298	78396	1648	109750	5303	41944	211822	1046
....	....	....	6	2	....	....	....	8632	....	....	....	616	....	....
....	....	....	4	....	4	....	....	1690	....	....	....	122	2	....
68	3396	1215	1039	161	2888	299	668	125288	19	24522	112	31022	82657	254
....	....	....	1227	97	24	....	2	954	....	....	....	279	320	124
....	2	....	318	23	69	....	269	9825	2	....	....	311	....	....
....	2	....	104	36	54	....	195	2601	....	....	....	84	....	....
88	46	17	699	119	7077	1689	648	193749	88	256860	1210	76253	405402	1295
108	460	175	3269	1027	3890	667	6786	83971	468	66517	15	21298	38883	128
27	38	12	575	174	4645	571	480	133889	368	27630	....	22785	64967	4758
17	1439	313	410	91	1819	292	417	72429	6	1490	....	8558	15323	....
....	5	....	113	19	151	6	14	62073	313	....	....	5655	350	....
472	3932	1156	1428	235	9168	2177	789	81430	572	415700	20115	60270	261593	5771
....	2	....	80	16	228	22	310	26652	1	280	....	3576	2152	....
....	....	....	....	....	13	....	25	2796	....	....	....	142	....	....
10	....	....	1610	250	3327	276	2760	101554	29	3572	20	14901	38332	314
15	9	3	1198	117	2404	213	2846	153635	7	13360	205	21441	53107	374
17	1537	908	358	143	2378	389	454	81121	4	1800	....	10519	15681	56
15	226	29	215	56	1251	133	17	53288	10	2200	56	7665	8562	....
799	9447	2611	1408	409	17709	5756	773	114615	23	97020	1385	23107	118689	1185
354	1817	515	832	289	12077	3074	4281	106321	25	92000	2265	37026	169083	1276
24	303	21	346	81	3371	606	1159	178539	14	59400	29	44743	207878	550

TABLE V.—Continued.

Counties.	Sweet potatoes		Onions.		Number of bushels of turnips.	Number of bushels of beets.	Number of bushels of peas and beans.	Acres of natural timber.	Acres of planted timber.	Rods of hedge.	Apples.		Number of pear trees in bearing.
	Number of acres.	Number of bushels.	Number of acres.	Number of bushels.							Number of trees in bearing.	Bushels gathered in 1874.	
Washn'ton	16	2205	6	484	1837	696	775	38350	1759	309827	74502	48696	596
Wayne	2	954	30	735	6068	495	1250	24214	171	210880	23024	13688	213
Webster.....	......	33	......	135	4375	216	353	11330	652	23996	7627	1500	29
Win'ebago	......	2	......	87	567	62	67	2979	92	814	191	57	....
Win'shiek	31	244	2	691	10202	4984	610	39844	284	5059	10344	4000	....
Woodbur'y	3	325	7	716	1098	1769	309	7204	503	7640	101	90	2
Worth..	......	25	......	254	2504	552	158	5428	161	5882	698	67	20
Wright	......	3	1	386	3521	311	356	3232	574	24141	1452	176	1
Total	1134	128579	1386	152758	462165	111152	59327	2312659	65549	7396662	2440934	1451037	30507

TABLE V.—Continued.

Bushels of pears gathered in 1874.	PEACHES.		PLUMS.		CHERRIES		Number of other fruit trees in bearing.	Number of fruit trees not in bearing.	GRAPES IN VINEYARD.			GRAPES NOT IN VINEYARD.		
	Number of trees in bearing.	Bushels gathered in 1874.	Number of trees in bearing.	Bushels gathered in 1874.	Number of trees in bearing.	Bushels gathered in 1874.			Number of acres.	Pounds of grapes gathered.	Gallons of wine made.	Number of vines.	Pounds of grapes gathered.	Gallons of wine made.
231	842	101	875	263	14121	3003	2009	129979	51	119910	2670	32654	192000	2250
77	1803	372	472	160	5539	1005	644	132758	15	54855	462	16379	47741	64
....	....	....	583	37	551	27	124	38061	3	1805	63	3381	3016	9
....	....	....	20	32	....	1	20	1916	....	....	....	52	20	....
....	....	....	444	128	71	7	928	72796	4	920	150	4939	25690	528
....	....	60	674	80	100	7	177	12636	2	....	....	853	115	....
....	....	....	49	11	60	....	264	6390	1	1	....	339	368	40
....	....	....	165	24	522	21	48	11193	2	150	5	1245	1205	94
10061	110729	49843	89640	22418	409774	99051	135192	7135832	14343	3896154	196470	1514607	5504731	66284

TABLE VI.

Statistics concerning Horses, Mules, and Asses; Milch Cows, Milk, Butter, and Cheese; Work Oxen, thorough-bred Short-horns, and other improved breeds of Cattle; number of Hogs, together with improved breeds of same, and number slaughtered in 1874.

COUNTIES.	Number of horses of all ages.	Number of horses sold for export in 1874.	Number of mules and asses.	Number of same sold for export in 1874.	Number of milch cows.	Number of pounds of butter made in 1874.	Number of pounds of cheese made in 1874 not at factory.	Number of gallons of milk sold in 1874.	Number of work oxen.	Number of all other cattle.	No. of cattle slaughtered or sold for slaughter in 1874.	Number of thorough-bred short-horns.	Number of Devons.	Number of Herefords.	Number of Ayrshires.	Number of Jerseys.	Number of Holderness.	Other improved breeds.	IMPROVED BREEDS OF HOGS. Number of hogs.	Number of Berk-shires.	Number of Poland-China.	Number of Chester White.	Number of Magee.	Number of Essex.	Other improved breeds.	No. slaughtered or sold for slaughter in 1874.
Adair	3917	154	276	12	3184	177640	5876	490	111	7958	1973	21	....	....	....	....	....	....	20394	948	2156	216	....	....	1335	15187
Adams	4261	50	280	11	4055	189386	8013	10235	76	9272	1271	35	1	....	....	....	....	13	21002	581	1592	50	....	....	483	13393
Allamakee	7610	218	86	2	7294	400562	8194	14673	337	12021	2942	9	....	....	....	....	....	10	19770	97	441	330	....	....	217	18334
Appanoose	9109	321	702	36	9565	534115	6657	12823	82	20669	4305	67	21	....	....	....	....	39	57446	779	2016	379	32	1	315	43994
Audubon	1554	17	165	4	1480	59719	452	665	22	3277	634	18	....	....	....	....	....	20	7377	115	215	....	....	....	40	4585
Benton	13472	331	624	30	11152	776448	12846	20695	50	22681	3908	104	23	....	2	32	....	....	57947	563	2423	92	....	....	388	43460
Bla'k Hawk	10627	536	369	22	8969	663700	13848	80642	54	15527	3445	72	25	....	....	....	....	2	39332	1009	3284	280	....	....	54	31265
Boone	7780	167	490	32	7538	455468	14350	25043	102	17435	4435	20	....	....	....	....	....	3	37090	826	2760	444	1	....	4921	28898
Bremer	7185	398	98	6	7917	598191	11812	18408	55	14786	2300	13	....	....	....	....	....	2	25252	415	191	19	....	....	33	18116
Buchanan	8450	174	300	23	9407	719264	9446	24013	70	18690	3099	220	25	....	....	....	....	....	31445	473	1360	249	2	3	1286	26984
Buena Vista	1495	25	66	....	1208	69853	1377	1161	326	2016	233	1	1	....	....	....	....	....	3414	183	162	51	....	....	1	2044
Butler	7004	233	126	11	5936	433463	43554	6550	45	11795	1597	46	1	....	....	....	....	....	25860	743	998	163	....	....	301	18643
Calhoun	1411	14	90	15	1471	114858	1005	413	138	2871	155	2	....	....	....	....	....	....	5983	204	209	2	....	....	....	3180
Carroll	2808	27	192	93	1975	93420	634	2042	117	3604	290	8	43	....	....	....	....	....	10638	363	298	2	....	....	995	8281
Cass	6206	139	491	32	4806	242600	807	5400	90	10547	2707	28	82	....	....	....	....	....	27001	1447	3787	1777	....	....	....	19911
Cedar	12303	610	717	53	11009	683821	20096	67187	21	27565	6726	512	22	55	....	4	....	....	71259	5456	6369	746	141	....	940	59653
Cerro Gordo	3113	82	68	3	2693	168496	12500	7531	139	4367	1186	15	1	....	....	....	....	....	4015	227	48	27	....	....	....	3736
Cherokee	2074	44	116	9	7504	87504	291	3722	264	1941	220	1	....	....	....	....	....	....	5133	239	167	169	....	....	....	4391
Chickasaw	5600	323	120	6	6278	495496	8805	788	206	12294	1267	22	7	....	....	....	....	....	11912	143	387	32	....	....	15	10036

Clarke	6047	184	463	42	5894	322149	1739	1907	14	26688	3044	184	36						45616	746	3281	300				22354
Clay	1580	53	91	2	1342	92236	245		313	1629	147	3							2708	28	28	26				1666
Clayton	11041	631	620	36	11096	684568	14879	14237	182	16360	4549	78	2			1		6	41057	560	1345	1184			411	34011
Clinton	12928	724	364	38	14295	1031442	4202	45664	2	31768	8421	134	73					70	73096	1044	3119	641		19	195	74724
Crawford	3472	242	208	32	3511	140694	91090	37122	127	7371	2240	37	1						12394	358	736	280	77			8595
Dallas	7707	245	679	33	7249	453567	1896	4243	90	18289	2931	243							44690	658	2212	16	9		327	33912
Davis	9154	692	1035	105	7192	450954	10424	1663	16	18679	4671	116	53						50576	1468	1573	155	11		545	44337
Decatur	7808	440	581	57	7848	396243	7373	1197	53	18575	3839	94	2						37405	1007	2068	120	1		23	27573
Delaware	10461	622	310	52	11800	738205	64202	251331	26	28120	3522	65	23			1			40815	832	1193	557			322	33679
Des Moines	8098	471	603	48	7409	464483	4397	219344	52	16700	4011	55	14						39978	2477	6490	109				31740
Dickinson	766	35	31		851	70950	2224	92	166	1049	147	7	1			1			934	2	18	20			1	897
Dubuque	11563	520	523	38	12617	649056	6535	115867	60	18904	4154	117							52341	923	461	322		28		44210
Emmet	649	19	21		1073	83215	6493		151	2346	301	6							557	2	7	3				519
Fayette	9752	318	363	21	10554	806441	22276	11186	183	19775	3250	25	5						24979	303	207	152			14	21879
Floyd	7067	177	82	3	5858	499739	8806	15478	155	12333	1847	70	6			3			14314	452	911	123			198	12327
Franklin	3973	122	104	10	3208	222366	2470	8695	97	7907	1270	29	40						15244	635	745	100				12280
Fremont	6378	179	1009	48	6784	316787	3145	9812	103	20110	8031	50	80						44757	1068	8152	2[illegible]0				34973
Greene	3311	112	305	34	3694	238642	2455	1717	113	8205	3104	18	21	1					20187	2274	2429	76	10		650	14098
Grundy	6402	68	235	10	4727	280708	29670	1945	41	9431	1671	37			134				29963	918	3510	906			436	23939
Guthrie	5587	128	224	9	4984	278369	475	7525	25	11875	2726	22		6					25740	496	1285	95	1	1	29	24748
Hamilton	3866	143	162	12	4355	290044	2787	6970	126	10851	2178	16	4						13954	227	1152	91			2	10354
Hancock	564	4	33	6	805	39934	16590		75	1367	123	4							535	3	26					660
Hardin	6778	356	232	28	5892	425827	10720	194555	60	10649	1783	82	1			1		2	32249	3685	5172	80		9	692	21411
Harrison	6539	120	285	9	6978	315732	9907	5473	64	16227	4534	59							29365	217	1314	25		6	29	28496
Henry	9924	549	737	92	8552	546518	5581	17990	56	20261	8925	88	19						56324	1229	9530	337			1846	57107
Howard	3433	278	58	6	4358	323116	16671	5432	279	8018	876	16	4						5777	171	163	15				4838
Humboldt	1702	98	57		2268	135066	5365	430	158	3701	173	35							4698	133	63	37	1			3467
Ida	431	10	13	1	399	20835			66	980	107	3							1833	42	55	1		12	16	1159
Iowa	9602	393	475	1077	68478	471962	7190	8649	509	24828	4656	117	52						46475	1178	2701	1006				34753
Jackson	11551	774	404	44	11503	576161	15248	30444	18	26505	6537	42	17						47612	353	782	1908		5	18	50449
Jasper	13668	392	1040	49	10450	722369	7554	9673	73	29081	6140	363	1				2		75513	1668	2674				423	59026
Jefferson	9448	894	633	91	7428	523261	4233	32461	20	18326	5706	72						46	59083	1418	1519	147	345		261	46289
Johnson	11886	506	976	72	11357	614617	20520	42006	16	28374	6046	135	25	1		21			66594	1122	4347	2980	1		1	47862
Jones	10605	612	435	53	11864	682167	29426	289708	1395	20885	5399	111	5					32	61050	7653	2985	423		11	2076	43403
Keokuk	10961	564	649	86	9733	644465	6629	25032	37	23575	4846	81	3					258	55126	1718	8801	30	625		1181	46716
Kossuth	1748	7	47		2108	128510	3000		234	3788	797	12						5	2157	44	58				24	1940
Lee	10844	594	1073	136	9651	496719	98508	84134	9	20592	5680	127	51	4	2	18	2		43999	1133	1482	614		34	5	37729
Linn	14240	460	752	54	15776	1011869	18711	82618	26	27785	6686	125	3			4		12	74985	667	1618	878		4	108	54082
Louisa	7557	213	513	678	5656	347774	937	5271	8	21697	8275	90	15					13	43433	3112	4466	495	17		1647	35882
Lucas	6375	220	524	23	6103	402297	14645	6976	25	15448	3469	40	3					13	41976	698	1564	40			91	29742
Lyon	476	56	20	9	508	21330	852	243	211	444	272	1	7						509	20	19	7	14			699

TABLE VI.—CONTINUED.

COUNTIES.	Number of horses of all ages.	Number of horses sold for export in 1874.	Number of mules and asses.	Number of same sold for export in 1874.	Number of milch cows.	Number of pounds of butter made in 1874.	Number of pounds of cheese made in 1874 not at factory.	Number of gallons of milk sold in 1874.	Number of work oxen.	Number of all other cattle.	No. of cattle slaughtered and sold for slaughter in 1874.	Number of thoroughbred short horns.	Number of Devons.	Number of Herefords.	Number of Ayrshires.	Number of Jerseys.	Number of Holderness.	Other improved breeds.	IMPROVED BREEDS OF HOGS							
																			Number of hogs.	Number of Berkshires.	Number of Poland-China.	Number of Chester White.	Number of Magee.	Number of Essex.	Other improved breeds.	No. slaughtered or sold for slaughter in 1874.
Madison	8717	151	728	35	7424	426077	6030	13328	54	21025	4986	82	...	...	...	...	...	91	62835	696	2461	...	...	...	891	55717
Mahaska	11874	605	816	25	10489	726334	1115	151396	23	26060	6510	175	27	...	...	10	...	...	81120	1190	2582	42	27	...	8	60753
Marion	12328	284	870	14	8485	567050	6701	11984	31	22555	4813	48	4	...	...	...	...	...	73702	1058	1774	22	...	...	2761	57676
Marshall	10282	608	412	41	8135	625418	5083	66311	30	17567	8949	101	1	...	...	...	...	...	56553	2592	3318	3	...	1	1782	41509
Mills	6996	267	607	23	5341	288776	6442	10428	30	18750	6909	60	2	...	...	...	...	...	49780	627	5017	373	...	...	...	35763
Mitchell	6122	95	86	...	5212	364520	6270	12738	216	7859	1898	48	...	...	...	...	...	17	6594	95	218	60	...	1	8	6185
Monona	3571	39	172	10	4033	129818	2340	1025	169	12891	1991	40	...	...	...	...	...	...	14830	120	1068	1	...	...	2	11025
Monroe	6296	399	441	48	6075	375517	3175	56075	34	16471	3282	111	...	...	...	...	...	...	32934	509	684	30	...	...	303	27660
Montgom'y.	53170	134	430	23	4407	208034	7640	4675	93	11379	1742	109	...	...	...	...	...	...	32736	734	2359	10	...	...	...	22760
Muscatine	10102	394	627	27	8077	498968	3704	32030	2	19152	7447	290	...	...	4	...	...	...	40169	1846	4546	1180	...	...	1347	34418
O'Brien	1014	31	81	2	742	58146	410	320	231	940	77	1	...	...	...	...	...	...	1991	91	158	40	...	5	...	1113
Osceola	631	2	40	2	539	36145	700	296	294	484	175	...	...	...	...	...	...	...	348	2	41	...	...	...	6	326
Page	9602	241	922	33	6776	343107	3165	600	63	26130	8103	86	...	...	...	...	...	...	58049	1823	8362	189	...	..	...	67818
Palo Alto	1016	11	52	9	1914	134200	4151	213	196	5084	586	8	129	...	...	...	...	...	2109	88	17	66	...	...	...	1670
Plymouth	2367	111	143	7	1830	88846	410	3689	392	2876	607	4	...	...	...	...	...	...	3559	112	175	245	2	...	2	3179
Pocahontas	1120	5	31	...	1483	86172	7872	...	215	3230	...	...	...	...	...	...	...	...	2608	61	384	106	...	...	11	1947
Polk	10927	239	646	8	10594	606965	18207	125621	54	21186	4743	209	6	...	2	...	...	3	62318	603	1613	94	...	2	401	42829
Pottawat'e	8805	318	455	64	8180	432559	26033	106386	83	16869	2551	54	...	...	...	...	...	44	28626	431	1666	181	12	1	...	24513
Poweshiek	10411	608	627	17	8873	568668	9422	40860	31	23229	4809	3257	23	26	1	2	...	...	47852	2339	8222	39	5	1	1992	47197
Ringgold	4736	358	431	59	4864	238744	2593	1145	64	15299	2747	36	9	...	...	...	...	...	25462	548	1708	134	47	...	...	22557
Sac	1474	43	112	1	1242	84953	445	455	128	3071	510	8	...	...	...	...	...	...	4539	715	476	198	...	...	...	4192
Scott	10831	252	824	27	10696	710303	19680	277013	...	15929	3905	97	...	...	...	...	...	...	51025	184	1636	227	...	...	5	40530
Shelby	3529	60	192	4	3176	200305	1590	130	20	7137	1221	17	9	...	...	...	...	...	14456	288	832	...	...	...	...	7984
Sioux	1343	26	124	...	997	66905	1066	175	356	1177	163	5	1	...	...	...	...	...	1757	59	50	...	2	...	35	1610
Story	6715	344	430	23	9160	765098	20589	36507	48	18936	3111	55	3	...	...	...	...	12	38394	2550	10569	2451	...	91	384	31697

Tama	10419	635	479	29	8806	574998	13495	40570	43	18740	3654	64	......	...	....	.....	...	.....	46379	966	1260	322	39	3	2	34218
Taylor	6463	191	487	15	5850	290953	3534	321	66	15894	3595	33	......	...	.....	.....	...	.....	33071	191	1780	2	......	.....	25	28507
Union	3880	182	305	12	3987	195251	10382	7498	36	10143	2955	56	......	...	.....	.....	...	.....	17351	482	2158	24	......	.....	6	14161
Van Buren	8528	570	720	64	7324	504562	93417	27574	22	18312	4093	77	5	...	...	.....	...	15	50590	1005	888	421	436	29	2	35716
Wapello	8765	765	691	75	7073	469887	2222	78581	34	23440	4566	60	15	...	.....	.....	...	.....	48709	907	2836	374	88	.....	93	59694
Warren	10766	195	610	26	8529	515910	5055	14115	35	22470	7384	76	1	...	.....	5	...	.....	68105	670	2046	64	......	.....	1116	78935
Washington	10787	523	792	114	10047	629047	22036	13438	28	26452	5338	96	5	...	.....	.....	...	211	67076	1314	2532	92	214	73	805	52273
Wayne	7605	407	554	86	7200	402042	5500	2152	45	20974	4864	58	46	...	.....	.....	...	.....	45077	2036	1807	336	......	.....	181	52537
Webster	5241	130	345	20	6874	366304	13762	5377	193	12068	1784	31	......	...	1	.....	...	.....	14191	63	403	74	......	.....	15	12077
Winnebago	868	28	37	2	1498	100912	....	318	414	2926	353	2	......	...	.....	.....	...	.....	838	13	8	....	11	.....	....	924
Winneshiek	11473	419	108	5	11629	736619	20020	210178	394	16116	3594	17	......	..	.....	14	...	.....	21104	316	119	48	......	.....	58	17537
Woodbury	3375	47	148	3	3102	143505	17257	29542	242	7262	1510	22	......	...	.....	.....	...	.....	9356	259	686	233	4	.....	280	5812
Worth	2248	47	46	1	3039	226481	9862	2655	440	5736	769	6	21	...	....	.....	...	.....	2819	13	5	62	......	.....	....	2331
Wright	1887	66	81	....	2192	149040	4495	110	122	4378	606	11	......	...	2	....	...	....	4281	327	475	....	......	....	36	4415
Total	698205	27318	37937	4498	673523	37862540	1145803	3285400	12710	1389009	314677	9733	1126	93	148	117	4	939	3086161	85466	196063	27315	2175	340	35451	2534371

TABLE VII.

Statistics concerning Sheep; number of Pounds of Wool Shorn in 1874; *number of Sheep Killed by Dogs in* 1874; *number of Dogs; number of Stands of Bees, Pounds of Honey and Beeswax in* 1874; *Value of Products of Farm, Herd, Dairy, Orchard, Garden and Forest for* 1874.

COUNTIES.	SHEEP.																			
	No. on hand.	No. of Merino.	No. of Cotswold.	No. of Leicester.	No. of Southdown.	Other improved.	No. of pounds of wool obtained in 1874.	No. slaughtered or sold for slaughter in 1874.	No. killed by dogs in 1874.	No. of dogs.	No. stands of bees.	No. of pounds of honey and beeswax in 1874.	Value of products of the farm.	Value of market garden produce.	Value of products of the orchard.	Value of small fruit.	Value of products of the herd.	Value of products of the dairy.	Value of products of the forest.
Adair	3117	465	19	......	......	30	14689	148	119	1396	208	2483	$ 828171	$ 6700	$ 1537	$ 1001	$ 222062	$ 24916	$ 9241
Adams	3560	563	......	......	......	142	13824	364	191	1534	274	3321	695318	3854	2508	1731	193186	35668	16611
Allamakee	7372	508	......	......	......	351	23809	1097	528	2937	192	1950	1415769	7230	4113	593	247446	45095	29240
Appanoose	19690	145	19	22	22	40	63485	5444	795	2693	2772	14949	1611937	22512	24431	12107	712629	112297	53745
Audubon	41	....	......	......	......	....	930	27	5	554	124	1426	184153	2270	1067	1831	60244	17775	2476
Benton	2931	128	6	14	......	27	13242	586	166	3536	896	9547	2664995	11212	14181	6526	678379	141583	39738
Black Hawk	2391	267	77	1	3	....	14436	912	89	2590	911	6348	1898424	5033	7852	9682	466324	137294	39400
Boone	9122	842	......	......	......	385	19832	841	418	2498	1295	4152	1018453	3633	6363	6903	462260	82512	45314
Bremer	2504	106	......	20	.....	19	12132	745	208	1988	498	6169	1144620	5155	2494	2453	290180	112832	62813
Buchanan	5878	1686	......	83	......	75	20072	1092	223	2234	600	2861	2615949	3308	5678	2218	365027	149439	27397
Buena Vista	748	108	......	......	......	13	1532	31	1	524	3	20	207828	848	....	32	20695	10100	1460
Butler	6909	394	......	......	......	120	8228	296	92	1840	398	4255	1209785	1515	2472	699	245159	87980	45519
Calhoun	1020	278	......	......	......	34	1633	25	14	660	43	370	221316	3	....	....	37366	11561	....
Carroll	1964	798	......	......	......	....	5341	23	....	1034	3	10	451365	1266	570	140	74170	12034	12483
Cass	1430	61	......	......	......	29	3318	151	16	2033	161	3263	1284899	3574	1673	1020	363962	37551	18679
Cedar	3328	1774	419	43	29	92	33952	1378	287	2609	783	5418	2606149	7154	21059	14089	1043962	149373	67778
Cerro Gordo	2112	95	5	......	......	41	5379	162	45	821	114	829	591617	1766	153	117	59288	31613	19350
Cherokee	718	24	4	......	......	....	130	....	2	720	2	5	350197	306	....	65	29049	23812	2315
Chickasaw	4381	1290	10	......	......	447	14619	372	209	1723	356	4561	894656	444	569	399	165415	97279	22196

Clarke	33610	668				940	36617	2090	474	1751	550	4086	7054987	5270	10455	6062	964896	869454	195414
Clay	88						100	6	12	584			123343	792		10	15157	8602	8351
Clayton	9295	837				137	31949	2148	405	4449	391	4644	2081793	25895	20100	4503	546851	157373	93077
Clinton	8796	1048	104	234		106	22955	3805	298	4469	657	8273	3049019	13322	24583	12186	1162289	219182	14513
Crawford	4367	460	17			526	13566	966	98	1070	109	1302	483337	1138	323	1060	179516	32575	8859
Dallas	10089	524	1			743	24220	640	417	2219	698	5337	1502047	5222	21919	4492	584986	87791	24763
Davis	25144	2663	79	54		1516	78944	5602	836	2356	2162	14585	1603090	15541	34150	8536	834414	95455	52469
Decatur	21362	2021	88	114	1		55300	5793	660	2249	1033	7276	1024541	14364	15237	3482	538911	62789	41737
Delaware	11685	706				19	23314	1722	304	2582	729	7184	1690314	12984	82319	3642	605035	187303	65548
Des Moines	8128	1075	5			80	33530	2119	469	2604	850	3038	1772992	23464	63958	18710	624939	303125	112624
Dickinson	406	36					1387	17	39	304			45334	438		8	13145	7485	5098
Dubuque	12217	178	12		77	721	31602	2468	683	5854	349	9814	1636132	25240	8792	3450	646405	117905	127500
Emmet	1155	98		44			3220	197	51	237	62	303	15244	25		4	12497	13937	2693
Fayette	11353	3374	4	16	3	989	41655	1307	271	2851	720	7788	1503127	1295	4470	1637	309722	131546	73890
Floyd	4802	1612			37		19455	641	251	1767	522	.013	1367377	6327	4392	3025	230127	102657	66610
Franklin	1693	258	6			11	5682	74	57	1007	102	1275	777106	3072	116	377	194274	74416	7795
Fremont	9875	897	290				19263	368	176	2102	752	8403	1046066	4316	18161	3989	792768	42313	33901
Greene	6520	1397				310	12552	423	97	1373	209	1267	620905	3517	954	675	197581	43853	27703
Grundy	2595	462	19	1		2	8907	236	10	1476	64	972	1593977	6864	528	312	314510	52711	
Guthrie	4327	250	68			382	18310	646	199	1694	240	1815	792461	2673	4265	881	421466	47487	15197
Hamilton	833						2110	64	46	1165	112	1006	527672	1028	1648	1105	202010	53083	10011
Hancock	208	68					965	12	17	235	28	520	89405	160		20	5392	7292	6991
Hardin	4131	1264	307			140	14551	1194	117	1927	345	3276	1066627	3082	5653	2320	359871	86497	40841
Harrison	1605	29				21	6663	466	153	2049	733	15635	786627	727	1674	448	432066	58132	39402
Henry	16806	6081	114		35	809	70451	6413	1051	3123	729	4483	1765670	19301	58234	17091	1213418	117487	59003
Howard	1872	31				16	3547	293	62	1134	132	1728	734409	2004	164	140	72708	58777	10421
Humboldt	795	288					3593	93	6	621	86	117	200001	58	11	67	53428	25190	11298
Ida	91	10				79	900	6	4	165			74821	27			8689	4413	2216
Iowa	8199	914	17			2047	188334	1323	276	2764	1144	5638	2005049	30232	24708	5190	472004	68114	24897
Jackson	9034	1040	13	183	45	239	32445	1482	645	3570	517	7175	1750091	8585	19550	3067	813814	114954	78472
Jasper	15312	370	13		3	599	28526	1668	569	3779	2355	23767	2916838	10098	15607	6482	997329	126137	32390
Jefferson	21816	3462				4501	79972	5228	1130	2762	1018	4417	1530140	21314	46912	17448	912657	108218	45397
Johnson	21617	3710	11	86			56523	1790	588	3868	1102	4438	2447875	5602	30607	13321	853484	121805	75765
Jones	7743	2550	14		47	533	29055	1032	495	2751	480	5062	1896416	950	7861	5396	812089	151057	54376
Keokuk	14232	732	2	14		1536	43091	2101	732	3214	949	4891	1919728	9430	27850	10266	790467	111888	50635
Kossuth	697	91					1605	13	18	600	107	388	105306	89	6	55	36643	22563	2310
Lee	18859	3505	603	465	1458	100	62753	4743	1207	4640	1418	4279	1631518	26816	68362	16551	664410	103782	68068
Linn	7963	578	25		10	208	35541	1617	560	3850	1417	12034	2590052	19601	12259	8044	832337	212259	116166
Louisa	3986	321		4		491	16436	1023	361	1913	693	4398	1665739	6559	24085	10563	1007018	73505	66706
Lucas	7869	387		1	1	482	28383	2300	457	1836	826	5527	1030554	4004	8673	4475	515975	72644	31717
Lyon	186	4				3	810	35		182			32651	73		1	12244	3093	260

TABLE VII.—Continued.

COUNTIES.	SHEEP.																			
	No. on hand.	No. of Merino.	No. of Cotswold.	No. of Leicester.	No. of Southdown.	Other improved.	No. of pounds of wool obtained in 1874.	No. slaughtered or sold for slaughter in 1874.	No. killed by dogs in 1874.	No. of dogs.	No. stands of bees.	No. of pounds of honey and beeswax in 1874.	Value of products of the farm.	Value of market garden produce.	Value of products of the orchard.	Value of small fruit.	Value of products of the herd.	Value of products of the dairy.	Value of products of the forest.
Madison	13237	2185				16	49827	6244	676	2411	638	9099	1709030	12344	15968	9823	991296	79825	36737
Mahaska	38238	5908	50	1		2480	199384	5155	1228	3408	2301	14262	2195785	26771	32053	15408	1147967	155883	56566
Marion	22704	1566	155			2254	99591	3409	472	2048	1025	10920	2181346	8722	25062	8790	869614	103102	41315
Marshall	7062	784				182	13249	940	154	2502	608	4047	2368278	19152	15099	18528	590713	141945	34153
Mills	941	78			5		3940	312	4	2008	473	3218	1083509	7520	16170	5726	716952	46206	44101
Mitchell	3078	264	19			90	11828	528	86	1488	491	8690	1591878	1628	448	1038	949[illegible]8	64174	30822
Monona	3439	617	7				14287	297	28	1141	504	10851	447665	2972	661	869	223424	27443	17722
Monroe	15039	2975			88	1772	42090	3640	741	2100	1029	6867	938362	9702	13814	6320	434462	54798	25535
Montgomery	701						3191	45	57	1972	305		1072127	817	2404	683	304791	36453	12404
Muscatine	4550	2067	1		10	119	20317	1318	269	2865	616	1967	1747906	9795	22672	15112	694378	88909	31413
O'Brien	25	9			1		105	8	3	351	1		191542	10551			20278	13216	39
Osceola	180						300			249			69581	115			1435	5219	
Page	11574	133				157	22297	622	268	2907	805	3825	1293463	4221	17877	6283	714592	54708	27612
Palo Alto	587	94	49				505	5	1	504	1	30	96616	156		13	16158	22862	1643
Plymouth	680	1				12	436	9		865			434123	1273	25	33	33937	13008	2055
Pocahontas	644	24				49	126	6		470			112666	12			21877	15188	
Polk	8830	316	265	11			23465	1511	291	2965	1299	7944	2140023	22887	18926	17081	674011	109603	51134
Pottawattamie	1936	308	3			901	6847	524	76	3640	287	2777	1252629	17312	12183	10829	319836	116536	107852
Poweshiek	4547	1114					20913	525	440	2375	566	3013	2393022	3542	7963	4790	818917	114636	13668
Ringgold	6119	661		708			16686	1171	175	1420	288	2865	1115782	16408	3607	2349	339238	40254	43123
Sac	1248	438		783		100	2210	18		489	27	215	238880	142	89	32	110925	22026	6352
Scott	8406	415	260			7	13874	1465	122	5398	248	1473	3041873	15213	41037	22322	731742	192777	17382
Shelby	828	3					3530	514	39	1121	96	2620	573046	3347		406	91920	25853	13122
Sioux	89	12	29				438	4		629			166980	12			5756	9935	
Story	5490	790			20		15636	444	135	1970	1011	4716	1033743	6941	7440	7143	336715	125338	41126

Tama	3851	545	26	......	......	....	10874	449	71	3092	542	1785	316405	4383	8463	5142	478394	167025	37285
Taylor	5550	16	4	......	......	....	18787	566	254	1904	556	3020	908476	3799	7259	1061	441269	41780	25000
Union	3422	22	......	......	......	204	7802	716	60	1193	261	1755	624260	4977	3483	621	196328	29733	11451
48 Van Buren	83873	3427	271	16	13	....	138264	5821	1309	2460	1608	6802	1439586	15053	53789	10941	689620	120276	53882
Wapello	18790	506	8	3	5	1518	63295	4068	1721	3102	1077	4945	1455319	16633	24666	11039	944974	115723	54894
Warren	13081	322	26	221	......	25	45357	2575	734	2665	1213	10413	2208392	17861	27889	10173	888061	91392	70013
Washington	10673	1653	......	4	5	175	40534	2784	588	2935	1016	4063	2085264	7544	53709	21864	862506	113664	62292
Wayne	16862	387	1	......	......	497	43204	2274	433	2223	1270	12395	1366376	8472	12952	10493	703012	65276	13528
Webster	2306	713	102	......	24	6	7974	495	112	1773	508	11594	733342	1345	1036	1094	189104	72418	10326
Winnebago	750	53	......	......	......	....	3431	253	93	416	124	1965	140219	1919	84	116	8381	8373	....
Winneshiek	10627	12	......	......	......	1026	38865	2310	429	2695	214	2628	2265252	5016	2810	1543	350598	118314	127665
Woodbury	1258	103	7	......	......	....	2415	151	58	1269	95	1000	298209	7434	....	145	86217	23233	13782
Worth	2072	102	......	......	......	531	4592	353	83	774	18	240	396506	389	62	100	51620	40809	4632
Wright	340	55	....	......	......	....	1083	19	15	636	87	416	288685	67	150	126	70638	30644	5555
Total	724204	82209	3654	3146	1942	31460	2340914	129406	28934	197509	54836	432522	124407078	726229	1215659	488259	42261039	8398212	3467020

TABLE VIII.

Showing the average yield per acre of certain Agricultural Products, and pounds of Wool per Sheep, in the several counties, for the year 1874.

COUNTIES.	Bushels spring wheat.	Bushels winter wheat.	Bushels corn.	Bushels rye.	Bushels oats.	Bushels barley.	Bushels buckwheat.	Tons tame grass.	Bushels Irish potatoes.	Bushels sweet potatoes.	Bushels onions.	Gallons sorghum.	Lbs. of wool per sheep.
Adair	15.7	50.	45.4	18.7	35.4	24.2	12.	.7	87.	......	57.	108.5	4.7
Adams	15.6	25.	38.	18.7	35.7	21.7	10.3	1.1	62.	......	76.	84.3	3.8
Allamakee	15.1	10.8	37.2	14.	34.6	25.4	16.7	1.	101.1	......	......	100.	8.2
Appanoose	8.	10.3	36.7	10.	28.2	......	13.2	.7	94.7	120.	72.2	101.6	3.2
Audubon	12.9	10.	42.7	16.6	42.2	20.8	13.5	1.5	120.	103.3	......	114.	20.2
Benton	13.5	40.	40.	16.3	28.7	19.1	12.7	.3	94.5	106.4	68.	75.4	4.5
Black Hawk	12.3	......	35.3	12.3	32.	20.	10.5	.6	76.8	......	......	70.8	6.
Boone	13.2	7.6	34.5	16.7	40.	24.5	15.2	1.7	76.4	77.3	......	133.6	2.1
Bremer	13.1	......	35.4	11.9	36.3	20.2	10.3	.8	81.2	......	......	82.4	4.
Buchanan	12.6	......	37.	15.2	31.8	18.1	12.6	1.1	85.	......	......	92.7	3.5
Buena Vista	10.4	......	29.	9.2	24.	11.4	7.	.7	70.	......	......	70.	2.
Butler	13.4	35.	33.	13.3	30.4	21.3	11.5	.7	82.6	......	123.4	67.	1.2
Calhoun	9.9	15.	33.	11.5	24.5	15.	13.	.4	68.8	......	......	13.	1.6
Carroll	12.7	7.	34.3	9.	33.2	22.5	10.1	.7	65.5	......	......	68.	2.7
Cass	16.8	......	46.8	......	19.3	26.7	10.	.7	89.6	104.	154.4	98.3	2.3
Cedar	15.8	11.3	36.3	13.7	33.3	22.	7.	.8	96.7	26.4	74.1	77.7	2.5
Cerro Gordo	14.6	......	27.9	15.	31.6	23.	10.5	.8	74.	......	52.5	80.3	2.5
Cherokee	12.6	......	33.3	15.4	32.6	20.	7.	.3	72.8	......	......	104.7	2.8
Chickasaw	16.	21.	36.	18.3	38.	24.1	12.8	1.	80.7	......	50.	89.2	3.3
Clarke	12.	8.	40.4	13.8	29.8	23.	20.2	.7	52.9	56.	8.5	64.7	1.9
Clay	8.7	......	20.4	9.3	22.2	16.4	7.	1.1	59.7	......	......	50.7	1.2
Clayton	15.	15.6	39.6	13.4	33.4	24.8	15.3	1.1	102.2	......	36.	86.3	3.4
Clinton	14.7	35.6	34.2	15.5	30.	20.9	16.	.9	87.5	152.5	165.7	78.5	2.6
Crawford	13.5	......	36.1	17.9	52.1	19.8	9.4	.8	79.5	125.	......	93.6	3.1
Dallas	15.2	23.2	43.1	18.	33.7	24.	12.4	1.2	110.4	138.	49.5	107.6	2.4
Davis	5.7	10.4	34.	9.	25.3	......	11.6	.7	108.8	72.5	......	111.8	3.1
Decatur	9.3	15.	35.	12.6	33.2	19.	15.2	1.1	88.7	145.	67.	91.2	2.5
Delaware	12.2	10.	30.1	7.2	30.6	23.5	13.	1.2	97.5	136.	47.7	78.4	2.
Des Moines	10.6	13.5	22.4	10.2	31.	17.3	18.1	.7	96.6	95.5	12.3	17.1	4.1
Dickinson	4.5	......	13.9	10.	15.5	5.	6.5	...	36.2	......	......	53.4	3.4
Dubuque	13.	20.5	26.8	13.1	25.6	22.3	13.	1.5	79.9	......	151.6	66.2	2.5
Emmet	......	......	......	......	......	......	......	......	37.4	......	......	17.4	2.8
Fayette	14.2	21.	34.9	11.3	33.9	20.	13.6	1.	98.7	......	46.1	100.3	3.6
Floyd	15.1	......	24.2	15.2	31.5	20.3	10.5	1.	71.8	......	134.3	61.3	4.
Franklin	14.6	......	31.5	18.8	34.4	21.5	16.2	.7	84.	......	80.6	61.2	3.3
Fremont	15.6	19.7	23.	3.1	33.1	23.4	9.3	1.	61.	57.1	5.7	87.3	2.
Greene	13.2	22.	35.9	14.8	28.6	28.3	11.	.8	89.1	26.3	......	78.	2.
Grundy	14.4	......	36.8	13.7	34.1	19.4	11.3	.5	89.2	......	175.6	60.9	3.4
Guthrie	14.3	12.	43.	16.7	37.3	23.7	15.1	.9	96.1	126.7	139.	103.6	4.2
Hamilton	14.2	......	32.7	15.2	32.9	18.2	7.7	1.	68.8	......	......	88.8	2.5
Hancock	14.3	......	28.	...	36.	17.	10.	1.2	83.	......	......	68.7	4.6
Hardin	12.9	......	34.8	16.6	32.5	16.6	16.2	.9	77.4	......	......	96.9	3.5
Harrison	......	25.	36.2	7.7	20.	11.3	15.1	.8	68.6	112.1	......	88.8	4.1
Henry	11.9	12.5	35.8	11.7	26.7	25.5	17.1	.8	136.	320.5	59.	118.7	4.1
Howard	16.1	......	31.	......	33.3	28.2	13.6	1.1	120.5	......	......	......	2.
Humboldt	10.	......	30.	9.	22.8	13.6	6.2	......	80.7	70.5	......	104.5	4.5
Ida	15.7	......	47.1	......	30.9	20.7	......	1.3	87.1	......	......	......	9.8
Iowa	13.8	30.	43.4	17.5	27.1	21.8	14.	.9	102.	114.8	......	100.3	4.3

TABLE VIII.—Continued.

COUNTIES.	Bushels spring wheat.	Bushels winter wheat.	Bushels corn.	Bushels rye.	Bushels oats.	Bushels barley.	Bushels buckwheat.	Tons tame grass.	Bushels Irish potatoes.	Bushels sweet potatoes.	Bushels onions.	Gallons sorghum.	Lbs. of wool per sheep.
Jackson	12 6	16.2	30.8	12.	22.	19.1	13.7	.7	77.7	......	21.2	76.5	3.5
Jasper	13.8	......	45.1	19.8	34.8	23.4	15.6	.7	88.7	80.	359.5	112.8	1.8
Jefferson	10.1	10.7	30.7	12.6	31.8	19.4	17.8	.7	119.	88.	......	101.6	3.6
Johnson	14.9	12.7	40.9	13.1	29.4	21.6	15.	.8	100.8	91.5	114.8	81.5	2.6
Jones	12.8	13.	29.2	15.	25.4	21.6	9.2	.8	90.	......	......	69.	3.6
Keokuk	11.1	9.2	43.9	10.8	28.7	18.4	17.8	.9	112.2	106.1	43.2	110.6	3.
Kossuth	......	......	12.2	......	5.4	......	10.	1.2	35.8	......	......	55.3	2.3
Lee	6.6	13.	36.5	10.8	23.6	14.9	12.4	.7	81.4	100.	102.3	83.	3.3
Linn	12.6	......	37.4	11.6	25.8	19.3	13.	1.3	100.	171.	......	107.5	4.4
Louisa	12.1	11.7	44.	10.	25.8	23.5	11.8	.6	95.3	66.4	......	62.1	4.1
Lucas	11.	10.6	40.4	12.8	27.6	16.	17.8	.8	101.	84.2	......	123.2	3.6
Lyon	9.4	......	3.9	......	3.7	17.7	6.	......	13.7	......	......	59.5	4.3
Madison	16.7	19.4	42.5	20.3	32.6	27.4	13.1	1.	110.8	87.1	24.	89.1	3.7
Mahaska	11.5	13.1	44.9	13.1	29.8	17.5	13.9	.8	113.7	204.7	67.2	117.7	2.8
Marion	13.2	11.7	45.3	13.6	30.7	21.6	15.9	.9	112.1	110.3	157.5	99.3	2.6
Marshall	16.1	10.	41.4	15.8	34.2	21.	13.7	.6	87.2	116.	206.	38.7	1.8
Mills	14.	14.	25.7	13.6	35.6	21.2	11.2	.3	60.1	65.5	112.6	56.4	4.1
Mitchell	16.5	......	36.5	16.5	38.5	26.2	9.4	1.	120.7	......	......	162.	3.8
Monona	11.9	......	37.9	20.6	28.8	24.6	8.2	......	85.3	148.5	......	85.8	4.1
Monroe	8.7	21.5	38 1	8.6	20.9	...	8.6	1.2	106.9	......	......	109.	2.7
Montgomery	17.5	20.7	36.7	15.8	37.	25.7	......	1.1	71.5	108.1	65.	118.2	4.5
Muscatine	12.8	10.	31.3	11.5	30.5	25.	14.8	.7	90.2	68.	104.4	74.3	4.4
O'Brien	10.5	......	16 6	12.2	17.3	16.4	16.6	1.	62.3	......	......	25.	4.2
Osceola	8.5	......	6.8	......	19.3	10.9	......	......	75.3	......	......	......	1.6
Page	15.6	16.5	31.3	15.5	35.5	25.3	10.9	1.	64.4	90.	151.5	60.5	1.9
Palo Alto	2.7	......	21.5	......	15.6	......	......	......	56.7	......	......	47.	1.1
Plymouth	13.1	16.	17.4	9.1	28.9	20.	......	1.	44.5	67.	......	62.	......
Pocahontas	4.1	......	25.5	11.1	15.9	8.31	6.4	......	65.2	......	......	47.4	......
Polk	14.9	19.	42.2	16.4	35.4	23.6	13.2	1.1	106.7	126.9	72.1	97.	2.6
Pottawattamie	17.6	7.5	37.	20.	31.8	19.3	21.3	1.2	69.8	128.8	155.5	110.1	3.5
Poweshiek	13.3	......	41.1	12.2	29.2	16.5	10.	.7	110.2	15.7	145.1	113.5	4.8
Ringgold	7.2	14.4	32.1	13.8	27.9	19.	12.9	1.2	78.9	45.2	......	95.8	2.6
Sac	10.	......	32.2	10.1	21.6	16.2	7.6	.9	79.4	......	......	99.6	1.7
Scott	15.9	15.4	37.6	10.2	33.2	22.4	19.6	.9	72.9	136.	150.8	96.	1.6
Shelby	14.4	......	39.	16.4	31.8	22.1	9.7	3.3	72.6	......	......	79.1	4.2
Sioux	11.3	......	4.7	6.	9.8	15.5	......	2.	20.7	46.3	......	32.5	4.9
Story	12.4	......	34.7	12.5	30.4	19.2	14.6	.6	67.	77.5	52.	71.9	2.8
Tama	14.8	......	38.8	13.4	28.3	19.5	14.	.6	80.	......	......	68.5	2.8
Taylor	13.3	12.5	29.4	13.2	30.8	18.5	13.	1.	85.	97.	77.4	87.9	3.3
Union	8.4	18.1	47.	12.3	30.6	21.7	12.8	1.	95.3	......	......	128.1	2.2
Van Buren	7.8	11.1	38.3	8.9	28.	8.3	17.4	.7	101.3	107.	......	106.4	4.8
Wapello	9.	10.	37.5	10.1	25.3	18.5	18.1	.6	105.4	141.8	38.1	102.	3.3
Warren	13.8	15.	44.3	14.	33.5	22.7	14.5	1.	125.9	54.	......	111.4	3.4
Washington	11.2	9.8	38.6	12.8	28.8	20.5	16.	.7	109.6	85.4	62.3	97.8	3.9
Wayne	7.3	8.5	36.6	8.8	27.7	16.4	13.7	.7	99.	......	......	85.8	2.5
Webster	12.7	......	32.	11.3	27.7	21.4	15.	.9	83.1	......	......	86.	3.4
Winnebago	18.1	24.5	38.	13.2	33.9	20.	14.4	1.9	70.	......	......	120.	4.5
Winneshiek	16.1	......	33.1	14.	34.	22.6	13.6	.9	64.	......	......	......	3.6
Woodbury	14.3	......	33.4	15.	30.	11.1	......	.5	60 7	108.3	102.2	98.5	2.
Worth	17.7	......	34.6	......	36.3	22.4	17.1	1.2	81.9	......	......	72.7	2.2
Wright	14.3	......	27.8	11.3	32.7	18.9	11.	.7	70.6	......	......	86.5	3.4

TABLE IX.

Showing, by Counties, the Number and Character of Manufac-
Used, Average Number of Hands Employed, Raw Material
Assessors in 1875.

COUNTIES.	Number of manufacturing establishments.	CHARACTER OF ESTABLISHMENTS, OR OF GOODS MADE.																		
		Agricultural implements.	Blacksmithing.	Boots and Shoes.	Breweries.	Brick.	Carpentering.	Carriages and wagons.	Clothing.	Foundry.	Furniture.	Machinery.	Millinery and dress-making.	Printing.	Saddlery and harness.	Tin, copper, and sheet-iron ware.	Woolen goods.	Flouring and grist mills.	Lumber.	Miscellaneous.
Adair	3																			
Adams																				
Allamakee																				
Appanoose	44		4	2		2	5	3	1	1	3		4	2	4	2		3	1	7
Audubon																				
Benton	13		4	2				1								1		2		
Black Hawk	36	1		2	2			4	4			1			3	3	1	7	1	9
Boone	53	10	2	1	2		4	2			1		3		4	6	1	6	4	
Bremer	40	1		7		1		5	2		1				4	2	3	3	3	6
Buchanan																				
Buena Vista	6		1								1				1	2		1		
Butler																				
Calhoun	30		4	3			5				3		3	2	5			1	4	
Carroll	21		3	2	1	1		2			2		4	2	2	3		2		
Cass																				
Cedar																				
Cerro Gordo																				
Cherokee																				
Chickasaw																				
Clarke																				
Clay																				
Clayton	116	1	2	9	7	3		15	3	1	6				8	4	1	13	26	11
Clinton	67		3	3		1			2	2	3			1	4	3		13	4	
Crawford																				
Dallas	22	1		1				4							4		1	10	1	
Davis	63		16	7		3	5	4	2		3		4	5	6	2		4	2	
Decatur	30	1		2			4				1		2		1	1	1	6	4	
Delaware	14							13									1			
Des Moines	12		2	2		1		1			1				1					4
Dickinson	2																	2		
Dubuque	212		2	2	4			1									2	16	2	183
Emmet																				
Fayette	42		1	2	1	4		4		3	2				3		1	8	4	1
Floyd	67	4	3	9	3	3		6	4	1	2	2	2	1	5	5	1	7	3	
Franklin																				
Fremont	85	1	24	9	1	9	4	1		1			10	2	7			11	5	
Greene																				
Grundy																				
Guthrie	22			3				2			2				5	3	2	3		
Hamilton																				
Hancock																				
Hardin	26		1	3		1		6			3	1			2			5		
Harrison	15										1				1		1	7	4	1
Henry	100		10	14	2	3	1	10		1	5	3	19	2	6		1	11	6	
Howard																				
Humboldt	14		3	3				1					1	1	1	2		2		
Ida	1																	1		
Iowa																				

TABLE IX.

turing Establishments, the Kinds of Goods Made, Kinds of Power Consumed, and Value of Goods Made in 1874, *as returned by the*

STEAM POWER.		WATER POWER.		Average of hands employed in 1874.	RAW MATERIAL CONSUMED IN 1874.								Value of goods made in 1874.
Number of engines.	Horse power.	Number of wheels.	Horse power.		Tons pig and scrap iron.	Cubic feet of wood.	Pounds of wool.	Pounds of leather.	Bushels of flax seed.	Bushels of wheat.	Bushels of corn.	Bushels of barley.	
2	90	...	...	6	...	...	...	...	...	...	...	...	$ 1450
...	...	...	...	...	...	...	...	...	...	...	...	...	...
7	156	16	240	199	250	3539274	27020	8000	...	280000	10400	7000	745072
6	119	1	32	135	150	7420	7000	21800	...	55400	15700	4500	186799
...	...	...	...	...	...	...	...	...	...	...	...	...	...
2	60	1	30	18	...	500	...	1200	...	10149	4597	...	20822
5	87	38	216	194	1892	44900	22600	18800	...	489000	191000	3500	386090
12	134	3	25	141	...	133397	1201	21000	...	121865	42150	4500	238214
1	30	15	341	103	...	33570	3200	25600	...	110000	8000	3200	168010
...	...	...	...	...	...	...	...	...	...	...	...	...	...
1	40	...	...	11	9400	500	4000	1200	...	22500	2500	2500	27698
...	...	2	16	3	...	1200	...	...	...	3000	4000	1000	2900
...	...	...	...	...	...	...	...	...	...	...	...	...	...
...	...	1	20	9	...	2200	...	...	...	10000	500	250	6820
...	...	...	...	...	...	...	...	...	...	...	...	...	...
...	...	...	...	1	...	300	...	...	...	...	...	...	...
...	...	...	...	...	...	...	...	...	...	...	...	...	...
...	...	4	93	2	1	914643	...	...	...	14132	10060	10	10983
1	19	...	...	5	...	...	...	...	...	...	...	...	...
...	...	...	...	...	2560	...	...	...	...	...	...	...	1335
...	...	...	...	...	...	...	...	...	...	...	...	...	...
20	657	26	394	397	62	1051300	10000	16450	...	452223	15027	7590	945050
37	3177	11	188	1853	527	...	...	38900	...	154363	27198	...	2399435
...	...	...	...	...	...	...	...	...	...	...	...	...	...
3	67	16	265	44	21	9000	16000	8200	...	95650	31525	...	86750
7	210	...	...	36	...	5400	...	...	2000	48000	52000	...	25000
15	471	2	25	84	1	259720	6000	1019	...	20130	18700	...	59822
4	103	16	137	141	30	29012	...	22838	...	122592	62490	7000	281816
26	988	1	15	1048	25400	5955800	...	10680	3500	464061	7055	32760	2079029
...	...	4	59	4	...	...	...	...	...	45000	11000	100	6000
86	1039	24	286	2334	738	5754994	3000	222325	...	516610	104400	159900	6316635
...	...	...	...	...	...	...	...	...	...	...	...	...	...
7	118	17	470	148	50	210550	...	5500	...	242900	15400	6100	152150
6	138	10	210	168	32	97077	...	21119	...	241000	27000	19000	387771
...	...	...	...	21	1	45694	...	5000	...	1829	12445	...	17825
11	179	6	33	38	...	...	...	6300	...	70000	10500	...	836000
...	...	...	...	...	...	...	...	...	...	...	...	...	...
...	...	...	...	...	...	...	...	...	...	...	...	...	...
...	...	2	20	40	...	100	65000	7200	...	96000	22000	...	102250
...	...	...	...	...	...	...	...	...	...	...	...	...	...
...	...	...	...	...	...	...	...	...	...	...	...	...	...
1	10	10	...	80	1	6000	...	9000	...	52500	11000	900	139967
6	149	10	235	34	...	...	4000	1500	...	29623	20700	200	171500
18	375	20	147	302	26500	242300	85000	116200	...	237400	95850	3000	508490
...	...	...	...	...	...	...	...	...	...	...	...	...	...
...	...	1	...	...	1000	...	...	2375	...	11523	14800	500	6980
...	...	...	1	4	...	...	...	...	...	10000	500	...	200
4	140	6	185	103	250000	...	...	...	113175	...	...	...	242000

TABLE IX.—Continued.

COUNTIES.	Number of manufacturing establishments.	CHARACTER OF ESTABLISHMENTS, OR GOODS MADE.																		
		Agricultural implements.	Blacksmithing.	Boots and shoes.	Breweries.	Brick.	Carpentering.	Carriages and wagons.	Clothing.	Foundry.	Furniture.	Machinery.	Millinery and dress-making.	Printing.	Saddlery and harness.	Tin, copper, and sheet-iron ware.	Woolen goods.	Flouring and grist mills.	Lumber.	Miscellaneous.
Jackson	43			15	1	3		6	4	1	1				4			3	3	2
Jasper	119		21	14		5	11	7	2	1	8		12	7	15	8		10		
Jefferson																				
Johnson	147		10	8	3	2	15	9	3	1	4		14	4	8	7	3	5		35
Jones																				
Keokuk	68		4	4		2	3	4		1	2	1	2	2	3	1	2	9	7	9
Kossuth																				
Lee	305	5	44	61	6	7	55	17	20	1	8	3	40	6	12	7	4	7	6	
Linn	96	2	4	15	3	8	2	8	4		3			3	10	6	2	11	1	8
Louisa	23			3				1	3		1	1	3	2	2		1			1
Lucas					1															
Lyon	4																			
Madison	33	1	3	5				4			2		2	2	3	3	1	4		
Mahaska	47	1	1			4	1	2		1					1		1	9	3	19
Marion	47			9		1		2	2	1	3				6		2	7	2	
Marshall	61	1	2	6	3	2	1	8	3	2	3	1		2	3	3		5		9
Mills	57	1	5	4		4	4	5	5	1	1	1	6	3	7	4		4		
Mitchell	30	1		2	1			3	2	2				2	2	3	3	7	1	
Monona	5							1		1								2		1
Monroe	32		6	4			2	1	1		3	1	5	2	3	2		2		
Montgomery	15			2	1	2									4			5	1	
Muscatine	88	2	9	8	5	4		4	2	2	3	4		4	6	4	1	4		13
O'Brien																				
Osceola	9		2	1							1		1	1	1	2				
Page	31		2	4				2							4	3		2	4	10
Palo Alto																				
Plymouth	32		6	5		1	3	1	2				4	2	2	3		3		
Pocahontas																				
Polk	141	5	6	16	2		1	10	2	8	8		3	15	11	12	1	3	1	33
Pottawattamie	194	1	31	16	3	9	33	9	11	2	9	1	17	7	8	10		12	6	
Poweshiek	3																			
Ringgold																				
Sac	12		2	1			1	1	1		1		1	1	1			2		
Scott	139	6	1	20	4	3	2	4	15	2	4	3		5	8	3	1	4	5	50
Shelby																				
Sioux																				
Story	4																	4		
Tama	22			3	1	1		2	3		1		1		1	1		5		3
Taylor																				
Union																				
Van Buren	67			8				4			6				6	2	5	7	7	3
Wapello	77	1	1	9	2			4	5	2	2	4	3	5	2	2		8	4	19
Warren	29	1		4				1						3	4	2		4	4	1
Washington	42	1		7				5			5				5	2	2	4	1	7
Wayne	10		2					2			2							4		
Webster	10										1						1	3	1	4
Winnebago																				
Winneshiek																				
Woodbury																				
Worth	5																			
Wright																				
Total	3203	48	238	342	59	90	162	212	108	40	122	27	166	96	219	129	45	203	131	449

TABLE IX.—Continued.

Steam power.		Water power		Average of hands employed in 1874.	Raw material consumed in 1874.								Value of goods made in 1874.
Number of engines.	Horse power.	Number of wheels.	Horse power.		Tons pig and scrap iron.	Cubic feet of wood.	Pounds of wool.	Pounds of leather.	Bushels of flax seed	Bushels of wheat.	Bushels of corn.	Bushels of barley.	
11	304	31	450	271	16	506670	7684	11335	....	245961	59515	3450	961041
9	315	5	170	294	50	30200	....	2275	....	288000	110000	7000	507050
10	171	.....	.....	100	174	108000	103000	19110	....	50000	10000	....	172750
13	359	18	602	549	3396	308200	10000	60435	94000	157300	15483	41464	1058434
1	20	2	8	48	100	41900	....	13636	....	21000	6800	....	82560
13	262	15	266	161	50	1133200	24780	17200	....	169180	43200	....	357457
.....	....	.....	.....	....	....	....	....	....	....	....	....	....	....
37	1968	1	35	2956	704	1328885	7100	35455	....	253574	44236	12500	3339562
17	523	28	276	788	76	41536	80000	162400	63000	326000	125700	30000	3119100
5	165	4	40	74	20	300	7000	5600	....	78000	11000	....	201911
.....	....	.....	.....	....	....	....	....	....	....	....	....	....	....
.....	....	5	70	8	3	20000	....	....	....	26248	3689	676	20700
8	123	1	.....	131	42	270600	50000	22800	....	130000	1500	....	403290
10	269	15	75	201	176	4500	45000	800	....	92200	6000	....	472127
12	344	1	.....	72	50	385400	36300	26500	3000	135000	1000	....	832710
7	103	8	207	245	140	27000	2000	32400	60000	165000	27000	7000	609330
1	5	8	90	13	5	64048	....	1910	....	78434	52920	....	113850
3	26	20	255	102	100	55040	40000	15330	....	225000	18000	1500	326183
6	105	3	.....	21	....	....	....	....	....	30300	5100	....	57420
3	109	.....	.....	22	....	....	....	....	....	13500	1360	2000	23319
1	30	10	80	56	....	44800	....	7194	....	118009	48255	1400	162612
16	770	3	.....	623	1330	2700	....	40950	....	22500	10800	18400	799925
.....	....	.....	.....	....	....	....	....	....	....	80	574	....	....
.....	....	.....	.....	....	....	....	....	600	....	....	....	....	1500
4	90	8	98	43	5	13000	50000	11500	....	63800	6000	....	66350
.....	....	.....	.....	....	....	....	....	....	....	....	....	....	....
1	....	5	.....	....	....	....	....	....	....	....	....	....	....
.....	....	.....	.....	....	....	....	....	....	....	....	....	....	....
38	1179	1	17	991	732	346405	22610	76815	60000	334000	53000	13000	2556427
18	500	8	.....	510	650	35560	....	....	....	218500	25000	....	....
1	12	.....	1	7	1	898	....	2840	....	....	....	....	12863
.....	....	.....	.....	....	....	....	....	....	....	....	....	....	....
.....	....	2	57	18	7	500	200	1200	....	11500	700	....	....
29	1469	1	.....	1803	836	2890507	130000	141659	....	761500	21250	205750	4714871
.....	....	.....	.....	....	....	....	....	....	....	....	....	....	....
.....	....	.....	.....	....	....	....	....	....	....	....	....	....	....
3	120	2	.....	46	....	105160	....	6950	....	67400	9500	100	79403
.....	....	8	134	44	....	5020	....	6540	....	78500	13000	....	88895
.....	....	.....	.....	....	....	....	....	....	....	....	....	....	....
.....	....	.....	.....	....	....	....	....	....	....	....	....	....	....
17	333	25	280	246	4	318600	184095	17580	....	99080	32822	....	431922
21	586	.....	.....	453	....	213000	....	265	....	59000	31700	10200	1134815
6	165	4	117	76	....	593128	14400	....	....	163500	13000	66	179345
3	72	2	32	78	309	92060	15500	29350	....	37277	7065	....	104466
5	85	.....	.....	20	5	704	6000	....	....	24000	6500	....	25535
7	235	3	60	63	....	....	....	....	....	92000	28000	....	167000
.....	....	.....	.....	....	....	....	....	....	....	....	....	....	....
.....	....	.....	.....	....	....	....	....	....	....	....	....	....	....
2	115	.....	.....	....	63	100300	150	....	....	170000	10000	....	13275
.....	....	2	40	5	....	....	21	200	....	12940	3200	375	24458
.....	....	.....	.....	....	....	....	....	....	....	....	....	....	....
577	19498	512	7143	18854	327660	27432673	1089861	1263035	388675	8845730	1711306	618331	39263319

TABLE X.

Statistics of Mines and Quarries for 1874 *as returned by the Assessors in* 1875.

COUNTIES.	COAL MINES.				OTHER MINES AND QUARRIES.			
	Number banks open.	Number hands employed.	Number of tons mined in 1874.	Value of same.	Number.	Value of building stone.	Lime.	Aggregate.
Adair								
Adams	9	21	3000	11250				
Allamakee								
Appanoose	46	282	57358	110817			450	
Audubon								
Benton						2000		
Black Hawk						5000	3000	
Boone	10	326	955	2505				
Bremer					1	180		
Buchanan								
Buena Vista								
Butler					5			350
Calhoun								
Carroll								
Cass								
Cedar								
Cerro Gordo								
Cherokee								
Chickasaw								
Clarke								
Clay								
Clayton								
Clinton								2135
Crawford								
Dallas	2	20	27	8400	5	15290		
Davis	5	38	11430	25566		166		
Decatur								
Delaware						582		
Des Moines						13600		
Dickinson								
Dubuque								
Emmet								
Fayette								
Floyd					4	950		950
Franklin								
Fremont								
Greene								
Grundy						800		800
Guthrie	8	25	1183	4155				
Hamilton	5	21	787	1574		1000		
Hancock								
Hardin	6	46	7193	27340				
Harrison					2	5500		
Henry	2	2	120	1090	6	14450		15200
Howard								
Humboldt						2010		
Ida								
Iowa								

TABLE X.—Continued.

COUNTIES.	COAL MINES.				OTHER MINES AND QUARRIES.			
	Number banks open.	Number hands employed.	Number of tons mined in 1874.	Value of same.	Number.	Value of building stone.	Lime.	Aggregate.
Jackson				$		$		
Jasper	23	195	31132	70802		100		100
Jefferson	12	122	26605	63270	1	1000		
Johnson						54135		54135
Jones						1533		
Keokuk	17	94	17120	54150	23	9770		
Kossuth								
Lee								
Linn						3074		3074
Louisa						650		
Lucas	40	81	6997	17720	2	730		
Lyon								
Madison						100		
Mahaska	29	419	135502	239719	9	4270		
Marion	37	95		20791		5450		29777
Marshall	1	2	600	1800		27700		29500
Mills					1	2000		2000
Mitchell								
Monona								
Monroe	19	219	236077	487437	2	40		
Montgomery						6620		6640
Muscatine								
O'Brien								
Osceola								
Page								
Palo Alto								
Plymouth								
Pocahontas								
Polk	7	222	69327	180726				
Pottawattamie								
Poweshiek								
Ringgold								
Sac								
Scott	7	77	9884	20777				
Shelby								5250
Sioux								
Story						582		
Tama						200		
Taylor	3	22	1160	4320				
Union								
Van Buren	6	14	3000	4625	2	330		4925
Wapello	24	236	518644	1041198	9	20320	2000	22320
Warren	26	95	8472	24399	6	836		
Washington					6	1134		1134
Wayne	9	49	4034	9068				
Webster	19	227	78867	166641				
Winnebago								
Winneshiek								
Woodbury								
Worth								
Wright								
Total	372	2928	1231547	2600140	84	202102	5450	178290

TABLE XI.

Statistics of Colleges, Academies, and other Private Schools.

COUNTIES.	Number.	NAME OF COLLEGE OR OTHER SCHOOL.	POST OFFICE	CHARACTER OR DENOMINATION	Male instructors.	Female instructors.	SEMINARIES AND SCHOOLS OF LOWER GRADE. Male students.	SEMINARIES AND SCHOOLS OF LOWER GRADE. Female students.	COLLEGIATE DEPARTMENTS. Male students.	COLLEGIATE DEPARTMENTS. Female students.	OTHER DEPARTMENTS. Male students.	OTHER DEPARTMENTS. Female students.	Volumes in library.	Income in 1874.
Adair														
Adams														
Allamakee	1	Sisters' School	Lansing	Catholic		3	25	55						800
Appanoose														
Audubon														
Benton	1	Tilford Academy	Vinton	Independent	2	2	75	40	60	15	20	20	300	5100
Bla'k Hawk	1	Lady of Victory	Waterloo	Catholic		5	80	100					200	
Boone														
Bremer														
Buchanan														
Buena Vista														
Butler														
Calhoun														
Carroll														
Cass														
Cedar														
Cerro Gordo														
Cherokee														
Chickasaw	1	Bradford Academy	Bradford	Congregational	2	1	50	35						
Clarke														
Clay														
Clayton														
Clinton	2	Business College	Clinton	Business	2		*							
"		Roman Catholic Seminary	Lyons	Catholic		3	*							
Crawford														

Dallas														
Davis	2	Southern Iowa Normal Institute.	Bloomfield		2	1	20	30						
"		Troy Normal	Troy		2		65	50						
Decatur														
Delaware														
Des Moines	9	German Evangelical Zion	Burlington	German	1	1	60	48						750
"		First German Evangelical	"	"	2		70	45						750
"		German American	"	Germ. and Am.	1	1	44	47						
"		St. Patrick's	"	Catholic		3	60	70						
"		Burlington Business College	"	Business	3						37	3		4000
"		Burlington University	"	Baptist	3	4			30	52			2300	3200
"		R. J. Graff's	"	Private	1		30	20						900
"		St. Paul's Parish	"	Catholic		5	75	85						
"		Mrs. Darwin's	"	Private		1			25					800
Dickinson														
Dubuque	6	St. Martha's Parochial	Cascade	Catholic		4	59	61						500
"		St Peter's	Sherrill's Mt	"		1	26	25						125
"		St. Matthew's	"	Lutheran		1	7	16						20
"		St. Joseph	Farley	Catholic		1	35	25					200	300
"		Epworth Seminary	Epworth			3			40	85				1500
"			Dyersville	Catholic	1	1	40	30						400
Emmet														
Fayette	2	Norwegian Evangelical	Eldorado	Lutheran	1	1	61	81						
"		Upper Iowa University,	Fayette	Methodist	5	5			15	7	65	48	1500	3300
Floyd														
Franklin														
Fremont	1	Tabor College	Tabor	Congregational	6	3			150	75			2800	
Greene														
Grundy														
Guthrie														
Hamilton														
Hancock														
Hardin	1	Eldora Academy	Eldora	Private		3	30	30						
Harrison														
Henry	6	Iowa Wesleyan University	Mt. Pleasant	Methodist	19	10	19	13	74	45	26	26	2000	5458
"		High School and Fem. Sem.	"	Unsectarian	8	1	214	137						2000
"		German College	"	Methodist	2				32	5			500	3000
"		Mt. Pleasant Female Sem.	"	Presbyterian	2	5	3	57					300	
"		New London Academy	New Lond'n	Unsectarian	1	1	35	40						1125
"		Whittier College	Salem.	Friends.	3	3			81	91	39	25	500	2000
Howard														
Humboldt	1	Humboldt College	Humboldt	Unsectarian	4				33	23			1500	
Ida														
Iowa														

*Number of students not reported.

TABLE XI.—CONTINUED.

COUNTIES.	Number.	NAME OF COLLEGE OR OTHER SCHOOL.	POST-OFFICE	CHARACTER OR DENOMINATION	Male instructors.	Female instructors.	SEMINARIES AND SCHOOLS OF LOWER GRADE.		COLLEGIATE DEPARTMENTS.		OTHER DEPARTMENTS.		Volumes in library.	Income in 1874.
							Male students.	Female students.	Male students.	Female students.	Male students.	Female students.		
Jackson	3	Lutheran	Bellevue	Lutheran	1				13	4				
"		St. Donatus	St Donatus		1		42							420
"		St. Mary's Institute		Catholic		4		30						2500
Jasper														
Jefferson	1	Parsons College	Fairfield	Presbyterian			Just esta	blished						
Johnson		St. Agatha's Seminary	Iowa City	Catholic		12		300		25		275	200	5000
"		St. Joseph's Institute	"	"	3	4	170	103	27	25			500	3000
"		Parochial School	"	"	1		70							
"		Anawishe School	"	"		3	150	160						
"	1	*State University	"	Unsectarian										
"		Academy and Commercial	"	Private	1	3	105	30						3000
Jones	2	Olin Academy	Olin		1		22	15						
		Wyoming Independent	Wyoming			4	116	132						
Keokuk	1	Sigourney Conservatory of Music	Sigourney		1	3					17	42		
Kossuth	1	Algona College	Algona	Methodist	2	2			47	53				3300
Lee	2	Denmark Academy	Denmark	Congregational	3	4	142	130					400	2300
"		Ft. Madison Academy	Ft. Madison	Independent	2	3	44	24					800	1000
Linn	2	Cornell College	Mt. Pleas'nt	Methodist	9	9	252	207	38	15	214	192	4000	10000
"		Western College	Western	United Breth'n	7	3	103	58	38	24			1200	5412
Louisa	1	Eastern Iowa Normal	Grand View	Unsectarian	5	3	53	50			66	50	350	3214
Lucas	1	Simsons Academy	Chariton											
Lyon														
Madison														
Mahaska	3	Hopewell Academy	Hopewell		1		11	9						
"		Penn College	Oskaloosa	Friends	5	2	162	116	28	13	134	103	1100	5600
"		Oskaloosa College	"	Christian	7		39	9	12	16	134	58	500	6500
Marion	3	Caloma Academy	Caloma	Lutheran	1		5	9						

Marion		Knoxville Academy	Knoxville	Unsectarian			No Report.							
"		Iowa Central University	Pella	Baptist	3	4	78	92					780	
Marshall	4	Hanford Seminary	Hanford	Friends	2		22	26						
"		Albion Seminary	Albion	Methodist	6	4	110	140					300	3500
"		Le Grand Christian Ins.		Christian	1	1			50	50				500
"		Le Grand Friends' Seminary.		Friends	1	1			50	50				1500
Mills	3	Western Iowa Collegiate Ins.	Glenwood	Methodist	2	3			20	30				
"		Ladies Seminary	"	Congregational	1	1						10		
"		Miss Mary Bosbyshell's	"	"		1					4	10		
Mitchell	1	Cedar Valley Seminary	Osage	Baptist	2	2	56	74					100	1600
Monona														
Monroe														
Montgom'y.														
Muscatine	2	Holy Family	Muscatine	Catholic		7		200					150	
"		Wilton Collegiate Institute	Wilton	Baptist	2	1	17	17	10	4				370
O'Brien														
Osceola														
Page	1	Amity College	College Spr.		2	1	48	52						
Palo Alto														
Plymouth														
Pocahontas.														
Polk	6	Mitchell Seminary	Mitchelville	Universalist	1	4	32	40						1300
"		University of Des Moines	Des Moines	Baptist	4	2								
"		St. Ambrose	"	Catholic	1	6	130	166					200	
"		St. Mary's Ger. Cath. School	"	"		3	50	50					150	200
"			"	Swede	1		18	17						
"		Iowa Musical Institute	"	Musical	1	1					1	14		
Pot'wattmie														
Poweshiek	1	Iowa College	Grinnell	Congregational	10	2			32	37	157	101	6350	12439
Ringgold														
Sac														
Scott	9	Germon Free School	Davenport	Ger. Catholic	3		57	59						2100
"		St. Kunigunde	"	"		4	55	65					300	1500
"		Wm. Geerdt's School	"	Ger. Priv. Prim	1		40	36						1800
"		Bryant & Stratton Com. Col.	"	Commercial	8				475	25				30000
"		Academy of Im. Conception	"	Catholic		18		150				40	500	
"		St. Anthony's	"	Catholic Prim'y	1	5	160	160					400	2500
"		Miss Pretman's	"	Eng. Private	1		7	8						300
"		Griswold College	"	Episcopal	3	1					45		5000	1800
"		St. Marguerite's	"	Eng. Catholic	1	3	120	120					300	1800
Shelby														
Sioux														

* NOTE BY THE SECRETARY OF STATE.—The Iowa State University, located at Iowa City, has thirty male and four female instructors; with 180 male and 95 female students in the Preparatory Department; 112 male and 34 female students in the Collegiate Department, 87 male and 7 female students in the Medical Department, 104 male and 2 female students in the Law Department, 7000 volumes in its Library, and its income in 1874 was $54,000.

TABLE XI.—Continued.

COUNTIES.	Number.	NAME OF COLLEGE OR OTHER SCHOOL.	POST-OFFICE	CHARACTER OR DENOMINATION	Male instructors.	Female instructors.	Seminaries and schools of lower grade. Male students.	Seminaries and schools of lower grade. Female students.	Collegiate departments. Male students.	Collegiate departments. Female students.	Other departments. Male students.	Other departments. Female students.	Volumes in library.	Income in 1874.
Story	†1	State Agricultural College	Ames	Unsectarian										
Tama														
Taylor														
Union														
Van Buren	1	Birmingham Academy	Birming'am	Unsectarian	1	2	63	46						1000
Wapello	3	Sisters of Visitation	Ottumwa	Catholic		3		62		28		39	200	2600
"		St. Joseph	"	"	1	1	65							1500
"		Mrs. M. Squires'	"	Private		2	12	28			12	28	65	1200
Warren	2	Ackworth Institute	Ackworth	Friends	1	1	18		7		9	6	300	500
"		Simpson Centenary	Indianola	Methodist	9	3			104	70	10	29	400	7500
Washingt'n	1	Washington Academy	Washington	Unsectarian	3	1	101	89						2000
Wayne														
Webster	2	German Lutheran School	Fort Dodge	Ger. Lutheran	1		30	84						
"		Academy our Lady of Lourdes	"	Catholic		10	60	120						
Winnebago														
Winneshiek	2	Decorah Institute	Decorah		5		144	101						
"		Decorah Commerci'l Institute	"		3		36							
Woodbury														
Worth														
Wright														
Total	99				201	220	4198	4274	1491	812	990	1119	34645	166783

† Note by Secretary of State.—The Iowa Agricultural College, at Ames, is a State institution; has thirteen male and four female instructors, one hundred and ninety-nine male and ninety-six female students, 3,600 volumes in library, and its income in 1874, $35,000.

TABLE XII.

Showing the number of Acres of Land Assessed, the Average Value per Acre, and the Aggregate Valuation after Equalization. Also, the Aggregate Value of Town Property, Railroad Property, and of Personal Property, and Total Valuation of Taxable Property, and State Tax thereon in each County, for the year 1875.

COUNTIES.	Acres of land.	Reported value per acre.	Equalized value per acre.	Reported value of lands.	Reported value of town lots.	Increase per cent.	Decrease per cent.	Reported value of lands and town lots.	Equalized value of lands and town lots.	Value of personalty.	Value of Railroad property.	Reported total value.	Equalized total value.	State tax at two mills.
Adair	368120	$6.50	$6.50	$ 2391981	$ 86828	...	...	$ 2478809	$ 2478809	$ 426749	$ 70727	$ 2976285	$ 2976285	$ 5952.57
Adams	269532	5.64	6.76	1520709	143466	20	...	1664175	1997010	396230	338002	2398407	2731242	5462.48
Allamakee	407084	4.07	5.69	1657510	339798	40	...	1997308	2796231	580311	155583	2733202	3532125	7064.25
Appanoose	322142	7.23	7.95	2329034	310856	10	...	2639890	2903879	1305797	243970	4189657	4453646	8907.29
Audubon	278388	5.50	5.50	1521179	19458	...	...	1540637	1540637	179250	....	1719887	1719887	3439.77
Benton	450977	7.55	8.30	3406160	744739	10	...	4150899	4565988	1458182	402570	6011651	6426740	12853.48
Black Hawk	363841	6.97	8.36	2538807	921664	20	...	3460471	4152565	695835	297506	4453812	5145906	10291.81
Boone	365957	6.57	7.22	2405308	381818	10	...	2787126	3065838	716502	292559	3796187	4074899	8149.80
Bremer	274858	6.51	7.16	1789926	195471	10	...	1985397	2183936	480586	84029	2550012	2748551	5497.10
Buchanan	346627	8.34	8.34	2889977	684908	...	...	3574885	3574885	1022159	232955	4829999	4829999	9660.00
Buena Vista	327943	4.09	4.09	1341522	101304	...	...	1442826	1442826	142472	139755	1725053	1725053	3450.11
Butler	366265	5.58	6.69	2048051	196457	20	...	2244508	2693409	427261	217009	2888878	3337779	6675.56
Calhoun	338185	3.90	4.29	1319460	22197	10	...	1341657	1475822	149804	81675	1573136	1707301	3414.60
Carroll	366866	4.95	5.44	1817777	199535	...	10	2017312	2219043	184954	261723	2463989	2665720	5331.44
Cass	347984	8.06	8.06	2804040	257324	...	...	3061364	3061364	532445	293929	3887738	3887738	7775.48
Cedar	359177	11.24	10 68	4036796	381049	...	5	4417845	4196953	1203110	401024	6021979	5801087	11602.17
Cerro Gordo	358602	4.56	5.47	1639006	217050	20	...	1856056	2227267	256844	252370	2365770	2736981	5473.96
Cherokee	312004	4.59	4.59	1433685	106573	...	...	1540258	1540258	212467	163900	1916625	1916625	3833.25
Chickasaw	317349	4.43	5.31	1406034	119143	20	...	1525177	1830212	442510	118370	2086057	2391092	4782.18
Clarke	272916	6.99	6.99	1910237	259451	...	...	2169688	2169688	1023755	317388	3510831	3510831	7021.66

TABLE XII.—Continued.

COUNTIES.	Acres of land.	Reported value per acre.	Equalized value per acre.	Reported value of lands.	Reported value of town lots.	Increase per cent.	Decrease per cent.	Reported value of lands and town lots.	Equalized value of lands and town lots.	Value of personalty.	Value of Railroad property.	Reported total value.	Equalized total value.	State tax at two mills.
Clay	193251	3.93	3.93	760228	18594	..	...	778822	778822	131205	....	910027	910027	1820.05
Clayton	483988	6.25	7.18	3024214	633701	15	...	3657915	4206601	1297408	361425	5316748	5865134	11730.87
Clinton	430570	10.24	10 75	4408433	1750261	5	...	6158694	6466628	1771402	735371	8665467	8973401	17946.80
Crawford	459840	4.99	5.48	2295311	109303	10	...	2404614	2645075	242235	325068	2971917	3212378	6424.76
Dallas	372064	7.82	7.82	2911387	297214	...	...	3208601	3208601	1158537	268952	4636090	4636090	9272.18
Davis	315165	7.99	7.99	2518979	258935	...	...	2777914	2777914	1315516	239260	4332690	4332690	8665.38
Decatur	334716	5.18	6.47	1734999	150654	25	...	1885653	2357066	770143	60042	2715838	3187251	6374.50
Delaware	356759	8.95	8 51	3193195	311131	...	5	3504326	3329110	893211	244175	4641712	4466496	8932.99
Des Moines	257703	13 40	13.40	3453912	4156735	...	...	7610647	7610647	2692122	344049	10646818	10646818	21293 64
Dickinson	192136	3.09	3.09	563696	10835	...	...	574531	574531	57420	....	631951	631951	1263.90
Dubuque	376775	7.17	9.32	2701931	3486558	30	...	6188489	8045033	2668332	317590	9174411	11030955	22061.91
Emmet	222369	2.55	3.06	567078	9400	20	...	576478	691773	36181	....	612659	727954	1455.91
Fayette	460875	6.54	7.51	3016048	272425	15	...	3288473	3781743	970048	209360	4467881	4961151	9922.30
Floyd	314537	5.28	6.60	1661396	301357	25	...	1962753	2453441	416352	230940	2610045	3100733	6201.47
Franklin	365865	5.55	6.10	2020728	17792	10	...	2038520	2242372	234080	122537	2395137	2598989	5197.98
Fremont	314746	8.02	8,82	2524061	302151	10	...	2826212	3108833	873688	320932	4020832	4303453	8606.91
Greene	365134	5.37	5.63	1961844	180863	5	...	2142707	2249842	357784	321453	2821944	2929079	5858.16
Grundy	321067	5.29	6.07	1699351	9106	15	...	1708457	1964724	259468	935	1968860	2225127	4450 25
Guthrie	378219	5 27	6.32	1993860	162142	20	...	2156002	2587202	513992	226947	2896941	3328141	6656.28
Hamilton	352683	4.35	5.22	1535230	168901	20	...	1704131	2044957	362987	127600	2194718	2535544	5071.09
Hancock	361777	3.08	3.38	1114368	11330	10	...	1125698	1238267	41673	84840	1252211	1364780	2729 56
Hardin	359849	5.55	6.37	1998209	313835	15	...	2312044	2658850	369084	254988	2936116	3282922	6565 84
Harrison	439013	8.14	7.33	3571988	316612	...	10	3888600	3499740	823079	423734	5135413	4746553	9493.11
Henry	268689	10 56	10.56	2838070	859540	...	...	3697610	3697610	1528520	236400	5462530	5462530	10925.06
Howard	297082	5.05	5.80	1500523	170577	15	...	1671100	1921765	310916	109710	2091726	2342391	4684.78
Humboldt	259112	3.66	4.02	947970	50757	10	...	998727	1098599	102854	....	1101581	1201453	2402.91

Ida	263916	3.00	3.60	791739	1780	20	...	793519	952223	48720	....	842239	1000943	2001.89
Iowa	372608	8.38	7.97	3123389	208869	...	5	3332258	3165646	1020367	269212	4621837	4455225	8910.45
Jackson	401968	6.18	7.09	2484887	554053	15	...	3038940	3494781	1047511	250710	4337161	4793002	9586.00
Jasper	452040	9.25	10.17	4180559	577974	10	...	4758533	5234386	1690718	480150	6929401	7405254	14810.51
Jefferson	271660	10.17	10.17	2762932	361724	...	...	3124656	3124656	1002855	407048	4534559	4534559	9069.12
Johnson	384886	10.50	10.50	4042612	1320119	...	...	5362731	5362731	1504605	378088	7245424	7245424	14490.85
Jones	356694	8.38	8.38	2988445	427234	...	...	3415679	3415679	917483	290580	4623742	4623742	9247.48
Keokuk	363503	8.49	8.49	3087215	242699	...	...	3329914	3329914	1473649	41760	4845323	4845323	9690.65
Kossuth	501025	3.35	3.35	1677674	68196	...	...	1745870	1745870	106676	42000	1894546	1894546	3789.09
Lee	325755	9.14	9.14	2978650	3129987	...	...	6108637	6108637	2371894	355760	8736291	8836291	17672.58
Linn	455672	11.36	10.81	5178399	1890815	...	5	7069214	6715754	1795284	560266	9424764	9071304	18142.61
Louisa	249332	8.77	8.77	2188088	298484	...	...	2486572	2486572	881274	290383	3658229	3658229	7316.46
Lucas	276041	6.19	7.42	1708572	301029	20	...	2009601	2411521	792141	370144	3171886	3573806	7147.61
Lyon	322649	3.50	3.15	1130375	19108	...	10	1149483	1034535	97286	....	1246769	1131821	2263.64
Madison	356361	7.11	8.53	2532574	349773	20	...	2882347	3458816	1196307	124524	4203178	4779647	9559.29
Mahaska	360363	9.84	9.84	3546489	656835	...	...	4203324	4203324	1784018	221333	6208675	6208675	12417.35
Marion	370667	7.38	8.85	2736194	456399	20	...	3192593	3831111	1684074	76850	4953517	5592035	11184.07
Marshall	366124	6.62	8.60	2422795	663281	30	...	3086076	4011897	941487	395794	4423357	5349178	10698.36
Mills	264979	8.71	8.71	2309340	286698	...	...	2596038	2596038	1091099	510068	4197205	4197205	8394.41
Mitchell	296308	6.88	6.54	2038275	223674	...	5	2261949	2148852	447154	106645	2815748	2702651	5405.30
Monona	409802	3.39	4.74	1387415	145108	40	...	1532523	2145531	267922	90125	1890570	2503578	5007.16
Monroe	251418	7.73	7.73	1944454	300821	...	...	2245275	2245275	896227	390613	3532115	3532115	7064.23
Montgomery	267147	8.61	8.61	2301215	303961	...	...	2605176	2605176	614242	370070	3589488	3589488	7178.98
Muscatine	276994	11.38	11.38	3152046	1079157	...	...	4231203	4231203	1265158	628641	6125002	6125002	12250.00
O'Brien	282023	3.00	3.00	846069	5142	...	...	851211	851211	39464	19860	910535	910535	1821.07
Osceola	180932	3.79	3.24	685855	22439	...	15	708294	602051	69988	53970	832252	726009	1452.02
Page	347149	6.71	8.72	2330568	255136	30	...	2585704	3361414	1149338	94495	3829537	4605247	9210.49
Palo Alto	243000	3.00	3.30	736910	14940	10	...	751850	827035	94432	....	846282	921467	1842.93
Plymouth	465138	4.36	4.36	2029824	124891	...	...	2154715	2154715	126917	220575	2502207	2502207	5004.41
Pocahontas	323223	2.95	3.24	942799	9938	10	...	952737	1048010	67616	53900	1074253	1169526	2339.05
Polk	368670	13.41	13.41	4944447	3184497	...	...	8128944	8128944	2510504	485963	11125411	11125411	22250.82
Pottawattamie	586221	7.87	7.87	4611605	2143331	...	...	6754936	6754936	1480980	778526	9014442	9014442	18028.88
Poweshiek	368071	5.92	7.69	2178704	334574	30	...	2513278	3267259	1146972	371254	4031504	4785485	9570.97
Ringgold	348245	4.96	5.45	1727657	64786	10	...	1792443	1971687	580484	....	2372927	2552171	5104.34
Sac	373523	4.69	4.69	1751193	19584	...	...	1770777	1770777	111288	....	1882065	1882065	3764.13
Scott	279926	16.92	16.92	4736674	3317178	...	...	8053852	8053852	2305437	240597	10599886	10599886	21199.77
Shelby	375169	6.39	6.39	2399988	75498	...	...	2475486	2475486	286905	68587	2830978	2830978	5661.96
Sioux	406218	5.06	3.80	2054656	11009	...	25	2065665	1549249	63981	66210	2195856	1679440	3358.88
Story	354937	6.54	6.86	2321796	189382	5	...	2511178	2636731	589781	267569	3368528	3494081	6988.16
Tama	457429	8.14	8.14	3722735	456676	...	...	4179411	4179411	1144185	297802	5621398	5621398	11242.80
Taylor	338375	6.06	6.66	2050378	152210	10	...	2202588	2422846	613559	148564	2964711	3184969	6369.94

TABLE XII.—Continued.

COUNTIES.	Acres of land.	Reported value per acre.	Equalized value per acre.	Reported value of lands.	Reported value of town lots.	Increase per cent.	Decrease per cent.	Reported value of lands and town lots.	Equalized value of lands and town lots.	Value of personalty.	Value of Railroad property.	Reported total value.	Equalized total value.	State tax at two mills.
Union	$ 264605	6.83	6.83	$ 1807568	$ 380594	...	...	$ 2188162	$ 2188162	$ 660550	$ 366227	$ 3214939	$ 3214939	$ 6429.88
Van Buren	305441	11.01	10.46	3364556	530730	...	5	3895286	3700522	1478291	261850	5635427	5440663	10881.33
Wapello	269076	8.80	9.68	2369435	1230613	10	...	3600048	3960052	1578488	549027	5727563	6087567	12175.13
Warren	360569	9.53	9.53	3437936	326839	...	...	3764775	3764775	1318406	91805	5174986	5174986	10349.97
Washington	358297	9.39	9.39	3363327	409380	...	...	3772707	3772707	1446411	232740	5451858	5451858	10903.72
Wayne	333144	7.20	7.20	2397082	184039	...	...	2581121	2581121	940508	127592	3649221	3649221	7298.44
Webster	448978	5.34	5.87	2399964	392071	10	...	2792035	3071238	483028	223120	3498183	3777386	7554.77
Winnebago	246637	3.00	3.45	739911	2172	15	...	742083	853395	59257	....	801340	912652	1825.30
Winneshiek	436441	6.29	6.60	2746698	509559	5	...	3253257	3415919	1029784	242847	4525888	4688550	9377.10
Woodbury	495976	3.99	4.79	1977617	536737	20	...	2516654	3019985	355656	133765	3006075	3509406	7019.81
Worth	252546	4.08	4.08	1030605	37919	...	...	1068524	1068524	206620	97315	1372459	1372459	2744.92
Wright	361063	3.57	3.92	1288509	25000	10	...	1313509	1444860	120455	....	1433964	1565315	3130.63
Total	$34117735	....	....	$228413607	$48833740	...	...	$277247347	$294313368	$79032896	$22076876	$378357119	$395423140	$790847.26

Note by Secretary of State.—The above table was prepared by the Auditor of State, and containing as it does items of public interest, it is given a place in the State Census.

TABLE XIII.

Showing, for the years 1865 *and* 1875, *the Number of Acres of Land Assessed, Reported Value per Acre, Equalized Value per Acre, Reported Value of Lands, Reported Value of Town Lots, Reported Value of Lands and Town Lots, and Equalized Value of Lands and Town Lots.*

COUNTIES.	ACRES OF LAND ASSESSED.		REPORTED VALUE PER ACRE.		EQUALIZED VALUE PER ACRE.		REPORTED VALUE OF LANDS.		REPORTED VALUE OF TOWN LOTS.		REPORTED VALUE OF LANDS AND TOWN LOTS.		EQUALIZED VALUE OF LANDS AND TOWN LOTS.	
	1865.	1875.	1865	1875.	1865.	1875.	1865.	1875.	1865.	1875.	1865.	1875.	1865.	1875.
Adair	351880	368120	$ 4.07	$ 6.50	$ 3.05	$ 6.50	$ 1431767	$ 2391981	$ 11259	$ 86828	$ 1443026	$ 2478809	$ 1082270	$ 2478809
Adams	247152	269532	2.90	5.64	2.90	6.76	716463	1520709	35650	143466	752113	1664175	752113	1997010
Allamakee	397021	407084	3.45	4.07	3.45	5.69	1369228	1657510	168882	339798	1538110	1997308	1538110	2796231
Appanoose	297723	322142	5.43	7.23	4.89	7.95	1616445	2329034	80312	310856	1696757	2639890	1527082	2903879
Audubon	106197	278388	4.39	5.50	2.64	5.50	466744	1521179	9950	19458	476694	1540637	286016	1540637
Benton	4 56459	450977	5.64	7.55	5.64	8.30	2575387	3406160	165383	744739	2740770	4150899	2740770	4565988
Black Hawk	354533	363841	6.72	6.97	6.05	8.36	2381458	2538807	672910	921664	3054368	3460471	2748931	4152565
Boone	302199	365957	12.10	6.57	6.05	7.22	3657431	2405308	144521	381818	3801952	2787126	1900976	3065838
Bremer	276480	274858	4.81	6.51	3.61	7.16	1329738	1789926	114923	195471	1444661	1985397	1083496	2183936
Buchanan	355462	346627	7.00	8.34	5.83	8.34	2487597	2889977	345416	684908	2833013	3574885	2360844	3574885
Buena Vista	....	327943	....	4.09	2.00	4.09	....	1341522	....	101304	....	1342826	....	1442826
Butler	362175	366265	3.50	5.58	3.06	6.69	1268322	2048051	54918	196457	1323240	2244508	1157835	2693409
Calhoun	297486	338185	2.37	3.90	2.37	4.29	706913	1319460	2440	22197	709353	1341657	709353	1475822
Carroll	218919	366866	2.19	4.95	2.19	5.44	479882	1817777	5785	199535	485667	2017312	485667	2219043
Cass	341384	347984	2.81	8.06	2.81	8.06	958194	2804040	43418	257324	1001612	3061364	1001612	3061364
Cedar	361274	359177	9.10	11.24	6.82	10.68	3288763	4036796	290406	381049	3576169	4417845	2684377	4196953
Cerro Gordo	353571	358602	3.14	4.56	2.51	5.47	1108313	1639006	19271	217050	1127584	1856056	902067	2227267
Cherokee	65225	312004	1.52	4.59	2.03	4.59	99272	1433685	1720	106573	100992	1540258	134656	1540258
Chickasaw	315553	317349	3.08	4.43	3.08	5.31	971785	1406034	51607	119143	1023392	1525177	1023392	1830212
Clarke	269298	272916	3.73	6.99	3.73	6.99	1005053	1910237	89828	259451	1094881	2169688	1094881	2169688

TABLE XIII.—Continued.

COUNTIES.	ACRES OF LAND ASSESSED.		REPORTED VALUE PER ACRE.		EQUALIZED VALUE PER ACRE.		REPORTED VALUE OF LANDS.		REPORTED VALUE OF TOWN LOTS.		REPORTED VALUE OF LANDS AND TOWN LOTS.		EQUALIZED VALUE OF LANDS AND TOWN LOTS.	
	1865.	1875.	1865.	1875.	1865.	1875.	1865.	1875.	1865.	1875.	1865.	1875.	1865.	1875.
Clay	130284	193251	$ 2.00	$ 3.93	$ 2.00	$ 3.93	$ 260496	$ 760228	$	$ 18594	$ 260496	$ 778822	$ 260496	$ 778822
Clayton	482360	483988	5.92	6.25	6.51	7.18	2855289	3024214	547631	633701	3402920	3657915	3743212	4206601
Clinton	381298	430570	7.28	10.24	8.01	10.75	2777141	4408433	791267	1750261	3568408	6158694	3925248	6466628
Crawford	222782	459840	1.91	4.99	2.15	5.48	426286	2295311	10763	109303	437049	2404614	491680	2645075
Dallas	346578	372064	5.40	7.82	4.50	7.82	1871550	2911387	138179	297214	2009729	3208601	1674774	3208601
Davis	321063	315165	4.96	7.99	5.46	7.99	1595459	2518979	98957	258935	1694416	2777914	1803858	2777914
Decatur	333658	334717	3.75	5.18	3.75	6.47	1251981	1734999	52089	150654	1304070	1885653	1304070	2357066
Delaware	363108	356759	5.90	8.95	5.90	8.51	2140792	3193195	178260	311131	2319052	3504326	2319052	3329110
Des Moines	259178	257703	10.41	13.40	10.41	13.40	2697833	3453912	1919302	4156735	4617135	7610647	4617135	7610647
Dickinson	....	192136	......	3.09	1.50	3.09	....	563696	....	10835	....	574531	....	574531
Dubuque	381889	376775	6 67	9.17	8.00	9.32	2547299	2701931	2319292	3486558	4866594	6188489	5839915	8045033
Emmet	10633	222369	2.26	2.55	2.03	3.06	23988	567078	3617	9400	27605	576478	24845	691773
Fayette	457261	460875	4.82	6.54	5.06	7.51	2204393	3016048	166781	272425	2371174	3288473	2489732	3781743
Floyd	314486	314537	2.88	5.28	3.02	6.60	904538	1661396	111975	301357	1016513	1962753	1067339	2453441
Franklin	333968	365865	5.23	5.55	3.14	6.10	1744700	2020728	10489	17792	1755189	2038520	1053113	2242372
Fremont	303823	314746	2.99	8.02	3.49	8.82	909701	2524061	68490	302151	978191	2826212	1141223	3108833
Greene	308508	365134	3.03	5.37	3.03	5.63	935473	1961844	15867	180863	951340	2142702	951340	2249842
Grundy	313079	321067	3.09	5.29	3.09	6.07	970317	1699351	2546	9106	972863	1708457	972863	1964724
Guthrie	344854	378219	4.35	5.27	3.48	6.32	1500850	1993860	39935	162142	1540785	2156002	1232628	2587202
Hamilton	317450	352683	2.50	4.35	2.50	5.22	793911	1535230	62283	168901	856194	1704131	856194	2044957
Hancock	356184	361777	4.04	3.08	2.69	3.38	1440112	1114368	4517	11330	1444629	1125698	963086	1238267
Hardin	328439	359849	4.55	5.55	3.41	6.37	1494134	1998209	161682	313835	1655816	2312044	1241862	2658850
Harrison	325113	439013	2.05	8.14	3.07	7.33	967969	3571988	76079	316612	1044048	3888600	1566072	3499740
Henry	266791	268689	8.48	10.56	8.92	10.56	2262665	2838070	606510	859540	2869175	3697610	3012633	3697610
Howard	293351	297082	2.50	5.05	2.75	5.80	734558	1500523	23853	170577	758411	1671100	831252	1921765
Humboldt	137212	259112	2.88	3.66	2.88	4.02	394589	947970	2761	50757	397350	998727	397350	1098599

Ida	60525	263916	2.00	3.00	2.00	3 60	121051	791739	....	1780	121051	793519	121051	952223
Iowa	362520	372608	5.34	8.38	5.34	7.97	1937307	3123389	787137	208869	2724444	3332258	2724444	3165646
Jackson	391673	401968	5.21	6.18	6.51	7.09	2061221	2484887	376670	554053	2437891	3038940	3047364	3494781
Jasper	449174	452040	7.62	9.25	5.71	10.17	3414731	4180559	250257	577974	3664988	4758333	2748741	5234386
Jefferson	279409	271660	6.06	10.17	7.07	10.17	1693456	2762932	198011	361724	1891467	3124656	2206711	3124656
Johnson	391393	384886	6.25	10.50	7.03	10.50	2451537	4042612	551932	1320119	3003469	5362731	3378903	5362731
Jones	354484	356694	7.06	8.38	6.35	8 38	2503733	2988445	184606	427234	2688339	3415679	2419505	3415679
Keokuk	361175	363503	5.29	8.49	5.29	8.49	1909794	3087215	105004	242699	2014798	3329914	2014798	3329914
Kossuth	193378	501025	2.03	3.35	2.03	3.35	391184	1677674	8384	68196	399568	1745870	399568	1745870
Lee	313022	325755	7.32	9.14	8.05	9.14	2289951	2978650	3184984	3129987	5474935	6108637	6022428	6108637
Linn	448955	455672	7.02	11.36	7.02	10.81	3152517	5178399	786344	1890815	3938861	7069214	3938861	6715754
Louisa	247841	249332	5.81	8.77	6.97	8.77	1440743	2188088	153732	298484	1594475	2486572	1913370	2486572
Lucas	267708	276041	3.74	6.19	3.93	7.42	1001481	1708572	99471	301029	1100952	2009601	1156000	2411521
Lyon	....	322649	....	3.50	....	3.15	....	1130375	....	19108	....	1149483	....	1034535
Madison	357420	356361	5.07	7.11	4.56	8.53	1813520	2532574	145266	349773	1958786	2882347	1762907	3458816
Mahaska	361392	360363	7.91	9.84	6.92	9.84	2860029	3546489	362062	656835	3222091	4203324	2819330	4203324
Marion	354137	370667	8.62	7.38	6.04	8.85	3051367	2736194	389074	456399	3440441	3192593	2408309	3831111
Marshall	361726	366124	7.50	6.62	5.00	8.60	2711489	2422795	205796	663281	2917285	3086076	1944857	4011897
Mills	252128	264979	3.57	8.71	3.57	8.71	901226	2309340	87845	286698	989071	2596038	989071	2596038
Mitchell	301445	296308	2.92	6.88	2.92	6.54	879762	2038275	73110	223674	952872	2261949	952872	2148852
Monona	234257	409802	1.86	3.39	1.95	4.74	434844	1387415	28700	145108	463544	1532523	486721	2145531
Monroe	257974	251418	7.49	7.73	5.00	7.73	1932599	1944454	120315	300821	2052914	2245275	1368609	2245275
Montgomery	181433	267147	2.94	8.61	2.94	8.61	532581	2301215	15749	303961	548330	2605176	548330	2605176
Muscatine	258083	276994	11.00	11.38	9.60	11.38	2839482	3152046	1910410	1079157	4749892	4231203	4156156	4231203
O'Brien	....	282023	....	3.00	1.50	3.00	....	846069	....	5142	....	851211	....	851211
Osceola	....	180932	....	3.79	....	3.24	....	685855	....	22439	....	708294	....	602651
Page	315675	347149	2.82	6.71	3.44	8.72	1206072	2330568	85153	255136	1291225	2585704	1162103	3361414
Palo Alto	....	243000	....	3.00	2.00	3.30	....	736910	....	14940	....	751850	....	827035
Plymouth	46434	465138	2.00	4.36	2.00	4.36	92868	2029824	450	124891	93318	2154715	93318	2154715
Pocahontas	256854	323223	2.00	2.95	2.00	3.24	513308	942799	....	9938	513308	952737	513308	1048010
Polk	380740	368670	7.58	13.41	6.63	13.41	2885004	4944447	1886959	3184497	4771963	8128944	4175468	8128944
Pottawattamie	452558	586221	3.15	7.87	3.15	7.87	1426587	4611605	941090	2143331	2367677	6754936	2367677	6754936
Poweshiek	381822	368071	6.08	5.92	5.48	7.69	2077167	2178704	125647	334574	2202814	2513278	1982533	3267259
Ringgold	343521	348245	2.46	4.96	2.95	5.45	845846	1727657	26347	64786	872193	1792443	1046632	1971687
Sac	129216	373523	2.21	4.69	2.21	4.69	285994	1751193	11088	19584	297082	1770777	297082	1770777
Scott	278348	279926	11.10	16.92	9.89	16.92	3090009	4736674	2264668	3317178	5354677	8053852	4819209	8053852
Shelby	210300	375169	2.88	6.39	2.88	6.39	606632	2399988	13661	75498	620293	2475486	620293	2475486
Sioux	174140	406218	2.50	5.06	2.50	3.80	435350	2054656	....	11009	435350	2065665	348280	1549249
Story	321747	354937	3.64	6.54	3.64	6.86	1170001	2321796	63327	189382	1233328	2511178	1233328	2636731
Tama	451010	457429	4.21	8.14	5.05	8.14	1899004	3722735	89479	456676	1988483	4179411	2386180	4179411
Taylor	322523	338375	2.92	6.06	2.92	6.66	943605	2050378	31725	152210	975330	2202588	975330	2422846

TABLE XIII.—CONTINUED.

COUNTIES.	ACRES OF LAND ASSESSED.		REPORTED VALUE PER ACRE.		EQUALIZED VALUE PER ACRE.		REPORTED VALUE OF LANDS.		REPORTED VALUE OF TOWN LOTS.		REPORTED VALUE OF LANDS AND TOWN LOTS.		EQUALIZED VALUE OF LANDS AND TOWN LOTS.	
	1865.	1875.	1865.	1875.	1865.	1875.	1865.	1375.	1865.	1875.	1865.	1875.	1865.	1875.
Union	$ 270068	$ 264605	$ 4.28	$ 6·83	$ 2.85	$ 6.83	$ 1156351	$ 1807568	$ 35103	$ 380594	$ 1191454	$ 2188162	$ 794303	$ 2188162
Van Buren	297087	305441	7.25	11.01	6.85	10.46	2152661	3364556	324416	530730	2477077	3895286	2353224	3700522
Wapello	267227	269076	9.15	8.80	6.87	9.68	2446493	2369435	886437	1230613	3332930	3600048	2499698	3960052
Warren	359302	360569	7.13	9.53	4.99	9.53	3561852	3437936	139877	326839	2701729	3764775	1891210	3764775
Washington	349985	358297	5.96	9.39	6.56	9.39	2086340	3363327	345975	409380	2432315	3772707	2675546	3772707
Wayne	310643	333144	3.77	7.20	3.95	7.20	1170871	2397082	41348	184039	1212219	2581121	1272830	2581121
Webster	440967	448978	3.18	5.34	3.18	5.87	1401961	2399964	125200	392071	1527161	2792035	1527161	3071238
Winnebago	25076	246637	3.00	3.00	2.00	3.45	75228	739911	791	2172	76019	742083	50679	853395
Winneshiek	434974	436441	4.01	6.29	4.01	6.60	1745507	2746698	190530	509559	1936037	3253257	1936037	3415919
Woodbury	229681	495976	1.62	3.99	1.95	4.79	371928	1977617	90792	536037	462720	2516654	555264	3019985
Worth	240934	252546	2.60	4.08	1.95	4.08	625524	1030605	5125	37919	630649	1068524	472987	1068524
Wright	345628	361063	2.43	3.57	2.43	3.92	838658	1288509	9623	25000	848281	1313509	848281	1444860
Total	$28041051	$34117735	....	....	....	....	$140061205	$228413607	$27488397	$48833740	$167542602	$277247347	$157485285	$294313368

TABLE XIII.—Continued.

Showing value of Personalty, reported total Valuation, equalized total Value, and State Tax at two mills for the year 1865, *and* 1875.

COUNTIES.	VALUE OF PERSONALTY.		REPORTED TOTAL VALUE.		EQUALIZED TOTAL VALUE.		STATE TAX AT TWO MILLS.	
	1865.	1875.	1865.	1875.	1865.	1875.	1865.	1875.
Adair	$ 81156	$ 426749	$ 1524182	$ 2976285	$ 1163426	$ 2976285	$ 2326.85	$ 5952.57
Adams	155535	396230	907648	2398407	907648	2731242	1815.39	5462.48
Allamakee	576884	580311	2114994	2733202	2114994	3532125	4229 99	7064.25
Appanoose	933274	1305797	2630031	4189657	2460356	4453646	4920.71	8907.29
Audubon	166469	179250	643163	1719887	452485	1719887	904.97	3439.77
Benton	724101	1458182	3464871	6011651	3464871	6426740	6929.74	12853.48
Black Hawk	987434	695935	4041802	4453812	3736365	5145906	7472.73	10291.81
Boone	192045	716502	3993997	3796187	2093021	4074899	4186.04	8149.80
Bremer	331600	480586	1776261	2550012	1415096	2748551	2830.19	5497.10
Buchanan	641523	1022159	3474536	4829999	3002367	4829999	6004.73	9660.00
Buena Vista	....	142472	....	1725053	....	1725053	....	3450.11
Butler	250247	427261	1573487	2888878	1408082	3337779	2816.16	6675.56
Calhoun	20015	149804	729368	1573136	729368	1707301	1458.73	3414.60
Carroll	28219	184954	513886	2463989	513886	2665720	1027.77	5331.44
Cass	190950	532445	1192562	3887738	1192562	3887738	2385.12	7775.48
Cedar	1126590	1203110	4705759	6021979	3810967	5801087	7621.93	11602.17
Cerro Gordo	143762	256844	1171346	2365770	945829	2736981	1891.66	5473.96
Cherokee	4790	212467	105782	1916625	139446	1916625	278.89	3833.25
Chickasaw	223690	442510	1195475	2086057	1247082	3391092	2494.16	4782.18
Clarke	548663	1023755	1643544	3510831	1643544	3510831	3287.09	7021.66
Clay	7901	131205	268397	910027	268397	910027	536.79	1820.05
Clayton	1268483	1297408	4671393	5316748	5011685	5865434	10023.37	11730.87
Clinton	1261044	1771402	4829452	8665467	5186292	8973401	10372.58	17946.80
Crawford	39324	242235	476373	2971917	531004	3212378	1062.01	6424.76
Dallas	748094	1158537	2757823	4636090	2422868	4636090	4845.74	9272.18
Davis	980202	1315516	2674618	4332690	2844060	4332690	5688.12	8665.38
Decatur	477488	770143	1781558	2715838	1781558	3187251	3563.12	6374.50
Delaware	849781	893211	3168833	4641712	3168833	4466496	6337.67	8932.99
Des Moines	2302648	2692122	6919783	10646818	6919783	10646818	13839.56	21293.64
Dickinson	....	57420	....	631951	....	631951	....	1263.90
Dubuque	2669775	2668332	7536369	9174411	8509688	11030955	17019.38	22061.91
Emmet	26975	36181	54580	612659	51820	727954	103.64	1455.91
Fayette	579496	970048	2950670	4467881	3069228	4961151	6138.46	9922.30
Floyd	238297	416352	1254810	2610045	1305636	3100733	2611.27	6201.47
Franklin	69044	234080	1824233	2395137	1122157	2598989	2244.31	5197.98
Fremont	509172	873688	1487363	4020832	1650395	4303453	3300.79	8606.91
Greene	112959	357784	1064299	2821944	1064299	2929079	2128.60	5858.16
Grundy	91429	259468	1064292	1968860	1064292	2225127	2128.58	4450.25
Guthrie	204711	513992	1745496	2896941	1437339	3328141	2874.68	6656.28
Hamilton	157836	362987	1014030	2194718	1014030	2535544	2028.06	5071.09
Hancock	12706	41673	1457335	1252211	975792	1364780	1951.58	2729.56
Hardin	379433	369084	2035249	2936116	1621295	3282922	3242.59	6565.84
Harrison	439956	823079	1484004	5135413	2006028	4746553	4012.06	9493.11

TABLE XIII.—Continued.

Counties.	Value of personalty.		Reported total value.		Equalized total value		State tax of two mills.	
	1865.	1875.	1865.	1875.	1865.	1875.	1865.	1875.
Henry	$ 1338598	$ 1528520	$ 4207773	$ 5462530	$ 4351231	$ 5462530	$ 8702.46	$ 10925.06
Howard	119395	310916	877806	2091726	953647	2342391	.1907.29	4684.78
Humboldt	49275	102854	445625	1101581	446625	1201453	893.25	2402.91
Ida	4316	48720	125367	842239	125367	1000943	250.73	2001 89
Iowa	116056	1020367	2840500	4621837	2840500	4455225	5681.00	8910.45
Jackson	932945	1047511	3370836	4337161	3980309	4793002	7960.62	9586.00
Jasper	1548914	1690718	5213902	6929401	4297655	7405254	8595.31	14810.51
Jefferson	807490	1002855	2698957	4534559	3014201	4534559	6028.40	9069.12
Johnson	1263971	1504605	4267440	7245424	4642874	7245424	9285.75	14490.85
Jones	1059446	917483	3747785	4623742	3478951	4623742	6957.90	9247.48
Keokuk	1056328	1473649	3071126	4845323	3071126	4845323	6142.25	9690.65
Kossuth	37348	106676	436916	1894546	436916	1894546	873.83	3789.09
Lee	2215162	2371894	7690097	8836291	8237590	8836291	16475.18	17672.58
Linn	1495990	1795284	5434851	9424764	5434851	9071304	10869.70	18142.61
Louisa	862903	881274	2457378	3658229	2776273	3658229	5552.55	7316.46
Lucas	408721	792141	1509673	3171886	1564721	3573806	3129.44	7147.61
Lyon	......	97286	......	1246769	......	1131821	......	2263.64
Madison	755651	1196307	2714437	4203178	2518550	4479647	5037.12	9559.29
Mahaska	1655141	1784018	4877232	6208675	4474471	6208675	8948.94	12417.35
Marion	1535680	1684074	4976121	4953517	3943989	5592035	7887.98	11184.07
Marshall	743702	941487	3660987	4423357	2688559	5349178	5377.12	10698.36
Mills	624056	1091099	1613127	4197205	1613127	4197205	3226.25	8394 41
Mitchell	216397	447154	1169269	2815748	1169269	2702651	2338 54	5405,30
Monona	93953	267922	557497	1890570	580674	2503578	1161.35	5007.16
Monroe	831342	896227	2884256	3532115	2199951	3532115	4399.90	7064.23
Montgomery	77396	614242	625726	3589488	625726	3589488	1251.45	7178.98
Muscatine	1327818	1265158	6077710	6125002	5483974	6125002	10967.95	12250.00
O'Brien	......	39464	......	910535	......	910535	......	1821.07
Osceola	......	69988	......	832252	......	726009	......	1452.02
Page	469268	1149338	1760493	3829537	1631371	4605247	3262.74	9210.49
Palo Alto	......	94432	......	846282	......	921467	......	1842.93
Plymouth	7269	126917	100587	2502207	100587	2502207	201.17	5004.41
Pocahontas	11709	67616	525017	1074253	525017	1169526	1050.03	2339.05
Polk	1746862	2510504	6518825	11125411	5922330	11125411	11844.66	22250.82
Pottawattamie	789872	1480980	3147549	9014442	3147549	9014442	6295.10	18028.88
Poweshiek	862923	1146972	3065737	4031504	2845456	4785485	5690.91	9570.97
Ringgold	236395	580484	1108588	2372927	1283027	2552171	2566.05	5104.34
Sac	22534	111288	319616	1882065	319616	1882065	639.23	3764.13
Scott	1731599	2305437	7086276	10599886	6550808	10599886	13101.61	21199.77
Shelby	67271	286905	687564	2830978	687564	2830978	1375.13	5661.96
Sioux	1600	63981	436950	2195856	349880	1679440	699.76	3358 88
Story	504205	589781	1737533	3368528	1737533	3494081	3475.06	6988.16
Tama	535812	1144185	2524295	5621398	2921992	5621398	5843.98	11242.80
Taylor	361139	613559	1336469	2964711	1336469	3184969	2672.94	6369.94
Union	161504	660550	1352958	3214939	955807	3214939	1911.61	6429.88
Van Buren	1090314	1478291	3567391	5635427	3443538	5440663	6887.08	10881.33
Wapello	2364780	1578488	5697710	5727563	4864478	6087567	9728.96	12175.13
Warren	975108	1318406	3676937	5174986	2866418	5174986	5732.84	10349.97
Washington	1543397	1446411	3975712	5451858	4218943	5451858	843.789	10903.72
Wayne	301300	940508	1513519	3649221	1574130	3649221	3148.26	7298.44
Webster	234155	483028	1761316	3498183	1761316	3777386	3522.63	7554.77
Winnebago	12513	59257	88532	801340	63192	912652	126.38	1825.30
Winneshiek	1458008	1029784	3394045	4525888	3394045	4688550	6788.09	9377.10
Woodbury	175546	355656	638266	3006075	730810	3509406	1461.62	7019.81
Worth	46277	206620	676926	1372459	519264	1372459	1038.53	2744.92
Wright	44971	120455	893252	1433964	893252	1565315	1786.50	3130.63
Total	$57578116	$79032896	225120718	378357119	215063401	395423140	430126.83	790847.26

TABLE XIV.

Exhibiting the aggregate of certain items in the preceding Tables, and comparing them with those of the Census of 1865.

ITEMS.	1865.	1875.
Number of dwelling houses	114351	221568
Number of families	....	249624
Number of white males	379746	697057
Number of white females	371379	647420
Total white population	751125	1344568
Number of colored males	1804	3123
Number of colored females	1803	2853
Total colored population	3607	5976
Total population	754699	1350544
Number of inhabitants born in Iowa	....	552482
Number born in United States, but not in Iowa	....	581550
Number born in foreign countries	....	203501
Number whose parents were both foreign born	....	318159
Number whose father only was foreign born	....	25962
Number whose mother only was foreign born	....	10927
Number between 5 and 6 years of age	....	62144
Number between 6 and 16 years of age	....	317691
Number between 16 and 21 years of age	....	116636
Number between 5 and 21 years of age	....	496471
Number 16 and under 21 who cannot read	....	2513
Number of males over 21 who cannot read	....	3124
Number of females over 21 who cannot read	....	2511
Whole number over 16 who cannot read	....	8148
Number of deaf and dumb	*376	467
Number of blind	259	389
Number of insane	*613	542
Number of births in 1874	....	45421
Number of deaths in 1874	....	16146
Number of voters	146427	286282
Number of voters born in United States	....	257301
Number of voters born in British America	....	6117
Number of voters born in England and Wales	....	9620
Number of voters born in Ireland	....	18369
Number of voters born in Scotland	....	3403
Number of voters born in Germany	....	30696
Number of voters born in Austria, Hungary and Bohemia	....	2721
Number of voters born in Holland	....	1407
Number of voters born in Norway	....	6701
Number of voters born in Sweden	....	3164
Number of voters born in Denmark	....	758
Number of voters born in France	....	1154
Number of voters born in all other countries	....	1520
Number of foreigners not naturalized	10594	23929
Number of militia	94734	193918
Number of acres of improved land	....	12658495
Number of acres of unimproved land	....	9803184
Number of rods of fence	....	52164603
Number of acres in cultivation	....	9645961
Number of acres of spring wheat	827487	3176086
Number of bushels of spring wheat	7175784	43280918
Number of acres of winter wheat	116965	68868
Number of bushels of winter wheat	1108781	850889
Number of acres of corn	1727777	4019738
Number of bushels of corn	48471133	146993570
Number of acres of rye	48992	36827
Number of bushels of rye	662388	432008
Number of acres of oats	577540	956687
Number of bushels of oats	15928777	29213891
Number of acres of barley	51804	166252
Number of bushels of barley	950696	3534291
Number of acres of buckwheat	....	12154
Number of bushels of buckwheat	....	160805
Number of acres of flax	12111	72984

* Includes those in State Institution for Deaf and Dumb, and Hospital for the Insane.

TABLE XIV.—Continued.

ITEMS.	1865.	1875.
Number of bushels of flax seed	75721	559836
Number of acres in sorghum	21452	15768
Number of gallons of syrup from sorghum	1443605	1386908
Number of gallons of maple syrup	....	19613
Number of pounds of maple sugar	....	132204
Number of acres of blue grass for pasture	....	483200
Number of acres of tame grass	302899	1055730
Number of tons of hay from tame grass	225349	908011
Number of tons of hay from wild grass	713119	1506509
Number of bushels of grass seed	62114	322497
Number of bushels of clover seed	....	15978
Number of acres in Hungarian grass	....	32427
Number of tons of hay from Hungarian grass	....	51637
Number of bushels of Hungarian grass seed	....	44800
Number of acres of hops	....	426
Number of pounds of hops	27847	113314
Number of acres of tobacco	....	260
Number of pounds of tobacco	....	102782
Number of acres of broom corn	....	2203
Number of tons of broom corn	....	5036
Number of acres of Irish potatoes	40198	81729
Number of bushels of Irish potatoes	2730811	7289953
Number of acres of sweet potatoes	....	1134
Number of bushels of sweet potatoes	....	128579
Number of acres of onions	....	1386
Number of bushels of onions	207638	152758
Number of bushels of turnips	....	462165
Number of bushels of beets	....	111152
Number of bushels of peas and beans	....	59327
Acres of natural timber	....	2312659
Acres of planted timber	20285	65549
Rods of hedge	331741	7396662
Number of apple trees in bearing	....	2440934
Number of bushels of apples	....	1451037
Number of pear trees in bearing	....	30507
Number of bushels of pears	....	10061
Number of peach trees in bearing	....	110729
Number of bushels of peaches	....	49843
Number of plum trees in bearing	....	89640
Number of bushels of plums	....	22418
Number of cherry trees in bearing	....	409774
Number of bushels of cherries	....	99051
Number of other fruit trees in bearing	....	135192
Number of all fruit trees in bearing	636458	3216776
Number of fruit trees not in bearing	2523905	7135832
Number of acres of grapes in vineyard	....	14343
Number of pounds gathered	....	3896154
Gallons of wine made	....	196470
Number of vines not in vineyard	....	1514607
Number of pounds gathered	....	5504731
Gallons of wine made	....	66284
Number of horses of all ages	316702	698205
Number of horses sold for export	....	27318
Number of mules and asses	14303	37937
Number of mules and asses sold for export	....	4498
Number of milch cows	310137	673523
Number of pounds of butter made	14538216	37862540
Number of pounds of cheese made	*1000738	1145803
Number of gallons of milk sold	....	3285400
Number of work oxen	37717	12710
Number of all other cattle	901831	1389009
Number of cattle slaughtered or sold for slaughter	....	314677
Number of thoroughbred short-horns	....	9733
Number of Devons	....	1126
Number of Herefords	....	93
Number of Ayrshires	....	148
Number of Jerseys	....	117
Number of Holderness	....	4
Number of all other improved breeds	....	939
Number of hogs	1037117	3086161
Number of Berkshires	....	85466
Number of Poland-China	....	196063

* This includes number of pounds of cheese made at factory while the return for 1875 does not.

TABLE XIV.—Continued.

ITEMS.	1865.	1875.
Number of Chester-White	....	27315
Number of Magee	....	2175
Number of Essex	....	340
Number of other improved breeds	....	35451
Number of hogs slaughtered or sold for slaughter	....	2534371
Number of sheep on hand	....	724204
Number of Merino	....	82209
Number of Cotswold	....	3654
Number of Leicester	....	3146
Number of Southdown	....	1942
Number of all other improved breeds	....	31460
Number of pounds of wool sheared	....	2340914
Number of sheep slaughtered or sold for slaughter	....	129406
Number of sheep killed by dogs	....	28934
Number of dogs	86060	197509
Number of stands of bees	87118	54836
Number of pounds of honey and beeswax	† 1128399	432522
Value of products of the farm	....	$124407078
Value of market garden produce	....	726229
Value of products of the orchard	....	1215659
Value of small fruit	....	488259
Value of products of the herd	....	42261039
Value of products of the dairy	....	8398212
Value of products of the forest	....	3467020
Number of colleges, academies, universities, and private schools	41	99
Number of male instructors	....	201
Number of female instructors	....	220
Number of male students	....	6679
Number of female students	....	6205
Whole number of students	2337	12884
Volumes in library	....	34645
Amount of income	....	166783
Number of coal mines open	....	372
Number of hands employed	....	2928
Number of tons of coal mined	66663	1231547
Value of coal mined	....	$ 2600140
Number of other mines open	....	84
Value of building stone	....	$ 202102
Number of manufacturing establishments	....	3203
Number of steam engines	....	577
Number of water wheels	....	512
Average number of hands employed in 1874	....	18854
Value of manufactures	$ 7100465	$ 39263319
Number miles of railroad	793	3765

† Does not include beeswax.

TABLE XV.

Showing the Incorporated Towns and Cities in the State, their Population in 1870, 1873 and 1875, and the Counties in which they are located.

TOWNS AND CITIES.	COUNTIES.	1870.	1873.	1875.
Adel	Dallas	711	726	815
Afton	Union	961	940	1123
Agency City	Wapello	630	612	658
Albia	Monroe	1621	1082	1883
Albion	Marshall	475	641	508
Algona	Kossuth	860	1057	989
Allerton	Wayne	....	....	571
Ames	Story	636	678	820
Anamosa	Jones	2083	1656	1605
Andrew	Jackson	352	378	264
Anita	Cass	....	....	*526
Atlantic	Cass	1200	1230	1832
Avoca	Pottawattamie	....	....	846
Beacon	Mahaska	....	....	680
Belle Plaine	Benton	1488	1445	1645
Bellevue	Jackson	1353	1552	1623
Bentonsport	Van Buren	432	371	338
Birmingham	Van Buren	626	562	595
Blairstown	Benton	682	631	714
Bloomfield	Davis	1553	916	969
Boone	Boone	2415	2154	2332
Boonsboro	Boone	1518	1447	1532
Brighton	Washington	785	669	634
Buffalo	Scott	368	449	453
Burlington	Des Moines	*14930	*22047	19987
Camanche	Clinton	840	793	758
Carlisle	Warren	....	....	*869
Carroll	Carroll	384	563	812
Cedar Falls	Black Hawk	3070	3127	3270
Cedar Rapids	Linn	5940	4089	7179
Center Point	Linn	....	....	*1487
Centerville	Appanoose	1037	1271	1226
Chariton	Lucas	1728	1963	2174
Charles City	Floyd	2166	2225	2269
Cherokee	Cherokee	....	....	841
Cincinnati	Appanoose	....	....	*1093
Clarence	Cedar	726	672	664
Clarksville	Butler	....	....	699
Clear Lake	Cerro Gordo	775	550	622
Clermont	Fayette	....	....	*1566
Clinton	Clinton	6129	6149	7028
Colfax	Jasper	....	....	*955
College Springs	Page	....	....	*1152
Columbus City	Louisa	....	....	605
Columbus Junction	Louisa	....	....	517
Coralville	Johnson	....	....	297
Corning	Adams	....	885	995
Council Bluffs	Pottawattamie	10020	10525	9287
Cresco	Howard	912	1092	1201
Creston	Union	411	1087	1819
Davenport	Scott	20038	20550	21234
Decatur City	Decatur	... .	....	*1224
Decorah	Winneshiek	2110	2219	2597
Des Moines	Polk	12035	15061	14443
De Soto	Dallas	....	....	*1510
De Witt	Clinton	1749	1621	1754
Dexter	Dallas	....	....	660
Drakeville	Davis	207	275	286

* Includes the township in which the town is situated.

TABLE XV.—Continued.

TOWNS AND CITIES.	COUNTIES.	1870.	1873.	1875.
Dubuque	Dubuque	18434	22151	23605
Dunlap	Harrison	....	....	636
Durant	Cedar	373	318	370
Earlham	Madison	222	220	266
Eddyville	Wapello	1212	1195	1250
Eldon	Wapello	....	365	427
Elkader	Clayton	....	....	*1709
Fairfield	Jefferson	2226	2558	2343
Farmington	Van Buren	640	551	679
Fayette	Fayette	....	....	868
Fontanelle	Adair	....	....	416
Fort Dodge	Webster	3095	3333	3537
Fort Madison	Lee	4011	4372	4305
Fredonia	Louisa	....	....	123
Glidden	Carroll	....	....	*525
Grand Junction	Greene	444	404	479
Grinnell	Poweshiek	1482	1261	1480
Guttenberg	Clayton	1040	1340	1045
Hamburg	Fremont	1431	1018	2058
Hopkinton	Delaware	....	....	661
Independence	Buchanan	2945	2800	3424
Indianola	Warren	1428	1445	1884
Iowa City	Johnson	5914	6214	6371
Iowa Falls	Hardin	....	....	1074
Jefferson	Greene	779	806	895
Kellogg	Jasper	....	....	*827
Keokuk	Lee	12766	11761	11841
Keosauqua	Van Buren	869	772	788
Keota	Keokuk	....	....	646
Knoxville	Marion	800	1644	1699
Lansing	Allamakee	1755	2087	2280
La Porte City	Black Hawk	....	....	715
Lawler	Chickasaw	....	....	*1139
Le Claire	Scott	1093	1137	1121
Leon	Decatur	....	....	889
Lewis	Cass	....	....	*1008
Lineville	Wayne	....	....	465
Lisbon	Linn	....	....	561
Liscomb	Marshall	....	....	372
Louden	Cedar	486	441	439
Lynnville	Jasper	....	....	*1281
Lyons	Clinton	4088	3989	3784
McGregor	Clayton	2074	1995	1852
Malcom	Poweshiek	....	....	353
Malvern	Mills	....	....	493
Manchester	Delaware	1492	1469	1566
Maquoketa	Jackson	1756	1681	2112
Marengo	Iowa	1693	1137	1650
Marion	Linn	1822	2108	2047
Marshalltown	Marshall	3218	4062	4384
Mason City	Cerro Gordo	....	....	1703
Mechanicsville	Cedar	628	619	598
Mediapolis	Des Moines	....	....	*1626
Missouri Valley	Harrison	....	759	948
Mitchellville	Polk	....	....	*1692
Montezuma	Poweshiek	555	506	460
Monticello	Jones	1337	1335	1587
Montrose	Lee	905	671	782
Morning Sun	Louisa	314	445	785
Moscow	Muscatine	346	222	794
Moulton	Appanoose	....	....	753
Mount Ayr	Ringgold	....	....	*952
Mount Pleasant	Henry	4245	4065	4563
Mount Vernon	Linn	910	734	779
Muscatine	Muscatine	6718	6939	7537
Nashua	Chickasaw	....	....	852
Nevada	Story	982	942	1105
New Hampton	Chickasaw	....	....	623
New London	Henry	....	498	553
New Sharon	Mahaska	....	....	603
Newton	Jasper	1983	2000	2354
Nora Springs	Floyd	....	....	742
North McGregor	Clayton	....	....	478
Northwood	Worth	....	....	*1000

*Includes the township in which the town is situated.

TABLE XV.—Continued.

TOWNS AND CITIES.	COUNTIES.	1870.	1873.	1875.
Onawa City	Monona	478	676	719
Orford	Tama	....	....	*1059
Osage	Mitchell	1400	1295	1488
Osceola	Clarke	1298	1351	1701
Oskaloosa	Mahaska	3204	3425	4263
Ottumwa	Wapello	5214	5713	6326
Panora	Guthrie	....	....	526
Parkersburg	Butler	....	....	*513
Pella	Marion	1909	2467	2536
Perry	Dallas	....	....	*1142
Pleasantville	Marion	....	....	337
Polk City	Polk	....	....	*1631
Postville	Allamakee	....	....	712
Prairie City	Jasper	....	....	781
Quincy	Adams	283	209	265
Red Oak Junction	Montgomery	1315	1665	1823
Richland	Keokuk	....	....	492
Ringwood	Clinton	....	....	*363
Sabula	Jackson	920	1033	1003
Sac City	Sac	....	....	*811
Salem	Henry	....	449	479
Seymour	Wayne	....	....	408
Shell Rock	Butler	....	....	*594
Shellsburg	Benton	....	....	554
Shenandoah	Page	....	258	711
Sidney	Fremont	817	665	822
Sigourney	Keokuk	992	1290	1377
Sioux City	Woodbury	3401	3137	4290
Springdale	Cedar	....	1528	*1481
Springfield	Keokuk	....	....	*1254
State Center	Marshall	559	726	796
Steamboat Rock	Hardin	....	....	*1371
Storm Lake	Buena Vista	....	....	479
Strawberry Hill	Jones	....	....	130
Tabor	Fremont	310	256	293
Tama City	Tama	1161	1037	1197
Tipton	Cedar	1246	1150	1243
Toledo	Tama	888	918	1022
Union	Hardin	....	....	471
Victor	Iowa	....	420	496
Villisca	Montgomery	....	....	836
Vinton	Benton	2460	2400	2389
Wapello	Louisa	870	982	903
Washington	Washington	2575	2211	2189
Waterloo	Black Hawk	4337	5901	5508
Waverly	Bremer	....	2506	2405
Webster City	Hamilton	....	....	*2262
West Branch	Cedar	....	....	*1481
Western	Linn	....	....	238
Westfield	Plymouth	....	....	*246
West Liberty	Muscatine	....	908	937
West Mitchell	Mitchell	....	....	*1215
West Point	Lee	794	711	709
West Union	Fayette	*2032	*2208	1388
Wheatland	Clinton	....	....	*804
Wilton	Muscatine	1317	1280	1351
Winterset	Madison	1485	1944	2343
Wyoming	Jones	....	....	1689

* Includes the township in which the town is situated.

TABLE XVI.

Showing the Population of the several Counties of Iowa at each enumeration since the organization of the Territory.

COUNTIES.	WIS. TER.	IOWA TERRITORY.				STATE OF IOWA.															
	1836.	1838.	1840.	1844.	1846.	1847.	1849.	1850.	1851.	1852.	1854.	1856.	1859.	1860.	1863.	1865.	1867.	1869.	1870.	1873.	1875.
Adair	...	...	...	...	...	...	...	...	...	...	150	663	1011	984	900	1071	1594	2312	3982	5264	7045
Adams	...	...	...	...	...	...	...	...	...	...	339	1019	1413	1533	1638	1818	2317	3302	4614	5865	7772
Allamakee	...	...	...	...	...	...	227	777	1300	2000	4266	7709	10843	12237	13465	13957	16003	16766	17868	18304	19168
Appanoose	...	...	...	...	1300	948	1281	3131	3951	4243	6265	9075	11449	11931	11866	10748	13064	14625	16456	16474	17405
Audubon	...	...	...	...	...	...	...	...	...	...	...	283	365	454	388	510	790	1032	1212	1873	2370
Benton	...	...	...	...	297	312	312	673	753	1237	2623	6247	8063	8496	9561	11245	14772	19420	22454	22068	22807
Black Hawk	...	...	...	...	...	...	...	...	...	315	2514	5538	7095	8244	10014	12306	16036	18961	21706	23136	22913
Boone	...	...	...	...	...	...	419	756	890	1024	1678	3518	4018	4232	4607	5236	9861	13912	14584	15167	17351
Bremer	...	...	...	...	...	...	...	...	...	309	1095	3228	4336	4915	5404	7224	9337	11358	12528	12517	13220
Buchanan	...	...	...	...	149	250	406	519	1006	1023	2299	5125	6918	7906	8294	10037	12231	14973	17034	16329	17315
Buena Vista	...	...	...	...	...	...	...	...	...	...	...	...	...	57	...	...	151	242	1585	2669	3561
Butler	...	...	...	...	...	...	...	...	...	73	...	2141	3504	3724	4142	5006	6542	8139	9951	10760	11734
Calhoun	...	...	...	...	...	...	...	...	...	...	...	119	136	147	170	224	546	944	1602	2922	3185
Carroll	...	...	...	...	...	...	...	...	...	...	...	251	250	281	297	400	688	1450	2451	3601	5760
Cass	...	...	...	...	...	...	...	...	...	...	416	815	1489	1612	1623	1895	2479	3604	5464	7660	10552
Cedar	...	557	1225	2217	2862	2809	3183	3941	4084	4971	7643	9481	12175	12949	13274	14041	16076	18239	19731	17089	17879
Cerro Gordo	...	...	...	...	...	...	...	...	...	...	...	632	855	940	1007	1311	1988	2466	4722	5636	6685
Cherokee	...	...	...	...	...	...	...	...	...	...	...	...	85	58	20	64	209	459	1967	3297	4245
Chickasaw	...	...	...	...	...	...	...	...	...	400	588	2651	3816	4336	4397	5355	6220	8513	10180	10292	11400
Clarke	...	...	...	...	...	...	...	...	...	549	1626	3978	5006	5427	5693	5716	6244	8027	8735	8778	10118
Clay	...	...	...	...	...	...	...	...	...	...	...	...	...	52	...	...	369	450	1523	3585	3569
Clayton	...	274	1044	1200	1500	2176	3000	3873	5000	6318	9337	15187	18669	20728	21235	21922	22879	25832	27771	26946	27184
Clinton	...	445	800	1201	1300	1570	2044	2835	3001	3822	7306	13441	17395	18938	19821	22405	27234	31952	35357	33591	34295
Crawford	...	...	...	...	...	...	...	...	...	...	...	235	429	383	456	574	1070	1640	2530	3777	6038

TABLE XVI.—Continued.

COUNTIES.	WIS. TER.	IOWA TERRITORY.				STATE OF IOWA.															
	1836	1838	1840	1844.	1846	1847.	1849.	1850.	1851.	1852.	1854	1856.	1859.	1860.	1863.	1865.	1867.	1869.	1870.	1873	1875.
Dallas						164	635	812	925	1216	2392	3991	4058	5244	5088	5886	7538	10361	12019	12689	14386
Davis				2622	3400	4464	4939	7264	7454	7553	9787	11258	13323	13764	13959	13123	13517	14921	15565	15434	15757
Decatur								965	1016	1184	3025	6229	8238	8677	8373	8052	8501	10339	12018	11598	13249
Delaware			171	300	781	1111	1300	1759	2000	2615	4637	8099	10024	11024	11667	12508	14463	15557	17432	16522	16890
Des Moines	6257	4605	5546	9109	9391	10071	11649	12914	14488	12575	16700	20198	20781	19611	21213	19894	23444	25986	27256	34691	35106
Dickinson													121	180	189	309	509	562	1389	1743	1748
Dubuque	4274	2381	3056	4049	6030	7440	9185	10841	11000	12500	16662	25871	30581	31164	30839	33078	38860	36946	38969	41900	43845
Emmet														105		368	708	990	1392	1618	1436
Fayette								825	1200	2065	5042	8375	11391	12073	12739	13124	14992	16391	16973	18796	20518
Floyd												2448	3458	3744	4018	4886	6731	8465	10768	11271	13100
Franklin												780	1159	1309	1448	1899	2321	3075	4738	5669	6558
Fremont								1244	1600	2044	3006	3368	4327	5074	4778	5698	7013	8051	11174	12394	13719
Greene												1089	1424	1374	1416	1659	2353	3494	4627	5755	7028
Grundy												435	680	793	1024	1332	2119	3850	6399	7154	8134
Guthrie									222	300	772	2149	2754	3058	3205	3249	3906	5219	7061	8017	9638
Hamilton													655	1699	1602	2023	3154	4268	6055	6672	7701
Hancock													121	179	240	292	357	572	999	1397	1482
Hardin										300	1259	4033	3323	5440	5376	6813	9345	11007	13684	13855	15010
Harrison											1065	1900	3132	3621	3663	4265	5836	7411	8931	10348	11818
Henry		3058	3784	6017	6875	6759	7229	8707	8915	9633	10159	15395	16299	18701	16780	17816	20110	20971	21463	20754	21594
Howard												444	3017	3168	3382	3871	4401	5149	6282	7459	7875
Humboldt													519	332	394	606	1307	1810	2596	2783	3455
Ida													38	43			90	144	226	449	794
Iowa						435	600	822	1000	1323	2307	4873	7098	8029	8544	10258	12390	14738	16644	16572	17456
Jackson		881	1452	2000	4767	4689	5677	7210	7597	8231	12166	14077	17710	18493	19158	19097	19970	20579	22619	22284	23062
Jasper						560	1223	1288	1492	1674	3466	7490	9195	9883	10627	12095	16239	20148	22116	22340	24128
Jefferson			2780	5694	6000	8463	8825	9997	10081	10225	11117	13305	14478	15038	14649	14772	16420	16772	17839	16778	17127
Johnson		237	1504	2949	3000	3387	4010	4474	5061	5788	8467	14457	16900	17573	17184	18778	21641	23948	24898	24814	24654
Jones		241	475	1112	1758	1779	2140	3007	3400	4201	6075	9835	13475	13306	13495	14376	16228	18113	19731	18930	19166
Keokuk						2918	3953	4822	5105	5306	7299	10646	12329	13271	13412	13996	15429	17280	19434	19974	20488
Kossuth												377	310	416	365	694	1573	1949	3351	4252	3765

52

Lee		2839	6095	9830	12860	13231	15000	18783	17625	20360	22590	27273	31242	29232	28523	28063	31417	34127	37210	33644	33914
Linn		205	1385	2643	3411	3954	4762	5444	6160	6890	10802	14702	17720	18947	18700	20754	24549	27467	28852	30019	31815
Louisa		1180	1925	3238	3644	3648	4155	5067	5100	5476	7341	9568	10805	10370	10673	10948	11885	12219	12877	12377	12499
Lucas								471	1025	1046	1921	4408	5287	5766	6257	6352	7746	9185	10388	10742	11725
Lyon																			221	966	1232
Madison							701	1174	1492	1832	3122	5508	7071	7379	7934	8214	9764	11817	13884	14698	16030
Mahaska					2942	3774	5559	5986	6758	7479	9093	13050	14515	14816	16249	17082	18693	20076	22508	22054	23718
Marion					1360	2350	3797	5412	5809	6289	9315	14060	16167	16813	17318	18719	20181	23440	24436	24272	24094
Marshall								338	454	710	1607	4460	5713	6015	7550	8759	11513	15514	17576	18272	19629
Mills										1463	2171	3102	4381	4481	6287	5218	6994	6935	8718	9664	10555
Mitchell												1911	3291	3409	3375	4176	6150	7288	9582	9563	11523
Monona											222	459	885	832	931	1096	1664	2679	3654	4989	5967
Monroe				386	400	1222	2000	2886	3125	3430	4577	6860	8377	8612	9322	9435	10208	11990	12724	12302	12711
Montgomery											233	872	1094	1256	1218	1535	2072	2892	5934	8601	10839
Muscatine		1247	1942	2882	1485	3010	4516	5773	6170	6812	9555	12569	15503	16444	16989	17241	20699	24336	21688	21382	21623
O'Brien														8			20	51	715	1865	2349
Osceola																				1409	1778
Page								551	534	636	1148	1964	3674	4419	4662	5211	6025	7843	9975	11734	14274
Palo Alto													131	132	142	216	413	535	1386	2617	2735
Plymouth													112	148	93	105	214	179	2199	3884	5282
Pocahontas													126	133	122	215	453	637	1146	2175	2249
Polk					1301	1792	4214	4444	6000	5939	5368	9417	11238	11625	12956	16473	22630	26408	27857	30892	31558
Pottawattamie							6552	7828	5758	5055	3060	3498	5012	4968	4737	5388	8733	10974	16893	20171	21665
Poweshiek							443	615	752	915	1953	4460	5338	5668	6370	7796	9888	12936	15581	15275	16482
Ringgold												1472	2507	2923	3039	3089	3888	5029	5691	6850	7546
Sac												251	269	246	234	304	595	840	1411	1698	2873
Scott		1252	2193	2750	3000	3652	4837	5987	6016	8628	12671	21521	25861	25959	26327	28474	34362	37615	38599	38936	39736
Shelby											328	456	784	818	828	900	1213	1744	2540	3762	5664
Sioux														10			18		576	2872	3220
Story										214	836	2868	3826	4051	4368	5918	6888	9347	11651	11519	13311
Tama										262	1163	3520	5346	5285	7027	7882	11165	14254	16131	16343	18771
Taylor								204	393	479	891	2079	3468	3590	3757	4299	4546	5591	6989	8191	10418
Union										80	81	806	1993	2012	2420	2528	3010	3821	5986	6911	8827
Van Buren		3174	6166	9019	9870	10203	11577	12269	13000	12753	13843	15921	15879	17081	15862	15599	16292	16839	17672	16860	16980
Wapello				2814	4422	5660	7255	8479	8500	8888	10521	13246	15060	14518	16729	18794	18930	20672	22346	22261	23865
Warren							649	943	1193	1488	4446	8000	9150	10281	10932	11150	13162	15810	17980	17400	18528
Washington		283	1571	3120	3483	3518	4434	4991	5079	5881	7560	11113	13366	14235	15003	15739	17675	18648	18952	18975	19269
Wayne								341	500	794	1665	4182	5860	6409	6522	6327	7657	9566	11287	11797	13978
Webster										372	907	3088	2596	2504	2858	3772	5631	7812	10484	11603	13114
Winnebago													188	168	204	298	785	1072	1562	2488	2987
Winneshiek						182	300	546	800	1523	3315	7506	12211	13942	15421	15421	19302	21047	23570	23061	24233

TABLE XVI.—Continued.

COUNTIES.	WIS. TER.	IOWA TERRITORY.				STATE OF IOWA.															
	1836	1838.	1840	1844	1846	1847.	1849.	1850.	1851.	1852.	1854.	1856.	1859.	1860.	1863.	1865.	1867.	1869	1870.	1873.	1875.
Woodbury	......	......	......	......	......	......	......	......	......	......	170	2000	1100	1119	1106	1295	1970	......	6172	6988	8568
Worth	......	......	......	......	......	......	......	......	......	......	......	......	759	756	895	1143	1543	2135	2892	3913	4908
Wright	......	......	......	......	......	......	......	......	......	......	......	427	632	653	693	908	1332	1765	2392	2826	3244
Total	10531	22859	43114	75152	97588	116651	152988	191982	204774	230713	326013	519055	638775	674913	701732	754699	902040	1040819	1191792	1251333	1350544

Note.—Calhoun county was originally called Fox county; Lyon was called Buncombe; Monroe, Kishkehosh; Washington, Slaughter; and Woodbury, Wahkaw. Hamilton was created as Risley county, and subsequently formed a part of Webster. Humboldt county, originally erected under that name, was afterwards divided between Kossuth and Webster; more recently, the territory which had been annexed to Kossuth, with the northern half of that detached to Webster, was re-erected into the county of Humboldt. The northern part of Kossuth county was at first Bancroft county, which, with the northern half of Humboldt was united with Kossuth in 1855; subsequently the territory obtained from Humboldt was again detached. Webster county was at first called Yell county, which in 1855 was united with Risley and two tiers of townships in Humboldt to form Webster; in 1857, Hamilton county was detached, and also one tier of townships to Humboldt.

By an act of the General Assembly of 1870, the territory now embraced in Kossuth county lying north of the north line of township ninety-seven, was erected into the county of Crocker, but said act of the General Assembly was afterwards declared unconstitutional by the Supreme Court, and said territory reverted to the county of Kossuth.

TABLE XVII.

Showing the length of the several Railroads in the State of Iowa, January 1, 1875; also, the assessed valuation per mile, as fixed by the Executive Council, March 1, 1875, pursuant to the provisions of Chapter 5, Title 10, of the Code of 1873.

NAMES OF RAILROADS.	Number of miles January 1, 1875.	Assessed value per mile.	Aggregate assessed value.
Burlington, Cedar Rapids and Minnesota Railway	368.850	$ 3800	$ 1401630.00
Burlington and Missouri River Railroad	282.926	12000	3395112.00
*Brownville and Nodaway Valley Railroad	14.190	3000	42570.00
*Burlington and Missouri River Railroad—Creston Branch	42.675	5300	226177.50
*Burlington and Missouri River Railroad—Chariton Branch	37.760	3500	132160.00
*Burlington and Missouri River Railroad—Red Oak Branch	39.291	5000	196455.00
Burlington and Southwestern Railway	79.600	3000	238800.00
Chicago, Rock Island and Pacific Railroad	368.450	10700	3942415.00
†Chicago, R. I. and P. R. R.—Indianola and Winterset Branch	48.240	3500	168840.00
†Chicago, R. I. and P. R. R.—Sigourney Branch	28.390	3000	85170.00
†Chicago and Southwestern Railway	129.580	3000	388740.00
Chicago, Newton and Southwestern Railway	3.750	1500	5625.00
Chicago and Northwestern Railway	355.010	10300	3656603.00
‡Iowa Midland Railway	68.800	3000	206400.00
‡Stanwood and Tipton Railway	8.500	3000	25500.00
‡Toledo and Northwestern Railway	3.000	1500	4500.00
Chicago, Dubuque and Minnesota Railroad	109.000	3700	403300.00
Chicago, Clinton and Dubuque Railroad	45.200	5000	226000.00
Central Railroad of Iowa	189.140	4300	813302.00
Chicago, Milwaukee and St. Paul Railway	93.608	4500	421236.00
Chi., Mil. and St. P. R'y—Algona and Mason City Branches	153.582	3500	537537.00
‖Sabula, Ackley and Dakota Railroad	86.640	3000	259920.00
Davenport and St. Paul Railroad	156.460	3000	469380.00
Dakota Southern Railroad	5.300	3000	15900.00
Des Moines and Ft. Dodge	87.190	3000	261570.00
Des Moines and Minnesota Railroad—Narrow Gauge	36.000	1500	54000.00
Dubuque and Southwestern Railroad	54.760	3000	164280.00
Iowa Eastern Railroad—Narrow Gauge	16.000	1800	28800.00
Illinois Central Railroad	326.580	5500	1796190.00
¶Cedar Falls and Minnesota Railroad	75.580	3500	264530.00
§Keokuk and St. Paul Railroad	42.466	5000	212330.00
Kansas City, St. Jo. and Council Bluffs Railway	52.145	8000	417160.00
Keokuk and Des Moines Railroad	161.300	5300	854890.00
Missouri, Iowa and Nebraska Railway	14.790	3000	44370.00
Mississippi Valley and Western Railway	250	3000	750.00
St. Louis and Cedar Rapids Railroad	43.314	4000	173256.00
Sioux City and St. Paul Railroad	57.250	3000	171750.00
Sioux City and Pacific Railroad	79.860	3500	279510.00
Total	3765.421		$21986658.50

Average valuation per mile, 1874, $5844.40.
Average valuation per mile, 1873, 5828.96.
Increase of average valuation over 1873, $15.44.

*Operated by the Burlington and Missouri River Railroad.
†Operated by the Chicago, Rock Island and Pacific Railroad.
‡Operated by the Chicago and Northwestern Railway.
§Operated by the Chicago, Burlington and Quincy Railroad.
‖Operated by the Chicago, Milwaukee and St. Paul Railway.
¶Operated by the Illinois Central Railroad.

TABLE XVIII.

Showing classified statement of Gross Earnings, the Aggregate Gross Earnings, and Gross Earnings per mile, 1873 *and* 1874.

NAMES OF RAILROADS.	CLASSIFIED STATEMENT OF GROSS EARNINGS.					Aggregate gross earnings.	Gross earnings per mile, 1874.	Gross earnings per mile, 1873.
	From Passengers.	From Freights.	From Express Service.	From Mail Service.	Miscellaneous.			
Burlington, Cedar Rapids and Minnesota Railway	$321645.15	$ 884484.54	$14807.84	$ 15600.16	$ 374.21	$1236901.90	$ 3086.48	$2719.20
* Burlington and Missouri River Railroad	961293.71	2299895.98	....	....	....	3388015.29	8131.17	6759.71
Burlington and Missouri River Railroad—Main line only	....	....	....	....	....	3136082.95	11087.64	....
Brownville and Nodaway Valley Railroad	....	....	....	....	....	12161.57	857.05	....
Burlington and Missouri River Railroad—Creston Branch	....	....	....	....	....	115603.32	2708.92	....
Burlington and Missouri River Railroad—Chariton Branch	....	....	....	....	....	29994.22	794.33	....
Burlington and Missouri River Railroad—Red Oak Branch	....	....	....	....	....	94173.23	2396.81	....
Burlington and Southwestern Railway	25605.81	97027.45	1872.43	4818.50	....	126324.19	1090.42	920.20
* Chicago, Rock Island and Pacific Railroad	848717.81	2091973.67	43685.00	86085.00	6951.50	3077412.98	5968.14	5747.16
Chicago and Southwestern Railway	120013.13	215769.62	7435.00	7828.00	....	351045.75	2713.29	2215.31
Chicago, Newton and Southwestern Railroad	....	....	....	....	....	....	....	1200.00
* Chicago and Northwestern Railway	723730.20	2070911.77	59591.92	109582.22	3507.52	2967323.63	6861.56	6423.89
Iowa Midland Railway	26632.33	55093.37	3866.53	3500.30	208.97	89301.50	1297.98	1349.61
Stanwood and Tipton Railway	4914.67	5574.52	1173.75	833.90	8.53	12505.37	1471.22	1139.68
Toledo and Northwestern Railway	No	Report ...	....	....	....	....	....	....
Chicago, Dubuque and Minnesota Railroad	93423.44	198988.26	1943.66	5580.00	180.00	300115.36	2752.44	2615.32
Chicago, Clinton and Dubuque Railroad	44415.13	140870.25	1081.96	3600.00	....	189967.34	4202.81	2517.73
Central Railroad of Iowa	154686.80	439591.98	6341.40	9436.99	32642.33	642699.50	3396.00	3251.75
Chicago, Milwaukee and St. Paul Railway	183173.79	508667.45	22839.07	15613.00	2427.95	732721 26	2963.36	2191.64
Sabula, Ackley and Dakota Railroad	9433.44	63940.65	900.00	3514.00	572.44	78360.53	904.43	915.09
† Davenport and St. Paul Railroad	49828.47	108268.37	2527.36	7273.75	103.91	183335.00	1171.76	1210.33
Dakota Southern Railroad	5066.66	8909.71	199.85	393.17	83.39	14652.78	2570.66	2628.18
Des Moines and Fort Dodge Railroad	35798.05	63569.02	2587.50	4944.06	1932.19	108830.82	1248.20	....
‡ Des Moines and Minnesota Railroad—Narrow Gauge	10395.51	7535.24	2682.30	....	....	20613.05	551.91	....
Dubuque Southwestern Railroad	38046.84	70768.40	1491.79	2967.65	4608.31	117882.99	2171.31	2245.00
Iowa Eastern Railroad—Narrow Gauge	1617.45	28171.85	84.88	887.50	....	30761.68	2190.12	1621.31
Illinois Central Railroad	466545.52	195295.14	22201.53	36712.00	7143.98	1627898.17	4048.09	4170.72

§ Cedar Falls and Minnesota Railroad	....	....	....	....	....	....	....	....
Keokuk and St. Paul Railroad	61213.89	70671.22	....	....	5140.75	143025.86	3368.00	3163.80
Kansas City, St. Jo. and Council Bluffs Railway	No	Report.	....	....	....	....	....	....
Keokuk and Des Moines Railroad	183975.70	475343.90	17036.18	13239.85	16590.00	706185.63	4378.08	....
Missouri, Iowa and Nebraska Railway	4860.00	12048.72	244.65	620.00	134.00	17907.37	1210.77	1000.00
Mississippi Valley and Western Railway	1833.00	1312.00	199.00	96.00	....	3440.00	1250.90	1220.73
St. Louis and Cedar Rapids Railroad	29993.61	39453.25	1608.47	3384.66	....	74399.99	1718.77	1416.59
Sioux City and St. Paul Railroad	33890.45	96535.89	3070.83	4831.21	16284.90	154613.28	2700.66	2071.24
Sioux City and Pacific Railroad	75785.55	121975.00	2548.23	5950.00	6515.39	212774.17	2664.33	3301.05
Total	4522536.11	10372647.22	222021.13	346291.92	105411.27	15568907.65	....	....

* Includes main line and branches.

† The classified gross earnings are for eleven months only, while the total includes additional estimated earnings for December at $17333.14.

‡ Earnings are for six months only, the road having been operated only since July 1, 1874.

§ Gross earnings included in Illinois Central Railroad.

NOTE.—The average gross earnings per mile on mileage of 1873 is $4,138.99, and for 1874, $4,136.56, showing an apparent decrease of $4.29, but really there is an increase as compared with these years, when it is taken into account that the gross earnings of the Des Moines and Minnesota Railroad were only for six months.

SECRETARY OF STATE

TABLE XIX.

SCHOOL STATISTICS.

Abstract from the report of the Superintendent of Public Instruction for 1874.

COUNTIES.	DISTRICTS.		SCHOOLS.			TEACHERS.				SCHOLARS.		
	Number District Townships.	Number Independent Districts.	Number ungraded.	Number graded.	Average number months taught.	Number employ'd		Av. compensation per mo.		Whole number.	Number enrolled in public schools.	Total average attendance.
						Males.	Females.	Males.	Females.			
Adair	16	......	83	2	6.5	62	81	$34.31	$28.87	2365	1928	993
Adams	11	7	67	2	6.5	50	76	34.86	26.08	2540	2002	1460
Allamakee	16	25	123	3	7.1	61	158	34.42	23.20	7853	6209	3252
Appanoose	13	28	144	2	5.8	89	96	35.06	27.58	6944	5156	3165
Audubon	8	.....	30	1	6.0	11	26	36.00	29.28	890	596	320
Benton	15	50	178	6	7.0	112	231	36.85	27.53	8574	6570	3951
Black Hawk	15	30	133	5	7.3	97	122	33.32	27.20	8095	6525	3798
Boone	17	5	109	5	6.7	87	127	41.01	28.55	6130	4232	2725
Bremer	9	34	99	11	7.4	52	160	32.51	23.84	4717	4039	2120
Buchanan	16	21	129	7	6.3	73	168	39.30	22.11	6588	5014	3012
Buena Vista	14	7	54	1	5.7	28	56	34.89	28.31	1162	874	493
Butler	16	21	109	3	6.7	55	172	33.66	26.91	4297	3652	1942
Calhoun	8	......	49	1	7.4	36	52	33.17	29.71	1132	895	539
Carroll	15	1	53	5	6.0	47	43	40.25	30.62	1799	1210	619
Cass	16	2	88	2	7.0	63	94	42.60	31.03	3318	2503	1528
Cedar	15	23	130	9	7.4	104	169	43.39	29.92	7103	5991	3675
Cerro Gordo	9	3	63	4	7.2	31	84	48.00	28.60	2468	1963	1232
Cherokee	13	1	60	1	5.7	43	67	35.13	29.37	1302	1020	554
Chickasaw	6	43	87	4	6.1	52	97	31.73	22.94	4482	3283	1910
Clarke	10	15	78	3	6.6	53	95	34.15	26.51	3723	3286	1690
Clay	8	1	56	......	4.8	24	61	28.55	24.00	1241	930	600
Clayton	20	18	150	11	7.3	102	176	40.81	27.52	11164	7371	4052
Clinton	18	35	160	6	7.5	102	226	41.82	27.43	13153	9438	5549
Crawford	18	......	68	1	7.0	42	64	36.00	32.00	1957	1225	882
Dallas	15	11	119	3	6.4	90	146	38.57	35.54	5206	4358	2261
Davis	8	43	97	1	6.0	103	78	31.33	24.21	6596	5313	3160
Decatur	11	35	42	10	7.0	79	94	33.68	22.59	5304	4851	2169
Delaware	15	13	116	6	7.5	70	182	33.61	23.56	6441	5106	3215
Des Moines	7	50	85	9	6.8	67	142	50.33	32.30	11854	6635	4120
Dickinson	11	2	33	1	6.6	24	37	31.37	25.40	726	664	333
Dubuque	11	45	110	14	7.2	57	166	40.04	26.82	16245	7603	5384
Emmet	7	1	21	......	6.3	18	19	30.84	25.87	613	463	212
Fayette	18	28	151	17	7.6	71	226	33.57	23.87	7826	5656	3243
Floyd	12	2	95	5	7.4	61	138	38.99	27.12	4747	4219	2199
Franklin	12	7	71	1	7.3	35	86	34.57	25.43	2333	1804	1002
Fremont	12	5	89	4	8.0	82	77	41.14	30.15	5122	3910	2078
Greene	14	2	81	7	7.3	66	87	48.50	30.00	2397	1729	1057
Grundy	13	......	109	1	7.0	55	106	29.37	26.37	2814	2326	8449
Guthrie	15	3	111	4	5.8	95	116	30.15	29.61	3420	3167	1713
Hamilton	12	2	5	......	6.7	55	78	34.51	26.95	2739	2315	1289
Hancock	7	......	55	......	5.7	13	29	35.89	30.94	597	502	292
Hardin	11	40	113	4	6.9	59	154	33.98	29.38	6040	4481	3051
Harrison	17	18	94	6	7.1	81	104	39.49	33.87	4452	3242	2000
Henry	7	57	99	12	6.8	75	152	35.91	24.46	8019	7305	2548
Howard	11	9	68	2	7.6	30	112	40.08	26.75	2875	2338	1219
Humboldt	9	8	45	4	9.4	21	39	27.65	24.36	1340	919	586
Ida	4	......	12	......	5.7	6	9	33.37	28.63	235	44	25
Iowa	13	60	127	6	6.3	100	140	35.77	25.42	6835	5074	3122

TABLE XIX.—Continued.

SCHOOL STATISTICS.

Abstract from the report of the Superintendent of Public Instruction for 1874.

SCHOOL-HOUSES.					APPARATUS.	LIBRARIES.	EXPENDITURES.				PRIVATE SCHOOLS.		
Number.													
Frame.	Brick.	Stone.	Log.	Value.	Value.	No. of volumes.	Teachers' salaries.	School-houses and sites.	Fuel and other contingencies.	Total expenditures for school purposes.	Number.	Teachers employed.	Aggregate attendance.
81	.....	.....	.....	$ 44030	$ 1878	4	$14783	7251	$ 4871	$ 26905	.....	.....	....
66	1	.....	.....	42800	359	2	12272	5712	4188	22172	.....	.....	....
86	2	9	26	83155	1543	8	28742	8021	7431	44194	3	4	130
107	3	.....	3	85915	2516	....	24429	9052	5645	39126	.....	.....	....
30	....	.....	.....	16820	525	....	6231	6922	3266	16419	.....	.....	....
184	2	.....	.....	126870	1170	254	50438	9632	14638	74708	7	13	302
122	9	10	.....	158940	1271	78	45448	20006	16162	81616	3	10	210
105	6	.....	.....	90365	1886	111	26666	16313	8701	51680	.....	.....	....
86	9	7	....	80065	593	16	23432	8682	7937	40051	3	3	55
128	4	3	1	116995	1113	58	32342	15603	13345	61290	2	6	190
55	1	.....	.....	43560	1048	40	12007	12745	3904	28661	.....	.....	....
108	1	2	.....	68308	1630	18	22782	11613	8954	43349	....	.....	....
47	1	.....	.....	26875	1233	24	11194	4204	3632	19030	.....	.....	....
55	.....	.....	.....	33018	1093	24	14451	12921	6948	34320	.....	.....	....
87	2	.....	.....	44295	400	....	21450	11537	8993	41980	.....	.....	....
128	11	1	.....	106855	1988	87	37663	14723	11890	64276	.....	.....	....
49	.....	15	1	39575	1172	4	16948	19378	6913	43239	1	2	25
57	1	.....	2	38241	250	6	12286	17363	4593	34242	.....	.....	....
87	1	.....	2	59373	1586	....	18522	9930	6522	34974	1	2	100
56	21	.....	2	55525	1200	....	17202	14315	7995	39512	.....	.....	....
47	.....	.....	.....	17720	424	200	12171	7390	4397	23958	.....	.....	....
100	22	22	19	148270	3854	117	53340	16674	13493	73507	8	11	480
157	9	2	.....	223866	2712	105	74647	27047	18248	119942	6	15	416
60	4	.....	.....	58100	6470	....	16337	17136	7477	40950	.....	.....	....
113	2	....	1	87250	1238	....	29995	15153	11858	57006	.....	.....	....
83	5	.....	9	51355	195	....	19241	8214	3786	31241	3	6	290
69	15	.....	12	46935	575	133	17414	13716	4226	35356	.....	.....	....
100	17	5	.....	101900	1984	194	30881	9914	9353	50148	1	5	150
53	24	14	.....	182339	1492	30	48966	15022	18127	82115	9	33	1118
30	.....	.....	.....	19696	1090	....	5607	3807	2366	11780	.....	.....	....
74	14	24	11	236430	3964	283	63567	8354	21251	93172	14	49	1992
20	.....	....	3	16000	329	1	4693	3935	2170	10798	.....	.....	....
130	11	9	4	94183	1464	158	27984	8714	6057	42755	2	9	255
87	3	11	2	999825	1009	37	25085	13185	8526	46796	.....	.....	....
63	2	6	.....	56955	2089	4	15936	5209	6218	27363	.....	.....	....
89	4	.....	.....	75835	315	....	22594	8975	6432	38001	1	7	....
78	2	.....	.....	60525	425	....	18038	10738	6302	35078	.....	.....	....
100	.....	.....	.....	57051	2615	16	19521	13478	5821	38820	.....	.....	....
114	4	.....	.....	57875	1599	....	23024	8615	8013	39652	.....	.....	....
68	1	1	1	401135	470	27	17005	3377	7568	27950	.....	.....	....
33	2	.....	.....	19000	778	37	7213	4070	3358	14641	.....	.....	....
104	5	3	.....	85800	580	17	31391	12608	11645	55644	2	4	142
96	7	.....	.....	87091	1082	192	26896	10957	9874	47727	.....	.....	....
80	28	1	1	132920	743	57	30335	5872	9119	45326	6	19	456
66	1	3	....	45111	1176	187	16965	6615	6382	29962	.....	.....	....
39	2	3	.....	26100	558	125	6968	5044	2649	14661	1	4	80
12	.....	.....	.....	9175	387	2	1654	4063	767	6484	.....	.....	....
111	14	1	.....	77298	2445	596	29696	10564	13589	53849	3	3	79

TABLE XIX.—Continued.

COUNTIES.	DISTRICTS.		SCHOOLS.			TEACHERS.				SCHOLARS.		
						Number employ'd		Av. compensation per mo.				
	Number District Townships.	Number Independent Districts.	Number ungraded.	Number graded.	Average number months taught.	Males.	Females.	Males.	Females.	Whole number.	Number enrolled in public schools.	Total average attendance.
Jackson	15	38	140	7	7.2	89	159	$29.05	$23.57	8840	7002	3516
Jasper	18	19	157	7	7.6	128	225	33.34	28.34	9242	6951	4134
Jefferson	9	27	84	6	6.6	80	107	36.07	24.04	6692	5548	3209
Johnson	16	37	159	8	7.4	87	94	29.74	24.96	10129	7260	3914
Jones	10	54	131	3	6.7	86	175	29.64	21.84	8291	5993	3960
Keokuk	6	91	128	8	6.2	92	126	33.64	29.35	8042	5205	3553
Kossuth	8	1	1	1	6.5	51	62	34.60	26.44	1452	1030	509
Lee	12	33	108	35	6.4	64	150	40.67	25.05	13723	8512	5225
Linn	17	31	178	10	6.6	95	317	41.32	25.44	12349	9115	5811
Louisa	9	28	75	13	6.9	58	82	36.69	26.54	4933	3638	2203
Lucas	5	52	83	1	6.0	54	88	34.05	26.14	4415	3356	1946
Lyon	4	3	27	......	8.3	6	29	35.00	34.00	447	326	167
Madison	14	15	108	3	6.5	77	115	37.70	31.75	6008	4496	2699
Mahaska	11	51	125	8	7.2	102	155	36.44	29.36	8966	7271	4096
Marion	7	90	113	......	6.1	103	119	32.92	24.51	9861	5851	3417
Marshall	13	44	150	6	6.5	95	160	41.60	32.73	6846	....	5625
Mills	7	34	72	1	6.9	57	75	39.72	31.18	3922	2612	1333
Mitchell	10	41	79	4	6.7	45	101	38.39	24.92	4273	2670	1990
Monona	17	1	63	......	6.0	48	62	34.65	30.07	2198	1502	954
Monroe	9	32	88	3	6.1	62	96	35.41	23.26	5409	2772	2868
Montgomery	12	2	74	2	6.4	50	97	43.90	29.90	3562	2593	1644
Muscatine	11	21	88	11	7.9	74	122	42.97	30.92	7892	5835	3768
O'Brien	8	......	49	......	6.5	39	45	32.00	26.57	752	591	264
Osceola	6	......	30	......	5.8	3	29	28.33	23.69	620	407	230
Page	14	16	114	3	6.6	80	100	40.12	32.91	5067	3528	2182
Palo Alto	13	......	......	......	6.5	24	56	27.29	25.27	1137	980	479
Plymouth	14	1	66	......	6.5	49	52	35.67	32.61	1807	1161	654
Pocahontas	11	......	52	......	5.9	24	57	29.93	27.80	905	799	441
Polk	15	25	136	2	6.5	110	162	40.63	36.36	11218	7921	4803
Pottawattamie	22	1	110	9	7.1	80	114	39.21	34.41	7706	4493	3023
Poweshiek	14	22	123	4	7.3	105	152	42.10	27.17	6001	4504	2700
Ringgold	13	23	98	1	6.0	80	87	31.03	24.56	2767	1811	1162
Sac	7	......	37	1	7.2	31	39	36.02	27.52	1032	892	395
Scott	14	21	97	13	8 7	91	151	50.73	37.93	14352	8634	5384
Shelby	14	......	53	......	6.7	45	51	33.35	29.25	1832	1225	774
Sioux	9	......	47	......	4.6	26	38	29.73	28.08	1307	932	520
Story	15	12	108	5	6.2	84	126	33.93	26.25	4990	4227	2303
Tama	18	36	153	4	6.9	109	186	34.94	26.28	6405	5893	3186
Taylor	16	3	100	7	6.2	54	98	31.06	30.17	3642	3311	1870
Union	12	2	72	10	6.1	53	81	38.31	28.68	3020	2448	1390
Van Buren	9	37	102	7	7.3	95	127	32.26	20.60	6459	5466	3149
Wapello	9	44	83	17	6.8	82	112	40.70	29.40	9167	5852	3494
Warren	8	78	125	4	6.1	106	144	34.04	26.23	7513	6008	3499
Washington	7	76	72	8	6.7	92	219	34.03	23.80	7784	5526	3269
Wayne	14	22	91	3	6.4	76	91	35.14	26.79	5230	4362	2330
Webster	18	20	105	2	6.5	73	117	33.31	27.33	4589	3593	1880
Winnebago	6	......	20	2	6.5	26	12	33.50	26.50	897	414	191
Winneshiek	16	32	124	8	7.1	68	149	38.89	24.89	9264	6577	3890
Woodbury	17	2	66	4	6.7	37	73	40.60	32.84	2736	1797	1221
Worth	11	1	36	1	6.3	12	52	30.08	25.58	1700	1207	502
Wright	11	......	48	......	7 0	34	59	33.17	27.00	1222	1082	645
Total	1195	2030	8796	464	6.7	6280	10713	$35.98	$27.66	506381	365115	227159

TABLE XIX.—Continued.

SCHOOL-HOUSES.					APPARATUS.	LIBRARIES.	EXPENDITURES.				PRIVATE SCHOOLS.		
NUMBER.													
Frame.	Brick.	Stone.	Log.	Value.	Value.	No. volumes.	Teachers' salaries.	School-houses and sites.	Fuel and other contingencies.	Total expenditures for school purposes.	Number.	Teachers employed	Aggregate attendance.
98	15	23	11	109921	3128	91	34446	6459	9582	50487	.....	.....	.....
160	4	.....	.....	167595	1988	73	46212	17423	14419	78054	1	4	75
85	6	.....	1	102411	41	1	21218	9350	3624	34192	3	9	143
149	12	3	1	131487	2681	61	45288	9826	19210	74324	5	51	1116
117	7	4	5	96665	1637	202	32008	2593	13160	47761	.....	.....	.....
127	6	4	.....	100655	891	32	26986	11643	8282	46911	4	6	151
55	.....	.....	1	33530	499	412	14399	9873	4764	29036	1	3	150
65	40	12	4	227995	861	.....	49731	15115	17085	81931	2	8	.....
154	31	4	.....	235865	1951	695	54552	22716	21757	99025	2	27	571
72	4	1	1	55940	581	14	20884	5369	4452	30705	1	5	50
81	2	1	.....	55057	1002	.....	18128	11126	5538	34792	2	2	60
17	.....	.....	.....	29550	1448	.....	3345	5371	2739	11455	.....	.....	.....
86	.....	23	.....	100400	490	160	27636	13278	9036	49950	.....	.....	.....
115	17	.....	.....	166240	1090	79	42844	22218	9348	74410	3	12	460
120	9	.....	3	73885	554	.....	31197	6369	9354	46920	1	12	240
104	17	.....	.....	128525	2528	100	37631	19991	17076	74698	4	8	230
66	3	.....	.....	65422	896	26	19708	13628	5600	38936	2	3	123
67	12	6	2	81545	865	13	19970	11433	8118	39521	1	3	60
56	4	.....	.....	56659	1431	277	15005	18692	4939	38636	.....	.....	.....
83	4	1	5	67040	835	7	20527	14072	4528	39127	1	2	58
66	5	3	.....	71600	439	.....	17553	16340	5658	39551	.....	.....	.....
81	13	1	.....	134650	2485	64	39011	15641	12541	67193	4	12	285
30	7	.....	.....	11431	.....	.....	9447	5872	2673	17992	.....	.....	.....
26	.....	.....	.....	5794	3	.....	2249	1029	551	3829	1	2	40
99	3	.....	.....	82601	1800	591	27937	21801	9136	58874	1	1	20
50	.....	.....	3	21153	1019	204	8538	5212	3640	17390	.....	.....	.....
66	.....	.....	.....	37873	265	75	10299	13284	4881	28464	.....	.....	.....
45	1	1	1	30140	345	40	9668	5460	3590	18718	.....	.....	.....
131	8	.....	.....	350290	892	332	56202	48265	21092	125559	2	10	250
86	31	1	.....	177590	3695	1726	51584	37062	18644	107290	2	5	150
123	1	.....	.....	108345	879	29	33470	16661	11974	62105	1	8	.....
91	.....	.....	1	33947	752	95	15547	5418	3693	24658	2	2	42
33	5	.....	.....	32850	.....	.....	9648	8957	5504	24109	.....	.....	.....
93	10	6	.....	322420	3848	415	85650	16766	28447	130863	6	32	1740
47	7	.....	.....	28385	709	23	13227	9254	5799	28280	.....	.....	.....
43	.....	.....	.....	26306	568	425	8252	9764	2602	20618	.....	.....	.....
106	10	.....	.....	66945	1055	74	25977	11840	9370	47187	1	12	292
152	4	3	.....	111997	591	16	21343	17754	13412	52509	.....	.....	.....
88	1	1	.....	61555	321	140	18558	11784	6458	36800	1	2	60
75	.....	.....	.....	37773	1113	34	20441	10398	5835	36674	.....	.....	.....
84	18	4	1	132115	116	33	22192	10743	5120	38055	1	3	60
84	11	1	1	147420	1343	45	36590	9995	12511	59096	6	28	1026
125	3	.....	.....	75489	540	.....	28563	9550	6855	44968	6	14	318
123	6	.....	1	65693	1715	58	30091	4094	10931	45116	2	7	252
93	1	.....	1	47804	507	5	19217	7168	4702	31087	.....	.....	.....
94	3	.....	.....	83434	1215	321	27094	19738	10631	57463	2	6	243
13	3	.....	2	19610	250	10	4150	4146	1694	9990	.....	.....	.....
89	23	12	5	119985	952	29	27953	12094	8928	48975	2	18	353
58	7	.....	2	83233	1271	6	26517	13323	10287	50127	.....	.....	.....
35	1	1	1	21960	132	116	9610	8926	2400	20936	.....	.....	.....
48	2	.....	.....	29980	1575	250	10141	4083	3877	18101	.....	.....	.....
8154	650	268	153	9499075	122308	10651	2444886	1153336	821652	4429874	149	522	15089

IOWA IN XLIVTH CONGRESS.

SENATORS.

George G. Wright, Des Moines, term expires March 4, 1877.
William B. Allison, Dubuque, term expires March 4, 1879.

REPRESENTATIVES.

George W. McCrary, Keokuk, First District.
John Q. Tufts, Wilton, Second District.
L. L. Ainsworth, West Union, Third District.
H. O. Pratt, Charles City, Fourth District.
James Wilson, Buckingham, Fifth District.
E. S. Sampson, Sigourney, Sixth District.
John A. Kasson, Des Moines, Seventh District.
J. W. McDill, Afton, Eighth District.
Addison Oliver, Onawa, Ninth District.

FEDERAL OFFICERS IN IOWA.

UNITED STATES CIRCUIT JUDGES.

Hon. Samuel F. Miller, Associate Justice of the Supreme Court, Washington, D. C.
Hon. John F. Dillon, Judge United States Circuit Court, Davenport, Iowa.
Hon. J. M. Love, Judge United States District Court, Keokuk, Iowa.

OFFICERS.

Hon. Jas. T. Lane, United States District Attorney, Davenport.
Col. John W. Chapman, United States Marshal, Council Bluffs.
Hon. George B. Corkhill, Clerk United States Circuit Court, Des Moines.
Hon. Lee R. Seaton, Assistant United States District Attorney, Keokuk.
Gen. R. V. Ankeny, Des Moines, Deputy United States Marshal.
Hon. Geo. C. Heberling, Dubuque, Deputy United States Marshal.
Col. R. Root, Keokuk, Deputy United States Marshal.
Hon. John T. Stuart, Council Bluffs, Deputy United States Marshal.
Ed. R. Mason, Deputy Clerk United States Court, Des Moines.

TERMS OF COURT.

The United States Circuit Court for the District of Iowa meets in the United States Court House in Des Moines, on the second Monday in May and October in each year.

The United States District Court meets in Keokuk, third Tuesdays, of June and January; Council Bluffs, fourth Monday of March and September; Des Moines, second Tuesday of May and third Tuesday of October; Dubuque, third Tuesday of April and November.

OFFICERS UNITED STATES DISTRICT COURT.

Hon. James M. Love, Judge, Keokuk, Iowa.
Hon. H. K. Love, Clerk, Des Moines, Iowa.
Ed. R. Mason, Deputy Clerk at Des Moines.
Hon. Alfred Hobbs, Deputy Clerk at Dubuque.
Hon. Erie J. Leech, Deputy Clerk at Keokuk.
Hon. Fitz Henry Warren, Deputy Clerk at Council Bluffs.

OFFICIAL REGISTER FOR 1876.

EXECUTIVE OFFICERS.

Samuel J. Kirkwood, of Johnson county, Governor.

———————— Private Secretary to the Governor.

Joshua G. Newbold, of Henry county, Lieutenant-Governor; P. O., Hillsboro.

Josiah T. Young, of Monroe county, Secretary of State.

Fletcher W. Young, of Monroe county, Deputy Secretary of State.

Buren R. Sherman, of Benton county, Auditor of State.

John C. Parish, of Polk county, Deputy Auditor of State.

William Christy, of Clarke county, Treasurer of State.

J. D. Ingalls, of Warren county, Deputy Treasurer of State.

David Secor, of Winnebago county, Register of the State Land Office.

J. F. Thompson, of Winnebago county, Deputy Register of the State Land Office.

Alonzo Abernethy, of Crawford county, Superintendent of Public Instruction.

John W. Stewart, of Fayette county, Deputy Superintendent of Public Instruction.

M. E. Cutts, of Mahaska county, Attorney-General; P. O., Oskaloosa.

Richard P. Clarkson, of Polk county, State Printer.

Henry A. Perkins, of Woodbury county, State Binder.

Nathaniel B. Baker, of Clinton county, Adjutant and Inspector-General and acting Quarter-Master-General.

William L. Baker, Clerk.

Prof. Amos N. Currier, of Johnson county, Superintendent of Weights and Measures; P. O., Iowa City.

Mrs. Ada North, of Polk county, State Librarian.

NOTE.—Where not otherwise stated, the Post Office address of the State Officers is Des Moines.

JUDICIAL OFFICERS.

SUPREME COURT.

Chester C. Cole, Chief Justice, Des Moines; term expires December 31, 1876.

James G. Day, Judge, Sidney; term expires December 31, 1877.

Joseph M. Beck, Judge, Fort Madison; term expires December 31, 1879.

Austin Adams, Judge, Dubuque; term expires December 31, 1881.

Edward J. Holmes, Clerk, Des Moines; term expires January 5, 1879.

John S. Runnells, Des Moines, Reporter of the Decisions; term expires January 1879.

DISTRICT COURTS.

JUDGES.

1st JUDICIAL DISTRICT.—Thomas W. Newman, Burlington, Des Moines county.
2nd JUDICIAL DISTRICT.—Joseph C. Knapp, Keosauqua, Van Buren county.
3rd JUDICIAL DISTRICT.—Samuel Forrey, Leon, Decatur county.
4th JUDICIAL DISTRICT.—Charles H. Lewis, Cherokee, Cherokeo county.
5th JUDICIAL DISTRICT.—John Leonard, Winterset, Madison county.
6th JUDICIAL DISTRICT.—Horace S. Winslow, Newton, Jasper county.
7th JUDICIAL DISTRICT.—Walter I. Hayes, Clinton, Clinton county.
8th JUDICIAL DISTRICT.—James H. Rothrock, Tipton, Cedar county.
9th JUDICIAL DISTRICT.—David S. Wilson, Dubuque, Dubuque county.
10th JUDICIAL DISTRICT.—Reuben Noble, McGregor, Clayton county.
11th JUDICIAL DISTRICT.—Isaac J. Mitchell, Boonsboro, Boone county.
12th JUDICIAL DISTRICT.—George W. Ruddick, Waverly, Bremer county.
13th JUDICIAL DISTRICT.—Joseph R. Reed, Council Bluffs, Pottawattamie county.

The terms of all the Judges of the District Courts, except those for the 12th and 13th Districts, expire on the 31st of December, 1878. Those for the 12th and 13th expire on the 31st of December, 1876.

DISTRICT ATTORNEYS.

1st JUDICIAL DISTRICT.—Damon N. Sprague, Keokuk, Lee county.
2nd JUDICIAL DISTRICT.—Thomas M. Fee, Centerville, Appanoose county.
3rd JUDICIAL DISTRICT.—Smith McPherson, Red Oak, Montgomery county.
4th JUDICIAL DISTRICT.—George B. McCarty, Emmetsburg, Palo Alto county.
5th JUDICIAL DISTRICT.—Hiram Y. Smith, Des Moines, Polk county.
6th JUDICIAL DISTRICT.—George W. Lafferty, Oskaloosa, Mahaska county.
7th JUDICIAL DISTRICT.—Lyman A. Ellis, Lyons, Clinton county.
8th JUDICIAL DISTRICT.—Milo P. Smith, Marengo, Iowa county.
9th JUDICIAL DISTRICT.—Joseph B. Powers, Cedar Falls, Black Hawk county.
10th JUDICIAL DISTRICT.—Orlando J. Clark, Decorah, Winneshiek county.
11th JUDICIAL DISTRICT.—Maurice D. O'Connell, Fort Dodge, Webster county.
12th JUDICIAL DISTRICT.—Lindley S. Butler, Northwood, Worth county.
13th JUDICIAL DISTRICT.—H. K. McJunkin, Glenwood, Mills county.

The terms of office for all the District-Attorneys, except those for the 12th and 13th Districts, expire January 5, 1879. Those for the 12th and 13th Districts expire December 31, 1876.

SHORT-HAND REPORTERS.

1st JUDICIAL DISTRICT.—W. R. Sillon, Burlington, Des Moines county.
2nd JUDICIAL DISTRICT.—W. S. Briggs, Ottumwa, Wapello county.
3rd JUDICIAL DISTRICT.—J. M. Huston, Iowa City, Johnson county.
4th JUDICIAL DISTRICT.—C. E. Walker, Sioux City, Woodbury county.

5th JUDICIAL DISTRICT.—C. A. Mosier, Des Moines, Polk county.
6th JUDICIAL DISTRICT.—Dosh Bros., Davenport, Scott county.
7th JUDICIAL DISTRICT.—Dosh Bros. and Leffingwell, Davenport, Scott county.
8th JUDICIAL DISTRICT.—Hudson Burr, La Porte City, Black Hawk county.
9th JUDICIAL DISTRICT.—H. W. Holman, Dubuque, Dubuque county.
10th JUDICIAL DISTRICT.—A. M. May, Waukon, Allamakee county.
11th JUDICIAL DISTRICT.—W. H. Jayne, Boone, Boone county.
12th JUDICIAL DISTRICT.—Charles M. Adams, Mason City, Cerro Gordo county.
13th JUDICIAL DISTRICT.—C. H. Sholes, Council Bluffs, Pottawattamie county.

CIRCUIT COURTS.

JUDGES.

1st CIRCUIT.—John B. Drayer, Mt. Pleasant, Henry county.
2nd CIRCUIT.—Robert Sloan, Keosauqua, Van Buren county.
3rd CIRCUIT.—J. W. Hewitt, Red Oak, Montgomery county.
4th CIRCUIT.—J. R. Zuver, Magnolia, Harrison county.
5th CIRCUIT.—John Mitchell, Des Moines, Polk county.
6th CIRCUIT.—Lucian C. Blanchard, Oskaloosa, Mahaska county.
7th CIRCUIT.—Daniel W. Ellis, Lyons, Clinton county.
8th CIRCUIT.—John McKean, Anamosa, Jones county.
9th CIRCUIT.—Sylvester Bagg, Waterloo, Black Hawk county.
10th CIRCUIT.—Charles T. Granger, Waukon, Allamakee county.
11th CIRCUIT.—John H. Bradley, Marshalltown, Marshall county.
12th CIRCUIT.—Robert G. Reiniger, Charles City, Floyd county.
13th CIRCUIT.—Thomas R. Stockton, Council Bluffs, Pottawattamie county.

The official terms of all the Circuit Judges expire December 31, 1876.
The boundaries of the Circuits are the same as those of the Judicial Districts.

SHORT-HAND REPORTERS.

1st CIRCUIT.—Frank Abbott, Burlington, Des Moines county.
2nd CIRCUIT.—L. A. Wilkinson.
3rd CIRCUIT.—W. E. Butler, Leon, Decatur county.
4th CIRCUIT.—Eldon Moran, Sioux City, Woodbury county.
5th CIRCUIT.—Frank M. Van Pelt, Indianola, Warren county.
6th CIRCUIT.—..
7th CIRCUIT.—T. P. Leffingwell and Dosh Bros., Davenport, Scott county.
8th CIRCUIT.—C. W. Michener, Marengo, Iowa county.
9th CIRCUIT.—E. V. Hayden, Waterloo, Black Hawk county.
10th CIRCUIT.—A. M. May, Waukon, Allamakee county.
11th CIRCUIT.—Henry Wilcox, Independence, Buchanan county.
12th CIRCUIT.—Charles M. Adams, Mason City, Cerro Gordo county.
13th CIRCUIT.—John H. Clark, Jefferson, Greene county.

PUBLIC INSTITUTIONS.

STATE UNIVERSITY.

IOWA CITY, JOHNSON COUNTY.

BOARD OF REGENTS.

Samuel J. Kirkwood, Governor, *ex-officio*, President.
George Thacher, President of the Faculty, *ex-officio*.
First District—Christian W. Slagle, Fairfield; term expires 1876.
Second District—John McKean, Anamosa; term expires 1876.
Third District—Austin Adams, Dubuque; term expires 1878.
Fourth District—Arthur T. Reeve, Hampton; term expires 1878.
Fifth District—John W. Henderson, Cedar Rapids; term expires 1880.
Sixth District—Angus R. Campbell, Newton; term expires 1880.
Seventh District—Phineas M. Casady, Des Moines; term expires 1876.
Eighth District—Lewis W. Ross, Council Bluffs; term expires 1880.
Ninth District—John F. Duncombe, Fort Dodge; term expires 1878.

John N. Coldren, Iowa City, Treasurer.
William J. Haddock, Secretary.

The Regents are elected by the General Assembly for six years, one from each Congressional District; one-third being elected at each regular session.

IOWA STATE AGRICULTUAL COLLEGE AND FARM.

AMES, STORY COUNTY.

BOARD OF TRUSTEES.

Alvin Tracy, Spillville, Winneshiek county; term expires April 30, 1876.
Charles E. Whiting, Whiting, Monona county; term expires April 30, 1876.
Charles C. Warden, Ottumwa, Wapello county; term expires April 30, 1878.
Laurel Summers, Le Claire, Scott county; term expires April 30, 1878.
Samuel J. Kirkwood, Iowa City, Johnson county; term expires April 30, 1878, president.

A. S. Welch, President of the college; Wm. D. Lucas, Treasurer; E. W. Stanton, Secretary.

IOWA COLLEGE FOR THE BLIND.

VINTON, BENTON COUNTY.

BOARD OF TRUSTEES.

Jacob Springer, Florence, Benton county; term expires March 31, 1878.
Ezekiel B. Kephart, Western, Linn county; term expires January 31, 1876.
Jeremiah L. Gay, Waterloo, Black Hawk county; term expires January 31, 1876.
Samuel H. Watson, Vinton, Benton county; term expires January 31, 1876.
Christopher L. Flint, Hazel Green, Delaware county; term expires March 31, 1878.
Harmon C. Piatt, Tipton, Cedar county; term expires March 31, 1878.

PRESIDENT—E. B. Kephart.
SECRETARY—Orlando Clark.
TREASURER—Samuel H. Watson.

The Trustees are chosen by the General Assembly for four years, one-half being chosen at each regular session.

IOWA INSTITUTION FOR THE DEAF AND DUMB.

COUNCIL BLUFFS, POTTAWATTAMIE COUNTY.

BOARD OF TRUSTEES.

Nathan P. Dodge, Council Bluffs, Pottawattamie county; term expires January 31, 1877.
William Orr, Council Bluffs, Pottawattamie county; term expires March 18, 1878.
Paul Lange, Burlington, Des Moines county; term expires March 18, 1878.
Jonathan W. Cattell, Des Moines, Polk county; term expires January 31, 1879.
Dexter C. Bloomer, Council Bluffs, Pottawattamie county; term expires January 31, 1876.

PRESIDENT—Dexter C. Bloomer.
SECRETARY—Benjamin Talbot.
TREASURER—Nathan P. Dodge.

IOWA SOLDIERS' ORPHANS' HOME.

DAVENPORT, SCOTT COUNTY; CEDAR FALLS, BLACK HAWK COUNTY; AND GLENWOOD, MILLS COUNTY (CLOSED).

—

BOARD OF TRUSTEES.

Wm. H. Leas, Des Moines, Polk county, President.

Seth P. Bryant, Davenport, Scott county.

George B. Van Saun, Waterloo, Black Hawk county.

J. C. Otis, Glenwood, Mills county.

S. W. Pierce, Superintendent of the Home at Davenport.

Henry F. Tucker, Superintendent of the Home at Cedar Falls.

The Trustees are appointed by the General Assembly for two years, one from each county in which a home is located and one from the State at large.

—

STATE HISTORICAL SOCIETY.

IOWA CITY, JOHNSON COUNTY.

—

BOARD OF CURATORS.

C. W. Slagle, Fairfield. John McKean, Anamosa. Austin Adams, Dubuque. Arthur T Reeve, Hampton. A. R. Campbell, Newton, P. M. Casady, Des Moines. J. F. Duncombe, Fort Dodge. Lewis W. Ross, Council Bluffs. John W. Henderson, Cedar Rapids,	Appointed by the Governor for two years, term commencing on the last Wednesday of June, 1874.
Thomas M. Banbury. M. W. Lewis. William Emonds. William G. Hammond. Thomas Hughes. Robert Hutchinson. S. M. Osmond. S. E. Paine. S. C. Trowbridge.	Elected by the Society for the term of two years, ending on the last Wednesday of June, 1877.

William G. Hammond, President, Iowa City.

Frederick Lloyd, Recording Secretary, Iowa City.

Frederick Lloyd, Corresponding Secretary, Iowa City.

S. C. Trowbridge, Acting Librarian, Iowa City.

H. S. Welton, Treasurer, Iowa City.

IOWA HOSPITAL FOR THE INSANE AT MOUNT PLEASANT.

MOUNT PLEASANT, HENRY COUNTY.

BOARD OF TRUSTEES.

Luke Palmer, Burlington; term expires July 3, 1876.
Andrew McClure, Mount Pleasant; term expires July 3, 1876.
William C. Evans, West Liberty; term expires July 3, 1878.
L. E. Fellows, Lansing; term expires July 3, 1878.
Mrs. Ellen M. Elliott, Mount Pleasant; term expires July 3, 1878.

The Trustees are elected by the General Assembly for the term of four years.

IOWA HOSPITAL FOR THE INSANE AT INDEPENDENCE.

INDEPENDENCE, BUCHANAN COUNTY.

BOARD OF TRUSTEES.

Erastus G. Morgan, Fort Dodge; term expires July 3, 1876.
C. C. Parker, Fayette; term expires July 3, 1876.
Maturin L. Fisher, Farmersburg; term expires July 3, 1878.
Prudence A. Appelman, Clermont; term expires, July 3, 1878.
John G. House, Independence; term expires July 3, 1876.

The Trustees are elected by the General Assembly for the term of four years.

COMMITTEE TO VISIT HOSPITALS FOR THE INSANE.

Mary A. P. Darwin, Burlington.
Charles S. Watkins, Davenport.
Dr. Stephen B. Olney, Fort Dodge.

This Committee is appointed by the Governor.

IOWA REFORM SCHOOL.

ELDORA, HARDIN COUNTY.

BOARD OF TRUSTEES.

John A. Parvin, Muscatine; term expires 1880.
Mark A. Dashiell, Hartford; term expires 1876.
Thomas E. Corkhill, Centerville; term expires 1878.
Warner L. Vestal, Storm Lake; term expires 1876.
Eleazer Andrews, Providence; term expires 1880.

PRESIDENT—John A. Parvin.
SECRETARY—Mark A. Dashiell.
TREASURER—Warner L. Vestal.

The Trustees are appointed by the General Assembly for six years; no two from the same Congressional District.

IOWA PENITENTIARY.

FORT MADISON, LEE COUNTY.

Seth H. Craig, Warden; term expires 1876.
J. H. Reynolds, Deputy Warden.
H. Clay Stuart, Clerk.
Rev. C. F. Williams, Chaplain.
J. J. Angear, M. D., Physician.

The Warden is elected by the General Assembly at each regular session. The Warden appoints the Deputy, Clerk, Chaplain, and Guards, and with the concurrence of the Governor, the Physician, and on the nomination of the Physician appoints a Hospital Steward.

ADDITIONAL PENITENTIARY.

ANAMOSA, JONES COUNTY.

Martin Heisey, Warden, Anamosa, Jones county.
Lewis Kinsey, Clerk, Anamosa, Jones county.

BOARD OF COMMISSIONERS.

Foster L. Downing, Oskaloosa, Mahaska county.
Charles H. Lull, Anamosa, Jones county.
William Ure, Fairfax, Linn county.

The Commissioners are elected by the General Assembly, term not limited. See Section 2, Chapter 43, General and Public Laws 1872.

NEW CAPITOL.

DES MOINES, POLK COUNTY.

BOARD OF COMMISSIONERS.

Samuel J. Kirkwood, Governor, *ex officio* President.
Maturin L. Fisher, Farmersburg, Clayton county.
John G. Foote, Burlington, Des Moines county.
Robert S. Finkbine, Iowa City, Johnson county.
Peter A. Dey, Iowa City, Johnson county.

Ed Wright, Secretary of the Board, Des Moines, Polk county.
A. H. Piquenard, Architect.

Commissioners appointed by Chapter 35, General and Public Laws 1872.

FISH COMMISSIONERS.

Samuel B. Evans, Ottumwa, Wapello county, term expires April 7, 1876.
Benjamin F. Shaw, Anamosa, Jones county, term expires April 1, 1876.
Charles A. Haines, Waterloo, Black Hawk county, term expires April 1, 1876.

Commissioners appointed for two years by the Governor.

TABLE XXI.

Showing the Newspapers in the State by Counties as returned by the Census of 1875, with such additions and corrections as could be obtained by the Secretary of State since the returns were received.

COUNTIES.	NAMES OF NEWSPAPERS.	When established.	WHERE PUBLISHED.	DAY OF PUBLICATION.	BY WHOM PUBLISHED.	CHARACTER.
Adair	Adair County Register	1864	Fontanelle	Thursday	James Rany	Democratic
"	Adair County Reporter	1872	Fontanelle	Friday	Gow Bros.	Republican
"	Casey Clarion	1873	Casey	Saturday	L. H. Boydston	Republican
"	Greenfield Transcript	1875	Greenfield	Friday	Chas. Stuart and J. J. Flynn	Republican
"	Stuart Locomotive	1873	Stuart	Monday	Chas. Stuart and J. J. Flynn	Republican
Adams	Adams County Gazette	1867	Corning	Wednesday	W. H. Hoxie	Republican
"	Adams County Union	1874	Corning	Thursday	O. E. Paul	Republican
Allamakee	Die Nord Iowa Post	......	Lansing	Friday	Peter Karberg	Independent
"	Lansing Mirror	......	Lansing	Friday	James F. Metcalf	Republican
"	New Albin Spectator	......	New Albin	Thursday	E. S. Kilbourne	Independent
"	North Iowa Journal	......	Lansing	Wednesday	T. C. Medary	Democratic Lib'l.
"	Postville Review	......	Postville	Wednesday	W. N. Burdick	Republican
"	Waukon Standard	......	Waukon	Thursday	May & Hancock	Republican
Appanoose	Centerville Citizen	1863	Centerville	Friday	W. O. Crosby & Co.	Republican
"	Moulton Weekly Record	1872	Moulton	Thursday	Record Printing Co.	Republican
"	The Peoples Journal	1872	Centerville	Friday	H. S. Ehrman	Democratic
Audubon	Audubon Co. Defender	1872	Exira	Thursday	E. H. Kimball	......
Benton	Belle Plaine Review	......	Belle Plaine	Wednesday	S. S. Farrington	Independent
"	Belle Plaine Union	......	Belle Plaine	Thursday	D. H. Frost	Republican
"	Benton County Record	......	Shellsburg	Saturday	Smith Bros.	Republican
"	Blairstown Advocate	......	Blairstown	Saturday	L. H. Barnes	Opposition
"	Peoples Journal	......	Vinton	Friday	C. R. Wilkinson & Co.	Republican
"	Vinton Eagle	......	Vinton	Wednesday	Hanford & Rich	Republican
Black Hawk	Cedar Falls Gazette	......	Cedar Falls	Friday	C. W. & E. A. Snyder	Republican
"	Cedar Falls Recorder	......	Cedar Falls	Wednesday	H. C. Shaver	Democratic
"	*Der Deutsch Amerikaner*	......	Waterloo	Friday	Martin Blim	Democratic
"	Iowa State Reporter	......	Waterloo	Wednesday	Parrott, Girton & Sherman	Republican

TABLE XXI.—CONTINUED.

COUNTIES.	NAMES OF NEWSPAPERS.	When established.	WHERE PUBLISHED.	DAY OF PUBLICATION.	BY WHOM PUBLISHED.	CHARACTER.
Black Hawk	La Porte City Progress	......	La Porte City	Wednesday	Jesse Wasson	Liberal
"	Waterloo Courier	......	Waterloo	Wednesday	Felt & Hartman	Republican
Boone	Boone County Democrat	1867	Boone	Wednesday	John Hornstein	Democratic
"	Boone County Republican	1865	Boone	Wednesday	Wm. Means & Downing	Republican
"	Boone Standard	1864	Boone	Saturday	John M. Brainard	Republican
"	Boonsboro News	1874	Boonsboro	Wednesday	Chas. Evans	Republican
"	Ogden Reporter	1874	Ogden	Friday	Earl Billings	Neutral
Bremer	Bremer Co. Independent	1867	Waverly	Thursday	Daniel Fichthorn	Republican
"	*Deutsche Volk-Zeitung*	1874	Waverly	Thursday	John Weidmann	Independent
"	Waverly Republican	1856	Waverly	Thursday	Lucas & Tyrrell	Republican
Buchanan	Buchanan Co. Bulletin	......	Independence	Friday	Wm. Toman	Republican
"	Indep'nd'nce Conserv'tive	......	Independence	Wednesday	W. Barnhart	Opposition
"	Jesup Vindicator	......	Jesup	Thursday	Wm. Hatton	Neutral
Buena Vista	Newell Mirror	1874	Newell	Friday	Will White	Republican
"	Sioux Rapids Echo	1872	Sioux Rapids	Wednesday	Thomas Brothers	Republican
"	Storm Lake Pilot	1870	Storm Lake	Wednesday	Vestal & Young	Republican
Butler	Butler County Press	1872	Greene	Thursday	Wagner & Riner	Republican
"	Clarksville Star	1867	Clarksville	Thursday	James O. Stewart	Republican
"	Parkersburg Eclipse	1872	Parkersburg	Thursday	Dodge & Savage	Republican
"	Shell Rock Enterprise	1872	Shell Rock	Thursday	E. A. Kittell	Republican
Calhoun	Lake City Journal	1874	Lake City	Thursday	T. B. Hotchkiss	Republican
Carroll	Carroll Herald	1868	Carroll	Wednesday	Hasting & Gray	....
"	*Der Carroll Demokrat*	1874	Carroll	Friday	Schirck & Burkhardt	....
"	Glidden Express	1875	Glidden	Friday	J. L. Smith	....
Cass	Atlantic Telegraph	......	Atlantic	Wednesday	Lafayette Young	Republican
"	Cass County Messenger	......	Atlantic	Saturday	Johnson & Willey	Republican
Cedar	Mechanicsville Press	1866	Mechanicsville	Friday	F. H. Williams	Democratic
"	The Conservative	1875	Tipton	Wednesday	M. R. Jackson	Democratic
"	Tipton Advertiser	1853	Tipton	Thursday	Mulford & Longley	Republican
"	West Branch Times	1874	West Branch	Thursday	Raber Brothers	Republican
Cerro Gordo	Cerro Gordo Republican	1862	Mason City	Thursday	Geo. R. Lanning	Republican
"	Clear Lake Observer	1873	Clear Lake	Saturday	Geo. E. Frost	Republican
"	Mason City Express	1872	Mason City	Thursday	Henry R. Spink	Republican
Cherokee	Cherokee Leader	1871	Cherokee	Thursday	Johnson & Aldrich	Independent
"	Cherokee Times	1870	Cherokee	Friday	Robert Buchanan	Republican

County	Newspaper	Est.	Place	Day of issue	Publisher	Politics
Chickasaw	Chickasaw County Times	1875	Lawler	Wednesday	F. M. Haislet	Independent
"	New Hampton Courier	1860	New Hampton	Thursday	George M. Reynolds	Republican
"	Weekly Nashua Post	1866	Nashua	Friday	Joseph F. Grawe	Republican
Clarke	Osceola Beacon	1874	Osceola	Thursday	H. C. Ayers	Independent
"	Osceola Sentinel	1857	Osceola	Thursday	Steadman & Leach	Republican
"	The New Era	1874	Osceola	Wednesday	J. M. Estes	Democratic
Clay	Clay County News	......	Spencer	Saturday	Ford & Gillespie	Republican
Clayton	Clayton County Journal	1853	Elkader	Wednesday	Shannon & Co	Republican
"	McGregor News	......	McGregor	Wednesday	Willis L. Osborne	Republican
"	*Nord Iowa Herald*	1869	Elkader	Wednesday	Charles Reinecke	Liberal
"	North Iowa Times	1857	McGregor	Thursday	Andriek & Richardson	Liberal
"	Weekly Free Press	1874	Strawberry Point	Thursday	H. B. Taylor	Republican
Clinton	Clinton Age	......	Clinton	Friday	E. H. Thayer	Democratic
"	Clinton Daily Herald	......	Clinton	Daily	Josiah Russell	Republican
"	Clinton Weekly Herald	......	Clinton	Thursday	Josiah Russell	Republican
"	Delmar Journal	......	Delmar	Thursday	F. R. Bennett	Republican
"	De Witt Observer	......	De Witt	Friday	S. H. Shoemaker	Republican
"	Lyons Advertiser	......	Lyons	Wednesday	J. C. Hopkins	Anti-Monopolist.
"	Lyons Mirror	......	Lyons	Saturday	Beers & Eaton	Republican
"	*Volks Zeitung*	......	Clinton	......	F. G. Pfeifer	Democratic
"	Wheatland News	......	Wheatland	Friday	D. W. Corothers	Republican
Crawford	Crawford County Bulletin	......	Denison	Thursday	Stephen & Heith	Democratic
"	Denison Review	......	Denison	Friday	J. Fred Meyers	Republican
Dallas	Dallas County Gazette	1865	Adel	Thursday	J. E. Williams	Republican
"	Dallas County News	1873	Adel	Wednesday	J. M. Landis	"What is it."
"	Dexter Herald	1870	Dexter	Saturday	J. J. Davis	Republican
"	Perry Chief	1874	Perry	Saturday	Jones & Lunt	Republican
"	Dallas Center Mail	1875	Dallas Center	Wednesday	J. W. Jones	Neutral
Davis	Bloomfield Weekly Democrat	1869	Bloomfield	Thursday	T. O. Walker	Democratic
Davis	Commonwealth	1874	Bloomfield	Tuesday	Moore & Van Benthusen	Republican
"	Davis County Republican	1863	Bloomfield	Thursday	J. A. T. Hull	Republican
"	Drakeville Sun	1875	Drakeville	Saturday	V. B. Wood	Independent.
"	Odd Fellows Banner	1874	Bloomfield	Saturday	J. B. King	I. O. O. F.
Decatur	Decatur County Advocate	1874	Leon	Thursday	B. F. Knapp	Republican
"	Decatur County Journal	1868	Leon	Thursday	Mrs. M. E. James	Republican
Delaware	Delhi Monitor	1870	Delhi	Thursday	J. B. Swinburn	Republican
"	Manchester Democrat	1875	Manchester	Wednesday	Democrat Pub. Co.	Democratic
"	Manchester Press	1871	Manchester	Friday	H. L. Ronn	Republican
Des Moines	Burlington Evening Gazette	1837	Burlington	Daily	Gazette Printing Co	Democratic
Des Moines	Burlington Weekly Gazette	1837	Burlington	Weekly	Gazette Printing Co	Democratic
Des Moines	Burlington Daily Hawkeye	1839	Burlington	Daily	Hawkeye Publishing Co	Republican
Des Moines	Burlington Semi-Weekly Hawkeye	1839	Burlington	Tuesday and Thursday	Hawkeye Publishing Co	Republican,
Des Moines	Burlington Weekly Hawkeye	1839	Burlington	Thursday	Hawkeye Publishing Co	Republican

TABLE XXI.—Continued.

COUNTIES.	NAMES OF NEWSPAPERS.	When established.	WHERE PUBLISHED.	DAY OF PUBLICATION.	BY WHOM PUBLISHED.	CHARACTER.
Des Moines	Evening Star	1875	Burlington	Daily	Willis & Chamberlin	Independent
"	Mediapolis Enterprise	1875	Mediapolis		W. A. Brown	Republican
"	*Die Iowa Tribune*	1861	Burlington		Iowa Tribune Co.	Republican
Dickinson	Spirit Lake Beacon	1871	Spirit Lake	Thursday	Smith & Funk	Republican
Dubuque	Dubuque Daily News		Dubuque	Daily	W. J. Gannon	Neutral
"	*Dubuque National Demokrat*		Dubuque	Thursday	Frederick A. Gniffke	Democratic
Dubuque	Dubuque Telegraph		Dubuque	Daily	Telegraph Publishing Co.	Independent
"	Dubuque Telegraph		Dubuque		Telegraph Publishing Co.	Independent
"	Dyersville Commercial		Dyersville	Thursday	Jerome Rose	Neutral
"	*Luxemberger Gazette*		Dubuque	Tuesday	Ger. Catholic Printing Ass'n.	Catholic
"	The Dubuque Herald		Dubuque	Daily	Ham & Carver	Democratic
"	The Dubuque Herald		Dubuque	Wednesday	Ham & Carver	Democratic
"	The Dubuque Times		Dubuque	Daily	Perkins & Woodruff	Republican
"	The Dubuque Times		Dubuque	Wednesday	Perkins & Woodruff	Republican
"	The Iowa Commercial		Dub. and Davenport	Friday	McLaury & Saunders	Commercial
Emmet	Northern Vindicator	1868	Estherville	Saturday	C. W. Jarvis	Republican
Fayette	Brush Creek News	1874	Brush Creek	Wednesday	Lewis & Osburne	Independent
"	Elgin Weekly Times	1875	Elgin		H. C. Hammond	
"	Fayette County Union	1866	West Union	Wednesday	Frank McClintock	Democratic
"	The Fayette News	1874	Fayette	Wednesday	Burch & Scobey	Republican
"	The Peoples Paper	1870	Clermont	Wednesday	Clermont Printing Co	Independent
"	West Union Republican Gazette	1867	West Union	Friday	C. H. Talmadge	Republican
Floyd	Charles City Intelligencer	1856	Charles City	Tuesday	C. A. Slocum	Republican
"	Floyd County Advocate	1860	Charles City	Tuesday	V. Baltuff	Republican
"	Floyd County Press	1872	Nora Springs	Thursday	H. H. Colt	Republican
"	Rockford Reveille	1873	Rockford	Thursday	Robinson, Lyon & Gaylord	Republican
"	Western Patriarch	1873	Charles City	Semi-monthly	John Bardsley	I. O. O. F.
Franklin	Franklin County Recorder	1866	Hampton	Wednesday	Whitney & Harwood	Republican
"	Hampton Magnet	1873	Hampton	Tuesday	W. C. Eaton	Republican
Fremont	Fremont Times		Hamburg	Friday	W. W. Copeland	Republican
"	Hamburg Democrat		Hamburg	Thursday	W. A. Fulmer	Democratic
"	Riverton Advocate		Riverton	Friday	T. K. Tyson	Democratic
"	Sidney Union		Sidney	Friday	Robert Simons	Republican

Greene	Grand Junction Head-Light	1870	Grand Junction	Thursday	S. C. Maynard	Democratic
"	*Jefferson Bee	1866	Jefferson	Saturday	Rhoads & Alexander	Republican
"	Scranton Gazette	1874	Scranton	Friday	W. W. Yarham	Democratic
Grundy	Grundy County Atlas	1868	Grundy Center	Friday	Rea & Moffett	Republican
Guthrie	Guthrie Vedette	......	Panora	Thursday	Lew Apple	Republican
"	The Beacon-Light	......	Guthrie Center	Wednesday	F. A. Mann	Independent
Hamilton	Hamilton Freeman	1857	Webster City	Wednesday	T. E. McCracken	Republican.
"	Webster City Argus	1874	Webster City	Friday	Edwards & Bundy	Anti-Republican.
Hancock	Hancock Signal	......	Garner	Thursday	W. C. Hayward	Republican
Hardin	Ackley Enterprise	......	Ackley	Friday	White & Courtwright	......
"	Alden News	......	Alden	Friday	J. B. Mathews	......
"	Eldora Herald	1873	Eldora	Wednesday	I. L. Hart	......
"	Eldora Weekly Ledger	1866	Eldora	Friday	R. H. McBride	......
"	Iowa Falls Sentinel	1856	Iowa Falls	Wednesday	O. W. Garrison	......
"	Union Star	......	Union	Friday	R. L. Rowe	......
Harrison	Dunlap Reporter	1870	Dunlap	Saturday	L. F. Cook	Republican
"	Harrison County Courier	1875	Magnolia	Thursday	Alpheus Davison	Independent
"	Missouri Valley Times	1869	Missouri Valley	Friday	Gore & Cutter	Independent
Henry	Free Press	......	Mount Pleasant	Thursday	Vancise & Throop	Independent
"	Mount Pleasant Journal	......	Mount Pleasant	Thursday	Teesdale, McAdams & Leech	Republican
Howard	Howard County Times	......	Cresco	Wednesday	L. E. Smith	Republican
"	Iowa Plaindealer	1859	Cresco	Friday	W. R. & F. J. Mead	Independent
"	People's Representative	1873	Cresco	Wednesday	George F. Crouch	Republican
Humboldt	Humboldt County Independent	1867	Dakota	Thursday	A. M. Adams	......
Humboldt	Humboldt Kosmos	1866	Humboldt	Tuesday	F. H. Taft	......
Ida	Ida County Pioneer	1871	Ida	Thursday	Chaffee & Williams	......
Iowa	Marengo Democrat	......	Marengo	Friday	Sehorn & Cohick	Democratic
"	Marengo Republican	......	Marengo	Wednesday	Spering & Crenshaw	Republican
"	Victor Index	......	Victor	Wednesday	Mrs. H. M. Clapp	Neutral
Jackson	Bellevue Leader	1870	Bellevue	Thursday	W. O. Evans	Republican
"	Jackson Sentinel	1854	Maquoketa	Thursday	Swigart & Sargent	Democratic
"	Maquoketa Excelsior	1856	Maquoketa	Thursday	W. S. Belden	Republican
"	Preston Weekly Clipper	1873	Preston	Saturday	P. R. Bailey	Republican
"	Sabula Gazette	......	Sabula	Thursday	J. F. Fairbanks	Independent
Jasper	*Deutsche Fortschritt*	1874	Newton	Friday	C. W. Weiner	Neutral
"	Jasper County Independent	1868	Newton	Friday	C. A. Clark	Independent
Jasper	Kellogg News	1873	Kellogg	Thursday	N. C. McBride	Independent
"	Monroe Mirror	1872	Monroe	Saturday	L. W. Allum	Republican
"	Jasper County Head-Light	1874	Newton	Thursday	Campbell & Rogers	Republican
"	Newton Free Press and Republican	1858	Newton	Wednesday	W. S. Benham	Republican
Jasper	Prairie City News	1875	Prairie City	Friday	H. L. McGinitie	Republican

*"Jefferson Era."

TABLE XXI —CONTINUED.

COUNTY.	NAMES OF NEWSPAPERS.	When established.	WHERE PUBLISHED.	DAY OF PUBLICATION.	BY WHOM PUBLISHED.	CHARACTER.
Jasper	Prairie City Union	1870	Prairie City	Friday	George Miller	Republican
Jefferson	Fairfield Ledger	1849	Fairfield	Thursday	W. W. Junkin	Republican
"	Iowa Democrat	1874	Fairfield	Saturday	M. M. Bleakmore	Democratic
Johnson	Daily State Press	1871	Iowa City	Daily	John P. Irish	Democratic
"	Iowa City Republican	1840	Iowa City	Wednesday	Pryce & Wilson	Republican
"	Iowa State Press	1840	Iowa City	Wednesday	John P. Irish	Democratic
"	*Slovan Amerikansky*	1869	Iowa City	Wednesday	Letovsky & Co.	
"	*The Volkfreund*	1874	Iowa City	Friday	Henry Brede	
"	University Reporter	1869	Iowa City	Monthly	Students of the University	
Jones	Anamosa Eureka		Anamosa	Thursday	E. Booth & Son	Republican
"	Anamosa Journal		Anamosa	Friday	C. Munger & Bro	Democratic
"	Jones County Liberal		Monticello	Thursday	G. W. Hunt	Liberal
"	Monticello Express		Monticello	Thursday	J. W. Blanchard	Republican
"	Wyoming Journal		Wyoming	Thursday	P. D. Swigart	Neutral
Keokuk	Richland Herald	1875	Richland	Thursday	C. D. Leonard	Independent
"	Sigourney News	1860	Sigourney	Wednesday	Havens & Farra	Republican
"	Sigourney Review	1872	Sigourney	Wednesday	W. R. Hollingsworth	Liberal
"	Western Herald	1872	South English	Friday	Brown Brothers	Independent
Kossuth	Algona Collegian		Algona	Monthly	Students of Algona College	Literary
"	Algona Republican		Algona			Republican
"	Upper Des Moines		Algona			Republican
Lee	Daily Constitution	1862	Keokuk	Daily	T. W. Clagett	Democratic
"	Daily Gate City	1853	Keokuk	Daily	Howell & Clark	Republican
"	Fort Madison Democrat	1869	Fort Madison	Wednesday	Roberts & Schroeder	Democratic
"	Fort Madison Plaindealer		Fort Madison	Thursday	Willson & Rasnick	Republican
"	Weekly Constitution		Keokuk	Wednesday	T. W. Clagett	Democratic
"	Weekly Gate City		Keokuk	Wednesday	Howell & Clark	Republican
"	Weekly Keokuk Post	1869	Keokuk	Wednesday	Charles Norman	Independent
Linn	Cedar Rapids Daily Republican		Cedar Rapids	Daily	Republican Printing Co.	Republican
"	Cedar Rapids Weekly Republican		Cedar Rapids	Wednesday	Republican Printing Co.	Republican
"	Cedar Rapids Times		Cedar Rapids	Wednesday	Ayres & McClelland	Republican
"	Farmers Journal		Cedar Rapids	Monthly	Republican Printing Co.	Agricultural
"	Linn County Pilot	1873	Marion	Wednesday	A. Beaty	Anti-Monopolist
"	Lisbon Sun	1873	Lisbon	Saturday	W. T. Baker	Neutral

Linn	Marion Semi-Weekly Register	1873	Marion	Tuesday and Friday	S. W. Rathbun	Republican
"	Marion Weekly Register	1852	Marion	Wednesday	S. W. Rathbun	Republican
"	Mount Vernon Hawkeye	1868	Mt. Vernon	Friday	S. H. Bauman	Republican
"	Progressive Farmer	1874	Cedar Rapids	Monthly	T. G. Newman	Agricultural
"	Sabbath Advocate		Marion	Monthly	J. Brinkerhoof	Religious
"	The Collegian	1870	Mt. Vernon	Monthly	Cornell College Societies	Literary
"	The Lotus	1871	Center Point	Wednesday	H. Cook	Independent
"	The Standard		Cedar Rapids	Wednesday	T. G. Newman	Democratic
Louisa	Columbus City Nonpareil	1875	Columbus City	Tuesday	Allen Hickok	Republican
"	Columbus Junction Herald	1875	Columbus Junction	Friday	Crocker, Stine and Jarboc	Democratic
"	Columbus Safeguard	1870	Columbus Junction	Wednesday	R. H. Moore	Republican
"	Louisa County Record	1870	Wapello	Thursday	J. D. Barr & Co.	Republican
"	Morning Sun Reporter	1875	Morning Sun	Wednesday	T. N. Ives	Republican
"	Wapello Republican	1859	Wapello	Friday	S. W. Myers	Republican
Lucas	Chariton Leader	1871	Chariton	Saturday	Best & Baker	Democratic
"	Chariton Patriot	1857	Chariton	Wednesday	W. H. Maple	Republican
Lyon	Beloit Times	1874	Beloit	Saturday	Cyrus B. Ingham	Independent
"	Rock Rapids Review	1873	Rock Rapids	Saturday	Monlux & Dickinson	Republican
Madison	Winterset Madisonian	1856	Winterset	Thursday	Cummings & Springer	Republican
"	Winterset News	1871	Winterset	Friday	G. D. Palmer	Democratic
Mahaska	Eclectic Bible Lessons	1875	Oskaloosa	Monthly	Central Book Concern	Religious
"	New Sharon Star	1873	New Sharon	Friday	H. J. Vail	Republican
"	Oskaloosa College Vidette	1874	Oskaloosa	Monthly	Students of Oskaloosa College	Literary
"	Oskaloosa Standard	1865	Oskaloosa	Saturday	M. G. Carleton	Democratic
"	The Evangelist	1849	Oskaloosa	Thursday	Central Book Concern	Religious
"	Weekly Oskaloosa Herald	1850	Oskaloosa	Thursday	Leighton & Needham	Republican
"	Weekly Reform Leader	1854	Oskaloosa	Thursday	Porte C. Welch	Independent
Marion	Baptist Beacon	1874	Pella			Religious
"	Knoxville Journal		Knoxville	Thursday	F. C. Barker	Republican
"	Marion County Democrat		Knoxville	Tuesday	J. L. McCormack	Democratic
"	Marysville Miner	1871	Marysville		T. C. McConnell	Neutral
"	Pella Blade		Pella	Wednesday	Mastellar & Co.	Republican
"	*Pella Week Blad*		Pella		H. Neyenesch	Independent
"	Pleasantville Enquirer	1875	Pleasantville		McCormack & Duncan	Independent
Marshall	Marshall County Times	1875	Marshalltown	Daily	Chapin & Sower	Republican
"	Marshall County Times	1859	Marshalltown	Thursday	Chapin & Sower	Republican
"	Marshalltown Republican	1875	Marshalltown	Semi-Weekly	A. H. Neidig & Co.	Republican
"	Marshalltown Republican	1871	Marshalltown	Thursday	A. H. Neidig & Co.	Republican
"	State Center Enterprise		State Center	Thursday	Merrill	Republican
"	The Ladies Bureau	1875	Marshalltown		Mrs. Nettie Sanford	
Mills	Glenwood Opinion	1865	Glenwood	Saturday	Opinion Printing Co.	Republican
"	Mills County Chronicle	1870	Glenwood	Saturday	Aiton & Rist	Republican
"	Mills County Journal	1872	Glenwood	Friday	Sherman & Harmon	Independent
Mitchell	Mitchell County News		Osage	Thursday	S. A. Foster	Republican
"	Mitchell County Press		Osage	Thursday	T. M. Atherton	Republican

TABLE XXI.—Continued.

COUNTIES.	NAMES OF NEWSPAPERS	When established.	WHERE PUBLISHED.	DAY OF PUBLICATION.	BY WHOM PUBLISHED.	CHARACTER.
Monona	Monona County Gazette	1865	Onawa City	Saturday	Aldridge & Sain	Republican
"	Peoples' Press	1871	Onawa City	Wednesday	Bassett & Bassett	Anti-Monopolist
Monroe	Weekly Albia Union	.....	Albia	Thursday	Val Mendel	Republican
"	The Industrial Era	1874	Albia	Tuesday	J. T. Flint	Anti-Monopolist
Montgomery	Red Oak Express	1867	Red Oak Junction	Thursday	J. Mayne & Co.	Republican
"	Red Oak Weekly Record	1870	Red Oak Junction	Friday	J. S. Stidger	Anti-Monopolist
"	Villisca Weekly Review	1871	Villisca	Thursday	H. G. Thurman	Republican
Muscatine	*Deutsche Zeitung*	1874	Muscatine	Saturday	J. W. Weippiert	Liberal
"	Muscatine Daily Journal	1854	Muscatine	Daily	Mahin Bros.	Republican
"	Muscatine Tri-Weekly Journal	1861	Muscatine	Tues., Thur. and Sat.	Mahin Bros	Republican
"	Muscatine Weekly Journal	1840	Muscatine	Friday	Mahin Bros.	Republican
"	The Muscatine Daily Tribune	1874	Muscatine	Daily	Van Horn & Betts	Independent
"	The Muscatine Weekly Tribune	1840	Muscatine	Thursday	Van Horn & Betts	Independent
"	The Weekly Enterprise	1872	West Liberty	Thursday	J. W. McElravy	Independent
"	The Wilton Herald	1872	Wilton	Thursday	J. E. Stevenson	Republican
"	Wilton Exponent	1874	Wilton	Friday	J. M. Rider	Independent
O'Brien	O'Brien Pioneer	1871	Primghar	Friday	A. H. Willits & Son	Republican
"	Sheldon Republic	1873	Sheldon	Friday	F. T. Piper	Republican
Osceola	Sibley Gazette	1872	Sibley	Friday	Glover & Hawxhurst	Republican
Page	Clarinda Herald	.....	Clarinda	Saturday	Ralph Robinson	Republican
"	Page County Democrat	.....	Clarinda	Thursday	N. C. Ridenour	Democrat
"	Shenandoah Reporter	.....	Shenandoah	Friday	Geo. W. Gunnison	Neutral
Palo Alto	Palo Alto Pilot	1873	Emmetsburg	Wednesday	Palo Alto Printing Co	Republican
"	Palo Alto Reporter	1875	Emmetsburg	Saturday	Henry A. Jenkins	Neutral
Plymouth	Iowa Liberal	.....	Le Mars	Thursday	John R. Curry	.....
"	Le Mars Sentinel	.....	Le Mars	Friday	J. C. Buchanan	.....
Pocahontas	Northwestern Hawkeye	1873	Fonda	Thursday	White & Son	Republican
Polk	Herald of Liberty	.....	Des Moines	.....	Joseph Eibœck	Personal Liberty
"	Iowa School Journal	1859	Des Moines	Monthly	C. M. Greene	Educational
"	*Iowa Staats Anzeiger*	1869	Des Moines	Thursday	Joseph Eibœck	Personal Liberty

Polk	Iowa State Leader	1848	Des Moines	Daily	State Leader Co	Democratic
"	Iowa State Register	1856	Des Moines	Daily	Clarkson Bros	Republican
"	Iowa State Register		Des Moines	Friday	Clarkson Bros	Republican
"	Plain Talk	1869	Des Moines	Saturday	M. H. Bishard	Republican
"	Western Farm Journal	1854	Des Moines	Friday	Western Farm Journal Co	Agricultural
"	Western Jurist	1866	Des Moines	Monthly	Mills & Co	Legal
Pottawattamie	Avoca Delta		Avoca	Thursday	J. C. Adams	Republican
"	Christian Expositor		Council Bluffs	Semi-Monthly	T. D. Adams	Religious
"	Council Bluffs Daily Globe		Council Bluffs	Daily	Globe Printing Co	Democratic
"	Council Bluffs Daily Nonpariel		Council Bluffs	Daily	Nonpariel Printing Co	Republican
"	Council Bluffs Weekly Globe		Council Bluffs	Friday	Globe Printing Co	Democratic
"	Council Bluffs Weekly Nonpariel		Council Bluffs	Thursday	Nonpariel Printing Co	Republican
"	*Free Presse*		Council Bluffs		Robert P. Riegel	
"	Inland Christi'n Advocate		Council Bluffs	Friday	A. Knotts & Co	Religious
"	Weekly Bugle		Council Bluffs		Lysander W. Babbitt	Democratic
Poweshiek	Grinnell Herald	1867	Grinnell	Thursday	S. A. Cravath	Republican
"	Montezuma Republican	1856	Montezuma	Wednesday	John W. Cheshire	Republican
Ringgold	Mt. Ayr Journal		Mount Ayr	Friday	C. C. Bartruff	Democratic
"	Ringgold Record		Mount Ayr	Wednesday	D. D. Pratt	Republican
Sac	Sac Sun	1871	Sac City	Thursday	James N. Miller	Republican
Scott	Church Missionary	1870	Davenport	Monthly	Board of Missions	Episcopal
"	Common School	1874	Davenport	Monthly	W. E. Crosby	Educational
"	Daily Davenport Democr't	1855	Davenport	Daily	Richardson Bros	Democratic
"	Daily Davenport Gazette	1854	Davenport	Daily	Gazette Company	Republican
"	*Daily Demokrat*	1855	Davenport	Daily	H. Lischer	Independent
"	Davenport Times	1874	Davenport	Saturday	Eldridge & Bro	Neutral
"	Iowa Commercial	1875	Davenp't & Dubuque	Friday	McLaury & Sanders	Commercial
"	Weekly Davenport Democrat	1855	Davenport	Wednesday	Richardson Bros	Democratic
"	Weekly Davenport Gazette	1841	Davenport	Wednesday	Gazette Co	Republican
"	*Weekly Demokrat*	1851	Davenport	Thursday	H. Lischer	Independent
Shelby	Harlan Herald	1874	Harlan		George D. Ross	Republican
"	Shelby County Record	1870	Harlan		H. L. Wood	Republican
Sioux	*De Volksvriend*	1874	Orange City	Wednesday	Henry Hospers	Republican
"	Sioux County Herald	1871	Orange City	Thursday	C. W. Harmon	Republican
Story	Ames Intelligencer	1868	Ames	Friday	A. McFadden	Republican
"	Aurora	1874	Ames	Monthly	Students of Ag. College	Literary
"	Morning Glory	1875	Nevada	Friday	James W. Tanner	Amateur
"	Nevada Representative	1857	Nevada	Wednesday	W. H. Gallup	Republican
"	Nevada Watchman	1874	Nevada	Tuesday	R. H. Rodermeal	Independent
Tama	Chelsea Bugle	1874	Chelsea	Wednesday	Chelsea Publishing Co	
"	Tama Citizen	1866	Tama City	Friday	W. G. Cambridge	Republican

TABLE XXI.—CONTINUED.

COUNTIES.	NAMES OF NEWSPAPERS.	When established.	WHERE PUBLISHED.	DAY OF PUBLICATION.	BY WHOM PUBLISHED.	CHARACTER.
Tama	Tama County Independent	1874	Toledo	Thursday	Rudolph Reighman	Liberal
"	Tama Press	1874	Tama City	Friday	Chapman & Grove	Democratic
"	Toledo Chronicle	1855	Toledo	Thursday	Jas. B. Hedge	Republican
"	Traer Clipper	1874	Traer	Friday	Bernard Murphy	Republican
Taylor	Bedford Argus	1872	Bedford	Thursday	Hale Bros	Republican
"	Iowa South West	1857	Bedford	Saturday	S Lucas	Anti-Monopolist.
"	Lenox Time Table	1874	Lenox	Friday	Townsend & Lupton	Independent
Union	Afton Weekly News	1871	Afton	Wednesday	J F. Bishop	Independent
"	Afton Weekly Tribune	1867	Afton	Thursday	W. R. Roberts	Republican
"	Creston Independent	1872	Creston	Thursday	—— Hamilton	Republican
"	Creston Weekly Gazette	1874	Creston	Thursday	Shoultz & Oungst	Republican
Van Buren	Birmingham Enterprise	1869	Birmingham	Thursday	Sherwood & Parker	Republican
"	Farmington Gazette	1873	Farmington	Friday	L. M. Mooers	Ind. Republican
"	Keosauqua Republican	1856	Keosauqua	Thursday	George A. Henry	Republican
"	Van Buren Democrat	1869	Bonaparte	Wednesday	George F. Smith	Democratic
Wapello	Agency Independent	1873	Agency City	Thursday	C. L. Morehouse	Republican
"	Eddyville Advance	1875	Eddyville	Thursday	W. A. Fast	Democratic
"	Eddyville Advertiser	1860	Eddyville	Saturday	Wm. L. Palmer	Republican
"	Ottumwa Daily Courier	1865	Ottumwa	Daily	J. M. Hedrick & Co	Republican
"	Ottumwa Journal	1871	Ottumwa	Saturday	A Danguard	Independent
"	Ottumwa Weekly Courier	1848	Ottumwa	Wednesday	J. M. Hedrick & Co	Republican
"	Spirit of the Times	1874	Ottumwa	Tuesday	Ottumwa Printing Co	Independent
"	The Daily Democrat	1875	Ottumwa	Daily	Sam. B. Evans	Democratic
"	The Ottumwa Democrat	1868	Ottumwa	Thursday	Sam. B. Evans	Democratic
Warren	Indianola Tribune	1873	Indianola	Thursday	George F. Parker	Democratic
"	Warren Record	1870	Indianola	Thursday	John A. Everett	Republican
"	Weekly Indianola Herald	1857	Indianola	Thursday	Graham & Knox	Republican
Washington	Brighton Star	1874	Brighton	Thursday	L. B. Fleak	Republican
"	Riverside News	1875	Riverside	Thursday	S. C. Bruce	Neutral
"	Washington County Press	1855	Washington	Wednesday	H. A. Burrell	Republican
"	Washington Gazette	1868	Washington	Friday	J. Wiseman	Democratic
Wayne	Corydon Times	1875	Corydon	Thursday	S W. Miles	Independent
"	Lineville Tribune	1873	Lineville	Thursday	Charles H. Austin	Republican

Wayne	Seymour Head-Light	1875	Seymour	Thursday	H. M. Belvel	Independent
"	Wayne County News	1872	Allerton	Thursday	H. M. Belvel	Anti-Monopolist
"	Wayne County Republican	1872	Allerton	Thursday	B. S. Jones	Republican
Webster	Fort Dodge Messenger	......	Fort Dodge	Thursday	Al. & Pauline Swalm	Republican
"	Fort Dodge Semi-Weekly Times	......	Fort Dodge	Tuesday and Friday	L. R. Train	Democratic
Winnebago	Independent Herald	1875	Lake Mills	Thursday	Marcellus Halvorsen	Republican
"	Winnebago Summit	1867	Forest City	Thursday	A. H. Chase	Republican
Winneshiek	Decorah Independent	......	Decorah	Tuesday	Wood & Haislett	Anti-Monopolist
"	*Decorah Pastern*	......	Decorah	......	B. Anundson	......
"	Decorah Register	......	Decorah	Wednesday	Henry Woodruff & Co	Republican
"	Decorah Republican	......	Decorah	Friday	A. K. Bailey & Bro	Republican
"	Ossian Enterprise	1875	Ossian	Thursday	B. S. & W. B. Morey	......
Woodbury	Sioux City Daily Journal	1869	Sioux City	Daily	Geo. D. Perkins	Republican
"	Sioux City Weekly Journal	1864	Sioux City	Thursday	Geo. D. Perkins	Republican
Woodbury	Sioux City Weekly Courier	1869	Sioux City	Saturday	C. J. Krejci	Democratic
"	Sioux City Weekly Times	1869	Sioux City	Saturday	Chas. Collins	Democratic
Worth	Northwood Pioneer	1869	Northwood	Thursday	A. G. McCargar	Republican
"	Northwood Sentinel	1875	Northwood	Tuesday	P. D. Swick	Independent
Wright	Belmond Herald	......	Belmond	Friday	James H. Brayton	Republican
"	Wright County Monitor	......	Clarion	Tuesday	Gates & Hathaway	Republican

TABLE XXII.

Alphabetical list of Post Offices in the State, November 1st, 1875.

Offices with (c h) following them indicate county seats; those with a * prefixed, denote Money Order Offices.

NAMES OF POST-OFFICES.	COUNTIES.	NAMES OF POST-OFFICES.	COUNTIES.
Abbott	Hardin	Austin	Fayette
Abingdon	Jefferson	Avery	Monroe
*Ackley	Hardin	*Avoca	Pottawattamie.
Ackworth	Warren	Avondale	Adair
Adair	Adair	Avon Station	Polk
Adams	Muscatine	Bach Grove	Wright
Adison	Humboldt	Badger Hill	Tama
*Adel (c h)	Dallas	Baker	Jefferson
Adelphi	Polk	Baldwin	Jackson
Advance	Guthrie	Ballyclough	Dubuque
*Afton (c h)	Union	Bangor	Marshall
*Agency City	Wapello	Bankston	Dubuque
Agricola	Mahaska	Banner	Madison
*Ainsworth	Washington	Barclay	Black Hawk
Albany	Davis	Barnum	Webster
*Albia (c h)	Monroe	Barryville	Delaware
Albion	Marshall	Bartlett	Fremont
*Alden	Hardin	Bassett	Chickasaw
*Algona (c h)	Kossuth	*Batavia	Jefferson
Alice	Grundy	Baxter	Jasper
Allamakee	Allamakee	Beacon	Mahaska
Allen's Grove	Scott	Bear Grove	Guthrie
*Allerton	Wayne	*Bedford (c h)	Taylor
Allison	Dubuque	Beetrace	Appanoose
Almont Station	Clinton	Belfast	Lee
Almoral	Delaware	Belinda	Lucas
Alta	Buena Vista	Belknap	Davis
Alta Vista	Chickasaw	Belle Air	Johnson
*Altoona	Polk	Belle Fountain	Mahaska
Amboy	Jasper	*Belle Plaine	Benton
*Ames	Story	*Bellevue	Jackson
Amish	Johnson	*Belmond	Wright
Amity	Scott	Beloit	Lyon
Amityville	Des Moines	Belvidere	Monona
*Anamosa (c h)	Jones	Bennington	Marion
*Andrew	Jackson	Benson Grove	Winnebago
*Anita	Cass	Benton	Mills
Ankeny	Polk	*Bentonsport	Van Buren
Annieville	Clay	Berlin	Hardin
Aplington	Butler	Bertram	Linn
Arbor Hill	Adair	Bethel	Fayette
Arcadia	Carroll	Bethel City	Marion
Arcola	Monona	Bethlehem	Wayne
Argo	Lucas	Beulah	Clayton
Armstrong's Grove	Emmet	Bevington	Madison
Ashewa	Polk	Big Grove	Pottawattamie.
Ash Grove	Davis	Big Mound	Lee
Ashland	Wapello	Big Rock	Scott
*Atalissa	Muscatine	Big Springs	Wayne
Atlanta	Buchanan	*Birmingham	Van Buren
*Atlantic (c h)	Cass	Bismarck	Clayton
Attica	Marion	Biven's Grove	Marshall
Auburn	Mahaska	Bladensburgh	Wapello
Augusta	Des Moines	Blairsburgh	Hamilton
Aurelia	Cherokee	*Blairstown	Benton
Aurora	Keokuk	Blakesburg	Wapello

TABLE XXII.—Continued.

NAMES OF POST-OFFICES.	COUNTIES.	NAMES OF POST-OFFICES.	COUNTIES.
Blakeville	Black Hawk	Carlisle	Warren
Blencoe	Monona	Carpenter	Mitchell
*Bloomfield (c h)	Davis	*Carroll (c h)	Carroll
Bloomington	Ringgold	Carrollton	Carroll
Blue Cut	Jones	Casady's Corner	Boone
Blue Grass	Scott	*Cascade	Dubuque
Bluffton	Winneshiek	*Casey	Guthrie
Boltonville	Iowa	Cass Center	Cass
Bon Accord	Johnson	Castalia	Winneshiek
*Bonaparte	Van Buren	Castana	Monona
*Boone	Boone	Castle Grove	Jones
*Boonsboro (c h)	Boone	Castleville	Buchanan
Booneville	Dallas	Cedar	Mahaska
Border Plains	Webster	Cedar Bluff	Cedar
Bowen's Prairie	Jones	*Cedar Falls	Black Hawk
Boylan's Grove	Butler	Cedar Mines	Monroe
Boyleston	Henry	*Cedar Rapids	Linn
Bozaris	Ringgold	Cedar Valley	Black Hawk
Braddyville	Page	*Centerville (c h)	Appanoose
Bradford	Chickasaw	Central City	Linn
Brainard	Fayette	Centralia	Dubuque
Brandon	Buchanan	Centre	Page
Bridgeport	Jackson	Centredale	Cedar
*Brighton	Washington	Centre Junction	Jones
Bristol	Worth	*Centre Point	Linn
Britt	Hancock	Ceres	Clayton
Broken Kettle	Plymouth	Chandaller	Keokuk
*Brooklyn	Poweshiek	Chapin	Franklin
Brooks	Adams	*Chariton (c h)	Lucas
Brookville	Jefferson	*Charles City (c h)	Floyd
Brough	Dallas	Charleston	Lee
Browning	Carroll	*Charlotte	Clinton
Brown's Station	Clinton	Chase	Johnson
Brownville	Mitchell	Chatham	Buchanan
*Brush Creek	Fayette	Chelsea	Tama
Bryant	Clinton	*Cherokee (c h)	Cherokee
Buck Creek	Bremer	Chester	Howard
Buck Horn	Mahaska	Chickasaw	Chickasaw
Buckingham	Tama	Chillicothe	Wapello
Buda	Pocahontas	Cincinnati	Appanoose
Beuna Vista	Clinton	Clanton	Madison
Buffalo	Scott	*Clarence	Cedar
Buffalo Fork	Kossuth	*Clarinda (c h)	Page
Buffalo Grove	Buchanan	Clarion (c h)	Wright
Bunch	Davis	Clarksville	Butler
Buncombe	Dubuque	Clay	Washington
Burgess	Clinton	Clayford	Jones
Burk	Benton	Clay Mills	Jones
*Burlington (c h)	Des Moines	Clay's Grove	Lee
Burr Oak	Winneshiek	Clayton	Clayton
Busti	Howard	Clear Creek	Allamakee
Butler	Keokuk	*Clear Lake	Cerro Gordo
*Butler Center (c h)	Butler	*Clermont	Fayette
Butlerville	Tama	Cliffland	Wapello
Byron	Humboldt	Clifton	Louisa
		Climax	Montgomery
Cairo	Louisa	*Clinton (c h)	Clinton
Caldwell	Appanoose	Clipper	Ringgold
Caledonia	Ringgold	Clio	Wayne
Calliope	Sioux	Clyde	Jasper
*Calmar	Winneshiek	Coal Creek	Keokuk
Calmus	Clinton	Coalfield	Monroe
Caloma	Marion	Coalton	Monroe
Camackville	Lee	Coalville	Webster
*Camanche	Clinton	Coalburgh	Montgomery
Cambria	Wayne	Colbyville	Story
Cambridge	Story	Coldville	Tama
Campton	Delaware	Coldwater	Franklin
Canby	Adair	*Colesburgh	Delaware
Canton	Jackson	Colfax	Jasper
Cantril	Van Buren	*College Springs	Page
Carbon	Adams	Colo	Story
Cardiff	Mitchell	Columbia	Marion
Carl	Adams	*Columbus City	Louisa

TABLE XXII.—Continued.

NAMES OF POST-OFFICES.	COUNTIES.	NAMES OF POST-OFFICES.	COUNTIES.
Columbus Junction	Louisa	Discord	Woodbury
Commerce Mills	Polk	Dixon	Scott
Communia	Clayton	Dodge	Guthrie
Competine	Wapello	Dodgeville	Des Moines
Comstock	Wapello	Donahue	Scott
Concord (c h)	Hancock	Donelan	Dubuque
Conesville	Muscatine	Donnan	Fayette
Confidence	Wayne	Donnellson	Lee
Congress	Franklin	Doon	Lyon
Connell	Tama	Doran	Mitchell
Conwa	Taylor	Dorchester	Allamakee
Coon Rapids	Carroll	Doud Station	Van Buren
Cooper Springs	Marion	Douglas Centre	Clay
Coopersville	Wapello	Douglass	Fayette
Coralville	Johnson	Dover	Lee
*Corning (c h)	Adams	Downey	Cedar
Correctionville	Woodbury	Downsville	Pottawattamie
*Corydon (c h)	Wayne	Dowville	Crawford
Cottage	Hardin	*Drakesville	Davis
Cottage Hill	Dubuque	Dryden	Tama
Cotton Grove	Henry	Dry Lake	Wright
Cottonville	Jackson	*Dubuque (c h)	Dubuque
*Council Bluffs (c h)	Pottawattamie	Dudley	Wapello
Council Hill	Clayton	Duke	Dubuque
Counover	Winneshiek	Duncombe	Webster
Cox's Creek	Clayton	*Dunlap	Harrison
Crabb's Mills	Jackson	Durango	Dubuque
*Crawfordsville	Washington	*Durant	Cedar
Cresent City	Pottawattamie	Dutch Creek	Washington
*Cresco (c h)	Howard	*Dyersville	Dubuque
*Creston	Union	*Dysart	Tama
Creswell	Keokuk		
Cromwell	Union	Eagle Grove	Wright
Cromwell Centre	Clay	*Earlham	Madison
Cross	Ringgold	*Earlville	Delaware
Croton	Lee	East Melrose	Monroe
Crystal	Tama	East Nodaway	Adams
Crystal Lake	Hancock	East Orange	Sioux
		Eastport	Fremont
Dahlonega	Wapello	*Eddyville	Wapello
Dairy	Washington	Eden	Fayette
Dakota (c h)	Humboldt	Edenville	Marshall
Dalby	Allamakee	Edgewood	Clayton
Dale City	Guthrie	Elba	Carroll
Dallas	Marion	Eldon	Wapello
*Dallas Center	Dallas	*Eldora (c h)	Hardin
Dalmanutha	Guthrie	El Dorado	Fayette
Dan	Taylor	Eldridge	Scott
Danforth	Johnson	*Elgin	Fayette
*Danville	Des Moines	Elizabeth	Grundy
Darlington	Sioux	Elk	Decatur
*Davenport (c h)	Scott	*Elkader (c h)	Clayton
Davis City	Decatur	Elkhart	Polk
Dayton	Bremer	Elk Horn	Shelby
Dean	Appanoose	Elkport	Clayton
Decatur	Decatur	Ellington	Hancock
*Decorah (c h)	Winneshiek	Ellis	Hardin
Deep River	Poweshiek	Elon	Allamakee
Deer Creek	Fremont	Elvira	Clinton
Deerfield	Chickasaw	Elwood	Clinton
Defiance	Shelby	Ely	Linn
Delaware	Delaware	Emeline	Jackson
*Delhi (c h)	Delaware	Emerson	Mills
*Delmar	Clinton	Emmet	Emmet
Deloit	Crawford	Emmetsburg (c h)	Palo Alto
*Denison (c h)	Crawford	Empire	Wright
*Denmark	Lee	English Settlement	Marion
Dennis	Appanoose	Enterprise	Black Hawk
Denver	Bremer	*Epworth	Dubuque
Derby	Lucas	Erie	O'Brien
*Des Moines (c h)	Polk	Ernest	Lyon
*De Soto	Dallas	Essex	Page
*De Witt	Clinton	Estherville (c h)	Emmet
*Dexter	Dallas	Eugene	Ringgold

TABLE XXII.—Continued.

NAMES OF POST-OFFICES.	COUNTIES.	NAMES OF POST-OFFICES.	COUNTIES.
Eveland Grove	Mahaska	Gem	Clayton
Evergreen	Tama	Geneva	Franklin
*Exira (c h)	Audubon	Genoa	Wayne
		Genoa Bluff	Iowa
Fairbank	Buchanan	Georgetown	Monroe
*Fairfax	Linn	Germanville	Jefferson
*Fairfield (c h)	Jefferson	Girard	Clayton
Fairhaven	Tama	Gilbert	Scott
Fairmount	Marion	Gilbertville	Black Hawk
Fairport	Muscatine	Gillett's Grove	Clay
Fairview	Jones	Gilman	Marshall
*Farley	Dubuque	Givin	Mahaska
Farmers	Sioux	Glasgow	Jefferson
Farmersburg	Clayton	Glendale	Jefferson
Farmersville	Jasper	*Glen Roy	Howard
*Farmington	Van Buren	*Glenwood (c h)	Mills
Farragut	Fremont	Glidden	Carroll
Faulkner	Franklin	Godfrey	Wapello
*Fayette	Fayette	Golden Prairie	Delaware
Fenton	Kossuth	Goldfield	Wright
Fern Valley	Palo Alto	Goose Lake	Clinton
Ferry	Mahaska	Gopher	Osceola
Fertile	Worth	Gorden's Ferry	Jackson
Festina	Winneshiek	Goshen	Ringgold
Fifteen Mile Grove	Tama	Gosport	Marion
Fillmore	Dubuque	Gower's Ferry	Cedar
Finchford	Black Hawk	Gowrie	Webster
Fisk	Adair	Grand Junction	Greene
Flemingville	Linn	Grand Mound	Clinton
Flint	Mahaska	Grand View	Louisa
*Florence	Benton	Grant	Montgomery
Florenceville	Howard	Grant Center	Monona
Floris	Davis	Grant City	Sac
Floyd	Floyd	Granville	Mahaska
Flushing	Ringgold	Gravity	Taylor
Fonda	Pocahontas	Great Oak	Palo Alto
*Fontanelle	Adair	Greeley	Delaware
Foote	Iowa	*Greene	Butler
*Forest City (c h)	Winnebago	Green Bay	Clarke
Forest Home	Poweshiek	Greencastle	Jasper
Forestville	Delaware	Greenfield (c h)	Adair
Fort Atkinson	Winneshiek	Green Island	Jackson
*Fort Dodge (c h)	Webster	Green Mountain	Marshall
*Fort Madison (c h)	Lee	Greenvale	Dallas
Four Corners	Jefferson	Green Valley	Decatur
Frankfort	Montgomery	Greenville	Clay
Franklin	Decatur	Greenwood	Polk
Franklin Center	Lee	Greenwood Center	Kossuth
Franklin Grove	Page	Griffinsville	Appanoose
Franklin Mills	Des Moines	*Grinnell	Poweshiek
Frank Pierce	Johnson	Grove	Audubon
Frankville	Winneshiek	Grove Creek	Delaware
Fredericksburg	Chickasaw	Grove Hill	Bremer
Fredonia	Louisa	Groveland	Adair
Fredric	Monroe	*Grundy Center (c h)	Grundy
Fredricka	Bremer	*Guthrie	Guthrie
Freedom	Lucas	*Guthrie Center, (c h)	Guthrie
Freeman	Clay	*Guttenburg	Clayton
Freeport	Winneshiek		
Fremont	Mahaska	Hale	Kossuth
French Creek	Allamakee	Hale Village	Jones
Fryeburg	Wright	Half Way Prairie	Monroe
Fulton	Jackson	Hall Creek	Monona
Funk's Mill	Decatur	*Hamburg	Fremont
		Hamilton	Marion
Gale	Woodbury	Hamlin	Audubon
Galesburgh	Jasper	Hammondsburgh	Warren
*Garden Grove	Decatur	*Hampton (c h)	Franklin
Garden Prairie	Boone	Hanover	Allamakee
Garibaldi	Keokuk	Happy Hollow	Wapello
*Garnavillo	Clayton	Hardin	Clayton
Garner	Hancock	Hardin City	Hardin
Garrison	Benton	*Harlan (c h)	Shelby
Garry Owen	Jackson	Harper	Keokuk

TABLE XXII.—Continued.

NAMES OF POST-OFFICES.	COUNTIES.	NAMES OF POST-OFFICES.	COUNTIES.
Harper's Ferry	Allamakee	Irvington	Kossuth
Hartford	Warren	Irwin	Audubon
Hartland	Worth		
Hastings	Mills	Jackson	Adair
Hatch	Kossuth	Jacksonville	Chickasaw
Haven	Tama	James	Plymouth
Hawk-Eye	Fayette	*Jaynesville	Bremer
Hawleyville	Page	*Jefferson (c h)	Greene
Hawthorn	Montgomery	Jerome	Appanoose
Hayesville	Keokuk	*Jesup	Buchanan
Hazard	Cherokee	Jewell	Mills
Hazelton	Buchanan	Johnson	Jones
Hazle Green	Delaware		
Hebron	Adair	Kasson	Madison
Helena	Tama	Keg Creek	Pottawattamie
Hepburn	Page	Kelley	Story
Hesper	Winneshiek	*Kellogg	Jasper
Hesperian	Webster	Kendallville	Winneshiek
Hibbsville	Appanoose	Kensett	Worth
Hickory	Van Buren	Kent	Union
Higginsport	Jackson	*Keokuk	Lee
High Creek	Fremont	*Keosauqua (c h)	Van Buren
Highland	Clayton	*Keota	Keokuk
Highland Center	Wapello	Kesho	Webster
Highland Grove	Jones	Kier	Buchanan
Highlandville	Winneshiek	Kilbourne	Van Buren
High Point	Decatur	King	Dubuque
Hillsborough	Henry	Kingston	Des Moines
Hillsdale	Mills	Kirkville	Wapello
Hinsdale	Lee	Kirkwood	Appanoose
Hinton	Plymouth	Kiron	Crawford
Hire's Grove	Buena Vista	Kniffen	Wayne
Holaday's	Adair	*Knoxville (c h)	Marion
Holt	Taylor	Kossuth	Des Moines
Home	Van Buren	Kossuth Center	Kossuth
Homer	Hamilton	Koszta	Iowa
*Homestead	Iowa	Lacelle	Clarke
Honey Creek	Pottawattamie	Lacona	Warren
Hook's Point	Hamilton	Ladora	Iowa
*Hopeville	Clarke	La Fayette	Linn
Hopewell	Mahaska	La Grange	Lucas
*Hopkinton	Delaware	Lake City (c h)	Calhoun
Horn	Jasper	LakeMills	Winnebago
Horton	Bremer	Lake View	Palo Alto
Hosper	Sioux	Lakeville	Dickinson
Howard Center	Howard	Lakin's Grove	Hamilton
Hudson	Black Hawk	Lally	Des Moines
Hull	Boone	Lamoille	Marshall
*Humboldt	Humboldt	La Motte	Jackson
Humeston	Wayne	Lancaster	Keokuk
Hummaconna	Monroe	Langworthy	Jones
Huron	Des Moines	*Lansing	Allamakee
		*La Porte City	Black Hawk
Iconium	Appanoose	Larchwood	Lyon
Ida (c h)	Ida	Last Chance	Lucas
Illinois Grove	Marshall	Latham	Webster
Illyria	Fayette	Lattners	Dubuque
*Independence (c h)	Buchanan	Latty	Des Moines
Indianapolis	Mahaska	Laurel	Marshall
*Indianola (c h)	Warren	La Vega	Des Moines
Ingart Grove	Ringgold	*Lawler	Chickasaw
Ingham	Franklin	Lawrenceburgh	Warren
Ingleville	Clay	Lebanon	Van Buren
Inland	Cedar	*LeClaire	Scott
Ioka	Keokuk	Le Grand	Marshall
Iola	Marion	Leighton	Mahaska
Ion	Allamakee	*Lemars (c h)	Plymouth
Ionia	Chickasaw	Lenox	Taylor
Iowa Center	Story	*Leon (c h)	Decatur
*Iowa City (c h)	Johnson	Leroy	Bremer
*Iowa Falls	Hardin	Leroyville	Audubon
Iowa Lake	Emmet	Lester	Black Hawk
Irene	Sioux	Letts	Louisa
Iron Hills	Jackson	*Lewis	Cass

TABLE XXII.—Continued.

NAMES OF POST-OFFICES.	COUNTIES.	NAMES OF POST-OFFICES.	COUNTIES.
Lewisburg	Wayne	Martelle	Jones
Lexington	Washington	*Martinsburgh	Keokuk
Liberty	Clarke	Marysville	Marion
Liberty Center	Warren	*Mason City (c h)	Cerro Gordo
Libertyville	Jefferson	Masonville	Delaware
Lima	Fayette	Massillon	Cedar
Lime Spring	Howard	Mauch Chunk	Mahaska
Lincoln	Polk	Maudville	Butler
Lincoln Center	Grundy	Maxfield	Bremer
*Lineville	Wayne	Maynard	Fayette
Linton	Des Moines	Maysville	Franklin
*Lisbon	Linn	Mead	Clinton
Liscomb	Marshall	*Mechanicsville	Cedar
Listonville	Woodbury	Mederville	Clayton
Little Cedar	Mitchell	Mediapolis	Des Moines
Little Port	Clayton	Melleray	Dubuque
Little River	Decatur	Melpine	Muscatine
*Little Sioux	Harrison	Melrose	Grundy
Livingston	Appanoose	Memory	Taylor
Lockridge	Jefferson	Menoti	Buena Vista
Locust Lane	Winneshiek	Mentor	Bremer
Logan	Harrison	Menzie	Franklin
Lone Tree	Johnson	Meroa	Mitchell
Long Creek	Decatur	Merrill	Plymouth
Long Grove	Scott	Merrimac	Jefferson
Losh's Mills	Pottawattamie	Middleburgh	Washington
Lost Island	Palo Alto	Middlefield	Buchanan
Lost Nation	Clinton	Middle River	Madison
Lothrop	Warren	Middletown	Des Moines
Lott's Creek	Humboldt	Midland	Hardin
*Louden	Cedar	Mid Prairie	Louisa
Louisville	Audubon	Milan	Lucas
Loveland	Pottawattamie	Miles	Jackson
Lovilia	Monroe	Milford	Dickinson
Lowell	Henry	Mill	Fayette
Low Moore	Clinton	Milledgeville	Appanoose
Luana	Clayton	Millersburg	Iowa
Lucas	Lucas	Miller's Creek	Black Hawk
Lucas Grove	Marion	Millville	Clayton
Ludlow	Allamakee	Milton	Van Buren
Luni	Wright	Minburn	Dallas
*Luzerne	Benton	Minden	Pottawattamie
Lycurgus	Allamakee	Mineral Ridge	Boone
Lynnville	Jasper	Minerva	Marshall
*Lyons	Clinton	*Missouri Valley	Harrison
Lytle City	Iowa	*Mitchell	Mitchell
		*Mitchellville	Polk
*McGregor	Clayton	Modale	Harrison
McKnight's Point	Humboldt	Moffitt's Grove	Guthrie
McPaul	Fremont	*Moingona	Boone
Macedonia	Pottawattamie	Mona	Mitchell
Macksburgh	Madison	Mondamin	Harrison
Madora	Warren	Monmouth	Jackson
*Magnolia (c h)	Harrison	Monona	Clayton
*Malcom	Poweshiek	*Monroe	Jasper
Mallory	Shelby	Monterey	Davis
Malone	Clinton	*Montezuma (c h)	Poweshiek
*Malvern	Mills	*Monticello	Jones
*Manchester	Delaware	*Montour	Tama
Manhattan	Keokuk	*Montrose	Lee
Manson	Calhoun	Mooreville	Tama
Mantena	Shelby	Moorhead	Monona
Maple Grove	Madison	Moravia	Appanoose
Maple Landing	Monona	Moriah	Iowa
Mapleton	Monona	Mormontown	Taylor
*Maquoketa (c h)	Jackson	*Morning Sun	Louisa
Marble Rock	Floyd	Morse	Johnson
Marcus	Cherokee	Moscow	Muscatine
Marena	Ringgold	*Moulton	Appanoose
*Marengo (c h)	Iowa	*Mount Algor	Jackson
Marietta	Marshall	Mount Auburn	Benton
*Marion (c h)	Linn	Mount Ayr (c h)	Ringgold
*Marshall	Henry	Mount Carmel	Carroll
*Marshalltown (c h)	Marshall	Mount Etna	Adams

TABLE XXII.—Continued.

NAMES OF POST-OFFICES.	COUNTIES.	NAMES OF POST-OFFICES.	COUNTIES.
Mount Joy	Scott	Oasis	Johnson
Mount Pisgah	Harrison	O'Brien	O'Brien
*Mount Pleasant (c h)	Henry	Ocheyedan	Osceola
Mount Sterling	Van Buren	Oelwein	Fayette
Mount Valley	Winnebago	Ogden	Boone
*Mount Vernon	Linn	Ohio	Madison
Mount Zion	Van Buren	Ola	Lucas
Moville	Woodbury	Old Mission	Winneshiek
Muchachinock	Mahaska	*Olin	Jones
Munterville	Wapello	Oliver	Sac
Murray	Clarke	*Onawa City (c h)	Monona
*Muscatine (c h)	Muscatine	Onslow	Jones
Musquaka	Iowa	Ontario	Story
Myron	Allamakee	Oran	Fayette
		Orange	Clinton
*Nashua	Chickasaw	*Orange City (c h)	Sioux
Nashville	Jackson	Orchard	Mitchell
National	Clayton	Orient	Adair
Nautrill	Black Hawk	Orleans	Appanoose
Navan	Winneshiek	Ormanville	Wapello
Neola	Pottawattamie	*Osage (c h	Mitchell
*Nevada (c h)	Story	*Osceolo (c h)	Clarke
Nevinville	Adams	Oshkosh	Sioux
New Alba	Winneshiek	*Oskaloosa	Mahaska
New Albin	Allamakee	*Ossian	Winneshiek
New Bergen	Emmet	Otho	Webster
Newbern	Marion	Otisville	Franklin
New Boston	Lee	Otley	Marion
New Buda	Decatur	Oto	Woodbury
Newell	Buena Vista	Otranto	Mitchell
New Hampton (c h)	Chickasaw	Otter Creek	Jackson
New Hartford	Butler	Otterville	Buchanan
New Liberty	Scott	*Ottumwa (c h)	Wapello
*New London	Henry	*Oxford	Johnson
Newlon's Grove	Cass	Oxford Mills	Jones
New Oregon	Howard	Oxford Junction	Jones
Newport	Johnson	Ozark	Jackson
New Providence	Hardin		
*New Sharon	Mahaska	Pacific City	Mills
*Newton (c h)	Jasper	Pacific Junction	Mills
Newtonville	Buchanan	Page City	Page
New Vienna	Dubuque	Palermo	Grundy
New Virginia	Warren	Palmer	Polk
New York	Wayne	Palmyra	Warren
Nichol Station	Muscatine	Palo	Linn
Nobleton	Polk	Palo Alto	Louisa
Nodaway Mills	Page	*Panora	Guthrie
Noebla	Kossuth	Paralta	Linn
Nora	Humboldt	Paris	Linn
Nora Springs	Floyd	*Parkersburg	Butler
Nordyke	Dallas	Park Grove	Humboldt
North Branch	Guthrie	Parma	Pottawattamie
North Buena Vista	Clayton	Parrish	Des Moines
North English	Iowa	Paton	Greene
Northfield	Des Moines	Patriot	Decatur
North Liberty	Johnson	Patterson	Madison
North McGregor	Clayton	Paul	Benton
North River	Madison	Pearl Rock	Chickasaw
Northville	Greene	Pedee	Cedar
North Washington	Chickasaw	*Pella	Marion
*Northwood (c h)	Worth	Peoria	Mahaska
Nortonville	Clarke	Peoria City	Polk
Norwalk	Warren	Peosta	Dubuque
Norwood	Lucas	Percival	Fremont
Nugent's Grove	Linn	Perlee	Jefferson
Numa	Appanoose	Perry	Dallas
		Peru	Madison
Oak	Marion	Petersburg	Delaware
Oakfield	Audubon	Peterson	Clay
Oakland Mills	Henry	Pierceville	Van Buren
Oakland Valley	Franklin	Pilot Grove	Lee
Oak Point	Van Buren	Pilot Mound	Boone
Oak Spring	Davis	Pilot Rock	Cherokee
Oak Wood Station	Polk	Pine Mills	Muscatine

TABLE XXII.—Continued.

NAMES OF POST-OFFICES.	COUNTIES.	NAMES OF POST-OFFICES.	COUNTIES.
Pin Oak	Dubuque	Rock Branch	Woodbury
Pittsburgh	Van Buren	Rock Creek	Mitchell
Plainfield	Bremer	Rock Dale	Dubuque
Plain View	Scott	Rock Falls	Cerro Gordo
Platteville	Taylor	Rockford	Floyd
Pleasant Grove	Des Moines	Rock Rapids (c h)	Lyon
Pleasant Hill	Cedar	Rockville	Delaware
Pleasanton	Decatur	Rockwell	Cerro Gordo
Pleasant Plain	Jefferson	Roland	Story
Pleasant Prairie	Muscatine	Rolfe (c h)	Pocahontas
Pleasant Valley	Scott	Rome	Henry
Pleasant View	Madison	Rosbach	Plymouth
Pleasantville	Marion	Rose Grove	Hamilton
Plum Hollow	Fremont	Rose Mount	Warren
Plymouth	Cerro Gordo	Rossville	Allamakee
Plymouth Rock	Winneshiek	Round Grove	Scott
Pocahontas Center	Pocahontas	Rousseau	Marion
Point Pleasant	Hardin	Rowley	Buchanan
Polk City	Polk	Royal Ridge	Sioux
Pomeroy	Calhoun	Rudd	Floyd
Ponona	Plymouth	Rural	Linn
Port Allen	Louisa	Russell	Lucas
Portland	Cerro Gordo	Rutland	Humboldt
Portlandville	Plymouth		
Port Louisa	Louisa	*Sabula	Jackson
Port Richmond	Wapello	Sac City (c h)	Sac
*Postville	Allamakee	Saint Ansgar	Mitchell
Prairieburg	Linn	Saint Charles	Madison
*Prairie City	Jasper	Saint Clair	Monona
Prairie Grove	Clarke	Saint Donatus	Jackson
Prairie Hill	Boone	Saint Gilman	Osceola
Prescott	Adams	Saint Mary's	Warren
*Preston	Jackson	Saint Olaf	Clayton
Primrose	Lee	Saint Paul	Lee
*Princeton	Scott	Saint Sebald	Clayton
Primghar (c h)	O'Brien	*Salem	Henry
Promise City	Wayne	Salina	Jefferson
Pulaski	Davis	Salix	Woodbury
Putnam	Fayette	Sand Spring	Delaware
		Sandusky	Lee
Quarry	Marshall	Sandyville	Warren
Quasqueton	Buchanan	Saratoga	Howard
*Quincy	Adams	Savannah	Davis
		Saylorville	Polk
Randall	Hamilton	Schoharie	Sac
Randolph	Humboldt	Schonberg	Warren
Raymond	Black Hawk	Sciola	Montgomery
Read	Clayton	Scotch Grove	Jones
Redding	Ringgold	Scott Center	Fayette
Redfield	Dallas	Scranton Station	Greene
*Red Oak (c h)	Montgomery	Searsborough	Poweshiek
Red Rock	Marion	Seaton	Fayette
Reeder's Mills	Harrison	Sedgewick	Decatur
Reed's Ridge	Allamakee	Selma	Wayne
Reinbeck	Grundy	Seneca	Kossuth
Riceville	Mitchell	Seney	Plymouth
Richfield	Fayette	Sergeant Bluffs	Woodbury
*Richland	Keokuk	Seventy-Eight	Johnson
*Richmond	Washington	*Seymour	Wayne
Rickardsville	Dubuque	Sharon	Warren
Ridgedale	Polk	Sheffield	Franklin
*Ridgeway	Winneshiek	Shelby	Shelby
Riggs	Clayton	Shelbyville	Shelby
Ringgold	Ringgold	*Sheldon	O'Brien
Rippey	Greene	Shell Rock	Bntler
Rising Sun	Polk	*Shellsburg	Benton
Riverdale	Iowa	*Shenandoah	Page
River Junction	Johnson	Sheridan	Van Buren
Riverside	Washington	Sherman	Poweshiek
Riverton	Fremont	Sherrill's Mount	Dubuque
Riverview	Lyon	Shiloh	Cedar
Robin	Benton	Shoo Fly	Johnson
Rochester	Cedar	Shueyville	Jonnson
Rock	Cerro Gordo	Siam	Taylor

TABLE XXII.—CONTINUED.

NAMES OF POST-OFFICES.	COUNTIES.	NAMES OF POST-OFFICES.	COUNTIES.
*Sibley (c h)	Osceola	Taunton	Warren
*Sidney	Fremont	Taylor's Station	Pottawattamie.
Sigel	Clayton	Taylorsville	Fayette
*Sigourney	Keokuk	Teed's Grove	Clinton
Silver Creek.	Ida	Terre Haute	Decatur
Silver Lake	Worth	Thayer	Union
*Sioux City (c h)	Woodbury	Thompson	Audubon
*Sioux Rapids (c h)	Buena Vista	Ticonic	Monona
Slagle	Keokuk	Tiffin	Johnson
Sloan	Woodbury	Tilton	Poweshiek
Smithland	Woodbury	Timber Creek	Marshall
Smyrna	Clarke	Tingley	Union
Snow Hill	Page	*Tipton (c h)	Cedar
Snyder	Dallas	Tipton Grove	Hardin
Soda Bar	Palo Alto	Tivoli	Dubuque
Soldier	Monona	Toddville	Linn
Soldier Valley	Harrison	*Toledo (c h)	Tama
*Solon	Johnson	Toolsborough	Louisa
South Amana	Iowa	Toronto	Clinton
South English	Keokuk	Tower Hill	Delaware
South Flint	Des Moines	*Traer	Tama
*Spencer (c h)	Clay	Tranquility	Appanoose
Spencer Grove	Benton	Trent	Polk
Sperry	Des Moines	Trenton	Henry
Spillville	Winneshiek	Tremello	Clay
Spinneyville	Scott	Tripoli	Bremer
*Spirit Lake (c h)	Dickinson	Troy	Davis
Spragueville	Jackson	Troy Mills	Linn
Spring Brook	Jackson	Turkey River	Clayton
Spring Creek	Tama	Turner	Mills
*Springdale	Cedar	Tuskeega	Decatur
Springfield	Keokuk	Tuttle Grove	Guthrie
Spring Grove	Linn	Twin Lakes	Calhoun
Spring Hill	Warren	Twin Oak	Louisa
Spring Valley	Decatur	Tyrone	Monroe
*Springville	Linn	Tyson's Mills	Webster
Springwater	Winneshiek		
Staceyville	Mitchell	Ulster	Floyd
Stanford	Marshall	*Union	Hardin
Stanton	Montgomery	Unionburgh	Harrison
*Stanwood	Cedar	Union Center	Jackson
Stapleton	Chickasaw	Union Grove	Page
Star	Marion	Union Hill	Ringgold
*State Center	Marshall	Union Mills	Mahaska
*Steamboat Rock	Hardin	Union Ridge	Butler
Stelapolis	Iowa	Uniontown	Delaware
Sterling	Jackson	Unionville	Appanoose
Stiles	Davis	Unity	Johnson
Stillwater	Mitchell	Upper Grove	Hancock
Stockton	Muscatine	Upton	Van Buren
Stone City	Jones	Urbana	Benton
*Storm Lake	Buena Vista	Urbana City	Monroe
Story City	Story	Utica	Van Buren
*Strawberry Point	Clayton		
*Stuart	Guthrie	Vail	Crawford
Sugar Creek Mills	Cedar	Valley	Washington
Summers	Benton	Valley Junction	Polk
Summerset	Warren	Van Buren	Jackson
Summit	Clay	Vandalia	Jasper
Summitville	Lee	*Van Meter	Dallas
Sumner	Bremer	Vaughan	Fremont
Sunny Side	Black Hawk	Vega	Jefferson
Swanton	Butler	Vernon	Van Buren
Swea	Kossuth	Verona	Poweshiek
Swede Point	Boone	*Victor	Poweshiek
Swedesburgh	Henry	Viele	Lee
Sweetland Center	Muscatine	Vienna	Marshall
		Village Creek	Allamakee
*Tabor	Fremont	*Villisca	Montgomery
Tallahoma	Lucas	Vincennes	Lee
Talleyrand	Keokuk	Vineyard	Tama
*Tama City	Tama	Vino	Adair
Tara	Webster	*Vinton (c h)	Benton
Tarkio	Page	Viola	Linn

TABLE XXII.—Continued.

NAMES OF POST-OFFICES.	COUNTIES.	NAMES OF POST-OFFICES.	COUNTIES.
Viona	Humboldt	*West Mitchell	Mitchell
Viroqua	Jones	Weston	Pottawattamie
Volga City	Clayton	West Pilot	Iowa
Volney	Allamakee	*West Point	Lee
Von	Humboldt	West Prairie	Linn
		Westside	Crawford
Wacousta	Humboldt	West Troy	Iowa
Wadaloup	Grundy	*West Union (c h)	Fayette
Wagner	Clayton	Wever	Lee
Walden	Keokuk	What Cheer	Keokuk
Walker	Linn	*Wheatland	Clinton
Walkerville	Page	Wheeler's Grove	Pottawattamie
Wallace	Montgomery	Wheeling	Marion
Walnut City	Appanoose	White Ash	Washington
Walnut Creek Station	Pottawattamie	White Breast	Lucas
Waltham	Tama	White Cloud	Mills
*Wapello (c h)	Louisa	White Oak	Mahaska
Wardena	Fayette	White Pigeon	Keokuk
Ward's Corners	Buchanan	Whiting	Monona
Warren	Lee	Whitneyville	Cass
Warsaw	Wayne	Williams	Hamilton
*Washington (c h)	Washington	Williamstown	Chickasaw
Washington Prairie	Winneshiek	Willida	Lyon
Washta	Cherokee	Willitts	Van Buren
Wassonville	Washington	Willoughby	Butler
*Waterloo (c h)	Black Hawk	Willow Creek	Clay
Waterman	Wright	Willow Dale	Ida
Watertown	Floyd	Willow Grove	Story
Waterville	Allamakee	Wilson	Montgomery
Watkins	Benton	Willsonville	Van Buren
Watkyn's Glen	Clinton	*Wilton Junction	Muscatine
Watson	Allamakee	Winchester	Van Buren
Waubeck	Linn	Windham	Johnson
Waucoma	Fayette	Windsor	Fayette
Waukee	Dallas	Windfield	Henry
*Waukon (c h)	Allamakee	Winona	Henry
Waupaton	Dubuque	*Winterset (c h)	Madison
*Waverly (c h)	Bremer	Winthrop	Buchanan
Waveland	Pottawattamie	Wiota	Cass
Wayne	Henry	Wolcott	Scott
Webster	Keokuk	Wolf Dale	Woodbury
*Webster City (c h)	Hamilton	Woodbine	Harrison
Weller	Monroe	Woodburn	Clarke
Wells	Madison	Woodville	Winneshiek
Wellsburgh	Page	Woolstock	Wright
Wells' Mills	Appanoose	Wooster	Jefferson
Welton	Clinton	Worthington	Dubuque
Wentworth	Mitchell	*Wyoming	Jones
Wesley Station	Kossuth		
West Albany	Fayette	Xenia	Dallas
West Bend	Palo Alto		
*West Branch	Cedar	Yatton	Washington
West Chester	Washington	Yazoo	Harrison
West Dayton	Webster	York	Delaware
Western College	Linn	York Center	Iowa
Westerville	Decatur		
West Grove	Davis	Zero	Lucas
West Irving	Tama	Zwingle	Jackson
*West Liberty	Muscatine		

COUNTY GOVERNMENT.

Table Showing the Names of the County Auditors, Clerks of the District and Circuit Courts, Treasurers, Recorders, and Sheriffs, with the County Seats of the several Counties, for the Year 1876; Also the Number of the Senatorial and Representative Districts in which each County is Located.

Senatorial District.	Representative District.	COUNTIES.	COUNTY SEATS.	AUDITORS.	CLERKS OF DISTRICT AND CIRCUIT COURTS.	TREASURERS.	RECORDERS.	SHERIFFS.
17	21	Adair	Greenfield	William B. Martin	Jno. J. Hetherington	L. J. Gray	R. O. Brown	C. B Hunt
17	20	Adams	Corning	Walter E. McDuffee	James Widner	Westley Homan	Jonas P. Cupp	John W. Larimer
41	60	Allamakee	Waukon	Wm. C. Thompson	H. O. Dayton	John Ryan	David W. Reed	George Hewit
4	9	Appanoose	Centerville	John B. Maring	Walter S Johnson	William Evans	John B. Wright	B. F. Silknetler
49	21	Audubon	Exira	Thomas Walker	A. Lorenzo Campbell	Wm. F. Stotts	John S. Toft	Joseph L. Stotts
33	51	Benton	Vinton	Edward M. Evans	Horace E. Warner	Othniel Horne	James W. Smock	Peter S. Smith
44	50	Black Hawk	Waterloo	Daniel W. Foote	John C. Gates	David B. Washburn	Chester B. Stillson	George W. Hayzlett.
45	44	Boone	Boonsboro	John A. Head	Phil. Livingston	John W. Snell	John F. Bratt	S. N. Canfield
48	62	Bremer	Waverly	Herman Rust	Aaron H. McCracken	George Morehouse	Harmon S. Munger	Lewis S. Hanchett
37	52	Buchanan	Independence	D. A. McLeish	D. L. Smith	James A. Poor	John Hollett	W. S. Van Osdal
47	71	Buena Vista	Sioux Rapids	W. Byron Farrar	Edgar E. Mack	John W. Ayres	Talmadge W. Lee	Ed. E. Evans
43	67	Butler	Butler Center	Rufus L. Chase	Wm. H. Burdick	Edward S. Thomas	Elwood Wilson	John R. Jones
47	42	Calhoun	Lake City	A. N. Jack	H. H. Hutchinson	T. P. Gregg	S. T. Hutchinson	L. H. Chase
49	42	Carroll	Carroll	E. M. Betzer	William Lynch, Jr.	P. M. Guthrie	H. E. Russell	Louis Bechler
17	21	Cass	Atlantic	Wm. Gardner	H. E. Bacon	John T. Gerbenck	Frank Aylesworth	J. S. Pressnale
24	32	Cedar	Tipton	Mareau Carroll	Wm. H. Van Ness	Samuel Wampler	Charles W. Hawley	Arthur B. Maynard.
46	68	Cerro Gordo	Mason City	Henry H. Shepard	M. B. Schermerhorn	James Rule	Owen T. Denison	H. H. Schell
50	41	Cherokee	Cherokee	William B. Chick	Oscar Chase	M. Baumgardner	John E. Davis	Leon Moore
48	63	Chickasaw	New Hampton	Lee Chapman	John M. Gilliland	John Foley	Charles A. Harris	Rodolph O. Sheldon.
6	13	Clarke	Osceola	Philip L. Fowler	John H. Jamison	Jacob M. Linder	A. C. Johnson	Joseph N. Ballou
47	72	Clay	Spencer	L. M. Pemberton	Ackley Hubbard	Marion E. Griffin	A. H. Cheney	John E. Francis

39	58	Clayton	Elkader	Martin Garber	Marvin Cook	Henry Kellner	Robert L. Freeman	Willard A. Benton
23	31	Clinton	Clinton	A. A. Wagner	W. B. Leffingwell	Edwin R. Lucas	Daniel Correll	Michael Purcell
49	41	Crawford	Denison	A. D. Molony	W. S. Wilson	L. Cornwell	J. B. Poitevin	A. C. Smith
16	38	Dallas	Adel	Z. W. Kelley	A. C. Hotchkiss	Jesse Macy	J. H. Mattox	S. J. Ellis
3	7	Davis	Bloomfield	Joseph W. Clayton	Ambrose N. Hill	John M. Sloane	Wm. Votaw	John McKibben
7	12	Decatur	Leon	Wm. C. Jackson	Abel E. Chase	Francis Varga	Wm. J. Sullivan	Albert Dilsaver
36	57	Delaware	Delhi	Jeremiah B. Boggs	Jerome B. Satterlee	Joseph M. Holbrook	Henry C. Jackson	John W. Corbin
10	2	Des Moines	Burlington	Turton J. Copp	T. G. Foster	Aug. C. Hutchinson	Fisher Morrison	Wm. Schaffner
47	72	Dickinson	Spirit Lake	Samuel S. Pillsbury	John A. Smith	Albert W. Osborne	Albert A. Mosher	Albert L. Sawyer
35	56	Dubuque	Dubuque	Frank McLaughlin	Patrick J. Quigley	V. J. Williams	Warren Lewis	Peter Ferring
47	71	Emmet	Estherville	H, W. Halverson	John M. Barker	E. H. Ballard	Jesse Coverdale	Knut Espeset
40	59	Fayette	West Union	James H. Lakin	B. Morse	F. Y. Whitmore	R. W. McFarland	J. J. Welsh
43	66	Floyd	Charles City	Joseph S. Trigg	Harvey Kellogg	Eli Brownell	Jacob Baier	James M. Miner
46	68	Franklin	Hampton	John M. Wait	Thomas B. Taylor	Rufus S Benson	Guy C. Hayes	Abel N. Minor
8	17	Fremont	Sidney	Amos P. Stafford	H. Russell Laird	Aden D. King	John B. Gray	Wm. Weber Morgan
49	42	Greene	Jefferson	George G. Lawrence.	James F. Anderson.	Samuel Jay	James W. Fitz	John Ayers
34	48	Grundy	Grundy Center	W. C. Williams	F. G. Moffett	E. H. Beckman	S. Rea Raymond	Levi Dilly
49	39	Guthrie	Gnthrie Center	Henry K. Dewey	Charles W Hill	Elijah J. Reynolds	James H. Rogers	Jas. McMillan
29	70	Hamilton	Webster City	Charles Wickware	Albert A. Wicks	John Eckstein	John V. Kearns	Fred. A. Harris
46	69	Hancock	Concord	John Christie, Jr	C. C. Doolittle	L. B. Bailey	H. M. Bradstreet	A. R. Barnes
29	46	Hardin	Eldora	D. B. Morse	Zeeb Gilman	Elias Hauser	Job Stout	J. M. Boyd
50	40	Harrison	Magnolia	Wm. H. Eaton	Henry W. Gleason	Isaac P. Hill	J. Cutter Milliman	J. B. McArthur
11	3	Henry	Mt Pleasant	Robert M. Lehen	John N. Allen	Addison Roads	Horton J. Howard	Wm. T. Spearman
48	64	Howard	Cresco	Jeremiah Barker	Calvin F. Webster	Frank Kyte	Wm. H. Patterson	Sam'l S. Thompson
46	70	Humboldt	Dakota City	Harlan Miner	Wm. Thompson	Ira L. Welch	S. K. Winne	A. B. West
26	34	Ida	Marengo.	W. B. Taylor	A. B. Eshleman	C. Baumer.	L. Patterson	O. B. Bolton
47	41	Iowa	Ida	Mat. M. Gray	Isaac Bunn	Frank Burns	Manford Evans	Ed. H. Burns
30	55	Jackson	Maquoketa	Allen J. House	John S. Ray	John Donnelly	John Griffin	John O. Bard
27	36	Jasper	Newton	Geo. R. Ledyard	W. R. McCully	Geo. T. Anderson	W. H. Hough	J. R. Bollinger
12	4	Jefferson	Fairfield	Sanford M. Boling	Marshall S. Crawford	Louis P. Vance	Jno. A. Montgomery	James M. Hughes
25	33	Johnson	Iowa City	Aaron J. Hershire	Jacob C. Switzer	Lovell Swisher	Geo. W. Hand	Mathew Cavanagh
31	54	Jones	Anamosa	Robert Dott	Benj. H. White	Thos. E. Patterson	Ralph L. Duer	Perry O. Babcock
14	26	Keokuk	Sigourney	John Morrison	Minor Wightman	Louis Hollingsworth	John M. Jones	A. Stranahan
46	69	Kossuth	Algona	Victor H. Stough	John Wallace	M. D. Blanchard	H. M. Horton	John M. Pinkerton
1	1	Lee	Fort Madison	Jacob C. Blackburn	Wm. P. Staub	Herman Welsing	Henry Bank, Jr	George T. Higgins
32	53	Linn	Marion	Samuel Daniels	John L. Crawford	Stephen T. Berry	Charles E. Putnam	George D. Gillilan
15	28	Louisa	Wapello	James B. Gibboney	John Huff	Whitney S. Kremer	N. W. M'Kay	Albert Ellis
6	10	Lucas	Chariton	J. Lee Brown	N. B. Gardner	James B. Custer	J. B Smith	George F. Holmes
50	73	Lyon	Rock Rapids	A. Tolman	Harman Cook	J. Shade	O. B. Dupee	James McCollen
16	22	Madison	Winterset	C. C. Goodale,	E, O, Burt	M. A. Knight	J. W. Graham	D. G. Ratliff

COUNTY GOVERNMENT.—Continued.

Senatorial District.	Representative District.	Counties.	County Seats.	Auditors.	Clerks of District and Circuit Courts.	Treasurers.	Recorders.	Sheriffs.
18	25	Mahaska	Oskaloosa	Geo. A. Ross	D. R. Moore	H. R. Kendig	Wm. R. Cowan	Jas. E. Hetherington
19	24	Marion	Knoxville	C. H. Robinson	Allen Hamrick	Richard M. Faris	Peter K. Bonebrake	Lucien W. Crozier
34	47	Marshall	Marshalltown	Alfred N. French	Edwin R. Jones	Henry A. Gerhart	N. C. Messenger	George S. Hickox
9	18	Mills	Glenwood	Jason M. Powell	T. P. Ballard	Marshal M. Angell	J. L. Tryon	James S. Hendrie
43	65	Mitchell	Osage	John R. Prime	Melvin H. White	E. P. Shepherd	Edwin L. Sawyer	L. D. Piper
50	41	Monona	Onawa	John K. McCaskey	W. R. Hanscom	G. H. Bryant	M. W. Bacon	James Walker
5	8	Monroe	Albia	Samuel T. Craig	J. W. H. Griffin	H. Hickenlooper	James R. Castle	James M. Robb
8	20	Montgomery	Red Oak Junct'n	Henry Howard	Henry H. Palmer	Thos. C. Lundy	W. B. Kennedy	Hiram G. McMillan
21	29	Muscatine	Muscatine	R. H. McCampbell	John H. Munroe	Jos. Morrison	W. M. Kenedy	Robt. C. Jewett
50	72	O'Brien	Primghar	Geo. W. Schee	Alonzo H. Willetts	Stephen Harris	Andrew J Brock	Edward A. Nissen
50	72	Osceola	Sibley	W. W. Moore	J. F. Glover	Levi Shell	D. L. McCausland	John H. Douglass
8	16	Page	Clarinda	Wm. M. Alexander	Joseph E. Hill	Henry Loranz	Jas. L. Brown	Isaac Damewood
47	71	Palo Alto	Emmetsburg	Benjamin Franklin	Thos. J. Prouty	Michael L. Brown	Jeremiah L. Martin	James E. King
50	73	Plymouth	LeMars	Gustave Haerling	E. E. Blake	John Herron	Melancthon Hilbert	James Hopkins
47	71	Pocahontas	Rolfe	A. O. Garlock	J. W. Wallace	W. D. McEwen	Andrew Jackson	Jos. Brietenbach
28	37	Polk	Des Moines	George C. Baker	John H. McClellan	William Lowry	James C. Read	George Lendrum
9	19	Pottawattamie	Council Bluffs	John Bennett	Reuben T. Bryant	Thomas Bowman	M. Flamant	A. L. Kable
38	35	Poweshiek	Montezuma	H. B. Muscott	J. W. Carr	Thos. Rainsburg	S. S. Snider	J. W. Farmer
7	14	Ringgold	Mt. Ayr	R. F. Askrew	G. S. Allyn	Henry Todd	B. F. Day	H. A. White
47	42	Sac	Sac City	Wm. Chapin	John F. Moody	Wm. H. Hobbs	N. B. Flack	Christopher Waddle
22	30	Scott	Davenport	James Dooley	Wm. H. Gabbert	Matthias J. Rohlfs	Joseph A. LeClaire	Harvey Leonard
49	21	Shelby	Harlan	W. Wyland	Geo. D. Ross	Thos. McDonald	A. F. Holcomb	John L. Long
50	73	Sioux	Orange City	John E. Wyatt	Jelle Pelmulder	Antonie J. Betten, Jr	Francis Lecocq	Thos. H. Dunham
45	45	Story	Nevada	John R. Hays	J. A. Fitchpatrick	Jay A. King	Ole K. Hill	J. F. Gillespie
38	49	Tama	Toledo	Jos. A. Bowelle	Chancy J. Stevens	Leonard B. Blinn	John B. M. Bishop	Robt. E. Austin
7	15	Taylor	Bedford	W. T. Evans	H. H. Taylor	Alex John	E. G. Medford	J. T. Scott

17	14	Union	Afton	F. M. Emmerson	E. J. Emmons	A. Skinner	B. F. Marts	F. M. chey
2	5	Van Buren	Keosauqua	Bernard F. Rehkopf.	Russell Johnston	Robert L. Clarke	Daniel K. Kittle	John W. Shane
13	6	Wapello	Ottumwa	M. B. Myers	Leonidas M. Godley.	Wm. H. H. Asbury	Wade Kirkpatrick	Thos. P. Spillman
20	23	Warren	Indianola	Joseph L. Wilson	J. E. Lucas	W. H. Anderson	Miles W. Judkins	Joseph T. Meek
15	27	Washington	Washington	D. J. Palmer	J. A. Cunningham	Robert Fisher	T. S. Rowan	Abram Bunker
5	11	Wayne	Corydon	James A. Harper	George Albertson	Jacob Brown	Clark G. Nelson	William Robb
47	43	Webster	Fort Dodge	John B. Scott	Moses H. Bliss	J. Hutchison	Jared Fuller	Peter W. Chantland
46	69	Winnebago	Forest City	Eugene Secor	O. T. Severs	Robert Clark	E. L. Stilson	Peter Lewis
42	61	Winneshiek	Decorah	Florenzo G. Hale	Aaron W. Brownell	Edwin Klove	Charles Steen	Jacob H. Womeldorf.
50	73	Woodbury	Sioux City	D. W. Moffat	E. B. Spalding	Charles Kent	Wm. I. Hepburn	John M. McDonald
46	69	Worth	Northwood	O. D. Eno	L. L. Carter	S. O. Peterson	S. O. Peterson	George F. Mattson
6	70	Wright	Clarion	Nicholas F. Weber	Lemuel P. Davis	Joseph H. Rowen	Edward Hartsock	Nicholas Malvin

COUNTY GOVERNMENT.—Continued.

Table showing the names of the Superintendents of Common Schools, County Surveyors, Coroners and Members Boards of Supervisors.

COUNTIES.	SUPERINTENDENT OF COMMON SCHOOLS.	COUNTY SURVEYORS.	CORONERS.	MEMBERS BOARDS OF SUPERVISORS.	MEMBERS BOARDS OF SUPERVISORS.	MEMBERS BOARDS OF SUPERVISORS.
Adair	M. W. Haver	W. A. Pryor	A. G. Carmichael	J. T. Graham	J. W. Hastings	George A. Davis
Adams	Wm. W. Roberts	Wm. E. Dougherty	John P. Hanna	J. S. Martin	J. L. Adkins	Jesse Orme
Allamakee	John W. Hinchon	James McAnaney	James Farrell	Henry Bensch	H. S. Cooper	Robert Crawford
Appanoose	J. W. Carey	D. N. Minor	Miles A. Holshouser	Joseph B. Gedney	Robert K. Johnson	Wm. S. Llewellyn
Audubon	Benj. F. Thacker	Robert T. Smart	Frank P. Bradley	Isaac Thomas	John Noon	Thomas A. Miller
Benton	Miss S. Blackberry	James A. Brown	Moses Denman	Isaac N. Chenoweth	Nelson Hawley	Hyrcanus Guinn
Black Hawk	James S. George	Edwin Rodenberger	Walter O. Richards	Caleb May	J. C. Burnham	H. W. Jenney
Boone	Thomas A. Cutler	I. A. Worcester	Wm. D. Templin	John Smyth	D. F. Goodykunts	I. N. Baynels
Bremer	Henry H. Burrington	Henry S. Moore	Horace Nichols	Sidney H. Curtis	Marvin Potter	Albert L. Stevenson
Buchanan	W. E. Parker	J. L. Seeley	H. H. Hunt	H. Bryant	Samuel Miller	Wm. Bunce
Buena Vista	James D. Adams	Samual W. Hobbs	Thomas Whitley	Lewis T. Swezey	Stephen Olney, Sr.	Edwin C. Cowles
Butler	John W. Stewart	John G. Rockwell	Charles Murray	Alex. Chrystie	N. H. Larkin	G. Hazlet
Calhoun	Mrs. C. E. O. Donaghue	H. J. Griswold	T. E. Hosman	Byron Ellis	E. S Clow	H. Love
Carroll	C. I. Hinman	L. McCurdy	D. Wayne	Geo. P. Wetherill	D. J. McDougall	R. L. Wolfe
Cass	Hiram A. Disbrow	Samuel Harlan	David H. Stafford	E. E. Herbert	S. E. Huse	E. J. Shields
Cedar	Eunice E. Frink	Martin G. Miller	Lorenzo L. Sweet	Herman G. Coe	Charles P. Sheldon	Orlando H. Helmer
Cerro Gordo	Ira C. Kling	C. F. Vincent	D. B. Mason	Thomas Perrett	George L. Herrick	C. B. Leabury
Cherokee	Rodney L. Robie	Joel H. Davenport	Watson Pelton	Geo. W. Lebourveau	David J. Hayes	Hiram J. McManus
Chickasaw	Wm. D. Collins	Wm. R. Geeting	Ira K. Gardner	E. R. Dickinson	E. C. Abbott	Thomas Kenyon
Clarke	Henry A. Tallman	James Elliott	James Bonar	John McDonough	John Stephenson	Wm. T. Mathews
Clay	James F. Thompson	Emmet Brown	Joseph C. Hoxsie	Michael Ueriell	Wm. Thomas	Isaac Otis
Clayton	Josiah E. Chase	A. W. Drake	Jacob Rood	Wm. Harvey	Cyrus H. Wait	A. F. McConnell
Clinton	Kate Hudson	Allen Slack	Lyman P. Adams	Wm. Lake	Henry Nure	Arthur Lillie
Crawford	N. F. Smith	George W. Heston	Dr. Wm. Iseminger	Robert Hope	Robert Bell	J. D. Jones
Dallas	Amos Dilly	A. A. Nolan	Wesley Wright	Lem Warford	J. C. Goodson	L. D. Burns
Davis	Israel F. Jenkins	Thomas Duffield	John M. Duffield	Jesse P. Fortune	Henry N. Cramer	David J. McConnell
Decatur	J. C. Roberts	H. W. Peck	J. A. Snyder	G. W. Rudibaugh	G. W. Shoemaker	
Delaware	Robert M. Ewart	Oren E. Noble	Wm. H. Finley	Jesse B. Bailey	Ferdinand Dunham	Henry C. Merriem
Des Moines	Enoch S. Burrns	John Nau	Fabian Brydolf	George Robertson	Dennis Melchior	
Dickinson	Hunter C. Crary	Emmet F. Hill	Isaac Ames	W. A. Richards	J. R. Upton	Andrew D. Foster
Dubuque	Nicholas W. Boyes	Mathew Tschergi, Jr.	Charles C. Coakley	Wm. Coates	Mark Sullivan	Jacob Kessler

Emmet	Frank Davey	John M. Barker	E. B. Campbell	Mathew Richmond	Welcome Barber	Bryngle Kundson
Fayette	G. A. Mathews	F. S. Palmer	L. Armstrong	F. Snedigar	P. L. Champlin	H. Hoagland
Floyd	Helen R. Duncan	Horace Stearns	John Kellogg	W. B. Tonner	L. H. Waterbury	A. G. Merrill
Franklin	Orrilla M. Reeve	L. B. Raymond	O. B. Harriman	David W. Elliott	Lorenzo D. Lane	David Church
Fremont	Thos. J. Brant	John Wilson	Cyrus McCrackin	Wm. Blair	Moses Samuels	Hugh Gammon
Greene	David Heagle	Nathan P. Stilson	William Allinson	C. B. Park	Rensalaer Allen	Richard E. Witt
Grundy	G. Riley Stoddard	E. A. Crary	W. P. Penfield	L. D. Tracy	Henry Johns	Joseph Huse
Guthrie	Giles C. Miller	Arthem's M'Clowan	John Boblett	William Andirson		
Hamilton	Benjamin S. Baker	Myron L. Tracy	Joseph N. Medberry	H. Corbin	John W. Lee	Edmund Crabtree
Hancock	A. R. Barnes	W. C. Moak	Z. C. Greene	G. R. Maben	J. H Melins	John Burnside
Hardin	L. S. McCoy	Geo. M. Hunt	M. J. Upright	S. R. Edgington	J. S. Hadley	M. J. Davis
Harrison	Samuel G. Rogers	George Madison	Geo. H. McGavrun	A. S. Chase	H. B. Cox	H. V. Armstron
Henry	Samuel L. Howe	John A. Schreiner	Joseph B. Vernon	George Hammond	Wm. R. Crew	George H. Spaher
Howard	Osmond N. Hoyt	Laban Hussett	James McCollum	Thomas Griffin	James Oakley	Alonzo G. Hubbard
Humboldt	L. J. Anderson	T. E. Collins	W. M. D. Van Velsor	George R. Hartwell	O. F. Avery	A. H. Knowles
Ida	Thad S. Snell	O. C. Thompson	M. P. Baldwin	H. D. Squyer	George Henry	John S. Kittle
Iowa	George Ingram	A. Hickman	I. M. Lyon	R. Grimes	A. Cover	C. A. Schonborn
Jackson	Norman C. White	Alex. C. Simpson	James W. Eckles	James Dunn	George H. Trumbull	Daniel F. Farr
Jasper	Wm. G. Work	W. L. Le Fever	E. W. Mitchell	W. G. Romans	Jesse Slavers	C. N. Doune
Jefferson	McHenry Robinson	Isaac H. Crumley	Thos. D. Evans	J. H. Allender	Thomas Pollock	Henry B Mitchell
Johnson	James M. Curry	Henry N. Berry	Henry Murray	George W. Nelson	John A. Stevenson	Thomas Combe
Jones	O. E. Aldrich	Orson Burlingame	Geo. W. Birdsall	Joseph Cool	W. J. Brainard	G. G. Baughart
Keokuk	H. D. Todd	N. Warrington	James McConnell	Geo. W. Morgan	Levi Bower	Wm. Jackson
Kossuth	A. A. Bronson	C. B. Hutchins	Henry C. McCoy	Marcellus Taylor	D. Rice	Philip Dorweiler
Lee	William J. Meades	Richard H. Heath	William Stot's, Sr.	William Davis	Elias Overton	A. L. Conable
Linn	Eli Johnston	James E. Lyman	Alexand'r Laurance	Joseph Whitney	Daniel Travis	James Yuill
Louisa	James A. Kennedy	John M. Huston	Frank Tustison	Robert T. Newell	Cyril Carpenter	Edson F. Smith
Lucas	Andrew Day	F. C. Fearing	H. S. Millan	Stephen Julian	John Murray	Hugh Larimer
Lyon	O. A. Cheney	La F. Knight	S. B. Willard	W. M. Lee	J. W. Monk	John Albertson
Madison	H. W. Hardy	R. A. Patterson	A. Hood	W. H. Lewis	Milton Wilson	S. M. Creger
Mahaska	J. W. Johnson	Samuel Thompson	J. M. Byers	W. F. Schee	Wm. Stewart	Samuel Knowlton
Marion	Aaron Yetter	Nathan J. Watkins	Thos. G. Carr	Daniel Sherwood	Hamilton D. Lucas	Alonzo A. Welcher
Marshall	Abbie Gifford	William Bremner	L. E. Holt	William H. Steward	Ed. P. Thompson	John G. Brown
Mills	Frank E. Stephens	Gustave Seegar	Samuel F. Brothers	John Barbour	Horace A. Norton	Francis J. Taylor
Mitchell	Geo. D. Pattengill	Eugene Huntington	R. F. Judd	George Brown	C. Carpenter	S. W Hastings
Monona	C. N. Lyman	J. B. P. Day	David Handel	N. B Olson	George M. Scott	H. E. Colby
Monroe	J. M. Porter	T. R. Cole	Casper Dull	Joseph Nichol		
Montgomery	Wm. P. Pattison	B. J. Austin	Charles M. Mills	Winchell Stafford	Frank G. Bean	Samuel Ewing
Muscatine	R. W. Leverich	John A. Mathewson	John K. Scott	J. L. Graham	James E. Robb	Thomas Birkett
O'Brien	Israel B. Chrysler	John T. Stearnes	George F. Colcord	Warren Walker	William E. Welch	Horace E. Hoagland
Osceola	C. L. Gurney	H. G. Doolittle	Wm. R. Lawrence	D. L. Riley		

COUNTY GOVERNMENT.—Continued.

Counties.	Superintendents of Common Schools.	County Surveyors.	Coroners.	Members Boards of Supervisors.	Members Boards of Supervisors.	Members Boards of Supervisors.
Page	Elijah Miller	Leavorit A. Russell	Thomas Evans	John X. Griffith	George McCullough	Samuel Gorman
Palo Alto	John C. Bennett	LeRoy Grout	Thos. E. McMurtrie	Charles Gibbs	R. M. J. McFarland	Matt Ryan
Plymouth	Floyd B. Sibley	J. B. Wynn	Paul Stockfeld	Wm. Barrett	E. H. Shaw	Leonhard Koenig
Pocahontas	J. F. Claak	Wm. Marshall	J. H. Johnson	B. McCartan	Wm. Stenson	D. Slosson
Polk	Robert S. Hughes	Frank Pelton	Isaac W. Griffith	Nat Parmenter	T. T. Morris	Wm. Christy
Pottawattamie	F. C. Childs	J. F. Brodbeck	M. T. Palmer	Wooster Fay	R. L. Douglass	Robert Kirkwood
Poweshiek	W. R. Akers	Jno. A. Griffith	M. B. Johnson	Thomas Morgan	Henry Sherman	J. A. Sanders
Ringgold	W. J. Work	E. B. Heaton	Wm. Millsaps	James A. Millen	Wm. H. Barns	I. W. Keller
Sac	John Dobson	Wilfield S. Williams	A. T. Brenton	N. Prentice	S. E. Gordin	Phil. Schaller
Scott	Chas. H. Clemmer	Thos. Murray	Dr. W. W. Grant	George Murray	Julius Laughlin	John Madden
Shelby	Aaron N. Buckman	Philetus C. Truman		Horace Beckley	John Fritz	Lewis Shorett
Sioux	Simon Knyper	Henry Hazlett	J. O. Beals	Henry Hospers	Daniel O. Gardner	Marquis D. Burket
Story	Charles H. Balliett	George Giddings	C. P. Robinson	John Evanson	Silas I. Shearer	Walter Evans
Tama	Henry A. Brown	W. H. Holstead	J. C. Kendrick	S. M. Hutton	J. H. Landerdale	T. F. Clark
Taylor	J. B. Owens	W. C. Blackstone	A. M. Golliday	D. W. Hamblin	D. H. Hamilton	W. D. Blakemore
Union	Miss J. E. Lester	G. C. Kirby	W. M. Lock	G. A. Ide	I. K. White	C. G. Shull
Van Buren	John W. Rowley	Ira Claflin	W. P. L. Muir	Erastus Pitkin	Isaac Nixon	Benj. Wagner
Wapello	Clay Wood	Wm H. McGlashon	E. L. Lathrop	D. H. Michael		
Warren	Miss E. S. Cook	Levi Reeves	Wm. P. Judkins	Saml. Irwin	Richard Moore	W. Marshal
Washington	Mary M. Jerman	Joseph Dudley	Saml. Melony	J. A. Henderson	W. McKinnie	M. Goodspeed
Wayne	J. W. Walker	Burris Moore	Nelson Rogers	V. T. Riley		
Webster	Jabez A. Adams	Charles H. Pierce	Sidney J. Bennett	Chris. Kundson	David S. Coughlin	Norman H. Harris
Winnebago	W. A. Chapman	John W. Ambrose	V. A. Jones	S. D. Wadsworth	James W. Fisher	Peter H. Peterson
Winneshiek	Nels Kessey	James L. Cameron	Aclus H. Fannon	Morgan S. Drury	Geo. C. Winshik	Peter Morton
Woodbury	A. R. Wright	Frank W. Davis	W. O. Davis	James S. Horton	Judson L. Follett	Norman Patterson
Worth	Geo. H. Whitcomb	H. V. Dwelle	Gulbrand Oelson	Wm. Rhodes	Lemuel Dwelle	S. J. White
Wright	John Q. Hanna	M. H. Austin	Thomas Garth	D. M. Inman	N. B. Paine	Henry Parker

TABLE.

Showing the times of holding the District and Circuit Courts in all the Counties of the State for the years 1876 *and* 1877, *as officially reported under Section* 165 *of the Code.*

Number of Dist.	COUNTIES.	COUNTY SEATS.	DISTRICT COURTS.		CIRCUIT COURTS.	
			1873.	1877.	1876.	1877.
1	Des Moines	Burlington	Jan. 3	Jan. 1	Feb. 21	Feb. 19
1	Des Moines	Burlington	May 22	May 28	May 1	May 7
1	Des Moines	Burlington	Sept. 25	Sept. 24	Aug. 28	Aug. 27
1	Des Moines	Burlington	....	....	Dec. 4	Dec. 3
1	Henry	Mt. Pleasant	March 6	March 5	Jan. 24	Jan. 22
1	Henry	Mt. Pleasant	Nov. 20	Nov. 19	April 17	April 16
1	Henry	Mt. Pleasant	....	....	Aug. 14	Aug. 13
1	Henry	Mt. Pleasant	....	....	Oct. 23	Oct. 22
1	Lee	Keokuk	Aug. 28	Aug. 27	June 13	June 12
1	Lee	Keokuk	Feb. 7	Feb. 5	Nov. 14	Nov. 13
1	Lee	Fort Madison	April 24	April 23	Jan. 4	Jan. 2
1	Lee	Fort Madison	Dec. 11	Dec. 10	April 4	April 3
1	Lee	Fort Madison	....	....	Oct. 3	Oct. 2
1	Louisa	Wapello	Mar. 27	Mar. 26	Mar. 14	Mar. 13
1	Louisa	Wapello	Oct. 23	Oct. 22	May 22	May 28
1	Louisa	Wapello	....	....	Sept. 19	Sept. 18
1	Louisa	Wapello	....	....	Dec. 19	Dec. 18
2	Appanoose	Centerville	Feb. 28	Feb. 26	Jan. 3	Jan 1
2	Appanoose	Centerville	Oct. 9	Oct. 8	Aug. 14	Aug. 13
2	Davis	Bloomfield	Feb. 14	Feb. 12	April 24	April 23
2	Davis	Bloomfield	Sep. 25	Sept. 24	Nov. 20	Nov. 19
2	Lucas	Chariton	April 3	April 2	Feb. 7	Feb. 5
2	Lucas	Chariton	Nov. 6	Nov. 5	Sept. 11	Sept. 10
2	Monroe	Albia	April 17	April 16	Feb. 21	Feb. 19
2	Monroe	Albia	Nov. 20	Nov. 19	Sept. 25	Sept. 24
2	Van Buren	Keosauqua	Jan. 3	Jan. 1	April 3	April 2
2	Van Buren	Keosauqua	Aug. 14	Aug. 13	Oct. 9	Oct. 8
2	Wapello	Ottumwa	Jan. 17	Jan. 15	Mar. 6	Mar. 5
2	Wapello	Ottumwa	Aug. 28	Aug. 27	Oct. 23	Oct. 22
2	Wayne	Corydon	Mar. 20	Mar. 19	Jan. 24	Jan. 22
2	Wayne	Corydon	Oct. 23	Oct. 22	Aug. 28	Aug. 27
3	Adams	Corning	April 24	April 23	Jan. 17	Jan. 15
3	Adams	Corning	Oct. 23	Oct. 22	Aug. 7	Aug. 6
3	Clarke	Osceola	May 22	May 21	Feb. 14	Feb. 12
3	Clarke	Osceola	Nov. 20	Nov. 19	Sept. 4	Sept. 3
3	Decatur	Leon	Jan. 17	Jan. 15	April 24	April 23
3	Decatur	Leon	Aug. 7	Aug. 6	Oct. 23	Oct. 22
3	Montgomery	Red Oak	May 8	May 7	Jan. 31	Jan. 29
3	Montgomery	Red Oak	Nov. 6	Nov. 5	Aug. 21	Aug. 20
3	Page	Clarinda	Feb. 28	Feb. 26	June 5	June 4
3	Page	Clarinda	Sept. 18	Sept. 17	Dec. 4	Dec. 3
3	Ringgold	Mt. Ayr	Jan. 31	Jan. 29	May 8	May 7
3	Ringgold	Mt. Ayr	Aug. 21	Aug. 20	Nov. 6	Nov. 5
3	Taylor	Bedford	Feb. 14	Feb. 12	May 22	May 21
3	Taylor	Bedford	Sept. 4	Sept. 3	Nov. 20	Nov. 19
3	Union	Afton	June 5	June 4	Feb. 28	Feb. 26
3	Union	Afton	Dec. 4	Dec. 3	Sept. 18	Sept. 17

TIMES OF HOLDING COURTS.—Continued.

Number of Dist.	COUNTIES.	COUNTY SEATS.	DISTRICT COURTS. 1876.	DISTRICT COURTS. 1877.	CIRCUIT COURTS. 1876.	CIRCUIT COURTS. 1877.
4	Buena Vista	Sioux Rapids	Apr. 10	Apr. 9	Jan. 25	Jan. 23
4	Buena Vista	Sioux Rapids	Nov. 7	Nov. 6	Aug. 28	Aug. 27
4	Calhoun	Lake City	Mar. 23	Mar. 19	May 8	May 7
4	Calhoun	Lake City	Oct. 16	Oct. 15	Dec. 18	Dec. 17
4	Cherokee	Cherokee	Feb. 7	Feb. 5	Apr. 11	Apr. 10
4	Cherokee	Cherokee	Sept. 11	Sept. 10	Nov. 7	Nov. 6
4	Clay	Spencer	Apr. 13	Apr. 16	Jan. 31	Jan. 29
4	Clay	Spencer	Nov. 13	Nov. 12	Aug. 31	Aug. 30
4	Dickinson	Spirit Lake	Apr. 17	Apr. 19	Feb. 7	Feb. 5
4	Dickinson	Spirit Lake	Nov. 16	Nov. 15	Sept. 4	Sept. 3
4	Emmet	Estherville	Apr. 20	Apr. 23	Feb. 10	Feb. 8
4	Emmet	Estherville	Nov. 20	Nov. 19	Sept. 7	Sept. 6
4	Harrison	Magnolia	Jan. 11	Jan. 9	Mar. 28	Mar. 27
4	Harrison	Magnolia	May 23	May 22	Oct. 24	Oct. 23
4	Humboldt	Dakota	May 8	May 10	Feb. 28	Feb. 26
4	Humboldt	Dakota	Dec. 7	Dec. 6	Sept. 25	Sept. 24
4	Ida	Ida	Mar. 16	Mar. 12	May 1	Apr. 30
4	Ida	Ida	Oct. 9	Oct. 8	Dec. 11	Dec. 10
4	Kossuth	Algona	May 1	Apr. 30	Feb. 21	Feb. 19
4	Kossnth	Algona	Nov. 27	Nov. 26	Sept. 18	Sept. 17
4	Lyon	Rock Rapids	Feb. 22	Feb. 22	Apr. 17	Apr. 16
4	Lyon	Rock Rapids	Sept. 21	Sept. 20	Nov. 14	Nov. 13
4	Monona	Onawa	Jan. 24	Jan. 22	Mar 13	Mar. 12
4	Monona	Onawa	Aug. 28	Aug. 27	Oct. 9	Oct. 8
4	O'Brien	Primghar	Mar. 6	Mar. 1	Apr. 24	April 23
4	O'Brien	Primghar	Sept. 28	Sept. 27	Nov. 27	Nov. 26
4	Osceola	Sibley	Feb. 28	Feb. 26	Apr. 20	Apr. 19
4	Osceola	Sibley	Sept. 25	Sept. 24	Nov. 20	Nov. 19
4	Palo Alto	Emmetsburg	Apr. 24	Apr. 26	Feb. 14	Feb. 12
4	Palo Alto	Emmetsburg	Nov. 23	Nov. 22	Sept. 11	Sept. 10
4	Plymouth	Le Mars	Jan. 31	Jan. 29	Mar. 20	Mar. 19
4	Plymouth	Le Mars	Sept. 4	Sept. 3	Oct. 16	Oct. 15
4	Pocahontas	Rolfe	Apr. 27	May 7	Feb. 17	Feb. 15
4	Pocahontas	Rolfe	Dec. 4	Dec. 3	Sept. 14	Sept. 13
4	Sac	Sac City	Mar. 20	Mar. 15	May 4	May 3
4	Sac	Sac City	Oct. 12	Oct. 11	Dec. 14	Dec. 13
4	Sioux	Orange City	Mar. 9	Mar. 5	Apr. 27	April 26
4	Sioux	Orange City	Oct. 2	Oct. 1	Dec. 4	Dec. 3
4	Woodbury	Sioux City	Mar. 27	Mar. 26	Jan. 3	Jan. 2
4	Woodbury	Sioux City	Oct. 23	Oct. 22	May 29	May 28
5	Adair	Greenfield	Feb. 28	Feb. 26	Apr. 24	April 23
5	Adair	Greenfield	Sept. 25	Sept. 24	Nov. 20	Nov. 19
5	Dallas	Adel	Mar. 20	Mar. 19	May 15	May 21
5	Dallas	Adel	Oct. 9	Oct. 8	Dec. 18	Dec. 17
5	Guthrie	Guthrie Center	Mar. 9	Mar. 8	May 8	May 7
5	Guthrie	Guthrie Center	Oct. 2	Oct. 1	Dec. 4	Dec. 3
5	Madison	Winterset	Jan. 31	Jan. 29	Apr. 3	April 2
5	Madison	Winterset	Sept. 4	Sept. 3	Oct. 30	Oct. 29
5	Polk	Des Moines	Apr. 10	Apr. 9	Jan. 3	Jan. 1
5	Polk	Des Moines	Oct. 30	Oct. 29	Sept. 4	Sept. 3
5	Warren	Indianola	Jan. 3	Jan. 2	Mar. 6	March 5
5	Warren	Indianola	Aug. 7	Aug. 6	Oct. 9	Oct. 8
6	Jasper	Newton	Jan. 17	Jan. 15	Mar. 20	Mar. 19
6	Jasper	Newton	May 15	May 21	Nov. 20	Nov. 19
6	Jefferson	Fairfield	Mar. 6	Mar. 5	Jan. 3	Jan. 1
6	Jefferson	Fairfield	Nov. 6	Nov. 5	Sept. 4	Sept. 3
6	Keokuk	Sigourney	Apr. 3	Apr. 2	Feb. 7	Feb. 5
6	Keokuk	Sigourney	Dec. 4	Dec. 3	Oct. 2	Oct. 1
6	Mahaska	Oskaloosa	Apr. 17	Apr. 16	Feb. 21	Feb. 19
6	Mahaska	Oskaloosa	Dec. 18	Dec. 17	Oct. 16	Oct. 15
6	Marion	Knoxville	Jan. 3	Jan. 1	Mar. 6	Mar. 5
6	Marion	Knoxville	May 1	May 7	Nov. 6	Nov. 5
6	Poweshiek	Montezuma	Feb. 7	Feb. 5	Apr. 3	April 2
6	Poweshiek	Montezuma	June 5	June 4	Dec. 4	Dec. 3
6	Washington	Washington	Mar. 20	Mar. 19	Jan. 17	Jan. 15

TIMES OF HOLDING COURTS.—Continued.

No. of District.	COUNTIES.	COUNTY SEATS.	DISTRICT COURTS.		CIRCUIT COURTS.	
			1876.	1877.	1876.	1877.
6	Washington	Washington	Nov. 20	Nov. 19	Sept. 18	Sept. 17
7	Clinton	Clinton	Feb. 28	Feb. 26	Jan. 3	Jan. 1
7	Clinton	Clinton	May 22	May 28	April 10	April 9
7	Clinton	Clinton	Nov. 6	Nov. 5	Sept. 4	Sept. 3
7	Jackson	Maquoketa	Mar. 21	Mar. 20	Jan. 25	Jan. 23
7	Jackson	Maquoketa	June 19	June 19	May 2	May 1
7	Jackson	Maquoketa	Dec. 5	Dec. 4	Oct. 3	Oct. 2
7	Muscatine	Muscatine	Jan. 4	Jan. 2	Feb. 15	Feb. 20
7	Muscatine	Muscatine	April 11	April 10	May 23	May 22
7	Muscatine	Muscatine	Aug. 22	Aug. 28	Oct. 24	Oct. 23
7	Scott	Davenport	Feb. 8	Feb. 6	Mar. 21	Mar. 20
7	Scott	Davenport	May 2	May 1	June 20	June 19
7	Scott	Davenport	Sept. 26	Sept. 25	Nov. 28	Nov. 27
8	Benton	Vinton	Mar. 6	Mar. 5	May 15	May 21
8	Benton	Vinton	Oct. 2	Oct. 1	Dec. 18	Dec. 17
8	Cedar	Tipton	May 1	May 7	Feb. 21	Feb. 19
8	Cedar	Tipton	Nov. 27	Nov. 26	Aug. 28	Aug. 27
8	Iowa	Marengo	Feb. 7	Feb. 5	April 17	April 16
8	Iowa	Marengo	Sept. 4	Sept. 3	Nov. 20	Nov. 19
8	Johnson	Iowa City	Jan. 3	Jan. 1	Mar. 20	Mar. 19
8	Johnson	Iowa City	June 5	June 4	Sept. 25	Sept. 24
8	Jones	Anamosa	May 15	May 21	Mar. 6	Mar. 5
8	Jones	Anamosa	Dec. 11	Dec. 10	Sept. 11	Sept. 10
8	Linn	Marion	Mar 20	Mar. 19	Jan. 3	Jan. 1
8	Linn	Marion	Oct. 16	Oct. 15	June 5	June 4
8	Tama	Toledo	Feb. 21	Feb. 19	May 1	May 7
8	Tama	Toledo	Sept. 18	Sept. 17	Dec. 4	Dec. 3
9	Black Hawk	Waterloo	Jan. 3	Jan. 1	Mar. 6	Mar. 5
9	Black Hawk	Waterloo	April 3	April 2	May 29	June 4
9	Black Hawk	Waterloo	Oct. 2	Oct. 1	Nov. 13	Nov. 12
9	Buchanan	Independence	Mar. 13	Mar. 12	Feb. 21	Feb. 19
9	Buchanan	Independence	Sept. 11	Sept. 10	May 15	May 21
9	Buchanan	Independence	....	....	Oct. 23	Oct. 22
9	Delaware	Delhi	Feb. 28	Feb. 26	Feb. 7	Feb. 5
9	Delaware	Delhi	Aug. 28	Aug. 27	May 1	May 7
9	Delaware	Delhi	....	....	Oct. 9	Oct. 8
9	Dubuque	Dubuque	Jan. 24	Jan. 22	Jan. 3	Jan. 1
9	Dubuque	Dubuque	May 1	May 7	Mar. 27	Mar. 26
9	Dubuque	Dubuque	Nov. 6	Nov. 5	Sept. 11	Sept. 10
9	Grundy	Grundy Center	April 24	April 23	Mar. 20	Mar. 19
9	Grundy	Grundy Center	Sept. 25	Sept. 24	June 12	June 11
9	Grundy	Grundy Center	....	....	Nov. 27	Nov. 26
10	Allamakee	Waukon	June 19	June 18	Jan. 31	Jan. 29
10	Allamakee	Waukon	Nov. 20	Nov. 19	June 5	June 4
10	Allamakee	Waukon	....	....	Oct. 2	Oct. 1
10	Chickasaw	New Hampton	May 1	April 30	Mar. 27	Mar. 26
10	Chickasaw	New Hampton	Nov. 6	Nov. 5	June 15	June 14
10	Chickasaw	New Hampton	....	....	Dec. 4	Dec. 3
10	Clayton	Elkader	Jan. 17	Jan. 15	Mar. 6	Mar. 5
10	Clayton	Elkader	May 15	May 14	June 8	June 7
10	Clayton	Elkader	Sept. 18	Sept. 17	Nov. 6	Nov. 5
10	Fayette	West Union	May 29	May 28	Feb. 14	Feb. 12
10	Fayette	West Union	Dec. 11	Dec. 10	May 18	May 17
10	Fayette	West Union	....	....	Oct. 16	Oct. 15
10	Howard	Cresco	April 24	April 23	Mar 20	Mar. 19
10	Howard	Cresco	Oct. 30	Oct. 29	June 12	June 11
10	Howard	Cresco	....	....	Nov. 27	Nov. 26
10	Winneshiek	Decorah	Feb. 21	Feb. 19	Jan. 3	Jan. 8
10	Winneshiek	Decorah	June 12	June 11	May 15	May 14
10	Winneshiek	Decorah	Oct. 16	Oct. 15	Sept. 11	Sept. 10
11	Boone	Boonsboro	June 14	June 13	April 13	April 12

TIMES OF HOLDING COURTS.—Continued.

Number of Dist.	COUNTIES.	COUNTY SEAT.	DISTRICT COURTS.		CIRCUIT COURTS.	
			1876.	1877.	1876.	1877.
11	Boone	Boonsboro	Dec. 13	Dec. 12	Oct. 12	Oct. 11
11	Franklin	Hampton	April 25	April 24	Feb. 14	Feb. 12
11	Franklin	Hampton	Oct. 24	Oct. 23	Aug. 14	Aug. 13
11	Hamilton	Webster City	April 4	April 3	Jan. 24	Jan. 22
11	Hamilton	Webster City	Oct. 3	Oct. 2	July 31	July 30
11	Hardin	Eldora	May 2	May 1	Feb. 24	Feb. 22
11	Hardin	Eldora	Oct. 31	Oct. 30	Aug. 24	Aug. 23
11	Marshall	Marshalltown	May 15	May 14	Mar. 13	Mar. 12
11	Marshall	Marshalltown	Nov. 13	Nov. 12	Sept. 11	Sept. 10
11	Story	Nevada	June 5	June 4	April 3	April 2
11	Story	Nevada	Dec. 4	Dec. 3	Oct. 2	Oct. 1
11	Webster	Fort Dodge	Mar. 21	Mar. 20	Jan. 4	Jan. 2
11	Webster	Fort Dodge	Sept 19	Sept. 18	July 5	July 5
11	Wright	Clarion	April 18	April 17	Feb. 8	Feb. 6
11	Wright	Clarion	Oct. 17	Oct. 16	July 25	July 24
12	Bremer	Waverly	Jan. 3	Jan. 1	Feb. 28	Feb. 26
12	Bremer	Waverly	April 17	April 16	June 19	June 18
12	Bremer	Waverly	Oct. 2	Oct. 1	Nov. 20	Nov. 19
12	Butler	Butler Center	April 10	April 9	May 22	May 28
12	Butler	Butler Center	Sept. 11	Sept. 10	Oct. 23	Oct. 22
12	Cerro Gordo	Mason City	Feb. 14	Feb. 12	Mar. 27	Mar. 26
12	Cerro Gordo	Mason City	June 19	June 18	May 15	May 21
12	Cerro Gordo	Mason City	Oct. 16	Oct. 15	Sept. 4	Sept. 3
12	Floyd	Charles City	Mar. 13	Mar. 12	Jan. 17	Jan. 15
12	Floyd	Charles City	July 24	July 23	June 5	June 4
12	Floyd	Charles City	Dec. 4	Dec. 3	Oct. 9	Oct. 8
12	Hancock	Concord	June 5	June 4	May 8	May 14
12	Hancock	Concord	Nov. 6	Nov. 5	Oct. 2	Oct. 1
12	Mitchell	Osage	May 8	May 14	Jan. 31	Jan. 29
12	Mitchell	Osage	July 17	July 16	June 26	June 25
12	Mitchell	Osage	Dec. 18	Dec. 17	Nov. 6	Nov. 5
12	Winnebago	Forest City	June 8	June 7	May 1	May 7
12	Winnebago	Forest City	Nov. 9	Nov. 8	Sept. 25	Sept. 24
12	Worth	Northwood	May 22	May 28	April 10	April 9
12	Worth	Northwood	Nov. 13	Nov. 12	Sept. 18	Sept. 17
13	Audubon	Exira	Jan. 10	Jan. 8	Mar. 20	Mar. 19
13	Audubon	Exira	Aug. 14	Aug. 13	Oct. 16	Oct. 15
13	Carroll	Carroll	April 3	April 2	Jan. 10	Jan. 8
13	Carroll	Carroll	Oct. 30	Oct. 29	July 31	July 30
13	Cass	Atlantic	Jan. 17	Jan. 15	Mar. 27	Mar. 26
13	Cass	Atlantic	Aug. 21	Aug. 20	Oct. 23	Oct. 22
13	Crawford	Denison	Mar. 27	Mar. 26	Jan. 3	Jan. 2
13	Crawford	Denison	Oct. 23	Oct. 22	July 24	July 23
13	Fremont	Sidney	Feb. 28	Feb. 26	May 8	May 14
13	Fremont	Sidney	Oct. 2	Oct. 1	Dec. 4	Dec. 3
13	Greene	Jefferson	April 10	April 9	Jan. 17	Jan. 15
13	Greene	Jefferson	Nov. 6	Nov. 5	Aug. 7	Aug. 6
13	Mills	Glenwood	Feb. 7	Feb. 5	April 17	April 16
13	Mills	Glenwood	Sept. 11	Sept. 10	Nov. 13	Nov. 12
13	Pottawattamie	Council Bluffs	April 24	April 23	Jan. 31	Jan. 29
13	Pottawattamie	Council Bluffs	Nov. 20	Nov. 19	Aug. 21	Aug. 20
13	Shelby	Harlan	Jan. 3	Jan. 2	Mar. 13	Mar. 12
13	Shelby	Harlan	Aug. 7	Aug. 6	Oct. 9	Oct. 8

ABSTRACT

Of votes cast at the General Election held on the 12*th day of October, A. D.* 1875, *by counties and townships for the offices of Governor and Lieutenant-Governor of Iowa.*

ADAIR COUNTY.

NAMES OF TOWNSHIPS.	GOVERNOR.			LIEUTENANT-GOVERNOR.	
	Samuel J. Kirkwood, *Republican.*	Shepherd Leffler, *Democrat.*	J. H. Lozier, *Prohibition.*	Joshua G. Newbold, *Republican.*	E. B. Woodward, *Democrat.*
Eureka	23	6	......	23	6
Grand River	34	16	......	35	16
Greenfield	131	30	......	131	30
Grove	44	7	......	43	8
Harrison	75	24	......	75	24
Jackson	25	42	......	32	36
Jefferson	79	15	......	79	15
Lincoln	97	13	......	98	12
Orient	42	13	......	42	13
Prussia	17	26	......	17	26
Richland	60	27	......	60	27
Summerset	93	52	......	93	52
Summit	47	7	......	47	7
Union	28	10	......	28	10
Walnut	28	21	......	29	21
Washington	53	46	......	53	46
Total	876	355	......	885	349
Majority	521	....	......	536	....

ADAMS COUNTY.

NAMES OF TOWNSHIPS.	Samuel J. Kirkwood	Shepherd Leffler	J. H. Lozier	Joshua G. Newbold	E. B. Woodward
Colony	66	4	......	66	4
Carl	97	25	......	97	25
Washington	119	36	......	119	36
Lincoln	81	10	......	81	10
Union	36	16	......	36	16
Prescott	106	31	......	106	31
Quincy	284	68	......	283	69
Douglas	73	37	......	72	38
Grant	48	18	......	48	18
Mercer	36	28	......	36	28
Jasper	100	15	......	100	15
Nodaway	80	70	......	81	69
Total	1126	358	......	1125	359
Majority	768	....	......	766	....

ALLAMAKEE COUNTY.

NAMES OF TOWNSHIPS.	GOVERNOR.			LIEUTENANT-GOVERNOR.	
	Samuel J. Kirkwood, *Republican.*	Shepherd Leffler, *Democrat.*	J. H. Lozier, *Prohibition.*	Joshua G. Newbold, *Republican.*	E. B. Woodward, *Democrat.*
Center	134	37	......	134	37
Fairview	28	75	......	28	75
Franklin	121	34	......	122	33
French Creek	16	115	......	16	115
Hanover	34	53	......	34	53
Iowa	37	126	......	56	111
Jefferson	116	98	......	116	98
Lafayette	67	189	......	67	190
Lansing	275	432	......	281	423
Linton	43	64	......	44	63
Ludlow	160	69	......	160	69
Makee	248	226	......	250	226
Paint Creek	124	106	......	124	106
Post	195	99	......	196	99
Taylor	40	167	......	40	167
Union City	61	45	......	61	45
Union Prairie	67	176	......	67	176
Waterloo	67	46	......	67	46
Total	1833	2157	3	18 3	2132
Majority	....	324	......	....	269

APPANOOSE COUNTY.

NAMES OF TOWNSHIPS.	Samuel J. Kirkwood, *Republican.*	Shepherd Leffler, *Democrat.*	J. H. Lozier, *Prohibition.*	Joshua G. Newbold, *Republican.*	E. B. Woodward, *Democrat.*
Beliair	76	37	......	77	36
Center	288	229	......	287	230
Chariton	70	70	......	70	70
Caldwell	76	104	......	75	106
Douglas	50	35	......	51	34
Franklin	85	35	......	86	34
Independence	76	70	......	77	69
Johns	67	68	......	66	60
Lincoln	44	68	......	46	68
Pleasant	83	64	......	87	65
Sharon	36	66	......	36	66
Taylor	85	86	......	88	85
Union	34	64	......	34	63
Udell	76	92	......	78	89
Washington	160	154	......	159	154
Wells	58	81	......	59	81
Walnut	65	47	......	65	47
Total	1429	1370	......	1441	1366
Majority	59	....	......	75	....

AUDUBON COUNTY.

NAMES OF TOWNSHIPS.	Samuel J. Kirkwood, *Republican.*	Shepherd Leffler, *Democrat.*	J. H. Lozier, *Prohibition.*	Joshua G. Newbold, *Republican.*	E. B. Woodward, *Democrat.*
Hamlin	34	21	......	34	21
Viola	24	20	......	23	21
Cameron	12	7	......	11	8
Douglas	6	15	......	6	17
Sharon	4	6	......	4	6
Leroy	28	17	......	28	17

AUDUBON COUNTY.—Continued.

NAMES OF TOWNSHIPS.	GOVERNOR. Samuel J. Kirkwood, *Republican.*	GOVERNOR. Shepherd Leffler, *Democrat.*	GOVERNOR. J. H. Lozier, *Prohibition.*	LIEUTENANT-GOVERNOR. Joshua G. Newbold, *Republican.*	LIEUTENANT-GOVERNOR. E. B. Woodward, *Democrat.*
Melville	5	7	......	5	7
Greeley	24	16	......	24	16
Aububon	27	34	......	23	38
Exira	126	127	......	124	129
Oakfield	27	5	......	26	6
Total	317	275	......	308	286
Majority	42	....	......	22	....

BENTON COUNTY.

Polk	81	101	......	83	100
Harrison	52	13	......	52	13
Cedar	101	28	......	101	28
Bruce	55	15	......	55	15
Benton	68	17	......	68	17
Taylor	533	110	......	534	110
Jackson	94	63	......	94	63
Monroe	23	13	......	22	14
Canton	126	67	......	124	68
Eden	56	21	......	56	21
Big Grove	58	24	......	58	24
Homer	60	22	......	60	22
Fremont	39	27	......	39	26
Eldorado	21	22	......	21	22
Union	20	60	......	18	62
Kane	25	30	......	25	30
Florence	106	30	......	106	30
St. Clair	62	43	......	59	44
Le Roy	148	115	......	150	116
Iowa	175	152	......	177	150
Total	1903	973	......	1902	975
Majority	930	....	......	927	....

BLACK HAWK COUNTY.

Lester	66	46	......	66	46
Bennington	49	31	......	43	38
Mt. Vernon	56	62	......	54	66
Washington	37	22	......	37	22
Union	28	21	......	28	21
Barclay	52	39	......	52	39
Poyner	70	57	......	74	57
East Waterloo	356	242	......	358	243
Waterloo	370	154	......	377	154
Cedar Falls	421	231	......	419	233
Fox	64	43	......	63	44
Cedar	49	32	......	50	31
Orange	70	19	......	71	18
Black Hawk	69	55	......	69	55
Spring Creek	41	61	......	41	61
ig Creek	193	115	......	193	117

BLACK HAWK COUNTY.—CONTINUED.

NAMES OF TOWNSHIPS.	GOVERNOR.			LIEUTENANT-GOVERNOR.	
	Samuel J. Kirkwood, *Republican.*	Shepherd Leffler, *Democrat.*	J. H. Lozier, *Prohibition.*	Joshua G. Newbold *Republican.*	E. B. Woodward, *Democrat.*
Eagle	47	45	......	47	45
Lincoln	65	19	......	65	19
Total	2103	1294	......	2107	1309
Majority	809	....	......	798	....

BOONE COUNTY.

NAMES OF TOWNSHIPS.	Samuel J. Kirkwood	Shepherd Leffler	J. H. Lozier	Joshua G. Newbold	E. B. Woodward
Amaqua	54	37	......	54	37
Boone	379	196	......	376	205
Boonsboro	277	144	......	277	146
Beaver	17	41	......	17	41
Cass	20	35	......	20	35
Colfax	42	30	......	44	28
Dodge	61	144	......	60	145
Douglass	70	43	......	69	43
Grant	46	5	......	46	5
Garden	79	25	......	79	25
Harrison	38	18	......	38	18
Jackson	90	45	......	89	46
Marcy	198	135	......	196	138
Pilot Mound	55	25	......	54	26
Peoples	67	25	......	67	25
Union	55	11	......	56	10
Worth	56	50	......	54	3
Yell	122	92	......	122	92
Total	1726	1101	......	1718	1118
Majority	625	....	......	600	....

BREMER COUNTY.

NAMES OF TOWNSHIPS.	Samuel J. Kirkwood	Shepherd Leffler	J. H. Lozier	Joshua G. Newbold	E. B. Woodward
Dayton	49	13	......	49	13
Douglas	73	39	......	74	39
Franklin	77	21	......	77	21
Frederika	58	19	......	58	19
Fremont	53	58	......	57	54
Jackson	133	46	......	138	46
Jefferson	64	65	......	65	65
La Fayette	82	60	......	83	58
Le Roy	32	32	......	34	31
Maxfield	14	76	......	15	75
Polk	196	37	......	199	36
Sumner	114	36	......	115	35
Warren	71	28	......	71	28
Washington	477	157	......	485	152
Totals	1493	687	......	1520	672
Majority	806	....	......	848	....

BUCHANAN COUNTY.

NAMES OF TOWNSHIPS.	GOVERNOR.			LIEUTENANT-GOVERNOR.	
	Samuel J. Kirkwood, *Republican.*	Shepherd Leffler, *Democrat.*	J. H. Lozier, *Prohibition.*	Joshua G. Newbold, *Republican.*	E. B. Woodward, *Democrat.*
Buffalo	66	27	......	65	28
Byron	105	80	......	106	79
Cono	47	23	......	50	21
Fairbank	68	83	......	67	84
Fremont	60	40	......	59	41
Hazelton	104	97	......	105	96
Homer	65	56	......	64	58
Jefferson	87	62	......	87	62
Liberty	114	116	......	117	114
Madison	61	33	......	60	34
Middlefield	49	70	......	50	71
Newton	77	49	......	77	49
Perry	150	105	......	150	106
Sumner	58	67	......	58	68
Washington	417	400	......	423	395
Westburg	56	51	......	57	50
Totals	1584	1359	......	1595	1356
Majority	225	......	......	239	......

BUENA VISTA COUNTY.

NAMES OF TOWNSHIPS.	Kirkwood	Leffler	Lozier	Newbold	Woodward
Elk	33	......	......	33	......
Lincoln	12	......	......	12	......
Fairfield	22	......	......	22	......
Coon	33	21	......	33	21
Barnes	49	......	......	49	......
Newell	103	30	......	103	30
Lee	67	5	......	68	4
Poland	13	1	......	13	1
Storm Lake	153	31	......	154	29
Scott	27	......	......	27	......
Providence	21	13	......	21	12
Brooks	12	......	......	12	......
Maple Valley	42	6	......	42	6
Grant	20	2	......	20	2
Nokomis	64	6	......	64	6
Totals	671	115	......	673	111
Majority	556	......	......	562	......

BUTLER COUNTY.

NAMES OF TOWNSHIPS.	Kirkwood	Leffler	Lozier	Newbold	Woodward
Fremont	49	39	......	49	39
Dayton	46	43	......	46	43
Cold Water	144	92	......	135	101
Bennezette	28	9	......	27	10
Pittsford	65	31	......	66	31
West Point	53	20	......	53	20
Jackson	65	64	......	65	64
Butler	208	84	......	208	84
Shell Rock	188	88	......	187	88
Jefferson	100	24	......	98	26
Ripley	31	13	......	31	13
Madison	28	3	......	28	3

BUTLER COUNTY.—CONTINUED.

NAMES OF TOWNSHIPS.	GOVERNOR.			LIEUTENANT-GOVERNOR.	
	Samuel J. Kirkwood, *Republican.*	Shepherd Leffler, *Democrat.*	J. H. Lozier, *Prohibition.*	Joshua G. Newbold, *Republican.*	E. B. Woodward, *Democrat.*
Washington	32	30	......	32	30
Monroe	79	30	...	80	29
Albion	122	32	......	125	31
Beaver	137	22	......	137	22
Totals	1375	624	......	1367	634
Majority	751	....	......	733	....

CALHOUN COUNTY.

NAMES OF TOWNSHIPS.	Samuel J. Kirkwood, *Republican.*	Shepherd Leffler, *Democrat.*	J. H. Lozier, *Prohibition.*	Joshua G. Newbold, *Republican.*	E. B. Woodward, *Democrat.*
Calhoun	97	20	......	101	21
Jackson	61	38	......	59	38
Lincoln	71	30	......	78	29
Sherman	49	3	......	49	3
Williams	21	2	......	25	2
Butler	38	15	......	38	16
Center	8	12	......	8	12
Greenfield	10	32	......	9	34
Reading	17	4	......	17	4
Totals	372	156	11	384	159
Majority	216	....	......	225	....

CARROLL COUNTY.

NAMES OF TOWNSHIPS.	Samuel J. Kirkwood, *Republican.*	Shepherd Leffler, *Democrat.*	J. H. Lozier, *Prohibition.*	Joshua G. Newbold, *Republican.*	E. B. Woodward, *Democrat.*
Arcadia	59	52	......	59	52
Carroll	145	142	......	147	143
Eden	23	14	......	23	14
Glidden	94	36	......	94	36
Grant	21	23	......	21	23
Jasper	40	10	......	40	10
Kniest	....	115	......	....	115
Newton	63	23	......	63	23
Pleasant Valley	19	16	......	19	16
Richland	21	8	......	21	8
Roselle	14	59	......	14	59
Sheridan	54	24	......	55	24
Union	50	17	......	49	18
Wheatland	....	44	......	....	44
Washington	19	13	......	19	13
Warren	10	....	......	9	1
Totals	632	596	......	633	599
Majority	36	....	......	34	....

CASS COUNTY.

NAMES OF TOWNSHIPS.	Samuel J. Kirkwood, *Republican.*	Shepherd Leffler, *Democrat.*	J. H. Lozier, *Prohibition.*	Joshua G. Newbold, *Republican.*	E. B. Woodward, *Democrat.*
Atlantic	386	191	......	416	187
Bear Grove	38	17	......	38	17
Benton	40	48	......	41	48
Brighton	51	51	......	52	51
Cass	103	55	......	106	55

CASS COUNTY.—Continued.

NAMES OF TOWNSHIPS.	GOVERNOR.			LIEUTENANT-GOVERNOR.	
	Samuel J. Kirkwood, *Republican.*	Shepherd Leffler, *Democrat.*	J. H. Lozier, *Prohibition.*	Joshua G. Newbold, *Republican.*	E. B. Woodward, *Democrat.*
Edna	47	32	......	47	32
Franklin	76	47	......	76	47
Grant	71	43	......	74	41
Lincoln	42	21	......	42	21
Massena	40	9	......	40	9
Noble	50	19	......	50	19
Pleasant	54	38	......	54	38
Pymosa	89	44	......	89	44
Union	41	33	......	41	33
Victoria	23	12	......	23	12
Washington	61	45	......	61	45
Totals	1212	705	30	1250	699
Majority	507	....	......	551	....

CEDAR COUNTY.

NAMES OF TOWNSHIPS.	Samuel J. Kirkwood	Shepherd Leffler	J. H. Lozier	Joshua G. Newbold	E. B. Woodward
Cass	33	75	......	33	75
Center	300	269	......	300	269
Dayton	153	81	......	152	81
Fremont	112	73	......	111	74
Fairfield	64	45	......	64	45
Farmington	69	63	......	69	63
Gower	65	41	......	65	41
Inland	70	48	......	70	48
Iowa	97	94	......	98	94
Linn	37	39	......	37	39
Massilon	57	62	......	57	61
Pioneer	132	116	......	131	117
Red Oak	40	35	......	40	35
Rochester	60	58	......	60	58
Springdale	209	15	......	215	15
Springfield	69	86	......	67	88
Sugar Creek	58	38	......	57	39
Totals	1625	1238	......	1626	1242
Majority	387	....	......	384	....

CERRO GORDO COUNTY.

NAMES OF TOWNSHIPS.	Samuel J. Kirkwood	Shepherd Leffler	J. H. Lozier	Joshua G. Newbold	E. B. Woodward
Mason	295	73	......	294	74
Falls	95	12	......	95	12
Clear Lake	101	53	......	100	11
Lake	69	15	......	69	15
Grant	36	1	......	36	1
Lime Creek	53	13	......	52	13
Portland	31	4	......	31	4
Dougherty	3	19	......	3	19
Owens	26	....	......	26	....
Geneseo	65	30	......	65	30
Lincoln	52	....	......	52	....
Totals	826	220	......	823	179
Majority	606	....	......	644	....

CHEROKEE COUNTY.

NAMES OF TOWNSHIPS.	GOVERNOR.			LIEUTENANT-GOVERNOR.	
	Samuel J. Kirkwood, *Republican.*	Shepherd Leffler, *Democrat.*	J. H. Lozier, *Prohibition.*	Joshua G. Newbold, *Republican.*	E. B. Woodward, *Democrat.*
Afton	50	36	......	50	36
Amherst	17	1	......	19	1
Cherokee	165	56	......	167	56
Cedar	26	33	......	24	35
Diamond	20	1	......	20	1
Marcus	6	3	......	6	3
Liberty	22	4	......	22	4
Pilot	55	23	......	55	23
Pitcher	60	3	......	60	3
Sheridan	50	6	......	50	6
Silver	28	8	......	31	8
Spring	11	3	......	11	3
Tilden	18	8	......	18	8
Willow	8	19	......	8	19
Totals	536	204	......	541	206
Majority	332	....	......	335	....

CHICKASAW COUNTY.

NAMES OF TOWNSHIPS.	Samuel J. Kirkwood, *Republican.*	Shepherd Leffler, *Democrat.*	J. H. Lozier, *Prohibition.*	Joshua G. Newbold, *Republican.*	E. B. Woodward, *Democrat.*
Bradford	204	132	......	206	130
Richland	69	14	......	70	14
Dresden	62	21	......	78	5
Fredericksburgh	123	22	......	125	22
Stapleton	84	163	......	84	163
New Hampton	163	93	......	164	92
Dayton	32	47	......	33	47
Chickasaw	102	79	......	102	79
Deerfield	51	23	......	52	22
Washington	31	101	......	32	99
Jacksonville	90	81	......	90	81
Utica	42	56	......	42	56
Totals	1053	832	......	1077	810
Majority	221	....	......	267	....

CLARKE COUNTY.

NAMES OF TOWNSHIPS.	Samuel J. Kirkwood, *Republican.*	Shepherd Leffler, *Democrat.*	J. H. Lozier, *Prohibition.*	Joshua G. Newbold, *Republican.*	E. B. Woodward, *Democrat.*
Liberty	69	71	......	70	70
Fremont	73	23	......	72	23
Washington	37	76	......	36	76
Madison	40	58	......	44	53
Troy	120	50	......	118	52
Ward	35	47	......	35	47
Osceola	287	147	......	293	174
Jackson	99	69	......	98	69
Franklin	66	45	......	67	45
Green Bay	73	34	......	73	34
Knox	58	52	......	58	52
Doyle	116	63	......	118	62
Totals	1073	763	......	1082	757
Majority	310	....	......	325	....

CLAY COUNTY.

NAMES OF TOWNSHIPS.	GOVERNOR.			LIEUTENANT-GOVERNOR.	
	Samuel J. Kirkwood, *Republican.*	Shepherd Leffler, *Democrat.*	J. H. Lozier, *Prohibition.*	Joshua G. Newbold, *Republican.*	E. B. Woodward, *Democrat.*
Bridgewater	56	8	......	55	8
Clay	106	1	......	107	....
Douglas	78	....	......	78	....
Gillett's Grove	43	....	......	43	....
Herdland	23	....	......	23	....
Lincoln	71	5	......	71	5
Riverton	68	3	......	68	....
Spencer	207	1	......	207	1
Summit	52	....	......	53	....
Totals	704	18	......	705	14
Majority	686	....	......	691	....

CLAYTON COUNTY.

NAMES OF TOWNSHIPS.	Kirkwood	Leffler	Lozier	Newbold	Woodward
Boardman	124	219	......	126	217
Buena Vista	12	40	......	13	40
Cass	132	100	......	132	98
Clayton	52	89	......	53	89
Cox Creek	59	85	......	63	85
Elk	105	28	......	105	28
Farmersburg	83	85	......	87	82
Garnavillo	50	124	......	47	127
Giard	59	79	......	58	81
Grand Meadow	29	54	......	29	54
Highland	64	72	......	64	72
Jefferson	90	241	......	74	239
Lodomillo	99	49	......	99	49
Mallory	48	95	......	49	94
Marion	60	19	......	60	19
Mendon	263	357	......	267	353
Millville	58	53	......	58	53
Monona	141	121	......	141	126
Read	18	88	......	20	86
Sperry	114	67	......	114	67
Volga	104	90	......	72	126
Wagner	75	16	......	75	16
Totals	1839	2171	......	1806	2198
Majority	....	332	......	....	392

CLINTON COUNTY.

NAMES OF TOWNSHIPS.	Kirkwood	Leffler	Lozier	Newbold	Woodward
Berlin	25	30	......	25	30
Bloomfield	132	101	......	132	100
Brookfield	58	32	......	58	32
Clinton, First Precinct	151	160	......	152	161
Clinton, Second Precinct	229	144	......	224	148
Clinton, Third Precinct	117	60	......	118	59
Clinton, Fourth Precinct	135	197	......	134	198
Camanche	155	93	......	148	99
Centre	30	98	......	30	98
De Witt	270	282	......	271	282
Deep Creek	61	57	......	65	54
Eden	71	40	......	72	41

CLINTON COUNTY.—Continued.

NAMES OF TOWNSHIPS.	GOVERNOR.			LIEUTENANT-GOVERNOR.	
	Samuel J. Kirkwood, *Republican.*	Shepherd Leffler, *Democrat.*	J. H. Lozier, *Prohibition.*	Joshua G. Newbold, *Republican.*	E. B. Woodward, *Democrat.*
Elk River	67	49	......	69	49
Hampshire	16	71	......	16	71
Lyons	241	383	......	242	384
Lincoln	29	18	......	30	18
Liberty	42	89	......	41	90
Olive	128	70	......	132	70
Orange	59	73	......	57	75
Spring Rock	102	113	......	103	112
Sharon	79	52	......	79	52
Welton	49	41	......	49	41
Waterford	48	109	...	47	110
Washington	12	117	......	11	118
Totals	2306	2479	......	2305	2492
Majority	....	173	......	....	187

CRAWFORD COUNTY.

NAMES OF TOWNSHIPS.	Samuel J. Kirkwood, *Republican.*	Shepherd Leffler, *Democrat.*	J. H. Lozier, *Prohibition.*	Joshua G. Newbold, *Republican.*	E. B. Woodward, *Democrat.*
Iowa	14	14	......	14	14
Nishnabotany	17	11	......	17	11
Washington	30	24	......	30	24
Union	41	64	......	42	64
Boyer	17	16	......	17	16
Hays	32	27	......	29	29
East Boyer	57	18	......	56	19
Denison	183	107	......	181	109
Paradise	21	19	......	21	19
Willow	13	4	......	13	4
West Side	108	54	......	108	54
Millford	71	48	......	71	48
Goodrich	27	20	......	27	20
Hanover	2	17	......	2	17
Charter Oak	11	11	......	11	11
Jackson	23	37	......	23	37
Stockholm	43	13	......	43	13
Otter Creek	35	19	......	35	19
Morgan	2	14	......	4	12
Soldier	6	16	......	6	16
Totals	753	553	......	750	556
Majority	200	....	......	194	....

DALLAS COUNTY.

NAMES OF TOWNSHIPS.	Samuel J. Kirkwood, *Republican.*	Shepherd Leffler, *Democrat.*	J. H. Lozier, *Prohibition.*	Joshua G. Newbold, *Republican.*	E. B. Woodward, *Democrat.*
Adel Precinct (Adel Township)	135	122	......	136	123
Dallas Center Precinct (Adel Township)	77	53	......	76	54
Adams Township	78	75	......	78	76
Colfax Township	52	49	......	51	48
De Soto Precinct (Van Meter Township)	99	57	......	102	55
Van Meter Township	84	33	......	85	33
Boone Township	68	35	......	68	34
Walnut Township	71	2[illegible]	......	67	24
Grant Township	26	33	......	26	32
Des Moines Township	18	28	......	17	28
Beaver Township	34	25	......	34	25

DALLAS COUNTY.—Continued.

COUNTIES.	GOVERNOR.			LIEUTENANT-GOVERNOR.	
	Samuel J. Kirkwood, *Republican.*	Shepherd Leffler, *Democrat.*	J. H. Lozier, *Prohibition.*	Joshua G. Newbold, *Republican.*	E. B. Woodward, *Democrat.*
Spring Valley Township	165	57	......	168	57
Dallas Township	22	29	......	24	28
Sugar Grove Township	76	51	......	76	51
Washington Township	37	49	......	36	50
Lincoln Township	35	25	......	35	25
Linn Township	82	16	......	83	16
Redfield Precinct (Union Tp.)	77	46	......	81	45
Dexter Precinct (Union Tp.	163	43	......	165	43
Totals	1399	847	......	1408	847
Majority	552	....	......	561	....

DAVIS COUNTY.

COUNTIES.	Kirkwood	Leffler	Lozier	Newbold	Woodward
Salt Creek	41	118	......	43	117
Lick Creek	86	184	......	87	183
Soap Creek	89	98	......	89	98
Marion	69	107	......	69	107
Fox River	83	46	......	82	46
Drakeville	92	45	......	92	45
Bloomfield	364	246	.....	368	243
Perry	62	80	......	61	81
Union	121	111	......	120	113
Prairie	70	48	......	69	50
Roscoe	31	44	......	32	43
Grove	92	100	......	94	98
Wyacondah	113	122	......	113	122
Fabius	87	117	......	88	117
West Grove	85	118	......	85	118
Totals	1485	1584	......	1492	1581
Majority	....	99	......	....	89

DECATUR COUNTY.

COUNTIES.	Kirkwood	Leffler	Lozier	Newbold	Woodward
Bloomington	84	18	......	83	18
Burrell	67	113	......	67	113
Center	84	61	......	84	61
Leon	145	109	......	143	112
Decatur	98	86	......	98	86
Eden	73	92	......	74	91
Fayette	34	13	......	32	13
Franklin	71	34	......	71	34
Garden Grove	132	100	......	133	99
Grand River	41	18	......	42	17
Hamilton	62	46	......	62	46
High Point	68	82	......	69	81
Long Creek	91	40	......	91	40
Morgan	68	32	......	68	32
New Buda	51	53	......	51	53
Richland	75	101	......	75	101
Woodland	25	93	......	25	97
Totals	1219	1091	......	1218	1094
Majority	128	....	......	124	....

DELAWARE COUNTY.

NAMES OF TOWNSHIPS.	GOVERNOR.			LIEUTENANT-GOVERNOR.	
	Samuel J. Kirkwood. *Republican.*	Shepherd Leffler, *Democrat.*	J. H. Lozier, *Prohibition.*	Joshua G. Newbold, *Republican.*	E. B. Woodward, *Democrat.*
Colony	100	81	......	100	81
Elk	109	68	......	110	68
Honey Creek	105	37	......	104	37
Richland	84	39	......	84	39
Bremen	9	76	......	11	74
Oneida	158	62	......	160	61
Delaware	369	195	......	369	195
Coffins Grove	88	63	......	89	63
North Fork	47	63	......	47	63
Delhi	136	103	......	138	102
Milo	79	54	......	79	54
Prairie	52	11	......	52	11
South Fork	181	104	......	181	102
Union	66	46	......	67	46
Hazel Green	67	45	......	67	45
Adams	38	37	......	38	37
Totals	1688	1084	2	1696	1078
Majority	604	....	......	618	....

DES MOINES COUNTY.

NAMES OF TOWNSHIPS.	Samuel J. Kirkwood.	Shepherd Leffler.	J. H. Lozier.	Joshua G. Newbold.	E. B. Woodward.
Augusta	41	47	......	40	47
Benton	48	91	......	53	86
Burlington, First Precinct	356	589	......	373	572
Burlington, Second Precinct	303	388	......	307	381
Burlington, Third Precinct	464	549	......	477	541
Danville	156	167	......	162	163
Flint River	80	112	......	92	102
Franklin	85	163	......	97	149
Huron	89	33	......	92	31
Jackson	5	18	......	7	18
Pleasant Grove	63	115	......	63	117
Union	105	78	......	100	74
Washington	59	69	......	55	68
Yellow Springs	250	66	......	250	65
Totals	2104	2485	......	2177	2414
Majority	....	381	......	....	237

DICKINSON COUNTY.

NAMES OF TOWNSHIPS.	Samuel J. Kirkwood.	Shepherd Leffler.	J. H. Lozier.	Joshua G. Newbold.	E. B. Woodward.
Center Grove	91	11	......	91	11
Diamond Lake	14	....	......	14	....
Excelsior	8	....	......	8	....
Lakeville	14	3	......	14	3
Lloyd	22	3	......	22	3
Milford	26	1	......	26	1
Okoboji	27	....	......	27	....
Richland	12	2	......	12	2
Superior	11	....	......	11	....
Spirit Lake	36	....	......	36	....
Silver Lake	5	2	......	5	2
Westport	15	....	......	15	....
Totals	281	22	......	281	22
Majority	259	....	......	259	....

DUBUQUE COUNTY.

NAMES OF TOWNSHIPS.	GOVERNOR.			LIEUTENANT-GOVERNOR.	
	Samuel J. Kirkwood, *Republican.*	Shepherd Leffler, *Democrat.*	J. H. Lozier, *Prohibition.*	Joshua G. Newbold, *Republican.*	E. B. Woodward, *Democrat.*
Cascade	44	116	......	43	117
Concord	53	150	......	53	150
Center	47	98	......	45	100
Dodge	79	71	......	89	66
Iowa	30	111	......	31	110
Jefferson	83	133	......	83	134
Julien, First Precinct	159	506	...	157	509
Julien, Second Precinct	78	184	......	85	178
Julien, Third Precinct	233	339	......	232	341
Julien, Fourth Precinct	499	327	......	511	316
Julien, Fifth Precinct	232	350	......	240	341
Julien, Sixth Precinct	93	84	......	94	83
Liberty Township	1	171	......	1	171
Mosalem	7	127	......	7	127
New Wine, Precinct	....	138	......	....	138
Dyersville	89	164	......	100	162
Peru, Township	27	101	......	30	98
Prairie Creek	4	203	......	5	202
Taylor	176	152	......	174	153
Table Mound	57	136	......	61	132
Vernon	59	111	......	59	111
Whitewater	56	138	......	57	137
Washington	18	137	......	18	137
To als	2124	4047	18	2175	4013
Majority	....	1923	......	....	1838

EMMET COUNTY.

NAMES OF TOWNSHIPS.	Kirkwood	Leffler	Lozier	Newbold	Woodward
Estherville	76	5	......	78	3
Emmet	32	4	......	32	4
Ellsworth	15	3	......	15	3
Iowa Lake	8	2	......	8	2
Armstrong Grove	25	7	......	25	7
Swan Lake	10	2	......	10	2
High Lake	44	6	......	44	6
Center	24	2	......	24	2
Twelve Mile Lake	12	....	......	12	....
Totals	246	31	.....	248	29
Majority	215	....	......	219	....

FAYETTE COUNTY.

NAMES OF TOWNSHIPS.	Kirkwood	Leffler	Lozier	Newbold	Woodward
Auburn	78	104	1	79	104
Banks	37	8	......	37	8
Bethel	75	13	1	76	13
Center	92	44	......	92	44
Clermont	98	146	8	104	148
Dover	105	37	......	105	37
Eden	106	92	15	121	90
Fairfield	161	104	......	166	99
Fremont	52	26	......	52	26
Harlan	85	35	......	87	34
Illyria	94	127	......	91	127

FAYETTE COUNTY.—Continued.

NAMES OF TOWNSHIPS.	GOVERNOR.			LIEUTENANT GOVERNOR.	
	Samuel J. Kirkwood, *Republican.*	Shepherd Leffler, *Democrat.*	J. H. Lozier, *Prohibition.*	Joshua G. Newbold, *Republican.*	E. B. Woodward, *Democrat.*
Jefferson	96	89	......	101	86
Oran	61	34	......	61	34
Pleasant Valley	164	92	......	166	92
Putnam	103	13	......	103	13
Scott	32	11	......	32	11
Smithfield	83	36	......	85	35
Westfield	260	96	11	281	98
West Union	342	183	19	364	180
Windsor	89	54	......	92	52
Totals	2213	1344	55	2295	1331
Majority	869	....	......	964	....

FLOYD COUNTY.

NAMES OF TOWNSHIPS.	Samuel J. Kirkwood, *Republican.*	Shepherd Leffler, *Democrat.*	J. H. Lozier, *Prohibition.*	Joshua G. Newbold, *Republican.*	E. B. Woodward, *Democrat.*
St. Charles	390	159	......	392	159
Floyd	153	36	......	153	36
Rock Grove	107	49	......	114	45
Rudd	61	25	......	61	25
Rockford	133	54	......	133	54
Ulster	68	10	......	68	10
Scott	50	24	......	50	24
Union	157	51	......	153	51
Pleasant Grove	68	15	......	67	16
Riverton	74	26	......	76	24
Niles	43	69	......	44	68
Cedar	38	7	......	38	7
Totals	1342	525	......	1349	519
Majority	817	....	......	830	....

FRANKLIN COUNTY.

NAMES OF TOWNSHIPS.	Samuel J. Kirkwood, *Republican.*	Shepherd Leffler, *Democrat.*	J. H. Lozier, *Prohibition.*	Joshua G. Newbold, *Republican.*	E. B. Woodward, *Democrat.*
Oakland	54	....	......	54	....
Osceola	34	63	......	34	63
Clinton	69	17	......	69	17
Ingham	51	16	......	51	16
Washington	295	53	......	295	53
Hamilton	33	....	......	33	....
Richland	30	....	......	30	....
Morgan	44	4	......	44	4
Geneva	87	17	......	87	17
West Fork	43	14	......	43	14
Grant	35	13	......	35	13
Reeve	101	2	......	101	2
Marion	11	14	......	11	14
Lee	36	1	......	36	1
Totals	923	214	......	923	214
Majority	709	....	......	709	....

FREMONT COUNTY.

NAMES OF TOWNSHIPS.	GOVERNOR.			LIEUTENANT-GOVERNOR.	
	Samuel J. Kirkwood, *Republican.*	Shepherd Leffler, *Democrat.*	J. H. Lozier, *Prohibition.*	Joshua G. Newbold, *Republican.*	E. B. Woodward, *Democrat.*
Sidney	196	341	......	196	341
Franklin	195	366	......	195	366
Scott	117	179	......	110	180
Madison	82	120	......	82	120
Riverton	116	99	......	116	99
Prairie	36	67	......	35	68
Walnut	40	55	......	40	55
Monroe	72	53	......	71	54
Ross	146	163	......	148	100
Benton, No. 1	66	87	......	67	86
Benton, No. 2	30	45	......	30	45
Locust Grove	49	25	......	49	25
Fisher	81	60	......	80	61
Totals	1226	1660	......	1219	1600
Majority	....	434	......	....	381

GREENE COUNTY.

NAMES OF TOWNSHIPS.	Kirkwood	Leffler	Lozier	Newbold	Woodward
Washington	75	48	......	75	48
Junction	99	56	......	102	53
Payton	6	9	......	6	9
Franklin	30	30	......	32	29
Jefferson	251	106	......	250	105
Hardin	31	24	......	31	24
Dawson	10	2	......	9	3
Greenbriar	29	9	......	29	9
Jackson	54	29	......	49	35
Bristol	36	38	......	36	38
Highland	9	10	......	9	10
Willow	14	8	......	14	8
Scranton	79	26	......	77	27
Kendrick	64	12	......	61	15
Cedar	29	27	......	29	27
Totals	816	434	......	809	440
Majority	382	....	......	369	....

GRUNDY COUNTY.

NAMES OF TOWNSHIPS.	Kirkwood	Leffler	Lozier	Newbold	Woodward
Fairfield	55	2	......	55	2
Beaver	31	1	......	31	1
Pleasant Valley	32	3	......	32	3
German	3	35	......	3	35
Shiloh	38	17	......	38	17
Colfax	46	....	......	46	....
Lincoln	31	4	......	31	4
Grant	25	26	......	25	26
Black Hawk	37	42	......	37	42
Palermo	161	13	......	162	12
Melrose	49	5	......	49	5
Felix	50	8	......	50	8
Clay	44	4	......	44	4
Totals	602	160	......	603	159
Majority	442	....	......	444	....

GUTHRIE COUNTY.

NAMES OF TOWNSHIPS.	GOVERNOR.			LIEUTENANT-GOVERNOR.	
	Samuel J. Kirkwood, *Republican.*	Shepherd Leffler, *Democrat.*	J. H. Lozier, *Prohibition.*	Joshua G. Newbold, *Republican.*	E. B. Woodward, *Democrat.*
Bear Grove	63	42	......	62	42
Beaver	95	28	......	96	28
Cass	206	112	......	206	111
Center	136	55	......	135	55
Dodge	23	9	......	23	9
Grant	27	25	......	27	25
Highland	45	14	......	45	13
Jackson	72	54	......	69	59
Orange	13	16	......	13	16
Penn	171	87	......	166	95
Richland	47	26	......	47	26
Thompson	82	52	......	82	52
Union	24	23	......	25	23
Valley	35	67	......	34	68
Victory	57	39	......	56	40
Totals	1096	649	......	1086	662
Majority	447	....	......	424	....

HAMILTON COUNTY.

NAMES OF TOWNSHIPS.	Samuel J. Kirkwood, *Republican.*	Shepherd Leffler, *Democrat.*	J. H. Lozier, *Prohibition.*	Joshua G. Newbold, *Republican.*	E. B. Woodward, *Democrat.*
Boone	329	112	......	344	109
Blairsburg	61	16	......	65	17
Cass	59	31	......	58	30
Clear Lake	28	10	......	27	11
Ellsworth	22	11	......	22	11
Fremont	52	28	......	54	28
Hamilton	57	35	......	57	35
Lincoln	11	4	......	12	4
Lyon	32	22	......	32	22
Marion	68	57	......	70	47
Rose Grove	11	14	......	11	14
Scott	52	1	......	52	1
Webster	83	28	......	86	31
Totals	865	369	......	890	360
Majority	496	....	......	530	....

HANCOCK COUNTY.

NAMES OF TOWNSHIPS.	Samuel J. Kirkwood, *Republican.*	Shepherd Leffler, *Democrat.*	J. H. Lozier, *Prohibition.*	Joshua G. Newbold, *Republican.*	E. B. Woodward, *Democrat.*
Avery	26	5	......	26	5
Amsterdam	30	15	......	30	15
Britt	13	2	......	13	2
Concord	86	14	......	86	14
Crystal	14	4	......	14	4
Ellington	75	26	......	75	26
Madison	20	11	......	21	10
Totals	264	77	......	265	76
Majority	187	....	......	189	....

HARDIN COUNTY.

NAMES OF TOWNSHIPS.	GOVERNOR. Samuel J. Kirkwood, *Republican.*	GOVERNOR. Shepherd Leffler, *Democrat.*	GOVERNOR. J. H. Lozier, *Prohibition.*	LIEUTENANT-GOVERNOR. Joshua G. Newbold, *Republican.*	LIEUTENANT-GOVERNOR. E. B. Woodward, *Democrat.*
Alden	99	49	......	100	49
Buckeye	28	12	......	28	12
Clay	130	91	......	129	92
Concord	15	....	......	15	....
Ellis	17	22	......	71	22
Etna	157	172	......	161	166
Eldora	353	135	......	356	136
Grant	47	1	......	48	1
Hardin	282	77	......	286	75
Jackson	78	64	......	78	64
Providence	126	14	......	160	14
Pleasant	73	54	......	73	54
Sherman	6	21	......	6	21
Tipton	24	34	......	24	34
Union	199	47	......	202	46
Totals	1688	793	32	1737	786
Majority	895	....	......	951	....

HARRISON COUNTY.

NAMES OF TOWNSHIPS.	Samuel J. Kirkwood, *Republican.*	Shepherd Leffler, *Democrat.*	J. H. Lozier, *Prohibition.*	Joshua G. Newbold, *Republican.*	E. B. Woodward, *Democrat.*
Harrison	173	110	......	171	111
Lincoln	8	17	......	8	17
Douglas	35	31	......	35	31
Cass	34	24	......	33	25
Union	32	53	......	30	55
Washington	3	42	......	6	39
Cincinnati	46	50	......	46	50
Raglan	17	56	......	17	56
Allen	12	7	......	12	7
St. Johns	167	282	......	165	285
Clay	46	63	......	47	63
Jefferson	150	141	......	152	143
Magnolia	122	82	......	124	81
Taylor	70	63	......	72	61
Calhoun	35	29	......	35	29
Morgan	80	42	......	80	43
Jackson	31	31	......	31	32
Boyer	102	64	......	105	65
Lagrange	46	48	......	46	48
Little Sioux	97	60	......	99	60
Totals	1306	1295	......	1314	1301
Majority	11	....	......	13	....

HENRY COUNTY.

NAMES OF TOWNSHIPS.	Samuel J. Kirkwood, *Republican.*	Shepherd Leffler, *Democrat.*	J. H. Lozier, *Prohibition.*	Joshua G. Newbold, *Republican.*	E. B. Woodward, *Democrat.*
Baltimore	42	139	......	42	
Canaan	97	63	......	96	
Center	687	360	......	690	
Jackson	88	89	......	90	
Jefferson	76	90	......	76	
Marion	131	78	......	131	

HENRY COUNTY.—Continued.

NAMES OF TOWNSHIPS.	GOVERNOR.			LIEUTENANT-GOVERNOR.	
	Samuel J. Kirkwood, *Republican.*	Shepherd Leffler, *Democrat.*	J. H. Lozier, *Prohibition.*	Joshua G. Newbold, *Republican.*	E. B. Woodward, *Democrat.*
New London	222	159	....	221	163
Salem	216	87	....	218	84
Scott	127	66	....	133	69
Tippecanoe	106	118	....	107	117
Trenton	68	100	....	66	98
Wayne	133	20	....	133	22
Totals	1993	1369	....	2003	1386
Majority	624	....	....	617	....

HOWARD COUNTY.

NAMES OF TOWNSHIPS.	Kirkwood	Leffler	Lozier	Newbold	Woodward
Albion	63	27	....	60	30
Forest City	131	50	....	131	50
Chester	57	28	....	57	28
Oak Dale	44	7	....	45	7
Jamestown	52	12	....	52	12
Saratoga	33	5	....	33	5
Howard Center	44	25	....	44	25
Vernon Springs	254	119	....	254	119
New Oregon	91	41	....	91	41
Paris	50	58	....	50	58
Howard	34	34	....	34	34
Afton	29	71	....	29	71
Totals	882	477	....	880	480
Majority	405	....	....	400	....

HUMBOLDT COUNTY.

NAMES OF TOWNSHIPS.	Kirkwood	Leffler	Lozier	Newbold	Woodward
Avery	21	6	....	23	6
Dakota	46	14	....	48	17
Delana	36	....	....	36	....
Humboldt	23	27	....	23	27
Grove	24	16	....	24	16
Lake	3	4	....	5	4
Norway	24	6	....	23	6
Rutland	44	9	....	46	9
Springvale	124	10	....	114	10
Weaver	10	4	....	10	4
Vernon	20	22	....	20	22
Wacousta	13	4	....	13	4
Totals	388	122	....	385	125
Majority	266	....	....	260	....

IDA COUNTY.

NAMES OF TOWNSHIPS.	Kirkwood	Leffler	Lozier	Newbold	Woodward
Corwin	78	1	....	80	....
Maple	47	17	....	47	17

IDA COUNTY.—Continued.

NAMES OF TOWNSHIPS.	GOVERNOR.			LIEUTENANT-GOVERNOR.	
	Samuel J. Kirkwood, *Republican.*	Shepherd Leffler, *Democrat.*	J. H. Lozier, *Prohibition.*	Joshua G. Newbold, *Republican.*	E. B. Woodward, *Democrat.*
Silver Creek	33	3	......	34	2
Douglas	19	9	......	19	9
Totals	177	30	......	180	28
Majority	147	......	......	152	......

IOWA COUNTY.

NAMES OF TOWNSHIPS.	Samuel J. Kirkwood, *Republican.*	Shepherd Leffler, *Democrat.*	J. H. Lozier, *Prohibition.*	Joshua G. Newbold, *Republican.*	E. B. Woodward, *Democrat.*
Amana	28	1	......	26	2
Cono	33	14	......	33	14
Dayton	103	56	......	106	54
English	187	128	......	188	127
Filmore	59	125	......	60	124
Greene	56	91	......	54	93
Hartford	190	96	......	191	95
Honey Creek	115	104	......	114	105
Hilton	53	53	......	55	52
Iowa	52	88	......	51	90
Lenox	41	30	......	39	30
Lincoln	55	16	......	55	16
Marengo	281	234	......	282	235
Pilot	74	53	......	74	53
Sumner	78	54	......	80	54
Troy	125	45	......	125	45
Washington	25	65	......	25	65
York	47	74	......	47	74
Totals	1602	1327	......	1605	1328
Majority	275	......	......	277	......

JACKSON COUNTY.

NAMES OF TOWNSHIPS.	Samuel J. Kirkwood, *Republican.*	Shepherd Leffler, *Democrat.*	J. H. Lozier, *Prohibition.*	Joshua G. Newbold, *Republican.*	E. B. Woodward, *Democrat.*
Bellevue	151	268	......	164	255
Brandon	58	83	......	60	81
Butler	4	183	......	4	183
Fairfield	27	78	......	28	77
Farmers' Creek	136	119	......	136	119
Iowa	90	80	......	95	79
Jackson	30	118	......	30	118
Maquoketa	195	189	......	204	186
Monmouth	138	85	......	139	84
Otter Creek	27	101	......	28	101
erry	148	85	......	151	82
[illegible] Spring	26	164	......	26	164
Richland	83	108	......	83	108
South Fork	226	171	......	227	170
Tete des Morts	15	105	......	14	106
Union	104	112	......	104	112
Van Buren	118	103	......	122	100
Washington	21	108	......	21	108
Totals	1597	2260	6	1636	2233
Majority	......	663	......	......	597

JASPER COUNTY.

NAMES OF TOWNSHIPS.	GOVERNOR.			LIEUTENANT-GOVERNOR.	
	Samuel J. Kirkwood, *Republican.*	Shepherd Leffler, *Democrat.*	J. H. Lozier, *Prohibition.*	Joshua G. Newbold, *Republican.*	E. B. Woodward, *Democrat.*
Newton	387	103	......	389	102
Fairview	272	172	......	273	172
Des Moines	209	130	......	208	128
Washington	83	69	......	85	68
Mound Prairie	69	42	......	76	41
Poweshiek	125	81	......	126	80
Clear Creek	70	73	......	70	74
Independence	74	21	......	74	21
Sherman	74	42	......	75	41
Palo Alto	86	44	......	85	45
Malaka	76	34	......	79	33
Mariposa	23	36	......	23	36
Kellogg	114	100	......	115	100
Buena Vista	74	44	......	75	44
Elk Creek	86	78	......	86	78
Lynn Grove	129	53	......	128	53
Richland	72	3	......	71	4
Rock Creek	21	32	......	21	34
Hickory Grove	34	9	......	34	9
Totals	2078	1166	......	2093	1163
Majority	912	....	......	930	....

JEFFERSON COUNTY.

NAMES OF TOWNSHIPS.	Samuel J. Kirkwood, *Republican.*	Shepherd Leffler, *Democrat.*	J. H. Lozier, *Prohibition.*	Joshua G. Newbold, *Republican.*	E. B. Woodward, *Democrat.*
Walnut	33	145	....	38	145
Penn	157	91	....	157	91
Black Hawk	92	56	....	93	55
Polk	129	99	....	131	98
Locust Grove	117	150	....	121	151
Fairfield	482	327	....	484	322
Buchanan	105	97	....	106	98
Lockridge	132	57	....	131	57
Round Prairie	88	60	....	84	61
Cedar	51	81	....	56	77
Liberty	120	64	....	120	64
Des Moines	92	104	....	92	104
Totals	1598	1331	....	1613	1323
Majority	267	....	....	290	....

JOHNSON COUNTY.

NAMES OF TOWNSHIPS.	Samuel J. Kirkwood, *Republican.*	Shepherd Leffler, *Democrat.*	J. H. Lozier, *Prohibition.*	Joshua G. Newbold, *Republican.*	E. B. Woodward, *Democrat.*
Cedar	61	71	....	60	72
Big Grove	78	154	....	75	156
Jefferson	32	103	....	32	103
Monroe	37	94	....	35	96
Oxford	119	174	....	115	178
Hardin	57	93	....	56	94
Madison	58	61	....	58	62
Penn	95	40	....	86	48
Clear Creek	69	64	....	63	70
Newport	35	88	....	36	87
Graham	84	75	....	84	77
Scott	119	38	....	117	40

JOHNSON COUNTY.—CONTINUED.

NAMES OF TOWNSHIPS.	GOVERNOR.			LIEUTENANT-GOVERNOR.	
	Samuel J. Kirkwood, *Republican.*	Shepherd Leffler, *Democrat.*	J. H. Lozier, *Prohibition.*	Joshua G. Newbold, *Republican.*	E. B. Woodward, *Democrat.*
Union	66	59	......	65	63
Washington	101	35	......	101	35
Sharon	105	43	......	102	44
Liberty	24	74	......	24	74
Fremont	110	91	......	102	99
Lincoln	67	41	......	66	41
Pleasant Valley	65	58	......	63	60
Lucas, East Precinct	141	134	......	129	147
Lucas, West Precinct	116	44	......	104	55
Iowa City	648	507	......	596	568
Total	2287	2141	1	2169	2269
Majority	146	....	......	....	100

JONES COUNTY.

NAMES OF TOWNSHIPS.	Samuel J. Kirkwood, *Republican.*	Shepherd Leffler, *Democrat.*	J. H. Lozier, *Prohibition.*	Joshua G. Newbold, *Republican.*	E. B. Woodward, *Democrat.*
Cass	90	68	......	90	68
Castle Grove	92	76	......	62	76
Clay	02	44	......	92	44
Fairview	324	296	......	330	290
Greenfield	79	100	......	84	98
Hale	110	30	......	109	31
Jackson	52	107	......	52	107
Monticello	250	239	......	257	240
Madison	167	28	......	168	27
Oxford	70	82	......	70	82
Rome	159	71	......	159	71
Richland	73	37	......	73	37
Scotch Grove	98	20	......	98	20
Wyoming	225	90	......	223	92
Wayne	144	34	......	145	33
Washington	6	78	......	6	78
Totals	2000	1400	6	2018	1394
Majority	600	....	......	624	....

KEOKUK COUNTY.

NAMES OF TOWNSHIPS.	Samuel J. Kirkwood, *Republican.*	Shepherd Leffler, *Democrat.*	J. H. Lozier, *Prohibition.*	Joshua G. Newbold, *Republican.*	E. B. Woodward, *Democrat.*
Richland	195	52	......	192	53
Jackson	70	159	......	70	159
Steady Run	119	62	......	118	62
Benton	102	99	......	102	99
Warren	35	109	....	35	109
Lancaster	63	149	......	63	149
Clear Creek	66	89	......	65	90
Lafayette, Keota Precinct	139	56	......	133	62
Lafayette, Harper Precinct	44	66	......	44	66
German	69	138	......	68	137
Sigourney	248	161	......	251	162
Van Buren	49	72	......	49	72
Washington	114	89	......	113	91
Prairie	91	16	......	91	17
Adams	71	40	......	69	42

KEOKUK COUNTY.—Continued.

Names of Townships.	Governor.			Lieutenant-Governor.	
	Samuel J. Kirkwood, *Republican.*	Shepherd Leffler, *Democrat.*	J. H. Lozier, *Prohibition.*	Joshua G. Newbold, *Republican.*	E. B. Woodward, *Democrat.*
English River	133	44	......	135	44
Liberty	24	65	......	24	65
Totals	1632	1466	......	1622	1481
Majority	166	....	......	141	....

KOSSUTH COUNTY.

Names of Townships.	Samuel J. Kirkwood, *Republican.*	Shepherd Leffler, *Democrat.*	J. H. Lozier, *Prohibition.*	Joshua G. Newbold, *Republican.*	E. B. Woodward, *Democrat.*
Algona	241	38	......	243	3[illegible]
Fenton	21	1	......	21	1
Wesley	39	7	......	39	7
Cresco	73	13	......	76	13
Irvington	71	6	......	72	5
Greenwood	33	1	......	33	1
Lott's Creek	34	....	......	34	....
Portland	70	5	......	71	5
Total	582	71	1	589	68
Majority	511	....	......	521	....

LEE COUNTY.

Names of Townships.	Samuel J. Kirkwood, *Republican.*	Shepherd Leffler, *Democrat.*	J. H. Lozier, *Prohibition.*	Joshua G. Newbold, *Republican.*	E. B. Woodward, *Democrat.*
Green Bay	38	69	......	36	69
Denmark	122	45	......	121	47
Pleasant Ridge	82	78	......	83	78
Marion	81	130	......	81	130
Cedar	94	69	......	95	68
Harrison	69	129	......	71	125
Franklin	66	182	......	64	184
West Point	84	245	......	85	244
Washington	78	109	......	79	109
Madison	234	475	......	231	480
Jefferson	56	105	......	56	105
Charleston	79	140	......	76	142
Van Buren	70	90	......	70	91
Des Moines	111	75	......	114	75
Montrose	153	260	......	154	259
Jackson	892	926	......	894	930
Totals	2309	3127	......	2310	3136
Majority	....	818	......	....	826

LINN COUNTY.

Names of Townships.	Samuel J. Kirkwood, *Republican.*	Shepherd Leffler, *Democrat.*	J. H. Lozier, *Prohibition.*	Joshua G. Newbold, *Republican.*	E. B. Woodward, *Democrat.*
Bertram	23	120	......	22	121
Brown	169	67	1	169	68
Boulder	64	77	......	65	76
Buffalo	26	55	......	26	55
Clinton	98	78	......	100	76
College	91	102	......	93	100
Fairfax	111	103	......	113	105

LINN COUNTY.—Continued.

NAMES OF TOWNSHIPS.	GOVERNOR.			LIEUTENANT-GOVERNOR.	
	Samuel J. Kirkwood, *Republican.*	Shepherd Leffler, *Democrat.*	J. H. Lozier, *Prohibition.*	Joshua G. Newbold, *Republican.*	E. B. Woodward, *Democrat.*
Fayette	121	46	......	121	46
Franklin	288	149	1	292	149
Grant	45	38	......	45	38
Jackson	113	29	......	113	29
Linn	85	89	......	86	88
Maine	126	95	......	128	96
Marion	431	238	34	462	242
Monroe	62	58	......	62	58
Otter Creek	79	41	......	79	41
Putnam	47	79	......	48	78
Rapids—1st Precinct	218	160	......	216	162
" 2d Precinct	269	122	1	271	121
" 3d Precinct	191	164	......	191	164
" 4th Precinct	193	91	......	191	93
Spring Grove	82	18	......	83	17
Washington	87	140	......	91	137
Totals	3019	2159	37	3067	2160
Majority	860	....	......	907	....

LOUISA COUNTY.

NAMES OF TOWNSHIPS.	Samuel J. Kirkwood, *Republican.*	Shepherd Leffler, *Democrat.*	J. H. Lozier, *Prohibition.*	Joshua G. Newbold, *Republican.*	E. B. Woodward, *Democrat.*
Columbus City	497	217	......	496	217
Concord	78	98	......	78	98
Eliot	50	32	......	50	32
Elm Grove	108	13	......	109	13
Grand View	258	81	......	264	77
Jefferson	132	74	......	132	74
Marshall	129	69	......	129	69
Morning Sun	220	136	......	236	120
Oakland	75	55	......	76	55
Port Louisa	106	62	......	105	63
Union	79	58	......	78	59
Wapello	265	256	......	266	254
Totals	1997	1151	......	2019	1131
Majority	846	....	......	888	....

LUCAS COUNTY.

NAMES OF TOWNSHIPS.	Samuel J. Kirkwood, *Republican.*	Shepherd Leffler, *Democrat.*	J. H. Lozier, *Prohibition.*	Joshua G. Newbold, *Republican.*	E. B. Woodward, *Democrat.*
Benton	168	55	......	168	52
Cedar	90	40	......	91	37
Chariton	354	277	......	332	290
English	61	69	......	61	67
Jackson	37	91	......	38	90
Liberty	53	56	......	53	56
Otter Creek	66	57	......	66	56
Pleasant	70	33	......	70	33
Union	50	81	......	54	79
Warren	77	54	......	75	54
Washington	81	83	......	81	81
White Breast	51	44	......	51	41
Totals	1058	940	......	1040	936
Majority	118	....	......	104	....

LYON COUNTY.

NAMES OF TOWNSHIPS.	GOVERNOR.			LIEUTENANT-GOVERNOR.	
	Samuel J. Kirkwood, *Republican.*	Shepherd Leffler *Democrat.*	J. H. Lozier, *Prohibition.*	Joshua G. Newbold, *Republican.*	E. B. Woodward, *Democrat.*
Grant	26			27	
Rock	52	6		52	6
Larchwood	25			25	
Lyon	86	1		86	1
Doon	36			36	
Dale	75			75	
Totals	300	7		301	7
Majority	293			294	

MADISON COUNTY.

NAMES OF TOWNSHIPS.	Samuel J. Kirkwood, *Republican.*	Shepherd Leffler *Democrat.*	J. H. Lozier, *Prohibition.*	Joshua G. Newbold, *Republican.*	E. B. Woodward, *Democrat.*
Center	352	187		354	187
Lee	48	88		48	88
Jefferson	113	62		113	62
Madison	131	85		131	85
Penn	101	61		101	61
Jackson	59	69		61	69
Douglas	89	117		88	119
Union	109	108		109	108
Crawford	95	63		96	62
South	132	69		135	70
Scott	103	122		103	121
Lincoln	109	96		109	86
Webster	62	63		61	64
Grand River	97	50		98	50
Monroe	38	68		38	68
Walnut	57	66		57	66
Ohio	84	38		84	38
Totals	1779	1412	8	1786	1404
Majority	367			382	

MAHASKA COUNTY.

NAMES OF TOWNSHIPS.	Samuel J. Kirkwood, *Republican.*	Shepherd Leffler *Democrat.*	J. H. Lozier, *Prohibition.*	Joshua G. Newbold, *Republican.*	E. B. Woodward, *Democrat.*
Cedar	136	93		136	93
Harrison	139	69	1	140	69
Des Moines	101	97		101	97
Jefferson	51	79		52	78
Scott	70	82		83	72
Oskaloosa	917	534	17	940	531
White Oak	86	120		86	121
Monroe	90	116		90	116
Adams	82	68		83	67
Madison	80	64	1	82	64
Black Oak	69	73		69	74
Richland	105	134		106	134
Prairie	259	93	4	264	94
Union	123	60	2	124	61
Pleasant Grove	60	60	2	60	61
Totals	2368	1742	27	2416	1732
Majority	626			684	

MARION COUNTY.

NAMES OF TOWNSHIPS.	GOVERNOR.			LIEUTENANT-GOVERNOR.	
	Samuel J. Kirkwood, *Republican.*	Shepherd Leffler, *Democrat.*	J. H. Lozier, *Prohibition.*	Joshua G. Newbold, *Republican.*	E. B. Woodward, *Democrat.*
Clay	108	56	......	108	56
Dallas	69	83	......	73	83
Franklin	68	70	......	67	67
Indiana	139	77	......	140	77
Knoxville	558	371	......	560	370
Lake Prairie	245	548	......	243	550
Liberty	118	120	......	119	120
Perry	18	57	......	18	57
Polk	15	101	......	15	100
Pleasant Grove	124	138	......	125	138
Red Rock	117	116	......	119	116
Swan	100	64	......	100	64
Summit	136	89	......	136	89
Union	66	76	......	66	76
Washington	139	82	......	140	82
Total	2020	2048	......	2026	2045
Majority	....	28	......	....	19

MARSHALL COUNTY.

NAMES OF TOWNSHIPS.	Samuel J. Kirkwood, *Republican.*	Shepherd Leffler, *Democrat.*	J. H. Lozier, *Prohibition.*	Joshua G. Newbold, *Republican.*	E. B. Woodward, *Democrat.*
Marshall	467	156	......	475	149
Logan	33	6	......	33	6
Marietta	80	21	......	86	22
Minerva	18	30	......	18	30
Liberty	46	19	......	46	19
Timber Creek	51	41	......	56	37
*Washington	....	....	......	....	....
Jefferson	38	22	......	38	22
Green Castle	90	58	......	92	58
State Center	170	34	......	176	31
Le Grand	162	32	......	166	33
Liscomb	142	18	......	141	19
Bangor	82	6	......	86	6
Iowa	119	36	......	138	34
Taylor	63	6	......	63	6
Marion	54	34	......	60	32
Eden	72	7	......	72	7
Vienna	49	16	......	49	16
Total	1736	542	32	1795	527
Majority	1194	....	......	1268	....

* Canvassers rejected the vote because not certified.

MILLS COUNTY.

NAMES OF TOWNSHIPS.	Samuel J. Kirkwood, *Republican.*	Shepherd Leffler, *Democrat.*	J. H. Lozier, *Prohibition.*	Joshua G. Newbold, *Republican.*	E. B. Woodward, *Democrat.*
Anderson	86	78	......	84	79
Ingraham	46	63	......	46	64
Oak	30	119	......	24	120
St. Mary	14	39	......	15	38
Platteville	48	84	......	49	83
Glenwood	256	209	3	255	213
Silver Creek	213	78	1	214	76
Indian Creek	148	74	......	148	74
Deer Creek	73	40	......	72	41

MILLS COUNTY.—Continued.

NAMES OF TOWNSHIPS.	GOVERNOR.			LIEUTENANT-GOVERNOR.	
	Samuel J. Kirkwood, *Republican.*	Shepherd Leffler, *Democrat.*	J. H. Lozier, *Prohibition.*	Joshua G. Newbold, *Republican.*	E. B. Woodward, *Democrat.*
White Cloud	63	22	......	62	23
Rawles	86	50	......	86	50
Lyons	36	77	......	35	79
Total	1099	933	4	1090	940
Majority	166	....	......	150	....

MITCHELL COUNTY.

NAMES OF TOWNSHIPS.	Samuel J. Kirkwood, *Republican.*	Shepherd Leffler, *Democrat.*	J. H. Lozier, *Prohibition.*	Joshua G. Newbold, *Republican.*	E. B. Woodward, *Democrat.*
Osage	299	54	......	303	54
Mitchell	204	31	......	204	30
St. Ansgar	83	20	......	83	20
Stacyville	39	32	......	39	32
Cedar	82	2	......	82	2
Burr Oak	64	18	......	64	18
Rock	64	32	......	64	32
Douglas	35	40	......	35	40
Otranto	54	13	......	54	13
Newburg	44	26	......	44	26
Union	30	6	......	30	6
Lincoln	103	7	......	103	7
Jenkins	61	17	......	61	17
Liberty	40	4	......	40	4
Wayne	49	27	......	48	20
Total	1251	329	......	1254	321
Majority	922	....	......	933	....

MONONA COUNTY.

NAMES OF TOWNSHIPS.	Samuel J. Kirkwood, *Republican.*	Shepherd Leffler, *Democrat.*	J. H. Lozier, *Prohibition.*	Joshua G. Newbold, *Republican.*	E. B. Woodward, *Democrat.*
Ashton	12	14	......	12	14
Belvidere	13	11	......	13	11
Center	28	23	......	29	22
Fairview	45	12	......	44	13
Franklin	156	54	......	157	58
Grant	49	9	......	45	9
Jordan	17	17	......	17	17
Kennebec	34	24	......	35	24
Lake	18	22	......	18	22
Lincoln	60	41	......	58	43
Maple	35	46	......	36	45
Sherman	27	18	......	26	20
Spring Valley	23	19	......	23	20
Soldier	9	23	......	11	20
St. Clair	22	18	......	20	20
West Fork	15	9	......	14	10
Willow	7	3	......	7	3
Total	570	363	......	565	371
Majority	207	....	......	194	....

MONROE COUNTY.

NAMES OF TOWNSHIPS.	GOVERNOR.			LIEUTENANT-GOVERNOR.	
	Samuel J. Kirkwood, *Republican.*	Shepherd Leffler, *Democrat.*	J. H. Lozier, *Prohibition.*	Joshua G. Newbold, *Republican.*	E. B. Woodward, *Democrat.*
Pleasant	75	101	......	77	100
Mantua	124	23	......	124	23
Urbana	30	76	......	31	75
Monroe	71	47	......	70	48
Troy	370	179	......	374	176
Bluff Creek	101	30	......	103	31
Union	87	84	......	87	84
Guilford	19	84	......	19	84
Franklin	34	57	......	34	57
Jackson	86	70	......	86	70
Wayne	21	27	......	21	27
Cedar	46	69	......	47	69
Totals	1064	847	......	1073	844
Majority	217	....	......	229	....

MONTGOMERY COUNTY.

NAMES OF TOWNSHIPS.	Samuel J. Kirkwood, *Republican.*	Shepherd Leffler, *Democrat.*	J. H. Lozier, *Prohibition.*	Joshua G. Newbold, *Republican.*	E. B. Woodward, *Democrat.*
Douglas	91	34	......	91	34
Pilot Grove	82	26	......	81	27
Sherman	61	63	......	60	64
Lincoln	75	38	......	75	38
Walnut	81	20	......	84	18
Red Oak	422	180	......	429	179
Frankfort	60	9	......	60	9
Washington	77	16	......	79	15
Jackson	218	139	......	219	139
Scott	55	15	......	55	15
Grant	125	14	......	125	14
West	98	42	......	98	42
Totals	1445	596	......	1456	594
Majority	849	....	......	862	....

MUSCATINE COUNTY.

NAMES OF TOWNSHIPS.	Samuel J. Kirkwood, *Republican.*	Shepherd Leffler, *Democrat.*	J. H. Lozier, *Prohibition.*	Joshua G. Newbold, *Republican.*	E. B. Woodward, *Democrat.*
Bloomington	675	801	9	677	810
Cedar	33	37	......	83	37
Fulton	46	74	1	46	76
Goshen	168	89	......	167	89
Lake	54	56	1	57	53
Montpelier	38	30	......	44	34
Moscow	41	100	10	41	100
Orono	47	64	......	45	66
Pike	72	126	......	71	127
Sweetland	127	79	8	136	78
Seventy Six	72	88	......	74	85
Wapsinonoc	270	62	25	292	64
Wilton	200	151	9	209	152
Totals	1843	1757	63	1892	1771
Majority	86	....	......	121	....

O'BRIEN COUNTY.

NAMES OF TOWNSHIPS.	GOVERNOR.			LIEUTENANT-GOVERNOR.	
	Samuel J. Kirkwood, *Republican.*	Shepherd Leffler, *Democrat.*	J. H. Lozier, *Prohibition.*	Joshua G. Newbold *Republican.*	E. B. Woodward, *Democrat.*
Waterman	28			28	
Grant	66	2		66	2
Center	68			68	
Highland	42	1		42	
Liberty	60			60	
Baker	48			48	
Carroll	48	1		49	1
Floyd	90	18		90	18
Summit	28			28	
Totals	478	22		479	21
Majority	456			458	

OSCEOLA COUNTY.

NAMES OF TOWNSHIPS.	Samuel J. Kirkwood	Shepherd Leffler	J. H. Lozier	Joshua G. Newbold	E. B. Woodward
Holman	131			131	
Ocheydan	26			26	
Gilman	35			35	
Goewey	49			49	
Baker	12	9		12	9
Viola	33			33	
Wilson	24			24	
Horton	13			13	
Fairview	15			15	
Totals	338	9		338	9
Majority	329			329	

PAGE COUNTY.

NAMES OF TOWNSHIPS.	Samuel J. Kirkwood	Shepherd Leffler	J. H. Lozier	Joshua G. Newbold	E. B. Woodward
Valley	43	61		43	61
Douglas	40	30		40	30
Fremont	54	22		55	21
Pierce	76	48		77	47
Grant	147	60		148	59
Tarkio	64	25		64	25
Nodaway	299	133		302	130
Nebraska	53	36		53	35
East River	43	47		43	47
Harlan	55	9		55	9
Lincoln	53	19		53	20
Morton	37	26		37	26
Washington	43	19		43	19
Colfax	65	13		65	13
Amity	164	2		166	1
Buchanan	54	59		53	60
Totals	1290	609		1297	603
Majority	581			584	

PALO ALTO COUNTY.

NAMES OF TOWNSHIPS.	GOVERNOR.			LIEUTENANT-GOVERNOR.	
	Samuel J. Kirkwood, *Republican.*	Shepherd Leffler, *Democrat.*	J. H. Lozier, *Prohibition.*	Joshua G. Newbold, *Republican.*	E. B. Woodward, *Democrat.*
Ellington	10	24	......	10	24
Emmetsburg	46	47	......	46	47
Fairfield	13	4	......	13	4
Fern Valley	15	8	......	15	9
Freedom	46	32	......	46	32
Great Oak	10	40	......	10	40
Highland	27	19	......	27	19
Lost Island	27	4	......	27	4
Nevada	2	27	......	2	27
Rush Lake	28	13	......	28	13
Silver Lake	56	8	......	56	8
Vernon	11	12	......	11	12
Walnut	15	30	......	15	30
West Bend	18	32	......	18	32
Totals	324	300	......	324	301
Majority	24	....	......	23	....

PLYMOUTH COUNTY.

NAMES OF TOWNSHIPS.	Samuel J. Kirkwood, *Republican.*	Shepherd Leffler, *Democrat.*	J. H. Lozier, *Prohibition.*	Joshua G. Newbold, *Republican.*	E. B. Woodward, *Democrat.*
America	261	62	......	*104	62
Marion	29	26	......	29	26
Fredonia	39	9	......	39	9
Elgin	49	2	......	49	2
Grant	55	1	......	55	1
Preston	22	15	......	22	15
Portland	21	1	......	21	1
Sioux	14	10	......	14	10
Johnson	48	20	......	47	22
Washington	43	5	......	46	4
Perry	67	25	......	67	25
Hungerford	51	2	......	62	1
Lincoln	41	6	......	43	6
Union	23	5	......	23	5
Stanton	50	24	......	52	22
Plymouth	43	2	......	43	2
Totals	866	215	......	716	213
Majority	651	....	......	503	....

* J. J. Newbold, 159.

POCAHONTAS COUNTY.

NAMES OF TOWNSHIPS.	Samuel J. Kirkwood, *Republican.*	Shepherd Leffler, *Democrat.*	J. H. Lozier, *Prohibition.*	Joshua G. Newbold, *Republican.*	E. B. Woodward, *Democrat.*
Bellville	38	3	......	38	3
Colfax	31	22	......	32	22
Cedar	50	26	......	50	26
Clinton	21	3	......	21	3
Center	....	16	......	....	16
Des Moines	56	5	......	56	5
Dover	21	8	......	21	8
Grant	18	2	......	18	2
Jackson	36	....	......	36	....
Lizard	42	41	......	44	39

POCAHONTAS COUNTY.—Continued.

NAMES OF TOWNSHIPS.	GOVERNOR.			LIEUTENANT-GOVERNOR.	
	Samuel J. Kirkwood, *Republican.*	Shepherd Leffler, *Democrat.*	J. H. Lozier, *Prohibition.*	Joshua G. Newbold, *Republican.*	E. B. Woodward, *Democrat.*
Lincoln	11	4	......	11	4
Swan Lake	8	....	......	8	....
Totals	332	332	......	335	128
Majority	202	....	......	207	....

POLK COUNTY.

NAMES OF TOWNSHIPS.	Samuel J. Kirkwood, *Republican.*	Shepherd Leffler, *Democrat.*	J. H. Lozier, *Prohibition.*	Joshua G. Newbold, *Republican.*	E. B. Woodward, *Democrat.*
Allen	46	23	......	43	24
Beaver, First Precinct	138	66	......	139	67
Beaver, Second Precinct	69	35	......	70	34
Bloomfield	93	67	......	95	68
Camp	104	118	......	104	118
Crocker	105	74	......	105	74
Des Moines, First Precinct	346	343	......	342	345
Des Moines, Second Precinct	537	254	......	536	255
Delaware	98	68	......	98	68
Douglass	96	36	......	96	36
Elkhart	58	61	......	59	60
Franklin	79	45	......	80	45
Four Mile	41	65	......	42	64
Grant	31	43	......	32	42
Jefferson	59	109	......	59	109
Lee	618	348	......	622	346
Lincoln	69	46	......	68	42
Madison	176	127	......	174	128
Saylor	71	36	......	71	35
Valley	68	52	......	66	54
Walnut	138	113	......	138	113
Washington	82	45	......	82	46
Totals	3122	2174	......	3121	2173
Majority	948	....	......	948	....

POTTAWATTAMIE COUNTY.

NAMES OF TOWNSHIPS.	Samuel J. Kirkwood, *Republican.*	Shepherd Leffler, *Democrat.*	J. H. Lozier, *Prohibition.*	Joshua G. Newbold, *Republican.*	E. B. Woodward, *Democrat.*
Boomer	13	59	......	13	59
Belknap	17	15	......	17	15
Crescent	22	55	3	25	55
Center	88	29	......	88	29
Grove	72	30	......	70	32
Harden	30	21	......	30	21
Hazel Dell	41	55	6	46	56
James	19	24	......	19	24
Keg Creek	20	35	......	20	36
Kane, First Precinct	163	255	4	169	254
Kane, Second Precinct	335	267	7	340	266
Kane, Third Precinct	202	257	......	202	255
Knox	252	197	......	247	202
Layton	108	138	......	105	141
Macedonia	67	31	1	65	34
Neola	46	55	......	46	55
Norwalk	12	47	......	12	47
Pleasant	45	25	......	43	27
Rockford	60	74	......	61	74

POTTAWATTAMIE COUNTY.—Continued.

NAMES OF TOWNSHIPS.	GOVERNOR.			LIEUTENANT-GOVERNOR.	
	Samuel J. Kirkwood, *Republican.*	Shepherd Leffler, *Democrat.*	J. H. Lozier, *Prohibition.*	Joshua G. Newbold, *Republican.*	E. B. Woodward, *Democrat.*
Silver Creek	35	12	......	35	12
Washington	16	29	......	16	19
Wright	56	11	......	56	11
Waveland	41	20	......	38	23
York	7	26	......	7	26
Totals	1767	1757	21	1770	1773
Majority	10	....	......	....	3

POWESHIEK COUNTY.

NAMES OF TOWNSHIPS.	Kirkwood	Leffler	Lozier	Newbold	Woodward
Chester	74	2	.....	75	2
Deep River	89	47	......	92	47
Bear Creek	195	126	......	201	125
Jefferson	55	51	......	55	51
Jackson	146	91	......	147	90
Lincoln	40	33	......	41	32
Malcolm	100	45	......	101	45
Madison	67	45	......	67	45
Pleasant	37	28	......	37	28
Sheridan	38	36	......	39	35
Sugar Creek	86	103	......	89	100
Scott	47	12	......	45	10
Union	66	24	......	66	24
Washington	42	30	......	42	30
Warren	35	58	......	35	58
Grinnell	376	49	......	378	50
Totals	1493	780	......	1510	775
Majority	713	....	......	735	....

RINGGOLD COUNTY.

NAMES OF TOWNSHIPS.	Kirkwood	Leffler	Lozier	Newbold	Woodward
Union	21	41	......	23	40
Tingley	27	16	......	26	16
Jefferson	66	35	......	67	35
Lincoln	37	16	......	32	22
Grant	38	40	......	39	40
Washington	59	31	......	58	32
Liberty	36	3	......	36	3
Monroe	54	9	......	54	9
Athens	28	37	......	28	37
Mount Ayr	148	33	......	149	33
Rice	38	19	......	38	19
Benton	40	47	......	40	47
Clinton	50	9	......	50	9
Middle Fork	31	41	......	31	41
Lots Creek	70	20	......	70	20
Riley	32	5	......	32	5
Totals	775	402	......	773	408
Majority	373	....	......	365	....

SAC COUNTY.

NAMES OF TOWNSHIPS.	GOVERNOR.			LIEUTENANT-GOVERNOR.	
	Samuel J. Kirkwood, *Republican.*	Shepherd Leffler, *Democrat.*	J. H. Lozier, *Prohibition.*	Joshua G. Newbold, *Republican.*	E. B. Woodward, *Democrat.*
Boyar Valley	42	18	......	43	17
Cedar	26	5	......	26	5
Clinton	46	6	......	46	6
Delaware	12	11	......	12	11
Douglas	35	11	......	35	11
Edin	31	7	......	30	7
Eureka	8	1	......	8	1
Jackson	138	59	2	141	59
Levey	24	9	......	25	9
Sack	59	27	......	59	27
Viola	20	1	......	20	1
Wall Lake	42	30	......	42	30
Wheeler	32	....	......	32	....
Totals	515	185	2	519	184
Majority	330	....	......	335	....

SCOTT COUNTY.

NAMES OF TOWNSHIPS.	Samuel J. Kirkwood, *Republican.*	Shepherd Leffler, *Democrat.*	J. H. Lozier, *Prohibition.*	Joshua G. Newbold, *Republican.*	E. B. Woodward, *Democrat.*
First Precinct, City of Davenport	52	453	......	52	453
Second Precinct, City of Davenport	40	226	......	37	228
Third Precinct, City of Davenport	63	234	......	57	240
Fourth Precinct, City of Davenport	204	187	......	199	....
Fifth Precinct, City of Davenport	168	222	......	168	222
Sixth Precinct, City of Davenport	158	108	......	158	107
First Precinct, Davenport Township	73	87	......	74	86
Second Precinct, Davenport Township	31	103	......	31	103
Rockingham	22	32	......	22	32
Buffalo	63	124	......	65	124
Blue Grass	15	70	......	15	70
Cleona	5	32	......	5	33
Liberty	78	69	......	73	69
Allen Grove	40	41	......	40	41
Hickory Grove	20	62	......	20	63
Winfield	24	73	......	24	73
Sheridan	30	53	....	31	52
Butler	36	56	......	36	56
Lincoln	35	56	......	35	56
Princeton	113	66	......	112	68
Le Claire	155	127	......	153	129
Pleasant Valley	79	38	......	79	38
Totals	1499	2519	......	1486	2343
Majority	....	1020	......	....	857

SHELBY COUNTY.

NAMES OF TOWNSHIPS.	Samuel J. Kirkwood, *Republican.*	Shepherd Leffler, *Democrat.*	J. H. Lozier, *Prohibition.*	Joshua G. Newbold, *Republican.*	E. B. Woodward, *Democrat.*
Harlan	132	80	......	133	81
Lincoln	53	30	......	53	30
Union	18	14	......	18	13
Monroe	29	13	......	29	13
Greeley	13	1	......	14	1
Westphalia	....	34	......	....	34
Grove	26	39	......	26	39

SHELBY COUNTY.—Continued.

NAMES OF TOWNSHIPS.	GOVERNOR.			LIEUTENANT-GOVERNOR.	
	Samuel J. Kirkwood, *Republican.*	Shepherd Leffler, *Democrat.*	J. H. Lozier, *Prohibition.*	Joshua G. Newbold, *Republican.*	E. B. Woodward, *Democrat.*
Jackson	22	7	......	21	8
Douglas	31	33	......	32	32
Cass	11	15	......	10	15
Shelby	59	33	......	59	33
Jefferson	24	4	......	24	4
Clay	31	18	......	34	17
Polk	23	12	......	23	12
Washington	13	23	......	14	21
Fairview	64	50	......	64	50
Totals	549	406	2	554	403
Majority	143	....	......	151	....

SIOUX COUNTY.

NAMES OF TOWNSHIPS.	Kirkwood	Leffler	Lozier	Newbold	Woodward
Settler	21	....	......	21	....
Rock	15	9	......	15	19
Lincoln	32	....	......	42	....
Sheridan	27	3	......	28	3
Grant	36	6	......	36	4
Floyd	41	5	......	41	5
Holland	164	5	......	163	5
Buncombe	18	24	......	19	23
Reading	35	8	......	35	8
Nassau	52	11	......	52	11
East Orange	18	19	......	18	19
Totals	470	90	......	470	97
Majority	380		......	373	

STORY COUNTY.

NAMES OF TOWNSHIPS.	Kirkwood	Leffler	Lozier	Newbold	Woodward
Collins	74	32	......	73	34
Franklin	92	35	......	90	37
Grant	61	28	......	61	29
Howard	83	13	......	83	13
Indian Creek	120	68	......	120	68
Lincoln	26	5	......	26	5
Lafayette	37	22	......	37	22
Milford	63	21	......	64	20
Nevada	186	145	......	185	147
New Albany	82	59	......	84	59
Palestine	75	10	......	77	10
Richland	54	18	......	55	18
Sherman	18	18	......	18	18
Union	98	67	......	95	68
Washington	260	58	......	255	62
Warren	17	4	......	17	4
Totals	1346	603	......	1340	614
Majority	743	....	......	726	....

TAMA COUNTY.

NAMES OF TOWNSHIPS.	GOVERNOR.			LIEUTENANT-GOVERNOR.	
	Samuel J. Kirkwood, *Republican.*	Shepherd Leffler, *Democrat.*	J. H. Lozier, *Prohibition.*	Joshua G. Newbold, *Republican.*	E. B. Woodward, *Democrat.*
Geneseo	69	15	......	70	15
Buckingham	50	36	......	50	36
Grant	20	6	......	20	6
Lincoln	16	14	......	16	14
Spring Creek	41	35	......	41	35
Crystal	44	28	......	44	28
Perry	208	76	......	209	77
Clarke	50	41	......	49	41
Oneidia	63	23	......	63	23
Carroll	21	29	......	20	30
Howard	65	31	......	65	31
Carlton	61	24	......	61	24
Indian Village	143	81	......	139	85
Toledo	192	107	......	190	109
Tama	113	109	......	116	111
Otter Creek	62	59	......	63	59
York	40	38	......	40	38
Salt Creek	59	75	......	59	75
Richland	67	59	......	67	59
Columbia	40	65	......	40	66
Highland	42	27	......	43	28
Totals	1466	978	......	1465	990
Majority	488	....	......	475	....

TAYLOR COUNTY.

NAMES OF TOWNSHIPS.	Samuel J. Kirkwood, *Republican.*	Shepherd Leffler, *Democrat.*	J. H. Lozier, *Prohibition.*	Joshua G. Newbold, *Republican.*	E. B. Woodward, *Democrat.*
Benton	302	130	2	303	133
Clayton	43	47	......	43	47
Dallas	62	16	......	62	16
Gay	25	22	......	25	22
Grove	80	20	......	30	20
Grant	45	31	......	45	31
Holt	40	53	......	40	53
Jackson	46	20	......	47	19
Jefferson	115	33	......	114	34
Mason	25	60	......	24	60
Marshall	89	27	......	89	27
Nodaway	50	17	......	50	17
Platte	80	41	......	81	42
Polk	40	72	......	39	73
Ross	42	39	......	41	40
Washington	48	41	......	48	41
Totals	1082	669	2	1081	675
Majority	413	....	......	406	....

UNION COUNTY.

NAMES OF TOWNSHIPS.	Samuel J. Kirkwood, *Republican.*	Shepherd Leffler, *Democrat.*	J. H. Lozier, *Prohibition.*	Joshua G. Newbold, *Republican.*	E. B. Woodward, *Democrat.*
Dodge	18	38	....	19	40
Douglas—Creston	234	184	....	234	184
Grant	23	38	....	24	37
Highland	64	44	....	44	65

UNION COUNTY.—Continued.

Names of Townships.	Governor. Samuel J. Kirkwood, *Republican.*	Governor. Shepherd Leffler, *Democrat.*	Governor. J. H. Lozier, *Prohibition.*	Lieutenant-Governor. Joshua G. Newbold, *Republican.*	Lieutenant-Governor. E. B. Woodward, *Democrat.*
Jones	70	76	......	69	77
Lincoln	38	25	......	39	24
New Hope	33	34	......	33	34
Platte	42	44	......	42	44
Pleasant	45	49	......	25	49
Sand Creek	31	35	......	31	36
Spaulding	40	5	......	40	5
Union	212	158	......	215	158
Douglas—Cromwell	35	45	......	35	45
Totals	885	775	.....	860	798
Majority	110	....	......	62	....

VAN BUREN COUNTY.

Names of Townships.	Kirkwood	Leffler	Lozier	Newbold	Woodward
Farmington	114	122	......	115	122
Bonaporte	93	157	......	95	157
Harrisburg	68	109	......	68	108
Cedar	110	40	......	99	43
Fremont	77	17	......	95	17
Winchester	60	60	......	60	60
Washington	80	76	......	83	76
Henry	77	52	......	79	52
Vernon	81	62	......	85	62
Des Moines	86	73	......	91	72
Keosauqua	170	104	......	192	102
Pittsburg	73	64	......	74	63
Lick Creek	95	61	......	95	61
Portland	29	46	......	29	46
Village	110	47	......	111	46
Chequest	44	87	......	44	87
Cantril	84	65	......	84	65
Milton	83	148	......	97	149
Totals	1534	1390	68	1596	1388
Majority	144	....	......	208	....

WAPELLO COUNTY.

Names of Townships.	Kirkwood	Leffler	Lozier	Newbold	Woodward
Agency	124	96	......	125	97
Adams	58	139	......	58	139
Center—1st Precinct	449	393	......	444	398
" 2d Precinct	325	300	......	324	298
Columbia	190	142	......	191	142
Cass	49	91	......	49	91
Competine	92	94	......	92	94
Dahlonega	68	44	......	69	43
Green	68	143	......	68	143
Highland	108	75	......	108	75
Keokuk	54	64	......	54	64
Polk	51	99	......	57	94
Pleasant	106	106	......	107	106

WAPELLO COUNTY.—Continued.

NAMES OF TOWNSHIPS.	GOVERNOR.			LIEUTENANT-GOVERNOR.	
	Samuel J. Kirkwood, *Republican.*	Shepherd Leffler, *Democrat.*	J. H. Lozier, *Prohibition.*	Joshua G. Newbold, *Republican.*	E. B. Woodward, *Democrat.*
Richland	152	84	......	156	84
Washington	130	132	......	132	130
Totals	2024	2002	......	2034	1998
Majority	25	....	......	36	....

WARREN COUNTY.

NAMES OF TOWNSHIPS.	Samuel J. Kirkwood, *Republican.*	Shepherd Leffler, *Democrat.*	J. H. Lozier, *Prohibition.*	Joshua G. Newbold, *Republican.*	E. B. Woodward, *Democrat.*
Washington	565	225	......	565	228
Palmyra	115	68	......	114	61
Richland	121	88	......	122	88
Allen	86	49	......	87	51
Greenfield	136	60	......	135	65
Linn	69	48	......	70	48
Jefferson	61	122	......	62	121
Union	98	73	......	98	73
Belmont	106	87	......	102	90
Otter	60	92	......	60	92
White Oak	71	56	......	71	56
Jackson	48	62	......	48	62
Virginia	80	41	......	81	41
Squaw	55	76	......	54	77
Liberty	105	56	......	406	56
White Breast	72	94	......	72	95
Totals	1848	1297	......	1847	1304
Majority	551	....	......	543	....

WASHINGTON COUNTY.

NAMES OF TOWNSHIPS.	Samuel J. Kirkwood, *Republican.*	Shepherd Leffler, *Democrat.*	J. H. Lozier, *Prohibition.*	Joshua G. Newbold, *Republican.*	E. B. Woodward, *Democrat.*
Washington	461	240	......	489	246
Clay	51	51	......	52	51
Brighton	108	62	......	122	59
Marion	38	76	......	35	79
Crawford	146	61	......	147	64
Oregon	153	58	......	153	61
Franklin	75	44	......	75	44
Dutch Creek	91	88	......	91	88
Seventy Six	92	37	......	93	38
Cedar	67	39	......	67	39
Jackson	77	49	......	71	51
Highland	54	39	......	57	40
Iowa	61	130	......	56	134
English River	64	139	......	62	141
Linn Creek	106	84	......	105	84
Totals	1644	1197	27	1675	1219
Majority	447	....	......	456	....

WAYNE COUNTY.

NAMES OF TOWNSHIPS.	GOVERNOR.			LIEUTENANT-GOVERNOR.	
	Samuel J. Kirkwood, *Republican.*	Shepherd Leffler, *Democrat.*	J. H. Lozier, *Prohibition.*	Joshua G. Newbold, *Republican.*	E. B. Woodward, *Democrat.*
Wright	55	76	......	56	76
Union	73	89	......	75	89
Washington	54	66	......	54	66
Richman	49	30	......	49	30
Clay	63	41	......	63	42
Benton	73	61	......	71	63
Corydon	151	132	......	151	132
South Fork	68	71	......	68	71
Walnut	132	100	......	132	100
Jackson	31	47	......	31	48
Warren	173	102	......	175	101
Jefferson	42	64	......	42	64
Grand River	65	93	......	65	93
Clinton	53	38	......	53	38
Howard	32	51	......	35	48
Monroe	48	24	......	48	24
Totals	1162	1085	......	1168	1085
Majority	77	....	......	83	....

WEBSTER COUNTY.

NAMES OF TOWNSHIPS.	Samuel J. Kirkwood, *Republican.*	Shepherd Leffler, *Democrat.*	J. H. Lozier, *Prohibition.*	Joshua G. Newbold, *Republican.*	E. B. Woodward, *Democrat.*
Badger	14	66	....	14	66
Clay	22	3	....	22	3
Colfax	13	14	....	13	14
Dayton	141	47	3	143	48
Deer Creek	21	34	....	21	34
Douglas	31	50	1	31	51
Elkhorn	13	46	....	15	44
Fulton	21	12	....	21	12
Gowrie	30	24	....	30	24
Hardin	16	12	....	24	7
Jackson	14	42	....	15	42
Johnson	15	44	....	16	43
Lost Grove	43	....	....	43	....
Newark	11	9	....	11	9
Otho	60	21	2	62	21
Pleasant Valley	23	72	....	24	72
Roland	11	1	....	11	1
Sumner	64	43	9	70	44
Wahkonsa	273	312	68	333	324
Washington	62	64	2	64	68
Webster	32	25	......	35	22
Yell	20	23	......	21	26
Totals	950	964	85	1039	975
Majority	....	14	......	64	....

WINNEBAGO COUNTY.

NAMES OF TOWNSHIPS.	Samuel J. Kirkwood, *Republican.*	Shepherd Leffler, *Democrat.*	J. H. Lozier, *Prohibition.*	Joshua G. Newbold, *Republican.*	E. B. Woodward, *Democrat.*
Forest	202	51	......	202	51
Center	136	7	......	136	7
Norway	45	4	......	45	4
Totals	383	62	......	383	62
Majority	321	....	......	321	....

WINNESHIEK COUNTY.

NAMES OF TOWNSHIPS.	GOVERNOR.			LIEUTENANT-GOVERNOR.	
	Samuel J. Kirkwood, *Republican.*	Shepherd Leffler, *Democrat.*	J. H. Lozier, *Prohibition.*	Joshua G. Newbold, *Republican.*	E. B. Woodward, *Democrat.*
Bloomfield	100	50	......	99	51
Military	101	149	......	103	149
Washington	24	188	......	24	189
Jackson	10	48	......	10	48
Frankville	81	84	......	79	84
Springfield	115	3	......	115	3
Calmar	106	121	......	106	121
Sumner	14	46	......	14	46
Glenwood	84	30	......	84	30
Decorah	439	329	......	441	328
Madison	83	7	......	83	7
Lincoln	76	26	......	76	26
Pleasant	77	13	......	77	13
Canoe	54	49	......	54	49
Bluffton	48	86	......	48	86
Orleans	90	10	......	90	10
Highland	69	3	......	69	3
Hesper	135	12	......	135	12
Burr Oak	101	62	......	101	62
Fremont	66	38	......	66	38
Totals	1873	1354	......	1874	1355
Majority	519	....	......	519	....

WOODBURY COUNTY.

NAMES OF TOWNSHIPS.	Samuel J. Kirkwood, *Republican.*	Shepherd Leffler, *Democrat.*	J. H. Lozier, *Prohibition.*	Joshua G. Newbold, *Republican.*	E. B. Woodward, *Democrat.*
Arlington	17	4	......	17	4
Concord	29	25	......	30	26
Floyd	8	4	......	12	....
Grant	29	39	......	29	40
Grange	11	5	......	11	5
Kedron	44	16	......	43	17
Lakeport	33	8	......	33	8
Liston	12	13	......	12	13
Liberty	63	41	......	63	41
Little Sioux	73	63	......	72	64
Moville	6	4	......	6	4
Rock	25	4	......	25	4
Rutland	13	5	......	14	4
Sioux City	510	415	2	512	415
Sloan	19	3	......	19	3
Union	67	11	......	67	11
Woodbury	65	24	3	70	24
West Fork	22	10	......	22	10
Wolf Creek	37	15	......	37	15
Willow	16	10	......	16	10
Totals	1099	719	5	1110	718
Majority	380	....	......	392	....

WORTH COUNTY.

NAMES OF TOWNSHIPS.	Samuel J. Kirkwood, *Republican.*	Shepherd Leffler, *Democrat.*	J. H. Lozier, *Prohibition.*	Joshua G. Newbold, *Republican.*	E. B. Woodward, *Democrat.*
Union	29	8	......	29	8
Deer Creek	18	10	......	18	10
Kensett	31	7	......	31	7

WORTH COUNTY.—Continued.

NAMES OF TOWNSHIPS.	GOVERNOR.			LIEUTENANT-GOVERNOR.	
	Samuel J. Kirkwood, *Republican.*	Shepherd Leffler, *Democrat.*	J. H. Lozier, *Prohibition.*	Joshua G. Newbold, *Republican.*	E. B. Woodward, *Democrat.*
Northwood	167	30	......	167	31
Danville	15	11	......	15	11
Brookfield	43	....	......	43	....
Hartland	58	2	......	58	2
Fertile	53	6	......	53	6
Bristol	71	19	......	71	19
Silver Lake	38	....	......	38	....
Totals	523	93	......	523	94
Majority	430	....	......	429	....

WRIGHT COUNTY.

NAMES OF TOWNSHIPS.	Kirkwood	Leffler	Lozier	Newbold	Woodward
Troy	53	8	......	52	9
Eagle Grove	44	3	......	44	3
Liberty	60	12	......	60	12
Boone	10	16	......	10	16
Belmond	54	32	......	54	32
Pleasant	60	38	......	57	39
Iowa	57	9	......	57	9
Vernon	30	....	......	30	....
Wall Lake	37	11	......	36	11
Clarion	63	13	......	63	13
Woolstock	25	4	......	25	4
Totals	493	146	......	488	148
Majority	347	....	......	340	....

Total vote cast for Governor 218,982
Kirkwood received 125,058
Leffler received 93,359
Lozier received 565
Kirkwood over Leffler 31,699
Kirkwood over Leffler and Lozier 31,134

Majorities in above table by counties are computed as between Kirkwood and Leffler. Full returns of the vote for Lozier not having been received at date of this publication.

Total vote cast for Lieutenant Governor 219,047
Newbold received 125,892
Woodward received 93,155
Newbold over Woodward 32,737

TABLE

Showing the population of Iowa by Congressional Districts for 1870, 1873, *and* 1875; *vote in* 1875 *for Judge of the Supreme Court and Superintendent of Public Instruction; and number entitled to vote in* 1875.

FIRST CONGRESSIONAL DISTRICT.

COUNTIES	Population, 1875.	Population, 1873.	Population, 1870.	VOTE IN 1875 FOR JUDGE OF SUPREME COURT.		VOTE IN 1875 FOR SUPERINTEDENT OF PUBLIC INSTRUCTION		Number entitled to vote.
				Austin Adams, *Republican.*	Wm. J. Knight, *Democrat.*	A. Abernethy, *Republican.*	Isaiah Doane, *Democrat.*	
Des Moines	35106	34691	27256	2204	2406	2206	2404	6654
Henry	21594	20754	21463	1993	1407	2000	1396	4641
Jefferson	17127	16778	17839	1620	1323	1624	1318	3721
Lee	33914	33644	37210	2328	3132	2323	3133	7509
Louisa	12499	12377	12877	2023	1129	2026	1124	2899
Van Buren	16980	16860	17672	1613	1383	1614	1380	3893
Washington	19269	18975	18952	1654	1213	1662	1221	4168
Totals	156489	154079	153269	13435	11993	13455	11976	33485
Majority	....	....	....	1442	....	1479	....	....

SECOND CONGRESSIONAL DISTRICT.

COUNTIES	Population, 1875.	Population, 1873.	Population, 1870.	Austin Adams, *Republican.*	Wm. J. Knight, *Democrat.*	A. Abernethy, *Republican.*	Isaiah Doane, *Democrat.*	Number entitled to vote.
Cedar	17879	17089	19731	1626	1243	1626	1244	3934
Clinton	34295	33591	35357	2317	2480	2314	2482	5569
Jackson	23062	22284	22619	1636	2333	1636	2234	4901
Jones	19166	18930	19731	1982	1427	1968	1435	4180
Muscatine	21623	21382	21688	1896	1766	1897	1772	6588
Scott	39736	38936	38599	1488	2534	1494	2533	7109
Totals	155761	152212	157725	10945	11683	10935	11700	32281
Majority	....	....	....	....	738	....	765	....

THIRD CONGRESSIONAL DISTRICT.

COUNTIES	Population, 1875.	Population, 1873.	Population, 1870.	Austin Adams, *Republican.*	Wm. J. Knight, *Democrat.*	A. Abernethy, *Republican.*	Isaiah Doane, *Democrat.*	Number entitled to vote.
Allamakee	19168	18304	17868	1863	2135	1815	2128	3653
Buchanan	17315	16329	17034	1596	1356	1603	1344	3890
Clayton	27184	26946	27771	1841	2176	1848	2165	5272
Delaware	16890	16522	17432	1699	1077	1700	1079	3662

THIRD CONGRESSIONAL DISTRICT.—CONTINUED.

COUNTIES.	Population, 1875.	Population, 1873.	Population, 1870.	VOTE IN 1875 FOR JUDGE OF SUPREME COURT.		VOTE IN 1875 FOR SUPERINTENDENT OF PUBLIC INSTRUCTI'N		Number entitled to vote.
				Austin Adams, *Republican.*	Wm. J. Knight, *Democrat.*	A. Abernethy, *Republican.*	Isaiah Doane, *Democrat.*	
Dubuque	43845	41900	38969	2123	4068	2205	3986	8759
*Fayette	20518	18796	16973	2298	1335	2294	1295	4637
Winneshiek	24233	23061	23570	1876	1349	1879	1343	4117
Totals	169153	161858	159617	13296	13496	13344	13340	33990
Majority	....	....	....	....	200	3	....	....

* *Isiah* Doane received one vote.

FOURTH CONGRESSIONAL DISTRICT.

COUNTIES.	Population, 1875.	Population, 1873.	Population, 1870.	Austin Adams, *Republican.*	Wm. J. Knight, *Democrat.*	A. Abernethy, *Republican.*	Isaiah Doane, *Democrat.*	Number entitled to vote.
Black Hawk	22913	23136	21706	2105	1312	2107	1304	4867
Bremer	13220	12517	12528	1526	666	1525	669	2656
Butler	11734	10760	9951	1372	631	1366	630	2598
Cerro Gordo	6685	5636	4722	826	221	825	220	1526
Chickasaw	11400	10292	10180	1078	811	1078	810	2392
Floyd	13100	11271	10768	1347	520	1356	517	2884
Franklin	6558	5669	4738	923	213	924	213	1374
*Grundy	8134	7154	6399	604	158	603	142	1525
Hancock	1482	1397	999	265	75	266	70	303
Hardin	15010	13855	13684	1737	785	1726	784	3215
Howard	7875	7459	6282	878	481	879	23	1712
Mitchell	11523	9563	9582	1255	329	1256	329	2338
Winnebago	2987	2488	1562	383	62	383	56	406
Worth	4908	3913	2892	523	93	522	94	763
Wright	3244	2826	2392	493	146	489	148	694
Totals	140773	127936	118385	15315	6503	15305	6009	29253
Majority	....	....	....	8812	....	9279	....	....

* Seventeen votes were cast for *Josiah* Doane.

FIFTH CONGRESSIONAL DISTRICT.

COUNTIES.	Population, 1875.	Population, 1873.	Population, 1870.	Austin Adams, *Republican.*	Wm. J. Knight, *Democrat.*	A. Abernethy, *Republican.*	Isaiah Doane, *Democrat.*	Number entitled to vote.
Benton	22807	22068	22454	1906	974	1903	977	4770
Iowa	17456	16572	16644	1608	1327	1610	1325	3576
Johnson	24654	24814	24898	2166	2276	2171	2269	5225
Linn	31815	30019	28852	3093	2155	3067	2153	7274
Marshall	19629	18272	17576	1803	524	1804	521	4445
*Poweshiek	16482	15275	15581	1513	778	1514	123	3634
Tama	18771	16343	16131	1466	980	1464	991	3911
Totals	151614	143363	142136	13555	9014	13533	8359	32835
Majority	....	....	....	4541	....	4522	....	....

* A. R. Wright received 652 votes for Superintendent of Public Instruction.

SIXTH CONGRESSIONAL DISTRICT.

COUNTIES.	Population, 1875.	Population, 1873.	Population, 1870.	Austin Adams, *Republican.*	Wm. J. Knight, *Democrat.*	A. Abernethy, *Republican.*	Isaiah Doane, *Democrat.*	Number entitled to vote.
Appanoose	17405	16474	16456	1447	1364	1442	1367	3679
Davis	15757	15434	15565	1492	1583	1492	1582	3448
Jasper	24128	22340	22116	2103	1158	2102	1160	5239
Keokuk	20488	19974	19434	1618	1482	1622	1475	4202
Mahaska	23718	22054	22508	2415	1734	2420	1726	5287
Marion	24094	24272	24436	2029	2052	2032	2050	4988

SIXTH CONGRESSIONAL DISTRICT.—Continued.

Counties.	Population, 1875.	Population, 1873.	Population, 1870.	Vote in 1875 for Judge of Supreme Court.		Vote in 1875 for Superintendent of Public Instructi'n		Number entitled to vote.
				Austin Adams, *Republican.*	Wm. J. Knight, *Democrat.*	A. Abernethy, *Republican.*	Isaiah Doane, *Democrat.*	
Monroe	12711	12302	12724	1081	834	1081	835	2743
Wapello	23865	22261	22346	2041	1986	2036	1979	5346
Total	162166	155112	155585	14226	12193	14227	12174	34932
Majority	....	....	....	2033	....	2053	....	....

SEVENTH CONGRESSIONAL DISTRICT.

Counties.	Population, 1875.	Population, 1873.	Population, 1870.	Austin Adams, *Republican.*	Wm. J. Knight, *Democrat.*	A. Abernethy, *Republican.*	Isaiah Doane, *Democrat.*	Number entitled to vote.
Adair	7045	5264	3982	888	346	887	346	1616
Clarke	10118	8778	8735	1084	760	1080	763	2213
Dallas	14386	12689	12019	1422	839	1414	845	3170
Decatur	13249	11598	12018	1220	1092	1218	1091	2882
Guthrie	9638	8017	7061	1082	662	1080	666	2239
Lucas	11725	10742	10388	1066	916	1065	934	2497
Madison	16030	14698	13884	1785	1414	1788	1419	3632
Polk	31558	30892	27857	3134	2163	3136	2156	6842
Warren	18528	17400	17980	1854	1305	1848	1303	3923
Wayne	13978	11797	11287	1166	1084	1168	1082	2947
Total	146255	131875	125211	14701	10581	14684	10605	31961
Majority	....	....	....	4120	....	4079	....	....

EIGHTH CONGRESSIONAL DISTRICT.

Counties.	Population, 1875.	Population, 1873.	Population, 1870.	Austin Adams, *Republican.*	Wm. J. Knight, *Democrat.*	A. Abernethy, *Republican.*	Isaiah Doane, *Democrat.*	Number entitled to vote.
Adams	7772	5865	4614	1126	357	1129	354	1727
Audubon	2370	1873	1212	307	286	305	285	527
Cass	10552	7660	5464	1250	697	1253	689	2422
Fremont	13719	12394	11174	1218	1601	1218	1600	2998
Harrison	11818	10348	8931	1317	1298	1321	1290	2658
Mills	10555	9664	8718	1088	950	1095	946	2365
Montgomery	10839	8601	5934	1454	595	1458	591	2485
Page	14274	11734	9975	1296	604	1292	608	3223
Pottawattamie	21665	20170	16893	1776	1772	1789	1770	4392
Ringgold	7546	6850	5691	777	404	775	403	1496
Shelby	5664	3762	2540	555	405	556	402	1084
Taylor	10418	8191	6989	1081	675	1085	670	2282
Union	8827	6911	5986	906	765	906	767	1924
Total	136019	114023	94121	14151	10409	14182	10370	29583
Majority	....	....	....	3742	....	3812	....	....

NINTH CONGRESSIONAL DISTRICT.

Counties.	Population, 1875.	Population, 1873.	Population, 1870.	Austin Adams, *Republican.*	Wm. J. Knight, *Democrat.*	A. Abernethy, *Republican.*	Isaiah Doane, *Democrat.*	Number entitled to vote.
Boone	17351	15167	14584	1717	1119	1719	1116	3515
Buena Vista	3561	2669	1585	670	119	675	116	817
Calhoun	3185	2922	1602	386	159	387	158	681
Carroll	5760	3601	2451	633	599	635	593	1197
Cherokee	4245	3297	1967	536	211	537	210	1001
*Clay	3569	3585	1523	706	14	714	....	868
Crawford	6038	3777	2530	754	554	1245	44	1254
Dickinson	1748	1743	1389	281	22	281	22	394
Emmet	1436	1618	1392	248	29	248	29	299

* Five votes for A. R. Wright.

NINTH CONGRESSIONAL DISTRICT.—Continued.

COUNTIES.	Population, 1875.	Population, 1873.	Population, 1870.	VOTE IN 1875 FOR JUDGE OF SUPREME COURT.		VOTE IN 1875 FOR SUPERINTENDENT OF PUBLIC INSTRUCTI'N		Number entitled to vote.
				Austin Adams, *Republican.*	Wm. J. Knight, *Democrat.*	A. Abernethy, *Republican.*	Isaiah Doane, *Democrat.*	
Greene	7028	5755	4627	806	444	760	442	1622
Hamilton	7701	6672	6055	892	362	883	374	1455
Humboldt	3455	2783	2596	387	123	387	124	695
Ida	794	449	226	177	30	198	10	172
Kossuth	3765	4252	3351	589	68	588	68	773
Lyon	1232	966	221	300	7	301	2	287
Monona	5967	4989	3654	569	368	570	367	1292
O'Brien	2349	1865	715	479	21	479	21	595
Osceola	1778	1409	....	289	9	347	....	498
Palo Alto	2735	2617	1336	324	301	323	301	556
Plymouth	5282	3884	2199	886	215	878	213	1136
Pocahontas	2249	2175	1446	336	126	333	126	464
Sac	2873	1698	1411	520	183	522	181	657
Sioux	3220	2872	576	470	90	476	87	637
Story	13311	11519	11651	1343	614	1351	605	2574
Webster	13114	11603	10484	1040	973	1035	988	2747
Woodbury	8568	6988	6172	1113	715	1113	713	1776
Total	132314	110875	85743	16451	7475	16985	6910	27962
Majority	....	....	....	8976	....	10075	....	....

RECAPITULATION.

First District	156489	154079	153269	13435	11993	13455	11976	33485
Second District	155761	152212	157725	10945	11683	10935	11700	32281
Third District	169153	161858	159617	13296	13496	13344	13340	33990
Fourth District	140773	127936	118385	15315	6503	15305	6009	29253
Fifth District	151614	143363	142136	13555	9014	13533	8359	32835
Sixth District	162166	155112	155585	14226	12193	14227	12174	34932
Seventh District	146255	131875	125211	14701	10581	14684	10605	31961
Eighth District	136019	114023	94121	14151	10409	14182	10370	29583
Ninth District	132314	110875	85743	16451	7475	16985	6910	27962
Total	1350544	1251333	1191792	126075	93347	126650	91443	286283

Total vote cast for Judge Supreme Court 219,422
Adams received 126,075
Knight received 93,347
Adams over Knight 32,728

Total vote cast for Superintendent of Public Instruction 218,093
Abernethy received 126,650
Doane received 91,443
Scattering 675
Abernethy over Doane 35,207
Abernethy over all 34,532

SIXTEENTH GENERAL ASSEMBLY.

To Convene at Des Moines, January 10, 1876.

SENATE.

No. of Dist.	COUNTIES.	Population in 1875.	NAMES OF MEMBERS.	POST-OFFICE.
1	Lee	33914	Henry W. Rothert	Keokuk
2	Van Buren	16980	James B. Pease	Big Mound
3	Davis	15757	Horatio A. Wonn	Drakeville
4	Appanoose	17405	Joshua Miller	Centerville
5	Monroe and Wayne	26689	Henry L. Dashiell	Albia
6	Clarke and Lucas	21843	Samuel L. Bestow	Chariton
7	Taylor, Ringgold, and Decatur	31213	Fred Teale	Decatur City
8	Fremont, Page, and Montgomery	38832	Alfred Hebard	Red Oak
9	Pottawattamie and Mills	32220	George F. Wright	Council Bluffs
10	Des Moines	35106	J. Wilson Williams	Huron
11	Henry	21594	John S. Woolson	Mt. Pleasant
12	Jefferson	17127	Moses A. McCoid	Fairfield
13	Wapello	23865	Joseph H. Merrill	Ottumwa
14	Keokuk	20488	Hosea N. Newton	Keota
15	Washington and Louisa	31768	William Wilson	Washington
16	Madison and Dallas	30416	Henry Thornburg	Perry
17	Adair, Cass, Adams, and Union	34196	Lafayette Young	Atlantic
18	Mahaska	23718	Thomas R. Gilmore	Kirkville
19	Marion	24094	John L. McCormack	Knoxville
20	Warren	18528	William Graham	Indianola
21	Muscatine	21623	Gilbert H. Wood	Muscatine
22	Scott	39736	Jeremiah H. Murphy	Davenport
23	Clinton	34295	N. A. Merrell	De Witt
24	Cedar	17879	Henry C. Carr	Tipton
25	Johnson	24654	Ezekiel Clark	Iowa City
26	Iowa	17456	John N. W. Rumple	Marengo
27	Jasper	24128	Frank T. Campbell	Newton
28	Polk	31558	Thomas Mitchell	Mitchellville
29	Hamilton and Hardin	22711	Elias Jessup	N. Providence
30	Jackson	23062	William A. Maginnis	Bellevue
31	Jones	19166	George W. Lovell	Monticello
32	Linn	31815	Stephen L. Dows	Cedar Rapids
33	Benton	22807	John Shane	Vinton
34	Marshall and Grundy	27763	Delos Arnold	Marshalltown
35	Dubuque	43845	Dennis N. Cooley	Dubuque
36	Delaware	16890	Lewis G. Hersey	Earlville
37	Buchanan	17315	Merritt W. Harmon	Independence
38	Poweshiek and Tama	35253	John Conaway	Brooklyn
39	Clayton	27184	John T. Stoneman	McGregor
40	Fayette	20518	William Larrabee	Clermont
41	Allamakee	19168	Samuel H. Kinne	Lansing
42	Winneshiek	24233	George R. Willett	Decorah
43	Mitchell, Floyd, and Butler	36357	Arad Hitchcock	Osage
44	Black Hawk	22913	Edward G. Miller	Waterloo
45	Boone and Story	30662	William H. Gallup	Nevada
46	Worth, Winnebago, Kossuth, Hancock, Cerro Gordo, Humboldt, Wright, and Franklin	33084	Lemuel Dwelle	Northwood
47	Dickinson, Emmet, Clay, Palo Alto, Buena Vista, Pocahontas, Ida, Sac, Calhoun, and Webster	35264	Eldin J. Hartshorn	Emmetsburg
48	Howard, Chickasaw, and Bremer	32495	Hiram Bailey	Williamstown
49	Greene, Carroll, Crawford, Shelby, Audubon, and Guthrie	36498	Samuel D. Nichols	Panora
50	Lyon, Osceola, O'Brien, Sioux, Plymouth, Cherokee, Woodbury, Monona, and Harrison	44459	George D. Perkins	Sioux City

SIXTEENTH GENERAL ASSEMBLY.

To Convene at Des Moines, January 10, 1876.

HOUSE OF REPRESENTATIVES.

No. of Dist.	COUNTIES.	Population in 1875.	NAMES OF MEMBERS.	POST-OFFICE.
1	Lee	33914	Wesley C. Hobbs	Fort Madison
		....	John Gibbons	Keokuk
		....	John N. Irwin	Keokuk
2	Des Moines	35106	John H. Gear	Burlington
		....	William Lynch	Burlington
3	Henry	21594	William Allen	New London
		....	Jacob Kauffman	Mt. Pleasant
4	Jefferson	17127	W. L. S. Simmons	Brookville
5	Van Buren	16980	Thomas Christy	Bonaparte
6	Wapello	23865	Jacob W. Dixon	Ottumwa
		......	G. A. Madson	Ottumwa
7	Davis	15757	L. D. Hotchkiss	Bloomfield
8	Monroe	12711	A. M. Giltner	Albia
9	Appanoose	17405	James B. Stuckey	Unionville
10	Lucas	11725	Dan M. Baker	Chariton
11	Wayne	13978	Elijah Glendenning	Lineville
12	Decatur	13249	Stanfield P. McNeill	Garden Grove
13	Clarke	10118	Jacob Proudfoot	Liberty
14	Ringgold and Union	16373	Samuel W. McElderry	Afton
15	Taylor	10418	John Madden	Lenox
16	Page	14274	Edwin B. Hoag	College Springs
17	Fremont	13719	William M. Brooks	Tabor
18	Mills	10555	John Y. Stone	Glenwood
19	Pottawattamie	21665	Daniel Hunt	Avoca
20	Montgomery and Adams	18611	George A. Morse	Corning
21	Audubon, Shelby, Adair and Cass	25631	Milton K. Campbell	Harlan
22	Madison	16030	J. J. Smith	Van Meter
23	Warren	18528	Samuel Irwin	New Virginia
24	Marion	24094	Green T. Clark	Pella
		....	John B. Elliott	Knoxville
25	Mahaska	23718	W. H. Seevers	Oskaloosa
		....	Hardin Tice	Pella
26	Keokuk	20488	B. A. Cleveland	Harper
		....	Sanford Harned	Sigourney
27	Washington	19269	William Said	Valley
		....	G. T. Auld	Crawfordsville
28	Louisa	12499	Robert E. Benton	Wapello
29	Muscatine	21623	Charles C. Horton	Muscatine
		....	Frank A. J. Gray	Sweetl'ndCentr
30	Scott	39736	Ernst Mueller	Davenport
		....	Eugene Birchard	Pleasant Valley
		....	Joseph A. Crawford	Davenport
31	Clinton	34295	Edward H. Thayer	Clinton
		....	John A. Young	Elvira
		....	Henry Horstman	Toronto
32	Cedar	17879	Robert G. Scott	Pleasant Hill
		....	Alexander Moffit	Mechanicsville
33	Johnson	24654	Rush Clark	Iowa City
		....	Charles W. McCune	Solon
34	Iowa	17456	John L. Williams	North English
35	Poweshiek	16482	Charles F. Craver	Grinnell
36	Jasper	24128	George M. Wilson	Greencastle
		....	Joel W. Deweese	Prairie City
37	Polk	31558	William G. Madden	Greenwood
		... .	Josiah Given	Des Moines
38	Dallas	14386	T. C. Norris	Perry
39	Guthrie	9638	George J. Maris	Guthrie Center
40	Harrison	11818	Lemuel R. Bolter	Woodbine

HOUSE OF REPRESENTATIVES.—CONTINUED.

No. of Dist.	COUNTIES.	Population in 1875.	NAMES OF MEMBERS.	POST-OFFICES.
41	Monona, Crawford, Ida and Cherokee	17044	George Rae	Dowville
42	Greene, Carroll, Calhoun and Sac	18846	Orlando H. Manning	Carroll City
43	Webster	13114	Samuel Rees	Ft. Dodge
44	Boone	17351	Levi Colvin	Moingona
45	Story	13311	Milton Evans	Ames
46	Hardin	15010	John Hall	Eldora
47	Marshall	19629	William D. Mills	Marshalltown
48	Grundy	8134	James Underwood	Eldora
49	Tama	18771	Gamaliel Jaqua	Traer
50	Black Hawk	22913	Herman C. Hemenway	Cedar Falls
			Harlan P. Homer	Blakeville
51	Benton	22807	E. Smyth Johnson	Belle Plaine
			John McCartney	Vinton
52	Buchanan	17315	John Calvin	Newtonville
53	Linn	31815	Moses C. Jordan	Central City
			William Ure	Fairfax
54	Jones	19166	William T. Shaw	Anamosa
			George W. Lathrop	Oxford Mills
55	Jackson	23062	Lewis W. Stuart	Monmouth
			William H. Reed	Bellevue
56	Dubuque	43845	Thomas W. Johnston	Rockdale
			Theophilus Crawford	Peosta
			Julius K. Graves	Dubuque
57	Delaware	16890	Joseph Chapman	Colesburg
58	Clayton	27184	Charles Mentzel	Elkader
			Thos. D. White	National
59	Fayette	20518	William E. Fuller	West Union
60	Allamakee	19168	Luther Brown	Postville
61	Winneshiek	24233	Warren Danforth	Cresco
			Martin N. Johnson	Decorah
62	Bremer	13220	Louis Case	Waverly
63	Chickasaw	11400	John McHugh	Lawler
64	Howard	7875	Henry T. Reed	Cresco
65	Mitchell	11523	Jesse P. Brush	Osage
66	Floyd	13100	Jared B. Shepardson	Marble Rock
67	Butler	11734	John Palmer	Clarksville
68	Franklin and Cerro Gordo	13243	Lorenzo D. Lane	Hampton
69	Worth, Winnebago, Kossuth and Hancock	13142	Henry H. Bush	Garner
70	Humboldt, Hamilton and Wright	14400	John L. Morse	Belmond
71	Pocahontas, Buena Vista, Palo Alto and Emmet	9981	Gifford S. Robinson	Storm Lake
72	Clay, Dickinson, Osceola and O'Brien	9444	John F. Glover	Sibley
73	Woodbury, Plymouth, Sioux and Lyon	18302	Samuel B. Gilliland	James

ERRATA.

Clayton county, PAGES 15, 82, 142. 200, 261, and 317 for "Girard" read "Giard."

PAGE 6.—Number of voters in Black Hawk county should be "4867," instead of "4877."

PAGE 24.—Franklin county, Geneva Township, "No. of dwelling houses" should be "122 instead of 132."

PAGE 31.—Humboldt county, for "Delano" read "Delana."

PAGE 69.—Wright county, for "Woodstock" read "Woolstock."

PAGE 71.—Allamakee county, Makee Township returns include those for Waukon.

PAGE 87.—Des Moines county, in "Total number of acres of corn" read "102,924" instead of "802,924."

PAGE 95.—Hardin county, in "Total number bushels of corn" read "1,379,961" instead " of 137,996."

PAGE 108.—Marshall county, in "Total number bushels of Spring Wheat" read "1,125,-382" instead of "112,582."

PAGE 115.—Polk county, for "Taylor" read "Saylor."

PAGE 131.—Allamakee county, in "Total number acres of Tame Grass" read "15,608 instead of 1,568."

PAGE 143.—Clinton county, in "Total number Bushels of Potatoes," read "138,361" instead of 1,318,361.

PAGE 148.—Dubuque county, in "Total number Acres in Sorghum," read "142" instead of 42.

PAGE 151.—Fremont county, in "Total number Acres of Potatoes," read "553" instead of "53." Also, in "Total number Acres of Onions," read "52" instead of "25."

PAGE 164.—Louisa county, in "Total number Gallons of Sorghum," read "20,760" instead of "207,060."

PAGE 172.—Page county, in "Total number Acres of Potatoes," read "793" instead of "4,793."

PAGE 182.—Wapello county, in "Total number Bushels of Potatoes," read "154,473" instead of "15,447."

PAGE 183.—At top of page read "Warren County."

PAGE 187.—Wright county, "Wall Lake," which has no returns, should be followed by "Woolstock" with the figures credited to "Wall Lake."

PAGE 211.—Guthrie county, in "Total number of Vines," read "12,186" instead of "2,186."

www.ingramcontent.com/pod-product-compliance
Lightning Source LLC
LaVergne TN
LVHW021310110826
845150LV00003B/543

* 9 7 8 1 4 2 5 5 5 8 6 7 3 *